Mike Meyers'

CompTIA Network+™ Guide to M[illegible] and Troubleshooting Networks

About the Series Editor

Michael Meyers is the industry's leading authority on CompTIA Network+ certification. He is the president and founder of Total Seminars, LLC, a member of CompTIA, and a major provider of IT fundamentals, PC and network repair, and computer security training and training materials for thousands of organizations throughout the world.

Mike has written numerous popular textbooks, including the best-selling *Mike Meyers' CompTIA A+™ Guide to Managing and Troubleshooting PCs, Mike Meyers' CompTIA Network+™ Guide to Managing and Troubleshooting Networks*, and *Mike Meyers' CompTIA Security+™ Certification Guide.*

Mike has attained numerous industry certifications, including CompTIA A+, CompTIA Network+, CompTIA Security+, CompTIA Cybersecurity Analyst (CySA+), and Microsoft Certified Professional.

About the Author

Scott Jernigan wields a mighty red pen as Editor in Chief for Total Seminars. With a Master of Arts in Medieval History, Scott feels as much at home in the musty archives of London as he does in the crisp IPS glow of Total Seminars' Houston HQ. After fleeing a purely academic life, he dove headfirst into IT, working as an instructor, editor, and writer.

Scott has written, edited, and contributed to dozens of books on computer literacy, hardware, operating systems, networking, security, and certification, including *Computer Literacy—Your Ticket to IC³ Certification*, and co-authoring with Mike Meyers the *CompTIA IT Fundamentals+™ All-in-One Exam Guide* and *Mike Meyers' CompTIA Security+™ Certification Guide.*

Scott has taught computer classes all over the United States, including stints at the United Nations in New York and the FBI Academy in Quantico. Practicing what he preaches, Scott is a CompTIA ITF+, CompTIA A+, CompTIA Network+, and CompTIA Security+ certified technician, a Microsoft Certified Professional, a Microsoft Office User Specialist, and Certiport Internet and Computing Core Certified.

About the Technical Editor

Jonathan S. Weissman is a senior lecturer (Department of Computing Security) at Rochester Institute of Technology, where he was awarded the RIT Outstanding Teaching Award in 2014, the RIT GCCIS Outstanding Educator Award in 2018, and RIT Distinguished Teacher Recognition Program Honors in 2019. Weissman developed and teaches three courses for the edX RITx Cybersecurity MicroMasters program to more than 300,000 students worldwide.

Jonathan is also a tenured associate professor and the Networking and Cybersecurity program coordinator (Department of Computing Sciences) at Finger Lakes Community College, where he was awarded the State University of New York Chancellor's Award for Excellence in Teaching in 2021. He has a Master of Arts in Computer Science from Brooklyn College and holds 44 industry certifications, including CCNP Enterprise, Cisco Certified Specialist – Enterprise Core, Cisco Certified Specialist – Enterprise Advanced Infrastructure Implementation, CCNA Security, CCNA, CompTIA Security+, CompTIA Network+, CompTIA A+, CompTIA Linux+, CompTIA Server+, EC-Council Certified Ethical Hacker™, EC-Council Computer Hacking Forensic Investigator™, and IPv6 Forum Certified Network Engineer (Gold), among many others. He was inducted into the IPv6 Forum's New Internet IPv6 Hall of Fame as an IPv6 Evangelist in 2021.

Jonathan is the coauthor of *Mike Meyers' CompTIA Network+™ Guide to Managing and Troubleshooting Networks Lab Manual* (fourth, fifth, and sixth editions) and *Mike Meyers' CompTIA Network+™ Certification Passport* (fifth, sixth, and seventh editions). He also serves as technical editor for many industry textbooks.

Follow Jonathan S. Weissman on LinkedIn at www.linkedin.com/in/jonathan-s-weissman-058b649b, Twitter at https://twitter.com/CSCPROF, and Instagram at www.instagram.com/cscprof. Subscribe to his YouTube channel at https://youtube.com/weissman52.

Mike Meyers'

CompTIA Network+™ Guide to Managing and Troubleshooting Networks

Sixth Edition

(Exam N10-008)

Mike Meyers, Series Editor
Scott Jernigan

New York Chicago San Francisco
Athens London Madrid Mexico City
Milan New Delhi Singapore Sydney Toronto

McGraw Hill books are available at special quantity discounts to use as premiums and sales promotions, or for use in corporate training programs. To contact a representative, please visit the Contact Us pages at www.mhprofessional.com.

Mike Meyers' CompTIA Network+™ Guide to Managing and Troubleshooting Networks, Sixth Edition (Exam N10-008)

1 2 3 4 5 6 7 8 9 LWI 25 24 23 22

Library of Congress Control Number: 2021953078

ISBN 978-1-264-26903-7
MHID 1-264-26903-X

Sponsoring Editor
Tim Green

Editorial Supervisor
Janet Walden

Project Editor
Rachel Fogelberg

Acquisitions Coordinator
Emily Walters

Technical Editor
Jonathan S. Weissman

Copy Editor
William McManus

Proofreader
Rick Camp

Indexer
Ted Laux

Production Supervisor
Thomas Somers

Composition
KnowledgeWorks Global Ltd.

Illustration
KnowledgeWorks Global Ltd.

Art Director, Cover
Jeff Weeks

Acknowledgments

To Katie, Maggie, and Simon for reminding me what's most important in life!

I'd like to acknowledge the many people who contributed their talents to make this book possible:

To Tim Green, my acquisitions editor at McGraw Hill: Your encouragement and support during our pandemic edition kept the sanity in place. Love working with you!

To my series editor, Mike Meyers: I couldn't have done it without you, amigo. Truthfully, has there ever been a better combo than a wizard and a paladin?

To Jonathan S. Weissman, technical editor: Great fun working with you on another book. Thanks for keeping me on my toes and technically on point!

To Bill McManus, copy editor: I would say that "people say" you're the best in the business, but that people is me. Love working with you!

To Travis Everett, writer and editor: Hand in glove on this one, Travis. Love your words and the meticulous attention to nuances that I missed. Great working with you and look forward to more. Qatar next winter?

To Michael Smyer, technologist and photographer: Enjoyed the process on this book, my friend. Yes, even the arguments, because they made the final product much better than anything I could have done on my own.

To Dave Rush, senior instructor and top researcher: Thank you for everything you contributed to this book, from research to sounding board to more research . . . . No idea how you can know so much about so much, but I'm very happy you're on my team!

To Andrew Hutz, security specialist and wordsmith: Awesome having you on board for this project! Great writing and editing! I look forward to many more with you.

To Dudley Lehmer, CEO of Total Seminars: Thanks for keeping the ship afloat while I got to play on this book! You are awesome.

To Emily Walters, acquisitions coordinator at McGraw Hill: What a joy to share this project with you! Thanks for keeping us moving and filling in pieces. Good luck with that epic cat and…surf 's up!

To Rachel Fogelberg, project editor: So fun to work with you! (I hope I didn't add any gray hair with my chronic lateness.) Let's do another one soon.

To Janet Walden, editorial supervisor: Thanks for jumping in and donning several hats during vacations and the like. Always enjoy working with you!

To Rick Camp, proofreader: You picked up some great stuff, amigo. This was a new process for us where we got to see your edits and suggestions before we did our own proof. Wow! Thank you.

To the KGL compositors and illustrators: The layout was excellent, thanks! And thanks for pushing through at crunch time, too.

ABOUT THIS BOOK

Important Technology Skills

Information technology (IT) offers many career paths, leading to occupations in such fields as PC repair, network administration, telecommunications, Web development, graphic design, and desktop support. To become competent in any IT field, however, you need certain basic computer skills. Mike Meyers' CompTIA Network+™ Guide to Managing and Troubleshooting Networks *builds a foundation for success in the IT field by introducing you to fundamental technology concepts and giving you essential computer skills.*

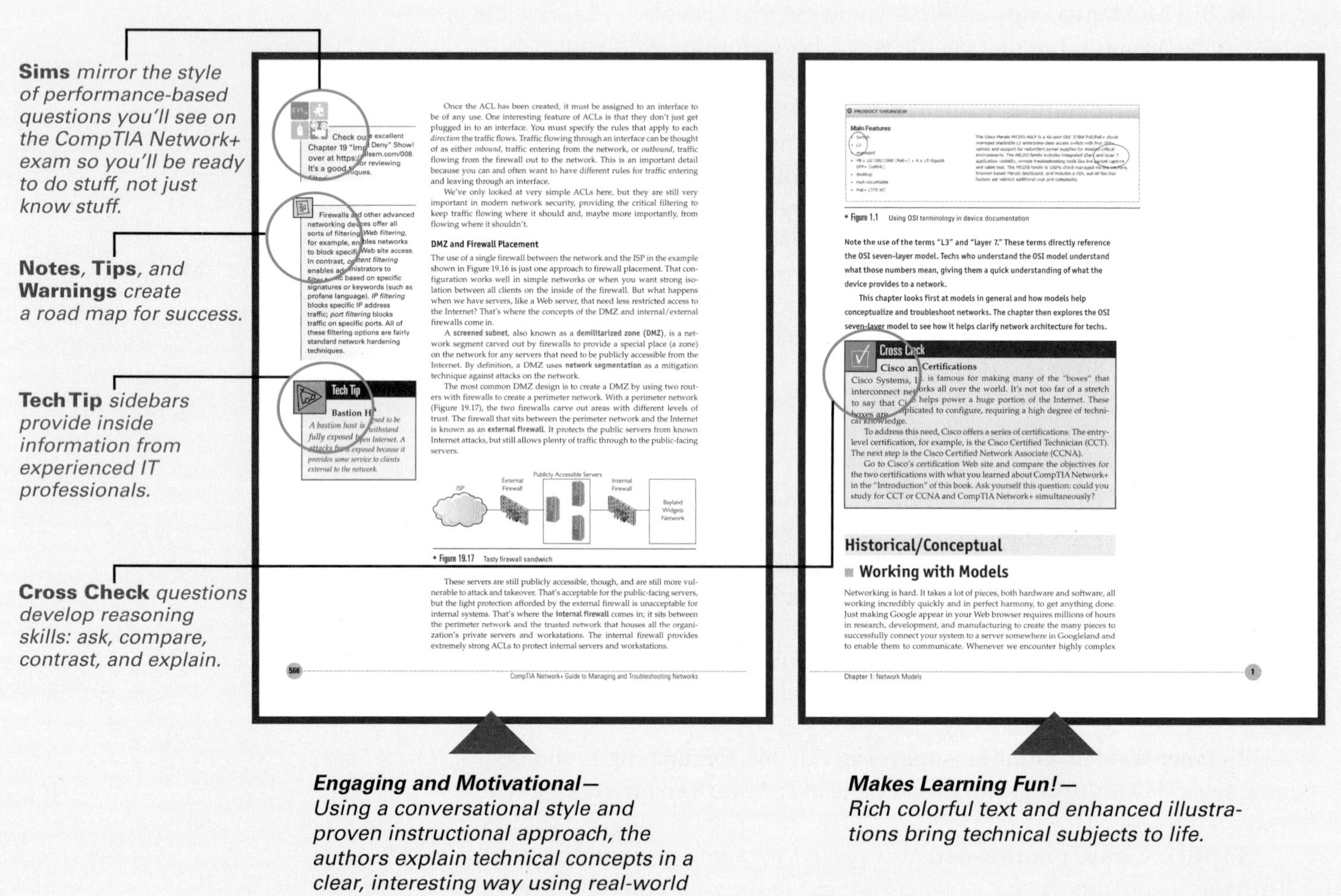

Sims *mirror the style of performance-based questions you'll see on the CompTIA Network+ exam so you'll be ready to do stuff, not just know stuff.*
Notes, **Tips**, *and* **Warnings** *create a road map for success.*
Tech Tip *sidebars provide inside information from experienced IT professionals.*
Cross Check *questions develop reasoning skills: ask, compare, contrast, and explain.*
Engaging and Motivational—
Using a conversational style and proven instructional approach, the authors explain technical concepts in a clear, interesting way using real-world examples.
Makes Learning Fun!—
Rich colorful text and enhanced illustrations bring technical subjects to life.

Proven Learning Method Keeps You on Track

Mike Meyers' CompTIA Network+ Guide to Managing and Troubleshooting Networks is structured to give you comprehensive knowledge of computer skills and technologies. The textbook's active learning methodology guides you beyond mere recall and—through thought-provoking activities, labs, and sidebars—helps you develop critical-thinking, diagnostic, and communication skills.

Effective Learning Tools

This pedagogically rich book is designed to make learning easy and enjoyable and to help you develop the skills and critical-thinking abilities that will enable you to adapt to different job situations and troubleshoot problems.

Mike Meyers' proven ability to explain concepts in a clear, direct, even humorous way makes this book interesting, motivational, and fun.

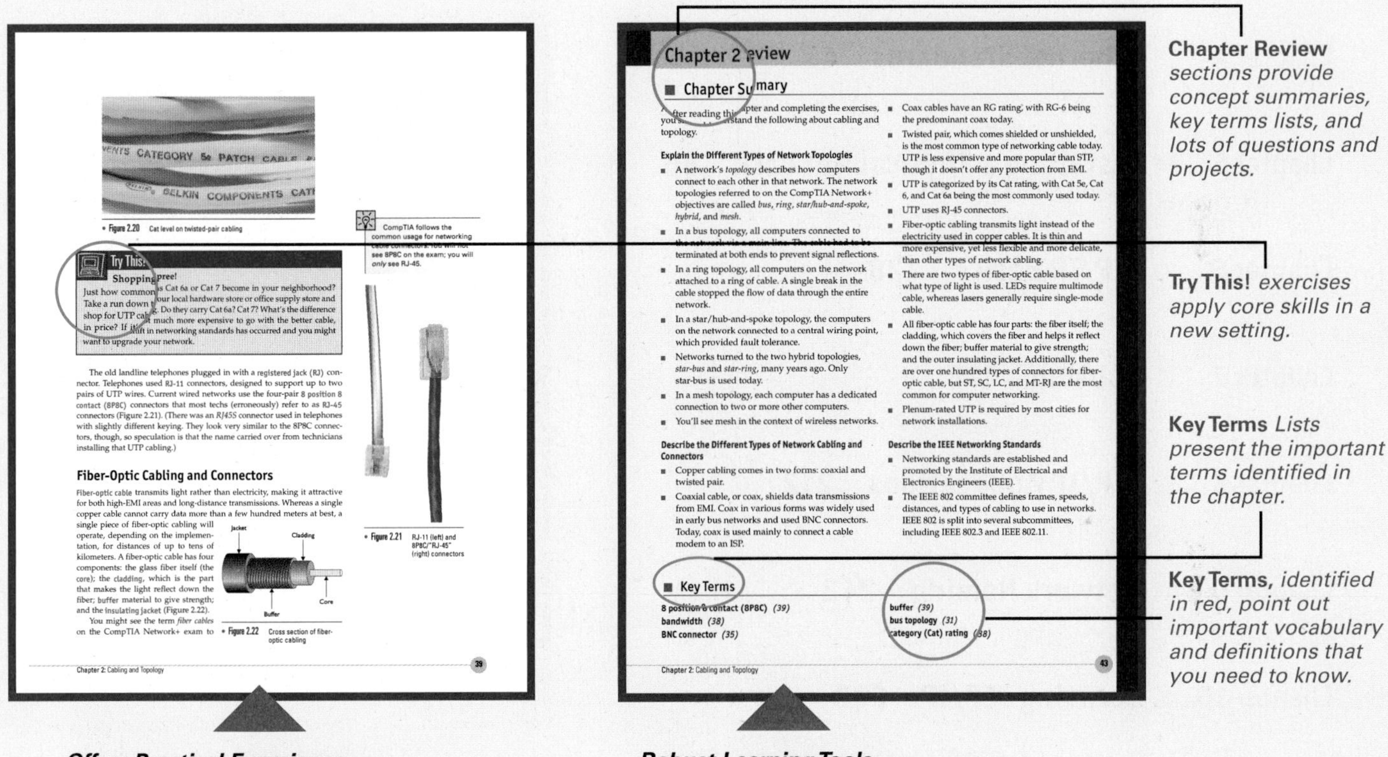

Chapter Review *sections provide concept summaries, key terms lists, and lots of questions and projects.*
Try This! *exercises apply core skills in a new setting.*
Key Terms *Lists present the important terms identified in the chapter.*
Key Terms, *identified in red, point out important vocabulary and definitions that you need to know.*

Offers Practical Experience—
Tutorials and lab assignments develop essential hands-on skills and put concepts in real-world context.

Robust Learning Tools—
Summaries, key terms lists, quizzes, essay questions, and lab projects help you practice skills and measure progress.

The chapters in this book include the following elements:

- **Learning objectives** that set measurable goals for chapter-by-chapter progress
- **Illustrations** that give you a clear picture of the concepts and technologies
- **Tutorials** that teach you to perform essential tasks and procedures hands-on
- **Try This!, Cross Check,** and **Tech Tip** sidebars that encourage you to practice and apply concepts in real-world settings
- **Notes, Tips,** and **Warnings** that guide you through difficult areas
- **Sims** links to practical simulations that prepare you for the performance-based questions on the CompTIA exams
- **Chapter Summaries** and **Key Terms Lists** that provide you with an easy way to review important concepts and vocabulary
- **Challenging End-of-Chapter Tests** that include vocabulary-building exercises, multiple-choice questions, essay questions, and on-the-job lab projects

CONTENTS AT A GLANCE

CONTENTS

Chapter 6
TCP/IP Basics 128

Chapter 7
Routing 172

Chapter 8
TCP/IP Applications 212

Chapter 9
Network Naming 242

Chapter 10
Securing TCP/IP 270

Chapter 11
Switch Features 306

Chapter 12
IPv6 332

Chapter 13
WAN Connectivity 352

Chapter 14
Wireless Networking 380

Chapter 19
Protecting Your Network 528

Chapter 20
Network Monitoring 576

Chapter 21
Network Troubleshooting 596

Appendix A
Exam Objective Map 638

Appendix B
Create Your Study Plan 655

Appendix C
About the Online Content 656

PREFACE

I was a teacher long before I was ever an author. I started writing computer books for the simple reason that no one wrote the kind of books I wanted to read. The books were either too simple (Chapter 1, "Using Your Mouse") or too complex (Chapter 1, "TTL Logic and Transistors") and none of them provided a motivation for me to learn the information. I guessed that there were geeky readers just like me who wanted to know *why* they needed to know the information in a computer book.

Good books motivate the reader to learn what he or she is reading. If a book discusses binary arithmetic but doesn't explain why I need to learn it, for example, that's not a good book. Tell me that understanding binary makes it easier to understand how an IP address works or why we're about to run out of IP addresses and how IPv6 can help, then I get excited, no matter how geeky the topic. If I don't have a good reason, a good motivation to do something, then I'm simply not going to do it (which explains why I haven't jumped out of an airplane!).

In this book, I teach you why you need to understand the wide world of networking. You'll learn everything you need to start building, configuring, and supporting networks. In the process, you'll gain the knowledge you need to pass the CompTIA Network+ certification exam.

Enjoy, my fellow geek.

Michael D. Meyers

INTRODUCTION

By picking up this book, you've shown an interest in learning about networking. But be forewarned. The term *networking* describes a vast field of study, far too large for any single certification, book, or training course to cover. Do you want to configure routers and switches for a living? Do you want to administer a large Windows network at a company? Do you want to install wide area network connections? Do you want to set up Web servers? Do you want to secure networks against attacks?

If you're considering a CompTIA Network+ certification, you probably don't yet know exactly what aspect of networking you want to pursue, and that's okay! You're going to *love* preparing for the CompTIA Network+ certification.

Attaining CompTIA Network+ certification provides you with four fantastic benefits. First, you get a superb overview of networking that helps you decide what part of the industry you'd like to pursue. Second, it acts as a prerequisite toward other, more advanced certifications. Third, the amount of eye-opening information you'll gain just makes getting CompTIA Network+ certified plain old *fun*. Finally, you'll significantly enhance your opportunity to get a job. Everything is networked today, putting network techs in demand.

Nothing comes close to providing a better overview of networking than CompTIA Network+. The certification covers local area networks (LANs), wide area networks (WANs), the Internet (the world's largest WAN), security, cabling, and applications in a wide-but-not-too-deep fashion that showcases the many different parts of a network and hopefully tempts you to investigate the aspects that intrigue you by looking into follow-up certifications.

The process of attaining CompTIA Network+ certification will give you a solid foundation in the whole field of networking. Mastering the competencies will help fill in gaps in your knowledge and provide an ongoing series of "a-ha!" moments of grasping the big picture that make being a tech so much fun.

Ready to learn a lot, grab a great certification, and have fun doing it? Then welcome to CompTIA Network+ certification!

Who Needs CompTIA Network+? I Just Want to Learn about Networks!

Whoa there, amigo! Are you one of those folks who either has never heard of the CompTIA Network+ exam or just doesn't have any real interest in certification? Is your goal only to get a solid handle on networks and a jump start on the basics? Are you looking for that "magic bullet" book that you can read from beginning to end and then start installing and troubleshooting a network? Do you want to know what's involved with running network cabling in your walls or getting your new wireless network working? Are you tired of not knowing enough about TCP/IP and how it works? If these types of questions are running through your mind, then rest easy—you have the right book. Like every book with the Mike Meyers name, you'll get solid concepts without pedantic details or broad, meaningless overviews. You'll look at real-world networking as performed by real techs. This is a book that understands your needs and goes well beyond the scope of a single certification.

If the CompTIA Network+ exam isn't for you, you can skip the rest of this introduction, shift your brain into learn mode, and dive into Chapter 1. But then, if you're going to have the knowledge, why *not* get the certification?

What Is CompTIA Network+ Certification?

CompTIA Network+ certification is an industry-wide, vendor-neutral certification program developed and sponsored by the Computing Technology Industry Association (CompTIA). The CompTIA Network+ certification shows that you have a basic competency in the physical support of networking systems and knowledge of the conceptual aspects of networking. To date, many hundreds of thousands of technicians have become CompTIA Network+ certified.

CompTIA Network+ certification enjoys wide recognition throughout the IT industry. It is considered the obvious next step after CompTIA A+ certification. (CompTIA A+ is the certification for PC technicians.)

What Is CompTIA?

CompTIA is a nonprofit, industry trade association based in Oakbrook Terrace, Illinois, on the outskirts of Chicago. Tens of thousands of computer resellers, value-added resellers, distributors, manufacturers, and training companies from all over the world are members of CompTIA.

CompTIA was founded in 1982. The following year, CompTIA began offering the CompTIA A+ certification exam. CompTIA A+ certification is now widely recognized as the *de facto* requirement for entrance into the PC industry. Because the CompTIA A+ exam initially covered networking only lightly, CompTIA decided to establish a vendor-neutral test covering basic networking skills. So, in April 1999, CompTIA unveiled the CompTIA Network+ certification exam.

CompTIA provides certifications for a variety of areas in the computer industry, offers opportunities for its members to interact, and represents its members' interests to government bodies. CompTIA certifications include CompTIA A+, CompTIA Network+, and CompTIA Security+, to name a few. Check out the CompTIA Web site at www.comptia.org for details on other certifications.

CompTIA is *huge*. Virtually every company of consequence in the IT industry is a member of CompTIA: Microsoft, Dell, Cisco… Name an IT company and it's probably a member of CompTIA.

The Current CompTIA Network+ Certification Exam Release

CompTIA constantly works to provide exams that cover the latest technologies and, as part of that effort, periodically updates its certification objectives, domains, and exam questions. This book covers all you need to know to pass the N10-008 CompTIA Network+ exam released in 2021.

How Do I Become CompTIA Network+ Certified?

To become CompTIA Network+ certified, you simply pass one computer-based exam. There are no prerequisites for taking the CompTIA Network+ exam, and no networking experience is needed. You're not required to take a training course or buy any training materials. The only requirements are that you pay a testing fee to an authorized testing facility and then sit for the exam. Upon completion of the exam, you will immediately know whether you passed or failed.

Once you pass, you become CompTIA Network+ certified for three years. After three years, you'll need to renew your certification by taking the current exam or completing approved Continuing Education activities. By completing these activities, you earn credits that (along with an annual fee) allow you to keep your CompTIA Network+ certification. For a full list of approved activities, check out CompTIA's Web site (www.comptia.org) and search for **CompTIA Continuing Education Program**.

> The American National Standards Institute (ANSI) has accredited the CompTIA Network+ certification as compliant with the ISO/IEC 17024 standard. That makes it special.

Now for the details: CompTIA recommends that you have at least nine to twelve months of networking experience and CompTIA A+ knowledge, but this is not a requirement. Note the word "recommends." You may not need experience or CompTIA A+ knowledge, but each helps! The CompTIA A+ certification competencies have a degree of overlap with the CompTIA Network+ competencies, such as types of connectors and how networks work.

As for experience, keep in mind that CompTIA Network+ is mostly a practical exam. Those who have been out there supporting real networks will find many of the questions reminiscent of the types of problems they have seen on LANs. The bottom line is that you'll probably have a much easier time on the CompTIA Network+ exam if you have some CompTIA A+ experience under your belt.

What Is the Exam Like?

The CompTIA Network+ exam contains a maximum of 90 questions, and you have 90 minutes to complete the exam. To pass, you must score at least 720 on a scale of 100–900, at the time of this writing. Check the CompTIA Web site when you get close to testing to determine the current scale: www.comptia.org/certifications/network.

CompTIA uses two types of questions: multiple choice and performance based. *Multiple-choice questions* offer four or five answer options; you select the correct answer and proceed to the next question. The majority of the questions follow this format.

Performance-based questions require you to do something. You might need to arrange a wireless access point in an office for maximum coverage, for example, or properly align the colored wires on a network connector. You need to have appropriate command-line skills to respond at a command prompt. These are all things that good network techs should be able to do without blinking. I'll cover all the topics in the book, and you'll get practical experience as well in the various extra design elements and labs.

The exam questions are divided into five areas that CompTIA calls domains. This table lists the CompTIA Network+ domains and the percentage of the exam that each represents.

CompTIA Network+ Domain	Percentage
1.0 Networking Fundamentals	24%
2.0 Network Implementations	19%
3.0 Network Operations	16%
4.0 Network Security	19%
5.0 Network Troubleshooting	22%

The CompTIA Network+ exam is extremely practical. Questions often present real-life scenarios and ask you to determine the best solution. The CompTIA Network+ exam loves troubleshooting. Let me repeat: many of the test objectives deal with direct, *real-world troubleshooting*. Be prepared to troubleshoot both hardware and software failures and to answer both "What do you do next?" and "What is most likely the problem?" types of questions.

A qualified CompTIA Network+ certification candidate can install and configure a PC to connect to a network. This includes installing and testing a network card, configuring drivers, and loading all network software. The exam will test you on the different topologies, standards, and cabling.

Expect conceptual questions about the Open Systems Interconnection (OSI) seven-layer model. You need to know the functions and protocols for each layer to pass the CompTIA Network+ exam. You can also expect questions on most of the protocol suites, with heavy emphasis on the TCP/IP

CompTIA occasionally makes changes to the content of the exam, as well as the score necessary to pass it. Always check the Web site of my company, Total Seminars (www.totalsem.com), before scheduling your exam.

suite. If you've never heard of the OSI seven-layer model, don't worry! This book will teach you all you need to know.

How Do I Take the Test?

To take the test, you may go to an authorized testing center or take it over the Internet. Pearson VUE administers the actual CompTIA Network+ exam. You'll find thousands of Pearson VUE testing centers scattered across the United States and Canada, as well as in over 186 other countries around the world. You may take the exam at any testing center. To locate a testing center and schedule an exam, call Pearson VUE at 877-551-7587. You can also visit their Web site at https://home.pearsonvue.com. To schedule an Internet-based exam through OnVUE, go to www.onvue.com. You'll need a solid Internet connection and a webcam, such as one built into most portable computers.

How Much Does the Test Cost?

CompTIA fixes the price, no matter what testing center you use. The cost of the exam depends on whether you work for a CompTIA member. At press time, the cost for non-CompTIA members is $338 (U.S.).

If your employer is a CompTIA member, you can save money by obtaining an exam voucher. In fact, even if you don't work for a CompTIA member, you can purchase a voucher from member companies (like mine) and take advantage of significant member savings. You simply buy the voucher and then use the voucher to pay for the exam. Vouchers are delivered to you on paper and electronically via e-mail. The voucher number is the important thing. That number is your exam payment, so protect it from fellow students until you're ready to schedule your exam.

If you're in the United States or Canada, you can visit www.totalsem.com or call 800-446-6004 to purchase vouchers. As I always say, "You don't have to buy your voucher from us, but for goodness' sake, get one from somebody!" Why pay full price when you have a discount alternative?

You must pay for the exam when you schedule, whether online or by phone. If you're scheduling by phone, be prepared to hold for a while. Have your Social Security number (or the international equivalent) ready and either a credit card or a voucher number when you call or begin the online scheduling process. If you require any special accommodations, Pearson VUE will be able to assist you, although your selection of testing locations may be a bit more limited.

International prices vary; see the CompTIA Web site for international pricing. Of course, prices are subject to change without notice, so always check the CompTIA Web site for current pricing!

How to Pass the CompTIA Network+ Exam

The single most important thing to remember about the CompTIA Network+ certification exam is that CompTIA designed it to test the knowledge of a technician with as little as nine months of experience—so keep it simple! Think in terms of practical knowledge. Read this book, answer the questions at the end of each chapter, take the practice exams on the media accompanying this book, review any topics you missed, and you'll pass with flying colors.

Is it safe to assume that it's probably been a while since you've taken an exam? Consequently, has it been a while since you've had to study for an exam? If you're nodding your head yes, you'll probably want to read the next sections. They lay out a proven strategy to help you study for the CompTIA Network+ exam and pass it. Try it. It works.

Obligate Yourself

The first step you should take is to schedule the exam. Ever heard the old adage that heat and pressure make diamonds? Well, if you don't give yourself a little "heat," you might procrastinate and unnecessarily delay taking the exam. Even worse, you may end up not taking the exam at all. Do yourself a favor. Determine how much time you need to study (see the next section), and then call Pearson VUE and schedule the exam, giving yourself the time you need to study—and adding a few extra days for safety. Afterward, sit back and let your anxieties wash over you. Suddenly, turning off the smartphone and cracking open the book will become a lot easier!

Set Aside the Right Amount of Study Time

After helping thousands of techs get their CompTIA Network+ certification, we at Total Seminars have developed a pretty good feel for the amount of study time needed to pass the CompTIA Network+ exam. Table 1 will help you plan how much study time you must devote to the exam. Keep in mind that these are averages. If you're not a great student or if you're a little on the nervous side, add another 10 percent. Equally, if you're the type who can learn an entire semester of geometry in one night, reduce the numbers by 10 percent. To use this table, just circle the values that are most accurate for you and add them up to get the number of study hours.

Table 1 Determining How Much Study Time You Need

Type of Experience	Amount of Experience: None	Once or Twice	On Occasion	Quite a Bit
Installing a SOHO wireless network	4	2	1	1
Installing an advanced wireless network (802.1X, RADIUS, etc.)	2	2	1	1
Installing structured cabling	3	2	1	1
Configuring a home router	5	3	2	1
Configuring a Cisco router	4	2	1	1
Configuring a software firewall	3	2	1	1
Configuring a hardware firewall	2	2	1	1
Configuring an IPv4 client	8	4	2	1
Configuring an IPv6 client	3	3	2	1
Working with a SOHO WAN connection (DSL, cable, fiber)	2	2	1	0
Working with an advanced WAN connection (Ethernet, MPLS, SD-WAN)	3	3	2	2
Configuring a DNS server	2	2	2	1
Configuring a DHCP server	2	1	1	0
Configuring a Web application server (HTTPS, SFTP, SSH, etc.)	4	4	2	1
Configuring a VLAN	3	3	2	1
Configuring a VPN	3	3	2	1
Configuring a dynamic routing protocol (RIP, EIGRP, OSPF)	2	2	1	1

A complete neophyte may need 120 hours or more of study time. An experienced network technician already CompTIA A+ certified should only need about 24 hours.

Study habits also come into play here. A person with solid study habits (you know who you are) can reduce the number by 15 percent. People with poor study habits should increase that number by 20 percent.

The total hours of study time you need is ________________.

Study for the Test

Now that you have a feel for how long it's going to take to study for the exam, you need a strategy for studying. The following has proven to be an excellent game plan for cramming the knowledge from the study materials into your head.

This strategy has two alternate paths. The first path is designed for highly experienced technicians who have a strong knowledge of PCs and networking and want to concentrate on just what's on the exam. Let's call this group the Fast Track group. The second path, and the one I'd strongly recommend, is geared toward people like me: the ones who want to know why things work, those who want to wrap their arms completely around a concept, as opposed to regurgitating answers just to pass the CompTIA Network+ exam. Let's call this group the Brainiacs.

To provide for both types of learners, I have broken down most of the chapters into two parts:

- **Historical/Conceptual** Although not on the CompTIA Network+ exam, this knowledge will help you understand more clearly what is on the CompTIA Network+ exam.
- **Test Specific** These topics clearly fit under the CompTIA Network+ certification domains.

The beginning of each of these areas is clearly marked with a large banner that looks like the following.

Historical/Conceptual

If you consider yourself a Fast Tracker, skip everything but the Test Specific sections in each chapter. After reading the Test Specific sections, jump immediately to the Chapter Review questions, which concentrate on information in the Test Specific sections. If you run into problems, review the Historical/Conceptual sections in that chapter. After going through every chapter as described, take the free practice exams on the media that accompanies the book. First, take them in Practice Mode, and then switch to Exam Mode. Once you start scoring in the 80–85 percent range, go take the test!

Brainiacs should first read the book—the whole book. Read it as though you're reading a novel, starting on Page 1 and going all the way through. Don't skip around on the first read-through, even if you are a highly experienced tech. Because there are terms and concepts that build on each other, skipping around might confuse you, and you'll just end up closing the book and firing up your favorite PC game. Your goal on this first read is to understand concepts—to understand the whys, not just the hows.

Having a network available while you read through the book helps a lot. This gives you a chance to see various concepts, hardware, and configuration screens in action as you read about them in the book. Plus, you'll need some gear to do all the hands-on exercises sprinkled throughout the book. Nothing beats doing it yourself to reinforce a concept or piece of knowledge!

You will notice a lot of historical information—the Historical/Conceptual sections—that you may be tempted to skip. Don't! Understanding how some of the older stuff worked or how something works conceptually will help you appreciate the reason behind current networking features and equipment, as well as how they function.

After you have completed the first read-through, cozy up for a second. This time, try to knock out one chapter per sitting. Concentrate on the Test Specific sections. Get a highlighter and mark the phrases and sentences that make major points. Look at the pictures and tables, noting how they illustrate the concepts. Then, answer the end-of-chapter questions. Repeat this process until you not only get all the questions right, but also understand *why* they are correct!

Once you have read and studied the material in the book, check your knowledge by taking the practice exams included on the media accompanying the book. The exams can be taken in Practice Mode or Exam Mode. In Practice Mode, you are allowed to check references in the book (if you want) before you answer each question, and each question is graded immediately. In Exam Mode, you must answer all the questions before you are given a test score. In each case, you can review a results summary that tells you which questions you missed, what the right answer is to each, and where to study further.

Use the results of the exams to see where you need to bone up, and then study some more and try them again. Continue retaking the exams and reviewing the topics you missed until you are consistently scoring in the 80–85 percent range. When you've reached that point, you are ready to pass the CompTIA Network+ exam!

If you have any problems or questions, or if you just want to argue about something, feel free to send an e-mail to me at scottj@totalsem.com or to the series editor, Mike Meyers, at michaelm@totalsem.com.

For additional information about the CompTIA Network+ exam, contact CompTIA directly at its Web site: www.comptia.org.

Good luck!

–Scott Jernigan

ADDITIONAL RESOURCES FOR TEACHERS

Instructors who have adopted this book for a course can access the support materials outlined here. Contact your McGraw Hill sales representative for details on how to access the materials.

Instructor Materials

A companion Web site provides resources for teachers in a format that follows the organization of the textbook. This site includes the following:

- Answer keys to the end-of-chapter activities in the textbook
- Answer keys to the activities in Mike Meyers' Lab Manual (available separately)
- Instructor's Manual that contains learning objectives, classroom preparation notes, instructor tips, and a lecture outline for each chapter
- Engaging PowerPoint slides on the lecture topics that include full-color artwork from the textbook
- Access to test bank files and software that allows you to generate a wide array of paper- or network-based tests and that feature automatic grading. The test bank includes hundreds of practice questions and a wide variety of question types and difficulty levels, enabling you to customize each test to maximize student progress.

Please contact your McGraw Hill sales representative for details.

Network Models

"Each person must live their life as a model for others."

—Rosa Parks

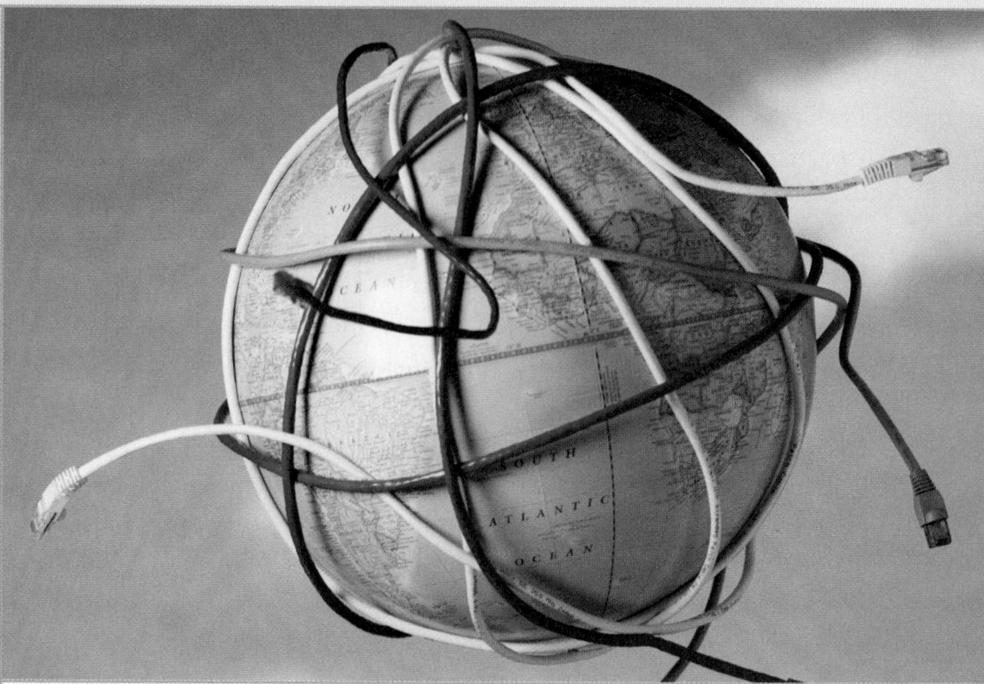

In this chapter, you will learn how to

- **Describe how the OSI seven-layer model helps technicians understand and troubleshoot networks**
- **Explain the major functions of networks with the OSI seven-layer model**

Networks enable connected hosts—computers—to share resources and access resources. The sharing host—a server—runs special software to enable the accessing host—a client—to get the desired resource. That resource can be any number of things, from a Web page on the Internet to files on a server in your office. It might even be a printer or a camera. Networking professionals need to know how all the connections happen and all the hardware and software that enables that exchange of resources.

The CompTIA Network+ certification challenges you to understand virtually every aspect of networking—not a small task. Networking professionals use models to conceptualize the many parts of a network, relying primarily on the **Open Systems Interconnection (OSI) seven-layer model**.

The OSI model provides two tools that makes it essential for networking techs. First, the OSI model provides a powerful mental tool for diagnosing problems. Understanding OSI enables a tech to determine quickly at what layer a problem can occur and helps the tech zero in on a solution without wasting a lot of time on false leads. Second, the OSI model provides a common language techs use to describe specific network functions. Figure 1.1 shows product information for a Cisco-branded advanced networking device.

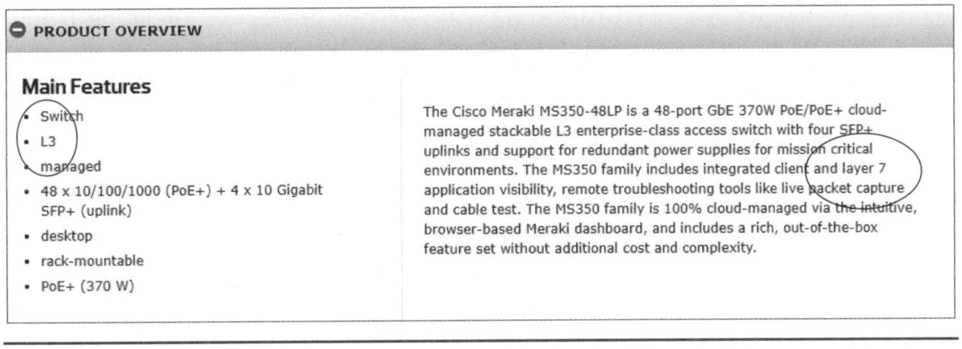

PRODUCT OVERVIEW

Main Features

- Switch
- L3
- managed
- 48 x 10/100/1000 (PoE+) + 4 x 10 Gigabit SFP+ (uplink)
- desktop
- rack-mountable
- PoE+ (370 W)

The Cisco Meraki MS350-48LP is a 48-port GbE 370W PoE/PoE+ cloud-managed stackable L3 enterprise-class access switch with four SFP+ uplinks and support for redundant power supplies for mission critical environments. The MS350 family includes integrated client and layer 7 application visibility, remote troubleshooting tools like live packet capture and cable test. The MS350 family is 100% cloud-managed via the intuitive, browser-based Meraki dashboard, and includes a rich, out-of-the-box feature set without additional cost and complexity.

• **Figure 1.1** Using OSI terminology in device documentation

Note the use of the terms "L3" and "layer 7." These terms directly reference the OSI seven-layer model. Techs who understand the OSI model understand what those numbers mean, giving them a quick understanding of what the device provides to a network.

This chapter looks first at models in general and how models help conceptualize and troubleshoot networks. The chapter then explores the OSI seven-layer model to see how it helps clarify network architecture for techs.

Cross Check

Cisco and Certifications

Cisco Systems, Inc. is famous for making many of the "boxes" that interconnect networks all over the world. It's not too far of a stretch to say that Cisco helps power a huge portion of the Internet. These boxes are complicated to configure, requiring a high degree of technical knowledge.

To address this need, Cisco offers a series of certifications. The entry-level certification, for example, is the Cisco Certified Technician (CCT). The next step is the Cisco Certified Network Associate (CCNA).

Go to Cisco's certification Web site and compare the objectives for the two certifications with what you learned about CompTIA Network+ in the "Introduction" of this book. Ask yourself this question: could you study for CCT or CCNA and CompTIA Network+ simultaneously?

Historical/Conceptual

Working with Models

Networking is hard. It takes a lot of pieces, both hardware and software, all working incredibly quickly and in perfect harmony, to get anything done. Just making Google appear in your Web browser requires millions of hours in research, development, and manufacturing to create the many pieces to successfully connect your system to a server somewhere in Googleland and to enable them to communicate. Whenever we encounter highly complex technologies, we need to simplify the overall process by breaking it into discrete, simple, individual processes. We do this using a network **model**.

Biography of a Model

What does the word "model" mean to you? Does the word make you think of a person walking down a catwalk at a fashion show in some outrageous costume or another showing off the latest style of blue jeans on a huge billboard? Maybe it makes you think of a plastic model airplane? What about those computer models that try to predict weather? We use the term "model" in a number of ways, but each use shares certain common themes.

All models are a simplified representation of the real thing. The human model ignores the many different types of body shapes, using only a single "optimal" figure. The model airplane lacks functional engines or the internal framework, and the computerized weather model might disregard subtle differences in wind temperatures or geology (Figure 1.2).

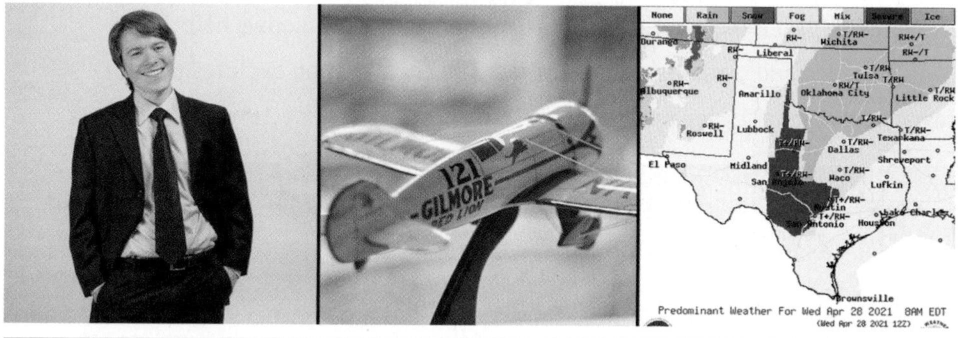

• **Figure 1.2** Types of models

• **Figure 1.3** Simple model airplane

Additionally, a model must have at least all the major functions of the real item, but what constitutes a major rather than a minor function is open to opinion. Figure 1.3 shows a different level of detail for a model. Does it contain all the major components of an airplane? There's room for argument that perhaps the model should have landing gear to go along with the propeller, wings, and tail.

Network Models

Network models face similar challenges. What functions define all networks? What details can you omit without rendering the model inaccurate? Does the model retain its usefulness when describing a network that does not employ all the layers?

In the early days of networking, different manufacturers made unique types of networks that functioned well. Part of the reason the networks worked was that every network manufacturer made everything. Back then, a single manufacturer provided everything for a customer when the customer purchased a network solution: all the hardware and all the software in one complete and expensive package. Although these networks worked fine as stand-alone networks, the proprietary nature of the hardware and software made it difficult—to put it mildly—to connect networks of multiple manufacturers. To interconnect networks and therefore improve the networking industry, someone needed to create a guide, a model, that described the functions of a network. Using this model, the people who made hardware and software could work together to make networks that worked together well.

The best way to learn the OSI model is to see it in action. For this reason, I'll introduce you to a small, simplified network that needs to copy a file from one computer to another. This example goes through each of the OSI layers needed to copy that file, and I explain each step and why it is necessary. The next part of the chapter explores a Web-centric enterprise version of a company so you can see how the OSI model applies to the latest networks. By the end of the chapter, you should have a definite handle on using the OSI model as a tool to conceptualize networks. You'll continue to build on this knowledge throughout the book and turn your OSI model knowledge into a powerful troubleshooting tool.

The International Organization for Standardization (ISO) created the OSI seven-layer model. ISO may look like a misspelled acronym, but it's actually a word, derived from the Greek word *isos*, which means "equal." The International Organization for Standardization sets standards that promote *equality* among network designers and manufacturers, thus ISO.

The OSI Seven-Layer Model on a Simple Network

Each layer in the OSI seven-layer model defines an important function in computer networking, and the protocols that operate at that layer offer solutions to those functions. **Protocols** are sets of clearly defined rules, regulations, standards, and procedures that enable hardware and software developers to make devices and applications that function properly at a particular layer. The OSI seven-layer model encourages modular design in networking, meaning that each layer has as little to do with the operation of other layers as possible. Think of it as an automobile assembly line. The guy painting the car doesn't care about the gal putting doors on the car—he expects the assembly line process to make sure the cars he paints have doors. Each layer on the model trusts that the other layers on the model do their jobs.

Be sure to memorize both the name and the number of each OSI layer. Network techs use OSI terms such as "Layer 4" and "Transport layer" synonymously. Students have long used mnemonics for memorizing such lists. One of my favorites for the OSI seven-layer model is "Please Do Not Throw Sausage Pizza Away." Yum! Another great mnemonic that helps students to memorize the layers from the top down is "All People Seem To Need Data Processing." Go with what works for you.

The OSI seven layers are

- **Layer 7** Application
- **Layer 6** Presentation
- **Layer 5** Session
- **Layer 4** Transport
- **Layer 3** Network
- **Layer 2** Data Link
- **Layer 1** Physical

The OSI seven layers are not laws of physics—anybody who wants to design a network can do it any way he or she wants. Although many protocols fit neatly into one of the seven layers, others do not.

Now that you know the names of the layers, let's see what each layer does. The best way to understand the OSI layers is to see them in action. Let's see them at work at the fictional company of MHTechEd, Inc.

This section is a conceptual overview of the hardware and software functions of a network. Your network may have different hardware or software, but it will share the same functions.

Welcome to MHTechEd!

Mike's High-Tech Educational Supply Store and Post Office, or MHTechEd for short, has a small network of PCs running Windows, a situation typical of many small businesses today. Windows comes with all the network software it needs to connect to a network. All the computers in the MHTechEd network are connected by special network cabling.

As in most offices, everyone at MHTechEd has his or her own PC. Figure 1.4 shows two workers, Shannon and Scott, who handle all the administrative functions at MHTechEd. Because of the kinds of work they do, these two often need to exchange data between their two PCs. At the moment, Shannon has just completed a new employee handbook in Microsoft Word, and she wants Scott to check it for accuracy. Shannon could transfer a copy of the file to Scott's computer by the tried-and-true Sneakernet method—saving the file on a flash drive and walking it over to him—but thanks to the wonders of computer networking, she doesn't even have to get up from her chair. Let's watch in detail each piece of the process that gives Scott direct access to Shannon's computer, so he can copy the Word document from Shannon's system to his own.

• **Figure 1.4** Shannon and Scott, hard at work

Long before Shannon ever saved the Word document on her system—when the systems were first installed—someone who knew what they were doing set up and configured all the systems at MHTechEd to be part of a common network. All this setup activity resulted in multiple layers of hardware and software that can work together behind the scenes to get that Word document from Shannon's system to Scott's. Let's examine the different pieces of the network.

• **Figure 1.5** UTP cabling

Test Specific

Let's Get Physical—Network Hardware and Layers 1–2

Clearly the network needs a physical channel through which it can move bits of data between systems. Most networks use a cable like the one shown in Figure 1.5. This cable, known in the networking industry as

unshielded twisted pair (UTP), usually contains four pairs of wires that can transmit and receive data.

Another key piece of hardware the network uses is a special box-like device that handles the flow of data from each computer to every other computer (Figure 1.6). This box is often tucked away in a closet or an equipment room. (The technology of the central box has changed over time. For now, let's just call it the "central box." I'll get to variations in a bit.) Each system on the network has its own cable that runs to the central box.

• **Figure 1.6** Typical central box

Layer 1 of the OSI model defines the method of moving data between computers, so the cabling and central box are part of the **Physical layer** (Layer 1). Anything that moves data from one system to another, such as copper cabling, fiber optics, even radio waves, is part of the OSI Physical layer. Layer 1 doesn't care what data goes through; it just moves the data from one system to another system. Figure 1.7 shows the MHTechEd network in the OSI seven-layer model thus far. Note that each system has the full range of layers, so data from Shannon's computer can flow to Scott's computer. (I'll cover what a "hub" is shortly.)

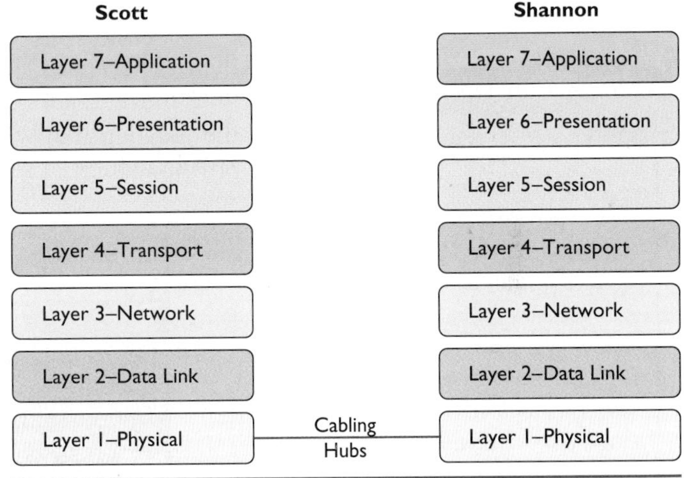

• **Figure 1.7** The network so far, with the Physical layer hardware installed

The real magic of a network starts with the **network interface card**, or **NIC** (pronounced "nick"), which serves as the interface between the PC and the network. While NICs come in a wide array of shapes and sizes, the ones at MHTechEd look like Figure 1.8.

On older systems, a NIC truly was a separate card that snapped into a handy expansion slot, which is why they were called network interface *cards*. Even though they're now built into the motherboard, they are still called NICs.

Figure 1.9 shows a typical modern laptop with a dongle providing an Ethernet port. Note the cable runs from the NIC into the wall; inside that wall is another cable running all the way back to the central box.

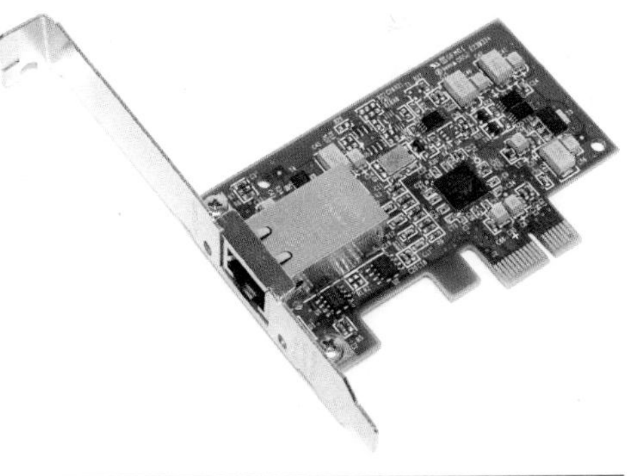

• **Figure 1.8** Typical NIC

• **Figure 1.9** Dongle NIC with cable connecting the laptop to the wall jack

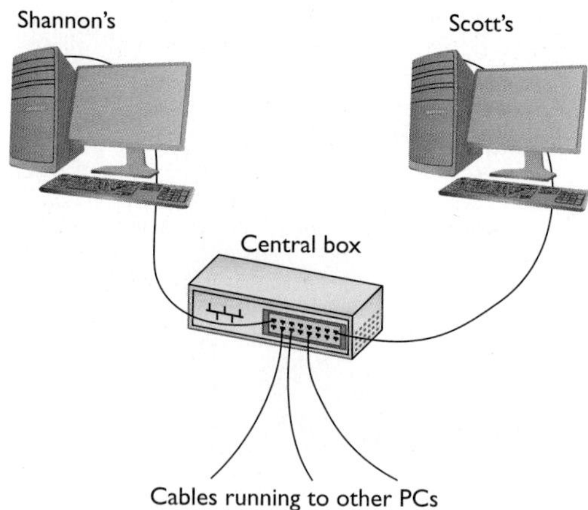

• **Figure 1.10** The MHTechEd network

Cabling and central boxes define the Physical layer of the network, and NICs provide the interface to the PC. Figure 1.10 shows a diagram of the network cabling system. I'll build on this diagram as I delve deeper into the network process.

You might be tempted to categorize the NIC as part of the Physical layer at this point, and you'd have a valid argument. The NIC clearly is necessary for the physical connection to take place. Many authors put the NIC in OSI Layer 2, the Data Link layer, though, so clearly something else is happening inside the NIC. Let's take a closer look.

Tech Tip

Hexadecimal

A hexadecimal numbering system uses base 16 to represent numbers—that would be 0–15 (in base 10 values). Contrast this with the more common decimal numbering system, numbered 0–9. Just as with decimal, people who work with hexadecimal need a single character to represent each number for the 16 values. Using 0–9 makes sense, but then hex is represented in letter form for the values 10–15 (A, B, C, D, E, F).

Hexadecimal works great with binary. Four bits provide the values of 0–15. 0001, for example, is the value 1; 1000 in binary is 8; 1111 is 15. When we work with MAC addresses, it's far easier to break each 4-bit section of the 48-bit address and translate that into hex. Humans work better that way!

Windows uses the dash as a delimiter for the MAC address. Linux and macOS use a colon.

The NIC

To understand networks, you must understand how NICs work. The network must provide a mechanism that gives each system a unique identifier—like a telephone number—so data is delivered to the right system. That's one of the NIC's most important jobs. Inside every NIC, burned onto some type of ROM chip, is special firmware containing a unique identifier with a 48-bit value called the **media access control address**, or **MAC address**.

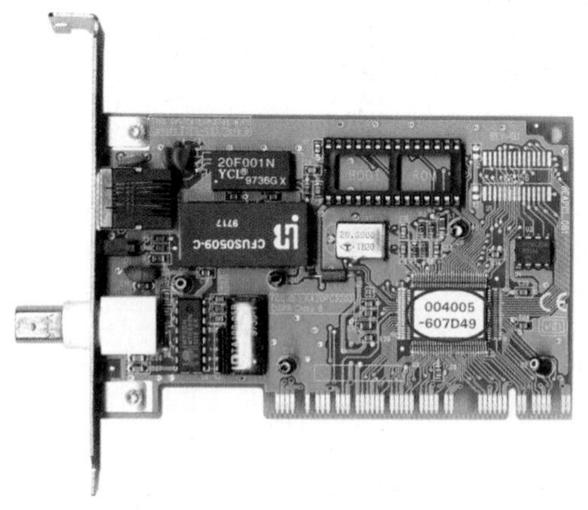

• **Figure 1.11** MAC address

No two NICs ever share the same MAC address—ever. Any company that makes NICs must contact the Institute of Electrical and Electronics Engineers (IEEE) and request a block of MAC addresses, which the company then burns into the ROMs on its NICs. Many NIC makers also print the MAC address on the surface of each NIC, as shown in Figure 1.11. Note that the NIC shown here displays the MAC address in hexadecimal notation. Count the number of hex characters—because each hex character represents 4 bits, it takes 12 hex characters to represent 48 bits. MAC addresses are always written in hex.

The MAC address in Figure 1.11 is 004005-607D49, although in print, we represent the MAC address as 00–40–05–60–7D–49. The first six digits, in this example 00–40–05, represent the number of the NIC manufacturer. Once the IEEE issues those six hex digits to a manufacturer—referred to as the **Organizationally Unique Identifier (OUI)**—no other manufacturer may use them. The last six digits, in this example 60–7D–49, are the manufacturer's unique serial number for that NIC; this portion of the MAC is often referred to as the **device ID**.

Would you like to see the MAC address for your NIC? If you have a Windows system, type **`ipconfig /all`** from a command prompt to display the MAC address (Figure 1.12). Note that `ipconfig` calls the MAC address the **physical address**, which is an important distinction, as you'll see a bit later in the chapter. For macOS, type **`ifconfig`** from a terminal;

```
C:\Users\michaels

Wireless LAN adapter Wi-Fi 2:

   Connection-specific DNS Suffix  . :
   Description . . . . . . . . . . . : Intel(R) Dual Band Wireless-AC 3168 #2
   Physical Address. . . . . . . . . : 48-A4-72-F6-A2-ED
   DHCP Enabled. . . . . . . . . . . : Yes
   Autoconfiguration Enabled . . . . : Yes
   Link-local IPv6 Address . . . . . : fe80::74a3:b54:eae3:1f5%35(Preferred)
   IPv4 Address. . . . . . . . . . . : 192.168.50.15(Preferred)
   Subnet Mask . . . . . . . . . . . : 255.255.255.0
   Lease Obtained. . . . . . . . . . : Tuesday, April 27, 2021 20:47:06
   Lease Expires . . . . . . . . . . : Wednesday, April 28, 2021 20:46:50
   Default Gateway . . . . . . . . . : 192.168.50.1
   DHCP Server . . . . . . . . . . . : 192.168.50.1
   DHCPv6 IAID . . . . . . . . . . . : 256418930
   DHCPv6 Client DUID. . . . . . . . : 00-01-00-01-23-EA-32-B0-48-A4-72-F6-A2-ED
   DNS Servers . . . . . . . . . . . : 192.168.50.1
   NetBIOS over Tcpip. . . . . . . . : Enabled
```

• **Figure 1.12** Output from `ipconfig /all`

```
scott@kali: ~
File  Actions  Edit  View  Help
scott@kali:~$ ip a
1: lo: <LOOPBACK,UP,LOWER_UP> mtu 65536 qdisc noqueue state UNKNOWN group d
efault qlen 1000
    link/loopback 00:00:00:00:00:00 brd 00:00:00:00:00:00
    inet 127.0.0.1/8 scope host lo
       valid_lft forever preferred_lft forever
    inet6 ::1/128 scope host
       valid_lft forever preferred_lft forever
2: eth0: <BROADCAST,MULTICAST,UP,LOWER_UP> mtu 1500 qdisc mq state UP group
 default qlen 1000
    link/ether 00:15:5d:38:01:01 brd ff:ff:ff:ff:ff:ff
    inet 192.168.1.2/24 brd 192.168.1.255 scope global noprefixroute eth0
       valid_lft forever preferred_lft forever
    inet6 fe80::215:5dff:fe38:101/64 scope link noprefixroute
       valid_lft forever preferred_lft forever
scott@kali:~$
```

• **Figure 1.13** Output from `ip a` in Kali Linux

for Linux, type **`ip a`** from a terminal to get similar results. Figure 1.13 shows a Kali Linux terminal; the link/ether line shows the MAC address.

Okay, so every NIC in the world has a unique MAC address, but how is it used? Ah, that's where the fun begins! Recall that computer data is binary, which means it's made up of streams of ones and zeroes. NICs send and receive this binary data as pulses of electricity, light, or radio waves. Let's consider the NICs that use electricity to send and receive data. The specific process by which a NIC uses electricity to send and receive data is

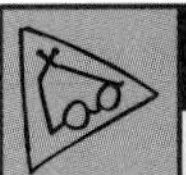

Tech Tip

MAC-48 and EUI-48

The IEEE forms MAC addresses from a numbering name space originally called **MAC-48**, *which simply means that the MAC address is 48 bits, with the first 24 bits defining the OUI, just as described here. The current term for this numbering name space is* **EUI-48**. *EUI stands for* Extended Unique Identifier. *(IEEE apparently went with the latter term because they could trademark it.)*

Most techs just call them MAC addresses, as you should, but you might see MAC-48 or EUI-48 on the CompTIA Network+ exam.

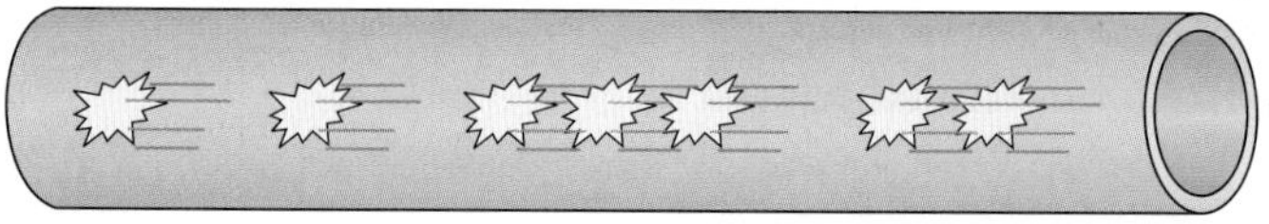

• **Figure 1.14** Data moving along a wire

exceedingly complicated but, luckily for you, not necessary to understand. Instead, just think of a *charge* on the wire as a *one* and *no charge* as a *zero*. A chunk of data moving in pulses across a wire might look something like Figure 1.14.

Try This!

What's Your MAC Address?

You can readily determine your MAC address on a desktop computer.

1. On macOS systems, open a terminal, type **`ifconfig`**, and press the ENTER key.
2. On Linux systems, open a terminal, type **`ip a`**, and press the ENTER key.
3. In Windows, type **`cmd`** at the Start screen and press ENTER when the Command Prompt option appears on the right. At the command prompt, type the command **`ipconfig /all`** and press the ENTER key.

The unit of data specified by a protocol at each layer of the OSI seven-layer model is called a **protocol data unit (PDU)**. A frame is the PDU for Layer 2.

Different frame types are used in different networks. All NICs on the same network must use the same frame type, or they will not be able to communicate with other NICs.

If you put an oscilloscope on the wire to measure voltage, you'd see something like Figure 1.15. An oscilloscope is a powerful tool that enables you to see electrical pulses.

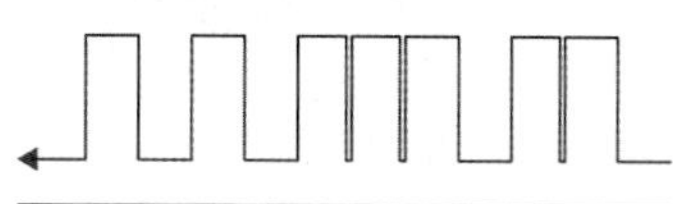

• **Figure 1.15** Oscilloscope of data

Now, remembering that the pulses represent binary data, visualize instead a string of ones and zeroes moving across the wire (Figure 1.16).

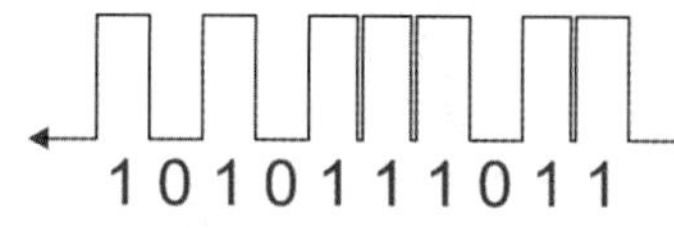

• **Figure 1.16** Data as ones and zeroes

Once you understand how data moves along the wire, the next question is, how does the network get the right data to the right system? All networks transmit data by breaking whatever is moving across the Physical layer (such as files, print jobs, Web pages, and so forth) into discrete chunks called frames. A **frame** is basically a container for a chunk of data moving across a network. A frame *encapsulates*—puts a wrapper around—information and data for easier transmission. (More on this later in the chapter.) The NIC creates and sends, as well as receives and reads, these frames.

I like to visualize an imaginary table inside every NIC that acts as a frame creation and reading station. I see frames as those pneumatic canisters you see when you go to a drive-in teller at a bank. A little guy inside the network card—named Nick, of course—builds these pneumatic canisters (the frames) on the table and then shoots them out on the wire to the central box (Figure 1.17).

• **Figure 1.17** Inside the NIC

Recipient's MAC address	Sender's MAC address	Type	Data	FCS

• **Figure 1.18** Generic frame

Here's where the MAC address becomes important. Figure 1.18 shows a representation of a generic frame, a simplified version of the wired network technology for home/office use, called *Ethernet*. (Chapter 3 covers Ethernet in great detail. For now just go with the frame described here as a generic wired thing.)

Even though a frame is a string of ones and zeroes, we often draw frames as a series of rectangles, each rectangle representing a part of the string of ones and zeroes. You will see this type of frame representation used quite often, so you should become comfortable with it (even though I still prefer to see frames as pneumatic canisters).

Note that the frame begins with the MAC address of the NIC to which the data is to be sent, followed by the MAC address of the sending NIC. Next comes the *Type* field, which indicates what's encapsulated in the frame. Then comes the *Data* field that contains what's encapsulated, followed by a special piece of checking information called the **frame check sequence (FCS)**. The FCS uses a type of binary math called a **cyclic redundancy check (CRC)** that the receiving NIC uses to verify that the data arrived intact.

You can think of a frame in a different way as having three sections. The **header** (MAC addresses and Type) starts, followed by the **payload** (whatever is encapsulated in the frame); this is followed by the **trailer** (the FCS).

So, what's inside the data part of the frame? The NIC neither knows nor cares. The data may be a part of a file, a piece of a print job, or part of a Web page. NICs aren't concerned with content! The NIC simply takes whatever data is passed to it via its device driver and addresses it for the correct system. Special software will take care of *what* data gets sent and what happens to that data when it arrives. This is the beauty of imagining frames as little pneumatic canisters (Figure 1.19). A canister can carry anything from dirt to diamonds—the NIC doesn't care one bit (pardon the pun).

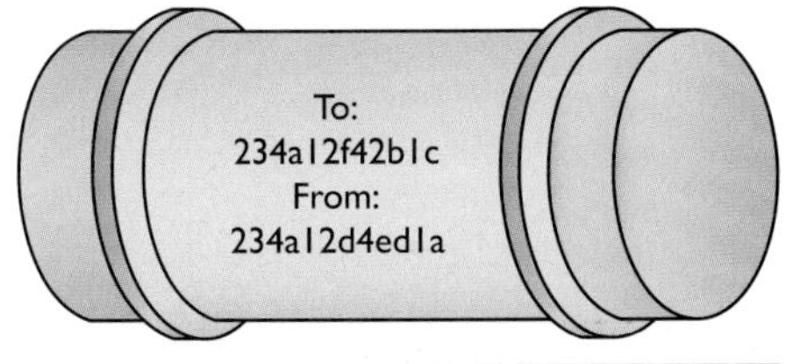

• **Figure 1.19** Frame as a canister

Like a canister, a frame can hold only a certain amount of data. Different types of networks use different sizes of frames, but the frames used in Ethernet networks hold at most 1500 bytes of data. This raises a new question: what happens when the data to be sent is larger than the frame size? Well, the sending system's software must chop the data up into nice, frame-sized chunks, which it then hands to the NIC for sending. As the receiving system begins to accept the incoming frames, the receiving system's software recombines the data chunks as they come in from the network. I'll show how this disassembling and reassembling is done in a moment—first, let's see how the frames get to the right system!

Into the Central Box

When a system sends a frame out on the network, the frame goes into the central box. What happens next depends on the technology of the central box.

In the early days of networking, the central box was called a **hub**. A hub was a dumb device, essentially just a repeater. When it received a frame, the hub made an exact copy of that frame, sending a copy of the original frame out of all connected ports except the port on which the message originated.

The interesting part of this process was when the copy of the frame came into all the other systems. I like to visualize that a frame slid onto the

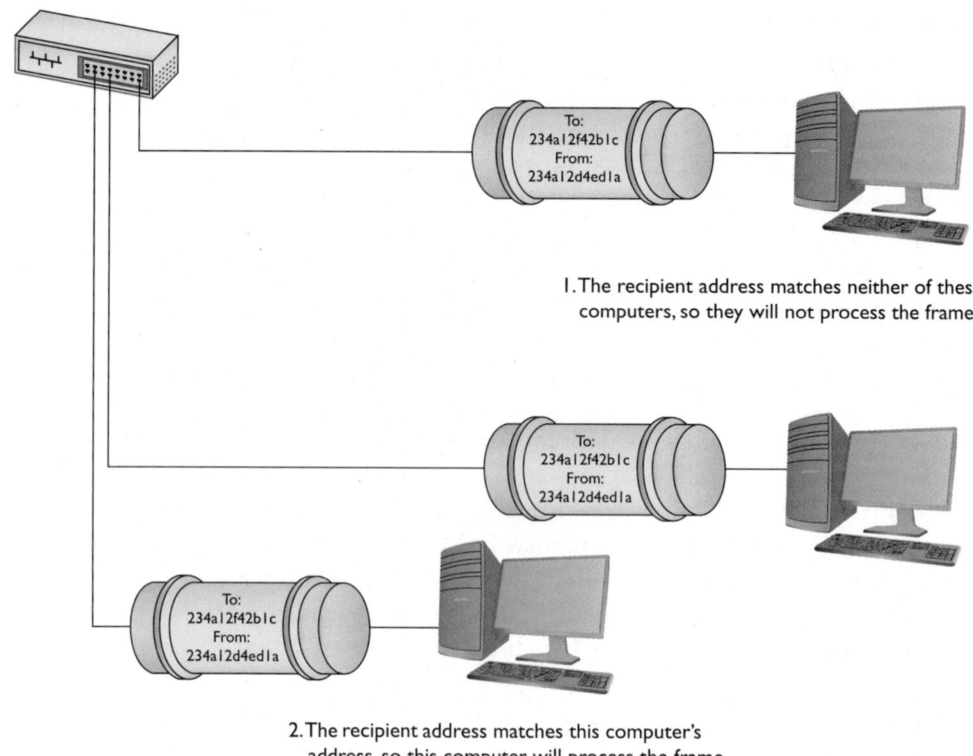
To:
234a12f42b1c
From:
234a12d4ed1a
1. The recipient address matches neither of these computers, so they will not process the frame.
To:
234a12f42b1c
From:
234a12d4ed1a
To:
234a12f42b1c
From:
234a12d4ed1a
2. The recipient address matches this computer's address, so this computer will process the frame.

• **Figure 1.20** Incoming frame!

receiving NIC's "frame assembly table," where the electronics of the NIC inspected it. (This doesn't exist; use your imagination!) Here's where the magic took place: only the NIC to which the frame was addressed would process that frame—the other NICs simply dropped it when they saw that it was not addressed to their MAC address. This is important to appreciate: with a hub, *every* frame sent on a network was received by *every* NIC, but only the NIC with the matching MAC address would process that frame (Figure 1.20).

Later networks replaced the hub with a smarter device called a **switch**. Switches, as you'll see in much more detail as we go deeper into networking, filter traffic by MAC address. Rather than sending all incoming frames to all network devices connected to it, a switch sends the frame only to the interface associated with the destination MAC address.

Tech Tip

FCS in Depth

All FCSs are only 4 bytes long, yet the wired frame carries at most 1500 bytes of data. How can 4 bytes tell you if all 1500 bytes in the data are correct? That's the magic of the math of the CRC. Without going into the grinding details, think of the CRC as just the remainder of a division problem. (Remember learning remainders from division back in elementary school?) The NIC sending the frame does a little math to make the CRC. The receiving NIC applies the same math. If the receiving NIC's answer is the same as the CRC, it knows the data is good; if it's not good, the frame is dropped.

Getting the Data on the Line

The process of getting data onto the wire and then picking that data off the wire is amazingly complicated. For instance, what would happen to keep two NICs from speaking at the same time? Because all the data sent by one NIC is read by every other NIC on the network, only one system could speak at a time in early wired networks. Networks use frames to restrict the amount of data a NIC can send at once, giving all NICs a chance to send data over the network in a reasonable span of time. Dealing with this and many other issues requires sophisticated electronics, but the NICs handle these issues completely on their own without our help. Thankfully, the folks who design NICs worry about all these details, so we don't have to!

Getting to Know You

Using the MAC address is a great way to move data around, but this process raises an important question. How does a sending NIC know the MAC address of the NIC to which it's sending the data? In most cases, the sending system already knows the destination MAC address because the NICs had probably communicated earlier, and each system stores that data. If it doesn't already know the MAC address, a NIC may send a **broadcast** onto the network to ask for it. The MAC address of FF-FF-FF-FF-FF-FF is the Layer 2 **broadcast address**—if a NIC sends a frame using the broadcast address, every single NIC on the network will process that frame. That broadcast frame's data will contain a request for a system's MAC address. Without knowing the MAC address to begin with, the requesting computer will use an IP address to pick the target computer out of the crowd. The system with the MAC address your system is seeking will read the request in the broadcast frame and respond with its MAC address. (See "IP—Playing on Layer 3, the Network Layer" later in this chapter for more on IP addresses and packets.)

The Complete Frame Movement

Now that you've seen all the pieces used to send and receive frames, let's put these pieces together and see how a frame gets from one system to another. The basic send/receive process is as follows.

First, the sending system's operating system hands some data to its NIC. The NIC builds a frame to transport that data to the receiving NIC (Figure 1.21).

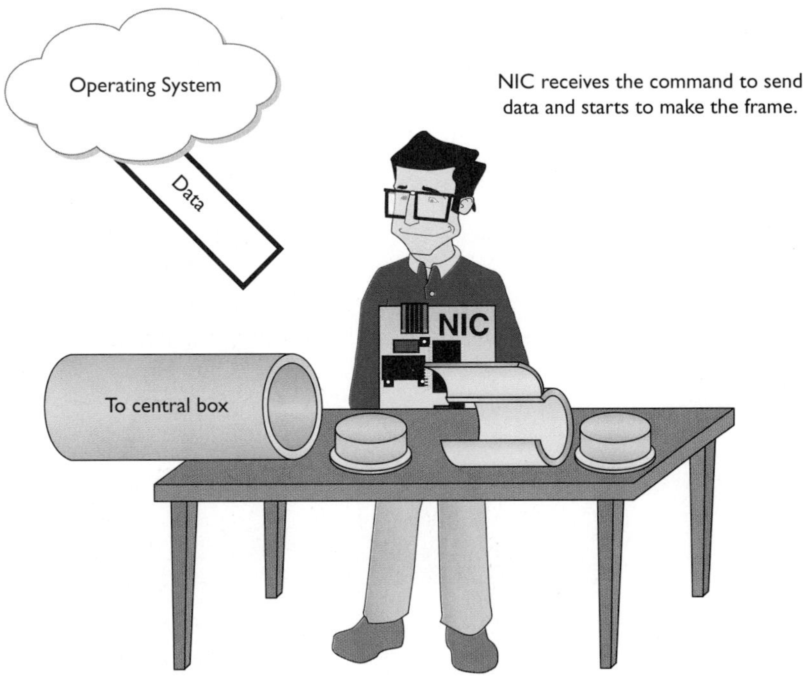

• **Figure 1.21** Building the frame

Any frame addressed specifically to another device's MAC address is called a *unicast frame*. The one-to-one addressing scheme is called *unicast addressing*; you'll see it in other layers as well as Layer 2.

• **Figure 1.22** Adding the data and FCS to the frame

• **Figure 1.23** Sending the frame

After the NIC creates the frame, it adds the FCS, and then dumps it and the data into the frame (Figure 1.22).

Next, the NIC puts both the destination MAC address and its own MAC address onto the frame. It then sends the frame through the cable to the network (Figure 1.23).

The frame propagates down the wire into the central box. The switch sends unicast frames to the destination address and sends broadcast frames to every system on the network. The NIC receives the frame (Figure 1.24). The NIC strips off all the framing information and sends the data to the

• **Figure 1.24** Reading an incoming frame

software—the operating system—for processing. The receiving NIC doesn't care what the software does with the data; its job stops the moment it passes on the data to the software.

Any device that deals with a MAC address is part of the OSI **Data Link layer**, or Layer 2 of the OSI model. Let's update the OSI model to include details about the Data Link layer (Figure 1.25).

Sending NICs break frames down into ones and zeroes for transmission; receiving NICs rebuild the frame on receipt. You get the idea.

The CompTIA Network+ exam tests you on the details of the OSI seven-layer model, so remember that the Data Link layer is the only layer that has sublayers.

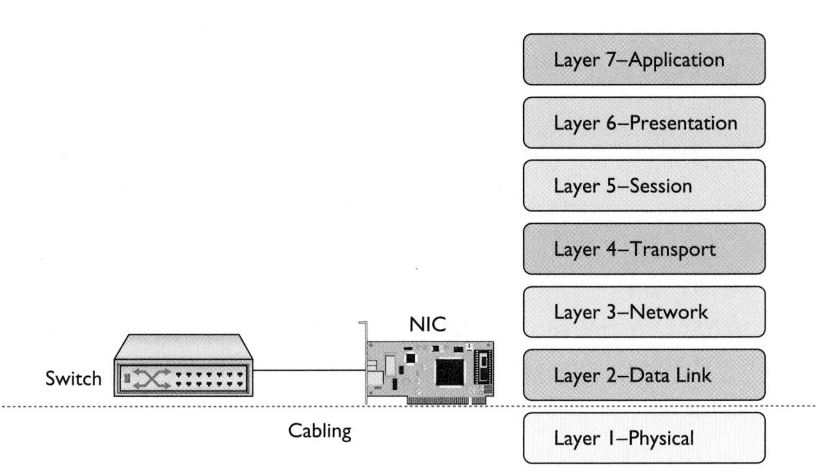

• **Figure 1.25** Layer 1 and Layer 2 are now properly applied to the network.

Note that the cabling (and hubs) are in the Physical layer. Switches handle traffic using MAC addresses, so they operate at Layer 2. That's the way modern wired networks work. The NIC is in the Data Link layer and the Physical layer.

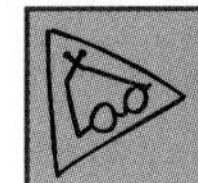

Tech Tip

NIC and Layers

Most networking materials that describe the OSI seven-layer model put NICs squarely into the Data Link layer of the model. It's at the MAC sublayer, after all, that data gets encapsulated into a frame, destination and source MAC addresses get added to that frame, and error checking occurs. What bothers most students with placing NICs solely in the Data Link layer is the obvious other duty of the NIC—putting the ones and zeroes on the network cable for wired networks and in the air for wireless networks. How much more physical can you get?

Many teachers will finesse this issue by defining the Physical layer in its logical sense—that it defines the rules for the ones and zeroes—and then ignore the fact that the data sent on the cable has to come from something. The first question when you hear a statement like that—at least to me—is, "What component does the sending?" It's the NIC, of course, the only device capable of sending and receiving the physical signal.

NICs, therefore, operate at both Layer 2 and Layer 1 of the OSI seven-layer model.

The Two Aspects of NICs

Consider how data moves in and out of a NIC. On one end, frames move into and out of the NIC's network cable connection. On the other end, data moves back and forth between the NIC and the network operating system software. The many steps a NIC performs to keep this data moving—sending and receiving frames over the wire, creating outgoing frames, reading incoming frames, and attaching MAC addresses—are classically broken down into two distinct jobs.

The first job is called the **Logical Link Control (LLC)**. The LLC is the aspect of the NIC that talks to the system's operating system (usually via device drivers). The LLC handles multiple network protocols and provides flow control.

The second job is called the **Media Access Control (MAC)**, which creates and addresses the frame. It adds the NIC's own MAC address and attaches MAC addresses to the frames. Recall that each frame the NIC creates must include both the sender's and recipient's MAC addresses. The MAC sublayer adds or checks the FCS. The MAC also ensures that the frames, now complete with their MAC addresses, are then sent along the network cabling. Figure 1.26 shows the Data Link layer in detail.

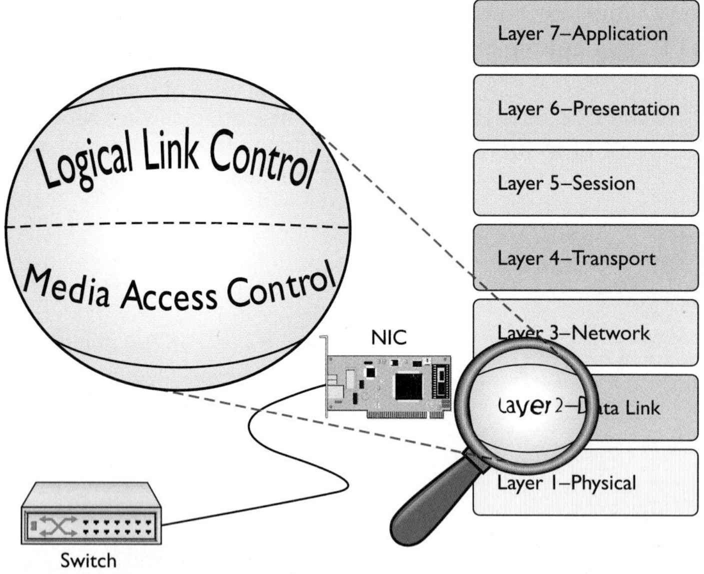

• **Figure 1.26** LLC and MAC, the two parts of the Data Link layer

Beyond the Single Wire—Network Software and Layers 3–7

Getting data from one system to another in a simple network (defined as one in which all the computers connect to one switch) takes relatively little effort on the part of the NICs. But one problem with simple networks is that computers need to broadcast to get MAC addresses. It works for small networks, but what happens when the network gets big, like the size of the entire Internet? Can you imagine millions of computers all broadcasting? No data could get through.

Equally important, data flows over the Internet using many technologies, not just Ethernet. These technologies don't know what to do with Ethernet MAC addresses. When networks get large, you can't use the MAC addresses anymore.

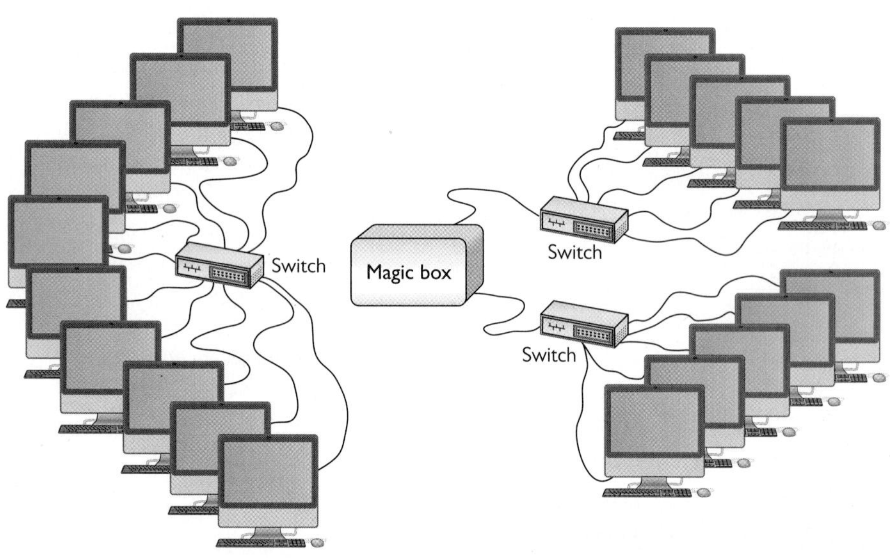

• **Figure 1.27** Large LAN complete (left) and broken up into two subnets (right)

Large networks need a **logical addressing** method, like a postal code or telephone numbering scheme, that ignores the hardware and enables you to break up the entire large network into smaller networks called **subnets**. Figure 1.27 shows two ways to set up a network. On the left, all the computers connect to a single switch. On the right, however, the LAN is separated into two five-computer subnets.

To move past the physical MAC addresses and start using logical addressing requires some special software called a **network protocol**. Network protocols exist in every operating system. A network protocol not only has to create unique identifiers for each system but also must create a set of communication rules for issues like how to handle data chopped up into multiple packets and how to ensure those packets get from one subnet to another. Let's take a moment to learn a bit about the most famous collection of network protocols—TCP/IP—and its unique universal addressing system.

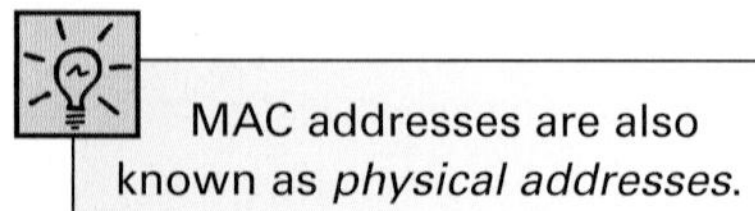

MAC addresses are also known as *physical addresses*.

To be accurate, TCP/IP is really several network protocols designed to work together—better known as a *protocol suite*—but two protocols, TCP and IP, do so much work that the folks who invented all these protocols named the whole thing TCP/IP. **TCP** stands for **Transmission Control Protocol**, and **IP** stands for **Internet Protocol**. IP is the network protocol I need to discuss first; rest assured, however, I'll cover TCP in plenty of detail later.

IP—Playing on Layer 3, the Network Layer

At the **Network layer**, Layer 3, containers called **packets** get created and addressed so they can go from one network to another. The Internet Protocol is the primary logical addressing protocol for TCP/IP. IP makes sure that a piece of data gets to where it needs to go on the network. It does this by giving each device on the network a unique numeric identifier called an **IP address**. An IP address is known as a **logical address** to distinguish it from the physical address, the MAC address of the NIC.

IP uses a rather unique dotted decimal notation based on four 8-bit numbers. Each 8-bit number ranges from 0 to 255, and the four numbers are separated by three periods. (If you don't see how 8-bit numbers can range from 0 to 255, don't worry—by the end of this book, you'll understand these numbering conventions in more detail than you ever believed possible!) A typical IP address might look like this: 192.168.4.232

No two systems on the same network share the same IP address; if two machines accidentally receive the same address, unintended side effects may occur. These IP addresses don't just magically appear—they must be configured by the network administrator.

What makes logical addressing powerful is another magic box—called a **router**—that connects each of the subnets, as previously shown in Figure 1.27. Routers use the IP address, not the MAC address, to forward data. This enables networks to connect across data lines that don't use Ethernet, like the telephone network. Each network type (such as Ethernet, SONET, and others that we'll discuss later in the book) uses a unique frame. Figure 1.28 shows a typical router.

A packet is the PDU for Layer 3.

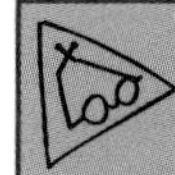

Tech Tip

The Origin of TCP/IP

TCP/IP dominates networking today, and although it might be fun to imagine that it had humble beginnings in someone's garage lab, that's not the case.

In the early 1970s, two researchers at the U.S. Defense Advanced Research Projects Agency (DARPA), Robert E. Kahn and Vinton Cerf, worked out the basic parameters of what would become TCP/IP. TCP/IP offered amazing robustness in its design and eventual implementation. Government research at its most profound and world shaping!

• **Figure 1.28** Typical small router

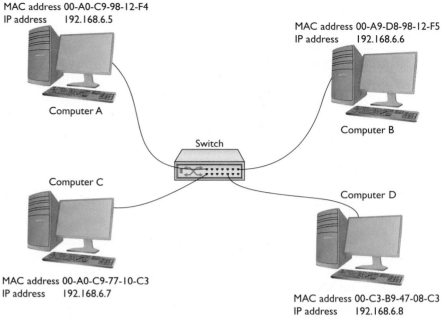

MAC address 00-A0-C9-98-12-F4
IP address 192.168.6.5

Computer A

MAC address 00-A9-D8-98-12-F5
IP address 192.168.6.6

Computer B

Switch

Computer C

MAC address 00-A0-C9-77-10-C3
IP address 192.168.6.7

Computer D

MAC address 00-C3-B9-47-08-C3
IP address 192.168.6.8

• **Figure 1.29** MHTechEd addressing

> Try to avoid using redundant expressions. Even though many techs will say "IP protocol," for example, you know that "IP" stands for "Internet Protocol." It wouldn't be right to say "Internet Protocol protocol" in English, so it doesn't work in network speak either. (Also, don't say "NIC card" for the same reason!)

> This is a highly simplified IP packet. I am not including lots of little parts of the IP packet in this diagram because they are not important to what you need to understand right now—but don't worry, you'll see them later in the book!

In a TCP/IP network, each system has two unique identifiers: the MAC address and the IP address. The MAC address (the physical address) is literally burned into the chips on the NIC, whereas the IP address (the logical address) is simply stored in the system's software. MAC addresses come with the NIC, so you don't configure MAC addresses, whereas you must configure IP addresses using software. Figure 1.29 shows the MHTechEd network diagram again, this time with the MAC and IP addresses displayed for each system.

Destination IP address	Source IP address	Data

• **Figure 1.30** IP packet

• **Figure 1.31** IP packet in a frame (as a canister)

Packets Within Frames

For a TCP/IP network to send data successfully, the data must be wrapped up in two distinct containers. A frame of some type enables the data to move from one device to another. Inside that frame are both an IP-specific container that enables routers to determine where to send data—regardless of the physical connection type—and the data itself. In TCP/IP, that inner container is the *packet*.

Figure 1.30 shows a typical IP packet; notice the similarity to the frames you saw earlier.

But IP packets don't leave their PC home without any clothes on! Each IP packet is handed to the NIC, which then encloses the IP packet in a regular frame, creating, in essence, a *packet within a frame*. I like to visualize the packet as an envelope, with the envelope in the pneumatic canister frame, as depicted in Figure 1.31. A more conventional drawing would look like Figure 1.32.

When you send data from one computer to another on a TCP/IP network such as the Internet, that data can go through many routers before it reaches its destination. Each router strips off the incoming frame, determines where to send the data according to the IP address in the packet, creates a new frame, and then sends the packet within a frame on its merry way. The new frame type will be the appropriate technology for whatever connection technology connects to the next router. That could be a cable or DSL network connection, for example (Figure 1.33). The IP packet, on the other hand, remains unchanged.

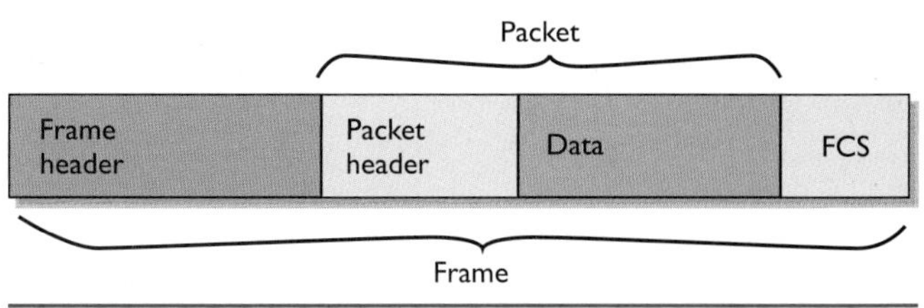

• **Figure 1.32** IP packet in a frame

Once the packet reaches the destination subnet's router, that router strips off the incoming frame—no matter what type—looks at the destination IP address, and then adds a frame with the appropriate destination MAC address that matches the destination IP address.

The receiving NIC strips away the Ethernet frame and passes the remaining packet off to the software. The networking software built into your operating system handles all the rest of the work. The NIC's driver software is the interconnection between the hardware and the software. The NIC driver knows how to communicate with the NIC to send and receive frames, but it can't do anything with the packet. Instead, the NIC driver hands the packet off to other services that know how to deal with all the separate packets and turn them into Web pages, e-mail messages, files, and so forth.

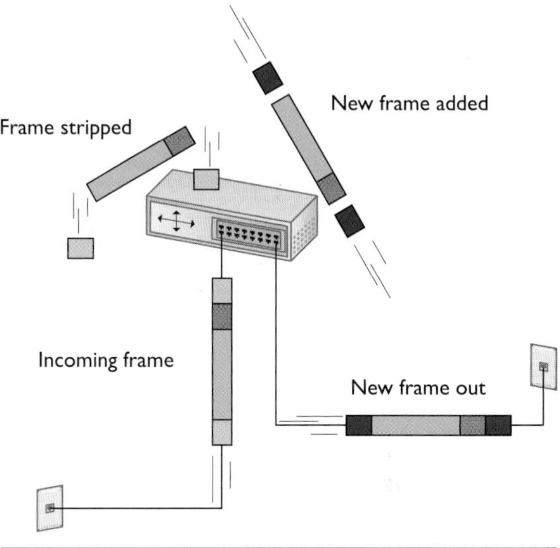

• **Figure 1.33** Router removing network frame and adding one for the outgoing connection

Segmentation and Reassembly—Layer 4, the Transport Layer

Because most chunks of data are much larger than a single packet, they must be chopped up before they can be sent across a network. When a serving computer receives a request for some data, it must be able to chop the requested data into chunks that will fit into a packet (and eventually into the NIC's frame), organize the packets for the benefit of the receiving system, and hand them to the NIC for sending. This is called **segmentation**. The receiving system does the **reassembly** of the packets. It must recognize a series of incoming packets as one data transmission, reassemble the packets correctly based on information included in the packets by the sending system, and verify that all the packets for that piece of data arrived in good shape.

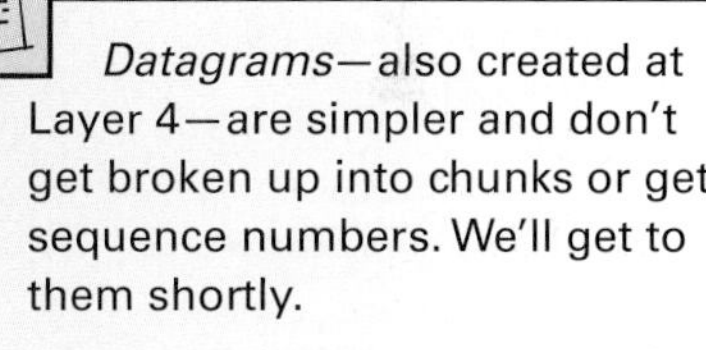

Datagrams—also created at Layer 4—are simpler and don't get broken up into chunks or get sequence numbers. We'll get to them shortly.

This part is relatively simple—the transport protocol breaks up the data into chunks called *segments* and gives each segment some type of sequence number.

I like to compare this sequencing process to the one that my favorite international shipping company uses. I receive boxes from UPS almost every day; in fact, some days I receive many, many boxes from UPS. To make sure I get all the boxes for one shipment, UPS puts a numbering system, like the one shown in Figure 1.34, on the label of each box. A computer sending data on a network does the same thing. Embedded into the data of each packet containing a segment is a sequencing number. By reading the sequencing numbers, the receiving system knows both the total number of segments and how to put them back together.

• **Figure 1.34** Labeling the boxes

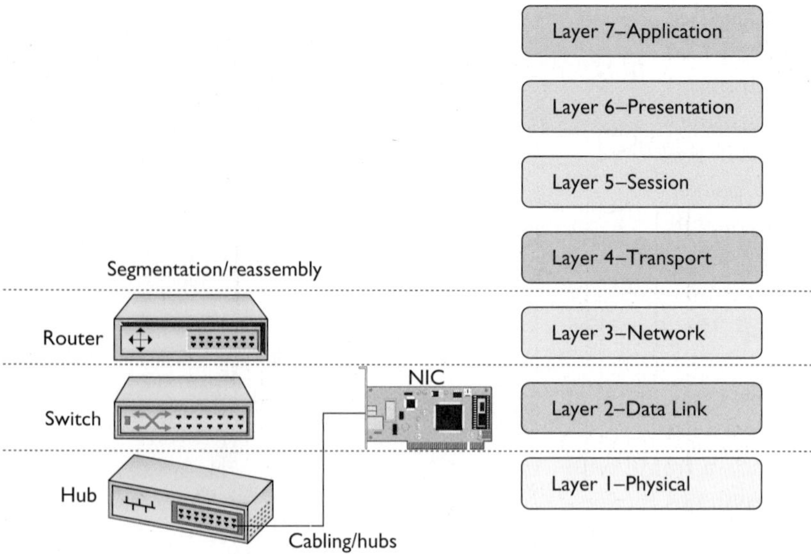

• **Figure 1.35** OSI updated

The MHTechEd network just keeps getting more and more complex, doesn't it? And the Word document still hasn't been copied, has it? Don't worry; you're almost there—just a few more pieces to go!

Layer 4, the **Transport layer** of the OSI seven-layer model, has a big job: it's the segmentation/reassembly software. As part of its job, the Transport layer also initializes requests for packets that weren't received in good order (Figure 1.35).

Connection-oriented vs. Connectionless Communication Some protocols, like the Simple Mail Transfer Protocol (SMTP) used for sending e-mail messages, require that the e-mail client and server verify that they have a connection before a message is sent (Figure 1.36). This makes sense because you don't want your e-mail message to be a corrupted mess when it arrives.

Alternatively, a number of TCP/IP protocols simply send data without first waiting to verify that the receiving system is ready (Figure 1.37). When using Voice over IP (VoIP), for example, the call is made without verifying first whether another device is there.

The connection-oriented protocol is *Transmission Control Protocol (TCP)*. The connectionless protocol is **User Datagram Protocol (UDP)**.

Everything you can do on the Internet, from Web browsing to Skype phone calls to playing World of Warcraft, is predetermined to be either connection-oriented or connectionless. It's simply a matter of knowing your applications.

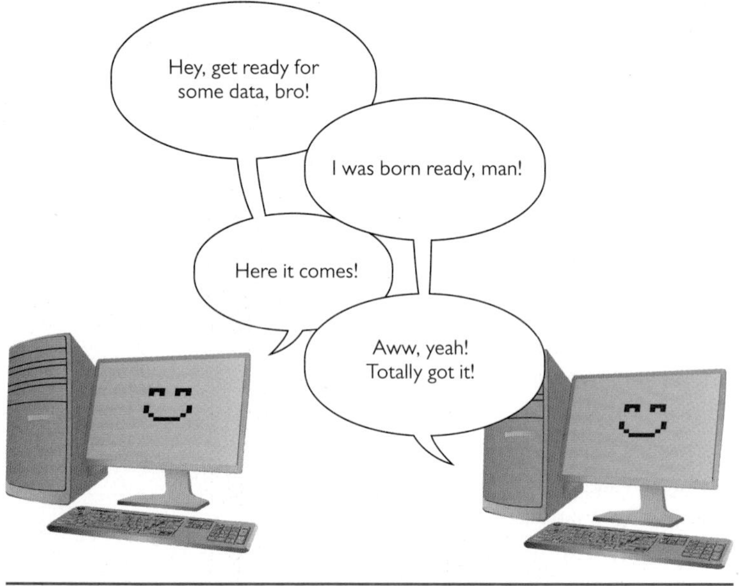

• **Figure 1.36** Connection between e-mail client and server

Chapter 6 covers TCP, UDP, and all sorts of other protocols in detail.

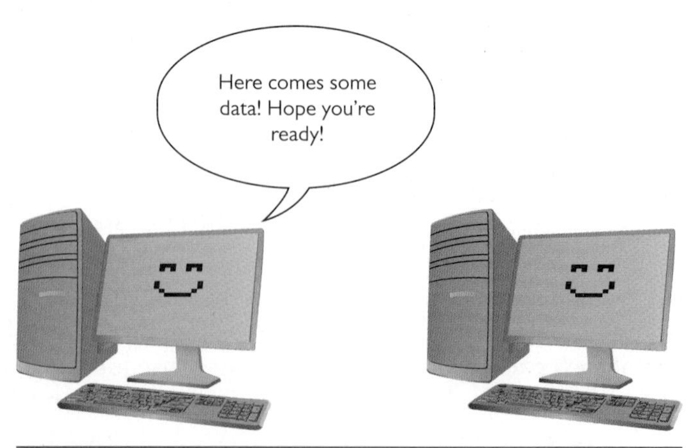

• **Figure 1.37** Connectionless communication

Source port	Destination port	Sequence number	Acknowledgment number	(and a bunch more)	Data

• **Figure 1.38** TCP segment

Segments Within Packets To see the Transport layer in action, strip away the IP addresses from an IP packet. What's left is a chunk of data in yet another container called a **TCP segment**. TCP segments have many other fields that ensure the data gets to its destination in good order. These fields have names such as Source port, Destination port, Sequence number, and Acknowledgment number. Figure 1.38 shows a typical (although simplified) TCP segment.

Chapter 6 goes into more detail on TCP segments, but let's look at source and destination ports as an example. You saw physical ports earlier in the chapter, but this use of the word "port" means something completely different. In this context, a **port**—a number between 1 and 65,536—is a logical value assigned to specific applications or services. A quick example will make this clear. Many TCP segments come into any computer. The computer needs some way to determine which TCP segments go to which applications. A Web server, for example, sees a lot of traffic, but it "listens" or looks for TCP segments with the destination port numbers 80 or 443, grabs those segments, and processes them. Equally, every TCP segment contains another port number—the source port—so the client knows what to do with returning information.

Data comes from the Application layer (with perhaps some input from Presentation and Session). The Transport layer breaks that data into chunks, adding port numbers and sequence numbers, creating the TCP segment. The Transport layer then hands the TCP segment to the Network layer, which, in turn, creates the IP packet.

Although a lot of traffic on a TCP/IP network uses TCP at the Transport layer, like Yoda said in *The Empire Strikes Back*, "There is another," and that's UDP. Following the same process, the Transport layer adds port and length numbers plus a checksum as a header and combines with data to create a container called a **UDP datagram**. A UDP datagram lacks most of the extra fields found in TCP segments, simply because UDP doesn't care if the receiving computer gets its data. Figure 1.39 shows a UDP datagram.

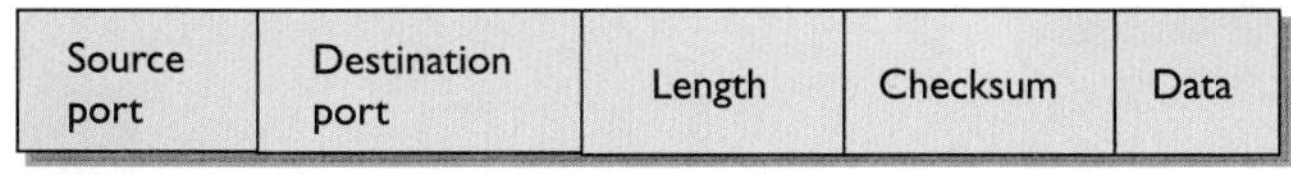

• **Figure 1.39** UDP datagram

Talking on a Network—Layer 5, the Session Layer

Now that you understand that the system uses software to segment and reassemble data packets, what's next? In a network, any one system may be talking to many other systems at any given moment. For example, Shannon's PC has a printer used by all the MHTechEd systems, so there's a

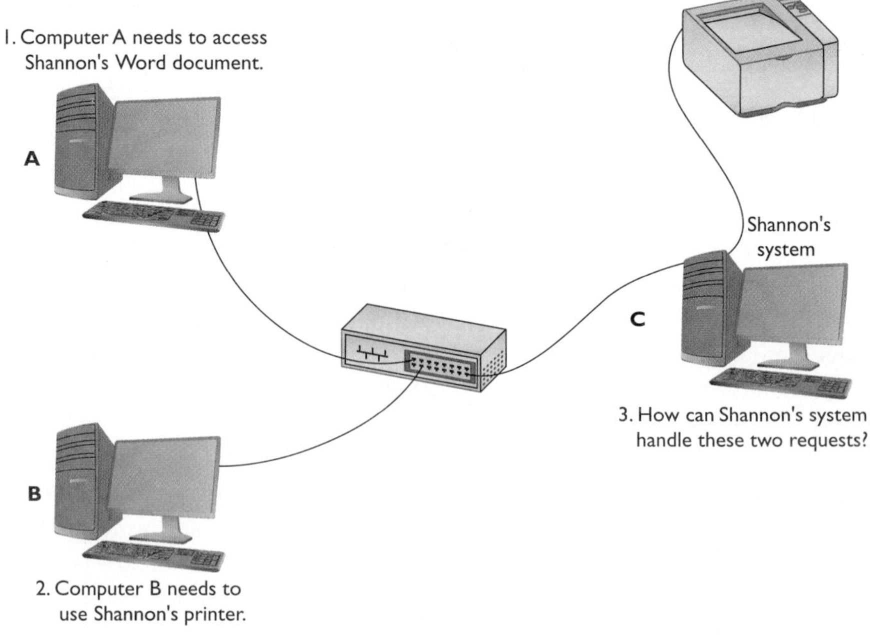
1. Computer A needs to access Shannon's Word document.
A
Shannon's system
C
3. How can Shannon's system handle these two requests?
B
2. Computer B needs to use Shannon's printer.

• **Figure 1.40** Handling multiple inputs

better than average chance that, as Scott tries to access the Word document, another system will be sending a print job to Shannon's PC (Figure 1.40).

Shannon's system must direct these incoming files, print jobs, Web pages, and so on, to the right programs (Figure 1.41). Additionally, the operating system must enable one system to make a connection to another system to verify that the other system can handle whatever operation the initiating system wants to perform. If Bill's system wants to send a print job to Shannon's printer, it first contacts Shannon's system to ensure that

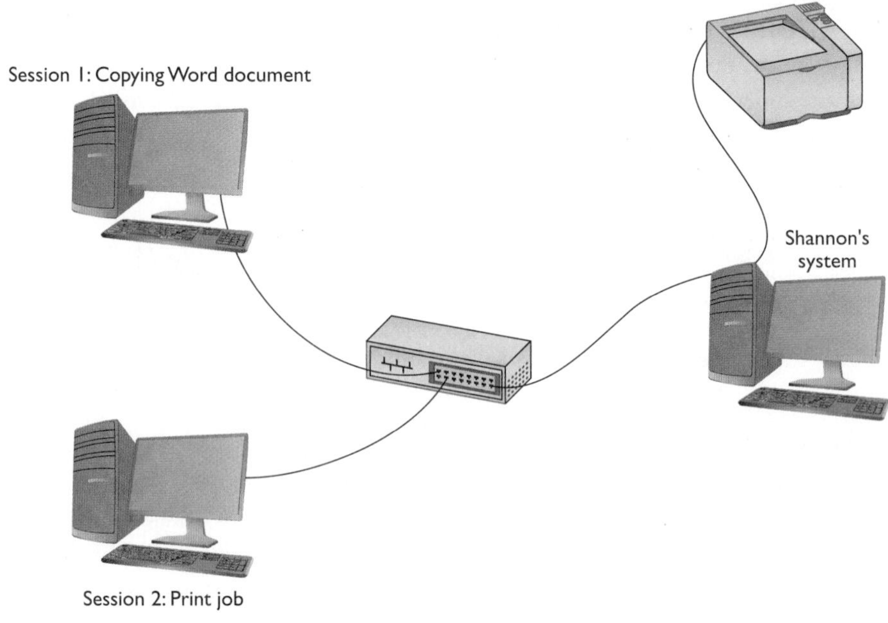
Session 1: Copying Word document
Shannon's system
Session 2: Print job

• **Figure 1.41** Each request becomes a session.

it is ready to handle the print job. The **session software** handles this part of networking, connecting applications to applications.

Try This!

See Your Sessions

How many sessions does a typical system have running at one time? Well, if you have a TCP/IP network (and who doesn't these days), you can run the netstat program from a command prompt to see all of them. Open a command prompt and type the following:

```
netstat -a
```

Then press the ENTER key to see your sessions. Don't worry about trying to interpret what you see—Chapter 8 covers netstat in detail. For now, simply appreciate that each line in the netstat output is a session. Count them! (You can also try the `ss` command in Linux to view sessions.)

Layer 5, the **Session layer** of the OSI seven-layer model, handles all the sessions for a system (Figure 1.42). The Session layer initiates sessions, accepts incoming sessions, and opens and closes existing sessions.

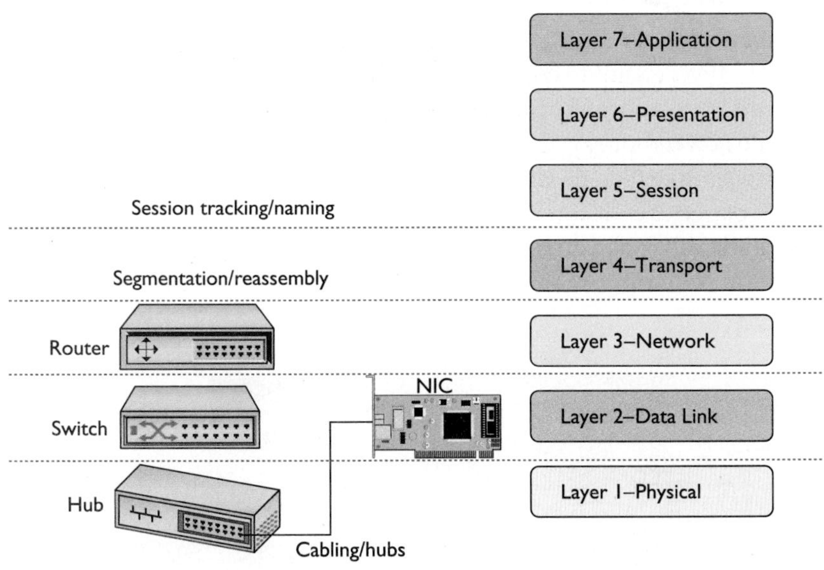

• **Figure 1.42** OSI updated

Many operating systems represent a session using the combination of the IP address and port numbers for both sides of a TCP or UDP communication. You can see a Web browser's session connecting to a Web server, for example, by running `netstat -n`. It'll return many lines like this:

```
TCP    192.168.4.34:45543         11.12.13.123:80         Established
```

The numbers describe the session. A Web client with IP address 192.168.4.34, using port number 45543, is in a TCP session with a Web server (we know it's a Web server because port 80 is dedicated to Web servers) using IP address 11.12.13.123.

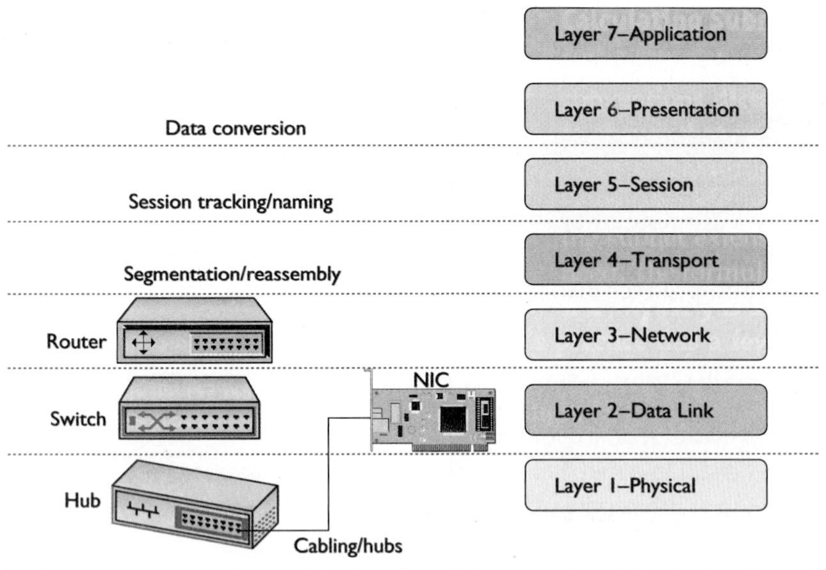

• **Figure 1.43** OSI updated

Translation—Layer 6, the Presentation Layer

The **Presentation layer** translates data from lower layers into a format usable by the Application layer, and vice versa (Figure 1.43). This manifests in several ways and isn't necessarily clear-cut. The messiness comes into play because TCP/IP networks don't necessarily map directly to the OSI model.

A number of protocols function on more than one OSI layer and can include Layer 6, Presentation. The encryption protocol used in e-commerce, Transport Layer Security (TLS), for example, seems to initiate at Layer 5 and then encrypt and decrypt at Layer 6. But even one of the authors of the protocol disputes that it should even be included in any OSI chart! It makes for some confusion.

Network Applications—Layer 7, the Application Layer

The last and most visible part of any network is the software applications that use it. If you want to copy a file residing on another system in your network, you need an applet like Network in Windows 10 that enables you to access files on remote systems. If you want to view Web pages, you need a Web browser like Google Chrome or Mozilla Firefox. The people who use a network experience it through an application. A user who knows nothing about all the other parts of a network may still know how to open an e-mail application to retrieve mail (Figure 1.44).

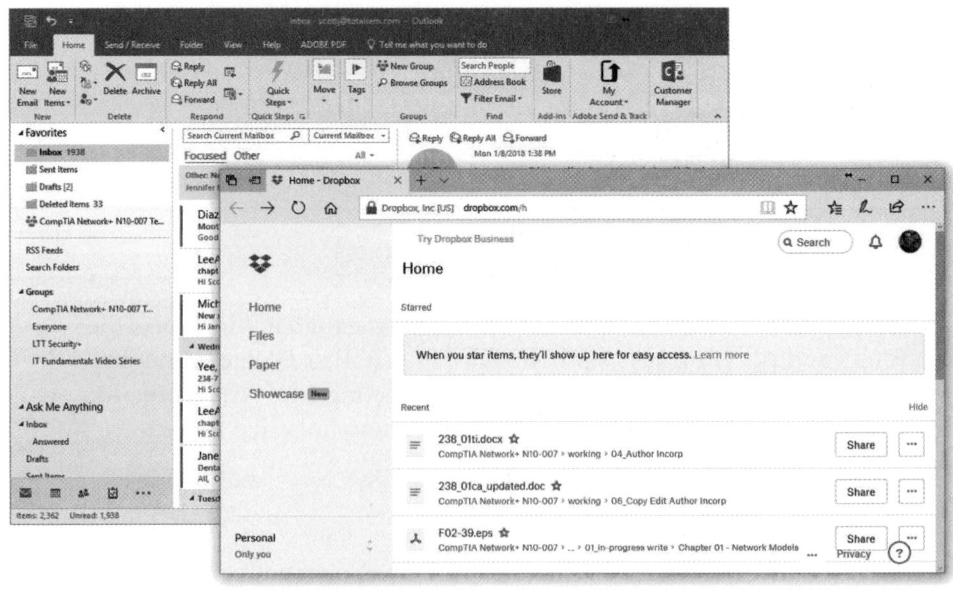

• **Figure 1.44** Network applications at work

Applications may include additional functions, such as encryption, user authentication, and tools to control the look of the data. But these functions are specific to the given applications. In other words, if you want to put a password on your Word document, you must use the password functions in Word to do so.

The **Application layer** is Layer 7 in the OSI seven-layer model. Keep in mind that the Application layer doesn't refer to the applications themselves. It refers to the code built into all operating systems that enables network-aware applications. All operating systems have **Application Programming Interfaces (APIs)** that programmers can use to make their programs network aware (Figure 1.45). An API, in general, provides a standard way for programmers to enhance or extend an application's capabilities.

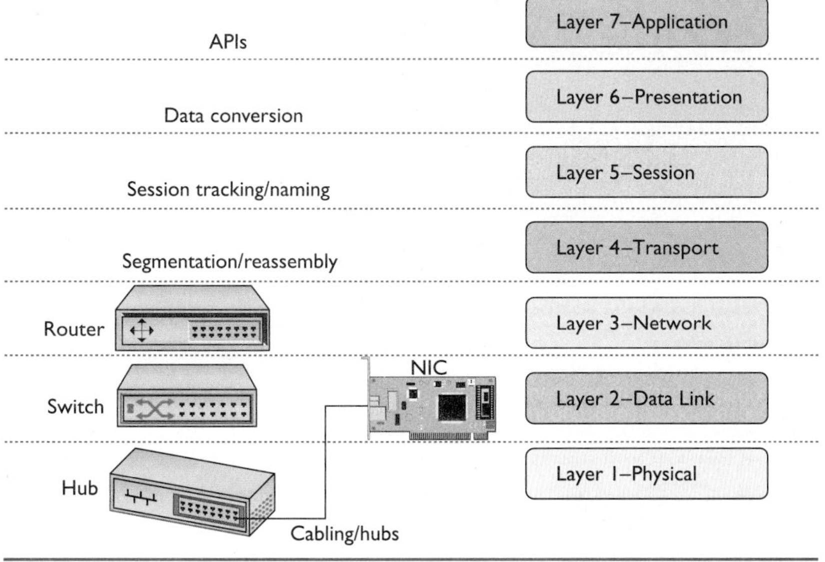

• **Figure 1.45** OSI updated

Tech Tip

Encapsulation and Decapsulation

The term **encapsulation** *encompasses the entire process of preparing data to go onto a network. This includes all the steps from the application to the Application, Presentation, Session, Transport, Network, and Data Link layers. Each layer adds more information so that the data gets to the correct recipient and the recipient knows what to do with the data.*

The receiving computer reverses the process, stripping all the extra header information out as the data goes up the stack. This reverse process is called **decapsulation.**

The Transport layer creates a segment or datagram and hands it down to the Network layer. That layer adds IP information, encapsulating the segment or datagram. The Data Link layer wraps up all that goodness, encapsulating the packet in a frame for delivery over the network. The NIC turns the frame into bits and bytes for transmission over the network medium.

The OSI Seven-Layer Model and Remote Work

Beth works remotely for a large company as a data analyst, putting her advanced degree in information science to good use. Let's explore her typical workflow in this section to see how the OSI seven-layer model applies.

Beth connects to the Internet wirelessly with her laptop. Her company, like so many these days, uses a number of different online services to help coordinate its far-flung workforce. These services go by names like Microsoft 365, Dropbox, GitHub, and so forth, but fundamentally these services

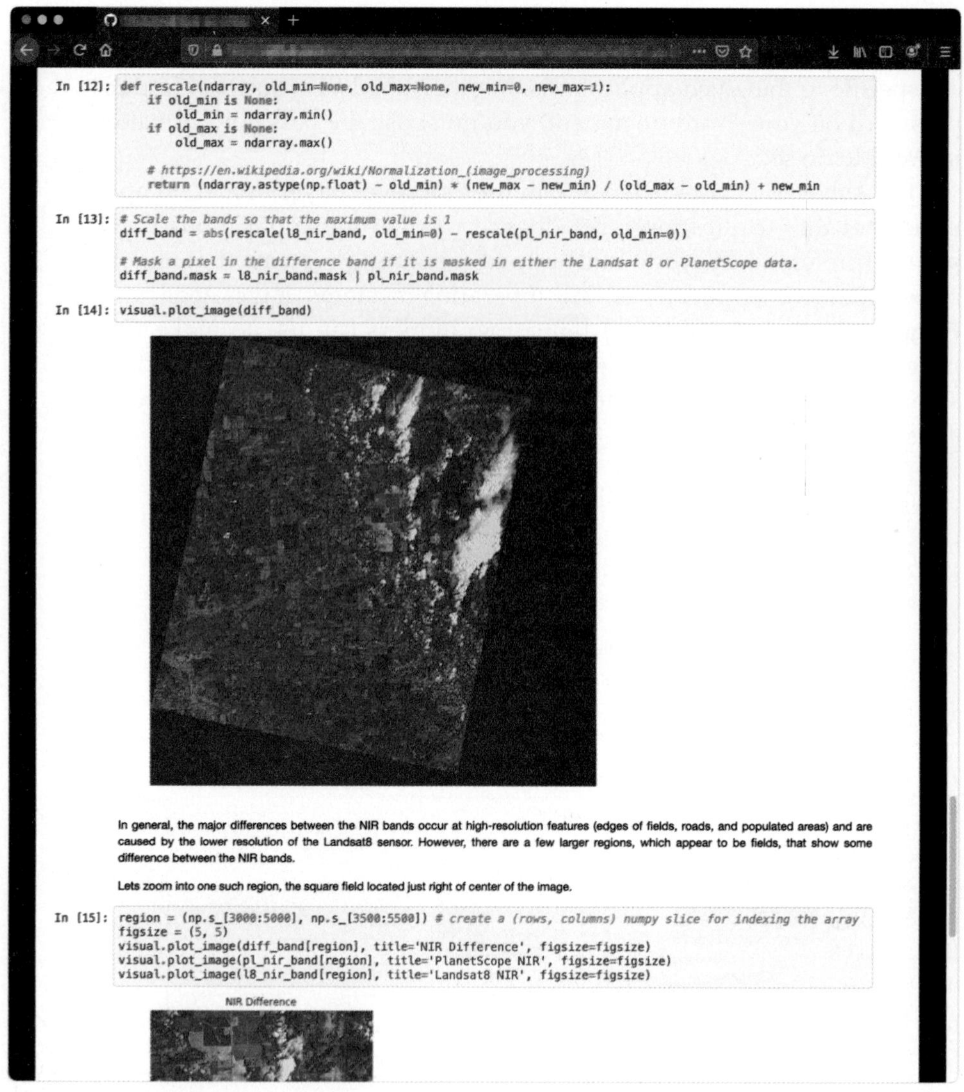

In [12]: def rescale(ndarray, old_min=None, old_max=None, new_min=0, new_max=1):
if old_min is None:
old_min = ndarray.min()
if old_max is None:
old_max = ndarray.max()
# https://en.wikipedia.org/wiki/Normalization_(image_processing)
return (ndarray.astype(np.float) - old_min) * (new_max - new_min) / (old_max - old_min) + new_min
In [13]: # Scale the bands so that the maximum value is 1
diff_band = abs(rescale(l8_nir_band, old_min=0) - rescale(pl_nir_band, old_min=0))
# Mask a pixel in the difference band if it is masked in either the Landsat 8 or PlanetScope data.
diff_band.mask = l8_nir_band.mask | pl_nir_band.mask
In [14]: visual.plot_image(diff_band)
In general, the major differences between the NIR bands occur at high-resolution features (edges of fields, roads, and populated areas) and are caused by the lower resolution of the Landsat8 sensor. However, there are a few larger regions, which appear to be fields, that show some difference between the NIR bands.
Lets zoom into one such region, the square field located just right of center of the image.
In [15]: region = (np.s_[3000:5000], np.s_[3500:5500]) # create a (rows, columns) numpy slice for indexing the array
figsize = (5, 5)
visual.plot_image(diff_band[region], title='NIR Difference', figsize=figsize)
visual.plot_image(pl_nir_band[region], title='PlanetScope NIR', figsize=figsize)
visual.plot_image(l8_nir_band[region], title='Landsat8 NIR', figsize=figsize)
NIR Difference

• **Figure 1.46** Reviewing some analysis on GitHub

all live on the Web and so Beth spends much of her workday in her browser of choice, Firefox (Figure 1.46).

• **Figure 1.47** Wireless is "physical" too!

In this scenario, Beth's computer isn't plugged into an Ethernet port. There are no local wires. Her laptop doesn't even have an Ethernet port (because it's modern and skinny). Do OSI layers even apply? If you answered, "Of course," then you win a prize because they most definitely apply.

The wireless radio waves that connect Beth's laptop to a wireless access point (WAP) operate at Layer 1 (Figure 1.47). So too do all the physical wires connecting the WAP to her router, Internet service provider (ISP), and all the routers in between there and her corporate network and other Internet-based services.

The wireless NIC in Beth's laptop most certainly has a MAC address and connects to the WAP with frames; the WAP uses MAC addresses to connect to the local switch. That's all clearly Layer 2 happiness.

Beth conducts almost all of her work via the Web and thus relies almost exclusively on TCP/IP for connections and interactions. By definition, her laptop must have a valid IP address or two (Layer 3) and must encapsulate/decapsulate segments and datagrams at the Transport layer (Layer 4). But the heavy lifting happens at Layer 7 with HTTP and TLS (HTTPS), because Web-based tools today rely on those protocols (as well as others). Figure 1.48 shows that the tools Beth uses all work with Layer 7.

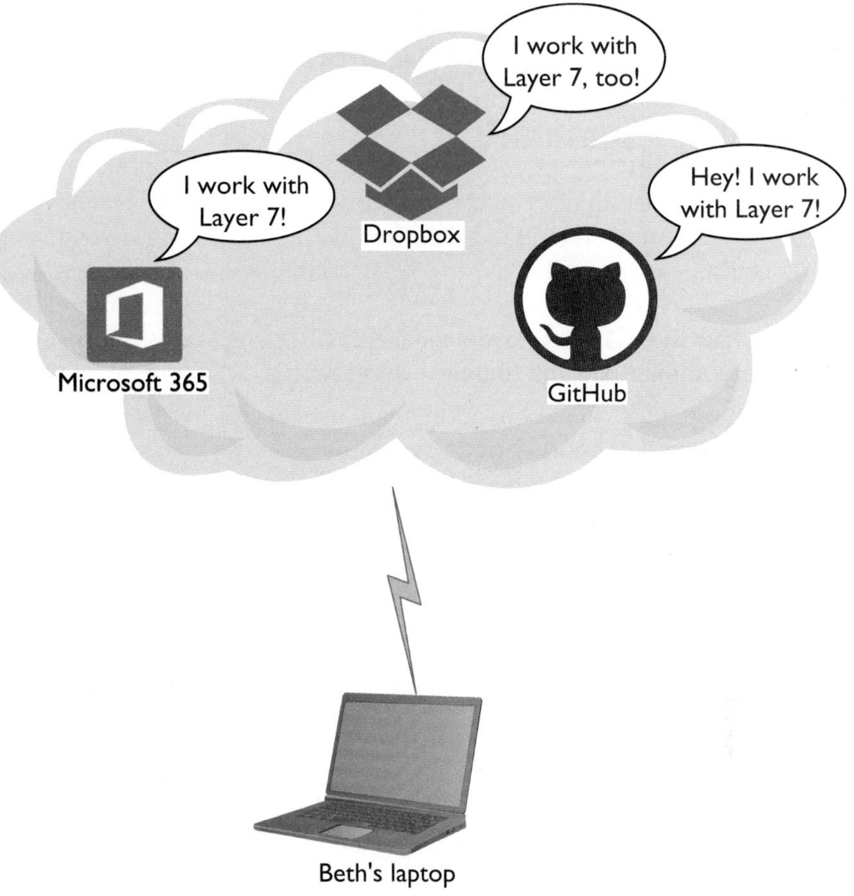

• **Figure 1.48** Beth's productivity tools

The bottom line is that the OSI seven-layer model provides you with a way to conceptualize a network to determine what could cause a specific problem when the inevitable problems occur. Good techs always use a model to troubleshoot their networks. The OSI model can apply to a simple network or a more advanced network.

If Beth can't print to a networked printer, for example, a model can help solve the problem. If her NIC shows activity, then, using the OSI model, you can set aside both the Physical layer (Layer 1) and Data Link layer (Layer 2). You'll find yourself moving up the layer ladder to the OSI model's Network layer (Layer 3). If her computer has a proper IP address, then you can set that layer aside too, and you can move on up to check other layers to solve the problem.

Understanding the OSI model is important. It is the primary diagnostic tool for troubleshooting networks and also the communication tool for talking with your fellow techs.

> Beth accesses servers to do her job; her laptop is a client of those servers. Thus, the previous scenario describes a classic *client-server network type*. In some circumstances, however, Beth might access resources distributed on many computers. In turn, her computer might share some of those resources with others. This alternative network type, typified by the BitTorrent file sharing protocol, is called *peer-to-peer*. Look for a question on the CompTIA Network+ exam that contrasts client-server and peer-to-peer networking.

Chapter 1 Review

Chapter Summary

After reading this chapter and completing the exercises, you should understand the following about networking.

Describe how the OSI seven-layer model helps technicians understand and troubleshoot networks

- Modeling is critical in networking. You use models to understand networks and to communicate with other techs about networks.
- All models are a simplified representation of the real thing. The human model ignores the many different types of body shapes, using only a single "optimal" figure. The model airplane lacks functional engines or the internal framework, and the computerized weather model might disregard subtle differences in wind temperatures or geology.
- In the early days of networking, different manufacturers made unique types of networks that functioned fairly well. But each network had its own cabling, hardware, drivers, naming conventions, applications, and many other unique features. To interconnect networks and improve networking as a whole, someone needed to create a guide—a model that described the functions of a network—so people who made hardware and software could work together to make networks that worked together well.
- The OSI seven-layer model defines the role played by each protocol. The OSI model also provides a common jargon that network techs can use to describe the function of any network protocol.

Explain the major functions of networks with the OSI seven-layer model

- OSI Layer 1, the Physical layer, includes anything that moves data from one system to another, such as cabling or radio waves.
- OSI Layer 2, the Data Link layer, defines the rules for accessing and using the Physical layer. The Data Link layer is divided into two sublayers: Media Access Control (MAC) and Logical Link Control (LLC).
- The LLC sublayer handles multiple network protocols and provides flow control. The MAC sublayer creates and addresses the frame. It adds the NIC's own MAC address and attaches MAC addresses to the frames and adds or checks the FCS.
- OSI Layer 3, the Network layer, creates and addresses packets. The IP addressing enables routers to make sure the packets get to the correct system without worrying about the type of hardware used for transmission. Anything having to do with logical addressing works at the Network layer.
- OSI Layer 4, the Transport layer, breaks up data received from the upper layers into smaller pieces for transport and adds sequencing numbers for TCP segments to make sure the receiving computer can reassemble the data properly. UDP datagrams get created here too.
- Session software at OSI Layer 5 handles the process of differentiating between various types of connections on a PC. The Session layer initiates sessions, accepts incoming sessions, and opens and closes existing sessions. You can use the netstat program to view existing sessions. Try the `ss` command in Linux to do the same thing.
- OSI Layer 6, the Presentation layer, translates data from the lower layers into formats usable by the Application layer; it also translates from the Application layer to lower layers. Several important functions occur here, including some encryption.
- OSI Layer 7, the Application layer, defines a set of tools that programs can use to access the network. APIs provide services to the programs that the users see.

Key Terms

Application layer *(23)*
Application Programming Interface (API) *(23)*
broadcast *(11)*
broadcast address *(11)*
cyclic redundancy check (CRC) *(9)*
Data Link layer *(13)*
decapsulation *(23)*
device ID *(6)*
encapsulation *(23)*
EUI-48 *(7)*
frame *(8)*
frame check sequence (FCS) *(9)*
header *(9)*
hub *(9)*
Internet Protocol (IP) *(14)*
IP address *(15)*
logical address *(15)*
logical addressing *(14)*
Logical Link Control (LLC) *(13)*
MAC-48 *(7)*
MAC address *(6)*
Media Access Control (MAC) *(13)*
media access control address *(6)*
model *(2)*
network interface card (NIC) *(5)*
Network layer *(15)*
network protocol *(14)*
Open Systems Interconnection (OSI) seven-layer model *(1)*
Organizationally Unique Identifier (OUI) *(6)*
packet *(15)*
payload *(9)*
physical address *(6)*
Physical layer *(5)*
port *(19)*
Presentation layer *(22)*
protocol *(3)*
protocol data unit (PDU) *(8)*
reassembly *(17)*
router *(15)*
segmentation *(17)*
Session layer *(21)*
session software *(21)*
subnet *(14)*
switch *(10)*
TCP segment *(19)*
trailer *(9)*
Transmission Control Protocol (TCP) *(14)*
Transport layer *(18)*
UDP datagram *(19)*
unshielded twisted pair (UTP) *(5)*
User Datagram Protocol (UDP) *(18)*

Key Term Quiz

Use the Key Terms list to complete the sentences that follow. Not all terms will be used.

1. The ______________ is an example of software that creates packets for moving data across networks.
2. Most often, the ______________ provides the physical connection between the PC and the network.
3. Using the ______________ enables a computer to send a packet that every other PC on the network will process.
4. You can connect two very different networks by using a(n) ______________.
5. Every NIC has a hard-coded identifier called a(n) ______________.
6. The ______________ provides an excellent tool for conceptualizing how a TCP/IP network works.
7. On a sending machine, data gets broken up at the ______________ of the OSI seven-layer model.
8. NICs encapsulate data into a(n) ______________ for sending that data over a network.
9. A(n) ______________ enables multiple machines to connect over a network.
10. The ______________ provides the key interface between the Physical and Network layers.

Multiple-Choice Quiz

1. Which of the following OSI layers converts the ones and zeroes to electrical signals and places these signals on the cable?
   - A. Physical layer
   - B. Transport layer
   - C. Network layer
   - D. Data Link layer
2. The term "unshielded twisted pair" describes which of the following network components?
   - A. Cable
   - B. Switch
   - C. Router
   - D. NIC
3. From the options that follow, select the one that best describes the contents of a typical network frame.
   - A. Sender's MAC address, recipient's MAC address, data, FCS
   - B. Recipient's MAC address, sender's MAC address, data, FCS
   - C. Recipient's IP address, sender's IP address, data, FCS
   - D. Recipient's e-mail address, sender's e-mail address, data, FCS
4. Which of the following is most likely to be a MAC address assigned to a NIC?
   - A. 192.168.1.121
   - B. 24-17-232-7B
   - C. 23-4F-17-8A-4C-10
   - D. 713-555-1212
5. Which layer of the OSI model involves routing?
   - A. Application layer
   - B. Network layer
   - C. Presentation layer
   - D. Transport layer
6. How much data can a typical frame contain?
   - A. 500 bytes
   - B. 1500 bytes
   - C. 1500 kilobytes
   - D. 1 megabyte
7. Which of the following best describes an IP address?
   - A. A unique dotted decimal notation burned into every NIC
   - B. A unique 48-bit identifying number burned into every NIC
   - C. A dotted decimal notation assigned to a NIC by software
   - D. A 48-bit identifying number assigned to a NIC by software
8. Which layer of the OSI model makes sure the data is in a readable format for the Application layer?
   - A. Application layer
   - B. Presentation layer
   - C. Session layer
   - D. Transport layer
9. At which layer of the OSI model are UDP datagrams created?
   - A. Physical
   - B. Network
   - C. Transport
   - D. Application
10. Which protocol creates the packet?
    - A. NIC
    - B. IP
    - C. TCP
    - D. UDP
11. Which OSI layer enables Web browsers to interact with operating system code?
    - A. Application layer
    - B. Data Link layer
    - C. Presentation layer
    - D. Transport layer
12. At which OSI layer is the frame created?
    - A. Application layer
    - B. Data Link layer
    - C. Session layer
    - D. Transport layer

13. Which component works at Layer 1 of the OSI seven-layer model?

    A. Cable

    B. Switch

    C. Network protocol

    D. Session software

14. Andalyn says complete 48-bit MAC addresses are allocated to NIC manufacturers from the IEEE. Buster says the IEEE only assigns the first 24 bits to manufacturers. Carlos says the IEEE assigns only the last 24 bits to manufacturers. Who is correct?

    A. Only Andalyn is correct.

    B. Only Buster is correct.

    C. Only Carlos is correct.

    D. No one is correct.

15. If a sending system does not know the MAC address of the intended recipient system, it sends a broadcast frame with what MAC address?

    A. 192.168.0.0

    B. FF-FF-FF-FF-FF-FF

    C. 11-11-11-11-11-11

    D. 00-00-00-00-00-00

Essay Quiz

1. Some new techs at your office are confused by the differences between a NIC's frame and an IP packet. Write a short essay describing the two encapsulations, including the components that do the encapsulating.

2. Your boss has received a set of files with the file extension .wp and is worried because he's never seen that extension before. He wants people to have access to the information in those files from anywhere in the network. Write a short memo describing how Microsoft Word can handle these files, including a discussion of how that fits with the OSI seven-layer model.

Lab Projects

• Lab Project 1.1

Examine your classroom network. What components does it have? How would you classify those components according to the OSI seven-layer model?

• Lab Project 1.2

Create a mnemonic phrase to help you remember the OSI seven-layer model. With two layers beginning with the letter *P*, how will you differentiate in your mnemonic between Presentation and Physical? How will you incorporate the two sublayers of the Data Link layer?

Cabling and Topology

"I'm not crazy. My mother had me tested!"

—Sheldon, *Big Bang Theory*

In this chapter, you will learn how to

- **Explain the different types of network topologies**
- **Describe the different types of network cabling and connectors**
- **Describe the IEEE networking standards**

Every network must provide some method to get data from one system to another. In most cases, this method consists of some type of cabling running between systems, although most networks today incorporate wireless methods to move data as well. Stringing those cables brings up a number of critical issues you need to understand to work on a network. How do all these cables connect the computers? Does every computer on the network run a cable to a central point? Does a single cable snake through the ceiling, with all the computers on the network connected to it? These questions need answering!

Furthermore, manufacturers need standards so they can make networking equipment that works well together. While we're talking about standards, what about the cabling itself? What type of cable? What quality of copper or fiber? How thick should it be? Who defines the standards for cables so they all work in the network?

This chapter answers these questions in three parts. First, you will learn about the **network topology**—the way that pieces of hardware connect to one another, via wires or wirelessly. Second, you will tour the most common standardized cable types used in networking. Third, you will learn about the IEEE committees that create network technology standards.

Test Specific

Network Topologies

Computer networks employ many different *topologies*, or ways of connecting computers and other devices like switches and printers together. This section looks at both the historical topologies (bus, ring, and star—all long dead) and the modern topologies (hybrid and mesh). In addition, we will look at what parameters are used to make up a network topology.

Wireless networks employ topologies too, just not with wires. We'll cover the common wireless topologies—infrastructure and ad hoc—in Chapter 14.

Bus and Ring

The first generation of wired networks used one of two topologies, both shown in Figure 2.1. A **bus topology** network used a single cable (i.e., the *bus*) that connected all the computers in a line. A **ring topology** network connected all computers on the network with a ring of cable.

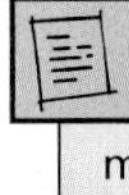

Topologies are diagrams, much like an electrical circuit diagram. Real network cabling doesn't go in perfect circles or perfect straight lines.

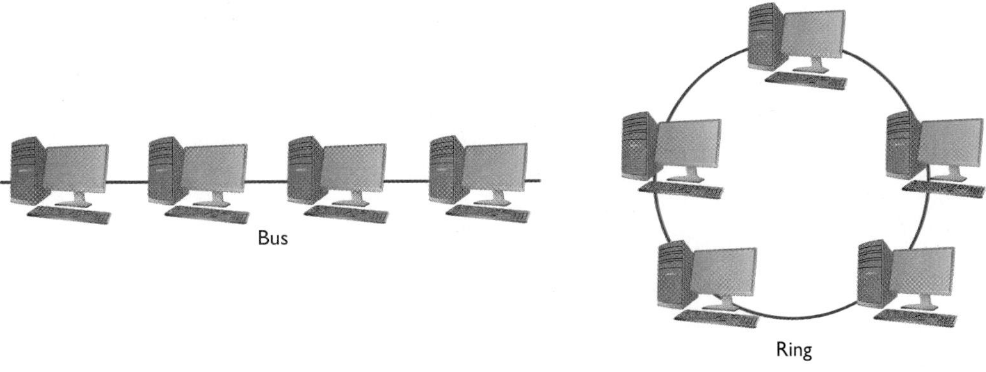

• **Figure 2.1** Bus and ring topologies

Data flowed differently between bus and ring networks, creating different problems and solutions. In bus topology networks, data from each computer simply went out on the whole bus. A network using a bus topology needed termination at each end of the cable to prevent a signal sent from one computer from reflecting at the ends of the cable, quickly bringing the network down (Figure 2.2).

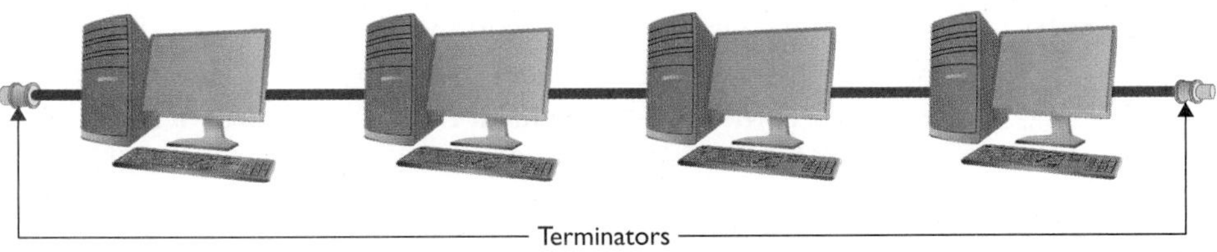

• **Figure 2.2** Terminated bus topology

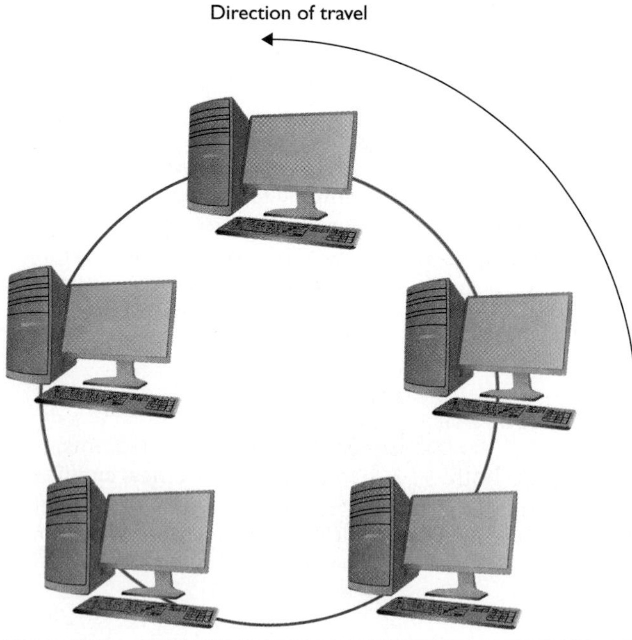

• **Figure 2.3** Ring topology moving in a certain direction

In a ring topology network, in contrast, data traffic moved in a circle from one computer to the next in the same direction (Figure 2.3) using a token. With no end to the cable, ring networks required no termination.

Bus and ring topology networks worked well but suffered from the same problem: the entire network stopped working if the cable broke at any point (Figure 2.4). The broken ends on a bus topology network didn't have the required termination, which caused reflection between computers that were still connected. A break in a ring topology network simply broke the circuit, stopping the data flow.

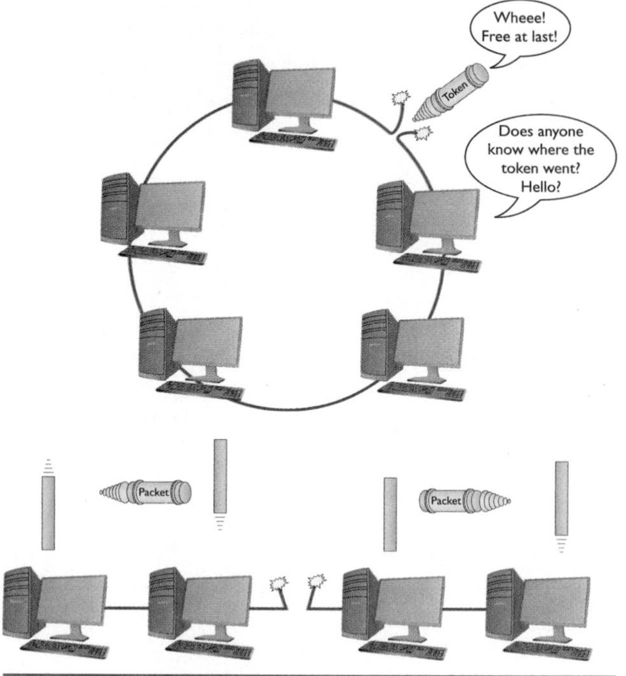

• **Figure 2.4** Nobody is talking!

Star

The **star topology**, also called **hub-and-spoke**, used a central connection box for all the computers on the network (Figure 2.5). Star topologies had a huge benefit over ring and bus topologies by offering **fault tolerance**—if one of the cables broke, all of the other computers could still communicate. Bus and ring topology networks were popular and inexpensive to implement, however, so the old-style star topology networks weren't very successful. Network hardware designers couldn't easily redesign their existing networks to use a star topology.

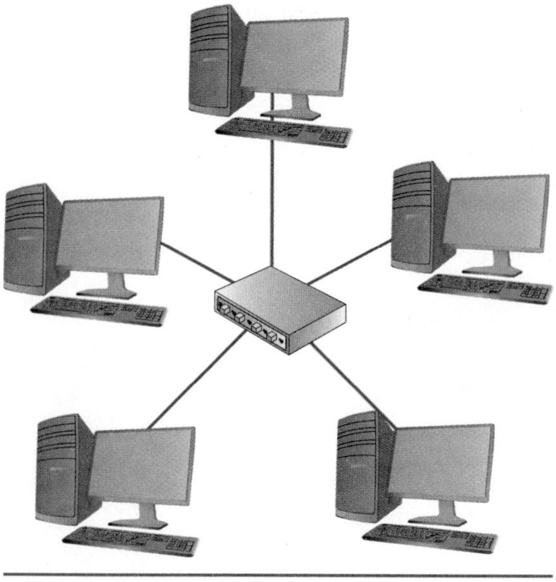

• **Figure 2.5** Star topology

Hybrid

Even though network designers couldn't easily use a star topology, the benefits of star topologies were overwhelming, motivating smart people to come up with a way to use star topologies without requiring a major redesign—and the way they did so was ingenious. The ring topology network designers struck first by taking the entire ring and shrinking it into a small box, as shown in Figure 2.6.

This was quickly followed by the bus topology folks, who, in turn, shrunk their bus (better known as the **segment**) into their own box (Figure 2.7).

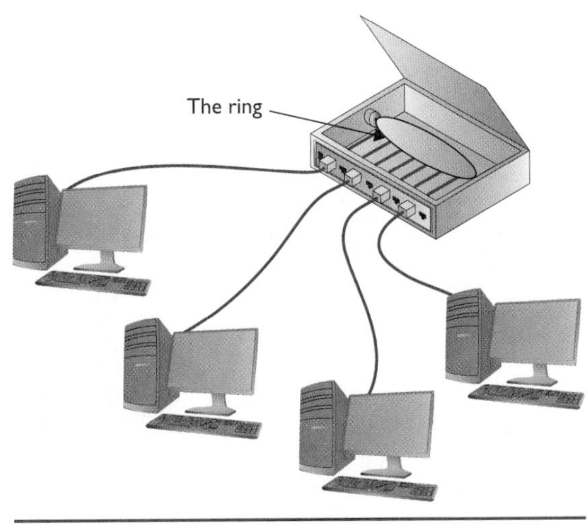

• **Figure 2.6** Shrinking the ring

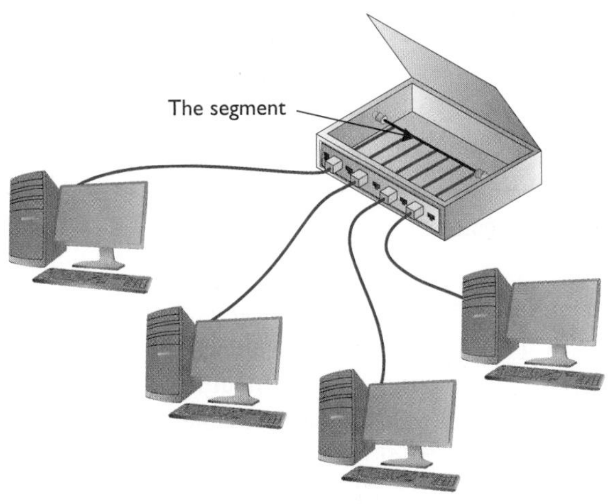

• **Figure 2.7** Shrinking the segment

Most techs refer to the signaling topology as the logical topology today. That's how you'll see it on the CompTIA Network+ exam as well. Look for a question on the exam that challenges you on logical versus physical topology.

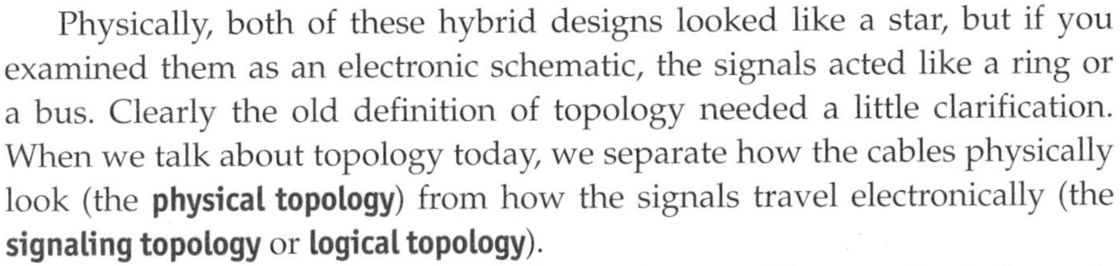

Physically, both of these hybrid designs looked like a star, but if you examined them as an electronic schematic, the signals acted like a ring or a bus. Clearly the old definition of topology needed a little clarification. When we talk about topology today, we separate how the cables physically look (the **physical topology**) from how the signals travel electronically (the **signaling topology** or **logical topology**).

Any form of networking technology that combines a physical topology with a signaling topology is called a **hybrid topology**. Hybrid topologies have come and gone since the earliest days of networking. Only two hybrid topologies, **star-ring topology** and **star-bus topology**, ever saw any amount of popularity. Eventually, star-ring lost market share, and star-bus reigns as the undisputed "star" (pun intended) of wired network topologies.

The most successful of the star-ring topology networks was called Token Ring, manufactured by IBM.

Mesh

Topologies aren't just for wired networks. Wireless networks also need topologies to get data from one machine to another, but using radio waves instead of cables involves somewhat different topologies. Wireless devices can connect in a **mesh topology** network, where every computer connects to every other computer via two or more routes. Some of the routes between two computers may require traversing through another member of the mesh network. (See Chapter 14 for the scoop on wireless network types.)

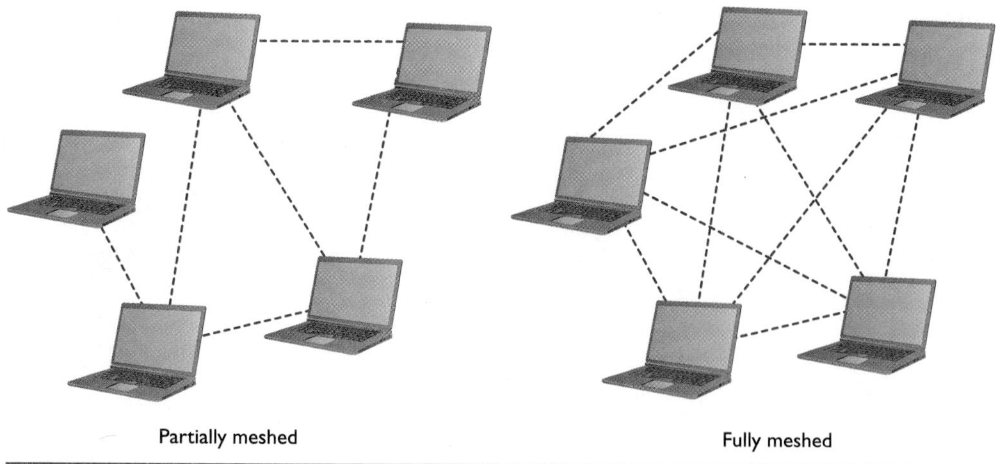

• **Figure 2.8** Partially and fully meshed topologies

There are two types of meshed topologies: partially meshed and fully meshed (Figure 2.8). In a **partially meshed topology** network, at least two machines have redundant connections. Every machine doesn't have to connect to every other machine. In a **fully meshed topology** network, every computer connects directly to every other computer.

Parameters of a Topology

Make sure you know the topologies: bus, ring, star/hub-and-spoke, hybrid, and mesh.

Although a topology describes the method by which systems in a network connect, the topology alone doesn't describe all of the features necessary to enable those networks. The term *bus topology*, for example, describes a network that consists of machines connected to the network via a single linear piece of cable. Notice that this definition leaves a lot of questions unanswered. What is the cable made of? How long can it be? How do the machines decide which machine should send data at a specific moment? A network based on a bus topology can answer these questions in several ways—but it's not the job of the topology to define issues like these. A functioning network needs a more detailed standard.

Check out the excellent Chapter 2 "Topology Matching" Challenge! over at **http://totalsem.com/008**. It's a good tool for reinforcing the topology variations.

Over the years, manufacturers and standards bodies have created network technologies based on different topologies. A **network technology** is a practical application of a topology and other critical tools that provides a method to get data from one computer to another on a network. These network technologies have names like 100BASE-T, 1000BASE-LX, and 10GBASE-T. You will learn all about these in the next two chapters.

Cabling and Connectors

Most networked systems link together using some type of cabling. Different types of networks over the years have used different types of cables—and you need to learn about all these cables to succeed on the CompTIA Network+ exam. This section explores scenarios where you would use common network cabling.

All cables used in the networking industry can be categorized in two distinct groups: copper and fiber-optic. All styles of cables have distinct connector types that you need to know.

Copper Cabling and Connectors

The most common form of cabling uses copper wire wrapped up in some kind of protective sheathing, thus the term *copper cables*. The two primary types of copper cabling used in the industry are coaxial and twisted pair.

Both cable types sport a variety of connector types. I'll cover the connector types as I discuss the cable varieties.

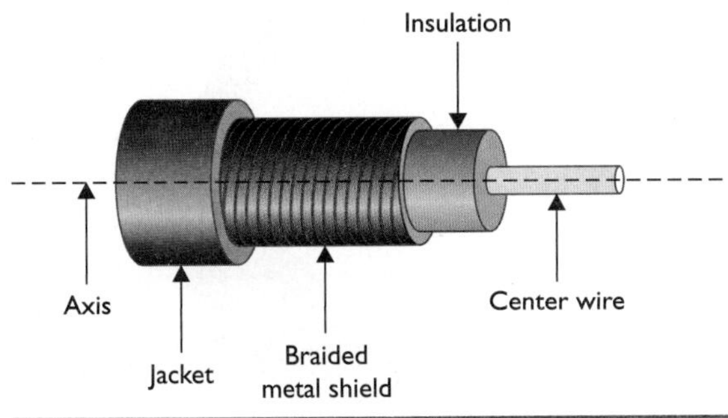

• **Figure 2.9** Cutaway view of coaxial cable

Coaxial Cable

Coaxial cable contains a central copper conductor wire surrounded by an insulating material, which, in turn, is surrounded by a braided metal shield. The cable is referred to as coaxial (coax for short) because the center wire and the braided metal shield share a common axis or centerline (Figure 2.9).

Techs all around the globe argue over the meaning of BNC. A solid percentage says with authority that it stands for "British Naval Connector." An opposing percentage says with equal authority that it stands for "Bayonet Neill-Concelman," after the stick-and-twist style of connecting and the purported inventors of the connector. The jury is still out, though this week I'm leaning toward Neill and Concelman and their bayonet-style connector.

Coaxial cable shields data transmissions from interference. Many devices in the typical office environment—including lights, fans, copy machines, and refrigerators—generate magnetic fields. When a metal wire encounters these magnetic fields, electrical current is generated along the wire. This extra current, called **electromagnetic interference (EMI)**, can shut down a network because it is easily misinterpreted as a signal by devices like NICs. To prevent EMI from affecting the network, the outer mesh layer of a coaxial cable shields the center wire (on which the data is transmitted) from interference (Figure 2.10).

• **Figure 2.10** Coaxial cable showing braided metal shielding

Early bus topology networks used coaxial cable to connect computers together. Back in the day, the most popular cable used special bayonet-style connectors called **BNC connectors** (Figure 2.11).

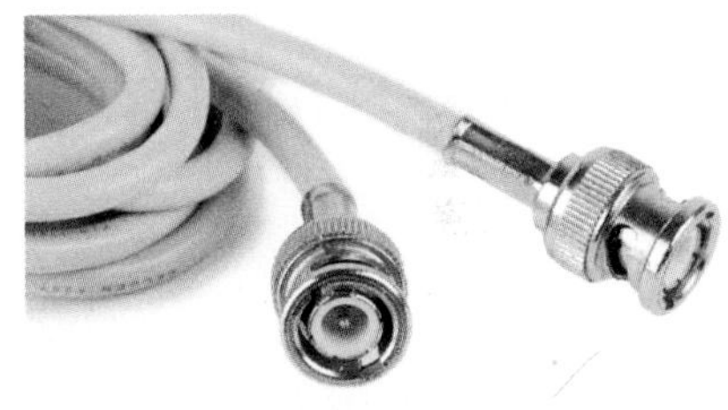

• **Figure 2.11** BNC connector on coaxial cable

You'll find coaxial cable used today primarily to enable a cable modem to connect to an Internet service provider (ISP). That's the typical scenario for using coaxial cable: connecting a computer to the cable modem enables that computer to access the Internet. This cable is the same type used to connect televisions to cable boxes or to satellite receivers. These cables use an **F connector** (or **F-type connector**) that screws on, making for a secure connection (Figure 2.12).

• **Figure 2.12** F-type connector on coaxial cable

Coaxial cabling is also very popular for use with satellite dishes, over-the-air antennas, and even some home video devices. This book covers cable and other Internet connectivity options in great detail in Chapter 13.

Cable modems connect using one of two coaxial cable types.

• **Figure 2.13** RG-6 cable

The Ohm rating of a piece of cable describes the impedance of that cable. *Impedance* describes a set of characteristics that define how much a cable resists the flow of electricity. This isn't simple resistance, though. Impedance is also a factor in such things as how long it takes the wire to get a full charge—the wire's *capacitance*—and more.

RG-59 was used primarily for cable television rather than networking. Its thinness and the introduction of digital cable motivated the move to the more robust **RG-6**, the predominant cabling used today (Figure 2.13).

All coax cables have a **Radio Guide (RG) rating**. The U.S. military developed these ratings to provide a quick reference for the different types of coax. The only important measure of coax cabling is its **Ohm rating**, a relative measure of the resistance (or more precisely, characteristic impedance) on the cable. You may run across other coax cables that don't have acceptable Ohm ratings, although they look just like network-rated coax. Both RG-6 and RG-59 cables are rated at 75 Ohms.

Given the popularity of cable for television and Internet in homes today, you'll run into situations where people need to take a single coaxial cable and split it. Coaxial handles this quite nicely with coaxial splitters like the one shown in Figure 2.14. You can also connect two coaxial cables together easily using a barrel connector when you need to add some distance to a connection (Figure 2.15). Table 2.1 summarizes the coaxial standards.

• **Figure 2.14** Coaxial splitter

• **Figure 2.15** Barrel connector

Table 2.1 Coaxial Cables

Rating	Ohms	Use	Connector
RG-59	75	Cable TV	F Type
RG-6	75	Cable TV	F Type

Twinaxial

Twinaxial cable is a type of coaxial cable that contains two central copper conductors wrapped around a single shield (Figure 2.16). You'll see it used as a substitute for short fiber connections, generally between equipment within a rack, like switches. For such uses, it's substantially cheaper than fiber and associated hardware. Twinaxial cable used this way is called a *direct attached cable (DAC)*.

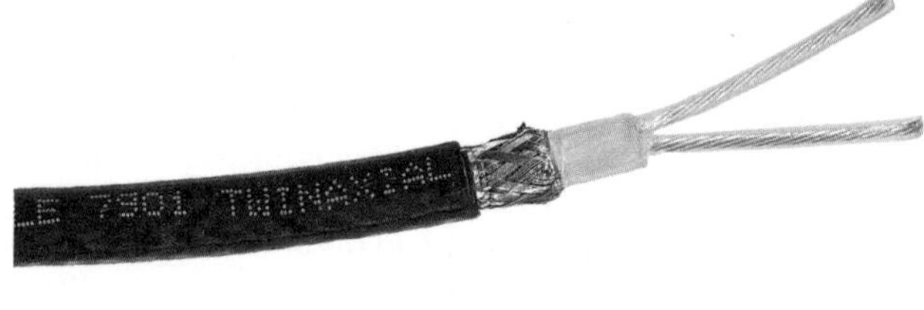

• **Figure 2.16** Twinaxial cable

Twisted Pair

The most common type of cabling used in networks consists of twisted pairs of cables, bundled together into a common jacket. Each pair in the cable works as a team either transmitting or receiving data. Using a pair of twisted wires rather than a single wire to send a signal reduces a specific type of interference, called **crosstalk**. The more twists per foot, the less crosstalk. Two types of twisted-pair cabling are manufactured: shielded and unshielded.

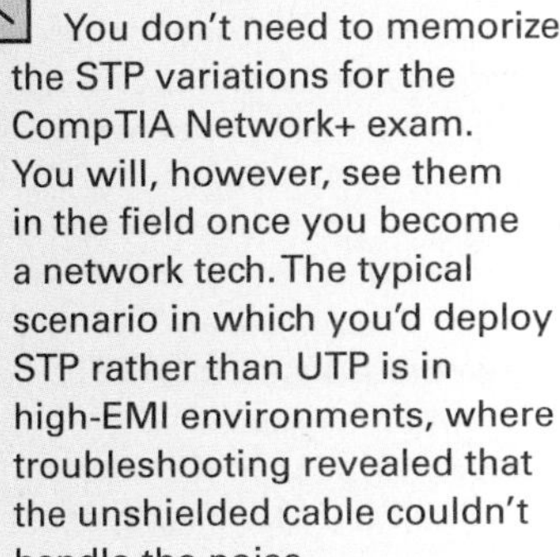

You don't need to memorize the STP variations for the CompTIA Network+ exam. You will, however, see them in the field once you become a network tech. The typical scenario in which you'd deploy STP rather than UTP is in high-EMI environments, where troubleshooting revealed that the unshielded cable couldn't handle the noise.

Shielded Twisted Pair **Shielded twisted pair (STP)** consists of twisted pairs of wires surrounded by shielding to protect them from EMI. There are six types, differentiated by which part gets shielding, such as the whole cable or individual pairs within the cable. Table 2.2 describes the six types. Figure 2.17 shows a typical piece of STP with the cladding partly removed so you can see the internal wiring.

Table 2.2 STP Standards

Name	Description
F/UTP	Foil shields the entire cable; inside, the wires are just like UTP.
S/UTP	A braid screen shields the entire cable; inside, the wires are just like UTP.
SF/UTP	A braid screen and foil shield the entire cable; the wires inside are just like UTP.
S/FTP	A braid screen shields the entire cable; foil shields each wire pair inside.
F/FTP	A foil screen shields the entire cable; foil shields each wire pair inside.
U/FTP	No overall shielding; each pair inside is shielded with foil screens.

• **Figure 2.17** Shielded twisted pair

Unshielded Twisted Pair **Unshielded twisted pair (UTP)** consists of twisted pairs of wires surrounded by a plastic jacket (Figure 2.18). This jacket does not provide any protection from EMI, just a slightly protective skin, so when installing UTP cabling, you must be careful to avoid interference from fluorescent lights, motors, and so forth. UTP costs much less than STP but, in most environments, performs just as well.

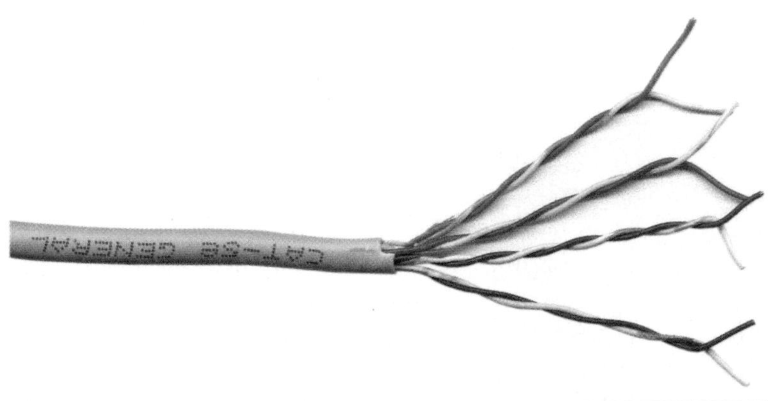

• **Figure 2.18** Unshielded twisted pair

Twisted-pair cabling has been around since the 1970s and evolving technologies demanded higher speeds. Over the years, manufacturers increased the number of twists per foot, used higher gauge cable, and added shielding to make twisted pair able to handle higher data speeds.

Several international groups set the standards for cabling and networking in general. Ready for alphabet soup? At or near the top is the International Organization for Standardization (ISO). The American National Standards Institute (ANSI) is both the official U.S. representative to ISO and a major international player. ANSI checks the standards and accredits other groups, such as the Telecommunications Industry Association (TIA).

To help network installers get the right cable for the right network technology, the cabling industry developed a variety of grades called **category (Cat) ratings**. Cat ratings are officially rated in *megahertz (MHz)*, indicating the highest frequency the cable can handle. Table 2.3 shows the most common categories along with their status with the TIA (see the subsequent Note for more information).

Table 2.3 Cat Ratings for Twisted Pair

Cat Rating	Max Frequency	Max Bandwidth	Status with TIA
Cat 3	16 MHz	16 Mbps	Recognized
Cat 4	20 MHz	20 Mbps	No longer recognized
Cat 5	100 MHz	100 Mbps	No longer recognized
Cat 5e	100 MHz	1 Gbps	Recognized
Cat 6[1]	250 MHz	10 Gbps	Recognized
Cat 6a[2]	500 MHz	10 Gbps	Recognized
Cat 7	600 MHz	10+ Gbps	Not recognized
Cat 7a[3]	1000 MHz	40–100 Gbps	Not recognized
Cat 8	2000 MHz	25–40 Gbps	Not recognized

[1] Cat 6 cables can use the full 100-meter length when used with 10/100/1000BASE-T networks. With 10GBASE-T networks, Cat 6 is limited to 55 meters.
[2] Cat 6a cables can use the full 100-meter length with networks up to 10GBASE-T.
[3] Cat 7a cables can theoretically support 40 Gbps at 50 meters; 100 Gbps at 15 meters.

The CompTIA Network+ exam is only interested in your knowledge of Cat 5, Cat 5e, Cat 6, Cat 6a, Cat 7, and Cat 8 cables. (In the field you'll see category represented lowercase and uppercase, so Cat 6a or CAT 6a.)

UTP cables handle a certain frequency or cycles per second, such as 100 MHz or 1000 MHz. You could take the frequency number in the early days of networking and translate that into the maximum throughput for a cable. Each cycle per second (or hertz) basically accounted for one bit of data per second. A 10 million cycle per second (10 MHz) cable, for example, could handle 10 million bits per second (10 Mbps). The maximum amount of data that goes through the cable per second is called the **bandwidth**.

For current networks, developers have implemented *bandwidth-efficient encoding schemes*, which means they can squeeze more bits into the same signal as long as the cable can handle it. Thus, the Cat 5e cable can handle a throughput of up to 1000 Mbps, even though it's rated to handle a frequency of only up to 100 MHz.

• Figure 2.19 Cat level marked on box of twisted-pair cabling

Because most networks can run at speeds of up to 1000 Mbps, most new cabling installations use Category 6 (Cat 6) cabling, although a large number of installations use Cat 6a or Cat 7 to future-proof the network.

Make sure you can look at twisted pair and know its Cat rating. There are two places to look. First, twisted pair is typically sold in boxed reels, and the manufacturer will clearly mark the Cat level on the box (Figure 2.19). Second, look on the cable itself. The category level of a piece of cable is usually printed on the cable (Figure 2.20).

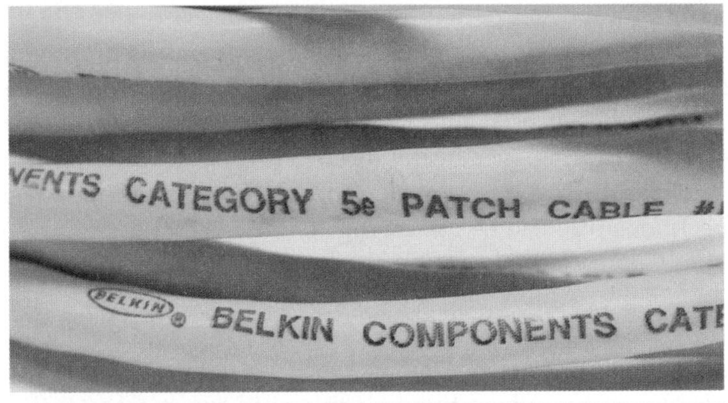

• **Figure 2.20** Cat level on twisted-pair cabling

Try This!

Shopping Spree!

Just how common has Cat 6a or Cat 7 become in your neighborhood? Take a run down to your local hardware store or office supply store and shop for UTP cabling. Do they carry Cat 6a? Cat 7? What's the difference in price? If it's not much more expensive to go with the better cable, the expected shift in networking standards has occurred and you might want to upgrade your network.

CompTIA follows the common usage for networking cable connectors. You will *not* see 8P8C on the exam; you will *only* see RJ-45.

The old landline telephones plugged in with a **registered jack (RJ)** connector. Telephones used **RJ-11** connectors, designed to support up to two pairs of UTP wires. Current wired networks use the four-pair **8 position 8 contact (8P8C)** connectors that most techs (erroneously) refer to as **RJ-45** connectors (Figure 2.21). (There was an *RJ45S* connector used in telephones with slightly different keying. They look very similar to the 8P8C connectors, though, so speculation is that the name carried over from technicians installing that UTP cabling.)

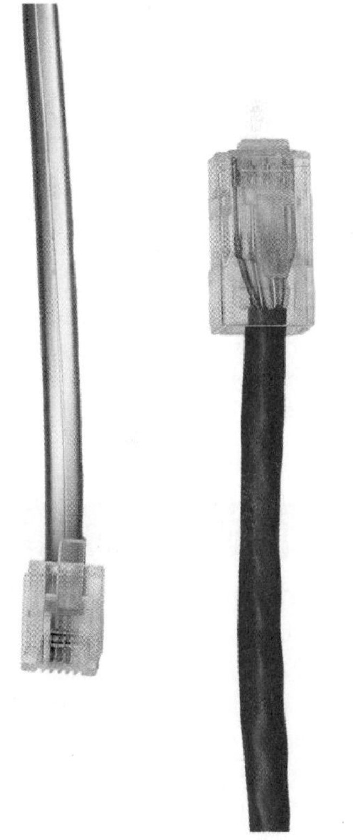

• **Figure 2.21** RJ-11 (left) and 8P8C/"RJ-45" (right) connectors

Fiber-Optic Cabling and Connectors

Fiber-optic cable transmits light rather than electricity, making it attractive for both high-EMI areas and long-distance transmissions. Whereas a single copper cable cannot carry data more than a few hundred meters at best, a single piece of fiber-optic cabling will operate, depending on the implementation, for distances of up to tens of kilometers. A fiber-optic cable has four components: the glass fiber itself (the **core**); the **cladding**, which is the part that makes the light reflect down the fiber; **buffer** material to give strength; and the **insulating jacket** (Figure 2.22).

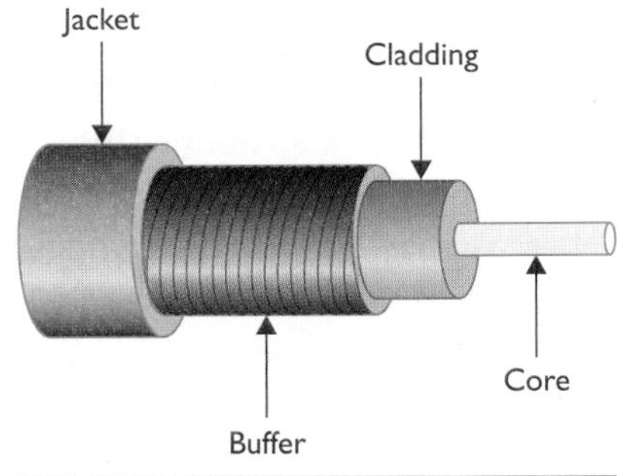

• **Figure 2.22** Cross section of fiber-optic cabling

You might see the term *fiber cables* on the CompTIA Network+ exam to describe the two varieties of fiber-optic cables discussed in this section. Just as copper cables don't have copper connectors, fiber cables don't have *fiber connectors*, but that's the term used in the CompTIA Network+ Spare Parts list. I'll discuss cables and connector types shortly.

Fiber-optic cabling is manufactured with many different diameters of core and cladding. Cable manufacturers use a two-number designator to define fiber-optic cables according to their core and cladding measurements. Common fiber-optic cable sizes are 9/125 µm, 50/125 µm, and 62.5/125 µm. Almost all network technologies that use fiber-optic cable require pairs of fibers. One fiber is used for sending, the other for receiving. In response to the demand for two-pair cabling, manufacturers often connect two fibers together to create *duplex* fiber-optic cabling (Figure 2.23).

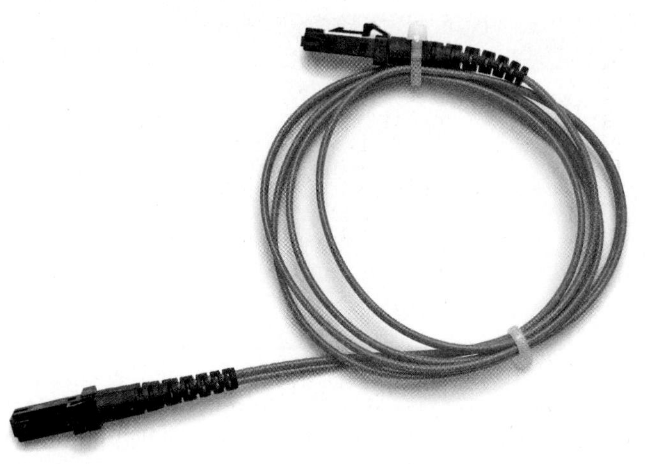

• **Figure 2.23** Duplex fiber-optic cable

Light can be sent down a fiber-optic cable as regular light or as laser light. The two types of light require totally different fiber-optic cables. Network technologies that use fiber optics use LEDs (light emitting diodes) to send light signals. A fiber-optic cable that uses LEDs is known as **multimode fiber (MMF)**.

A fiber-optic cable that uses lasers is known as **single-mode fiber (SMF)**. Using laser light and single-mode fiber-optic cables prevents a problem unique to multimode fiber optics called **modal distortion** (signals sent at the same time don't arrive at the same time because the paths differ slightly in length) and enables a network to achieve phenomenally high transfer rates over incredibly long distances.

Fiber optics also defines the wavelength of light used, measured in nanometers (nm). Multimode cables transmit 850-nm or 1300-nm wavelengths, whereas single-mode transmits either 1310 nm or 1550 nm, depending on the laser.

Fiber-optic cables come in a broad choice of connector types. There are over one hundred different connectors, but the four you need to know for the CompTIA Network+ exam are ST, SC, LC, and MT-RJ. Figure 2.24 shows the first three; Figure 2.25 shows an MT-RJ connector.

For those of you unfamiliar with it, the odd little u-shaped symbol describing fiber cable size (µ) stands for *micro*, or 1/1,000,000. It's the Greek letter mu.

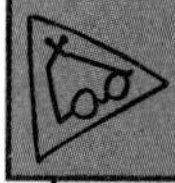

Tech Tip

VCSEL

MMF can use a form of laser called a vertical-cavity surface-emitting laser (VCSEL), *which differs substantially from the lasers used in SMF. You'll find VCSELs in computer mice and laser printers, among other uses. And in case you're curious, VCSELs are not on the CompTIA Network+ exam.*

A *nano*—abbreviated as *n*—stands for 1/1,000,000,000, or one-billionth of whatever. Here you'll see it as a nanometer (nm), one-billionth of a meter. That's one tiny wavelength!

Tech Tip

OM Nomenclature and Colors

The ANSI/TIA-568.3-D standard defines the nomenclature for fiber. The multimode standard prefix is OM (single-mode is OS). OM1 and OM2 are used in shorter runs with LEDs. OM3, OM4, and OM5 can use lasers and run at higher bandwidths, thus providing faster speed and greater distances.

The ANSI/TIA 598-C standard provides guidelines for color-coding various fiber types. Single-mode fiber is yellow. OM1 and OM2 are both orange. OM3 and OM4 sport aqua, and OM5 appears in a spectacular lime green.

• **Figure 2.24** From left to right: ST, SC, and LC fiber-optic connectors

• **Figure 2.25** MT-RJ fiber-optic connector

Although all fiber connectors must be installed in pairs, the ST and SC connectors traditionally have unique ends. The LC and MT-RJ connectors are always duplex, meaning both the send and receive cables are attached. You can certainly find SC connectors or sleeves to make them duplex too, so don't get too caught up with which can be which. We'll revisit fiber-optic connectors in Chapter 4 when we discuss implementation of specific networking standards.

> Most technicians call common fiber-optic connectors by their initials—such as ST, SC, or LC—perhaps because there's no consensus about what words go with those initials. ST probably stands for *straight tip*, although some call it *snap and twist*. But SC and LC? How about *subscriber connector*, *standard connector*, or *Siemon connector* for the former, and *local connector* or *Lucent connector* for the latter? If you want to remember the connectors for the exam, try these: *snap and twist* for the bayonet-style ST connectors; *stick and click* for the straight push-in SC connectors; and *little connector* for the ... little ... LC connector.

Fire Ratings

Did you ever see the movie *The Towering Inferno?* Don't worry if you missed it—*The Towering Inferno* was one of the better disaster movies of the 1970s, although it was no *Airplane!* Anyway, Steve McQueen stars as the fireman who saves the day when a skyscraper goes up in flames because of poor-quality electrical cabling. The burning insulation on the wires ultimately spreads the fire to every part of the building. Although no cables made today contain truly flammable insulation, the insulation is made from plastic, and if you get any plastic hot enough, it will create smoke and noxious fumes. The risk of burning insulation isn't fire—it's smoke and fumes.

To reduce the risk of your network cables burning and creating noxious fumes and smoke, Underwriters Laboratories and the National Electrical Code (NEC) joined forces to develop cabling *fire ratings*. The two most common fire ratings are PVC and plenum. Cable with a **polyvinyl chloride (PVC)** rating has no significant fire protection. If you burn a **PVC-rated cable**, it creates lots of smoke and noxious fumes. Burning **plenum-rated cable** creates much less smoke and fumes, but plenum-rated cable costs about three to five times as much as PVC-rated cable. Most city ordinances require the use of plenum cable for network installations. The bottom line in such scenarios? Get plenum!

The space between the acoustical tile ceiling in an office building and the actual concrete ceiling above is called the **plenum**—hence the name for the proper fire rating of cabling to use in that space. A third type of fire rating, known as **riser**, designates the proper cabling to use for vertical runs between floors of a building. **Riser-rated** cable provides less protection than plenum cable, though, so most installations today use plenum for runs between floors.

> Look for a troubleshooting scenario question on the CompTIA Network+ exam that asks you to compare plenum versus PVC cable best use. If it goes in the wall, make it plenum!

Networking Industry Standards—IEEE

The **Institute of Electrical and Electronics Engineers (IEEE)** defines industry-wide standards that promote the use and implementation of technology. In February 1980, a committee called the 802 Working Group took over from the private sector the job of defining network standards. The IEEE 802 committee defines frames, speeds, distances, and types of cabling to use in a network environment. Concentrating on cables, the IEEE recognizes that no single cabling solution can work in all situations and, therefore, provides a variety of cabling standards.

IEEE committees define standards for a wide variety of electronics. The names of these committees are often used to refer to the standards they publish. The **IEEE 1284** committee, for example, set standards for parallel communication, so you would see parallel cables marked "IEEE 1284 compliant," as in Figure 2.26.

• **Figure 2.26** Parallel cable marked IEEE 1284-compliant

The IEEE 802 committee sets the standards for networking. Although the original plan was to define a single, universal standard for networking, it quickly became apparent that no single solution would work for all needs. The 802 committee split into smaller subcommittees, with names such as IEEE 802.3 and IEEE 802.11. Table 2.4 shows the currently recognized IEEE 802 subcommittees and their areas of jurisdiction. The missing numbers, such as 802.2 and 802.12, were used for committees long-ago disbanded. Each subcommittee is officially called a Working Group, except the few listed as a Technical Advisory Group (TAG) in the table.

Table 2.4	Some IEEE 802 Subcommittees
IEEE 802.1	Higher Layer LAN Protocols (with many subcommittees, like 802.1X for port-based network access control)
IEEE 802.3	Ethernet (with a ton of subcommittees, such as 802.3ae for 10-Gigabit Ethernet)
IEEE 802.11	Wireless LAN (WLAN); specifications, such as Wi-Fi, and many subcommittees
IEEE 802.15	Wireless Personal Area Network (WPAN)
IEEE 802.18	Radio Regulatory Technical Advisory Group
IEEE 802.19	Wireless Coexistence Working Group
IEEE 802.24	Vertical Applications Technical Advisory Group

Chapter 2 Review

Chapter Summary

After reading this chapter and completing the exercises, you should understand the following about cabling and topology.

Explain the Different Types of Network Topologies

- A network's *topology* describes how computers connect to each other in that network. The network topologies referred to on the CompTIA Network+ objectives are called *bus*, *ring*, *star/hub-and-spoke*, *hybrid*, and *mesh*.
- In a bus topology, all computers connected to the network via a main line. The cable had to be terminated at both ends to prevent signal reflections.
- In a ring topology, all computers on the network attached to a ring of cable. A single break in the cable stopped the flow of data through the entire network.
- In a star/hub-and-spoke topology, the computers on the network connected to a central wiring point, which provided fault tolerance.
- Networks turned to the two hybrid topologies, *star-bus* and *star-ring*, many years ago. Only star-bus is used today.
- In a mesh topology, each computer has a dedicated connection to two or more other computers.
- You'll see mesh in the context of wireless networks.

Describe the Different Types of Network Cabling and Connectors

- Copper cabling comes in two forms: coaxial and twisted pair.
- Coaxial cable, or coax, shields data transmissions from EMI. Coax in various forms was widely used in early bus networks and used BNC connectors. Today, coax is used mainly to connect a cable modem to an ISP.
- Coax cables have an RG rating, with RG-6 being the predominant coax today.
- Twisted pair, which comes shielded or unshielded, is the most common type of networking cable today. UTP is less expensive and more popular than STP, though it doesn't offer any protection from EMI.
- UTP is categorized by its Cat rating, with Cat 5e, Cat 6, and Cat 6a being the most commonly used today.
- UTP uses RJ-45 connectors.
- Fiber-optic cabling transmits light instead of the electricity used in copper cables. It is thin and more expensive, yet less flexible and more delicate, than other types of network cabling.
- There are two types of fiber-optic cable based on what type of light is used. LEDs require multimode cable, whereas lasers generally require single-mode cable.
- All fiber-optic cable has four parts: the fiber itself; the cladding, which covers the fiber and helps it reflect down the fiber; buffer material to give strength; and the outer insulating jacket. Additionally, there are over one hundred types of connectors for fiber-optic cable, but ST, SC, LC, and MT-RJ are the most common for computer networking.
- Plenum-rated UTP is required by most cities for network installations.

Describe the IEEE Networking Standards

- Networking standards are established and promoted by the Institute of Electrical and Electronics Engineers (IEEE).
- The IEEE 802 committee defines frames, speeds, distances, and types of cabling to use in networks. IEEE 802 is split into several subcommittees, including IEEE 802.3 and IEEE 802.11.

Key Terms

8 position 8 contact (8P8C) *(39)*
bandwidth *(38)*
BNC connector *(35)*
buffer *(39)*
bus topology *(31)*
category (Cat) rating *(38)*

cladding *(39)*
coaxial cable *(35)*
core *(39)*
crosstalk *(37)*
electromagnetic interference (EMI) *(35)*
F (F-type) connector *(35)*
fault tolerance *(32)*
fiber-optic cable *(39)*
fully meshed topology *(34)*
hub-and-spoke *(32)*
hybrid topology *(33)*
Institute of Electrical and Electronics Engineers (IEEE) *(42)*
IEEE 1284 *(42)*
insulating jacket *(39)*
logical topology *(33)*
mesh topology *(33)*
modal distortion *(40)*
multimode fiber (MMF) *(40)*
network technology *(34)*
network topology *(30)*
Ohm rating *(36)*
partially meshed topology *(34)*
physical topology *(33)*
plenum *(41)*
plenum-rated cable *(41)*
polyvinyl chloride (PVC) *(41)*
PVC-rated cable *(41)*
Radio Guide (RG) rating *(36)*
registered jack (RJ) *(39)*
ring topology *(31)*
riser *(41)*
riser-rated *(41)*
RG-6 *(36)*
RG-59 *(36)*
RJ-11 *(39)*
RJ-45 *(39)*
segment *(33)*
shielded twisted pair (STP) *(37)*
signaling topology *(33)*
single-mode fiber (SMF) *(40)*
star topology *(32)*
star-bus topology *(33)*
star-ring topology *(33)*
twinaxial *(36)*
unshielded twisted pair (UTP) *(37)*

Key Term Quiz

Use the Key Terms list to complete the sentences that follow. Not all terms will be used.

1. The _______________ is a network topology that relies on a main line of network coaxial cabling.
2. The _______________ of a cable determines its speed.
3. A(n) _______________ provides more fault tolerance than any other basic network topology.
4. When your network has all computers connected to a centrally located wiring closet, you have a physical _______________ network.
5. _______________ networks use more than one type of basic network topology.
6. Cat 6a cable is a type of _______________ wiring.
7. Coaxial cable uses a braided metal shield to protect data from _______________.
8. Network cabling can use either light or electricity to transmit data. The faster of these types uses light along _______________.
9. _______________-grade UTP must be installed in ceilings, whereas _______________-grade UTP is often used to connect one floor to another vertically in a building.
10. The twisting of the cables in UTP and STP reduces _______________.

Multiple-Choice Quiz

1. Which of the following are classic network topologies? (Select three.)
   - **A.** Bus
   - **B.** Star
   - **C.** Ring
   - **D.** Dual-ring
2. John was carrying on at the water cooler the other day, trying to show off his knowledge of networking. He claimed that the company had installed special cabling to handle the problems of crosstalk on the network. What kind of cabling did the company install?
   - **A.** Coaxial
   - **B.** Shielded coaxial
   - **C.** Unshielded twisted pair
   - **D.** Fiber-optic
3. Jill needs to run some UTP cable from one office to another. She found a box of cable in the closet and wants to make sure it's Cat 5e or better. How can she tell the Cat level of the cable? (Select two.)
   - **A.** Check the box.
   - **B.** Scan for markings on the cable.
   - **C.** Check the color of the cable—gray means Cat 5e, yellow means Cat 6a, and so on.
   - **D.** Check the ends of the cable.
4. What topology provides the most fault tolerance?
   - **A.** Bus
   - **B.** Ring
   - **C.** Star-bus
   - **D.** Mesh
5. What organization is responsible for establishing and promoting networking standards?
   - **A.** Institute of Electrical and Electronics Engineers (IEEE)
   - **B.** International Networking Standards Organization (INSO)
   - **C.** Federal Communications Commission (FCC)
   - **D.** International Telecommunications Association (ITA)
6. What aspects of network cabling do the IEEE committees establish? (Select three.)
   - **A.** Frame size
   - **B.** Speed
   - **C.** Color of sheathing
   - **D.** Cable types
7. What types of coax cabling have been used in computer networking? (Select two.)
   - **A.** RG-6
   - **B.** RG-11
   - **C.** RG-45
   - **D.** RG-59
8. What applications are best suited for fiber-optic cabling? (Select two.)
   - **A.** Short distances
   - **B.** Wireless networks
   - **C.** High-EMI areas
   - **D.** Long distances
9. What are the main components of fiber-optic cabling? (Select three.)
   - **A.** Cladding
   - **B.** Insulating jacket
   - **C.** Copper core
   - **D.** Fiber
10. What is the most popular size of fiber-optic cabling?
    - **A.** 62.5/125 µm
    - **B.** 125/62.5 µm
    - **C.** 50/125 µm
    - **D.** 125/50 µm
11. Most fiber-optic installations use LEDs to send light signals and are known as what?
    - **A.** Single-mode
    - **B.** Multimode
    - **C.** Complex mode
    - **D.** Duplex mode

12. Why was the main cable in a bus topology terminated at both ends?
    - A. To allow the signal to be amplified so it could reach both ends of the network
    - B. To prevent the signal from dropping off the network before reaching all computers
    - C. To prevent the signal from bouncing back and forth
    - D. To convert the signal to the proper format for a bus network
13. Where are you most likely to encounter a mesh network?
    - A. On any network using fiber-optic cable
    - B. On any network using plenum cable
    - C. On wireless networks
    - D. On wired networks
14. You are asked by your boss to research upgrading all the network cable in your office building. The building manager requires the safest possible cabling type in case of fire, and your boss wants to future-proof the network so cabling doesn't need to be replaced when network technologies faster than 1 Gbps come on the market. You decide to use Cat 5e plenum cabling throughout the building. Which objective have you satisfied?
    - A. Neither the building manager's nor your boss's requirements have been met.
    - B. Only the building manager's requirement has been met.
    - C. Only your boss's requirement has been met.
    - D. Both the building manager's and your boss's requirements have been met.
15. Which committee is responsible for wireless networking standards?
    - A. IEEE 802.2
    - B. IEEE 802.3
    - C. IEEE 802.5
    - D. IEEE 802.11

Essay Quiz

1. Your boss has decided to have cable run to every computer in the office, but doesn't know which type to use. To help bring the company into the 21st century, write a short essay comparing the merits of UTP and fiber-optic cabling.
2. Your company has hired a group of new network techs, and you've been tasked to do their training session on networking standards organizations. Write a brief essay detailing the IEEE and its various committees.

Lab Projects

• Lab Project 2.1

This lab project requires you to demonstrate knowledge of the four classic network topologies. Obtain four blank pieces of paper. Proceed to draw six boxes on each page to represent six computers—neatness counts! At the top of each sheet, write one of the following: bus topology, mesh topology, ring topology, or star topology. Then draw lines to represent the physical network cabling required by each network topology.

• Lab Project 2.2

In your studies of network cabling for the CompTIA Network+ certification exam, you realize you could use a simplified chart to study from and memorize. Build a reference study chart that describes the features of network cabling.

Create your completed chart using a spreadsheet program, or simply a sheet of paper, with the column headings and names shown in this table. If you wish, you can start by writing your notes here.

Cable Type	Description	Benefits	Drawbacks
Cat 5			
Cat 5e			
Cat 6			
Cat 6a			
Fiber-optic			

• Lab Project 2.3

In this lab project, you will demonstrate knowledge of the different IEEE committees that are most prevalent today. Use the Internet to research both of these subcommittees: IEEE 802.3 and IEEE 802.11. Give an example of where each type of technology might best be used.

Ethernet Basics

"In theory there is no difference between theory and practice. In practice there is."
—Yogi Berra

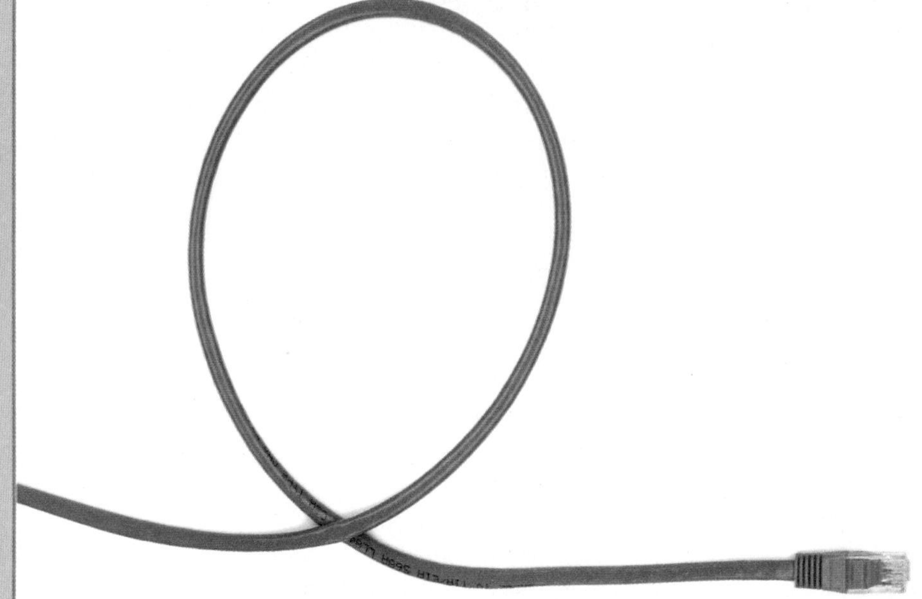

In this chapter, you will learn how to

- **Define and describe Ethernet**
- **Explain early Ethernet implementations**
- **Describe ways to enhance and extend Ethernet networks**

In the beginning, there were no networks. Computers were isolated, solitary islands of information in a teeming sea of proto-geeks who banged out binary messages with wooden clubs and wore fur pocket protectors. Okay, maybe it wasn't that bad, but if you wanted to move a file from one machine to another, you had to use **Sneakernet**, which meant you saved the file on a disk, laced up your tennis shoes, and hiked over to the other system.

All that walking no doubt produced lots of health benefits, but frankly, proto-geeks weren't all that into health benefits—they were into speed, power, and technological coolness in general. (Sound familiar?) It's no wonder, then, that geeks everywhere agreed on the need to replace walking with some form of networking technology that connects computers together to transfer data at very high speeds.

This chapter explores the networking technology that eventually took control of the industry, Ethernet. We'll start with basic terminology, then look at two early forms of Ethernet. The chapter finishes with a discussion on enhancing and expanding Ethernet networks.

Historical/Conceptual

Ethernet

In 1973, Xerox answered the challenge of moving data without sneakers by developing **Ethernet**, a networking technology standard based on a bus topology. The original Ethernet used a single piece of coaxial cable to connect several computers, enabling them to transfer data at a rate of up to three million bits per second (3 Mbps). Although slow by today's standards, this early version of Ethernet was a huge improvement over manual transfer methods and served as the foundation for all later versions of Ethernet.

Ethernet remained a largely in-house technology within Xerox until 1979, when Xerox decided to look for partners to help promote Ethernet as an industry standard. Xerox worked with Digital Equipment Corporation (DEC) and Intel to publish what became known as the Digital/Intel/Xerox (DIX) standard. The DIX Ethernet standard improved on the original Ethernet standard, increasing speed to a screaming 10 Mbps.

These companies then did something visionary: they transferred (one might also say gave away) control of the Ethernet standard to the Institute of Electrical and Electronics Engineers (IEEE), which, in turn, created the **802.3 (Ethernet)** working group that continues to control the Ethernet standard to this day. By transferring control to IEEE, Ethernet became an open standard, enabling anyone to make interchangeable Ethernet equipment. Making Ethernet an open standard made Ethernet much cheaper than any alternative technology and certainly contributed to Ethernet winning the marketplace.

802.3 Standards

The 802.3 working group defines wired network standards that share the same basic frame type and network access method. Each of these variants is under the IEEE 802.3 standard, each with its own identifier. Here's a small selection of 802.3 standards:

- **802.3i** 10 Mbps Ethernet using twisted pair cabling (1990)
- **802.3ab** Gigabit Ethernet over twisted pair (1999)
- **802.3by** 25 Gigabit Ethernet over fiber (2016)
- **802.3cm** 400 Gigabit Ethernet over multimode fiber (2020)
- **802.3cu** 100 Gigabit and 400 Gigabit Ethernet over single mode fiber using 100-Gbps lanes (2021)

Because the technologies share essential components, you can communicate among them just fine. The implementation of the network might be different, but *the frames remain the same.*

Ethernet's designers faced the same challenges as the designers of any network: how to send data across the wire, how to identify the sending and receiving computers, and how to determine which computer should use the shared cable at what time. The engineers resolved these issues by using data frames that contain MAC addresses to identify computers on the network and by using a process called CSMA/CD (discussed shortly)

The source for all things Ethernet is but a short click away on the Internet. For starters, check out www.ieee802.org.

to determine which machine should access the wire at any given time. You saw some of this in action in Chapter 1, but now I need to introduce you to a bunch of additional terms.

Test Specific

Ethernet Frames

All network technologies break data transmitted between computers into segments or datagrams, placed into packets that in turn get placed into **frames**, as you'll recall from Chapter 1. Using frames addresses two networking issues. First, frames prevent any single machine from monopolizing the shared bus cable. Second, they make the process of retransmitting lost data more efficient.

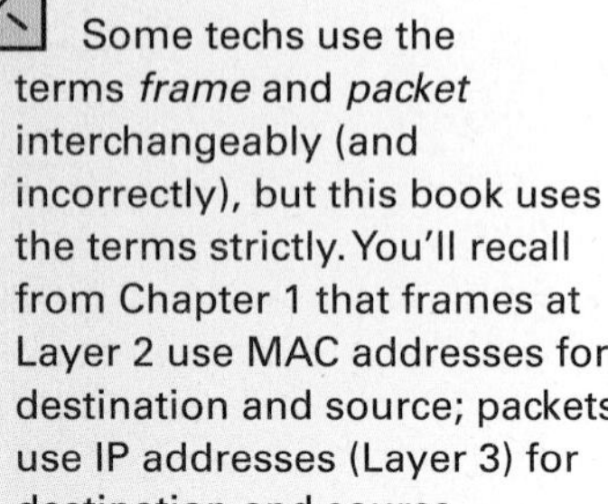

Some techs use the terms *frame* and *packet* interchangeably (and incorrectly), but this book uses the terms strictly. You'll recall from Chapter 1 that frames at Layer 2 use MAC addresses for destination and source; packets use IP addresses (Layer 3) for destination and source.

The process you saw in Chapter 1 of transferring a word processing document between two computers illustrates these two issues. First, if the sending computer sends the document as a single huge frame, the frame will monopolize the cable and prevent other machines from using the cable until the entire file gets to the receiving system. Using relatively small frames enables computers to share the cable easily—each computer listens on the **network segment**, sending a few frames of data whenever it detects that no other computer is transmitting. Second, in the real world, bad things can happen to good data. When errors occur during transmission, the sending system must retransmit the frames that failed to reach the receiving system in good shape. If a word processing document were transmitted as a single massive frame, the sending system would have to retransmit the entire frame—in this case, the entire document. Breaking the file up into smaller frames enables the sending computer to retransmit only the damaged frames. Because of these benefits—shared access and more efficient retransmission—all networking technologies use frames.

In Chapter 1, you saw a generic frame. Let's take what you know of frames and expand on that knowledge by inspecting the details of an Ethernet frame. A basic Ethernet frame contains five fields: the *destination address*—the MAC address of the frame's recipient; the *source address*—the MAC address of the sending system; the *type* of the data; the *data* itself; and a *frame check sequence*. Figure 3.1 shows these components. Transmission of a frame starts with a *preamble* and can also include some extra filler called a *pad*. Let's look at each piece.

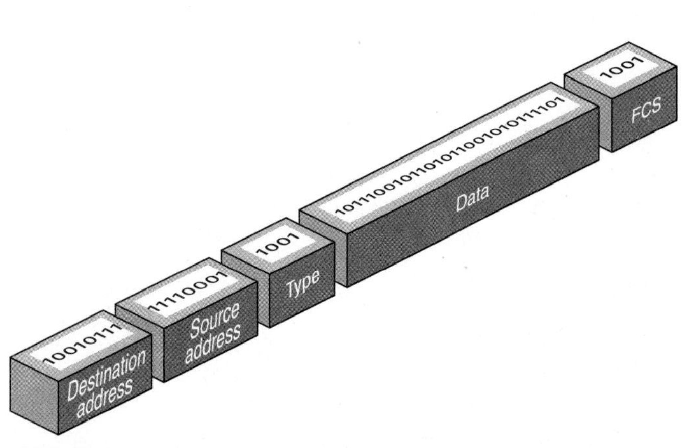

• **Figure 3.1** Ethernet frame

Preamble

A **preamble**, a 7-byte series of alternating ones and zeroes followed by a 1-byte **start frame delimiter** or an 8-byte series of alternating ones and zeroes, always precedes a frame. The preamble gives a receiving NIC time to realize a frame is coming and to know exactly where the frame starts. The preamble is added by the sending NIC.

MAC Addresses

Each NIC on an Ethernet network must have a unique identifying address. Ethernet identifies the NICs on a network using special 48-bit (6-byte) binary addresses known as **MAC addresses**.

The CompTIA Network+ exam might describe MAC addresses as 48-bit binary addresses or 6-byte binary addresses.

In a bus network, all the connected computers could see all traffic. The **destination address** in the frame enabled NICs to examine each frame and process only frames intended for them. The **source address** in the frame enabled the recipient to respond accurately.

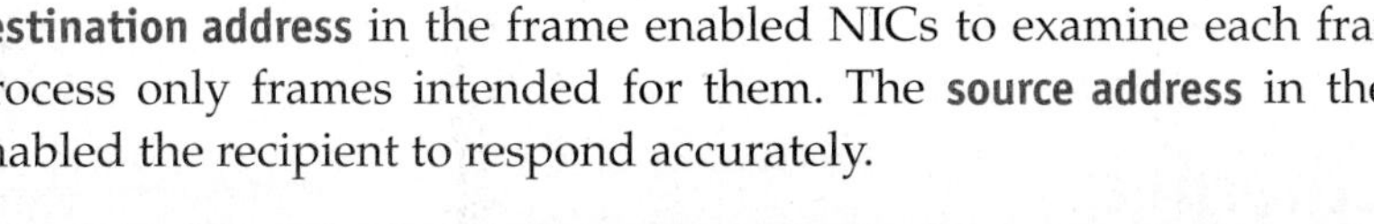

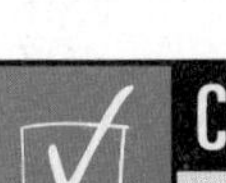

Cross Check

NICs and OSI

You learned about NICs and MAC addresses in Chapter 1, so check your memory with these questions: Where does the NIC get its MAC address? How does the MAC address manifest on the card? At what layer or layers of the OSI seven-layer model does the NIC operate?

Type

An Ethernet frame may carry one of several types of data. The **type** field helps the receiving computer interpret the frame contents at a very basic level. This way the receiving computer can tell if the frame contains IPv4 data, for example, or IPv6 data. (See Chapter 6 for more details on IPv4; I cover IPv6 in Chapter 12.)

The type field does *not* tell you if the frame carries higher-level data, such as an e-mail message or Web page. You have to dig deeper into the data section of the frame to find that information.

Data

The **data** part of the frame contains whatever payload the frame carries. If the frame carries an IP packet, that packet will include extra information, such as the IP addresses of the source and destination systems.

Pad

The minimum Ethernet frame is 64 bytes in size, but not all of that has to be actual data. If an Ethernet frame has fewer than 64 bytes of data to haul, the sending NIC automatically adds extra data—a **pad**—to bring the data up to the minimum 64 bytes. Padding is used all the time in modern networking.

Frame Check Sequence

The **frame check sequence (FCS)** enables Ethernet nodes to recognize when bad things happen to good data. Machines on a network must be able to detect when data has been damaged in transit. To detect errors, the computers on an Ethernet network attach a special code to each frame. When creating an Ethernet frame, the sending machine runs the data through a special mathematical formula called a **cyclic redundancy check (CRC)** and attaches the result, the FCS, to the frame as the trailer. The receiving machine opens the frame, performs the same calculation, and compares its answer with the one included with the frame. If the answers do not match, the receiving machine drops the frame.

Early Ethernet Standards

Contemplating the physical network brings up numerous questions. What kind of cables should you use? What should they be made of? How long can they be? For these answers, turn to the IEEE 802.3 standard, both true bus and star-bus versions.

Bus Ethernet

The original Ethernet networks employed a true bus topology, meaning every computer on a network connected to the same cable, the bus. Every version of Ethernet invented since the early 1990s uses a hybrid star-bus topology. At the center of these early networks was a **hub**. A hub was nothing more than an electronic **repeater**—it interpreted the ones and zeroes coming in from one port and repeated the same signal out to the other connected ports. Hubs did not send the same signal back down the port that originally sent it (Figure 3.2). Any scenario involving these early networks found the placement of a hub at the center of the network.

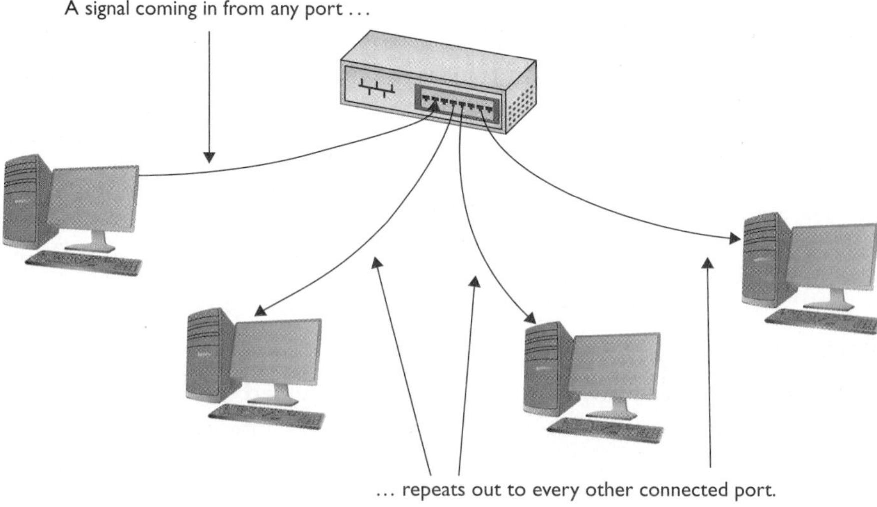

A signal coming in from any port . . .
. . . repeats out to every other connected port.

• **Figure 3.2** Ethernet hub

10BASE-T

In 1990, the IEEE 802.3 committee created a version of Ethernet called **10BASE-T** that rapidly became the most popular network technology in the world, replacing competing and now long-gone competitors with names like Token Ring and LocalTalk. The classic 10BASE-T network consisted of two or more computers connected to a central hub. The NICs connected with wires as specified by the 802.3 committee.

The name 10BASE-T follows roughly the same naming convention used for earlier Ethernet cabling systems. The number *10* refers to the speed: 10 Mbps. The word *BASE* refers to the signaling type: baseband. (*Baseband* means that the cable carries only one signal. Contrast this with *broadband*—as in cable television—where the cable carries multiple signals or channels.) The letter *T* refers to the type of cable used: twisted pair. 10BASE-T used unshielded twisted pair (UTP) cabling.

Cross Check

Physical vs. Logical

You might be tempted at this moment to define 10BASE-T in terms of physical topology versus logical topology—after all, 10BASE-T uses a physical star, but a logical bus. Refer to Chapter 2, "Cabling and Topology," however, and cross-check your memory. What's a physical topology? And a logical topology? What would you say if you were sent back in time and walked into an office building that implemented a 10BASE-T network? Yes, if you actually *walked into* it, you'd probably say "Ouch!" But beyond that, think about how you would describe the wires and connectors you would see in terms of physical or logical topology.

UTP

Officially, 10BASE-T required the use of Cat 3 (or higher), two-pair, UTP cable. One pair of wires sent data to the hub while the other pair received data from the hub. Even though 10BASE-T only required two-pair cabling, everyone installed four-pair cabling to connect devices to the hub as insurance against the possible requirements of newer types of networking (Figure 3.3). Not surprisingly, this came in handy very soon. See Chapter 4 for more details.

Most UTP cables (then and now) come with stranded Kevlar fibers to give the cable added strength, which, in turn, enables installers to pull on the cable without excessive risk of literally ripping it apart.

10BASE-T also introduced the networking world to the **RJ-45 connector** (Figure 3.4). Each pin on the RJ-45 connects to a single wire inside the cable; this enables devices to put voltage on the individual wires within the cable. The pins on the RJ-45 are numbered from 1 to 8, as shown in Figure 3.5.

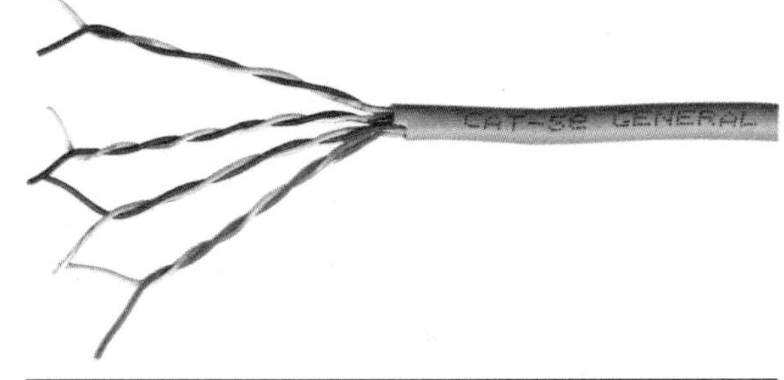

• **Figure 3.3** A typical four-pair Cat 5e unshielded twisted pair cable

• **Figure 3.4** Two views of an RJ-45 connector

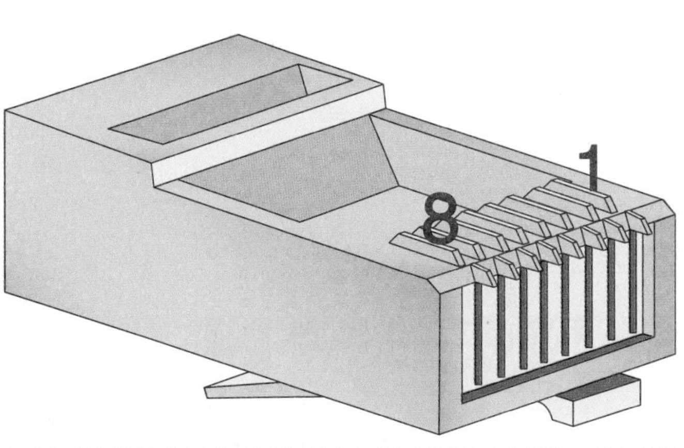

• **Figure 3.5** The pins on an RJ-45 connector are numbered 1 through 8.

As noted in Chapter 2, the real name for RJ-45 is *8 position 8 contact (8P8C)* modular plug. The term RJ-45 is so prevalent, however, that nobody but the nerdiest of nerds calls it by its real name. Stick to RJ-45.

The current twisted pair cabling standard includes the same wiring standards as TIA/EIA 568A and TIA/EIA 568B. It's all just wrapped up in a slightly different name: *ANSI/TIA-568-D*. When the EIA left the planet in 2011, the names of the standards changed. CompTIA continues to use the older names on exams.

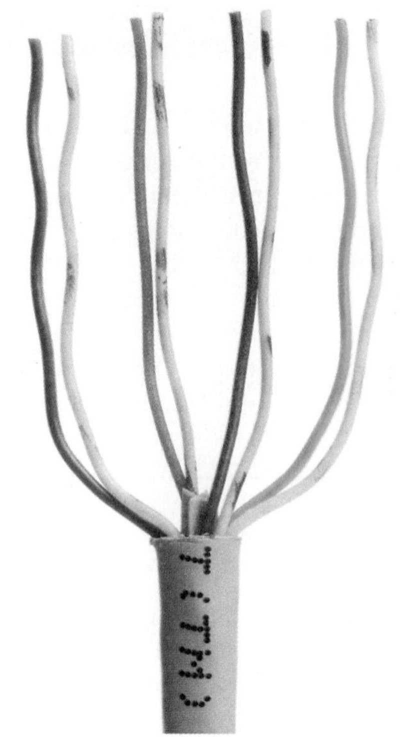

• **Figure 3.6** Color-coded pairs (note the alternating solid and striped wires)

The 10BASE-T standard designates some of these numbered wires for specific purposes. As mentioned earlier, although the cable has four pairs, 10BASE-T used only two of the pairs. 10BASE-T devices used pins 1 and 2 to send data, and pins 3 and 6 to receive data. Even though one pair of wires sent data and another received data, a 10BASE-T device that was connected to a hub could not send and receive simultaneously. See "CSMA/CD" later in this chapter for details about collisions and using a shared bus.

NICs that can communicate in only one direction at a time run in **half-duplex** mode. Later advances (as you'll see shortly) enabled NICs to send and receive at the same time, thus running in **full-duplex** mode.

An RJ-45 connector is sometimes called a *crimp*, and the act (some folks call it an art) of installing a crimp onto the end of a piece of UTP cable is called *crimping*. The tool used to secure a crimp onto the end of a cable is a **crimper**. Each wire inside a UTP cable must connect to the proper pin inside the crimp. Manufacturers color-code each wire within a piece of four-pair UTP to assist in properly matching the ends. Each pair of wires consists of a solid-colored wire and a striped wire: blue/blue-white, orange/orange-white, brown/brown-white, and green/green-white (Figure 3.6).

The Telecommunications Industry Association/Electronics Industries Alliance (TIA/EIA) defines the industry *termination standard* for correct crimping of four-pair UTP. You'll find two standards mentioned on the CompTIA Network+ exam: **TIA/EIA 568A** and **TIA/EIA 568B**. Figure 3.7 shows the TIA/EIA 568A and TIA/EIA 568B color-code standards. Note that the wire pairs used by 10BASE-T (1 and 2, 3 and 6) come from the same color pairs (green/green-white

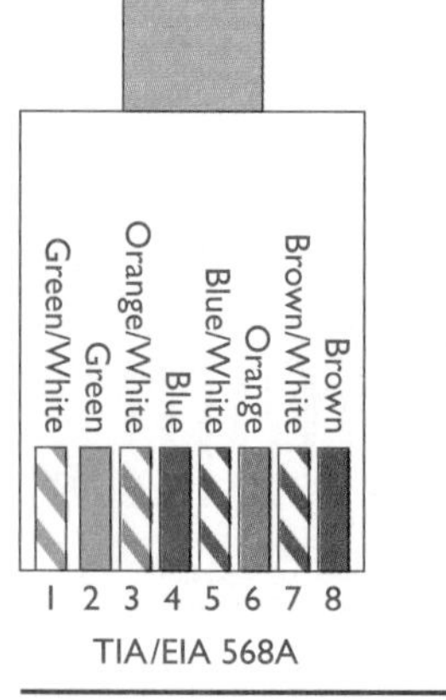

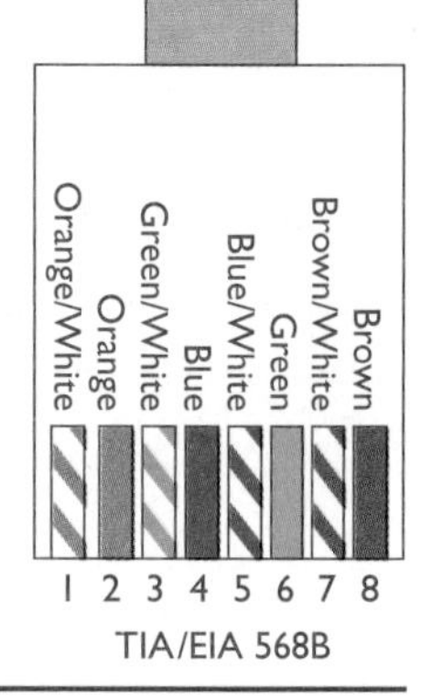

• **Figure 3.7** The TIA/EIA 568A and 568B standards

and orange/orange-white). Following an established color-code scheme, such as TIA/EIA 568A, ensures that the wires match up correctly at each end of the cable.

The ability to make your own Ethernet cables is a real plus for a network tech. With a reel of Cat 5e, a bag of RJ-45 connectors, a moderate investment in a crimping tool, and a little practice, you can kiss those mass-produced cables goodbye! You can make cables to your own length specifications, replace broken RJ-45 connectors that would otherwise mean tossing an entire cable, and, in the process, save your company or clients time and money.

An easy trick to remembering the difference between 568A and 568B is the word "GO." The green and orange pairs are swapped between 568A and 568B, whereas the blue and brown pairs stay in the same place!
For the CompTIA Network+ exam, you will be tested on the TIA/EIA 568A or 568B color codes. Memorize them. You'll see the standards listed as EIA/TIA 568A, TIA/EIA568A, T568A, or just 568A. Know the A and B and you'll be fine.

10BASE-T Limits and Specifications

Like any other Ethernet standard, 10BASE-T had limitations, both on cable distance and on the number of computers. The key distance limitation for 10BASE-T was the distance between the hub and the computer. The twisted pair cable connecting a computer to the hub could not exceed 100 meters in length. A 10BASE-T hub could connect no more than 1024 computers, although that limitation rarely came into play. It made no sense for vendors to build hubs that large—or more to the point, that *expensive*.

10BASE-T Summary

- **Speed** 10 Mbps
- **Signal type** Baseband
- **Distance** 100 meters between the hub and the node
- **Node limit** No more than 1024 nodes per hub
- **Topology** Star-bus topology: physical star, logical bus
- **Cable type** Cat 3 or better UTP cabling with RJ-45 connectors

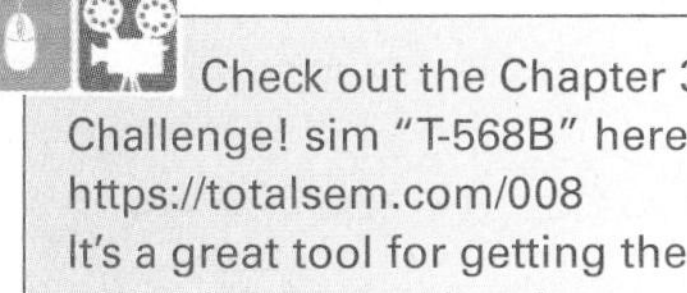

Check out the Chapter 3 Challenge! sim "T-568B" here: https://totalsem.com/008
It's a great tool for getting the colors set in your head.

10BASE-FL

Just a few years after the introduction of 10BASE-T, a fiber-optic version, called **10BASE-FL**, appeared. As you know from the previous chapter, fiber-optic cabling transmits data using pulses of light instead of using electrical current. Using light instead of electricity addresses the three key weaknesses of copper cabling. First, optical signals can travel much farther. The maximum length for a 10BASE-FL cable was up to 2 kilometers, depending on how you configured it. Second, fiber-optic cable is immune to electrical interference, making it an ideal choice for high-interference environments. Third, the cable is much more difficult to tap into, making fiber a good choice for environments with security concerns. 10BASE-FL used **multimode** 62.5/125 µm (OM1) fiber-optic cabling and employed either an SC or ST connector.

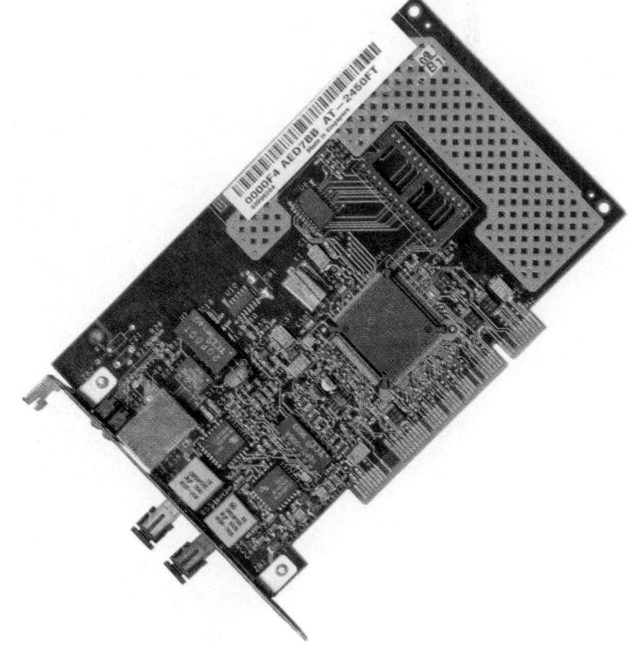

• **Figure 3.8** Typical 10BASE-FL card

Figure 3.8 shows a typical 10BASE-FL card. Note that it uses two fiber connectors—one to send and

10BASE-FL is *not* on the CompTIA Network+ exam. Its successor, 100BASE-FX is on the exam; we'll get there in Chapter 4.

CSMA/CD was a network access method that mapped to the IEEE 802.3 standard for Ethernet networks. It's disabled in modern full-duplex networks, but still shows up on the objectives for an exam in your near future.

one to receive. All fiber-optic networks use at least two fiber-optic cables. Although 10BASE-FL enjoyed some popularity for a number of years, most networks today are using the same fiber-optic cabling to run far faster network technologies.

10BASE-FL Summary

- **Speed** 10 Mbps
- **Signal type** Baseband
- **Distance** 2000 meters between the hub and the node
- **Node limit** No more than 1024 nodes per hub
- **Topology** Star-bus topology: physical star, logical bus
- **Cable type** Multimode 62.5/125 µm (OM1) fiber-optic cabling with ST or SC connectors

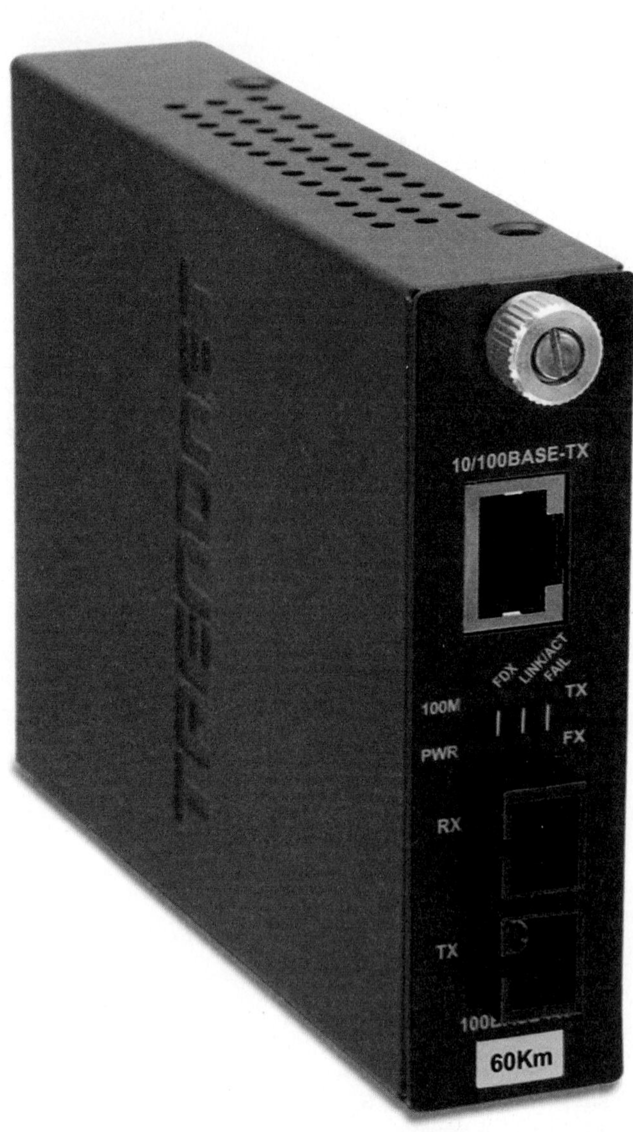

• **Figure 3.9** Typical copper-to-fiber Ethernet media converter (photo courtesy of TRENDnet)

So far you've seen two different flavors of star-bus Ethernet, 10BASE-T and 10BASE-FL. Even though these used different cabling and hubs, they used Ethernet frames. As a result, interconnecting flavors of Ethernet were (and still are) common. Because 10BASE-T and 10BASE-FL used different types of cable, you could use a **media converter** (Figure 3.9) to interconnect different Ethernet types.

CSMA/CD

One of the issues with bus communication is that devices essentially share the same cable. This applies to pure bus networks and hybrid star-bus networks as well. The NICs need some way to determine which machine should send data at which time. Ethernet designers came up with a clever way to handle the issue of potential collisions.

Ethernet networks used a system called **carrier-sense multiple access with collision detection (CSMA/CD)** to determine which computer should use a shared cable at a given moment. *Carrier sense* meant that each node using the network examined the cable before sending a data frame (Figure 3.10). If another machine was using the network, the node detected traffic on the segment, waited a few milliseconds, and then rechecked. If it detected no traffic, the node sent out its frame.

Multiple access meant that all machines had equal access to the wire. If the line was free, any Ethernet node could send a frame. From Ethernet's point of view, it didn't matter what function the node performed: it could have been a desktop system running Windows 98 or a file server running Windows Server or Linux. As far as early Ethernet was concerned,

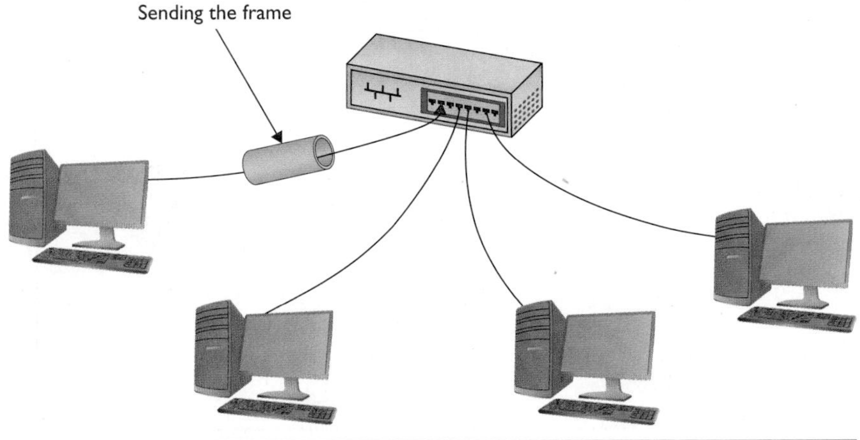

• **Figure 3.10** No one else is talking—send the frame!

a node was a node was a node and access to the cable was assigned strictly on a first-come, first-served basis.

So what happened if two machines, both listening to the cable, simultaneously decided that it was free and tried to send a frame? A collision occurred, and both of the transmissions were lost (Figure 3.11). A collision resembled the effect of two people talking at the same time: the listener hears a mixture of two voices and can't understand either one.

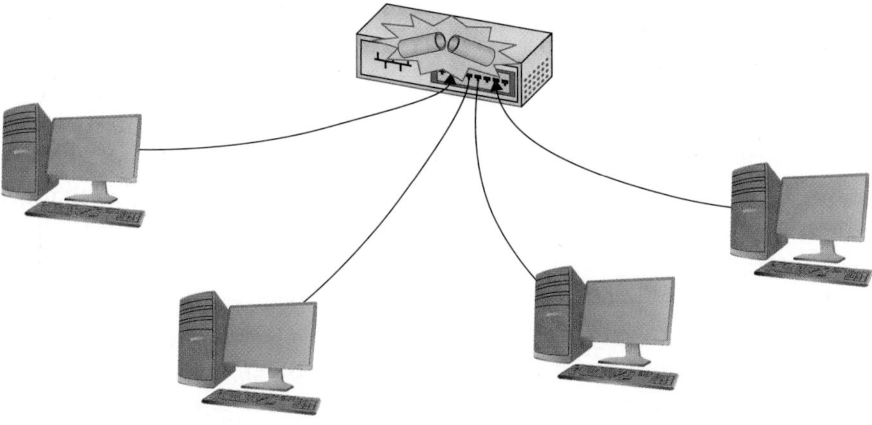

• **Figure 3.11** Collision!

When two NICs sent at the same time, they'd sense the overlapping signals and immediately know that a collision occurred. When they detected a collision, both nodes stopped transmitting.

They then each generated a random number to determine how long to wait before trying again. If you imagine that each machine rolled its magic electronic dice and waited for that number of seconds, you wouldn't be too far from the truth, except that the amount of time an Ethernet node waited to retransmit was much shorter than one second (Figure 3.12). Whichever node generated the lowest random number began its retransmission first, winning the competition to use the wire. The losing node then saw traffic on the wire and waited for the wire to be free again before attempting to retransmit its data.

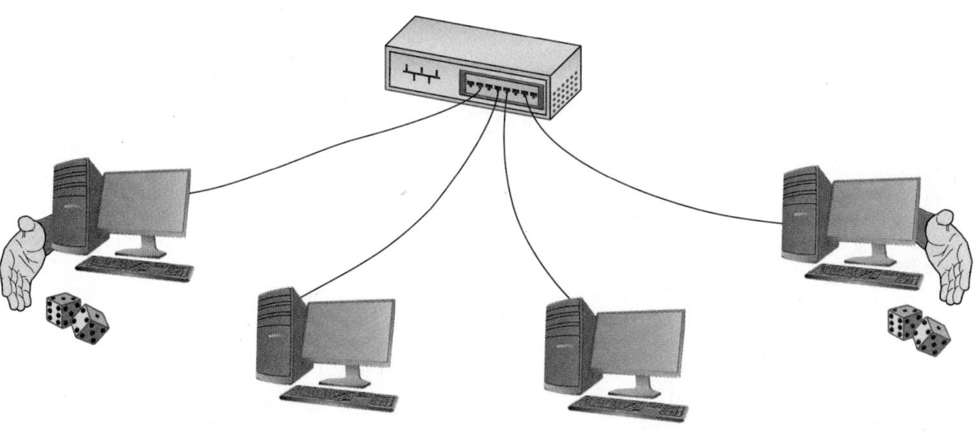

• **Figure 3.12** Rolling for timing

Collisions were a normal part of the operation of early Ethernet networks, because every device shared a bus. A group of nodes that have the capability of sending frames at the same time as each other, resulting in collisions, is called a **collision domain**. Better technology today eliminates collisions.

Enhancing and Extending Ethernet Networks

While plain-vanilla 10BASE-T Ethernet performed well enough for first-generation networks (which did little more than basic file and print sharing), by the early 1990s networks used more-demanding applications, such as Lotus Notes, SAP business management software, and Microsoft Exchange, which quickly saturated a 10BASE-T network. Fortunately, those crazy kids over at the IEEE kept expanding the standard, giving the network tech in the trenches a new tool that provided additional bandwidth—the switch.

Adding another hub or two to an early Ethernet network enabled you to add more devices, but also compounded the problem with collisions. In such a scenario, you could connect networks using a bridge. A **bridge** acted like a repeater to connect two networks, but then went a step further—filtering and forwarding traffic between those segments based on the MAC addresses of the computers on those segments. This placement between two segments preserved bandwidth, making larger Ethernet networks possible. You'll see the term "bridge" applied to modern devices, primarily in wireless networking. The interconnectedness of network segments is similar, but the devices are fundamentally different. See Chapter 14 for the scoop on wireless.

Additionally, more companies and organizations adopted Ethernet, leading to a demand for larger networks, both geographically and in the number of nodes that could interconnect. Hubs were cranky and creaky; switches brought much better scalability.

The Trouble with Hubs

A classic 10BASE-T network with a hub could only have one message on the wire at any time. When two computers sent at the same time, the hub dutifully repeated both signals. The nodes recognized the collision and, following the rules of CSMA/CD, attempted to resend. Add in enough computers and the number of collisions increased, lowering the effective transmission speed for the whole network. A busy network became a slow network because all the computers shared the same collision domain.

Switches to the Rescue

An Ethernet **switch** looks like a hub, because all nodes plug into it (Figure 3.13). But switches don't function like hubs inside. Switches come with extra smarts that enable them to take advantage of MAC addresses, effectively creating point-to-point connections between two conversing computers. This gives every conversation between two computers the full bandwidth of the network.

• **Figure 3.13** Hub (top) and switch (bottom) comparison

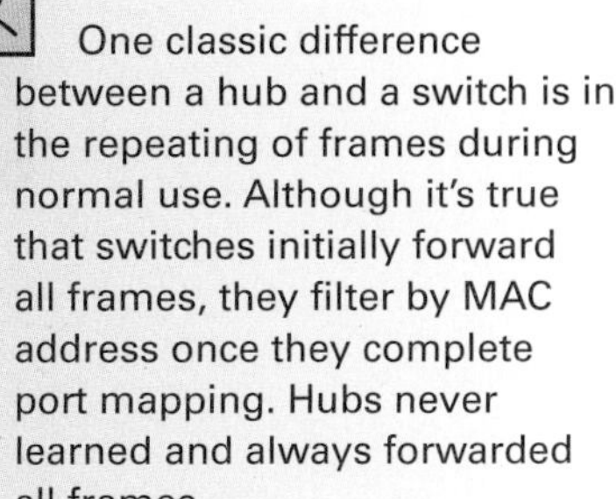

One classic difference between a hub and a switch is in the repeating of frames during normal use. Although it's true that switches initially forward all frames, they filter by MAC address once they complete port mapping. Hubs never learned and always forwarded all frames.

To see a switch in action, check out Figure 3.14. When you first turn on a switch, it acts like a hub, passing all incoming frames right back out to all the other ports. As it forwards all frames, however, the switch copies the source MAC addresses and quickly creates a table of the MAC addresses of each connected computer, called a **media access control (MAC) address table**.

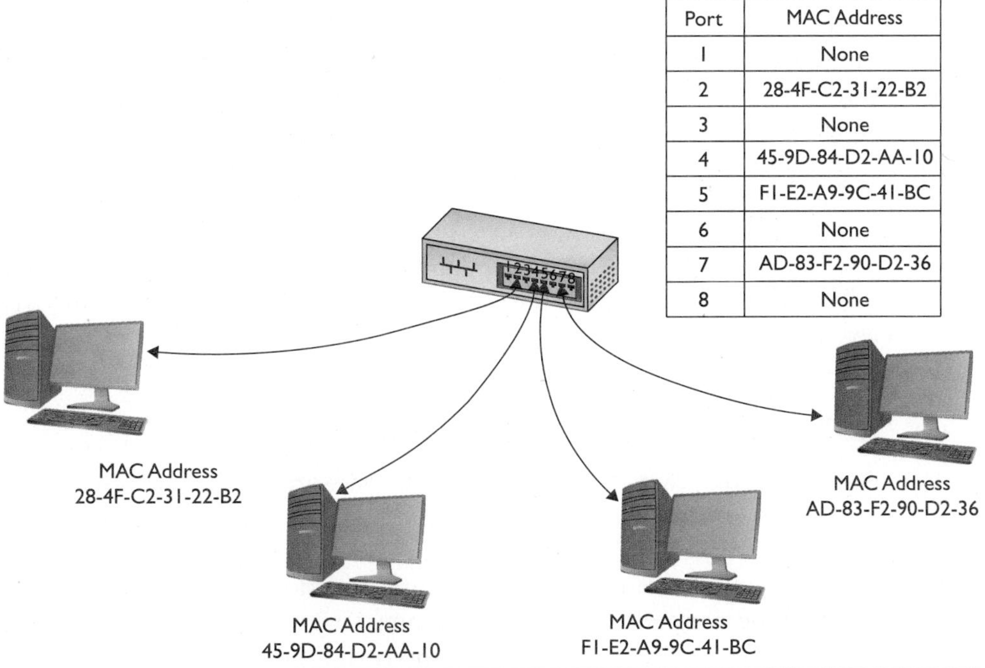

Port	MAC Address
1	None
2	28-4F-C2-31-22-B2
3	None
4	45-9D-84-D2-AA-10
5	F1-E2-A9-9C-41-BC
6	None
7	AD-83-F2-90-D2-36
8	None

• **Figure 3.14** A switch tracking MAC addresses

As soon as this table is created, the switch begins to do something amazing. When a computer sends a frame into the switch destined for another computer on the same switch, the switch acts like a telephone operator, creating an on-the-fly connection between the two devices. While these two devices communicate, it's as though they are the only two computers on the network. Figure 3.15 shows this in action. Because the switch handles each conversation individually, each conversation runs at the full network speed.

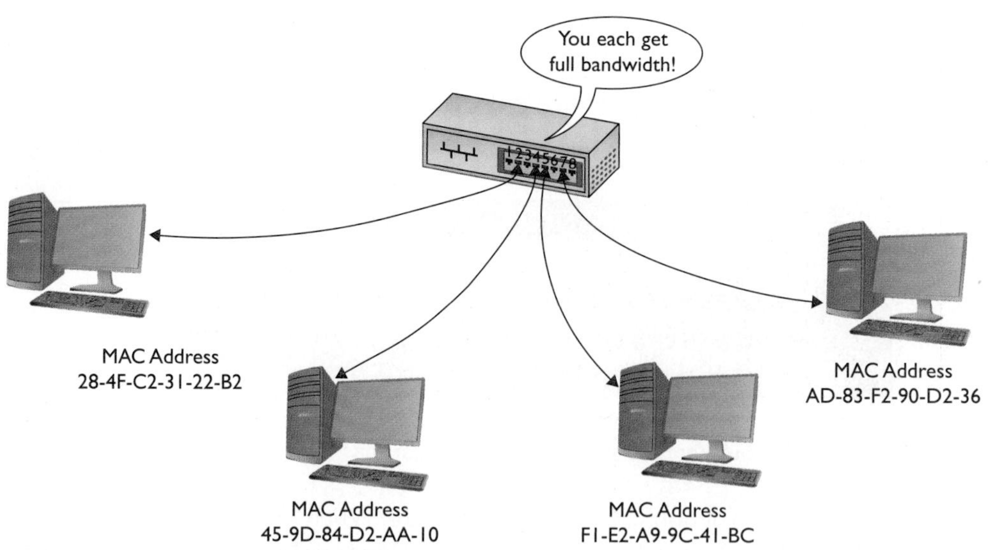

• **Figure 3.15** A switch making four separate connections

> Because a switch filters traffic on MAC addresses (and MAC addresses run at Layer 2 of the OSI seven-layer model), they are sometimes called *Layer 2 switches.*

Each port on a switch is in its own collision domain, plus the switch can buffer incoming frames. That means that two nodes connected to the switch can send data at the same time and the switch will handle it without any collision.

Unicast messages always go only to the intended recipient when you use a switch and the switch knows the destination address. The switch sends all broadcast messages to all the ports (except the port on which the frame originated). You'll commonly hear a switched network called a **broadcast domain** to contrast it to the ancient hub-based networks with their collision domains.

Connecting Ethernet Segments

Sometimes, one switch is just not enough. Once an organization uses every port on its existing switch, adding more nodes requires adding switches. Physical distance requirements also lead to the need for more switches. Even fault tolerance can motivate an organization to add more switches. If every node on the network connects to the same switch, that switch becomes a single point of failure—if it fails, everybody drops off the network. You can connect switches in two ways: via an uplink port or a crossover cable.

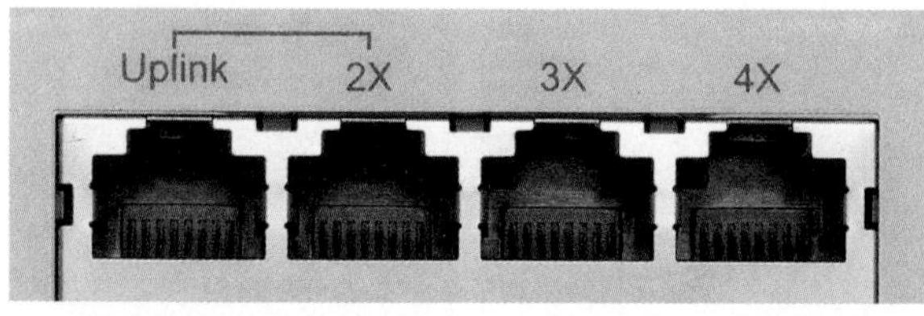

• **Figure 3.16** Typical uplink port

Uplink Ports

Uplink ports enable you to connect two switches using a **straight-through cable**. They're clearly marked on older switches, as shown in Figure 3.16. To connect two switches, insert one end of a cable in the uplink port and the other end of the cable in any one of the regular ports on the other switch.

Modern switches do not have a dedicated uplink port, but instead auto-sense when another switch is plugged in. You can plug into any port.

The technical term for an uplink port and the auto-sensing feature of ports in modern switches is **auto-medium-dependent interface crossover (MDI-X)**.

Crossover Cables

Switches can also connect to each other via special twisted pair cables called crossover cables. A **crossover cable** reverses the sending and receiving pairs on one end of the cable. One end of the cable is wired according to the TIA/EIA 568A standard, whereas the other end is wired according to the TIA/EIA 568B standard (Figure 3.17). With the sending and receiving pairs reversed, the switches can hear each other; hence the need for two standards for connecting RJ-45 jacks to UTP cables.

A crossover cable connects to a regular port on each switch. Modern switches with auto-sensing ports don't require a crossover cable.

In a pinch, you can use a crossover cable to connect two computers together using Ethernet NICs with no switch between them at all. This is handy for quickie connections, although not used much anymore because we mostly go wireless now.

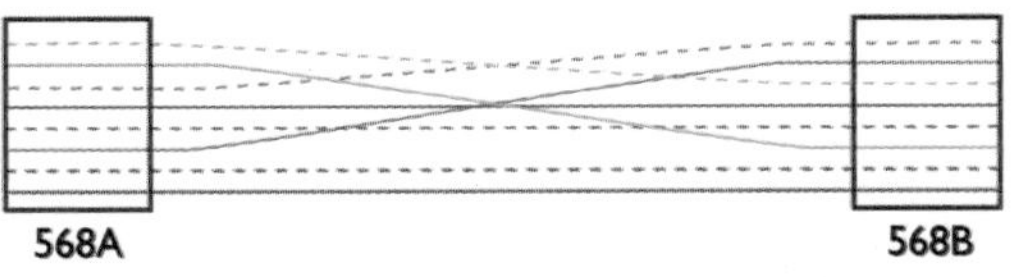

• **Figure 3.17** A crossover cable reverses the sending and receiving pairs.

Spanning Tree Protocol

Because you can connect switches together in any fashion, you can create redundant connections in a network. These are called **switching loops** or *bridge loops* (Figure 3.18).

In the early days of switches, making a bridge loop in a network setup would bring the network crashing down. A frame could get caught in the loop, so to speak, and not reach its destination.

The Ethernet standards body adopted the **Spanning Tree Protocol (STP)** to eliminate the problem of accidental switching loops. For decades, switches have had STP enabled by default, and can detect potential loops before they happen. Using special STP frames known as *bridge protocol data units (BPDUs)*, switches communicate with other switches to prevent loops from happening in the first place.

The CompTIA Network+ exam objectives list using a crossover cable in a troubleshooting scenario, presumably meaning you'd need to add an additional switch to a network to test ports. Modern switches auto-sense, so this isn't a thing anymore. If you're asked about interconnecting ancient switches (10BASE-T/100BASE-T), *crossover* might be the correct answer.

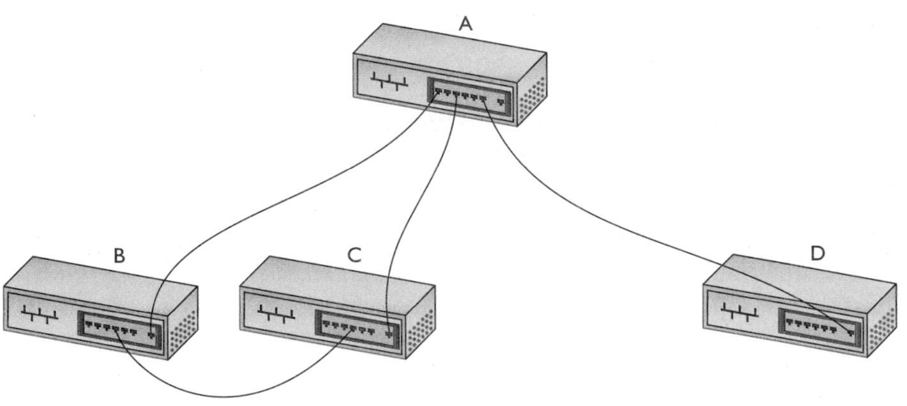

• **Figure 3.18** A switching loop

Configuration BPDUs establish the topology, where one switch is elected *root bridge* and acts as the center of the STP universe. Each switch then uses the root bridge as a reference point to maintain a loop-free topology. There will be redundant links, for fault tolerance, that would ordinarily cause a switching loop, but certain ports will be placed in a "blocking" state and will not send or receive data frames. Ports in the blocking state will still hear the configuration BPDUs, which are sourced by the root bridge and forwarded downstream to the other switches every 2 seconds.

If a link or device goes down, STP springs into action with another type of BPDU, called a *topology change notification (TCN) BPDU*, that enables the switches to rework themselves around the failed interface or device. The blocked ports, listening to the BPDUs, will realize they're needed and eventually move to a forwarding state.

Administrators can manually change STP settings for a switch. A switch port directly connected to a PC, for example, should never participate in STP, and could be configured with a setting called *PortFast* that enables the interface to come up right away, without the normal latency introduced by STP. Another reason to configure switch ports with PortFast is to prevent TCN BPDUs being sent out of that switch every time a PC is powered on and off, which has severe side effects, like causing all switches to flush their source address table, and relearn MAC addresses.

> The preceding terms used to describe functions within a switch apply specifically to Cisco switches. Cisco creates many of the network boxes (switches, routers, and more) that power a zillion networks, including much of the Internet. Other companies, notably Juniper, compete with Cisco and use different terms for the same actions.

BPDU guard will move a port configured with PortFast into an errdisable state (i.e., error occurred, disabled) if a BPDU is received on that port. This requires an administrator to manually bring the port back up.

Ports configured with PortFast should never receive a BPDU, and if they do, it could start a switching loop. Another mechanism, *root guard*, will move a port into a root-inconsistent state if BPDUs coming from a certain direction indicate another switch is trying to become the root bridge. The root-inconsistent port will automatically return to its forwarding state once these BPDUs stop. This helps define locations where the root bridge should never be located.

The original Spanning Tree Protocol, introduced by IEEE as 802.1d, was replaced a long time ago (2001) by the Rapid Spanning Tree Protocol (RSTP), 802.1w. RSTP offers significantly faster convergence time following some kind of network change. STP could take up to 50 seconds to get back to a steady state, for example, whereas an RSTP network could return to convergence in 6 seconds.

Troubleshooting Switches

The simple switches described in this chapter generally function flawlessly for years without any need for a tech to do more than wipe dust off the top. Very occasionally you'll run into a switch that has problems. These problems often fall into two categories:

- Obvious physical damage
- Dead ports

Diagnosing any of these problems follows a similar pattern. First, you recognize that a switch might have problems because a device you've plugged in can't connect to the network. Second, you examine the switch for obvious damage. Third, you look for link lights. If they're not flashing, try a different port. Fourth, you look at your cables. If anything looks bent, broken, or stepped on, you should replace it. A bad cable or improper cable type can lead to problems that point to a "failed" switch when the true culprit is really the cable. Finally, you use the tried-and-true method of replacing the switch or the cable with a known-good device.

When we get to modern higher-end switches in Chapter 11, you'll need to follow other procedures to do proper diagnostic work. We'll get there soon enough!

Chapter 3 Review

Chapter Summary

After reading this chapter and completing the exercises, you should understand the following about Ethernet.

Define and describe Ethernet

- Ethernet is based on a family of network technologies from a bus topology. Ethernet enables computers to send data across a network, identify sending and receiving computers, and determine which computer should use the cable at which time. Early Ethernet networks originally used a single coax cable as a physical bus.
- The IEEE 802.3 committee controls the Ethernet standard.
- Ethernet frames prevent any single computer from monopolizing the cable while making the retransmission of lost data efficient.
- A basic Ethernet frame contains five fields: the destination address (the MAC address of the frame's recipient), the source address (the MAC address of the sending system), the type of the data, the data itself, and a frame check sequence. At the front of the frame is the preamble. A pad is added if necessary.

Explain early Ethernet implementations

- Star-bus topology Ethernet connected all nodes with a hub at the center. Hubs repeated the incoming signal to every connected port.
- Early Ethernet networks used 10BASE-T cabling.
- The physical topology of 10BASE-T was a star; however, the data used a logical bus topology with a central hub. Therefore, 10BASE-T actually used a hybrid star-bus topology to accomplish moving data frames through the network.
- 10BASE-T supported speeds up to 10 Mbps over baseband.
- 10BASE-T required the use of Cat 3 or higher, two-pair, UTP cable. These cables used RJ-45 connectors crimped to the cable.
- Correct crimping (then and now) follows either the TIA/EIA 568A or the TIA/EIA 568B color-code standard.
- 10BASE-FL was a fiber-optic version of 10BASE-T that used multimode fiber-optic cable and SC or ST connectors. One major advantage of 10BASE-FL was its increased maximum distance between hub and node.
- CSMA/CD stands for carrier-sense multiple access with collision detection. Carrier sense meant that the node checked the network cable before sending to see if anyone else was transmitting. Multiple access meant all computers had equal access to the network cable. Collision detection was when nodes detected that a transmission did not complete.

Describe ways to extend and enhance Ethernet networks

- Busy networks suffered decreased bandwidth when using hubs. A switch solves this problem by managing the connection, based on MAC addresses, between the sending and receiving nodes. Switches break up collision domains.
- You can connect additional switches to increase the size and capacity of a network. Connect a straight-through cable to the uplink port on one switch and a regular port on the other. With modern auto-sensing ports, this is pretty straightforward. You can also connect two switches using a crossover cable.
- Connecting switches can lead to bridge loops, which caused early switched networks trouble. Switches that support the Spanning Tree Protocol are immune to bridge loops, even if wired in a physical loop.
- Switches fail from physical abuse or from electrical surges. Troubleshoot by checking link lights, trying different ports, or swapping out the switch or cable for a known-good replacement.

Key Terms

10BASE-FL *(55)*
10BASE-T *(52)*
802.3 (Ethernet) *(49)*
auto-medium-dependent interface crossover (MDI-X) *(61)*
bridge *(58)*
broadcast domain *(60)*
carrier-sense multiple access with collision detection (CSMA/CD) *(56)*
collision domain *(58)*
crimper *(54)*
crossover cable *(61)*
cyclic redundancy check (CRC) *(51)*
data *(51)*
destination address *(51)*
Ethernet *(49)*
frame *(50)*
frame check sequence (FCS) *(51)*
full-duplex *(54)*
half-duplex *(54)*
hub *(52)*
MAC address *(51)*
media access control (MAC) address table *(59)*
media converter *(56)*
multimode *(55)*
network segment *(50)*
pad *(51)*
preamble *(50)*
repeater *(52)*
RJ-45 connector *(53)*
Sneakernet *(48)*
source address *(51)*
Spanning Tree Protocol (STP) *(61)*
start frame delimiter *(50)*
straight-through cable *(60)*
switch *(58)*
switching loop *(61)*
TIA/EIA 568A *(54)*
TIA/EIA 568B *(54)*
type *(51)*
uplink port *(60)*

Key Term Quiz

Use the Key Terms list to complete the sentences that follow. Not all terms will be used.

1. The _______________ is unique to each individual NIC.
2. When extra "filler" data is needed in a packet, a(n) _______________ is added.
3. A network connection that can send and receive at the same time is called a(n) _______________ connection.
4. The _______________ in an Ethernet frame describes the protocol used in that frame.
5. At the front of the frame is the _______________.
6. A hub acted as a(n) _______________ in that it copied all incoming signals to every connected port.
7. Connecting switches incorrectly can create a(n) _______________, which can make the whole network stop working.
8. The _______________ enables Ethernet nodes to recognize receiving bad data.
9. _______________ had a maximum distance between node and hub of 100 meters, whereas _______________ had a maximum distance of 2000 meters.
10. A(n) _______________ can be used to interconnect different Ethernet types.

Multiple-Choice Quiz

1. How are the connectors wired on a crossover cable?
   - **A.** One end is TIA/EIA 568A; the other end is TIA/EIA 568B.
   - **B.** Both ends are TIA/EIA 568A.
   - **C.** Both ends are TIA/EIA 568B.
   - **D.** One end is an RJ-45; the other end is an RG-6.
2. What items made up the CSMA/CD system used in early Ethernet networks? (Select three.)
   - **A.** Collision avoidance
   - **B.** Carrier sense
   - **C.** Multiple access
   - **D.** Collision detection
3. What happened when two computers transmitted through a hub simultaneously?
   - **A.** Nothing happened.
   - **B.** The terminators prevented any transmission problems.
   - **C.** Their signals reflected back down the cable to their points of origin.
   - **D.** A collision occurred.
4. What is a group of nodes that can at any point send messages at the same time, causing a collision?
   - **A.** Collision domain
   - **B.** Ethernet
   - **C.** Fast Ethernet
   - **D.** Sneakernet
5. Which committee is responsible for Ethernet standards?
   - **A.** IEEE 803.2
   - **B.** IEEE 803.3
   - **C.** IEEE 802.2
   - **D.** IEEE 802.3
6. What type of cabling did the first star-bus topology Ethernet networks use?
   - **A.** FTP
   - **B.** SFTP
   - **C.** STP
   - **D.** UTP
7. What is the purpose of a preamble in an Ethernet frame?
   - **A.** It gives the receiving NIC time to realize a frame is coming and to know when the frame starts.
   - **B.** It provides the receiving NIC with the sending NIC's MAC address so communication can continue.
   - **C.** It provides error-checking to ensure data integrity.
   - **D.** It contains a description of the data that is to follow so the receiving NIC knows how to reassemble it.
8. Which ports must you use to interconnect two switches in early Ethernet with a crossover cable?
   - **A.** Regular ports on both switches.
   - **B.** Uplink port on one switch; regular port on the other switch.
   - **C.** Regular port on the root bridge switch; uplink port on the branch switch.
   - **D.** You can't do this; you need to use a straight-through cable.
9. For what purpose is a crimping tool used?
   - **A.** To splice a 10BASE-T cable with a 10BASE-FL cable
   - **B.** To attach an RJ-45 connector to a UTP cable
   - **C.** To attach a 10BASE-T cable to a media converter
   - **D.** To connect two switches together
10. Which of the following is not a limitation on 10BASE-T cable?
    - **A.** Maximum speed of 10 Mbps
    - **B.** Maximum distance between hub and node of 100 feet
    - **C.** Maximum of 1024 nodes per hub
    - **D.** Minimum Cat 3 or better UTP with RJ-45 connectors

11. Which of the following is not a limitation on 10BASE-FL cable?

    A. Maximum speed of 10 Mbps

    B. Maximum distance between hub and node of 2000 meters

    C. Maximum of 1024 nodes per hub

    D. Minimum Cat 3 or better UTP with RJ-45 connectors

12. Which field of an Ethernet frame enables a switch to send the frame only to the intended recipient?

    A. Preamble

    B. Destination MAC address

    C. Source MAC address

    D. Type

13. Which part of the frame will a NIC automatically add to make the Ethernet frame up to the 64-byte minimum size?

    A. Preamble

    B. Type

    C. Data

    D. Pad

14. What feature of switches prevents the problem of switching loops?

    A. STP

    B. TCP/IP

    C. IEEE 802.3

    D. UTP

15. What feature of switches keeps track of which MAC address goes to each port?

    A. frame address table

    B. MAC address table

    C. STP

    D. UTP

Essay Quiz

1. Describe two ways that using frames helps move data along a network.
2. Define the term *CSMA/CD*, using simple descriptions to explain each of the three parts: CS, MA, and CD.
3. Describe what a hub did and some of its limitations. Then explain how a switch works to overcome the problems of a hub.

Lab Project

• Lab Project 3.1

In this chapter, you learned about the basic functionality of switches. Use the Internet to delve deeper and research the difference among a managed switch, an unmanaged switch, and a smart switch. Create a chart to compare their similarities and differences. In addition to the differences in features and functionality, research and report on the pricing differences for similarly sized switches. For example, what is more expensive, a 24-port managed, unmanaged, or smart switch? What do you get for the extra money? Is it worth it?

Ethernet Standards

"To expect the unexpected shows a thoroughly modern intellect."
—Oscar Wilde

In this chapter, you will learn how to

- **Describe the varieties of 100-megabit Ethernet**
- **Discuss copper- and fiber-based Gigabit Ethernet**
- **Discover and describe Ethernet varieties beyond Gigabit**

Within a few years of its introduction, 10BASE-T proved inadequate to meet the growing networking demand for speed. As with all things in the computing world, bandwidth is the key. Even with switching, the 10-Mbps speed of 10BASE-T, seemingly so fast when first developed, quickly found a market clamoring for even faster speeds. This chapter looks at the improvements in Ethernet since 10BASE-T. You'll read about the 100-megabit standards and the Gigabit Ethernet standards. The chapter finishes with a look at Ethernet standards that exceed Gigabit speeds.

Test Specific

100-Megabit Ethernet

The quest to break 10-Mbps network speeds in Ethernet started in the early 1990s. By then, 10BASE-T Ethernet had established itself as the most popular networking technology (although other standards, such as IBM's Token Ring, still had some market share). The goal was to create a new speed standard that made no changes to the Ethernet frames. By doing this, the 802.3 committee ensured that different speeds of Ethernet could interconnect, assuming you had something that could handle the speed differences and a media converter if the connections differed. This standardization ensures communication and scalability.

100BASE-T

When it came time to come up with a new standard to replace 10BASE-T, network hardware makers forwarded a large number of potential standards, all focused on the prize of leading the new Ethernet standard. As a result, two twisted-pair Ethernet standards appeared: *100BASE-T4* and **100BASE-TX**. 100BASE-T4 used Cat 3 cable, whereas 100BASE-TX used Cat 5 and Cat 5e. By the late 1990s, 100BASE-TX became the dominant 100-megabit Ethernet standard. 100BASE-T4 disappeared from the market and today has been forgotten. As a result, we never say 100BASE-TX, simply choosing to use the term **100BASE-T**.

100BASE-T was at one time called **Fast Ethernet**. The term still sticks to the 100-Mbps standards even though there are now much faster versions of Ethernet.

A **baseband** network means that only a single signal travels over the wires of the network at one time, occupying the lowest frequencies. Ethernet networks are baseband. Contrast this with **broadband**, where you can get multiple signals to flow over the same wire at the same time, modulating to higher frequencies. The latter is how cable television and cable Internet work.

100BASE-T Summary

- **Speed** 100 Mbps
- **Signal type** Baseband
- **Distance** 100 meters between the hub/switch and the node
- **Node limit** No more than 1024 nodes per hub/switch
- **Topology** Star-bus topology: physical star, logical bus
- **Cable type** Cat 5 or better UTP or STP cabling with RJ-45/8P8C connectors

Upgrading a 10BASE-T network to 100BASE-T was not a small process. First, you needed Cat 5 cable or better. Second, you had to replace all 10BASE-T NICs with 100BASE-T NICs. Third, you had to replace the 10BASE-T hub or switch with a 100BASE-T hub or switch. Making this upgrade cost a lot in the early days of 100BASE-T, so people clamored for a way to make the upgrade a little easier and less expensive. This was accomplished via multispeed, auto-sensing NICs and hubs/switches.

Figure 4.1 shows a typical multispeed, auto-sensing 100BASE-T NIC from the late 1990s. When this NIC first connected to a network, it negotiated automatically with the hub or switch to determine the other device's highest speed. If they

• **Figure 4.1** PCI 100BASE-T NIC

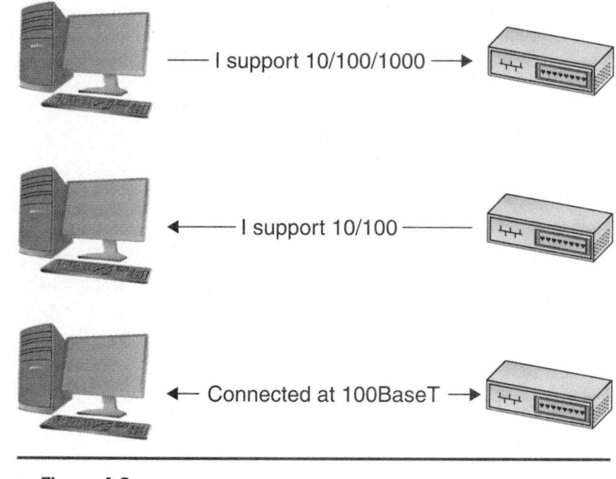

• **Figure 4.2** Auto-negotiation in action

both did 100BASE-T, then you got 100BASE-T. If the hub or switch only did 10BASE-T, then the NIC did 10BASE-T. All of this happened automatically (Figure 4.2).

Distinguishing a 10BASE-T NIC from a 100BASE-T NIC without close inspection was impossible. You had to look for something on the card to tell you its speed. Some NICs had extra link lights to show the speed (see Chapter 5, "Installing a Physical Network," for the scoop on link lights). Of course, you could always simply install the card, as shown in Figure 4.3, and see what the operating system says it sees.

• **Figure 4.3** 100BASE-T NIC in Windows 8.1

You'll also have trouble finding a true 10BASE-T or 100BASE-T NIC any longer because multispeed NICs have been around long enough to have replaced any single-speed NIC. All modern NICs are multispeed and auto-sensing.

100BASE-FX

Most Ethernet networks use unshielded twisted pair (UTP) cabling, but quite a few use fiber-based networks instead. In some networks, using fiber simply makes more sense.

UTP cabling cannot meet the needs of every organization for three key reasons. First, the 100-meter distance limitation of UTP-based networks is inadequate for networks covering large buildings or campuses. Second, UTP's lack of electrical shielding makes it a poor choice for networks functioning in locations with high levels of **electromagnetic interference (EMI)**—disturbance in electrical signals caused by electrical radiation coming from nearby devices. Finally, the Jason Bournes and James Bonds of the world find UTP cabling (and copper cabling in general) easy to tap, making it an inappropriate choice for high-security environments. To address these issues, the IEEE 802.3 standard provides for a flavor of 100-megabit Ethernet using fiber-optic cable, called 100BASE-FX.

The **100BASE-FX** standard saw quite a bit of interest for years, as it combined the high speed of 100-megabit Ethernet with the reliability of fiber optics. Outwardly, 100BASE-FX looked exactly like its predecessor, 10BASE-FL (introduced in Chapter 3). 100BASE-FX uses multimode fiber-optic cabling and *subscriber connector (SC)* or *straight tip (ST)* connectors. 100BASE-FX offers improved data speeds over 10BASE-FL and equally long cable runs, supporting a maximum cable length of 2 kilometers.

Multimode fiber comes in varying core sizes and capabilities. You'll see these as *optical multimode (OM)* types, such as OM1, OM2, OM3, and OM4). The key is to match the fiber to the technology.

100BASE-FX Summary

- **Speed** 100 Mbps
- **Signal type** Baseband
- **Distance** Two kilometers between the hub/switch and the node
- **Node limit** No more than 1024 nodes per hub/switch
- **Topology** Star-bus topology: physical star, logical bus
- **Cable type** Multimode fiber-optic cabling (generally OM1) with ST or SC connectors

There is no scenario today where you would install 100BASE- networking components, except perhaps to make use of donated equipment. You will definitely find 100BASE- gear installed and functioning in many organizations.

100BASE-SX

100BASE-SX was a short-distance, LED-based alternative to 100BASE-FX. It ran on OM1 or OM2 fiber at 850 nm (nanometer) and used ST, SC, or LC connectors. It was completely backwardly compatible to 10BASE-FL, so was touted as a viable upgrade from the even older tech. 100BASE-SX is long gone but appears in the CompTIA Network+ N10-008 objectives for some reason, so I've included it here for completeness.

Full-Duplex Ethernet

Full-duplex doesn't increase network speed directly, but it doubles network bandwidth. Imagine a one-lane road expanded to two lanes while keeping the speed limit the same. It also prevents those cars from crashing (colliding) into each other.

Early 100BASE-T NICs, just like 10BASE-T NICs, could send and receive data, but not at the same time—a feature called **half-duplex** (Figure 4.4). The IEEE addressed this characteristic shortly after adopting 100BASE-T as a standard. By the late 1990s, most 100BASE-T cards could auto-negotiate for full-duplex. With **full-duplex**, a NIC can send and receive at the same time, as shown in Figure 4.5.

All NICs today run full-duplex. The NIC and the attached switch determine full- or half-duplex during the auto-negotiation process. The vast

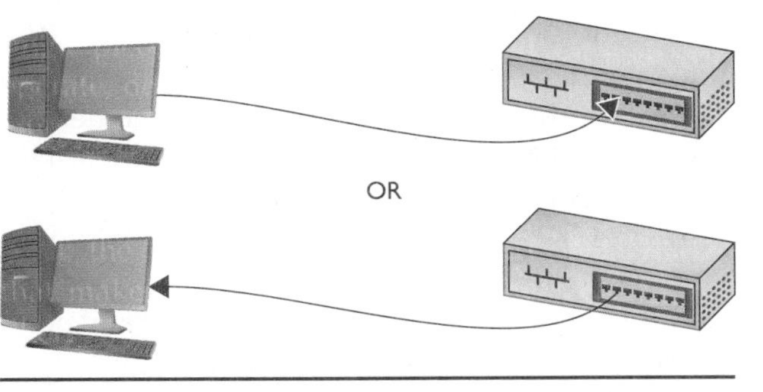

• **Figure 4.4** Half-duplex; sending at the top, receiving at the bottom

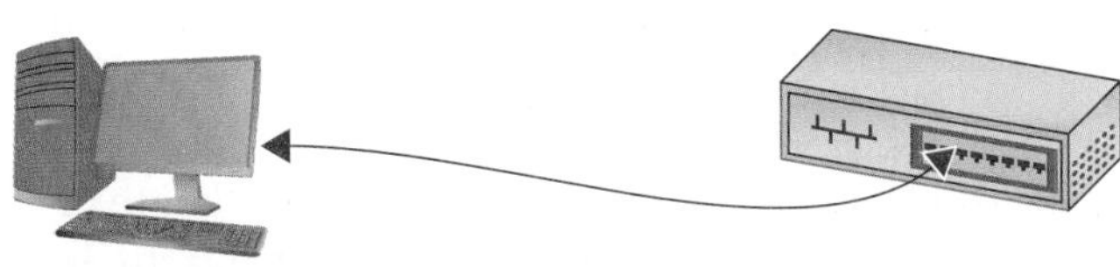

• **Figure 4.5** Full-duplex

majority of the time you simply let the NIC do its negotiation. Every operating system has some method to force the NIC to a certain speed/duplex, as shown in Figure 4.6.

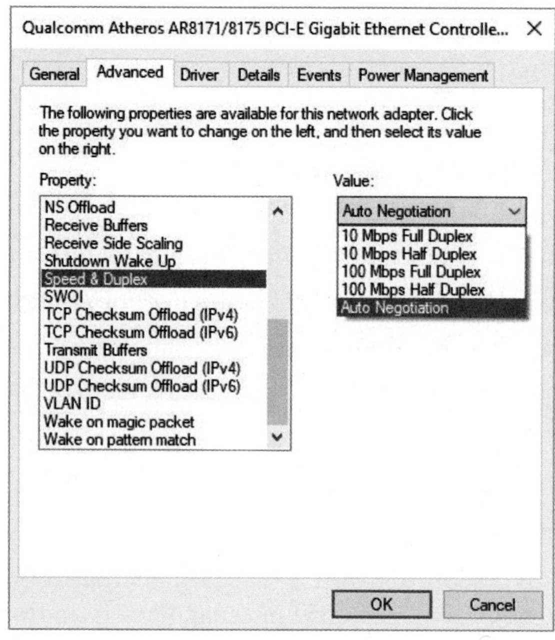

• **Figure 4.6** Forcing speed and duplex in Windows 10

Fast Ethernet at 100 Mbps makes sense for *local area networks (LANs)*—with computers interconnected in a defined space, like a home or office—where you share small data, like documents and spreadsheets. Plenty of LANs around the world continue to soldier on at 100-megabit speeds. A lot of network-connected devices, such as printers, function just fine on Fast Ethernet as well. Still, Fast Ethernet is dead in new installations, so let's turn to the current standard.

Gigabit Ethernet

The term *Gigabit Ethernet* is more commonly used than *1000BASE-T*.

The vast majority of network rollouts in offices use 1000BASE-T connections (or *drops*, as you'll hear them called). You can imagine any number of appropriate scenarios for using 1000BASE-T. Many offices also add in wireless today. We'll get there in Chapter 14.

By the end of the 1990s, Fast Ethernet was not enough for networking needs. In response, the IEEE created **Gigabit Ethernet**, which today is the most common type of Ethernet found on new NICs.

The IEEE approved two different versions of Gigabit Ethernet. The most widely implemented solution, published under the IEEE **802.3ab** standard, is called **1000BASE-T**. The other version, published under the **802.3z** standard and known as **1000BASE-X**, is divided into a series of standards, with names such as 1000BASE-SX and 1000BASE-LX.

1000BASE-T uses four-pair UTP or STP cabling to achieve gigabit performance. Like 10BASE-T and 100BASE-T, 1000BASE-T has a maximum cable length of 100 meters on a segment. 1000BASE-T connections and ports look exactly like the ones on a 10BASE-T or 100BASE-T network.

The 802.3z standards require a bit more discussion. Let's look at each of these solutions in detail to see how they work.

1000BASE-SX

Many networks upgrading to Gigabit Ethernet use the **1000BASE-SX** standard. 1000BASE-SX uses multimode fiber-optic cabling to connect systems, with a generous maximum cable length of 220 to 500 meters; the exact length is left up to the various manufacturers. 1000BASE-SX uses an 850-nm wavelength LED to transmit light on the fiber-optic cable. 1000BASE-SX devices look similar to 100BASE-FX devices, and although both standards can use several types of connectors, 1000BASE-SX devices commonly use LC, while 100BASE-FX devices frequently use SC. (See "SFF Fiber Connectors" later in the chapter for the scoop on LC connectors.)

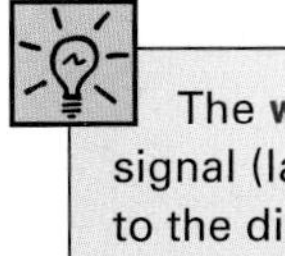

The **wavelength** of a particular signal (laser, in this case) refers to the distance the signal has to travel before it completes its particular shape and starts to repeat. The different colors of the laser signals feature different wavelengths.

Cross Check

SC and ST

You learned about the common fiber-optic cable SC and ST connectors in Chapter 2, so cross-check your knowledge here. What distinguishes the two connectors? Can 100BASE-FX NICs use either one? Which do you need to twist like a bayonet?

1000BASE-LX

1000BASE-LX is the long-distance carrier for Gigabit Ethernet. 1000BASE-LX uses lasers on single-mode cables to shoot data at distances up to 5 kilometers—and some manufacturers use special repeaters to increase that to distances as great as 70 kilometers! The Ethernet folks are trying to position this as the Ethernet backbone of the future, and already some large carriers are beginning to adopt 1000BASE-LX. You may live your whole life and never see a 1000BASE-LX device, but odds are good that you will encounter connections that use such devices in the near future. 1000BASE-LX connectors look like 1000BASE-SX connectors.

SFF Fiber Connectors

Around the time that Gigabit Ethernet first started to appear, two problems began to surface with ST and SC connectors. First, ST connectors are relatively large, twist-on connectors, requiring the installer to twist the cable when inserting or removing it. Twisting is not a popular action with fiber-optic cables, as the delicate fibers may fracture. Also, big-fingered techs have a problem with ST connectors if the connectors are too closely packed: they can't get their fingers around them.

SC connectors snap in and out, making them much more popular than STs. SC connectors are also large, however, and the folks who make fiber networking equipment wanted to pack more connectors onto their boxes.

This brought about two new types of fiber connectors, known generically as **small form factor (SFF)** connectors, both of which were introduced in Chapter 2. The first SFF connector—the **Mechanical Transfer Registered Jack (MT-RJ)**, shown in Chapter 2 in Figure 2.25—gained popularity with important companies like Cisco and is still quite common. The second, the **local connector (LC)**, is shown in Figure 4.7. LC-type connectors are very popular,

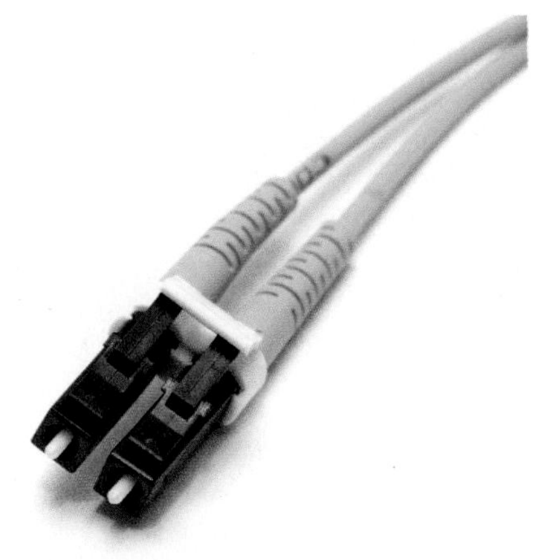

• **Figure 4.7** LC-type connector

particularly in the United States, and many fiber experts consider the LC-type connector to be the predominant fiber connector.

LC and MT-RJ are the most popular types of SFF fiber connectors, but many others exist. The fiber industry has no standard beyond ST and SC connectors, which means that different makers of fiber equipment may have different connections. Table 4.1 summarizes common Gigabit Ethernet standards.

Table 4.1 Gigabit Ethernet Summary

Standard	Cabling	Cable Details	Connectors	Length
1000BASE-SX	OM2 or better multimode fiber (although OM1 works for short distances)	850 nm	Variable, commonly LC	220–500 m
1000BASE-LX	OS1 or OS2 single-mode fiber	1300 nm	Variable, commonly LC and SC	5 km
1000BASE-T	Cat 5e/6 UTP	Four-pair/ full-duplex	RJ-45	100 m

Mechanical Connection Variations

Aside from the various connection types (LC, MT-RJ, and so on), fiber connectors vary in the connection point. The standard connector type today is called a **physical contact (PC) connector** because the two pieces of fiber touch when inserted. These connectors replace the older **flat-surface connector** that left a little gap between the connection points due to imperfections in the glass. PC connectors are highly polished and slightly spherical, reducing the signal loss at the connection point.

Two technologies have dropped in price and have replaced PC connectors in some implementations: UPC and APC. **Ultra-physical contact (UPC) connectors** are polished extensively for a superior finish. These reduce signal loss significantly over PC connectors. **Angled physical contact (APC) connectors** add an 8-degree angle to the curved end, lowering signal loss further. Plus, their connection does not degrade from multiple insertions, unlike earlier connection types.

So, note that when you purchase fiber cables today, you'll see the connector type and the contact type, plus the type of cable and other physical dimensions. A typical patch cable, for example, would be an SC/UPC single-mode fiber of a specific length.

Implementing Multiple Types of Gigabit Ethernet

Because Ethernet frames don't vary among the many flavors of Ethernet, network hardware manufacturers have long built devices capable of supporting more than one flavor right out of the box.

You can also use dedicated **media converters** to connect any type of Ethernet cabling together. Most media converters are plain-looking boxes with a port or dongle on either side with placement between two segments. They come in all flavors:

- Single-mode fiber (SMF) to UTP/STP
- Multimode fiber (MMF) to UTP/STP
- Fiber to coaxial
- SMF to MMF

Eventually, the Gigabit Ethernet folks created a standard for modular ports called a **gigabit interface converter (GBIC)**. With many Gigabit Ethernet switches and other hardware, you can simply pull out a **transceiver**—the connecting module, commonly referred to as an **optic**—that supports one flavor of Gigabit Ethernet and plug in another. You can replace an RJ-45 GBIC, for example, with an SC GBIC, and it'll work just fine. In this kind of scenario, electronically, the switch or other gigabit device is just that—Gigabit Ethernet—so the physical connections don't matter. Ingenious!

A *transceiver* or *optic* is a removable module that enables connectivity between a device and a cable. A *media converter* enables connection between two different types of network, such as copper and optical fiber.

Switches and other network equipment today use a much smaller modular transceiver, called a **small form-factor pluggable (SFP)**. Hot-swappable like the GBIC transceivers, the SFPs take up a lot less space and support all the same networking standards.

Ethernet Evolutions

The vast majority of wired networks today feature Gigabit Ethernet, which seems plenty fast for current networking needs. That has not stopped developers and manufacturers from pushing well beyond those limits. This last section looks at high-speed Ethernet standards: 10/40/100 gigabit.

10 Gigabit Ethernet

Developers continue to refine and increase Ethernet networking speeds, especially in the LAN environment and in backbones. **10 Gigabit Ethernet (10 GbE)** offers speeds of up to 10 gigabits per second, as its name indicates.

10 GbE has a number of fiber standards and two copper standards. While designed with fiber optics in mind, copper 10 GbE can still often pair excellent performance with cost savings. As a result, you'll find a mix of fiber and copper in data centers today.

Fiber-Based 10 GbE

When the IEEE members sat down to formalize specifications on Ethernet running at 10 Gbps, they faced an interesting task in several ways. First, they had to maintain the integrity of the Ethernet frame. Data is king, after all, and the goal was to create a network that could interoperate with any other Ethernet network. Second, they had to figure out how to transfer those frames at such blazing speeds. This second challenge had some interesting ramifications because of two factors. They could use the traditional Physical layer mechanisms defined by the Ethernet standard. But a perfectly usable ~10-Gbps fiber network, called **Synchronous Optical Network (SONET)**, was already in place and being used for wide area networking (WAN) transmissions. What to do?

The IEEE created a whole set of 10 GbE standards that could use traditional LAN Physical layer mechanisms, plus a set of standards that could take advantage of the SONET infrastructure and run over the WAN fiber. To make the 10-Gbps jump as easy as possible, the IEEE also recognized the need for different networking situations. Some implementations require data transfers that can run long distances over single-mode fiber, for example, whereas others can make do with short-distance transfers over multimode fiber. This led to a lot of standards for 10 GbE.

The 10 GbE standards are defined by several factors: the type of fiber used, the wavelength of the laser or lasers, and the Physical layer signaling type. These factors also define the maximum signal distance.

The IEEE uses specific letter codes with the standards to help sort out the differences so you know what you're implementing or supporting. All the standards have names in the following format: "10GBASE-" followed by two other characters, what I'll call *xy*. The *x* stands for the type of fiber (usually, though not officially) and the wavelength of the laser signal; the *y* stands for the Physical layer signaling standard. The *y* code is always either *R* for LAN-based signaling or *W* for SONET/WAN-based signaling. The *x* differs a little more, so let's take a look.

10GBASE-S*y* uses a short-wavelength (850 nm) signal over multimode fiber. The maximum fiber length is 400 meters, although this length will vary depending on the type of multimode fiber used. (OM1 offers a super-short 33 m range, for example, whereas with OM4 the distance extends to 400 m.) **10GBASE-SR** is used for Ethernet LANs, and **10GBASE-SW** is used to connect to SONET devices.

Standard	Fiber Type	Wavelength	Physical Layer Signaling	Maximum Signal Length
10GBASE-SR	Multimode	850 nm	LAN	33–400 m
10GBASE-SW	Multimode	850 nm	SONET/WAN	33–400 m

10GBASE-L*y* uses a long-wavelength (1310 nm) signal over single-mode fiber. The maximum fiber length is 10 kilometers, although this length will vary depending on the type of single-mode fiber used. **10GBASE-LR** connects to Ethernet LANs and **10GBASE-LW** connects to SONET equipment. 10GBASE-LR is the most popular and least expensive 10 GbE media type.

Standard	Fiber Type	Wavelength	Physical Layer Signaling	Maximum Signal Length
10GBASE-LR	Single-mode	1310 nm	LAN	10 km
10GBASE-LW	Single-mode	1310 nm	SONET/WAN	10 km

10GBASE-E*y* uses an extra-long-wavelength (1550 nm) signal over single-mode fiber. The maximum fiber length is 40 kilometers, although this length will vary depending on the type of single-mode fiber used. **10GBASE-ER** works with Ethernet LANs and **10GBASE-EW** connects to SONET equipment.

Standard	Fiber Type	Wavelength	Physical Layer Signaling	Maximum Signal Length
10GBASE-ER	Single-mode	1550 nm	LAN	40 km
10GBASE-EW	Single-mode	1550 nm	SONET/WAN	40 km

The 10 GbE fiber standards do not define the type of connector to use and instead leave that to manufacturers (see the upcoming section "10 GbE Physical Connections").

The Other 10 GbE Fiber Standards

Manufacturers have shown both creativity and innovation in taking advantage of both existing fiber and the most cost-effective equipment. This has led to a variety of standards that are not covered by the CompTIA Network+ exam objectives, but that you should know about nevertheless. The top three as of this writing are 10GBASE-L4, 10GBASE-RM, and 10GBASE-ZR.

The *10GBASE-L4* standard uses four lasers at a 1300-nanometer wavelength over legacy fiber. On multimode cable, 10GBASE-L4 can support up to 300-meter transmissions. The range increases to 10 kilometers over single-mode fiber.

The **10GBASE-LRM** standard uses the long-wavelength signal of 10GBASE-LR but over legacy multimode fiber. The standard can achieve a range of up to 220 meters, depending on the grade of fiber cable.

Finally, some manufacturers have adopted the *10GBASE-ZR* "standard," which isn't part of the IEEE standards at all (unlike 10GBASE-L4 and 10GBASE-LRM). Instead, the manufacturers have created their own set of specifications. 10GBASE-ZR networks use a 1550-nanometer wavelength over single-mode fiber to achieve a range of a whopping 80 kilometers. The standard can work with both Ethernet LAN and SONET/WAN infrastructure.

The 802.3bz standard (2014) specifies support for Ethernet over twisted pair between 1 Gbps and 10 Gbps, notably 2.5 Gbps (*2.5 GBASE-T* running over Cat 5e or better cable) and 5 Gbps (*5 GBASE-T* running over Cat 6 or better cable). You'll see both standards in the wild, but not on the CompTIA Network+ exam.

Copper-Based 10 GbE

It took until 2006 for IEEE to come up with a standard for 10 GbE running on twisted pair cabling—called, predictably, 10GBASE-T. **10GBASE-T** looks and works exactly like the slower versions of UTP Ethernet. The only downside is that 10GBASE-T running on Cat 6 has a maximum cable length of only 55 meters. The Cat 6a standard enables 10GBASE-T to run at the standard distance of 100 meters.

Table 4.2 summarizes the 10 GbE standards.

Table 4.2 10 GbE Summary

Standard	Cabling	Wavelength/ Cable Details	Connectors	Length
10GBASE-SR/SW	Multimode fiber (generally OM3 or better)	850 nm	Not defined	26–300 m
10GBASE-LR/LW	Single-mode fiber (OS2 required to reach the full distance)	1310 nm	Variable, commonly LC	10 km
10GBASE-ER/EW	Single-mode fiber	1550 nm	Variable, commonly LC and SC	40 km
10GBASE-T	Cat 6/6a UTP	Four-pair/ full-duplex	RJ-45	55/100 m

10 GbE Physical Connections

This hodgepodge of 10 GbE types might have been the ultimate disaster for hardware manufacturers. All types of 10 GbE send and receive the same signal; only the physical medium is different. Imagine a single switch that had to come out in seven different versions to match all these types! Instead, the 10 GbE industry simply chose not to define the connector types and devised a very clever, very simple concept called *multisource agreements (MSAs)*: agreements among multiple manufacturers to make interoperable devices and standards. A transceiver based on an MSA plugs into your 10 GbE equipment, enabling you to convert from one media type to another media type.

• **Figure 4.8** SFP+ transceiver (Photo courtesy of D-Link)

Characteristics of Fiber Transceivers

Up to this point, the book has described the most common forms of fiber-optic networking, where fiber is installed in pairs, with one cable to send and the other to receive. This is still the most common fiber-based networking solution out there. All the transceivers used in these technologies have two connectors, a standard **duplex** format. A typical transceiver used in 10 GbE is called the **enhanced small form-factor pluggable (SFP+)**, shown in Figure 4.8.

Manufacturers have developed technology that relies on *wave division multiplexing (WDM)* to differentiate wave signals on a single fiber, creating *single strand fiber transmission*. **Bidirectional (BiDi) transceivers** (Figure 4.9) have only a single optical port designed inside to send on one wavelength, such as 1310 nm, and receive on a different wavelength, such as 1550 nm. A corresponding BiDi transceiver must be installed on the other end of the fiber for this to work.

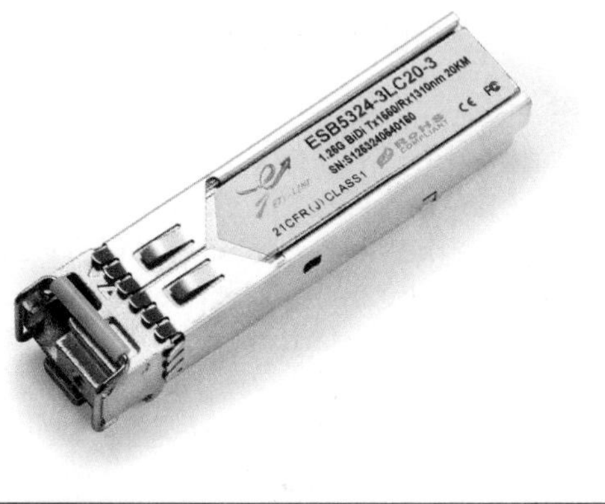

• **Figure 4.9** BiDi transceiver

BiDi technology has a couple of notable advantages over its dual-fiber predecessors. First, it costs less to deploy in a new network. You can establish the same level of network performance using half the number of fiber runs. Second, you can use existing fiber runs to rapidly double the capacity of a network. Replace the duplex transceivers with twice the number of BiDi transceivers and plug in the fiber.

Gigabit BiDi transceivers typically use SFP optics. Most 10 GbE BiDi transceivers use SFP+ connectors. 40 GbE BiDi transceivers use **quad small form-factor pluggable (QSFP)** optics.

Backbones

The beauty and the challenge of the vast selection of Ethernet flavors is deciding which one to use in your network. The goal is to give your users the fastest network response time possible while keeping costs reasonable. To achieve this balance, most network administrators find that a multispeed Ethernet network works best. In a multispeed network, a series of high-speed (relative to the rest of the network) switches maintain a backbone network. No computers, other than possibly servers, attach directly to this backbone. Figure 4.10 shows a typical backbone network. Each floor has its own switch that connects to every node on the floor. In turn, each of these switches also has a separate high-speed connection to a main switch that resides in the office's computer room.

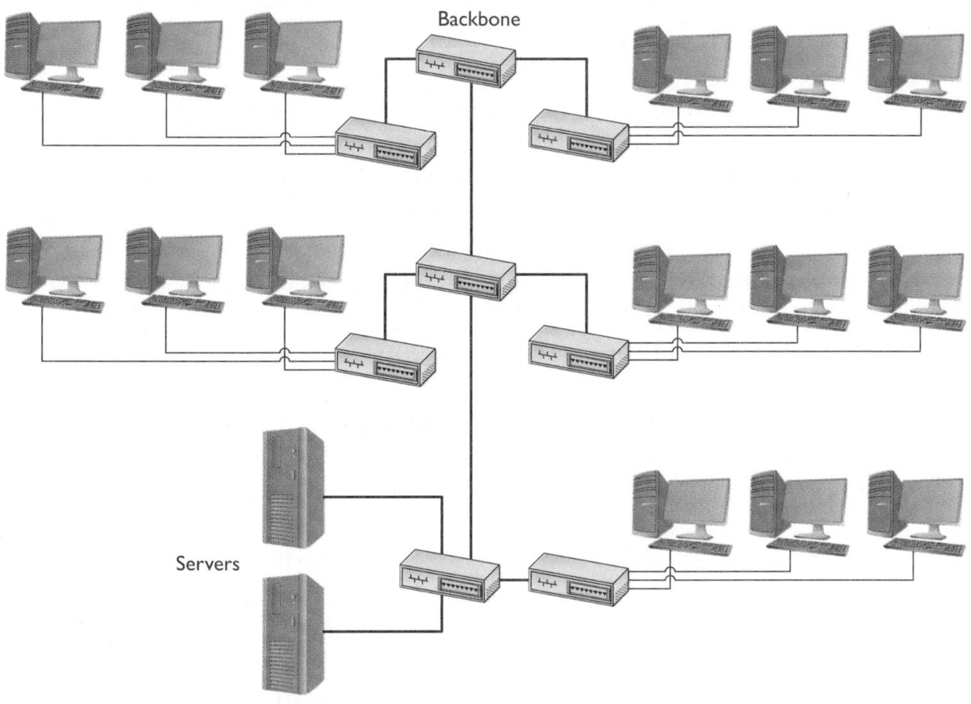

• **Figure 4.10** Typical network configuration showing backbone (pun intended)

To make this work, you need switches with separate, dedicated, high-speed ports like the ones shown in Figure 4.11. The ports (often fiber) on the switches run straight to the high-speed backbone switch.

• **Figure 4.11** Switch with dedicated, high-speed ports

Try This!

Shopping for Switches

Cisco, one of the industry leaders for Ethernet switches, has a great Web site for its products. Imagine that you are setting up a network for your school or business (keep it simple and pick a single building if you're in a large organization). Decide what type of switches you'd like to use, including both the backbone and local switches. If you're really motivated, decide where to locate the switches physically. Don't be afraid to try a fiber backbone—almost every Cisco switch comes with special ports (such as SFP+) to enable you to pick the type of Ethernet you want to use for your backbone.

40 GbE and 100 GbE

Way back in 2010, the IEEE 802.3ba committee approved standards for 40- and 100-Gb Ethernet, **40 Gigabit Ethernet (40 GbE)** and **100 Gigabit Ethernet (100 GbE)**, respectively. Both standards, in their many varieties, use the same frame as the slow-by-comparison earlier versions of Ethernet, so with the right switches, you've got perfect interoperability. The 40 GbE and 100 GbE standards are primarily used when lots of bandwidth is needed, such as connecting servers, switches, and routers.

Common 40 GbE runs on OM3 or better multimode fiber, uses laser light, and uses various four-channel connectors. A typical connector is called an **enhanced quad small form-factor pluggable (QSFP+)**, essentially taking four SFP+ transceivers and squashing them into a single, wider transceiver. Other 40 GbE standards run on single-mode fiber and can do distances up to 10 km. Still other 40 GbE connections run on Cat 8 UTP for an underwhelming 30 meters. This is **40GBASE-T** and shows up in the CompTIA Network+ objectives.

The CompTIA Network+ exam does *not* include 100 GbE or its faster variants 200 GbE and 400 GbE.

100 GbE standards employ both MMF and SMF with various connectors. A typical connector is the *QSFP28* that has four channels of 25 Gb each. You'll sometimes see this connector referred to as a QSFP100 or 100G QSFP.

Chapter 4 Review

Chapter Summary

After reading this chapter and completing the exercises, you should understand the following about Ethernet.

Describe the varieties of 100-megabit Ethernet

- Fast Ethernet includes two UTP/STP variations, both arranged in a physical star, but operating in a logical bus—100BASE-TX and 100BASE-T4. The latter standard has disappeared into the dustbins of history.
- In 100BASE-TX Ethernet cabling systems, speeds are 100 Mbps, wires are twisted copper pairs, signals are baseband, and distance is limited to 100 meters from the node to the switch, with a limit of 1024 nodes per switch. The cabling used must be Cat 5 or better UTP/STP crimped with RJ-45 connectors.
- Limitations of Fast Ethernet over UTP include distance (only
100 meters), inadequate shielding for some installations, and relative ease of intruder break-ins on the physical cable.
- The fiber-optic variation of Fast Ethernet, 100BASE-FX, overcomes these limitations, offering immunity to electrical interference and
a range of up to 2 kilometers from node to switch.
- A half-duplex NIC could only send or receive at any one time.
Full-duplex NICs can send and receive at the same time, thereby doubling the bandwidth.

Discuss copper- and fiber-based Gigabit Ethernet

- Two Gigabit Ethernet standards have been approved by the IEEE: 802.3ab (1000BASE-T) and 802.3z (1000BASE-X).
- 1000BASE-T uses four-pair UTP/STP cabling and has a maximum length of 100 meters.
- 1000BASE-X is divided into a number of standards, such as 1000BASE-SX and 1000BASE-LX.
- 1000BASE-SX uses multimode fiber-optic cable with a maximum length between 220 and 500 meters, depending on the manufacturer.
- 1000BASE-LX uses single-mode fiber-optic cable with a maximum length of 5 kilometers. Some manufacturers use repeaters to extend the maximum length to 70 kilometers.
- The small form factor (SFF) fiber connector includes the Mechanical Transfer Registered Jack (MT-RJ) and the LC, both of which were created to overcome problems with the ST and SC connectors.
- Aside from the various connection types (LC, MT-RJ, and so on), fiber connectors vary in the connection point. The standard connector type today is called a Physical Contact (PC) connector because the two pieces of fiber touch when inserted. Ultra-physical contact (UPC) connectors are polished extensively for a superior finish. These reduce signal loss significantly over PC connectors. Angled physical contact (APC) connectors add an 8-degree angle to the curved end, lowering signal loss further.
- The gigabit interface converter (GBIC) is a standard for modular Gigabit Ethernet transceivers. With GBICs, you can switch out the module and replace it with a different Gigabit transceiver type.

Discover and describe Ethernet varieties beyond Gigabit

- 10 Gigabit Ethernet (10 GbE) has several fiber standards and two copper standards.
- SONET is the networking standard for long-distance optical connections that serve as the main backbone for the Internet.
- 10 GbE is organized into six different standards: 10GBASE-SR, 10GBASE-SW, 10GBASE-LR, 10GBASE-LW, 10GBASE-ER, and 10GBASE-EW.
- 10GBASE-Sy uses multimode fiber with a maximum length of 300 meters. 10GBASE-LR is used for Ethernet LANs, whereas 10GBASE-SW is used to connect to SONET devices.
- 10GBASE-L*y* uses single-mode fiber with a maximum length of 10 kilometers. 10GBASE-LR is for Ethernet LANs, whereas 10GBASE-LW is used to connect to SONET devices. 10GBASE-LR is the most popular and least expensive 10 GbE media type.
- 10GBASE-E*y* uses single-mode fiber with a maximum length of 40 kilometers. 10GBASE-ER

is used for Ethernet LANs, whereas 10GBASE-EW is used to connect to SONET devices.

- 10GBASE-T defines 10 Gigabit Ethernet over UTP/STP cable. It is capable of a maximum distance of 55 meters with Cat 6; however, using Cat 6a, it can achieve 100 meters.
- All types of 10 GbE send and receive the exact same signal. Network devices, such as routers, that need to support different 10 GbE cable types use multisource agreements (MSAs) to create interchangeable transceivers.
- Bidirectional transceivers use WDM to differentiate light waves, enabling communication using a single fiber-optic cable. Although dual-fiber cable runs are currently the norm, single-fiber seems a more cost-effective solution for new installations.
- IEEE 802.3ba defines the 40 GbE and 100 GbE standards, most using multimode fiber with QSFP+ and QSFP28 connectors, respectively. The 40GBASE-T standard uses Cat 8 twisted pair cabling and RJ-45 connectors.

Key Terms

10GBASE-ER *(76)*
10GBASE-EW *(76)*
10GBASE-LR *(76)*
10GBASE-LW *(76)*
10GBASE-SR *(76)*
10GBASE-SW *(76)*
10GBASE-T *(77)*
10 Gigabit Ethernet (10 GbE) *(75)*
100BASE-FX *(70)*
100BASE-T *(69)*
100BASE-TX *(69)*
1000BASE-LX *(73)*
1000BASE-SX *(73)*
1000BASE-T *(72)*
1000BASE-X *(72)*
40 Gigabit Ethernet (40 GbE) *(80)*
40GBASE-T *(80)*
100 Gigabit Ethernet (100 GbE) *(80)*
802.3ab *(72)*
802.3z *(72)*
Angled Physical Contact (APC) connector *(74)*
baseband *(69)*
bidirectional (BiDi) transceiver *(78)*
broadband *(69)*
duplex *(78)*
electromagnetic interference (EMI) *(70)*
enhanced quad small form-factor pluggable (QSFP+) *(80)*
enhanced small form-factor pluggable (SFP+) *(78)*
Fast Ethernet *(69)*
flat-surface connector *(74)*
full-duplex *(71)*
Gigabit Ethernet *(72)*
gigabit interface converter (GBIC) *(75)*
half-duplex *(71)*
local connector (LC) *(73)*
Mechanical Transfer Registered Jack (MT-RJ) *(73)*
media converter *(75)*
optic *(75)*
physical contact (PC) connector *(74)*
quad small form-factor pluggable (QSFP) *(78)*
small form factor (SFF) *(73)*
small form-factor pluggable (SFP) *(75)*
Synchronous Optical Network (SONET) *(76)*
transceiver *(75)*
ultra-physical contact (UPC) connector *(74)*
wavelength *(73)*

Key Term Quiz

Use the Key Terms list to complete the sentences that follow. Not all terms will be used.

1. When a network device can both send and receive data at the same time, it is said to be ______________.
2. ______________ has a maximum cable length of 2 kilometers and uses multimode fiber with ST or SC connectors.
3. 100BASE-T is also known as ______________.

4. You can use a(n) ______________ to connect any type of Ethernet cabling together.
5. 802.3z and 802.3ab are both ______________ standards.
6. ______________ supports the longest maximum distance for Gigabit Ethernet.
7. The ______________ and ______________ IEEE standards support the longest maximum distance for 10 Gigabit Ethernet.
8. Many fiber experts consider the ______________ to be the predominant fiber connector.
9. ______________ is the least expensive and most popular 10 GbE media type.
10. Switches that support a(n) ______________ transceiver can connect a variety of Gigabit types.

Multiple-Choice Quiz

1. Which of the following are 100BASE-T cable types? (Select two.)
   - **A.** Cat 3
   - **B.** Cat 5
   - **C.** Cat 5e
   - **D.** 10BASE-FL
2. Which IEEE standard covers 1000BASE-X?
   - **A.** 802.3a
   - **B.** 802.3ab
   - **C.** 802.3z
   - **D.** 802.11x
3. Which type of connector would you typically find with a 40 GbE installation?
   - **A.** LC
   - **B.** SFP
   - **C.** QSFP+
   - **D.** XSFP+
4. What important technology is also known as Gigabit Ethernet?
   - **A.** 100BASE-T
   - **B.** 100BASE-FL
   - **C.** 100BASE-FX
   - **D.** 1000BASE-T
5. Which term represents an agreement among multiple manufacturers to make interoperable devices and standards?
   - **A.** BiDi
   - **B.** MSA
   - **C.** QSFP
   - **D.** SFF
6. Which technology enables duplex communication over a single fiber connection?
   - **A.** BiDi
   - **B.** MSA
   - **C.** MT-RJ
   - **D.** UPC
7. Which standard defines Fast Ethernet using fiber cabling?
   - **A.** 10BASE-FL
   - **B.** 100BASE-FX
   - **C.** 100BASE-T4
   - **D.** 100BASE-TX
8. Which of the following are fiber connector types? (Select three.)
   - **A.** LC
   - **B.** LS
   - **C.** MT-RJ
   - **D.** ST
9. Which standard defines Gigabit Ethernet over twisted pair copper wire?
   - **A.** 802.3ab
   - **B.** 802.3e
   - **C.** 802.3GbUTP
   - **D.** 802.3z
10. You've lost the manual to your router. How can you tell the difference between a 1000BASE-T port and a 100BASE-T port on a router just by looking?
    - **A.** The 1000BASE-T ports are noticeably larger.
    - **B.** The 100BASE-T ports are green, whereas the 1000BASE-T ports are gray.

C. 1000BASE-T ports are reversed with the clip on the top.

D. You can't tell the difference by looking. They look exactly the same.

11. What is a big advantage to using fiber-optic cable?

A. Fiber is common glass; therefore, it's less expensive.

B. Fiber is not affected by EMI.

C. Making custom cable lengths is easier with fiber.

D. All that orange fiber looks impressive in the network closet.

12. Which of the following is one of the most popular transceivers currently used in 10 GbE?

A. LC

B. MT-RJ

C. GBIC

D. SFP+

13. What is the big physical difference between 1000BASE-SX and 100BASE-FX?

A. 1000BASE-SX commonly uses the LC connector, whereas 100BASE-FX frequently use the SC connector.

B. 1000BASE-SX is single-mode, whereas 100BASE-FX is multimode.

C. 1000BASE-SX uses the ST connector exclusively.

D. There is no physical difference.

14. What is the difference between the *R* and *W* designations in 10GBASE- standards, such as 10GBASE-LR and 10GBASE-LW, or 10GBASE-ER and 10GBASE-EW?

A. The *R* indicates "regular," or half-duplex. The *W* indicates "wide mode," which is the 10 Gigabit Ethernet version of full-duplex.

B. The *R* indicates "read," or the ability to receive signals; the *W* indicates "write," or the ability to send signals.

C. The *R* and *W* indicate differences in the circuitry, with the *W* versions used to connect to SONET equipment.

D. The *R* indicates the use of UTP, whereas the *W* indicates the use of fiber optics.

15. Which of the following is a standard fiber connector type?

A. AC

B. BC

C. EC

D. PC

Essay Quiz

1. Which types of computer network cable connections are you familiar with already? Write a short paragraph describing your experience.

2. Your manager has just informed you that several departments at your company will be switching over to fiber-optic NICs. How many and what type of connectors will be needed for each node on the new segment? Document your recommendations.

3. Compose a letter to the network administrator of a nearby telecommunications company or ISP (Internet service provider). Introduce yourself in the top part of the letter as a networking student. Then ask if the company ever gives tours or holds open houses for the public. Close the letter by thanking the person reading it for his or her time. Spell-check and have others proofread your letter. Consider mailing the letter if you are serious about your visit and your instructor approves your final copy.

4. Prepare a list of questions you would ask a large organization's network administrator regarding cabling, connections, hubs, switches, and even routers. Use the situation described in Essay 3 to help you create your list of questions.

Lab Projects

• Lab Project 4.1

Find a switch at your school or company. Examine the wiring closely to determine what cable connections it uses. Try to determine whether the cabling was placed neatly and in an organized manner, whether the ports are clearly labeled, and whether all the ends were crimped well. Be prepared to discuss your findings with the rest of the class.

• Lab Project 4.2

Use the Internet to research prices to order 100 each of the connectors from the following list. Don't forget to include basic shipping and handling to your organization's location, as these are a price factor in real life.

- RJ-45 connectors
- SC connectors
- ST connectors
- MT-RJ connectors
- LC connectors

From your research, which connectors would be the least costly?

• Lab Project 4.3

All these standards! How can you remember them?

Make a chart that compares the features (cabling, connectors, data throughput, and so on) of the following Ethernet technologies:

- 100BASE-T
- 100BASE-FX
- 1000BASE-T
- 1000BASE-LX
- 1000BASE-SX
- 10GBASE-SR/10GBASE-SW
- 10GBASE-LR/10GBASE-LW
- 10GBASE-ER/10GBASE-EW

Installing a Physical Network

"I am rarely happier than when spending an entire day programming my computer to perform automatically a task that it would otherwise take me a good ten seconds to do by hand."

—Douglas Adams

In this chapter, you will learn how to

- **Recognize and describe the functions of basic components in a structured cabling system**
- **Explain the process of installing structured cable**
- **Install a network interface card**
- **Perform basic troubleshooting on a structured cable network**

Armed with the knowledge of previous chapters, it's time to construct a physical network. This might seem easy; after all, the most basic network is nothing more than a switch with cables snaking out to all of the PCs on the network (Figure 5.1).

On the surface, such a network setup is absolutely correct, but if you tried to run a network using only a switch and cables running to each system, you'd have some serious practical issues. In the real world, you need to deal with physical obstacles like walls and ceilings. You also need to deal with *people*. People are incredibly adept at destroying physical networks. They unplug switches, trip over cables, and rip connectors out of NICs with incredible consistency unless you protect the network from their destructive ways. Although the simplified switch-and-a-bunch-of-cables type of network can function in the real world, the network clearly has some problems that need addressing before it can work safely and efficiently (Figure 5.2).

This chapter takes the abstract discussion of network technologies from previous chapters into the concrete reality of real networks. To achieve this goal, it marches you through the process of installing an entire network system from the beginning. The chapter starts by introducing you to *structured cabling*, the critical set of standards used all over the world to install physical cabling in a safe and orderly fashion. It then delves into the world of larger networks—those with more than a single switch—and shows you some typical methods used to organize them for peak efficiency and reliability. Next, you'll take a quick tour of the most common NICs used in PCs, and see what it takes to install them. Finally, you'll look at how to troubleshoot cabling and other network devices, including an introduction to some fun diagnostic tools.

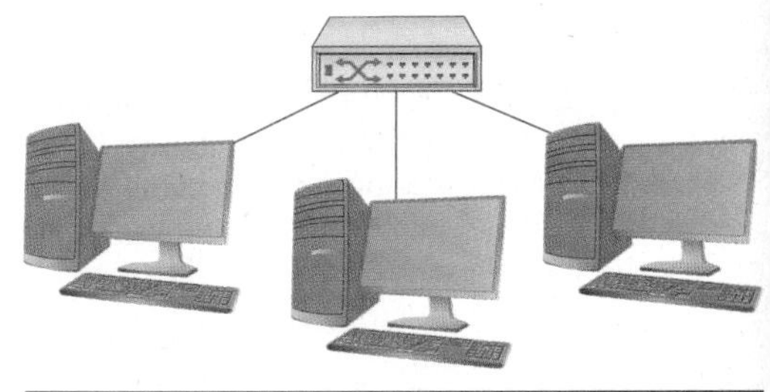

• **Figure 5.1** What an orderly looking network!

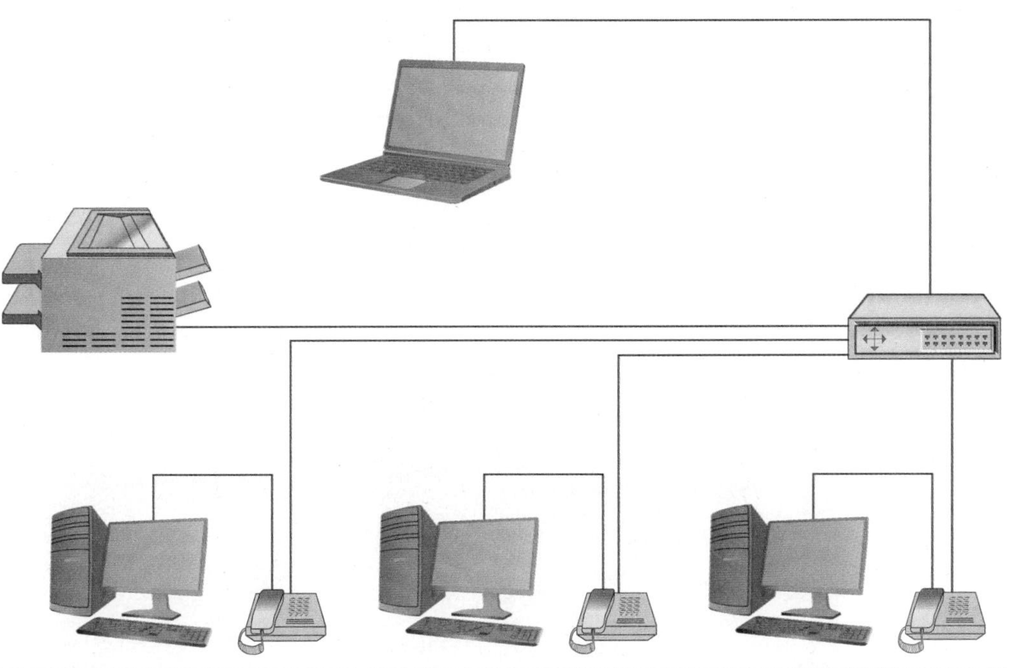

• **Figure 5.2** A real-world network

Historical/Conceptual

Understanding Structured Cabling

If you want a functioning, dependable, real-world network, you need a solid understanding of a set of standards and proprietary systems, collectively called **structured cabling**. In the United States, the Telecommunications Industry Association (TIA) gives professional cable installers detailed standards on every aspect of a cabled network, from the type of cabling to use to the position of wall outlets. The European Union has adopted some of the TIA standards, but publishes versions with various bodies such as Europe Norm (EN) and CENELEC.

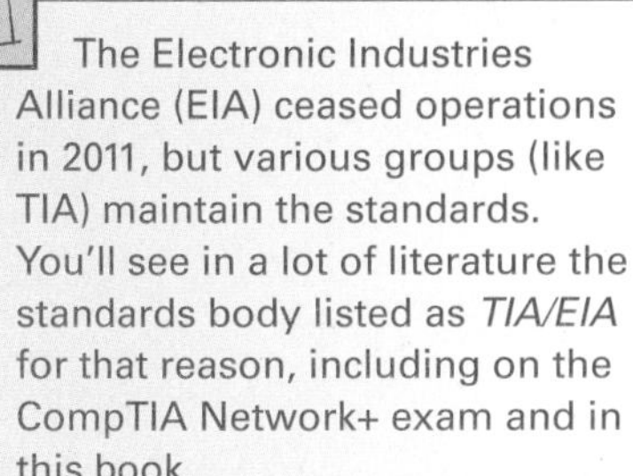

The Electronic Industries Alliance (EIA) ceased operations in 2011, but various groups (like TIA) maintain the standards. You'll see in a lot of literature the standards body listed as *TIA/EIA* for that reason, including on the CompTIA Network+ exam and in this book.

The CompTIA Network+ exam requires you to understand the basic concepts involved in designing a network and installing network cabling and to recognize the components used in a real network. The CompTIA Network+ exam does not, however, expect you to be as knowledgeable as a

A structured cabling system is useful for more than just computer networks. You'll find structured cabling defining telephone networks and video conferencing setups, for example.

Tech Tip

Integrating Wi-Fi

Most networks today have a wireless component in addition to a wired infrastructure. The switches, servers, and workstations rely on wires for fast and stable networking, but the wireless component supports the large number of laptops, phones, and other devices found in a modern network.

This chapter focuses on the wired infrastructure. Once we get through Wi-Fi in Chapter 14, I'll add that component to our networking conversation.

professional network designer or cable installer. Your goal is to understand enough about real-world cabling systems to communicate knowledgeably with cable installers and to perform basic troubleshooting. Granted, by the end of this chapter, you'll have enough of an understanding to try running your own cable (I certainly run my own cable), but consider that knowledge a handy bit of extra credit.

The idea of structured cabling is to create a safe, reliable cabling infrastructure for all of the devices that may need interconnection. Certainly this applies to computer networks, but also to telephone, video—anything that might need low-power, distributed cabling.

You should understand three issues with structured cabling. Cable basics start the picture, with switches, cabling, and PCs. You'll then look at the components of a network, such as how the cable runs through the walls and where it ends up. This section wraps up with an assessment of connections leading outside your network.

Cable Basics—A Star Is Born

This exploration of the world of connectivity hardware starts with the most basic of all networks: a switch, some UTP cable, and a few PCs—in other words, a physical star network (Figure 5.3).

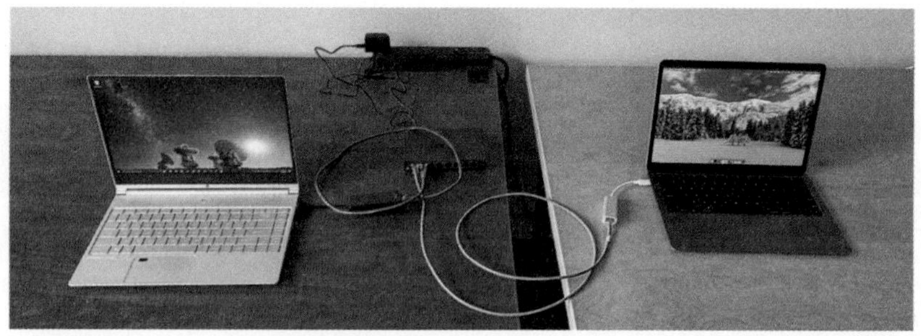

• **Figure 5.3** A switch connected by UTP cable to two PCs

No law of office decor prevents you from installing a switch in the middle of your office and running cables on the floor to all the computers in your network. This setup works, but it falls apart spectacularly when applied to a real-world environment. Three problems present themselves to the network tech. First, the exposed cables running along the floor are just waiting for someone to trip over them, damaging the network and giving that person a wonderful lawsuit opportunity. Possible accidents aside, simply moving and stepping on the cabling will, over time, cause a cable to fail due to wires breaking or RJ-45 connectors ripping off cable ends. Second, the presence of other electrical devices close to the cable can create interference that confuses the signals going through the wire. Third, this type of setup limits your ability to make any changes to the network. Before you can change anything, you have to figure out which cables in the huge rat's nest of cables connected to the switch go to which machines. Imagine *that* troubleshooting nightmare!

"Gosh," you're thinking, "there must be a better way to install a physical network." A better installation would provide safety, protecting the star from vacuum cleaners, clumsy coworkers, and electrical interference. It would have extra hardware to organize and protect the cabling. Finally, the new and improved star network installation would feature a cabling standard with the flexibility to enable the network to grow according to its needs and then to upgrade when the next great network technology comes along.

As you have no doubt guessed, I'm not just theorizing here. In the real world, the people who most wanted improved installation standards were the ones who installed cable for a living. In response to this demand, TIA and other standards bodies developed standards for cable installation. The TIA/EIA 568 standards you learned about in Chapter 3 are only some of the standards all lumped together under the umbrella of structured cabling.

Cross Check

TIA/EIA Standards

You should remember the TIA/EIA 568 standards from Chapter 3, but do you remember how to tell the difference between 568A and 568B? Why were the standards considered necessary?

Tech Tip

Professional Cabling Certifications with BICSI

Installing structured cabling properly takes a startlingly high degree of skill. Thousands of pitfalls await inexperienced network people who think they can install their own network cabling. Pulling cable requires expensive equipment, a lot of hands, and the ability to react to problems quickly. Network techs can cost employers a lot of money—not to mention losing their good jobs—by imagining they can do it themselves without the proper knowledge.

If you are interested in learning more details about structured cabling, an organization called the Building Industry Consulting Service International (BICSI; www.bicsi.org) provides a series of widely recognized certifications and training courses for the cabling industry.

Test Specific

Structured Cable—Network Components

Successful implementation of a basic structured cabling network requires three essential ingredients: a telecommunications room, horizontal cabling, and a work area. Let's zero in on one floor of Figure 4.10 from the previous chapter. All the cabling runs from individual PCs to a central location, the **telecommunications room** (Figure 5.4). What equipment goes in there—a switch or a telephone system—is not important. What matters is that all the cables concentrate in this one area.

All cables run horizontally (for the most part) from the telecommunications room to the PCs. This cabling is called, appropriately, **horizontal cabling**. A single piece of installed horizontal cabling is called a **run**. At the opposite end of the horizontal cabling from the telecommunications room is the work area. The **work area** is often simply an office or cubicle that potentially contains a PC and a telephone. Figure 5.5 shows both the horizontal cabling and work areas.

Each of the three parts of a basic star topology network—the telecommunications room, the horizontal cabling, and the work area(s)—must follow a series of

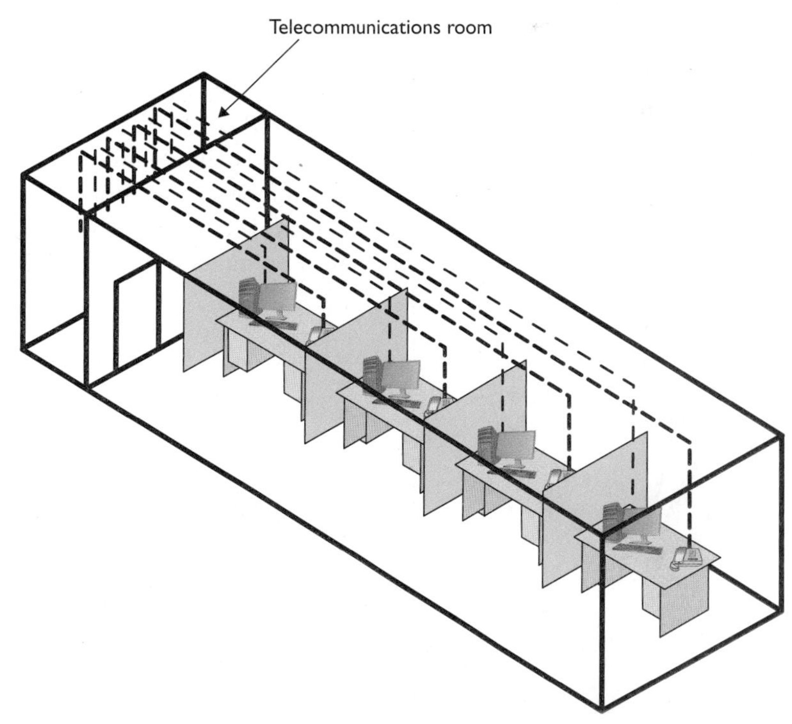

• **Figure 5.4** Telecommunications room

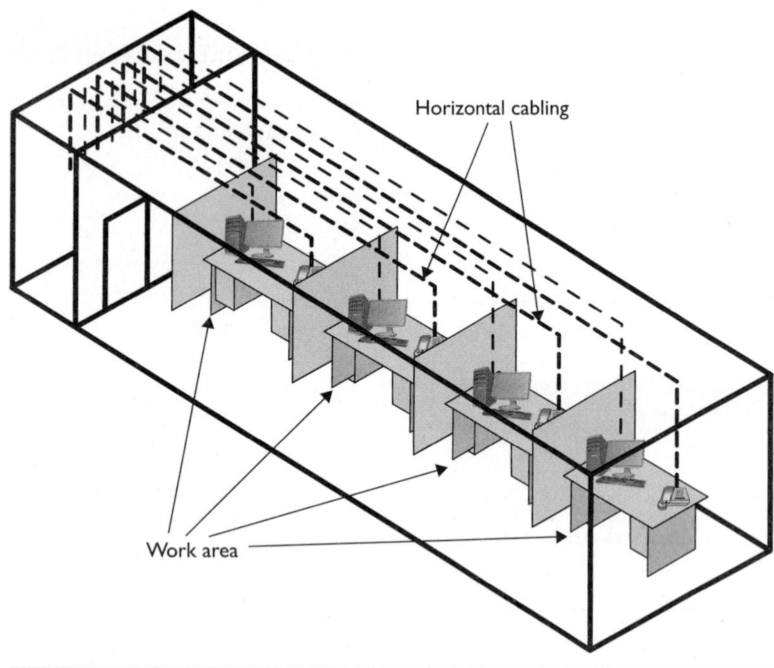

• **Figure 5.5** Horizontal cabling and work area

strict standards designed to ensure that the cabling system is reliable and easy to manage. The cabling standards set by TIA/EIA enable techs to make sensible decisions on equipment installed in the telecommunications room, so let's tackle horizontal cabling first, and then return to the telecommunications room. We'll finish up with the work area.

Horizontal Cabling

A horizontal cabling run is the cabling that goes more or less horizontally from a work area to the telecommunications room. In most networks, this cable is Cat 5e or better UTP for copper-based standards, such as 1000BASE-T. (Fiber-based standards, such as 1000BASE-SX, would use multimode fiber-optic cabling, also in a star topology.) When you move into structured cabling, the TIA/EIA standards define a number of other aspects of the cable, such as the type of wires, number of pairs of wires, and fire ratings.

A single piece of cable that runs from a work area to a telecommunications room is called a *run*.

Solid Core vs. Stranded Core All UTP cables come in one of two types: solid core or stranded core. Each wire in **solid core** UTP uses a single solid wire. With **stranded core**, each wire is actually a bundle of tiny wire strands. Each of these cable types has its benefits and downsides. Solid core is a better conductor, but it is stiff and will break if handled too often or too roughly. Stranded core is not quite as good a conductor, but it will stand up to substantial handling without breaking. Figure 5.6 shows a close-up of solid and stranded core UTP.

TIA/EIA specifies that horizontal cabling should always be solid core. Remember, this cabling is going into your walls and ceilings, safe from the harmful effects of shoes and vacuum cleaners. The ceilings and walls enable you to take advantage of the better conductivity of solid core without the risk of cable damage. Stranded core cable also has an important function in a structured cabling network, but I need to discuss a few more parts of the network before I talk about where to use stranded core UTP cable.

• **Figure 5.6** Solid and stranded core UTP

Number of Pairs Pulling horizontal cables into your walls and ceilings is a time-consuming and messy business, and not a process you want to repeat, if at all possible. For this reason, most cable installers recommend using the highest Cat rating you can afford. Many years ago, I would also mention that you should use four-pair UTP, but today, four-pair is assumed. Four-pair UTP is so common that it's difficult, if not impossible, to find two-pair UTP. Cat 5e, Cat 6, Cat 6a, Cat 7, etc., all use four-pair UTP.

You'll find larger bundled UTP cables in legacy telephone installations. These cables hold 25 or even 100 pairs of wires (Figure 5.7). These cables are not used for Ethernet.

• **Figure 5.7** 25-pair UTP

Cross Check

Fire Ratings

You saw another aspect of cabling way back in Chapter 2, so check your memory here. What are fire ratings? When should you use plenum-grade cabling and when should you use riser-grade cabling? What about PVC? What are the differences?

Choosing Your Horizontal Cabling Network installations today favor at least Cat 6. Installing higher-rated cabling—Cat 6a, 7, etc.—is done either as a hedge against new network technologies that may require a more advanced cable or simply adoption of the faster 10+ Gigabit standards.

The Telecommunications Room

The telecommunications room is the heart of the basic star topology network. This room—technically called the **intermediate distribution frame (IDF)**—is where all the horizontal runs from all the work areas come together. The concentration of all this gear in one place makes the telecommunications room potentially one of the messiest parts of the basic star topology network. Even if you do a nice, neat job of organizing the cables when they are first installed, networks change over time. People move computers, new work areas are added, network topologies are added or improved, and so on. Unless you impose some type of organization, this conglomeration of equipment and cables decays into a nightmarish mess.

The telecommunications room is also known as the *intermediate distribution frame (IDF)*, as opposed to the main distribution frame (MDF), which we will discuss later in the chapter.

Fortunately, the TIA/EIA structured cabling standards define the use of specialized components in the telecommunications room that make organizing a snap. In fact, it might be fair to say that there are too many options! To keep it simple, we're going to stay with the most common telecommunications room setup and then take a short peek at some other fairly common options.

Equipment racks evolved out of the railroad signaling racks from the 19th century. The components in a rack today obviously differ a lot from railroad signaling, but the 19-inch width has remained the standard for well over 100 years.

Equipment Racks The central component of every telecommunications room is one or more equipment racks. An **equipment rack** provides a safe, stable platform for all the different hardware components. All equipment racks are 19 inches wide, but they vary in height from two- to three-foot-high models that bolt onto a wall (Figure 5.8) to the more popular floor-to-ceiling free-standing models (Figure 5.9).

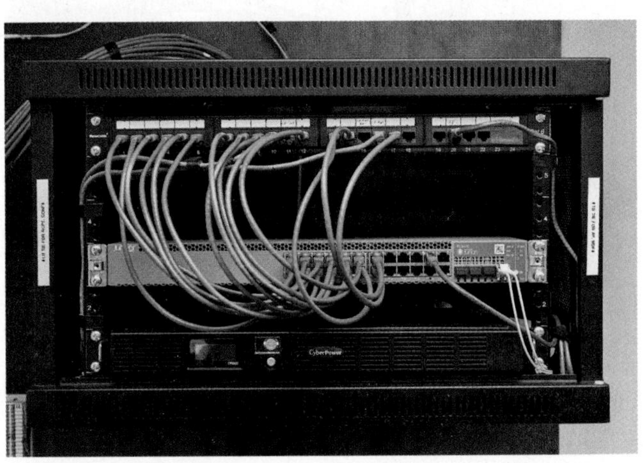

• **Figure 5.8** A short equipment rack

You can mount almost any network hardware component into a rack. All manufacturers make rack-mounted switches that mount into a rack with a few screws. These switches are available with a wide assortment of ports and capabilities. There are even rack-mounted servers, complete with slide-out keyboards, and rack-mounted uninterruptible power supplies (UPSs) to power the equipment (Figure 5.10). A UPS provides backup power to the devices on the rack. (See "Problems in the Telecommunication Room" later in this chapter for more details.)

• **Figure 5.9** A free-standing rack

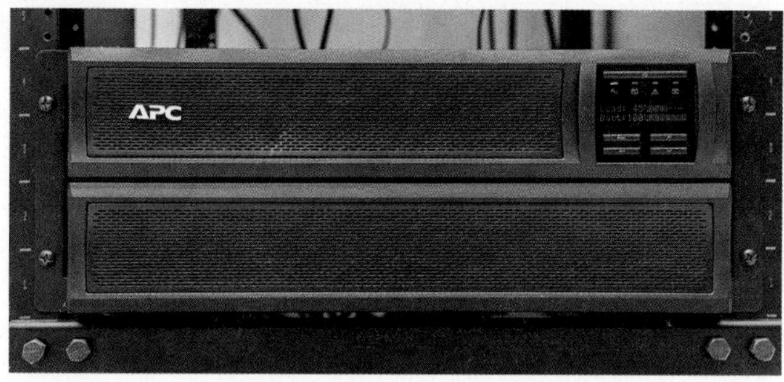

• **Figure 5.10** A rack-mounted UPS

All rack-mounted equipment uses a height measurement known simply as a **unit (U)**. A U is 1.75 inches. A device that fits in a 1.75-inch space is called a 1U; a device designed for a 3.5-inch space is a 2U; and a device that goes into a 7-inch space is called a 4U. Most rack-mounted devices are 1U, 2U, or 4U. A typical full-size rack is called a 42U rack to reflect the total number of Us it can hold.

The key when planning a rack system is to determine what sort of rack-mounted equipment you plan to have and then get the rack or racks for your space. For example, if your rack will have only patch panels (see the next section), switches, and routers, you can get away with a *two-post rack*. The pieces are small and easily supported.

If you're going to install big servers, on the other hand, then you need to plan for a *four-post rack* or a *server rail rack*. A four-post rack supports all four corners of the server. The server rail rack enables you to slide the server out so you can open it up. This is very useful for swapping out dead drives for new ones in big file servers.

Bigger installations incorporate a **power distribution unit (PDU)** for centralized power management (Figure 5.11). On the surface, a PDU works like a power strip, providing multiple outlets for components, drawing electricity directly from a wall socket or indirectly from an UPS. Better PDUs enable remote connectivity and management for monitoring power levels.

• **Figure 5.11** PDU in server rack

When planning how many racks you need in your rack system and where to place them, take proper air flow into consideration. You shouldn't cram servers and gear into every corner. Even with good air conditioning systems, bad air flow can cook components.

Finally, make sure to secure the telecommunications room. Rack security is a must for protecting valuable equipment. Get a lock! Figure 5.12 shows a server lock on a rack.

Server enclosure manufacturers incorporate all sorts of locking mechanisms. You'll see plenty of physical locks on doors, for example, but also keypad locks,

• **Figure 5.12** Lock on a rack-mounted server

Expect a question on the CompTIA Network+ exam about *physical security* access *prevention methods*. Locking racks and cabinets might feature in. We'll get to a lot more physical security concepts in Chapter 19.

biometric locks, smart card locks, and more. The terms *locking racks* and *locking cabinets* refer to a chassis (rack or cabinet) plus a door with a locking mechanism.

We'll revisit UPSes, PDUs, generators, and other elements of *facilities and infrastructure support* when we explore techniques for keeping datacenter infrastructure up and running (called *high availability*) and handling potential disasters in Chapters 16 and 18.

Patch Panels and Cables Ideally, once you install horizontal cabling, you should never move it. As you know, UTP horizontal cabling has a solid core, making it pretty stiff. Solid core cables can handle some rearranging, but if you insert a wad of solid core cables directly into your switches, every time you move a cable to a different port on the switch, or move the switch itself, you will jostle the cable. You don't have to move a solid core cable many times before one of the solid copper wires breaks, and there goes a network connection!

Luckily for you, you can easily avoid this problem by using a patch panel. A **patch panel** is simply a box with a row of female ports in the front and permanent connections in the back, to which you connect the horizontal cables (Figure 5.13).

Make sure you insert the wires according to the same standard (TIA/EIA 568A or TIA/EIA 568B) on both ends of the cable. If you don't, you might end up swapping the sending and receiving wires (known as *transmit and receive TX/RX reversed*) and inadvertently creating a crossover cable.

• **Figure 5.13** Typical patch panels

The most common type of patch panel today uses a special type of connector called a **110 block**, or sometimes called a *110-punchdown block*. UTP cables connect to a 110 block using a **punchdown tool**. Figure 5.14 shows a typical punchdown tool, and Figure 5.15 shows the punchdown tool punching down individual strands.

The punchdown block has small metal-lined grooves for the individual wires. The punchdown tool has a blunt end that forces the wire into the groove. The metal in the groove slices the cladding enough to make contact.

• **Figure 5.14** Punchdown tool

• **Figure 5.15** Punching down a 110 block

• **Figure 5.16** 66-block patch panels

At one time, the older 66-punchdown block patch panel (a **66 block**), found in just about every commercial telephone installation (Figure 5.16), saw some use in PC networks. The 110 block introduces less crosstalk than 66 blocks, so most high-speed network installations use the former for both telephone service and LANs. Given their large installed base, it's still common to find a group of 66-block patch panels in a telecommunications room separate from the network's 110-block patch panels.

• **Figure 5.17** Typical patch panels with labels

Not only do patch panels prevent the horizontal cabling from being moved, but they are also your first line of defense in organizing the cables. All patch panels have space in the front for labels, and these labels are the network tech's best friend! Simply place a tiny label on the patch panel to identify each cable, and you will never have to experience that sinking feeling of standing in the telecommunications room of your nonfunctioning network, wondering which cable is which. If you want to be a purist, there is an official, and rather confusing, ANSI/TIA naming convention called **ANSI/TIA-606-C**, but a number of real-world network techs simply use their own internal codes (Figure 5.17).

Patch panels are available in a wide variety of configurations that include different types of ports and numbers of ports. You can get UTP, STP, or fiber ports, and some manufacturers combine several different types on the same patch panel. Panels are available with 8, 12, 24, 48, or even more ports.

UTP patch panels, like UTP cables, come with Cat ratings, which you should be sure to check. Don't blow a good Cat 6 cable installation by buying a cheap patch panel—get a Cat 6 patch panel! A Cat 6 panel can handle the 250-MHz frequency used by Cat 6 and offers lower crosstalk and network interference. A higher-rated panel supports earlier standards, so you can use a Cat 6 or even Cat 6a rack with Cat 5e cabling. Most manufacturers proudly display the Cat level right on the patch panel (Figure 5.18).

• **Figure 5.18** Cat level on patch panel

Once you have installed the patch panel, you need to connect the ports to the switch through **patch cables**. Patch cables are short straight-through UTP cables. Patch cables use stranded core rather than solid core cable, so they can tolerate much more handling. Even though you can make your own patch cables, most people buy premade ones. Buying patch cables enables you to use different-colored cables to facilitate organization (yellow for accounting, blue for sales, or whatever scheme works for you). Most prefabricated patch cables also come with a reinforced (booted) connector specially designed to handle multiple insertions and removals (Figure 5.19).

• **Figure 5.19** Typical patch cable

Alternative Cable Connection Points Although you'll most likely encounter 110 blocks today, some cable installations—especially outside the United States—incorporate proprietary cable interconnects. The **BIX block**, for example, is a proprietary networking interconnect developed by Nortel Networks. (BIX stands for *Building Industry Cross-connect*, in case you're curious.) Similar in function to a 110-punchdown block, a BIX block is installed on a wall rather than in a rack. Figure 5.20 shows BIX blocks and connectors.

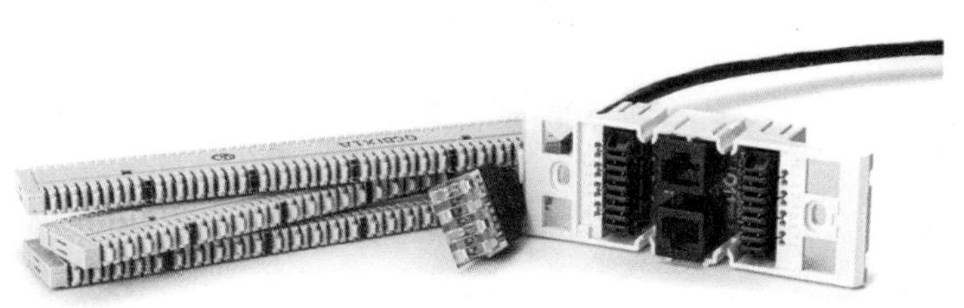

• **Figure 5.20** BIX blocks and connectors

The *Krone LSA-PLUS* proprietary European telecommunication connector—**Krone block**—offers another alternative to the 110-punchdown block. Developed by the German telecommunications company The Krone Group in the 1970s, Krone connectors enable networking as well as audio interconnections. Figure 5.21 shows a couple of Krone blocks.

• **Figure 5.21** Krone blocks

Networks that include audio/video components (like with the Total Seminars video production studio, where I make awesome training videos for you) have a second set of wires for the A/V connections running to the telecommunications room. These runs of coaxial or fiber connect to a **patch bay**, a dedicated block with A/V connections rather than twisted pair and fiber network connections. Expect a question on the CompTIA Network+ exam that explores patch bays.

Finishing the Telecommunications Room Portion A telecommunications room doesn't have to be a special room dedicated to computer equipment. You can use specially made cabinets with their own little built-in equipment racks that sit on the floor or attach to a wall, or you can use a storage room if the equipment can be protected from the other items stored there. Fortunately, the demand for telecommunications rooms has been around for so long that most office spaces have premade telecommunications rooms, even if they are no more than closets in smaller offices.

At this point, the network is taking shape (Figure 5.22). The horizontal cabling is installed, and the telecommunications room is configured. Now it's time to address the last part of the structured cabling system: the work area.

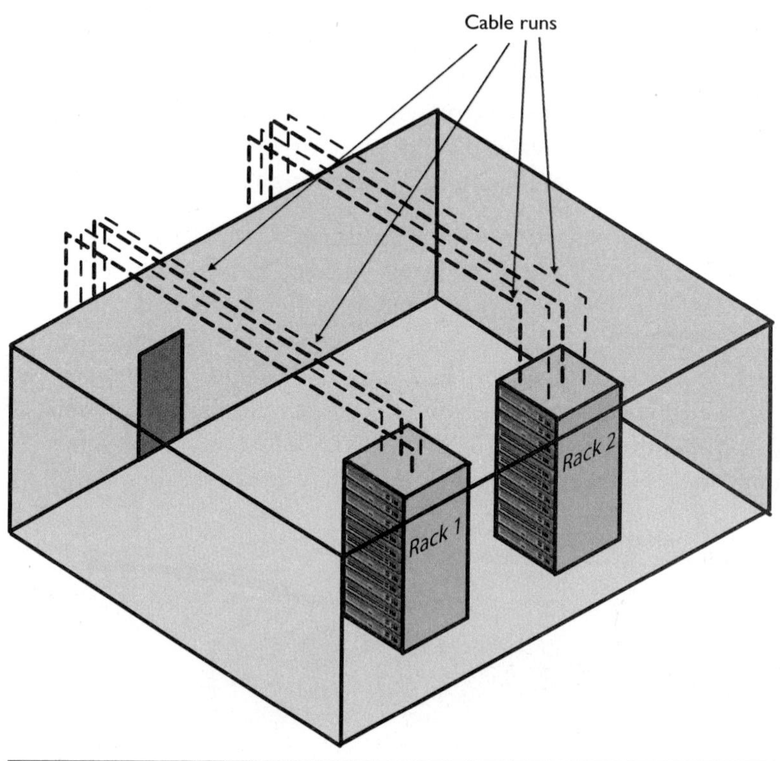

• **Figure 5.22** Network taking shape, with racks installed and horizontal cabling runs

The Work Area

From a cabling standpoint, a work area is nothing more than a wall outlet that serves as the termination point for horizontal network cables: a convenient insertion point for a PC and a telephone. (In practice, of course, the term "work area" includes the office or cubicle.) A wall outlet itself consists of one or two female jacks to accept the cable, a mounting bracket, and a faceplate. You connect the PC to the wall outlet with a patch cable (Figure 5.23).

• **Figure 5.23** Typical work area outlet

The female RJ-45 jacks in these wall outlets also have Cat ratings. You must buy Cat-rated jacks for wall outlets to go along with the Cat rating of the cabling in your network. In fact, many network connector manufacturers use the same connectors in the wall outlets that they use on the patch panels. These modular outlets significantly increase ease of installation.

Make sure you label the outlet to show the job of each connector (Figure 5.24). A good outlet will also have some form of label that identifies its position on the patch panel. Proper documentation of your outlets will save you an incredible amount of work later.

The last step is connecting the PC to the wall outlet. Here again, most folks use a patch cable. Its stranded core cabling stands up to the abuse caused by moving PCs, not to mention the occasional kick.

You'll recall from Chapter 4 that most Ethernet networks specify a limit of 100 meters between a switch and a node. Interestingly, though, the TIA/EIA 568 specification allows only UTP cable lengths of 90 meters. What's with the missing 10 meters? Have you figured it out? Hint: The answer lies in the discussion we've just been having. Ding! Time's up! The answer is … the patch cables! Patch cables add extra distance between the switch and the PC, so TIA/EIA compensates by reducing the horizontal cabling length.

The work area may be the simplest part of the structured cabling system, but it is also the source of most network failures. When a user can't access the network and you suspect a broken cable, the first place to look is the work area.

• **Figure 5.24** Properly labeled outlet

> Structured cabling goes beyond a single building and even describes methods for interconnecting multiple buildings. The CompTIA Network+ certification exam does not cover interbuilding connections.

Structured Cable—Beyond the Star

Thus far you've seen structured cabling as a single star topology on a single floor of a building. Let's now expand that concept to an entire building and learn the terms used by the structured cabling folks, such as the demarc and NIU, to describe this much more complex setup.

You can hardly find a building today that isn't connected to both the Internet and the telephone company. In many cases, this is a single connection, but for now, let's treat them as separate connections.

As you saw in Chapter 4, a typical building-wide network consists of a high-speed backbone that runs vertically through the building and connects to multispeed switches on each floor that, in turn, service the individual PCs on that floor. A legacy telephone cabling backbone that enabled the distribution of phone calls to individual telephones might run alongside the network cabling. While every telephone installation varies, most commonly you'll see one or more strands of 25-pair UTP cables running to a 66 block in the telecommunications room on each floor (Figure 5.25).

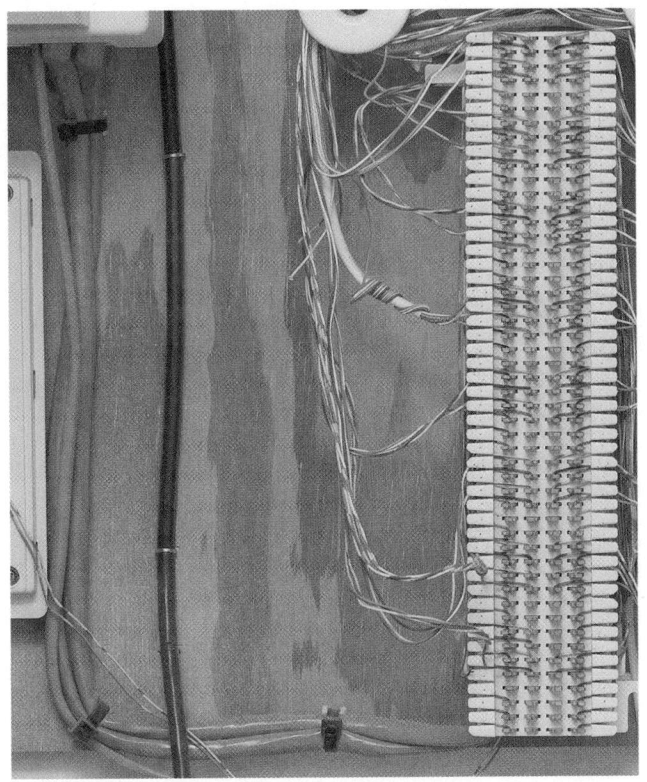

• **Figure 5.25** 25-pair UTP cables running to local 66 block

Demarc

Connections from the outside world—whether network or telephone—come into a building at a location called a **demarcation point (demarc)**. The demarc refers to the physical location of the connection and marks the dividing line of responsibility for the functioning of the network. You take care of the internal functioning; the company that supplies the upstream service to you must support connectivity and function on the far side of the demarc.

You might get a question about the location of a demarc on the CompTIA Network+ exam. You'll find the demarc located in the *service-related entry point* for a network.

One challenge to companies that supply Internet services is the need to diagnose faults in the system. Early systems used an NIU called a *smartjack* to set up a remote loopback—critical for loopback testing when you were at one end of the connection and the other connection was blocks or even miles away. Traditional smartjacks no longer exist, but CompTIA left them in the Network+ objectives.

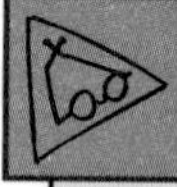

Tech Tip

NIU=NIB=NID: Huh?

The terms used to describe the devices that mark the demarcation point in a home or office often get tossed about with wild abandon. Various manufacturers and technicians call them network interface units, network interface boxes, or network interface devices. (Some techs call them demarcs, just to muddy the waters further, but we won't go there.) By name or by initial—NIU, NIB, or NID—it's all the same thing, the box that marks the point where your responsibility begins.

The best way to think of a demarc is in terms of responsibility. If something breaks on one side of the demarc, it's your problem; on the other side, it's the ISP's problem.

In a private home, the equipment (cable modem, optical network terminal, etc.) supplied by your ISP is a **network interface unit (NIU)** that serves as a demarc between your home network and your ISP, and most homes have a network interface box, like the one shown in Figure 5.26.

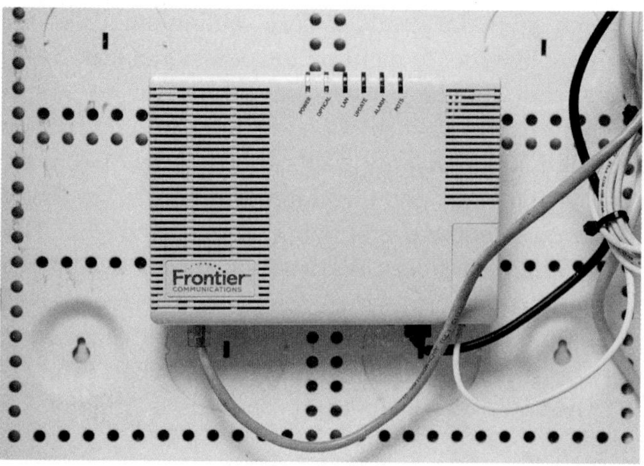

• **Figure 5.26** Typical home network interface box for home fiber Internet service

In an office environment, the demarc is usually more complex, given that a typical building simply has to serve a much larger number of computers. Figure 5.27 shows the demarc for a midsized building, showing both Internet and legacy telephone connections coming in from the outside.

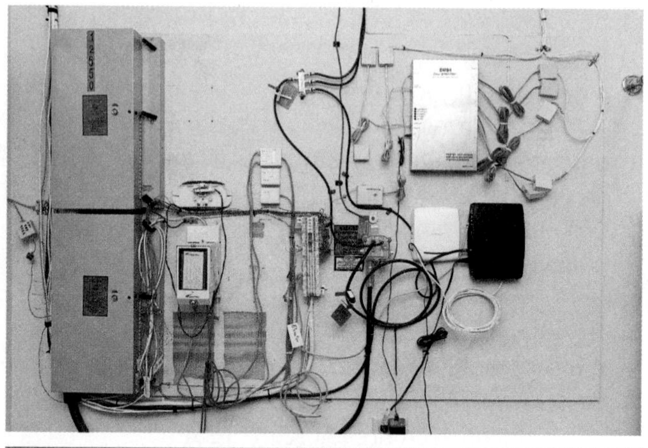

• **Figure 5.27** Messy office demarcs for Internet and legacy phone

Connections Inside the Demarc

After the demarc, network and telephone cables connect to some type of box, owned by the customer, that acts as the primary distribution tool for the building. That box is called the **customer-premises equipment (CPE)**. Any cabling that runs from the NIU to whatever CPE is used by the customer is the **demarc extension**. The cabling connects to a powerful switch or other network box (that we'll cover in detail in later chapters). This switch usually connects to a patch panel. This patch panel, in turn, leads to every telecommunications room in the building. This main patch panel is called a **vertical cross-connect**. Figure 5.28 shows an example of a **fiber distribution panel** (fiber patch panel) acting as a vertical cross-connect for a building.

The combination of demarc and LAN cross-connects needs a place to live in a building. The room that stores all of this equipment is known as a **main distribution frame (MDF)** to distinguish it from the multiple IDF rooms (aka telecommunications rooms) that serve individual floors.

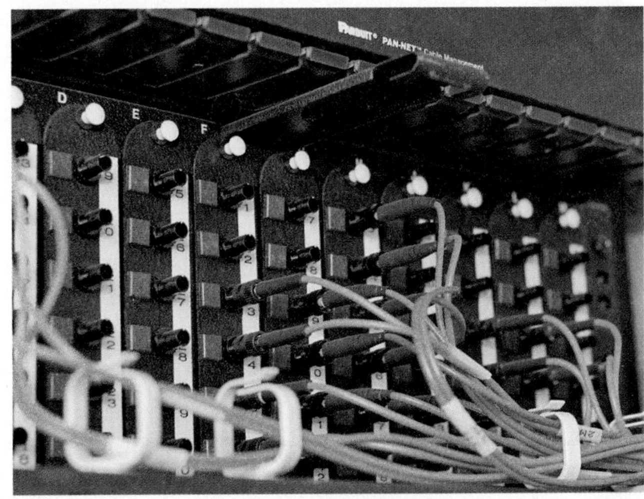

• **Figure 5.28** LAN vertical cross-connect

The ideal that every building should have a single demarc, a single MDF, and multiple IDFs is only that—an ideal. Every structured cabling installation is unique and must adapt to the physical constraints of the building provided. One building may serve multiple customers, creating the need for multiple NIUs each serving a different customer. A smaller building may combine a demarc, MDF, and IDF into a single room. With structured cabling, the idea is to appreciate the terms while, at the same time, appreciating that it's the actual building and the needs of the customers that determine the design of a structured cabling system.

Installing Structured Cabling

A professional installer always begins a structured cabling installation by first assessing your site and planning the installation in detail before pulling a single piece of cable. As the customer, your job is to work closely with the installer. That means locating floor plans, providing access, and even putting on old clothes and crawling along with the installer as he or she combs through your ceilings, walls, and closets. Even though you're not the actual installer, you must understand the installation process to help the installer make the right decisions for your network.

Structured cabling requires a lot of planning. You need to know if the cables from the work areas can reach the telecommunications room—is the distance less than the 90-meter limit dictated by the TIA/EIA standard? How will you route the cable? What path should each run take to get to the wall outlets? Don't forget that just because a cable looks like it will reach, there's no guarantee that it will. Ceilings and walls often include hidden surprises like firewalls—big, thick, concrete walls designed into buildings that require a masonry drill or a jackhammer to punch through. Let's look at the steps that go into proper planning.

Getting a Floor Plan

First, you need a blueprint of the area. If you ever contact an installer who doesn't start by asking for a floor plan, fire the installer immediately and get one who does. The floor plan is the key to proper planning; a good

> A *floor plan* is a key component of organizational documents, part of the physical network diagram of an organization. You might see it as one of the correct options for important documentation on the CompTIA Network+ exam.

floor plan shows you the location of closets that could serve as telecommunications rooms, alerts you to any firewalls in your way, and gives you a good overall feel for the scope of the job ahead.

If you don't have a floor plan—and this is often the case with homes or older buildings—you'll need to create your own. Go get a ladder and a flashlight—you'll need them to poke around in ceilings, closets, and crawl spaces as you map out the location of rooms, walls, and anything else of interest to the installation. Figure 5.29 shows a typical do-it-yourself floor plan.

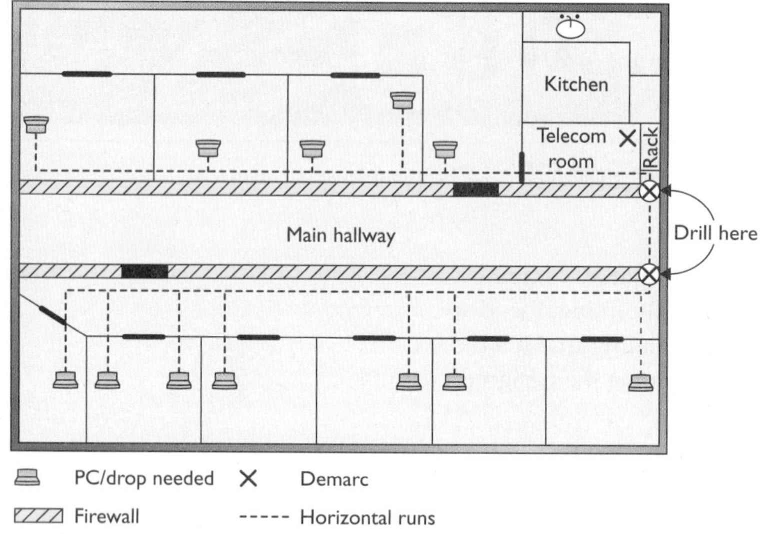

• **Figure 5.29** Network floor plan

Mapping the Runs

Now that you have your floor plan, you need to map the cable runs. Here's where you survey the work areas, noting the locations of existing or planned systems to determine where to place each cable drop. A **cable drop** is the location where the cable comes out of the wall in the work area. You should also talk to users, management, and other interested parties to try to understand their plans for the future. Installing a few extra drops now is much easier than installing them a year from now when those two unused offices suddenly find themselves with users who immediately need networked computers!

> Watch out for the word *drop,* as it has more than one meaning. A single run of cable from the telecommunications room to a wall outlet is often referred to as a "drop." The word "drop" is also used to define a new run coming through a wall outlet that does not yet have a jack installed.

At this point, cost first raises its ugly head. Face it: cables, drops, and the people who install them cost money! The typical price for a network installation in Houston, Texas, for example, is around US $50–150 per drop. Cost will vary in different locales. Find out how much you want to spend and make some calls. Most network installers price their network jobs by quoting a per-drop cost.

While you're mapping your runs, you have to make another big decision: Do you want to run the cables in the walls or outside them? Many companies sell wonderful external **raceway** products that adhere to your walls, making for a much simpler, though less neat, installation than running cables in the walls (Figure 5.30). Raceways make good sense in older buildings or when you don't have the guts—or the rights—to go into the walls.

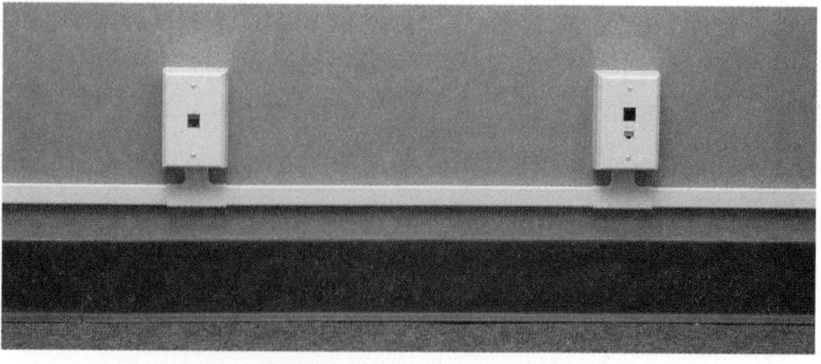

• **Figure 5.30** A typical raceway

Determining the Location of the Telecommunications Room

While mapping the runs, you should decide on the location of your telecommunications room. When deciding on this location, keep five issues in mind:

- **Distance** The telecommunications room must be located in a spot that won't require cable runs longer than 90 meters. In most locations, keeping runs under 90 meters requires little effort, as long as the telecommunications room is placed in a central location.
- **Power** Many of the components in your telecommunications room need power. Make sure you provide enough! If possible, put the telecommunications room on its own dedicated circuit; that way, when someone blows a circuit in the kitchen, it doesn't take out the entire network.
- **Humidity** Electrical components and water don't mix well. (Remind me to tell you about the time I installed a rack in an abandoned bathroom and the toilet that later exploded.) Remember that dryness also means low humidity. Avoid areas with the potential for high humidity, such as a closet near a pool or the room where the cleaning people leave mop buckets full of water. Of course, any well air-conditioned room should be fine—which leads to the next big issue…
- **Cooling** Telecommunications rooms tend to get warm, especially if you add a couple of server systems and a UPS. Make sure your telecommunications room has an air-conditioning outlet or some other method of keeping the room cool. Figure 5.31 shows how I monitor the temp of my equipment rack.

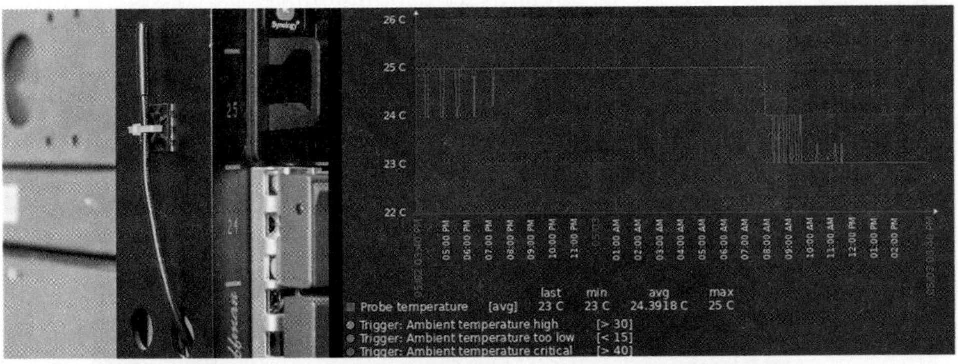

• **Figure 5.31** Temperature probe (left) with a graph of the temperature (right)

- **Access** Access involves two different issues. First, it means preventing unauthorized access. Think about the people you want and don't want messing around with your network, and act accordingly. In my small office, the equipment closet literally sits eight feet from me, so I don't concern myself too much with unauthorized access. You, on the other hand, may want to consider placing a lock on the door of your telecommunications room if you're concerned that unscrupulous or unqualified people might try to access it.

One other issue to keep in mind when choosing your telecommunications room is expandability. Will this telecommunications room be able to grow with your network? Is it close enough to be able to service any additional office space your company may acquire nearby? If your company decides to take over the floor above you, can you easily run vertical cabling to another telecommunications room on that floor from this room? While the specific issues will be unique to each installation, keep thinking "expansion" or *scalability* as you design—your network will grow, whether or not you think so now!

So, you've mapped your cable runs and established your telecommunications room—now you're ready to start pulling cable!

Pulling Cable

Pulling cable is easily one of the most thankless and unpleasant jobs in the entire networking world. It may not look that hard from a distance, but the devil is in the details. First of all, pulling cable requires two people if you want to get the job done quickly; having three people is even better. Most pullers like to start from the telecommunications room and pull toward the drops. In an office area with a drop ceiling, pullers often feed the cabling along the run by opening ceiling tiles and stringing the cable via hooks or **cable trays** that travel above the ceiling (Figure 5.32). Professional cable pullers have an arsenal of interesting tools to help them move the cable horizontally, including telescoping poles, coiled flat steel wire (called fish tape) for snaking through conduit, special nylon pull ropes, and even nifty little crossbows and pistols that can fire a pull rope long distances!

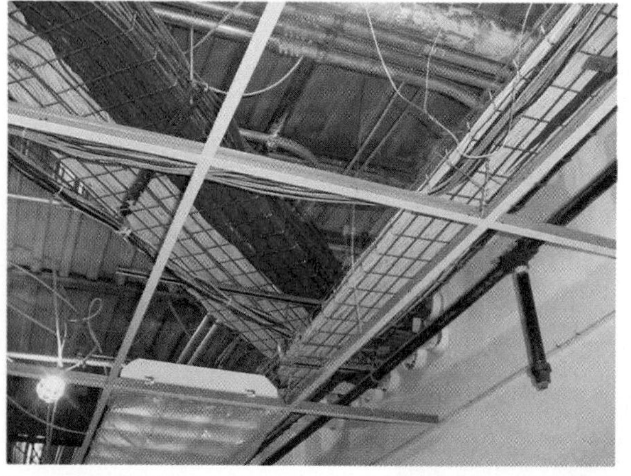

• **Figure 5.32** Cable trays over a drop ceiling

Cable trays are standard today, but a previous lack of codes or standards for handling cables led to a nightmare of disorganized cables in drop ceilings all over the world. Any cable puller will tell you that the hardest part of installing cables is the need to work around all the old cable installations in the ceiling (Figure 5.33).

• **Figure 5.33** Messy cabling nightmare

Local codes, TIA, and the National Electrical Code (NEC) all have strict rules about how you pull cable in a ceiling. A good installer uses either hooks or trays, which provide better cable management, safety, and protection from electrical interference. The faster the network, the more critical good cable management (Figure 5.34) becomes.

Running cable horizontally requires relatively little effort, compared to running the cable down from the ceiling to a pretty faceplate at the work area, which often takes a lot of skill. In a typical office area with sheetrock walls, the installer first decides on the position for the outlet, generally using a stud finder to avoid cutting on top of a stud. Once the worker cuts the hole (Figure 5.35), most installers drop a line to the hole using a weight tied to the end of a nylon pull rope (Figure 5.36). They can then attach the network cable to the pull rope and pull it down to the hole. Once the cable is pulled through the new hole, the installer puts in an outlet box or a low-voltage **mounting bracket** (Figure 5.37). This bracket acts as a holder for the faceplate.

• **Figure 5.34** Nicely run cables

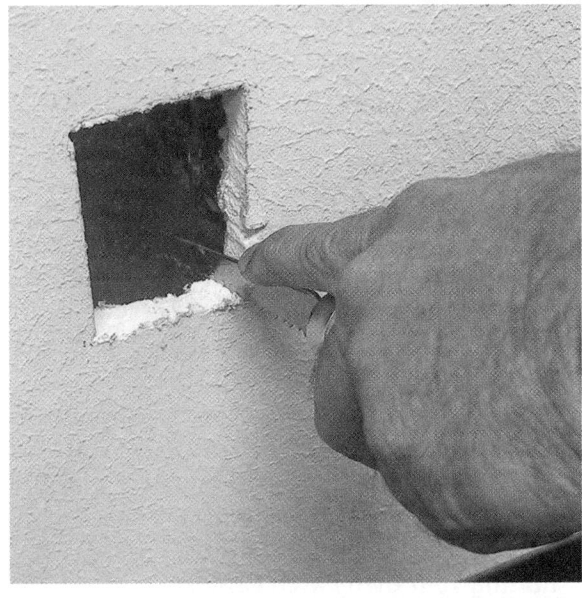

• **Figure 5.35** Cutting a hole

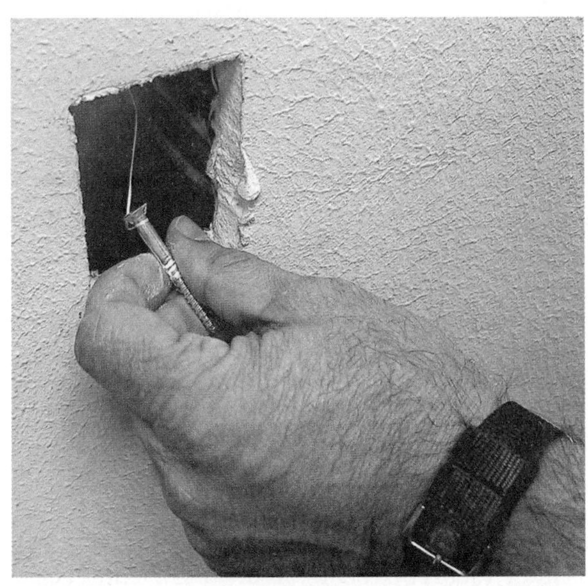

• **Figure 5.36** Locating a dropped pull rope

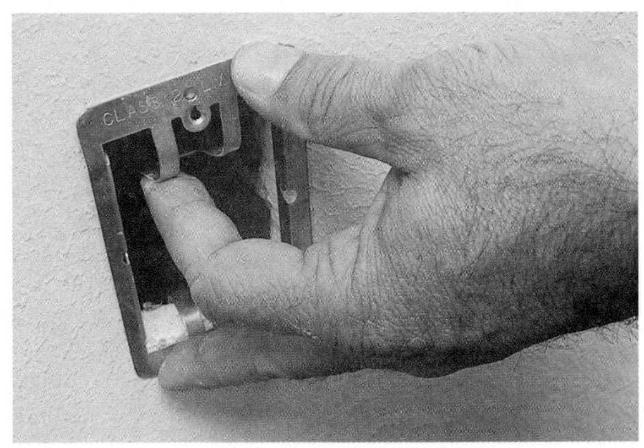

• **Figure 5.37** Installing a mounting bracket

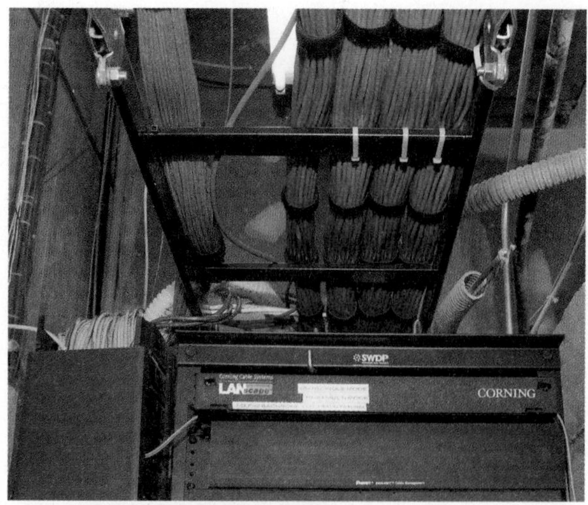

• **Figure 5.38** End of cables guided to rack

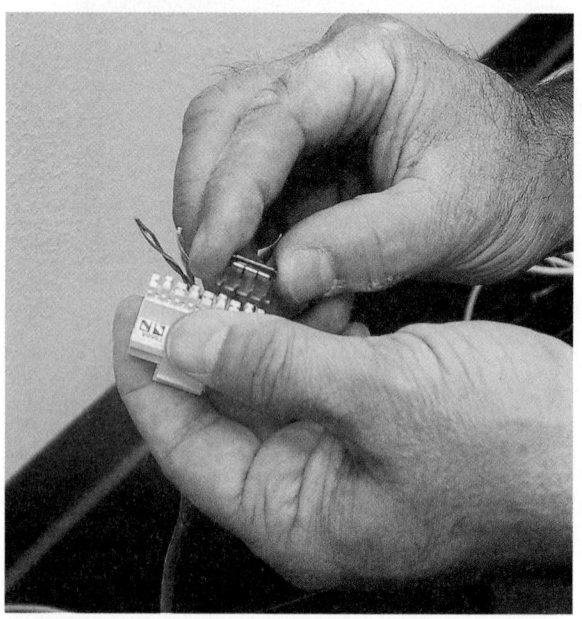

• **Figure 5.39** Punching down a jack

Back in the telecommunications room, the many cables leading to each work area are consolidated and organized in preparation for the next stage: making connections. A truly professional installer takes great care in organizing the equipment closet. Figure 5.38 shows a typical installation using special cable guides to bring the cables down to the equipment rack.

Making Connections

Making connections consists of connecting both ends of each cable to the proper jacks. This step also includes the most important step in the entire process: testing each cable run to ensure that every connection meets the requirements of the network that will use it. Installers also use this step to document and label each cable run—a critical step too often forgotten by inexperienced installers, and one you need to verify takes place!

Connecting the Work Areas

In the work area, the cable installer terminates a cable run by adding a jack to the end of the wire and mounting the faceplate to complete the installation (Figure 5.39). Note the back of the jack shown in Figure 5.39. This jack uses the popular 110-punchdown connection just like the one shown earlier in the chapter for patch panels. All 110-punchdown connections have a color code that tells you which wire to punch into which connection on the back of the jack.

Rolling Your Own Patch Cables

Although most people prefer simply to purchase premade patch cables, making your own is fairly easy. To make your own, use stranded core UTP cable that matches the Cat level of your horizontal cabling. Stranded core cable also requires specific crimps, so don't use crimps designed for solid core cable. Crimping is simple enough, although getting it right takes some practice.

Figure 5.40 shows the two main tools of the crimping trade: an RJ-45 crimper with built-in cable stripper and a pair of wire snips/cutters. Professional cable installers naturally have a wide variety of other tools as well.

Here are the steps for properly crimping an RJ-45 onto a UTP cable. If you have some crimps, cable, and a crimping tool handy, follow along!

1. Cut the cable square using RJ-45 crimpers or scissors.
2. Strip at least ½ inch of plastic jacket from the end of the cable (Figure 5.41) with a dedicated cable stripper or the one built into the crimping tool.
3. Slowly and carefully insert each individual wire into the correct location according to either T568A or T568B (Figure 5.42). Unravel as little as possible.

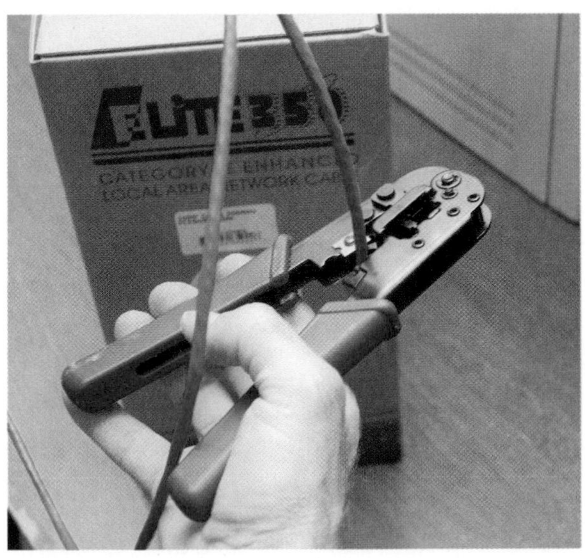

• **Figure 5.40** Crimper and snips/cutters

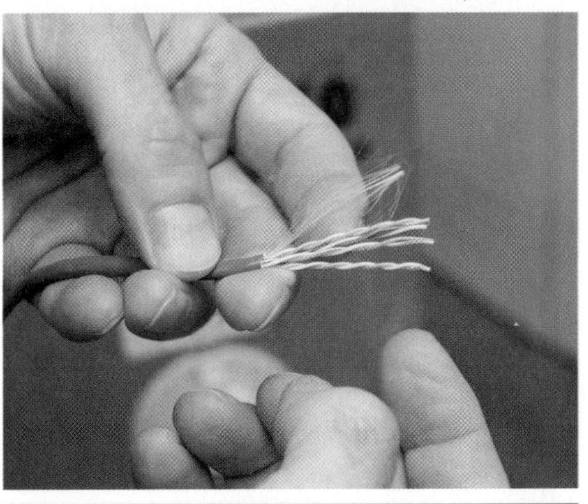

• **Figure 5.41** Properly stripped cable—it doesn't hurt to leave room for mistakes!

4. Insert the crimp into the crimper and press (Figure 5.43). Don't worry about pressing too hard; the crimper has a stop to prevent you from using too much pressure.

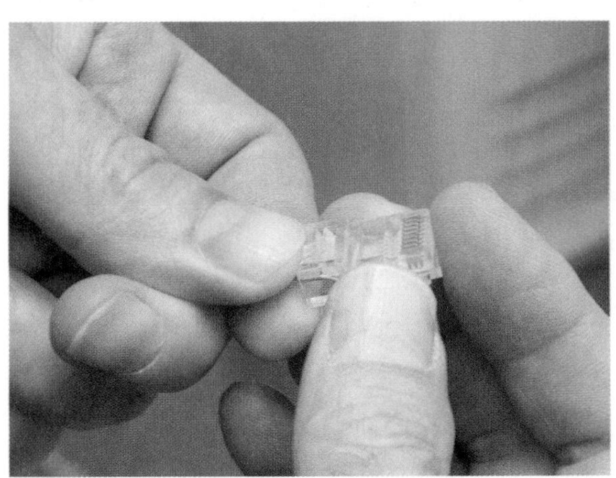

• **Figure 5.42** Inserting the individual strands

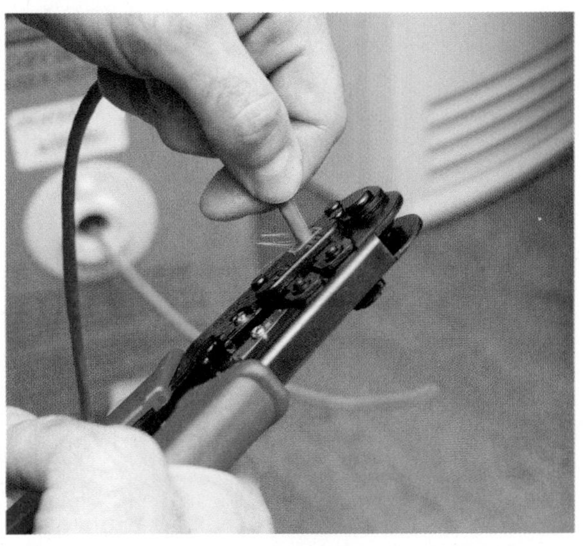

• **Figure 5.43** Crimping the cable

Figure 5.44 shows a nicely crimped cable. Note how the plastic jacket goes into the crimp.

A good patch cable should include a boot. Figure 5.45 shows a boot being slid onto a newly crimped cable. Don't forget to slide each boot onto the patch cable *before* you crimp both ends!

After making a cable, you need to test it to make sure it's properly crimped. Read the section on testing cable runs later in this chapter to see how to test them.

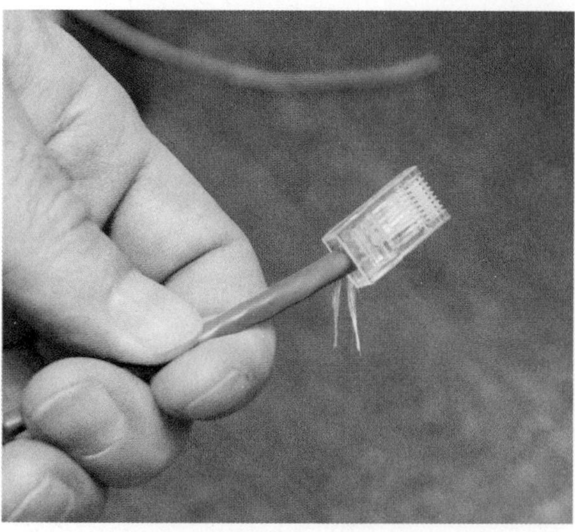

• **Figure 5.44** Properly crimped cable

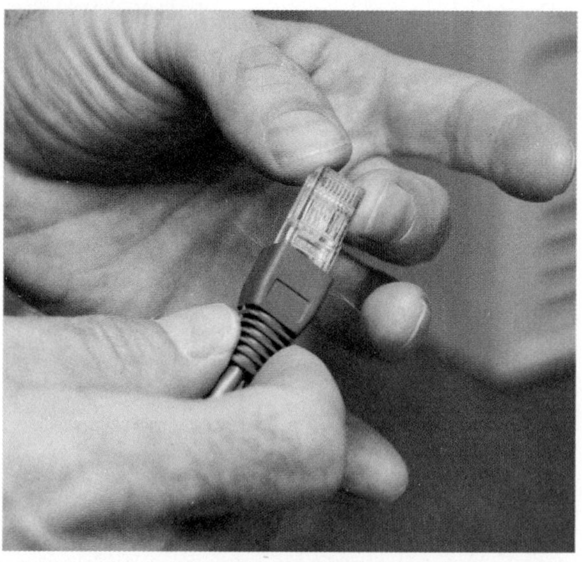

• **Figure 5.45** Adding a boot

Try This!

Crimping Your Own Cable

If you've got some spare UTP lying around (and what tech enthusiast doesn't?) as well as a cable crimper and some crimps, go ahead and use the previous section as a guide and crimp your own cable. This skill is essential for any network technician. Remember, practice makes perfect!

Connecting the Patch Panels

Connecting the cables to patch panels requires you to deal with three issues. The first issue is patch cable management. Figure 5.46 shows the front of a small network's equipment rack—note the complete lack of cable management!

Managing patch cables means using the proper cable management hardware. Plastic D-rings guide the patch cables neatly along the sides and front of the patch panel. Finger boxes are rectangular cylinders with slots in the front; the patch cables run into the open ends of the box, and individual cables are threaded through the fingers on their way to the patch panel, keeping them neatly organized.

Creativity and variety abound in the world of cable-management hardware—there are as many different solutions to cable management as there are ways to screw it up. Figure 5.47 shows a rack using good cable management—these patch cables are well secured using cable-management hardware, making them much less susceptible to damage from mishandling. Plus, it looks much nicer!

The second issue to consider when connecting cables is the overall organization of the patch panel as it relates to the organization of your network. Organize your patch panel so it mirrors the layout of your network.

• **Figure 5.46** Bad cable management

• **Figure 5.47** Good cable management

You can organize according to the physical layout, so the different parts of the patch panel correspond to different parts of your office space—for example, the north and south sides of the hallway. Another popular way to organize patch panels is to make sure they match the logical layout of the network, so the different user groups or company organizations have their own sections of the patch panel.

Finally, proper patch panel cable management means documenting everything clearly and carefully. This way, any competent technician can follow behind you and troubleshoot connectivity problems. Good techs draw diagrams!

Testing the Cable Runs

Well, in theory, your horizontal cabling system is now installed and ready for a switch and some systems. Before you do this, though, you must test each cable run. Someone new to testing cable might think that all you need to do is verify that each jack has been properly connected. Although this is an important and necessary step, the interesting problem comes after that: verifying that your cable run can handle the speed of your network.

The basic Layer 1 issues with network connections boil down to three factors: signal degradation, lack of connection, and interference. A host of factors can cause overall degradation, which in turn slows or stops network communication. A lack of connection can be caused by many things, detailed below, but the effect is that the networked device(s) can't communicate.

Interference means any disruption on a medium (wired or wireless) that intentionally or inadvertently prevents valid signals from being read by an intended recipient.

Copper- and fiber-based network runs have different causes for loss of connectivity, interference, and degradation, and thus require different tools to resolve. Let's look at copper, then fiber.

Before I go further, let me be clear: a typical network admin/tech cannot properly test a new cable run. TIA provides a series of incredibly complex and important standards for testing cable, requiring a professional cable installer. The testing equipment alone totally surpasses the cost of most smaller network installations. Advanced network testing tools easily cost over $5000, and some are well over $10,000! Never fear, though—a number of lower-end tools work just fine for basic network testing.

The test tools described here also enable you to diagnose network problems.

Copper Challenges

Most network admins staring at a scenario with a potentially bad copper cable want to know the following:

- How long is this cable? If it's too long, the signal will degrade to the point that it's no longer detectable on the other end.
- Every signal—copper, fiber, and wireless—has noise. Too much noise and the signal will degrade, the network will slow down or even stop. You'll see this in action with cable Internet connections, so we'll pick it up in Chapter 13.
- Are any of the wires broken or not connected in the crimp (*open*)? If a wire is broken or a connection is open, it no longer has **continuity** (a complete, functioning connection). Are there bent pins on the RJ-45 or in the jack?
- Is there any place where two bare wires touch? This creates a *short*. Shorts can take place when cables are damaged, but you can also get a short when improperly crimping two cables into the same place on a crimp.
- If there is a break, where is it? It's much easier to fix if the location is detectable.
- Are all of the wires terminated in the right place in the plug or jack? Does each termination match to the same standard? In other words, am I looking at an *incorrect pinout* scenario?
- Is there electrical or radio *interference* from outside sources? UTP is susceptible to electromagnetic interference (EMI), as introduced in Chapter 4.
- Is the signal from any of the pairs in the same cable interfering with another pair? This common problem in UTP installations is called a **split pair**.

The CompTIA Network+ objectives lump *open/short* together as a common issue with cable connectivity. They're different problems, as noted here, but have the same effect, which is no connectivity.

To answer these questions, you must verify that both the cable and the terminated ends are correct. Making these verifications requires a **cable tester**. Various models of cable testers can answer some or all of these questions, depending on the amount of money you are willing to pay. At the low end of the cable tester market are devices that only test for continuity. These inexpensive (under $100) testers are often called **continuity testers**

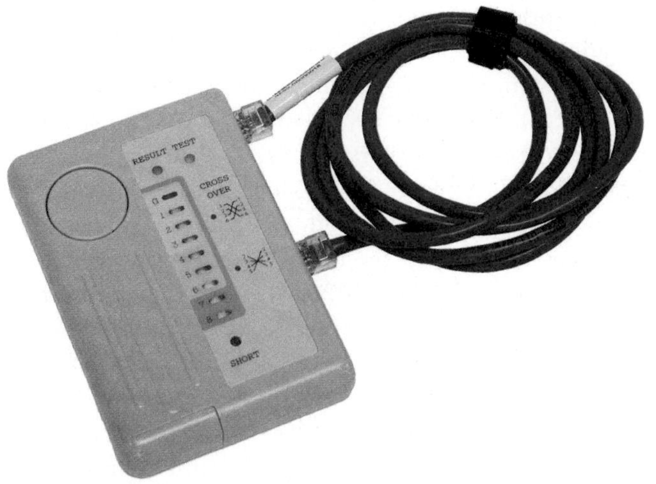

• **Figure 5.48** Continuity tester

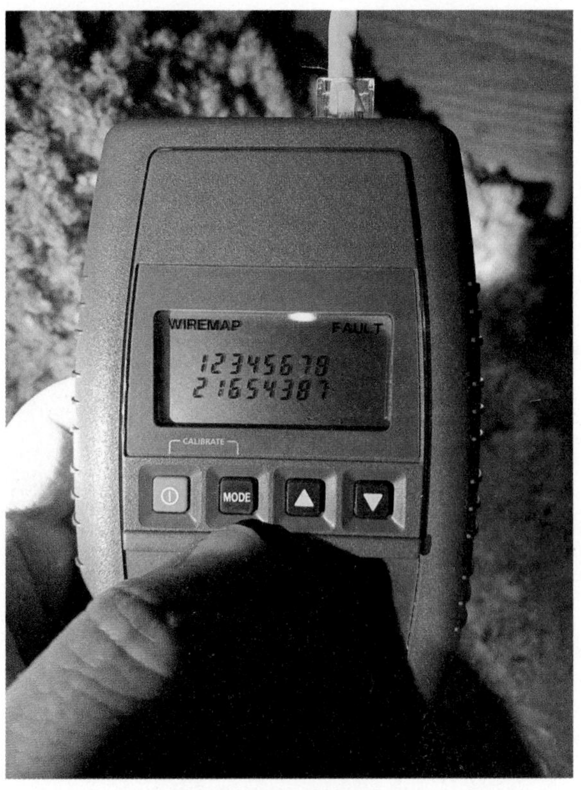

• **Figure 5.49** MicroScanner readout

(Figure 5.48). Many of these testers require you to insert both ends of the cable into the tester. Of course, this can be a bit of a problem if the cable is already installed in the wall!

Better testers can run a **wire map** test that goes beyond mere continuity, testing that all the wires on both ends of the cable connect to the right spot. A wire map test will pick up shorts, crossed wires, and more. Figure 5.49 shows a MicroScanner diagnosing a wire map problem.

To check continuity, you can also use a **multimeter,** a device to test AC and DC voltage and current as well as continuity and resistance. Some advanced models can test other components such as transistors and capacitors. Set the multimeter (Figure 5.50) to continuity mode (if it has one), or to the lowest Ohm range on the device. In the latter mode, zero Ohms indicate continuity and infinite Ohms indicate no connection.

Many techs and network testing folks use the term *wire map* to refer to the proper connectivity for wires, as in, "Hey Joe, check the wire map!"

• **Figure 5.50** Multimeter

• Figure 5.51 A vintage MicroScanner TDR

Medium-priced testers (~$400) certainly test continuity and wire map and include the additional capability to determine the length of a cable; they can even tell you where a break is located on any of the individual wire strands. This type of cable tester (Figure 5.51) is generically called a **time-domain reflectometer (TDR)**. Most medium-priced testers come with a small loopback device to insert into the far end of the cable, enabling the tester to work with installed cables. This is the type of tester you want to have around!

If you want a device that fully tests a cable run to the very complex TIA standards, the price shoots up fast. These higher-end testers can detect things the lesser testers cannot, such as crosstalk and attenuation.

Crosstalk poses a threat to properly functioning cable runs. Today's UTP cables consist of four pairs of wires, all squished together inside a plastic tube. When you send a signal down one of these pairs, the other pairs pick up some of the signal, as shown in Figure 5.52. This is called **crosstalk**.

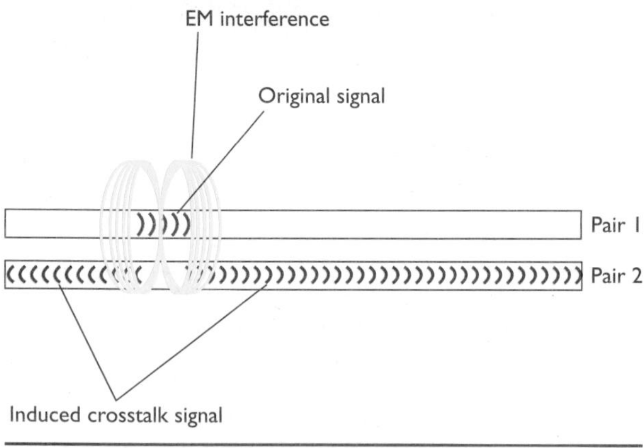

• Figure 5.52 Crosstalk

Every piece of UTP in existence generates crosstalk. Worse, when you crimp the end of a UTP cable to a jack or plugs, crosstalk increases. A poor-quality crimp creates so much crosstalk that a cable run won't operate at its designed speed. To detect crosstalk, a normal-strength signal is sent down one pair of wires in a cable. An electronic detector, connected on the same end of the cable as the end emanating the signal, listens on the other three pairs and measures the amount of interference, as shown in Figure 5.53. This is called **near-end crosstalk (NEXT)**.

If you repeat this test, sending the signal down one pair of wires, but this time listening on the other pairs on the far end of the connection, you test for **far-end crosstalk (FEXT)**, as shown in Figure 5.54.

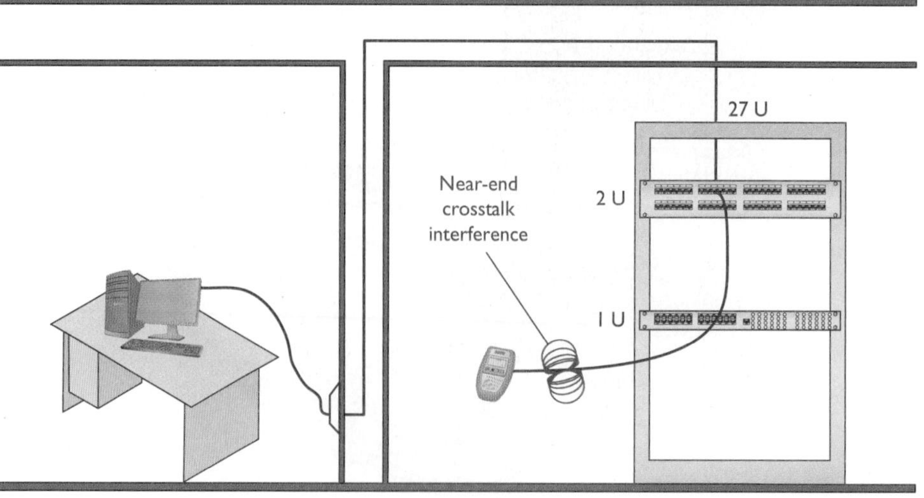

• Figure 5.53 Near-end crosstalk

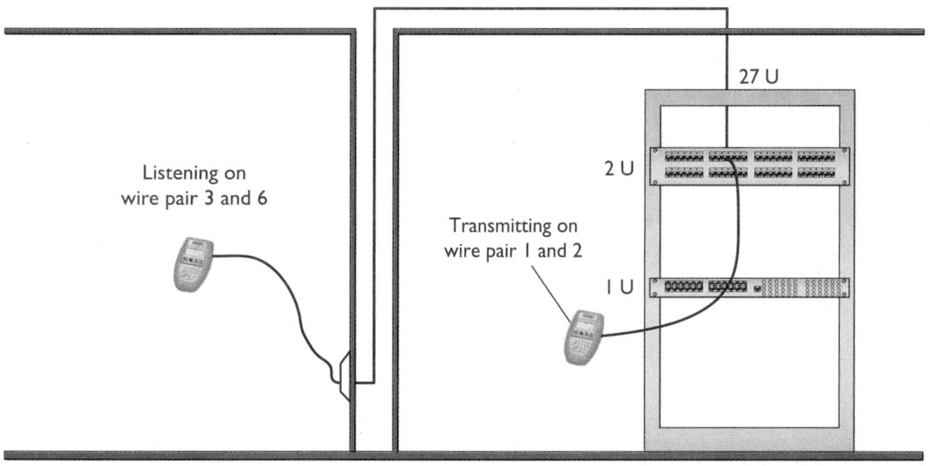

• **Figure 5.54** Far-end crosstalk

If that's not bad enough, as a signal progresses down a piece of wire, it becomes steadily weaker; this is called **attenuation**. As a cable run gets longer, the attenuation increases, and the signal becomes more susceptible to crosstalk. A tester must send a signal down one end of a wire, test for NEXT and FEXT on the ends of every other pair, and then repeat this process for every pair in the UTP cable.

This process of verifying that every cable run meets the exacting TIA standards requires very powerful testing tools, generally known as **cable certifiers** or just certifiers. Cable certifiers can both do the high-end testing and generate a report that a cable installer can print out and hand to a customer to prove that the installed cable runs pass TIA standards. Cable certifiers cost a lot and are thus reserved for cable installation experts rather than network techs.

Both NEXT and FEXT are measured in decibels (dB).

Every network—copper or otherwise—experiences data loss or lag over distances and with enough traffic. Ethernet network frame traffic has **latency**, a delay between the time the sending machine sends a message and the time the receiving machine can start processing those frames.

Add in a lot of machines and the network will also experience **jitter**, a delay in completing a transmission of all the frames in a message. This is perfectly normal and modern network technologies handle jitter fine. This does not affect moving files around much, but becomes a serious problem in real-time voice communication. Excessive jitter generally sounds like, "Dude, you're totally breaking up." We'll explore voice communication in Chapter 17 in some detail.

Tech Tip

Measuring Signal Loss

Signal loss in networking is measured in a unit called a decibel (dB). This applies to both electrical signals in copper wires and light signals in fiber cables. Unfortunately for a lot of network techs, a decibel is tough to grasp without a lot of math. I'm going to skip the technical details and give you a shorthand way to understand the numbers to troubleshoot a cable connectivity scenario with decibel (dB) loss.

When referring to a signal traveling from one end of a cable to another, you really care about how much information on that signal gets to the end, right? In a simple sense, if you have some interference, some imperfections in the cable or fiber, you'll get some loss from beginning to end. Most people think about that loss in terms of percentage or even in more common terms, like "a little" or "a lot of" loss. No problem, right?

The problem when you take that same concept to networking is that the percentages lost can be gigantic or really, really small. When you start talking about a 10,000% loss or a .00001% loss, most folks eyes glaze over. The numbers are simply too big or small to make intuitive sense.

Technicians use the term decibel to describe those numbers in a more digestible format. When a tech looks at a signal loss of 3 dB, for example, he or she should be able to know that that number is a lot smaller than a signal loss of 10 dB.

Fiber Challenges

Fiber cable runs offer similar challenges to copper cable runs, but there are also some very specific differences. Just like with copper, signal loss is important and measured in decibels. But the causes of loss can differ a lot. Also, the many competing standards can catch techs running fiber by surprise.

Signal Loss/Degradation Just like with copper wire, various imperfections in the media—the glass fiber, in this case—cause signal loss over distance. A lot of factors come into play.

Damaged cables or *open connections* obviously stop signals. The typical small form-factor pluggable (SFP) or gigabit interface converter (GBIC) can have problems. When you're checking for a *bad SFP/GBIC*, you'll need to check both the connector and the cable going into that connector. Either or both could cause the signal loss.

A *dirty connector*—CompTIA calls these **dirty optical cables**—can cause pretty serious signal loss with fiber. It's important not to smudge the glass!

When you think about fiber-optic cables, you need to remember that the part that carries the signal is really tiny, only a few microns. When you're connecting two pieces of fiber, even a small *connector mismatch* in either the cladding (the outside) or the core (the inside) can cause serious losses.

Attenuation is the weakening of a signal as it travels long distances, as you'll recall from earlier in the chapter.

Dispersion is when a signal spreads out over long distances. Both attenuation and dispersion are caused when wave signals travel too far without help over fiber-optic media. This is also called *modal dispersion*.

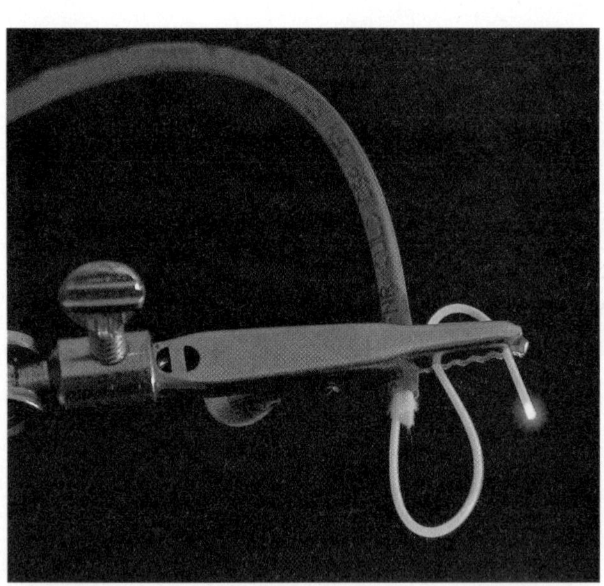

• **Figure 5.55** Light leakage—note the colored glow at the bends but the dark cable at the straight.

Every piece of fiber has a certain *bend radius limitation*. If you bend a fiber-optic cable too much, you get **light leakage**, as shown in Figure 5.55. Light leakage means that part of the signal goes out the cable rather than arriving at the end. That's not a good thing.

Physical or Signal Mismatch Fiber networks have a relatively small number of connectors but offer a pretty wide variety of signal types that use those connectors. These variations come into play in several ways. First, just because you can connect to a particular SFP or GBIC, that doesn't mean the signal will work. Plugging an *incorrect transceiver* into a Cisco switch might work in a physical sense, but if the switch won't play with anything but Cisco technology, you'll get a *transceiver mismatch*.

Likewise, you can find fiber connectors like SC or LC that will attach to single-mode or multimode fiber. Plugging a single-mode cable into a switch that expects multimode? Such a *cable mismatch* or *fiber mismatch*—an *incorrect cable type*—means your network—at least that portion of it—won't work.

Finally, different runs of fiber use different wavelength signals. You might be able to plug an LC connector into a switch just fine, for example, but if the signal starts at 1310 nm and the switch expects 1530 nm, that sort of *wavelength mismatch* will stop the transmission cold.

Cross Check

Wavelength

You explored fiber wavelengths back in Chapter 4, so cross-check your knowledge here. Which type of fiber operates at 850 nm? What about 1300 nm? If two fiber ports require LC connectors, are they guaranteed to work if connected together?

Fiber Tools A fiber technician uses a large number of tools (Figure 5.56) and an almost artistic amount of skill. Over the years, easier terminations have been developed, but putting an ST, SC, LC, or other connector on the end of a piece of fiber is still very challenging.

• **Figure 5.56** Fiber splicing kit in the field

> One of the common tools for fiber-optic cable installers is a *fusion splicer* that enables the tech to combine two fiber-optic cables without losing quality.

A fiber-optic run has problems that are both similar to and different from those of a UTP run. Fiber-optic runs don't experience crosstalk or interference (as we usually think of it) because they use light instead of an electrical current.

Fiber-optic cables still break, however, so a good tech always keeps an **optical time-domain reflectometer (OTDR)** handy (Figure 5.57) for just such scenarios. OTDRs determine continuity and, if there's a break, tell you exactly how far down the cable to look for the break.

TIA has very complex requirements for testing fiber runs, and the cabling industry sells fiber certifiers to make sure a fiber will carry its designed signal speed.

The three big issues with fiber are light leakage, attenuation, and dispersion. You read about all three earlier in the chapter.

The process of installing a structured cabling system is rather involved, requires a great degree of skill, and should be left to professionals. By understanding the process, however, you can tackle

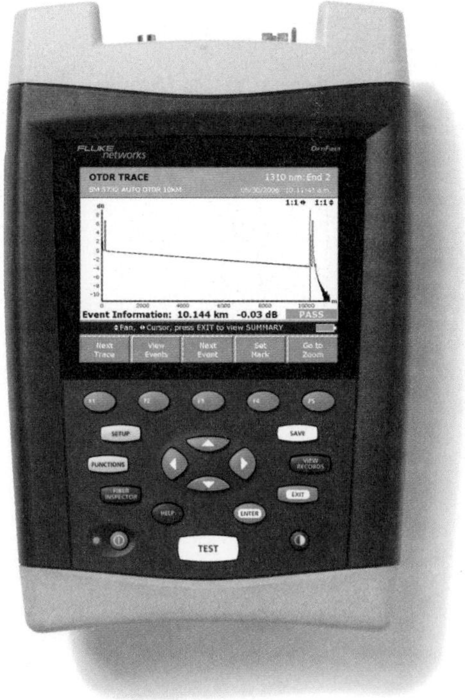

• **Figure 5.57** An optical time-domain reflectometer (photo courtesy of Fluke Networks)

most of the problems that come up in an installed structured cabling system. Most importantly, you'll understand the lingo used by the structured cabling installers so you can work with them more efficiently.

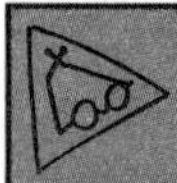

Tech Tip

Onboard NICs

Motherboards these days include an onboard NIC. This, of course, completely destroys the use of the acronym "NIC" to represent network interface card because no card is actually involved. But heck, we're nerds and, just as we'll probably never stop using the term "RJ-45" when the correct term is "8P8C," we'll keep using the term "NIC." I know! Let's just pretend it stands for network interface connection!

NICs

Now that the network is completely in place, it's time to turn to the final part of any physical network: the NICs. A good network tech must recognize different types of NICs by sight and know how to install and troubleshoot them. Let's begin by reviewing the differences between UTP and fiber-optic NICs.

All UTP Ethernet NICs use the RJ-45 connector. The cable runs from the NIC (Figure 5.58) to a switch.

• **Figure 5.58** Typical UTP NIC

Fiber-optic NICs come in a wide variety and can support multiple standards. Figure 5.59 shows a typical fiber-optic network card.

• **Figure 5.59** Typical NIC supporting fiber
Copyright © Intel Corporation

Buying NICs

Some folks may disagree with me, but I always purchase name-brand NICs. For NICs, I recommend sticking with big names, such as Intel. The NICs are better made, have extra features, and are easy to return if they turn out to be defective.

Plus, replacing a missing driver on a name-brand NIC is easy, and you can be confident the drivers work well. The type of NIC you should purchase depends on your network. Try to stick with the same model of NIC. Every different model you buy means another set of drivers. Using the same model of NIC makes driver updates easier, too.

• **Figure 5.60** PCI NIC

Physical Connections

I'll state the obvious here: if you don't plug the NIC into the computer, the NIC won't work! If you're buying a NIC, physically inserting the NIC into one of the PC's expansion slots is the easiest part of the job. Most PCs today have two types of expansion slots. The older expansion slot is the Peripheral Component Interconnect (PCI) type (Figure 5.60).

The PCI Express (PCIe) expansion slots are now widely adopted by NIC suppliers (Figure 5.61). PCIe NICs usually come in either one-lane (×1) or two-lane (×2) varieties. You would add a NIC if you wanted to connect a PC to a fiber-based network, for example, and only had onboard copper-based NIC.

• **Figure 5.61** PCIe NIC

If you're not willing to open a PC case, you can get NICs with USB connections (Figure 5.62). USB NICs are handy to keep in your toolkit. If you walk up to a machine that might have a bad NIC, test your suspicions by inserting a USB NIC and moving the network cable from the potentially bad NIC to the USB one. (USB NICs are also commonly used with super-thin laptops that don't come with built-in Ethernet ports.)

Drivers

A modern OS might have a driver included for the NIC. If not, installing a NIC's driver into a Windows, macOS, or Linux system is easy: just insert a driver disc when prompted by the system. Many current systems don't sport optical drives, so installing a new NIC requires access to the Internet. Have a spare machine and copy drivers to a USB flash drive, then install drivers from there.

Every operating system has some method to verify that the computer recognizes the NIC and is ready to use it. Windows systems have the Device Manager; Ubuntu Linux users have the Network applet under the Administration menu; and macOS users get the Network utility in System Preferences. Actually, most operating systems have multiple methods to show that the NIC is in good working order. Learn the various ways to verify the NIC for your OS, as this is the ultimate test of a good NIC installation.

• **Figure 5.62** USB NIC

Port Aggregation

Most switches enable you to use multiple NICs for a single machine, a process called **port aggregation**, *bonding*, or *link aggregation*. Bonding doesn't necessarily increase the speed of the network connection, but instead adds another lane of equal speed. In cases where you're sending multiple files over the network, bonding enables more than one file to copy or move at full speed. This effectively increases the overall bandwidth of the connection. If you want to add link aggregation to your network to increase performance, use identical NICs and switches from the same companies to avoid incompatibility.

The *Link Aggregation Control Protocol (LACP)* controls how multiple network devices send and receive data as a single connection.

Link Lights

All NICs and switches made today have some type of light-emitting diodes (LEDs) that give information about the state of the link to whatever is on the other end of the connection. Even though you know the lights are actually LEDs, get used to calling them **link lights**, as that's the term all network techs use. NICs and switches can have between one and four different link lights, and the LEDs can be any color. These lights give you clues about what's happening with the link and are one of the first items to check whenever you think a system is disconnected from the network (Figure 5.63).

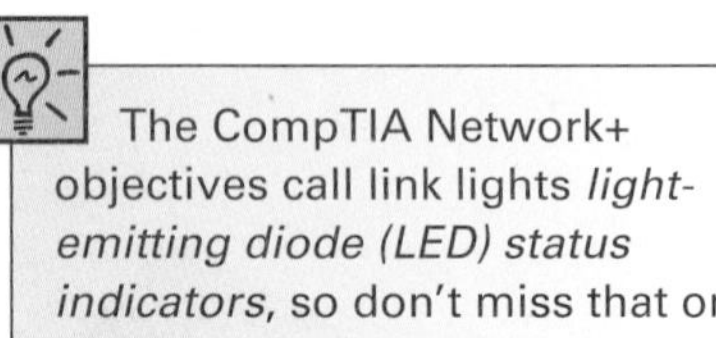

The CompTIA Network+ objectives call link lights *light-emitting diode (LED) status indicators*, so don't miss that on the exam. In the real world, call them link lights.

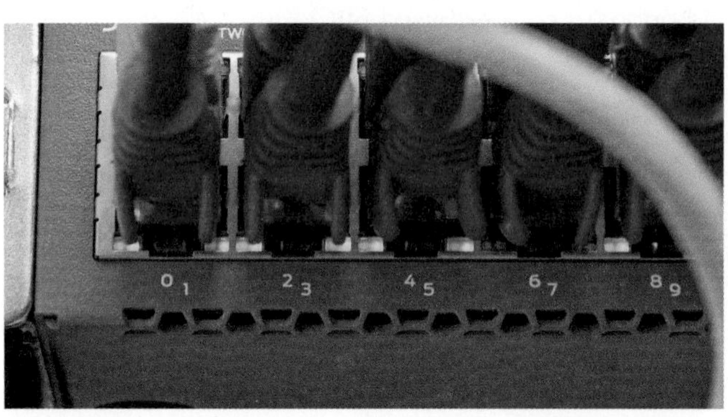

• **Figure 5.63** Ooooh, pretty lights!

A link light displays connectivity. If a PC can't access a network and is acting disconnected, always check the link lights first. Multispeed devices usually have a link light that tells you the speed of the connection. In Figure 5.64, the left link light for port 2 is lit, but the right link light is not, signifying that the other end of the cable is plugged into a 100BASE-T NIC. Port 1, on the other hand, has both link lights lit. It's clearly Gigabit.

• **Figure 5.64** Multispeed lights

Another light is the **activity light**. This little guy turns on when the card detects network traffic, so it intermittently flickers when operating properly. The activity light is a lifesaver for detecting problems, because in the real world, the connection light will sometimes lie to you. If the connection light says the connection is good, the next step is to try to copy a file or do something else to create network traffic. If the activity light does not flicker, there's a problem.

On many NICs, a properly functioning link light is on and steady when the NIC is connected to another device. *On* with no flickering indicates a good connection. On NICs that use a single LED to display both the link and activity status, on the other hand, the single LED will flicker with activity. That's how the NIC in Figure 5.63 works. Read the online documentation from the NIC manufacturer's Web site to determine the meaning of the lights and their steadiness or flickering.

No standard governs how NIC or switch manufacturers use their lights, and, as a result, they come in an amazing array of colors and layouts. When you encounter a NIC or switch with a number of LEDs, take a moment to try to figure out what each one means. Although different NICs and switches have various ways of arranging and using their LEDs, the functions are always the same: link, activity, and speed.

Diagnostics and Repair of Physical Cabling

"The network's down!" is easily the most terrifying phrase a network tech will ever hear. Networks fail for many reasons, and the first thing to know is that good-quality, professionally installed cabling rarely goes bad. Chapter 20 covers principles of network diagnostics and support that apply to all networking scenarios, but let's take a moment now to discuss how to troubleshoot common cable connectivity issues when faced with a scenario that points to a problem with your physical network.

Diagnosing Physical Problems

Look for errors that point to physical disconnection. A key clue that you may have a physical problem is that a user gets a "No server is found" error, or tries to use the operating system's network explorer utility (like Network in Windows) and doesn't see any systems besides his or her own. First, try to eliminate software errors: If one application fails, try another. If the user can't browse the Internet, but can get e-mail, odds are good that the problem is with software, not hardware—unless someone unplugged the e-mail server!

Multiple systems failing to access the network often points to hardware problems. This is where knowledge of your network cabling helps. If all the systems connected to one switch suddenly no longer see the network, but all the other systems in your network still function, you not only have a probable hardware problem but also a suspect—the switch.

Check Your Lights

If you suspect a hardware problem, first check the link lights on the NIC and switch. If they're not lit, you know the cable isn't connected somewhere. If you're not physically at the system in question (if you're on a tech call, for example), you can have the user check his or her connection status through the link lights or through software. Every operating system has some way to tell you on the screen if it detects the NIC is disconnected. The network status icon in the notification area in Windows, for example,

• **Figure 5.65** Disconnected NIC in Windows

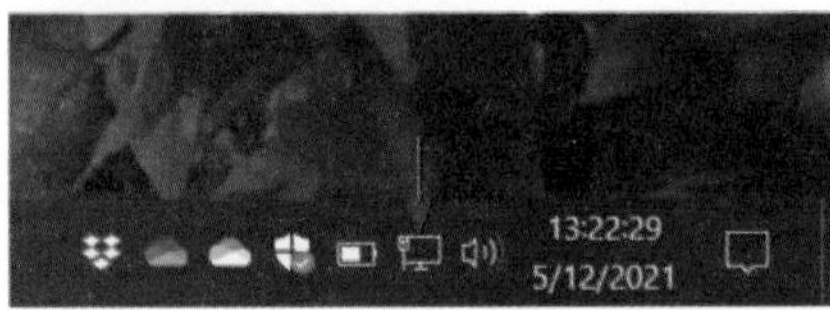

• **Figure 5.66** Connected NIC in Windows

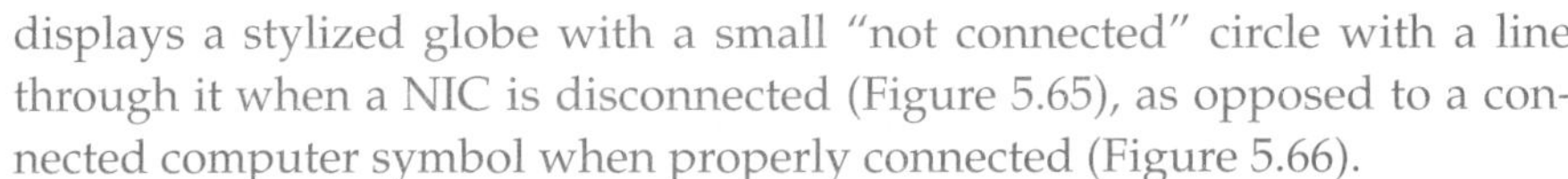

displays a stylized globe with a small "not connected" circle with a line through it when a NIC is disconnected (Figure 5.65), as opposed to a connected computer symbol when properly connected (Figure 5.66).

If a problem system has no connection, eliminate the possibility of a failed switch or other larger problem by checking to make sure other people can access the network, and that other systems can access the shared resource (server) that the problem system can't see. Make a quick visual inspection of the cable running from the back of the PC to the outlet.

Finally, if you can, plug the system into a known-good outlet and see if it works. A good network tech always keeps a long patch cable for just this purpose. If you get connectivity with the second outlet, you should begin to suspect bad wiring in structured cable running from the first outlet to the switch. Or, it could be a bad connector. Assuming the cable is installed properly and has been working correctly before this event, a simple continuity test will confirm your suspicion in most cases.

Check the NIC

> Onboard NICs on laptops are especially notorious for breaking due to constant plugging and unplugging. On some laptops, the NICs are easy to replace; others require a motherboard replacement.

Be warned that a bad NIC can also generate this "can't see the network" problem. Use the utility provided by your OS to verify that the NIC works. If you've got a NIC with diagnostic software, run it—this software checks the NIC's circuitry. The NIC's female connector is a common failure point, so NICs that come with diagnostic software often include a special test called a **loopback test**. A loopback test sends data out of the NIC and checks to see if it comes back. Some NICs perform only an internal loopback, which tests the circuitry that sends and receives, but not the actual connecting pins. A true external loopback requires a **loopback adapter** or *loopback plug* inserted into the NIC's port (Figure 5.67). If a NIC is bad or has a *bad port*, replace it—preferably with an identical NIC so you don't have to reinstall drivers!

Cable Testing

The vast majority of network disconnect problems occur at the work area. If you've tested those connections, though, and the work area seems fine, it's time to consider deeper issues.

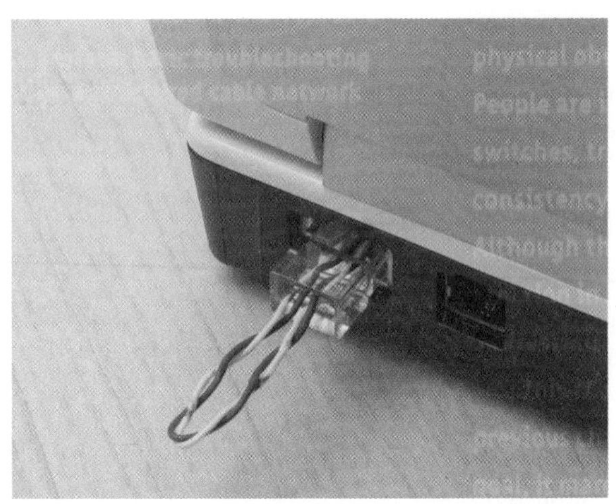

• **Figure 5.67** Loopback adapter or plug

With the right equipment, diagnosing a bad horizontal cabling run is easy. Anyone with a network should own a midrange tester with TDR such as the Fluke MicroScanner. With a little practice, you can easily determine not only whether a cable is disconnected but also where the disconnection takes place. Sometimes patience is required, especially if the cable runs aren't labeled, but you will find the problem.

When you're testing a cable run, always include the patch cables as you test. This means unplugging the patch cable from the PC, attaching a tester, and then going to the telecommunications room. Here you'll want to unplug the patch cable from the switch and plug the tester into that patch cable, making a complete test, as shown in Figure 5.68.

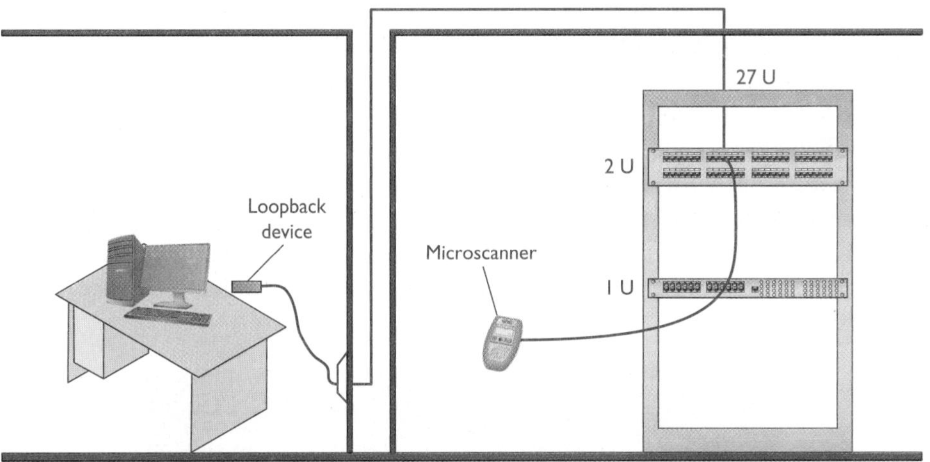

• **Figure 5.68** Loopback adapter in action

Testing in this manner gives you a complete test from the switch to the system. In general, a broken cable must be replaced. Fixing a bad patch cable is easy, but what happens if the horizontal cable is to blame? In these cases, I get on the phone and call my local installer. If a cable's bad in one spot, the risk of it being bad in another is simply too great to try anything other than total replacement.

Finally, check the coupler if one is used to extend a cable run. *Couplers* are small devices with two female ports that enable you to connect two pieces of cable together to overcome *distance limitations*. UTP couplers are most common, but you can find couplers for every type of network: fiber couplers, even coaxial or BNC couplers. The plastic UTP couplers are relatively easily broken.

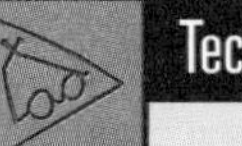

Tech Tip

Online vs. Standby Power Supplies

You can purchase two different types of UPSs—online and standby. An online UPS continuously charges a battery that, in turn, powers the computer components. If the telecommunications room loses power, the computers stay powered up without missing a beat, at least until the battery runs out.

A standby power supply (SPS) also has a big battery but doesn't power the computer unless the power goes out. Circuitry detects the power outage and immediately kicks on the battery.

Problems in the Telecommunications Room

Even a well-organized telecommunications room is a complex maze of equipment racks, switches, and patch panels. The most important issue to remember as you work is to keep your diagnostic process organized and documented. For example, if you're testing a series of cable runs along a patch panel, start at one end and don't skip connections. Place a sticker as you work to keep track of where you are on the panel.

Your biggest concerns in the telecommunications room are *facilities and infrastructure support* areas such as power and air quality.

All those boxes in the rack need good-quality power. Even the smallest rack should run off of a good **uninterruptible power supply (UPS)**, a battery backup that plugs into the wall. Make sure you get one that can handle the amount of wattage used by all the equipment in the rack.

A UPS provides several benefits. First, it acts as an inverter. It stores power as direct current in its battery, then inverts that power to alternating current as the servers and other boxes in the rack system require. A good UPS acts as a *power monitoring tool* so it can report problems when there's any fluctuation in the electrical supply. All UPS boxes can provide security from power spikes and sags.

A UPS enables you to shut down in an orderly fashion. It does *not* provide enough power for you to continue working. The device that handles the latter service is called a *generator.*

Pay attention to how often your UPS kicks in. Don't assume the power coming from your physical plant (or power company) is okay. If your UPS comes on too often, it might be time to install a voltage event recorder (Figure 5.69). As its name implies, a **voltage event recorder** plugs into your power outlet and tracks the voltage over time. These devices often reveal interesting issues.

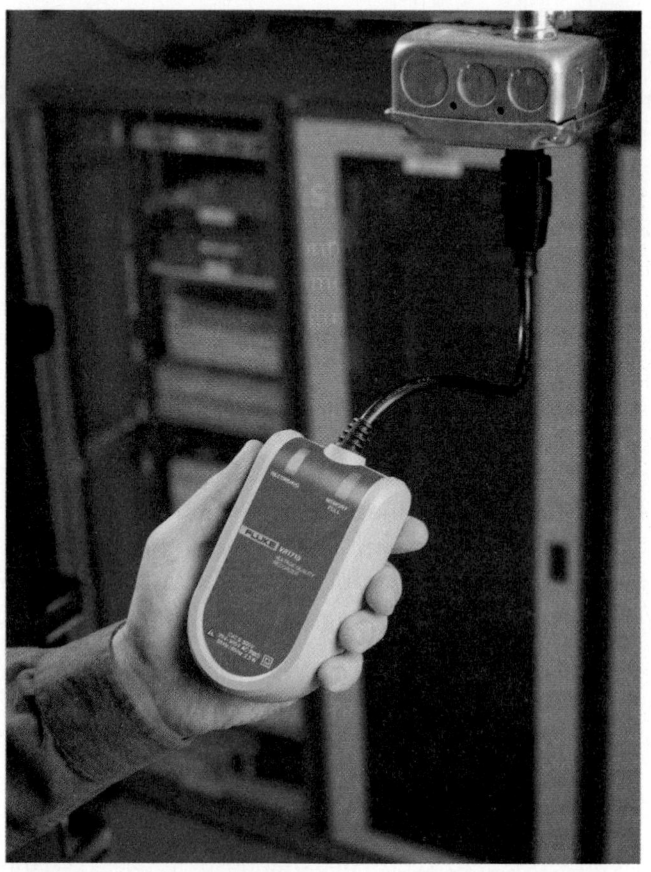

• **Figure 5.69** A voltage event recorder (photo courtesy of Fluke Networks)

The temperature in the telecommunications room should be maintained and monitored properly. If you lose the air conditioning, for example, and leave systems running, the equipment will overheat and shut down—sometimes with serious damage. To prevent this, all serious telecommunications rooms should have a UPS with a **temperature monitor**.

Likewise, you need to control the level of humidity in a telecommunications room. You can install **environmental monitors** that keep a constant watch on humidity, temperature, and more, for just a few hundred dollars. The devices cost little in comparison to the equipment in the telecommunications room that you're protecting.

Toners

It would be nice to say that all cable installations are perfect and that over the years they won't tend to grow into horrific piles of spaghetti-like, unlabeled cables. In the real world, though, you might eventually find yourself having to locate or *trace* cables. Even in the best-planned networks, labels fall off ports and outlets, mystery cables appear behind walls, new cable runs are added, and mistakes are made counting rows and columns on patch panels. Sooner or later, most network techs will have to be able to pick out one particular cable or port from a stack.

When the time comes to trace cables, network techs turn to a device called a toner for help. **Toner** is the generic term for two separate devices that are used together: a tone generator and a tone probe. The **tone generator** connects to the cable using alligator clips, tiny hooks, or a network jack, and it sends an electrical signal along the wire at a certain frequency. The **tone probe** emits a sound when it is placed near a cable connected to the tone generator. These two devices are often referred to by the brand-name Fox and Hound (Figure 5.70), a popular model of toner made by the Triplett Corporation.

• **Figure 5.70** Fox and Hound

To trace a cable, connect the tone generator to the known end of the cable in question, and then position the tone probe next to the other end of each of the cables that might be the right one. The tone probe makes a sound when it's placed next to the right cable. Some toners have one tone probe that works with multiple tone generators. Each generator emits a separate frequency, and the probe sounds a different tone for each one. Even good toners are relatively inexpensive ($75); although inexpensive toners can cost less than $25, they don't tend to work well, so spending a little more is worthwhile. Just keep in mind that if you have to support a network, you'd do best to own a decent toner.

A good, medium-priced cable tester and a good toner are the most important tools for folks who must support, but not install, networks. A final tip: Be sure to bring along a few extra batteries—there's nothing worse than sitting on the top of a ladder holding a cable tester or toner that has just run out of juice!

Chapter 5 Review

Chapter Summary

After reading this chapter and completing the exercises, you should understand the following about installing a physical network.

Recognize and describe the functions of basic components in a structured cabling system

- Structured cabling refers to a set of standards established by the TIA in the United States and other agencies elsewhere in the world regarding network cabling. The three basic structured cabling network components are the telecommunications room, the horizontal cabling, and the work area (or the actual workers' office space).
- Although wireless networks are popular, they lack the reliability and speed of wired networks.
- All cabling should run from individual PCs to a telecommunications room, called the *intermediate distribution frame (IDF)*.
- A telecommunications room should have one or more sturdy equipment racks, used to hold mountable network devices (switches and routers); this space also houses server PCs, patch panels, UPSs, and monitors.
- Horizontal cabling usually refers to the cabling that runs from the telecommunications room out to the work areas of a single office building floor.
- The work area is where PCs and printers connect to the ends of the horizontal cabling. In other words, the work area is the actual office space where the jacks should be located for connecting to the network.
- UTP cable comes in one of two types: solid core and stranded core. Horizontal cabling should always be solid core.
- Solid core UTP is a better conductor than stranded core but breaks easily if handled roughly. Stranded core holds up better to substantial handling.
- Equipment racks are 19 inches wide and come in a variety of heights. Rack-mounted equipment is manufactured to fit in the 19-inch width, but the equipment height can vary.
- Rack-mounted equipment heights are measured in units (Us), each U being equal to just under 1.75 inches.
- UTP cables can be connected to a 110 block in a patch panel by using a punchdown tool.
- The ANSI/TIA-606-C labeling standard can help a technician keep track of cables.
- Patch cables are used to connect the ports on a patch panel to a switch. Although solid core horizontal runs typically connect to the 110 block, patch cables are usually stranded core.
- You might run into BIX blocks or Krone blocks—alternatives to 110 blocks—outside of the United States. They serve the same function as 110 blocks, but differ a bit.
- Patch cables are also used in the work area to connect a PC to the RJ-45 wall jack.
- TIA/EIA 568 limits horizontal runs to 90 meters, allowing 10 meters for patch cables before the 100-meter UTP cable limit is reached.
- The demarc location is where the connection is made from the outside world to a private network. An Internet service provider provides service through its demarc.
- A network interface unit, such as a cable modem, may sit between the demarc and local network.
- Demarcs and cross-connects typically reside in a room called the main distribution frame.

Explain the process of installing structured cable

- A good installation entails planning the cabling runs with an actual floor plan, as well as poking around in walls and ceilings.
- Raceway products may be used to run cable externally rather than inside walls.
- When planning cable runs, keep five things in mind: distance, power, dryness, temperature, and access.
- Cable trays may be used to aid in pulling cable within a drop ceiling.

- If you make your own patch cables, be sure to use the correct crimp, as the crimps differ for solid core and stranded core UTP.
- A variety of cable testers, including time-domain reflectometers and optical time-domain reflectometers, can be used to test for continuity, shorts, split pairs, attenuation, and crosstalk.
- Big issues with fiber include signal degradation through broken, bad, or dirty connectors; attenuation or light leakage; and physical or signal mismatches.

Install a network interface card

- All UTP Ethernet NICs use an RJ-45 connector. Fiber-optic NICs use a variety of connectors, depending on the manufacturer.
- Many motherboards now include an onboard NIC.
- Using the same model of NIC for all the PCs on your network makes installing and updating drivers much easier.
- The most common type of expansion card for NICs is PCI express (PCIe), but legacy PCI cards are installed in some systems. USB NICs are convenient, and you don't have to open the computer case to install one.
- The link lights on a NIC indicate the status of the NIC, such as if it's connected to a network and if there is any network activity.

Perform basic troubleshooting on a structured cable network

- A "No server is found" error is likely caused by a physical connection problem. If one program (such as a Web browser) works but another (such as e-mail) does not, the problem is likely software related.
- If you suspect a hardware problem, check the link lights on the NIC and the switch. If the lights are not on, the cable is probably disconnected or the port may be faulty.
- A loopback test can check a NIC's circuitry, but not the actual connecting pins.
- When testing cables, be sure to test the entire run, including the patch cable in the work area, the cable leading from the work area wall back to the telecommunications room, and the patch cable from the patch panel to the switch.
- Tools that are helpful for troubleshooting a structured cable network include a voltage event recorder and a toner.

Key Terms

66 block *(94)*
110 block *(93)*
activity light *(116)*
ANSI/TIA-606-C *(94)*
attenuation *(111)*
BIX block *(95)*
cable certifier *(111)*
cable drop *(100)*
cable tester *(108)*
cable tray *(102)*
continuity *(108)*
continuity tester *(108)*
crosstalk *(110)*
customer-premises equipment (CPE) *(98)*
demarc extension *(98)*
demarcation point (demarc) *(97)*
dirty optical cable *(112)*
dispersion *(112)*
environmental monitor *(120)*
equipment rack *(91)*
far-end crosstalk (FEXT) *(110)*
fiber distribution panel *(99)*
floor plan *(100)*
horizontal cabling *(89)*
interference *(108)*
intermediate distribution frame (IDF) *(91)*
jitter *(111)*
Krone block *(95)*
latency *(111)*
light leakage *(112)*
link light *(116)*
loopback adapter *(118)*
loopback test *(118)*
main distribution frame (MDF) *(99)*
mounting bracket *(103)*
multimeter *(109)*

near-end crosstalk (NEXT) *(110)*
network interface unit (NIU) *(98)*
optical time-domain reflectometer (OTDR) *(113)*
patch bay *(96)*
patch cable *(95)*
patch panel *(93)*
port aggregation *(116)*
power distribution unit (PDU) *(92)*
punchdown tool *(93)*
raceway *(100)*
run *(89)*
solid core *(90)*
split pair *(108)*
stranded core *(90)*
structured cabling *(87)*
telecommunications room *(89)*
temperature monitor *(120)*
time-domain reflectometer (TDR) *(110)*
tone generator *(121)*
tone probe *(121)*
toner *(121)*
unit (U) *(92)*
uninterruptible power supply (UPS) *(119)*
vertical cross-connect *(99)*
voltage event recorder *(120)*
wire map *(109)*
work area *(89)*

Key Term Quiz

Use the Key Terms list to complete the sentences that follow. Not all terms will be used.

1. All the cabling from individual work areas runs via _______________ to a central location.
2. The central location that all cabling runs to is called the _______________.
3. A single piece of installed horizontal cabling is called a(n) _______________.
4. The set of standards established by the TIA/EIA regarding network cabling is called _______________.
5. You use a(n) _______________ to connect a strand of UTP to a 110 block or 66 block.
6. A short UTP cable that uses stranded core, rather than solid core, cable is called a(n) _______________ and can tolerate much more handling near a patch panel.
7. A(n) _______________ is a proprietary European telecommunication connector that is an alternative to a 110 block.
8. The spot where a cable comes out of the wall at the work area is called a(n) _______________.
9. The height measurement known as U is used for devices that fit into a(n) _______________.
10. The term _______________ describes the process of a signal weakening as it progresses down a piece of wire.

Multiple-Choice Quiz

1. Which item describes the length of cable installed within walls from a telecommunications room out to a jack?
   A. Cable drop
   B. Cable run
   C. Cable tester
   D. Cable tray
2. What is the term used to describe where the network hardware and patch panels are kept?
   A. Drop room
   B. Telecommunications room
   C. Routing room
   D. Telecloset room

3. Aside from outright breakage, what's the primary worry with bending a fiber-optic cable too much?
   A. Attenuation
   B. Light leakage
   C. Near-end crosstalk
   D. Port aggregation
4. When connecting a cable run onto a patch panel, which tool should you use?
   A. 110-punchdown tool
   B. Crimper
   C. TDR
   D. Tone generator
5. What is the structured cabling name for the end user's office space where network computers are set up?
   A. Backbone
   B. Building entrance
   C. Cable drop
   D. Work area
6. Which of the following enables you to use multiple NICs in a computer to achieve a much better network bandwidth?
   A. Linking
   B. Port aggregation
   C. SLI
   D. Xing
7. Why would network techs use stranded core cabling from a patch panel's ports to a switch?
   A. Cost
   B. Fire rating
   C. Flexibility
   D. Safety
8. What is the first thing a professional cable installer should request when providing an estimate at a site?
   A. Wiring diagram
   B. Network map
   C. Floor plan
   D. Liability forms
9. What component best enables you to install more servers in the limited space of a telecommunications room?
   A. Cable tray
   B. Outlet box
   C. Patch panel
   D. Equipment rack
10. How tall is a network router that is 8U?
    A. 8 inches
    B. 8 centimeters
    C. 14 inches
    D. 14 centimeters
11. On your first day on the job, you get a call from the owner complaining that her network connection is down. A quick check of the central switch verifies that it's in good working order, as is the boss's PC. As luck would have it, your supervisor calls at just that time and tells you not to worry; she'll be by in a jiffy with her TDR to help root out the problem. What is she talking about?
    A. Tune-domain resonator, her network tone generator
    B. Time-detuning resonator, her network tester
    C. Time-domain reflectometer, her network tester
    D. Time-detail resource, her network schematic
12. Jenny's office building recently had sections renovated, and now some users are complaining that they can't see the network. She suspects that the workers might have inadvertently broken wires when they did ceiling work. George suggests she use a toner to figure out which wires go to the complaining users. Erin disagrees, saying that Jenny should use a Fox and Hound. Who's right?
    A. Only George is right.
    B. Only Erin is right.
    C. Both George and Erin are right.
    D. Neither George nor Erin is right.

13. What is generated by every piece of UTP cable in existence?
    - **A.** Modal dispersion
    - **B.** Crosstalk
    - **C.** EMI
    - **D.** ESD
14. Which statement about structured cable is correct?
    - **A.** The term "demarc" refers to a physical location, whereas the phrase "network interface unit" refers to a piece of equipment provided by an ISP.
    - **B.** The term "demarc" refers to a piece of equipment provided by an ISP, whereas the phrase "network interface unit" refers to a piece of equipment provided by the customer.
    - **C.** The terms "demarc" and "network interface unit" refer to pieces of equipment provided by an ISP.
    - **D.** A demarc is used for fiber cabling, whereas a network interface unit is used for UTP.
15. Bill the fiber inspector comes back after reviewing a fiber run and says there's too much *attenuation*. What does he mean?
    - **A.** The signal gets weak as it travels long distances.
    - **B.** The signal spreads as it travels long distances.
    - **C.** The signal amplifies as it travels long distances.
    - **D.** He doesn't mean anything. "Attenuation" is technobabble.

Essay Quiz

1. Sketch a rough draft of your classroom, office, or the room you are in right now. Indicate any doors, windows, closets, lights, plumbing fixtures, desks or tables, and even any visible electrical wall outlets. Then indicate with a large letter *X* where you would place a new cable drop. Jot down some notes explaining why you would choose the location you did.
2. Your boss mentions "demarc" when discussing his recent interaction with an ISP salesman, but it seems like he doesn't understand the concept at all. Write a quick note to your boss describing the true meaning of a structured cabling building entrance, so you can put it on his desk before you leave for the day.
3. The youth group at a local community organization has received funding to help with creating a computer network. They have already purchased the required number of 10/100/1000 NICs. You have been asked by one of the group's leaders to assist with installing the NICs. You want to help, but time doesn't permit you to volunteer any more hours in a week than you already do. It makes better sense to organize a step-by-step fact sheet that describes installing a NIC into an open slot on a computer. When you have finished, e-mail the fact sheet you created to your instructor (or a friend) for comments.

Lab Projects

• Lab Project 5.1

You are a recently hired network technician at a local business. During the interview phase with the company, some questions were raised about installing cable. You made it clear that professional cable installation was the way to go. You justified your statements and impressed the interviewers with your knowledge and honesty, so they hired you.

Now you need to research which professional cable installers are available in your area and what each charges as a "per drop" price. Use the Internet to gather research from at least two companies. Prepare a PowerPoint presentation to present your findings to management. Be sure to use color, graphics, and slide transitions (as time permits) to further impress your new bosses!

• Lab Project 5.2

You have become the de facto network administrator for your employer at a nearby tax preparation company. The owner of this small business closely monitors all expenses. She realizes that you could use additional tools to help with installing cable for her soon-to-be-expanded office network. You see this as the opportunity to purchase a cable tester and a tone generator. Your boss casually says to check out some prices. You know that well-laid-out numbers could mean approval on the toys you'd like!

Prepare a spreadsheet that shows three levels, including prices, for each of these items. Arrange your spreadsheet in a "good/better/best" layout, with "best" listed on top for the most attention. Use the following chart as a guide:

"BEST"	**Brand/Model**	**Price**
Cable Tester A		$.
Tone Generator A		$.
Total for A Items		$.
"BETTER"	**Brand/Model**	**Price**
Cable Tester B		$.
Tone Generator B		$.
Total for B Items		$.
"GOOD"	**Brand/Model**	**Price**
Cable Tester C		$.
Tone Generator C		$.
Total for C Items		$.

TCP/IP Basics

"If it's sent by ship then it's a cargo, if it's sent by road then it's a shipment."

—Dave Allen

In this chapter, you will learn how to

- **Describe how the TCP/IP protocol suite works**
- **Explain CIDR and subnetting**
- **Describe the functions of static and dynamic IP addresses**

The mythical MHTechEd network (remember that from Chapter 1?) provided an overview of how networks work. The foundation of every physical network is hardware: wires, network interface cards, and other stand-alone network devices that move data from one computer to another. This hardware corresponds to OSI Layers 1 and 2—the Physical and Data Link layers (though some devices may also perform higher-layer functions). The higher layers of the model—from Network up to Application—work with this hardware to make network magic.

Chapters 2 through 5 provided details of the hardware at the Physical and Data Link layers of the OSI model. You learned about the network protocols, such as Ethernet, which standardize networking so that data sent by one NIC can be read correctly by another NIC.

This chapter begins a fun journey into the software side of networking. You'll learn the details about the IP addressing scheme that enables computers on one network to communicate with each other and with computers on other networks. You'll get the full story of how TCP/IP networks divide into smaller units—subnets—to make management of a large TCP/IP network easier. And you won't just get it from a conceptual standpoint. This chapter provides the details you've undoubtedly been craving—it teaches you how to set up a network properly. The chapter finishes with an in-depth discussion on implementing IP addresses.

Historical/Conceptual

The early days of networking, roughly the 1980s, exposed a problem in the way the software developers created the programs that powered networks at the time. Unlike the hardware organizations that worked together to make solid standards, the different organizations developing network software worked separately, secretly, and competitively. The four major players—Microsoft, Apple, Novell, and UNIX developers such as AT&T—created network software solutions that were mostly incompatible and had very different answers to the question "What do we share on a network?"

Microsoft, Apple, and Novell created networking software that for the most part did nothing more than share different computers' folders and printers (and they all did this sharing differently). AT&T and the universities developing the UNIX operating system saw networks as a way to share terminals, send e-mail messages, and transfer files. As a result, everyone's software had its own set of Rules of What a Network Should Do and How to Do It. These sets of rules—and the software written to follow these rules—were broken down into individual rules or languages called **protocols**. No single protocol could do everything a network needed to do, so companies lumped together all their necessary protocols under the term **protocol suite**. Novell called its protocol suite IPX/SPX; Microsoft's was called NetBIOS/NetBEUI; Apple called its protocol suite AppleTalk; and the UNIX folks used this wacky protocol suite called TCP/IP.

It took about 20 very confusing years, but eventually TCP/IP replaced every other protocol suite in all but the most rare and unique situations. To get ahead today, to get on the Internet, and to pass the CompTIA Network+ exam, you only need to worry about TCP/IP. Microsoft, Apple, and Linux developers no longer actively support anything but TCP/IP. You live in a one-protocol-suite world, the old stuff is forgotten, and you kids don't know how good you've got it!

Test Specific

The TCP/IP Protocol Suite

If you recall from Chapter 1, the first two layers of the OSI seven-layer model deal with physical connectivity—wires and such—and protocols that interact with the physical. These are Layer 1, Physical, and Layer 2, Data Link. The TCP/IP protocol suite operates at Layers 3–7 of the OSI seven-layer model. This chapter explores Layer 3, Network, for the most part, though I'll remind you about Layer 4, Transport protocols, and Layer 7, Application protocols, before the deep dive into the Network layer.

Network Layer Protocols

Internet Protocol (IP) works at the Network layer, where it takes data chunks from the Transport layer (which become the packet's *payload*), adds addressing, and creates the final IP packet. IP then hands the IP packet to the Data Link layer for encapsulation into a frame.

Let's look at the addressing in more depth. I think it's safe to assume that most folks have seen IP addresses before. Here's a typical example:

192.168.1.115

This type of address—four values ranging from 0 to 255, separated by three periods—is known officially as an **Internet Protocol version 4 (IPv4)** address.

This chapter introduces you to IPv4 addresses. You should understand the correct name for this older type of address because the world is in a slow transition to a newer, longer type of IP address called IPv6. Here's an example of an IPv6 address:

2001:0:4137:9e76:43e:2599:3f57:fe9a

IPv4 and IPv6 aren't the only TCP/IP protocols that work at the Network layer. **Internet Control Message Protocol (ICMP)**, for example, plays a role in IP error reporting and diagnostics. TCP/IP users rarely start a program that uses ICMP (or its IPv6 counterpart, ICMPv6). For the most part, software automatically uses ICMP as needed without direct user action. There are exceptions to every rule: the ping utility, a popular network diagnostic tool, directly uses ICMP. You can use ping to answer a question like, "can my computer communicate with any device at the IP address 192.168.1.15?"

When thinking about the Network layer, remember the following three protocols:

Chapter 12 goes into IPv6 in detail.

- IPv4 (normally referred to as simply "IP")
- IPv6
- ICMP

Figure 6.1 shows a highly simplified *Internet Protocol (IP) header*.

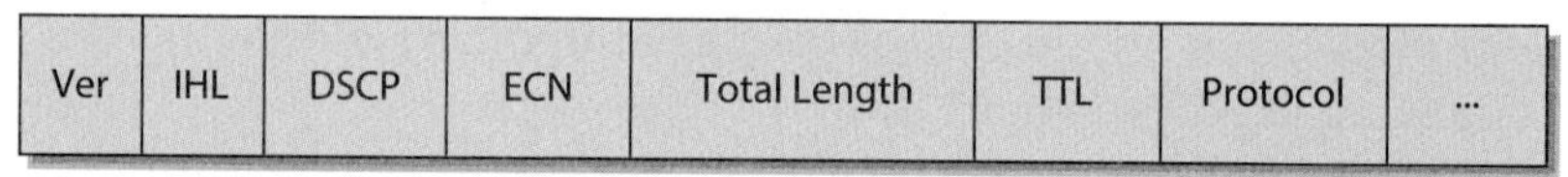

• **Figure 6.1** Simplified IPv4 header

The full IPv4 packet header has 14 different fields. As discussed in Chapter 1, "Network Models," the destination and source IP address fields are critical for getting packets to their destination. Dissecting the entire set of fields isn't important this early in the discussion, but here are a few to whet your appetite:

- **Version** The version (Ver) field defines the IP address type: 4, for IPv4. If you're thinking, "Hey, Mike, what about 6?" I've got a surprise for you. The IPv6 packet header also starts with a version field (which is "6"), but the formats differ after that field. We'll look at the IPv6 header format separately in Chapter 12.

- **Total Length** The total size of the IP packet in octets. This includes the IP header and its payload. This field is 16 bits, which limits the packet size to 65 KB.
- **Time to Live (TTL)** Implementations of routers on the Internet are not perfect and engineers sometimes create loops. The TTL field prevents an IP packet from indefinitely spinning through the Internet by using a counter that decrements by one every time a packet goes through a router. This number cannot start higher than 255; many operating systems start at 128.
- **Protocol** In most cases, the protocol field is either TCP or UDP and identifies what's encapsulated inside the packet. See the next section for more information.

Transport Layer Protocols

When moving data from one system to another, the TCP/IP protocol suite needs to know if the communication is connection-oriented or connectionless. If the data moving between two systems must get there in good order, a connection-oriented application is the safe bet. If it's not a big deal for data to miss a bit or two, then connectionless is the way to go. The connection-oriented protocol used with TCP/IP is called the **Transmission Control Protocol (TCP)**. The connectionless one is called the **User Datagram Protocol (UDP)**.

Let me be clear: *you* don't *choose* TCP or UDP. The people who develop an application decide which protocol to use. The people who build Discord or Twitch or Firefox or Zoom pick (and sometimes even design) one or more protocols that they think will meet their application's needs. These protocols are, in turn, designed to use TCP, UDP, or both.

TCP

Most TCP/IP applications use TCP—that's why the protocol suite is called "TCP/IP" and not "UDP/IP." TCP gets an application's data from one machine to another reliably and completely. As a result, TCP comes with communication rules that require both the sending and receiving machines to acknowledge the other's presence and readiness to send and receive data. This process is referred to as the TCP *three-way handshake* of SYN, SYN-ACK, and ACK (Figure 6.2). TCP also chops up data into **segments**, gives the segments a sequence number, and then verifies that all sent segments were received. If a segment goes missing, the receiving system must request the missing segments.

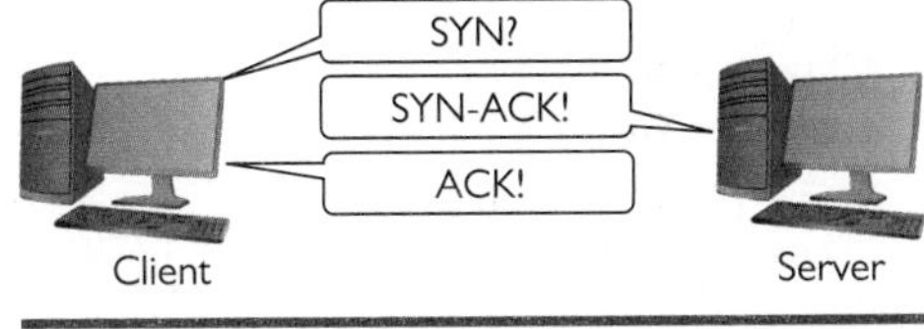

• **Figure 6.2** TCP three-way handshake in action

Figure 6.3 shows a simplified TCP header. Notice the source port and the destination port. Port numbers, which range from 1 to 65,535, are used by systems to determine what application needs the received data. Each application is assigned a specific port number on which to listen/send. Web servers use port 80 (HTTP) or 443 (HTTPS), for example, whereas port 143 is used to receive e-mail messages from e-mail servers (IMAP4).

You might be required to select the fully spelled-out version of "TCP header" on the CompTIA Network+ exam, as in *Transmission Control Protocol (TCP) header.*

Source port	Destination port	Sequence number	Acknowledgment number

• **Figure 6.3** TCP header

The client uses the source port number to remember which client application requested the data. The rest of this book dives much deeper into ports. For now, know that the TCP or UDP header inside an IP packet stores these values.

Ports aren't the only items of interest in the TCP header. The header also contains these fields:

- **Sequence number and acknowledgment number** These numbers enable the sending and receiving computers to keep track of the various pieces of data flowing back and forth.
- **Flags** These individual bits give both sides detailed information about the state of the connection. (These appear in the CompTIA Network+ objectives as *TCP flags*.)
- **Checksum** The recipient can use the checksum to check the TCP header for errors such as bits flipped or lost during transmission.

> You might be required to select the fully spelled-out version of "UDP header" on the CompTIA Network+ exam, as in *User Datagram Protocol (UDP) header*.

UDP

UDP is the "fire and forget" missile of the TCP/IP protocol suite. As you can see in Figure 6.4, a UDP **datagram** header doesn't possess any of the extra fields TCP segment headers carry to make sure the data is received intact. UDP works best when you have a lot of data that doesn't need to be perfect or when the systems are so close to each other that the chances of a problem occurring are too small to bother worrying about. A few dropped frames on a Voice over IP call, for example, won't make much difference in the communication between two people. So, there's a good reason to use UDP: it's smoking fast compared to TCP. Two of the most important networking protocols, Domain Name System (DNS) and Dynamic Host Configuration Protocol (DHCP), use UDP.

> You saw this back in Chapter 1, but I'll mention it again here. Data gets chopped up into chunks at the Transport layer when using TCP. The chunks are called *segments* with TCP. UDP *datagrams* don't get chopped up at the Transport layer; they just get a header.

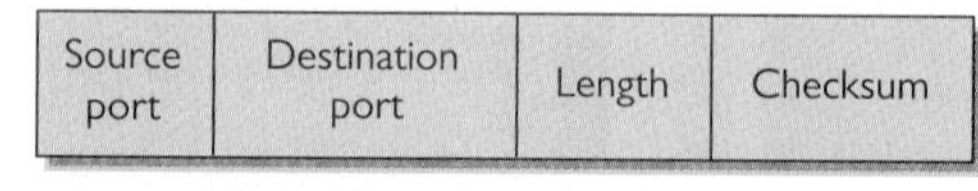

• **Figure 6.4** UDP header

Application Layer Protocols

TCP/IP applications use TCP/IP protocols to move data back and forth between clients and servers. Because every application has different needs, I can't show you a generic application header. Instead, we'll look at a sample header from a pillar of the World Wide Web—the Hypertext Transfer Protocol (HTTP).

Web servers and Web browsers use HTTP (or, more accurately, HTTPS, a secure version of HTTP wrapped in encryption—we'll take a closer look at it in Chapter 10, "Securing TCP/IP") to communicate. Figure 6.5 shows a sample header for HTTP. Specifically, this header is a response from a Web server containing a resource the client previously requested. This header—it's just text—begins with "HTTP/1.1," which indicates the version of the HTTP protocol in use. The "200 OK" indicates a successful request. The first blank line separates the end of the header from the beginning of the response body (which contains the requested Web page).

> I'm simplifying the call-and-response interaction between a Web server and a Web client. The explanation here is only part of the process of accessing a Web page.

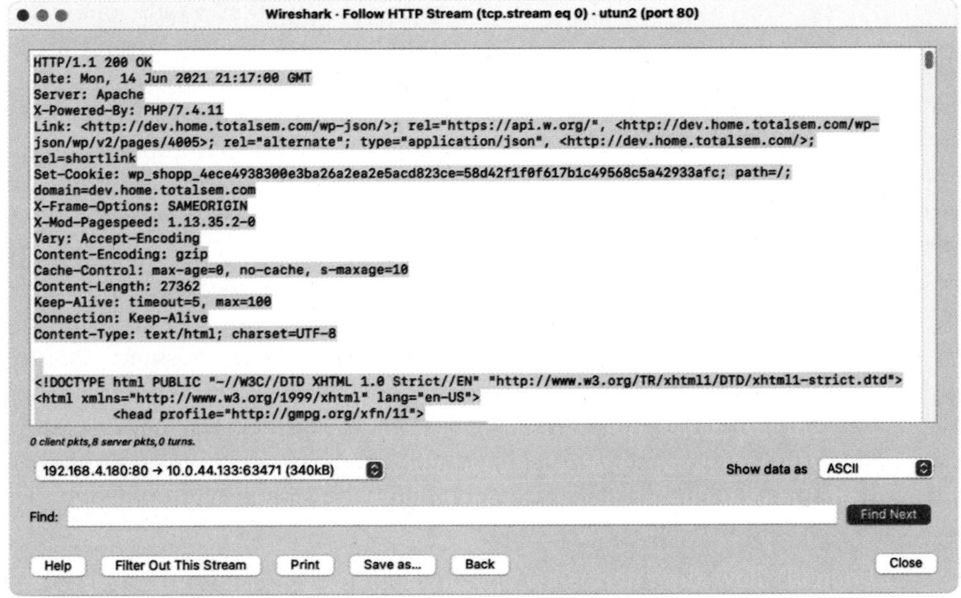

Wireshark · Follow HTTP Stream (tcp.stream eq 0) · utun2 (port 80)
HTTP/1.1 200 OK
Date: Mon, 14 Jun 2021 21:17:00 GMT
Server: Apache
X-Powered-By: PHP/7.4.11
Link: <http://dev.home.totalsem.com/wp-json/>; rel="https://api.w.org/", <http://dev.home.totalsem.com/wp-json/wp/v2/pages/4005>; rel="alternate"; type="application/json", <http://dev.home.totalsem.com/>; rel=shortlink
Set-Cookie: wp_shopp_4ece4938300e3ba26a2ea2e5acd823ce=58d42f1f0f617b1c49568c5a42933afc; path=/; domain=dev.home.totalsem.com
X-Frame-Options: SAMEORIGIN
X-Mod-Pagespeed: 1.13.35.2-0
Vary: Accept-Encoding
Content-Encoding: gzip
Cache-Control: max-age=0, no-cache, s-maxage=10
Content-Length: 27362
Keep-Alive: timeout=5, max=100
Connection: Keep-Alive
Content-Type: text/html; charset=UTF-8
<!DOCTYPE html PUBLIC "-//W3C//DTD XHTML 1.0 Strict//EN" "http://www.w3.org/TR/xhtml11/DTD/xhtml1-strict.dtd">
<html xmlns="http://www.w3.org/1999/xhtml" lang="en-US">
<head profile="http://gmpg.org/xfn/11">
0 client pkts, 8 server pkts, 0 turns.
192.168.4.180:80 → 10.0.44.133:63471 (340kB)
Show data as
ASCII
Find:
Find Next
Help
Filter Out This Stream
Print
Save as...
Back
Close

• **Figure 6.5** HTTP header

Super! Now that you're comfortable with how the TCP/IP protocols fit into clear points on the OSI seven-layer model, let's head back to the Network layer and explore IP addressing.

> We say LAN so often in networking that you might assume it has a crystal-clear definition, but there's a bit of art in it. A LAN generally (but not always) belongs to one household or organization. A LAN covers a limited place—but that can mean anything from two devices in an apartment up to thousands of devices on a multi-building school or business campus.
>
> A WAN in a basic sense means a collection of interconnected LANs. Most authors also add a geographical context to the term, such as "spread out over a large area."

IP and Ethernet

TCP/IP supports simple networks and complex networks. You can use the protocol suite and a switch to connect a handful of computers in the same place into a **local area network (LAN)**. TCP/IP also enables you to interconnect multiple LANs into a **wide area network (WAN)**. Let's start by examining how **IP addressing** works in a simple network, a LAN.

At the LAN level, every host runs TCP/IP software over Ethernet hardware, creating a situation where every host has two addresses: an IP address and an Ethernet MAC address (Figure 6.6). While at first this seems redundant, it's the power behind TCP/IP's ability to support both LANs and WANs. But again, we're only talking about LANs at this point.

• **Figure 6.6** Two addresses

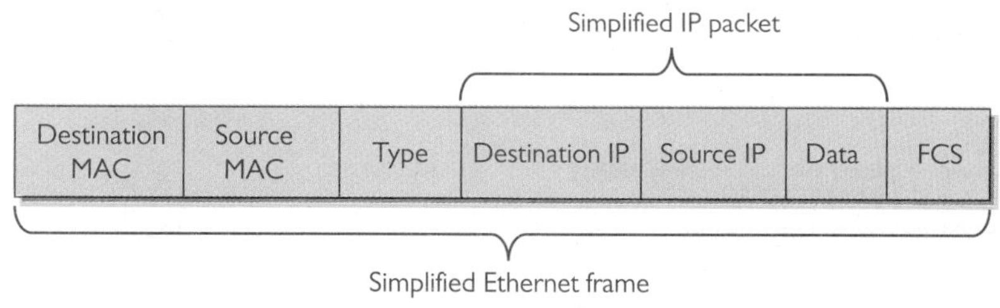

• **Figure 6.7** Encapsulation of an IP packet inside an Ethernet frame

Imagine a situation where one computer, Computer A, wants to send an IP packet to another computer, Computer B, on the LAN. To send an IP packet to another computer, the sending computer (Computer A) must insert the IP packet into an Ethernet frame, as shown in Figure 6.7.

Note that the IP packet is completely encapsulated inside the Ethernet frame. Also note that the *Ethernet header*—the initial portion of the frame—has both a destination MAC address and a source MAC address, while the IP packet encapsulated in the Ethernet frame has both a source IP address and a destination IP address. This encapsulation idea works great, but there's a problem: Computer A knows Computer B's IP address, but how does Computer A know the MAC address of Computer B? (See Figure 6.8.)

> The Ethernet header includes the destination and source MAC addresses, plus the *Type* field. The latter can indicate the size of the payload in octets or the protocol of the encapsulated payload.

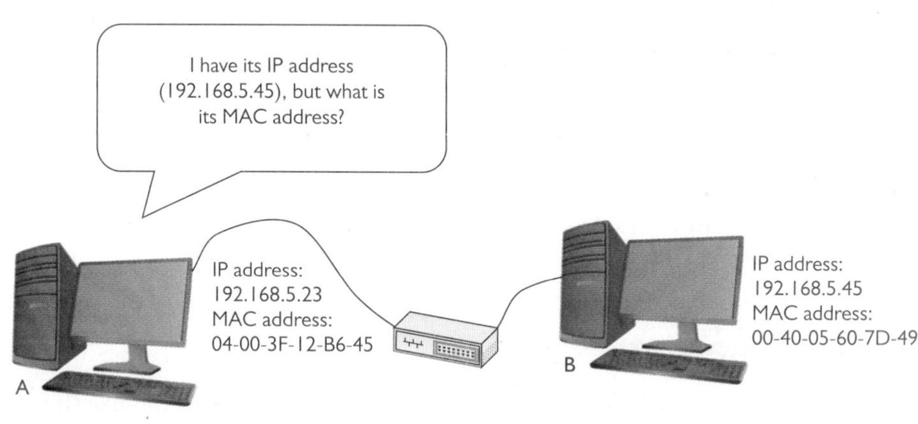

• **Figure 6.8** What is its MAC address?

> The process and protocol used in resolving an IP address to an Ethernet MAC address is called **Address Resolution Protocol (ARP)**.

To get Computer B's MAC address, Computer A sends a special query called an *ARP request* to MAC address FF-FF-FF-FF-FF-FF, the universal MAC address for broadcast (Figure 6.9). The switch forwards the broadcast to every connected node.

Computer B responds to the ARP request by sending Computer A an ARP reply (Figure 6.10) through the switch. Once Computer A has

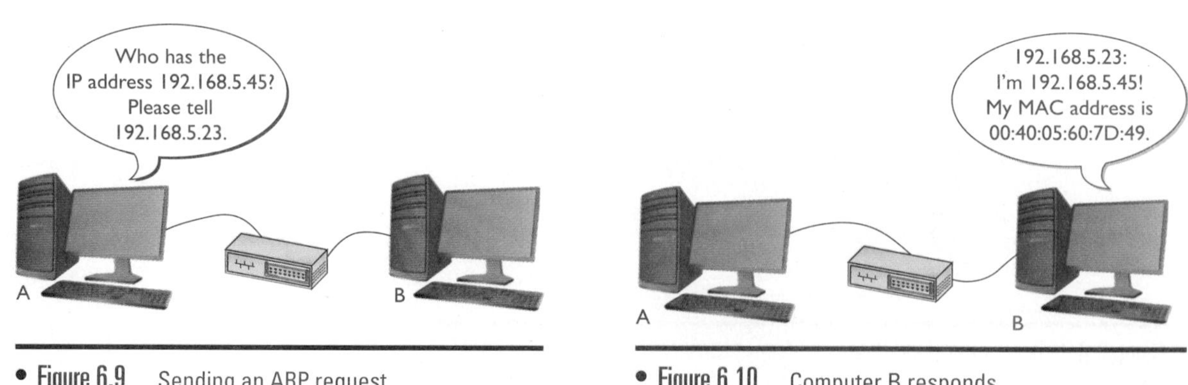

• **Figure 6.9** Sending an ARP request

• **Figure 6.10** Computer B responds.

Computer B's MAC address, it starts sending unicast Ethernet frames to Computer B through the switch.

Try This!

ARP in Windows

To show a Windows system's current ARP cache, open a command line and type

```
arp -a
```

You should see results like this:

```
Interface: 192.168.4.71 --- 0x4

Internet Address Physical Address Type
192.168.4.76   00-1d-e0-78-9c-d5  dynamic
192.168.4.81   00-1b-77-3f-85-b4  dynamic
```

Now delete one of the entries in the ARP table with this command:

```
arp -d [ip address from the previous results]
```

Run the `arp -a` command again. The line for the address you specified should be gone. Now ping the address you deleted and check the ARP table again. Did the deleted address return?

IP addresses provide several benefits that MAC addresses alone cannot offer. First, IP addresses are not a fixed part of the NIC. They can be changed to suit the needs of the network designer. Second, IP addresses group together sets of computers into logical networks, so you can, for example, distinguish one LAN from another. Finally, because TCP/IP network equipment understands the IP addressing scheme, computers can communicate with each other across all of the LANs that make up a WAN. Let's go into more detail on IP addresses.

IP Addresses

The most common type of IP address (officially called IPv4, but usually simplified to just "IP") consists of a 32-bit value. Here's an example of an IP address:

11000000101010000000010000000010

Whoa! IP addresses are just strings of 32 binary digits? Yes, they are, but to make IP addresses easier for humans to use, the 32-bit binary value is broken down into four groups of eight, separated by periods, or *dots*, like this:

11000000.10101000.00000100.00000010

Each of these 8-bit values is, in turn, converted into a decimal number between 0 and 255. If you took every possible combination of eight binary values and placed them in a spreadsheet, it would look something like the list in the left column. The right column shows the same list with a decimal value assigned to each.

00000000	00000000 = 0
00000001	00000001 = 1
00000010	00000010 = 2
00000011	00000011 = 3
00000100	00000100 = 4
00000101	00000101 = 5
00000110	00000110 = 6
00000111	00000111 = 7
00001000	00001000 = 8
(skip a bunch in the middle)	*(skip a bunch in the middle)*
11111000	11111000 = 248
11111001	11111001 = 249
11111010	11111010 = 250
11111011	11111011 = 251
11111100	11111100 = 252
11111101	11111101 = 253
11111110	11111110 = 254
11111111	11111111 = 255

Converted, the original value of 11000000.10101000.00000100.00000010 is displayed as 192.168.4.2 in IPv4's **dotted decimal notation**. Note that dotted decimal is simply a shorthand way for people to discuss and configure the binary IP addresses computers use.

> Check out two excellent Chapter 6 "Binary Calculator" sims over at https://totalsem.com/008. Watch the Show! and then practice on the Click!

People who work on TCP/IP networks must know how to convert dotted decimal to binary and back. You can convert easily using any operating system's calculator. Every OS has a calculator (UNIX/Linux systems have about 100 different ones to choose from) that has a scientific or programmer mode like the ones shown in Figure 6.11.

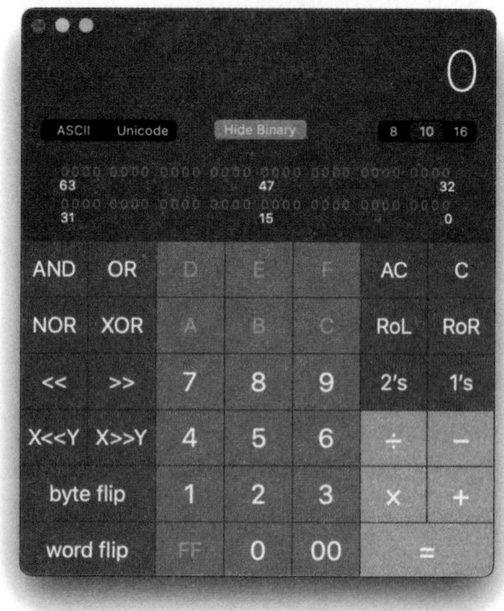

• **Figure 6.11** Windows (left) and macOS (right) calculators in Programmer mode

To convert from decimal to binary, go to decimal view, enter the decimal value, and then switch to binary view to get the result. To convert from binary to decimal, go to binary view, enter the binary value, and switch to decimal view to get the result. Figure 6.12 shows the result of Windows 10 Calculator converting the decimal value 42 into binary. Notice the result is 101010—the leading two zeroes do not appear. When you work with IP addresses, you must always have eight digits, so just add two more to the left to get 00101010.

Just as every MAC address must be unique on a network, every IP address must be unique as well. For logical addressing to work, no two computers on the same network may have the same IP address. In a small network running TCP/IP, every computer has both an IP address and a MAC address (Figure 6.13), as you know from earlier in the chapter.

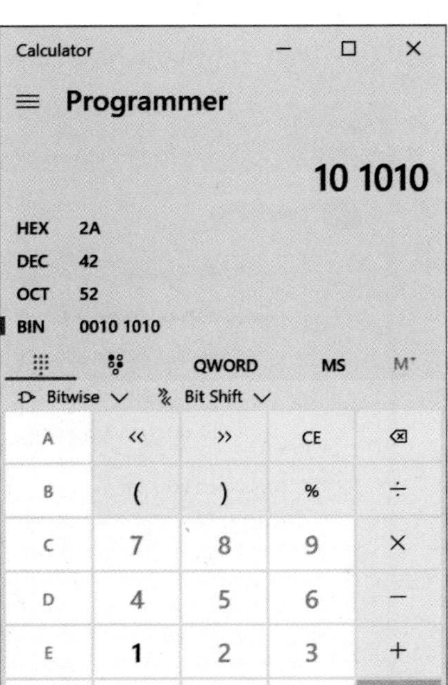

• **Figure 6.12** Converting decimal to binary with Windows 10 Calculator

> Using a calculator utility to convert to and from binary/decimal is a critical skill for a network tech. Later on you'll do this again, but by hand!

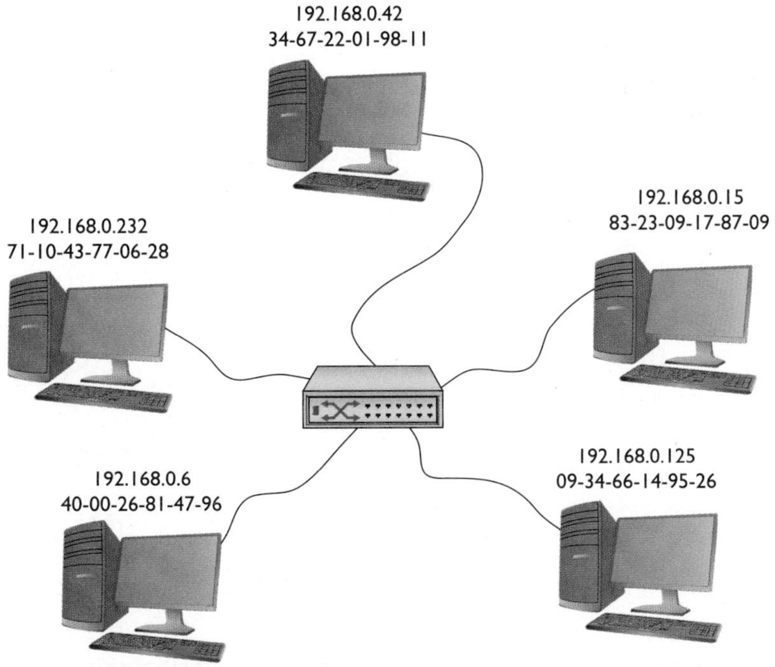

• **Figure 6.13** A small network with both IP and MAC addresses

Every operating system comes with utilities to display a system's IP address and MAC address. Figure 6.14 shows a macOS system's Network utility with TCP/IP information displayed. Note the IP address

(192.168.50.157). Figure 6.15 shows the Hardware information in the same utility, which shows the MAC address.

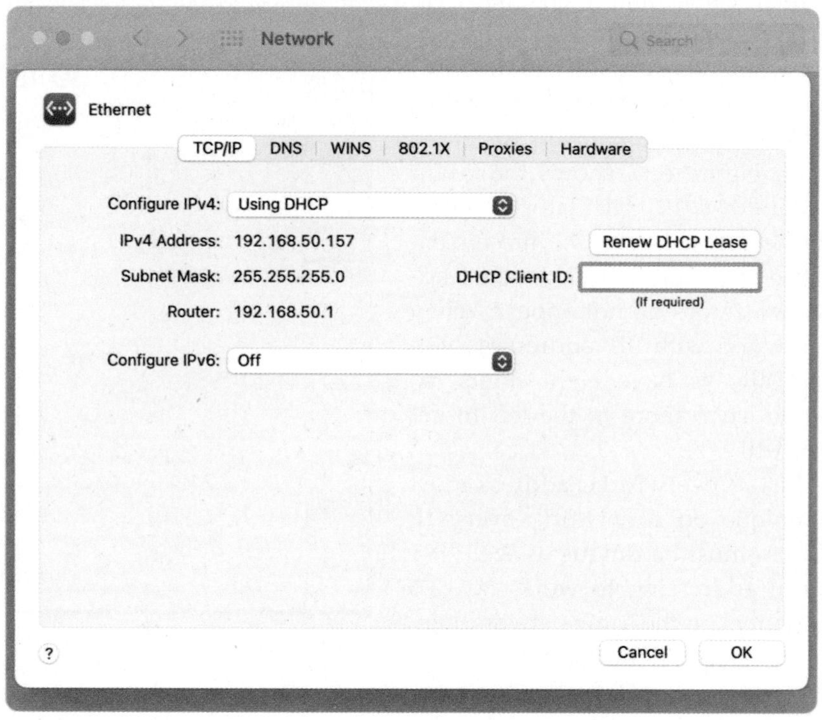

• **Figure 6.14** macOS Network utility

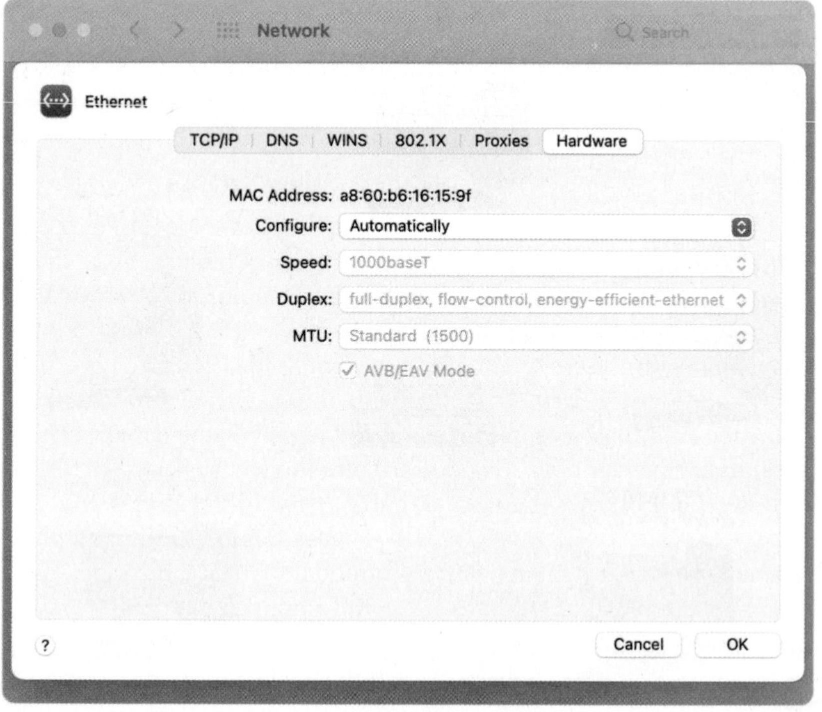

• **Figure 6.15** macOS Network utility displaying a MAC address

Every operating system also has a command-line utility that gives you this information. In Windows, for example, the **ipconfig** command can display the IP and MAC addresses. (The latter requires the /all switch.) Run `ipconfig /all` to see the results shown in Figure 6.16.

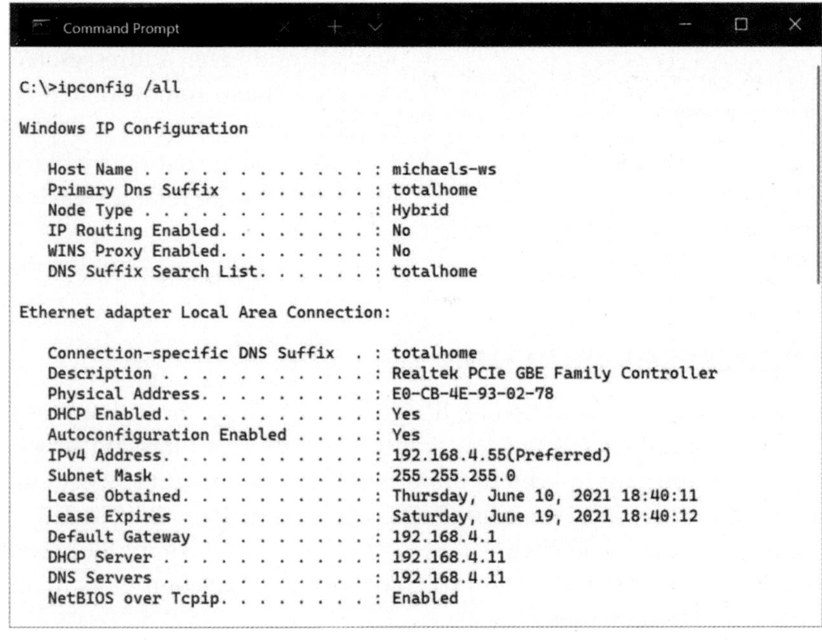

```
C:\>ipconfig /all

Windows IP Configuration

   Host Name . . . . . . . . . . . . : michaels-ws
   Primary Dns Suffix  . . . . . . . : totalhome
   Node Type . . . . . . . . . . . . : Hybrid
   IP Routing Enabled. . . . . . . . : No
   WINS Proxy Enabled. . . . . . . . : No
   DNS Suffix Search List. . . . . . : totalhome

Ethernet adapter Local Area Connection:

   Connection-specific DNS Suffix  . : totalhome
   Description . . . . . . . . . . . : Realtek PCIe GBE Family Controller
   Physical Address. . . . . . . . . : E0-CB-4E-93-02-78
   DHCP Enabled. . . . . . . . . . . : Yes
   Autoconfiguration Enabled . . . . : Yes
   IPv4 Address. . . . . . . . . . . : 192.168.4.55(Preferred)
   Subnet Mask . . . . . . . . . . . : 255.255.255.0
   Lease Obtained. . . . . . . . . . : Thursday, June 10, 2021 18:40:11
   Lease Expires . . . . . . . . . . : Saturday, June 19, 2021 18:40:12
   Default Gateway . . . . . . . . . : 192.168.4.1
   DHCP Server . . . . . . . . . . . : 192.168.4.11
   DNS Servers . . . . . . . . . . . : 192.168.4.11
   NetBIOS over Tcpip. . . . . . . . : Enabled
```

• **Figure 6.16** Result of running `ipconfig /all` in Windows

In macOS, you can run the very similar **ifconfig** command. Figure 6.17, for example, shows the result of running `ifconfig` ("en0" is the NIC) from the terminal.

```
mikesmyer@michaels-mac-ws:~

~
> ifconfig
lo0: flags=8049<UP,LOOPBACK,RUNNING,MULTICAST> mtu 16384
        options=1203<RXCSUM,TXCSUM,TXSTATUS,SW_TIMESTAMP>
        inet 127.0.0.1 netmask 0xff000000
        inet6 ::1 prefixlen 128
        inet6 fe80::1%lo0 prefixlen 64 scopeid 0x1
        nd6 options=201<PERFORMNUD,DAD>
gif0: flags=8010<POINTOPOINT,MULTICAST> mtu 1280
stf0: flags=0<> mtu 1280
en0: flags=8863<UP,BROADCAST,SMART,RUNNING,SIMPLEX,MULTICAST> mtu 1500
        options=50b<RXCSUM,TXCSUM,VLAN_HWTAGGING,AV,CHANNEL_IO>
        ether a8:60:b6:16:15:9f
        inet 192.168.50.157 netmask 0xffffff00 broadcast 192.168.50.255
        nd6 options=201<PERFORMNUD,DAD>
        media: autoselect (1000baseT <full-duplex,flow-control,energy-efficient-ethernet>)
        status: active
en1: flags=8863<UP,BROADCAST,SMART,RUNNING,SIMPLEX,MULTICAST> mtu 1500
        options=400<CHANNEL_IO>
        ether 28:f0:76:69:e7:d6
        media: autoselect (<unknown type>)
        status: inactive
bridge0: flags=8863<UP,BROADCAST,SMART,RUNNING,SIMPLEX,MULTICAST> mtu 1500
        options=63<RXCSUM,TXCSUM,TSO4,TSO6>
        ether 82:19:0a:ee:b2:c0
        Configuration:
                id 0:0:0:0:0:0 priority 0 hellotime 0 fwddelay 0
                maxage 0 holdcnt 0 proto stp maxaddr 100 timeout 1200
                root id 0:0:0:0:0:0 priority 0 ifcost 0 port 0
                ipfilter disabled flags 0x0
        member: en2 flags=3<LEARNING,DISCOVER>
                ifmaxaddr 0 port 7 priority 0 path cost 0
        member: en3 flags=3<LEARNING,DISCOVER>
                ifmaxaddr 0 port 8 priority 0 path cost 0
        media: <unknown type>
        status: inactive
en2: flags=8963<UP,BROADCAST,SMART,RUNNING,PROMISC,SIMPLEX,MULTICAST> mtu 1500
        options=460<TSO4,TSO6,CHANNEL_IO>
        ether 82:19:0a:ee:b2:c0
        media: autoselect <full-duplex>
        status: inactive
```

• **Figure 6.17** Result of running `ifconfig` in macOS

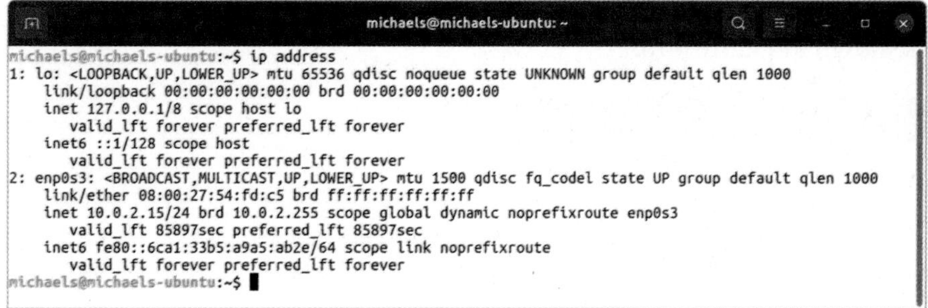

michaels@michaels-ubuntu: ~
michaels@michaels-ubuntu:~$ ip address
1: lo: <LOOPBACK,UP,LOWER_UP> mtu 65536 qdisc noqueue state UNKNOWN group default qlen 1000
link/loopback 00:00:00:00:00:00 brd 00:00:00:00:00:00
inet 127.0.0.1/8 scope host lo
valid_lft forever preferred_lft forever
inet6 ::1/128 scope host
valid_lft forever preferred_lft forever
2: enp0s3: <BROADCAST,MULTICAST,UP,LOWER_UP> mtu 1500 qdisc fq_codel state UP group default qlen 1000
link/ether 08:00:27:54:fd:c5 brd ff:ff:ff:ff:ff:ff
inet 10.0.2.15/24 brd 10.0.2.255 scope global dynamic noprefixroute enp0s3
valid_lft 85897sec preferred_lft 85897sec
inet6 fe80::6ca1:33b5:a9a5:ab2e/64 scope link noprefixroute
valid_lft forever preferred_lft forever
michaels@michaels-ubuntu:~$

• **Figure 6.18** Result of running `ip address` in Ubuntu

On Linux systems, you can run either the newer `ip address` (see Figure 6.18) or the older `ifconfig` from a terminal to display a system's IP and MAC addresses. (A lot of distros have removed net-tools, so `ifconfig` won't be an option.) Note that most distros enable you to shorten the command switch and will fill in the word "address." So `ip addr` or even `ip a` will work.

> Make sure you know that running `ipconfig`, `ifconfig`, and `ip` provides a tremendous amount of information regarding a system's TCP/IP settings.

IP Addresses in Action

Now that you understand that an IP address is nothing more than a string of 32 ones and zeroes, it's time to (finally) see how IP addressing supports WANs. It's important to keep in mind that the IP numbering system must support both WANs and the many LANs connected by the WANs. This can create problems in some circumstances, such as when a computer needs to send data both to computers in its own network and to computers in other networks at the same time.

To make all this work, the IP numbering system must do three things:

- Create network IDs, a way to use IP addresses so that each LAN has its own identification.
- Interconnect the LANs using routers and give those routers some way to use the network ID to send packets to the right network.
- Use a subnet mask to give each computer on the network a way to recognize if a packet is for the LAN or for a computer on the WAN, so it knows how to handle the packet.

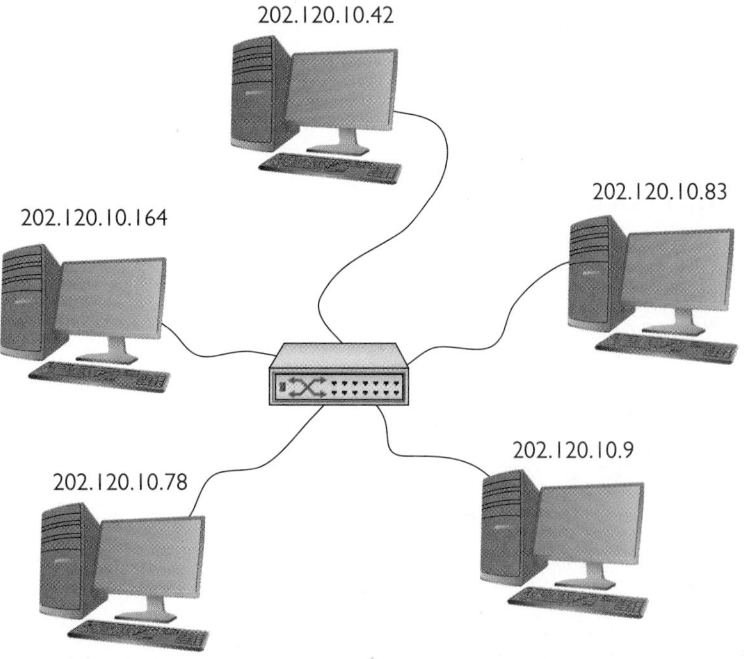

• **Figure 6.19** IP addresses for a LAN

Network IDs

A WAN is nothing more than a group of two or more interconnected LANs. For a WAN to work, each LAN needs some form of unique identifier called a network ID.

To differentiate LANs from one another, each computer on a single LAN must share a very similar, but not identical, IP address. Some parts of the IP address will match all the others on the LAN. Figure 6.19 shows a LAN where all the computers share the first three numbers of the IP address, with only the last number being unique on each system.

In this example, every computer has an IP address of 202.120.10.x, where the x value is unique for every host, but every host's IP address starts with 202.120.10. That means the **network ID** is 202.120.10.0. The x part of the

IP address is the **host ID**. Combine the network ID (after dropping the ending 0) with the host ID to get an individual system's IP address. No individual computer can have an IP address that ends with 0 because that is reserved for network IDs.

> Two things to note here. First, the network ID and the host ID are combined to make a system's IP address. Second, a host ID *can* end in 0—as long as it isn't *all* zeroes—but we have to discuss subnetting before any of this will make sense. Read on!

Interconnecting LANs

To organize all those individual LANs into a larger network, every TCP/IP LAN that wants to connect to another TCP/IP LAN must have a router connection. There is no exception to this critical rule. A router, therefore, needs an IP address on every LAN that it interconnects (Figure 6.20), so it can correctly send (route) the packets to the correct LAN.

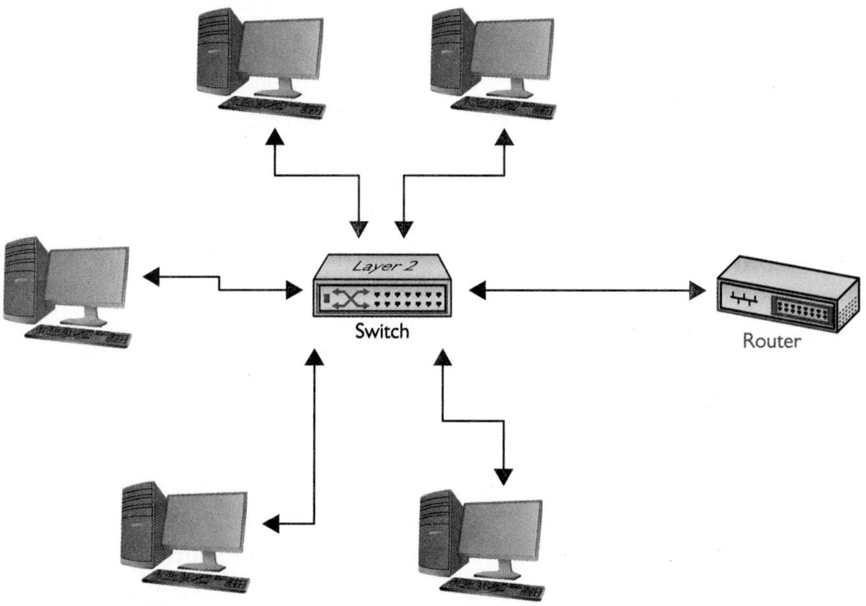

When you have a router that routes traffic out to other networks, both the router's interface on a LAN and the router itself are called the **default gateway**. In a typical scenario configuring a client to access the network beyond the router, you use the IP address of the default gateway. The default gateway is in the same network ID as the host. The network administrator who sets up the router must make sure to configure the router's LAN interface to have an address in the LAN's network ID. By convention, most network administrators give the LAN-side NIC on the default gateway the lowest or highest host address in the network. Therefore, if a network ID is 22.33.4.*x*, the router might be configured to use the address 22.33.4.1 or 22.33.4.254.

• **Figure 6.20** LAN with router

Routers use network IDs to determine network traffic. Figure 6.21 shows a diagram for a small, two-NIC router similar to the ones you see in many homes. Note that one port (202.120.10.1) connects to the LAN and the other port connects to the Internet service provider's network (14.23.54.223). Built into this router is a **routing table**: the actual instructions that tell the router what to do with incoming packets and where to send them.

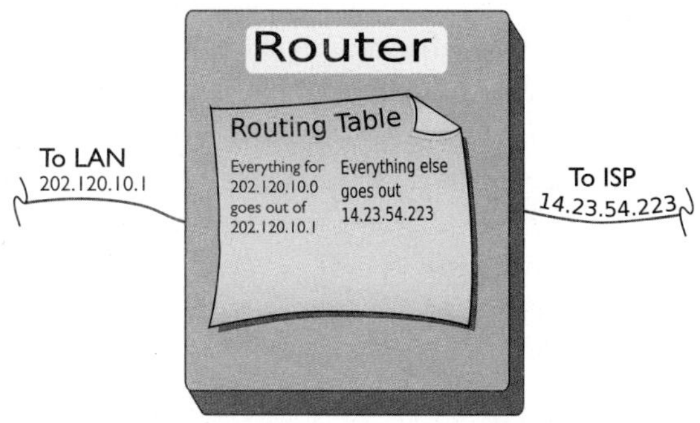

• **Figure 6.21** Router diagram

Routing tables are covered in more detail in Chapter 7, "Routing."

Now let's add in the LAN and the Internet (Figure 6.22). When discussing networks in terms of network IDs (especially with illustrations in books) the common practice is to draw a circle around an illustrated network. Here, you should concentrate on the IDs—not the specifics of the networks.

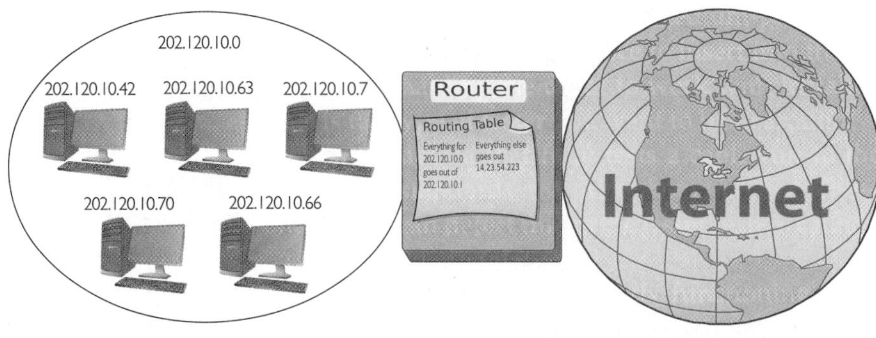

• Figure 6.22 LAN, router, and the Internet

Network IDs are very flexible, as long as no two interconnected networks share the same network ID. If you wished, you could change the network ID of the 202.120.10.0 network to 202.155.5.0, or 202.21.8.0, but only if you can guarantee that no other LAN on the WAN shares the same network ID. On the Internet, powerful governing bodies carefully allocate network IDs to ensure no two LANs share the same network ID. I'll talk more about how this works later in the chapter.

So far, you've only seen examples of network IDs where the last value is zero. This is common for small networks, but it creates a limitation. With a network ID of 202.120.10.0, for example, a network is limited to IP addresses from 202.120.10.1 to 202.120.10.254. (202.120.10.255 is a broadcast address used to talk to every computer on the LAN.) This provides only 254 IP addresses: enough for a small network, but many organizations need many more IP addresses. No worries! You can simply use a network ID with more zeroes, such as 170.45.0.0 (for a total of 65,534 hosts) or even 12.0.0.0 (for around 16.7 million hosts).

Network IDs enable you to connect multiple LANs into a WAN. Routers then connect everything together, using routing tables to keep track of which packets go where. So that takes care of the second task: interconnecting the LANs using routers and giving those routers a way to send packets to the right network.

Now that you know how IP addressing works with LANs and WANs, let's turn to how IP enables each computer on a network to recognize if a packet is going to a computer on the LAN or to a computer on the WAN. The secret to this is something called the subnet mask.

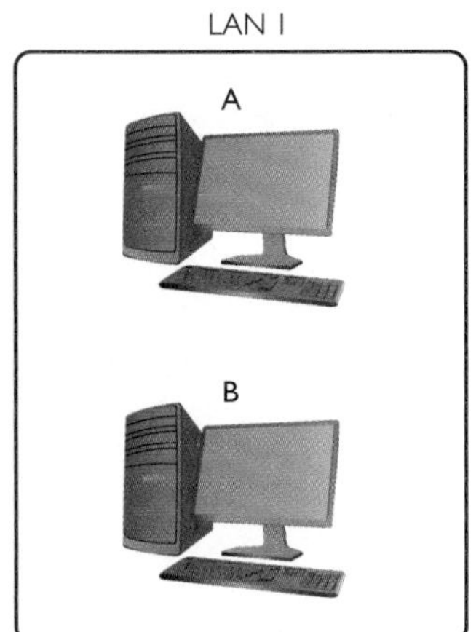

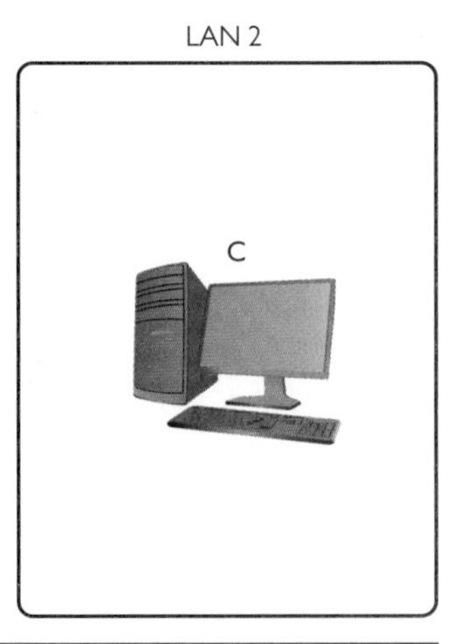

• Figure 6.23 The three amigos, separated by walls or miles

Subnet Mask

Picture this scenario. Three friends sit at their computers—Computers A, B, and C—and want to communicate with each other. Figure 6.23 illustrates the situation. You can tell from the drawing that Computers A and B are in the same LAN, whereas Computer C is on a completely different LAN. The IP addressing scheme can handle this communication, so let's see how it works.

The process to get a packet to a local computer is very different from the process to get a packet to a faraway computer. If one computer wants to send a packet to a local computer, it must send a broadcast to get the other computer's MAC address. (It's easy to forget about the MAC address, but remember that Layer 2 requires the MAC address to get the packet to the other computer.) If the packet is for some computer on a faraway network, the sending computer must send the packet to the default gateway (Figure 6.24).

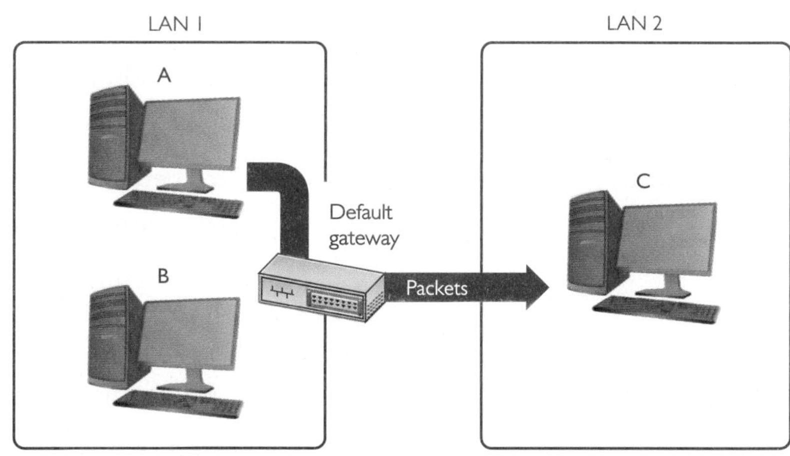

• **Figure 6.24** Sending a packet to a remote location

In the scenario illustrated in Figure 6.23, Computer A wants to send a packet to Computer B. Computer B is on the same LAN as Computer A, but that begs a question: How does Computer A know this? Every TCP/IP computer needs a tool to tell the sending computer whether the destination IP address is local or long distance. This tool is the subnet mask.

A **subnet mask** is nothing more than a string of ones followed by some number of zeroes, always totaling exactly 32 bits, set on every TCP/IP host. Here's an example of a typical subnet mask:

11111111111111111111111100000000

For the courtesy of the humans reading this (if any computers are reading this book, please call me—I'd love to meet you!), let's convert this to dotted decimal. First, add some dots:

11111111.11111111.11111111.00000000

Then convert each octet into decimal (use a calculator):

255.255.255.0

At this point, you should memorize that 0 = 00000000 and 255 = 11111111. You'll find knowing this very helpful throughout the rest of the book.

When you line up an IP address with a corresponding subnet mask in binary, the portion of the IP address that aligns with the ones of the subnet mask is the network ID portion of the IP address. The portion that aligns with the zeroes is the host ID. With simple IP addresses, you can see this with dotted decimal, but you'll want to see this in binary for a true understanding of how the computers work.

The IP address 192.168.5.23 has a subnet mask of 255.255.255.0. Convert both numbers to binary and then compare the full IP address to the ones and zeroes of the subnet mask:

	Dotted Decimal	**Binary**
IP address	192.168.5.23	11000000.10101000.00000101.00010111
Subnet mask	255.255.255.0	11111111.11111111.11111111.00000000
Network ID	192.168.5.0	11000000.10101000.00000101.*x*
Host ID	*x*.*x*.*x*.23	*x*.*x*.*x*.00010111

The explanation about comparing an IP address to a subnet mask simplifies the process, leaving out how the computer uses its routing table to accomplish the goal. We'll get to routing and routing tables in Chapter 7. For now, stick with the concept of the node using the subnet mask to determine the network ID.

Before a computer sends out any data, it first compares its network ID to the destination's network ID. If the network IDs match, then the sending computer knows the destination is local. If they do not match, the sending computer knows it's a long-distance call.

Let's head over to Computer A and see how the subnet mask works. Computer A's IP address is 192.168.5.23. Convert that into binary:

11000000.10101000.00000101.00010111

Now drop the periods because they mean nothing to the computer:

11000000101010000000010100010111

Let's say Computer A wants to send a packet to Computer B. Computer A's subnet mask is 255.255.255.0. Computer B's IP address is 192.168.5.45. Convert this address to binary:

11000000101010000000010100101101

Computer A compares its IP address to Computer B's IP address using the subnet mask, as shown in Figure 6.25. For clarity, I've added a line to show you where the ones end and the zeroes begin in the subnet mask. Computers certainly don't need the line!

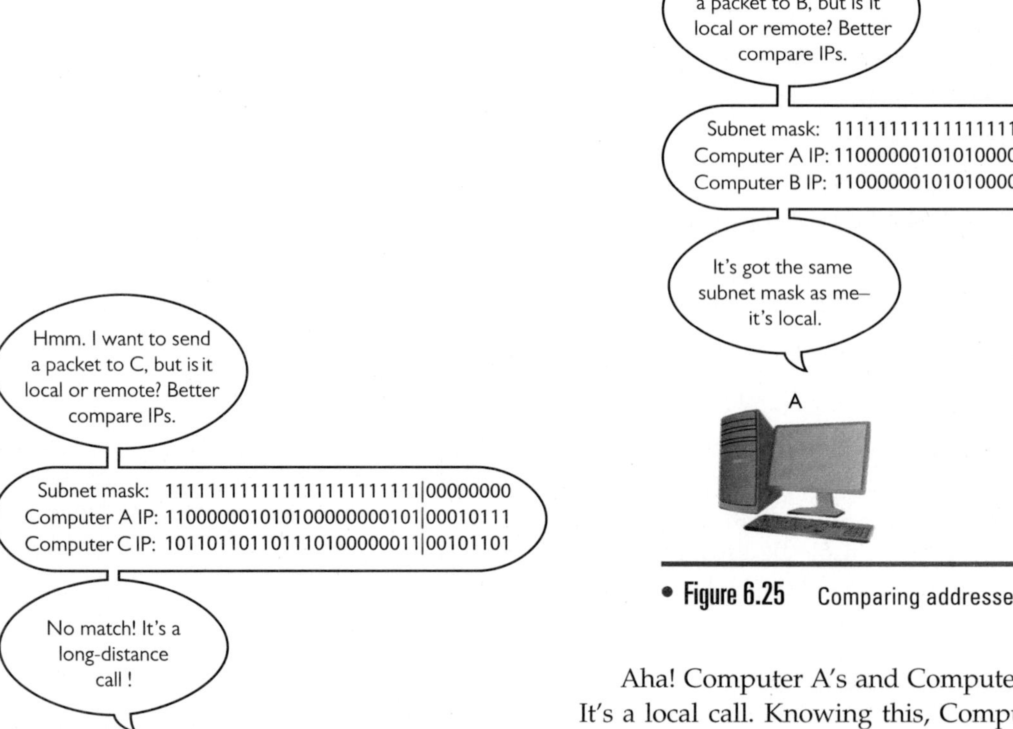

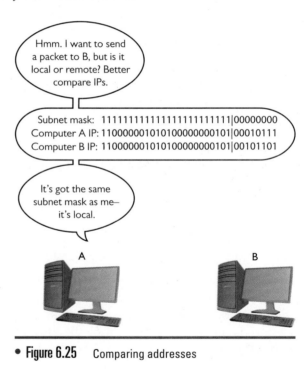

• **Figure 6.25** Comparing addresses

Aha! Computer A's and Computer B's network IDs match! It's a local call. Knowing this, Computer A can now send out an ARP request, which is a broadcast to determine Computer B's MAC address. Address Resolution Protocol (ARP) is how a TCP/IP network figures out the MAC address based on the destination IP address, as you'll recall from earlier in the chapter.

But what happens when Computer A wants to send a packet to Computer C? First, Computer A compares Computer C's IP address to its own using the subnet mask (Figure 6.26).

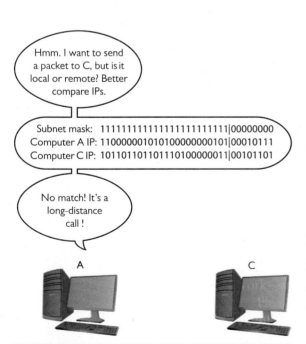

• **Figure 6.26** Comparing addresses again

It sees that the IP addresses do not match in the all-ones part of the subnet mask—meaning the network IDs don't match; therefore, this is a long-distance call.

Whenever a computer wants to send to an IP address on another LAN, it knows to send the packet to the default gateway. It still sends out an ARP broadcast, but this time it's to learn the MAC address for the default gateway (Figure 6.27). Once Computer A gets the default gateway's MAC address, it then begins to send packets.

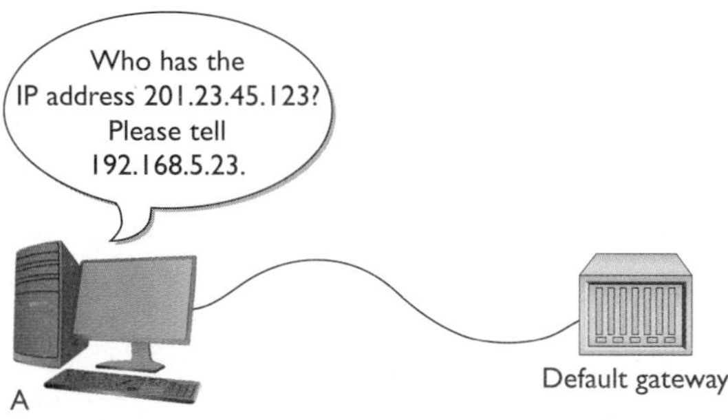
Who has the
IP address 201.23.45.123?
Please tell
192.168.5.23.
A
Default gateway

• **Figure 6.27** Sending an ARP request to the gateway

Subnet masks are represented in dotted decimal like IP addresses—just remember that both are really 32-bit binary numbers. All the following (shown in both binary and dotted decimal formats) can be subnet masks:

11111111111111111111111100000000 = 255.255.255.0
11111111111111110000000000000000 = 255.255.0.0
11111111000000000000000000000000 = 255.0.0.0

Most network folks represent subnet masks using shorthand called *CIDR notation*: a / character followed by a number equal to the number of ones in the subnet mask (CIDR is covered in more depth a bit later in the chapter). Here are a few examples:

11111111111111111111111100000000 = /24 (24 ones)
11111111111111110000000000000000 = /16 (16 ones)
11111111000000000000000000000000 = /8 (8 ones)

An IP address followed by the / and number tells you the IP address and the subnet mask in one statement. For example, 201.23.45.123/24 is an IP address of 201.23.45.123 with a subnet mask of 255.255.255.0. Similarly, 184.222.4.36/16 is an IP address of 184.222.4.36 with a subnet mask of 255.255.0.0.

By definition, all computers on the same network have the same subnet mask and network ID.

Class IDs

The Internet is by far the biggest and the most complex TCP/IP internetwork. Numbering over half a billion computers already a decade ago, it has grown so quickly that now it's nearly impossible to find an accurate number. One challenge for the Internet is to make sure no two devices share the same public IP address. To support the dispersion of IP addresses, an organization called the **Internet Assigned Numbers Authority (IANA)** was

This class system has long since gone the way of the dodo, but techs do still use these classes as shorthand for the private address ranges that organizations and households worldwide use for their internal networks. We'll take a closer look at these private address ranges in the "Special IP Addresses" section at the end of the chapter.

CompTIA and many techs use the term **classful** to describe the traditional class blocks. Thus, you'll see *classful A, B, C, D,* and *E addressing* on the exam. Keep reading and this will make sense.

The Internet Corporation for Assigned Names and Numbers (ICANN) indirectly manages IANA through an affiliate organization, Public Technical Identifiers (PTI). PTI was formed to perform IANA's technical work; ICANN is more focused on policy.

Make sure you memorize the IP class blocks! You should be able to look at any IP address and know its class block. Here's a trick to help: The first binary octet of a Class A address always begins with a 0 (0*xxxxxxx*); for Class B, it begins with a 10 (10*xxxxxx*); for Class C, with 110 (110*xxxxx*); for Class D, with 1110 (1110*xxxx*); and for Class E, it begins with 1111 (1111*xxxx*).

formed to track and disperse IP addresses to those who need them. Initially handled by a single person (Jon Postel) until his death in 1998, IANA has grown dramatically and now oversees five Regional Internet Registries (RIRs) that parcel out IP addresses to ISPs and corporations. The RIR for North America is called the **American Registry for Internet Numbers (ARIN)**. All end users get their IP addresses from their respective ISPs. IANA manages contiguous chunks called **network blocks** (or just **blocks**). Once upon a time, there was a "class" system for organizing and defining these blocks, which is outlined in the following table:

	First Decimal Value	Addresses	Hosts per Network ID
Class A	1–126	1.0.0.0–126.255.255.255	16,777,214
Class B	128–191	128.0.0.0–191.255.255.255	65,534
Class C	192–223	192.0.0.0–223.255.255.255	254
Class D	224–239	224.0.0.0–239.255.255.255	Multicast
Class E	240–255	240.0.0.0–255.255.255.255	Experimental

A typical Class A network block, for example, had a network ID starting between 1 and 126; hosts on that network had only the first octet in common, with any numbers for the other three octets. Having three octets to use for hosts means an enormous number of possible hosts, over 16 million different combinations. The corresponding subnet mask for a Class A network block would be 255.0.0.0, leaving 24 bits for host IDs.

Do you remember binary math? 2^{24} = 16,777,216. Because the host can't use all zeroes or all ones (those are reserved for the network ID and broadcast address, respectively), you should subtract two from the final number to get the available host IDs (both in this example, and in the ones below).

A Class B network block, which would correspond to a subnet mask of 255.255.0.0, used the first two octets to define the network ID. This left two octets to define host IDs, meaning each Class B network ID could have up to $2^{16} - 2$ = 65,534 different hosts. A Class C network block used the first three octets to define only the network ID. All hosts in network 192.168.35.0, for example, would have all three first numbers in common. Only the last octet defined the host IDs, leaving just $2^8 - 2$ = 254 possible unique addresses. The subnet mask corresponding to a Class C block is 255.255.255.0.

Multicast class blocks are used for one-to-many communication (though we don't really refer to them as classes anymore), such as in streaming video conferencing. There are four ways to send a packet: a **broadcast**, which is where every computer on the LAN hears the message; a **unicast**, where one computer sends a message directly to another; an **anycast**, where multiple computers share a single address and routers direct messages to the closest computer; and a **multicast**, where a single computer sends a message to a group of interested computers. Routers use multicast to talk to each other. Experimental addresses are reserved and never used except for occasional experimental reasons. These were originally called Reserved addresses.

IP class blocks worked well for the first few years of the Internet but quickly ran into trouble because they didn't quite fit for everyone. Early on, IANA gave away IP network blocks rather generously, perhaps too generously. Over time, unallocated IP addresses became scarce. Additionally, the IP class block concept didn't scale well. If an organization needed 2000 IP addresses, for example, it either had to take a single Class B network block (wasting 63,000 addresses) or eight Class C blocks. As a result, a new method of generating blocks of IP addresses, called **Classless Inter-Domain Routing (CIDR)**, was developed.

CIDR and Subnetting

The foundation of CIDR is a concept called **subnetting**: taking a single class of IP addresses and chopping it up into multiple smaller groups called subnets. Once upon a time, subnetting was just One Weird Trick organizations used to break up and organize their networks. CIDR makes it possible to extend this subnetting approach to the Internet as a whole. RIRs and ISPs play an important role in taking blocks of IP addresses, breaking them up into multiple subnets, and assigning those subnets to smaller organizations. Subnetting and CIDR have been around for quite a long time now and are a critical part of all but the smallest TCP/IP networks. Let's first discuss subnetting and then visit CIDR.

You need to know how to subnet to pass the CompTIA Network+ exam.

Subnetting

Subnetting enables a much more efficient use of IP addresses compared to class blocks. It also enables you to separate a network for security (separating a bank of publicly accessible computers from your more private computers) and for bandwidth control (separating a heavily used LAN from one that's not so heavily used).

The cornerstone to subnetting lies in the subnet mask. You take an existing /8, /16, or /24 subnet and extend the subnet mask by replacing zeroes with ones. For example, let's say you have a café with public Wi-Fi and two computers in the back office for accounting and monitoring the shop's security cameras (Figure 6.28). Your network ID is 192.168.4.0/24. You want to prevent people who are using the public systems from accessing your private machines, so you decide to set up two physically separate LANs—one for the guests, and one for your own systems—and then assign a subnet to each LAN.

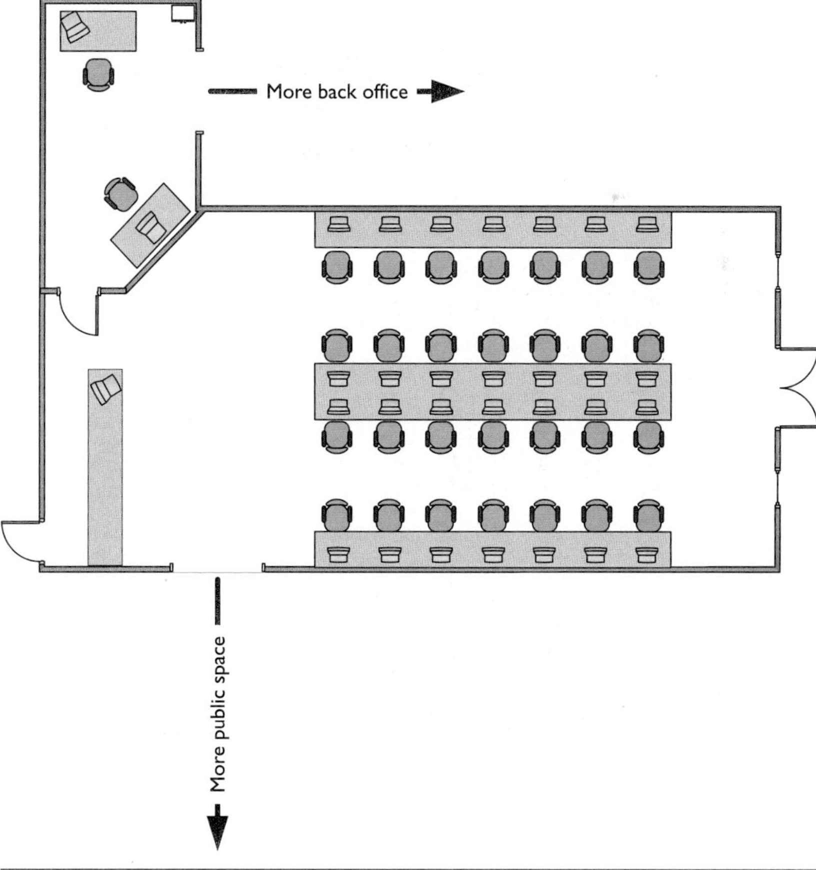

• **Figure 6.28** Layout of the network

You need to keep two things in mind about subnetting. First, start with the given subnet mask and move it to the right until you have the number of subnets you need. Second, forget the dots. They no longer define the subnets.

Classful subnets were always /8, /16, or /24.

Never try to subnet without first converting to binary. Too many techs are what I call "victims of the dots." They are so used to working only with class blocks that they forget there's more to subnets than just /8, /16, and /24 networks. There is no reason network IDs must end on the dots. The computers, at least, think it's perfectly fine to have subnets that end at points between the periods, such as /26, /27, or even /22. The trick here is to stop thinking about network IDs and subnet masks just in their dotted decimal format and instead return to thinking of them as binary numbers.

Let's begin subnetting the café's network of 192.168.4.0/24. Start by changing a zero to a one on the subnet mask so the /24 becomes a /25 subnet:

```
11111111111111111111111110000000
```

Calculating Hosts

Before going even one step further, you need to answer this question: On a /24 network, how many hosts can you have? If you used dotted decimal notation, you might answer as follows:

192.168.4.1 to 192.168.4.254 = 254 hosts

But do this from the binary instead. In a /24 network, you have eight zeroes that can be the host ID:

00000001 to 11111110 = 254

There's a simple piece of math here: $2^x - 2$, where x represents the number of zeroes in the subnet mask. Subtract two for the network ID and broadcast address, just as when calculating the number of hosts in classful addressing.

$2^8 - 2 = 254$

Use this formula to know precisely the number of hosts for a given subnet: 2^x-2, where x=number of zeroes in the subnet mask.

If you remember this simple formula, you can always determine the number of hosts for a given subnet. This is critical! Memorize this!

If you have a /16 subnet mask on your network, what is the maximum number of hosts you can have on that network?

1. Because a subnet mask always has 32 digits, a /16 subnet means you have 16 zeroes left after the 16 ones.
2. $2^{16} - 2$ = 65,534 total hosts.

If you have a /26 subnet mask on your network, what is the maximum number of hosts you can have on that network?

1. Because a subnet mask always has 32 digits, a /26 subnet means you have 6 zeroes left after the 26 ones.
2. $2^6 - 2$ = 62 total hosts.

Excellent! Knowing how to determine the number of hosts for a subnet mask will help you tremendously, as you'll see in a moment.

Making a Subnet

Let's now make a subnet. All subnetting begins with a single network ID. In this scenario, you need to convert the 192.168.4.0/24 network ID for the café into three network IDs: one for the public computers, one for the private computers, and one for the wireless clients.

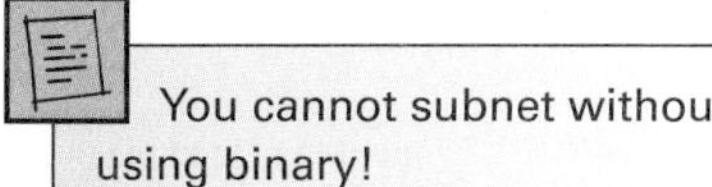

You cannot subnet without using binary!

The primary tool for subnetting is the existing subnet mask. Write it out in binary. Place a line at the end of the ones, as shown in Figure 6.29.

Subnet mask 111111111111111111111111|00000000

• **Figure 6.29** Step 1 in subnetting

Now draw a second line one digit to the right, as shown in Figure 6.30. You've now separated the subnet mask into three areas that I call (from left to right) the default subnet mask (DSM), the network ID extension (NE), and the hosts (H). These are not industry terms, so you won't see them on the CompTIA Network+ exam, but they're a handy Mike Trick that makes the process of subnetting a lot easier.

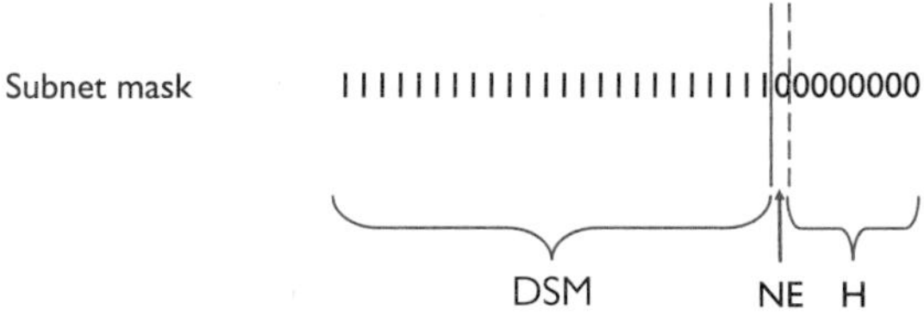

• **Figure 6.30** Organizing the subnet mask

You now have a /25 subnet mask. At this point, most people first learning how to subnet start to freak out. They're challenged by the idea that a subnet mask of /25 isn't going to fit into one of the three pretty subnets of 255.0.0.0, 255.255.0.0, or 255.255.255.0. They think, "That can't be right! Subnet masks are made of only 255s and 0s." That's not correct. A subnet mask is a string of ones followed by a string of zeroes. People only convert the masks into dotted decimal to enter them into computers. So, convert /25 into dotted decimal. First write out 25 ones, followed by 7 zeroes. (Remember, subnet masks are *always* 32 binary digits long.)

```
11111111111111111111111110000000
```

Insert the periods in between every eight digits:

```
11111111.11111111.11111111.10000000
```

Then convert them to dotted decimal:

```
255.255.255.128
```

Get used to the idea of subnet masks that use more than 255s and 0s. Here are some examples of perfectly legitimate subnet masks. Try converting these to binary to see for yourself:

```
255.255.255.224
255.255.128.0
255.248.0.0
```

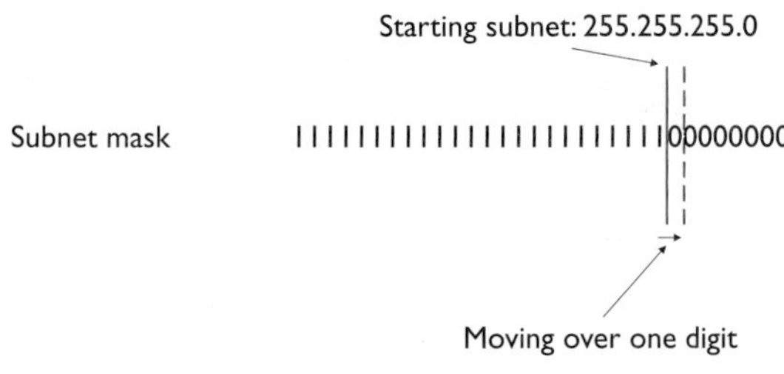

• **Figure 6.31** Initial subnetting

Original network ID: 192.168.4.0 /24
Translates to this in binary:
11000000.10101000.00000100.00000000

11000000101010000000010000000000
11000000101010000000010001000000
11000000101010000000010010000000
11000000101010000000010011000000

• **Figure 6.32** Creating the new network IDs

Calculating Subnets

When you subnet a network ID, you need to follow the rules and conventions dictated by the good folks who developed TCP/IP to ensure that your new subnets can interact properly with each other and with larger networks. All you need to remember for subnetting is this: start with a beginning subnet mask and extend the subnet extension until you have the number of subnets you need. The formula for determining how many subnets you create is 2^y, where y is the number of bits you add to the subnet mask.

Let's practice this a few times. Figure 6.31 shows a starting subnet of 255.255.255.0. If you move the network ID extension over one, it's only a single digit, 2^1.

That single digit is only a zero or a one, which gives you two subnets. You have only one problem—the café needs three subnets, not just two! So, let's take /24 and subnet it down to /26. Extending the network ID by two digits creates four new network IDs, $2^2 = 4$. To see each of these network IDs, first convert the original network ID—192.168.4.0—into binary. Then add the four different network ID extensions to the end, as shown in Figure 6.32.

Figure 6.33 shows all the IP addresses for each of the four new network IDs.

• **Figure 6.33** New network ID address ranges

Now convert these four network IDs back to dotted decimal:

Network ID	Host Range	Broadcast Address
192.168.4.0/26	(192.168.4.1–192.168.4.62)	192.168.4.63
192.168.4.64/26	(192.168.4.65–192.168.4.126)	192.168.4.127
192.168.4.128/26	(192.168.4.129–192.168.4.190)	192.168.4.191
192.168.4.192/26	(192.168.4.193–192.168.4.254)	192.168.4.255

Congratulations! You've just taken a single network ID, 192.168.4.0/24, and subnetted it into four new network IDs! Figure 6.34 shows how you can use these new network IDs in a network.

You may notice that the café only needs three subnets, but you created four—you're wasting one. Because subnets are created by powers of two, you will often create more subnets than you need—welcome to subnetting.

For a little more subnetting practice, let's create eight subnets on a /27 network. First, move the NE over three digits (Figure 6.35).

To help you visualize the address range, I'll calculate the first two subnets—using 000 and 001 (Figure 6.36). Please do the other six for practice.

Note that in this case you only get $2^5 - 2 = 30$ hosts per network ID! These better be small networks!

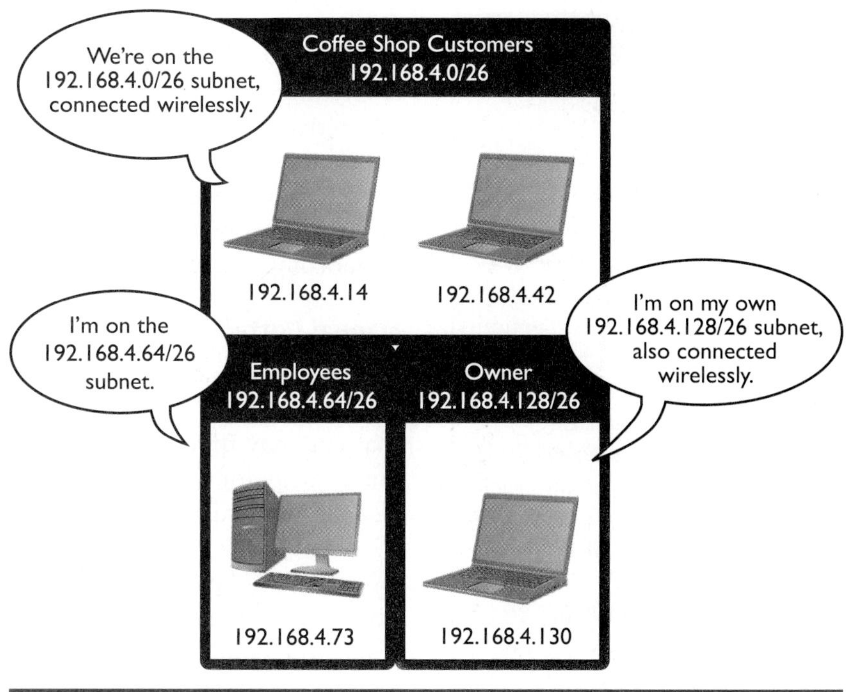

• **Figure 6.34** Three networks using the new network IDs

> If wasting subnets seems contrary to the goal of efficient use, keep in mind that subnetting has two goals: efficiency and making multiple network IDs from a single network ID. This example is geared more toward the latter goal.

```
Subnet mask   11111111111111111111111100000000
192.168.4.0   11000000101010000000010000000000

Add 000       11000000101010000000010000000000
Add 001       11000000101010000000010000100000
Add 010       11000000101010000000010001000000
Add 011       11000000101010000000010001100000
Add 100       11000000101010000000010010000000
Add 101       11000000101010000000010010100000
Add 110       11000000101010000000010011000000
Add 111       11000000101010000000010011100000
```

• **Figure 6.35** Moving the network ID extension three digits

```
11000000101010000000010000100000
11000000101010000000010000100001
11000000101010000000010000100010
:
11000000101010000000010000111101
11000000101010000000010000111110
11000000101010000000010000111111

11000000101010000000010001100000
11000000101010000000010001100001
11000000101010000000010001100010
:
11000000101010000000010001111101
11000000101010000000010001111110
11000000101010000000010001111111
```

• **Figure 6.36** Two of the eight network ID address ranges

Converting these to dotted decimal, you get the following:

192.168.4.0/27 (192.168.4.1–192.168.4.30)
192.168.4.32/27 (192.168.4.33–192.168.4.62)
192.168.4.64/27 (192.168.4.65–192.168.4.94)
192.168.4.96/27 (192.168.4.97–192.168.4.126)
192.168.4.128/27 (192.168.4.129–192.168.4.158)
192.168.4.160/27 (192.168.4.161–192.168.4.190)
192.168.4.192/27 (192.168.4.193–192.168.4.222)
192.168.4.224/27 (192.168.4.225–192.168.4.254)

> CompTIA and many techs refer to a CIDR address as a **classless** address, meaning the subnet used does not conform to the big three on the classful side: A, B, or C. When you see that term on the exam, you'll know you should look for subnetting.

These two examples began with a Class C address. However, you can begin with any starting network ID. Nothing changes about the process you just learned.

Tech Tip

ISPs and Classless Addresses

Assuming you could still order real, unique, ready-for-the-Internet IP addresses from your local ISP (you can't), you'd invariably get a classless set of IP addresses. More importantly, when you work with clients, you need to be able to explain why their subnet mask is 255.255.255.192, when all the books they read tell them it should be 255.255.255.0!

See Chapter 12, "IPv6," for the scoop on IPv6, the addressing scheme gradually replacing IPv4.

The examples used in this introduction to subnetting took a single network ID and chopped it into identically sized subnets. The simplest subnetting example, in other words, created four /26 subnets from one /24 network ID. You can vary the size of the subnets created, however, with classless **variable-length subnet masking (VLSM)**. ISPs might do this to accommodate different customer needs, taking a single network ID and handing out custom subnets. John's tiny company might get a /30 subnet; Jennie's larger company might get a /26 subnet to accommodate many more users.

Manual Dotted Decimal to Binary Conversion

The best way to convert from dotted decimal to binary and back is to use a calculator. It's easy, fast, and accurate. There's always a chance, however, that you may find yourself in a situation where you need to convert without a calculator. Fortunately, manual conversion, although a bit tedious, is also easy. You just have to remember a single number: 128.

Take a piece of paper and write the number **128** in the top-left corner. Now, what is half of 128? That's right, 64. Write **64** next to 128. Now keep dividing the previous number in half until you get to the number 1. The result will look like this:

```
128    64    32    16    8    4    2    1
```

Notice that you have eight numbers. Each of these numbers corresponds to a position of one of the eight binary digits. To convert an 8-bit value to dotted decimal, just take the binary value and put the numbers under the corresponding eight digits. Wherever there's a 1, add that decimal value.

Let's take the binary value 10010110 into decimal. Write down the numbers as shown, and then write the binary values underneath each corresponding decimal number:

```
128    64     32     16     8     4     2     1
  1     0      0      1     0     1     1     0
```

Add the decimal values that have a 1 underneath:

128 + 16 + 4 + 2 = 150

Converting from decimal to binary is a bit more of a challenge. You still start with a line of decimal numbers starting with 128, but this time, you place the decimal value above. If the number you're trying to convert is greater than or equal to the number underneath, subtract it and place a 1 underneath that value. If not, then place a 0 under it and move the number to the next position to the right. Let's give this a try by converting 221 to binary. Begin by placing 221 over the 128:

```
221
128    64    32    16    8    4    2    1
93
1
```

Now place the remainder, 93, over the 64:

```
       93
128    64    32    16    8    4    2    1
       29
1       1
```

Place the remainder, 29, over the 32. The number 29 is less than 32, so place a 0 underneath the 32 and move 29 again, over the 16:

```
                29
128   64   32   16   8   4   2   1
                13
  1    1    0    1
```

Then move to the 8:

```
                    13
128   64   32   16   8   4   2   1
                     5
  1    1    0    1   1
```

Then the 4:

```
                         5
128   64   32   16   8   4   2   1
                         1
  1    1    0    1   1   1
```

Then the 2. The number 1 is less than 2, so drop a 0 underneath and move to 1:

```
                             1
128   64   32   16   8   4   2   1
  1    1    0    1   1   1   0   1
```

Finally, the 1; 1 is equal to 1, so put a 1 underneath and you're done. The number 221 in decimal is equal to 11011101 in binary.

Make sure you can manually convert decimal to binary and binary to decimal.

CIDR: Key Takeaways

Subnetting is a competency everyone who's serious about networking understands in detail—it's a clear separation between those who know networks and those who do not. For the CompTIA Network+ exam, you need to be able to take any existing network ID and break it down into a given number of subnets. You need to know how many hosts the resulting network IDs possess. You need to be able to calculate the IP addresses and the new subnet masks for each of the new network IDs. You need to think of subnets in CIDR terms like /10, /22, /26, and so on.

Expect to see a question or two on the CompTIA Network+ exam that asks you to compare *Classless Inter-Domain Routing (CIDR) notation* (IPv4 vs. IPv6). The former should be familiar, with "notation" meaning the four octets and a /# for the subnet mask. See Chapter 12 for full coverage of IPv6.

You've done well, my little Padawan. Subnetting takes a little getting used to. Go take a break. Take a walk. Play some *World of Warcraft* (I just can't quit!), *Fortnite*, or maybe a few laps in *Forza Horizon*. After a good mental break, dive back into subnetting and *practice*. Take any old network ID and practice making multiple subnets—lots of subnets!

IP Address Assignment

Whew! After all that subnetting, you've reached the point where it's time to start using some IP addresses. That is, after all, the goal of going through all that pain. There are two ways to configure a host's IP settings (for our purposes here, its IP address, subnet mask, and default gateway): either by

The CompTIA Network+ exam objectives use the terms *static assignment* and *dynamic assignment* to describe these static and dynamic addressing methods for setting device IP addresses.

typing in all the information (called **static addressing**) or by having a server program running on a system that automatically passes out all the IP information to systems as they boot up on or connect to a network (called **dynamic addressing**). Additionally, you must learn about several specialty IP addresses that have unique meanings in the IP world to make this all work.

Static IP Addressing

Static addressing means typing all the IP information into each of your hosts. But before you type in anything, you must answer two questions: What are you typing in and where do you type it? Let's visualize a four-node network like the one shown in Figure 6.37.

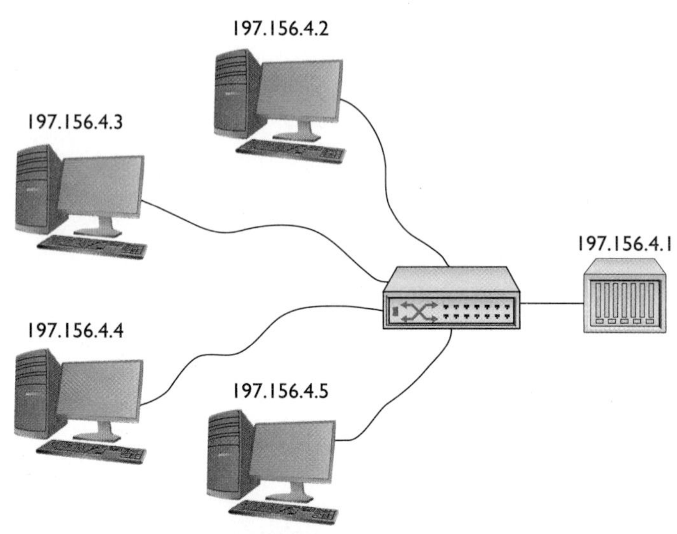

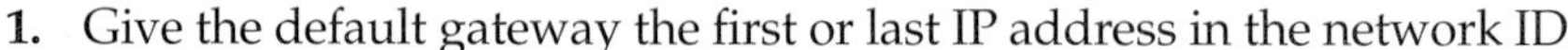

• **Figure 6.37** A small network

To make this network function, each computer must have an IP address, a subnet mask, and a default gateway. First, decide what network ID to use. In the old days, your ISP gave you a block of IP addresses to use. Assume that's still the method and you've been allocated a Class C network block for 197.156.4.0/24. The first rule of Internet addressing is…no one talks about Internet addressing. Actually, we can maul the *Fight Club* reference and instead say, "The first rule of Internet addressing is that you can do whatever you want with your own network ID." There are no rules other than to make sure every computer gets a legit IP address and subnet mask for your network ID and make sure every IP address is unique. You don't have to use the numbers in order, you don't have to give the default gateway the 192.156.4.1 address—you can do it any way you want. That said, most networks follow a common set of principles:

1. Give the default gateway the first or last IP address in the network ID.
2. Try to use the remaining IP addresses in sequential order.
3. Try to separate servers from clients. For example, servers could have the IP addresses 197.156.4.10 to 197.156.4.19, whereas the clients range from 197.156.4.200 to 197.156.4.254.
4. Document whatever you choose to do so the person who comes after you understands.

These principles have become unofficial standards for network techs, and following them will make you very popular with whoever has to manage your network in the future.

Now you can give each of the computers an IP address, subnet mask, and default gateway. Every operating system has some method for you to enter the static IP information. Let's look at how the same configuration looks on Windows, macOS, and Ubuntu Linux. In Windows, you use the Internet Protocol Version 4 (TCP/IPv4) Properties dialog (the older way) or the Edit IP Settings dialog in the Settings app, as shown in Figure 6.38.

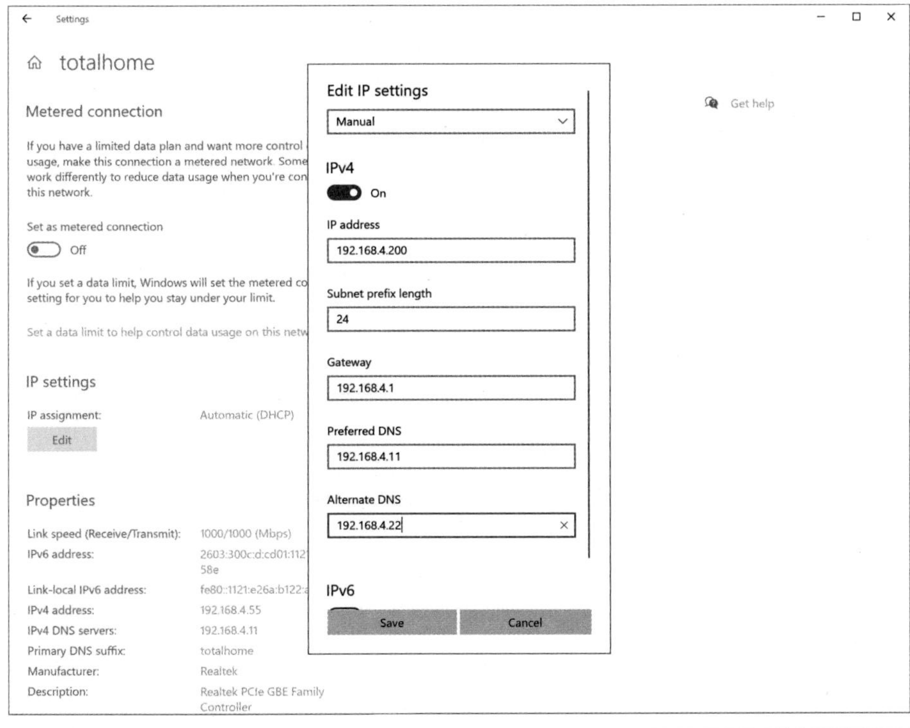

• **Figure 6.38** Entering static IP information in Windows Settings

In macOS, run the Network utility in System Preferences to enter in the IP information (Figure 6.39).

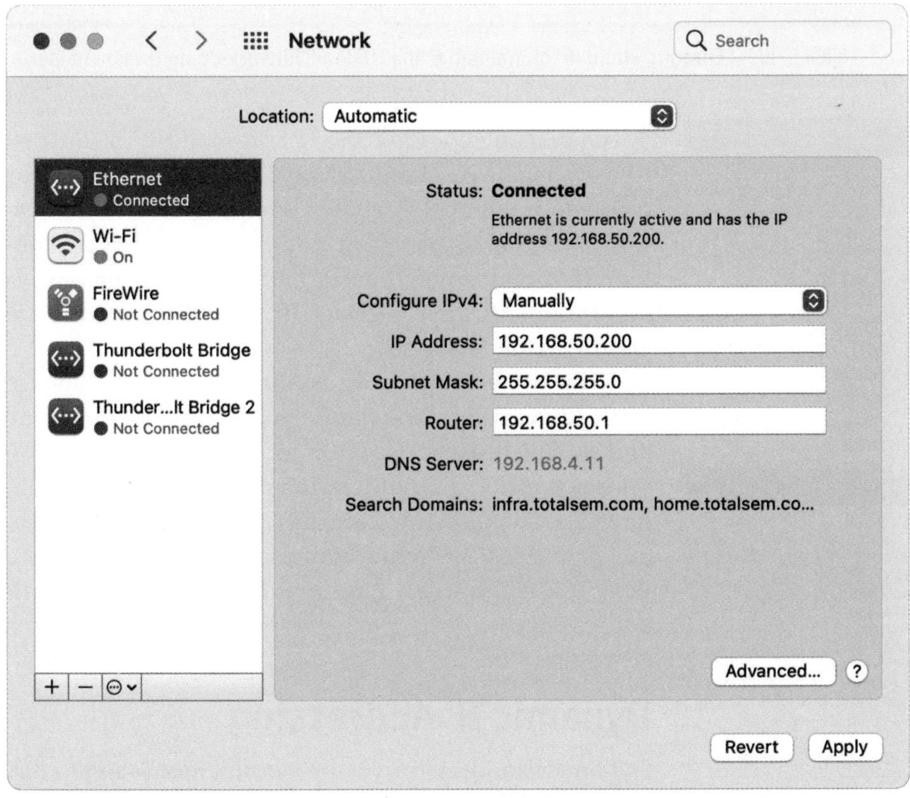

• **Figure 6.39** Entering static IP information in the macOS Network utility

You might get a question about setting a static IP address in Linux where `ip` *isn't* one of the choices. Go with the deprecated `ifconfig` command in that case.

Check out the excellent "Static IP in Linux" Show! over at https://totalsem.com/008. It'll take you through the process of setting up a static IP in a typical Linux distro.

Always verify with ping—it's too easy to make a typo when entering static IP addresses.

The universal tool for entering IP information on UNIX/Linux systems is the command-line `ip` command:

```
# ip addr add 192.168.4.10 dev eth1
```

A warning about setting static IP addresses with `ip`: any address entered will not be permanent and will be lost on reboot. To make the new IP address permanent, you need to find and edit your network configuration files. Fortunately, modern distros make your life a bit easier. Almost every flavor of UNIX/Linux comes with some handy graphical program, such as Network Configuration in the popular Ubuntu Linux distro (Figure 6.40).

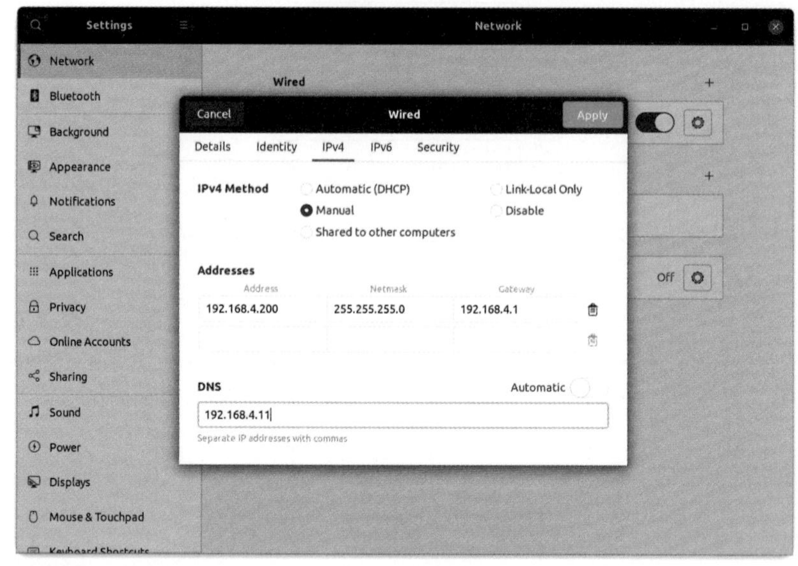

• **Figure 6.40** Entering static IP information in the Ubuntu Network Configuration utility

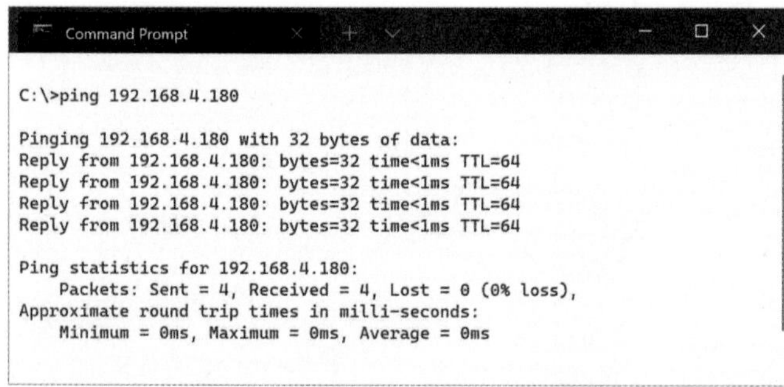

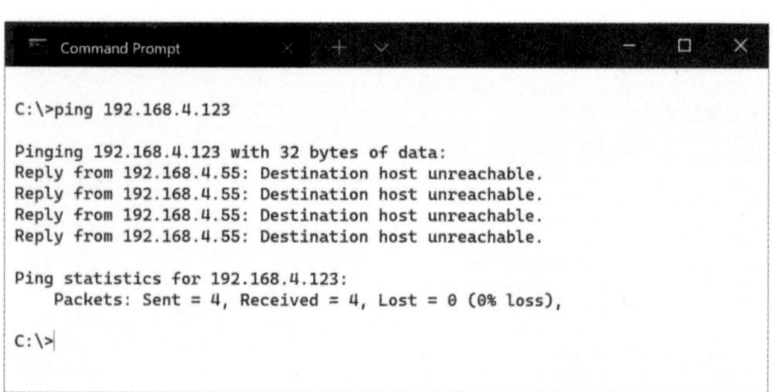

• **Figure 6.41** Successful ping (top) and unsuccessful ping (bottom)

Once you've added the IP information for at least two systems, you should always verify using the `ping` command. Figure 6.41 shows what to expect if the system is reachable and what you'll see if there's a problem. If you've entered an IP address and your ping is not successful, first check your IP settings. Odds are good you made a typo.

Otherwise, check your connections, driver, and so forth. Static addressing has been around for a long time and is still heavily used for more-critical systems on your network. Static addressing poses one big problem, however: making any changes to the network is a serious pain. Most systems today use a far easier and more flexible method to get their IP information: dynamic IP addressing.

Dynamic IP Addressing

Dynamic IP addressing via the **Dynamic Host Configuration Protocol (DHCP)** automatically assigns an IP address whenever a computer connects to the network. DHCP works very simply. Any network using DHCP consists of a DHCP server and DHCP clients. Clients request IP information from DHCP servers. DHCP servers in turn pass out IP information to the clients (Figure 6.42). In most networks, most hosts—desktops, laptops, and mobile devices—are DHCP clients. Most networks have a single DHCP server. It is often built into a router for small office/home office (SOHO) networks, but in enterprise networks the DHCP server program may be one of many running on a rack-mounted server.

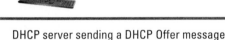

DHCP server

DHCP clients

• **Figure 6.42** DHCP server and clients

How DHCP Works

When a DHCP client boots up, it automatically broadcasts a *DHCP Discover* message. This DHCP Discover message asks, "Are there any DHCP servers out there?" (See Figure 6.43.)

The DHCP server hears the request and then sends the DHCP client a *DHCP Offer* message (Figure 6.44). This message includes an IP address, subnet mask, and gateway (as well as other information not yet covered in this book).

Is there a DHCP server out there? I'm wrestling with tough identity issues and need help.

• **Figure 6.43** Computer sending out a DHCP Discover message

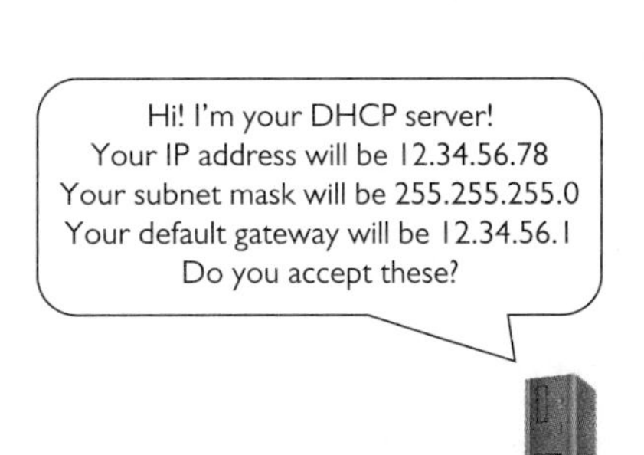
Hi! I'm your DHCP server!
Your IP address will be 12.34.56.78
Your subnet mask will be 255.255.255.0
Your default gateway will be 12.34.56.1
Do you accept these?

• **Figure 6.44** DHCP server sending a DHCP Offer message

The DHCP client sends out a *DHCP Request*—a poor name choice as it is really accepting the offer—verifying that the offer is still valid. The DHCP Request is very important as it tells the network that this client is accepting IP information from this and only this DHCP server.

The DHCP server then sends a *DHCP ACK (Acknowledgment)* and lists the client's MAC address as well as the IP information given to the DHCP client in a database (Figure 6.45).

Now that I'm secure with my identity, I can face the cruel world without fear. Thanks, DHCP server!
No problem. By the way, you've got those addresses for five days. Don't get too comfortable.

• **Figure 6.45** DHCP Request and DHCP Acknowledgment

Using the acronym DORA—for Discover, Offer, Request, and Acknowledgment—will help you remember the DHCP four-way handshake.

DHCP servers use *UDP* port 67 and DHCP clients use port 68. And yes, memorize the numbers.

Check out the excellent Chapter 6 "DHCP Client Setup" Click! over at https://totalsem.com/008. It walks you through the process of setting up DHCP in Windows.

At the end of this four-step DHCP dance (called the **DHCP four-way handshake**, or **DORA**, for Discover, Offer, Request, and Acknowledgment), the DHCP client gets a **DHCP lease** from the pool of *available leases*. A DHCP lease is set for a fixed amount of time, often one to eight days. Near the end of the *lease time*, the DHCP client sends another DHCP Request message.

The DHCP server looks at the MAC address information and always gives the DHCP client the same IP information, including the same IP address.

Configuring DHCP

A properly functioning DHCP network requires properly configured DHCP clients and DHCP servers. Let's look at the configuration of both a client and a server.

Configuring a DHCP client is simple and, in most cases, every host is preconfigured as a DHCP client by default. Every OS has some method to tell the computer to use DHCP, as in the Windows example shown in Figure 6.46.

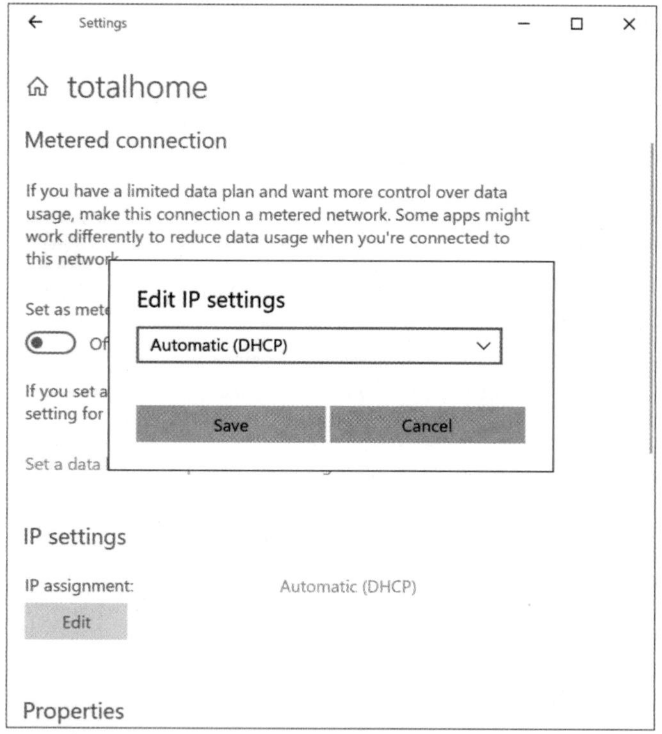

• **Figure 6.46** Setting up for DHCP

DHCP servers, on the other hand, require some hands-on configuration. Consider what a DHCP server requires:

- It needs a pool of legitimate IP addresses that it can pass out to clients.
- It needs to know the subnet mask for the network.
- It needs to know the IP address for the default gateway for the network.

When a technician installs a range (or *pool*) of IP addresses, this is called a **DHCP scope**. Figure 6.47 shows a typical home router's DHCP settings. Note that it is passing out a DHCP scope of 192.168.50.2 to 192.168.50.254. It also passes out other information, known as *scope options*, that cover many choices, such as the default gateway, DNS server, Network Time server, and so on. So why is the Default Gateway setting blank? This home router assumes that it is the default gateway (a fairly safe guess), so it automatically passes out its own IP address (configured on a different screen).

Note the settings to enable or disable the DHCP server in Figure 6.47. Since in all but the rarest cases there should only be one DHCP server on a small LAN, it's handy to have an option to disable the DHCP server on this router.

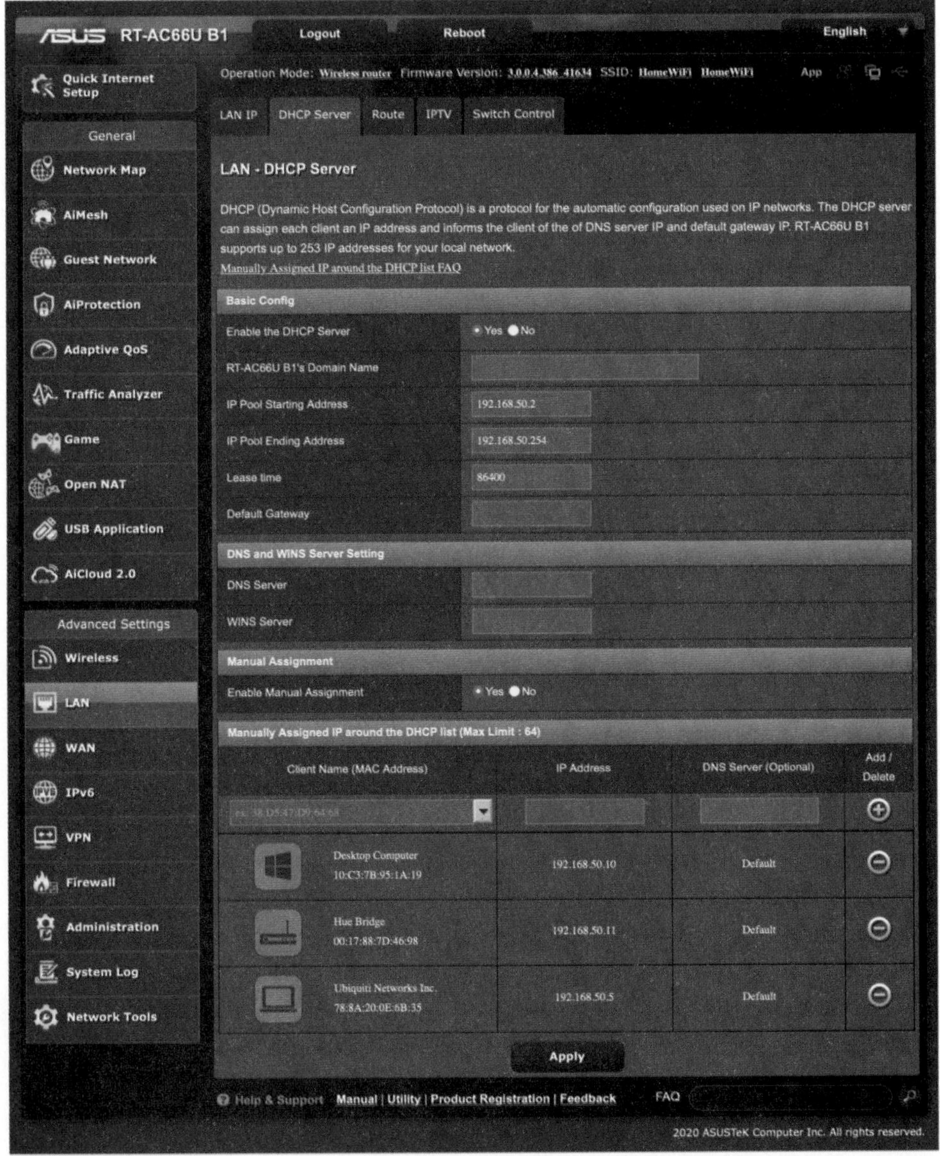

• **Figure 6.47** SOHO DHCP server main screen

DHCP relay is a bit more complex, so let's take some time to understand this powerful feature.

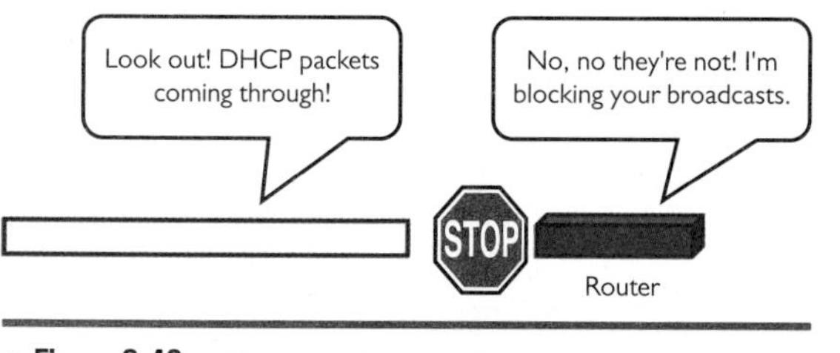

• **Figure 6.48** Routers block DHCP broadcasts.

DHCP Relay DHCP's initial four-way DORA handshake relies on broadcasting to work. (When a client renews its DHCP lease, everything's unicast because the client already has a valid IP address and knows the DHCP server's IP address.) Broadcasting works well within a broadcast domain, but all routers block broadcast traffic (if they didn't, the entire Internet would consist of nothing but broadcasts). See Figure 6.48.

There are situations, however, where it's difficult or impractical to place a DHCP server in the same LAN as the DHCP clients. A single organization with many individual LANs would also need many individual DHCP servers, an administrative nightmare. These cases require the use of a **DHCP relay** (or DHCP relay agent), which enables a router to accept DHCP broadcasts from clients and then use **UDP forwarding** to send them on via unicast addresses directly to the DHCP server (Figure 6.49).

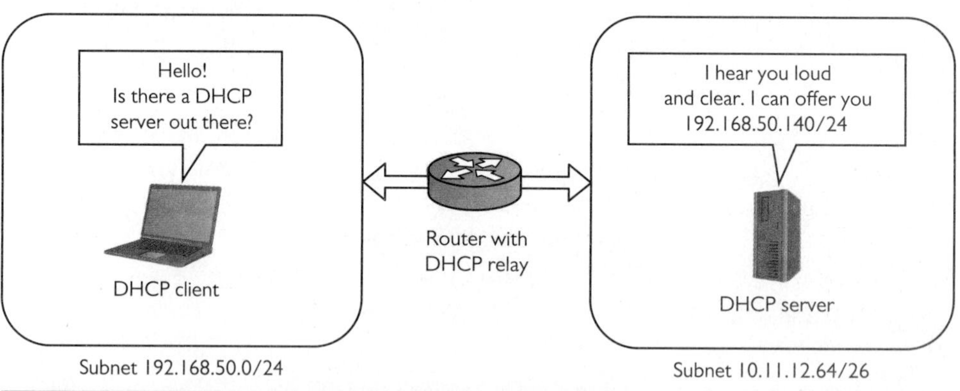

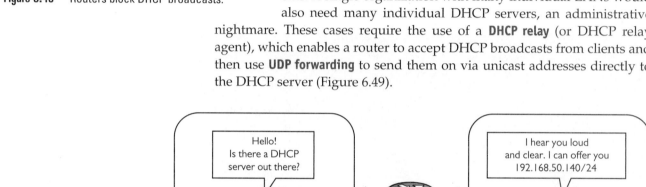

• **Figure 6.49** DHCP relays enable DHCP traffic to cross routers.

To make a DHCP relay–capable device work, you must give the relay the IP address of the real DHCP server. This address is variously known as the **IP helper** address or *UDP helper* address. (The approach you'll need to configure this can vary widely across routers.)

Reservation Many networks contain hosts that we need to be able to reach at a stable IP address. Some devices, such as routers, switches, file servers, printers, and cameras, should never use dynamic IP addresses; users need a permanent, fixed IP address to locate these devices easily (Figure 6.50).

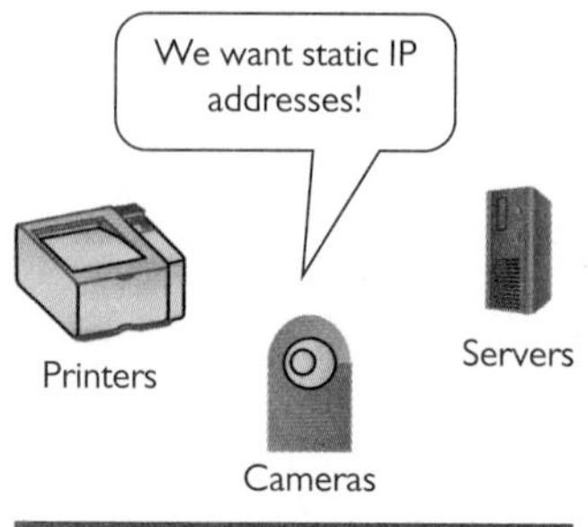

• **Figure 6.50** Many devices do not need DHCP.

When you set up a new network, it's a good idea to set aside IP addresses for these devices and then subdivide the set-aside addresses into chunks for each kind of device. You might, for example, set aside distinct address ranges for your network hardware, servers, workstations, printers, and Wi-Fi clients. Part of deciding how to carve up these addresses is deciding whether each range should be statically or dynamically assigned.

Where the rubber meets the road, there are two approaches to managing the static addresses. The first approach is to reserve the IP addresses to keep DHCP from assigning them and configure each host with a static address. One way to "reserve" some is to just reduce the size of the pool of assignable addresses to avoid that range. The other way is to knock out some of the addresses inside the pool by creating an **IP exclusion range**. Figure 6.51 shows the configuration screen for setting an IP exclusion range in the built-in DHCP tool that comes with Windows Server.

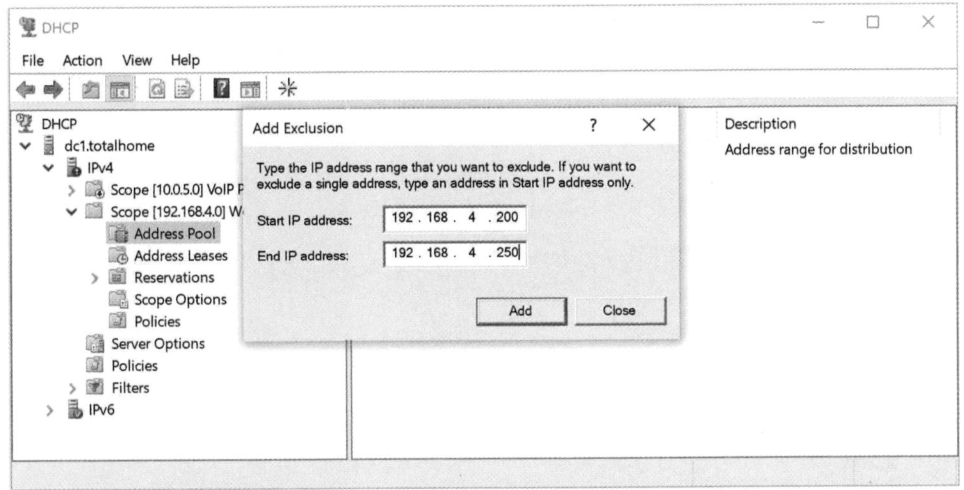

• **Figure 6.51** DHCP Server configuration screen showing IP exclusion range

The other approach is to use the DHCP server to set up **MAC reservations**—enabling DHCP to lease the same address to the same host each time. From then on, any time the system with that MAC address makes a DHCP Request, the reservation guarantees that that system will get the same IP address. Figure 6.52 shows Windows DHCP Server configuring a MAC reservation.

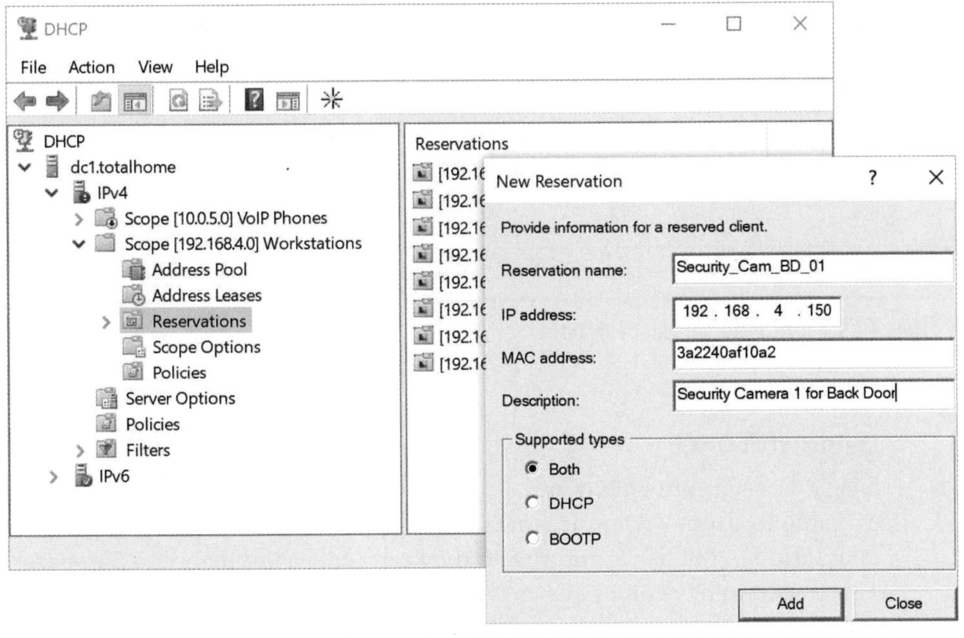

• **Figure 6.52** DHCP Server configuration screen showing a MAC reservation

Figure 6.53 shows Windows DHCP Server's general configuration screen. Note the single scope. Figure 6.54 shows the same DHCP Server tool, in this case detailing the Scope Options. At this point, you're probably not sure what any of these options are for. Don't worry. I'll return to these topics in later chapters.

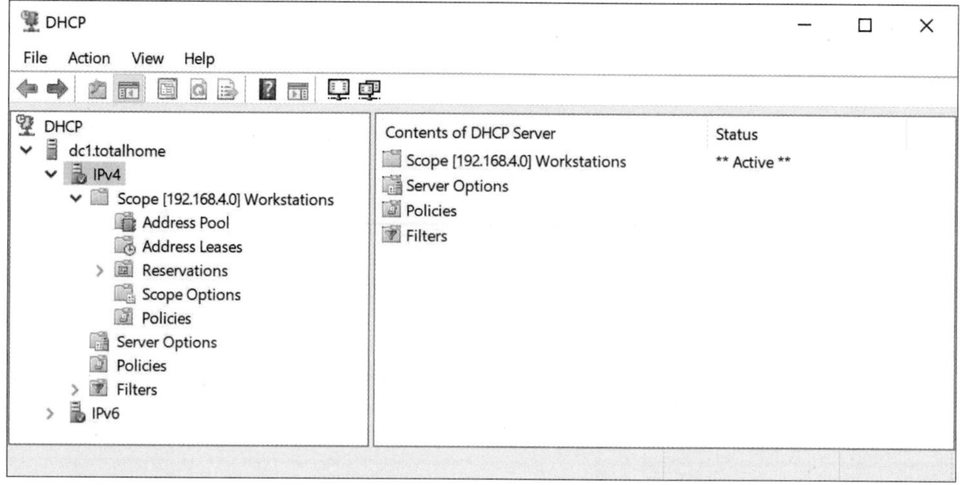

Figure 6.53 DHCP Server configuration screen showing single scope

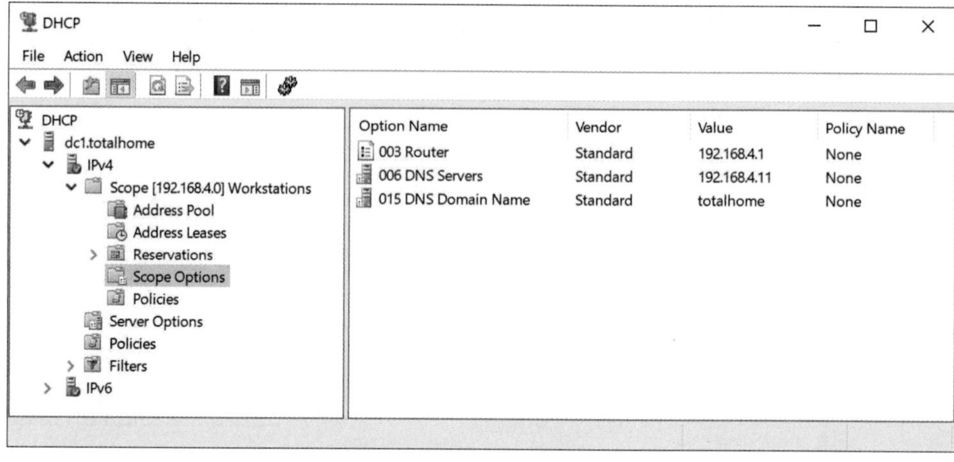

Figure 6.54 DHCP Server Scope Options

Living with DHCP

DHCP is very convenient and, as such, very popular. It's also completely invisible to users—when it works. They just turn on their devices, DHCP does its job in the background, and they can access Netflix or the file server. This transparency comes at a cost; when it breaks, the user may be clueless. Their systems won't get IP information and they won't get on the network. Taking the time to understand a few basic problems that come up with DHCP will help you quickly track down the cause.

No DHCP Server The single biggest issue is when a DHCP client tries to get a DHCP address and fails. You'll know when this happens because the operating system will post some form of error telling you there's a problem (Figure 6.55) and the DHCP client will have a rather strange address in the 169.254.0.0/16 network ID.

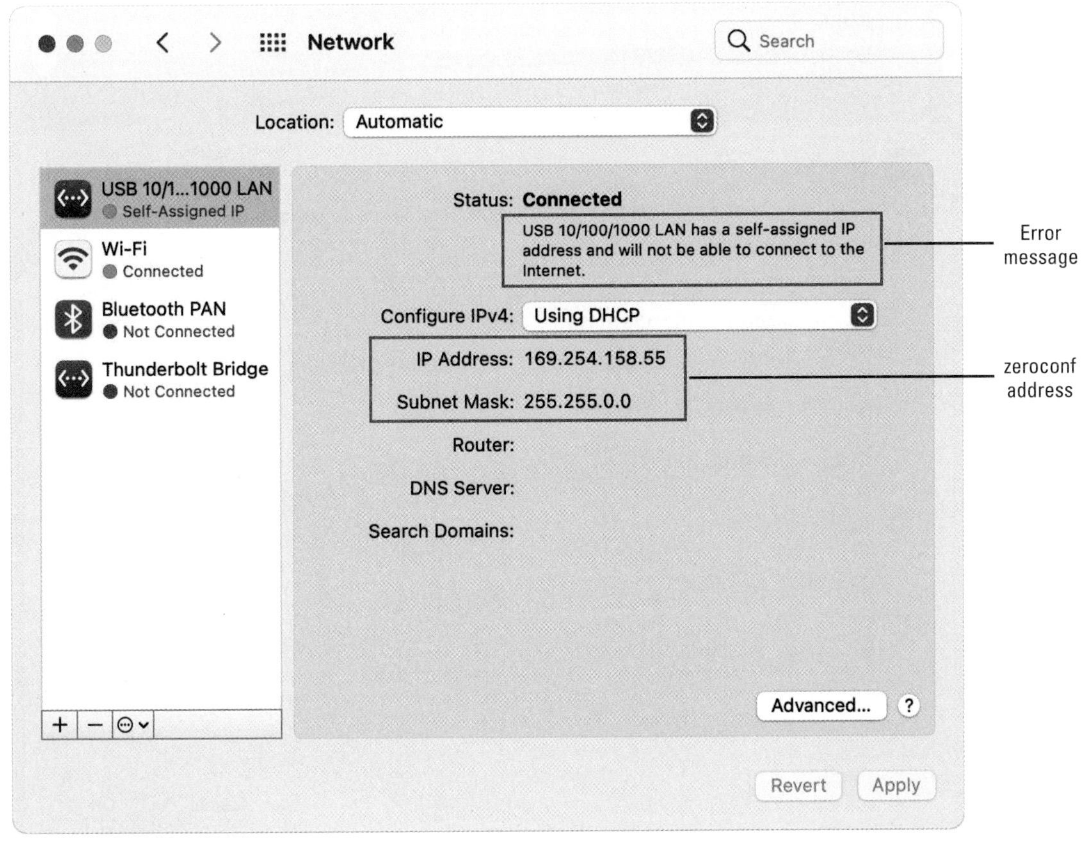

• **Figure 6.55** DHCP error in macOS

This special IP address is generated by a version of **zero-configuration networking (zeroconf)**. Microsoft's implementation is called **Automatic Private IP Addressing (APIPA)**. (That's the one you'll see on the exam.)

All DHCP clients are designed to generate an APIPA address automatically if they do not receive a response to a DHCP Discover message. The client only generates the last two octets of an APIPA address. This at least allows the dynamic clients on a single network to continue to communicate with each other because they are on the same network ID.

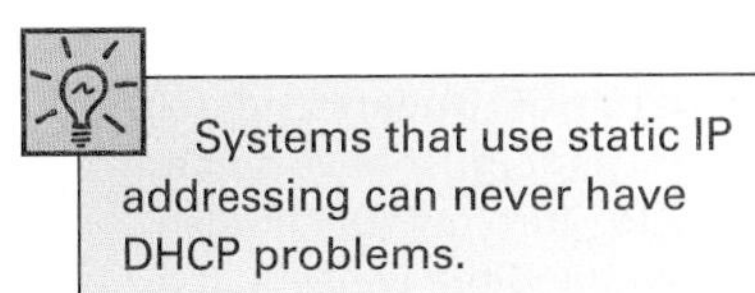

Systems that use static IP addressing can never have DHCP problems.

Unfortunately, APIPA cannot issue a default gateway, so you'll never get on the Internet using APIPA. That provides a huge clue to a DHCP problem scenario: you can communicate with other computers on your network that came up *after* the DHCP server went down, but you can't get to the Internet or access computers that retain the DHCP-given address.

If you can't get to the Internet, use whatever tool your OS provides to check your IP address. If it's an APIPA address, you know instantly that you have a DHCP problem. First, try to reestablish the lease manually.

Every OS has some way to do this. In Windows, you can type the following command:

```
ipconfig /renew
```

With macOS, go to System Preferences and use the Network utility (Figure 6.56).

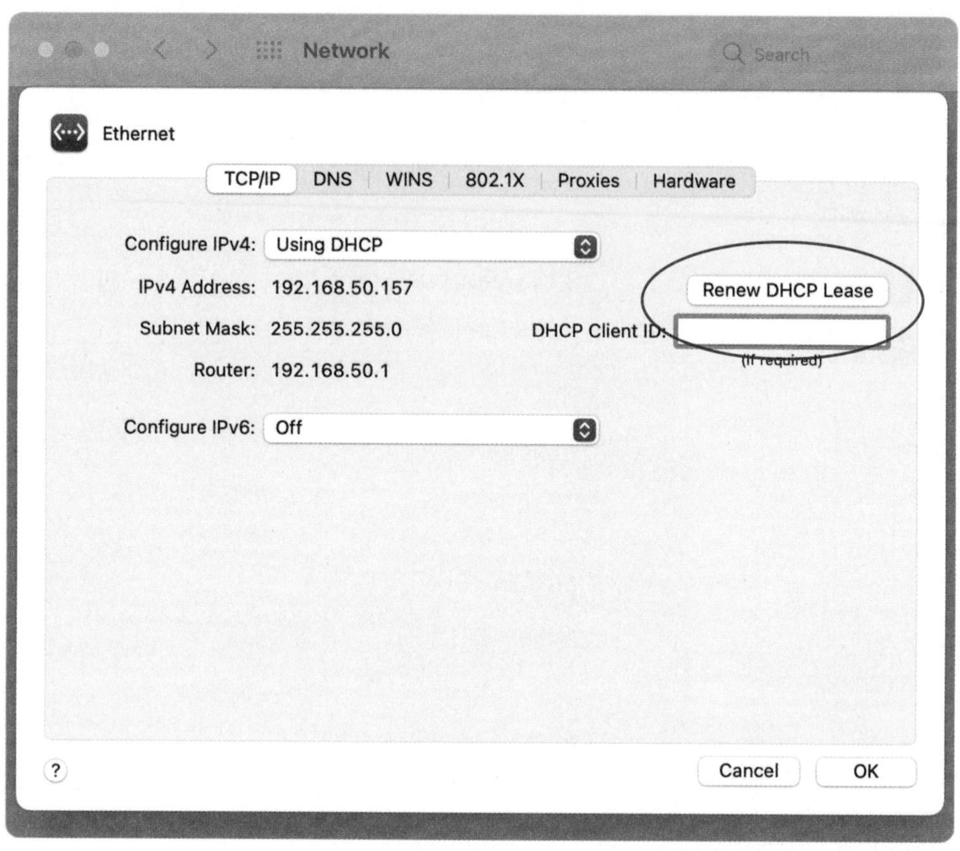

• **Figure 6.56** Network utility in System Preferences

> Make sure you know how to configure your computers to use static IP addressing and know that you use ping to ensure they can communicate. For dynamic IP addressing, make sure you know DHCP. Understand that each client must have some way to "turn on" DHCP. Also understand the concept of a DHCP client and a DHCP server. Be comfortable with APIPA and releasing and renewing a lease on a client.

Sometimes you might find yourself in a situation where your computer gets confused and won't grab an IP address no matter what you try. In these cases, you should first force the computer to release its lease. In Windows, get to a command prompt and type these two commands; follow each by pressing ENTER:

```
ipconfig /release
ipconfig /renew
```

In macOS, use the `ifconfig` command to release and renew a DHCP address. Here's the syntax to release:

```
sudo ifconfig eth0 down
```

And here's the syntax to renew:

```
sudo ifconfig eth0 up
```

Linux can use the deprecated `ifconfig` command with the same syntax as shown for macOS, but a better tool is `dhclient`. Here's the syntax to release, followed by the syntax to renew:

```
sudo dhclient -r
sudo dhclient
```

You might see a question on the CompTIA Network+ exam that asks you to contrast automatically generated IP addresses in IPv4 vs. IPv6. A zeroconf address in IPv4 points to a DHCP failure. IPv6 *always* generates IP addresses automatically. These are called *link-local* addresses and we'll go into detail on them in Chapter 12. Just note that they're normal and expected in IPv6.

Multiple DHCP Servers A lone DHCP server is a single point of failure for a network. If this server dies, at best no one can get on the Internet; at worst, no one can do anything at all. To avoid this problem, bigger networks—think enterprise—run more than one DHCP server. That way it doesn't matter which DHCP server answers. You can do this in a couple ways. Assume you have a network ID of 172.13.14.0. You could configure the two DHCP servers as such:

DHCP Server 1: Scope 172.13.14.200–172.13.14.225

DHCP Server 2: Scope 172.13.14.226–172.13.14.250

Each DHCP server would still use the same subnet mask, default gateway, and so on.

Running two independent DHCP servers doubles the administrative load, so a far more elegant solution is *DHCP failover*. In DHCP failover, two—and only two—DHCP servers work together to provide DHCP for the network. First widely implemented in Windows Server 2012, a DHCP failover pair consists of a primary DHCP server and a secondary DHCP server. As opposed to two independent DHCP servers, the DHCP failover pair shares a single scope. If either fails, the other picks up the load and the end users never notice a thing. DHCP failover is quite common in large networks.

Rogue DHCP Server A DHCP client will accept IP information from the first DHCP server that responds, creating a bit of a problem. It's too easy to add another DHCP server to a network, passing out incorrect IP information to clients. This is called a **rogue DHCP server**. Rogues happen in one of two ways: someone in the organization brings in a home router and innocently plugs it into the network or someone evil is trying to attack your network. In either case, a rogue DHCP server is bad.

An unintentional rogue server is usually easy to detect. Consider this scenario. A legitimate user in your network plugs a home router into a wall outlet in your location with the desire to provide a wireless network for their little corner of the world. Sadly, the router also has a DHCP server running by default. This DHCP server is invariably running a default IP address range such as 192.168.1.0/24, and your network ID should be anything *but* this default. As new DHCP clients request leases, the rogue DHCP server might respond before the legitimate DHCP server. Then the client can't get on the Internet or access local network resources. Anytime a network administrator notices that some users can access resources and some cannot, it's time to check for a rogue DHCP server. Usually a quick `ipconfig` will show DHCP clients with incorrect network IDs.

Let's assume that your network ID is 10.11.12.0/24. A user complains that they can't get on the Internet. You go to the user's machine, run the ipconfig command, and see the following:

```
Ethernet LAN adapter #1:
   Connection-specific DNS Suffix  . : mikemeyers.net
   IPv4 Address. . . . . . . . . . . : 172.18.13.110
   Subnet Mask . . . . . . . . . . . : 255.255.255.0
   Default Gateway . . . . . . . . . : 172.18.13.1
```

A good network administrator would quickly see that this system is gathering incorrect DHCP information from…somewhere. That somewhere is a rogue DHCP server.

Good network admins always know their network IDs!

Malicious rogue DHCP servers can be tougher to detect if they give out IP addresses in the same scope as the legitimate DHCP server, but change the default gateway. This enables the rogue server to intercept or capture incoming and outgoing traffic. What it does with this information depends on the nature of the attack. See Chapter 19, "Protecting Your Network," for the scoop on bad people doing bad things to good networks.

Special IP Addresses

Even though, by convention, you use 127.0.0.1 as the loopback address, the entire 127.0.0.0/8 subnet is reserved for loopback addresses! You can use any address in the 127.0.0.0/8 subnet as a loopback address.

The folks who invented TCP/IP created several special IP addresses you need to know about. The first special address is 127.0.0.1—the **loopback address**. When you tell a device to send data to 127.0.0.1, you're telling that device to send the packets to itself. The loopback address has several uses. One of the most common is to use it with the ping command. I use the command ping 127.0.0.1 to test a computer's network stack.

Make sure you can quickly tell the difference between a public IP address and a private IP address for the CompTIA Network+ exam. The objectives mention the distinction as *public vs. private*.

Lots of folks use TCP/IP in networks that either aren't connected to the Internet or include computers they want to hide from the rest of the Internet. The Engineering Task Force (IETF) set out specific ranges of IP addresses for such uses, known as **private IP addresses**, in *RFC1918*. (RFC is a *Request for Comments*; RFCs are used to define just about everything involving computer networking.) All routers block private IP addresses. Those addresses can never be used on the Internet, making them a handy way to hide systems. Anyone can use these private IP addresses, but they're useless for systems that need to access the Internet—unless you use the mysterious and powerful NAT, which I'll discuss in the next chapter. (Bet you're dying to learn about NAT now!) For the moment, however, let's just look at the ranges of addresses that are designated as private IP addresses:

- 10.0.0.0 through 10.255.255.255 (1 Class A network block)
- 172.16.0.0 through 172.31.255.255 (16 Class B network blocks)
- 192.168.0.0 through 192.168.255.255 (256 Class C network blocks)

All other IP addresses are public IP addresses.

Chapter 6 Review

Chapter Summary

After reading this chapter and completing the exercises, you should understand the following about TCP/IP.

Describe how the TCP/IP protocol suite works

- Whereas MAC addresses are physical addresses burned into the NIC, IP addresses are logical and are assigned via software.
- An IP address consists of 32 binary digits, often written in dotted decimal notation to make it easier for humans to read.
- Every IP address must be unique on its network.
- Run the utilities `ipconfig` (Windows), `ifconfig` (macOS), and `ip` (Linux) to view IP address information.
- Every IP address contains both a network ID and a host ID. Computers on the same network will have the same network ID portion of an IP address, whereas the host ID portion will be unique.
- A network's default gateway is a router that routes traffic to other networks.
- The router uses an internal routing table and network IDs to determine where to send network packets.
- A subnet mask helps to define the network ID of an IP address. All computers on a specific network share the same subnet mask.
- An Address Resolution Protocol (ARP) broadcast is used to determine the MAC address of the destination computer or router based on its IP address.
- Subnet masks are often written with the IP address in slash notation, such as 201.23.45.123/24. In this example, the IP address is 201.23.45.123 and the subnet mask consists of 24 ones, or 11111111.11111111.11111111.00000000 (255.255.255.0).
- The Internet Assigned Numbers Authority (IANA) is the organization responsible for tracking and dispersing IP addresses to Regional Internet Registries (RIRs), which in turn disperse IP addresses to Internet service providers.
- A broadcast is sent to every node on the network. A unicast is sent from one node to one other node. A multicast is sent from one computer to multiple nodes.

Explain CIDR and subnetting

- Subnet masks enable NICs to determine whether incoming packets are being sent to a local network address or a remote network.
- A subnet mask is similar in form to an IP address. Subnet masks consist of some number of ones, followed by zeroes, for a total of 32 bits.
- Subnetting is done by organizations when they need to create multiple networks.
- Classless Inter-Domain Routing (CIDR) is when an ISP subnets a block of addresses and passes them out to smaller customers.
- Any subnet mask outside of the classic /8, /16, or /24 is called a custom subnet mask.
- Computers use subnet masks to distinguish (sub) network IDs from host IDs. Any bit on the full IP address that corresponds to a 1 on the subnet mask is part of the network ID. Any uncovered (turned off or = 0) bits show the host ID of an IP address.
- Assignable IP addresses come in three basic classful address types: Class A, Class B, and Class C.
- The Class A range of addresses has its first octet anywhere from 1 through 126. The default Class A subnet mask is 255.0.0.0.
- A Class B address has its first octet anywhere from 128 through 191. Class B subnets use a mask of 255.255.0.0.
- Class C addresses range from 192 through 223, with the standard Class C subnet mask set to 255.255.255.0.
- Classless subnets do away with neat subnet masks. These subnet masks employ other binary representations in the masking process. For example, 255.255.255.0 is a standard Class C subnet mask, allowing for one subnet of 254 systems. Contrast that example with using subnet mask 255.255.255.240, which would allow for 14 subnets with 14 systems each.

Describe the functions of static and dynamic IP addresses

- Static addressing requires the IP address, subnet mask, and default gateway to be entered manually.

- Dynamic addressing uses Dynamic Host Configuration Protocol (DHCP) to assign an IP address, subnet mask, and default gateway to a network client.
- A network client is assigned an IP address from a DHCP server by exchanging the following messages: DHCP Discover, DHCP Offer, DHCP Request, and DHCP ACK (Acknowledgement).
- The agreement accepted by the DHCP client is called the DHCP lease, which is good for a fixed period of time. The time varies based on how the DHCP server was configured.
- A DHCP client that fails to acquire a DHCP lease from a DHCP server self-generates an IP address and subnet mask via Automatic Private IP Addressing (APIPA). This address falls in the Class B range of 169.254.*x.x*/16.
- The 127.0.0.1 loopback address used in testing is a reserved IP address.
- Private IP addresses include the following ranges:

  10.0.0.0–10.255.255.255 (Class A)

  172.16.0.0–172.31.255.255 (Class B)

  192.168.0.0–192.168.255.255 (Class C)

Key Terms

Address Resolution Protocol (ARP) *(134)*
American Registry for Internet Numbers (ARIN) *(146)*
anycast *(146)*
Automatic Private IP Addressing (APIPA) *(163)*
block *(146)*
broadcast *(146)*
classful *(146)*
classless *(151)*
Classless Inter-Domain Routing (CIDR) *(147)*
datagram *(132)*
default gateway *(141)*
DHCP four-way handshake (DORA) *(158)*
DHCP lease *(158)*
DHCP relay *(160)*
DHCP scope *(159)*
dotted decimal notation *(136)*
dynamic addressing *(154)*
Dynamic Host Configuration Protocol (DHCP) *(156)*
host ID *(141)*
ifconfig *(139)*
Internet Assigned Numbers Authority (IANA) *(145)*
Internet Control Message Protocol (ICMP) *(130)*
Internet Protocol (IP) *(130)*
Internet Protocol version 4 (IPv4) *(130)*
IP addressing *(133)*
IP exclusion range *(161)*
IP helper *(160)*
ipconfig *(138)*
local area network (LAN) *(133)*
loopback address *(166)*
MAC reservation *(161)*
multicast *(146)*
network block *(146)*
network ID *(140)*
private IP addresses *(166)*
protocol *(129)*
protocol suite *(129)*
rogue DHCP server *(165)*
routing table *(141)*
segment *(131)*
static addressing *(154)*
subnet mask *(143)*
subnetting *(147)*
Transmission Control Protocol (TCP) *(131)*
unicast *(146)*
User Datagram Protocol (UDP) *(131)*
variable-length subnet masking (VLSM) *(152)*
wide area network (WAN) *(133)*
zero-configuration networking (zeroconf) *(163)*

Key Term Quiz

Use the Key Terms list to complete the sentences that follow. Not all terms will be used.

1. The _______________ resembles 192.168.17.0.
2. The _______________ portion of an IP address corresponding with the 0 bits in the subnet mask.

3. The single organization that distributes IP addresses to RIRs is called ______________.

4. The IP address 10.11.12.13 is a valid ______________ address.

5. The command ______________ is a utility that comes with Microsoft Windows to show TCP/IP settings.

6. The command ______________ is a utility for UNIX/macOS used to show TCP/IP settings.

7. ______________ is used to resolve IP addresses to MAC addresses.

8. Computers set for dynamic addressing that cannot locate a DHCP server use ______________ to assign themselves an IP address.

9. The router interface on your subnet is commonly known as the ______________.

10. The ______________ is a 32-bit binary number common to all computers on a network that is used to determine to which network a computer belongs.

Multiple-Choice Quiz

1. What is the result of converting 11110000.1011100 1.00001000.01100111 to dotted decimal notation?

   A. 4.5.1.5
   B. 240.185.8.103
   C. 15.157.16.230
   D. 103.8.185.240

2. Eric sits down at a client's Windows computer that's having some network connectivity issues. He wants to start troubleshooting by viewing both the system's IP address and MAC address. What command should he use?

   A. ifconfig
   B. ip addr
   C. ipconfig
   D. ipconfig /all

3. Which of the following describe IPv4? (Select three.)

   A. Uses decimal, not hexadecimal numbers
   B. Uses periods, not colons, as separators
   C. Uses four octets
   D. Uses eight sets of characters

4. What is the result of converting 192.168.0.1 to binary?

   A. 11000000.10101000.00000000.00000001
   B. 11000000.10101000.00000000.10000000
   C. 11000000.10101000.00000000.1
   D. 11.10101.0.1

5. Which of the following are *not* valid IP addresses to assign to a Windows-based system? (Select two.)

   A. 10.1.1.1/24
   B. 127.0.0.1/24
   C. 250.250.250.255/24
   D. 192.168.0.1/24

6. Which of the following is a valid assignable Class A IP address?

   A. 22.33.44.55
   B. 127.0.0.1
   C. 250.250.250.250
   D. 192.168.0.1

7. Phyllis has a service ticket for one of the latest Apple Macs that's having network connectivity problems. What tool could she use to quickly see the IP address and MAC address for that computer?

   A. ifconfig
   B. ip addr
   C. ipconfig
   D. ipconfig /all

8. Which of the following is a valid Class C IP address?

   A. 50.50.50.50
   B. 100.100.100.100
   C. 192.168.0.254
   D. 250.250.250.250

9. Which method sends a packet from a single computer to a group of interested computers? Select the best answer.
   A. Broadcast
   B. Unicast
   C. Multicast
   D. Omnicast
10. What processes are used to take a single class of IP addresses and chop it up into multiple smaller groups? (Select two.)
   A. CIDR
   B. ping
   C. Subnetting
   D. Subnitting
11. Which statements about subnet masks are true? (Select two.)
   A. Every network client has a unique subnet mask.
   B. Every client on a network shares the same subnet mask.
   C. A subnet mask consists of a string of zeroes followed by a string of ones.
   D. A subnet mask consists of a string of ones followed by a string of zeroes.
12. In which order are packets created and sent when a client requests an IP address from a DHCP server?
   A. DHCP Discover, DHCP Offer, DHCP Request, DHCP ACK
   B. DHCP Discover, DHCP Request, DHCP Offer, DHCP ACK
   C. DHCP Request, DHCP Offer, DHCP Discover, DHCP ACK
   D. DHCP Request, DHCP Offer, DHCP ACK, DHCP Discover
13. Which of the following is a valid classful subnet mask?
   A. 255.0.0.0
   B. 255.252.0.0
   C. 255.255.255.192
   D. 255.255.255.255
14. Which command would you use to force a DHCP request on a Windows computer?
   A. ifconfig /all
   B. ifconfig /renew
   C. ipconfig /release
   D. ipconfig /renew
15. Which of the following IP addresses indicates a computer configured for dynamic addressing was unable to locate a DHCP server?
   A. 255.255.255.255
   B. 192.168.1.1
   C. 127.0.0.1
   D. 169.254.1.30

Essay Quiz

1. Use your Web browser to go to the www.webopedia .com Web site. Search for the full term TCP/IP. Write down its definition on a piece of paper, being sure to cite the exact Web site link to give credit to where you obtained the information.
2. You and a classmate are trying to calculate the number of possible IPv4 addresses versus IPv6 addresses. (The TCP/IP powers that be created the IPv6 addressing system to replace the IPv4 system discussed in this chapter. Because I feel IPv6 is extremely important for all techs to understand, this book devotes a full chapter to the subject—Chapter 12.) Research the Internet to discover exactly how many addresses are available for each of these numbering schemes. Document your findings in a short essay.
3. A new intern is confused about the CIDR notation for subnets, such as 192.168.1/26. In your own words, explain to him why the part in front of the slash represents only three of the four octets in an IP address and what the number after the slash is.

Lab Projects

• Lab Project 6.1

Use the Internet to research the components of what an individual TCP packet and an IP packet might look like. You can search on keywords such as "sample," "TCP," "IP," "session," and "packet." Create a reference document that has links to five sites with appropriate information. Save the document, so the links contain hyperlinks that you can click. Then write an additional paragraph describing your overall findings. Print one copy as well.

• Lab Project 6.2

Starting with the IP address 192.42.53.12, create a list of IP address ranges for six subnets.

• Lab Project 6.3

Log in to any available networked Windows computer. Select Start | Run or just Start, type **cmd**, and press ENTER to open a command prompt; from the command prompt, type `ipconfig /all`, and then press ENTER. Fill in as much information as you can from your screen onto a sheet like the following (or create one as directed by your instructor):

Host Name:
Primary DNS Suffix:
Node Type:
IP Routing Enabled:
WINS Proxy Enabled:
DNS Suffix Search List:
Connection-specific DNS Suffix:
Description: Physical Address:
DHCP Enabled:
Autoconfiguration Enabled:
IP Address:
Subnet Mask:
Default Gateway:
DHCP Server:
DNS Servers:
Primary WINS Server:
Lease Obtained:
Lease Expires:

Routing

"Youngsters read it, grown men understand it, and old people applaud it."

—Miguel de Cervantes

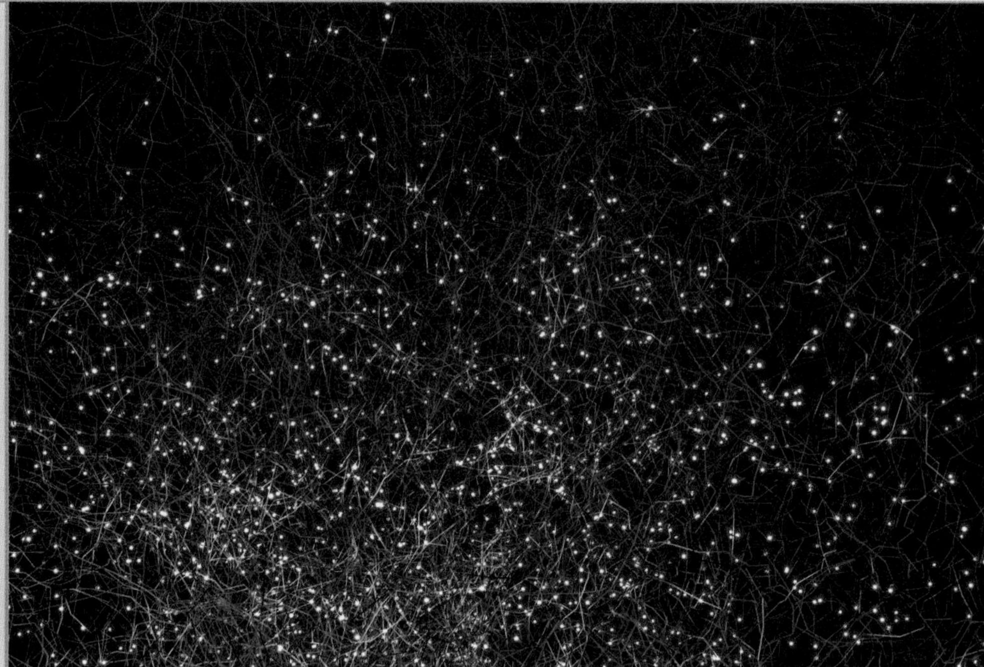

In this chapter, you will learn how to

- **Explain how routers work**
- **Describe dynamic routing technologies**
- **Install and configure a router successfully**

The true beauty and amazing power of TCP/IP lies in one word: routing. Routing enables us to interconnect individual LANs into WANs. Routers, the magic boxes that act as the interconnection points, have all the built-in smarts to inspect incoming packets and forward them toward their eventual LAN destination. Routers are, for the most part, automatic. They require very little in terms of maintenance once their initial configuration is complete because they can talk to each other to determine the best way to send IP packets.

This chapter discusses how routers work, including an in-depth look at different types of network address translation (NAT), and then dives into an examination of various dynamic routing protocols such as Open Shortest Path First (OSPF) and Border Gateway Protocol (BGP). The chapter finishes with the nitty-gritty details of installing and configuring a router successfully. Not only will you understand how routers work, you should be able to set up a router and diagnose common router issues by the end of this chapter.

Historical/Conceptual

How Routers Work

A **router** is any piece of hardware or software that forwards packets based on their destination IP address. Routers work, therefore, at the Network layer (Layer 3) of the OSI model.

• **Figure 7.1** Ubiquiti EdgeRouter Pro router

Classically, routers are dedicated boxes that contain at least two connections, although many routers contain many more connections. The Ubiquiti EdgeRouter Pro shown in Figure 7.1 has eight connections (the Console connection is used for maintenance and configuration). The two "working" connections—labeled WAN and LAN—provide connection points between the line that goes to the Internet service provider (in this case through a cable modem) and the local network. The router reads the IP addresses of the packets to determine where to send the packets. (I'll elaborate on how that works in a moment.) The port marked LTE, by the way, is a failover to a cellular modem connection in case the cable service goes down.

• **Figure 7.2** Business end of a typical home router

Most techs today get their first exposure to routers with the ubiquitous home routers that enable PCs to connect to a cable or fiber service (Figure 7.2). The typical home router, however, serves multiple functions, often combining a router, a switch, a Wi-Fi WAP, and other features like a firewall (for protecting your network from intruders), a DHCP server, and much more into a single box.

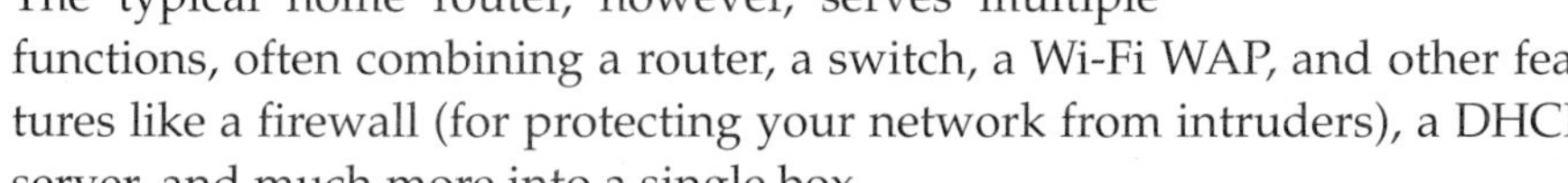

See Chapter 19 for an in-depth look at firewalls and other security options.

Figure 7.3 shows the logical diagram for a two-port router, whereas Figure 7.4 shows the diagram for a home router.

Note that both boxes connect two networks. They differ in that one side of the home router connects directly to a built-in switch. That's convenient! You don't have to buy a separate switch to connect multiple computers to the home router.

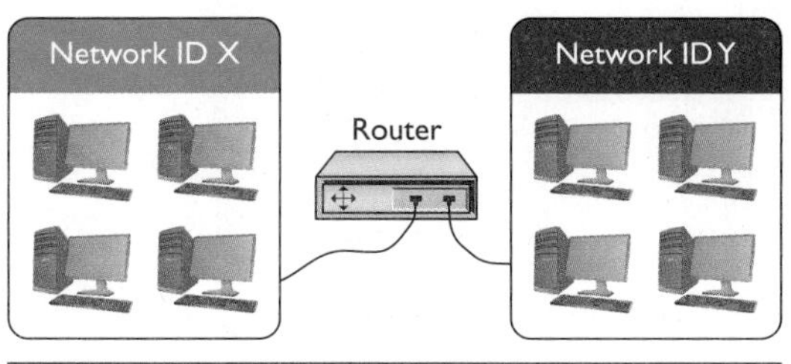

• **Figure 7.3** Router diagram

A switch that works at more than one layer of the OSI model is called a *multilayer switch (MLS)*. An MLS that handles routing is often called a *Layer 3 switch* because it can understand and route IP traffic. The CompTIA Network+ objectives use the term *Layer 3 capable switch*.

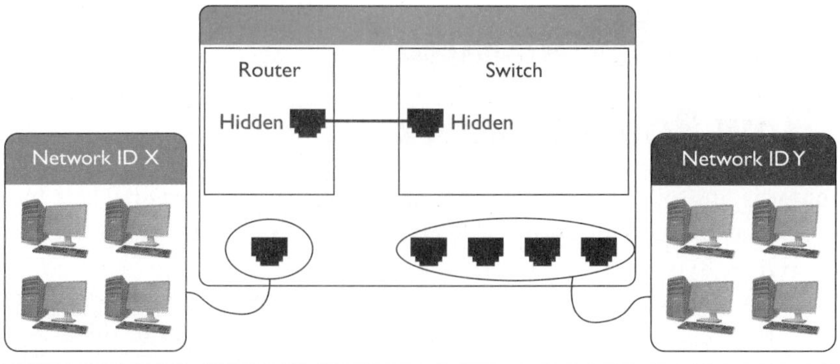

• **Figure 7.4** Home router diagram

All routers—big and small, plain or bundled with a switch—examine packets and then send the packets to the proper destination. Let's look at that process in more detail now.

• **Figure 7.5** Incoming packets

Test Specific

Routing Tables

Routing begins as packets come into the router for handling (Figure 7.5). The router immediately strips off any of the Layer 2 information and queues the resulting IP packet (Figure 7.6) based on when it arrived (unless it's using Quality of Service [QoS], in which case it can be prioritized by a wide array of factors—Chapter 11 takes a closer look at QoS).

• **Figure 7.6** All incoming packets stripped of Layer 2 data and queued for routing

Cross Check

What's Up with Layer 2?

You first read about routers stripping incoming frames of all their Layer 2 (OSI) information way back in Chapter 1, so check your memory now. What defines the Layer 2 information? How is it assigned?

The router inspects each packet's destination IP address and then sends the IP packet out the correct port. To perform this inspection, every router comes with a **routing table** that tells the router exactly where to send the packets. This table is the key to understanding and controlling the process of forwarding packets to their proper destination. Figure 7.7 shows a routing table for a typical home router. Each row in this routing table defines a single route. Each column identifies one of two specific criteria. Some columns define which packets are for the route and other columns define which port to send them out. (We'll break these down shortly.)

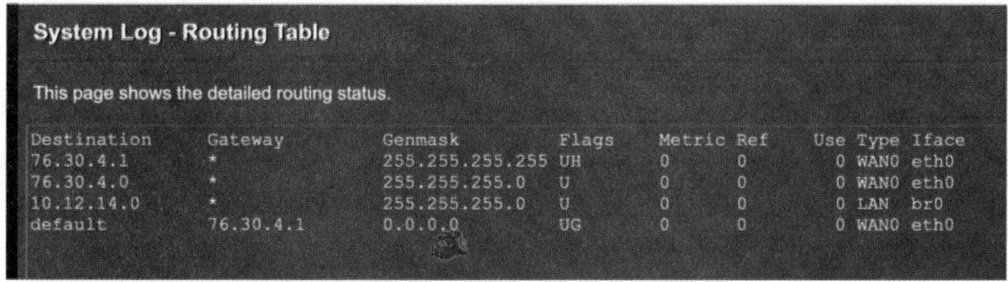

System Log - Routing Table

This page shows the detailed routing status.

Destination	Gateway	Genmask	Flags	Metric	Ref	Use	Type	Iface
76.30.4.1	*	255.255.255.255	UH	0	0	0	WAN0	eth0
76.30.4.0	*	255.255.255.0	U	0	0	0	WAN0	eth0
10.12.14.0	*	255.255.255.0	U	0	0	0	LAN	br0
default	76.30.4.1	0.0.0.0	UG	0	0	0	WAN0	eth0

• **Figure 7.7** Routing table from a home router

The router in this example has only two ports internally: one port that connects to an Internet service provider, labeled as WAN0 eth0 in the Iface and Type columns of the table, and another port that connects to the router's built-in switch, labeled LAN br0 in the table. Due to the small number of ports, this little router table has only four routes. Wait a minute: four routes and only two ports? No worries, there is *not* a one-to-one correlation of routes to ports, as you will soon see. Let's inspect this routing table.

Reading Figure 7.7 from left to right shows the following:

- **Destination** A defined network ID. Every network ID directly connected to one of the router's ports is always listed here.
- **Gateway** The IP address for the **next hop** router—in other words, where the packet should go. If the outgoing packet is for a network ID that's not directly connected to the router, the Gateway column tells the router the IP address of a router to which to send this packet. That router then handles the packet, and your router is done. (Well-configured routers ensure a packet gets to where it needs to go.) If the network ID is directly connected to the router, then you don't need a gateway. If there is no gateway needed, most routing tables put either *, 0.0.0.0, or *On-link* in this column.
- **Genmask** To define a network ID, you need a subnet mask (described in Chapter 6), which this router calls *Genmask*.

(I know, I know, but I have no idea who or what decided to replace the standard term "subnet mask" with "genmask.")

- **Flags** Describes the destination. For instance, U means that the route is up and working. H means this route is a host, or in other words, a complete IP address for a system on the network, not a subnet. G means this is the route to the gateway.
- **Metric, Ref, and Use** Most small networks are simple enough that these values (which are used for picking the best route to a destination) will all be 0. We'll take a closer at these values in the "Routing Metrics" section.
- **Type and Iface** Tell the router which of its ports to use and what type of port it is. This router uses the Linux names for interfaces, so eth0 and br0. Other routing tables use the port's IP address or some other description. Some routers, for example, use Gig0/0 or Gig0/1, and so on.

The router uses the combination of the destination and subnet mask (*genmask*, here) to see if a packet matches a route. For example, if you had a packet with the destination IP address of 10.12.14.26 coming into the router, the router would use the subnet mask to discover the network ID. It would quickly determine that the packet matches the third route shown in Figure 7.8.

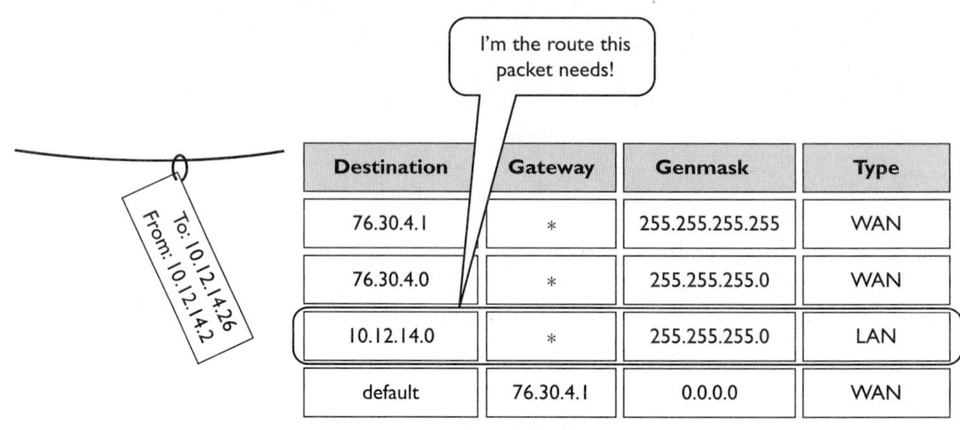

• **Figure 7.8** Routing table showing the route for a packet

A routing table looks like a table, so there's an assumption that the router will start at the top of the table and march down until it finds the correct route. That's not accurate. The router compares the destination IP address on a packet to every route listed in the routing table and only then sends the packet out. If a packet matches more than one route, the router uses the better route (we'll discuss this more in a moment).

The most important trick to reading a routing table is to remember that a zero (0) means "anything." For example, in Figure 7.7, the third route's destination network ID is 10.12.14.0. You can compare that to the subnet mask (255.255.255.0) to confirm that this is a /24 network. This tells you that any value (between 1 and 254) is acceptable for the last value in the 10.12.14.0/24 network ID.

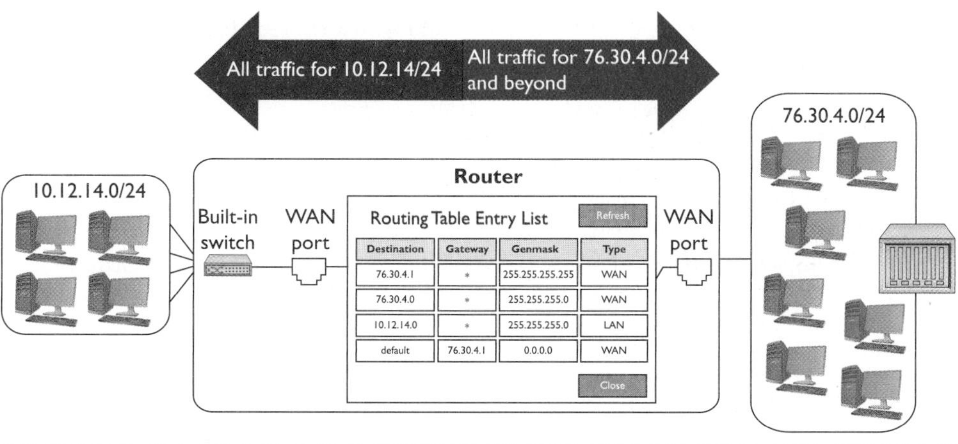

• **Figure 7.9** The network based on the routing table in Figure 7.7

A properly configured router must have a route for any packet it might encounter. Routing tables tell you a lot about the network connections. From just this single routing table, for example, the diagram in Figure 7.9 can be drawn.

Take another look at Figure 7.8. Notice the last route. How do I know the 76.30.4.1 port connects to another network? The fourth line of the routing table shows the default route for this router, and (almost) every router has one. In this case it's labeled "default" so you can't miss it. You'll also commonly see the default destination listed as 0.0.0.0. You can interpret this line as follows:

> *(Any destination address) (with any subnet mask) (forward it to 76.30.4.1) (using my WAN port)*

```
Destination          Gateway        Genmask            Type
    default          76.30.4.1      0.0.0.0            WAN
```

The *default route* is very important because this tells the router exactly what to do with every incoming packet *unless* another line in the routing table gives another route. Excellent! Interpret the other lines of the routing table in Figure 7.7 in the same fashion:

> *(Any packet for the 10.12.14.0) (/24 network ID) (don't use a gateway) (just ARP on the LAN interface to get the MAC address and send it directly to the recipient)*

```
Destination          Gateway        Genmask            Type
 10.12.14.0          *              255.255.255.0      LAN
```

> *(Any packet for the 76.30.4.0) (/24 network ID) (don't use a gateway) (just ARP on the WAN interface to get the MAC address and send it directly to the recipient)*

```
Destination          Gateway        Genmask            Type
  76.30.4.0          *              255.255.255.0      WAN
```

I'll let you in on a little secret. Routers aren't the only devices that use routing tables. In fact, every node (computer, printer, TCP/IP-capable soda dispenser, whatever) on the network also has a routing table. The main difference is that these routing tables also include rules for routing broadcast and multicast packets.

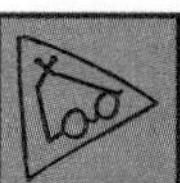

Tech Tip

Top o' the Internet

There are two places where you'll find routers that do not have default routes: isolated (as in not on the Internet) internetworks, where every router knows about every connected network, and the monstrous "Tier One" backbone, where you'll find the routers that make the main connections of the Internet.

At first, this may seem silly—doesn't every computer have a single connection that all traffic has to flow through? Every packet sent out of your computer uses the routing table to figure out where the packet should go, whether directly to a node on your network or to your gateway. Here's an example of a routing table in Windows. This machine connects to the home router described earlier, so you'll recognize the IP addresses it uses. (The results screen of the `route print` command is very long, even on a basic system, so I've deleted a few parts of the output for the sake of brevity.)

```
C:\>route print

IPv4 Route Table
===========================================================================
Active Routes:
Network Destination        Netmask          Gateway       Interface  Metric
          0.0.0.0          0.0.0.0      10.12.14.1    10.12.14.201     25
        127.0.0.0        255.0.0.0         On-link       127.0.0.1    306
        127.0.0.1  255.255.255.255         On-link       127.0.0.1    306
  127.255.255.255  255.255.255.255         On-link       127.0.0.1    306
       10.12.14.0    255.255.255.0         On-link    10.12.14.201    281
     10.12.14.201  255.255.255.255         On-link       127.0.0.1    281
     10.12.14.255  255.255.255.255         On-link    10.12.14.201    281
        224.0.0.0        240.0.0.0         On-link       127.0.0.1    306
        224.0.0.0        240.0.0.0         On-link    10.12.14.201    281
  255.255.255.255  255.255.255.255         On-link       127.0.0.1    306
  255.255.255.255  255.255.255.255         On-link    10.12.14.201    281
===========================================================================
Persistent Routes:
None
```

Tech Tip

Viewing Routing Tables in Linux and macOS

Every modern operating system gives you tools to view a computer's routing table. Most techs use the command line or terminal window interface—often called simply terminal—because it's fast. You can run `ip route` *to show your routing table on Linux, or* `netstat -r` *to show it on both macOS and Windows (and* `route print` *as an alternative on Windows).*

Unlike the routing table for the typical home router you saw in Figure 7.7, this one seems a bit more complicated. My PC has only a single NIC, though, so it's not quite as complicated as it might seem at first glance.

Take a look at the details. First note that my computer has an IP address of 10.12.14.201/24 and 10.12.14.1 as the default gateway. The interface entries have actual IP addresses—10.12.14.201, plus the loopback of 127.0.0.1—instead of the word "LAN." Second—and this is part of the magic of routing—is something called the metric.

A **metric** is a relative value that defines the desirability of a route. Routers often know more than one route to get a packet to its destination. If a route suddenly goes down, then the router could use an alternative route to deliver a packet. Figure 7.10 shows a networked router with two routes to the same network: a route to Network B with a metric of 1 using Route 1, and a second route to Network B using Route 2 with a metric of 10.

When a router has more than one route to the same network, it's up to the person in charge of that router to assign a different metric for each route. With dynamic routing protocols (discussed in detail later in the chapter in "Dynamic Routing"), the routers determine the proper metric for each route.

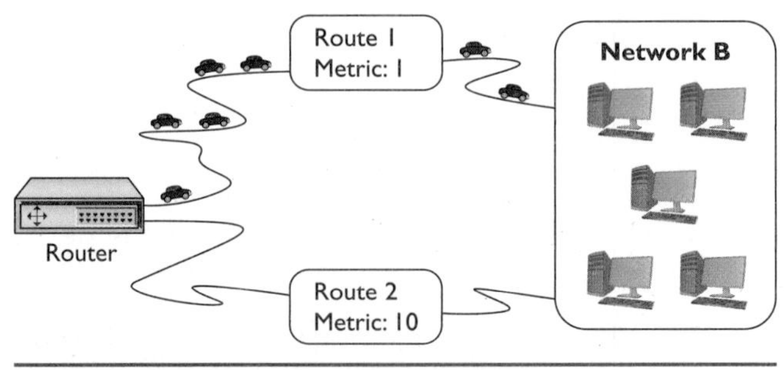

• **Figure 7.10** Two routes to the same network

The route with the lowest metric always wins. In this case, the router will always use the route with the metric of 1, unless that route suddenly stopped working. In that case, the router would automatically switch to the route with the 10 metric (Figure 7.11). This is how the Internet works! The entire Internet is nothing more than a whole bunch of big, powerful routers connected to lots of other big, powerful routers. Connections go up and down all the time, and routers (with multiple routes) constantly talk to each other, detecting when a connection goes down and automatically switching to alternate routes.

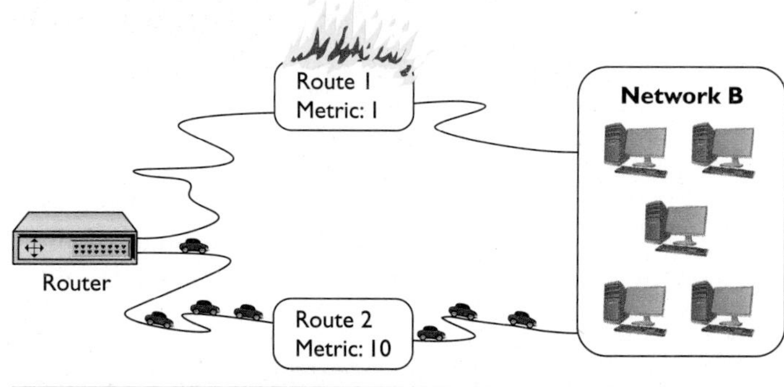

• **Figure 7.11** When a route no longer works, the router automatically switches.

I'll go through this routing table one line at a time. Every address is compared to every line in the routing table before the packet goes out, so it's no big deal if the default route is at the beginning or the end of the table.

The top line defines the default route: (*Any destination address*) (*with any subnet mask*) (*forward it to my default gateway*) (*using my NIC*) (*Metric of* 25 *to use this route*). Anything that's not local goes to the router and from there out to the destination (with the help of other routers).

```
Network Destination        Netmask          Gateway       Interface  Metric
          0.0.0.0          0.0.0.0       10.12.14.1    10.12.14.201      25
```

The next three lines tell your system how to handle the loopback address. The second line is straightforward, but examine the first and third lines carefully. Earlier you learned that only 127.0.0.1 is the loopback, and according to the first route, any packet with a network ID of 127.0.0.0/8 will be sent to the loopback. The third line handles the broadcast traffic for the loopback.

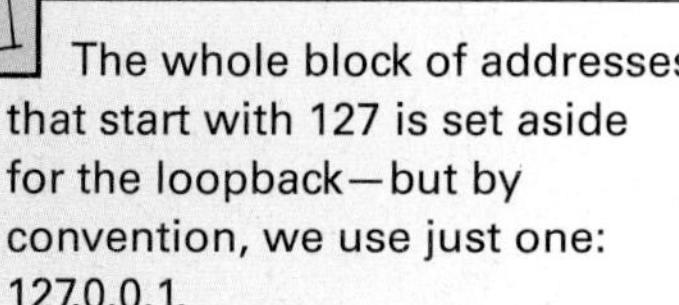

The whole block of addresses that start with 127 is set aside for the loopback—but by convention, we use just one: 127.0.0.1.

```
Network Destination            Netmask    Gateway     Interface    Metric
        127.0.0.0            255.0.0.0    On-link     127.0.0.1       306
        127.0.0.1      255.255.255.255    On-link     127.0.0.1       306
  127.255.255.255      255.255.255.255    On-link     127.0.0.1       306
```

The next line defines the local connection: (*Any packet for the* 10.12.14.0) (/24 *network ID*) (*don't use a gateway*) (*just ARP on the LAN interface to get the MAC address and send it directly to the recipient*) (*Metric of* 1 *to use this route*).

```
Network Destination          Netmask        Gateway       Interface       Metric
       10.12.14.0      255.255.255.0        On-link    10.12.14.201          281
```

Okay, on to the next line. This one's easy. Anything addressed to this machine should go right back to it through the loopback (127.0.0.1).

```
Network Destination            Netmask        Gateway   Interface  Metric
     10.12.14.201      255.255.255.255        On-link   127.0.0.1     281
```

The next line, a *directed* broadcast, is for broadcasting to the other computers on the same network ID (in rare cases, you could have more than one network ID on the same LAN).

```
Network Destination          Netmask        Gateway       Interface  Metric
     10.12.14.255    255.255.255.255        On-link    10.12.14.201     281
```

The next two lines are for the multicast address range. Windows and macOS put these lines in automatically.

```
Network Destination        Netmask         Gateway       Interface    Metric
          224.0.0.0      240.0.0.0         On-link       127.0.0.1       306
          224.0.0.0      240.0.0.0         On-link    10.12.14.201       281
```

The bottom lines each define a limited broadcast.

When you send a limited broadcast (255.255.255.255), it will reach every node on the local network—even nodes with differing network IDs.

```
Network Destination             Netmask         Gateway       Interface    Metric
    255.255.255.255     255.255.255.255         On-link       127.0.0.1       306
    255.255.255.255     255.255.255.255         On-link    10.12.14.201       281
```

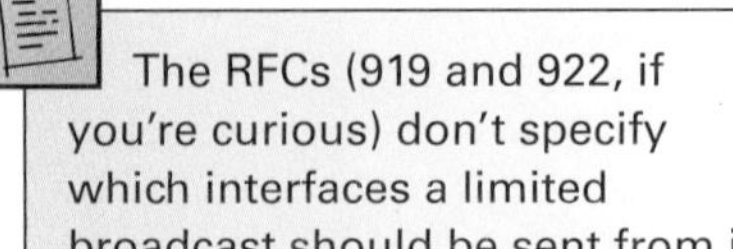

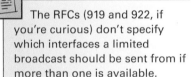

The RFCs (919 and 922, if you're curious) don't specify which interfaces a limited broadcast should be sent from if more than one is available.

Try This!

Getting Looped

Try pinging any 127.0.0.0/8 address to see if it loops back like 127.0.0.1. What happens?

Just for fun, let's add one more routing table—this time from my Ubiquiti EdgeMax router, which is doing a great job of connecting me to the Internet! I access the EdgeMax router remotely from my system using SSH, log in, and then run this command:

```
show ip route
```

Don't let all the output shown next confuse you. The first part, labeled Codes, is just a legend to let you know what the letters at the beginning of each row mean.

```
ubnt@gateway:~$ show ip route
Codes: K - kernel, C - connected, S - static, R - RIP, B - BGP
       O - OSPF, IA - OSPF inter area
       N1 - OSPF NSSA external type 1, N2 - OSPF NSSA external type 2
       E1 - OSPF external type 1, E2 - OSPF external type 2
       > - selected route, * - FIB route, p - stale info
IP Route Table for VRF "default"
S     *> 0.0.0.0/0 [1/0] via 73.155.122.1, eth0
C     *> 73.155.122.0/23 is directly connected, eth0
C     *> 127.0.0.0/8 is directly connected, lo
C     *> 192.168.4.0/24 is directly connected, eth1
```

These last four lines are the routing table. The router has two active Ethernet interfaces called eth0 and eth1. This is how the EdgeMax (which is based on Linux) names Ethernet interfaces.

Reading from the bottom, you see that eth1 is directly connected (the C at the beginning of the line—and it explicitly reveals this as well) to the network 192.168.4.0/24. Any packets that match 192.168.4.0/24 go out on eth1. Next line up, you can see the entry for the loopback device, lo, taking all packets matching 127.0.0.0/8. Second from the top, any packets for the connected 73.155.122.0/23 network go out on eth0. Finally, the top route gets an S for static because it was manually set, not inserted by a routing protocol like OSPF. This is the default route because its route is 0.0.0.0/0.

In this section, you've seen three different types of routing tables from three different types of devices. Even though these routing tables have different ways to list the routes and different ways to show the categories, they all perform the same job: moving IP packets to the correct interface to ensure they get to where they need to go.

Freedom from Layer 2

Routers enable you to connect different types of network technologies. You now know that routers strip off all of the Layer 2 data from the incoming packets, but thus far you've only seen routers that connect to different Ethernet networks—and that's just fine with routers. But routers can connect to almost anything that stores IP packets. Not to take away from some very exciting upcoming chapters, but Ethernet is not the only networking technology out there. Once you want to start making long-distance connections, Ethernet is not the only choice, and technologies with names like Data-Over-Cable Service Interface Specification (DOCSIS) for cable modems or passive optical network (PON) for fiber to the premises enter the mix. These technologies are not Ethernet, and they all work very differently than Ethernet. The only common feature of these technologies is they all carry IP packets inside their Layer 2 encapsulations.

Most enterprise (that is, not home) routers enable you to add interfaces. You buy the router and then snap in different types of interfaces depending on your needs. Note the Cisco router in Figure 7.12. Like many Cisco routers, you can buy and add removable modules. If you want to connect to an LTE (cellular phone) network, you buy an LTE module.

• **Figure 7.12** Modular Cisco router

Network Address Translation

Many regions of the world have depleted their available IPv4 addresses already and the end for everywhere else is in sight. Although you can still get an IP address from an Internet service provider (ISP), the days of easy availability are over. Routers running some form of **network address translation (NAT)** hide the IP addresses of computers on the LAN but still enable those computers to communicate with the broader Internet. NAT extended the useful life of IPv4 addressing on the Internet for many years. NAT is extremely common and heavily in use, so learning how it works is important. Note that many routers offer NAT as a feature *in addition* to the core capability of routing. NAT is not routing, but a separate technology. With that said, you are ready to dive into how NAT works to protect computers connected by router technology and conserve IP addresses as well.

The Setup

Here's the situation. You have a LAN with five computers that need access to the Internet. With classic TCP/IP and routing, several things have to happen. First, you need to get a block of legitimate, unique, expensive

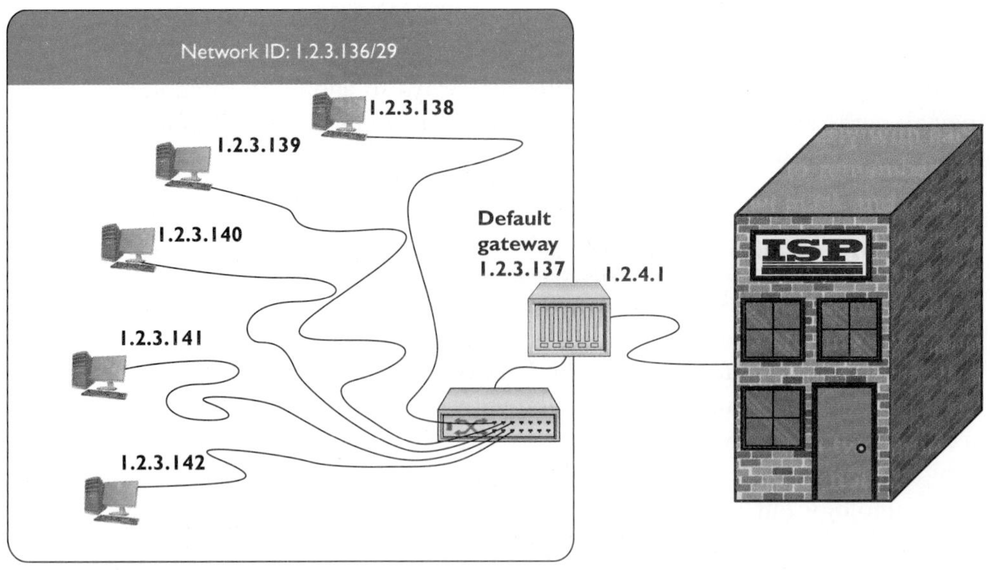

• **Figure 7.13** Network setup

IP addresses from an ISP. You could call up an ISP and purchase a network ID—say, 1.2.3.136/29. Second, you assign an IP address to each computer and to the LAN connection on the router. Third, you assign the IP address for the ISP's router to the WAN connection on the local router, such as 1.2.4.1. After everything is configured, the network looks like Figure 7.13. All of the clients on the network have the same default gateway (1.2.3.137). This router, called a **gateway**, acts as the default gateway for a number of client computers.

This style of network mirrors how computers in LANs throughout the world connected to the Internet for the first 20+ years, but the major problem of a finite number of IP addresses worsened as more and more computers connected.

NAT replaces the source IP address of a computer with the source IP address from the outside router interface on outgoing packets. NAT is performed by NAT-capable routers.

Port Address Translation

Most internal networks today don't have one machine, of course. Instead, they use a block of private IP addresses for the hosts inside the network. They connect to the Internet through one or more public IP addresses.

The most common form of NAT that handles this one-to-many connection—called **port address translation (PAT)**—uses port numbers to map traffic from specific machines in the network. Let's use a simple example to make the process clear: John has a network at his office that uses the private IP addressing space of 192.168.1.0/24. All the computers in the private network connect to the Internet through a single router using PAT with the global IP address of 208.190.121.12/24. See Figure 7.14.

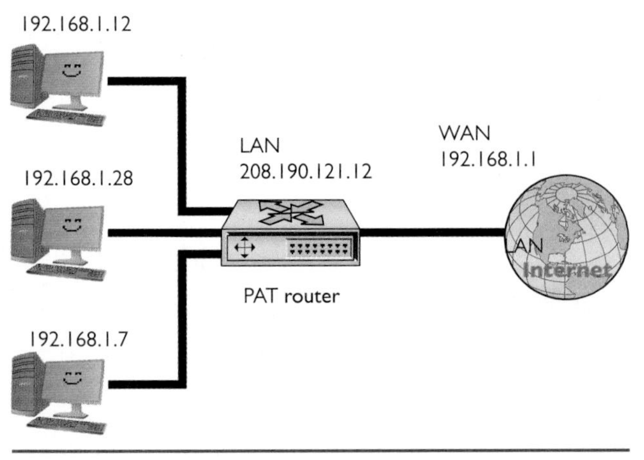

• **Figure 7.14** John's network setup

When an internal machine initiates a session with an external machine, such as a Web browser accessing a Web site, the source and destination IP addresses and port numbers for the TCP segment or UDP datagram are recorded in the NAT device's translation table, and the

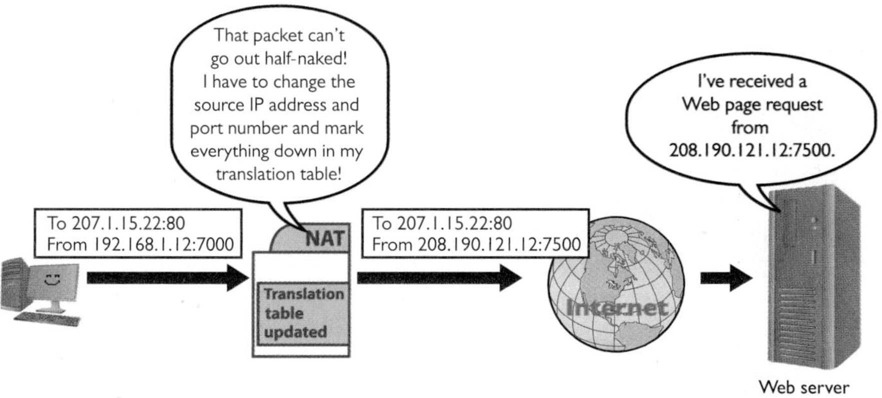

• **Figure 7.15** PAT in action—changing the source IP address and port number to something usable on the Internet

private IP address is swapped for the public IP address on each packet. The port number used by the internal computer for the session may also be translated into a unique port number, in which case the router records this as well. See Figure 7.15.

Table 7.1 shows a sample of the translation table inside the PAT router. Note that more than one computer translation has been recorded.

Table 7.1 Sample NAT Translation Table

Source	Translated Source	Destination
192.168.1.12:52331	208.190.121.12:55030	
192.168.1.24:61324	208.190.121.12:65321	17.5.85.11:80

Chapter 8 goes into port numbers in great detail.

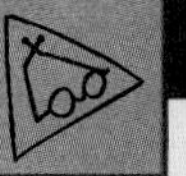

Tech Tip

Dynamic NAT

With **dynamic NAT (DNAT)***, many computers can share a pool of routable IP addresses that number fewer than the computers. The NAT translation table might have 10 routable IP addresses, for example, to serve 40 computers on the LAN. LAN traffic uses the internal, private IP addresses. When a computer requests information beyond the network, the NAT doles out a routable IP address from its pool for that communication. Dynamic NAT is also called pooled NAT. This works well enough—unless you're the unlucky 11th person to try to access the Internet from behind the company NAT—but has the obvious limitation of still needing many true, expensive, routable IP addresses.*

When the receiving system sends the packet back, it reverses the IP addresses and ports. The router compares the incoming destination port and source IP address to the entry in the **NAT translation table** to determine which IP address to put back on the packet. It then sends the packet to the correct computer on the network.

This mapping of internal IP address and port number to a translated IP address and port number enables perfect tracking of packets out and in. PAT can handle many internal computers with a single public IP address because the TCP/IP port number space is big, as you'll recall from previous chapters, with values ranging from 1 to 65535. Some of those port numbers are used for common protocols, but many tens of thousands are available for PAT to work its magic.

PAT takes care of many of the problems facing IPv4 networks exposed to the Internet. You don't have to use legitimate Internet IP addresses on the LAN, and the IP addresses of the computers behind the routers are somewhat isolated (but *not* safe) from the outside world.

Since the router is revising the packets and recording the IP address and port information already, why not enable it to handle ports more aggressively? Enter port forwarding, stage left.

Port Forwarding

The obvious drawback to relying exclusively on PAT for network address translation is that it only works for outgoing communication, not incoming

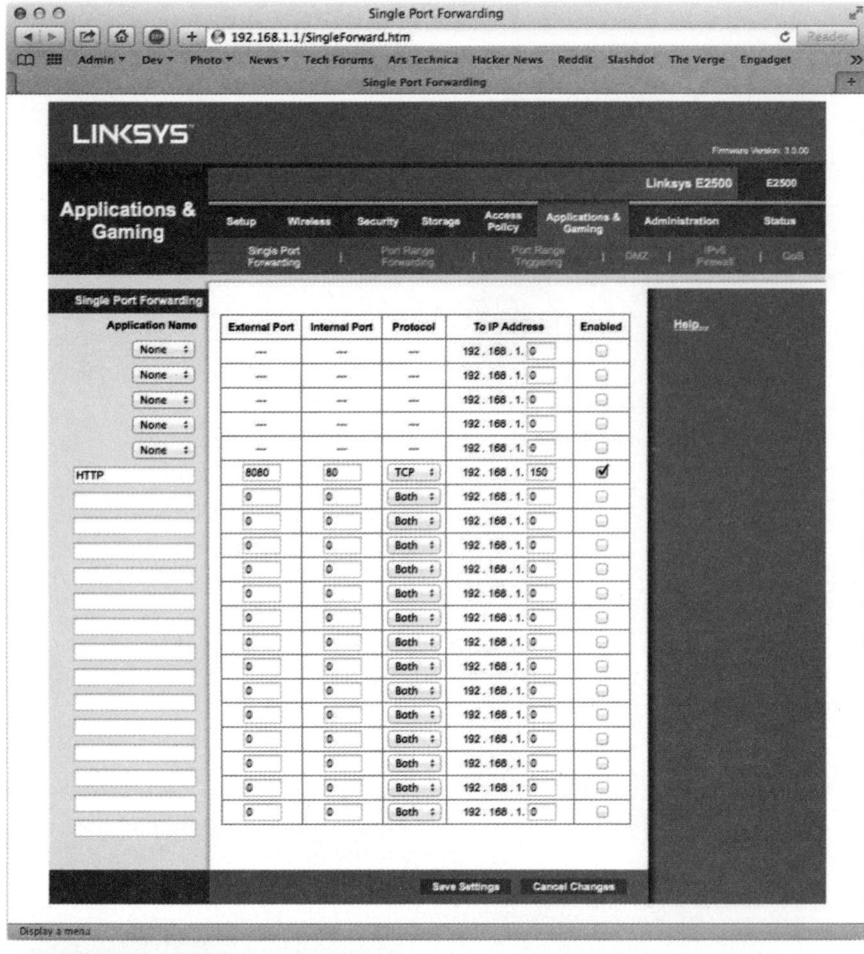

• **Figure 7.16** Setting up port forwarding on a home router

communication. For traffic originating *outside* the network to access an *internal* machine, such as a Web server hosted inside your network, you need to use other technologies.

Static NAT (SNAT) maps a single routable (that is, not private) IP address to a single machine, enabling you to access that machine from outside the network and *vice versa*. The NAT router keeps track of the IP address or addresses and applies them permanently on a one-to-one basis with computers on the network. With **port forwarding**, you can designate a specific local address for various network services. Computers outside the network can request a service using the public IP address of the router and the port number of the desired service. The port-forwarding router would examine the packet, look at the list of services mapped to local addresses, and then send that packet along to the proper recipient.

If you'd like users outside of your network to have access to an internal Web server, for example, you can set up a port forwarding rule for it. The router in Figure 7.16 is configured to forward all port 8080 packets to an internal Web server at port 80.

To access that internal Web site from outside your local network, you would have to change the URL in the Web browser by specifying the port request number. Figure 7.17 shows a browser that has :5000 appended to

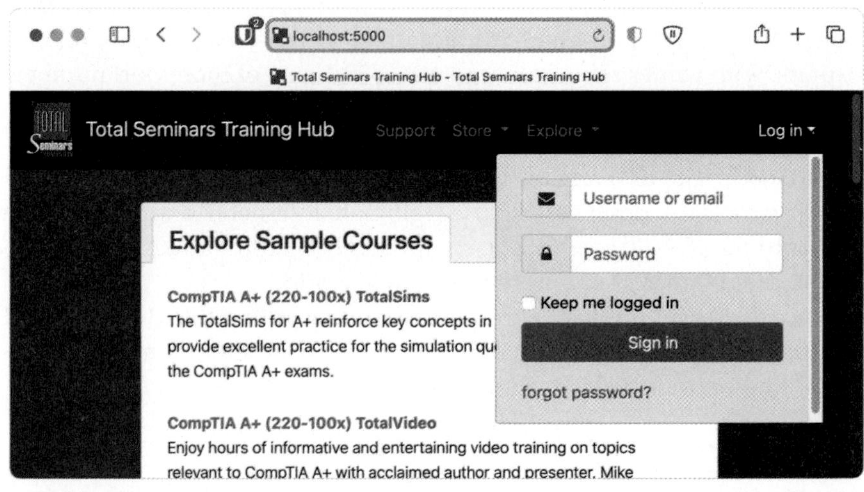

• **Figure 7.17** Changing the URL to access a Web site using a nondefault port number

the URL, which tells the browser to make the HTTP request to port 5000 rather than port 80.

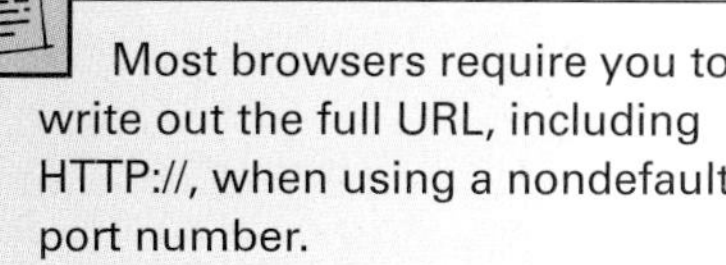

Most browsers require you to write out the full URL, including HTTP://, when using a nondefault port number.

Configuring NAT

Configuring NAT on home routers is a no-brainer as these boxes invariably have NAT turned on automatically. Figure 7.18 shows the screen on my home router for NAT. Note the radio buttons that say Gateway and Router.

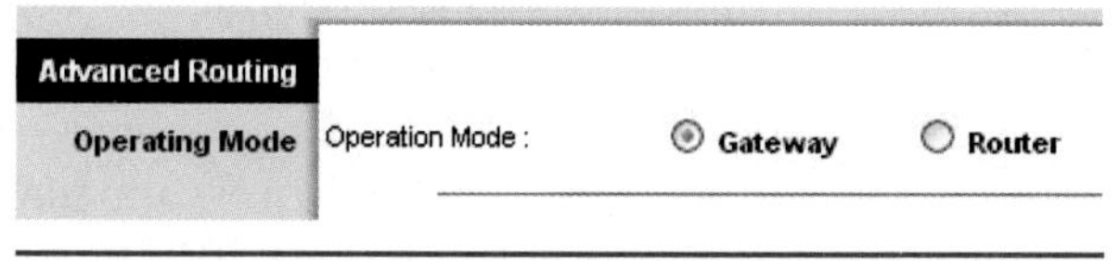

• **Figure 7.18** NAT setup on home router

Expect a question on the CompTIA Network+ exam that explores *public vs. private IP addressing schemes* and when you should use NAT or PAT. (Use them almost always with IPv4 networks.)

By default, the router is set to Gateway, which is Linksys-speak for "NAT is turned on." If I wanted to turn off NAT, I would set the radio button to Router.

Figure 7.19 shows a router configuration screen on a Cisco router. Commercial routers enable you to do a lot more with NAT.

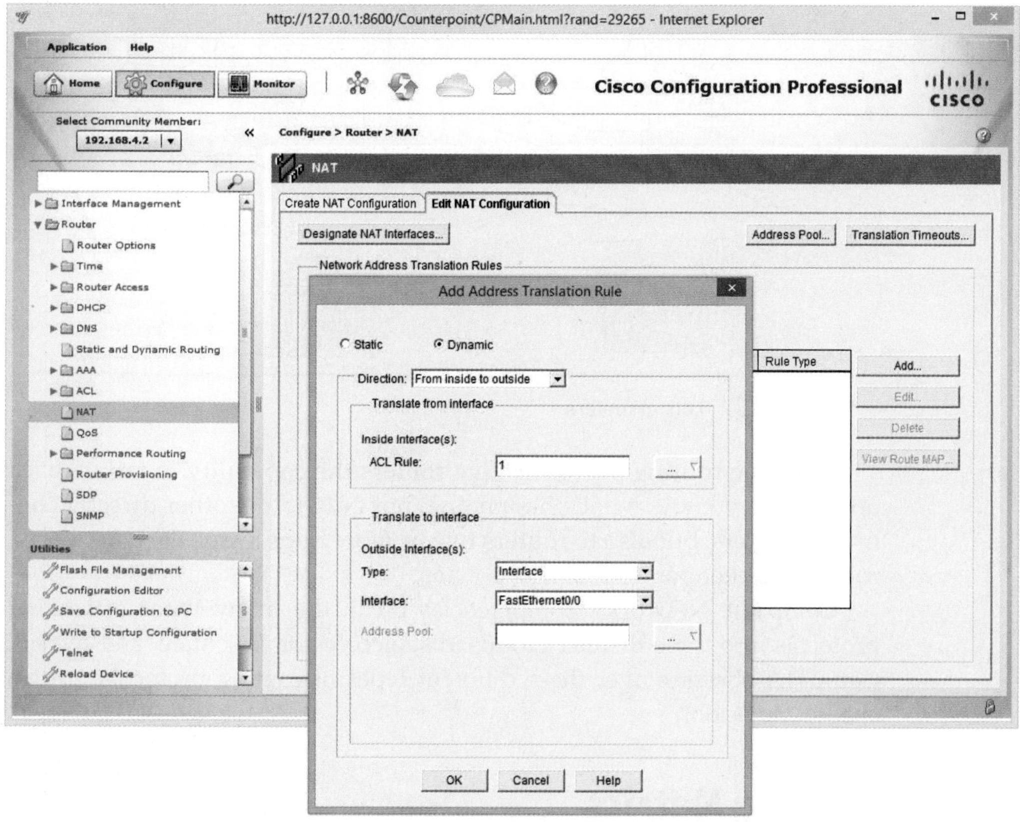

• **Figure 7.19** Configuring NAT on a commercial-grade router

Dynamic Routing

Based on what you've read up to this point, it would seem that routes in your routing tables come from two sources: either they are manually entered or they are detected at setup by the router. In either case, a route seems *static*, just sitting there and never changing. And based on what you've seen so far, that's true. Routers can have **static routes**—routes that do not change. But most routers also have the capability to update their routes *dynamically* with *dynamic routing protocols* (both IPv4 and IPv6). **Dynamic routing** is a process that routers use to update routes to accommodate conditions, such as when a line goes down because of an electrical blackout. Dynamic routing protocols enable routers to work around such problems.

Dynamic routing protocols really shine when you manage a complex network. What if your routers look like Figure 7.20? Do you really want to try to set up all these routes statically? What happens when something changes? Can you imagine the administrative nightmare?

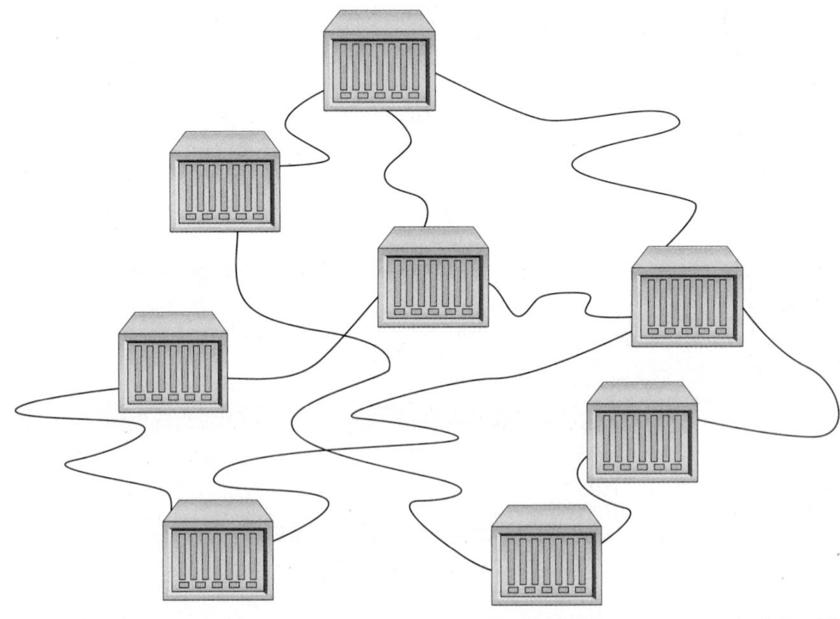

• **Figure 7.20** Lots of routers

Dynamic routing protocols give routers the capability to talk to each other so they know what's happening, not only to the other directly connected routers, but also to routers two or more hops away. Each network/router a packet passes through is a **hop**.

CompTIA Network+ competencies break the many types of routing protocols into three distinct groups: distance vector, link state, and hybrid. CompTIA obsesses over these different types of routing protocols, so this chapter does too!

Routing Metrics

Earlier in the chapter, you learned that routing tables contain a factor called a *metric*. A metric is a relative value that routers use when they have more than one route to get to another network. Unlike the gateway routers in our homes, a more serious router often has multiple connections to get to a particular network. This is the beauty of routers combined with dynamic protocols. If a router suddenly loses a connection, it has alternative routes to the same network. It's the role of the metric setting for the router to decide which route to use.

There is no single rule to set the metric value in a routing table. The various types of dynamic protocols use different criteria. Here are some common criteria for determining a metric.

- **Hop count** The **hop count** is a fundamental metric value for the number of routers a packet will pass through on the way to its destination network. For example, if Router A needs to go through three intermediate routers to reach a network connected to Router C, the hop count is 3. The hop occurs when the packet is handed off to each subsequent router. (I'll go a lot more into hops and hop count in "Distance Vector and Path Vector," next.)
- **Bandwidth** Some connections handle more data than others. An ancient 10BASE-T interface tops out at 10 Mbps. A 40GBASE-LR4 interface flies along at up to 40 Gbps.
- **Delay** Suppose you have a race car that has a top speed of 200 miles per hour, but it takes 25 minutes to start the car. If you press the gas pedal, it takes 15 seconds to start accelerating. If the engine runs for more than 20 minutes, the car won't go faster than 50 miles per hour. These issues prevent the car from doing what it should be able to do: go 200 miles per hour. *Delay* is like that. Hundreds of issues occur that slow down network connections between routers. These issues are known collectively as *latency*. A great example is a cross-country fiber connection. The distance between New York and Chicago causes a delay that has nothing to do with the bandwidth of the connection.
- **Cost** Some routing protocols use **cost** as a metric for the desirability of that particular route. A route through a low-bandwidth connection, for example, would have a higher cost value than a route through a high-bandwidth connection. A network administrator can also manually add cost to routes to change the route selection.

Different dynamic routing protocols use one or more of these criteria to calculate their own routing metric. As you learn about these protocols, you will see how each of these calculates its own metrics differently.

If a routing table has two or more valid routes for a particular IP address destination, it always chooses the route with the lowest metric.

I want to apologize now on behalf of the people who created the language used to describe various routing protocol features, most notably with metrics. The *metric* of a route enables a router to determine the *preferred route* to get a packet to its destination. The *criteria* or *information variables* used to determine the metric of a route are called . . . *metrics.* I've used *criteria* here in hopes of making this less confusing, but you'll see the term *metrics* in networking to mean both the route desirability numbers and the information variables to get to those numbers. Nice, no?

Distance Vector and Path Vector

Distance vector routing protocols were the first to appear in TCP/IP routing. The cornerstone of all distance vector routing protocols is the *metric*. The simplest metric sums the hops (the hop count) between a router and a network, so if you had a router one hop away from a network, the metric for that route would be 1; if it were two hops away, the metric would be 2.

All network connections are not equal. A router might have two one-hop routes to a network—one using a fast connection and the other using a slow connection. Administrators set the metric of the routes in the routing table to reflect the speed. The slow single-hop route, for example, might be given the metric of 10 rather than the default of 1 to reflect the fact that it's slow. The total metric for this one-hop route is 10, even though it's only one hop. Don't assume a one-hop route always has a metric of 1.

Distance vector routing protocols calculate the metric number to get to a particular network ID and compare that metric to the metrics of all the other routes to get to that same network ID. The router then chooses the route with the lowest metric.

For this to work, routers using a distance vector routing protocol transfer their entire routing table to other routers in the WAN. Each distance vector routing protocol has a maximum number of hops that a router will send its routing table to keep traffic down.

Assume you have four routers connected as shown in Figure 7.21. All of the routers have routes set up between each other with the metrics shown. You add two new networks, one that connects to Router A and the other to Router D. For simplicity, call them Network ID X and Network ID Y. A computer on one network wants to send packets to a computer on the other network, but the routers in between Routers A and D don't yet know the two new network IDs. That's when distance vector routing protocols work their magic.

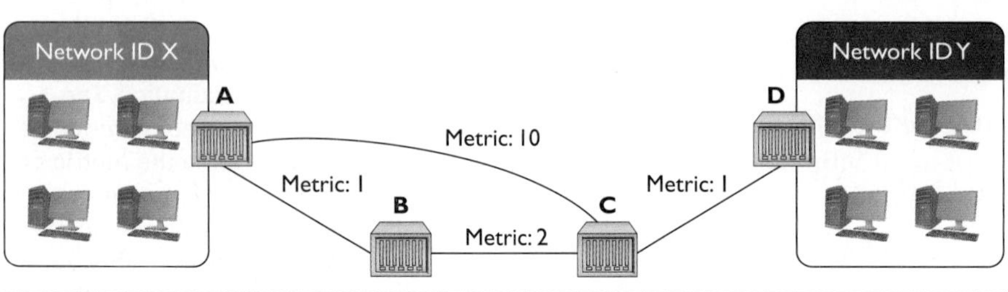

• **Figure 7.21** Getting a packet from Network ID X to Network ID Y? No clue!

Because all of the routers use a distance vector routing protocol, the problem gets solved quickly. At a certain defined time interval (usually 30 seconds or less), the routers begin sending each other their routing tables (the routers each send their entire routing table, but for simplicity just concentrate on the two network IDs in question). On the first iteration, Router A sends its route to Network ID X to Routers B and C. Router D sends its route to Network ID Y to Router C (Figure 7.22).

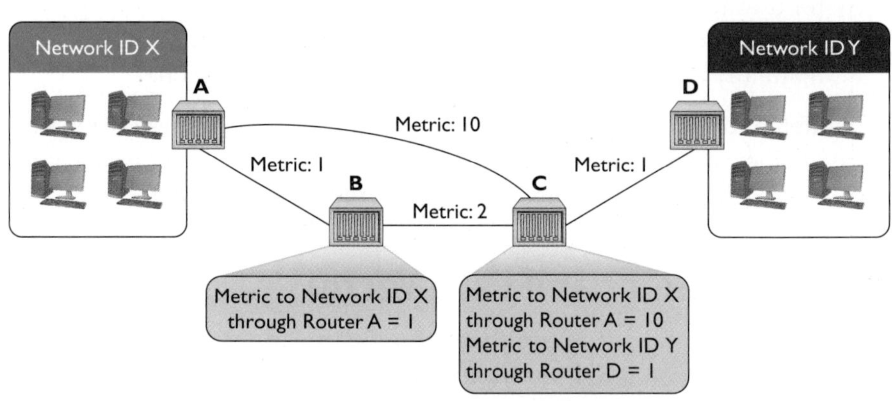

• **Figure 7.22** Routes updated

This is great—Routers B and C now know how to get to Network ID X, and Router C can get to Network ID Y. There's still no complete path, however, between Network ID X and Network ID Y. That's going to take another interval. After another set amount of time, the routers again send their now updated routing tables to each other, as shown in Figure 7.23.

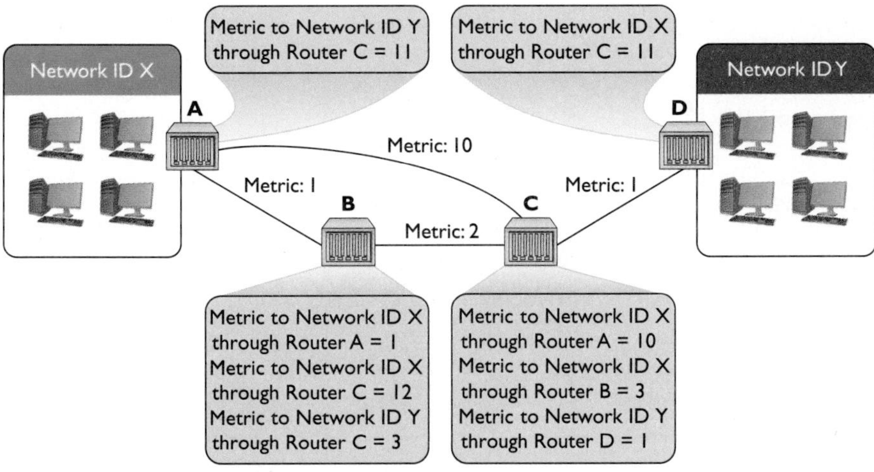

• **Figure 7.23** Updated routing tables

Router A knows a path now to Network ID Y, and Router D knows a path to Network ID X. As a side effect, Router B and Router C have two routes to Network ID X. Router B can get to Network ID X through Router A and through Router C. Similarly, Router C can get to Network ID X through Router A and through Router B. What to do? In cases where the router discovers multiple routes to the same network ID, the distance vector routing protocol deletes all but the route with the lowest metric (Figure 7.24).

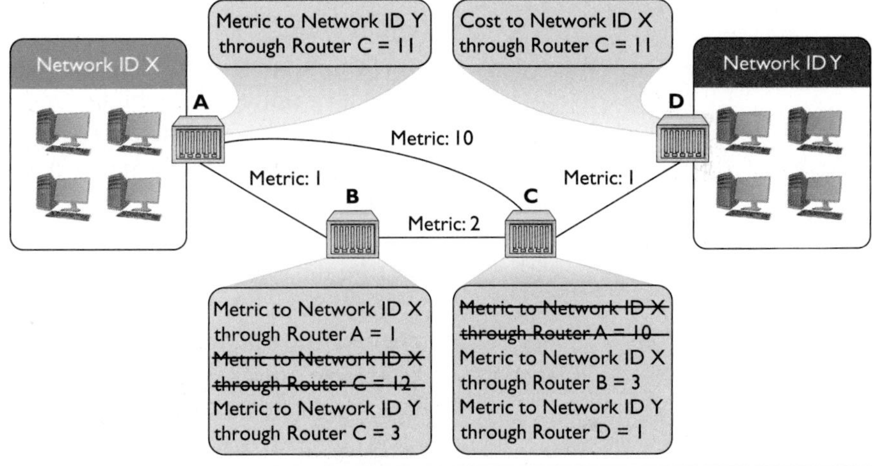

• **Figure 7.24** Deleting routes with higher metrics

On the next iteration, Routers A and D get updated information about the lower metric to connect to Network IDs X and Y (Figure 7.25).

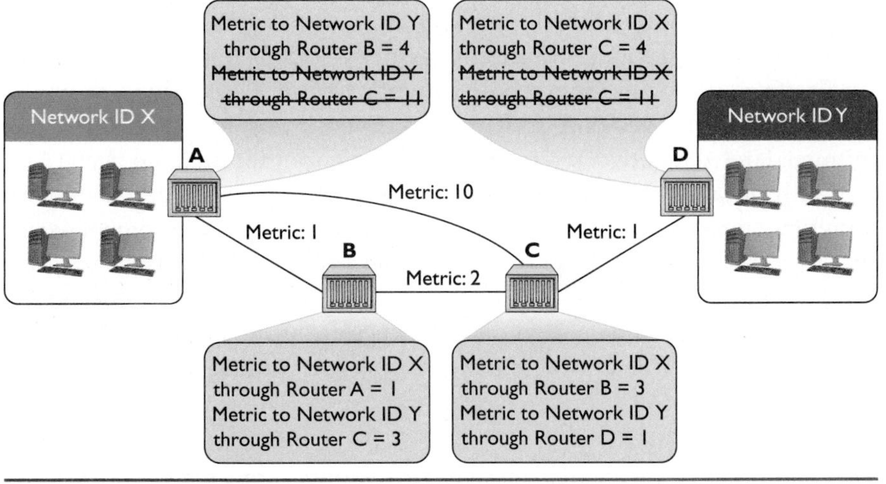

• **Figure 7.25** Argh! Multiple routes!

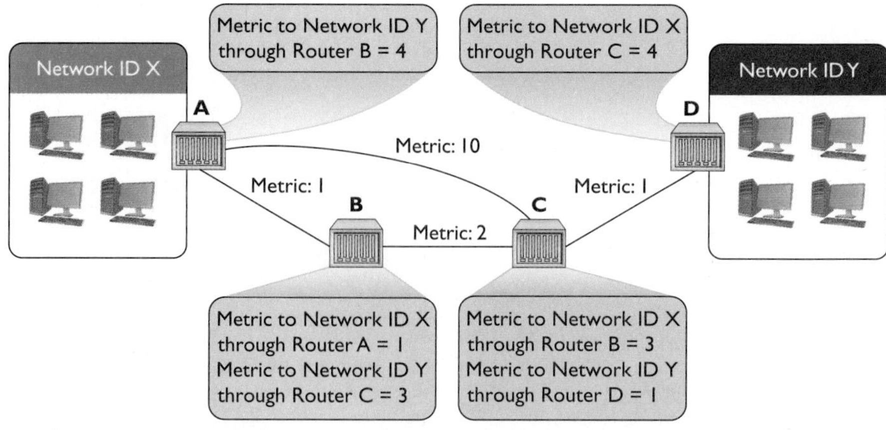

• **Figure 7.26** Last iteration

Just as Routers B and C only kept the routes with the lowest metrics, Routers A and D keep only the lowest-metric routes to the networks (Figure 7.26).

Now Routers A and D have a lower-metric route to Network IDs X and Y. They've removed the higher-metric routes and begin sending data.

At this point, if routers were human they'd realize that each router has all the information about the network and stop sending each other routing tables. Routers using distance vector routing protocols, however, aren't that smart. The routers continue to send their complete routing tables to each other, but because the information is the same, the routing tables don't change.

At this point, the routers are in **convergence** (also called *steady state*), meaning the updating of the routing tables for all the routers has completed. Assuming nothing changes in terms of connections, the routing tables will not change. In this example, it takes three iterations to reach convergence.

So what happens if the route between Routers B and C breaks? The routers have deleted the higher-metric routes, only keeping the lower-metric route that goes between Routers B and C. Does this mean Router A can no longer connect to Network ID Y and Router D can no longer connect to Network ID X? Yikes! Yes, it does. At least for a while.

Routers that use distance vector routing protocols continue to send to each other their entire routing table at regular intervals. After a few iterations, Routers A and D will once again know how to reach each other, although they will connect through the once-rejected slower connection.

Distance vector routing protocols work fine in a scenario such as the previous one that has only four routers. Even if you lose a router, a few minutes later the network returns to convergence. But imagine if you had tens of thousands of routers (the Internet). Convergence could take a very long time indeed. As a result, a pure distance vector routing protocol works fine for a network with a few (less than ten) routers, but it isn't good for large networks.

Routers can use one of two distance vector routing protocols: RIPv1 or RIPv2. Plus there's an option to use a path vector routing protocol, BGP.

RIPv1

The granddaddy of all distance vector routing protocols is the **Routing Information Protocol (RIP)**. The first version of RIP—called **RIPv1**—dates from the 1980s, although its predecessors go back all the way to the beginnings of the Internet in the 1960s. RIP (either version) has a maximum hop count of 15, so your router will not talk to another router more than 15 routers away. This plagues RIP because a routing table request can literally loop all the way around back to the initial router.

RIPv1 sent out an update every 30 seconds. This also turned into a big problem because every router on the network would send its routing table at the same time, causing huge network overloads.

As if these issues weren't bad enough, RIPv1 didn't know how to use *variable-length subnet masking (VLSM)*, where networks that are connected through the router use different subnet masks. Plus, RIPv1 routers had no authentication, leaving them open to hackers sending false routing table information. RIP needed an update.

RIPv2

RIPv2, adopted in 1994, is the current version of RIP. It works the same way as RIPv1, but fixes many of the problems. RIPv2 supports VLSM, includes built-in authentication, swaps broadcasting for multicast, and increases the time between updates from 30 seconds to 90 seconds.

Most routers still support RIPv2, but RIP's many problems, especially the time to convergence for large WANs, make it obsolete for all but small, private WANs that consist of a few routers. The increase in complexity of networks since the 1990s demanded a far more robust dynamic routing protocol. That doesn't mean RIP rests in peace! RIP is both easy to use and simple for manufacturers to implement in their routers, so most routers, even home routers, can use RIP (Figure 7.27). If your network consists of only two, three, or four routers, RIP's easy configuration often makes it worth putting up with slower convergence.

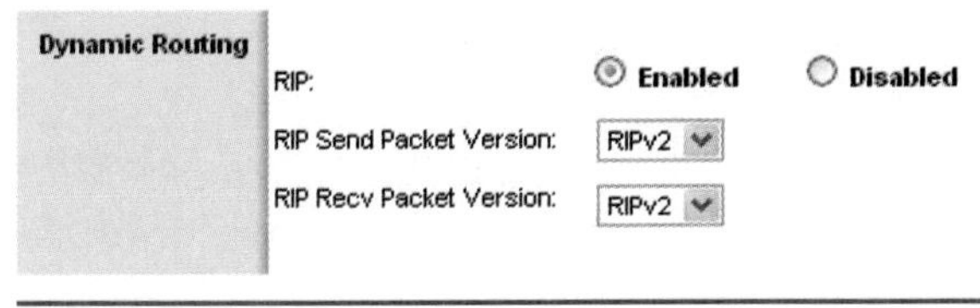

• **Figure 7.27** Setting RIP in a home router

BGP

The explosive growth of the Internet in the 1980s required a fundamental reorganization in the structure of the Internet itself, and one big part of this reorganization was the call to make the "big" routers use a standardized dynamic routing protocol. Implementing this was much harder than you might think because the entities that govern how the Internet works do so in a highly decentralized fashion. Even the organized groups, such as the Internet Society (ISOC), the Internet Assigned Numbers Authority (IANA), and the Internet Engineering Task Force (IETF), are made up of many individuals, companies, and government organizations from across the globe. This decentralization made the reorganization process take time and many meetings.

What came out of this process was an organizational concept called Autonomous Systems. An **Autonomous System (AS)** is one or more networks

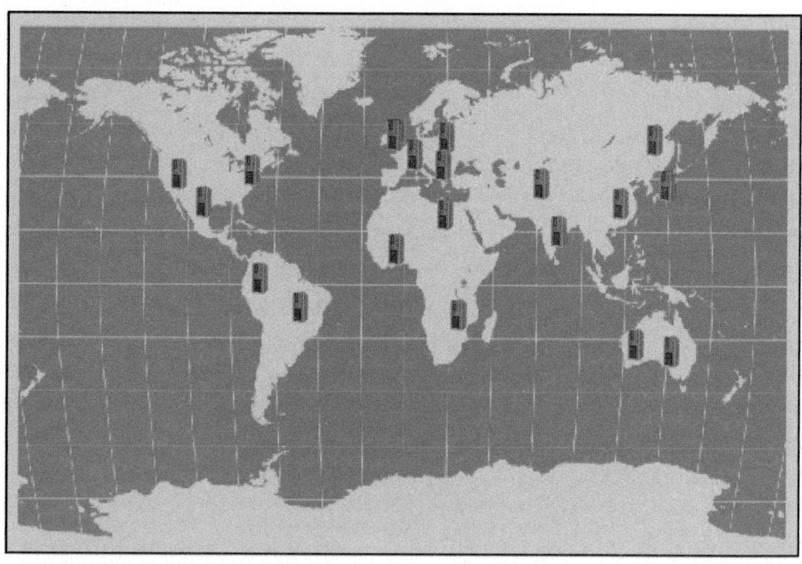

• **Figure 7.28** The Internet

that share a unified "policy" regarding how they exchange traffic with other Autonomous Systems. (These policies are usually economic or political decisions made by whoever administers the AS.) Figure 7.28 illustrates the decentralized structure of the Internet.

Each Autonomous System must have a special globally unique Autonomous System Number (ASN) assigned by IANA.

```
Router2811(config)#router bgp ?
  <1-65535>   Autonomous system number

Router2811(config)#router bgp 1902
```

• **Figure 7.29** Configuring a Cisco router to use an ASN

Originally a 16-bit number, the current ASNs are 32 bits, displayed as two 16-bit numbers separated by a dot. So, 1.33457 would be a typical ASN. This isn't work the computers do for us like DHCP—the routers that comprise the AS have to be configured to use the ASN assigned by IANA. See Figure 7.29.

When routers in one AS need to communicate with routers in another AS, they use an *Exterior Gateway Protocol (EGP)*. The network or networks within an AS communicate with protocols as well: *Interior Gateway Protocols (IGPs)*.

I use EGP and IGP generically to categorize specific protocols. In *Ye Olde Days*, there was a specific Exterior Gateway Protocol. It was replaced with BGP in the 1990s, but you may see EGP refer to that specific protocol in old RFCs and documentation.

The easy way to keep these terms separate is to appreciate that although many protocols can be used *within* each Autonomous System, the Internet uses a single protocol for AS-to-AS communication: the **Border Gateway Protocol (BGP)**. BGP is the glue of the Internet, connecting all of the Autonomous Systems. Other dynamic routing protocols such as OSPF are, by definition, IGPs. The current version of BGP is BGP-4.

Try This!

Discovering the Autonomous System Numbers

You can discover the ASN for almost any IP or company with this great little site:

https://mxtoolbox.com/asn.aspx/

It might not work for every IP, but it's still interesting.

A lot of authors refer to BGP as a *hybrid routing protocol*, but it's more technically a **path vector** routing protocol. BGP routers advertise information passed to them from different Autonomous Systems' **edge routers**—that's what the AS-to-AS routers are called.

BGP also knows how to handle a number of situations unique to the Internet. If a router advertises a new route that isn't reliable, most BGP routers will ignore it. BGP also supports policies for limiting which and how other routers may access an ISP.

BGP implements and supports *route aggregation*, a way to simplify routing tables into manageable levels. Rather than trying to keep track of every router on the Internet, the backbone routers track the shortest common network ID(s) of all of the routes managed by each AS.

Route aggregation is complicated, but an analogy should make its function clear. A computer in Prague in the Czech Republic sends a packet intended to go to a computer in Chicago, Illinois, USA. When the packet hits one of the BGP routers, the router doesn't have to know the precise location of the recipient. It knows the router for the United States and sends the packet there. The U.S. router knows the Illinois router, which knows the Chicago router, and so on.

BGP is the obvious (only) choice for edge routers, but distance vector protocols aren't the only game in town when it comes to the inside of your network. Let's look at another family: link state routing protocols.

The CompTIA Network+ objectives in the past have listed BGP as a hybrid routing protocol. Read the question carefully and if BGP is your only answer as hybrid, take it.

I've focused closely on BGP's role as the exterior gateway protocol that glues the Internet together because I think that's how CompTIA sees it. Technically, you can also use BGP as an interior protocol. If you get a question about an interior network, BGP is probably the last answer you should consider.

Link State

The limitations of RIP motivated the demand for a faster protocol that took up less bandwidth on a WAN. The basic idea was to come up with a dynamic routing protocol that was more efficient than routers that simply sent out their entire routing table at regular intervals. Why not instead simply announce and forward individual route changes as they appeared? That is the basic idea of a **link state** dynamic routing protocol. There are only two link state dynamic routing protocols: OSPF and IS-IS.

OSPF

Open Shortest Path First (OSPF) is the most commonly used IGP in the world. Most large enterprises use OSPF on their internal networks. Even an AS, while still using BGP on its edge routers, will use OSPF internally because OSPF was designed from the ground up to work within a single AS. OSPF converges dramatically faster and is much more efficient than RIP. Odds are good that if you are using dynamic routing protocols, you're using OSPF.

OSPF offers a number of improvements over RIP. OSPF-capable routers initially send out *Hello packets*, looking for other OSPF routers (see Figure 7.30). After two adjacent routers form a *neighborship* through the Hello

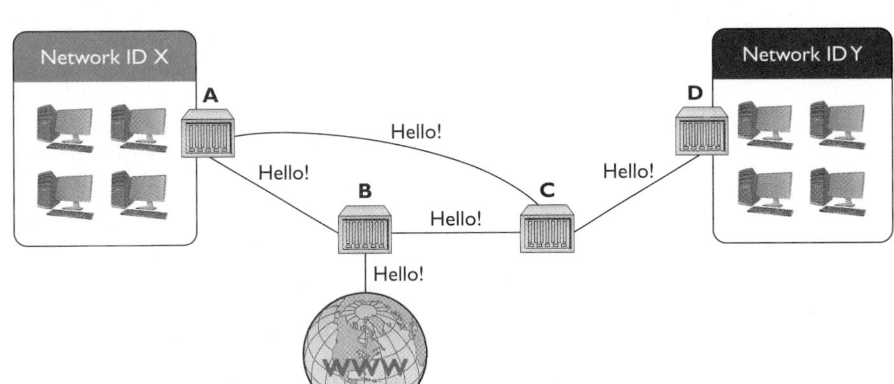

• **Figure 7.30** Hello!

packets, they exchange information about routers and networks through *link state advertisement (LSA)* packets. LSAs are sourced by each router and are flooded from router to router through each OSPF area.

Once all the routers communicate, they individually decide their own optimal routes, and convergence happens almost immediately. If a route goes down, OSPF routers quickly recompute a new route with stored LSAs.

OSPF's metric is *cost*, which is a function of bandwidth. All possible ways to get to a destination network are computed based on cost, which is proportional to bandwidth, which is in turn proportional to the interface type (Gigabit Ethernet, 10-Gigabit Ethernet, and so on). The routers choose the lowest total cost route to a destination network.

In other words, a packet could go through more routers (hops) to get to a destination when OSPF is used instead of RIP. However, more hops doesn't necessarily mean slower. If a packet goes through three hops where the routers are connected by fiber, for example, as opposed to a slow 1.544-Mbps link, the packet would get to its destination quicker. We make these decisions everyday as humans, too. I'd rather drive more miles on the highway to get somewhere quicker, than fewer miles on local streets where the speed limit is much lower. (Red lights and stop signs introduce driving latency as well!)

> OSPF corrects link failures and creates convergence almost immediately, making it the routing protocol of choice in most large enterprise networks. OSPF Version 2 is used for IPv4 networks, and OSPF Version 3 includes updates to support IPv6.

OSPF uses *areas*, administrative groupings of interconnected routers, to help control how routers reroute traffic if a link drops. All OSPF networks use areas, even if there is only one area. When you interconnect multiple areas, the central area—called the backbone—gets assigned the Area ID of 0 or 0.0.0.0. (Note that a single area also gets Area ID 0.) All traffic between areas has to go through the backbone.

OSPF isn't popular by accident. It scales to large networks quite well and is supported by all but the most basic routers. By the way, did I forget to mention that OSPF also supports authentication and that the shortest-path-first method, by definition, prevents loops?

IS-IS

If you want to use a link state dynamic routing protocol and you don't want to use OSPF, your only other option is **Intermediate System to Intermediate System (IS-IS)**. IS-IS is extremely similar to OSPF. It uses the concept of areas and send-only updates to routing tables. IS-IS was developed at roughly the same time as OSPF and had the one major advantage of working with IPv6 from the start. IS-IS is the *de facto* standard for ISPs. Make sure you know that IS-IS is a link state dynamic routing protocol, and if you ever see two routers using it, call me as I've never seen IS-IS in action.

EIGRP

There is exactly one protocol that doesn't really fit into either the distance vector or link state camp: Cisco's proprietary **Enhanced Interior Gateway Routing Protocol (EIGRP)**. Back in the days when RIP was dominant, there was a huge outcry for an improved RIP, but OSPF wasn't yet out. Cisco, being the dominant router company in the world (a crown it still wears to this day), came out with the Interior Gateway Routing Protocol (IGRP), which was quickly replaced with EIGRP.

> The CompTIA Network+ objectives in the past have listed EIGRP as a distance vector protocol, right along with RIP. Read questions carefully and if EIGRP is the only right answer as a distance vector protocol, take it.

EIGRP has aspects of both distance vector and link state protocols, placing it uniquely into its own "hybrid" category. Cisco calls EIGRP an *advanced distance vector protocol*.

Dynamic Routing Makes the Internet

Without dynamic routing, the complex, self-healing Internet we all enjoy today couldn't exist. So many routes come and go so often that manually updating static routes would be impossible. Review Table 7.2 to familiarize yourself with the differences among the different types of dynamic routing protocols.

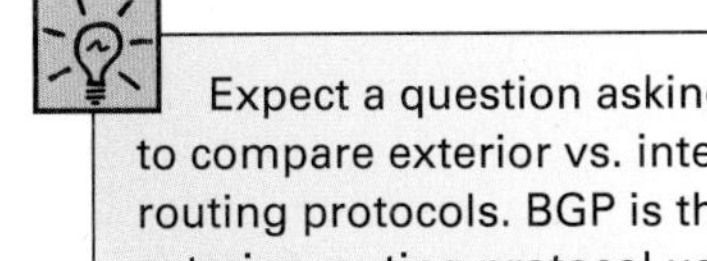

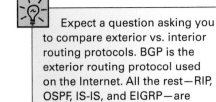

Expect a question asking you to compare exterior vs. interior routing protocols. BGP is the exterior routing protocol used on the Internet. All the rest—RIP, OSPF, IS-IS, and EIGRP—are interior protocols.

Table 7.2 Dynamic Routing Protocols

Protocol	Type	IGP or EGP?	Notes
RIPv1	Distance vector	IGP	Old; only used variable subnets within an AS
RIPv2	Distance vector	IGP	Supports VLSM and discontiguous subnets
BGP	Path vector	EGP	Used on the Internet, connects Autonomous Systems
OSPF	Link state	IGP	Fast, popular, uses Area IDs (Area 0/backbone)
IS-IS	Link state	IGP	Alternative to OSPF
EIGRP	Hybrid	IGP	Cisco-developed; less common on non-Cisco routers

Route Redistribution and Administrative Distance

Wow, there sure are many routing protocols out there. It's too bad they can't talk to each other…or can they?

The routers cannot use different routing protocols to communicate with each other, but many routers can speak multiple routing protocols simultaneously. When a router takes routes it has learned by one method, say, RIP or a statically set route, and announces those routes over another protocol such as OSPF, this is called **route redistribution**. This feature can come in handy when you have a mix of equipment and protocols in your network, such as occurs when you switch vendors or merge with another organization.

When a multilingual router has two or more protocol choices to connect to the same destination, the router uses a feature called **administrative distance** to determine which route is the most reliable. You'll see this feature called *route preference* as well.

Working with Routers

Understanding the different ways routers work is one thing. Actually walking up to a router and making it work is a different animal altogether. This section examines practical router installation. Physical installation isn't very complicated. With a home router, you give it power and then plug in connections. With a business-class router, you insert it into a rack, give it power, and plug in connections.

The complex part of installation comes with the specialized equipment and steps to connect to the router and configure it for your network needs. This section, therefore, focuses on the many methods and procedures used to access and configure a router.

The single biggest item to keep in mind here is that although there are many different methods for connecting, hundreds of interfaces, and probably millions of different configurations for different routers, the functions are still the same. Whether you're using an inexpensive home router or a hyper-powerful Internet backbone router, you are always working to do one main job: connect different networks.

• **Figure 7.31** Cisco console cable

The term *Yost cable* comes from its creator's name, Dave Yost. For more information visit http://yost.com/computers/RJ45-serial.

Expect a question on the CompTIA Network+ exam that explores *cable application* scenarios where you would use a rollover cable/console cable. That's a lot of words that simply describe a situation where you need to communicate with a router.

Connecting to Routers

When you take a new router out of the box, it's not good for very much. You need to somehow plug into that shiny new router and start telling it what you want to do. There are a number of different methods, but one of the oldest (yet still very common) methods is to use a special serial connection. Figure 7.31 shows the classic Cisco console cable, more commonly called a *rollover* or **Yost cable**.

At this time, I need to make an important point: switches as well as routers often have some form of configuration interface. Granted, you have nothing to configure on a basic switch, but in later chapters, you'll discover a number of network features that you'll want to configure more advanced switches to use. Both routers and these advanced switches are called **managed devices**. In this section, I use the term *router*, but it's important for you to appreciate that all routers and many better switches are all managed devices. The techniques shown here work for both!

When you first unwrap a new router, you plug the rollover cable into the console port on the router (Figure 7.32) and a serial port on a PC. If you don't have a serial port, then buy a USB-to-serial adapter.

• **Figure 7.32** Console port

Once you've made this connection, you need to use a terminal emulation program to talk to the router. Two common graphical programs are PuTTY (www.chiark.greenend.org.uk/~sgtatham/putty) and HyperTerminal (www.hilgraeve.com/hyperterminal). Using these programs requires that you to know a little about serial ports, but these basic settings should get you connected:

- 9600 baud
- 8 data bits
- 1 stop bit
- No parity

Every terminal emulator has some way for you to configure these settings. Figure 7.33 shows these settings using PuTTY.

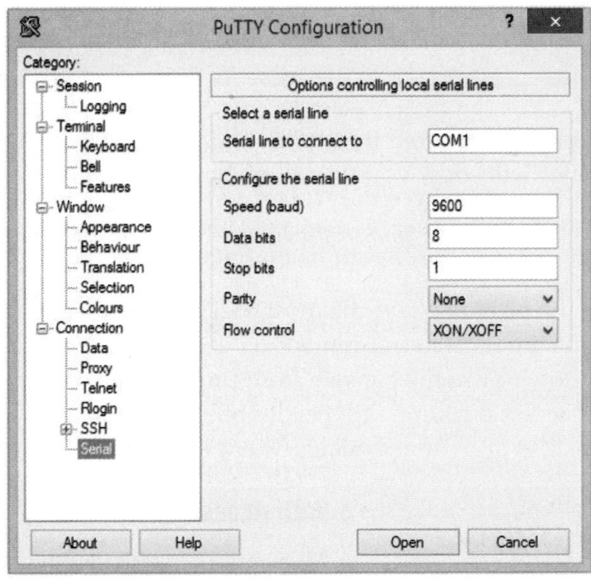

• **Figure 7.33** Configuring PuTTY

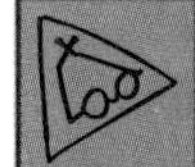

Tech Tip

Terminals and Consoles

Much initial router configuration harkens back to the methods used in the early days of networking, when massive mainframe computers were the computing platform available. Researchers used dumb terminals—machines that were little more than a keyboard, monitor, and network connection—to connect to the mainframe and interact. You connect to and configure many modern routers using software that enables your PC to pretend to be a dumb terminal. These programs are called terminal emulators; the screen you type into is called a console.

IOS used to stand for *Internetwork Operating System*, but it's just IOS now with a little trademark symbol.

Now it's time to connect. Most Cisco products run **Cisco IOS**, Cisco's proprietary operating system. If you want to configure Cisco routers, you must learn IOS. Learning IOS in detail is a massive job and outside the scope of this book. No worries, because Cisco provides a series of certifications to support those who wish to become "Cisco People." Although the CompTIA Network+ exam won't challenge you in terms of IOS, it's important to get a taste of how this amazing operating system works.

Once you've connected to the router and started a terminal emulator, you should see the initial router prompt, as shown in Figure 7.34.

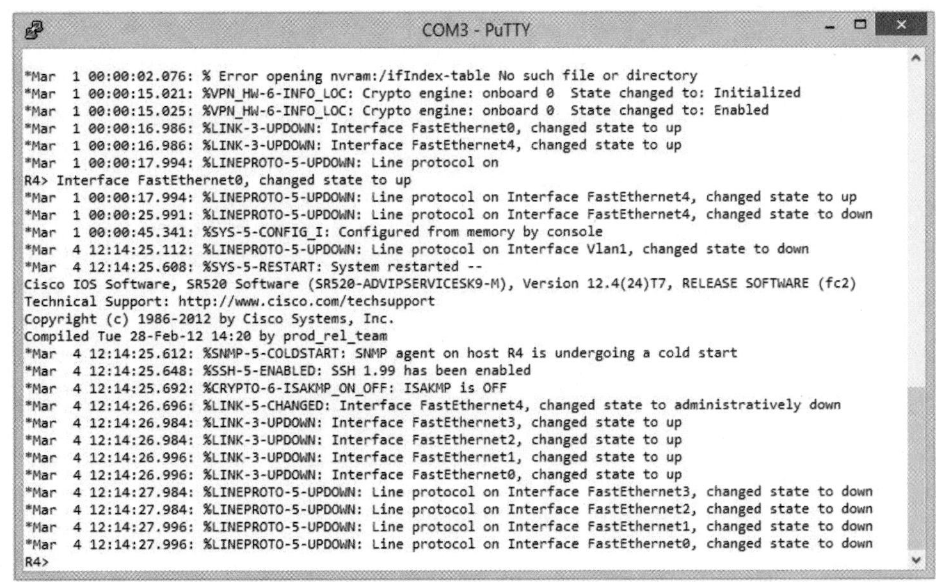

• **Figure 7.34** Initial router prompt

A new Cisco router often won't have a password, but all good admins know to add one.

(If you plugged in and then started the router, you can actually watch the router boot up first.)

This is the IOS user mode prompt—you can't do too much here. To get to the fun, you need to enter privileged EXEC mode. Type **enable**, press ENTER, and the prompt changes to

```
Router#
```

From here, IOS gets very complex. For example, the commands to set the IP address for one of the router's ports look like this:

```
Router# configure terminal
Router(config)# interface GigabitEthernet 0/0
Router(config-if)# ip address 192.168.4.10 255.255.255.0
Router(config-if)# ^Z
Router# copy run start
```

Cisco has long appreciated that initial setup is a bit of a challenge, so a brand-new router will show you the following prompt:

```
Would you like to enter the initial configuration dialog?
[yes/no]?
```

Simply follow the prompts, and the most basic setup is handled for you.

You will run into Cisco equipment as a network tech, and you will need to know how to use the console from time to time. For the most part, though, you'll access a router—especially one that's already configured—through Web access or network management software.

Web Access

Most routers come with a built-in Web interface that enables you to do everything you need on your router and is much easier to use than Cisco's command-line IOS. For a Web interface to work, however, the router must have a built-in IP address from the factory, or you have to enable the Web interface after you've given the router an IP address. Bottom line? If you want to use a Web interface, you have to know the router's IP address. If a router has a default IP address, you will find it in the documentation, as shown in Figure 7.35.

Never plug a new router into an existing network! There's no telling what that router might start doing. Does it have DHCP? You might now have a rogue DHCP server. Are there routes on that router that match up to your network addresses? Then you see packets disappearing into the great bit bucket in the sky. Always fully configure your router before you place it online.

How to open the browser-based utility

For ALL

To access some advanced settings, you need to open the browser-based utility.

CAUTION

If you change settings in the browser-based utility, you might not be able to run Cisco Connect later.

To open the browser-based utility:

1. Run Cisco Connect, click **Change** under *Router settings*, click **Advanced settings**, then click **OK**.

   – or –

   Open a web browser on a computer connected to your network, then go to **192.168.1.1**. If your router is version 2 (look for **V2** on router's bottom label), you can go to **myrouter.local** instead.

   The router prompts you for a user name and password.

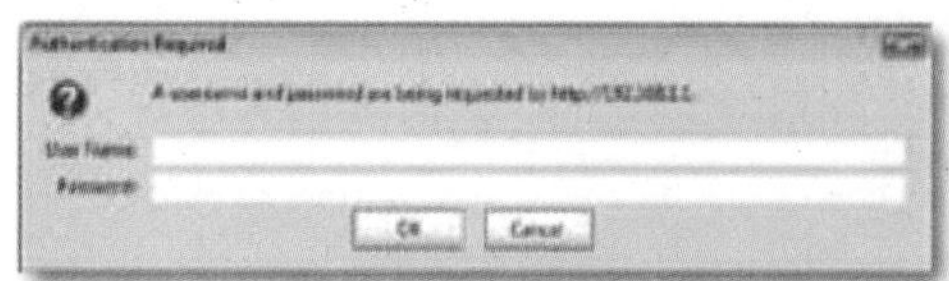

• **Figure 7.35** Default IP address

Most router people use a laptop and a crossover cable to connect to the new router. To get to the Web interface, first set a static address for your computer that will place your PC on the same network ID as the router. If, for example, the router is set to 192.168.1.1/24 from the factory, set your computer's IP address to 192.168.1.2/24. Then connect to the router (some routers tell you exactly where to connect, so read the documentation first), and check the link lights to verify you're properly connected. Open a Web browser and type in the IP address, as shown in Figure 7.36.

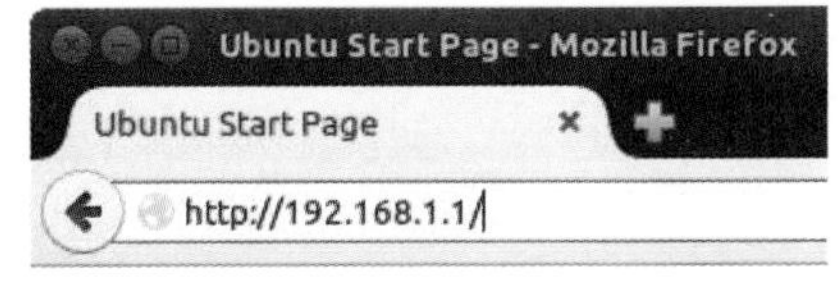

• **Figure 7.36** Entering the IP address

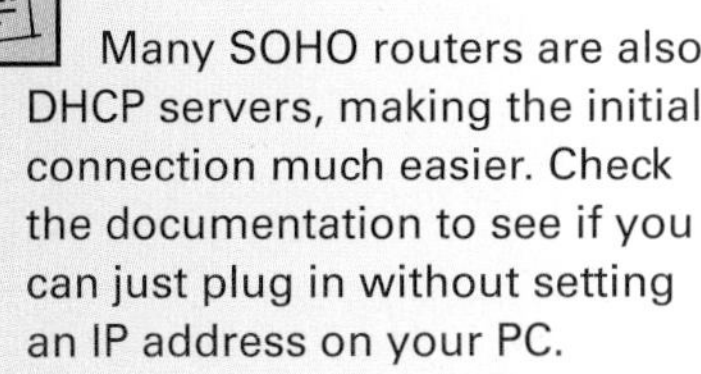

Many SOHO routers are also DHCP servers, making the initial connection much easier. Check the documentation to see if you can just plug in without setting an IP address on your PC.

Assuming you've done everything correctly, you almost always need to enter a default username and password, as shown in Figure 7.37.

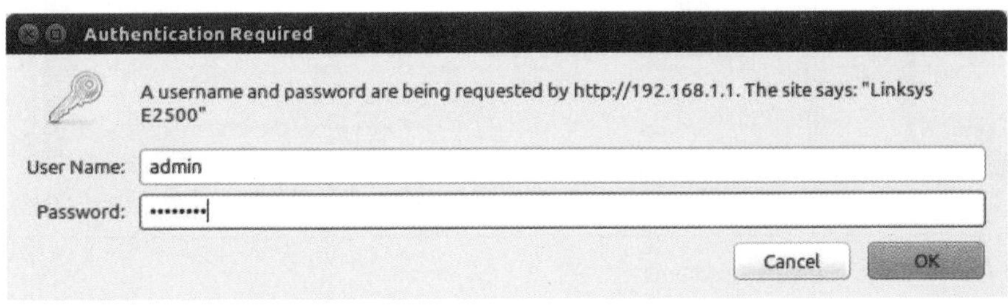

• **Figure 7.37** Username and password

The default username and password come with the router's documentation. If you don't have that information, plenty of Web sites list this data. Do a Web search on "**default username password**" to find one.

Once you've accessed the Web interface, you're on your own to poke around to find the settings you need. There's no standard interface—even between different versions of the same router make and model. When you encounter a new interface, take some time and inspect every tab and menu to learn about the router's capabilities. You'll almost always find some really cool features!

Network Management Software

The idea of a "Web-server-in-a-router" works well for single routers, but as a network grows into lots of routers, administrators need more advanced tools that describe, visualize, and configure their entire network. These tools, known as **Network Management Software (NMS)**, know how to talk to your routers, switches, and even your computers to give you an overall view of your network. In most cases, NMS manifests as a Web site where administrators may inspect the status of the network and make adjustments as needed.

I divide NMS into two camps: proprietary tools made by the folks who make managed devices (known as *original equipment manufacturers*, or *OEMs*), and third-party tools. OEM tools are generally very powerful and easy to use, but only work on that OEM's devices. Figure 7.38 shows an example of Cisco Network Assistant, one of Cisco's NMS applications. Others include the Cisco Configuration Professional and Cisco Prime Infrastructure, an enterprise-level tool.

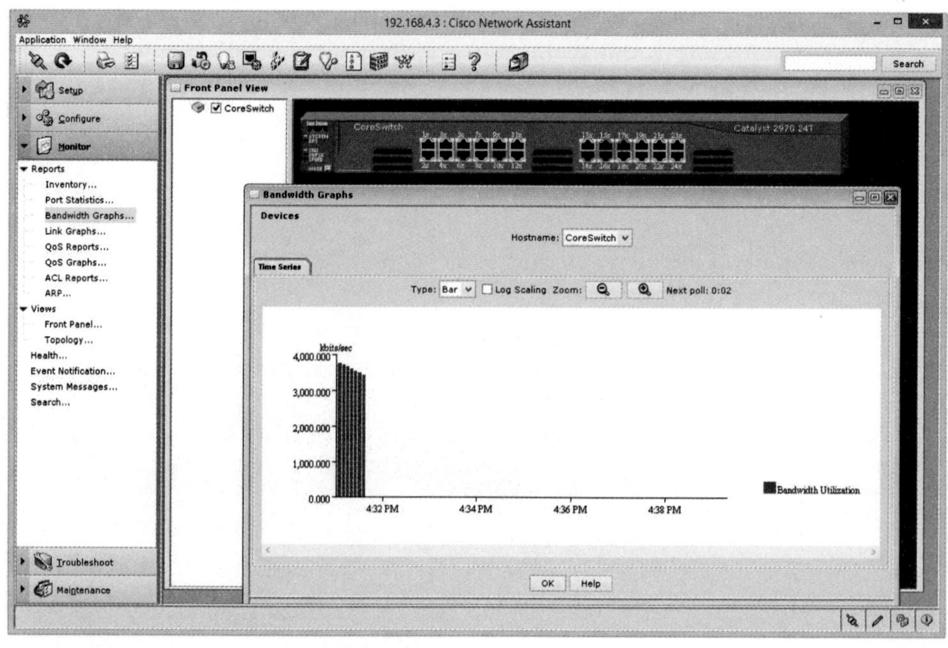

• **Figure 7.38** Cisco Network Assistant

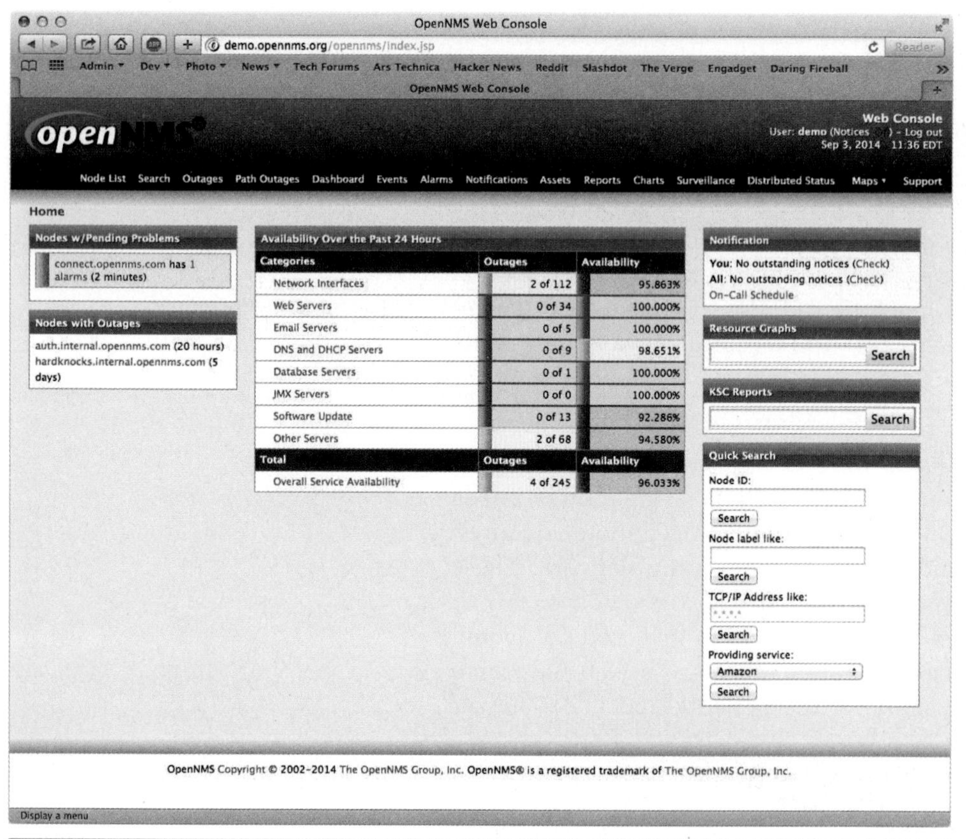

• **Figure 7.39** OpenNMS

A number of third-party NMS tools are out there as well; you can even find some pretty good freeware NMS options. These tools are invariably harder to configure and must constantly be updated to try to work with as many devices as possible. They usually lack the amount of detail you see with OEM NMS and lack interactive graphical user interfaces. For example, various Cisco products enable you to change the IP address of a port, whereas third-party tools only let you see the current IP settings for that port. Figure 7.39 shows OpenNMS, a popular open source NMS.

Unfortunately, no single NMS tool works perfectly. Network administrators are constantly playing with this or that NMS tool in an attempt to give themselves some kind of overall picture of their networks.

Other Connection Methods

Be aware that most routers have even more ways to connect. More powerful routers may enable you to connect using the ancient Telnet protocol or its newer and safer equivalent Secure Shell (SSH). These are terminal emulation protocols that look exactly like the terminal emulators seen earlier in this chapter but use the network instead of a serial cable to connect (see Chapter 8 for details on these protocols).

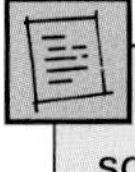

You can even configure some devices by popping in a USB drive with the correct configuration settings saved to it.

Basic Router Configuration

A router, by definition, must have at least two connections. When you set up a router, you must configure every port on the router properly to talk to its connected network IDs, and you must make sure the routing table sends packets to where you want them to go. As a demonstration, Figure 7.40 uses an incredibly common setup: a single gateway router used in a home or small office that's connected to an ISP.

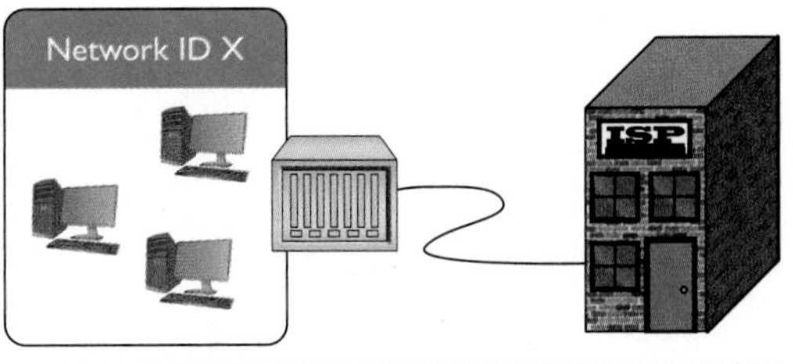

• **Figure 7.40** The setup

Step 1: Set Up the WAN Side

To start, you need to know the network IDs for each side of your router. The WAN side invariably connects to an ISP, so you need to know what the ISP wants you to do. If you bought a static IP address, type it in now. However—brace yourself for a crazy fact—most home Internet connections use DHCP! That's right, DHCP isn't just for your PC. You can set up your router's WAN connection to use it too. DHCP is by far the most common connection to use for home routers. Access your router and locate the WAN connection setup. Figure 7.41 shows the setup for my home router set to DHCP.

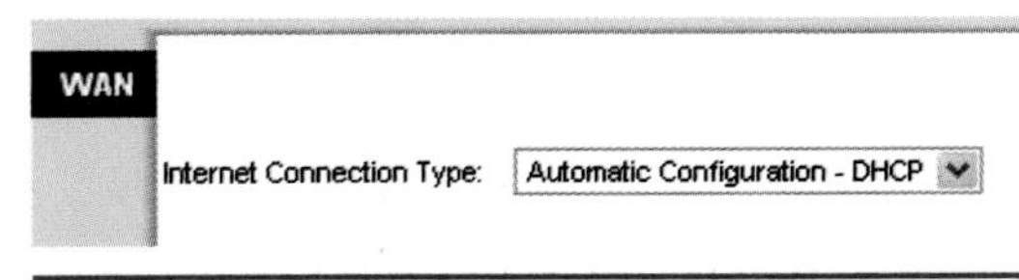

• **Figure 7.41** WAN router setup

I'm ignoring a number of other settings here for the moment. I'll revisit most of these in later chapters.

But what if I called my ISP and bought a single static IP address? This is rarely done anymore, but virtually every ISP will gladly sell you one (although you will pay three to four times as much for the connection). If you use a static IP address, your ISP will tell you what to enter, usually in the form of an e-mail message like the following:

```
Dear Mr. Meyers,
Thank you for requesting a static IP address from
totalsem.com!
Here's your new static IP information:
IP address: 1.151.35.55
Default Gateway: 1.151.32.132
Subnet Mask: 255.255.128.0
Installation instructions can be found at:
http://totalsem.com/setup/
Support is available at:
http://helpdesk.totalsem.com or by calling (281)922-4166.
```

In such a case, I would need to change the router setting to Static IP (Figure 7.42). Note how changing the drop-down menu to Static IP enables me to enter the information needed.

Once you've set up the WAN side, it's time to head over to set up the LAN side of the router.

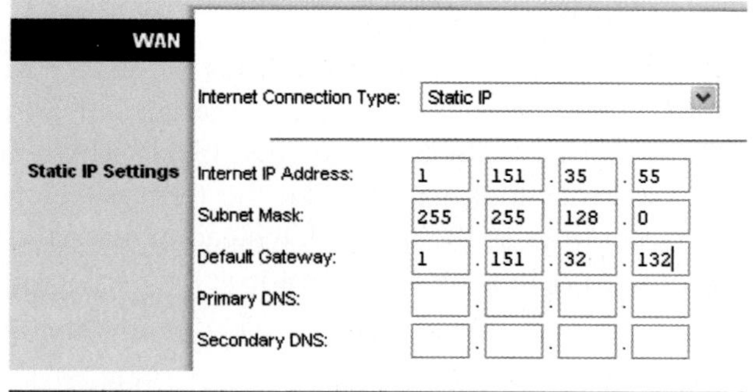

• **Figure 7.42** Entering a static IP

Step 2: Set Up the LAN Side

Unlike the WAN side, you usually have total control on the LAN side of the router. You need to choose a network ID, almost always some arbitrarily chosen private range unless you do not want to use NAT. This is why so many home networks have network IDs of 192.168.1.0/24, 192.168.2.0/24, and so forth. Once you decide on your LAN-side network ID, you need to assign the correct IP information to the LAN-side NIC. Figure 7.43 shows the configuration for a LAN NIC on my home router.

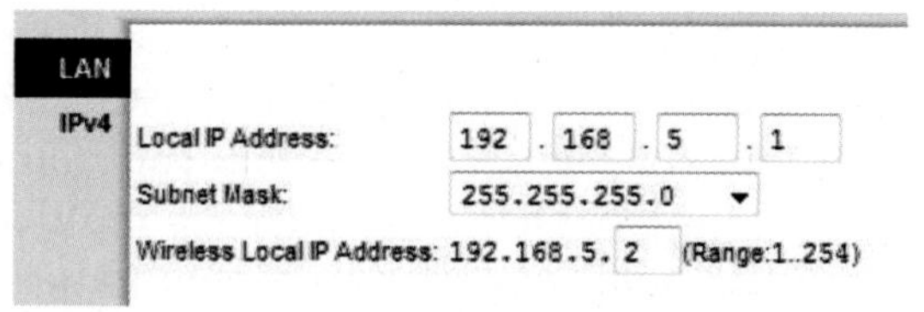

• **Figure 7.43** Setting up an IP address for the LAN side

Step 3: Establish Routes

Most routers are pretty smart and use the information you provided for the two interfaces to build a routing table automatically. If you need to add more routes, every router provides some method to add routes. The following shows the command entered on a Cisco router to add a route to one of its Ethernet interfaces. The term "gig0/0" is how Cisco describes Ethernet NICs in its device software. It is short for GigabitEthernet, which you may remember as being the common name (when you add a space) for 1000BaseT.

```
ip route 192.168.100.0 255.255.255.0 gig0/0 192.168.1.10
```

Step 4 (Optional): Configure a Dynamic Protocol

The rules for using any dynamic routing protocol are fairly straightforward. First, dynamic routing protocols are tied to individual interfaces, not the entire router. Second, when you connect two routers together, make sure those two interfaces are configured to use the same dynamic routing protocol. Third, unless you're in charge of two or more routers, you're probably not going to use any dynamic routing protocol.

The amazing part of a dynamic routing protocol is how easy it is to set up. In most cases you just figure out how to turn it on and that's about it. It just starts working.

Step 5: Document and Back Up

Once you've configured your routes, take some time to document what you've done. A good router works for years without interaction, so by that time in the future when it goes down, odds are good you will have forgotten why you added the routes. Last, take some time to back up the configuration. If a router goes down, it will most likely forget everything and you'll need to set it up all over again. Every router has some method to back up the configuration, however, so you can restore it later.

Router Problems

The CompTIA Network+ exam will challenge you on some basic router problems. All of these questions should be straightforward for you as long as you do the following:

- Consider other issues first because routers don't fail very often.
- Keep in mind what your router is supposed to do.
- Know how to use a few basic tools that can help you check the router.

Any router problem starts with someone not connecting to someone else. Even a small network has a number of NICs, computers, switches, and routers between you and whatever it is you're not connecting to. Compared to most of these, a router is a pretty robust device and shouldn't be considered as the problem until you've checked out just about everything else first.

In their most basic forms, routers route traffic. Yet you've seen in this chapter that routers can do more than just plain routing—for example, NAT. As this book progresses, you'll find that the typical router often handles a large number of duties beyond just routing. Know what your router is doing and appreciate that you may find yourself checking a router for problems that don't really have anything to do with routing at all.

Routing Tables and Missing Routes

Be aware that routers have some serious but rare potential problems. One place to watch is your routing table. For the most part, today's routers automatically generate directly connected routes, and dynamic routing takes care of itself, leaving one type of route as a possible suspect: the static routes. This is the place to look when packets aren't getting to the places you expect them to go. Look at the following sample static route:

```
Network Destination       Netmask          Gateway          Interface          Metric
    22.46.132.0    255.255.255.255   22.46.132.1      22.46.132.11             1
```

No incoming packets for the network ID are getting out on interface 22.46.132.11. Can you see why? Yup, the Netmask is set to 255.255.255.255, and there are no computers that have exactly the address 22.46.132.0. Entering the wrong network destination, subnet mask, gateway, and so on, is very easy. If a new static route isn't getting the packets moved, first assume you made a typo.

Make sure to watch out for missing routes. These usually take place either because you've forgotten to add them (if you're entering static routes) or, more commonly, there is a convergence problem in the dynamic routing protocols. For the CompTIA Network+ exam, be ready to inspect a routing table to recognize these problems.

MTUs and PDUs

The developers of TCP/IP assumed that traffic would move over various networking technologies and packet size would vary. Each technology has a maximum size of a single *protocol data unit (PDU)* that can transmit, called the **maximum transmission unit (MTU)**. The PDU for TCP at Layer 4, for example, is a segment that gets encapsulated into an IP packet (the PDU for Layer 3). The IP packet in turn gets encapsulated in some medium at Layer 2. Ethernet frames encapsulate IP packets, for example.

At each layer of encapsulation, other information gets added (such as source and destination IP or MAC address) and the PDU for that layer gets larger. Going from one network technology to another can cause a packet or frame to exceed the MTU for the receiving system, which is not a big deal. The network components know to split the packet or frame into two or more pieces to get below the MTU threshold for the next hop. The problem is that this *fragmentation* can increase the number of packets or frames needed to move data between two points—gross inefficiency.

Path MTU describes the largest packet size transmissible without fragmentation through all the hops in a route. Devices can use *Path MTU Discovery* to determine the path MTU, that maximum size. MTU size can be adjusted at the source to eliminate fragmentation.

Tools

When it comes to tools, networking comes with so many utilities and magic devices that it staggers the imagination. You've already seen some, like good old ping and route, but let's add two more tools: traceroute and mtr.

The **traceroute** tool, as its name implies, records the route between any two hosts on a network. On the surface, traceroute is something like ping in that it sends a single packet to another host, but as it progresses, it returns information about every router between them.

Every operating system comes with traceroute, but the actual command varies among them. In Windows, the command is `tracert` and looks like this (I'm running a traceroute to the router connected to my router—a short trip):

```
C:\>tracert 96.165.24.1

Tracing route to 96.165.24.1 over a maximum of 30 hops:

   1     1 ms     1 ms     1 ms    10.12.14.1
    2    10 ms    10 ms     8 ms   96.165.24.1
Trace complete.
```

The macOS/UNIX/Linux command is `traceroute` and looks like this:

```
michaelm@ubuntu:~$ traceroute 96.165.24.1
traceroute to 96.165.24.1 (96.165.24.1), 30 hops max, 40 byte
packets
1     10.12.14.1 (10.12.14.1)   0.763 ms 0.432 ms  0.233 ms
2     96.165.24.1 (96.165.24.1) 12.233 ms 11.255 ms 14.112 ms
michaelm@ubuntu:~$
```

The traceroute tool is handy, not so much for what it tells you when everything's working well, but for what it tells you when things are not working. Look at the following:

```
:\>tracert 96.165.24.1

Tracing route to 96.165.24.1 over a maximum of 30 hops
  1      1 ms      1 ms      1 ms  10.12.14.1
   2      *         *         *      Request timed out
   3  96.165.24.1  reports: Destination host unreachable.
```

If this traceroute worked in the past but now no longer works, you know that something is wrong between your router and the next router upstream. You don't know what's wrong exactly. The connection may be down; the router may not be working; but at least traceroute gives you an idea where to look for the problem and where not to look.

You might get a question on troubleshooting routers and connection choices. Typically you should use SSH to connect and configure a router over the LAN, but if that connection doesn't work, connect directly using a rollover cable/console cable.

My traceroute (mtr) is very similar to traceroute, but it's dynamic, continually updating the route that you've selected (Figure 7.44). You won't find mtr in Windows; mtr is a Linux tool. Instead, Windows users can use pathping. This utility pings each node on the route just like mtr, but instead of showing the results of each ping in real time, running `pathping` computes the performance over a set time and then shows you the summary after it has finished.

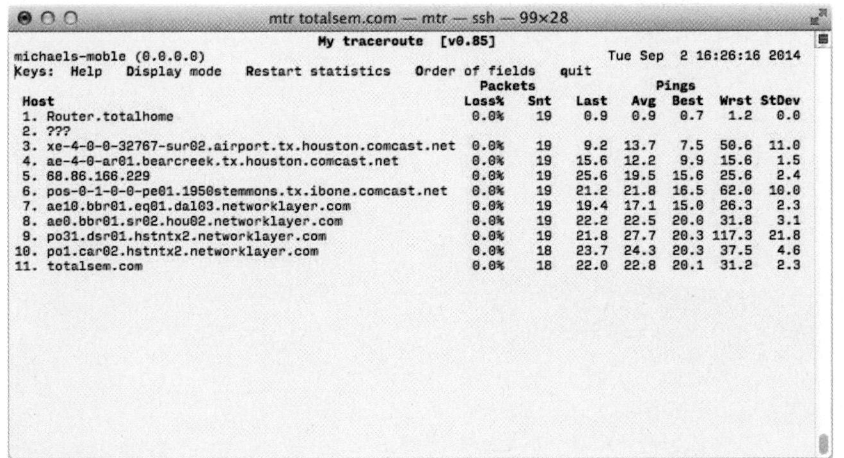

• **Figure 7.44** mtr in action

Packets used by tools like traceroute and mtr have a default number of hops they'll go before being discarded by a router. At every hop, a router decreases the **time to live (TTL)** number in a packet until the packet reaches its destination or hits zero. This stops packets from going on forever. The final router will discard the packet and send an ICMP message to the original sender.

Each tool for doing tracing (and that includes ping and pathping) enables you to set the maximum hop count; most default at 30, as you can see in the various "over a maximum of 30 hops" notes in the screen outputs above. To set a tracert to go for many hops, for example, you'd use the -h switch and a number, like in Figure 7.45.

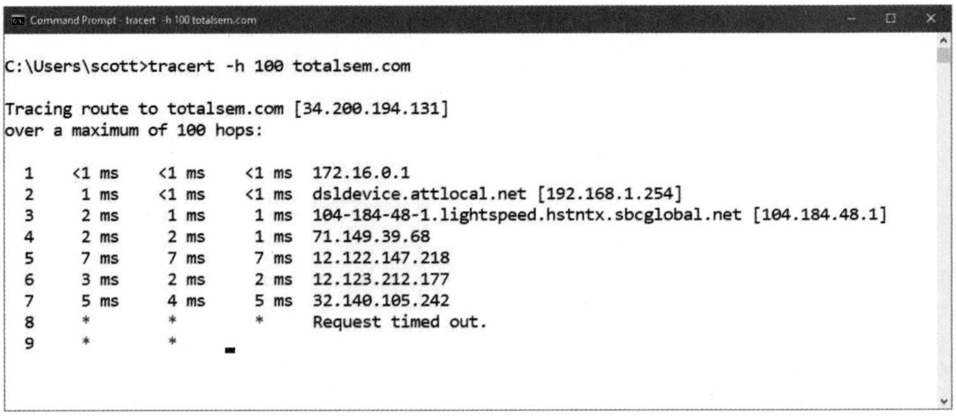
Command Prompt - tracert -h 100 totalsem.com
C:\Users\scott>tracert -h 100 totalsem.com
Tracing route to totalsem.com [34.200.194.131]
over a maximum of 100 hops:
1 <1 ms <1 ms <1 ms 172.16.0.1
2 1 ms <1 ms <1 ms dsldevice.attlocal.net [192.168.1.254]
3 2 ms 1 ms 1 ms 104-184-48-1.lightspeed.hstntx.sbcglobal.net [104.184.48.1]
4 2 ms 2 ms 1 ms 71.149.39.68
5 7 ms 7 ms 7 ms 12.122.147.218
6 3 ms 2 ms 2 ms 12.123.212.177
7 5 ms 4 ms 5 ms 32.140.105.242
8 * * * Request timed out.
9 * *

• **Figure 7.45** Adjusting TTL in tracert

Chapter 7 Review

Chapter Summary

After reading this chapter and completing the exercises, you should understand the following about routing.

Explain how routers work

- A router is any piece of hardware that forwards network packets based on their destination IP addresses.
- A routing table is the chart of information kept on a router to aid in directing the flow of packets through computer networks.
- Routers learn new routes as they go, interacting with each other by exchanging routing table information. The routing tables are checked and can be updated dynamically as data flows across a network, with routers chatting with each other for the latest network and IP address information periodically.
- Routers can connect dissimilar networks, such as Ethernet, DOCSIS, and PON.
- NAT saves a table of information, so it knows which system is communicating with which external site. NAT solutions can be software based or included as part of a hardware device such as a router.
- PAT is the most common form of NAT that handles a one-to-many connection, using port numbers to map traffic from specific machines in the network.
- Dynamic NAT can share a pool of routable IP addresses with multiple computers.
- Static NAT maps a single IP address to a single machine, enabling you to access that machine from outside the network.
- Port forwarding hides port numbers from the public side of a network. The router simply forwards packets from one port number to another as the packet passes from the public to the private side of the router.

Describe dynamic routing technologies

- Routing table entries are entered manually on static routers and do not change. Dynamic routers, in contrast, automatically update their routing table. This is accomplished by using special routing protocols.
- The CompTIA Network+ exam objectives focus on three distinct groups of routing protocols: distance vector, link state, and hybrid.
- Routing tables are shared with other routers, and routers automatically choose the complete route with the lowest metric.
- Distance vector routing protocols are not recommended for networks with more than ten routers because of the time it takes for the routers to reach convergence.
- Distance vector routing protocols include RIPv1 and RIPv2.
- RIPv1 has a maximum hop count of 15, with routing table updates sent every 30 seconds. Because RIPv1 lacked authentication and experienced network overloads as every router sent its routing table at the same time, the RIPv2 update was developed.
- RIPv2, which also has a maximum hop count of 15, supports VLSM and discontiguous subnets and provides authentication to prevent hackers from sending false routing table information. RIPv2's lengthy time to convergence for large networks led to the development of better routing protocols such as OSPF.
- An Autonomous System (AS) is one or more networks that share a unified "policy" regarding how they exchange traffic with other Autonomous Systems. Each AS must have a globally unique Autonomous System Number (ASN) assigned by IANA.
- The protocol used by Autonomous Systems to communicate with each other is generically called an Exterior Gateway Protocol (EGP). Networks within an Autonomous System use an Interior Gateway Protocol (IGP). Edge routers connect an AS network to another AS network.
- Interior Gateway Protocols include OSPF and other protocols.

- Border Gateway Protocol (BGP) is the only Exterior Gateway Protocol used on the Internet. It connects all of the Autonomous Systems.
- BGP implements and supports route aggregation, a way to simplify routing tables into manageable levels.
- Link state protocols include OSPF and IS-IS. Link state protocols overcome the relatively slow and bandwidth-heavy usage of distance vector protocols.
- The Open Shortest Path First (OSPF) routing protocol is the most commonly used Interior Gateway Protocol in the world. It is more efficient than RIP, converges dramatically faster than RIP, and supports IPv6 as of OSPF Version 3.
- OSPF sends Hello packets when an OSPF-enabled router first boots up. An OSPF router then sends link state advertisements (LSAs) to known connections.
- Intermediate System to Intermediate System (IS-IS) is another link state dynamic routing protocol, similar to OSPF. It has supported IPv6 from the start.
- Enhanced Interior Gateway Routing Protocol (EIGRP) is a hybrid Cisco protocol that has aspects of both distance vector and link state protocols.

Install and configure a router successfully

- A Yost cable (rollover cable) is a special serial cable used to connect directly to a Cisco router for configuration purposes.
- Once a direct connection has been made to a router, use a terminal emulation program such as PuTTY or HyperTerminal to communicate.
- Most Cisco products run Cisco's proprietary operating system, Cisco IOS. Although not covered on the CompTIA Network+ certification exam, understanding IOS is a must for anyone who wants to become Cisco Certified.
- Most routers include a built-in Web interface for configuration. You must know the router's IP address to make this type of connection.
- Many techs use a laptop and a crossover cable to connect to a Web server–enabled router for the initial configuration. This method also requires setting a static IP address on the connected laptop, unless the router includes a DHCP server.
- Network Management Software (NMS) is used to describe, visualize, and configure an entire network. NMS is made both by the OEMs that make managed devices and by third-party companies.
- In general, NMS made by the OEMs that make managed devices is easy to use but only works on specific hardware. Much third-party NMS is available as freeware, but is typically harder to use and must be constantly updated to work with as many devices as possible.
- Some routers may be connected to via USB, Telnet, or SSH.
- When you set up a router, you must configure every port on the router properly to talk to its connected network IDs and to make sure the routing table sends packets to where you want them to go.
- Setting up a router can be broken down into five steps: set up the WAN side, set up the LAN, establish routes, optionally configure a dynamic routing protocol, and document and back up your settings.
- The traceroute utility records the route between any two hosts on a network and can be used to troubleshoot routing problems.

Key Terms

administrative distance *(195)*
Autonomous System (AS) *(191)*
Border Gateway Protocol (BGP) *(192)*
Cisco IOS *(197)*
convergence *(190)*
cost *(187)*
distance vector *(188)*
dynamic NAT (DNAT) *(183)*
dynamic routing *(186)*
edge router *(193)*
Enhanced Interior Gateway Routing Protocol (EIGRP) *(194)*
gateway *(182)*
hop *(186)*
hop count *(187)*
Intermediate System to Intermediate System (IS-IS) *(194)*
link state *(193)*

managed device *(196)*
maximum transmission unit (MTU) *(204)*
metric *(178)*
My traceroute (mtr) *(205)*
NAT translation table *(183)*
network address translation (NAT) *(181)*
Network Management Software (NMS) *(199)*
next hop *(175)*
Open Shortest Path First (OSPF) *(193)*
path vector *(193)*
port address translation (PAT) *(182)*
port forwarding *(184)*
RIPv1 *(190)*
RIPv2 *(191)*
route redistribution *(195)*
router *(173)*
Routing Information Protocol (RIP) *(190)*
routing table *(175)*
static NAT (SNAT) *(184)*
static route *(186)*
time to live (TTL) *(205)*
traceroute *(204)*
Yost cable *(196)*

Key Term Quiz

Use the Key Terms list to complete the sentences that follow. Not all the terms will be used.

1. A device called a(n) _______________ is also called a Layer 3 switch.
2. The external routing protocol used on the Internet is _______________.
3. The variety of _______________ protocols would include RIP, OSPF, EIGRP, and BGP.
4. A(n) _______________ is normally entered manually into a router.
5. A(n) _______________ connects one Autonomous System to another Autonomous System.
6. _______________ is a routing protocol that updates routing tables every 30 seconds, resulting in overloaded network traffic.
7. When all routers can communicate with each other efficiently, they are said to have reached _______________.
8. One or more networks with a unified traffic-exchange policy is known as a(n) _______________.
9. You can use the _______________ utility to troubleshoot routing problems.
10. _______________ uses IP addresses and port numbers to enable many internal computers to share a single public IP address.

Multiple-Choice Quiz

1. How many IP addresses should a router have?
   - **A.** One
   - **B.** One or more
   - **C.** Two
   - **D.** Two or more
2. Choose the Cisco Systems routing protocol from the following items.
   - **A.** BGP
   - **B.** EIGRP
   - **C.** RIP
   - **D.** OSPF
3. If specialty accounting software being used at your company requires that packet headers remain unchanged, which item cannot be used on your network?
   - **A.** RIP
   - **B.** NAT
   - **C.** OSPF
   - **D.** traceroute

4. How does a router use a routing table to determine over which path to send a packet?
   - A. The first line in the routing table is used if the path is available; otherwise, the router tries the next line down, and so on.
   - B. The last line in the routing table is used if the path is available; otherwise, the router tries the next line up, and so on.
   - C. After examining all rows in the routing table, the router sends the packet along the path with the highest metric.
   - D. After examining all rows in the routing table, the router sends the packet along the path with the lowest metric.
5. Which version of NAT maps a single routable IP address to a single network node?
   - A. Static NAT
   - B. Dynamic NAT
   - C. Pooled NAT
   - D. Private NAT
6. What technology enables you to designate a specific local address for various network services?
   - A. Dynamic NAT
   - B. Port Address Translation
   - C. Port forwarding
   - D. Port filtering
7. Which of the following is a distance vector routing metric?
   - A. Meters
   - B. Hops
   - C. Routes
   - D. Segments
8. Which of the following is a path vector routing protocol?
   - A. RIP
   - B. OSPF
   - C. BGP
   - D. ASN
9. Which of the following are benefits of RIPv2 over RIPv1? (Select two.)
   - A. Longer convergence times
   - B. Support for authentication
   - C. Support for VLSM
   - D. Support for metrics
10. Which of the following router protocols uses link state advertisements?
    - A. RIPv1
    - B. RIPv2
    - C. OSPF
    - D. BGP
11. Which of the following is an exterior routing protocol?
    - A. BGP
    - B. IS-IS
    - C. OSPF
    - D. RIPv2
12. What does OSPF do, initially?
    - A. It floods the network with Hello packets as it looks for other OSPF routers.
    - B. It floods the network by requesting routing tables from every computer on the network.
    - C. It is unavailable for several hours as it builds its default routing table.
    - D. It runs a self-test to determine if it should run in hybrid mode (RIP and OSPF) or native mode (OSPF only).
13. Which of the following is a valid Area ID for an OSPF backbone?
    - A. 0.1
    - B. 0
    - C. 1.0
    - D. 255
14. How can you connect a PC directly to a router for configuration purposes? (Select two.)
    - A. Parallel cable
    - B. USB cable
    - C. Crossover cable
    - D. Rollover cable
15. Once you have made a physical direct connection to a router, what utility/program can you use to issue commands and instructions? (Select three.)
    - A. PuTTY
    - B. HyperTerminal
    - C. IOS
    - D. Web browser

Essay Quiz

1. You have been introduced to a lot more "alphabet soup" in this chapter. Quickly jot down what each of the following stands for: BGP, NAT, RIP, OSPF, NMS, PAT, EIGRP, IS-IS, AS, ASN, EGP, and IGP.
2. Explain why a router is sometimes called a Layer 3 switch.
3. Write a short essay about OSPF and its uses, as well as its benefits over using RIPv2.

Lab Projects

• Lab Project 7.1

A classmate of yours is all excited about some upcoming classes available at your school that will cover Cisco routing. He keeps talking about EIGRP and its importance in the workplace, as well as how much cash can be earned if you know EIGRP. Use the Internet to research EIGRP—its history, its uses, and what devices run using EIGRP—and to research what salaries Cisco Certified professionals earn (possibly your next certification after passing the CompTIA Network+ exam). Then share this information with your instructor and your classmate to compare your findings. What does EIGRP do for corporate networks? What salaries are realistically possible? What were your sources?

• Lab Project 7.2

Start a command prompt at your computer and enter **`netstat -nr`** to view its routing table. Create a screenshot of the output and paste it into a word processing document. Under the pasted screenshot, briefly explain what each column is for. Compare your routing table to your classmates' routing tables and explain to each other what the differences are and why differences occur.

TCP/IP Applications

"The World Wide Web is the only thing I know of whose shortened form—www—takes three times longer to say than what it's short for."

—Douglas Adams

In this chapter, you will learn how to

- **Describe common Transport and Network layer protocols**
- **Explain the power of port numbers**
- **Define common TCP/IP applications such as Telnet, SSH, e-mail (SMTP, POP3, and IMAP4), FTP, HTTP, and HTTPS**

We network to get work done. Okay, sometimes that "work" involves a mad gaming session in which I lay some smack down on my editors, but you know what I mean. Thus far in the book, everything you've read about networking involves connecting computers together. This chapter moves further up the OSI seven-layer model to look at applications such as e-mail messaging, Web browsers, and more.

To understand the applications that use TCP/IP networks, a tech needs to know the structures below those applications. Have you ever opened multiple Web pages on a single computer? Have you ever run multiple Internet apps, such as a Web browser, an e-mail client, and a remote connectivity app, all at the same time? Clearly, a lot of data is moving back and forth between your computer and many other computers. With packets coming in from two, three, or more computers, there has to be a mechanism or process that knows where to send and receive that data.

In this chapter, you'll discover the process used by TCP/IP networks to ensure the right data gets to the right applications on your computer. This process uses very important Transport and Network layer protocols—TCP, UDP,

and ICMP—and port numbering. When used together, TCP and UDP along with port numbers enable you to get work done on a network.

Historical/Conceptual

Transport Layer and Network Layer Protocols

I hate to tell you this, but you've been lied to. Not by me. Even though I've gone along with this Big Lie, I need to tell you the truth.

There is no such thing as TCP/IP. *TCP over IP* is really many other things, such as *HTTP*, *DHCP*, *POP*, and about 500 more terms over *TCP*, plus *UDP* and *ICMP* over *IP*. Given that this overly complex but much more correct term is too hard to use, the people who invented this network protocol stack decided to call it *TCP/IP*, even though that term is way too simplistic to cover all the functionality involved. One way to refer to all the aspects and protocols that make up TCP/IP is to call it the **TCP/IP suite** or the **Internet Protocol suite**.

There is a strong movement toward using the term *Internet Protocol* instead of the term *TCP/IP*.

This chapter explores many of the protocols used in TCP/IP networks and shows how they help make applications work. This section looks at the big three—TCP, UDP, and ICMP, plus IGMP for fun. (Subsequent sections of this chapter explore many more protocols.) Let's start the process with an analogy, by considering how humans communicate. You'll see some very interesting commonalities between computers and people.

How People Communicate

Imagine you walk into a school cafeteria to get some lunch. You first walk up to the guy making custom deli sandwiches (this is a great cafeteria!) and say, "Hello!" He says, "How may I help you?" You say, "I'd like a sandwich please." He says, "What kind of sandwich would you like?" and you order your sandwich. After you get your sandwich you say, "Thanks!" and he says, "You're welcome." What a nice guy! In the networking world, we would call this a **connection-oriented** communication. Both you and the lunch guy first acknowledge each other. You then conduct your communication; finally, you close the communication.

While you're in line, you see your friend Janet sitting at your usual table. The line is moving fast so you yell out, "Janet, save me a seat!" before you rush along in the line. In this case, you're not waiting for her to answer; you just yell to her and hope she hears you. We call this a **connectionless** communication. There is no acknowledgment or any closing.

In networking, any single communication between a computer and another computer is called a **session**. When you open a Web page, you make a session. When you call your buddy (using the Internet, not the cellular networks), you create a session. All sessions must begin and eventually end.

Test Specific

TCP

All of the segments described here—such as SYN segment and ACK segment—are *TCP segments* with the appropriate *flag* set. So a "SYN segment" is a TCP segment with the SYN flag set. I used common shorthand for the segments to use fewer words and avoid repetition.

Transmission Control Protocol (TCP) enables connection-oriented communication in networks that use the TCP/IP protocol suite. Figure 8.1 shows two computers. One computer (Server) runs a Web server and the other (Client) runs a Web browser. When you enter a computer's address in the browser running on Client, it sends a single SYN (synchronize) segment to the Web server. If Server gets that segment, it returns a single SYN, ACK (synchronize, acknowledge) segment. Client then sends Server a single ACK (acknowledge) segment and immediately requests that Server begin sending the Web page. This process is called the **TCP three-way handshake**.

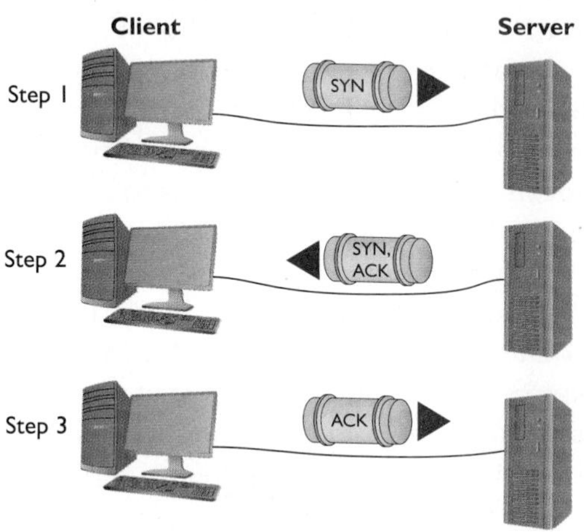

• **Figure 8.1** A connection-oriented session starting

Once Server finishes sending the Web page, it sends a FIN (final) segment. Client responds with an ACK segment and then sends its own FIN segment. The server then responds with an ACK; now both parties consider the session closed (Figure 8.2).

Most TCP/IP applications use TCP because connection-oriented sessions are designed to check for errors. If a sending computer doesn't see an ACK for an outstanding segment, the sender takes the initiative to send it again.

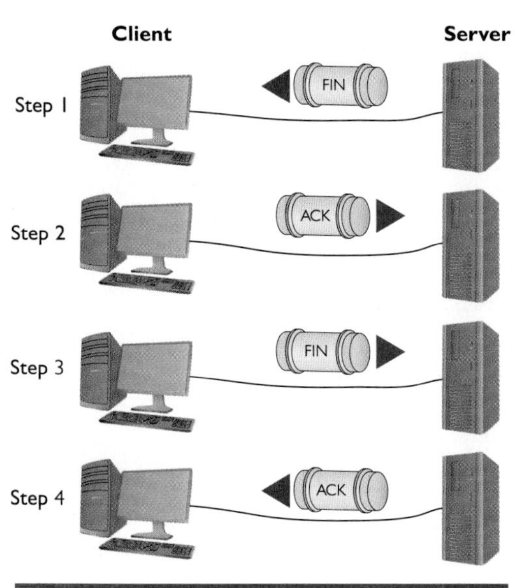

• **Figure 8.2** A connection-oriented session ending

UDP

User Datagram Protocol (UDP) is perfect for the types of sessions that don't require the overhead of all that connection-oriented stuff. These include sessions that use important protocols such as DNS, DHCP, NTP/SNTP, and TFTP.

DNS

Domain Name System (DNS) enables the use of names associated with IP addresses for devices connected to IP networks, such as the Internet and private intranets. In a nutshell, DNS is why you can type www.google.com into a Web browser to get to Google search engine servers and not have to try to remember the numbers of the IP address. DNS uses UDP on port 53 by default.

DNS is so important that I've devoted an entire chapter to the topic, Chapter 9.

DHCP

Dynamic Host Configuration Protocol (DHCP) uses UDP and provides a good example of connectionless communication. DHCP can't assume another computer is ready on either side of the session, so each step of a DHCP session just sends the information for that step without any confirmation (Figure 8.3). Sending a connectionless datagram also makes sense because the client won't have an IP address to begin the three-way handshake. Plus, if the server doesn't respond, the client can simply ask again.

As you learned in Chapter 6, DHCP uses two port numbers. DHCP clients use port 68 for sending data to and receiving data from the DHCP server, and DHCP servers use port 67 for sending and receiving data to and from DHCP clients.

• **Figure 8.3** DHCP steps

NTP/SNTP

The **Network Time Protocol (NTP)** and his lightweight little brother, *Simple Network Time Protocol (SNTP)*, use UDP to synchronize the clocks of devices on a network. Computers need to use the same time so services like Kerberos authentication work properly. If a device requires NTP/SNTP, you will be able to enter the IP address for an NTP/SNTP server. NTP/SNTP uses port 123.

NTP operates in a hierarchical fashion or **clock strata**. At the highest end, *stratum 0* devices—like atomic clocks or the Global Positioning System (GPS) satellites—keep near perfect time. The servers that connect to stratum 0 devices, called *stratum 1* servers, synchronize to within a few milliseconds of the stratum 0 time. Stratum 1 servers in turn enable connection by *stratum 2* clients—which are a little less perfectly synchronized—that enable connection by *stratum 3* clients. This hierarchy continues until stratum 15; after that, devices are not synchronized with the clock.

NTP usually employs the *client/server* hierarchy described here, but also enables *peer-to-peer* connections at each stratum level for backup and sanity checks.

TFTP

You might also be tempted to think that UDP wouldn't work for any situation in which a critical data transfer takes place—untrue! **Trivial File Transfer Protocol (TFTP)** enables you to transfer files from one machine to another. TFTP, using UDP, doesn't have any data protection, so you would never use TFTP between computers across the Internet. The typical scenario for using TFTP is updating software and configurations on routers, switches, VoIP phones, and other devices on a LAN, where the chances of losing packets is very small. TFTP uses port 69.

Expect to get a question that compares *connectionless* vs. *connection-oriented* communication in general, or the protocols commonly used in each.

ICMP

While TCP and UDP differ dramatically—the former connection-oriented and the latter connectionless—both are encapsulated in packets in the classic sense with a destination IP address, source IP address, destination port

A *firewall* is a device or software that filters all the packets between two computers (or groups of computers) and acts like a club bouncer deciding who gets in and who gets blocked. Firewalls are vital for securing all networks and will be discussed in Chapter 19.

numbers, and source port numbers. A single session can consist of a packet or a series of packets with the Layer 4 protocol inside.

On the other hand, sometimes applications are so simple that they don't need the overhead and complexity of TCP. **Internet Control Message Protocol (ICMP)** works at Layer 3 to handle low-level housekeeping tasks such as host unreachable messages and router advertisements (see Chapter 12).

The ping utility works by sending a single ICMP message called an *echo request* to an IP address you specify. All computers running TCP/IP (assuming no firewall is involved) respond to echo requests with an *echo reply*, as shown in Figure 8.4.

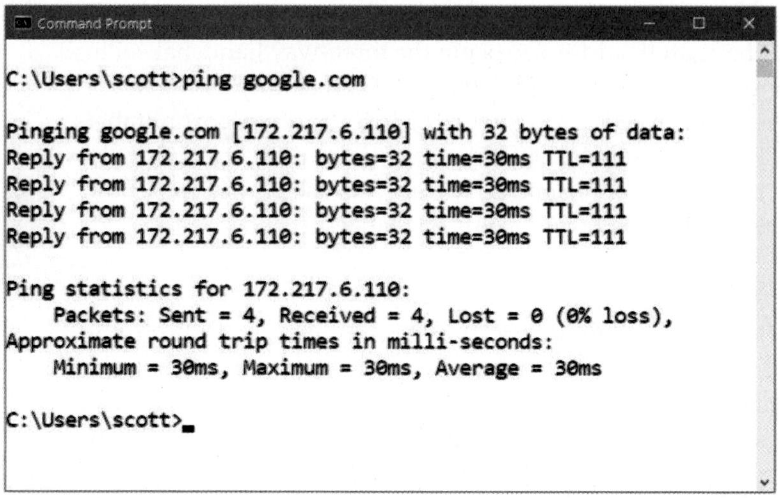

```
C:\Users\scott>ping google.com

Pinging google.com [172.217.6.110] with 32 bytes of data:
Reply from 172.217.6.110: bytes=32 time=30ms TTL=111
Reply from 172.217.6.110: bytes=32 time=30ms TTL=111
Reply from 172.217.6.110: bytes=32 time=30ms TTL=111
Reply from 172.217.6.110: bytes=32 time=30ms TTL=111

Ping statistics for 172.217.6.110:
    Packets: Sent = 4, Received = 4, Lost = 0 (0% loss),
Approximate round trip times in milli-seconds:
    Minimum = 30ms, Maximum = 30ms, Average = 30ms

C:\Users\scott>_
```

• **Figure 8.4** `ping` in action

The ping utility provides a couple of responses that indicate problems locating the remote computer. If your computer has no route to the address listed, ping displays *destination host unreachable*. You might get the same message from a router upstream if that router can't go forward. If you ping a device and no echo reply comes back before the default time, `ping` responds with *request timed out*. (The default time varies by platform, but within a few seconds.) This can be caused by a slow network, excess traffic, a downed router, and more. Ping responses, for example, could be disabled on the target computer.

Many years ago, operating systems had a bug that allowed malicious users to send malformed packets to a destination, with ping packets being the most common type. This *ping of death* would cause the recipient computer to crash. This bug was fixed long ago, but you might still hear this term used by grizzled, veteran techs.

IGMP

Do you remember the idea of IP multicast addresses, described in Chapter 6? The challenge to multicasting is determining who wants to receive the multicast and who does not. **Internet Group Management Protocol (IGMP)** enables routers to communicate with hosts and switches to determine a "group" membership. As you might remember from Chapter 6, multicast is in the

Class D range (224.0.0.0–239.255.255.255). Just about all multicast addresses will start with 224.0.0.*x*, although the range goes up to 239.255.255.255. IP multicast traffic is not addressed to unique IP addresses assigned to individual hosts in the same manner as you've seen thus far. Instead, multicast traffic (called an *IGMP group*) is assigned to an address in the Class D range, and those who wish to receive this multicast must tell their upstream router or switch (which must be configured to handle multicasts) that they wish to receive it. To do so, they join the IGMP group (Figure 8.5).

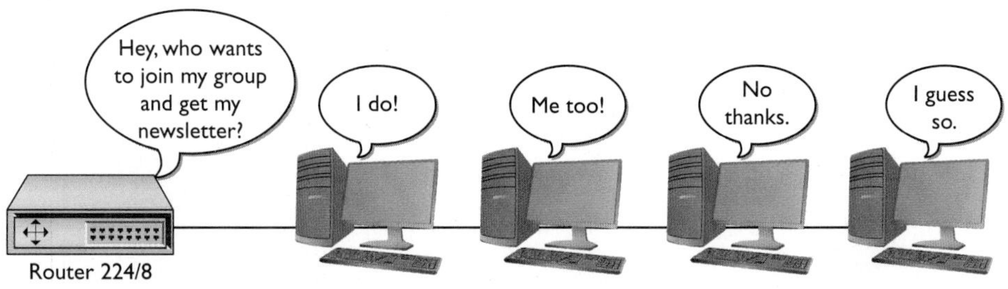

• **Figure 8.5** IGMP in action

Cross Check

Multicast

You first saw multicast in Chapter 6, when you learned about classful IP addressing. Refer to that chapter and see if you can answer this question. What is the difference between unicast and multicast?

The Power of Port Numbers

If you want to understand the power of TCP/IP, you have to get seriously into port numbers. If you want to pass the CompTIA Network+ exam, you need to know how TCP/IP uses port numbers and you have to memorize a substantial number of common port numbers. As you saw in Chapter 7, port numbers make NAT work. As you progress through this book, you'll see a number of places where knowledge of port numbers is critical to protect your network, make routers work better, and address a zillion other issues. There is no such thing as a successful network administrator who isn't deeply into the magic of port numbers and who cannot manipulate them for his or her network's needs.

Let's review and expand on what you learned about port numbers in Chapters 1 and 7. Thus far, you know that every TCP/IP application requires a server and a client. Clearly defined port numbers exist for every popular or *well-known* TCP/IP application. A port number is a 16-bit value between 0 and 65535. Web servers, for example, use port number 80 (for nonsecure connections). Port numbers from 0 to 1023 are called **well-known ports** and are reserved for specific TCP/IP applications.

TCP/IP port numbers between 0 and 1023 are the well-known ports. You'll find them at every party.

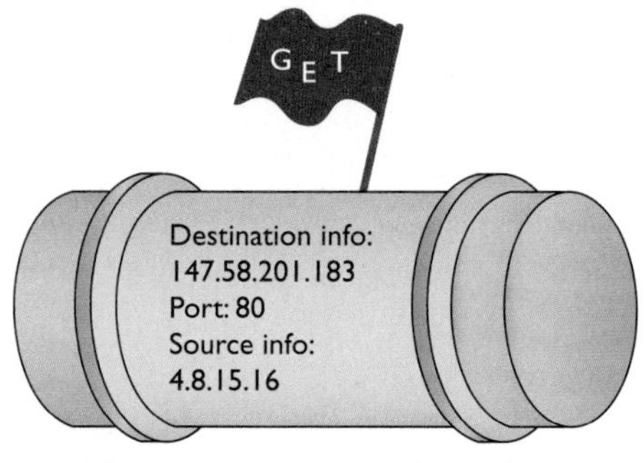

• **Figure 8.6** HTTP GET request

When a client (let's say your computer running the Mozilla Firefox Web browser) sends an HTTP GET request to a Web server to request the Web page, your computer's request packet looks like Figure 8.6.

As you can see, the destination port number is 80. The computer running the Web server reads the destination port number, telling it to send the incoming segment to the Web server program (Figure 8.7).

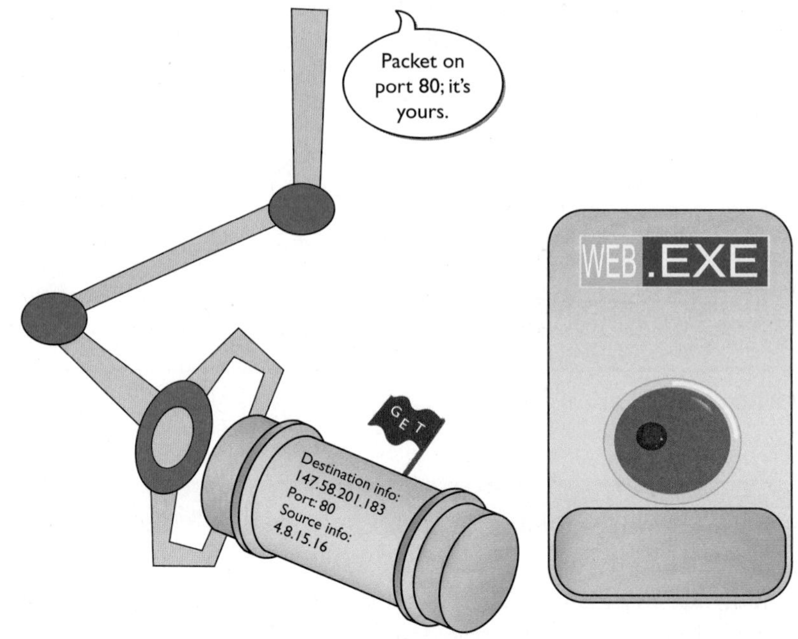

• **Figure 8.7** Dealing with the incoming packet

The Web client's source port number is generated pseudo-randomly by the Web client computer. This value has varied by operating system over the decades, but generally falls within the values 1024–5000 and 49152–65535, the **dynamic ports** (also called **ephemeral ports** and **private ports**).

The Internet Assigned Numbers Authority (IANA) today recommends using only ports 49152–65535 as ephemeral ports. Let's redraw Figure 8.6 to show the more complete packet (Figure 8.8).

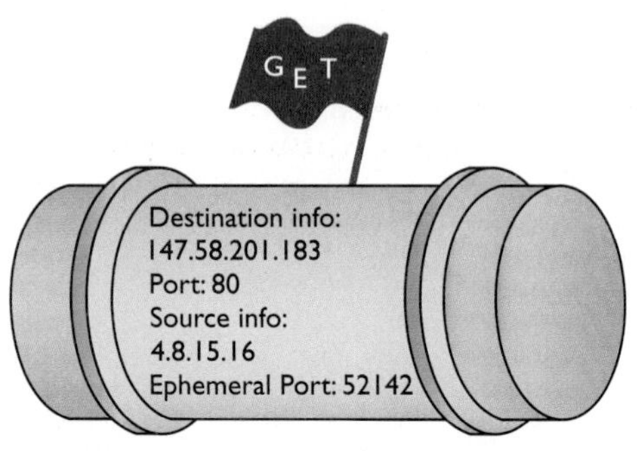

• **Figure 8.8** A more complete IP packet

When the serving system responds to the Web client, it uses the ephemeral port as the destination port to get the information back to the Web client running on the client computer (Figure 8.9).

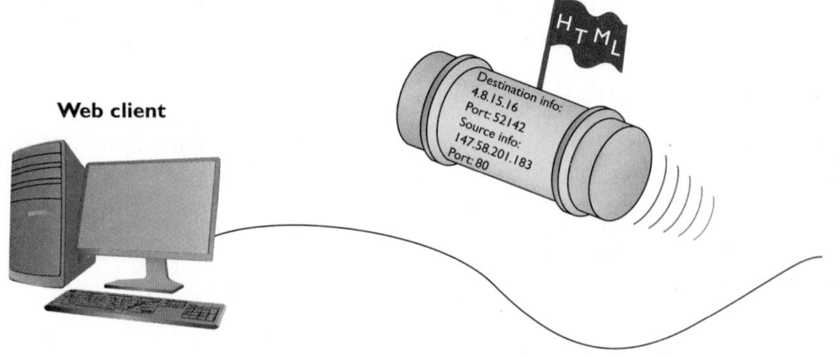

• **Figure 8.9** Returning a response packet

Registered Ports

The port numbers from 1024 to 49151 are called **registered ports**. Less-common TCP/IP applications can register their ports with the IANA. Unlike well-known ports, anyone can use these port numbers for their servers or for ephemeral numbers on clients. Here's the full list of ports:

0–1023	Well-known ports
1024–49151	Registered ports
49152–65535	Dynamic, ephemeral, or private ports

Each computer on each side of a session must keep track of the status of the communication. In TCP/IP, the session information (a combination of the IP address, port number, and Layer 4 protocol—TCP or UDP) held in memory is called a **socket** or **endpoint**. When discussing the session information each computer holds in memory about the connection between two computers' TCP/IP applications, the term to use is **socket pairs** or **endpoints**. A *session* refers to the connection in general, rather than anything specific to TCP/IP. Here's a summary of the terms used:

- Terms for the session information (IP address, port number, and Layer 4 protocol) held in memory on a single computer—*socket* or *endpoint*
- Terms for the session information held in memory on two computers about the same connection—*socket pairs* or *endpoints*
- Term for the whole interconnection—*session*

As two computers begin to communicate, they store the information about the session—the endpoints—so they know where to send and receive data. At any given point in time, your computer is probably connected to many servers all around the Internet. If you want to know your computer's communication partners, you need to see this list of endpoints. As you'll recall from Chapter 7, Windows, macOS, and older Linux distros come with **netstat**, the universal "show me the endpoint" utility. (Current Linux distros use ss rather than netstat.)

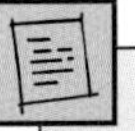

Even though almost all desktop operating systems use netstat, there are differences in options and output among the different versions. The examples in this section are based on the Windows version.

The netstat utility works at the command line, so open one up and type **`netstat -n`** to see something like this:

```
C:\>netstat -n
Active Connections
  Proto  Local Address          Foreign Address         State
   TCP    192.168.4.27:1271      192.168.4.12:445        ESTABLISHED
   TCP    192.168.4.27:1183      192.168.4.251:443       ESTABLISHED
C:\>
```

When you run `netstat -n` on a typical computer, you'll see many more than just two connections! The preceding example is simplified for purposes of discussing the details. It shows two connections: My computer's IP address is 192.168.4.27. The top connection (port 445) is to my file server (192.168.4.12). The second connection is an open Web page (port 443) to a server running GitLab at https://192.168.4.251. Looking on my Windows Desktop, you could confirm that at least these two windows

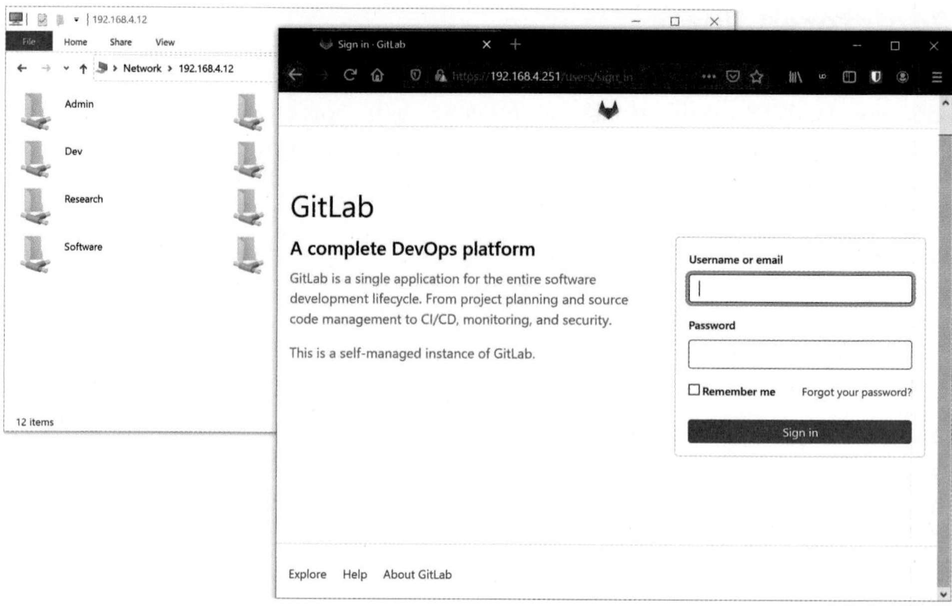

• **Figure 8.10** Two open windows

are open (Figure 8.10). (The file server is the background window; the GitLab server is the foreground window.)

Don't think that a single open application always means a single connection. The following example shows what `netstat -n` looks like when I open the well-known www.microsoft.com Web site (I removed lines unrelated to the Web browser's connections to www.microsoft.com):

```
C:\>netstat -n
Active Connections
  Proto  Local Address          Foreign Address        State
  TCP    192.168.4.27:1240      172.217.14.164:443     ESTABLISHED
  TCP    192.168.4.27:1241      23.203.17.160:443      ESTABLISHED
  TCP    192.168.4.27:1242      151.101.1.192:443      ESTABLISHED
  TCP    192.168.4.27:1243      199.187.116.153:443    ESTABLISHED
  TCP    192.168.4.27:1244      54.69.39.99:443        ESTABLISHED
  TCP    192.168.4.27:1245      20.190.154.19:443      ESTABLISHED
  TCP    192.168.4.27:1246      20.190.154.19:443      ESTABLISHED
  TCP    192.168.4.27:1247      72.21.91.29:80         ESTABLISHED
  TCP    192.168.4.27:1248      151.139.128.14:80      ESTABLISHED
  TCP    192.168.4.27:1249      40.64.101.146:443      ESTABLISHED
  TCP    192.168.4.27:1251      199.187.116.91:443     ESTABLISHED
  TCP    192.168.4.27:1253      151.139.128.14:80      ESTABLISHED
  TCP    192.168.4.27:1255      199.187.116.90:443     ESTABLISHED
  TCP    192.168.4.27:1256      13.77.160.237:443      ESTABLISHED
  TCP    192.168.4.27:1257      208.89.12.87:443       ESTABLISHED
```

The netstat utility enables you to see active TCP/IP connections at a glance.

A single simple Web page may need only a single connection, but this Web page is a bit more complex. Different elements in the Web page, such as advertisements, can have their own connection.

Because netstat is such a powerful tool, you will see it used throughout this book. The CompTIA Network+ exam also tests your netstat skills. On the other hand, connections come and go constantly on your computer, and netstat, being a command-line utility, can't update to reflect changes automatically. While all of the cool, hip, network techs live in the terminal, sometimes you just want a pretty GUI tool. Take a moment right now and

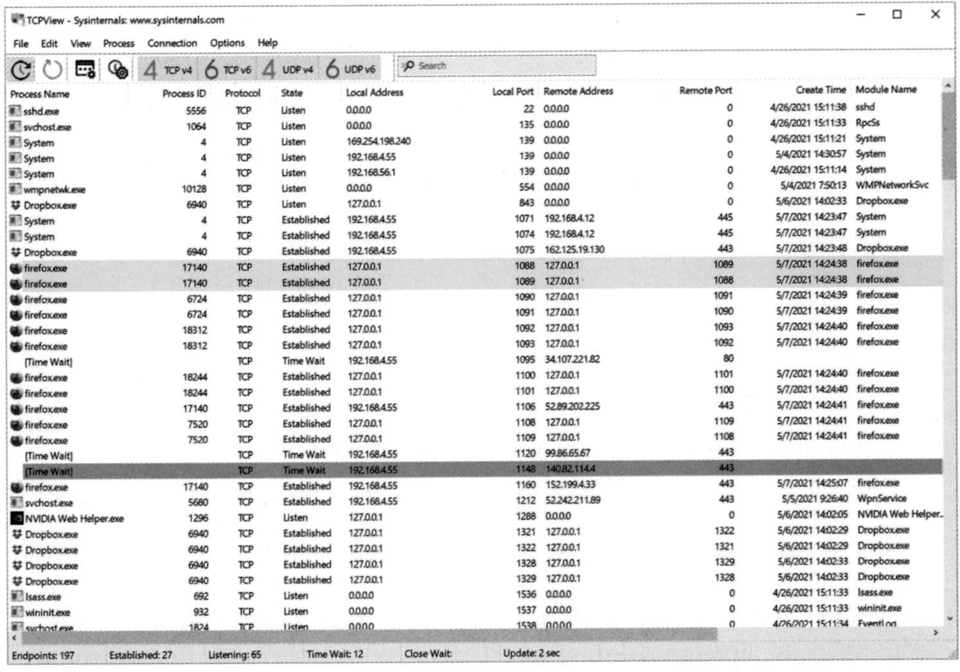

• **Figure 8.11** TCPView in action

download the popular, powerful, and completely free TCPView, written by Mark Russinovich of Sysinternals, the Guru of Windows utilities. Just type **TCPView** into your search engine to find the download page or go here: https://docs.microsoft.com/en-us/sysinternals/. Expand Networking Utilities in the navigation pane on the left icon to find TCPView. Figure 8.11 shows TCPView in action.

Connection Status

Connection states change continually, and it's helpful when using tools such as netstat or TCPView to understand the status of a connection at any given moment. Let's look at the various connection statuses so you understand what each means—this information is useful for determining what's happening on networked computers.

> The `-a` switch tells netstat to show all used ports, including "listening" ports not engaged in active communications. The `-n` switch instructs netstat to show port numbers and IP addresses.

A socket that is prepared to respond to any traffic destined for that socket's port number is called a **listening port** or *open port*; **in other words, a port with the status of** *listening*. Every serving application has a listening port. If you're running a Web server on a computer, for example, it will classically have listening port 80. That's easy enough to appreciate, but you'll be amazed at the number of open ports on just about *any* computer. Fire up a command prompt or terminal and type **`netstat -an`** to see all your listening ports. Running `netstat -an` gives a lot of information, so let's just look at a small amount:

```
C:\>netstat -an
Active Connections
  Proto  Local Address          Foreign Address        State
  TCP    0.0.0.0:7              0.0.0.0:0              LISTENING
  TCP    0.0.0.0:135            0.0.0.0:0              LISTENING
  TCP    0.0.0.0:445            0.0.0.0:0              LISTENING
```

```
TCP    0.0.0.0:912            0.0.0.0:0              LISTENING
TCP    0.0.0.0:990            0.0.0.0:0              LISTENING
TCP    127.0.0.1:27015        0.0.0.0:0              LISTENING
TCP    127.0.0.1:52144        127.0.0.1:52145        ESTABLISHED
TCP    127.0.0.1:52145        127.0.0.1:52144        ESTABLISHED
TCP    127.0.0.1:52146        127.0.0.1:52147        ESTABLISHED
TCP    127.0.0.1:52147        127.0.0.1:52146        ESTABLISHED
TCP    192.168.4.27:139       0.0.0.0:0              LISTENING
TCP    192.168.4.27:52312     74.125.47.108:80       TIME_WAIT
TCP    192.168.4.27:57913     63.246.140.18:80       CLOSE_WAIT
TCP    192.168.4.27:61707     192.168.4.10:445       ESTABLISHED
```

First look at this line:

```
TCP    0.0.0.0:445            0.0.0.0:0              LISTENING
```

This line shows a listening port ready for incoming packets that have a destination port number of 445. Notice the local address is 0.0.0.0. This is how Windows tells you that the listening port works on all NICs on this PC. In this case, my PC has only one NIC (192.168.4.27), but even if you have only one NIC, netstat still shows it this way. This computer is sharing some folders on the network. At this moment, no one is connected, so netstat shows the Foreign Address as 0.0.0.0. Incoming requests use port number 445 to connect to those shared folders. If another computer on my network (192.168.4.83) was accessing the shared folders, this line would look like

```
TCP    192.168.4.27:445       192.168.4.83:1073      ESTABLISHED
```

Established ports are active, working endpoint pairs.

Eventually, one side of the connection will initiate the close with a FIN signal and the other side will go into passive close:

```
TCP    192.168.4.27:57913     63.246.140.18:80       CLOSE_WAIT
```

This line shows that a Web server has initiated a close with the client.

If data's going to move back and forth between computers, some program must always be doing the sending and/or receiving. Take a look at this line from `netstat -an`:

```
TCP    192.168.4.27:52312     74.125.47.108:80       ESTABLISHED
```

You see the 80 and might assume the connection is going out to a Web server. But what program on the computer is sending it? Enter the command **`netstat -ano`** (the `-o` switch tells netstat to show the process ID). Although you'll see many lines, the one for this connection looks like this:

```
Proto  Local Address          Foreign Address        State          PID
TCP    192.168.4.27:1065      104.16.249.249:443     ESTABLISHED    9796
```

Every running program on your computer gets a process ID (PID), a number used by the operating system to track all the running programs. Numbers aren't very helpful to you, though, because you want to know the name of the running program. In most operating systems, finding this out is fairly easy to do. In Windows, run a command prompt as an administrator and type **`netstat -anob`**:

```
Proto  Local Address          Foreign Address        State          PID
TCP    192.168.4.27:1065      104.16.249.249:443     ESTABLISHED    9796
[firefox.exe]
```

You might be tempted to say, "Big whoop, Mike—what else would use port 443?" Then consider the possibility that you run netstat and see a line like the one just shown, but *you don't have a browser open!* You determine the PID and discover the name of the process is "Evil_Overlord.exe." Something is running on your computer that should not be there.

Understanding how TCP/IP uses ports is a base skill for any network tech. To pass the CompTIA Network+ exam, you need to memorize a number of different well-known ports and even a few of the more popular registered ports. You must appreciate how the ports fit into the process of TCP/IP communications and know how to use netstat and other tools to see what's going on inside your computer.

Determining what's supposed to be running and what's not presents a challenge. No one on Earth can run a netstat command and instantly recognize every connection and why it's running, but a good network tech should know most of them. For those connections that a tech doesn't recognize, he or she should know how to research them to determine what they are.

Rules for Determining Good vs. Bad Communications

Here is the general list of rules I follow for determining good versus bad communications (as far as networking goes, at least!):

1. Memorize a bunch of known ports for common TCP/IP applications. The next section in this chapter will get you started.
2. Learn how to use netstat to see what's happening on your computer. Learn to use switches such as `-a`, `-n`, `-o`, and `-b` to help you define what you're looking for.
3. Take the time to learn the ports that normally run on your operating system. When you see a connection using ports you don't recognize, figure out the process running the connection using a utility such as `tasklist` or Process Explorer (another awesome Mark Russinovich tool) in Windows.
4. Take the time to learn the processes that normally run on your operating system. Most operating systems have their own internal programs (such as Windows' svchost.exe) that are normal and important processes.
5. When you see a process you don't recognize, just enter the filename of the process in a Web search. Hundreds of Web sites are dedicated to researching mystery processes that will tell you what the process does.
6. Get rid of bad processes.

Common TCP/IP Applications

Finally! You now know enough about the Transport layer, port numbering, and sockets to get into some of the gritty details of common TCP/IP applications. There's no pretty way to do this, so let's start with some older ones, namely Telnet and SSH, e-mail protocols, databases, and FTP. We'll finish

All the port numbers listed here for applications refer to the server side of the connection. Servers respond to clients using the client's dynamic/ephemeral port. The CompTIA Network+ exam questions, on the other hand, most likely will just ask, "What port number is used by the *x* protocol?" Always assume the question means the default *server side*.

A dumb terminal is a local system—generally a monitor, keyboard, and mouse—that enables you to access a distant system that has all the computing power. The dumb terminal can't do any work on its own, even though it might look like a personal computer. Think of it like the command-line window in hardware form.

Telnet only enables command-line remote access; it does not enable GUI access. If you want to access another computer's desktop remotely, you need another type of program.

this section with the application everyone on the planet knows these days, the Web, and applications that use HTTP and HTTPS.

Telnet and SSH

Roughly one billion years ago, there was no such thing as the Internet or even networks… Well, maybe it was the 1960s, but as far as nerds like me are concerned, a world before the Internet was filled with brontosauruses and palm fronds. The only computers were huge monsters called mainframes and to access them required a "dumb" terminal.

Operating systems didn't have windows and pretty icons. The interface to the mainframe was a command line, but it worked just fine for the time. Then the cavemen who first lifted their heads up from the computer ooze known as mainframes said to themselves, "Wouldn't it be great if we could access each other's computers from the comfort of our own caves?" That was what started the entire concept of a network. Back then the idea of sharing folders or printers or Web pages hadn't been considered yet. The entire motivation for networking was so people could sit at their terminals and, instead of accessing only their local mainframes, access totally different mainframes. The protocol to do this was called the *Telnet Protocol* or simply **Telnet**.

Modern PCs can (but shouldn't) use Telnet to connect remotely to another computer via the command line. Telnet servers run on TCP port 23, enabling you to connect to a Telnet server and run commands on that server as if you were sitting right in front of it.

Telnet enables you to administer a server remotely and communicate with other servers on your network. As you can imagine, this is sort of risky. If you can remotely control a computer, what is to stop others from doing the same? Thankfully, Telnet does not allow just *anyone* to log on and wreak havoc with your network. The Telnet server can be configured to require a username and password.

Unfortunately, Telnet does not have any form of encryption. If someone intercepted the conversation between a Telnet client and Telnet server, he or she would see all the commands typed as well as the results from the Telnet server, including things like passwords (see Figure 8.12). As a result, in *no*

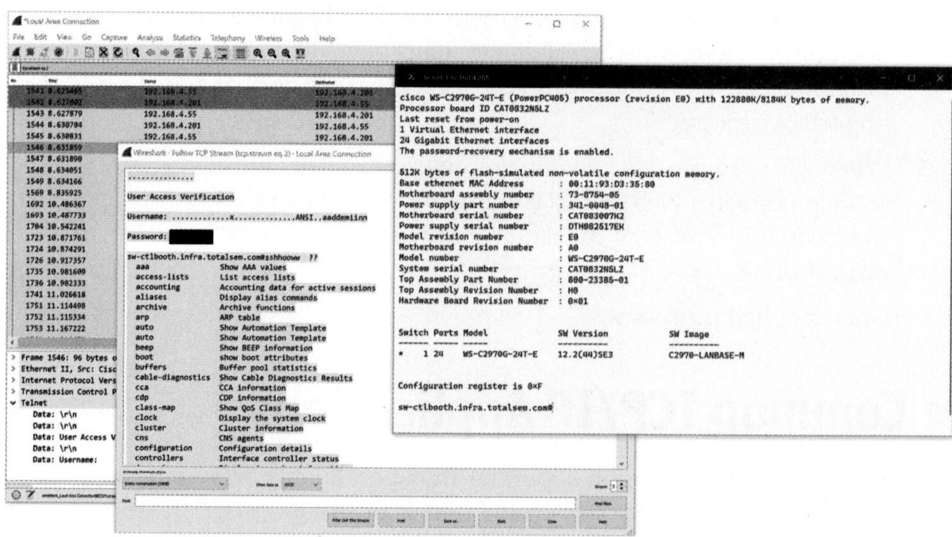

• **Figure 8.12** Telnet client and Wireshark recording every keystroke

scenario should you use Telnet on the Internet for administering a system today. Instead, use **Secure Shell (SSH)**, a protocol that works on the surface exactly like Telnet, but has security with encryption and authentication, plus a few other tricks up its sleeve.

SSH has replaced Telnet for every serious remote access via terminal emulation. In terms of what it does, SSH is extremely similar to Telnet in that it creates a terminal connection to a remote host. Every aspect of SSH, however, including both login and data transmittal, is encrypted. To get the full SSH understanding, we need to talk about encryption standards, which we'll get to in Chapter 10. SSH uses TCP port 22 instead of Telnet's port 23.

SSH enables you to control a remote computer from a local computer over a network, just like Telnet. Unlike Telnet, SSH enables you to do it securely!

E-mail

Electronic mail (e-mail) has been a major part of the Internet revolution, and not just because it streamlined the junk mail industry. E-mail provides a quick way for people to communicate with one another, letting them send messages and attachments (like documents and pictures) over the Internet. Let's look at traditional e-mail based on dedicated client software and then explore the Web-based e-mail that's probably much more familiar to you.

Traditional e-mail consists of e-mail clients and e-mail servers. When a message is sent to your e-mail address, it is normally stored in an electronic mailbox on your e-mail server until you tell the e-mail client to download the message. Once you read an e-mail message, you can reply to it, archive it, forward it, print it, or delete it.

E-mail programs use Layer 7 (Application) protocols to send and retrieve information. Specifically, the e-mail you find on the Internet uses SMTP to send e-mail, and either POP3 or IMAP4 to retrieve e-mail.

SMTP, POP3, and IMAP4, Oh My!

The following is a list of the different protocols that the Internet uses to transfer and retrieve traditional e-mail:

SMTP The **Simple Mail Transfer Protocol (SMTP)** is used to send e-mail from clients and between e-mail servers. SMTP travels over TCP port 25 by default.

POP3 **Post Office Protocol version 3 (POP3)** is one of the two protocols that retrieve e-mail from e-mail servers. POP3 uses TCP port 110. POP3 is on its way out today, though you'll see it on the exam.

IMAP4 **Internet Message Access Protocol version 4 (IMAP4)** is a preferred alternative to POP3. Like POP3, IMAP4 retrieves e-mail from an e-mail server. IMAP4 uses TCP port 143 and supports some features that are not supported in POP3. For example, IMAP4 enables synchronization of mail among many devices, meaning you can access e-mail messages at your Windows workstation, your Mac laptop, and your Android phone. (It works for any combination; I used those three as an example.) IMAP4 also supports the concept of folders that you can place on the IMAP4 server to organize your e-mail. Some POP3 e-mail clients have folders, but that's not a part of POP3, just a nice feature added to the client.

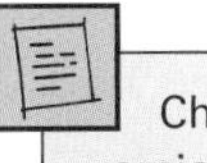

Chapter 10 explores secure versions of e-mail protocols.

E-mail Servers

Two mail server types dominate the once-fragmented e-mail server space: **Exim** and Postfix. With well over 50 percent market share, Exim runs on just about everything, from Unix/Linux to Windows. It even runs on the tiny Raspberry Pi! Exim, at heart, is a configuration file that you can manage by hand or through a graphical tool like cPanel (Figure 8.13).

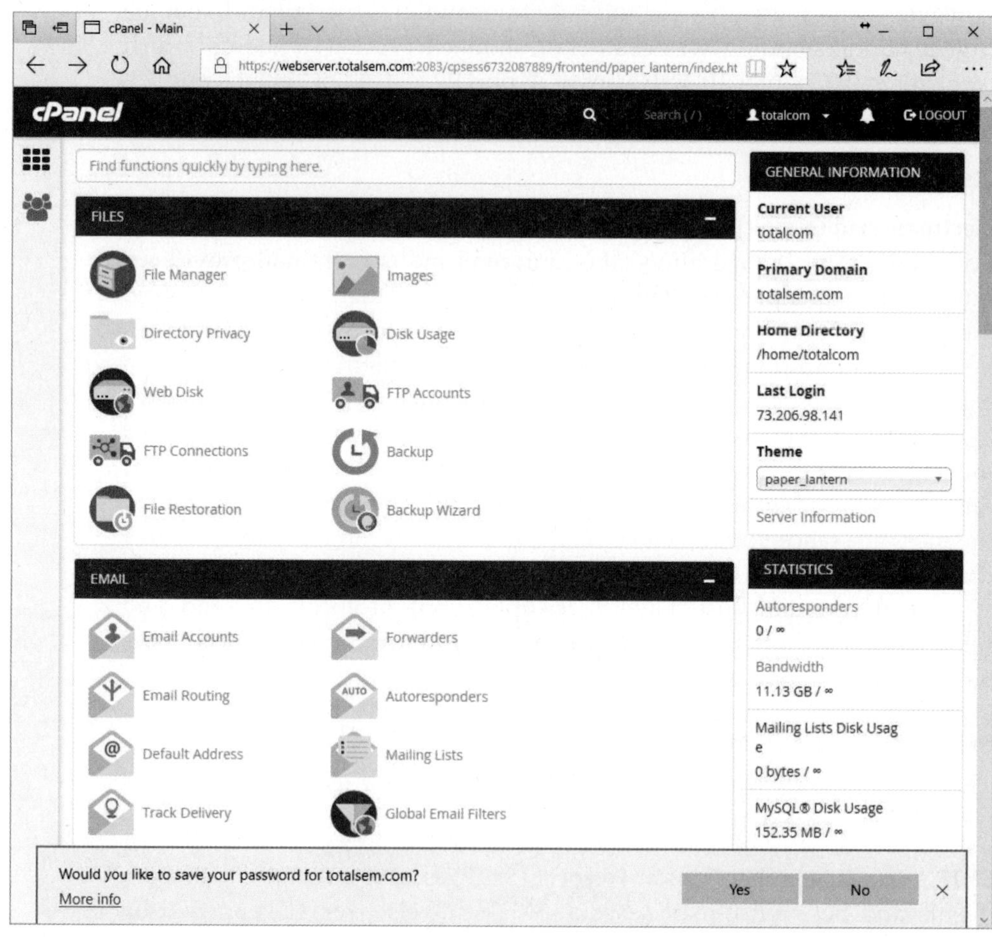

• **Figure 8.13** cPanel used to manage Exim mail server

Microsoft, of course, has its own Windows-based e-mail server, Microsoft Exchange Server. Figure 8.14 shows the Exchange admin center for Microsoft 365. Exchange Server is both an SMTP and a POP3/IMAP4/Exchange ActiveSync/MAPI/etc. server in one package.

E-mail servers accept incoming mail and sort out the mail for recipients into individual storage area mailboxes. These **mailboxes** are special separate folders or directories for each user's e-mail. An e-mail server works much like a post office, sorting and arranging incoming messages, and kicking back those messages that have no known recipient.

E-mail servers are difficult to manage. E-mail servers store user lists, user rights, and messages, and are constantly involved in Internet traffic and resources. Setting up and administering an e-mail server takes a lot of planning, and it's getting harder. Beyond simply setting up the software, running your own server requires a solid understanding of modern Internet security

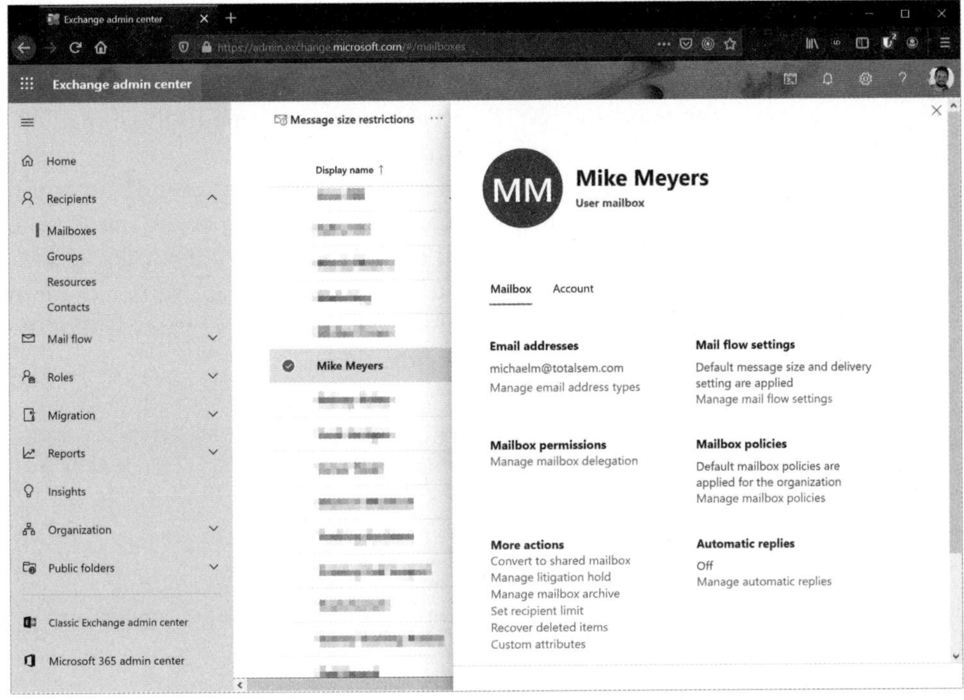

• **Figure 8.14** Exchange admin center for Microsoft 365

so you don't end up being a sitting duck for hackers to turn your server into a spam-spewing machine.

E-mail Client

An **e-mail client** is a program that runs on a computer and enables you to send, retrieve, and organize e-mail. There used to be dozens of desktop e-mail clients, but that number has dwindled greatly. Of the survivors, Microsoft Outlook (Figure 8.15) is probably the one with the most users.

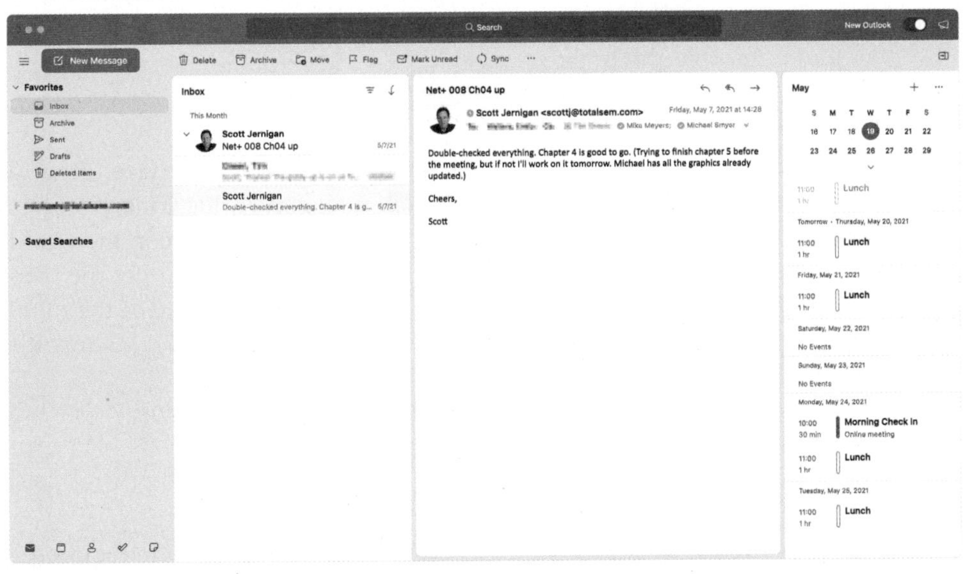

• **Figure 8.15** Microsoft Outlook

Configuring an E-mail Client Configuring a client is an easy matter. Your mail administrator will give you the server's domain name and your mailbox's username and password. You need to enter the POP3 or IMAP4 server's domain name and the SMTP server's domain name to the e-mail client (Figure 8.16). Every e-mail client has a different way to add the server domain names or IP addresses, so you may have to poke around, but you'll find the option there somewhere! In many cases, this may be the same name or address for both the incoming and outgoing servers—the folks administering the mail servers will tell you. Besides the e-mail server domain names or addresses, you must also enter the username and password of the e-mail account the client will be managing.

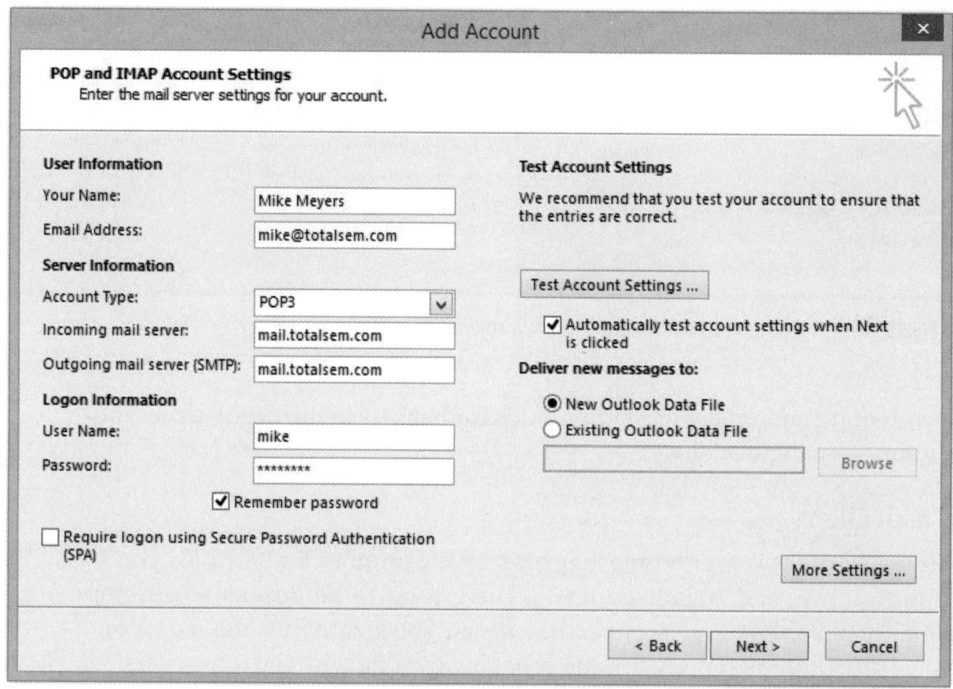

• **Figure 8.16** Entering server information in Microsoft Outlook

Web Mail

Web-based mail, as the name implies, requires a Web interface. From a Web browser, you simply surf to the Web-mail server, log in, and access your e-mail. The cool part is that you can do it from anywhere in the world where you find a Web browser and an Internet hookup! You get the benefit of e-mail without even needing to own a computer. Some of the more popular Web-based services are Google's Gmail (Figure 8.17), Microsoft's Outlook.com/Outlook Mail, and Yahoo!'s Yahoo! Mail.

The key benefits of Web-based e-mail services are as follows:

- You can access your e-mail from anywhere.
- They're free.
- They're handy for throw-away accounts (like when you're required to give an e-mail address to download something, but you know you're going to get spammed if you do).

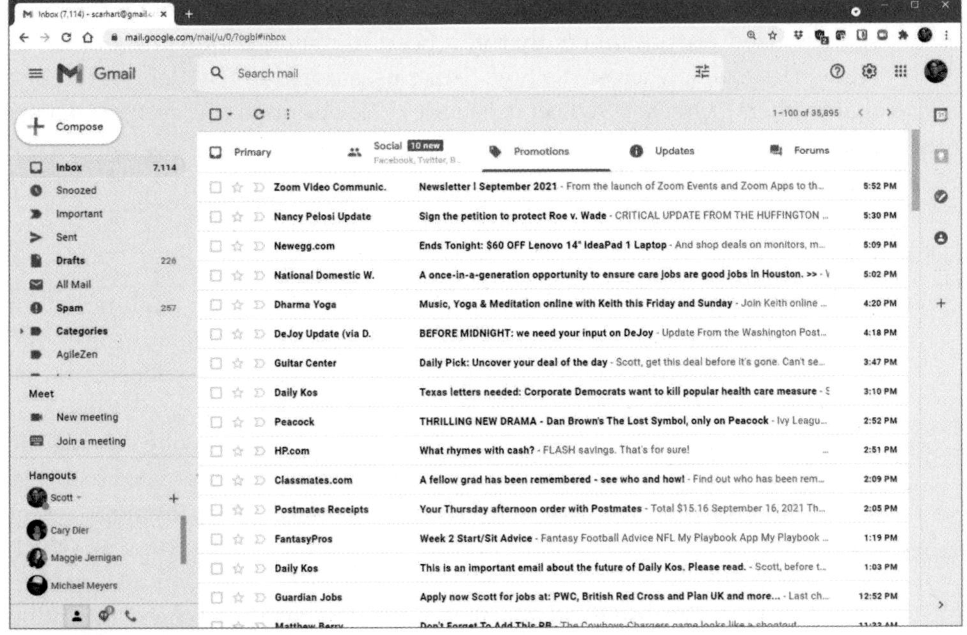

• **Figure 8.17** Gmail in action

SQL

Databases store data in an organized manner for quick searching and retrieval. Database server software hosts database files so that people can access them directly on the computer or, more commonly, across a network. Database servers handle simultaneous access from multiple users without breaking a sweat and provide data for many applications.

A *relational database* stores individual records in tables and those tables can refer to the data in other tables to enable users to mine rich information from that database. For example, School Principal Edwina has a relational database that tracks the grades and standing of all the students in her school. The students are in the Students table. Each teacher in each subject has a table in the database that lists grades for specific exams and refers to the Students table for specific student relationships with that class. Other tables in the database provide different information sets. Principal Edwina can run various queries to see how individual students are doing, which group of students are struggling with which subjects, and so on. The various tables connect in some fashion—they relate to each other—thus a *relational database*.

A relational database's *schema* describes all of its tables, the fields in each table, and how fields in different tables relate. The database can enforce these relationships to prevent nonsense records such as a grade for a class a student isn't even enrolled in.

Databases can store enormous amounts of information, so database developers use a *query language* to describe exactly which bits they want the database server to find. Different kinds of database need their own distinct query language. Every major relational database, for example, uses the **Structured Query Language (SQL)**.

> The servers described here are generically called *database management systems*; prepend *relational* and you get *RDBMS* as the general descriptor for the genre.

Microsoft uses SQL as a name in its database software, SQL Server. The CompTIA Network+ exam objectives spell out SQL in the description, so you might see *Structured Query Language (SQL) server* on the exam as a generic description for any of the relational database servers that use SQL (though the industry uses *RDBMS*).

Database servers play well on TCP/IP networks and, therefore, have standardized port numbers that you need to memorize for the CompTIA Network+ exam. Microsoft's *SQL Server* uses port 1433 by default (among many others). Oracle's *SQLnet* uses port 1521. The open source *MySQL* uses port 3306.

FTP

File Transfer Protocol (FTP) was the original protocol used on the Internet for transferring files. Active FTP uses TCP ports 21 and 20 by default, although passive FTP only uses port 21 by default. (The following subsection discusses active versus passive FTP.)

FTP sites are either anonymous sites, meaning that anyone can log on, or secured sites, meaning that you need a username and password to access the site and transfer files. A single FTP site can offer both anonymous access and protected access, but you'll see different resources depending on which way you log in.

The FTP server does all the real work of storing the files, accepting incoming connections, verifying usernames and passwords, and transferring the files. The client logs onto the FTP server (either from a Web site, a command line, or a special FTP application) and downloads the requested files onto the local hard drive.

Although FTP is still used, you should avoid it. FTP is not very secure because data transfers are not encrypted by default, so you don't want to use straight FTP for sensitive data. You can add usernames and passwords to prevent all but the most serious hackers from accessing an FTP server, but the usernames and passwords, like with Telnet, are sent over the network in cleartext.

Trivial File Transfer Protocol (TFTP), introduced earlier in the chapter, is used for transferring files and has a similar-sounding name to FTP, but beyond that it is very different. TFTP uses UDP port 69 and does not use usernames and passwords, although you can usually set some restrictions based on the client's IP address. TFTP is not at all secure, so never use it on any network that's less than trustworthy.

Active vs. Passive FTP

FTP has two ways to transfer data: *active* and *passive* FTP. Traditionally, FTP used the active process—let's see how this works. Remember that FTP uses TCP ports 20 and 21? Well, when your client sends an FTP request, it goes out on port 21. When your FTP server responds, however, it sends the data back using an ephemeral destination port and port 20 as a source port.

Active FTP works great unless your client uses NAT. Since your client didn't initiate the source port 20, your NAT router has no idea where to send this incoming packet. Additionally, any good firewall sees this incoming connection as something evil because it doesn't have anything inside the network that started the connection on port 20. No problem! Good FTP clients all support passive FTP. With passive FTP, the server doesn't use port 20. Instead, the client sends an FTP request on port 21, just like active FTP. But then the server sends back a random port number, telling the client which port it's listening on for data requests. The client, in turn, sends data to the port specified by the FTP server. Because the client initiates all conversations, the NAT router knows where to send the packet. The only trick to passive FTP is that the client needs to expect this other incoming data.

Check out the excellent Chapter 8 "Ports and Protocols" Challenge! over at http://totalsem.com/008. It'll help greatly in memorizing the port numbers that each protocol uses.

When you configure an FTP client for passive, you're telling it to expect these packets.

HTTP and HTTPS

Where would we be without the World Wide Web? If you go up to a non-nerd and say, "Get on the Internet," most of them will automatically open a Web browser, because to them the Web *is* the Internet. The Internet is the infrastructure that enables the Web to function, but it's certainly more than just the Web. This section looks at the Web and the tools that make it function, specifically the protocols that enable communication over the Internet. It also discusses other applications that use HTTPS that aren't in the CompTIA Network+ objectives but are used all around the world, like Microsoft Teams.

The Web is composed of servers running Web server software, such as NGINX (pronounced "engine ex"), Apache HTTP Server, or Microsoft Internet Information Services (IIS), that speak the Hypertext Transfer Protocol (HTTP) and, traditionally, serve up documents written in the Hypertext Markup Language (HTML). Figure 8.18 shows the Web interface built into my wireless access point.

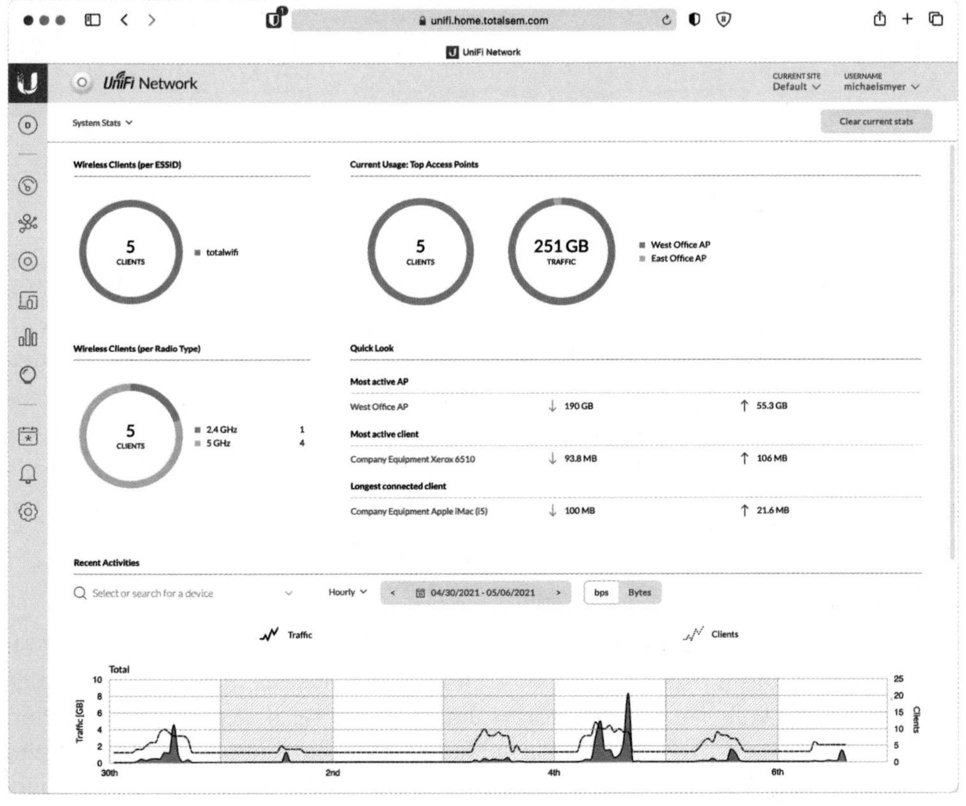

• **Figure 8.18** My wireless access point's Web interface

HTML has been around since the early 1990s and, as a result, has gone through many versions. Today many developers use the latest HTML version called HTML5. See Figure 8.19.

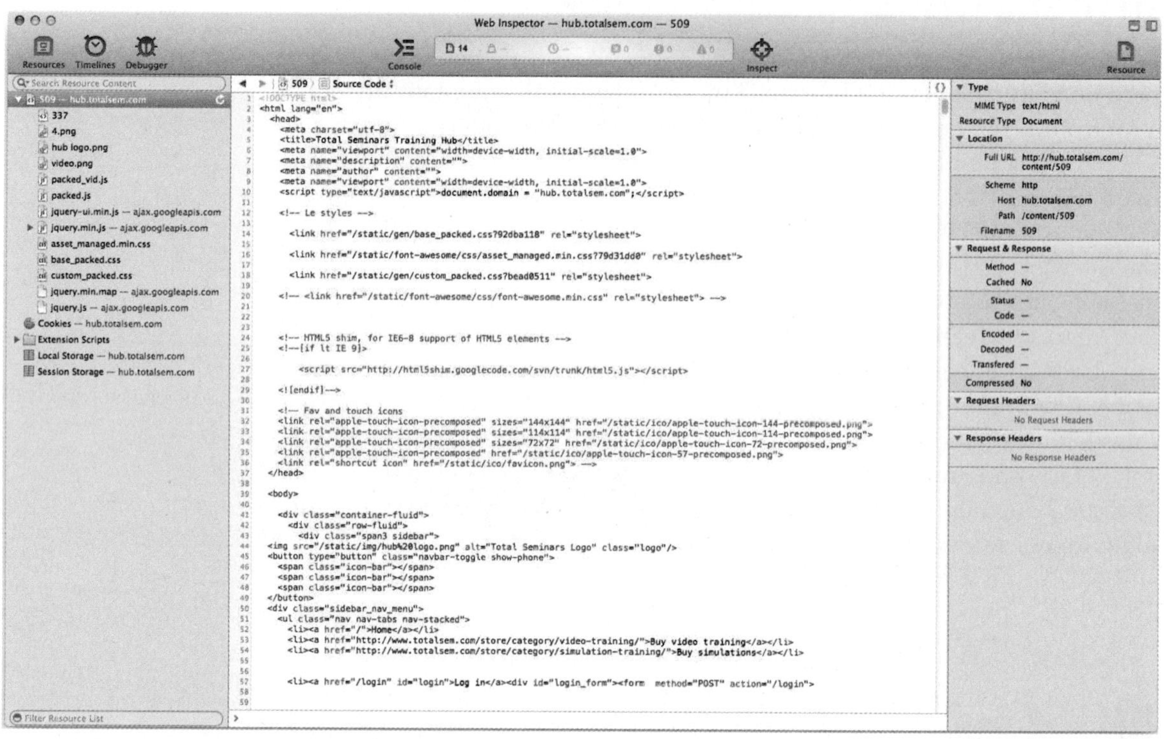

• **Figure 8.19** HTML5 source code

> Today, typing in an IP address for a Web server, especially on the Internet, won't work. For many sites, you need to type the name of the server and let DNS enable your computer to connect to the proper resource. I'll go much deeper into this in Chapter 9.

Web browsers are designed to request HTML pages from Web servers and then open them. To access a Web page, you *could* enter **http://** plus the IP address of the Web server. When you type the address of a Web server, such as **http://192.168.4.1**, you tell the browser to go to 192.168.4.1 and ask for a Web page.

Granted, most people don't enter IP addresses into browsers, but rather enter text like totalsem.com or google.com. Memorizing text addresses is much easier than memorizing IP addresses. Web site text addresses use the DNS naming protocol, covered in depth in the next chapter.

HTTP

Hypertext Transfer Protocol (HTTP) is the underlying protocol used by Web servers, and it runs, traditionally, on TCP port 80. The http:// at the beginning of a Web server's IP address tells the browser that you are connecting to a Web server with HTTP. HTTP defines the commands that browsers (and other software) use to ask Web servers for things, such as a Web page, and how the server will format what it sends back to the browser. If you want to see the gory details, you can use the developer tools in any modern browser to peek under the hood (see Figure 8.20).

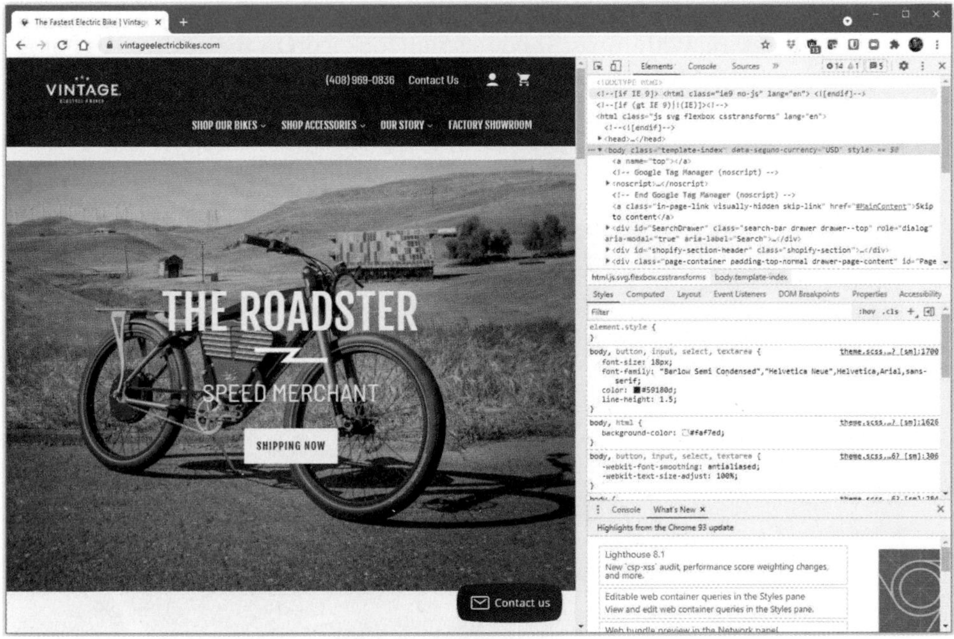

• **Figure 8.20** Vintage Electric Bikes homepage open with the Google Chrome developer tools revealing the code underlying the site (on the right)

HTTP has a general weakness in its handling of Web pages: it relays commands executed by users without reference to any commands previously executed. The problem with this is that Web designers continue to design more complex and truly interactive Web pages. HTTP is pretty dumb when it comes to remembering what people have done on a Web site. Luckily for Web designers everywhere, other technologies exist to help HTTP relay commands and thus support more interactive, intelligent Web sites. These technologies include JavaScript/AJAX, server-side scripting, and cookies.

SSL/TLS and HTTPS

Any nosy person who can plug into a network can see and read the HTTP packets moving between a Web server and a Web client. Less than nice people can easily create a fake Web site to trick people into thinking it's a legitimate Web site and then steal their usernames and passwords. For these and other reasons, the Internet has moved away from HTTP.

For an Internet application to be secure, it must have the following:

- **Authentication** Usernames and passwords
- **Encryption** Stirring up the data so others can't read it
- **Nonrepudiation** Source is not able to deny a sent message

The CompTIA Network+ exam objectives use Hypertext Transfer Protocol *Secure* for HTTPS, though you'll hear the older terms—HTTP over SSL and HTTP over TLS—used by many techs.

All of Chapter 10 is dedicated to these concepts, but the Web side of things requires mention here. Almost every Web site today uses the secure version of HTTP, called **Hypertext Transfer Protocol Secure (HTTPS)**, to enable connections between clients and servers that hackers can't break. HTTPS uses **Transport Layer Security (TLS)**, the latest version of **Secure Sockets Layer (SSL)**, although techs use the terms interchangeably. SSL/TLS uses encryption to set up a secure private connection.

HTTP enables you to access the Web, but HTTPS gets you there securely. HTTPS uses TLS to provide the security. The exam objectives list HTTPS twice. The first is *Hypertext Transfer Protocol Secure (HTTPS) [Secure Sockets Layer (SSL)]*. The second time is *HTTPS [Transport Layer Security (TLS)]* to reinforce that modern HTTPS uses TLS rather than SSL.

HTTPS uses TCP port 443. You can tell a Web page is using HTTPS by the URL (starts with https://) or a small lock icon in the address bar of the browser. Figure 8.21 shows a typical secure Web page.

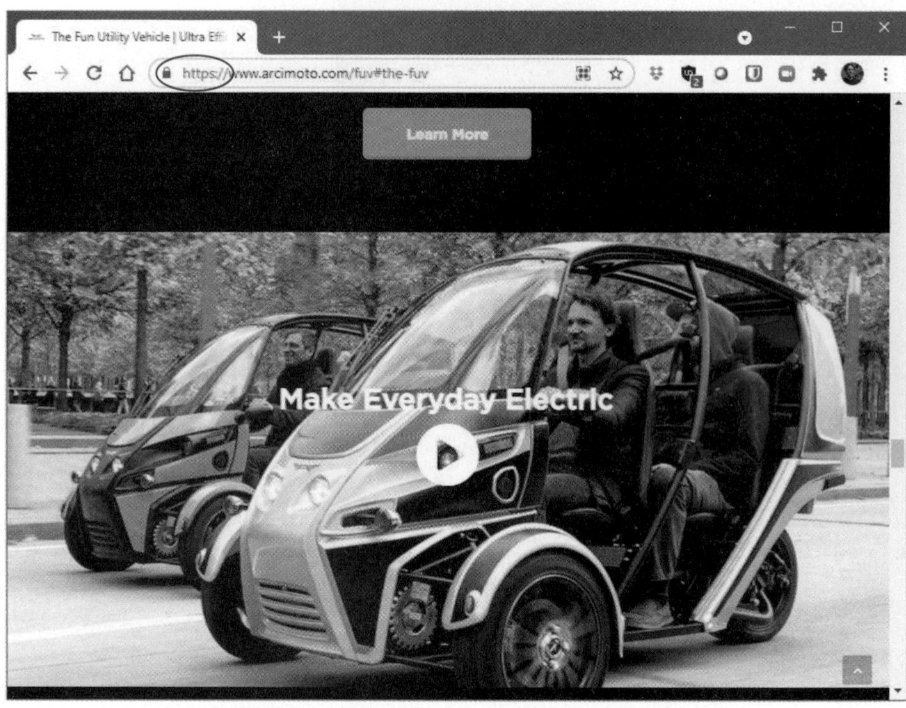

• **Figure 8.21** Secure Web page

Table 8.1	Internet Application Ports and Protocols		
Application	**TCP/UDP**	**Port**	**Notes**
FTP	TCP	20/21 (active) 21 (passive)	File transfer
SSH	TCP	22	Secure remote control
Telnet	TCP	23	Remote control
SMTP	TCP	25	Sending e-mail
DNS	UDP[1]	53	Naming
DHCP	UDP	67 (server), 68 (client)	Assigns IP information
TFTP	UDP	69	File transfer
HTTP	TCP	80	The Web
POP3	TCP	110	E-mail retrieval
NTP/SNTP	UDP	123	Timing
IMAP4	TCP	143	E-mail retrieval
HTTPS	TCP	443	The Web, securely
SQL Server[2]	TCP	1433	Database server
SQLnet	TCP	1521	Database server
MySQL	TCP	3306	Database server

[1] DNS uses TCP for some actions; see Chapter 9.
[2] SQL Server typically uses TCP ports 1433, 4022, 135, 1434; and UDP ports 1433, 1434. TCP port 1433 is the official IANA-designated port.

TCP/IP Applications Chart

Use Table 8.1 as a review tool to help you remember each TCP/IP application covered in this chapter, arranged by ascending default port number. And yes, memorize the port numbers for the exam.

Beyond Network+

Other Layer 7 Applications

Although the CompTIA Network+ exam tests you on classic TCP/IP applications, such as knowing that you can use SSH to connect and control a remote computer securely and HTTPS is used for secure Web sites, you should know that many other Application layer programs ride the same train. Let's look at two widely used applications as examples, Zoom and Teams.

Millions of people use the *Zoom* videotelephony program (created by Zoom Video Communications) for both work and socializing. Zoom offers robust video, audio, and text interaction over computing devices of all sorts and the Internet (Figure 8.22). Although the initial release was a while ago (2012), the global pandemic that started in 2020 propelled Zoom to rock star status and a central part in the workflow and playflow for many people.

The Zoom client uses UDP and HTTPS over port 443 to connect to Zoom servers initially, then connects to the various multimedia aspects (video, voice, etc.) using Zoom's proprietary protocol and UDP over port 8801. If UDP fails, Zoom will connect using TCP over port 8801.

• **Figure 8.22** Zoom meeting

Microsoft Teams offers a full working environment for videotelephony, data exchange, and integration with other Microsoft Cloud services like Office 365 for productivity tools (like Word, Excel, and so on). Figure 8.23 shows a typical Teams interface. Teams is wildly complex and uses a lot of protocols and ports for its many components, but the initial connectivity relies on UDP and HTTPS over port 443. Just like Zoom, though, Teams will use TCP if UDP doesn't work.

I'm simplifying the initial Zoom connection process. Zoom has a great whitepaper detailing the many steps in the process at https://zoom.us. Check it out!

The takeaway here is that a lot of modern programs that aren't the Web use protocols like HTTPS for secure connectivity on the Internet. While you won't be tested on them, you will be working with them. They function at heart like the traditional TCP/IP applications, relying on TCP or UDP (usually the latter, these days), protocols like HTTPS, and both standard and unique port numbers.

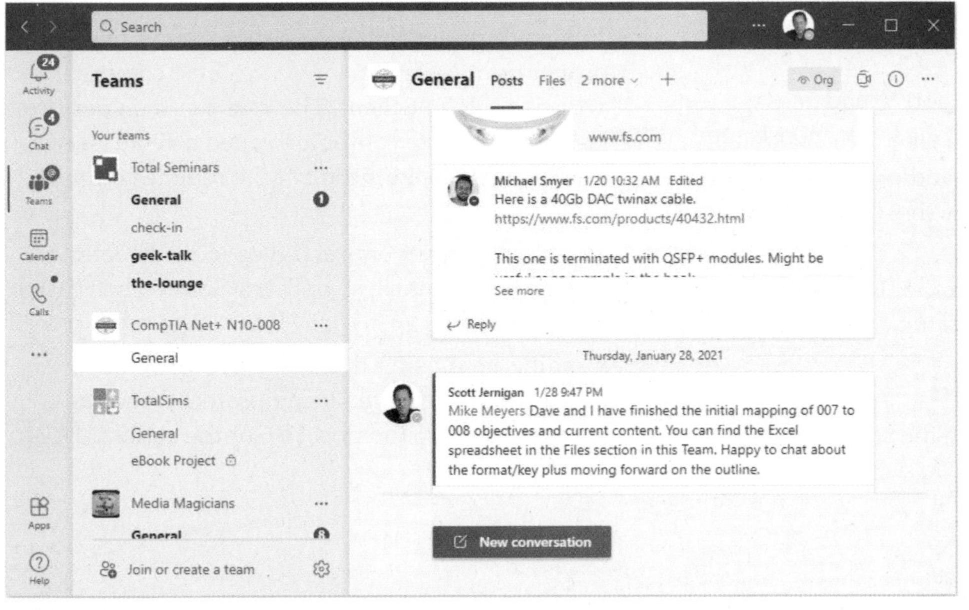

• **Figure 8.23** Teams interface

Chapter 8 Review

Chapter Summary

After reading this chapter and completing the exercises, you should understand the following about the basics of TCP/IP.

Describe common Transport and Network layer protocols

- TCP/IP involves many more protocols other than just TCP over IP. HTTP, DHCP, POP, and about 500 more terms over TCP, plus UDP and ICMP over IP.
- If every communication requires an acknowledgment from the receiving computer, the session is said to be connection-oriented. Otherwise, the session is connectionless.
- TCP is a connection-oriented protocol, whereas UDP is connectionless. Many TCP/IP applications use TCP because connection-oriented sessions are designed to check for errors. If a sending computer doesn't see an ACK for an outstanding segment, it sends the segment again.
- Domain Name System (DNS) enables the use of names associated with IP addresses for devices connected to IP networks. DNS uses UDP port 53 by default, but see Chapter 9 for all the details.
- Dynamic Host Configuration Protocol (DHCP) uses UDP ports 67 and 68 to provide IP configuration information to clients. Network Time Protocol (NTP) and its little brother, Simple Network Time Protocol (SNTP) use port 123 to synchronize time on a network.
- Trivial FTP (TFTP) uses UDP port 69 and does not use usernames or passwords, making it very nonsecure.
- ICMP works at Layer 3 to handles mundane issues such as disconnect messages (host unreachable) and router advertisements.
- IGMP enables devices to share a multicast address and thus receive multicast traffic.

Explain the power of port numbers

- Well-known ports fall within the range 0–1023. Web servers use port 80 or port 443, for example.
- Dynamic ports fall within the ranges 1024–5000 and 49152–65535. These are also called ephemeral or private ports.
- Registered ports are those that have been registered with the Internet Assigned Numbers Authority and fall within the range 1024–49151.
- Information about a session is held in memory and is called a socket. The sockets held in memory by two computers in a session with each other are called socket pairs or endpoints.
- The netstat command-line utility is used to view a list of endpoints. It can't automatically update to display real-time information, however.
- A listening port is a socket prepared to respond to incoming IP packets. Type `netstat -an` to see all of your listening ports.
- You can use the `netstat -anob` command at an elevated prompt to identify which application is using a specific port, allowing you to identify malicious software.
- The netstat switches `-a`, `-n`, `-b`, and `-o` are important for any tech to know.

Define common TCP/IP applications, such as Telnet, SSH, e-mail (SMTP, POP3, and IMAP4), databases, FTP, HTTP, and HTTPS

- Telnet is a protocol that enables a user with the proper permissions to log onto a host computer, acting as a Telnet client. The user can then perform tasks on a remote computer, called a Telnet server, as if he or she were sitting at the remote computer itself.
- Telnet sends passwords and data in easily detected cleartext or plaintext, so only use Secure Shell (SSH) today.
- E-mail is sent using the SMTP protocol on port 25 and is retrieved using protocols such as the ancient POP3 (on port 110) or the better IMAP4 (on port 143).

- E-mail servers are needed to help forward, store, and retrieve e-mail messages for end users, who need a valid username and password to gain access. E-mail can also contain attachments like pictures or small programs or data files.
- Exim is the leading e-mail server with over 50 percent market share and runs on just about everything. Exchange Server is the e-mail server software from Microsoft, and it supports SMTP and POP3, IMAP4, Exchange ActiveSync, MAPI, etc.
- A mailbox is a folder or directory within an e-mail server that holds all the e-mail for a specific user.
- An e-mail client enables you to send, retrieve, and organize e-mail. Popular e-mail clients include Microsoft Outlook and not many others these days.
- Many companies produce relational database software that uses SQL for queries. Microsoft's SQL Server uses TCP port 1433 (among others). Oracle's SQLnet uses port 1521. The open source MySQL uses port 3306.
- FTP stands for File Transfer Protocol, which uses ports 20 and 21, and efficiently transmits large files. FTP lacks security and should not be used today.
- Active FTP uses both ports 20 and 21 and can be problematic if you are using NAT. The incoming connection from the server can appear to be unsolicited. This makes firewalls unhappy.
- Passive FTP uses port 21 and works fine with NAT.
- HTTP stands for the Hypertext Transfer Protocol. HTTP uses port 80 to transmit the common data used in Web pages.
- To make Web pages available to the public, the Web pages must reside on a computer with Web server software—such as NGINX, Apache, or IIS—installed and configured.
- HTTPS stands for Hypertext Transfer Protocol Secure, with the security provided originally with Secure Sockets Layer (SSL). The current version of SSL is Transport Layer Security (TLS). HTTPS uses port 443.
- HTTPS uses TLS to protect sensitive data, like credit card numbers and personal information.
- A good network tech knows the port numbers for Internet applications and protocols such as Telnet, SSH, SMTP, POP3, IMAP4, FTP, TFTP, HTTP, and HTTPS.

Key Terms

clock strata *(215)*
connectionless *(213)*
connection-oriented *(213)*
dynamic port *(218)*
electronic mail (e-mail) *(225)*
e-mail client *(227)*
endpoint *(219)*
endpoints *(219)*
ephemeral port *(218)*
Exim *(226)*
File Transfer Protocol (FTP) *(230)*
Hypertext Transfer Protocol (HTTP) *(232)*
Hypertext Transfer Protocol Secure (HTTPS) *(233)*
Internet Control Message Protocol (ICMP) *(216)*
Internet Group Management Protocol (IGMP) *(216)*
Internet Message Access Protocol version 4 (IMAP4) *(225)*
Internet Protocol suite *(213)*
listening port *(221)*
mailbox *(226)*
netstat *(219)*
Network Time Protocol (NTP) *(215)*
Post Office Protocol version 3 (POP3) *(225)*
private port *(218)*
registered port *(219)*
Secure Shell (SSH) *(225)*
Secure Sockets Layer (SSL) *(233)*
session *(213)*

Simple Mail Transfer Protocol (SMTP) *(225)*
socket *(219)*
socket pairs *(219)*
Structured Query Language (SQL) *(229)*
TCP three-way handshake *(214)*
TCP/IP suite *(213)*
Telnet *(224)*
Transport Layer Security (TLS) *(233)*
Transmission Control Protocol (TCP) *(214)*
Trivial File Transfer Protocol (TFTP) *(215)*
User Datagram Protocol (UDP) *(214)*
well-known port *(217)*

■ Key Term Quiz

Use the Key Terms list to complete the sentences that follow. Not all terms will be used.

1. A TCP port number that falls in the range of 0–1023 is called a(n) _______________.
2. A TCP port number within the range of 1024–49151 is called a(n) _______________.
3. The protocol used to transmit large files over the Internet using both ports 21 and 22 is called _______________.
4. The protocol that replaced POP3 for receiving e-mail is _______________.
5. Port 443 is used by _______________ to enable secure Web traffic.
6. _______________ is used to send e-mail from clients and between e-mail servers..
7. A traditional way to send information about an upcoming meeting to a few co-workers would be to send a(n) _______________.
8. The _______________ utility can be used to view the endpoints of your computer's sessions.
9. Telnet has been replaced by _______________, which provides better security through data encryption.
10. TCP is _______________ in that it requires computers to acknowledge each other, whereas UDP is _______________ in that it provides no guarantee packets were successfully received.

■ Multiple-Choice Quiz

1. What port number is the well-known port used by Web servers to distribute Web pages to Web browsers?
   - **A.** Port 20
   - **B.** Port 21
   - **C.** Port 25
   - **D.** Port 80
2. What nonsecure protocol handles large file transfers between Internet users?
   - **A.** FTP
   - **B.** IMAP4
   - **C.** POP3
   - **D.** SMTP
3. How can you tell that a secure Web page transaction is taking place?
   - **A.** The URL in the address bar starts with https.
   - **B.** The URL in the address bar starts with http/ssl.
   - **C.** The URL in the address bar starts with ssl.
   - **D.** The URL in the address bar starts with tls.
4. Jane has been tasked to find and implement an application that will enable her boss to log into and control a server remotely and securely. Which of the following applications would work best?
   - **A.** E-mail
   - **B.** FTP
   - **C.** Telnet
   - **D.** SSH

5. SSH uses which port?
   - **A.** TCP port 22
   - **B.** TCP port 23
   - **C.** UDP port 22
   - **D.** UDP port 23
6. What is the session information—IP address, port number, and Layer 4 protocol—held in memory called? (Select two.)
   - **A.** Endpoint
   - **B.** Port
   - **C.** Session
   - **D.** Socket
7. Which protocol enables synchronization of communication among connected computing devices?
   - **A.** FTP
   - **B.** IMAP4
   - **C.** NTP
   - **D.** TFTP
8. Which port does Microsoft SQL Server use by default?
   - **A.** 80
   - **B.** 443
   - **C.** 1433
   - **D.** 1521
9. What do DHCP, NTP, SNTP, and TFTP have in common?
   - **A.** They all use ICMP.
   - **B.** They all use IGMP.
   - **C.** They all use TCP.
   - **D.** They all use UDP.
10. When using Windows, which command shows all ports being used and the IP addresses using them?
    - **A.** `telnet localhost 25`
    - **B.** `telnet -ano`
    - **C.** `netstat -an`
    - **D.** `netstat -ao`
11. What is the main difference between TCP and UDP?
    - **A.** TCP is connection-oriented, whereas UDP is connectionless.
    - **B.** TCP supports HTTPS, whereas UDP supports SSL.
    - **C.** TCP sessions can be encrypted, whereas UDP sessions cannot.
    - **D.** TCP is used on Windows, whereas UDP is used on Linux/UNIX/macOS.
12. Which connectionless protocol handles chores such as disconnect messages and router advertisements?
    - **A.** TCP
    - **B.** UDP
    - **C.** ICMP
    - **D.** IGMP
13. John says he's concerned that listening ports on the server make it vulnerable to attacks. What does he mean by "listening ports"?
    - **A.** A "listening port" is a socket prepared to respond to any traffic destined for that socket's port number.
    - **B.** A "listening port" is a socket prepared to respond to any traffic on the network.
    - **C.** A "listening port" is a socket prepared to respond to any traffic destined for an "open" command on port 80.
    - **D.** A "listening port" is a socket unavailable to respond to any traffic destined for that socket's port number.

14. Which port does SMTP use?
    A. TCP port 22
    B. TCP port 25
    C. TCP port 80
    D. UDP port 81

15. What could you do if you are having difficulty transferring files with your FTP client when your router supports NAT?
    A. Configure your FTP client to use active FTP.
    B. Configure your FTP client to use passive FTP.
    C. Use SSH to transfer your files instead.
    D. Use Telnet to connect to the server and then use netstat to transfer the files.

Essay Quiz

1. Your company is interested in setting up secure Web pages for credit card transactions. The company currently does have a Web presence. Write two short paragraphs describing the two different port numbers that would be used on the company's improved Web site.
2. After checking various e-mail settings, a colleague of yours mentions port numbers. Write down some quick notes about which TCP ports would handle e-mail.
3. Write down a few notes explaining why some Web pages have an extra *s* after the http in their Web addresses. Be prepared to discuss your findings in class.
4. Write a paragraph that describes what a Web server does. Write a second paragraph that describes what an e-mail server does.

Lab Projects

• Lab Project 8.1

Start some Internet programs, such as a Web browser, an e-mail or FTP client, and an instant messenger. Open a command prompt and type **`netstat -ano`** or **`netstat -b`**. Make a list of the well-known ports in use and the process ID using each port. Then write the actual name of the application identified by the process ID. Linux users can type **`ps`** to learn the application name of a process ID, but Windows users have to use a third-party tool like Process Explorer.

• Lab Project 8.2

Using a word processing program or a spreadsheet program, create a chart that lists all the port numbers mentioned in this chapter, similar to the following list in the leftmost column. Use the Internet to look up other commonly used port numbers as well. Fill in the Abbreviation column, the Full Name column, and the Brief Description column. Repeat this lab exercise several times until you have memorized it fully. This activity will help you pass the CompTIA Network+ exam!

Port #	Abbreviation	Full Name	Brief Description of What This Port Does...
20			
21			
22			
23			
25			
53			
67			
68			
69			
80			
110			
123			
143			
443			

Network Naming

"It's not DNS
There's no way it's DNS
It was DNS"

—u/SSBroski

In this chapter, you will learn how to

- **Analyze and configure early name resolution solutions**
- **Describe the function and capabilities of DNS**
- **Use common TCP/IP utilities to diagnose problems with DNS**

Every host on the Internet has a unique IP address. Then why do we use *names* such as www.totalsem.com to access hosts, such as a Web server, instead of an IP address?

Although computers use IP addresses to communicate with each other over a TCP/IP network, people need easy-to-remember names. To resolve this conflict, long ago, even before TCP/IP and the Internet took over, network developers created a process called **name resolution** that automatically converts computer names to logical addresses or physical addresses (MAC addresses) to make it easier for people to communicate with computers (Figure 9.1).

Like any process that's been around for a long time, name resolution has evolved over the years. Ancient networking protocols would resolve a computer name such as MIKESDESKTOP to a MAC address. As TCP/IP gained dominance, name resolution concentrated on resolving names to IP addresses. Even within TCP/IP, there have been many changes in name resolution. Entire TCP/IP applications have been written, only to be supplanted (but never totally abandoned) by newer name resolution protocols.

All TCP/IP networks, including the Internet, use a name resolution protocol called **Domain Name System (DNS)**. DNS is a powerful, extensible, flexible system that supports name resolution on networks, from tiny in-house ones up to the entire Internet. Most of this chapter covers DNS, but be warned: your brand-new system, running the latest version of whatever operating system, still fully supports a few older name resolution protocols that predate DNS. This makes name resolution in contemporary networks akin to a well-run house that's also full of ghosts—ghosts that can do very strange things if you don't understand how those ghosts behave.

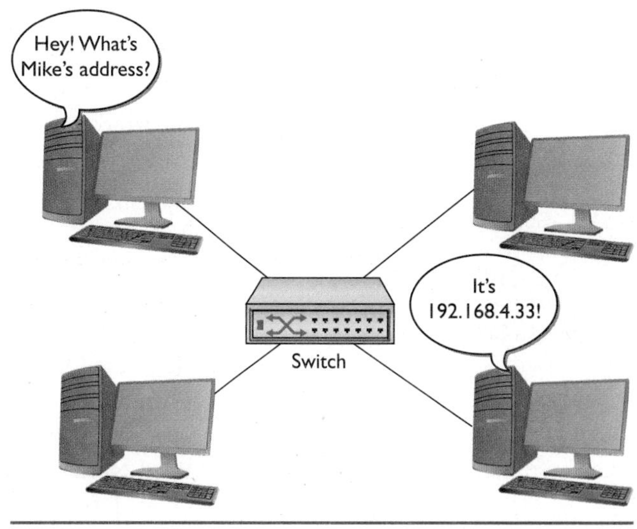

• **Figure 9.1** Turning names into numbers

In this chapter, you'll take an in-depth tour of name resolution, starting with a discussion of two ghostly precursors to DNS: Microsoft's ancient NetBIOS protocol and the even older hosts file. The chapter then turns to DNS, explaining how it works, and how DNS servers and clients are used today. The chapter wraps up with a discussion of diagnosing TCP/IP network issues.

Odds are good you have a system connected—or that at least can connect—to the Internet. If I were you, I'd fire up that system and use it while you read this chapter. Most of the programs you're going to learn about here come free with every operating system.

Historical/Conceptual

Before DNS

Early name resolution solutions offered simple but effective network naming. While most of these are long dead, there are two name resolution solutions that continue to work in modern systems: Microsoft's NetBIOS names and the hosts file found on every network operating system.

• **Figure 9.2** NetBIOS broadcast

NetBIOS

Even though TCP/IP was available back in the 1980s, Microsoft developed and popularized a light and efficient networking protocol called **NetBIOS/NetBEUI**. It had a simple naming convention (the NetBIOS part) that used broadcasts for name resolution. When a computer booted up, it broadcast its name (Figure 9.2) along with its MAC address. Every other NetBIOS/NetBEUI system heard the message and stored the information in a cache. Any time a system was missing a NetBIOS name, the broadcasting started all over again.

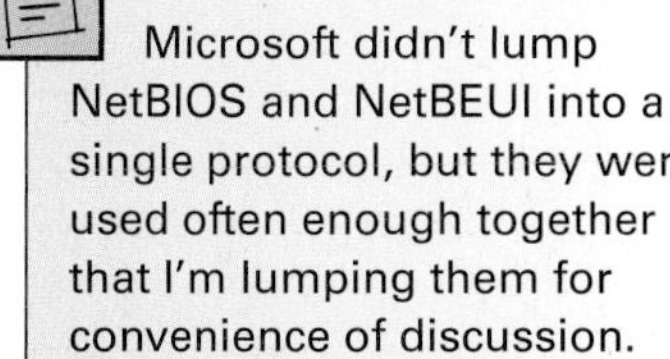
Microsoft didn't lump NetBIOS and NetBEUI into a single protocol, but they were used often enough together that I'm lumping them for convenience of discussion. You *won't* see NetBEUI on the CompTIA Network+ exam.

NetBIOS was suitable only for small networks for two reasons. First, it provided no logical addressing like IP addresses; each system had to remember the NetBIOS name and the MAC address. Without a logical address, there was no way to support routing. Second, all the broadcasting made it unacceptable for large networks.

Microsoft's networking was designed for small, unrouted networks of no more than around 40 hosts. There was no such thing as Telnet, e-mail, Minecraft, or the Web with NetBIOS, but it worked well for what it did at the time.

Getting NetBIOS to play nicely with TCP/IP requires proper protocols. NetBIOS over TCP/IP uses TCP ports 137 and 139, and UDP ports 137 and 138.

By the mid-1990s, Microsoft realized the world was going with TCP/IP and DNS, and it needed to switch too. The problem was that there was a massive installed base of Windows networks that needed NetBIOS. Microsoft's solution was to design a new TCP/IP protocol that enabled it to keep using the NetBIOS names but dump the NetBEUI protocol. The new protocol, **NetBIOS over TCP/IP (NetBT)**, runs NetBIOS on top of TCP/IP. In essence, Microsoft created its own name resolution protocol that had nothing to do with DNS.

NetBT made things weird on Windows systems. Windows systems used NetBT names for local network jobs such as accessing shared printers or folders, but they also used DNS for everything else. It basically meant that every Windows computer had one name used on the local network—like MIKES-PC—and a DNS name for use on the Internet.

SMB uses TCP port 445 by default.

To be more accurate, NetBIOS only handled host names and didn't do any of the resource sharing. Microsoft used another Layer 7 protocol called **Server Message Block (SMB)** that ran on top of NetBT to support sharing folders and files. SMB used NetBIOS names to support the sharing and access process. SMB isn't dependent on NetBIOS and today runs by itself using TCP port 445.

hosts

Before the Internet even existed and its predecessor, the ARPANET, was populated with only a few dozen computers, name resolution was simple, if not tedious. The ARPANET implemented name resolution using a special text file called *hosts*. A copy of this file was stored on every computer system on the ARPANET. The **hosts file** contained a list of IP addresses for every computer on the network, matched to the corresponding system names. Part of an old hosts file might look something like this:

```
140.247.21.53        HARVARD
128.2.0.1            CARNEGIE
23.54.122.103        AMES
129.55.0.1           MIT
```

If your system wanted to access the system called MIT, it looked up the name MIT in its hosts file and then used the corresponding IP address to contact MIT. Every hosts file on every system on the ARPANET was updated every morning at 2 A.M.

Not only was the ARPANET a lot smaller then, but also there weren't yet rules about how to compose names, such as that they must end in .com or .org. People could name computers pretty much anything they wanted (there were a few restrictions on length and allowable characters) as long as nobody else had snagged the name first. All you had to do was call up the Stanford Research Institute and talk to *Elizabeth Feinler*. She and her team would then add you to the master hosts file. It really was a simpler time.

This hosts file naming system worked fine when the ARPANET was still the province of a few university geeks and some military guys, but as the ARPANET grew, by the early 1980s it became impractical to make every system use and update a hosts file and keep it manually updated. This created the motivation for a more scalable name resolution process, but the hosts file did not go away.

While the ARPANET did not survive the '80s, believe it or not, the hosts file did and is still alive and well in every computer. You can find the hosts file in C:\Windows\System32\drivers\etc in Windows. On macOS and Linux systems, you'll find hosts in the /etc directory.

The hosts file is just a text file that you can open with any text editor. Here are a few lines from the default hosts file that comes with Windows:

```
# Additionally, comments (such as these) may be inserted on individual
# lines or following the machine name denoted by a '#' symbol.
#
# For example:
#
#          102.54.94.97     rhino.acme.com    # source server
#           38.25.63.10     x.acme.com  #    x client host
# localhost name resolution is handled within DNS itself.
#     127.0.0.1       localhost
#     ::1             localhost
```

See the # signs? Those are *remark* symbols that designate lines as comments (for humans to read) rather than code. Windows ignores any line that begins with #. Remove the # and Windows will read the line and try to act on it. Although all operating systems continue to support the hosts file, few users will actively modify and employ it in the day-to-day workings of most TCP/IP systems.

> Tablets and smartphones have hosts files as well. You can readily access and edit hosts on Android devices. Apple has the hosts file on iOS devices locked down.

Test Specific

DNS

When the ARPANET folks decided to dump the hosts file for name resolution and replace it with something better, they needed a flexible naming system that worked across cultures, time zones, and different sizes of networks. They needed something that was responsive to thousands, millions, even billions of requests. They built the Domain Name System (DNS) to solve these problems. This section looks at how DNS works, then examines the servers that make the magic happen. The DNS discussion wraps up with troubleshooting scenarios.

How DNS Works

To serve users and resolve names all around the world, DNS relies on that time-tested bureaucratic solution: delegation! The top-dog DNS system delegates parts of the job to subsidiary DNS systems that, in turn, delegate part of their work to other systems, and so on.

DNS servers need some way to decide how to divide the work. Toward this end, DNS is split into two halves: resolvers and name servers (often just called **DNS servers**). **Resolvers** query name servers with a name to get its associated IP address. **Name servers** hold the actual name and IP **DNS records** in a kind of database called a **zone**.

> DNS servers primarily use UDP port 53 (and sometimes TCP port 53 for zone transfers and responses larger than 512 bytes).

The DNS root for the entire Internet consists of over a thousand powerful systems grouped together as 13 root server "identities" scattered all over the world. Go to https://root-servers.org to see exactly where all the root servers are located.

The original top-level domain names were .com, .org, .net, .edu, .gov, .mil, and .int.

The **Internet Corporation for Assigned Names and Numbers (ICANN)** has the authority to create new TLDs. ICANN has added hundreds of generic TLDs, such as .biz for businesses and .rodeo for—you guessed it—the rodeo industry.

These name servers are arranged in a hierarchal, interlinked fashion to help distribute the work of storing and translating all those names to IP addresses. The top-dog DNS name server is actually a system—a bunch of powerful computers dispersed around the world—that forms the "root" of a **global hierarchy** that covers every name accessible on the public Internet. They work as a team known collectively as **DNS root servers** (or simply as the *DNS root*). (The CompTIA Network+ exam objectives list them as *root DNS servers*.)

The DNS root servers have only one job: to delegate name resolution to more specific DNS systems. Just below the DNS root in the global hierarchy is a set of DNS systems—called the **top-level domain servers**—that handle the **top-level domain (TLD) names**, such as .com, .org, .net, .edu, .gov, .mil, .int; international country code names such as .us and .eu; and a more recent crowd of less-well-known generic names.

The TLD name servers delegate to domain-specific name servers that handle the 300 million+ names—like totalsem.com and wikipedia.org—registered under each top-level domain. These domain-specific name servers are the authoritative source for the IP addresses a computer needs to communicate with a domain's servers. For example, the name server for totalsem.com has a record that includes information like:

```
www   34.200.194.131
```

This means any computer trying to visit *www*.totalsem.com needs to connect to the server at 34.200.194.131. Only the name server controlling the totalsem.com domain—the domain's **authoritative name server**—holds the zone that stores the actual IP address for *www*.totalsem.com. The name servers above this one in the global hierarchy enable any DNS resolver to find totalsem.com's authoritative name server.

Name Spaces

Networks that use DNS rely on an **hierarchical name space**. That's a fancy phrase for describing a tree structure for naming network resources so they interconnect but have unique names or paths within that network.

You work with hierarchical structures all the time. PCs store data that way. The root of a hard drive, such as C:\, can have many folders. Those folders can store data files or subfolders (or both). The subfolders can in turn store files or subfolders.

Figure 9.3 shows a simple root/folder/subfolder/file hierarchy. The root is C:\, which has two folders, Windows and Program1. Program1 has two subfolders, Current and Backup, which contain two files, both named Data.txt and Data.xlsx. The two pairs of files can have the same names because they're stored in different sections of the drive.

Drive storage displays hierarchy from left to right, with the root at the far left. You'd write the path to Data.txt in the Current subfolder like this:

C:\Program1\Current\Data.txt

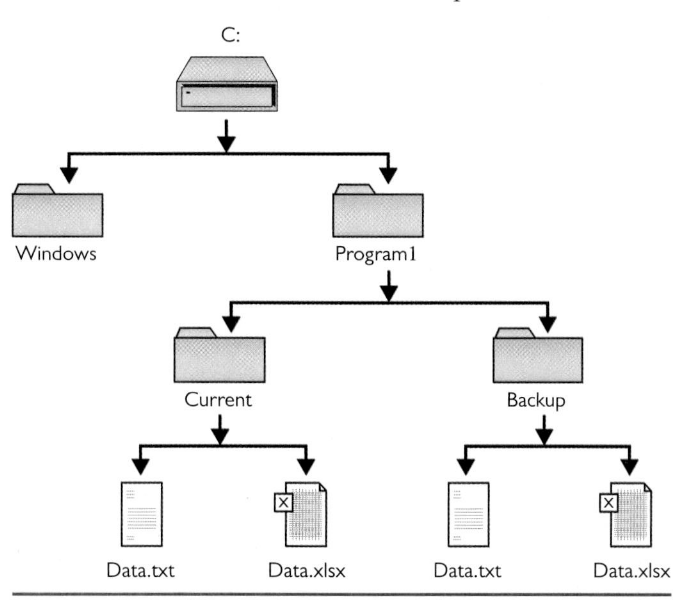

• **Figure 9.3** Hierarchical data storage in a PC

In contrast, Data.txt in the Backup folder's path looks like this:

C:\Program1\Backup\Data.txt

The hierarchical storage structure of the drive keeps the files separated and the paths to each file unique. DNS works similarly in both private networks and the Internet.

The top of the DNS hierarchy in a network is the **root**. The root can have domains, which can in turn have subdomains. Those domains and subdomains can have individual hosts that also have names, called **host names**.

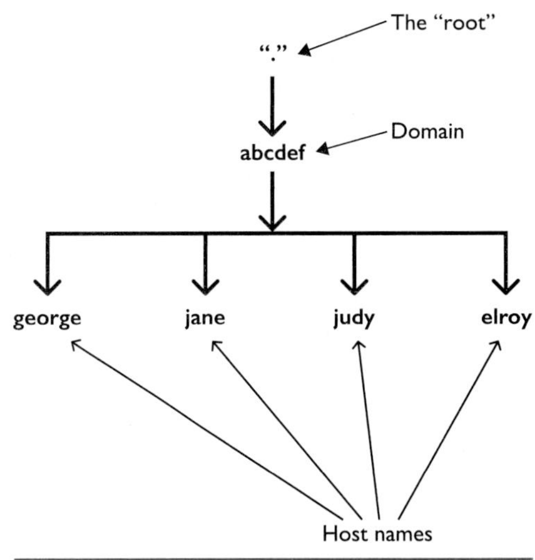

• **Figure 9.4** Private DNS network

Figure 9.4 shows a sample DNS tree for a small network that is not attached to the Internet. In this case, there is only one domain: `abcdef`. Each computer on the network has a host name, as shown in the figure.

A complete DNS name, including the host name and all its domains (in order), is called a **fully qualified domain name (FQDN)**, and it's written with the root on the far right, followed by the names of the domains (in order) added to the left of the root, and the host name on the far left. Each name is separated by a period symbol. Here are the FQDNs for two systems in the `abcdef` domain. Note the period for the root is on the far *right* of each FQDN!

```
george.abcdef.
judy.abcdef.
```

This "." signifies the root—you almost never see it outside of configuring name servers because the presence of the root is assumed and we drop it like so:

```
george.abcdef
judy.abcdef
```

Tech Tip

It's Not Always .com

Don't get locked into thinking FQDNs always end with names like ".com" or ".net." True, DNS names on the Internet must always end with them, but private networks can (and often do) ignore this and use whatever naming scheme they want with their DNS names.

If you're used to seeing DNS names on the Internet, you're probably wondering about the lack of ".com," ".net," or other common DNS domain names. Those conventions are enforced for computers that are visible on the Internet, such as Web servers, but they're not technically required for DNS names on a private network. If you know you won't need these DNS names to be visible on the Internet, you can skip the Internet top-level domains.

Let's look at another DNS name space example but make it a bit more complex. This network is not on the Internet. The network has two domains, *houston* and *dallas*, as shown in Figure 9.5. Note that each domain has a *server* subdomain. They don't clash because each node in the tree has its own name space, just as you can have two files with the same name in different folders on your PC.

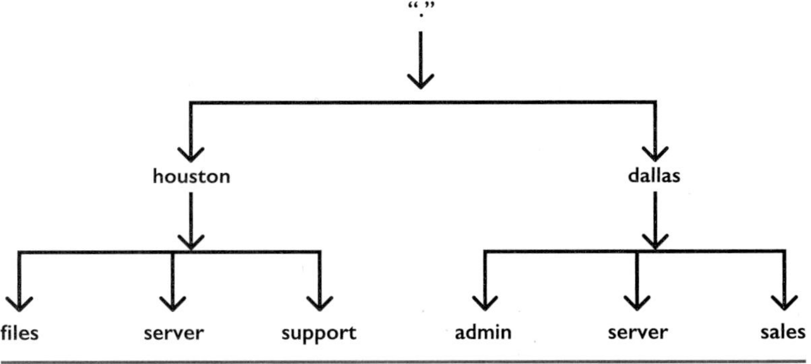

• **Figure 9.5** Two DNS domains

The *support* subdomain has two client machines, one used by Tom (named tom-wks) and the other used by Rita (named rita-wks). It's common to use a system's name as its DNS subdomain so

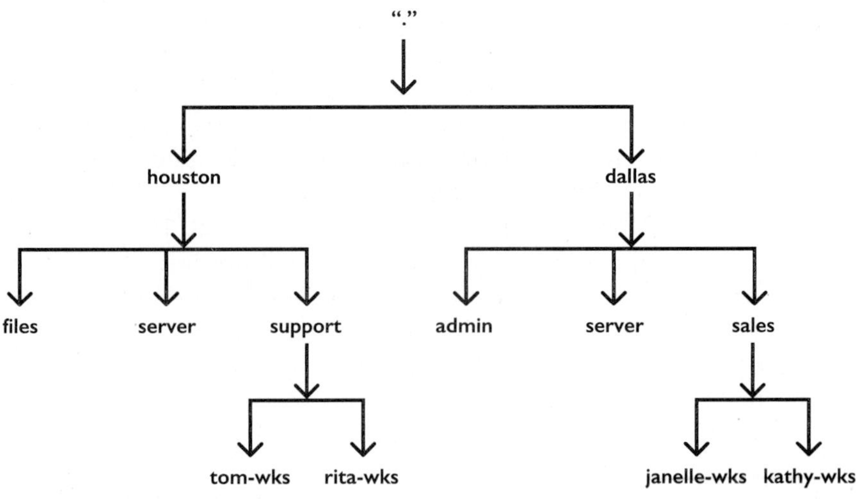

• **Figure 9.6** Subdomains added

The term "host name" can refer to only the leftmost label of a DNS name (which is often the computer name) or the whole FQDN.

that it looks like Figure 9.6. You don't *have* to use the host names—but it's a common pattern that you'll almost certainly see in the real world.

Here's how you would write out the FQDNs (without the root ".") of a few nodes in this tree. Since most people write in English from left to right, start with the host name and move up to the top of the DNS tree, adding all domains until you get to the top of the DNS tree:

```
tom-wks.support.houston
rita-wks.support.houston
janelle-wks.sales.dallas
server.dallas
```

Scaling up to the Internet, the DNS hierarchical naming structure includes the top-level domain of a resource as well as domains and subdomains. When describing the Web server www.totalsem.com, for example, the root is the implied period on the far right; com is the TLD; totalsem is a domain under com; and www is a subdomain under totalsem. "www" might also be the host name of the physical Web server machine, but in the DNS naming scheme, it's just a subdomain name. So www.totalsem.com is the FQDN for the Total Seminars Web server.

Name Servers

So where does this massive database of DNS names reside and how does it work? The power of DNS comes from its incredible flexibility. Because of its distributed nature, DNS works as well on a small, private network as it does on the biggest network of all—the Internet. We've gone over this terminology already but let's review the three key players:

- **Record** A record attaches a piece of data to a name in the DNS tree, such as its IP address. Records store the names you see between the dots in an FQDN.
- **Zone** A zone is a container for a single domain that gets filled with records. In other words, a zone is a collection of records about a name in the DNS tree.
- **Name server** A name server is software that responds to queries about DNS zones.

Name servers may store their own zones or copies of zones from other name servers. A simple network might have one name server with a single zone that lists all its names and their corresponding IP addresses. As previously introduced, it's known as the *authoritative name server* for the domain. If you've got more complex naming needs, your name server can be authoritative for multiple domain zones without a problem (Figure 9.7).

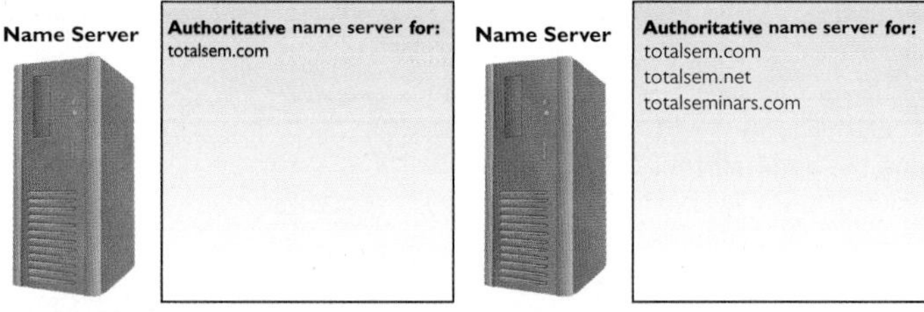

• **Figure 9.7** A single name server can be authoritative for one or more domains.

On the opposite end of the spectrum, a single domain can use more than one DNS server. Imagine how busy the google.com domain is—it needs lots of name servers to support all the incoming DNS queries.

A larger-scale network starts with a **primary name server** and one or more **secondary name servers**. The secondary servers are subordinate to the primary server, but all support the same domain (Figure 9.8). Let's go into a little more detail on how these two types of servers work together to support a domain.

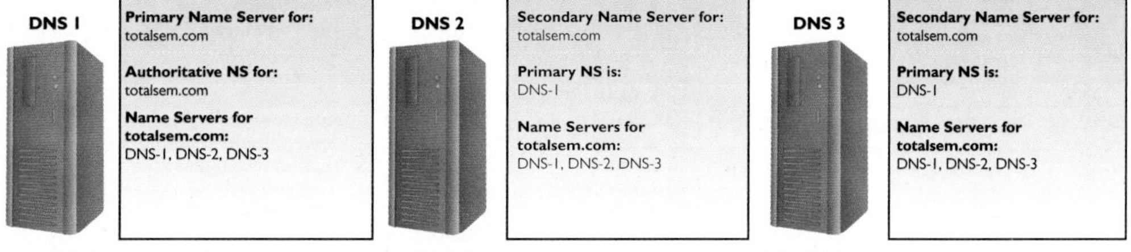

• **Figure 9.8** DNS flexibility

Primary/Secondary Servers and Zones If you have a lot of servers all supporting the same domain, they need to be able to talk to each other frequently. If one server gets a new record, that record must propagate to all the name servers through a process called **zone transfer**. Every name server for this domain must know the name and address of the primary name server as well as the name and address of every secondary name server. The primary name server's job is to make sure that all the other name servers can discover the latest changes.

Let's say you add a new server called git.totalsem.com to the totalsem .com domain with the IP address 34.200.194.132. As an administrator, you add this data to the primary name server. The primary name server then advances a special value called a **serial field** that secondary name servers regularly check. If the secondary servers see that their serial field is lower than the one on the primary server, they request a zone transfer of the DNS zone from the primary server (Figure 9.9).

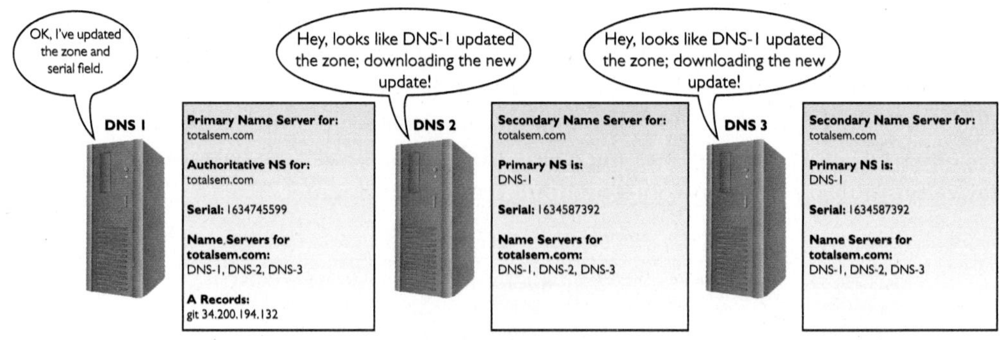

• **Figure 9.9** Distributing the updated zone information

For clarity, a regular lookup is also sometimes called a **forward lookup**. If you need even more clarity in your life, Windows Server uses the term *Forward Lookup Zones* for normal zones and *Reverse Lookup Zones* for zones that map IP addresses to names.

Reverse Zones One cool thing about DNS is that it can drive backward, so to speak—converting an IP address back into a name—through a process called **reverse lookup**. It isn't essential for using DNS, but it can make a network easier to troubleshoot and may be more or less required for things like verifying e-mail server ownership.

Reverse lookups are enabled by separate zones that focus on IP addresses instead of labels. A reverse lookup zone (Figure 9.10) takes a network ID, reverses it, and adds a unique domain called "in-addr.arpa" to create the zone.

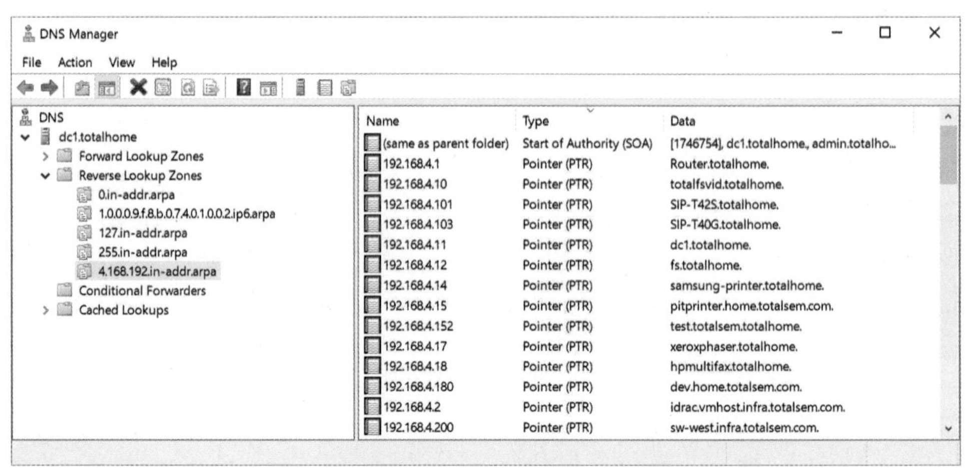

• **Figure 9.10** Reverse lookup zone

Make sure you know the difference between forward and reverse lookup zones. Forward lookup enables a system to determine an IP address by knowing the FQDN; reverse lookup enables a system to determine an FQDN by knowing the IP address. Also, the exam might ask about *reverse DNS*, meaning the process of using reverse lookup.

A few low-level functions (like mail) and some security programs depend on reverse lookup zones, so DNS servers provide them. When in doubt, make one. If you don't need it, it won't cause any trouble.

Name Resolution

That was a lot of information about how DNS stores FQDNs, but how do client systems use that web of name servers? Well, when you whip out your phone and enter the address of your favorite Web site, your phone doesn't directly query all the name servers it needs to contact to resolve the name. All these name servers exist to enable us to resolve names to IP addresses, but the real work is done by a *resolver*, as mentioned in the beginning of this section. Let's look at how this process works.

When you type in a Web address, your browser must resolve that name to the Web server's IP address to make a connection to that Web server. First, your browser uses the operating system's built-in resolver. The operating system's resolver consults its local DNS **resolver cache**—a memory area that also includes recently resolved addresses—or queries remote servers for the answer. Getting the address locally is much more efficient than asking a remote server. It also includes records from the hosts file (your system won't ask an external resolver about names and addresses from the hosts file).

> **Tech Tip**
>
> **Taking a Peek in the Local DNS Cache**
>
> *From time to time, you may need to pop the hood of a host's DNS cache to see its list of recently resolved FQDNs (plus entries from the hosts file). In Windows, for example, open a command prompt and type* ***ipconfig /displaydns*** *to see them. Here are some sample results:*

```
    news.ycombinator.com

    ----------------------------------------
    Record Name . . . . . : news.ycombinator.com
    Record Type . . . . . : 1
    Time To Live  . . . . : 203
    Data Length . . . . . : 4
    Section . . . . . . . : Answer
    A (Host) Record . . . : 209.216.230.240
     www.totalsem.com
     --------------------
    Record Name . . . . . : www.totalsem.com
     Record Type . . . . . : 1
     Time To Live  . . . . : 1697
     Data Length . . . . . : 4
     Section . . . . . . . : Answer
     A (Host) Record . . . : 34.200.194.131
C:\>
```

Setting down the phone, let's say you type **www.totalsem.com** in a Web browser for the first time on your PC. To resolve the name www.totalsem.com, the host contacts its DNS resolver and requests the IP address, as shown in Figure 9.11. The resolver is responsible for querying the name servers needed to answer a given request. This resolver may have its own cache, and it might be running on the host itself, running on the local router/gateway, or combined with a network's local name server.

Client
1. The client asks its DNS server for the www.totalsem.com IP address.

Client's DNS server
2. The DNS server doesn't know the IP address, so it asks the DNS root server.

• **Figure 9.11** A host contacts its local DNS resolver.

To request the IP address of www.totalsem.com, your operating system's built-in DNS resolver needs the IP address of a DNS server. You must enter DNS information into your system. DNS server data is part of the critical basic IP information such as your IP address, subnet mask, and default gateway, so you usually enter it at the same time as the other IP information. You configure DNS in Windows using the Internet Protocol Version 4 (TCP/IPv4) Properties dialog box. Figure 9.12 shows the DNS settings for my system. Note that I have more than one DNS server setting; the second one is a backup in case the first one isn't working. Two DNS settings is not a rule, however, so don't worry if your system shows only one DNS server setting.

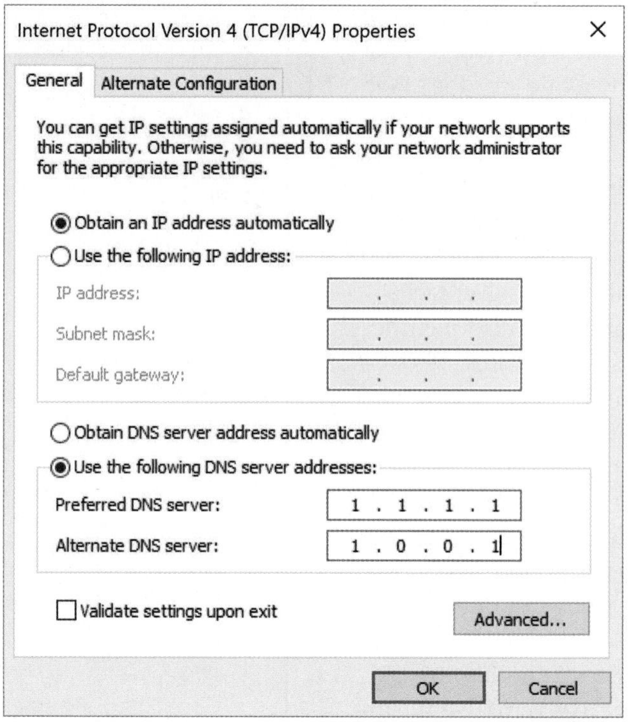

• **Figure 9.12** DNS information in Windows

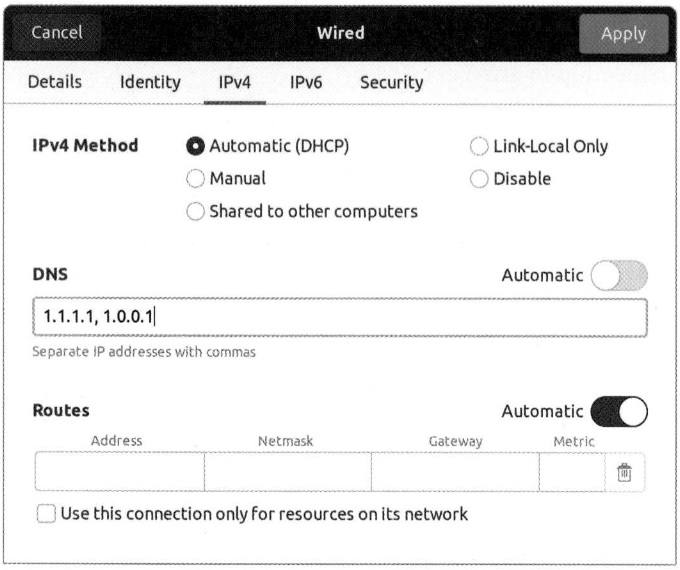

• **Figure 9.13** Entering DNS information in Ubuntu

Every operating system has a way for you to enter DNS server information. Just about every version of Linux has some form of graphical editor, for example, to make this an easy process. Figure 9.13 shows Ubuntu's Network Configuration utility.

Every operating system also comes with a utility you can use to verify the DNS server settings. The tool in Windows, for example, is called **ipconfig**. You can see your current DNS server settings in Windows by typing **`ipconfig /all`** at the command prompt (Figure 9.14). In UNIX/Linux, type the following at a terminal: **`cat /etc/resolv.conf`**.

Now that you understand how your system knows the DNS server's IP address, let's return to the DNS process.

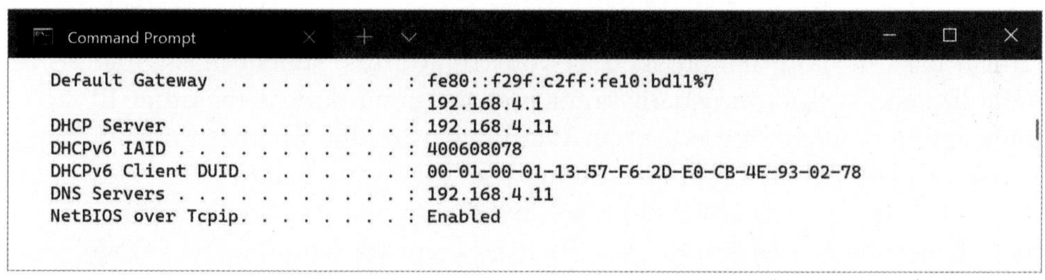

• **Figure 9.14** Output from the `ipconfig /all` command showing DNS information in Windows

Your client will send its DNS resolver a **recursive lookup** request for the IP address of www.totalsem.com, which means the resolver will query other servers with the full requested FQDN as needed to answer your query. At this point, your DNS server checks its resolver cache of previously resolved FQDNs to see if www.totalsem.com is there. In this case, www.totalsem.com is not in the server's DNS resolver cache—so your DNS server needs to perform an iterative lookup to find the answer.

Your local DNS server may not know the IP address for www.totalsem.com, but it does know the addresses of the DNS root servers. The root servers know all the addresses of the top-level domain name servers (.com, .org, .rodeo). The root servers send your DNS server an IP address for a .com server (Figure 9.15).

• **Figure 9.15** Talking to a root server

• **Figure 9.16** Talking to the .com server

A local DNS server, like the one connected to a LAN, is not authoritative, but rather is used just for internal queries from internal clients, and caching.

The .com server also doesn't know the address of www.totalsem.com, but it knows the IP address of the totalsem.com authoritative name server. It sends that IP address to your DNS server (Figure 9.16).

The authoritative totalsem.com name server does know the IP address of www.totalsem.com and can send that information back to the local DNS server. This whole process of asking each name server from the root down is an **iterative lookup**. Figure 9.17 shows the process of resolving an FQDN into an IP address.

Now that your DNS server has the IP address for www.totalsem.com, it stores a copy in its cache and answers your client's recursive query. Your Web browser then begins the HTTP request to get the Web page.

You might be asked to compare *internal vs. external DNS servers*, but the objective stops short of mentioning resolvers or name servers. That's kind of a huge distinction to fail to make. Let's look at both. First, *internal DNS* refers to private networks, so the name server hosts zones for those private networks only, like totalhome used as an example in this chapter. The local resolver would query the local name server for local resources.

Second, *external DNS* refers to things outside your network, like the Internet. External DNS name servers would have zones for Internet sites. And the local resolver might also have an Internet-ready aspect to query those name servers.

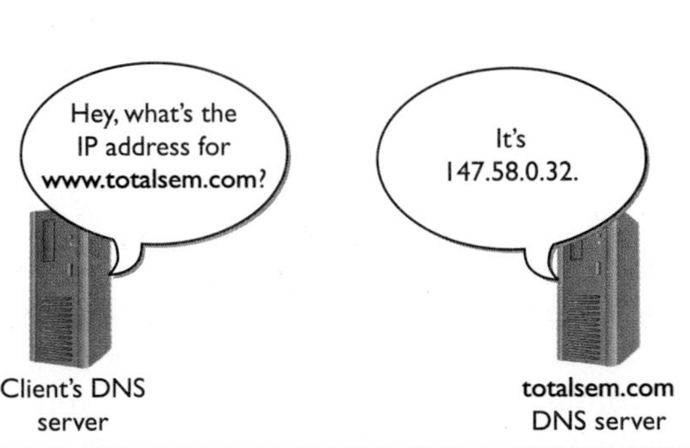

• **Figure 9.17** Talking to the totalsem.com DNS server

Cross Check

HTTP Process

You learned the specifics of HTTP in Chapter 8, so check your memory now. Is the HTTP process connectionless or connection-oriented? At what OSI layers does the process happen?

Administering DNS Servers

I've been talking about DNS servers for so long, I feel I'd be untrue to my vision of a Mike Meyers book unless I gave you at least a quick peek at a DNS server in action. Lots of operating systems come with built-in DNS server software, including Windows Server and just about every version of UNIX/Linux. Several third-party DNS server programs are also available for virtually any operating system. I'm going to use the DNS server program that comes with Microsoft Windows Server, primarily because it takes the prettiest screenshots and is the one I use here at the office.

The most popular DNS server used in UNIX/Linux systems is called BIND.

Although you can use it independently if you like, Windows DNS server is the default resolver and name server for **Active Directory**—Microsoft's batteries-included approach to managing enterprise networks. Unfortunately, Microsoft decided to use the word *domain* to mean something specific in Active Directory. Buckle up! This is *not* the same as a DNS domain. The Windows Server system that manages an Active Directory domain is called a *domain controller*. With that bit of backstory out of the way, let's dive in! Figure 9.18 shows the DNS Manager for my company's domain controller, imaginatively named dc1.totalhome.

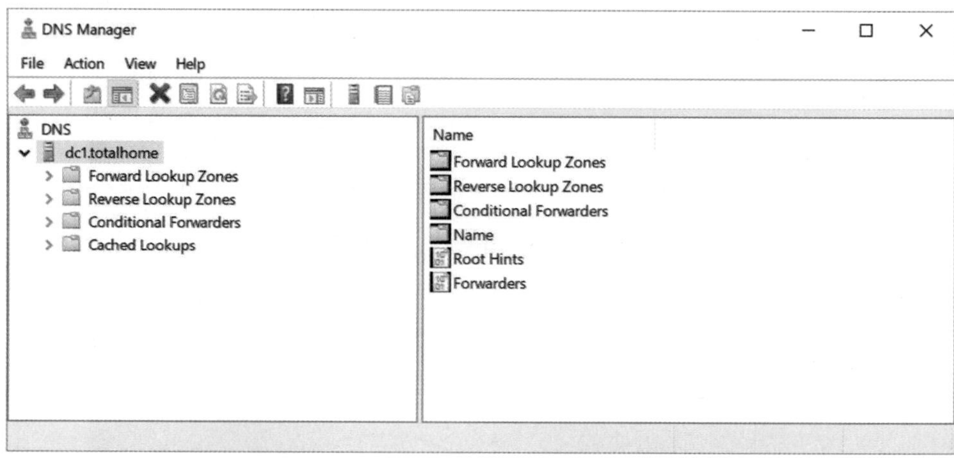

• **Figure 9.18** DNS Manager main screen

Windows DNS server, which uses a folder analogy to show DNS zones and records, has (at least) three folder icons visible: Forward Lookup Zones, Reverse Lookup Zones, and Cached Lookups. Depending on the version of Windows Server you're running and the level of customization, your server might have more than three folder icons. Let's look at Cached Lookups and Forward Lookup Zones here.

DNS Caching

Because this DNS server also acts as the recursive resolver for my office, it performs **DNS caching** for my network, temporarily storing information about previous DNS lookups. As we discussed when talking about name resolutions, servers acting as recursive resolvers cache the results of DNS queries to speed up future requests. This is an important feature of DNS servers and keeps the whole system running fast.

Windows does a nice job of visualizing these cached records by placing all cached lookups in folders that share the first name of the top-level domain, with subfolders that use the name of the second-level domain (Figure 9.19). This sure makes it easy to see where folks have been Web browsing!

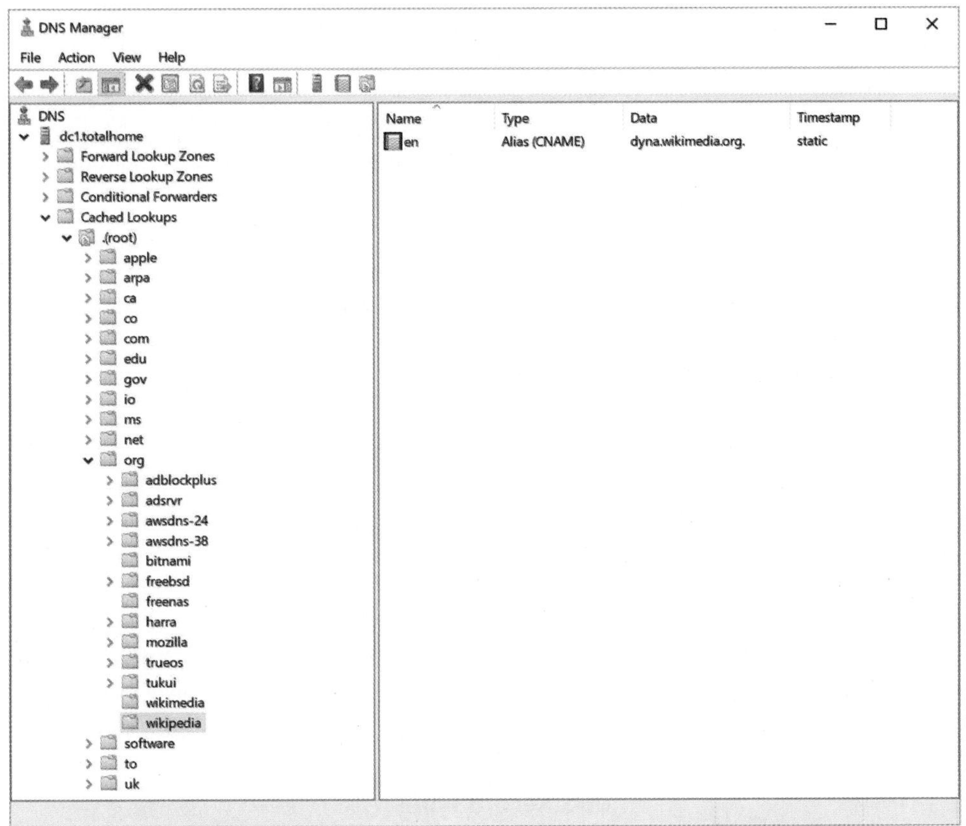

• **Figure 9.19** Inspecting the DNS cache

One question you might be thinking about now is, "How do all these DNS servers know to refresh the records they store in their cache with fresh information from the authoritative name servers?" That is controlled by a **time to live (TTL)** field on every DNS record. This field indicates the number of seconds that administrators want DNS resolvers to hold records in their caches before removing the cached record.

A short TTL time means that people will see DNS record updates faster (for instance, if you have moved your Web site to a new server). A longer TTL means the records will be held in caches longer, but this can be a good thing if, say, your DNS name server gets hacked and the bad guys point your Web site to a server they control! A longer TTL gives you more time to react and fix the damage without the public being directed to the hacker server.

Forward Lookup Zones

Next up let's look at the zones for my corporate network. Figure 9.20 shows the Forward Lookup Zones folder expanded. You can see the records for my "totalhome" domain. I can get away with a domain name that's not Internet-legal because none of these computers are visible on the Internet. The totalhome domain only works on my local network for local computers to find each other.

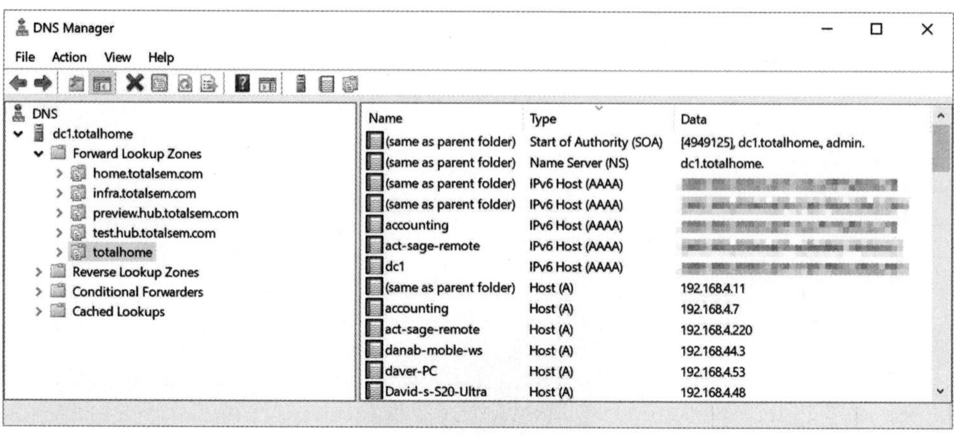

• **Figure 9.20** Forward lookup zone totalhome

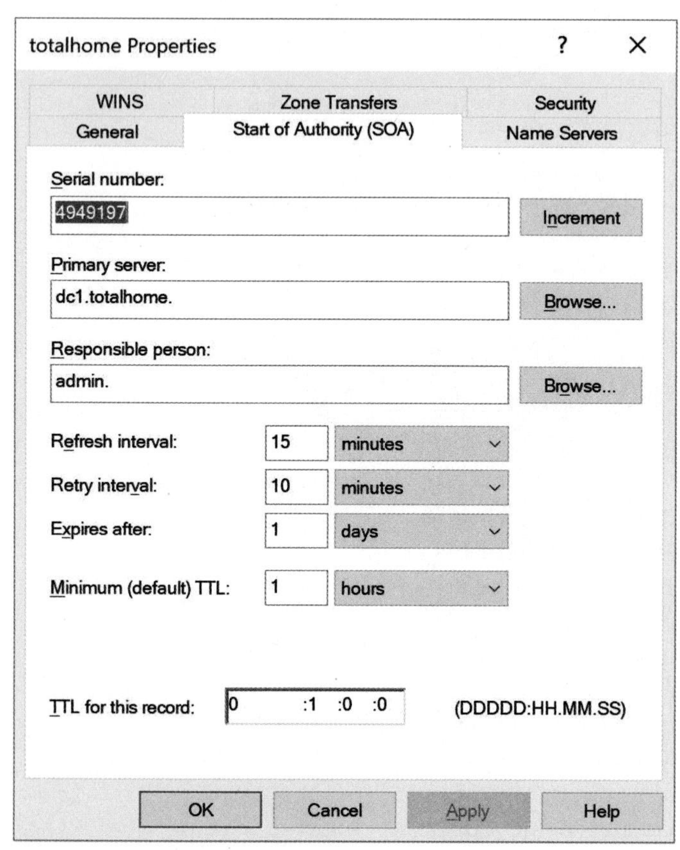

• **Figure 9.21** Details of the SOA record for totalhome

Let's look at the contents of the totalhome zone and concentrate on the individual rows of data. Each row defines a zone record. Each record consists of Name, Type, and Data (TTL is only visible from the record's Properties dialog box). While Name and Data (showing IPv6 and IPv4 addresses, for the most part) are obvious, the DNS record type—Type—needs a bit of discussion.

DNS Record Types

Part of the power and flexibility of DNS comes from the use of record types. Each record type helps different aspects of DNS do their jobs. Let's take a moment and review all the DNS record types you'll see on the CompTIA Network+ exam. These are, in no specific order: SOA, NS, A, AAAA, CNAME, PTR, MX, SRV, and TXT.

SOA Every zone requires an **SOA record** that defines the primary name server in charge of the zone. The SOA record in the totalhome zone in Figure 9.21, for example, indicates that my server is the primary DNS server for a domain called totalhome. You can also see the serial number that secondary name servers use to check if they need to update their copy of the zone information. (The SOA record clearly has a lot more information, as you can see, but this is good enough for our current discussion.)

In the official RFC language, an SOA record "marks the start of a zone of authority." You'll see the record called a *start of authority (SOA) record* on the CompTIA Network+ exam.

NS An **NS record** points to the server that holds the records (zone) for a part of the DNS tree. The NS record in Figure 9.22 shows the primary name server for totalhome. My network could have a secondary name server to provide redundancy. This secondary name server is also authoritative for the totalhome domain. Having two DNS servers ensures that if one fails, the totalhome domain will continue to have a DNS server, plus it provides load balancing for efficiency.

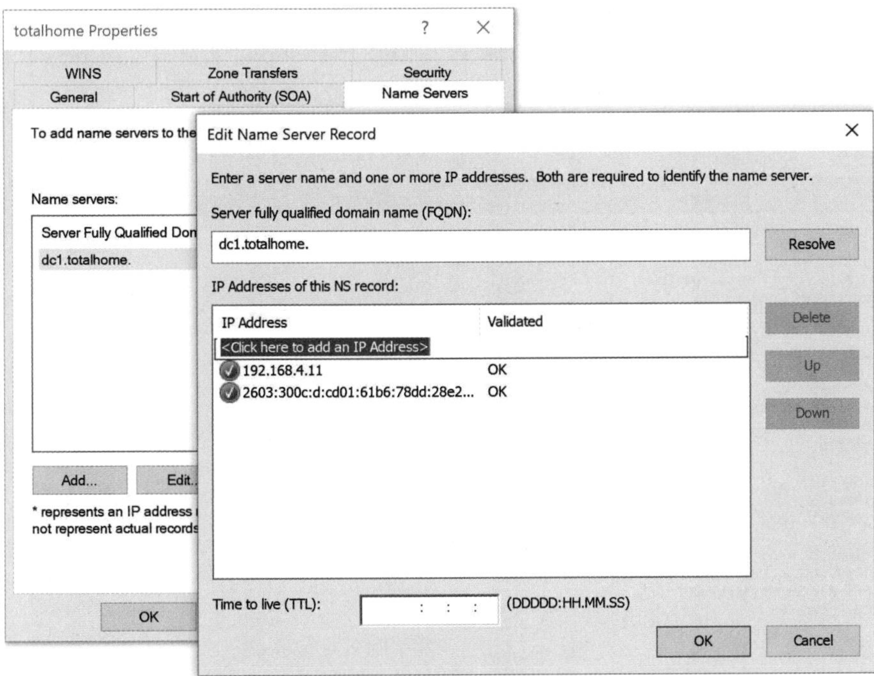

• **Figure 9.22** NS record

In the official RFC language, an NS record is for "name server." You'll see the record called a *name server (NS) record* on the CompTIA Network+ exam.

While in my network the NS records don't look like anything special, NS (and SOA) records link the DNS hierarchy together. NS records enable the name servers to know where to point the resolvers to find the authoritative name servers for a specific domain below them in the DNS hierarchy.

In the official RFC language, an A record is for "a host address." You'll see the record called an *address (A) record* on the CompTIA Network+ exam.

A Individual hosts each get their own unique **A record**. A records are the workhorse records in the zone that hold the IPv4 addresses for hosts. There are some common conventions here. A Web server on a forward lookup zone, for example, often has a host name of www, if for no other reason than users expect a Web site URL to start with www.

AAAA **AAAA records** ("quad A" when spoken) are the equivalent of A records, but they hold IPv6 addresses. You'll learn a lot more about IPv6 in Chapter 12. The reason this type of record is called AAAA is that 128-bit IPv6 addresses are four times the length of 32-bit IPv4 addresses.

The AAAA DNS record is *not* an initialism. The four A letters signify that IPv6 addresses are four times longer than IPv4 addresses. *AAA* in computer security, on the other hand, stands for *authentication, authorization, and accounting.* The CompTIA Network+ exam objectives merge these terms erroneously in the Acronym list by identifying AAAA (not AAA) as representing authentication, authorization, accounting, and *auditing.* You will only see the AAAA DNS record, not the security (mis)usage term, on the exam.

CNAME A **CNAME record** acts like an alias and holds an FQDN, not an IP address. My computer's name is mikesdesktop.totalhome, but I can also use mike.totalhome to reference that computer. The Linux/Mac `host` command shows this very clearly. Running `host mike.totalhome` returns the following:

```
$ host mike.totalhome
mike.totalhome is an alias for mikesdesktop.totalhome.
mikesdesktop.totalhome has address 192.168.4.96
```

> In the official RFC language, a CNAME record is for "the canonical name for an alias." You'll see the record called a *canonical name (CNAME) record* on the CompTIA Network+ exam.

You can also use other commands like `nslookup`, `dig`, and even `ping` to inspect CNAME records. (I cover `dig` more completely in the "Troubleshooting DNS on Clients" section, later in this chapter.) Figure 9.23 shows the text output of a `dig` query. The query `dig mike.totalhome`—making an A record query for a specific name—returns the CNAME (mikesdesktop.totalhome), and then the A record that shows the IP address for the host.

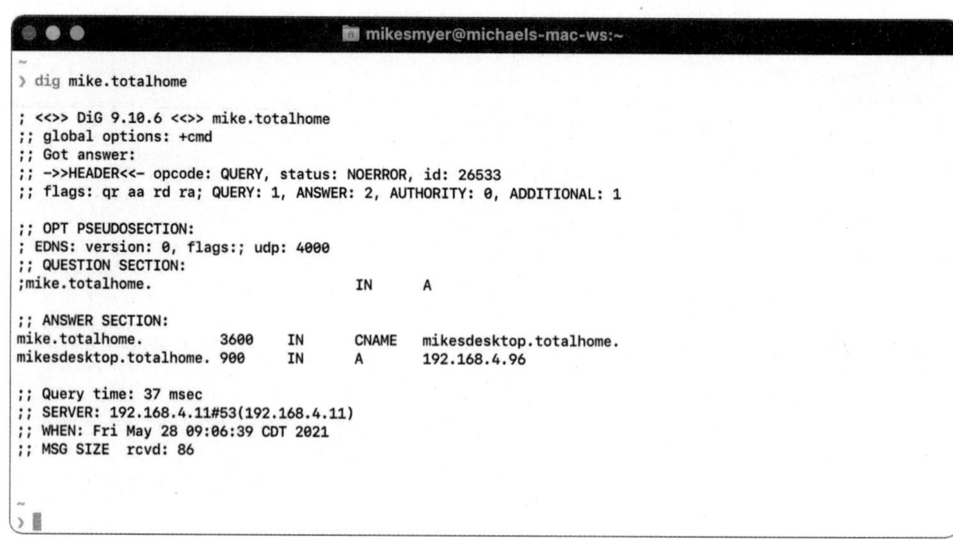

mikesmyer@michaels-mac-ws:~
› dig mike.totalhome
; <<>> DiG 9.10.6 <<>> mike.totalhome
;; global options: +cmd
;; Got answer:
;; ->>HEADER<<- opcode: QUERY, status: NOERROR, id: 26533
;; flags: qr aa rd ra; QUERY: 1, ANSWER: 2, AUTHORITY: 0, ADDITIONAL: 1
;; OPT PSEUDOSECTION:
; EDNS: version: 0, flags:; udp: 4000
;; QUESTION SECTION:
;mike.totalhome. IN A
;; ANSWER SECTION:
mike.totalhome. 3600 IN CNAME mikesdesktop.totalhome.
mikesdesktop.totalhome. 900 IN A 192.168.4.96
;; Query time: 37 msec
;; SERVER: 192.168.4.11#53(192.168.4.11)
;; WHEN: Fri May 28 09:06:39 CDT 2021
;; MSG SIZE rcvd: 86

• **Figure 9.23** Results of running `dig` on a CNAME

> In the official RFC language, a PTR record is "a domain name pointer." You'll see the record called a *pointer (PTR) record* on the CompTIA Network+ exam.

PTR A **PTR record** reverses the functions of A or AAAA records. PTR records are found only in reverse lookup zones; they use an IP address for their names and hold the FQDN of a host at that address. One quirk of PTR records is that a PTR record can only point a single IP address to a single FQDN. In contrast, A or AAAA records can have many FQDNs pointing to a single IP address.

> In the official RFC language, an MX record is for "mail exchange." You'll see the record called a *mail exchange (MX) record* on the CompTIA Network+ exam.

MX SMTP servers use **MX records** exclusively to determine where to send mail. They hold the FQDN of the server that handles mail for the domain. As an example, my company uses Microsoft 365 for our corporate e-mail. Microsoft has provided an FQDN to which to point my MX records (see Figure 9.24). Now when someone mails me at mike@totalsem.com, their SMTP server will know to send the mail on to Microsoft's servers.

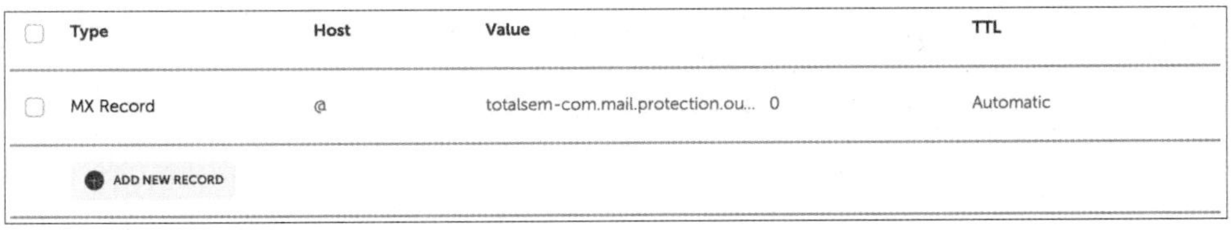

Type	Host	Value	TTL
MX Record	@	totalsem-com.mail.protection.ou... 0	Automatic

ADD NEW RECORD

• **Figure 9.24** MX record for totalsem.com

SRV The idea of creating MX records to directly support e-mail motivated the Elders of the Internet to develop a generic DNS record that supports any type of server, the **SRV record**. SRV records have a different look than most other DNS records. The basic format of an SRV record is as follows:

```
_service._proto.name. TTL IN SRV priority weight port target.
```

- *service* Name of the service supported by this record
- *proto* TCP or UDP
- *name* The domain name for this server (ends with a period)
- *TTL* Time to live, in seconds
- *IN* DNS class field (always IN)
- *SRV* Type of Record (always SRV)
- *priority* The priority of the target host; used when multiple servers are present (value is 0 when only one server)
- *weight* An arbitrary value to give certain services priority over others
- *port* The TCP or UDP port on which the service is to be found
- *target* The FQDN of the machine providing the service, ending in a dot

Here is an example of an SRV record for a Session Initiation Protocol (SIP) service:

```
_sip._tcp.testserve.com. 86400 IN SRV 0 5 5060 sipserver.mikemeyers.com.
```

Several common services use SRV records. These include Kerberos servers, Lightweight Directory Access Protocol (LDAP), SIP, and, surprisingly, the popular game *Minecraft*!

> In the official RFC language, an SRV record is for "specifying the location of services." You'll see the record called a *service (SRV) record* on the CompTIA Network+ exam.

TXT A **TXT record** is a freeform type of record that can be used for… anything. TXT records allow any text to be added to a zone. Early on, one proposed use of TXT records was documentation. An example from the original RFC was this:

```
"printer=lpr5"
```

While using TXT records as general documentation didn't really catch on, one place it has become popular is helping to secure against e-mail spoofing. Solutions such as DomainKeys Identified Mail (DKIM), Sender Policy Framework (SPF), and Domain-based Message Authentication, Reporting, and Conformance (DMARC) use TXT records that enable domains to verify that e-mail being received by a third-party e-mail server is sent by a legitimate server within the domain. The following is the SPF TXT record from my totalsem.com domain:

> In the official RFC language, a TXT record is for "text strings." You'll see the record called a *text (TXT) record* on the CompTIA Network+ exam.

```
v=spf1 include:spf.protection.outlook.com include:servers.mcsv.net -all
```

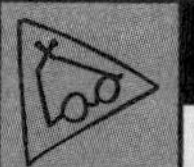

Tech Tip

Public DNS Servers

Every DNS server that resolves legitimate, registered Internet domains is public, but there is also a type of public DNS server that's designed to handle all requests for any FQDN equally, known as **public DNS servers**. *These public DNS servers often offer faster DNS resolution, are all but guaranteed to never go down, and many times avoid DNS redirections that some ISPs do to their customers. Here's a small sampling of the more famous public DNS servers:*

Provider	Primary Name Server	Secondary Name Server
Cloudflare	1.1.1.1	1.0.0.1
Google	8.8.8.8	8.8.4.4
Quad9	9.9.9.9	149.112.112.112
OpenDNS	208.67.222.222	208.67.220.220
SafeDNS	195.46.39.39	195.46.39.40

All DHCP servers provide an option called *DNS server* that tells clients the IP address of the DNS server to use as their resolver.

Dynamic DNS

In the early days of TCP/IP networks, DNS servers required manual updates of their records. This was not a big deal until the numbers of computers using TCP/IP exploded in the 1990s. Then every office had a network and every network had a DNS server to update. DHCP helped to some extent. You could add a special option to the DHCP server, which is generally called the *DNS suffix*. This way the DHCP clients would know the name of the DNS domain to which they belonged, automatically appending a suffix when a bare name was used. It didn't help the manual updating of DNS records, but clients don't need records. No one accesses the clients! The DNS suffix helped the clients access network resources more efficiently.

Today, manual updating of DNS records is still the norm for most Internet-serving systems like Web servers and e-mail servers. DNS has moved beyond Internet servers; even the smallest Windows networks that run Active Directory use it. Whereas a popular Web server might have a phalanx of techs to adjust DNS settings, small networks in which most of the computers run DHCP need an alternative to old-school DNS. Luckily, the solution was worked out decades ago.

The TCP/IP folks came up with a protocol called **Dynamic DNS (DDNS)** in 1997 that enabled DNS servers to get automatic updates of IP addresses of computers in their forward lookup zones, mainly by talking to the local DHCP server. All modern DNS servers support DDNS, and all but the most primitive DHCP servers support DDNS as well.

Active Directory leans heavily on DDNS. Active Directory use DDNS for the DHCP server to talk to the DNS server. When a DHCP server updates its records for a DHCP client, it reports to the DNS server. The DNS server then updates its A or AAAA records accordingly. DDNS simplifies setting up and maintaining a LAN tremendously. If you need to force a Windows client to update its records on the Active Directory's DNS server, use the `ipconfig /registerdns` command from the command prompt.

DNS Security Extensions

If you think about what DNS does, you can appreciate that it can be a big security issue. Simply querying a DNS server gives you a list of every computer name and IP address that it serves. The big fix is called *DNS Security Extensions (DNSSEC)*. DNSSEC is an authorization and integrity protocol designed to prevent bad guys from impersonating legitimate DNS servers. It's implemented through *Extension Mechanisms for DNS (EDNS)*, a specification that expands several parameter sizes but maintains backward compatibility with earlier DNS servers.

Troubleshooting DNS on Clients

Many DNS problems result from issues with client systems, but DNS servers occasionally fail. Thus, you need be able to determine whether a DNS problem is attributable to the client system or to the DNS server. All the tools you're about to see come with every operating system that supports TCP/IP, with the exception of the previously introduced `ipconfig` commands, which I'll also mention in the next section.

So how do you know when to suspect DNS is causing the problem on your network? Well, just about everything you do on an IP network depends on DNS to find the right system to talk to for whatever job the application does. Desktop clients use DNS to find their servers; phone apps use DNS for their servers; even smart watches use DNS to find their servers; and so on. The first clue something is wrong is generally when a user calls and says he's getting a "server not found" error. Server not found errors look different depending on the app, but you can count on something being there that says in effect "server not found." Figure 9.25 shows how this error appears in a file transfer client.

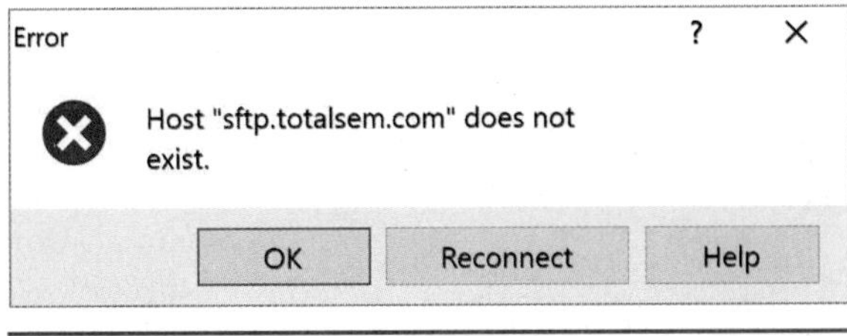

• **Figure 9.25** DNS error

Before you start testing, you need to eliminate any DNS caches on the local system. If you're running Windows, run the **`ipconfig /flushdns`** command now.

Your best friend when testing DNS is often **ping**. Run `ping` from a command prompt, followed by the name of a well-known Web site, such as **`ping www.totalsem.com`**. Watch the output carefully to see if you get an IP address. You may get a "request timed out" message, but that's fine; you just want to see if DNS is resolving FQDNs into IP addresses (Figure 9.26).

> When troubleshooting, ping is your friend. If you can ping an IP address but not the name associated with that address, check DNS.

```
Administrator: Command Prompt

C:\WINDOWS\system32>ipconfig /flushdns

Windows IP Configuration

Successfully flushed the DNS Resolver Cache.

C:\WINDOWS\system32>ping www.totalsem.com

Pinging www.totalsem.com [34.200.194.131] with 32 bytes of data:
Request timed out.
Request timed out.
Request timed out.
Request timed out.

Ping statistics for 34.200.194.131:
    Packets: Sent = 4, Received = 0, Lost = 4 (100% loss),

C:\WINDOWS\system32>_
```

• **Figure 9.26** Using ping to check DNS

If ping can't resolve the IP address with an Internet-based host, you know DNS is the problem at some level. The next step is to determine if it's the local DNS server that's down or if the problem is farther down the line.

If you get a "server not found" error on a local network where you know the IP addresses as well as the names, you need to ping again using just an IP address. If ping works with the IP address but not with the Web site name, you know you have a DNS problem.

Once you've determined that DNS is the problem, check to make sure your system has the correct DNS server entry. Again, this information is something you should keep around for local networks. If that isn't the problem, run **ipconfig /all** to see if those DNS settings are the same as the ones in the server; if they aren't, you may need to refresh your DHCP settings.

Make sure you know how to use nslookup to determine if a DNS server is active!

If you have the correct DNS settings for your DNS server and the DNS settings in the `ipconfig /all` output match those settings, you can assume the problem is with the DNS server itself. The **nslookup** (name server lookup) tool enables DNS server queries. All operating systems have a version of nslookup.

You run `nslookup` from a command prompt. With nslookup, you can (assuming you have the permission) query all types of information from a DNS server and change how your system uses DNS. Although most of these commands are far outside the scope of the CompTIA Network+ exam, you should definitely know nslookup. You can run nslookup in noninteractive or interactive mode. If you just want a quick query, use the former. Type **nslookup** followed by the desired IP address or name; if you want to, you can specify a DNS server by adding that after. Here's the output querying the Google DNS server (with the IP address 8.8.8.8):

```
C:\>nslookup www.totalsem.com 8.8.8.8
Server:    dns.google
Address:    8.8.8.8

Non-authoritative answer:
Name:      www.totalsem.com
Addresses:    2600:1f18:12fd:4801:2c7d:a10:237b:2fc1
          34.200.194.131

C:\>
```

If you want to make multiple queries, run in interactive mode. You can get there by typing **nslookup** and pressing ENTER or by using the hyphen followed by a desired IP address or name. For instance, just running `nslookup` alone from a command prompt shows you some output similar to the following:

```
C:\>nslookup
Default Server:  dc1.totalhome
Address:  192.168.4.11

>
```

Running `nslookup` gives me the IP address and the name (from an automatically executed PTR query) of my default DNS server. If I got an error at this point, perhaps a "server not found" error, I would know that either my primary name server is down or I might not have the correct DNS server information in my DNS settings.

The `nslookup` command can run a recursive lookup on other DNS resolvers, too, if you know the IP address or name. At the nslookup prompt, for example, type **`server`**, followed by the IP address or the domain name of the DNS server:

```
> server dns.google
Default Server:  dns.google
Addresses:  2001:4860:4860::8888
          2001:4860:4700::8844
          8.8.8.8
          8.8.4.4
```

This new server has four IP addresses (two v4 and two v6). This provides load balancing and redundancy in case one system fails. Type **`exit`** to leave interactive mode.

Those using UNIX/Linux have an extra DNS tool called **domain information groper (dig)**. The dig tool is similar to nslookup, but it only runs noninteractively—you ask it a question, it answers the question, and it puts you back at a regular command prompt. When you run dig, you tend to get a large amount of information. The following is a sample of a dig doing a reverse lookup run from macOS:

Check out the excellent Chapter 9 "Name Resolution" Type! over at http://totalsem.com/008. Working with the command line is cool!

```
$dig -x 192.168.4.251

; <<>> DiG 9.10.6 <<>> -x 192.168.4.251
;; global options: +cmd
;; Got answer:
;; ->>HEADER<<- opcode: QUERY, status: NOERROR, id: 22770
;; flags: qr aa rd ra; QUERY: 1, ANSWER: 1, AUTHORITY: 0, ADDITIONAL: 1

;; OPT PSEUDOSECTION:
; EDNS: version: 0, flags:; udp: 4000
;; QUESTION SECTION:
;251.4.168.192.in-addr.arpa.   IN      PTR

;; ANSWER SECTION:
251.4.168.192.in-addr.arpa. 3600 IN   PTR     gitlab.home.totalsem.com.

;; Query time: 34 msec
;; SERVER: 192.168.4.11#53(192.168.4.11)
;; WHEN: Thu May 27 13:30:51 CDT 2021
;; MSG SIZE  rcvd: 93
```

Diagnosing TCP/IP Network Issues

I've dedicated all of Chapter 21 to network diagnostic procedures, but TCP/IP has a few little extras that I want to talk about here. TCP/IP is a robust protocol suite, and in good networks, it runs like a top for years without problems. Most of the TCP/IP problems you'll see come from improper configuration, so I'm going to assume for purposes of this discussion that you've run into problems with a new TCP/IP install, and I'll show you some classic screw-ups common in this situation. I want to concentrate on making sure you can ping anyone you want to ping.

I've done thousands of IP installations over the years, and I'm proud to say that, in most cases, they worked right the first time. My users jumped on the newly configured systems, fired up their network, e-mail software, and Web browsers, and were last seen typing away, smiling from ear to ear. But I'd be a liar if I didn't also admit that plenty of setups didn't work so well. Let's start with the hypothetical case of a user who can't see something on the network. You get a call: "Help!" he cries. The first troubleshooting point to remember here is this: it doesn't matter *what* the user can't see. It doesn't matter if he can't see other systems in his network or can't see the home page on his browser—you go through the same steps in any event.

Remember to use common sense wherever possible. If the problem system can't ping by DNS name but all the other systems can, is the DNS server down? Of course not! If something—*anything*—doesn't work on one system, *always* try it on another one to determine whether the problem is specific to one system or affects the entire network.

One thing I always do is check the network connections and protocols. I'm going to cover those topics in greater detail later in the book, so, for now, assume the problem systems are properly connected and have good protocols installed. Here are some steps I recommend taking:

1. *Diagnose the NIC.* If you're lucky enough to own a higher-end NIC that has its own Control Panel applet, use the diagnostic tool to see if the NIC is working.
2. *Check your NIC's driver.* Replace it if necessary.
3. *Diagnose locally.* If the NIC's okay, diagnose locally by pinging a few neighboring systems, by both IP address and DNS name. If you can't ping by DNS, check your DNS settings. If you can't see the network using `net view`, you may have a problem with your NetBIOS settings.
4. *Check IP address and subnet mask.* If you're having a problem pinging locally, make sure you have the right IP address and subnet mask. Oh, if I had a nickel for every time I entered those incorrectly! If you're on DHCP, try renewing the lease—sometimes that does the trick. If DHCP fails, call the person in charge of the server.
5. *Run netstat.* At this point, another little handy program comes into play called **netstat**. The netstat program offers several options. The two handiest ways to run `netstat` are with no options at all and with the `-s` option. Running `netstat` with no options shows you all the current connections to your system. Look for a connection here that isn't working with an application—that's often a clue to an application problem, such as a broken application or a sneaky application running in the background. Figure 9.27 shows a `netstat` command running.

> netstat on Windows can display the executable the connection goes to using the –b option. This requires elevated privileges, but is better than –s.

6. *Run netstat –s.* Running `netstat` with the `-s` option displays several statistics that can help you diagnose problems. For example, if the display shows you are sending but not receiving, you almost certainly have a bad cable with a broken receive wire.
7. *Diagnose to the gateway.* If you can't get on the Internet, check to see if you can ping the router. Remember, the router has two interfaces, so try both: first the local interface (the one on your subnet) and then the one to the Internet. You *do* have both of those IP addresses memorized, don't you? If not, run `ipconfig` to display the LAN interface address.

```
# michaels @ michaels-ws in ~ [13:51:06] C:2
$ netstat

Active Connections

  Proto  Local Address          Foreign Address        State
  TCP    127.0.0.1:1294         michaels-ws:1295       ESTABLISHED
  TCP    127.0.0.1:1295         michaels-ws:1294       ESTABLISHED
  TCP    127.0.0.1:1297         michaels-ws:1298       ESTABLISHED
  TCP    127.0.0.1:1298         michaels-ws:1297       ESTABLISHED
  TCP    192.168.4.55:1117      52.230.222.68:https    ESTABLISHED
  TCP    192.168.4.55:1171      fs:microsoft-ds        ESTABLISHED
  TCP    192.168.4.55:1177      fs:microsoft-ds        ESTABLISHED
  TCP    192.168.4.55:1253      52.242.211.89:https    ESTABLISHED
  TCP    192.168.4.55:1261      52.242.211.89:https    ESTABLISHED
  TCP    192.168.4.55:2106      162.125.19.131:https   ESTABLISHED
  TCP    192.168.4.55:2115      162.125.19.9:https     ESTABLISHED
  TCP    192.168.4.55:2128      52.167.253.237:https   TIME_WAIT
  TCP    192.168.4.55:3389      10.0.44.130:50362      ESTABLISHED
  TCP    192.168.4.55:7680      MACH5:58363            TIME_WAIT

# michaels @ michaels-ws in ~ [13:54:54]
$
```

• **Figure 9.27** The `netstat` command in action

If you can't ping the router, either it's down or you're not connected to it. If you can only ping the near side, something in the router itself is messed up, like the routing table.

8. *Diagnose to the Internet.* If you can ping the router, try to ping something on the Internet. If you can't ping one address, try another—it's always possible that the first place you try to ping is down. If you still can't get through, you can try to locate the problem using the **tracert** (in Windows) or **traceroute** (every other OS) utility. Run either command to explore the route between you and whatever you were trying to ping. It may even tell you where the problem lies (see Figure 9.28).

```
Default Shell (Light) (-zsh) — mikesmyer
┌─[mikesmyer in ~][17:25:32]
└─>$ traceroute 8.8.8.8
traceroute to 8.8.8.8 (8.8.8.8), 64 hops max, 52 byte packets
 1  rt-ac66u_b1-6468 (192.168.50.1)  0.493 ms  0.304 ms  0.235 ms
 2  * * *
 3  172.102.49.68 (172.102.49.68)  6.326 ms * *
 4  * ae8---0.scr01.dlls.tx.frontiernet.net (74.40.3.21)  13.894 ms *
 5  ae0---0.cbr03.dlls.tx.frontiernet.net (45.52.201.113)  14.926 ms *  11.678 ms
 6  * 74.40.26.234 (74.40.26.234)  12.032 ms *
 7  108.170.252.129 (108.170.252.129)  15.051 ms
    108.170.240.193 (108.170.240.193)  11.850 ms
    108.170.240.129 (108.170.240.129)  13.210 ms
 8  * 142.250.62.203 (142.250.62.203)  11.628 ms *
 9  dns.google (8.8.8.8)  11.897 ms  13.883 ms *
```

• **Figure 9.28** Using `tracert` to identify packet loss in my ISP's network

Chapter 9 Review

Chapter Summary

After reading this chapter and completing the exercises, you should understand the following about network naming.

Analyze and configure early name resolution solutions

- Windows used a simple networking protocol for a long time, called NetBIOS/NetBEUI. It was designed primarily for sharing files and folders in a local network. The protocol didn't work when scaled up because it wasn't routable and relied too much on broadcasts.
- Microsoft created a TCP/IP protocol called NetBT to support systems that relied on NetBIOS but needed to use DNS. Every Windows computer had one name used on the local network and a DNS name for use on the Internet.
- The hosts file provided name resolution in the early days of TCP/IP networking. Although all operating systems continue to support the hosts file, few users will actively modify and employ it in the day-to-day workings of most TCP/IP systems.

Describe the function and capabilities of DNS

- DNS (Domain Name System) is vital to IP networking, whether on the Internet or within the smallest of networks. DNS functions as a hierarchical naming system for computers on a network. DNS is split into two kinds of server: resolvers that end-user computers use to ask to translate DNS names to IP addresses, and name servers that hold the actual name and IP address DNS records in a database called a zone.
- The DNS root for the Internet consists of over a 1000 powerful systems grouped together as 13 root server identities scattered all over the world.
- If one DNS resolver cannot find out (resolve) the IP address of a computer, the request gets passed along to another name server. The process continues until the request reaches the destination domain's name server. (Note that root servers and top-level domain servers just pass requests down the line.)
- Name resolution can be accomplished through consulting the host's DNS resolver cache or by contacting a DNS name server.
- Run `ipconfig /all` to view your DNS server settings. Run `ipconfig /displaydns` to display a cache of recently resolved FQDNs.
- An authoritative name server stores IP addresses and FQDNs of all systems for a particular domain.
- Forward lookup zones are the most important part of any DNS server because they contain the IP addresses and FQDNs, among other records such as A, AAAA, MX, NS, and so on.
- DNS uses many record types for various services. A records, SOA records, NS records, CNAME records, AAAA records, MX records, SRV records, and TXT records must be properly configured on any DNS server.
- Reverse lookup zones resolve an IP address to an FQDN using PTR records.
- The Dynamic DNS (DDNS) protocol enables DNS servers to update their records automatically when they receive changed IP address information from a DHCP server or clients on the network.
- The ipconfig utility is useful for troubleshooting TCP/IP settings. Running `ipconfig /flushdns` clears the local cache of DNS entries.
- The ping utility is essential in establishing connectivity to a destination PC. If you can ping a host computer by IP address (for example, `ping 192.168.4.55`) but not by name (`ping acctngpc2`), then you have a DNS resolution issue. Check the DNS servers listed under each NIC's settings; check to see that the DNS server is truly up and operational.
- The nslookup utility enables you to research which name servers are being used by a particular computer. Advanced variations of nslookup can query information from a DNS server and even change how your system uses DNS.
- UNIX/Linux users have an additional DNS tool called dig, which enables you to do more than with nslookup.

Use common TCP/IP utilities to diagnose problems with DNS

- Always try to connect from another system to determine the extent of the problem. You can then begin the steps to diagnose TCP/IP errors on a single system.

- Remember to work "from the inside out"—that is, check for connectivity problems on the local system before moving on to check the larger network structure.
- Running `netstat` shows all the current connections on your system. Running `netstat -s` displays useful statistical information.
- The tracert/traceroute utility enables you to mark the entire route an ICMP or UDP packet travels, telling you exactly where a problem lies.

Key Terms

A record *(257)*
AAAA record *(257)*
Active Directory *(254)*
authoritative name server *(246)*
CNAME record *(258)*
DNS caching *(255)*
DNS record *(245)*
DNS root server *(246)*
DNS server *(245)*
domain information groper (dig) *(263)*
Domain Name System (DNS) *(243)*
Dynamic DNS (DDNS) *(260)*
forward lookup *(250)*
fully qualified domain name (FQDN) *(247)*
global hierarchy *(246)*
hierarchical name space *(246)*
host name *(247)*
hosts file *(244)*
Internet Corporation for Assigned Names and Numbers (ICANN) *(246)*
ipconfig *(252)*
iterative lookup *(253)*
MX record *(258)*
name resolution *(242)*
name server *(245)*
NetBIOS over TCP/IP (NetBT) *(244)*
NetBIOS/NetBEUI *(243)*
netstat *(264)*
nslookup *(262)*
NS record *(257)*
ping *(261)*
primary name server *(249)*
PTR record *(258)*
public DNS server *(260)*
recursive lookup *(253)*
resolver *(245)*
resolver cache *(251)*
reverse lookup *(250)*
root *(247)*
secondary name server *(249)*
serial field *(249)*
Server Message Block (SMB) *(244)*
SOA record *(256)*
SRV record *(259)*
time to live (TTL) *(255)*
top-level domain (TLD) name *(246)*
top-level domain server *(246)*
tracert *(265)*
traceroute *(265)*
TXT record *(259)*
zone *(245)*
zone transfer *(249)*

Key Term Quiz

Use the Key Terms list to complete the sentences that follow. Not all the terms will be used.

1. The ______________ utility is used to establish connectivity.
2. The ______________ protocol originally ran on top of NetBT, but today runs by itself and uses port 445.
3. A name server holds DNS records in a(n) ______________.
4. A helpful command that displays TCP/IP naming information is ______________ (with extra switches).
5. A DNS forward lookup zone uses a(n) ________ for individual host records.
6. To connect to systems on the Internet using domain names, your network needs the name of at least one ______________.

7. The (host) ______________ gets precedence over querying a DNS server.
8. You can use the diagnostic utility called ______________ in Windows to trace the progress of an ICMP packet between your system and a remote computer.
9. To avoid having to re-resolve an FQDN that it has already checked, a Windows DNS server performs _________ to keep a list of IP addresses it has already resolved.
10. The single DNS server that has a list of all the host names on the domain and their corresponding IP addresses—and actively distributes that zone list—is the ______________.

Multiple-Choice Quiz

1. Which DNS component holds DNS records?
   A. FQDN
   B. ICANN
   C. Name server
   D. Resolver
2. What do DNS servers use to help resolve IP addresses to FQDNs?
   A. Authentication
   B. Authorization
   C. Backward lookup
   D. Reverse lookup
3. What do DNS servers use to help resolve FQDNs to IP addresses?
   A. Accounting
   B. Administration
   C. Backward lookup
   D. Forward lookup
4. Running what command can give you the IP address and the name of your system's default DNS server?
   A. `nbtstat`
   B. `nslookup`
   C. `ping`
   D. `winword`
5. What's the process through which records propagate among name servers?
   A. hosts file
   B. Recursive transfer
   C. Resolver cache
   D. Zone transfer
6. Which record type acts like an alias and returns an FQDN rather than an IP address?
   A. A
   B. CNAME
   C. MX
   D. SOA
7. Which DNS record field signals a DNS resolver to remove cached records?
   A. A
   B. SOA
   C. TTL
   D. zone
8. Which record type holds the IPv6 address for a host?
   A. A
   B. AAAA
   C. A6
   D. SOA
9. Domain names with subdomains, like folders with subfolders on a system, are said to have a structure resembling what?
   A. Branch
   B. Forest
   C. Root
   D. Tree
10. Running which of the following commands clears the local cache of DNS entries?
   A. `ipconfig /clear`
   B. `ipconfig /cls`
   C. `ipconfig /flushdns`
   D. `ipconfig /renew`
11. What port do DNS servers use?
   A. 53
   B. 137
   C. 138
   D. 445

12. Which DNS component can perform a recursive lookup to determine an IP address?
   A. FQDN
   B. ICANN
   C. Name server
   D. Resolver

13. Which of the following are valid DNS record entry types? (Select three.)
   A. A
   B. M
   C. NS
   D. SOA

14. Which of the following is an example of a top-level domain?
   A. .com
   B. totalsem.com
   C. support.totalsem.com
   D. houston.support.totalsem.com

15. Which record type defines the primary name server in charge of a zone?
   A. A
   B. AAAA
   C. NS
   D. SOA

Essay Quiz

1. Your boss comes into your office in a panic. He can't reach the company's internal Web server from his office. It worked yesterday. Write an essay describing what you'd do to troubleshoot the situation. Which tool or tools would you use? Why?

2. Jot down some brief notes about how you would troubleshoot and diagnose a TCP/IP issue on one of the systems on your network. You can list the actual commands if you like, too. Choose an interesting Web site that you would ping on the Internet as your final step.

Lab Projects

• Lab Project 9.1

This chapter has presented many variations of common network troubleshooting commands. You have decided it would be beneficial to create an alphabetized chart of these commands, including their variations and what they do. Using either a word processing program or spreadsheet program, create a chart like the following—you fill in the rightmost column:

Command	Switch or Second-level Command	What It Does . . .
ipconfig	(blank)	
ipconfig	/all	
ipconfig	/release	
ipconfig	/renew	
ipconfig	/flushdns	
ping	127.0.0.1	
ping	disney.com	
ping	localhost	

• Lab Project 9.2

A request must potentially make many trips when trying to resolve a fully qualified domain name to an IP address. Aside from the hosts file, you have primary name servers, secondary name servers, authoritative name servers, DNS root servers, top-level domain servers, and second-level domain servers.

On a piece of paper, sketch a diagram/flowchart showing how a request for www.example.com gets resolved to an IP address.

Securing TCP/IP

"Better to be despised for too anxious apprehensions than ruined by too confident a security."

—Edmund Burke

In this chapter, you will learn how to

- **Discuss the standard methods for securing TCP/IP networks**
- **Compare TCP/IP security standards**
- **Implement secure TCP/IP applications**

TCP/IP wasn't designed with any real security in mind. Oh sure, you can put usernames and passwords on FTP, Telnet, and other TCP/IP applications, but everything else is basically wide open. Every device with a public IP address on the Internet is constantly bombarded with malicious packets trying to gain some level of access to precious data. Even data moving between two hosts is relatively easily intercepted and read. Bad guys make millions by stealing data in any of hundreds of thousands of different ways, and TCP/IP in its original form is all but powerless to stop them.

Happily, TCP/IP has a tremendous amount of flexibility. Over time, this has enabled developers to bolt on substantial security for pretty much anything you want to send in an IP packet. This chapter takes you on a tour of the many ways smart people have built on top of TCP/IP to protect data from those who wish to do evil things to or with it. First, we'll look at security concepts, and then we'll turn to specific standards and protocols. The chapter wraps with a discussion of secure TCP/IP applications.

Historical/Conceptual

Making TCP/IP Secure

While we'll take a closer look at risk management and security concepts in later chapters, it will be easier to understand how we secure TCP/IP connections if you know a little about the following five important concepts:

- **Encryption** means to scramble, mix up, or change data in such a way that bad guys can't read it. Of course, this scrambled-up data must also be easily descrambled by the person receiving the data.
- **Integrity** is the process that guarantees that the data received is the same as originally sent. Integrity is designed to cover situations in which someone intercepts your data on-the-fly and makes changes.
- **Nonrepudiation** means that a person cannot deny he or she took a specific action. Mike sends a message; that message can be traced back specifically to Mike.
- **Authentication** means to verify that whoever is trying to access the data is the person you want accessing that data. The most classic form of authentication is the username and password combination, but there are plenty more ways to authenticate.
- **Authorization** defines what an authenticated person can do with that data. Different operating systems and applications provide different schemes for authorization, but the classic scheme for Windows is to assign permissions to a user account. An administrator, for example, can do a lot more after being authenticated than a limited user can do.

Encryption, integrity, nonrepudiation, authentication, and authorization may be separate issues, but they play a big role in modern TCP/IP security practices. For example, you shouldn't send a credit card number or password over the Internet without encrypting it to keep the bad guys from reading it. Similarly, if you send someone the "secret decoder ring" she needs to unscramble the encryption, she'll need a way to confirm that the decoder ring actually came from you. When it comes to TCP/IP security, *protocols* combine encryption, integrity, nonrepudiation (sometimes), authentication, and authorization to create complete security solutions in a way that makes sense for their specific purpose.

Encryption

All data on your network is nothing more than ones and zeroes. Identifying what type of data the strings of ones and zeroes in a packet represent usually is easy. A packet of data on the Internet often comes with a port number encapsulated in the segment or datagram, for example, so a bad guy quickly knows what type of data he's reading.

All data starts as **cleartext**, which roughly means the data hasn't been encrypted yet. If you want to take some data and make figuring out what it means difficult for other people, you need a cipher. A **cipher** is a general term for a way to encrypt data. An **algorithm** is the mathematical formula

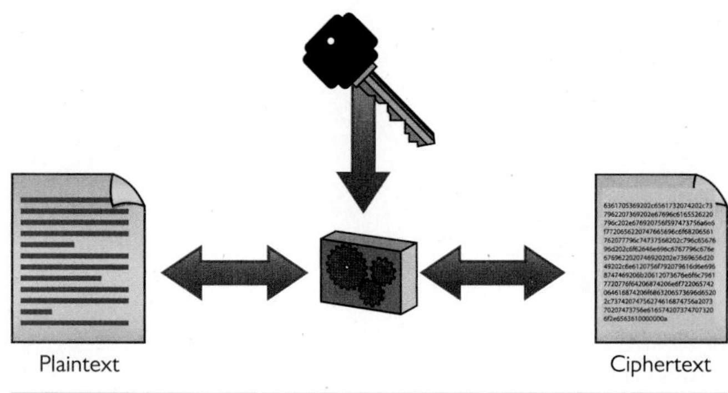

• **Figure 10.1** Encryption process

that underlies the cipher. In cryptography, any data you pass through a cipher—even if it is already encrypted—is called the **plaintext**. When you run plaintext through a cipher algorithm using a key, you get the encrypted **ciphertext** (Figure 10.1).

Substitution

One of the earliest forms of cryptography used **substitution**, swapping letters of the alphabet for other letters of the alphabet. How early? Julius Caesar used substitution to secure communication during his military campaigns; thus this kind of encryption is often called a *Caesar cipher*. Here's how it works.

See if you can crack the following code:

```
WKH TXLFN EURZQ IRA MXPSV RYHU WKH ODCB GRJ
```

> Outside of encryption, the term "plain text" means something you could open and read in Notepad. Even though they are cleartext, binary files (such as a .jpg or .exe) will look like gibberish in Notepad because they're designed for computers—not for us.

This is a classic example of the Caesar cipher. You just take the letters of the alphabet and transpose them:

```
Real Letter: ABCDEFGHIJKLMNOPQRSTUVWXYZ
Code letter: DEFGHIJKLMNOPQRSTUVWXYZABC
```

Caesar ciphers are very easy to crack by using word patterns, frequency analysis, or brute force. The code "WKH" shows up twice, which means it's the same word (*word patterns*). The letters *W* and *H* show up fairly often too. Certain letters of the alphabet are used more than others, so a code-breaker can use that to help decrypt the code (*frequency analysis*). Assuming that you know this is a Caesar cipher, a computer can quickly go through every different code possibility and determine the answer (*brute force*). Incredibly, even though it's not as obvious, binary code also suffers from the same problem.

So let's solve the code:

W=T; K=H; H=E; first word: The
T=Q; X=U; L=I; F=C; N=K; second word: quick
E=B; U=R; R=O; Z=W; Q=N; third word: brown

Get it yet? The full text is "The quick brown fox jumps over the lazy dog." Use this simple Caesar cipher to amaze your friends and family, and baffle your instructors!

Substitution is used in modern computing encryption, although in a much more sophisticated way than in a Caesar cipher. Let's go on.

XOR

Let's say you have a string of ones and zeroes that looks like this:

```
01001101010010010100101101000101
```

This string may not mean much to you, but if it is part of an HTTP segment, a Web browser instantly knows that this is Unicode—that is, numbers representing letters and other characters—and converts it into text:

```
01001101 01001001 01001011 01000101
M        I        K        E
```

So let's create a cipher to encrypt this cleartext. All binary encryption requires some interesting binary math. You could do something really simple such as add 1 to every value (and ignore carrying the 1):

```
0 + 1 = 1 and 1 + 1 = 0 10110010101101101011010010111010
```

No big deal; that just reversed the values. Any decent hacker would see the pattern and break this code in about three seconds. Let's try something harder to break by bringing in a second value (a key) of any eight binary numbers (let's use 10101010 for this example) and doing some math with every sequence of eight binary values using this algorithm:

If plaintext is...	And key value is...	Then the result is...
0	0	0
0	1	1
1	0	1
1	1	0

This calculation (also called an *operation*) is known as a bitwise **XOR (eXclusive OR)**. Line up the key against the first eight values in the cleartext:

```
10101010
01001101010010010100101101000101
11100111
```

Then do the next eight binary values:

```
1010101010101010
01001101010010010100101101000101
1110011111100011
```

Then the next eight:

```
101010101010101010101010
01001101010010010100101101000101
111001111110001111100001
```

Then the final eight:

```
10101010101010101010101010101010
01001101010010010100101101000101
11100111111000111110000111101111
```

If you want to decrypt the data, you need to know the algorithm and the key. This is a very simple example of how to encrypt binary data. At first glance, you might say this is good encryption, but the math is simple, and a simple XOR is easy for someone to decrypt.

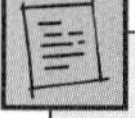

As a bitwise operation, XOR operates on each pair of corresponding bits. At this level, letters and numbers are all just binary ones and zeroes—XOR works on any data you can throw at it.

In computing, you need to make a cipher hard for anyone to break, yet make it accessible to the people you want to read the data. Luckily, computers do more complex algorithms very quickly (it's just math), and you can use longer keys to make the code much harder to crack.

Over the years, cryptographers have developed hundreds of different complete algorithms for encrypting binary data. Only a few of these were (or still are) commonly used in TCP/IP networks. The math behind all of these complete algorithms is incredibly complex and way beyond the scope of the CompTIA Network+ exam, but all of them have two items in common: a complex algorithm underlying the cipher and a key or keys used to encrypt and decrypt the text.

Any encryption that uses the same key for both encryption and decryption is called symmetric-key encryption or a **symmetric-key algorithm**. If you want someone to decrypt what you encrypt, you have to make sure they have some tool that can handle the algorithm and you have to give them the key. Any encryption that uses different keys for encryption and decryption is called asymmetric-key encryption or an **asymmetric-key algorithm**. Let's look at symmetric-key encryption first, and then turn to asymmetric-key encryption.

Symmetric-Key Encryption

Symmetric-key algorithms are either block ciphers or stream ciphers. **Block ciphers**, which encrypt data in single "chunks" of a certain length at a time, are the most common. Let's say you want to encrypt a 100,000-byte Microsoft Word document. An approach that uses a block cipher would take the file, split it into 128-bit chunks, and encrypt each one separately (Figure 10.2).

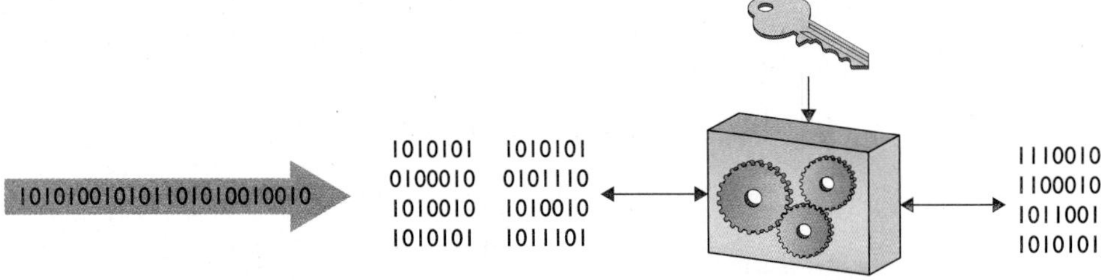

• **Figure 10.2** Block cipher

Advanced Encryption Standard (AES), the most-common block cipher, uses a 128-bit block size and 128-, 192-, or 256-bit key size. AES is incredibly secure, practically uncrackable (for now at least), and so fast even applications that traditionally used stream ciphers are switching to AES.

The alternative to a block cipher is the much quicker **stream cipher**, which takes a single bit at a time and encrypts on-the-fly (Figure 10.3). Stream ciphers used to be very popular for data that comes in long streams (such as with older wireless networks or cell phones), but they've been largely displaced by block ciphers (with the help of faster hardware) and are rare in the wild.

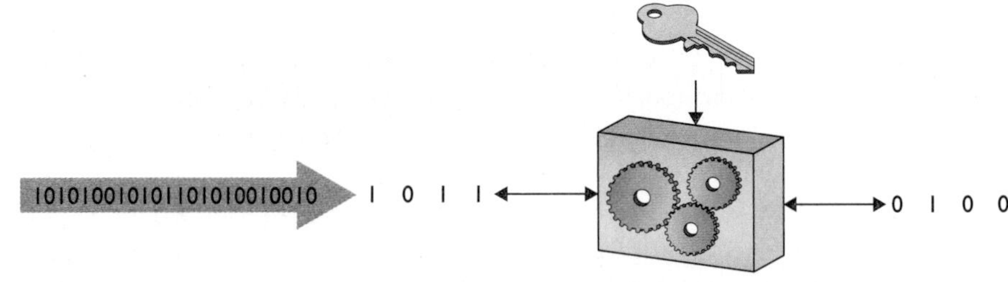

• **Figure 10.3** Stream cipher

Asymmetric-Key Cryptography

Symmetric-key encryption has one serious weakness: anyone who gets a hold of the key can encrypt or decrypt data with it. The nature of symmetric-key encryption forces us to send the key to the other person in one way or another, making it a challenge to use symmetric-key encryption safely by itself.

As a result, folks have been strongly motivated to create a way for the encryptor to send a symmetric key to the decryptor without fear of interception (Figure 10.4). The answer is to bundle the symmetric key up inside another encrypted message via an asymmetric-key algorithm that uses two different keys—one to encrypt and one to decrypt.

• **Figure 10.4** How do we safely deliver the key?

Here's how **public-key cryptography**—the primary asymmetric implementation—works. Imagine two people, Bob and Alice, want to exchange Alice's symmetric key (Figure 10.5).

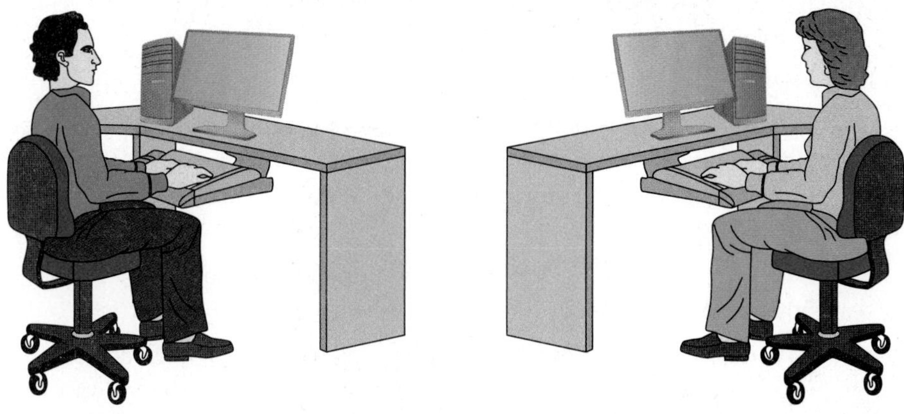

• **Figure 10.5** Bob and Alice, wanting to share a symmetric key

Before Alice can send her symmetric key to Bob, Bob first generates *two* keys. Bob keeps one of these keys (the *private* key) on his computer, and sends the other key (the *public* key) to Alice (Figure 10.6). These two keys—called a **key pair**—are generated at the same time and are designed to work together. Data encrypted with the public key, for example, must be decrypted with the private key, and vice versa.

Alice encrypts her symmetric key with Bob's public key, enabling her to send it to Bob securely for him to decrypt with his private key. Now that Bob and Alice have the same symmetric key, they can establish a connection and exchange encrypted data using symmetric encryption.

Some asymmetric cryptographic algorithms you will see these days are *RSA* (for its creators—*Rivest, Shamir, and Adleman*), DSA (Digital Signature Algorithm), and ECDSA (Elliptic Curve DSA).

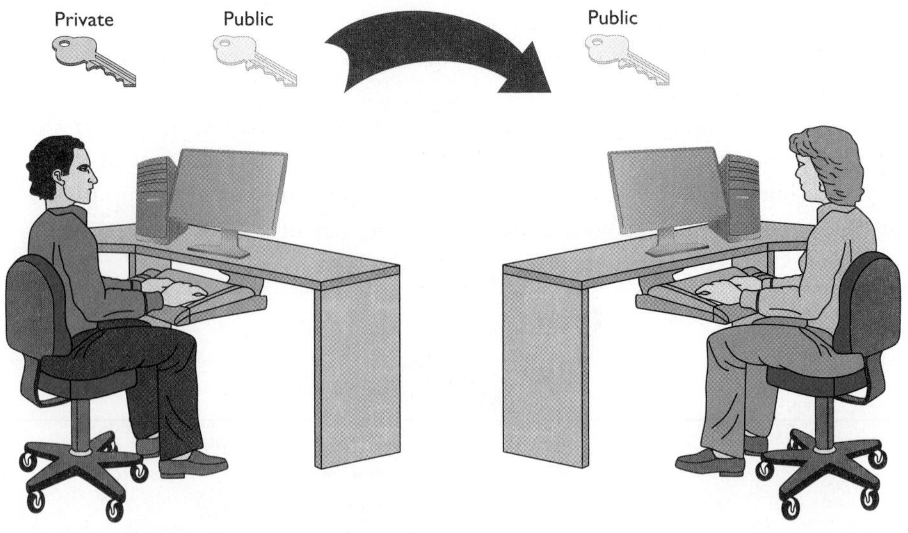

• **Figure 10.6** Sending a public key

Encryption and the OSI Model

The process of encryption varies dramatically depending on what you want to encrypt. To make life a bit easier, let's look at how you encrypt using the OSI seven-layer model:

- **Layer 1** Encryption is not common at this layer, until you get to some of the bigger WAN technologies, like SONET.
- **Layer 2** Encryption is not common at this layer.
- **Layer 3** Only one common protocol encrypts at Layer 3: IPsec. IPsec is typically implemented via software that encrypts the IP packet. A new outer packet completely encapsulates and encrypts the inner packet.
- **Layer 4** Neither TCP nor UDP offers any encryption methods, so nothing happens security-wise at Layer 4.
- **Layers 5, 6, and 7** Important encryption standards (such as TLS used in e-commerce) happen within these layers, but they don't fit cleanly into the OSI model.

Integrity

It's important to know that you receive the same data that was sent. It's not too terribly hard for bad luck and bad players to maul data, however, so several tools ensure data has the integrity needed. The one of greatest interest for CompTIA certifications is the hash function.

Hash

In computer security, a **hash** (or more accurately, a *cryptographic hash function*) is a mathematical function that you run on a string of binary digits of any length that results in a value of some fixed length (often called a *checksum* or a *message digest*). No matter how long or how short the input, the hash's message digest will always be the same length (usually around 100 to 500 bits long, depending on the type of hash used).

A cryptographic hash function is a one-way function. One-way means the hash is irreversible in that you cannot recreate the original data from the hash, even if you know the hashing algorithm and the checksum. A cryptographic hash function should also have a unique message digest for any two different input streams (Figure 10.7).

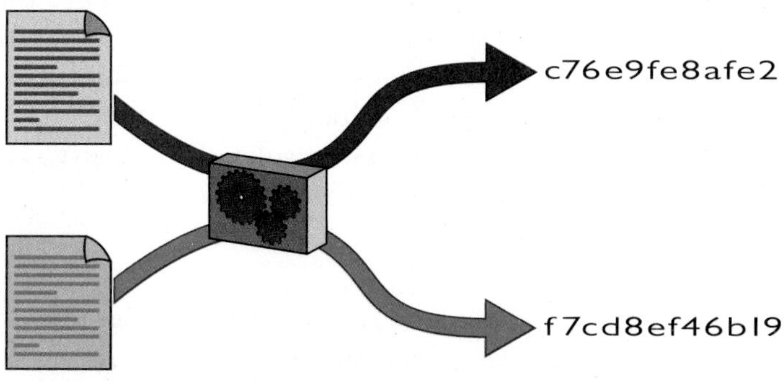

• **Figure 10.7** A hash at work

Cryptographic hash functions have a huge number of uses, but a common one is for verifying file integrity. If you download a file from a reputable source, there are two main threats to its integrity: accidental damage caused by networking/storage issues, and tampering by an attack that has compromised the site or your connection.

When the download provider hashes the contents of the file—called **file hashing**—and publishes the resulting message digest, you can hash the copy downloaded and compare the digests to verify the file on your system is most likely identical (Figure 10.8). This provides the best protection from accidental damage; an attacker capable of altering the file downloaded might also be able to alter the message digest published on the site. You can increase confidence in its integrity by verifying the digest with more than one reputable source.

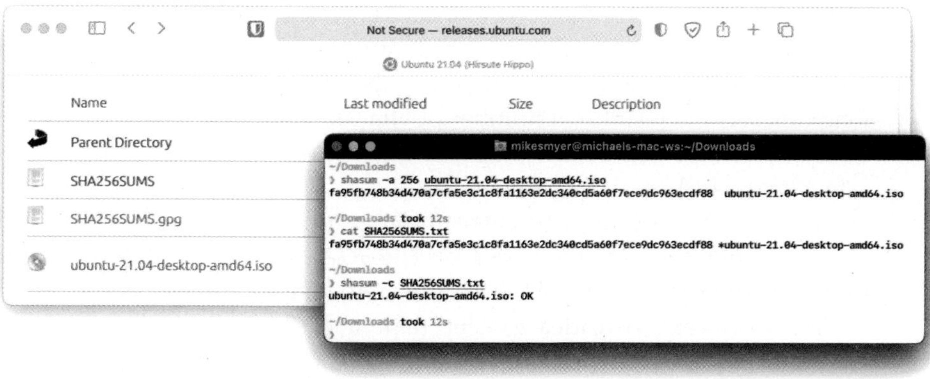

• **Figure 10.8** Using hashes to verify a downloaded file

Operating systems and applications store hashes of passwords. It's not a good idea to store plaintext passwords, and encrypting a password always leaves a chance that a bad actor can find the key and decrypt it. When a user creates a password, the operating system hashes the password and only stores the hash. From then on, when anyone provides a password, the operating system just hashes the value entered and compares the hash to the stored hash. If they match, the password is correct.

Operating systems (especially old ones, or ones using legacy compatibility settings) may use hashes that are much easier to reverse.

The main way to recover (or crack) a hashed password is to guess a password, hash it, and see if the hash matches. Attackers speed this up by saving each guess and hash and looking up hashes they find to see if they already know the answer. Modern password hashing builds on lessons learned when hackers compromise online services with zillions of users and start cracking password hashes. In particular, the industry is trending toward hash algorithms designed to slow down cracking.

Hash Algorithms

There have been quite a few different hash algorithms over the years. The first commonly used hash algorithm was called *Message-Digest Algorithm version 5*—best known as *MD5*. MD5 was introduced in 1991, creating a 128-bit message digest.

These days, **Secure Hash Algorithm (SHA)** is the primary family of cryptographic hash functions. It includes SHA-1, SHA-2, and SHA-3. SHA-1 produces a 160-bit message digest. SHA-2 has six variants:

- **SHA-224** SHA-2 with a 224-bit message digest
- **SHA-256** SHA-2 with a 256-bit message digest
- **SHA-384** SHA-2 with a 384-bit message digest
- **SHA-512** SHA-2 with a 512-bit message digest
- **SHA-512/224** SHA-2 with a 512-bit message digest truncated to 224 bits
- **SHA-512/256** SHA-2 with a 512-bit message digest truncated to 256 bits

There have been many popular hash functions over the years, and this part of the industry can change rapidly once a problem with a widely deployed hash is identified. In simpler uses like verifying file integrity, you're more likely to encounter older hashes.

One thing to keep in mind about cryptographic functions is that we err on the side of caution. Once someone demonstrates a practical attack against an algorithm, recommendations shift quickly to newer functions with improved security. Still, existing uses of the old functions can linger for a long time. As the result of a number of attacks, MD5 and SHA-1 have both ended up on this list of hash functions that are no longer recommended as safe. Don't use them in the real world.

SHA-2 is the most popular set of cryptographic hash functions used and SHA-2 continues to resist any attacks. The SHA-256 variant is used all over the place, such as in TLS, SSH, IPsec, even Bitcoin!

Yet it's never a bad idea to keep making hashes more robust. To that end, the U.S. National Institute of Standards (NIST) adopted a new family of hash algorithms called SHA-3. Like SHA-2, SHA-3 comes in six variants, each with a different message digest length. SHA-3 variants include SHA3-224, SHA3-256, SHA3-384, SHA3-512, SHAKE128, and SHAKE256. SHA-3 is not widely used yet.

Try This!

Is This the File I Think It Is?

Let's download a common program—the latest version of Mozilla's Firefox browser—and use the trustworthy hash functions that come with our operating system to confirm our copy matches the hashes Mozilla has published. We'll use the SHA-512 algorithm for this exercise.

1. Download a copy of the latest Firefox (for Windows, English language) from https://download.mozilla.org/?product=firefox-latest&os=win&lang=en-US, but don't install it when the download completes.
2. Make sure to note the version you have downloaded.
3. Navigate to https://download-origin.cdn.mozilla.net/pub/firefox/releases/<version you downloaded> and look for the files ending with SUMS. Each of these contains a long list of hashes computed using a given algorithm for all of the files in the directory. The part of the file name before SUMS specifies the algorithm used.
4. Click the SHA512SUMS file. The left-hand column contains hashes, and the right-hand column contains relative file paths.
5. The way we actually calculate the hash varies a bit from platform to platform. Pick your platform below and type the appropriate command, replacing `<filename>` with the name or path of the file downloaded in step 1.

   Linux and macOS:

   a. Open a terminal window and navigate to the directory you downloaded the file to.

   b. At the prompt, type this command:

   ```
   shasum -a 512 "<filename>"
   ```

   c. This command outputs a single line in the same format as the SHA512SUMS file. Select and copy the hash.

   Windows 8 or newer:

   a. Open Windows PowerShell—not to be confused with the regular Windows command line—and navigate to the directory where you downloaded the file.

   b. At the PowerShell prompt, type this sequence of commands:

   ```
   (Get-FileHash -Algorithm SHA512 '<filename>').hash | clip
   ```

   c. This command generates and copies the hash directly to your clipboard.
6. Switch back to your browser and use **Find** to search the SHA512SUMS document for the hash you copied in step 4. If your file downloaded properly, you'll usually get a single match. Since there are unique installer files for different platforms and languages, the file path on the matched line should specify your platform, language, and the name of the file you downloaded in step 1 and hashed in step 4.

Nonrepudiation

Nonrepudiation, as mentioned earlier, simply means that a person cannot deny (repudiate) that he or she took a specific action. Sometimes nonrepudiation isn't an important property in a system—or may even undermine your goals—and other times it's critical. For example, nonrepudiation isn't a good fit for a system that manages anonymous employee complaints. On the other hand, the property of nonrepudiation can create confidence in exactly who made every change in a system that manages purchase orders or patient records.

In network security, nonrepudiation is typically enabled by a combination of encryption and hashing called a *digital signature*. Digital signatures—much like the signatures put on contracts and other legal documents—play a role in bringing nonrepudiation to IT contexts where older approaches like physical signatures aren't practical. Let's take a closer look at how they work.

Digital Signatures

To create a **digital signature**, the sender hashes a message (or part of one) and then encrypts the hash with their private key. The receiver decrypts the signature with the sender's public key and computes the hash of the message itself. If the hash the receiver computes matches the one inside the digital signature, all is well. The sender can't deny sending the signed message (at least, not without claiming someone stole their private key), because the computed hash matches the hash decrypted with their public key—the signature could only have been encrypted with the sender's private key.

Digital signatures have multiple uses—for example, most modern operating systems use digital signatures to verify installed programs came from their registered developers. Figure 10.9 shows information about the digital signature for Firefox on Windows including who signed it, when it was signed, and how. Digital signatures also play an important role in how a browser makes basic decisions about which Web sites are secure.

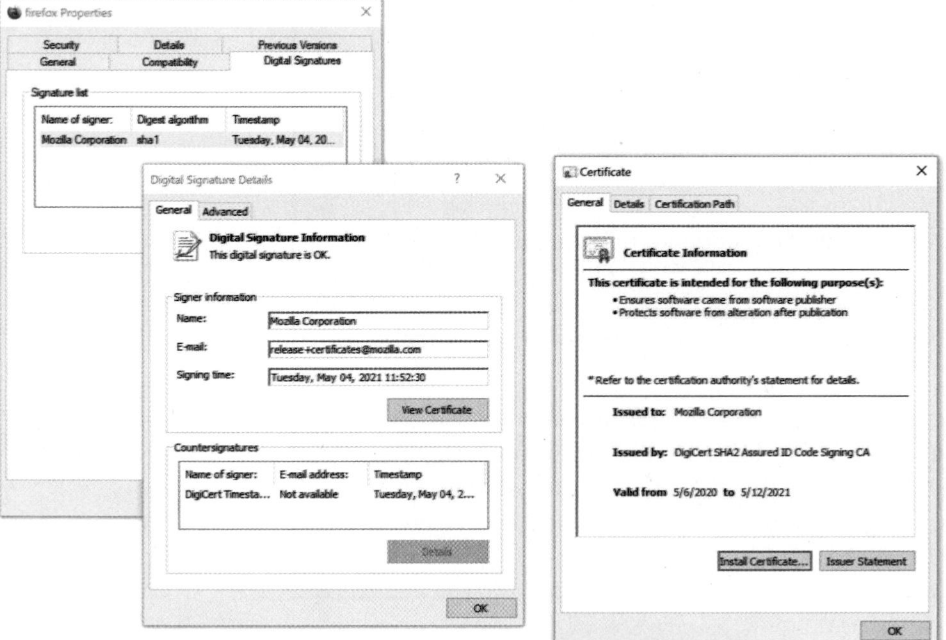

• **Figure 10.9** Information about the digital signature on a copy of Firefox

PKI

Imagine you develop a breakthrough open source app that enables whistleblowers and journalists worldwide to communicate securely, and host it on GitHub. When you click on a message notifying you of a newly posted user issue, there's a small chance the link isn't from GitHub. It might be from an enemy you've made—one who would love nothing more than to compromise your app, figure out who told the world about their bad behavior, and destroy your reputation in the process. Every time you visit GitHub, your reputation and the safety of your users depends on ensuring you're securely connected to GitHub's official servers.

To address this need, the industry came up with the idea of certificates. A **certificate** is a standardized type of file that includes a public key, some information about the certificate, and the digital signature of a *trusted third party*—a person or a company that vouches for the identity of whoever requested the certificate. The information about the certificate includes goodies like the exact date and time, who is issuing it, who they're issuing it to, when it will expire, and so on. Let's see how this looks on GitHub.

Go to https://github.com and click **Sign In** (you don't even need a GitHub account to do this). In the background, several actions take place (all before the secure Web page loads). First, the Web server automatically sends a copy of its certificate. Built into that certificate is the Web server's public key and a signature from the third party that asserts that they issued this certificate to GitHub.

Modern Web browsers generally help out with the first step of ensuring you ended up in the right place: they'll show some kind of indicator or warning if the page isn't secure, the certificate is expired, or the details otherwise don't add up. Once you clear this hurdle, you can confirm you're on a secure page by looking for the lock icon at the bottom of the screen or in the address bar (Figure 10.10) or by checking the address bar

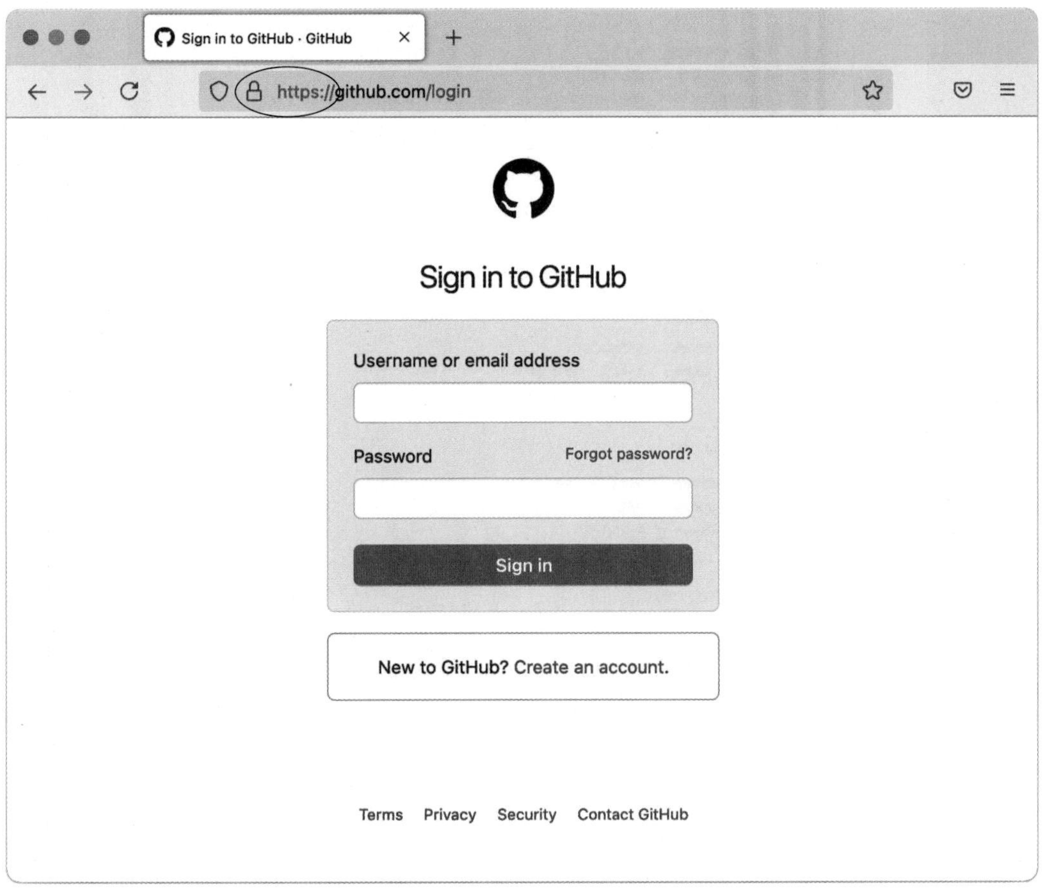

• **Figure 10.10** Secure Web page

to ensure the URL starts with https:// (instead of http://). You might need to click, double-click, or tap into the bar to access the full URL. While you're here, you should verify the URL itself—especially if you opened the page from a link elsewhere. There's always a chance you're really on a look-alike site hosted by the bad guys—and bad guys can apply for certificates, too!

Now look at the certificate for the current session. Different Web browsers have different ways to access this. Try clicking the little lock icon in the address bar (or anywhere else you found it), as this usually works. Figure 10.11 shows the certificate for this session.

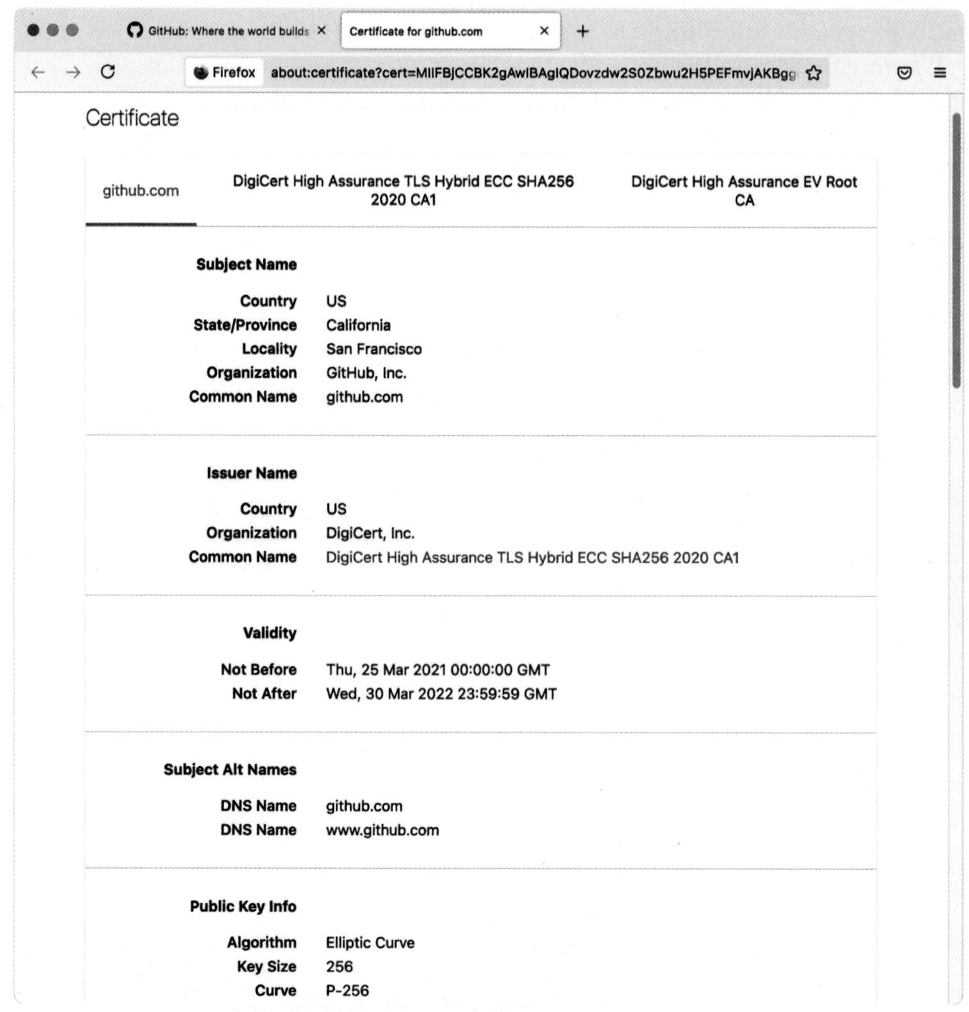

• **Figure 10.11** GitHub site certificate

> Becoming a root certificate authority with enough respect to have Web browsers install your certificate is very difficult!

A company called DigiCert issued this certificate. That's great, but how does your computer check all this? DigiCert is a certificate authority (CA). Every Web browser keeps a list of CA certificates that it checks against when it receives a digital certificate. Figure 10.12 shows the CA certificates stored on my system.

When an organization wants to create a secure Web site, the organization buys a certificate signed by a certificate authority, such as DigiCert. DigiCert acts as the root, and the new Web site's certificate contains

DigiCert's signature. In most situations, DigiCert doesn't directly sign these certificates with its root certificate—it keeps that under lock and key (we hope). Instead, they'll use an intermediate certificate, which they've signed with their own root certificate, to sign the buyer's certificate. This creates a tree of certificate authorization, with the root certificate authorities at the top and issued certificates at the bottom.

You can also have additional intermediate certificate authorities, although these are not as heavily used. A CA that directly issues certificates to organizations or devices is also sometimes called an issuing certificate authority. Together, this hierarchy is called a **public-key infrastructure (PKI)** (Figure 10.13).

Name	Kind	Expires	Keychain
Chambers of Commerce Root	certificate	Sep 30, 2037 at 11:13:44	System Roots
Chambers of Commerce Root - 2008	certificate	Jul 31, 2038 at 07:29:50	System Roots
Cisco Root CA 2048	certificate	May 14, 2029 at 15:25:42	System Roots
COMODO Certification Authority	certificate	Dec 31, 2029 at 17:59:59	System Roots
COMODO ECC Certification Authority	certificate	Jan 18, 2038 at 17:59:59	System Roots
COMODO RSA Certification Authority	certificate	Jan 18, 2038 at 17:59:59	System Roots
ComSign CA	certificate	Mar 19, 2029 at 10:02:18	System Roots
ComSign Global Root CA	certificate	Jul 16, 2036 at 05:24:55	System Roots
ComSign Secured CA	certificate	Mar 16, 2029 at 10:04:56	System Roots
D-TRUST Root CA 3 2013	certificate	Sep 20, 2028 at 03:25:51	System Roots
D-TRUST Root Class 3 CA 2 2009	certificate	Nov 5, 2029 at 02:35:58	System Roots
D-TRUST Root Class 3 CA 2 EV 2009	certificate	Nov 5, 2029 at 02:50:46	System Roots
Developer ID Certification Authority	certificate	Feb 1, 2027 at 16:12:15	System Roots
DigiCert Assured ID Root CA	certificate	Nov 9, 2031 at 18:00:00	System Roots
DigiCert Assured ID Root G2	certificate	Jan 15, 2038 at 06:00:00	System Roots
DigiCert Assured ID Root G3	certificate	Jan 15, 2038 at 06:00:00	System Roots
DigiCert Global Root CA	certificate	Nov 9, 2031 at 18:00:00	System Roots
DigiCert Global Root G2	certificate	Jan 15, 2038 at 06:00:00	System Roots
DigiCert Global Root G3	certificate	Jan 15, 2038 at 06:00:00	System Roots
DigiCert High Assurance EV Root CA	certificate	Nov 9, 2031 at 18:00:00	System Roots
DigiCert Trusted Root G4	certificate	Jan 15, 2038 at 06:00:00	System Roots
DST Root CA X3	certificate	Sep 30, 2021 at 09:01:15	System Roots
E-Tugra Certification Authority	certificate	Mar 3, 2023 at 06:09:48	System Roots
Echoworx Root CA2	certificate	Oct 7, 2030 at 05:49:13	System Roots
EE Certification Centre Root CA	certificate	Dec 17, 2030 at 17:59:59	System Roots
Entrust Root Certification Authority	certificate	Nov 27, 2026 at 14:53:42	System Roots
Entrust Root Certification Authority - EC1	certificate	Dec 18, 2037 at 09:55:36	System Roots
Entrust Root Certification Authority - G2	certificate	Dec 7, 2030 at 11:55:54	System Roots
Entrust.net Certification Authority (2048)	certificate	Jul 24, 2029 at 09:15:12	System Roots
ePKI Root Certification Authority	certificate	Dec 19, 2034 at 20:31:27	System Roots
GDCA TrustAUTH R5 ROOT	certificate	Dec 31, 2040 at 09:59:59	System Roots
GeoTrust Global CA	certificate	May 20, 2022 at 23:00:00	System Roots
GeoTrust Primary Certification Authority	certificate	Jul 16, 2036 at 18:59:59	System Roots
GeoTrust Primary Certification Authority - G2	certificate	Jan 18, 2038 at 17:59:59	System Roots

• **Figure 10.12** Certificate authority certificates on a system

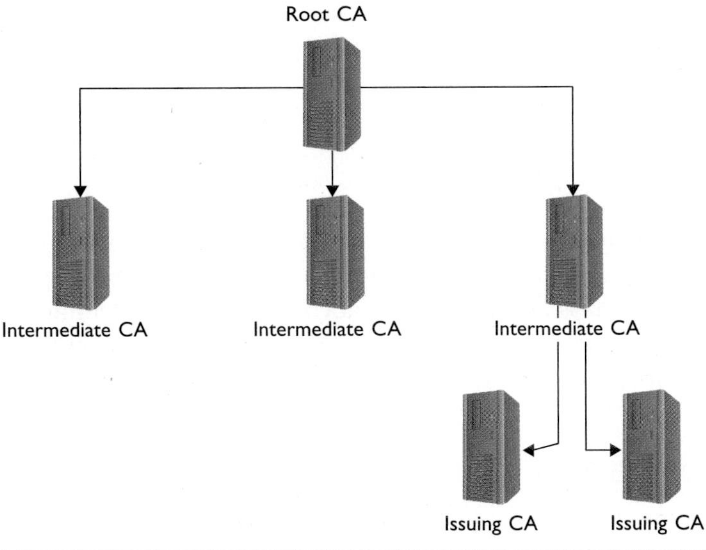

• **Figure 10.13** PKI tree

You don't have to use PKI to use certificates. First, you can create and self-sign your own certificates. These are perfectly fine for lower-security situations (such as e-mail among friends), but don't expect anyone to buy products on a Web site or send highly sensitive e-mail without a signed

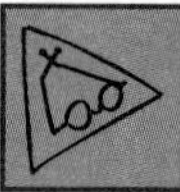

Tech Tip

Attributes

Authentication protocols can also use other characteristics to provide additional levels of security, what CompTIA calls attributes *(in the CompTIA Security+ SY0-601 exam objectives). There are three:*

Somewhere you are *(a location attribute) requires you to be in a space to authenticate. You might have to be at the computer in a specific office, for example.*

Something you do *(an action attribute) is a little vague, but CompTIA used to include it in the objectives. Using a pattern to log into a smartphone, for example, is an action. (But it's also something you* know.*) Other examples are how you walk or write your signature.*

Some when you are *(a temporal attribute) factors into various authentication criteria. You could restrict access to a certain time of day, for example.*

Network access control (NAC) defines a newer series of protection applications that combine the features of what traditionally was done by separate applications. There is no perfect single definition for NAC. There are, however, certain functions that a NAC application often does. A NAC application usually prevents computers lacking anti-malware and patches from accessing the network. NACs also create policies (their own policies, not Windows policies) that define what individual systems can do on the network, including network access, segregation of portions of the network, etc.

certificate from a well-known certificate authority like Sectigo, DigiCert, or Let's Encrypt. Digital certificates and asymmetric cryptography are closely linked because digital certificates verify the ownership of public keys.

Test Specific

Authentication

As mentioned at the beginning of this chapter, authentication is the process of positively identifying users trying to access data. The first exposure to authentication for most users is **local authentication**, coming across a login screen prompting you to enter a username and password, to log into a Windows or macOS computer. But there are many other ways to authenticate, especially when networking is added into the mix. A network technician should understand not only how different authentication methods control usernames and passwords, but also some of the authentication standards used in today's TCP/IP networks.

Passwords create as many problems as they solve—especially the problems of how to store, transfer, and verify passwords securely. Because of these problems, passwords get compromised *all* the time. And because passwords are always getting compromised, some systems require a second form of authentication. Some second forms of authentication include items you carry (like a smart card) or something physical that uniquely identifies you (such as your retinal patterns or fingerprints—*biometrics*).

Multifactor authentication (MFA) means using two or more distinctly different methods for authentication. (When only two authentication methods are used, you'll see the term **two-factor authentication**.) These methods fall into one of three categories. The CompTIA Network+ N10-008 exam objectives do not list specific factors, but it's a good idea to be able to recognize examples of all of them:

- Something you know
- Something you have
- Something you are

Something you know (a knowledge factor) is a username, a password, a passphrase, or a personal identification number (PIN). *Something you have* (a possession factor) is an object, like a key fob you scan to get into your gym at night. *Something you are* (an inherent or inherence factor) indicates some distinguishing, unique characteristic, like the biometrics just mentioned.

Authorization

At a high level, networking exists to enable one computer to request something from another computer. A Web client, for example, might ask for a Web page. A computer far away might ask another computer for access to a private network. Whatever the scenario, you should carefully assign levels of access to your resources. This is authorization and an essential part of network hardening techniques. To help define how to assign levels of access, you use an access control list.

An **access control list (ACL)** is a clearly defined list of permissions that specifies what an authenticated user may perform on a shared resource. Over the years the way to assign access to resources has changed dramatically. To help you to understand these changes, the security industry likes to use the idea of *ACL access models*. There are three types of ACL access models: mandatory, discretionary, and role based.

In a **mandatory access control (MAC)** security model, every resource is assigned a label that defines its security level. If the user lacks that security level, he or she does not get access. The MAC security model is the oldest and least common of the three.

Discretionary access control (DAC) is based on the idea that a resource has an owner who may at his or her discretion assign access to that resource. DAC is considered much more flexible than MAC.

Role-based access control (RBAC) is the most popular model used in file sharing. RBAC defines a user's access to a resource based on the roles the user plays in the network environment. This leads to the idea of creating groups. A group in most networks is nothing more than a name that has clearly defined access to different resources. User accounts are placed into various groups.

Keep in mind that these three types of access control are models. Every TCP/IP application and operating system has its own set of rules that sometimes follows one of these models, but in many cases does not. But do make sure you understand these three models for the CompTIA Network+ exam!

TCP/IP Security Standards

Now that you have a conceptual understanding of encryption, integrity, nonrepudiation, authentication, and authorization, it's time to see how the TCP/IP folks have put it all together to create standards so you can secure just about anything in TCP/IP networks.

TCP/IP security standards are a rather strange mess. Some are authentication standards, some are encryption standards, and some are so unique to a single application that I'm not even going to talk about them in this section and instead will wait until the "Secure TCP/IP Applications" discussion at the end of this chapter. There's a reason for all this confusion: TCP/IP was never really designed for security. As you read through this section, you'll discover that almost all of these standards either predate the whole Internet, are slapped-together standards that have some serious issues, or, in the case of the most recent standards, are designed to combine a bunch of old, confusing standards. So hang tight—it's going to be a bumpy ride!

User Authentication Standards

Authentication standards are some of the oldest standards used in TCP/IP. Many are so old they predate the Internet itself. Once upon a time, nobody had fiber-optic, cable, or DSL connections to their ISPs. For the most part, if you wanted to connect to the Internet you had a choice: go to the computer center or use dial-up.

Dial-up, using telephone lines for the most part, predates the Internet, but the nerds of their day didn't want just anybody dialing into their computers. To prevent unauthorized access, they developed some excellent authentication methods that TCP/IP adopted for itself. A number of authentication methods were used back in those early days, but, for the most part, TCP/IP authentication started with something called Point-to-Point Protocol.

PPP

Point-to-Point Protocol (PPP) enables two devices to connect, authenticate with a username and password, and negotiate the network protocol the two devices will use (Figure 10.14). Today that network protocol is almost always TCP/IP.

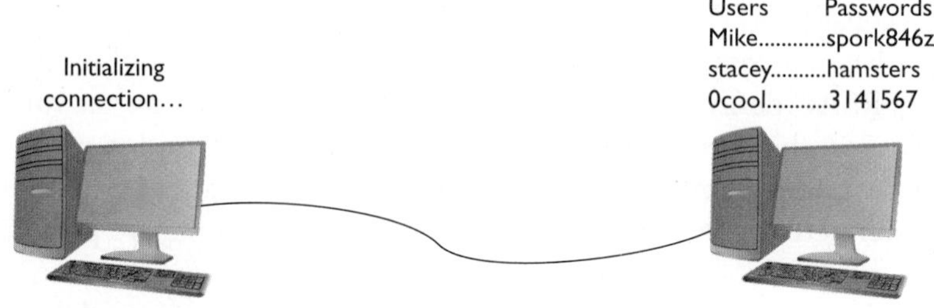

• **Figure 10.14** A point-to-point connection

PPP came with two methods of *user authentication*, the process of authenticating a username and password. The original way—called **Password Authentication Protocol (PAP)**—simply transmits the username and password over the connection in plaintext. Unfortunately, that means anyone who can tap the connection can learn the username and password (Figure 10.15).

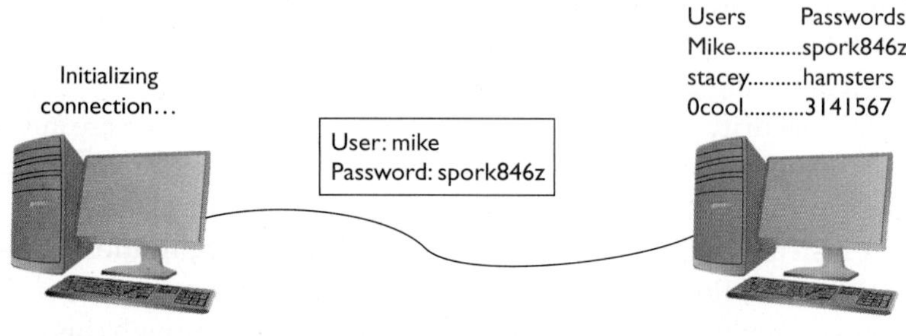

• **Figure 10.15** PAP in action

Fortunately, PPP also includes the safer **Challenge Handshake Authentication Protocol (CHAP)** to provide a more secure authentication routine. CHAP relies on hashes based on a shared secret, usually a password that both ends of the connection know. When the initiator of the connection makes the initial connection request, the authenticator creates some form of challenge message. The initiator then makes a hash using the password and sends that to the authenticator. The authenticator, in turn, compares that value to its own hash calculation based on the password. If they match, the initiator is authenticated (Figure 10.16).

Once the connection is up and running, CHAP keeps working by periodically repeating the entire authentication process. This prevents *man-in-the-middle* attacks, where a third party inserts an independent connection, intercepts traffic, reads or alters it, and then forwards it on without either the sender or recipient being aware of the intrusion.

CHAP works nicely because it never sends the actual password over the link. The CHAP standard leaves a number of issues undefined, however, like "If the hash doesn't match, what do I do?" The boom in dial-up connections to the Internet in the 1990s led Microsoft to invent a more detailed version of CHAP called **MS-CHAP**. The current version of MS-CHAP is called MS-CHAPv2. MS-CHAPv2 is still the most common authentication method for the few using dial-up connections. Dial-up is still used and even the latest operating systems support it. Figure 10.17 shows the dial-up connection options for Windows 10.

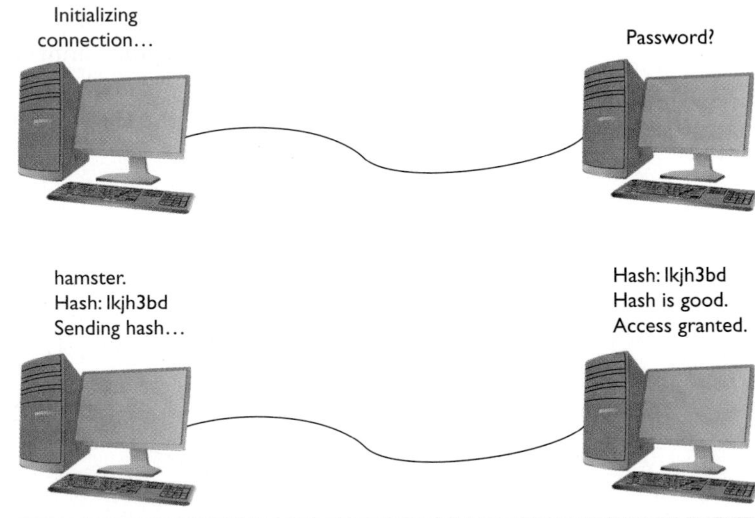

• **Figure 10.16** CHAP in action

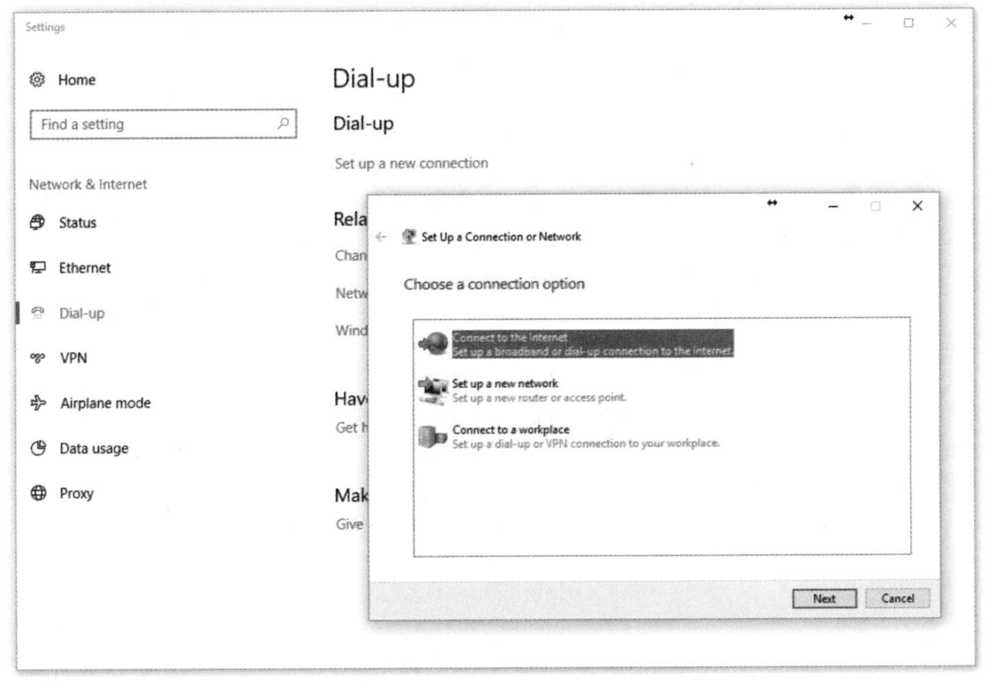

• **Figure 10.17** MS-CHAP is alive and well.

AAA

PPP does a great job of handling authentication for point-to-point connections, but it has some limitations. The biggest problem is that, in many cases, a network might have more than one point for an initiator to enter. PPP assumes that the authenticator at the endpoint has all the username and password information, but that's not necessarily true. In traditional modem communication, for example, an ISP has a large bank of modems to

> If you get a question on PAP, CHAP, and MS-CHAP on the CompTIA Network+ exam, remember that MS-CHAPv2 offers the most security.

support a number of users. When a user dials in, the modem bank provides the first available connection, but that means that any modem in the bank has to support any of the users. You can't put the database containing all usernames and passwords on every modem (Figure 10.18).

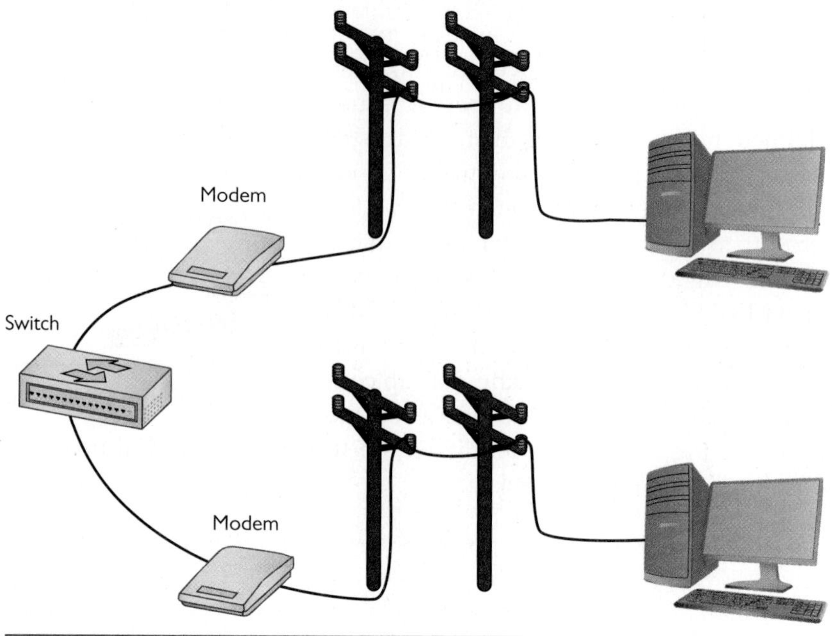

• **Figure 10.18** Where do you put the usernames and passwords?`

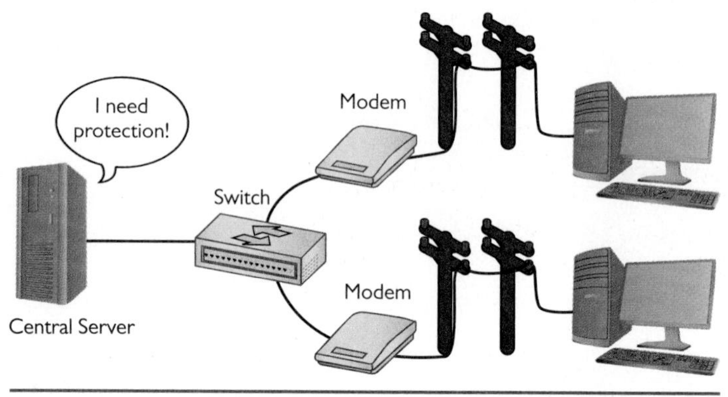

• **Figure 10.19** Central servers are vulnerable to attack.

In this use case, you need a central database of usernames and passwords. That's simple enough, but it creates another problem—anyone accessing the network can see the passwords unless the data is somehow protected and encrypted (Figure 10.19). PPP is good at the endpoints, but once the data gets on the network, it's unencrypted.

Thus, the folks overseeing central databases full of usernames and passwords needed to come up with standards to follow to protect that data. They first agreed upon a philosophy called **Authentication, Authorization, and Accounting (AAA)**. AAA is designed for the idea of port authentication—the concept of allowing remote users authentication to a particular point of entry (a port) to another network.

- **Authentication** A computer that is trying to connect to the network must present some form of credential for access to the network. This credential most commonly starts with identification via a username and password, which is then checked against a credentials database. If the credentials match up, the user is authenticated. Username and password are common for identification, but the credential might also be a security token such as a smart card, fingerprint, or digital certificate. It might even be a combination of some of these. The authentication gives the computer the right to access the network.

- **Authorization** Once authenticated, the computer determines what it can or cannot do on the network. It might only be allowed to use a certain amount of bandwidth. It might be limited to working only certain times of day or might be limited to using only a certain set of applications.
- **Accounting** The authenticating server should log events, such as logins, session action, user bandwidth usage, and so on.

NAS stands for either *network access server* or *network attached storage*. The latter is a type of dedicated file server used in many networks. Make sure you read the question to see which NAS it's looking for!

Once the idea of AAA took shape, those smart Internet folks developed two standards: RADIUS and TACACS+. Both standards offer authentication, authorization, and accounting.

RADIUS **Remote Authentication Dial-In User Service (RADIUS)** is the better known of the two AAA standards and, as its name implies, was created to support ISPs with hundreds if not thousands of modems in hundreds of computers to connect to a single central database. While originally designed for dial-up connections, RADIUS still works hard in a huge number of different types of networks, both wired and wireless, and I'm sure there are a few ancient dial-up networks still working somewhere as well. RADIUS consists of three devices: the RADIUS server that has access to a database of usernames and passwords, a number of **network access servers (NASs)** that control the modems or wireless access points, and a group of systems that in some way connect to the network (Figure 10.20).

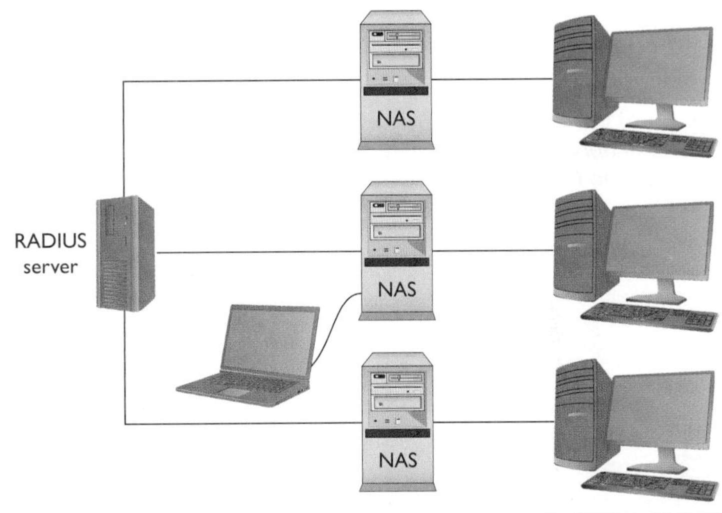

• **Figure 10.20** RADIUS setup

To use RADIUS, you need a RADIUS server. A popular choice for Microsoft environments is **Internet Authentication Service (IAS)**, which comes built in with most versions of Microsoft Windows Server operating systems. For the UNIX/Linux crowd, the popular (yet, in my opinion, difficult to set up) **FreeRADIUS** is the best choice.

A single RADIUS server can support multiple NASs and provide a complete PPP connection from the requesting system, through the NAS, all the way to the RADIUS server. Like any PPP connection, the RADIUS server supports PAP, CHAP, and MS-CHAP. Even if you use PAP, RADIUS hashes the password so at no time is the username/password exposed. Newer versions of RADIUS support even more authentication methods, as you will soon see. RADIUS performs this authentication on either UDP port 1812 or port 1645. (RADIUS also uses UDP ports 1813 and 1646 for accounting.)

TACACS+ Routers and switches need administration. In a simple network, you can access the administration screen for each router and switch by entering a username and password for each device. When a network becomes complex, with many routers and switches, logging into each device separately starts to become administratively messy. The answer is to make a single server store the ACL for all the devices in the network. To make this secure, you need to follow the AAA principles.

Kerberos uses UDP or TCP port 88 by default.

The TGT is sometimes referred to as *Ticket to Get Tickets.*

You'll see TGS referred to as the Ticket-Granting *Server* in a lot of documentation. Microsoft uses *Service*, which is what we're following here.

Terminal Access Controller Access Control System Plus (TACACS+) is a protocol developed by Cisco to support AAA in a network with many routers and switches. TACACS+ is very similar to RADIUS in function, but uses TCP port 49 by default and separates authorization, authentication, and accounting into different parts. TACACS+ uses PAP, CHAP, and MD5 hashes, but can also use Kerberos as part of the authentication scheme.

Kerberos

Almost all the authentication schemes discussed up to this point are based on PPP or at least take the idea of PPP and expand upon it. Of course, every rule needs an exception, and Kerberos is the exception here.

Kerberos is an authentication protocol for TCP/IP networks with many clients all connected to a single authenticating server—no point-to-point here! Kerberos is an authentication protocol that has no connection to PPP. Kerberos works nicely in a network, so nicely that Microsoft adopted it as the authentication protocol for all Windows networks using a domain controller.

Microsoft Windows domains rely on Kerberos for authentication. A Windows domain is a group of computers that defers all authentication to a *domain controller*, a special computer running some version of Windows Server (with the appropriate role installed). The Windows domain controller stores a list of all usernames and password hashes in Active Directory. When you log on at a computer that is a member of a Windows domain, your username and password hash go directly to the domain controller, which uses Kerberos for authentication.

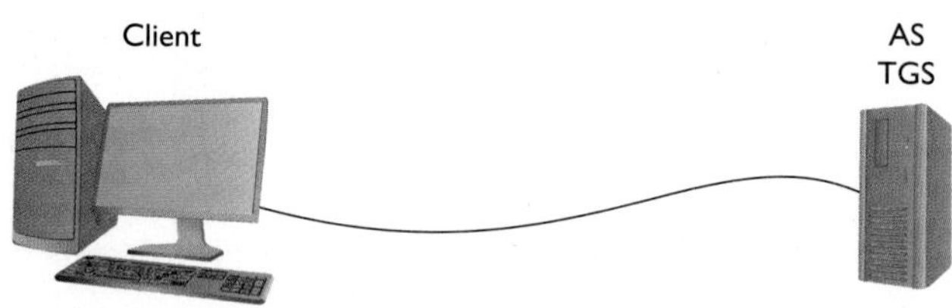

• **Figure 10.21** Windows Kerberos setup

The Kerberos **Key Distribution Center (KDC)** service supplies both session tickets and session keys in an Active Directory domain. In Windows Server environments, the KDC is installed on the domain controller (Figure 10.21). KDC relies on two components: the Authentication Server and the Ticket-Granting Service.

When a client logs onto the domain, it sends a request that includes a hash of the username and password to the Authentication Server. The **Authentication Server (AS)** compares the results of that hash to its own hash (as it also stores the username and password hash) and, if they match, sends a **Ticket-Granting Ticket (TGT)** and a timestamp (Figure 10.22). The ticket has a default lifespan in Windows of ten hours. The client is now authenticated but not yet authorized.

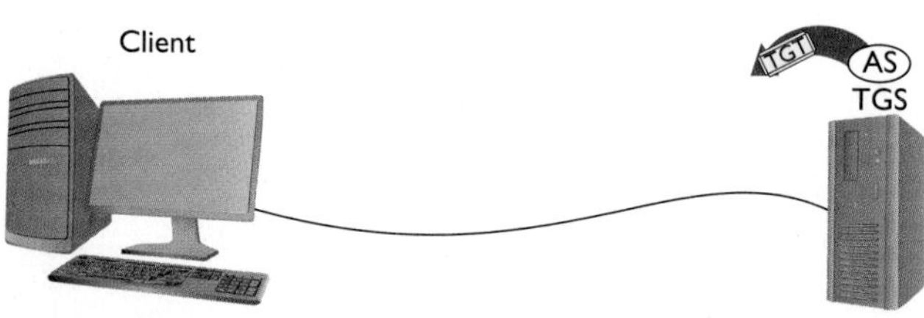

• **Figure 10.22** AS sending a TGT back to client

The client then sends the timestamped TGT to the **Ticket-Granting Service (TGS)** for authorization. The TGS sends a timestamped service ticket (also called a *token* or *access token*) back to the client (Figure 10.23).

This token is the key that the client uses to access any single resource on the entire domain. The access token contains the *security identifier (SID)* for the user's account, plus SIDs for the groups of which the user is a member. This is where authorization takes place.

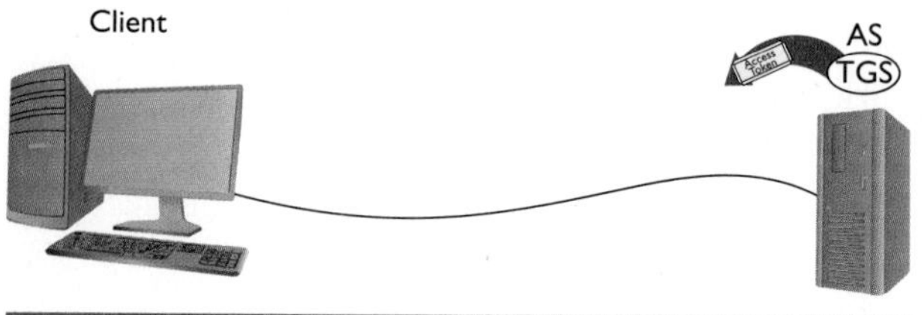

• **Figure 10.23** TGS sending token to client

The token authorizes the user to access resources without reauthenticating. Any time the client attempts to access a folder, printer, or service anywhere in the domain, the server sharing that resource uses the token to see exactly what access the client may have to that resource. If the client tries to access some other feature under Windows, such as retrieve e-mail via Microsoft Exchange Server, it won't need to log in again. The ability to log in only one time and use the same token to access any resource (that you're allowed to access) on an entire network is called **single sign-on (SSO)**.

Timestamping is important for Kerberos because it forces the client to request a new token every eight hours. This prevents third parties from intercepting the tokens and attempting to crack them. Kerberos tokens can be cracked, but it's doubtful this can be done in under eight hours.

Kerberos is very popular but has some serious weaknesses. First, if the KDC goes down, no one has access. That's why Microsoft and other operating systems that use Kerberos always stress the importance of maintaining a backup KDC. In Windows, it is standard practice to have at least two domain controllers. Second, timestamping requires that all the clients and servers are synchronized, typically within two minutes. This is fairly easy to do in a wired network (such as a Windows domain or even a bunch of connected switches or routers using TACACS+).

Wireless networks make extensive use of authentication protocols. Chapter 14 explores the varieties of the Extensible Authentication Protocol (EAP) and the 802.1X standard.

The book goes further into authentication and authorization in due time, but this section provided the basics of the popular authentication and authorization protocols and standards. You have more protocols to learn, but all of them are rather specialized for specific uses and thus are covered at various places throughout the book.

Encryption Standards

The Internet had authentication long before it had encryption. As a result, almost all encryption came out as a knee-jerk reaction to somebody realizing that a TCP/IP application wasn't secure. For years, there were new secure versions of just about every protocol in existence. New "secure" versions of all the classics—HTTP, FTP, SMTP, and even POP—started to appear. They worked, but there were still hundreds of not-yet-secured protocols and the specter of redoing all of them was daunting. Fortunately, some new, all-purpose encryption protocols were developed that enable a client to connect to a server in a secure way while still using the corresponding older, unsecure protocols—and it all started because of Telnet.

SSH

The broad adoption of the Internet by the early 1990s motivated programmers to start securing their applications. Telnet had a big problem. It was incredibly useful and popular, but it was a completely unsecure protocol. Telnet credentials were (and are) sent in plaintext, an obvious vulnerability.

SSH servers listen and respond on TCP port 22.

Telnet needed to be fixed. As the story goes, Tatu Ylonen of the Helsinki University of Technology, reacting to an attack that intercepted Telnet usernames and passwords on his network, invented a new *secure protocol* replacement for Telnet called **Secure Shell (SSH)**. You've already seen SSH in action (in Chapter 8) as a secure version of Telnet, but now that you know more about security, let's look at a scenario where you implement network device hardening via SSH.

SSH servers can use a number of public-key algorithms such as RSA or ECDSA, to name a couple. The first time a client tries to log into an SSH server, the server sends its public key to the client (Figure 10.24).

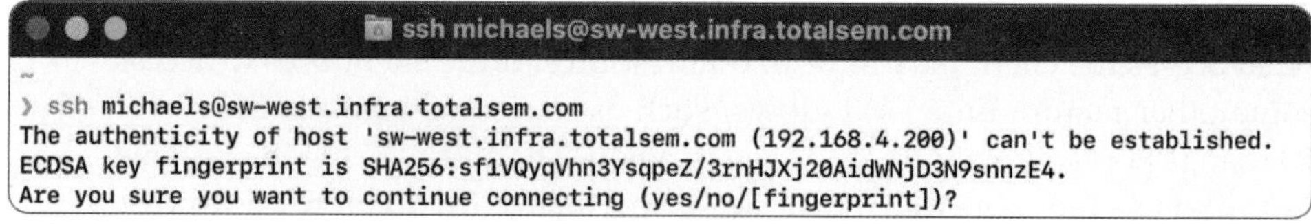

ssh michaels@sw-west.infra.totalsem.com
> ssh michaels@sw-west.infra.totalsem.com
The authenticity of host 'sw-west.infra.totalsem.com (192.168.4.200)' can't be established.
ECDSA key fingerprint is SHA256:sf1VQyqVhn3YsqpeZ/3rnHJXj20AidWNjD3N9snnzE4.
Are you sure you want to continue connecting (yes/no/[fingerprint])?

• **Figure 10.24** PuTTY getting an ECDSA key

After the client receives this key, it creates a session ID, encrypts it using the public key, and sends it back to the server. The server decrypts this session ID and uses it in all data transfers going forward. Only the client and the server know this session ID. Next, the client and server negotiate the type of encryption to use for the session, generally AES. The negotiation for the cipher is automatic and invisible to the user.

This handshake process makes a very safe connection, but the combination doesn't tell the server who is using the client. All SSH servers, therefore, need to authenticate (usually with usernames and passwords) the client (Figure 10.25). Once a user logs in, he or she has access to the system.

User: mike
Password: egGs!

User: sarah
Password: bAcon!

SSH Authorized Users
User: mike
Pass: egGs!
User: sarah
Pass: bAcon!

• **Figure 10.25** Users on an SSH server

In addition to using a password for authentication, SSH also can use public keys to identify clients. This opens up some interesting possibilities such as noninteractive logins. You can also turn off password login altogether, hardening your server even further. To use public/private keys for authentication, you must first generate a pair of keys with a tool such as ssh-keygen or PuTTYgen (Figure 10.26). The public key is then copied to the server, and the private key is kept safe on the client.

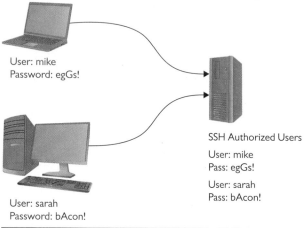

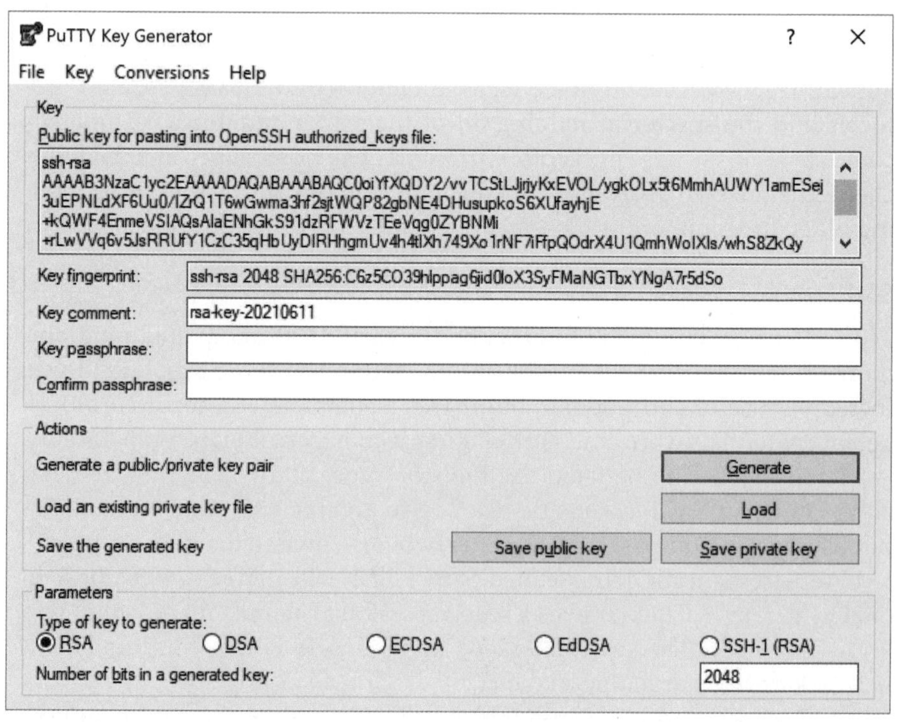

• **Figure 10.26** Generated RSA keys in PuTTY Key Generator

When you connect to the server, your client generates a signature using its private key and sends it to the server. The server then checks the signature with its copy of the public key, and if everything checks out, you will be authenticated with the server.

If SSH stopped here as a secure replacement for Telnet, that would be fantastic, but SSH has another trick up its sleeve: the capability to act as a *tunnel* for *any* TCP/IP application. Let's see what tunnels are and how they work.

Tunneling

Simply, an **SSH tunnel** is an encrypted link between SSH processes on two separate computers. Once an SSH link between a server and a client is established, anything you enter into the client application is encrypted, sent to the server, decrypted, and then acted upon (Figure 10.27).

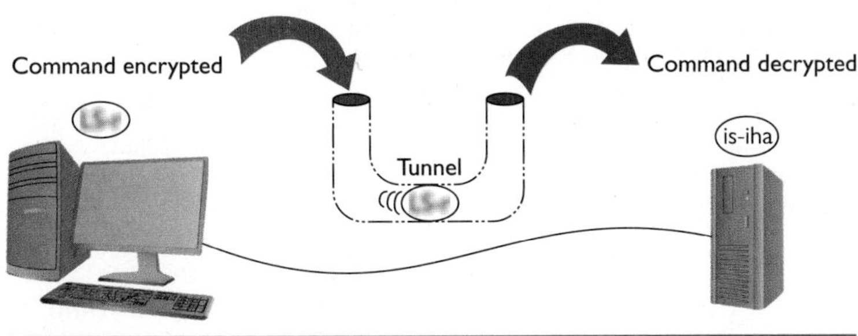

• **Figure 10.27** SSH in action

The nature of SSH is such that it took very little to extend the idea of SSH to accept input from any source, even another program (Figure 10.28). As long as the program can redirect to the SSH client and then the SSH server can redirect to the server application, anything can go through an SSH connection encrypted. This is an SSH tunnel.

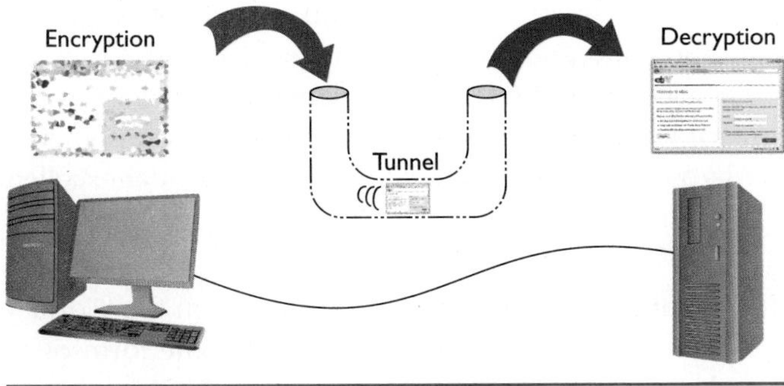

• **Figure 10.28** Encrypting a Web client

SSH tunnels are useful tools and fairly easy to set up. Equally, all of the popular SSH clients and servers are designed to go into tunnel mode, usually with no more than a few extra flags when connecting (Figure 10.29).

Many tunneling protocols and standards are used in TCP/IP. SSH is one of the simplest types of tunnels, so it's a great first exposure to tunneling. As the book progresses, you'll see more tunneling protocols, and you'll get the basics of tunneling. For now, make sure you understand that a tunnel is an encrypted connection between two endpoints. Any packet that enters

```
bitnami@dev: ~
> ssh -R 9000:localhost:9000 bitnami@dev.home.totalsem.com
Linux dev 4.19.0-14-amd64 #1 SMP Debian 4.19.171-2 (2021-01-30) x86_64

The programs included with the Debian GNU/Linux system are free software;
the exact distribution terms for each program are described in the
individual files in /usr/share/doc/*/copyright.

Debian GNU/Linux comes with ABSOLUTELY NO WARRANTY, to the extent
permitted by applicable law.
       ___ _ _                   _
      | _ |_) |_ _ _  __ _ _ __ (_)
      | _ \ |  _| ' \/ _` | '  \| |
      |___/_|\__|_|_|\__,_|_|_|_|_|

  *** Welcome to the Bitnami WordPress 5.5.3-0                            ***
  *** Documentation:  https://docs.bitnami.com/virtual-machine/apps/wordpress/ ***
  ***                 https://docs.bitnami.com/virtual-machine/               ***
  *** Bitnami Forums: https://community.bitnami.com/                      ***

###########################################################
###    For frequently used commands, please run:       ###
###        sudo /opt/bitnami/bnhelper-tool              ###
###########################################################

Last login: Wed Jun  2 14:20:20 2021
bitnami@dev:~$
```

• **Figure 10.29** Creating a tunnel for port 9000 over SSH

the encrypted tunnel, including a packet with unencrypted data, is automatically encrypted, goes through the tunnel, and is decrypted on the other endpoint.

SSH may be popular, but it's not the only option for encryption. All of the other encryption standards are built into combined authentication/encryption standards, as covered in the next section.

Combining Authentication and Encryption

The rest of the popular authentication and encryption standards include both authentication and encryption in a single standard. Lumping together authentication and encryption into the same standard does not make it weaker than the standards already discussed. These are some of the most popular standards on the Internet today, because they offer excellent security.

SSL/TLS

The introduction and rapid growth of e-commerce on the World Wide Web in the mid-1990s made it painfully obvious that some form of authentication and encryption was needed. Netscape Corporation took the first shot at a new standard. At the time, the dominant Web browser was Netscape Navigator. Netscape created a standard called **Secure Sockets Layer (SSL)**. SSL requires a server with a certificate. When a client requests access to an SSL-secured server, the server sends to the client a copy of the certificate (Figure 10.30). The SSL client checks this certificate (all Web browsers come with an exhaustive list of CA root certificates preloaded), and if the certificate checks out, the server is authenticated and the client negotiates a symmetric-key cipher for use in the session. The session is now in a very secure encrypted tunnel between the SSL server and the SSL client.

• **Figure 10.30** Fetching the server's certificate

The **Transport Layer Security (TLS)** protocol was designed as an upgrade to SSL. TLS is very similar to SSL, working in almost the same way. TLS is more robust and flexible and works with just about any TCP application. SSL is limited to HTTP, FTP, SMTP, and a few older TCP applications. TLS has no such restrictions and is used in securing Voice over IP (VoIP) and virtual private networks (VPNs), but it is still most heavily used in securing Web pages. Every Web browser today uses TLS for HTTPS-secured Web sites, and EAP-TLS (discussed in Chapter 14) is common for more secure wireless networks.

SSL/TLS also supports mutual authentication, but this is relatively rare.

The *Internet Engineering Task Force (IETF)* oversees the IPsec protocol suite, managing updates and revisions. One of those specifications regards the acronym for the protocol suite, calling it *IPsec* with a lowercase "s" rather than IPS or IPSec (the form CompTIA prefers). Go figure.

IPsec

Every authentication and encryption protocol and standard you've learned about so far works *above* the Network layer of the OSI seven-layer model. **Internet Protocol Security (IPsec)** is an authentication and encryption protocol suite that works at the Network layer.

IPsec works in two different modes: Transport mode and Tunnel mode. In Transport mode, only the actual payload of the IP packet is encrypted: the destination and source IP addresses and other IP header information are still readable. In Tunnel mode, the entire IP packet is encrypted and is encapsulated inside another IP packet at an endpoint. The mode you use depends on the application (Figure 10.31).

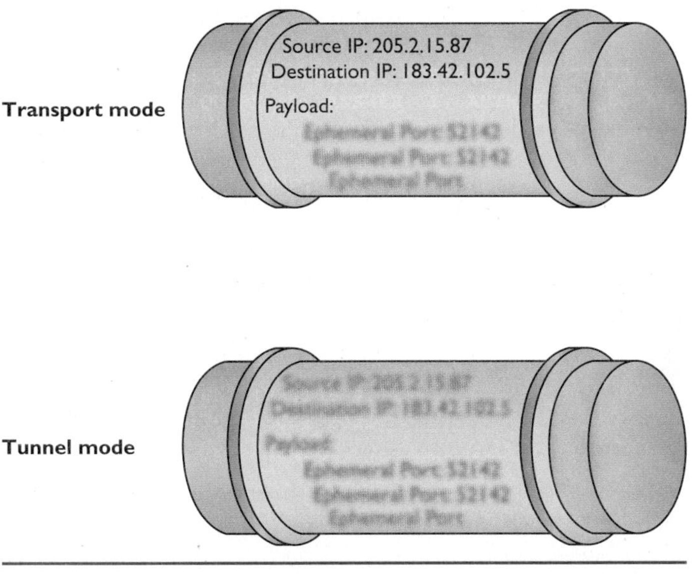

• **Figure 10.31** IPsec's two modes

IPsec provides authentication, integrity, and confidentiality through two protocols, AH and ESP. *Authentication Header (AH)* handles authentication and data integrity, but provides no encryption. *Encapsulating Security Payload (ESP)* encrypts the TCP segment, thus providing confidentiality as well as integrity and authentication. Because ESP can do everything that AH can do, plus provide encryption, ESP is the primary protocol used in IPsec for authentication, integrity, and confidentiality. AH has almost never been used.

IPsec is an incredibly powerful authentication/encryption protocol suite for creating secure tunnels between two computers. (See the discussion of VPNs in Chapter 13 for the scoop.)

Secure TCP/IP Applications

I've covered quite a few TCP/IP security standards and protocols thus far in the chapter, but I really haven't put anything to work yet. Now is the time to talk about actual applications that use these tools to make secure connections. As mentioned earlier, this is in no way a complete list, as there are thousands of secure TCP applications; I'll stick to ones you will see on the CompTIA Network+ exam. Even within that group, I've saved discussion of some of the applications for other chapters that deal more directly with certain security aspects (such as remote connections).

HTTPS

You've already seen **Hypertext Transfer Protocol Secure (HTTPS)**, but let's do a quick review. HTTPS URLs start with https:// and most browsers also show a small lock icon somewhere around their address bar. HTTPS uses TLS for the actual authentication and encryption process. In most cases, all of this works very well, but what do you do when HTTPS has trouble?

Since you won't get an HTTPS connection without a good certificate exchange, the most common problems are caused by bad certificates. When a certificate comes in from an HTTPS Web site, your computer checks the expiration date to verify the certificate is still valid and checks the Web site's URL to make sure it's the same as the site you are on. If either of these is not correct, you get an error such as the one shown in Figure 10.32.

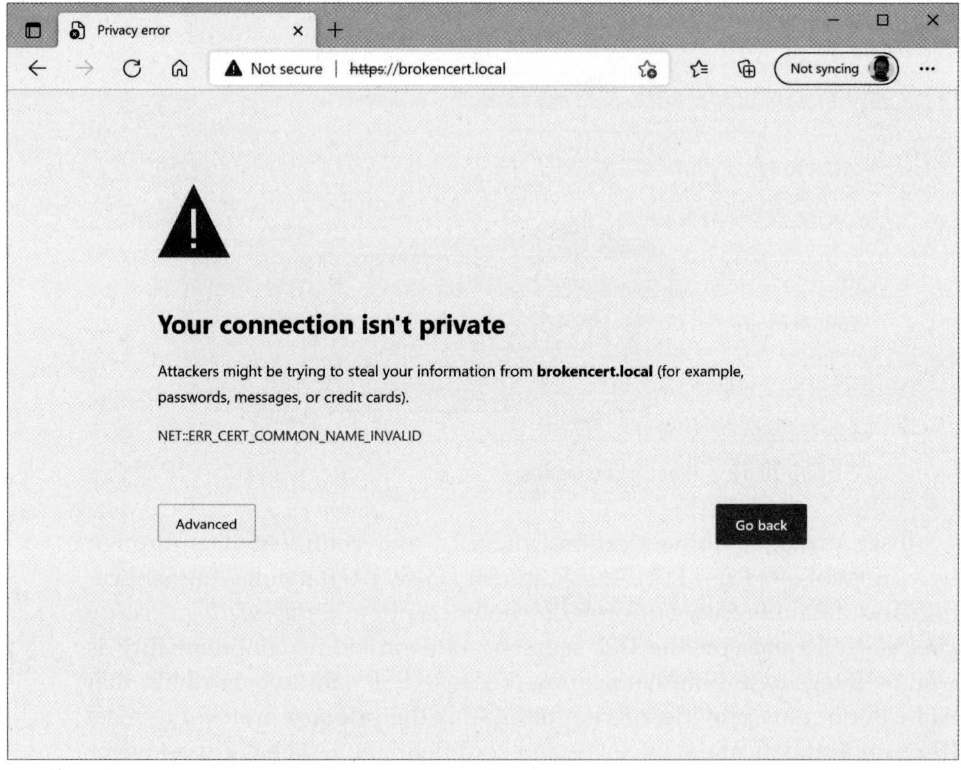

• **Figure 10.32** Certificate problem

If you get one of these errors, you need to decide what to do. Legitimate certificates do expire (this even happened on my own Web site once) and sometimes the URLs on the certificates are not exactly the same as the site using them. When in doubt, stop. On the other hand, if the risk is low (for example, you're not entering a credit card number or other sensitive information) and you know and trust the site, proceeding is safe in most cases. If there's a clear way to contact the site's operators, send a quick message to let them know their certificate has expired!

Invalid certificates aren't the only potential problems. After this basic check, the browser checks to see if the certificate has been revoked. Root authorities, like Sectigo, generate Certificate Revocation Lists (CRLs) that a Web browser can check against. Certificates are revoked for a number of reasons, but most of the time the reasons are serious, such as a compromised private key.

If you get a revoked certificate error, it's better to stay away from the site until the site's operators fix the problem.

Securing E-Mail Protocols

The traditional TCP/IP mail protocols Secure Mail Transfer Protocol (SMTP) for sending e-mail and Post Office Protocol (POP) or Internet Message Access Protocol (IMAP) for retrieving e-mail offered no effective security. Traffic of all sorts travels in cleartext that bad guys can easily intercept. Several techniques enable e-mail traffic to be wrapped within TLS to provide security.

The *STARTTLS* protocol command tells an e-mail server that an e-mail client wants to run over a secure connection, such as TLS. It's not on the exam, but it functions as a tool commonly used to secure e-mail communication.

The **Simple Mail Transport Protocol Secure (SMTPS)** uses TCP port 587 to wrap SMTP communication within TLS. SMTPS is not an extension of SMTP or a propriety protocol. Note that CompTIA refers to SMTPS as *SMTP TLS*.

The **Post Office Protocol 3 over SSL (POP3S)** extension adds a TLS wrap to POP3 e-mail retrieval. POP3S uses port 995. The **Internet Message Access Protocol over SSL (IMAPS)** works similarly, with a TLS wrap for encryption. IMAPS uses port 993.

SCP

The **Secure Copy Protocol (SCP)** enables secure data transfers between two hosts and thus might have replaced FTP. SCP works well but lacks features such as a directory listing. SCP still exists, especially with the well-known UNIX scp command-line utility, but the developers of the popular OpenSSH project encourage users to switch to other secure file-transfer protocols such as SFTP.

SFTP

You'll hear some techs refer to SSH FTP as *Secure FTP*. That's not technically correct, but it's common. If you see Secure FTP on the CompTIA Network+ exam, think SSH FTP and you'll be fine.

The IETF designed the **SSH File Transfer Protocol (SFTP)** to bring secure, full-featured FTP-style file transfer and management to SSH. Although SFTP and FTP have similar names and perform the same job of transferring files, the way in which they do that job differs greatly.

SFTP is not FTP over SSH—it's an entirely separate protocol designed as an extension of the SSH-2 protocol. It offers secure file transfers, resumption of interrupted file transfers, deletion of files on the server, and more. SFTP uses TCP port 22.

Cross Check

FTP and TFTP

You saw FTP and TFTP back in Chapter 8, so check your memory now. How do they differ from SFTP? Do they use the same ports? Would you use FTP and TFTP in the same circumstances? Finally, what's the difference between active and passive FTP?

SFTP is often incorrectly equated with FTPS, which is FTP using TLS to add security. They're very different animals! Just note that you'll find both running out there in the wild.

SNMP

The **Simple Network Management Protocol (SNMP)** is a great way to query the state of network devices—as long as they are SNMP-capable. SNMP can report whatever device-specific information the device provides—such as CPU usage, network utilization, or even detailed firewall hits.

SNMP uses *agents* (special client programs) to collect network information from a **Management Information Base (MIB)**, SNMP's version of a server. To use SNMP, you need SNMP-capable devices and some tool to query them. One tool is Zabbix (www.zabbix.com), shown in Figure 10.33. Zabbix, like most good monitoring tools, enables you to query an SNMP-capable device for hundreds of different types of information.

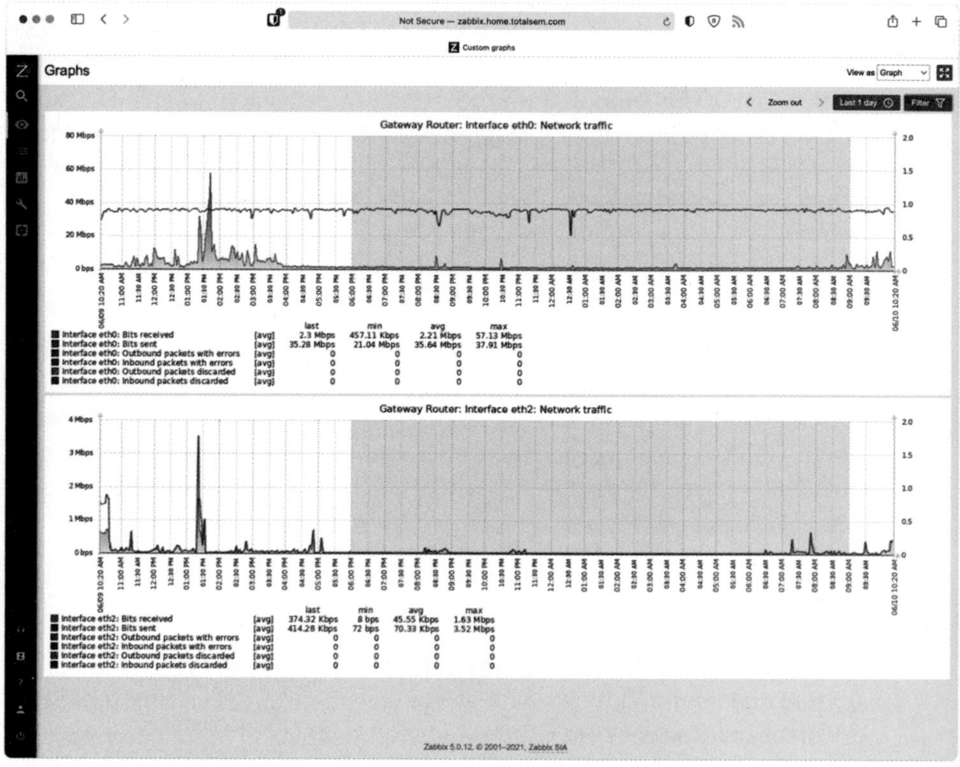

• **Figure 10.33** Zabbix at work

SNMP is a useful tool for network administrators, but the first version, SNMPv1, sent all data, including the passwords, unencrypted over the network. SNMPv2c still lacked encryption and was rather challenging to use. SNMPv3 is the standard version used today and combines solid, fairly easy-to-use authentication and encryption.

SNMP runs on UDP ports 161 and 162. Chapter 20 revisits SNMP.

LDAP

Programs use the **Lightweight Directory Access Protocol (LDAP)** to query and change a database used by the network. These databases track aspects of networks, such as users logged into the network, currently active DHCP clients, or the location of all the printers in the local network.

One of the most complex and also most used databases is Active Directory, the power behind single sign-on and network information (where's the closest printer to me?). Every Windows domain controller stores a copy of the Active Directory database. LDAP can talk to Active Directory and other directory service providers to query and modify items.

You will probably never use LDAP manually. Your domain controllers will use it automatically and transparently in the background to keep your databases in good order. LDAP uses TCP and UDP ports 389 by default.

The now-deprecated secure version of LDAP, *Lightweight Directory Access Protocol over SLL (LDAPS)*, used TCP port 636. You'll see it on the CompTIA Network+ exam, but LDAP version 3 made it obsolete.

NTP

As you'll recall from Chapter 8, the **Network Time Protocol (NTP)** does one thing: it gives you the current time. NTP is an old protocol and isn't in and of itself much of a security risk unless you're using some timestamping protocol like Kerberos. Make sure all of your computers have access to an NTP server so users don't run into problems when logging in. NTP uses UDP port 123.

Chapter 10 Review

Chapter Summary

After reading this chapter and completing the exercises, you should understand the following about securing TCP/IP.

Discuss the standard methods for securing TCP/IP networks

- TCP/IP security can be broken down into five areas: encryption, integrity, nonrepudiation, authentication, and authorization.
- Encryption means to scramble, mix up, or change the data in such a way that bad guys can't read the data.
- Integrity is the process that guarantees that the data received is the same as originally sent.
- Nonrepudiation means that a person cannot deny he or she took a specific action.
- Authentication means to verify that whoever is trying to access data is the person you want accessing that data.
- Authorization defines what data an authenticated person can access and what he or she can do with that data.
- All data starts as plaintext, meaning the data is in an easily read or viewed industry-wide standard format.
- A cipher is a general term for a way to encrypt data, and an algorithm is the cipher's underlying mathematical formula.
- A symmetric-key algorithm is any encryption algorithm that uses the same key for both encryption and decryption. There are two types of symmetric-key algorithms: block ciphers and stream ciphers.
- Block ciphers encrypt data in single chunks of a certain length. Stream ciphers encrypt a single bit at a time.
- Advanced Encryption Standard (AES) is the most secure TCP/IP symmetric-key algorithm and uses a 128-bit block with a 128-, 192-, or 256-bit key. AES has not been cracked.
- Symmetric-key encryption has one serious weakness: anyone who gets a hold of the key can encrypt or decrypt.
- Public-key cryptography is an implementation of asymmetric-key encryption, which uses one key to encrypt and a different key to decrypt.
- A key pair consists of a public key, which is shared and distributed to senders to use to encrypt data, and a private key, which is kept only by the recipient and used to decrypt data.
- Public-key cryptography works by encrypting a symmetric key with a public key and then decrypting the symmetric key with a private key. The connection, once made, exchanges encrypted data using symmetric encryption.
- A hash is a mathematical function that you run on a string of binary digits of any length that results in a value of some fixed length, often called a checksum or a message digest.
- A cryptographic hash function is a one-way function that produces a unique checksum that can be used to verify nonrepudiation and integrity. SHA-2 and SHA-3 are popular hashes for this type of work.
- A digital signature is a hash of a message encrypted by a private key.
- A certificate is a standardized type of file that includes a public key with a digital signature and the digital signature of a trusted third party—a person or a company that guarantees that who is passing out this certificate truly is who they say they are. Sectigo and DigiCert are popular certificate authorities.
- Multifactor authentication means using two or more distinctly different methods for authentication. These include something you know, have, or are; somewhere you are; something you do; or some when you are.
- An access control list (ACL) is used to control authorization, or what a user is allowed to do once they have been authenticated. There are three types of ACL access modes: MAC, DAC, and RBAC.
- In a mandatory access control (MAC) security model, every resource is assigned a label that defines its security level. If the user lacks that security level, he or she does not get access.

- Discretionary access control (DAC) is based on the idea that a resource has an owner who may, at his or her discretion, assign access to that resource.
- Role-based access control (RBAC) is the most popular model used in file sharing and defines a user's access to a resource based on the user's group membership.

Compare TCP/IP security standards

- Point-to-Point Protocol (PPP) enables two point-to-point devices to connect, authenticate with a username and password, and negotiate the network protocol the two devices will use.
- PPP includes two methods to authenticate a username and password: PAP and CHAP.
- The Password Authentication Protocol (PAP) transmits the username and password over the connection in plaintext, which is not secure.
- The Challenge Handshake Authentication Protocol (CHAP) provides a more secure authentication routine because it relies on hashes based on a shared secret, usually a password that both ends of the connection know. Microsoft created its own version called MS-CHAP.
- Authentication, Authorization, and Accounting (AAA) is a philosophy applied to computer security. RADIUS and TACACS+ are standard implementations of AAA.
- Remote Authentication Dial-In User Service (RADIUS) is the better known of the two AAA standards and was created to support ISPs with hundreds if not thousands of modems in hundreds of computers to connect to a single central database.
- Microsoft's RADIUS server is called Internet Authentication Service (IAS) and comes built in with most versions of Microsoft Windows Server. FreeRADIUS is a popular RADIUS server for UNIX/Linux.
- Terminal Access Controller Access Control System Plus (TACACS+) is a proprietary protocol developed by Cisco to support AAA in a network with many routers and switches.
- Kerberos, unlike PPP, is an authentication protocol for TCP/IP networks with many clients all connected to a single authenticating server.
- Kerberos, which is the authentication protocol for all Windows networks using a domain controller, uses a Key Distribution Center (KDC) that has two components: the Authentication Server (AS) and the Ticket-Granting Service (TGS).
- The Authentication Server authenticates users at login and, if successful, sends a Ticket-Granting Ticket (TGT; good for ten hours by default) allowing the user to access network resources without having to reauthenticate.
- The timestamped TGT is sent to the TGS, which returns an access token used by the client for authorization to a network resource.
- Secure Shell (SSH) is a secure replacement for Telnet. SSH uses PKI in the form of an RSA key. At login, the SSH server sends its public key to the client. The client then encrypts data using the public key and transmits the data, which is subsequently decrypted on the server with the server's private key.
- An SSH tunnel is an encrypted link between two programs on two separate computers. Once established, anything you enter into the client application is encrypted, sent to the server, decrypted, and then acted upon.
- Netscape created the Secure Sockets Layer (SSL) standard, which requires a server with a certificate. SSL has been updated to the Transport Layer Security (TLS) standard and TLS is used for secure Web transactions, such as online credit card purchases and just logging into a site.
- SSL is limited to HTTP, FTP, SMTP, and a few older TCP applications, whereas TLS is less restrictive and is used for everything SSL does in addition to VoIP and VPNs.
- IPsec is an encryption protocol that works in two different modes: Transport mode and Tunnel mode. IPv6 uses the IPsec Transport mode by default.
- In Transport mode, only the actual payload of the IP packet is encrypted; the destination and source IP addresses and other IP header information are still readable.
- In Tunnel mode, the entire IP packet is encrypted and then encapsulated inside another IP packet at an endpoint.

Implement secure TCP/IP applications

- HTTPS uses TLS for the actual authentication and encryption process. Most browsers show a small lock icon in the lower-right corner or in the address bar when an HTTPS connection is established.

- The most common problems with HTTPS connections are caused by bad or outdated certificates.
- The Secure Copy Protocol (SCP) is an SSH-enabled program or protocol used to copy files securely between a client and a server. It has been replaced by SSH File Transfer Protocol (SFTP).
- The Simple Network Management Protocol (SNMP) is a method for querying the state of SNMP-capable devices. SNMP can tell you a number of settings, like CPU usage, network utilization, and detailed firewall hits. SNMP uses agents and MIBs to capture and monitor network usage.
- SNMPv1 sent all data, including the passwords, unencrypted over the network. SNMPv2c also lacked encryption and was rather challenging to use. SNMPv3 is the standard version used today and combines solid, fairly easy-to-use authentication and encryption.
- Domain controllers running Active Directory and other servers use the Lightweight Directory Access Protocol (LDAP) to keep important databases updated.
- The Network Time Protocol (NTP) gives you the current time. It isn't much of a security risk unless you're using some timestamping protocol like Kerberos.

Key Terms

access control list (ACL) *(285)*
Advanced Encryption Standard (AES) *(274)*
algorithm *(271)*
asymmetric-key algorithm *(274)*
authentication *(271)*
Authentication, Authorization, and Accounting (AAA) *(288)*
Authentication Server (AS) *(290)*
authorization *(271)*
block cipher *(274)*
certificate *(281)*
Challenge Handshake Authentication Protocol (CHAP) *(286)*
cipher *(271)*
ciphertext *(272)*
cleartext *(271)*
digital signature *(280)*
discretionary access control (DAC) *(285)*
encryption *(271)*
file hashing *(277)*
FreeRADIUS *(289)*
hash *(276)*
Hypertext Transfer Protocol Secure (HTTPS) *(296)*
integrity *(271)*
Internet Authentication Service (IAS) *(289)*
Internet Message Access Protocol over SSL (IMAPS) *(297)*
Internet Protocol Security (IPsec) *(295)*
Kerberos *(290)*
Key Distribution Center (KDC) *(290)*
key pair *(275)*
Lightweight Directory Access Protocol (LDAP) *(299)*
local authentication *(284)*
Management Information Base (MIB) *(298)*
mandatory access control (MAC) *(285)*
MS-CHAP *(287)*
multifactor authentication (MFA) *(284)*
network access control (NAC) *(284)*
network access server (NAS) *(289)*
Network Time Protocol (NTP) *(299)*
nonrepudiation *(271)*
Password Authentication Protocol (PAP) *(286)*
plaintext *(272)*
Point-to-Point Protocol (PPP) *(286)*
Post Office Protocol 3 over SSL (POP3S) *(297)*
public-key cryptography *(275)*
public-key infrastructure (PKI) *(283)*
Remote Authentication Dial-In User Service (RADIUS) *(289)*
role-based access control (RBAC) *(285)*
Secure Copy Protocol (SCP) *(297)*
Secure Hash Algorithm *(278)*
Secure Shell (SSH) *(291)*
Secure Sockets Layer (SSL) *(294)*
Simple Mail Transport Protocol Secure (SMTPS) *(297)*
Simple Network Management Protocol (SNMP) *(298)*
single sign-on (SSO) *(291)*

SSH File Transfer Protocol (SFTP) *(297)*
SSH tunnel *(293)*
stream cipher *(274)*
substitution *(272)*
symmetric-key algorithm *(274)*
Terminal Access Controller Access Control System Plus (TACACS+) *(290)*
Ticket-Granting Service (TGS) *(290)*
Ticket-Granting Ticket (TGT) *(290)*
Transport Layer Security (TLS) *(295)*
two-factor authentication *(284)*
XOR (eXclusive OR) *(273)*

Key Term Quiz

Use the Key Terms list to complete the sentences that follow. Not all the terms will be used.

1. ________________ defines what a person accessing data can do with that data.
2. ________________ is the act of verifying you are who you say you are.
3. ________________ is the process of guaranteeing that data is as originally sent.
4. A(n) ________________ encrypts data in fixed-length chunks at a time.
5. ________________ is a secure replacement for Telnet.
6. A(n) ________________ uses one key to encrypt data and a different key to decrypt the same data.
7. SSL has been replaced by the more robust ________________.
8. The developers of SCP encourage users to switch to ________________, a secure protocol for copying files to a server.
9. ________________ is the default authentication protocol for Windows domains and is time sensitive.
10. ________________ uses a 128-bit block, up to a 256-bit key, and is an uncracked encryption algorithm.

Multiple-Choice Quiz

1. Justin wants his team to be able to send him encrypted e-mails. What protocol enables sending secure e-mail messages?
   - **A.** IMAPS
   - **B.** Kerberos
   - **C.** POP3S
   - **D.** SMTPS
2. Which of the following is a popular cryptographic hashing function?
   - **A.** SSH
   - **B.** SHA-256
   - **C.** RADIUS
   - **D.** TACACS+
3. A public and private key pair is an example of what?
   - **A.** Symmetric-key algorithm
   - **B.** Asymmetric-key algorithm
   - **C.** Certificate
   - **D.** RADIUS
4. Which authentication protocol is time sensitive and is the default authentication protocol on Windows domains?
   - **A.** PPP
   - **B.** MS-CHAP
   - **C.** IPsec
   - **D.** Kerberos

5. What helps to protect credit card numbers during online purchases? (Select two.)
   A. Certificates
   B. TLS
   C. SCP
   D. NTP
   E. HTTP
6. Emily wants to enter commands remotely and securely to run at a remote server. What application should she use?
   A. Telnet
   B. SSH
   C. SFTP
   D. RSA
7. A hash function is which of the following?
   A. A complex function
   B. A PKI function
   C. A one-way function
   D. A systematic function
8. To have a PKI, you must have which of the following?
   A. Web server
   B. Web of trust
   C. Root authority
   D. Unsigned certificate
9. Which term describes the process of guaranteeing that the sender of the data cannot later deny having sent it?
   A. Authentication
   B. Authorization
   C. Encryption
   D. Nonrepudiation
10. If you see some traffic running on TCP port 49, what AAA standard is running?
    A. PPP
    B. RADIUS
    C. MS-CHAP
    D. TACACS+
11. What is the difference between RADIUS and TACACS+?
    A. RADIUS is the authentication control for Windows networks, whereas TACACS+ is the authentication control for UNIX/Linux networks.
    B. RADIUS is an implementation of an authentication control, whereas TACACS+ is an implementation of authorization control.
    C. RADIUS is a protocol for authentication control, and there are implementations for Windows, UNIX, and Linux servers. TACACS+ is authentication control for Cisco routers and switches.
    D. RADIUS supports encryption; TACACS+ does not and, therefore, is less desirable in a network.
12. AES is a(n) ________________ cipher.
    A. block
    B. forwarding
    C. stream
    D. asymmetric
13. If you see some traffic running on UDP ports 1812 and 1813, what AAA standard is running?
    A. PPP
    B. RADIUS
    C. MS-CHAP
    D. TACACS+
14. Digital signatures and certificates help with which aspect of computer security?
    A. Accounting
    B. Authentication
    C. Authorization
    D. Integrity
15. Which authorization model grants privileges based on the group membership of network users?
    A. MAC
    B. DAC
    C. RBAC
    D. GAC

Essay Quiz

1. Explain the difference between symmetric-key and asymmetric-key algorithms and give examples of each. Which is more secure? Why?
2. Access control lists help to control the authorization of network resources. Explain the differences among the three ACL access models.
3. You receive a call from a distressed user telling you she was in the middle of an online purchase (just entering her credit card number) when she noticed a certificate warning on the screen saying the Web site's certificate has expired. What advice would you give the user?

Lab Projects

• Lab Project 10.1

Download a copy of GnuPG from www.gnupg.org and one of the frontends from www.gnupg.org/related_software/frontends.en.html. Generate a key pair and share your public key with a classmate. Have your classmate encrypt a file using your public key and e-mail it to you. Decrypt your file with your private key.

• Lab Project 10.2

You have learned many acronyms in this chapter! Make a list of the following acronyms, state what they stand for, and briefly describe them. Use this as a study sheet for the CompTIA Network+ certification exam: AES, RSA, MD5, SHA, PKI, ACL, MAC, DAC, RBAC, PPP, PAP, CHAP, MS-CHAP, AAA, RADIUS, TACACS+, KDC, AS, TGT, TGS, SID, SSH, SSL, TLS, HTTPS, SCP, SFTP, SNMP, and NTP.

Switch Features

"It followed from the special theory of relativity that mass and energy are both but different manifestations of the same thing. A somewhat unfamiliar conception for the average mind."

—Albert Einstein

In this chapter, you will learn how to

- **Define the capabilities and management of managed switches**
- **Configure and deploy VLANs**
- **Implement advanced switch features**

So far in this book we've looked at networks in a rather simplistic way. First, we explored network topologies. Second, we've seen a number of devices whose functions neatly align with the OSI model. From cabling humming along at Layer 1, switches at Layer 2, and routers at Layer 3, each performs specific services without overlap. This is a great way to begin learning about networking, but it's not a complete view of how many networks function. It's time to go into more depth.

This chapter starts by exploring how to manage devices that handle switching, security, and more. The second portion examines VLANs: technology built into better switches that segments a single network into multiple virtual networks. The chapter finishes with a discussion of multilayer switches—boxes that do pretty much everything from Layer 1 all the way to Layer 7.

Test Specific

Switch Management

The simple switches discussed so far in this book are also called **unmanaged switches**, which basically means techs have no control over how they work beyond what devices to plug in and which ports to use. This "simple" work is critical—it's the device's purpose—so the heavy lifting is traditionally done in highly optimized hardware. These optimized components are also known as the *data plane* or the *forwarding plane*.

Less simple **managed switches** have an operating system (running on hardware separate from the data plane) that enables device configuration. The device also uses the OS and hardware resources to run software that implements additional features. This extra layer of software and the hardware that supports it are also known as the *control plane*. What's there to configure? Pretty much everything in this chapter! Let's start with a look at how to access the configuration interface.

This distinction between the data and control planes doesn't just apply to switches. You may see these terms applied to other hardware devices such as routers, firewalls, and sometimes even entire networks. Likewise, these methods of switch management apply to any type of managed device (such as routers).

You can connect to a managed switch to tell it what you want it to do. Exactly how you do this varies from switch to switch, but generally there are three ways:

- Directly plug into a serial interface and use a virtual terminal program to connect to a command-line interface. Nowadays, you'd use a serial-to-USB converter to connect a laptop to the console port on the switch.
- Attach the switch to the network and then use a virtual terminal over SSH to connect to the same command-line interface.
- Connect the switch to the network and use the switch's built-in Web interface.

Let's look at the steps involved in each method.

First, many managed switches have a special serial port called a **console port**. Plug a laptop (or other computing device) into the console port on the back of the switch (Figure 11.1). Then, run a terminal program like PuTTY to access the command-line interface on the switch. As long as you speak the language of the switch's command prompt, you're good to go. It's very common to use a console port for initial configuration of a new managed switch.

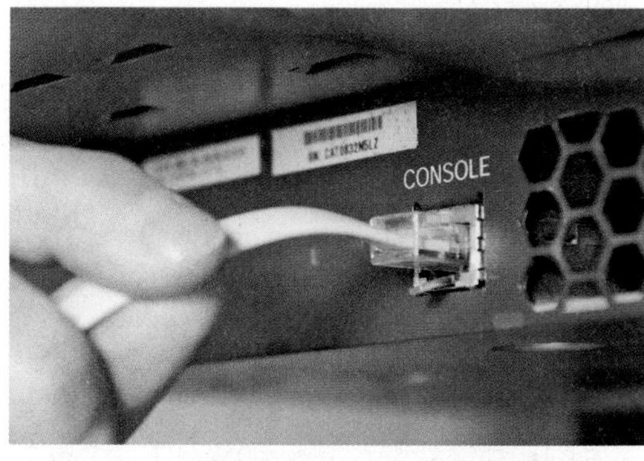

• **Figure 11.1** Plugging into a managed switch's console port using a console cable

The second and third methods require the managed switch to be connected to the network and have an accessible IP address. Connect to the switch over the network and run some sort of software—either PuTTY or a Web browser—to manage the switch.

Wait! It's a switch. Switches that we've discussed in the book so far operate at Layer 2 of the OSI model. IP addresses don't show up until Layer 3. Here's the scoop in a nutshell. A managed switch needs an IP address to enable configuration on Layer 3.

This means a new, out-of-the-box managed switch has all the same configuration issues a new router would have. Many new managed switches have a default IP address (but you should assign an IP address that's applicable to your network). Others require a proprietary configuration utility that discovers by MAC address. Switches with default IP addresses have default usernames and passwords (but you should change those!). Both types have a bunch of other default settings that you'll probably want to change once you know what they mean.

You configure a default gateway on a switch by telling the switch the IP address of the router.

Like any IP device, a managed switch needs good, basic maintenance. One example would be updating the firmware. Managed switches support firmware updates over the Internet. That's a nice idea, but it means your switch needs a default gateway, a DNS server, and so forth to be able to access content over the Internet.

Access Management

As you might imagine, it would be scary to let unauthorized people have access to your switch management configuration interface. When you configure a switch over the network—we call this **in-band management**—anyone who knows the IP addresses of the managed devices can access them if they know or guess the username and password. To reduce this risk, it's common to dedicate one port on every managed device as a *management port*. You can do *interface configuration* only by directly connecting to that port.

Look for a question that asks you to compare *in-band vs. out-of-band management*, specifically in the context of securing remote access. In-band management means managing the switch from the same network that moves data (whether you connect locally or remotely). Out-of-band management means managing the switch from outside the network, usually via a separate network just for managing and monitoring.

Alternatively, you can connect all those dedicated ports into a switch that's totally separate from the rest of the network, which will prevent unauthorized access to those ports. This is one example of **out-of-band management**.

If you have a switch in a far-flung location, it'll be much easier to manage with some method of remote management. Switches with Web management interfaces often provide a well-protected *HTTPS/management URL* that administrators can use to log into the switch via the Internet (another example of in-band management).

The CompTIA Network+ objectives call out some basic network platform commands—*show config*, *show interface*, and *show route*. These commands can be a big help when it comes to troubleshooting, so keep an eye out for all of them in Chapter 21!

Port Configuration

Over the years, switches have accumulated a number of situational port features that were built to make lemonade out of lemons when a network runs into some specific problems. The defaults are usually fine; we only fiddle with these to address specific problems (and, even then, only if they don't create more problems than they fix). Let's look at the settings for speed, duplex, flow control, and jumbo frames.

Before you start changing port settings, check the current status of the interface. You can do this in many ways, though most techs use the command line. Here are three command-line options on three different switches from three different providers. The command-line syntax and options differ between vendors and even OS versions. A lot of the commands are very similar, but you'll have to spend a little time getting used to the syntax and options available on any devices with which you work.

Figure 11.2 shows the output for `show interfaces` on all three switches (with the settings we're focusing on here highlighted when they are present).

Modern switches enable you to provide manual support for older hardware in terms of controlling network *speed* and *duplex* settings. A typical "Gigabit" switch, for example, automatically supports 1000-Gbps connections and the slower 100-Mbps "Fast Ethernet" connections and the super

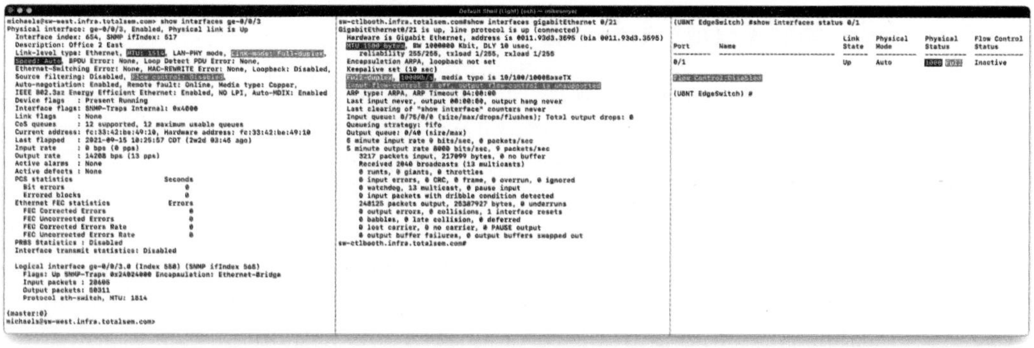

• **Figure 11.2** Interface status in Juniper JunOS (left), Cisco IOS (middle), and Ubiquiti EdgeSwitch (right)

slow 10-Mbps connections. In some rare circumstances, you can set a port manually to run at a specific speed.

Some truly ancient wired devices operate at *half duplex*, meaning they can send or receive, but not both at the same time. (The latter is *full duplex*.) The default switch port setting is autosensing, just like with speed, but you can force a port to half duplex if necessary to support an old device.

In theory, *flow control* can help with situations like a host that can't keep up with the flow of traffic. It enables the host to send an Ethernet *PAUSE* frame, which asks the switch to hold up for some amount of time so the host can catch its breath. If the switch can, it'll buffer transmissions until the pause expires, and then start sending again. If the host catches up early, it can send another PAUSE frame with a delay of zero to ask the switch to resume. In practice, flow control can cause latency trouble for modern real-time applications such as VoIP, and the same needs are usually met by QoS (which we'll take a closer look at later in the chapter).

Some special-purpose networks, such as those optimized for reading and writing to storage devices (we'll take a closer look at these in Chapter 16), require a lot of throughput. An inexpensive way to boost their performance is to enable them to use *jumbo frames* larger than the normal 1500-byte payload limit specified by IEEE 802.3, because it helps improve the payload-to-overhead ratio. You can't just enable jumbo frames for all purposes, especially if you're connected to the Internet. The rest of the WAN won't respect your hefty frames, and you'll just end up with fragmentation and dropped packets that actually hurt performance or prevent connections altogether.

Port Security

In a general sense, **port security** means to lock switch ports to a specific MAC address. The port will only work with a specific computer after configuration. This process is pretty time-intensive in larger networks.

With Cisco switches, you can configure MAC addresses to be *sticky*—also called *persistent MAC* by other switch makers. The MAC addresses can be dynamically learned or manually configured, stored in the address table, and added to the running configuration. If these addresses are saved in the configuration file, the interface does not need to dynamically relearn them when the switch restarts. Although sticky secure addresses can be manually configured, it is not recommended.

Virtual LANs

> The CompTIA objectives use the term *data virtual local area network (VLAN)* to describe the standard VLANs discussed here. This differentiates them from *voice VLANs*, discussed later in this chapter.

Today's LANs are complex places. It's rare to see any serious network that doesn't have remote incoming connections, public Web or e-mail servers, wireless networks, and a string of connected switches. Leaving all of these different features on a single broadcast domain creates a tremendous amount of broadcast traffic and creates security challenges. What if you could segment the network using the switches you already own? A **virtual local area network (VLAN)** enables you to segment a physical network into multiple discreet networks without having to add additional hardware.

To create a VLAN, you take a single physical broadcast domain made up of one or more switches and chop it up into multiple broadcast domains. This is most simply done by assigning each port to a specific VLAN. VLANs require switches with specific programming to create the virtual networks.

Imagine a single switch with a number of computers connected to it. Up to this point, a single switch creates a single broadcast domain, but that's about to change. You've decided to take this single switch and turn it into two VLANs. VLANs typically get the name "VLAN" plus a number, like VLAN1 or VLAN0275. The devices usually start at 1, although there's no law or rules on the numbering other than that enterprise switches require four digits (like VLAN0001 rather than VLAN1). In this example, I'll configure the ports on a single switch to be in one of two VLANs: VLAN1 or VLAN2 (Figure 11.3). I promise to show you how to configure ports for different VLANs shortly, but I've got a couple of other concepts to hit first.

> Most of the networking industry recommends changing your network's default VLAN to anything other than VLAN1 to harden your network against attacks that target the default setting. "Change default VLAN" is how this appears in the CompTIA N10-008 exam objectives.

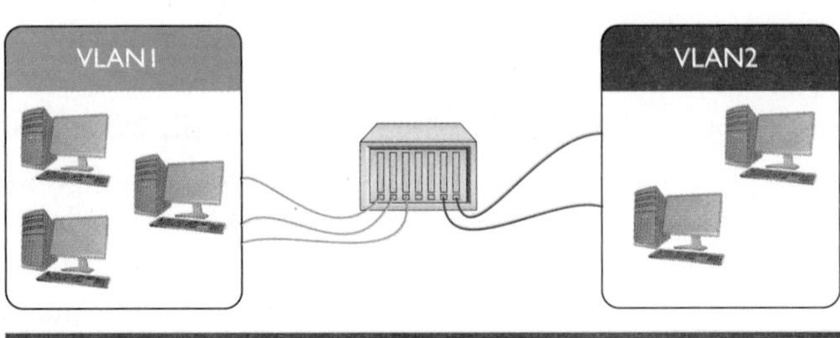

• **Figure 11.3** Switch with two VLANs

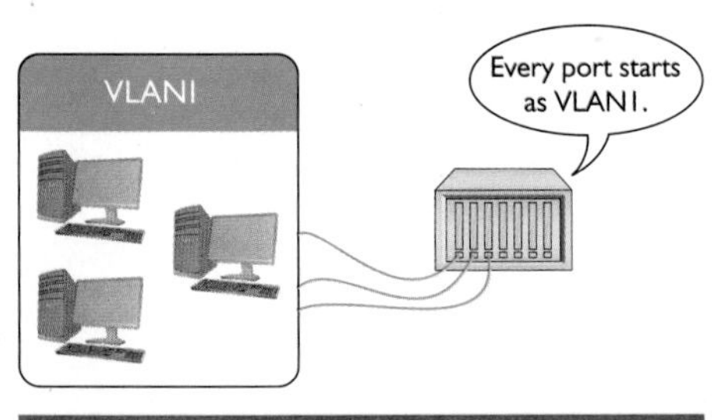

• **Figure 11.4** Every port is VLAN1 by default.

Figure 11.4 shows a switch configured to assign individual ports to VLANs. Managed switches can handle any number of VLANs. Every port starts with the *default VLAN*, VLAN1, so even if you don't specify multiple VLANs, you get one by default.

To set up a VLAN on a switch, create one or more VLANs, then assign ports to those VLANs. Any traffic sent from a host plugged into a port for VLAN1, therefore, becomes part of the broadcast domain of VLAN1.

Serious networks usually have more than one switch. Let's say you added a switch to a simple network. You'd like to keep VLAN1 and VLAN2 but use both switches. You can configure the new switch to use VLAN1 and VLAN2, but you've got to enable data to flow between the two switches, regardless of VLAN. That's where trunking comes into play.

Trunking

Trunking is the process of transferring VLAN traffic between two or more switches. Imagine two switches, each configured with a VLAN1 and a VLAN2, as shown in Figure 11.5.

You want computers connected to VLAN1 on one switch to talk to computers connected to VLAN1 on the other switch. Of course, you want to do this with VLAN2 also. To do this, configure a port on each switch as a **trunk port**, a port on a switch configured to carry all traffic, regardless of VLAN number, between all switches in a LAN (Figure 11.6).

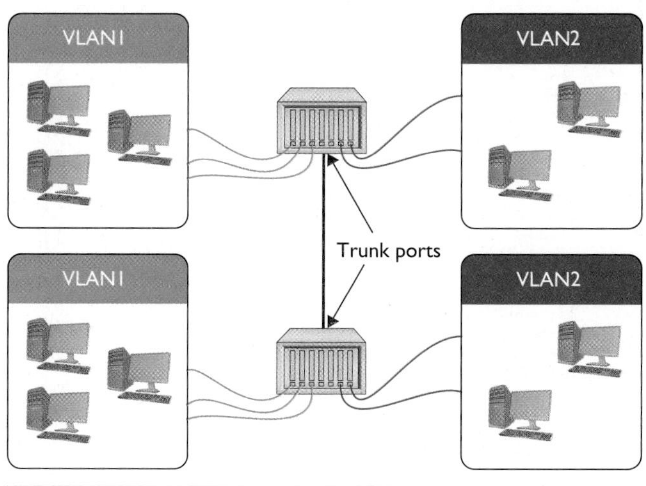

• **Figure 11.6** Trunk ports

• **Figure 11.5** Two switches, each with a VLAN1 and a VLAN2

Check out the excellent Chapter 11 Challenge! Sim, "Trunking," to test your understanding of trunking. You'll find it here: https://totalsem.com/008.

Every Ethernet switch uses the IEEE **802.1Q** trunk standard that enables you to connect switches from different manufacturers.

Configuring a VLAN-Capable Switch

If you want to configure a VLAN-capable switch, you need a method to perform that configuration. One method uses a console port like the one described in Chapter 7. The most common method is to log into the switch using SSH—not Telnet, because you need security—and use the command-line interface. Once you know what you're doing, the command line is fast, precise, and scriptable. Alternatively, you can access the switch with a Web browser interface, like the one shown in Figure 11.7.

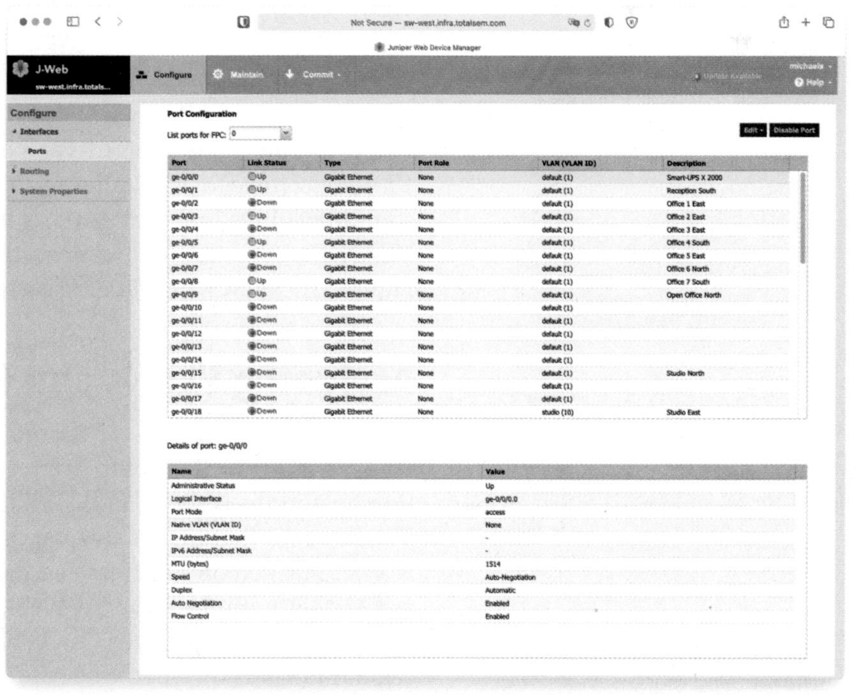

• **Figure 11.7** Browser interface for a switch

Every switch manufacturer has its own interface for configuring VLANs, but the interface shown in Figure 11.8 is a classic example. This is Cisco Network Assistant, a GUI tool that enables you to configure multiple Cisco devices through the same interface. Note that you first must define your VLANs.

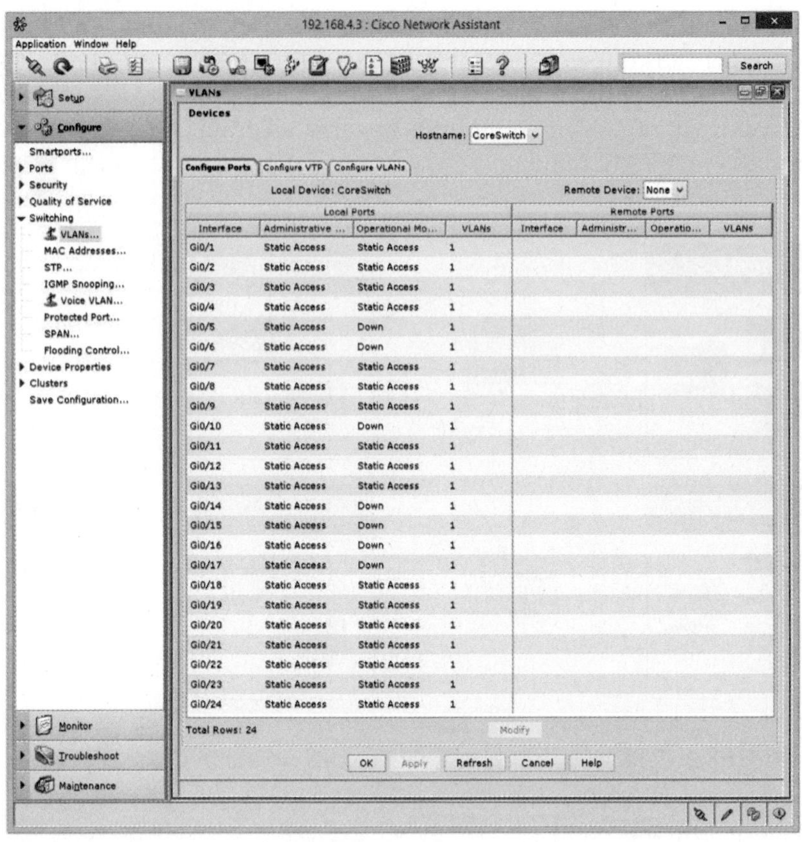

• **Figure 11.8** Defining VLANs in Cisco Network Assistant

After you create the VLANs, you assign ports to them, a process called *VLAN assignment*. Assigning each port to a VLAN means that whatever computer plugs into that port, its traffic will be associated with that port's VLAN ID. (See the following section, "Assigning VLANs and Tagging.") Figure 11.9 shows a port being assigned to a particular VLAN.

Assigning VLANs and Tagging

When you have a busy network with multiple switches and multiple VLANs, how does a frame from a host in VLAN100 make it to a destination host in the same VLAN? What if the hosts are several switches apart? The key tool that makes this happen is 802.1Q *port tagging*. An 802.1Q tag is a field tacked on to a frame's Ethernet header enabling the next switch to associate it with the correct VLAN. You'll only find tags on frames as they transit trunk lines between switches—not on lines between switches and regular hosts.

> VLANs based on ports are the most common type of VLAN and are commonly known as *static VLANs*. VLANs based on MAC addresses are called *dynamic VLANs*. The latter method is never used these days.

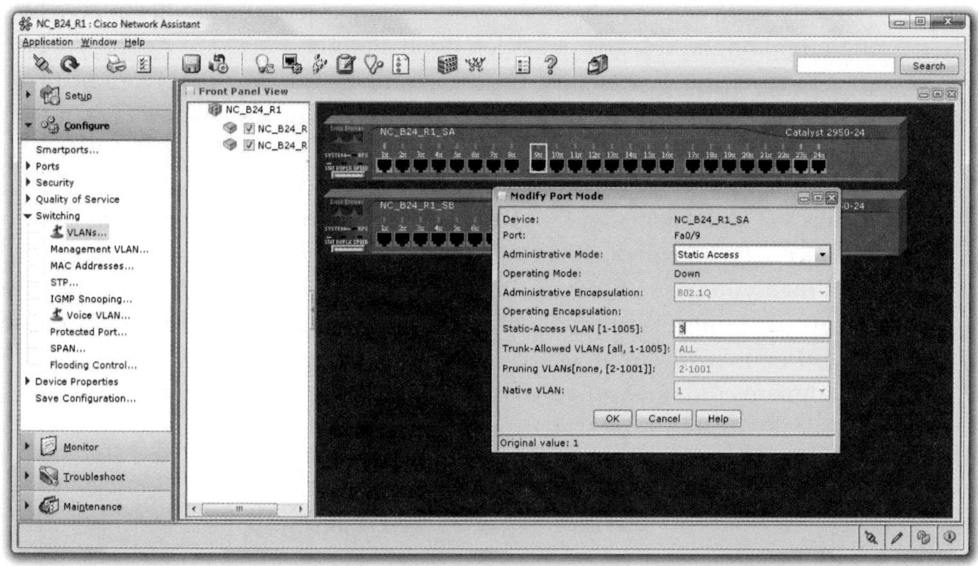

• **Figure 11.9** Assigning a port to a VLAN

Regular hosts plug into **access ports** (sometimes called untagged ports), standard switch ports that do the work of associating untagged traffic with their assigned VLAN as frames enter the switch. Access ports connect to hosts; trunk ports connect to other trunk ports on other switches.

When the data enters the access port, the switch associates the frames with the appropriate VLAN ID. If the destination host is connected to the same switch, the frames flow to that host's access port and out over the wire without a VLAN tag. If the destination host connects to a different switch, the initial switch sends the frames out its trunk port (sometimes called a tagged port). What happens next is determined by how the trunk port is configured.

If the trunk port's **native VLAN**—the VLAN ID it associates untagged traffic with—is the same as the VLAN the frame was associated with as it entered the access port, the switch sends the frame along to the next switch without adding a tag. If the frame is part of any other VLAN, then the trunk port adds the 802.1Q tag to the frame and sends it on its way.

Native VLANs exist to provide compatibility with older or simpler non-802.1Q switches, but there is a catch. The native VLAN opens your network to a nasty vulnerability called a *double-tagging attack* that lets the attacker access VLANs they should not be able to access. For this reason, in modern networks the native VLAN is set to an unused VLAN and the trunk port is configured to tag its native VLAN traffic as well.

VLAN Trunking Protocol

A busy network with many VLAN switches can require periods of intensive work to update. Imagine the work required to redo all the VLAN switches if you changed the VLAN configuration by adding or removing a VLAN. You'd have to access every switch individually, changing the port configuration to alter the VLAN assignment, and so on. The potential for errors is staggering. What if you missed updating one switch? Joe in Sales might wrongly have access to a sensitive accounting server or Phyllis in accounting might not be able to get her job done on time.

VTP offers *VTP pruning*, a tool for minimizing broadcast traffic. This can be a very useful tool on larger-scale networks.

VTP clients can update VTP servers the same way VTP servers update VTP clients. The difference is that VLAN info can only be changed on VTP servers.

Cisco uses a proprietary protocol called **VLAN Trunking Protocol (VTP)** to automate the updating of multiple VLAN switches. With VTP, you put each switch into one of three states: server, client, or transparent. When you make changes to the VLAN configuration of a VTP server switch, all the connected VTP clients and VTP servers update their configurations within minutes. The big job of changing every switch manually just went away.

When you set a VLAN switch to transparent, you tell it not to update but to hold onto its manual settings. You would use a transparent mode VLAN switch in circumstances where the overall VLAN configuration assignments did not apply. (VTP transparent switches still pass on updates to other switches in the VTP domain.)

Inter-VLAN Routing

Once you've configured a switch to support multiple VLANs, each VLAN is its own broadcast domain, just as if the two VLANs were on two completely separate switches and networks. There is no way for data to get from one VLAN to another unless you use a router or a multilayer switch. (See "Multilayer Switches" later in the chapter for the scoop on these devices.)

The process of passing traffic between two VLANs is called **inter-VLAN routing**. In principle, implementing inter-VLAN routing could be done using a router with multiple ports. Figure 11.10 shows a very simple example with two VLANs connected by a single router. Note that the router has one port connected to VLAN100 and another connected to VLAN200. Devices on VLAN100 may now communicate with devices on VLAN200.

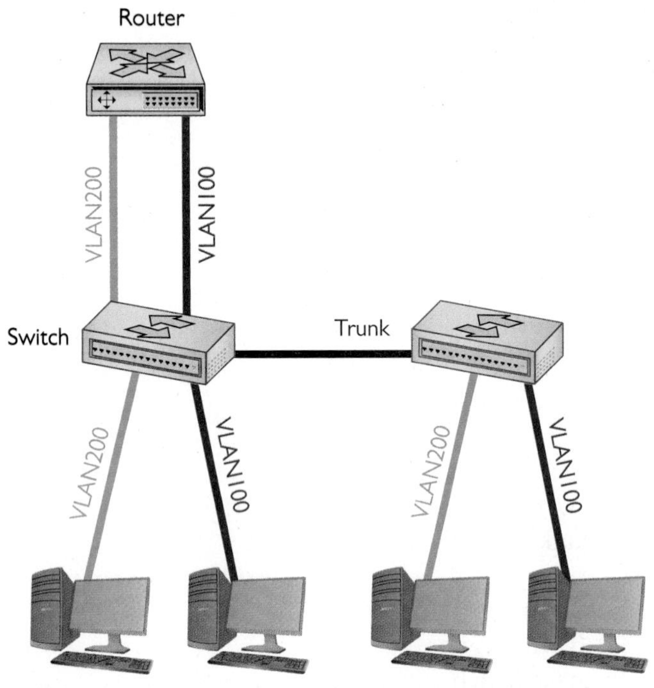

• **Figure 11.10** One router connecting multiple VLANs

More commonly, you see a router-on-a-stick configuration, which uses a single router interface to connect to multiple VLANs on a switch. The router interface is set up as a trunk port and then broken up into logical subinterfaces for each VLAN. The subinterfaces can handle different or unique Layer 3 information. Figure 11.11 shows a visual example, with eth1 as the physical interface, and eth1.5, eth1.10, and eth1.20 as the subinterfaces.

Cisco uses the term *subinterface* to refer to multiple logical interfaces created by dividing a single physical interface.

local	eth1	ethernet	192.168.4.1/24 2603:300c:d:cd01::1/64
voice	eth1.5	vlan	10.0.5.1/24
studio	eth1.10	vlan	10.0.10.1/24 2603:300c:d:cd03::1/64
guest	eth1.20	vlan	10.0.20.1/24 2603:300c:d:cd04::1/64

• **Figure 11.11** Subinterfaces in action

Adding a physical router isn't a very elegant way to connect VLANs. This forces almost all traffic to go through the router, and it's not a very flexible solution if you want to add more VLANs in the future. As a result, many VLAN-capable switches also do routing. Figure 11.12 shows an inter-VLAN routing–capable switch, the Juniper EX3400.

• **Figure 11.12** Juniper EX3400

From the outside, the EX3400 looks like any other switch. On the inside, it's a flexible device that not only supports VLANs but also provides routing to interconnect these VLANs.

If the Juniper EX3400 is a switch and a router, on what layer of the OSI seven-layer model does it operate? If it's a switch, then it works at Layer 2. But routers work at Layer 3. This isn't an ordinary switch. The Juniper EX3400 works at both Layers 2 and 3 at the same time.

DHCP and VLANs

DHCP is an awesome tool to automate, track, and manage *IP address assignments*, as you know from previous chapters. Unfortunately, the protocol is limited to a single subnet within a single broadcast domain. By default, DHCP requests (which are broadcasts) can't pass through a router. So, if you have broken up your network with VLANs and connected those VLANs with routers, you need some method for getting IP addresses and other TCP/IP information to hosts. Unless you want to go back to tediously applying static addresses one at a time!

When a *relay agent* (CompTIA calls this a **DHCP relay**—you might remember this from the discussion of DHCP in Chapter 6) is enabled and configured within a router, the router passes DHCP messages across the router interfaces. So now we can use a single DHCP server to serve addresses to multiple networks or subnetworks. Cisco implements DHCP relay through a configuration command called **IP helper** (the command is technically `ip helper-address`). IP helper enables DHCP relay support (port 67). It also enables relaying for TFTP (port 69), NTP (port 123), TACACS+ (port 49), DNS (port 53), NetBIOS (port 137), and NetBIOS Datagram (port 138).

Voice VLANs

VLANs optimized for voice data streams—voice VLANs—prioritize voice traffic over data traffic to ensure smooth voice communication. Voice VLANs can use MAC addresses to determine which devices on the network are phones or use VLAN-based tags in the received frame. The switch can prioritize the voice traffic and deprioritize data traffic as specified.

Private VLANs

The point of a network may seem to be interconnecting devices, but there *are* times when you don't want hosts on a switch to talk to one another. Think of a hotel where every room has Internet access. You wouldn't want the guests seeing each other's traffic—you just want each guest's Ethernet frames to flow to and from the hotel's gateway. For situations like this, it's a best practice to implement Private VLANs.

A *Private VLAN* only allows traffic from private ports (regular switch ports that are part of the private VLAN) to be switched to the uplink trunk port. It can't go to any other port on the switch, isolating hosts from each other at Layer 2.

Troubleshooting VLANs

At this level, troubleshooting a new VLAN is mostly about port assignment. If you give an incorrect VLAN assignment to a device, either you won't be able to see it or that device won't have access to resources it needs. The fix is the obvious one: change the VLAN assignment.

Multilayer Switches

At this point you must stop thinking (if you still are) that a "switch" always works at Layer 2. A *Layer 2 switch* forwards traffic based on MAC addresses, whereas a *Layer 3 switch* (also called a *Layer 3 capable switch*) forwards traffic based on IP addresses. A Layer 3 switch is a router that does what a traditional router does in software...in hardware. A Layer 3 switch, by definition, is a **multilayer switch**, functioning at both Layer 2 and Layer 3. From here on out, I will carefully address at what layer of the OSI seven-layer model a switch operates.

The challenge to multilayer switches comes with the ports. On a classic Layer 2 switch, individual ports don't have IP addresses. They don't need them. On a router, however, every port must have an IP address because the routing table uses the IP address to determine where to send packets.

A multilayer switch needs some option or feature for configuring ports to work at Layer 2 or Layer 3. Cisco uses the terms *switch port* and *router port* to differentiate between the two types of ports. You can configure any port on a multilayer switch to act as a switch port or a router port, depending on your needs. Multilayer switches are incredibly common and support a number of interesting features, clearly making them part of what I call *advanced networking devices.*

I'm going to show you four areas where multilayer switches are very helpful: load balancing, quality of service, port bonding, and network protection. (Each term is defined in its respective section.) These four areas aren't the only places where multiplayer switches solve problems, but they are popular (and covered on the CompTIA Network+ exam). Each section covers common use cases, in CompTIA speak, for these devices. In other words, I'll explain when and where to use each function.

Any device that works at multiple layers of the OSI seven-layer model, providing more than a single service, is called a *multifunction network device.*

Load Balancing

Popular Internet servers are exactly that—popular. So popular that a single system cannot possibly support the thousands, if not millions, of requests per day that bombard them. But from what you've learned thus far about servers, you know that a single server has a single IP address. Put this to the test. Go to a command prompt and type **`ping www.google.com`** and press enter.

```
C:\>ping www.google.com

Pinging www.l.google.com [74.125.95.147] with 32 bytes of data:
Reply from 74.125.95.147: bytes=32 time=71ms TTL=242
Reply from 74.125.95.147: bytes=32 time=71ms TTL=242
Reply from 74.125.95.147: bytes=32 time=70ms TTL=242
Reply from 74.125.95.147: bytes=32 time=70ms TTL=242
```

A seriously epic site like google.com will handle trillions of search requests per year. Let's throw hypothetical math into the mix. Imagine 2 trillion requests; the average would be well over 5 billion search requests a day and 60,000 per second. Each of those 60,000 requests might require the Web server to deliver thousands of HTTP segments. A single, powerful, dedicated Web server simply can't handle that load. A busy Web site often needs more than one Web server to handle all the requests. Let's say a Web site needs three servers to handle the traffic. How does that one Web site, using three different servers, use a single IP address? The answer is found in something called *load balancing*.

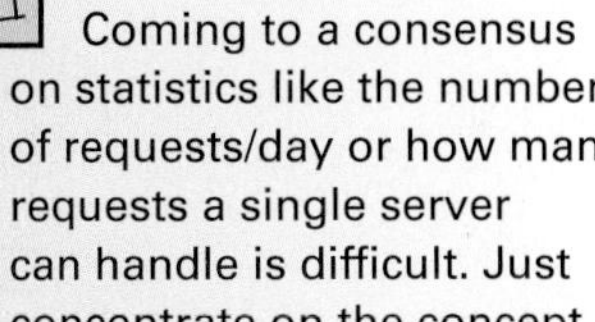

Coming to a consensus on statistics like the number of requests/day or how many requests a single server can handle is difficult. Just concentrate on the concept. If some nerdy type says your numbers are way off, nicely agree and walk away. Just don't invite them to any parties.

Load balancing means making a bunch of servers look like a single server, creating a *server cluster*. Not only do you need to make them look like one server, you need to make sure that requests to these servers are distributed evenly so no one server is bogged down while another is idle. There are a few ways to do this, as you are about to see. Be warned, not all of these methods require an advanced network device called a *load balancer*, but it's common to use one. Employing a device designed to do one thing really well is always much faster than using a general-purpose computer and slapping on software.

DNS Load Balancing

Using DNS for load balancing is one of the oldest and still very common ways to support multiple Web servers. In this case, each Web server gets its own (usually) public IP address. Each DNS server for the domain has multiple "A" DNS records, each with the same fully qualified domain name (FQDN). The DNS server then cycles around these records, so the same domain name resolves to different IP addresses. Figure 11.13 shows a DNS server with multiple A records for the same FQDN.

Now that the A records have been added, you need to tell the DNS server to cycle around these names. It should be fairly obvious where to do this. In a Windows DNS server, for example, you'll select a checkbox to do this, as shown in Figure 11.14.

When a computer comes to the DNS server for resolution, the server responds with all A records. Then next time DNS is queried, all A records are returned but in a different order. This is known as *round robin*.

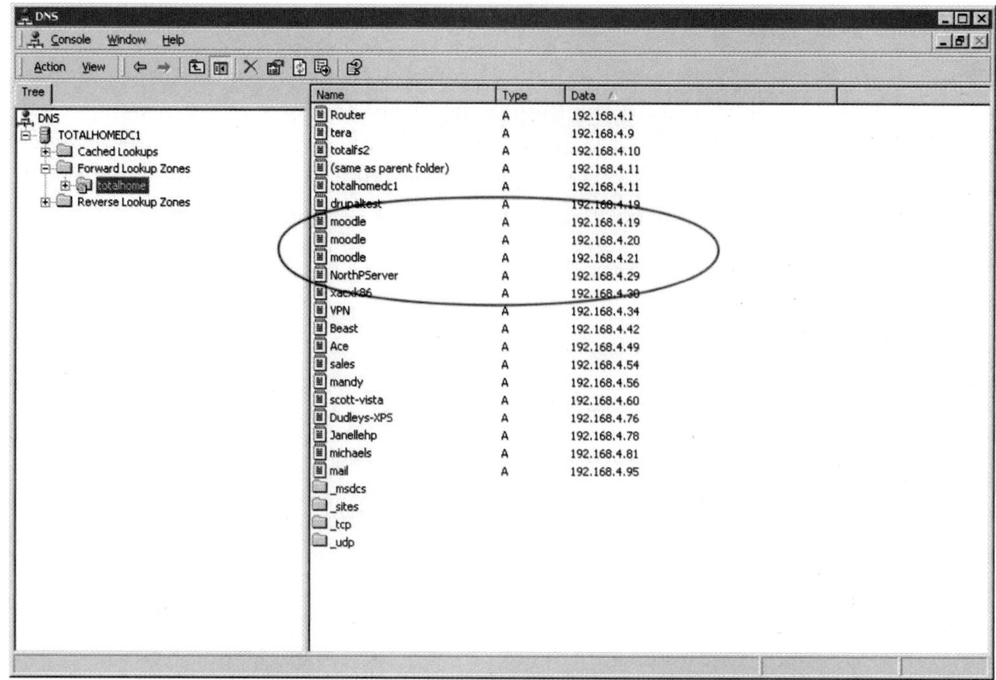

• **Figure 11.13** Multiple IP addresses, same name

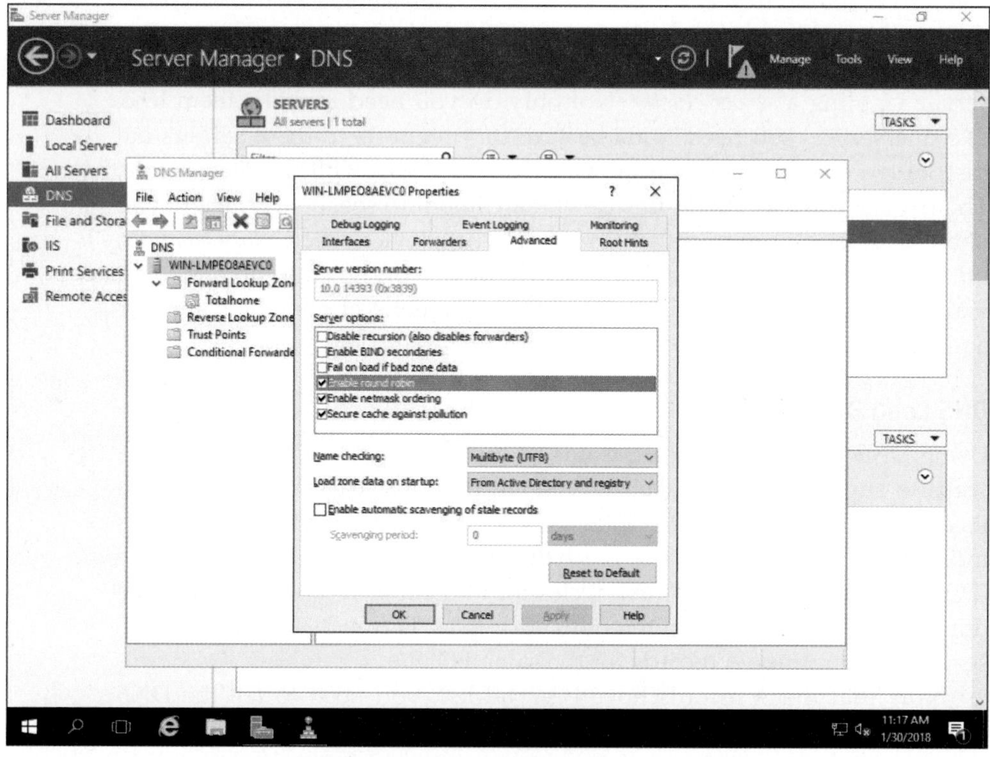

• **Figure 11.14** Enabling round robin

The popular BIND DNS server has a very similar process but adds even more power and features such as weighting one or more servers more than others or randomizing the DNS response.

Content Switch

Many multilayer switches handle load balancing by functioning at multiple layers. An alternative is a **content switch**. Content switches always work at Layer 7 (Application layer). Content switches designed to work with Web servers, for example, can read incoming HTTP and HTTPS requests. With this feature, you can perform very advanced actions, such as handling TLS certificates and cookies, on the content switch, removing the workload from the Web servers. Not only can these devices load balance in the ways previously described, but their HTTP savvy can actually pass a cookie to HTTP requesters—Web browsers—so the next time that client returns, it is sent to the same server.

QoS and Traffic Shaping

Just about any router you buy today has the capability to block packets based on port number or IP address, but these are simple mechanisms mainly designed to protect an internal network. What if you need to control how much of your bandwidth is used for certain devices or applications? In that case, you need **quality of service (QoS)** policies to prioritize traffic based on certain rules. These rules control how much bandwidth a protocol, PC, user, VLAN, or IP address may use. Figure 11.15 shows the QoS configuration on an Ubiquiti EdgeMAX router, what Ubiquiti calls *Smart Queue Management*.

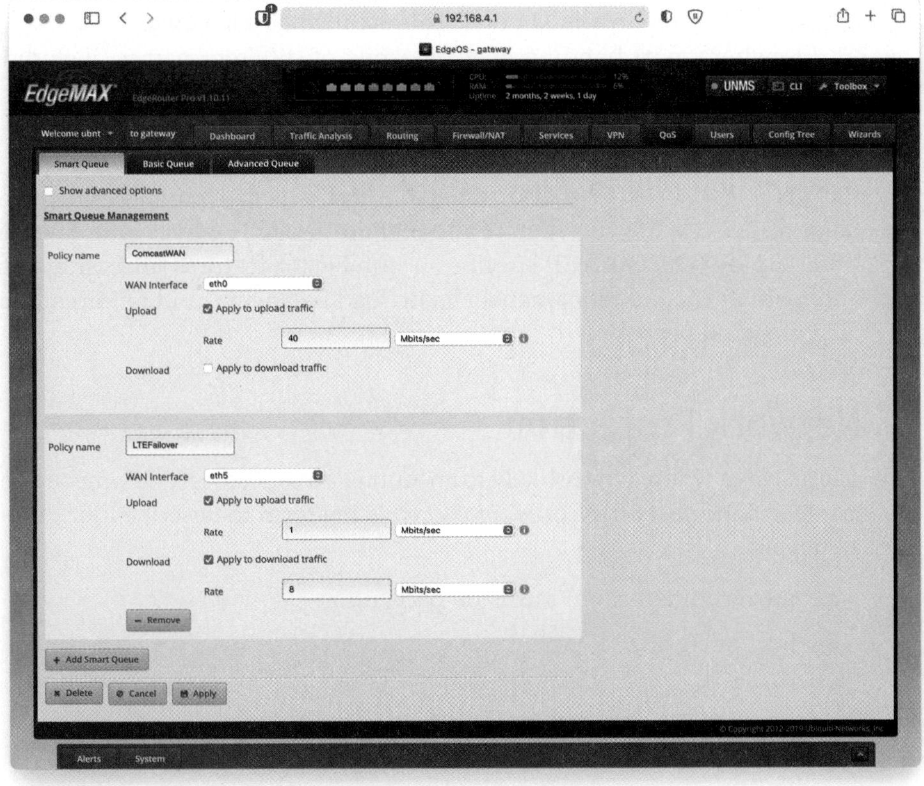

• **Figure 11.15** QoS configuration (Smart Queue Management) on a router

The term *bandwidth shaping* is synonymous with *traffic shaping.* The routers and switches that can implement traffic shaping are commonly referred to as *shapers.*

On many routers and switches, you can implement QoS through bandwidth management, such as **traffic shaping** where you control the flow of packets into or out of the network according to the type of packet or other rules.

Traffic shaping is very important when you must guarantee a device or application a certain amount of bandwidth and/or latency, such as with VoIP or video. Traffic shaping is also very popular in places such as schools, where IT professionals need to control user activities, such as limiting Web usage or blocking certain risky applications such as peer-to-peer file sharing.

Port Bonding

There are times when the data capacity of a connection between a switch and another device isn't enough to meet demand. Situations like these are encountered regularly in large data centers where tremendous amounts of data must be moved between racks of storage devices to vast numbers of users. Sometimes the solution is simple, like changing from a low-capacity standard like 100-megabit Ethernet to Gigabit Ethernet.

But there are other ways to achieve high-speed links between devices without having to upgrade the infrastructure. One of those ways is to join two or more connections' ports logically in a switch so that the resulting bandwidth is treated as a single connection and the throughput is multiplied by the number of linked connectors. All of the cables from the joined ports must go to the same device—another switch, a storage area network (SAN), a station, or whatever. That device must also support the logical joining of all of the involved ports. This is called **port bonding**.

Elsewhere, port bonding goes by a pile of different names, including *link aggregation, NIC bonding,* **NIC teaming**, **port aggregation**—the last two terms you'll see on the CompTIA Network+ exam—and a bunch of others. The Cisco protocol for accomplishing aggregation is called *Port Aggregation Protocol (PAgP).* You may also run across it in a very common implementation called **Link Aggregation Control Protocol (LACP)**, which is defined in IEEE 802.1AX-2020. LACP specifies a number of features and options to automate the negotiation, management, load balancing, and failure modes of aggregated ports.

Network Protection

The last area where you're likely to encounter advanced networking devices is network protection. *Network protection* is my term to describe four different areas:

- Intrusion detection/intrusion prevention
- Port mirroring
- Proxy serving
- AAA

Intrusion Detection/Intrusion Prevention

Intrusion detection and intrusion prevention detect that something has intruded into a network and then do something about it. Odds are good you've heard the term *firewall*. Firewalls are hardware or software tools that filter traffic based on various criteria, such as port number, IP address, or protocol. A firewall works at the border of your network, between the outside and the inside. (A *host-based firewall*, one installed on a single computer, similarly works on the border of that system.)

An **intrusion detection system (IDS)** is an application (often running on a dedicated IDS box) that inspects packets, looking for active intrusions. An IDS functions inside the network. A good IDS knows how to find attacks that a firewall might miss, such as viruses, illegal logon attempts, and other well-known attacks. Plus, because it inspects traffic inside the network, a good IDS can discover internal threats, like the activity of a vulnerability scanner smuggled in on a flash drive by a disgruntled worker planning an attack on an internal database server.

An IDS in promiscuous mode inspects a *copy* of every packet on a network. This placement outside the direct flow of traffic has three effects. First, there's a slight delay between something malicious hitting the network and the detection occurring. Second, there's no impact on network traffic flow. Third, if the IDS goes down, traffic keeps flowing normally.

An IDS always has some way to let the network administrators know if an attack is taking place: at the very least the attack is logged, but some IDSs offer a pop-up message, an e-mail, or even a text message to your phone.

An IDS can also respond to detected intrusions with action. The IDS can't stop the attack directly, but can request assistance from other devices—like a firewall—that can.

Modern IDS tools come in two flavors: network-based or host-based. A *network-based IDS (NIDS)* consists of multiple sensors placed around the network, often on one or both sides of the gateway router. These sensors report to a central application that, in turn, reads a signature file to detect anything out of the ordinary (Figure 11.16).

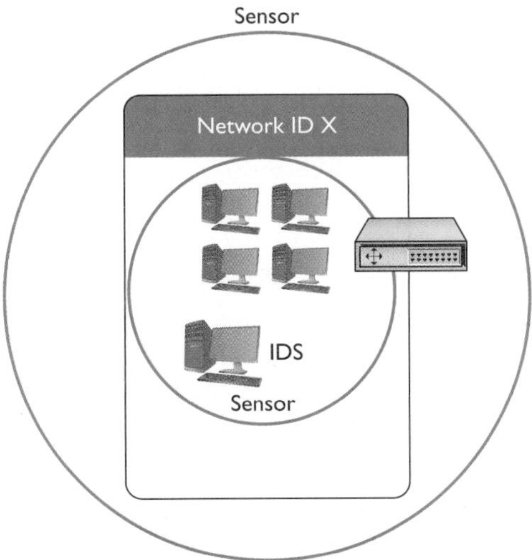

• **Figure 11.16** Diagram of network-based IDS

Different types of network traffic have detectable patterns, called *signatures*. Anti-malicious software (anti-malware) developers create *definition files*—collections of these signatures—for known malware. We'll see a lot more of this in Chapter 19, but for now note that many advanced networking devices can detect and filter traffic based on signatures.

A *host-based IDS (HIDS)* is software running on individual systems that monitors for events such as system file modification or registry changes (Figure 11.17). More expensive IDSs do all this and can provide a single reporting source—very handy when one person is in charge of everything that goes on throughout a network.

• **Figure 11.17** OSSEC HIDS

An **intrusion prevention system (IPS)** is very similar to an IDS, but an IPS sits directly in the flow of network traffic. This active monitoring has a trio of consequences. First, an IPS can stop an attack while it is happening. No need to request help from any other devices. Second, the network bandwidth and latency take a hit. Third, if the IPS goes down, the link might go down too.

Depending on what IPS product you choose, an IPS can block incoming packets on-the-fly based on IP address, port number, or application type. An IPS might go even further, literally fixing certain packets on-the-fly. A *host-based intrusion prevention system (HIPS)* is located on a host. As you might suspect, you can roll out an IPS on a network and it gets a new name: a *network-based intrusion prevention system (NIPS)*.

Port Mirroring

Many managed switches have the capability to copy data from any or all physical ports on a switch to a single physical port. This is called **port mirroring**. It's as though you make a customized, fully configurable promiscuous port. Port mirroring is incredibly useful for any type of situation where an administrator needs to inspect packets coming to or from certain computers.

There are two forms of port mirroring: local and remote. Local port mirroring copies data from one or more ports on a single switch to a specific port on that switch. To monitor this data, you have to plug directly into the switch with ports being monitored. Remote port mirroring enables you to access data copied from one or more specific ports on a switch without plugging directly into that switch.

Port mirroring isn't the only way to duplicate network traffic for monitoring and troubleshooting. You can also use a standalone *network tap*. (Some sources use TAP as an acronym for Traffic Access Port or Test Access Port.) These multi-port hardware devices literally copy 100% of the bits that they see—even errors—and send them out separate ports for monitoring. You'll see them in scenarios that require non-obtrusive data collection.

Some advantages of a tap over a mirrored port are that the tap will perform better under high load and won't require you to give up scarce switch ports. Plus, they're invisible to detection, because they have no MAC address or IP address.

Proxy Serving

A **proxy server** sits in between clients and external servers, essentially pocketing the requests from the clients for server resources and making those requests itself. The client computers never touch the outside servers and thus stay protected from any unwanted activity. A proxy server usually *does something* to those requests as well. Let's see how proxy servers work using HTTP, one of the oldest uses of proxy servers.

Since proxy serving works by redirecting client requests to a proxy server, you first must tell the Web client not to use the usual DNS resolution to determine the Web server and instead to use a proxy. Every Web client comes with a program that enables you to set the IP address of the proxy server, as shown in the example in Figure 11.18.

Once the proxy server is configured, HTTP requests move from the client directly to the proxy server. Built into every HTTP request is the URL of the target Web server, so the Web proxy knows where to get the requested data once it gets the request. In the simplest format, the proxy server simply forwards the requests using its own IP address and then forwards the returning packets to the client (Figure 11.19).

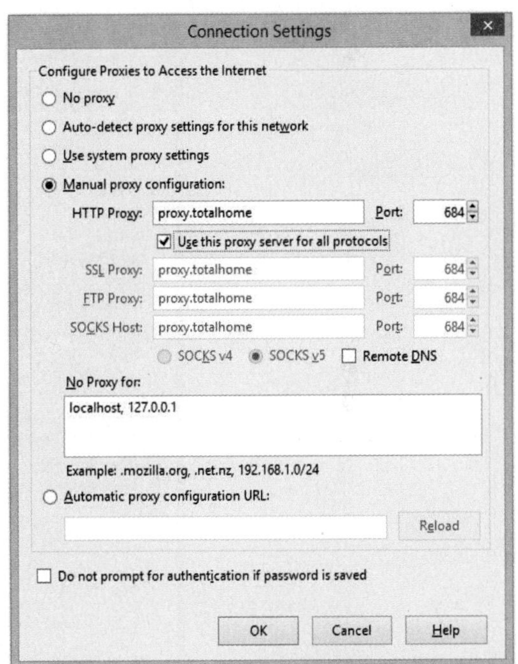

• **Figure 11.18** Setting a proxy server in Mozilla Firefox

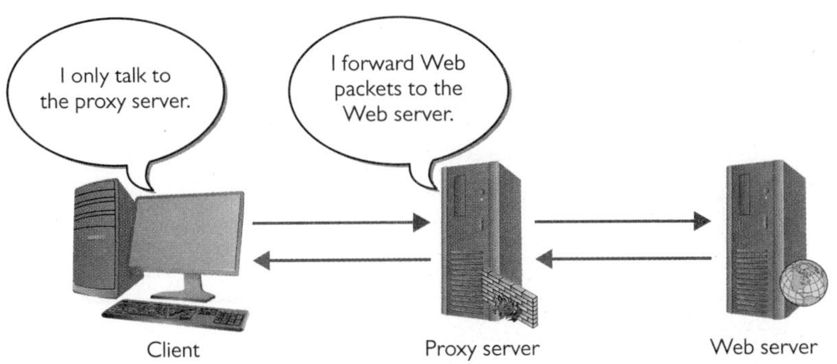

• **Figure 11.19** Web proxy at work

This simple version of using a proxy server prevents the Web server from knowing where the client is located—a handy trick for those who wish to keep people from knowing where they are coming from, assuming you can find a public proxy server that accepts your HTTP requests (there are plenty!). There are many other good reasons to use a proxy server. One big benefit is caching. A proxy server keeps a copy of the served resource, giving clients a much faster response.

Tech Tip

Proxy Caching

If a proxy server caches a Web page, how does it know if the cache accurately reflects the real page? What if the real Web page was updated? In this case, a good proxy server uses querying tools to check the real Web page to update the cache. The benefit of a caching proxy is that content can be retrieved without contacting sites over WAN links.

A **forward proxy server** acts on behalf of clients, getting information from various sources and handing that info to the clients. The sources (servers) don't know about the clients, only the proxy server.

A **reverse proxy server**, in contrast, acts on behalf of its servers. Clients contact the reverse proxy server, which gathers information from its associated server(s) and hands that information to the clients. The clients don't know about the servers behind the scenes. The reverse proxy server is the only machine with which they interact.

A proxy server might inspect the contents of the resource, looking for inappropriate content, viruses/malware, or just about anything else the creators of the proxy might desire it to identify.

HTTP proxy servers are the most common type of proxy server, but any TCP application can take advantage of proxy servers. Numerous proxy serving programs are available, such as Squid, shown in Figure 11.20. Proxy serving takes some substantial processing, so many vendors sell proxy servers in an integrated hardware solution, such as Broadcom's Symantec Secure Web Gateway Appliance.

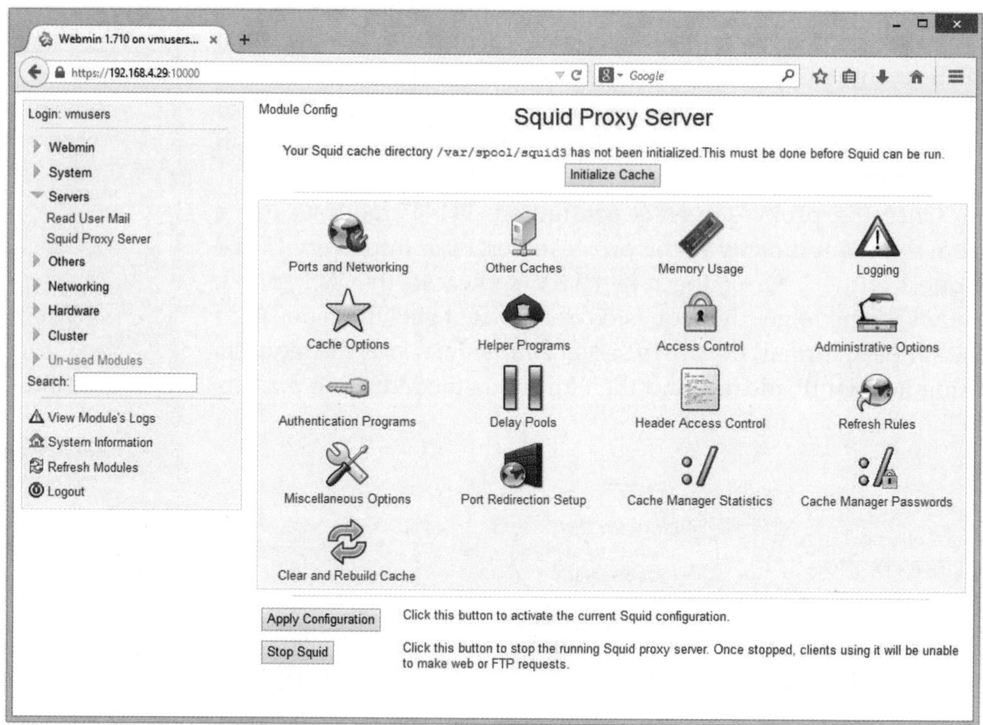

• **Figure 11.20** Squid Proxy Server software

Cross Check

AAA

You learned about AAA in Chapter 10, so cross-check your memory: Which jobs do they do to help lock down a TCP/IP network properly?

AAA

Authentication, Authorization, and Accounting (AAA—pronounce it "triple A"), as you'll recall from Chapter 10, are vitally important for security on switches to support **port authentication**. Port authentication gives us a way to protect our network from unwanted people trying to access the network. Let's say that someone wants to bypass network security by bringing in a laptop and plugging the Ethernet connection straight into a switch port, or using that same laptop to connect wirelessly into one of the network wireless access points (WAPs). To prevent these types of intrusions, we use intelligent switches that support AAA.

When someone attempts a connection, he or she must have something at the point of connection to authenticate, and that's where advanced networking devices come into play. Many switches, and almost every WAP, come with feature sets to support port authentication. My routers support RADIUS and 802.1X port authentication.

Configuring a switch for AAA is arguably one of the most complex configuration jobs a network tech may ever face. Before you get anywhere near the switch, you'll need to make a number of decisions, such as the version of AAA you want to use (RADIUS or TACACS+), the type of 802.1X authentication methods you will use (passwords, certificates, retina scanners), deciding on and setting up the authentication database system, and opening up security policies to make sure it all works. This list is long, to say the least.

Once your AAA infrastructure is set up, you then configure a AAA-capable switch to support one or more methods of authentication. This is complicated too! There are ten flavors and "subflavors" of authentication supported by Cisco, for example, ranging from simple passwords to a local database to a RADIUS server and a TACACS+ server.

One of the really cool things about switch- and router-level authentication is the ability to fall back or fail over to a "next method" of authentication. You can configure as many fallback methods as you like, as long as the method is supported by the switch you configure. The system attempts to authenticate using the first method in a list. If that first method isn't available (for instance, if the RADIUS server is down), it reverts to the second method in the list, and so forth.

Try This!

Exploring Switch Capabilities

If you have access to a managed switch of any kind, now would be a great time to explore its capabilities. Use a Web browser of choice and navigate to the switch. What can you configure? Do you see any options for proxy serving, load balancing, or other fancy capability? How could you optimize your network by using some of these more advanced capabilities?

Chapter 11 Review

Chapter Summary

After reading this chapter and completing the exercises, you should understand the following about networking devices.

Define the capabilities and management of managed switches

- You can manage switches by directly connecting via a serial console interface, or by accessing the terminal via a terminal emulator or Web interface.
- In-band management means to access the switch over a network. Out-of-band management refers to accessing the switch without also accessing the active LAN.
- You can configure modern switches to support older devices, such as forcing a port from autosensing to a lower speed (like 10 Mbps) or half duplex. This support for older devices can be useful in specific circumstances, but is increasingly irrelevant on anything other than a CompTIA exam. You can also configure features such as flow control and jumbo frames to address some situational issues with network throughput.

Configure and deploy VLANs

- A VLAN takes a single physical broadcast domain and splits it into multiple virtual broadcast domains, thereby reducing broadcast traffic.
- Trunking enables VLANs to work across multiple switches, so that multiple computers on the same LAN, but connected to different physical switches, can be members of the same VLAN.
- A trunk port carries all traffic, regardless of VLAN number, between all switches on a LAN. Today, every Ethernet switch prefers the IEEE 802.1Q trunk standard, enabling you to connect switches from different manufacturers.
- Many switches can be configured for VLANs via a console port connection, but the most common method is to log into the switch using SSH and use the command-line interface.
- Once the VLANs have been created on the switches, the next step is to assign switch ports to VLANs (static VLANs). This process is called VLAN assignment.
- Tagging enables messages to get to their proper destination. It lets trunk ports know which VLAN a frame belongs to.
- Switches running Cisco VTP can be set in client mode to update automatically when a switch set to server mode is updated.
- VLAN-capable multilayer switches also do routing, connecting different VLANs.
- A DHCP relay can enable a single DHCP server to serve clients separated by routers.
- Unlike data VLANs, voice VLANs prioritize voice traffic to ensure smooth communication.
- Private VLANs isolate hosts from each other, limiting their ability to see each other's traffic and communicate.

Implement advanced switch features

- A multilayer switch is one that operates at multiple layers of the OSI model, such as the Juniper EX3400 switch that functions at both Layer 2 and Layer 3.
- Layer 2 switches forward frames based on MAC addresses, whereas Layer 3 switches—routers—forward packets based on IP addresses.
- Load balancing involves configuring multiple servers to look like a single server, allowing multiple servers to handle requests sent to a single IP address. Additionally, load balancing spreads

the requests evenly across all the servers so that no one system is bogged down.

- With DNS load balancing, each Web server receives a unique IP address because the DNS servers hold multiple A records, each with the same FQDN, for each Web server. The DNS server then returns the IP addresses of all A records to requestors in different order for each new request so the same domain name resolves to different IP addresses.
- A content switch provides load balancing by reading the HTTP and HTTPS requests and acting upon them, taking the workload off the Web servers.
- Quality of service (QoS) sets priorities for how much bandwidth is used for certain protocols, PCs, users, VLANs, IP addresses, or other devices or applications. This is often implemented through traffic shaping.
- Port bonding, or link aggregation, enables you to join together two or more ports in a switch to improve bandwidth. A common implementation of port bonding is Link Aggregation Control Protocol (LACP).
- An intrusion detection system (IDS) inspects a copy of every packet on the network and actively monitors for attacks. A network-based IDS (NIDS) typically consists of sensors on one or both sides of the gateway router, whereas a host-based IDS (HIDS) consists of monitoring software installed on individual computers.
- An intrusion prevention system (IPS) proactively monitors for attacks and then reacts if an attack is identified. An IPS sits directly in the flow of network traffic. HIPS are host-based solutions; NIPS are network-based solutions.
- Port mirroring mirrors data from any or all physical ports on a switch to a single physical port, making it easy for administrators to inspect packets to or from certain computers.
- A proxy server intercepts client requests and acts upon them, usually by blocking the request or forwarding the request to other servers.
- Many switches support port authentication, a feature that requires network devices to authenticate themselves, protecting your network from rogue devices.

Key Terms

802.1Q *(311)*
access port *(313)*
console port *(307)*
content switch *(319)*
DHCP relay *(315)*
forward proxy server *(324)*
in-band management *(308)*
inter-VLAN routing *(314)*
intrusion detection system (IDS) *(321)*
intrusion prevention system (IPS) *(322)*
IP helper *(315)*
Link Aggregation Control Protocol (LACP) *(320)*
load balancing *(317)*
managed switch *(307)*
multilayer switch *(316)*
native VLAN *(313)*
NIC teaming *(320)*
out-of-band management *(308)*
port aggregation *(320)*
port authentication *(325)*
port bonding *(320)*
port mirroring *(323)*
port security *(309)*
proxy server *(323)*
quality of service (QoS) *(319)*
reverse proxy server *(324)*
traffic shaping *(320)*
trunk port *(311)*
trunking *(311)*
virtual local area network (VLAN) *(310)*
VLAN Trunking Protocol (VTP) *(314)*

Key Term Quiz

Use the Key Terms list to complete the sentences that follow. Not all terms will be used.

1. A(n) ______________ services client requests and forwards them to the appropriate server.
2. ______________ allows multiple VLANs to work across multiple switches.
3. The process of passing traffic between two VLANs is called ______________.
4. Routers that enable you to set QoS often use ______________ to limit the amount of bandwidth used by certain devices or applications.
5. Creating a(n) ______________ helps to reduce Layer 2 broadcast traffic by separating the one large broadcast domain into smaller ones, but it requires the use of a special switch.
6. Although it functions at Layer 2, you can connect to a(n) ______________ for configuration of things like VLANs.
7. Switches use the ______________ trunk standard to enable connection of switches from different manufacturers.
8. The VLAN designation for a trunk port is its ______________.
9. Maria has concerns about the nature of the traffic coming to and from a specific workstation. She can copy all that traffic by ______________.
10. Eduardo sets the priority of various packet types by implementing ______________.

Multiple-Choice Quiz

1. Which of the following enables direct access to configure a managed switch?
   - **A.** Console port
   - **B.** End port
   - **C.** Manage port
   - **D.** Switch port
2. Eduardo accesses a managed switch from his desktop computer on the far side of the campus. What type of access management enables this connection?
   - **A.** In-band management
   - **B.** LAN-band management
   - **C.** Out-of-band management
   - **D.** WAN-band management
3. Jellystone Industrial has recently upgraded a switch from Fast Ethernet to Gigabit Ethernet, but now the old large-sheet printer won't connect over the network. It worked with the old switch. What could Edith do to enable the printer to connect? (It's physically connected to port 7 on the switch.)
   - **A.** Access the managed switch and change the switch port settings for port 7 from Automatic to Full Duplex.
   - **B.** Access the managed switch and change the switch port settings for port 7 from Automatic to 1000 Mbps.
   - **C.** Access the managed switch and change the switch port settings for port 7 from Automatic to 100 Mbps.
   - **D.** Access the managed switch and change the switch port settings for port 7 from Automatic to 10 Mbps.

4. What is one benefit of a VLAN?
   A. It allows remote users to connect to a local network via the Internet.
   B. It reduces broadcast traffic on a LAN.
   C. It can create a WAN from multiple disjointed LANs.
   D. It provides encryption services on networks that have no default encryption protocol.
5. What type of port carries all traffic, regardless of VLAN ID, between all switches in a LAN?
   A. Access port
   B. Egress port
   C. Transport port
   D. Trunk port
6. Into which type of port should you plug a host into a VLAN switch?
   A. Access port
   B. Proxy port
   C. Trunk port
   D. VLAN port
7. Rashan's company has multiple servers from which remote users download files. What should Rashan implement on his servers to make them appear as a single server so that they receive similar amounts of requests?
   A. Load balancing
   B. Port authentication
   C. Port mirroring
   D. Trunking
8. Which function enables members of the same VLAN on different switches to communicate with each other?
   A. Content switching
   B. Port authentication
   C. Port mirroring
   D. Trunking
9. What is true of a multilayer switch?
   A. It can work at multiple OSI layers at the same time.
   B. It can work with one of several OSI layers at a time, depending on its configuration mode. Working at a different layer requires making a configuration change and resetting the switch.
   C. It can communicate with other switches that work at different OSI layers.
   D. It has twice the ports of a standard switch because it contains two regular switches, one stacked on top of the other.
10. Which IEEE protocol enables port bonding?
    A. LACP
    B. PAgP
    C. 802.1Q
    D. 802.1X
11. What are the benefits of caching on a Web proxy? (Select two.)
    A. Response time
    B. Virus detection
    C. Behavior-based scanning
    D. Authentication
12. Which are effective methods of implementing load balancing? (Select two.)
    A. Content switching
    B. DNS round robin
    C. Traffic shaping
    D. Proxy serving
13. Employees in the sales department complain that the network runs slowly when employees in the art department copy large graphics files across the network. What solution might increase network speed for the sales department?
    A. DNS load balancing
    B. Content switching
    C. Traffic shaping
    D. 802.1Q

14. Which of the following statements best applies to an IDS?

    A. An IDS inspects a copy of all traffic in a network and can respond to detected intrusions with actions.

    B. An IDS inspects all traffic as it enters a network and can respond to detected intrusions with actions.

    C. An IDS inspects a copy of all traffic in a network and reports intrusions to a configured user account.

    D. An IDS inspects all traffic as it enters a network and reports intrusions to a configured user account.

15. Allison wants to add a layer of protection to her network. She wants to actively monitor all network traffic and act immediately to stop any attacks. What should she install?

    A. Firewall

    B. IDS

    C. IPS

    D. NIDS

Essay Quiz

1. Your boss is becoming increasingly worried about hacking attempts on the company Web server. Write a letter explaining the various options for protecting against, and reacting to, attacks.

Lab Projects

• Lab Project 11.1

You have read quite a bit in this chapter about securing networks against attacks. Research at least three intrusion prevention systems and create a matrix comparing them. Include comparisons of features, cost, reliability, network/operating system support, and general user reviews.

• Lab Project 11.2

Your boss wants to reduce broadcast traffic and asks you to segment the network into multiple VLANs. Use your favorite e-commerce Web site for purchasing computer and networking devices and find at least three switches that support VLANs. Create a matrix comparing features and cost. Based on your research, which VLAN switch would you recommend to your employer and why?

chapter 12 IPv6

"Give a man a fish and he will eat for a day. Teach a man to fish and he will eat for a lifetime. Teach a man to create an artificial shortage of fish and he will eat steak."

—Jay Leno

In this chapter, you will learn how to

- **Discuss the fundamental concepts of IPv6**
- **Describe IPv6 practices**
- **Implement IPv6 in a TCP/IP network**

The Internet developers wanted to make a networking protocol that had serious longevity, so they had to define a large enough IP address space to last well beyond the foreseeable future. They had to determine how many computers might exist in the future and then make the IP address space even bigger. But how many computers would exist in the future? Keep in mind that TCP/IP development took place in the early 1970s. There were fewer than 1000 computers in the entire world at the time, but that didn't keep the IP developers from thinking big! They decided to go absolutely crazy (as many people considered at the time) and around 1979 created the **Internet Protocol version 4 (IPv4)** 32-bit IP address space, creating about four billion IP addresses. That should have held us for the foreseeable future.

It didn't. First, the TCP/IP folks wasted huge chunks of IP addresses due to classful addressing and a generally easygoing, wasteful method of parceling out IP addresses. Second, the Internet reached a level of popularity way beyond the original developers' imaginations. By the late 1980s the rate of consumption for IP addresses started to worry the Internet people and the writing was on the wall for IPv4's 32-bit addressing.

As a result, the Internet Engineering Task Force (IETF) developed the **Internet Protocol version 6 (IPv6)** addressing system. IPv6 extended the 32-bit IP address space to 128 bits, allowing up to 2^{128} (that's close to 3.4×10^{38}) addresses. Take all the grains of sand on earth and that will give you an idea of how big a number that is.

If you really want to know how many IP addresses IPv6 provides, here's your number: 340,282,366,920,938,463,463,374,607,431,768,211,456. Yes, that's 340 *undecillion*.

IPv6 has been the future of TCP/IP network addressing since the IETF published the IPv6 draft standard in 1995. Someday, we knew, we'd flip the switch from IPv4 to IPv6 and transform the Internet and TCP/IP networking forever. That switch started flipping rapidly in 2017. All the major ISPs in Japan, for example, deployed IPv6 in 2017. Mobile device networks and the Internet of Things (IoT) are all IPv6. The rollout and changes are happening throughout the globe as I type these words. And it's not just the ISPs flipping to IPv6.

As you read through this exam guide, more and more companies are making the switch from IPv4 to IPv6. This is very much cost driven, because you have to pay for addresses separately. Why roll out IPv4 today when IPv6 is ready to roll now and for the foreseeable future?

This chapter breaks the exploration of IPv6 into three parts. First, you need the basic concepts, such as how the numbers work. Second, you need to learn how to implement IPv6 in a variety of technologies, such as Dynamic Host Configuration Protocol (DHCP). Finally, you need answers on how to deploy IPv6 in a world where IPv4 is still alive and kicking.

Test Specific

IPv6 Concepts

Although they achieve the same function—enabling computers on IP networks to send packets to each other—IPv6 and IPv4 differ a lot where the rubber meets the road. The addresses work differently and don't look alike. IPv6 *always* uses link-local addressing for communicating on a local network. (The IPv4 version of an automatically generated local address, APIPA/zeroconf—169.254.0.0/16—usually means something's wrong!) Subnetting works differently as well. You also need to understand the concepts of **multicast**, global addresses, and neighbor discovery. Let's look at all these topics.

IPv6 Addresses

Up until now, you've been used to looking at IPv4's dotted decimal notation, with four simple numbers and three periods, like 10.11.12.13. But IPv6 moves from 32 bits to 128 bits—and a whole new way to write addresses.

At first, these addresses may look a little foreign. Instead of just making every address four times as long, designers of IPv6 worked out a number of ways to make the human form of each address—its *notation*—short enough for techs to work with. It'll take a bit of work to get used to reading IPv6 addresses, so buckle up!

You'll see the hexadecimal letters in IPv6 written both uppercase and lowercase. It doesn't matter to the computer, but the people behind IPv6 insist (per RFC 5952) that notation should be lowercase. That's the convention used here. You might see the letters uppercase on the CompTIA Network+ exam. It's all the same, so don't get thrown off!

IPv6 Address Notation

The 32-bit IPv4 addresses are written as 197.169.94.82, using four octets. IPv6 has 128 bits, so octets are gone. IPv6 addresses are written like this:

```
2001:0db8:0000:0000:0800:200c:00cf:1234
```

IPv6 uses a colon as a separator, instead of the period used in IPv4's dotted decimal format. Each 16-bit group—called a *quartet* or *hextet*—is a hexadecimal number between 0000 and ffff.

For those who don't play with hex regularly, one hexadecimal character (for example, *f*) represents 4 bits; so four hexadecimal characters make a 16-bit group.

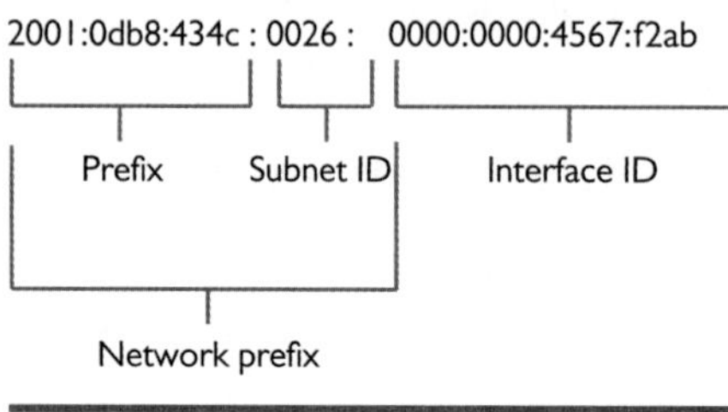

• **Figure 12.1** Typical IPv6 address components

An IPv6 address generally splits into two 64-bit sections: the **network prefix** is the first 64 bits and is used for routing. The second 64 bits is the user portion, called the **interface ID**. The network prefix further gets broken into a **routing prefix** and a **subnet ID**, as depicted in Figure 12.1 (I've added space between the sections for emphasis).

A complete IPv6 address always has eight groups of four hexadecimal characters. If this sounds like you're going to type in really long IP addresses, don't worry, IPv6 offers a *shorthand notation* that provides shortcuts.

First, leading zeroes can be dropped from any group, so 00cf becomes cf, 0db8 becomes db8, and 0000 becomes 0. Let's rewrite that IPv6 address using this shortcut:

```
2001:db8:0:0:800:200c:cf:1234
```

To write IPv6 addresses containing strings of zeroes, you can use a pair of colons (::) to represent one or more consecutive groups with a value of zero. For example, using the :: rule, you can write the IPv6 address

```
2001:db8:0:0:800:200c:cf:1234
```

as

```
2001:db8::800:200c:cf:1234
```

Double colons are very handy, but you have to be careful when you use them. Take a look at this IPv6 address:

```
fe80:0000:0000:0000:00cf:0000:ba98:1234
```

It can be converted as such:

```
fe80::cf:0:ba98:1234
```

Note that you *cannot* use a second :: to represent the last group of four zeroes—only one :: is allowed per address! There's a good reason for this rule. If more than one :: was used, how could you tell how many sets of zeroes were in each group? Answer: you couldn't.

IPv6 uses the "/*x*" **prefix length** naming convention to specify the number of bits in the network ID, similar to the Classless Inter-Domain Routing (CIDR) naming convention in IPv4. Here's how to write an IP address and prefix length for a typical IPv6 host:

```
fe80::cf:0:ba98:1234/64
```

The /64 tells the reader that the network prefix is 64 bits. The address starts with fe80 followed by some number of hextets of all zeroes: 0000. With the /64, you know to make the prefix thus:

```
fe80:0000:0000:0000
```

Here's an example of a very special IPv6 address that takes full advantage of the double colon, the IPv6 loopback address:

```
::1
```

Without using the double-colon notation, this IPv6 address would look like this:

```
0000:0000:0000:0000:0000:0000:0000:0001
```

The unspecified address (all zeroes) can never be used, and neither can an address that contains all ones (all *f*s in IPv6 notation).

Cross Check

Loopback

You learned about the IPv4 loopback address in Chapter 6, so check your memory as you read about the IPv6 loopback address here. What IP address or addresses could you use for a loopback address? When might you ping the loopback address? How would this differ from loopback testing, discussed in Chapter 5?

Although only the fe80::/10 denotes the link-local address, according to the Request for Comments that defined link-local addressing (RFC 4291), the next 54 bits have to be zeroes. That means in implementation, a link-local address will start with fe80::/64.

Link-Local Address

The folks who created IPv6 worked hard to make it powerful and easy to use, but you pretty much have to forget all the rules you learned about IPv4 addressing. The biggest item to wrap your mind around is that a host no longer has a single IP address unless the network isn't connected to a router. When a computer running IPv6 first boots up, it gives itself a **link-local address**. Think of a link-local address as IPv6's equivalent to IPv4's APIPA/zeroconf address. The first 64 bits of a link-local address are always fe80::/10, followed by 54 zero bits. That means every link-local address always begins with fe80:0000:0000:0000.

The second 64 bits of a link-local address, the interface ID, are generated in two ways. First, most consumer-oriented operating systems generate a 64-bit random number (Figure 12.2). Older operating systems (and also devices where this privacy is less critical) may use the

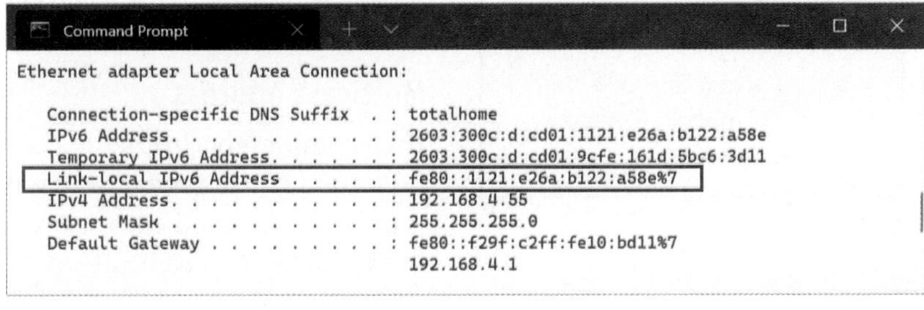

Command Prompt
Ethernet adapter Local Area Connection:
Connection-specific DNS Suffix . : totalhome
IPv6 Address. . . . . : 2603:300c:d:cd01:1121:e26a:b122:a58e
Temporary IPv6 Address. . . . . . : 2603:300c:d:cd01:9cfe:161d:5bc6:3d11
Link-local IPv6 Address . . . . . : fe80::1121:e26a:b122:a58e%7
IPv4 Address. . . . . : 192.168.4.55
Subnet Mask . . . . : 255.255.255.0
Default Gateway . . . . : fe80::f29f:c2ff:fe10:bd11%7
192.168.4.1

• **Figure 12.2** Link-local address in Windows

device's MAC address to create a 64-bit number called an **Extended Unique Identifier, 64-bit (EUI-64)**.

The link-local address does much of the hard work in IPv6, and, as long as you don't need an Internet connection, it's all you need. The old concepts of static and DHCP addressing don't really make much sense in IPv6 unless you have dedicated servers (even in IPv6, servers generally still have static IP addresses). Link-local addressing takes care of all your local network needs!

Link-local addressing appears on the CompTIA Network+ exam objectives as a standalone, non-hyphenated term, i.e., *link local*. If you're comparing IPv4 vs. IPv6, the automatically generated addresses show lack of DHCP server connectivity (APIPA/zeroconf) in the former, standard behavior in the latter.

Global Unicast Address

A system's IPv6 link-local address is a **unicast address**: a unique address exclusive to that system. To get on the Internet, devices need a second unicast address, often referred to as a "global address." A **global unicast address** is a fully routable public address (see Figure 12.3) that supports two-way connectivity between a device and the world (unless a firewall has anything to say about it). We'll take a closer look at the different ways a device can get its global address in the "IPv6 Implementations" section.

Tech Tip

Regional Internet Registries

Just like with globally routable IPv4 addresses, IANA manages IPv6 prefixes. It doesn't directly pass them out, though. It delegates this job to the five Regional Internet Registries (RIRs):

- American Registry for Internet Numbers (ARIN) *supports North America and many Caribbean and North Atlantic islands.*
- RIPE Network Coordination Centre (RIPE NCC) *supports Europe, the Middle East, and Central Asia.*
- Asia-Pacific Network Information Centre (APNIC) *supports Asia and the Pacific region.*
- Latin American and Caribbean Internet Addresses Registry (LACNIC) *supports Central and South America and parts of the Caribbean.*
- African Network Information Centre (AFRINIC) *supports Africa.*

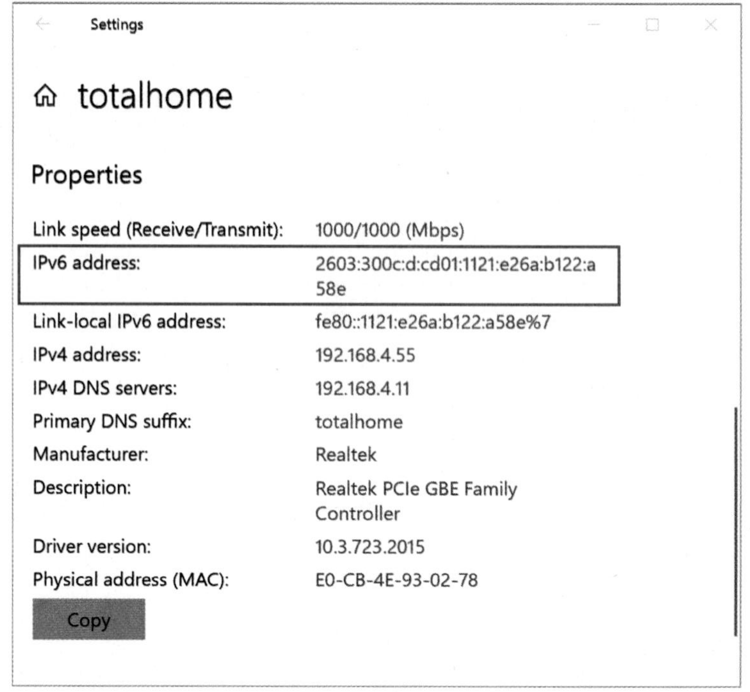

• **Figure 12.3** IPv6 global address on Windows 10

Multicast Address

IPv6 completely drops the concept of a broadcast address used in IPv4, in favor of a **multicast address**, where a single computer sends a message to a group of interested computers. IPv6 multicast addresses are a little surprising because they're built up from independent parts. This section focuses more on well-known multicast addresses than on these independent parts, but seeing how they work first may help.

IPv4 networks use broadcast and multicast addresses. IPv6 networks use the latter but not the former.

If an IPv6 system sends out a multicast to the address ff02::2, for example, only routers read the message while everyone else ignores it (Figure 12.4). The first "2" in this address is an independent part indicating that the *scope* of this message is the local network segment, and the last "2" indicates that it should go to the *group* of routers within that scope. (The group can be indicated by more than one hex digit. This is just an example.) Scope roughly means how widely or narrowly the message should be spread, while the group means what kind of hosts should listen. A multicast to ff08::02 is also intended for all routers—but over the much-wider scope of the entire organization.

The Ethernet address (MAC address) for IPv6 multicast traffic is 33-33-*xx-xx-xx-xx*. Here's a bit of geeky trivia for you. Why 33-33? Xerox PARC (Palo Alto Research Center), the birthplace of Ethernet and many other networking technologies used today, is at 3333 Coyote Hill Road.

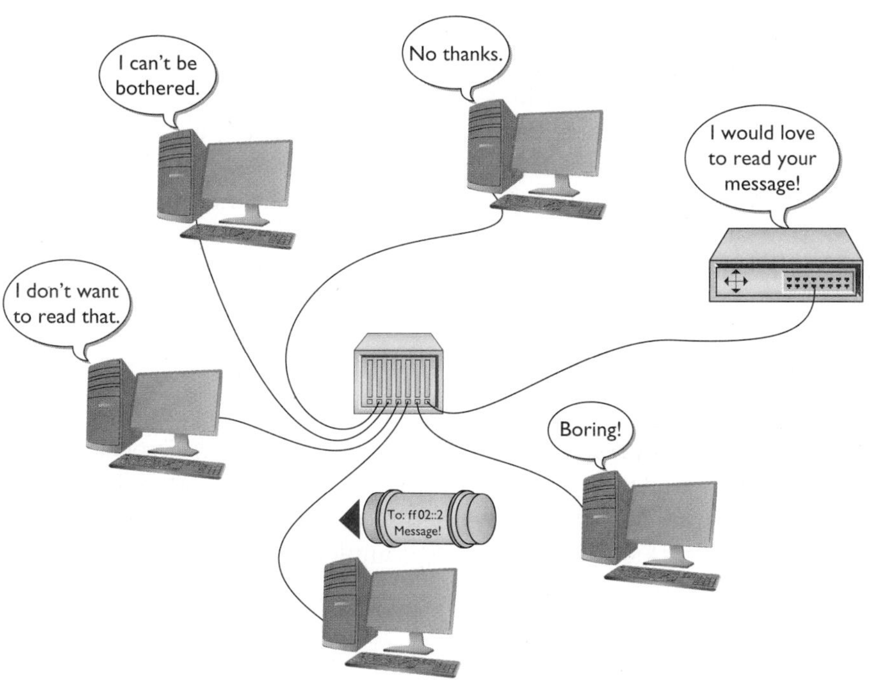

• **Figure 12.4** Multicast to routers

Every computer sees the multicast traffic, but they only take action on packets that are addressed to multicast groups to which they belong. Table 12.1 shows a few of the more useful IPv6 multicast addresses.

Table 12.1 A Few IPv6 Multicast Addresses

Address	Function
ff02::1	All-nodes multicast address
ff02::2	All-routers multicast address
ff02::1:ff*xx:xxxx*	Solicited-node multicast address (with variable hex digits)

Looking at the first listing, ff02::1, you might ask: "How is that different from a broadcast?" The answer lies more in the definition of multicast than in what really takes place. A computer must be configured as a member of a particular group to read a particular multicast. In the case of ff02::1, all systems on the network are members—a packet sent to that address will be much like a IPv4 broadcast. That same packet sent to ff02::2 will only reach routers on the network. These addresses become important in the upcoming discussion of the Neighbor Discovery Protocol.

Anycast Address

Beyond unicast and multicast, IPv6 also supports **anycast** addressing. An anycast address is a bit of a strange animal because it is a single IP address shared by multiple hosts. Routers are configured to direct traffic destined for that single address to the closest system based on what routing metrics were chosen by the network designers.

A common use for anycast addresses is in a globe-spanning content delivery network (CDN). These networks use servers placed in cities around the world to cache content—like videos for Netflix or YouTube—so that people can binge their favorite series from a data center just up the road. The CDN's servers share an anycast address. Then all the routers between you and the content will see that they can direct your request for that show to the CDN server in your city and not the one on the other side of the world. When it works like it's supposed to, the routers between your device and the content provider dynamically direct your traffic to a nearby server.

Neighbor Discovery

You'll see the term **neighbor discovery** in documentation about uses of the Neighbor Discovery Protocol. You'll also see the term on the CompTIA Network+ exam.

All the NDP control message types are encapsulated in a single packet, thus many techs use shorthand here and call each one of these a "packet type."

Just like with IPv4, IPv6 needs a utility protocol to do the low-level work of determining the Layer 2 MAC addresses that correspond to specific Layer 3 IPv6 addresses and performing other utility functions on the network. In IPv4, this protocol is ARP (as described in Chapter 6), and in IPv6 it is the **Neighbor Discovery Protocol (NDP)**. NDP is implemented using IPv6's version of ICMP—you guessed it: ICMPv6. NDP performs many of the same functions as IPv4 ARP, but does more as well.

NDP has five control message types: neighbor solicitation, neighbor advertisement, router solicitation, router advertisement, and redirect. Let's take a quick look at each.

Neighbor Solicitation

The **neighbor solicitation** message is part of this ARP-alike functionality. Hosts use these messages to request the MAC address of a target system, to inform the target system of their own MAC address, and to verify a system is still reachable. As you'll see later, these neighbor solicitations help IPv6 hosts detect duplicate addresses on the local network.

When a host needs to find the MAC address of a system it does not know, it sends a neighbor solicitation packet to the solicited-node multicast address. (This address is specified as ff02::1:ff*xx*:*xxxx*, where the last six digits of the multicast address are the last six hex digits of the corresponding unicast address.) When a host just wants to verify a neighbor is still reachable, it sends the message directly via unicast.

Neighbor Advertisement

Two things happen when a host receives a neighbor solicitation. The host adds the MAC address of the sending system to its **neighbor discovery cache**—a holding spot for such information, the equivalent of an ARP cache—because the sending system is clearly a reachable neighbor. The host also sends a

neighbor advertisement in response to a neighbor solicitation. The response tells the requesting system the MAC address of the system it solicited—and that this system is reachable. The advertiser responds directly to the soliciting system via unicast. The original sender adds the recipient's MAC address to its neighbor discovery cache.

Router Solicitation

Router solicitations are sent by nodes on the network to find any routers on the network. You can think of them like neighbor solicitations—but just for finding routers. These packets are always sent to the all-routers multicast address.

Router Advertisement

Router advertisements contain important information about routers available on a local network. Routers announce their presence periodically, but they'll also send a router advertisement in response to a router solicitation. Unlike neighbor advertisements, router advertisements are sent to the all-nodes multicast address or, in certain circumstances, to a unicast address.

One key thing about router advertisements is that they carry not only the MAC and link-local addresses of the router but also information about how hosts on the network should get a global unicast address. Furthermore, routers can be configured to give out DNS information in the router advertisements.

Redirect

A *redirect* packet enables a router to tell a host that there is a better router to use for traffic to a given destination. You don't see redirects used on a network segment with a single router, but they can come into play when multiple routers are available for hosts to use.

IPv6 Implementations

Once IPv6 replaces IPv4 for typical user traffic, we will find ourselves in a very different world from the one we left in terms of configuration. In this section, you will see what it takes to turn on IPv6 for a network. This section also assumes you've turned off IPv4—which isn't a realistic option right now because IPv4 is still prevalent, but it makes understanding some aspects of using IPv6 much easier. You'll also learn how IPv6 works (or doesn't work, as the case may be) with NAT, DHCP, and DNS. We'll cover the idea of running IPv6 and IPv4 at the same time in the next section.

Stateless Address Autoconfiguration (SLAAC)

One of the big ideas in IPv6 is to use autoconfiguration to make setting up most systems so easy that *it just works*. Big ideas like this aren't worth much without solid implementations that do what they say on the label, but IPv6 delivers on this promise for most users. This also means IPv6 has a slightly different relationship with DHCP. Let's take a look at how this autoconfiguration process works and where DHCP fits into the picture.

For a few different reasons, IPv6 systems often have multiple global addresses at any given time. In a common privacy-preserving scheme, hosts regularly generate a new global address. They'll recognize both addresses for a while before they stop recognizing the older address. You will see these labeled as "temporary" when running ipconfig in Windows.

The prefix isn't the only thing IPv6 hosts can get from the advertisement; they can also use it to discover their default gateway, DNS server addresses, whether to use DHCP (more on this in a moment), and so on.

Most SOHO routers these days are so easy to use out of the box that I've forgotten just how much network configuration was manual back when IPv6 was being designed. The designers of IPv6 imagined a **stateless address autoconfiguration (SLAAC)** process that enables network clients to figure out their own addresses—and the designers started before modern SOHO Wi-Fi routers with built-in DHCP servers even roamed the earth.

SLAAC leans on the neighbor-discovery process supported by NDP. Hosts in an IPv6 network can create their own link-local and global unicast addresses. We looked at how hosts generate their link-local address in the "Link-Local Address" section, but NDP also plays a crucial role in the process. After hosts generate their local address, they send a neighbor solicitation message to it to make sure it isn't already taken.

Hosts can generate a global address as soon as they get a crucial piece of the puzzle—the address prefix—from the router advertisements that their router sends out. When hosts join a network, they send out a router solicitation to request a fresh advertisement. When they receive it, hosts combine the network ID (/64 prefix length) it contains with the same interface identifier they used for the link-local address—and once again send a neighbor solicitation to the new address to verify that it is open.

DHCPv6

You'd think with router advertisements that we wouldn't need DHCP anymore, and in many ways you'd be right. DHCP is still important in IPv6, but in slightly different ways than it was in IPv4.

DHCPv6 still works like traditional DHCP in that you have to configure a DHCPv6 server. This DHCPv6 server works in one of two modes: stateful or stateless. A **stateful** DHCPv6 server works very similarly to an IPv4 DHCP server: it tells the host the full 128-bit address it should use and keeps track of the addresses it has passed out. Figure 12.5 shows the DHCPv6

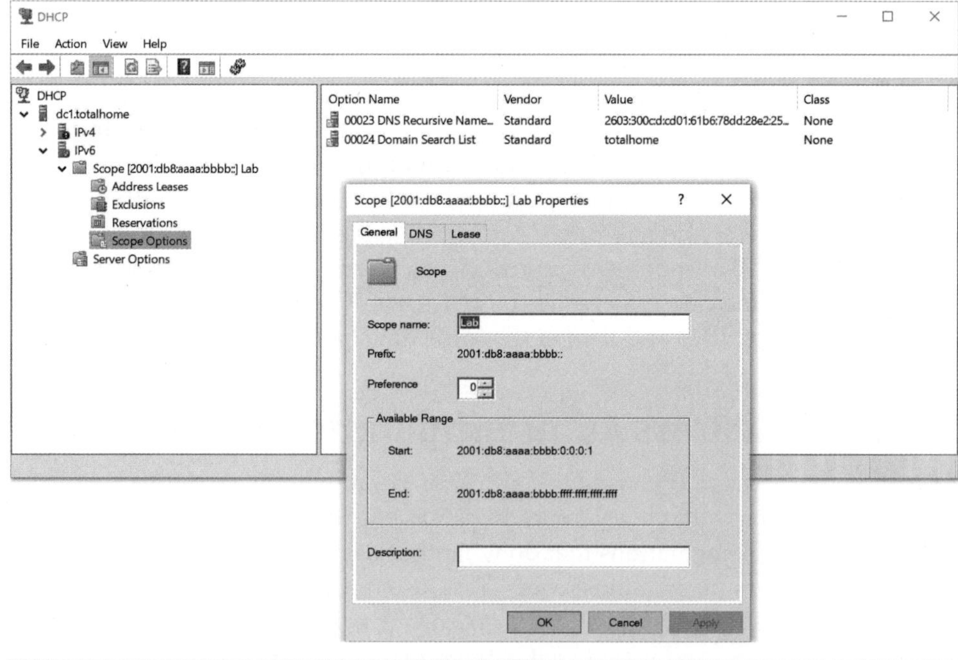

• **Figure 12.5** DHCPv6 server settings running on Windows Server 2019

server on Windows Server. A **stateless** DHCPv6 server lets the host pick its own address via SLAAC. In fact, stateless DHCPv6 is needed to give clients using SLAAC other information, like DNS server IP addresses. In both modes, DHCPv6 can pass along additional information, such as the addresses of DNS and time servers.

IPv6 DHCP servers use DHCPv6. This is not the sixth version of DHCP, mind you, just the name of DHCP for IPv6.

Since SLAAC is good at solving problems we address with DHCP in IPv4, far fewer networks need their own DHCPv6 server. DHCPv6 is super popular with ISPs, who use **prefix delegation**—specifically, *DHCPv6 Prefix Delegation (DHCPv6-PD)*—to hand out IPv6 prefixes to customer routers (if the corresponding setting, shown in Figure 12.6, is enabled). Inside most of those customer networks, SLAAC is just fine. You're more likely to find DHCPv6 servers, in stateless or stateful incarnations, in enterprise environments and networks with special needs, such as data centers.

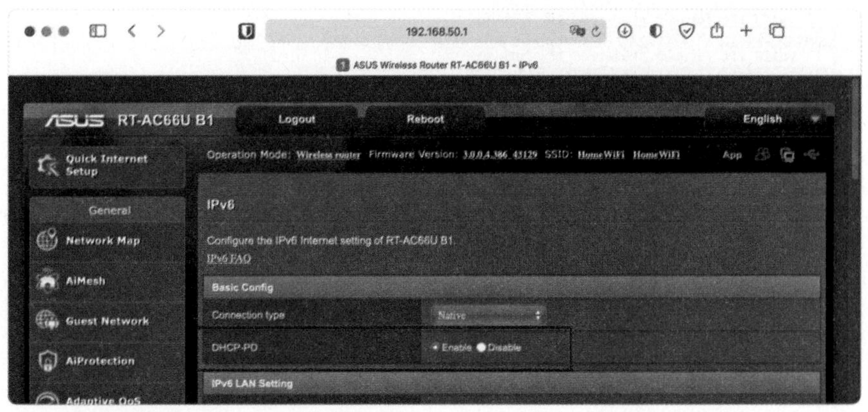

• **Figure 12.6** Enabling prefix delegation on a SOHO router (called DHCP-PD on this router)

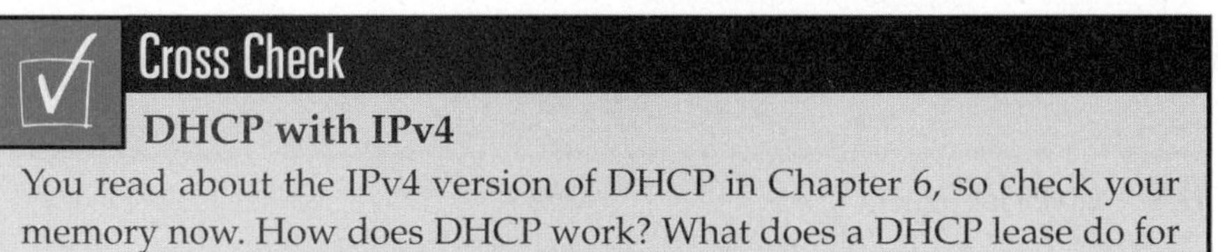

Cross Check

DHCP with IPv4

You read about the IPv4 version of DHCP in Chapter 6, so check your memory now. How does DHCP work? What does a DHCP lease do for you? What happens if your computer can't get to a DHCP server but is configured for DHCP?

Is IPv6 Working?

You can use the command line to see if your system runs IPv6. In Windows, go to a command prompt and type **`ipconfig`** and press ENTER (Figure 12.7). In Linux or macOS, go to a terminal and type **`ip address`** (Linux) or **`ifconfig`** (macOS) and press ENTER (Figure 12.8).

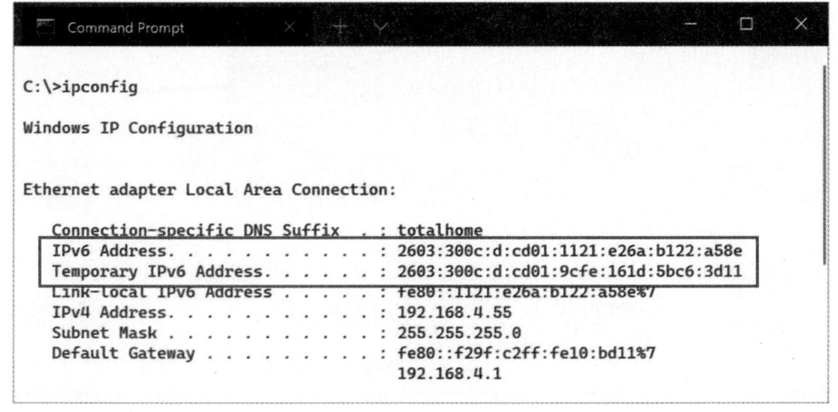

• **Figure 12.7** IPv6 enabled with SLAAC-generated addresses in Windows

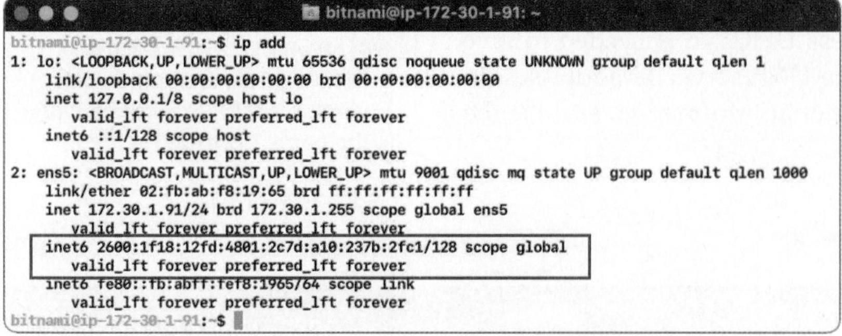

• **Figure 12.8** IPv6 enabled with DHCPv6-provided address in Ubuntu (via SSH)

Aggregation

As you'll recall from Chapter 7, routers need to know where to send every packet they encounter. Most routers have a default path on which they send packets that aren't specifically defined to go on any other route. As you get to the top of the Internet, the Tier 1 routers that connect to the other Tier 1 routers can't have any default route (Figure 12.9). These no-default routers make up the *default-free zone (DFZ)*.

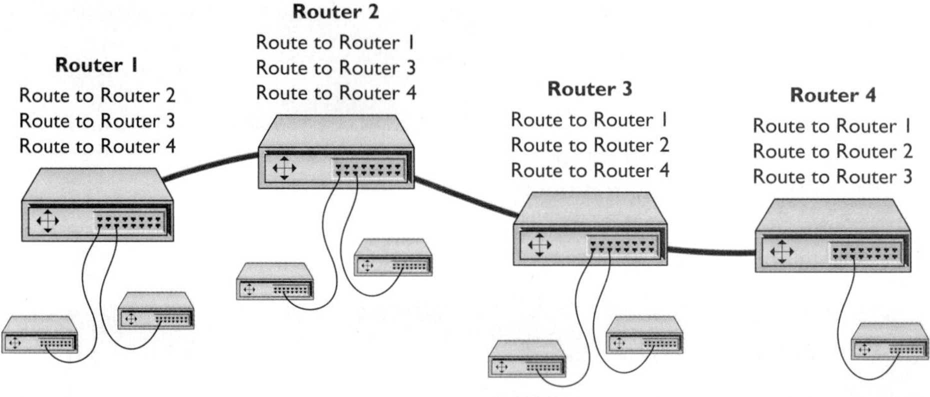

• **Figure 12.9** No-default routers

The current state of the Internet's upper tiers is rather messy. A typical DFZ router has over 850,000 routes in its routing table, requiring a router with massive firepower. But what would happen if the Internet was organized as shown in Figure 12.10? Note how every router underneath one router always uses a subset of that router's existing routes. This is called

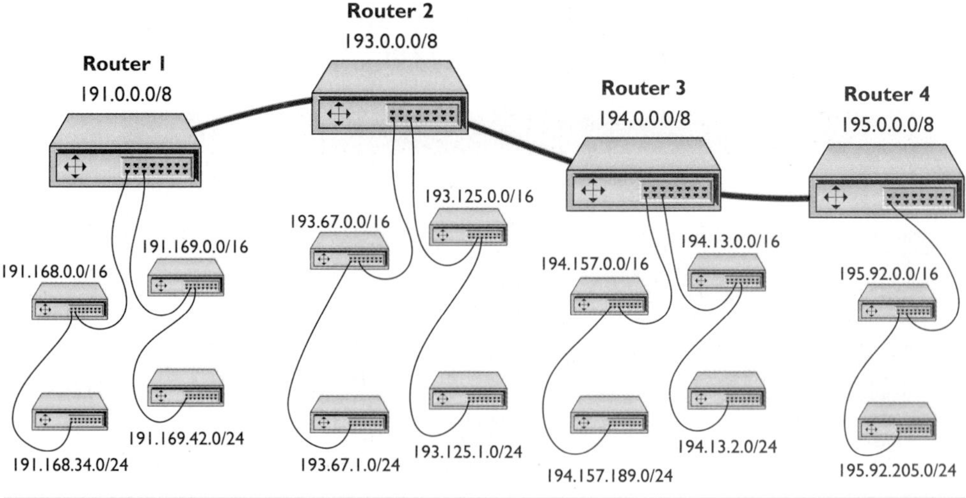

• **Figure 12.10** Aggregation

aggregation and it can drastically reduce the size and complexity of routing tables.

IPv4's address space is too *fragmented* to see the full benefits of this kind of aggregation. Some organizations that received /8 blocks in the 1980s and 1990s simply will not relinquish them. Newer organizations have had to cobble together bits and pieces of address space from whoever is willing to sell some. The amount of effort necessary to reach maximum aggregation throughout IPv4 would require unimaginable levels of cooperation and coordination. IPv6 provides a fresh start and enough address space to avoid the fragmentation issues that plague IPv4.

Remember, a computer gets the 64-bit prefix (its network ID) from a LAN router. The router, in turn, gets a prefix (usually between 48 and 64 bits) from its upstream router and adds a subnet ID if the delegated prefix is not 64 bits. This method enables the entire IPv6 network to change IP addresses on-the-fly to keep aggregation working. Imagine you have a default gateway connected to an upstream router from your ISP, as shown in Figure 12.11

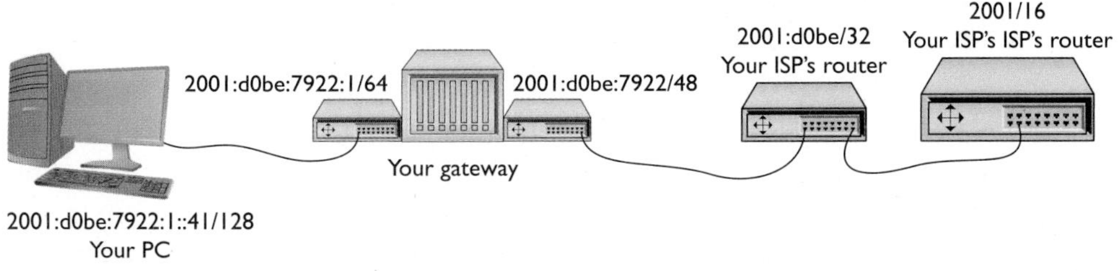

• **Figure 12.11** An IPv6 group of routers

Your PC's IPv6 address is 2001:d0be:7922:1::41/128. Let's cut out the interface ID and look at the prefix and see where this comes from:

Your network's prefix: 2001:d0be:7922:1/64

IPv6 addresses begin at the very top of the Internet with the no-default routers. We'll assume your *ISP's* ISP is one of those routers. Your ISP gets a shorter prefix (32-bit in this case) from an RIR or from its ISP if it is small. In this case, the prefix is 2001:d0be/32. This prefix is assigned by the RIR, and your ISP has no control over it. The person setting up the ISP's router, however, will add a 16-bit subnet ID to the prefix, as shown in Figure 12.12.

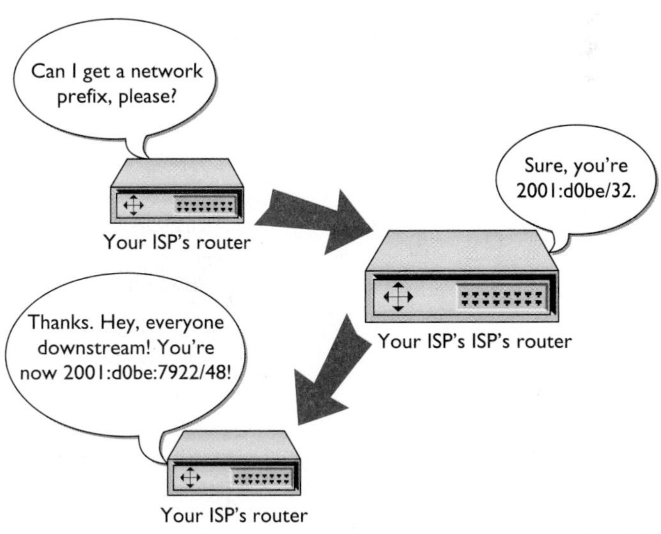

• **Figure 12.12** Adding the first prefix

Your router receives a 48-bit prefix (in this case, 2001:d0be:7922/48) from your ISP's router. Your router has no control over that prefix. The person setting up your gateway, however, adds a 16-bit subnet ID (in this case :0001, or :1) to the 48-bit prefix to make the 64-bit prefix for your network (Figure 12.13).

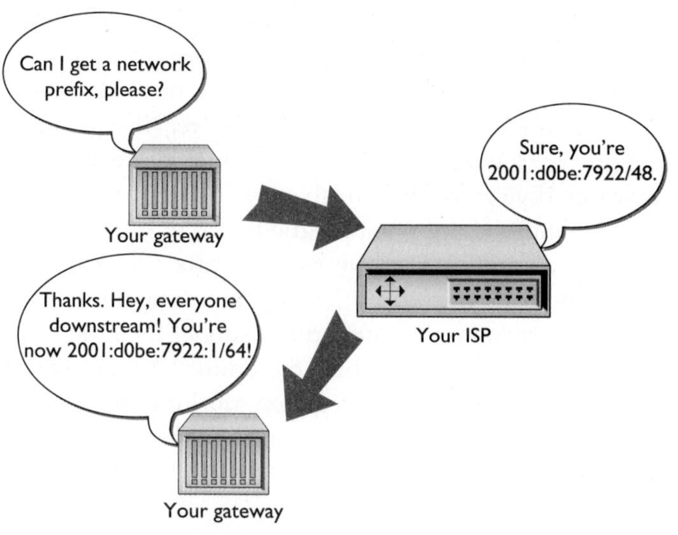

• **Figure 12.13** Adding the second prefix

What makes all this particularly interesting is that (at least in theory) upstream routers can change the prefix they send downstream, triggering downstream nodes to *renumber* (keeping aggregation intact). To see this in action, let's watch what happens if your ISP decides to change to another upstream ISP (Figure 12.14). In this case, your ISP moves from the old ISP (ISP1) to a new ISP (ISP2). When your ISP makes the new connection, the new ISP passes out a different 32-bit prefix (in this example, 2ab0:3c05/32). As quickly as this change takes place, all the downstream routers send a router advertisement to the "all nodes" multicast address; all clients get new IP addresses.

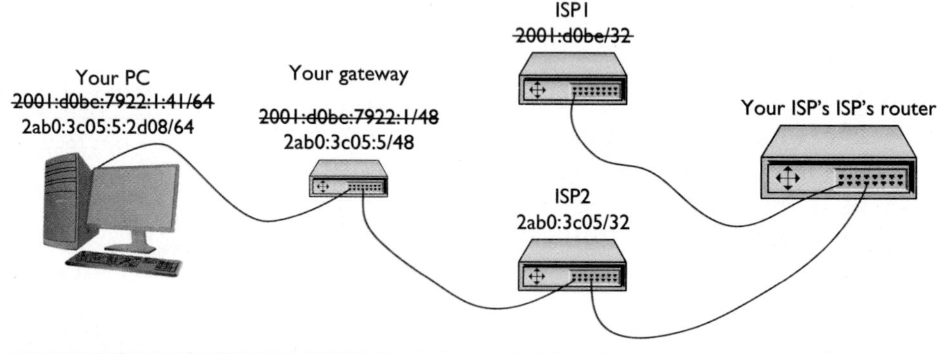

• **Figure 12.14** New IP address updated downstream

Aggregation is an intrinsic but for the most part completely transparent part of IPv6. Your IPv6 Internet addresses may suddenly change from time to time, and these changes are a fairly rare but normal aspect of using IPv6.

IPv6 and DNS

Most DNS servers support IPv6 addresses at this time, so setting up DNS requires little from network administrators. Just make sure that the router advertisements include the IPv6 DNS server if you are using SLAAC, or that your DHCPv6 server is properly configured if you are using DHCP. Zone records use the AAAA record (chosen because it's four times the length of IPv4 addresses) to map names to IPv6 addresses. Figure 12.15 shows some AAAA IPv6 records for my Web site.

Check out the excellent pair of Sims for Chapter 12 at https://hub.totalsem.com/008. You'll find both a Show! and a Click! called "IPv6 Configuration" that walk you through the process of configuring IPv6 in Windows.

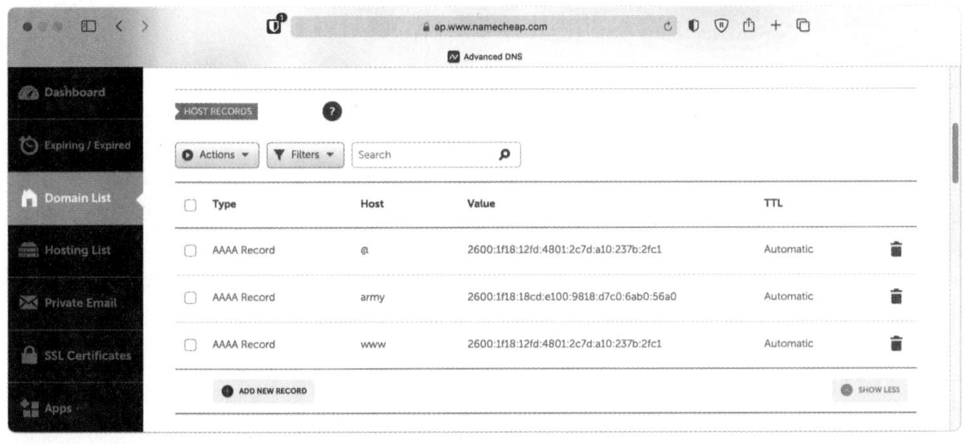

• **Figure 12.15** IPv6 AAAA records in a DNS zone

Moving to IPv6

There's no reason for you *not* to try running IPv6 today—like right now! At the very least, you can explore the world of IPv6-only Web sites that are out there. At the most, you may very well become the IPv6 expert in your organization. You almost certainly have an operating system ready to do IPv6; the only trick is to get you connected to the rest of us fun-loving IPv6-enabled folks.

IPv4 and IPv6

The first and most important point to make right now is that you can run a **dual stack**—both IPv4 and IPv6 on your computers and routers at the same time—as my computer does in Figure 12.16. This capability is a critical part of the process enabling the world to migrate slowly from IPv4 to IPv6.

All modern operating systems support IPv6, and almost all routers support IPv6. Not all routers on the Internet have IPv6 support turned on.

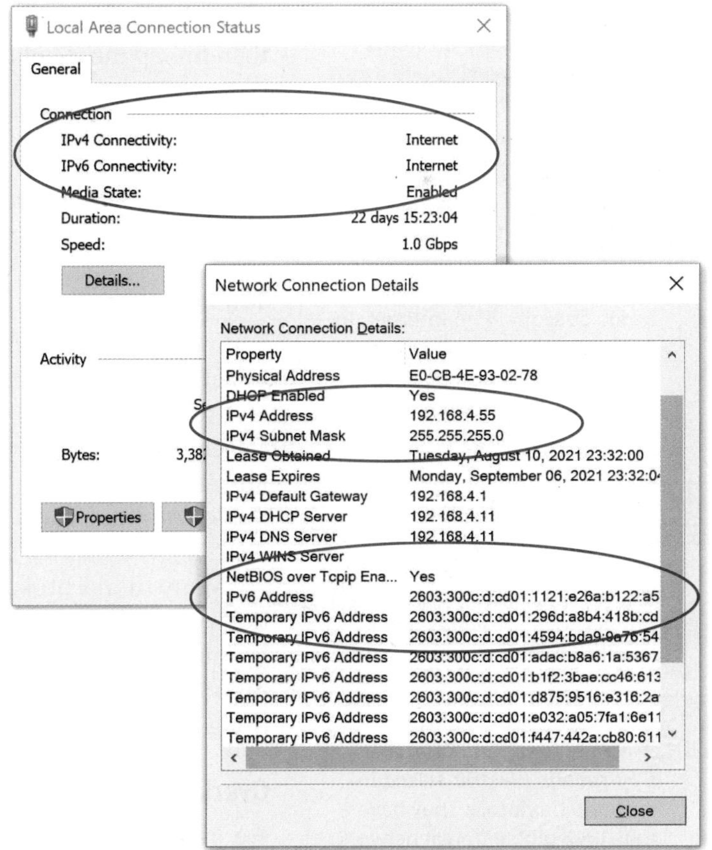

• **Figure 12.16** IPv4 and IPv6 on one computer

Tier I IPv6 enabled

Tier 2 Not IPv6 enabled

Tier 3 IPv6 enabled

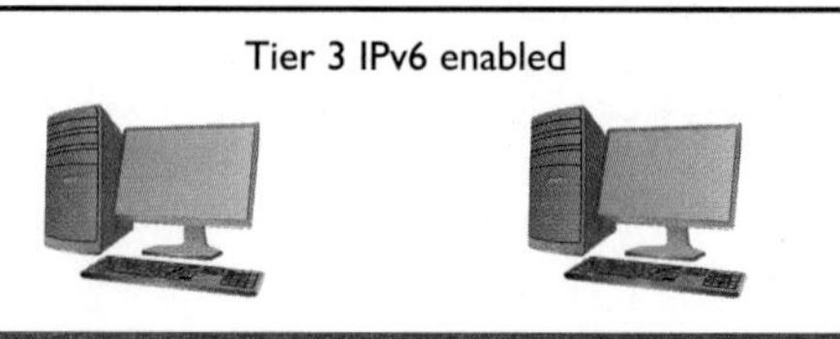

• **Figure 12.17** The IPv6 gap

Eventually, every router and every computer on the Internet will support IPv6, but the Internet is not yet there. Two critical parts of the Internet are ready, however:

- All the root DNS servers support IPv6 resolution.
- Almost all the Tier 1 ISP routers properly forward IPv6 packets.

The problem is that the routers and DNS servers between your IPv6-enabled computer and other IPv6-enabled computers to which you would like to connect are not yet IPv6-ready. How do you get past this IPv6 gap (Figure 12.17)?

Transition Mechanisms

To get on the IPv6 network, you need to leap over this gap, to implement an IPv4-to-IPv6 transition mechanism. The folks who developed IPv6 have several ways for you to do this using one of many IPv4-to-IPv6 *tunneling standards*, such as the one you'll see on the exam, **4to6**.

> Depending on when you're reading this chapter, you may not need a tunnel for typical Internet traffic because the gap won't exist. Read through this section specifically for items you'll find on the N10-008 exam.

4to6

An IPv4-to-IPv6 tunnel works like any other tunnel, encapsulating one type of data into another. In this case, you encapsulate IPv4 traffic into an IPv6 tunnel to get to an IPv6-enabled router. To make this tunnel, you would download a tunneling client and install it on your computer. You would then fire up the client and make the tunnel connection—it's very easy to do.

> You might see a now-deprecated tunneling protocol called 6to4 on the CompTIA Network+ exam. In theory, this protocol enabled IPv6 traffic over the IPv4 Internet. In practice, it proved unsuitable for widespread deployment. (See RFC 7526 for more information if you're curious.)

6in4

6in4 (also called IPv6-in-IPv4) is one of the most popular IPv6 tunneling standards. 6in4 is one of only two IPv6 tunneling protocols that can go through IPv4 NAT (called *NAT traversal*).

Tunnel Brokers

Setting up an IPv6 tunnel can be a chore. You have to find someone willing to act as the far endpoint, you have to connect to their system somehow, and then you have to know the tunneling standard they use. To make life easier, those who provide the endpoints have created the idea of the **tunnel broker**. Tunnel brokers create the actual tunnel and (usually) offer a custom-made endpoint client for you to use, although more advanced users can often make a manual connection.

> You rarely have a choice of tunneling protocol. The tunneling protocol you use is the one your tunnel broker provides and is usually invisible to you.

Many tunnel brokers take advantage of one of two automatic configuration protocols, called **Tunnel Setup Protocol (TSP)** and **Tunnel Information and Control (TIC) protocol**. These protocols set up the tunnel and handle configuration as well as login. If it wasn't for TSP and TIC, there would be no such thing as automatic third-party tunnel endpoint clients for you to use.

> The biggest tunnel broker is *Hurricane Electric*, based in Fremont, California. They have a huge IPv6 global transit network, offer IPv6 certifications, and more. Check them out at www.he.net.

Overlay Tunnels

An **overlay tunnel** enables two IPv6 networks to connect over an existing IPv4 infrastructure, such as the Internet. In more precise terms, the routers that connect the IPv6 networks to the IPv4 infrastructure encapsulate the traffic from the local network into IPv4 packets. Those IPv4 packets travel over the IPv4 infrastructure and the router at the other end (this can also be a single host) of the tunnel strips the IPv4 stuff off the packet and sends the remaining IPv6 packet on its merry way.

NAT64

IPv6 has no need or use for classic network address translation (NAT) implemented in IPv4 to mitigate the problem of address exhaustion. The massive IPv6 address space just renders it unnecessary. Don't think this means the idea of translating network addresses is dead and buried—it still plays an important role in the transition to IPv6.

NAT64 tacks the bytes of an IPv4 address onto the end of an IPv6 address for network traversal. Typically, you'll have a NAT64 gateway that handles the traffic between the IPv4 and IPv6 segments, doing the address translation on-the-fly and keeping track of who's who on either end.

NAT64, along with DNS64, was designed specifically to enable IPv6-only clients to access servers still running only IPv4. A NAT64 gateway can be installed in front of an IPv4 server to provide automatic translations—*stateless mapping*—or on the client side (or at the ISP) with manual translations—*stateful mapping*.

Chapter 12 Review

Chapter Summary

After reading this chapter and completing the exercises, you should understand the following about IPv6.

Discuss the fundamental concepts of IPv6

- IPv4 supports only about four billion addresses, which is no longer enough for the future. IPv6 supports 2^{128} (or ~ 3.4×10^{38}) IP addresses.
- IPv6 addresses are composed of 128 bits written in hexadecimal notation. Every 4 bits are separated by a colon. 2001:0db8:0000:0000:0800:200c:00cf:1234 is a valid IPv6 address.
- Leading zeroes can be dropped, and double colons may be used to represent one or more consecutive groups of zeroes to write an IPv6 address with fewer characters. 2001:db8::800:200c:cf:1234 is a valid IPv6 address.
- IPv6 prefix lengths are represented with the /*x* prefix length naming convention. fe80::cf:0:ba98:1234/64 translates to a 64-bit prefix.
- Computers using IPv6 that are on the Internet have (at least) two IPv6 addresses: a link-local address and a global unicast address.
- A link-local address is similar to an IPv4 APIPA/zeroconf address. The first 64 bits of a link-local address are always fe80::/10, followed by 54 zero bits.
- The last 64 bits of the link-local address are generated randomly in modern operating systems for privacy-conscious users. Otherwise, they may use the EUI-64 generated from the device's MAC address.
- IPv6 link-local addresses are unicast, or unique to a specific computer or network node.
- IPv6 relies heavily on multicasts for Neighbor Discovery Protocol.
- A multicast is a set of reserved addresses designed to go to only certain systems. Packets sent to addresses beginning with ff02::2 are sent only to routers.
- An IPv6 global unicast address is required for Internet access.
- IPv6 networks use Neighbor Discovery Protocol for translating MAC addresses to IPv6 addresses (among other things). NDP is implemented using ICMPv6.
- Hosts send neighbor solicitation messages to request a MAC address, inform of their MAC address, and verify system reachability. Hosts send neighbor advertisement messages in response to neighbor solicitation messages; the neighbor advertisement messages includes their MAC address and verifies reachability.
- Hosts send router solicitations to find routers on the network via the all-routers multicast address. Routers send router advertisements—both periodically and in response to router solicitations—that contain information about the router, how hosts can get a global unicast address, and more.

Describe IPv6 practices

- Automatic configuration via the stateless address autoconfiguration (SLAAC) process plays an important role in IPv6 by enabling hosts to figure out their own link-local and global unicast addresses.
- SLAAC describes the process a host uses to obtain information it needs to generate an address and then generate the address.
- SLAAC is supported by the Neighbor Discovery Protocol, which uses ICMPv6.
- Router advertisements may also tell hosts their prefix, prefix length, default gateway, DNS servers, whether to use DHCP, and so on.
- DHCPv6 plays a different role in IPv6 than DHCPv4 does in IPv4.
- Stateful DHCPv6 servers pass out full 128-bit IPv6 addresses and optional information such as DNS server addresses.
- Stateless DHCPv6 servers let hosts pick their own addresses via SLAAC, and pass out only the optional information (such as DNS server addresses).
- Since SLAAC is the most common way to configure hosts with a global unicast address, fewer networks need their own DHCPv6 servers.
- DHCPv6 is popular with ISPs who use DHCPv6-PD to delegate prefixes to customer routers.
- Aggregation reduces the size and complexity of routing tables by allowing downstream routers

to use a subset of an upstream router's routes to populate their routing tables rather than tens or hundreds of thousands of disjointed routes.

Implement IPv6 in a TCP/IP network

- Currently, all root DNS servers support IPv6 resolution and almost all Tier 1 ISP routers properly forward IPv6 packets. The routers between you and these root and Tier 1 servers, however, may not support IPv6 at the moment.
- An IPv4-to-IPv6 tunnel works like any other tunnel, encapsulating one type of data into another. In this case, you encapsulate IPv4 traffic into an IPv6 tunnel to get to an IPv6-enabled router. Tunneling standards include 4to6 and 6in4.
- A tunnel broker is a service provider that creates the tunnel, acts as the far endpoint, and often provides a tunneling client for easier setup.
- Tunnel Setup Protocol (TSP) and Tunnel Information and Control (TIC) protocol are two automatic configuration protocols for setting up IPv4-to-IPv6 tunnels.
- An overlay tunnel enables two IPv6 networks to connect over an existing IPv4 infrastructure, such as the Internet. Routers can use the same protocols used to connect an IPv4 client to an IPv6 network or can be configured manually.
- NAT64 translates addresses between IPv4 and IPv6 segments.

Key Terms

4to6 *(346)*
6in4 *(346)*
aggregation *(343)*
anycast *(338)*
DHCPv6 *(340)*
dual stack *(345)*
Extended Unique Identifier, 64-bit (EUI-64) *(336)*
global unicast address *(336)*
interface ID *(334)*
Internet Protocol version 4 (IPv4) *(332)*
Internet Protocol version 6 (IPv6) *(333)*
link-local address *(335)*
multicast *(333)*
multicast address *(336)*
NAT64 *(347)*
neighbor advertisement *(339)*
neighbor discovery *(338)*
neighbor discovery cache *(338)*
Neighbor Discovery Protocol (NDP) *(338)*
neighbor solicitation *(338)*
network prefix *(334)*
overlay tunnel *(346)*
prefix delegation *(341)*
prefix length *(335)*
router advertisement *(339)*
router solicitation *(339)*
routing prefix *(334)*
stateful *(340)*
stateless *(341)*
stateless address autoconfiguration (SLAAC) *(340)*
subnet ID *(334)*
tunnel broker *(346)*
Tunnel Information and Control (TIC) protocol *(346)*
Tunnel Setup Protocol (TSP) *(346)*
unicast address *(336)*

Key Term Quiz

Use the Key Terms list to complete the sentences that follow. Not all the terms will be used.

1. A(n) _______________ DHCPv6 server does not assign addresses.
2. A(n) _______________ enables two IPv6 networks to connect over an existing IPv4 infrastructure.
3. It is the practice of _______________ that greatly reduces the size of IPv6 routing tables by reducing them to a prefix length of an upstream router.
4. You must have a(n) _______________ to connect to the IPv6 Internet.
5. In a(n) _______________ infrastructure, devices have both IPv6 and IPv4 addresses.
6. All nodes see _______________ messages, but only the group members process the messages.

7. The first (usually) 64 bits of an IPv6 address, the ________________, is used for routing.

8. A host will respond with a(n) ________________ after receiving a neighbor solicitation.

9. IPv6 uses the /*x* ________________ to denote the number of bits in the network ID.

10. A host that receives a neighbor solicitation stores the sending system's MAC address in its ________________.

Multiple-Choice Quiz

1. How many bits comprise an IPv6 address?
   - A. 32
   - B. 48
   - C. 64
   - D. 128

2. Which of the following is a valid IPv6 address?
   - A. 192.168.0.1
   - B. 2001:376:bgp:0:3378:baaf:qr9:223
   - C. 2541:fdc::acdf:2770:23
   - D. 0000:0000:0000:0000:0000:0000:0000:0000

3. Which of the following IPv6 addresses are equivalent to accb:0876:0000:0000:fd87:0000:0000:0064? (Select two.)
   - A. accb:876::fd87:0:0:64
   - B. accb:876::fd87::64
   - C. accb:876:0:0:fd87::64
   - D. accb:876:0:fd87:0:64

4. Routers use what control message type to provide important information—such as the MAC and link-local addresses of the router—to network hosts?
   - A. Router advertisement
   - B. Router solicitation
   - C. Routing delegation
   - D. Routing prefix

5. Which of the following is a valid link-local address?
   - A. 2001:2323:cce:34ff:19:de3:2dba:52
   - B. fe80::1994:33dd:22ce:769b
   - C. fefe:0:0:0:fefe:0:0:0
   - D. ffff:ffff:ffff:ffff:232d:0:de44:cb2

6. What is true of link-local addresses?
   - A. They are passed out by the default gateway router.
   - B. They are completely randomly generated by each computer.
   - C. An OS may generate a random value for the second 64-bit portion.
   - D. They always start with 169.254.

7. What is a standard IPv6 prefix length?
   - A. /64
   - B. /72
   - C. /255
   - D. 255.255.255.0

8. Which of the following address types is a single IP address shared by multiple hosts?
   - A. Anycast
   - B. Multicast
   - C. Singlecast
   - D. Unicast

9. A newly installed host uses what NDP control message type to find available routers on the network?
   - A. Network advertisement
   - B. Network solicitation
   - C. Router advertisement
   - D. Router solicitation

10. A packet has been sent to the address ff02::2. What will process the sent packet?
    - A. The single computer with the address ff02::2.
    - B. Every network node.
    - C. Every router on the network.
    - D. Nothing will read the packet because it is an invalid address.

11. What must your computer have to access the IPv6 Internet?
    - A. An IPv4 address
    - B. A global multicast address
    - C. A link-local address
    - D. A global unicast address

12. What takes the place of ARP in IPv6 networks?

   A. Network Discovery Protocol (NDP)

   B. MAC Translation Protocol (MTP)

   C. Address Resolution Protocol v6 (ARPv6)

   D. Layer 2 Address Mapping Protocol (L2AMP)

13. What is the main benefit of IPv6 aggregation?

   A. It allows users to combine multiple IPv6 addresses to increase their bandwidth and overall Internet speed exponentially.

   B. It is backward-compatible and can be directly applied to IPv4 networks.

   C. It reduces the size and complexity of routing tables, allowing routers to work more efficiently.

   D. Signals are increased with each router the packet travels through, allowing for greater distances over wireless networks.

14. What kind of NDP message is sent to the solicited-node multicast address of a host?

   A. Neighbor solicitation

   B. Neighbor advertisement

   C. Router solicitation

   D. Router advertisement

15. As IPv6 clients can get a portion of their IP address from the default gateway server, what purpose do DHCPv6 servers serve?

   A. DHCPv6 servers can still distribute DNS server information.

   B. DHCPv6 servers provide link-local addresses.

   C. DHCPv6 servers provide the other half of the IPv6 address.

   D. There is no such thing as a DHCPv6 server.

Essay Quiz

1. Explain to a colleague the difference between link-local and global IPv6 addresses. Be sure to include when each one is necessary.
2. Explain how aggregation reduces the size and complexity of routing tables.
3. Explain how the SLAAC process works and what roles DHCPv6 may serve in the process.

Lab Projects

• Lab Project 12.1

The transition from IPv4 to IPv6 continues across the world. Assess the state of your school, work, and home Internet status. Ensure that IPv6 support is enabled on your wired or wireless network adapter. Then disable IPv4 (noting the steps taken so you can reenable it quickly). What can you access with a Web browser? https://google.com? https://totalsem.com? https://arstechnica.com? Reenable IPv4 to make sure you have full compatibility with any legacy sites out there.

• Lab Project 12.2

From a command prompt (Windows) run `ipconfig /all` to display any IPv6 address in shorthand. (In macOS run `ifconfig`; in Linux try `ip -addr`.) Find the shorthand IPv6 address(es) and practice writing them out in full. For example, find a link-local address like this:

```
fe80::fd83:e5a6:3b1d:5f58%39(Preferred)
```

And add in the missing pieces (and ignore the %#) to bring the address to full 128-bit glory:

fe80:0000:0000:0000:fd83:e5a6:3b1d:5f58

WAN Connectivity

"Gongs and drums, banners and flags, are means whereby the ears and eyes of the host may be focused on one particular point."

—Sun Tzu

In this chapter, you will learn how to

- Describe WAN telephony technologies
- Compare last-mile connections for connecting homes and businesses to the Internet
- Discuss and implement various remote access connection methods
- Troubleshoot various WAN scenarios

Computers connect to other computers locally in a *local area network (LAN)*—you've read about LAN connections throughout this book—and remotely through a number of different methods. Interconnecting computers over distances, especially when the connections cross borders or jurisdictions, creates a **wide area network (WAN)**, though the term is pretty flexible. For example, you can refer to a *campus area network (CAN)*—a bunch of interconnected LANs on a campus—as a WAN.

Remote connections have been around for a long time. Before the Internet, network users and developers created ways to take a single system or network and connect it to another faraway system or network. This wasn't the Internet! These were private interconnections of private networks. These connections were very expensive and, compared to today's options, pretty slow. As the Internet and WAN connectivity developed, most of the same technologies used to make the earlier private remote connections became the way the Internet itself interconnects.

This chapter first explores the technologies that enable WAN connections. The second portion examines the last-mile technologies that enable users and organizations to tap into both private WANs and the Internet. The third section explores the use of WAN technology to tap directly into a remote LAN through virtual private networking. The chapter wraps up with a discussion on troubleshooting WAN technologies.

Historical/Conceptual

WAN Technologies

We've discussed briefly the Tier 1 routers and ISPs of the Internet in Chapter 12 briefly, but let's look at them here more closely. Those of us in the instruction business invariably start this description by drawing a picture of the United States and then adding lines connecting big cities, as shown in Figure 13.1.

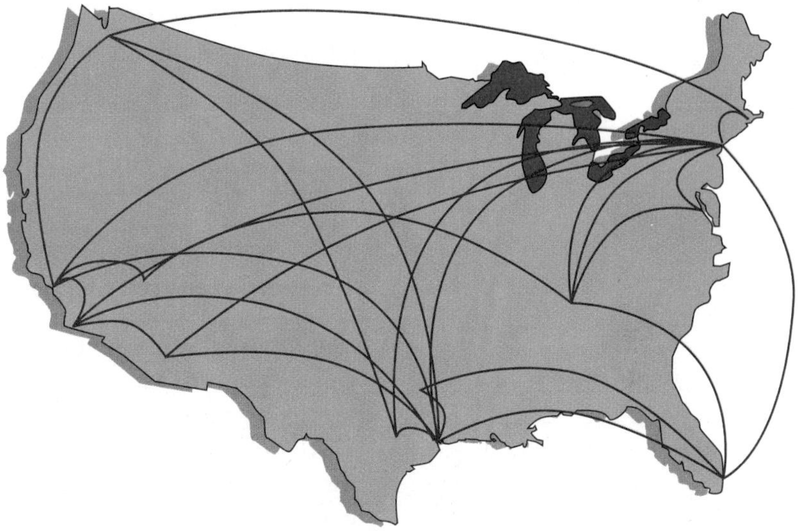

• **Figure 13.1** The Tier 1 Internet

But what are these lines and where did they come from? If the Internet is just a big TCP/IP network, wouldn't these lines be Ethernet connections? Maybe copper, maybe fiber, but surely they're Ethernet? Well, traditionally they're not. Many of the long-distance connections that make up the Internet use a unique type of signal called SONET. SONET was originally designed to handle special heavy-duty circuits with names like T1.

Technologies that connect the servers that form the backbone of the Internet—and private WAN networks—have evolved over the years, from standards created for telephony to current high-end Ethernet. And a lot of these standards coexist. This section explores the public and private WAN connections, from the fading SONET/SDH standards to more recent 100 Gigabit Ethernet (100GbE) and 400 Gigabit Ethernet (400GbE), and the private WAN connections featuring MPLS and SD-WAN.

Tech Tip

What's in a Name?

Students often wonder why two separate names exist for the same technology. In reality, SONET and SDH vary a little in their signaling and frame type, but routers and other magic boxes on the Internet handle the interoperability between the standards. The American National Standards Institute (ANSI) publishes the standard as SONET; the International Telecommunication Union (ITU) publishes the standard as SDH, but includes SONET signaling. For simplicity's sake, and because SONET is the more common term in the United States, this book uses SONET as the term for this technology.

SONET

By 1987, the primary fiber-optic cable carriers settled on a single international standard called **Synchronous Optical Network (SONET)** in the United States and **Synchronous Digital Hierarchy (SDH)** in Europe for handling the interconnections of long-distance Internet routers.

All of these carriers adopting the same standard created simple interconnections between competing voice and data carriers. This adoption defined the moment that truly made the Internet a universal network. Before SONET, interconnections happened, but they were outlandishly expensive, preventing the Internet from reaching many areas of the world.

SONET remains an important standard for long-distance, high-speed, fiber-optic transmission systems. SONET defines interface standards at the Physical and Data Link layers of the OSI seven-layer model. The physical aspect of SONET is partially covered by the Optical Carrier standards, but it also defines a ring-based topology that most SONET adopters use. SONET does not require a ring, but a SONET ring has fault tolerance in case of line loss. As a result, many of the big long-distance optical pipes for the world's telecommunications networks are SONET rings.

The **Optical Carrier (OC)** standards denote the optical data-carrying capacity (in bits per second) of fiber-optic cables in networks conforming to the SONET standard. The OC standards describe an escalating series of speeds, designed to meet the needs of medium-to-large corporations. SONET establishes OC speeds from 51.8 Mbps (OC-1) to 39.8 Gbps (OC-768).

Test Specific

Fiber Improvements

Still want more throughput? Many fiber devices use a very clever feature called **bidirectional wavelength division multiplexing (WDM or BWDM)** or its newer and more popular version, **dense wavelength division multiplexing (DWDM)**. DWDM enables an individual single-mode fiber to carry multiple signals by giving each signal a different wavelength (using different colors of laser light). The result varies, but a single DWDM fiber can support ~150 signals, enabling, for example, a 51.8-Mbps OC-1 line to run at 51.8 Mbps × 150 signals = 7.6 *gigabits per second!* DWDM has been very popular for long-distance lines as it's usually less expensive to replace older SONET/OC-*x* equipment with DWDM than it is to add more fiber lines.

> DWDM isn't just upgrading SONET lines; DWDM works just as well on long-distance fiber Ethernet.

A related technology, **coarse wavelength division multiplexing (CWDM)**, also relies on multiple wavelengths of light to carry a fast signal over long distances. It's simpler than DWDM, which limits the practical distances of CWDM to a mere 60 km. You'll see it used in higher-end LANs with 10GBASE-LX4 networks, for example, where its lower cost (compared to direct competitors) offers benefits.

In the mid-life of the Internet, backbone runs were largely composed of SONET links. Today, SONET has mostly been replaced with a mix of ever-improving optical links such as 100 Gigabit Ethernet, 400 Gigabit Ethernet, and others.

Private WANs

Many organizations connect far-flung network resources through private connections rather than across the Internet. The purchase of dedicated connections—*leased lines*—from telecommunication companies enables these organizations to secure network communication with no fear of hackers accessing network resources. These dedicated connections are expensive, as you might imagine, but ideal for many businesses. Several technologies provide the underpinnings for private WANs: MPLS, SD-WAN, and metro Ethernet.

MPLS

In an IP network, a router receives an incoming IP packet, checks the destination IP address, consults its routing table, and then forwards the packet to the next hop. Nothing in the IP packet tells the router details about how to get to that destination. This router-intensive analysis of where to send each packet happens at every hop that packet takes from its source to its destination. This works great for a typical IP network, but years ago applications like video conferencing suffered over distances. (This has changed a lot today, but go with me here on the motivation for something better.)

In a private network of dedicated leased lines, a few destinations can use a different switching technology to make direct or more efficient connections. **Multiprotocol Label Switching (MPLS)** provides a platform-agnostic labeling system to greatly improve performance compared to an IP network.

MPLS adds an MPLS label that sits between the Layer 2 header and the Layer 3 header. Layer 3 is always IP, so MPLS labels sit between Layer 2 and the IP headers. Figure 13.2 shows the structure of an MPLS header.

• **Figure 13.2** MPLS header

The MPLS header consists of four parts:

- **Label** A unique identifier, used by MPLS-capable routers to determine how to move data.
- **Experimental Bits (Exp)** A relative value used to determine the importance of the labeled packet to be able to prioritize some packets over others.
- **Bottom of Label Stack (S)** In certain situations, a single packet may have multiple MPLS labels. This single bit value is set to 1 for the initial label.
- **Time to Live (TTL)** A value that determines the number of hops the label can make before it's eliminated

• **Figure 13.3** MPLS header inserted in a frame

Figure 13.3 shows the location of the MPLS header.

The original idea for MPLS was to give individual ISPs a way to move traffic through their morass of different interconnections and switches more quickly and efficiently by providing network-wide quality of service (QoS). MPLS-capable routers avoid running IP packets through their full routing tables and instead use the header information to route packets quickly. Where "regular" routers use QoS on an individual basis, MPLS routers use their existing dynamic routing protocols to send each other messages about their overhead, enabling QoS to span an entire group of routers (Figure 13.4).

• **Figure 13.4** MPLS routers talk to each other about their overhead.

Cross Check

QoS

You learned about QoS back in Chapter 11, so see if you remember enough to answer these questions. What is the purpose of QoS? How does it speed up networks?

Let's see how the MPLS-labeled packets, combined with MPLS-capable routers, create improved throughput. To see this happen, I need to introduce a few MPLS terms:

- **Forwarding Equivalence Class (FEC)** FEC is a set of packets that can be sent to the same place, such as a single broadcast domain of computers connected to a router.
- **Label switching router (LSR)** An LSR looks for and forwards packets based on their MPLS label. These are the "MPLS routers" mentioned previously.
- **Label edge router (LER)** An LER is an MPLS router that has the job of adding MPLS labels to incoming packets that do not yet have a label, and stripping labels off outgoing packets.
- **Label Distribution Protocol (LDP)** LSRs and LERs use LDP to communicate dynamic information about their state.

Figure 13.5 shows a highly simplified MPLS network. Note the position of the LERs and LSRs.

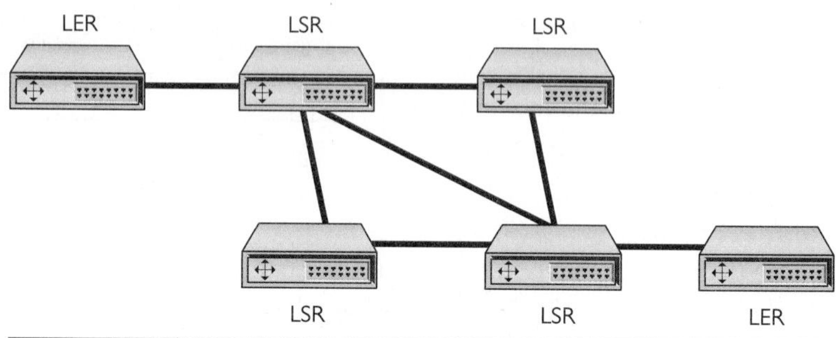

• **Figure 13.5** Sample MPLS network

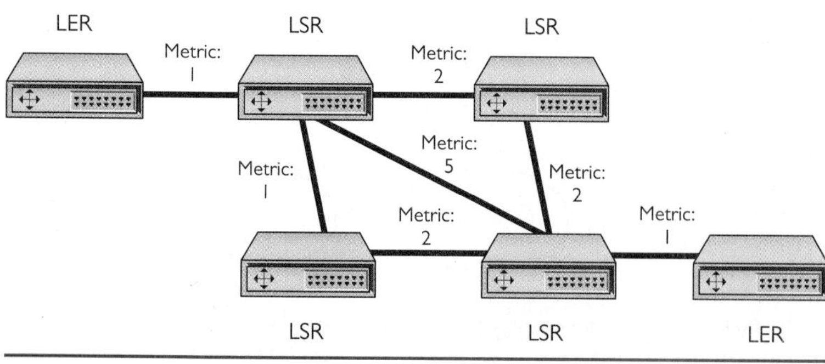

• **Figure 13.6** MPLS initial routes added

When an MPLS network comes online, administrators configure initial routing information, primarily setting metrics to routes (Figure 13.6).

LERs have the real power in determining routes. Because LERs are the entrances and exits for an MPLS network, they talk to each other to determine the best possible routes. As data moves from one FEC, the LERs add an MPLS label to every packet. LSRs strip

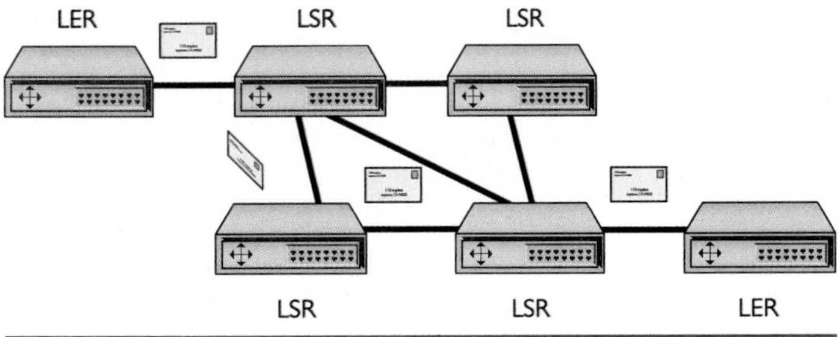

• **Figure 13.7** Data routing through an MPLS network

away incoming labels and add their own. This progresses until the packets exit out the opposing LER (Figure 13.7).

SD-WAN

One interesting use of MPLS networks is to provide Internet connectivity to a back office or satellite location via a public-facing router at the telephone company's central office, a *backhaul* connection. This keeps the full security in place (the good part about MPLS and private WANs), but the connection will most likely be slow compared to a direct Internet connection.

Another disadvantage of MPLS is that acquiring and installing dedicated connections between the central office and the various back offices or satellites is expensive. The public Internet eclipsed any performance advantage of dedicated networks, so the only thing superior in the latter is security.

Software-defined wide area networking (SD-WAN) enables traffic over the Internet that incorporates a lot of the features of MPLS, with efficient addressing and routing for a lot of traffic. SD-WAN maintains high security as well. SD-WAN relies on virtualization technologies covered more fully in Chapter 15. (Note also that the Network+ exam objectives drop the hyphen, so *SDWAN*.)

Metro Ethernet

A **metro Ethernet** network creates a secure, private network within a city using fiber-optic cabling and Ethernet technology. CompTIA refers to this networking technology as *metro-optical*. The *metropolitan area network (MAN)* created does not use the Internet to connect and thus doesn't require security. Use of Ethernet reduces the cost of implementing a metro Ethernet network substantially compared to an MPLS or SD-WAN network.

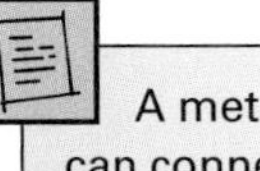

A metro Ethernet network can connect offices and individuals and provide Internet connectivity.

Last-Mile Technologies

Various technologies enable individuals and organizations to tap into wide area networks, such as the Internet. These technologies enable connections to ISPs, businesses that lease direct connections and in turn provide a public onramp—**provider links**—to the Internet. This section explores DSL, cable, fiber to the premises, satellite, and cellular, the connections most frequently termed the **last mile**—literally the connection options from a telco central office to the premises.

Tech Tip

VDSL

AT&T (along with other telecoms) uses a very fast DSL version in some of its Internet offerings called very-high-bit-rate DSL (VDSL). The current version, VDSL2, can provide simultaneous upload and download speeds in excess of 100 Mbps, though only at short distances (~300 meters). Typical speeds using this technology are a lot slower, in the range of 8 to 16 Mbps down and 1 to 2 Mbps up.

DSL

Many telephone companies offer a **digital subscriber line (DSL)** connection, a fully digital, dedicated (no phone number) connection. DSL represented the next great leap forward past Integrated Services Digital Network (ISDN) for telephone lines. A physical DSL connection manifests as just another Public Switched Telephone Network (PSTN) connection, using the same telephone lines and RJ-11 jacks as any regular phone line. DSL comes in a number of versions, but the two most important to know for the fundamental technologies are **symmetric DSL (SDSL)** and **asymmetric DSL (ADSL)**.

SDSL

SDSL provides equal upload and download speeds and, in theory, provides speeds up to 15 Mbps, although the vast majority of ISPs provide packages ranging from 192 Kbps to 9 Mbps.

ADSL

ADSL uses different upload and download speeds. ADSL download speeds are much faster than the upload speeds. Most small office and home office (SOHO) users are primarily concerned with fast *downloads* for things like Web pages and can tolerate slower upload speeds. ADSL provides theoretical maximum download speeds up to 15 Mbps and upload speeds up to 1 Mbps. Real-world ADSL download speeds vary from 384 Kbps to 15 Mbps, and upload speeds go from as low as 128 Kbps to around 768 Kbps. ADSL is less expensive than SDSL.

Try This!

Comparing Options in Your Neighborhood

So what do your local providers offer in terms of higher-speed service, if any? Try this! Call your local phone company or shop them on the Web (https://broadbandnow.com is an excellent reference). Does the company offer DSL? What speed options do you have? If you want to compare with other parts of the United States, check one of the national *speed test sites*, like MegaPath's Speakeasy Speed Test (www.speakeasy.net/speedtest/).

DSL Features

One nice aspect of DSL is that you don't have to run new phone lines. The same DSL lines you use for data can simultaneously transmit your voice calls.

All versions of DSL have the same central office–to–end user distance restrictions as ISDN—around 18,000 feet from your demarc to the central office. At the central office, your DSL provider has a device called a **DSL Access Multiplexer (DSLAM)** that connects multiple customers to the Internet.

The DSL modem in your house is considered a termination point, a demarc. Any DSL modem today is a **smart jack**, a network interface unit (NIU) that enables loopback testing so the ISP can remotely check your line and box.

Installing DSL

DSL operates using your preexisting telephone lines (assuming they are up to specification). This is wonderful but also presents a technical challenge. For DSL and your run-of-the-mill plain old telephone service (POTS) line to coexist, you need to filter out the DSL signal on the POTS line. A DSL line has three information channels: a high-speed downstream channel, a medium-speed duplex channel, and a POTS channel.

> **Tech Tip**
>
> **DSL POTS Filters**
>
> *If you install a telephone onto a line in your home with DSL and you forget to add a filter, don't panic. You won't destroy anything, though you won't get a dial tone either! Just insert a DSL POTS filter and the telephone will work.*

Segregating the two DSL channels from the POTS channel guarantees that your POTS line will continue to operate even if the DSL fails. You accomplish this by inserting a filter on each POTS line, or a splitter mechanism that allows all three channels to flow to the DSL modem but sends only the POTS channel down the POTS line. The DSL company should provide you with a few POTS filters for your telephones. If you need more, most computer/electronics stores stock DSL POTS filters.

A common early DSL installation consisted of a **DSL modem** connected to a telephone wall jack and to a standard network interface card (NIC) in your computer (Figure 13.8). The DSL line ran into a DSL modem via a standard phone line with RJ-11 connectors. Today you'd add a router in between the DSL modem and the wall jack.

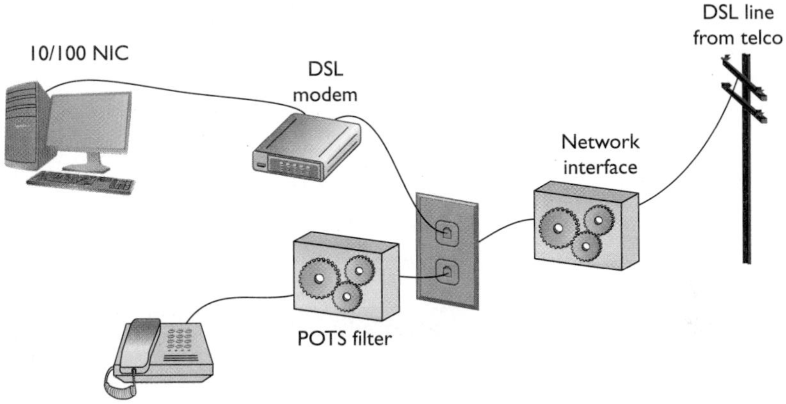

• **Figure 13.8** A DSL modem connection between a PC and telco

The DSL modem connects to the gateway router with a Cat 5/6 patch cable, which, in turn, connects to the company's switch. Figure 13.9 shows an ADSL modem and a router.

The first generation of DSL providers used a **bridged connection**; once the DSL line was running, it was as if you had snapped an Ethernet cable into your NIC. You were on the network. Those were good days for DSL. You just plugged your DSL modem into your NIC and, assuming your IP settings were whatever the DSL folks told you to use, you were running.

The DSL providers didn't like that too much. There was no control—no way to monitor who was using the DSL modem. As a result, the DSL folks started to use **Point-to-Point Protocol over Ethernet (PPPoE)**, a protocol that was originally designed to encapsulate PPP frames into Ethernet frames. The DSL people adopted it to make stronger controls over your DSL connection. In particular, you could no longer simply connect; you now had to log on with an account and a password to make the DSL connection. PPPoE is now predominant on DSL. If you get a DSL line, your operating system has software to enable you to log onto your DSL network. Most small office/home office (SOHO) routers come with built-in

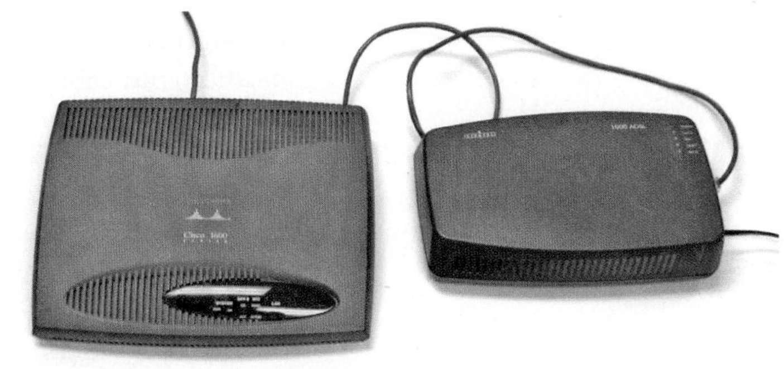

• **Figure 13.9** DSL connection

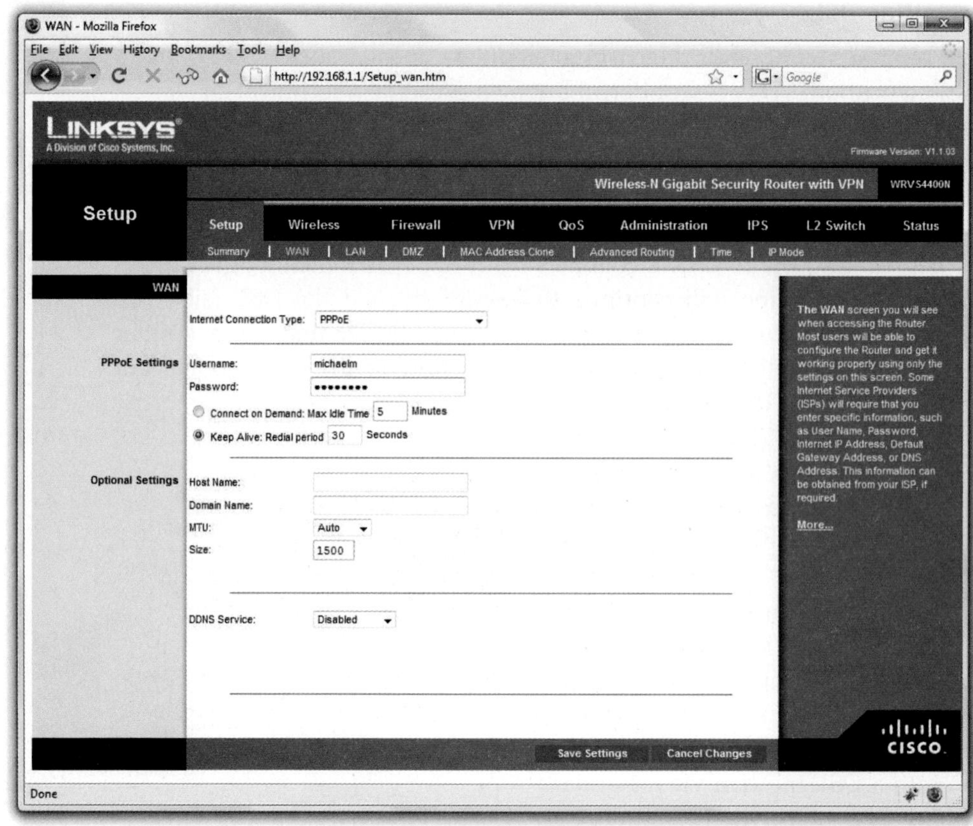

• **Figure 13.10** PPPoE settings in SOHO router

PPPoE support, enabling you to enter your username and password into the router itself (Figure 13.10).

Broadband Cable

The first big competition for ADSL came from the cable companies. A majority of houses in America have a coax cable for cable TV. In a moment of genius, the cable industry realized that if it could put the Home Shopping Network and the History Channel into every home, why not provide Internet access? The entire infrastructure of the cabling industry had to undergo some major changes to deal with issues like bidirectional communication, but cable modem service quickly became common in the United States. Cable modems are now as common as cable TV boxes.

Cable modems have the impressive benefit of phenomenal top speeds. These speeds vary from cable company to cable company, but most advertise speeds in the 5 Mbps to 1.2 Gbps range. Many cable modems provide a throughput speed of 30 Mbps to 1.2 Gbps for downloading and 5 Mbps to 35 Mbps for uploading—there is tremendous variance among different providers.

In a cable modem installation, the cable modem connects to an outlet via a coaxial cable. It's separate from the one that goes to the television. It's the same cable line, just split from the main line as if you were adding a second cable outlet for another television. A cable modem connects to a router, which in turn connects to a PC using a standard NIC and UTP cabling (Figure 13.11).

Cable modems connect using coax cable to a *headend*, similar to a telephone company's central office. Headends, in turn, connect to the cable company's network. This network uses a unique protocol called **Data Over Cable Service Interface Specification (DOCSIS)**. The current specification is DOCSIS 4.0.

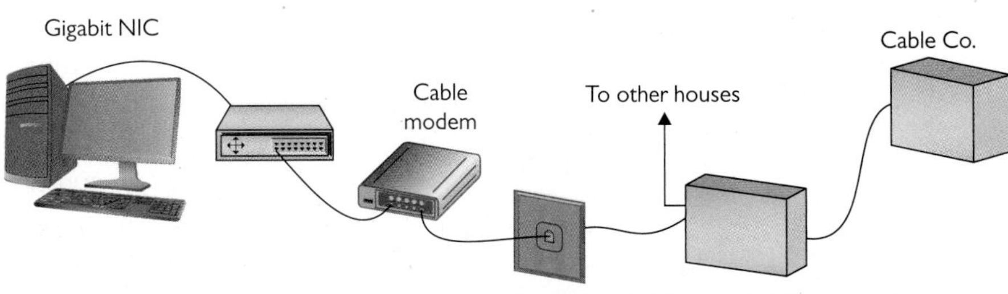

• Figure 13.11 Cable modem

You'll have a hard time telling a cable modem from a DSL modem. The only difference, other than the fact that one will have "cable modem" printed on it whereas the other will say "DSL modem," is that the cable modem has a coax F connector and an RJ-45 connector; the DSL modem has an RJ-11 connector and an RJ-45 connector.

Cable companies aggressively market high-speed packages to business customers, making cable a viable option for businesses.

Companies that design satellite communications equipment haven't given up on their technology. The standard HughesNet products advertise download speeds up to 25 Mbps. The SpaceX Starlink service claims potential download speeds of 1 Gbps worldwide, though it's still in beta as I type.

Satellite

Living in the countryside may have its charms, but you'll have a hard time getting high-speed Internet out on the farm. For those too far away to get anything else, satellite may be your only option. Satellite access comes in two types: one-way and two-way. *One-way* means that you download via satellite, but you must use a PSTN/dial-up modem connection for uploads. *Two-way* means the satellite service handles both the uploading and downloading.

Neither cable modems nor satellites use PPP, PPPoE, or anything else that begins with three Ps.

Satellite requires a small satellite antenna, identical to the ones used for satellite television. This antenna connects to a satellite modem, which, in turn, connects to your PC or your network (Figure 13.12).

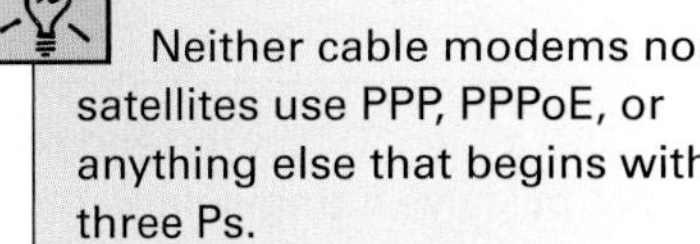

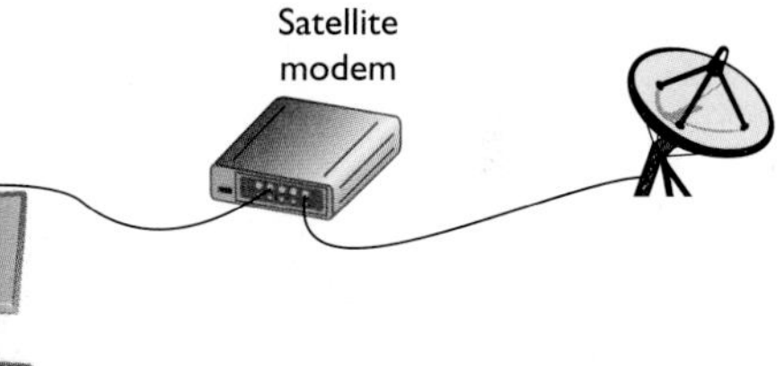

• Figure 13.12 Satellite connection

Fiber

DSL was the first popular last-mile WAN option, but over the years cable modems have taken the lead. In an attempt to regain market share, telephone providers rolled out fiber-to-the-home/fiber-to-the-premises options that have changed the game in many cities In the United States, two companies, AT&T and Verizon (Fios), offer Internet connectivity, television, and phone services at super speeds, such as bidirectional 1-Gbps throughput. Some markets also have Internet-only fiber offerings, such as Google Fiber, where users connect at 1 Gbps.

To make rollouts affordable, most fiber-to-the-home technologies employ a version of **passive optical network (PON)** architecture that uses a single fiber to the neighborhood splitter and then individual fiber runs to each final destination. PON uses WDM to enable multiple signals to travel on the same fiber and then passively splits the signal to send traffic to its proper recipient.

Most municipalities in the United States have very tight deals in place with telephone and cable companies, allowing little room for any other high-speed Internet service. A few cities have bucked the regional monopolies and done pretty well, such as Chattanooga, Tennessee. Their publicly owned electric utility—EPB—rolled out fiber to every home and business by 2011 and currently offers Internet speeds up to 10 Gbps.

Cellular WAN

• **Figure 13.13** Cellular tower

Anyone with a smartphone these days can enjoy the convenience of using wireless cellular technology. Who doesn't love firing up an Android phone or an iPhone and cruising the Internet from anywhere? As cell-phone technology converges with Internet access technologies, competent techs need to understand what's happening behind the scenes. That means tackling an alphabet soup of standards.

Regardless of the standard, the voice and data used on smartphones (unless you have 802.11 wireless turned on) moves through a cellular wireless network with towers that cover the world (Figure 13.13).

Mobile data services started in the mid-1980s and, as you might imagine, have gone through a dizzying number of standards and protocols, all of which have been revised, improved, abandoned, and reworked. Instead of trying to advertise these fairly complex and intimidating technologies, the industry instead came up with the marketing term *generations*, abbreviated by a number followed by the letter *G*: 2G, 3G, 4G, and 5G.

Salespeople and TV commercials use these terms to push mobile cellular services. The generation terms aren't generally used within the industry, and certainly not at a deeply technical level. As I go through the standards that you'll see on the exam and encounter in real life, I'll mention both the technical name and the generation where applicable. I'll cover six common terms here:

> There's no "C" on the end of GSM because it originally came from a French term, *Groupe Spécial Mobile.*

- GSM and EDGE
- CDMA
- HSPA+
- LTE
- 5G

GSM and EDGE

• **Figure 13.14** Original SIM card

The **Global System for Mobile Communications (GSM)**, the first group of networking technologies widely applied to mobile devices, relied on a type of time-division multiplexing called *time-division multiple access (TDMA)*. TDMA enabled multiple users to share the same channel more or less at the same time; and in this scenario, the switching from one user to another happened so quickly no one noticed.

GSM introduced the handy **subscriber identity module (SIM) card** that is now ubiquitous in smartphones (Figure 13.14). The SIM card identifies the phone, enabling access to the cellular networks, and stores some other information (contents differ according to many factors, none relevant for this discussion).

The GSM standard was considered a 2G technology. The standard continued to improve over the years, getting new names and better data speeds. One of the last of these was

Enhanced Data rates for GSM Evolution (EDGE), which offered data speeds up to 384 Kbps.

CDMA

Code-division multiple access (CDMA) came out not long after GSM, but used a spread-spectrum form of transmission that was totally incompatible with GSM's TDMA. Rather than enabling multiple users to share a single channel by splitting the channel into time slices, spread-spectrum transmission changed the frequencies used by each user.

CDMA was considered superior to GSM, and U.S. carriers adopted CDMA *en masse*, which created some problems later since the rest of the world went with GSM. Plus, CDMA lacked some key features, such as SIM cards.

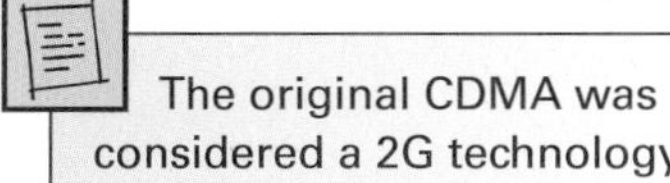

The original CDMA was considered a 2G technology.

HSPA+

In the late 1990s the International Telecommunication Union (ITU) forwarded a standard called International Mobile Telecommunications-2000 (IMT-2000) to address shortcomings in mobile technology. IMT-2000 defined higher speeds, support for full-time Internet connections, and other critical functions. The standard pushed support for multimedia messaging system (MMS) (so you can send cat pictures in your text messages) and IP-based telephony.

Both GSM and CDMA improved during the late 1990s to the mid-2000s to address IMT-2000: all these improvements were marketed under probably the most confusing marketing term ever used: *3G*. Ideally, **3G** meant a technology that supported IMT-2000, although the industry was very lax in how companies used this term. (This time period is so confusing that many technologies in this period were given decimal generations to clarify the situation. One example is GSM EDGE being called 2.9G due to its lack of full IMT-2000 support.)

Evolved High-Speed Packet Access (HSPA+) was the final 3G data standard, providing theoretical speeds up to 168 Mbps, although most HSPA+ implementations rarely exceeded 10 Mbps.

• **Figure 13.15** Modern nano-SIM

LTE

Devices and networks using **Long Term Evolution (LTE)** technology rolled out world-wide in the early 2010s and now dominate wireless services. Marketed as and now generally accepted as a true **4G** technology, LTE networks feature speeds of up to 300 Mbps download and 75 Mbps upload. All LTE services use SIM cards such as the one shown in Figure 13.15. Note the SIM size in Figure 13.15 compared to the much older SIM in Figure 13.14. The much smaller SIM in Figure 13.15 is a *nano-SIM*. The SIM in Figure 13.14 is an original, standard SIM.

Smartphones have LTE radios built in, but it's easy to add LTE to almost any device. Need LTE on a laptop or a desktop? No problem, get an LTE NIC and just plug it into a convenient USB port (Figure 13.16).

• **Figure 13.16** Cellular wireless NIC on USB stick

5G

The successor to 4G, called **5G** (for fifth generation), offers substantially upgraded technology and dramatically increased speeds over its predecessor. Cellular companies started rolling out 5G in 2019.

5G operates at three bands, low, medium, and high. Clever, huh? All three use a range of frequencies, with low-band running 600–800 MHz (similar to 4G), medium-band at 2.5–3.7 GHz, and high-band at 25–39 GHz. The higher the frequency, the faster the possible throughput speeds and the shorter the range. Depending on the radios installed in 5G towers and devices, expected speeds can range from 30 Mbps up to 1 Gbps.

The high-band 5G implementation will require dense saturation of transmitters/receivers and antennas, so will work best in dense settings, such as stadiums. Additionally, the exceptional speeds offered by 5G makes the technology a viable replacement for other technologies for mobile devices such as laptops and tablets, as well as smoking-fast speeds in the latest smartphones.

Which Connection?

With so many connection options for homes and small offices, making a decision is often a challenge. Your first question is availability: Which services are available in your area? The second question is: How much bandwidth do you need? The latter is a question of great debate. Most services are more than happy to increase service levels if you find that a certain level is too slow. I usually advise clients to start with a relatively slow level and then increase if necessary. After all, once you've tasted the higher speeds, going slower is hard, but the transition to faster is relatively painless!

Try This!

Going Connection Shopping

You've already checked the availability of DSL in your neighborhood, but now you have more choices! Try this! Do you have cable or satellite available? A great Web site to start your search is www.dslreports.com. It has a handy search feature that helps you determine the types of service and the costs for DSL, cable, and other services. Which one makes sense for you?

Remote Access

You'll see the term *extranet* more in books than in the day-to-day workings of networks and network techs. So what is an extranet? Whenever you allow authorized remote users to access some part of your private network, you have created an extranet.

Because most businesses are no longer limited to a simple little shop like you would find in a Dickens novel, many people need to be able to access files and resources over a great distance. Enter remote access. **Remote access** uses WAN and LAN connections to enable a computer user to log onto a network from the other side of a city, a state, or even the globe. As people travel, information has to remain accessible. Remote access enables users to connect a server at the business location and log into the network as if they were in the same building as the company. The only problem with remote access is that there are so many ways to do it! This section covers two of the most common forms, remote terminal and virtual private networking.

Remote Terminal

You can use a terminal emulation program to create a **remote terminal**, a connection on a faraway computer that enables you to control that computer as if you were sitting in front of it, logged in. Terminal emulation has been a part of TCP/IP from its earliest days, in the form of good-old Telnet. Because it dates from pre-GUI days, Telnet is a text-based utility; most modern operating systems are graphical, so there was a strong desire to come up with graphical remote terminal tools. Citrix Corporation made the first popular terminal emulation products—the *WinFrame/MetaFrame* products (Figure 13.17). (Their current product is called Citrix Virtual Apps and Desktop.)

From a security standpoint, all remote connections have *authentication and authorization considerations*. Connecting via Telnet, as you'll recall from Chapter 8, can require a username and password for authentication, but it lacks any real security because credentials are passed unencrypted. Most other remote connection types at least have encryption to make the authentication part more secure. Once logged into a remote system, the remote operating system handles authorization.

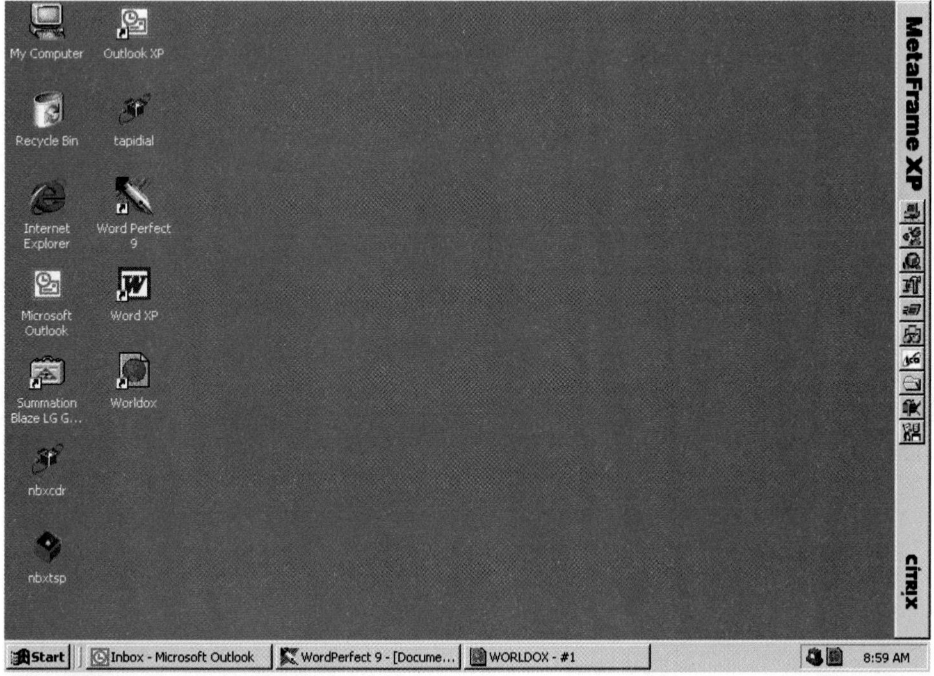

• **Figure 13.17** Citrix MetaFrame

Remote terminal programs all require a server and a client. The server is the computer to be controlled. The client is the computer from which you do the controlling. Citrix created a standard called **Independent Computing Architecture (ICA)** that defined how terminal information was passed between the server and the client. Citrix made a breakthrough product—so powerful that Microsoft licensed the Citrix code and created its own product called Windows Terminal Services. Not wanting to pay Citrix any more money, Microsoft then created its own standard called **Remote Desktop Protocol (RDP)** and unveiled a new remote terminal called *Remote Desktop Connection (RDC)* starting with Windows XP (so it's been around a long time). Figure 13.18 shows Windows Remote Desktop Connection running on a Windows 10 system, connecting to a Windows Server.

All RDP applications run on port 3389 by default.

Current versions of Windows Server can provide a secure tunnel via HTTPS for an RDC session. The server runs the *Remote Desktop Gateway (RDG)* component or role to supply security with TLS.

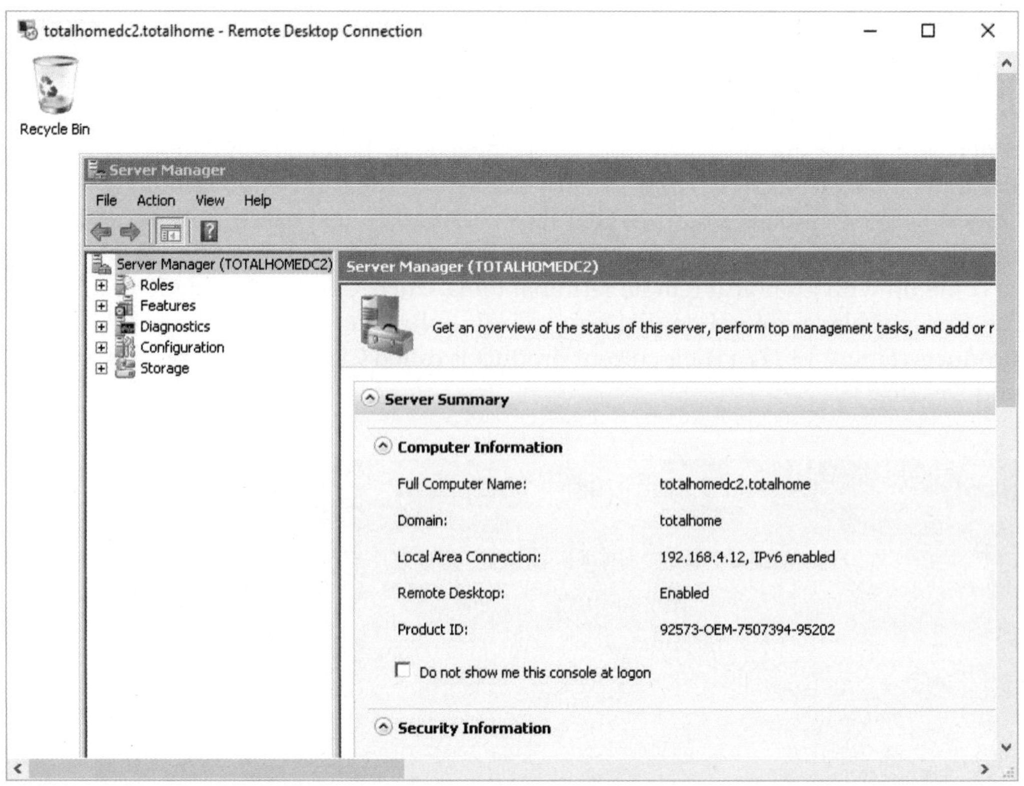

• **Figure 13.18** RDC in action

A number of third parties make absolutely amazing terminal emulation programs that run on any operating system. The best of these is **VNC** (which stands for **Virtual Network Computing**), shown in Figure 13.19. VNC doesn't let you share folders or printers, but it's solid as a rock, runs on every operating system, and you can even access it from a Web browser.

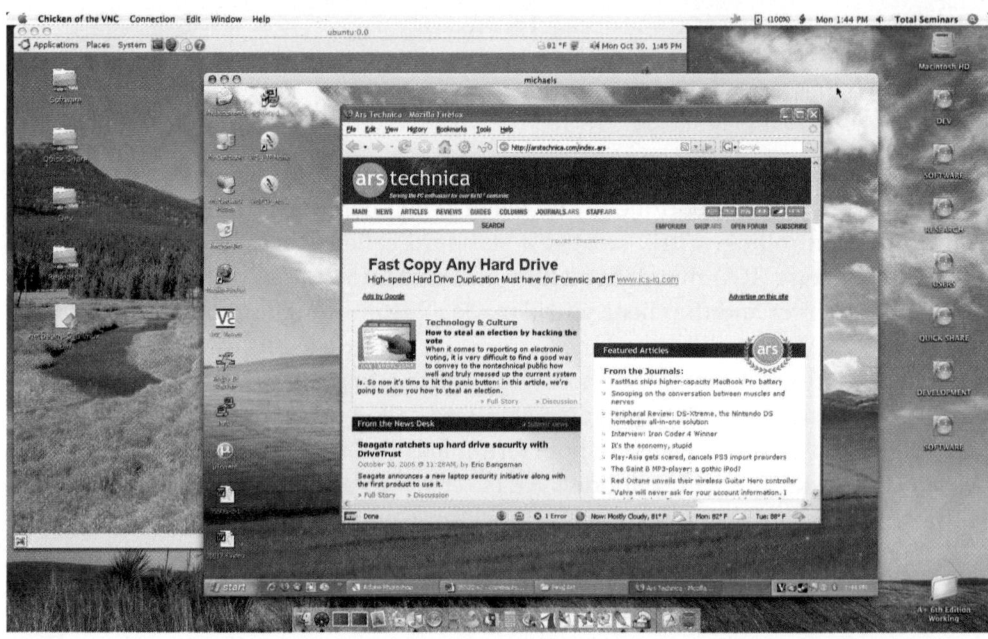

• **Figure 13.19** VNC in action

It works nicely in Secure Shell (SSH) tunnels for great security, plus it comes, by default, with every copy of macOS and almost every Linux distro. Why bother sharing if you can literally be at the screen? Oh, and did I mention that VNC is completely free?

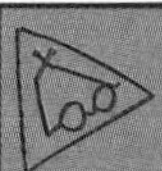

Tech Tip

In-Band Management

VNC and SSH enable in-band management of resources, meaning software installed on both the client and the remote system enables direct control over resources. The interaction uses the primary network connection for both devices, thus it's in-band and sharing resources (and traffic) with the regular network.

In-band management is fast and inexpensive but has a couple of drawbacks in a busy network. First, the remote system must be booted up with its operating system fully loaded for this to work. Second, putting management of a remote system on the main network doesn't provide as much security or control as a dedicated, alternative connection would provide.

Many servers employ lights-out-management (LOM) capabilities that enable out-of-band management to address these issues. We'll see a lot more of these technologies when we discuss network monitoring and management in Chapter 20.

Virtual Private Networks

Remote connections have been around for a long time, even before the Internet existed. The biggest drawback to remote connections was the cost to connect. If you were on one side of the continent and had to connect to your LAN on the other side of the continent, the only connection option was a telephone. Or, if you needed to connect two LANs across the continent, you ended up paying outrageous monthly charges for a private connection. The introduction of the Internet gave people wishing to connect to their home or work networks a very inexpensive connection option, but there was one problem—the whole Internet was (and is) open to the public. People wanted to stop using dial-up and expensive private connections and use the Internet instead, but they wanted to be able to do it securely.

If you read the previous chapter, you might think you could use some of the tools for securing TCP/IP to help, and you would be correct. Several standards use encrypted tunnels between a computer or a remote network and a private network through the Internet (Figure 13.20), resulting in what is called a **virtual private network (VPN)**.

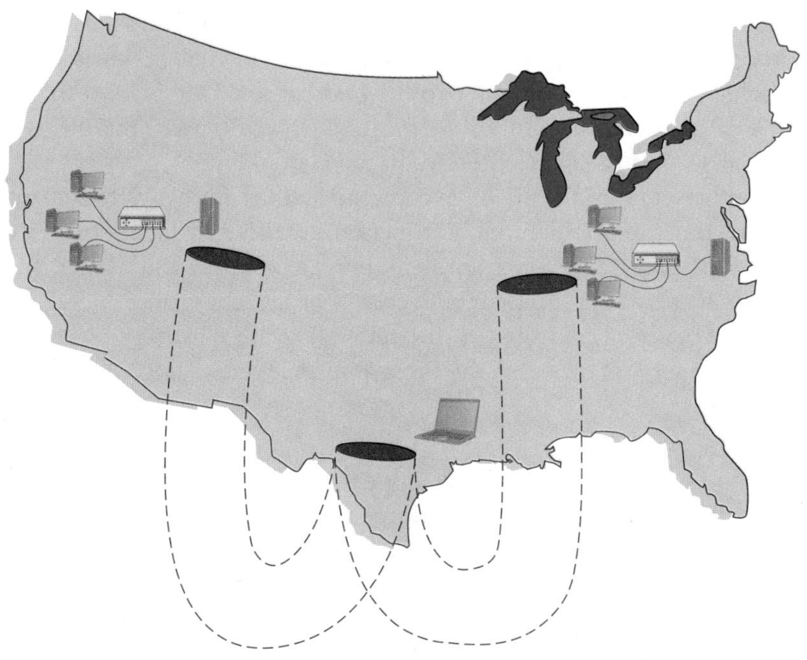

• **Figure 13.20** VPN connecting computers across the United States

An encrypted tunnel requires *endpoints*—the ends of the tunnel where the data is encrypted and decrypted. In the tunnels you've seen thus far, the client for the application sits on one end and the server sits on the other. VPNs do the same thing. Either some software running on a computer or, in some cases, a dedicated box must act as an endpoint for a VPN (Figure 13.21).

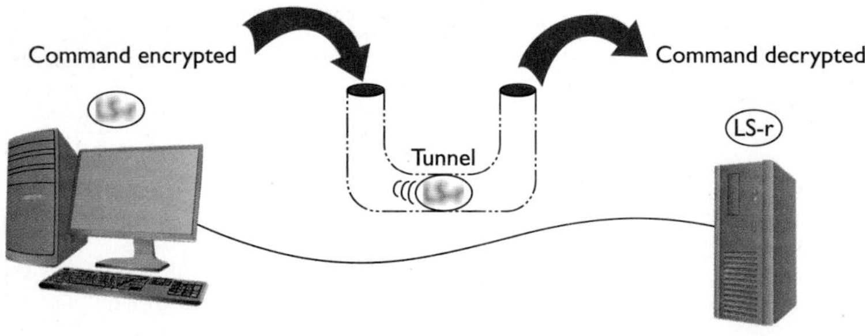

• **Figure 13.21** Typical tunnel

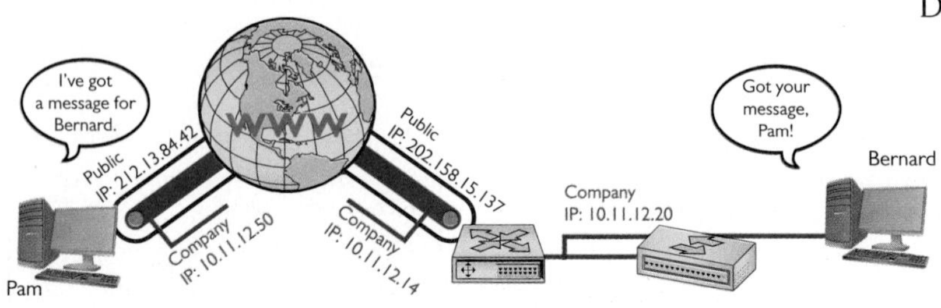

• **Figure 13.22** Endpoints must have their own IP addresses.

The key with the VPN is that the computers should be on the same network—and that means they must all have the same network ID. You would want the laptop that you use in the Denver airport lounge, for example, to have the same network ID as the computers in the LAN back at the office. But there's no simple way to do this. If it's a single client trying to access a network, that client is going to take on the IP address from its local DHCP server. In the case of your laptop in the airport, your network ID and IP address come from the DHCP server in the airport, not the DHCP server back at the office.

To make the VPN work, you need VPN client software installed on your local machine—the laptop at the Denver airport—and VPN server software or hardware at your office. You connect your laptop first to the Internet using the airport wireless network; it's just a normal Internet connection. Second, the VPN client software creates a virtual NIC on your laptop (endpoint 1), makes a connection with the VPN server at the office (endpoint 2), and then, in essence, creates a virtual direct cable from the virtual NIC to the office (Figure 13.22). That "virtual cable" is called a **VPN tunnel**. The laptop now has two IPv4 addresses. One is local from the airport DHCP server. The other is "local," but works with the office network. That second IP address goes with the virtual NIC.

Clever network engineers have come up with many ways to make this work, and those implementations function at different layers of the OSI model. PPTP and L2TP, for example, work at the Data Link layer. Many VPNs use IPsec at the Network layer to handle encryption needs. TLS VPNs don't really fit into the OSI model well at all, with some features in the Session layer and others in the Presentation layer.

PPTP VPNs

So how do you make IP addresses appear out of thin air? Point-to-Point Protocol (PPP) can make the connection.

Microsoft got the ball rolling with the **Point-to-Point Tunneling Protocol (PPTP)**, an advanced version of PPP that handles the connection right out of the box. Microsoft places the PPTP endpoints on the client and the server. The server endpoint is a special remote access server program on a Windows server, called **Routing and Remote Access Service (RRAS)**. Figure 13.23 shows Remote Access in Windows Server 2016.

On the Windows client side, you run **Add a VPN connection** (Figure 13.24) in Settings in the Control Panel. (With older versions of Windows, you'd run the **Create a new connection** option in the Network and Sharing Center applet.) This creates a virtual NIC that, like any other NIC, does a DHCP query and gets an IP address from the DHCP server on the private network.

> A system connected to a VPN looks as though it's on the local network but performs much slower than if the system were connected directly back at the office, because it's not local at all.

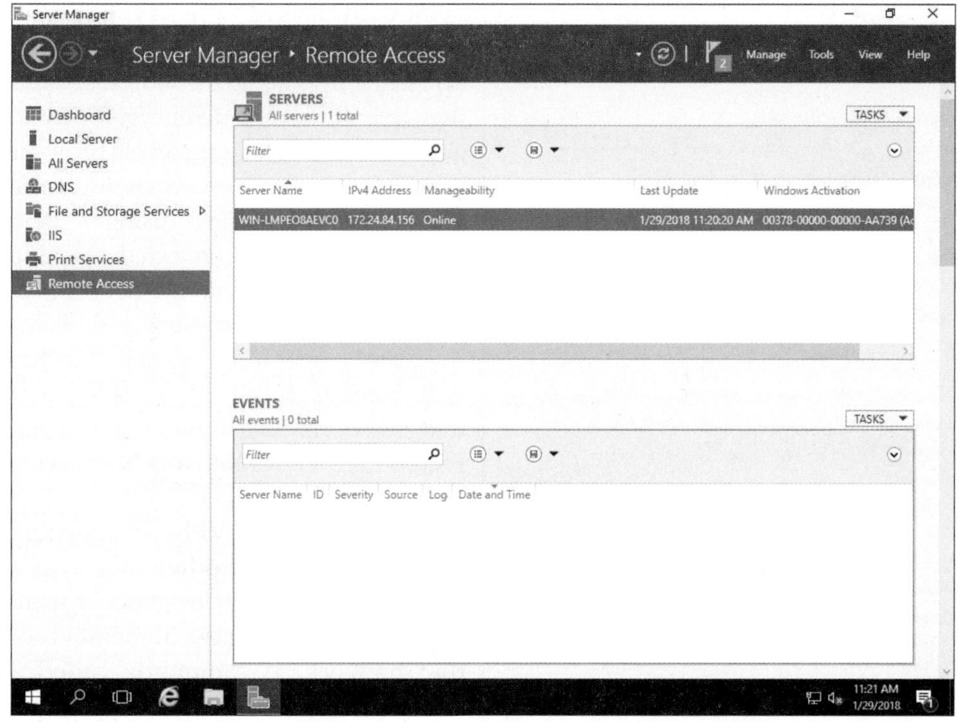

• **Figure 13.23** RRAS in action

When your computer connects to the RRAS server on the private network, PPTP creates a secure tunnel through the Internet to the private LAN. Your client takes on an IP address of that network, as if your computer is directly connected to the LAN at the office, even down to the default gateway.

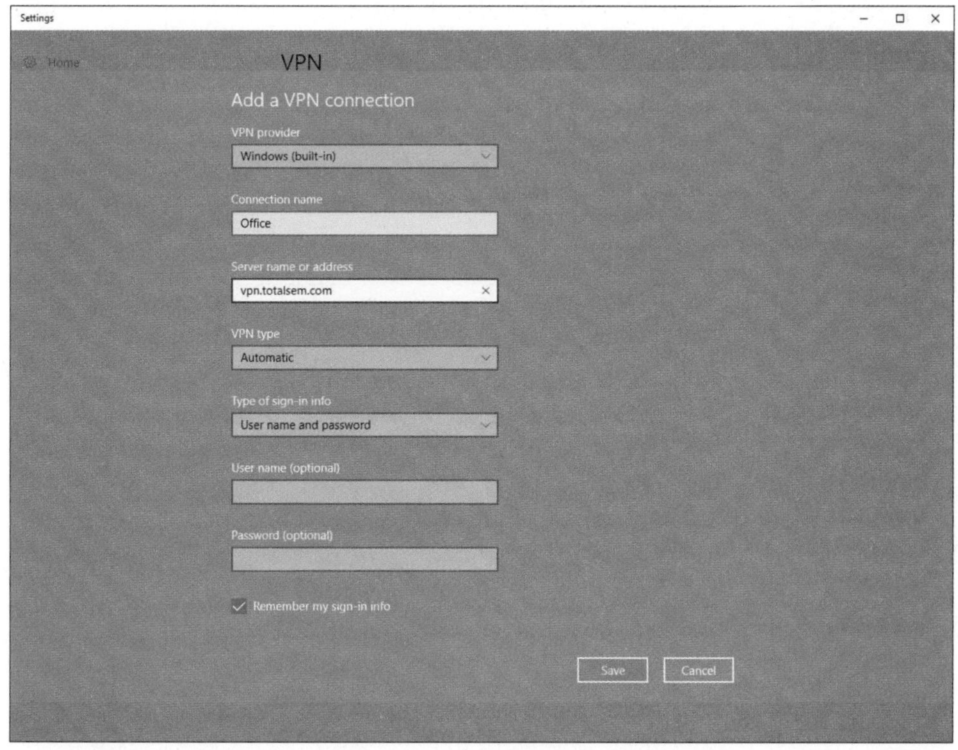

• **Figure 13.24** Setting up a VPN connection in Windows 10

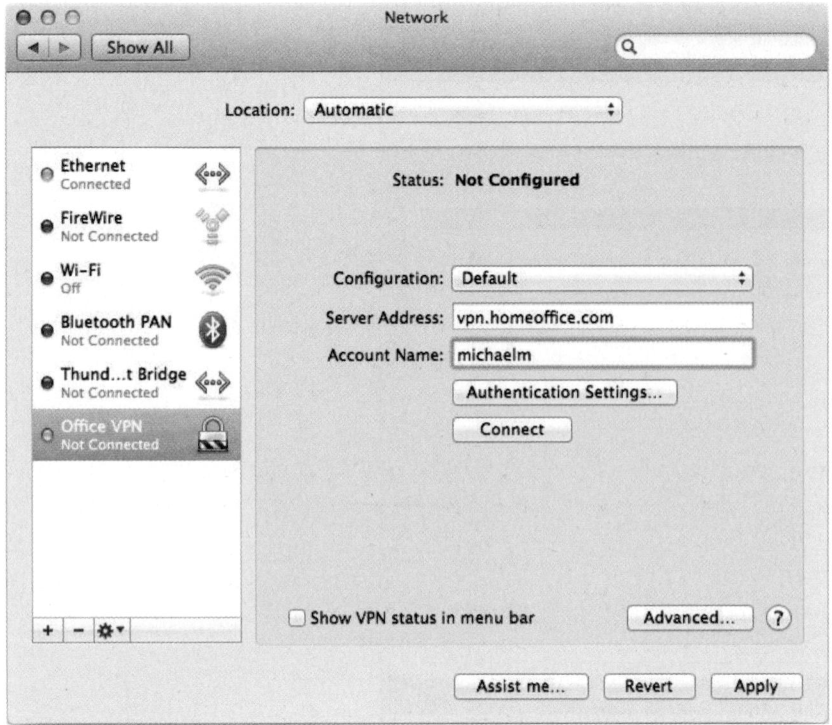

• **Figure 13.25** VPN on a macOS system

In the early days of VPNs, if you opened a Web browser, your client would go across the Internet to the local LAN and then use the LAN's default gateway to get to the Internet! Using a Web browser would be much slower when you were on a VPN. Nowadays, using a Web browser on a VPN-connected machine will use the faster local Internet connectivity, so this is not an issue.

Every operating system comes with some type of built-in VPN client that supports PPTP (among others). Figure 13.25 shows Network, the macOS VPN connection tool.

This type of VPN connection, where a single computer logs into a remote network and becomes, for all intents and purposes, a member of that network, is commonly called a **host-to-site VPN** connection.

> The focal point for VPN connections is called the *VPN headend*. This is often the VPN concentrator.

> A *split tunnel* VPN connection creates a secure connection to a remote network but leaves the rest of the Internet connection to the local connection. When you open a browser, in other words, and surf to www.google.com, you would go through the local, regular interface, not the VPN one. In a *full tunnel* VPN, in contrast, every connection goes through the remote connection. This offers security in exchange for performance; that is, full tunnel Internet connections are slug-like compared to split tunnel Internet connections.

L2TP VPNs

The VPN protocol called **Layer 2 Tunneling Protocol (L2TP)** took all the good features of PPTP and a Cisco protocol called *Layer 2 Forwarding (L2F)* and added support to run on almost any type of connection possible, from telephones to Ethernet to ultra-high-speed optical connections. The endpoint on the local LAN went from a server program to a VPN-capable router, called a **VPN concentrator**.

Cisco provides free client software to connect a single faraway PC to a Cisco VPN. This creates a typical host-to-site or **client-to-site VPN** connection. Network people often directly connect two Cisco VPN concentrators to connect two separate LANs permanently. It's slow, but inexpensive, compared to a dedicated high-speed connection between two faraway LANs. This kind of connection enables two LANs to function as a single network, sharing files and services as if in the same building. This is called a **site-to-site VPN** connection.

L2TP differs from PPTP in that it has no authentication or encryption. L2TP generally uses IPsec for all security needs. Technically, you should call an L2TP VPN an "L2TP/IPsec" VPN. L2TP works perfectly well in the single-client-connecting-to-a-LAN scenario, too. Every operating system's VPN client fully supports L2TP/IPsec VPNs.

SSL (Really TLS) VPNs

Cisco makes VPN hardware that enables **SSL VPNs**. These types of VPN offer an advantage over Data Link– or Network-based VPNs because they don't require any special client software. **Clientless VPN** clients connect to the VPN server using a standard Web browser, with the traffic secured using Transport Layer Security (TLS), requiring no specific client-based software. (TLS replaced Secure Sockets Layer, or SSL, many years ago, but the SSL VPN moniker stuck.) The two most common types of SSL VPNs are SSL portal VPNs and SSL tunnel VPNs.

With SSL portal VPNs, a client accesses the VPN and is presented with a secure Web page. The client gains access to anything linked on that page, be it e-mail, data, links to other pages, and so on.

With tunnel VPNs, in contrast, the client Web browser runs some kind of active control, such as Java, and gains much greater access to the VPN-connected network. SSL tunnel VPNs create a more typical host-to-site connection than SSL portal VPNs, but the user must have sufficient permissions to run the active browser controls.

Aside from client-to-site and site-to-site VPNs, you'll sometimes see *host-to-host* connections discussed. A **host-to-host VPN** deals with a specific single connection between two machines using VPN software or hardware.

DTLS VPNs

Datagram TLS (DTLS) VPNs optimize connections for delay-sensitive applications, such as voice and video over a VPN. After establishing a traditional TLS tunnel, DTLS VPNs use UDP datagrams rather than TCP segments for communication. This enhances certain types of VPN traffic. *Cisco AnyConnect DTLS VPN* is the prototypical example of this sort of VPN implementation.

Many VPN technologies use the terms *client* and *server* to denote the functions of the devices that make the connection. You'll also see the terms *host* and *gateway* to refer to the connections, such as a *host-to-gateway tunnel*.

DMVPN

Extending VPN access across a company with multiple locations can create some logistical problems. The (fictional) Bayland Widgets Corporation has a main office in Houston and two satellite offices for manufacturing, one in El Paso and the other in Laredo. A traditional VPN located at the center location would become a bottleneck for traffic. Site-to-site traffic follows a familiar pattern, with the El Paso-to-Houston and Laredo-to-Houston connections going to the central VPN. But what about connections between El Paso and Laredo? With a traditional VPN, all that traffic would route through the main VPN in Houston. That seems inefficient!

A **dynamic multipoint VPN (DMVPN)** fixes this problem by enabling direct VPN connections between multiple locations directly. With a DMVPN solution, traffic between El Paso and Laredo happens directly, with no need to travel through the main Houston VPN. The typical DMVPN solution, such as a Cisco DMVPN, employs standard security (IPsec) to make all the connections secure from unwanted prying.

Alternative VPNs

There are other popular VPN options beyond PPTP, L2TP, and SSL, such as OpenVPN and SSH. The most common VPN technologies today offer pure (no L2TP) IPsec solutions. These **IPsec VPN** technologies use IPsec tunneling for VPNs, such as Cisco IOS Easy VPN.

Another alternative is the Cisco-developed *Generic Routing Encapsulation (GRE)* protocol paired with IPsec for encryption. You can use GRE to make a point-to-point tunnel connection that carries all sorts of traffic over Layer 3, including multicast and IPv6 traffic. This works great for smaller implementations, but scaled up, having a unique tunnel for each node (or spoke) makes configuration of the main hub router excessive. The DMVPN solution discussed solves this by using *multipoint GRE (mGRE)* protocol for dynamically configured tunnels and tunnels to go to multiple destinations.

WAN Troubleshooting Scenarios

Competent network techs can recognize and deal with typical remote connectivity issues in a WAN setting. Sometimes the problem lies well beyond the job description, but that's when the tech knows to escalate the problem. This section looks at four very important CompTIA Network+ problem areas: loss of Internet connectivity, interface errors, DNS issues, and interference.

Loss of Internet Connectivity

Given that the core reason to use all these forms of remote connectivity is to get to the Internet in the first place, I don't look at loss of Internet connectivity as a problem. It's more a symptom. Be sure to watch for WAN scenarios on the CompTIA Network+ exam that really aren't always WAN scenarios.

If you want to connect a computer to the Internet, that computer needs a legitimate IP address, subnet mask, default gateway, and DNS address. These needs don't change whether you connect through a Gigabit Ethernet wired network or through a cable modem. Use the utilities already covered in the book in such a scenario, such as ping, ipconfig, netstat, nslookup, and so forth, to verify that the device has a solid IP connection.

Interface Errors

CompTIA loves to use the term *interface errors* as a catchall term to describe the many connections between your computer and the remote connection that enables you to get to the Internet. In a WAN scenario you'll have at least one more interface than in a native Ethernet world. Think about a typical office environment.

Local Ethernet Interface/LAN Interfaces

When you use DSL or cable or any other form of remote connection, it's very easy to forget all of the LAN connections that make connectivity possible. It's plausible, if you're anything like me, that you'll call an ISP like Comcast or AT&T and complain, only to find that you don't have a patch cable plugged into the right port on the back of the computer. (Not that I've ever done this. Twice.)

Before you blame Comcast or AT&T for losing your connection, make sure to verify that everything on your end is in order. Is the computer properly connected to the LAN? If you are using a router, is it providing good IP information? Can you access the router and see if it is reporting that it has a proper upstream connection? Before you blame the WAN interface, always first confirm everything on the LAN.

Modem Interface

It doesn't really matter what type of remote connection you use. There's always a "modem." Be careful here: "modem" is the term commonly used for any box that sits in your location and connects your LAN to the WAN, even if your ISP calls it something loftier like: cable modem, router, optical network terminal (ONT), or *customer premises equipment (CPE)*.

Everything said here that references "modem" works for whatever CPE device your ISP provides.

The modem's job is to connect your LAN to the WAN, so by definition it's going to have at least two interfaces: one to the LAN and one to the WAN. First of all, familiarize yourself with the lights on your modem, preferably before you have problems. Any modem is going to have a power LED, link LEDs to both the LAN and the WAN, and some form of activity LED. Study them first when you're looking for interface issues. In almost every case of a bad interface, you'll verify connections and reset the modem.

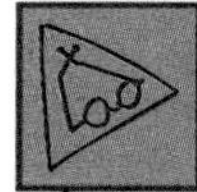

Tech Tip

Quad9

In 2017, the Global Cyber Alliance (a group dedicated to reducing cybercrime) and IBM and other players launched Quad9, a free public DNS server that blocks the bad domains and whitelists the good domains. Phishing and scammer domains are blocked; Google and Amazon, for example, are not. Check it out by changing your DNS server to 9.9.9.9. The computer you save might be your own!

DNS Issues

There is one specific DNS issue that comes up in WANs: choosing what DNS server to use. Every ISP has its own DNS server(s) and, in almost every case, your modem is going to propagate those DNS settings down to every device in your LAN. In most cases there isn't any problem with this, but there are two cases where you might want to consider manually adding DNS to your local devices or your local router. First, an ISP's DNS servers can fail.

Second, some ISPs will *help* and redirect your browser to advertising or to links of possible sites you meant when you type in an incorrect URL.

In either of these cases, the rules you learned back in Chapter 9 still apply. Get yourself a fast public DNS IP address—I love the Google 8.8.8.8 and 8.8.4.4 addresses—and at the very least load one of those as a secondary DNS server.

Interference

Interference at the WAN level—that CompTIA Network+ techs can fix—generally implies the connection between the LAN and the WAN. The point at which the ISP's responsibility ends and the customer's begins is the demarc. Let's look at both sides of the demarc for interference.

On the customer side, the CPE can create problems. In a busy office building, for example, new installations or connections can add electromagnetic interference (EMI) and create disturbances. New things added to old environments, in other words, can create interference in existing networks.

When my company changed locations, for example, the building we moved into had several offices, connected to Internet and corporate WANs with several dedicated (ancient) T1 lines (Figure 13.26). With the local cable company offering 100-Mbps connections, we opted to have cable installed in the building for us (T1 was the dedicated network connection that ran at a whopping 1.5 Mbps).

If the cable company had not been careful or not used properly shielded boxes and cables, this could have wreaked havoc on the other folks in the building.

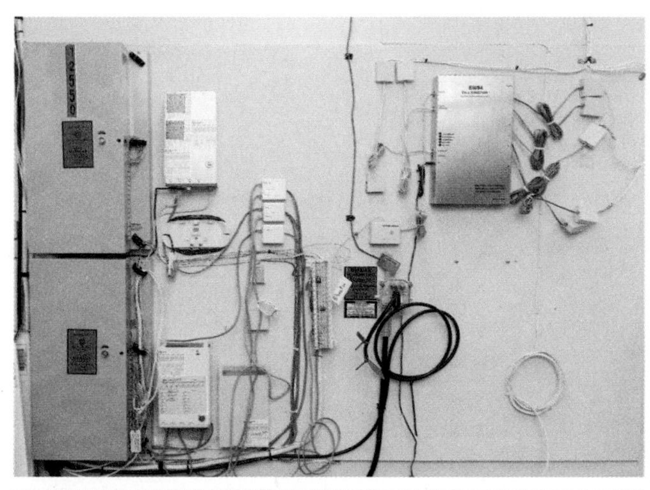

• **Figure 13.26** Demarc at my office building

In a consumer space, the CPE doesn't run into interference that would block connectivity at the demarc, unless you overly broaden the term "interference" to include "failure." Then you can point to the "modem" as the only major failure culprit.

Once you go to the ISP side of the demarc, there's not much interference involved, especially with existing, previously well-functioning networks. Again, WAN interference only happens if you extend the definition to include failure. Then storms, downed power lines, extraterrestrial activity, and so on, can cause problems.

In a home network, there are only two times you should worry about interference in a WAN outside the demarc: during installation and when changing the connection in any way. Every form of remote connection has very clear interference tolerances, and you should have the installation tech verify this. Cable and DSL self-installations are a big issue here as most people don't have access to the tools necessary to confirm their PSTN or coax cabling. If I'm installing a new DSL or cable modem, I refuse the self-install option and gladly pay the extra money to verify my cabling can handle the connection.

It's incredibly easy to introduce interference into an otherwise perfectly functioning wired WAN connection by adding splitters, noisy devices, splices, and so on. This is especially true for tech folks (like your humble author) who have learned this the hard way. In general, be conservative when disturbing your WAN connection and be ready to call support if needed.

Chapter 13 Review

■ Chapter Summary

After reading this chapter and completing the exercises, you should understand the following about remote connections.

Describe WAN telephony technologies

- Traditionally, long-distance connections that make up the Internet use a unique type of signaling called SONET. Newer technologies are gradually replacing SONET.
- The Optical Carrier (OC) specification defines speeds from 51.8 Mbps (OC-1) to 39.8 Gbps (OC-768) for fiber-optic cables used in networks conforming to the SONET standard.
- Many fiber devices utilize a very clever feature called bidirectional wavelength division multiplexing (WDM) or its newer and more popular version, dense WDM (DWDM). DWDM enables an individual single-mode fiber to carry multiple signals by giving each signal a different wavelength. A single DWDM fiber can support ~150 signals, enabling, for example, a 51.8-Mbps OC-1 line to run at 51.8 Mbps × 150 signals = 7.6 gigabytes per second.
- A related technology, course WDM (CWDM), offers a simpler and less expensive solution to DWDM, though it offers much shorter distances (a mere 60 km).
- MPLS is a router technique that labels certain data to use a desired connection.

Compare last-mile connections for connecting homes and businesses to the Internet

- DSL provides a fully digital dedicated connection. Two versions of DSL are SDSL and ADSL.
- SDSL supports speeds up to 15 Mbps, but most ISPs only provide SDSL up to 9 Mbps. SDSL provides equal upload and download speeds.
- ADSL provides download speeds up to 15 Mbps and upload speeds up to 1 Mbps, although ISPs offer varying combinations of download/upload speeds.
- All versions of DSL are limited to a maximum distance of around 18,000 feet between a user's demarc and the central office. The central office houses a DSLAM connecting multiple customers to the Internet.
- Because DSL runs over normal POTS lines, filtering out the DSL signal on the POTS line is necessary. This guarantees your POTS line will continue to work if the DSL fails.
- A DSL modem connects the telephone jack (with the DSL signal) to your computer.
- RJ-11 connectors connect the telephone jack to the DSL modem, whereas RJ-45 connectors connect the DSL modem to the computer's NIC.
- Early DSL providers used bridged connections, but these connections have been replaced by PPPoE, so providers can monitor modem usage and require users to log in with a valid account before they gain Internet access.
- Cable Internet providers offer plans ranging in speeds up to 1.2 Gbps.
- Download speeds are typically much faster than upload speeds.
- Cable modems use coaxial cable to connect to the headend and use regular UTP cabling to connect to the PC. The headend connects to the cable company's network using the DOCSIS protocol.
- Satellite Internet access is available as one-way or two-way. With a one-way connection, you download over the satellite connection but upload over PSTN. Two-way satellite service accommodates both downloads and uploads over the satellite connection. Satellite access sometimes is the only option for remote or geographically challenging areas.
- In an attempt to regain their share of the market from cable providers, some phone companies offering DSL are now offering fiber-to-the-home connections in the form of AT&T Fiber (AT&T) or Fios (Verizon).

- Global System for Mobile Communications (GSM) relied on a type of time-division multiplexing called time-division multiple access (TDMA).
- GSM introduced the handy and now common SIM card.
- Code-division multiple access (CDMA) was heavily adopted by U.S. carriers and does not use a SIM card. CDMA was rare outside the USA.
- Evolved High-Speed Packet Access (HSPA+), a 3G technology, provided theoretical speeds up to 168 Mbps, but practical speeds rarely exceeding 10 Mbps.
- Long Term Evolution (LTE) is the dominant cellular WAN technology today, commonly marketed as 4G technology.
- 5G is the cellular standard slowly replacing 4G, offering speeds up to 1 Gbps over three bands, low, medium, and high.

Discuss and implement various remote access connections

- Remote terminal emulation allows a user to take over a remote computer as if he or she were sitting in front of it, as opposed to simply accessing remote resources. Citrix Virtual Apps and Desktops is a popular terminal emulator.
- Microsoft's terminal emulator is called Remote Desktop Connection, which uses its own Remote Desktop Protocol. VNC is a cross-platform terminal emulator that comes with macOS and many Linux distributions.
- A VPN creates a tunnel that enables users to connect to remote LANs across the Internet.
- RRAS, a program available only on Windows servers, allows VPN connections using PPTP. PPTP creates the secure tunnel through the Internet to your private LAN.
- L2TP is a Cisco VPN protocol that was built on the best features of Microsoft's PPTP and Cisco's L2F. Rather than requiring special server software (such as Microsoft's RRAS), L2TP places a tunnel endpoint directly on a VPN-capable router.
- L2TP provides no authentication or encryption. It usually relies on IPsec for this.
- SSL VPNs come in two flavors: portal and tunnel. Both provide connectivity to the internal network through a standard Web browser and do not need special client software. All "SSL" VPNs today use the successor to SSL, Transport Layer Security (TLS), to enable security.
- Many VPN implementation these days implement IPsec directly, without using any of the older protocols.

Troubleshoot various WAN scenarios

- Competent network techs can recognize and deal with typical remote connectivity issues in a WAN setting. Issues include loss of Internet connectivity, interface errors, DNS problems, and interference.
- Loss of internet connectivity points to problems common to networks in general. Use standard command-line tools like ping and ipconfig to determine IP address, default gateway, and so on.
- Interface errors can be a lot of things. LAN settings can cause seemingly "WAN" errors, for example. The modem/cable box/CPE—i.e., the magic box that does routing as well as handling ingoing and outgoing traffic between the LAN and the WAN—can be the source of interface errors. Check the link lights, verify connections, and possibly reset the modem.
- DNS issues involve problems accessing an ISP's DNS servers. Keep a handy backup DNS server like 8.8.8.8 (Google) that you can plug in to bypass the local DNS servers if you experience problems.
- Interference at the WAN level generally falls into two categories: interference among the connectivity devices inside the demarc (the CPE), and changes to home cable or DSL installations outside the house (such as adding a splitter to a coaxial cable).

Key Terms

3G *(363)*
4G *(363)*
5G *(364)*
asymmetric DSL (ADSL) *(358)*
bidirectional wavelength division multiplexing (WDM or BWDM) *(354)*
bridged connection *(359)*
client-to-site VPN *(370)*

- **clientless VPN** *(370)*
- **coarse wavelength division multiplexing (CWDM)** *(354)*
- **code-division multiple access (CDMA)** *(363)*
- **Data Over Cable Service Interface Specification (DOCSIS)** *(361)*
- **datagram TLS (DTLS) VPN** *(371)*
- **dense wavelength division multiplexing (DWDM)** *(354)*
- **digital subscriber line (DSL)** *(358)*
- **DSL Access Multiplexer (DSLAM)** *(358)*
- **DSL modem** *(359)*
- **dynamic multipoint VPN (DMVPN)** *(371)*
- **Enhanced Data rates for GSM Evolution (EDGE)** *(363)*
- **Evolved High-Speed Packet Access (HSPA+)** *(363)*
- **Global System for Mobile Communications (GSM)** *(362)*
- **host-to-host VPN** *(371)*
- **host-to-site VPN** *(370)*
- **Independent Computing Architecture (ICA)** *(365)*
- **IPsec VPN** *(371)*
- **last mile** *(357)*
- **Layer 2 Tunneling Protocol (L2TP)** *(370)*
- **Long Term Evolution (LTE)** *(363)*
- **metro Ethernet** *(357)*
- **Multiprotocol Label Switching (MPLS)** *(355)*
- **Optical Carrier (OC)** *(354)*
- **passive optical network (PON)** *(361)*
- **Point-to-Point Protocol over Ethernet (PPPoE)** *(359)*
- **Point-to-Point Tunneling Protocol (PPTP)** *(368)*
- **provider link** *(357)*
- **remote access** *(364)*
- **Remote Desktop Protocol (RDP)** *(365)*
- **remote terminal** *(365)*
- **Routing and Remote Access Service (RRAS)** *(368)*
- **site-to-site VPN** *(370)*
- **smart jack** *(358)*
- **SSL VPN** *(370)*
- **subscriber identity module (SIM) card** *(362)*
- **symmetric DSL (SDSL)** *(358)*
- **Synchronous Digital Hierarchy (SDH)** *(353)*
- **Synchronous Optical Network (SONET)** *(353)*
- **Virtual Network Computing (VNC)** *(366)*
- **virtual private network (VPN)** *(367)*
- **VPN concentrator** *(370)*
- **VPN tunnel** *(368)*
- **wide area network (WAN)** *(352)*

Key Term Quiz

Use the Key Terms list to complete the sentences that follow. Not all the terms will be used.

1. _______________ is the primary standard in the United States for long-distance, high-speed, fiber-optic transmission systems.
2. In the world of DSL, _______________ provides equal upload and download speeds up to 15 Mbps.
3. _______________ is a routing technique that avoids running IP packets through their full routing tables and instead uses the header information to route packets quickly.
4. A(n) _______________ optimizes connections for delay-sensitive applications, such as voice and video over a VPN.
5. A(n) _______________ enables direct VPN connections between multiple locations directly.
6. A VPN connection where a single computer logs into a remote network and becomes a member of that network is commonly called a(n) _______________ connection.
7. A(n) _______________ is a network created by a secure tunnel from one network to another remote network.
8. _______________ is a special program running on Microsoft servers that enables remote users to connect to a local Microsoft network.
9. _______________ cellular technology does not use SIM cards.
10. _______________ is the most recent and most common cellular WAN technology.

Multiple-Choice Quiz

1. Janina needs to connect two office LANs in two different cities to function as a single network. She opts to use virtual private networking to connect the two LANs over the public Internet. What kind of VPN connection will she employ?
   - A. Client-to-site
   - B. Host-to-host
   - C. Point-to-point
   - D. Site-to-site
2. Sinjay's home office is 200 meters from his ISP's DSLAM. Which DSL version will provide him with, theoretically, up to 100 Mbps of both download and upload speeds?
   - A. DS3
   - B. ADSL
   - C. SDSL
   - D. VDSL
3. Which protocol is used by cable companies?
   - A. PPPoE
   - B. DOCSIS
   - C. PSTN
   - D. SIP
4. What is a reason to use a satellite Internet connection?
   - A. It offers speeds faster than both DSL and cable.
   - B. The upload and download speeds are always equal.
   - C. It is often available in remote locations where DSL and cable are not.
   - D. If offers better security than both DSL and cable.
5. Marcy is working from home, but she uses a VPN to connect to her network at work and is able to access files stored on the remote network just as if she were physically in the office. Which protocols make it possible for Marcy to receive an IP address from the DHCP server at work? (Select two.)
   - A. PPTP
   - B. IDS
   - C. L2TP
   - D. IPS
6. Which of the following describes a VPN?
   - A. A remote connection using a secure tunnel across the Internet
   - B. Segmenting a local network into smaller networks without subnetting
   - C. A network that is protected from viruses
   - D. A protocol used to encrypt L2TP traffic
7. Which is an advantage of SSL (really TLS) VPNs over Data Link layer or Network layer VPNs?
   - A. SSL VPNs use specialized client software for secure connections.
   - B. SSL VPNs function at Layer 1, the Physical layer, and thus run much faster than Layer 2 or Layer 3 VPNs.
   - C. SSL VPNs offer robust security features and, therefore, do not rely on other protocols or services to handle encryption.
   - D. SSL VPNs don't require specialized client software because they use Web browsers.
8. Which architecture enables fiber-to-the-home to connect the neighborhood switch to the premises?
   - A. DOCSIS
   - B. HSPA+
   - C. PON
   - D. PPPoE
9. Which technology enables a private optical network within a MAN?
   - A. DSL
   - B. DOCSIS
   - C. Metro Ethernet
   - D. VPN
10. Which technology runs at three bands and enables wireless data speeds up to 1 Gbps?
    - A. 2G
    - B. 3G
    - C. 4G
    - D. 5G

11. Aaron wants to connect to and control a remote computer via a GUI. Which Microsoft protocol would enable this connection?
    - **A.** Remote terminal
    - **B.** ICA
    - **C.** RDP
    - **D.** VNC
12. What technology enables single-mode fiber to carry multiple signals of varying wavelengths at the same time?
    - **A.** DWDM
    - **B.** HSPA+
    - **C.** MPLS
    - **D.** WDSL
13. Which last-mile technology employs an F connector?
    - **A.** Cable
    - **B.** DSL
    - **C.** Fiber
    - **D.** Satellite
14. Which last-mile technology enables bidirectional throughput of up to 1 Gbps?
    - **A.** Cable
    - **B.** DSL
    - **C.** Fiber
    - **D.** 4G
15. Abraham wants to connect his office to the Internet, but the building is historic, so he can't run wires. Which option would give him the most throughput?
    - **A.** Cable
    - **B.** DSL
    - **C.** Fiber
    - **D.** Satellite

■ Essay Quiz

1. Early DSL providers used bridged connections, but now they tend to use PPPoE instead. What is the difference between these connection types and why do you think DSL providers switched?

Lab Projects

• Lab Project 13.1

Which last-mile options do you have in your neighborhood? DSL, cable, fiber, satellite? How do they compare with the options of your classmates?

• Lab Project 13.2

Take a survey of your fellow students and ask them which mobile devices they use and why they chose those particular devices.

Wireless Networking

"Casting my fate to the heavens, quite literally, I decided to go wireless. Completely wireless. All wireless, all the time, everywhere."

—Kara Swisher, technology journalist; co-founder of Recode

In this chapter, you will learn how to

- **Explain wireless networking standards**
- **Describe the process for implementing Wi-Fi networks**
- **Describe troubleshooting techniques for wireless networks**

Every type of network covered thus far in the book assumes that your PCs connect to your network with some kind of physical cabling. Now it's time to cut the cord and look at the many technologies that collectively changed the way we use the Internet: wireless networking.

Historical/Conceptual

You need to be careful when talking about wireless networking. Wireless is everywhere. It's in our phones and in our laptops. It's at home, work, and school. Wireless is so transparent and handy we tend to forget that wireless isn't a single technology. There are a number of technologies that collectively make up wireless networking.

Let's start with the basics. Instead of a physical set of wires running among networked PCs, servers, printers, or what-have-you, a **wireless network** uses radio frequency (RF) waves to enable these devices to communicate with each other. Wireless technologies provide incredible flexibility and mobility.

For all their disconnected goodness, wireless networks share more similarities than differences with wired networks. With the exception of the first two OSI layers, wireless networks use the same protocols as wired networks. The thing that differs is the type of media—radio waves instead of cables—and the protocols for transmitting and accessing data. Different wireless networking solutions have come and gone in the past, but the wireless networking market these days is dominated by **Wi-Fi**, a family of protocols based on IEEE 802.11 standards.

Because the networking signal is freed from wires, you'll sometimes hear the term *unbounded media* to describe wireless networking.

This chapter looks first at the standards for modern wireless networks and then turns to implementing those networks. The chapter finishes with a discussion on troubleshooting Wi-Fi.

Test Specific

Wi-Fi Standards

Wi-Fi is by far the most widely adopted wireless networking type today, especially for accessing the Internet. You'd be hard-pressed to find a location—work or home—that doesn't have Wi-Fi. Millions of private businesses and homes have wireless networks, and most public places, such as coffee shops and libraries, offer Internet access through wireless networks.

A lot of folks think Wi-Fi originally stood for *wireless fidelity* to make it cutely equated with *high fidelity (Hi-Fi)*, but it doesn't really stand for anything. It's just a name.

Wi-Fi technologies have been around since the late 1990s, supported and standardized under the umbrella IEEE 802.11 standards. The 802.11 standard has been updated continually since then, manifested by a large number of amendments to the standard. These amendments have names such as 802.11g and 802.11ac. It's important for you to understand all of these 802.11 amendments in detail, as well as the original version, 802.11.

802.11

The **802.11** standard defines both how wireless devices communicate and how to secure that communication. The original 802.11 standard, now often referred to as *802.11-1997*, is no longer used, but it established the baseline features common to all subsequent Wi-Fi standards.

The 802.11-1997 standard defined certain features, such as a wireless network cards, special configuration software, and the capability to run in multiple styles of networks. In addition, 802.11-1997 defined how transmissions work, so we'll look at frequencies of radio signals, transmission methods, and collision avoidance.

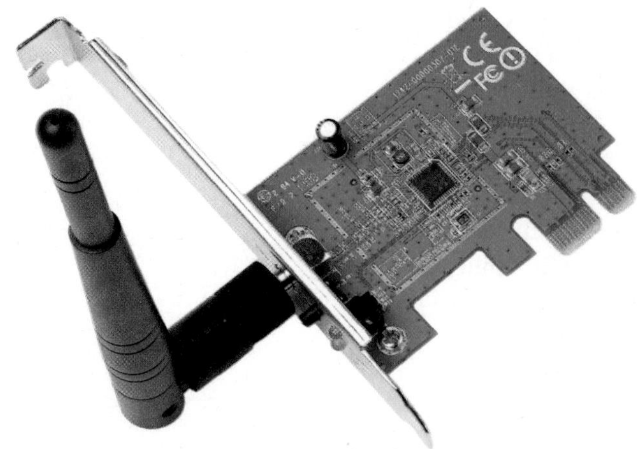

• **Figure 14.1** Internal PCIe wireless NIC

Hardware

Wireless networking hardware serves the same function as hardware used on wired PCs. Wireless Ethernet NICs take data passed down from the upper OSI layers, encapsulate it into frames, send the frames out on the network media in streams of ones and zeroes, and receive frames sent from other computing devices. The only difference is that instead of charging up a network cable with electrical current or firing off pulses of light, these devices transmit and receive radio waves.

Wireless networking capabilities of one form or another are built into many modern computing devices. Almost all portable devices have built-in wireless capabilities. Desktop computers can easily go wireless by adding an expansion card. Figure 14.1 shows a wireless PCI Express (PCIe) Ethernet card.

• **Figure 14.2** External USB wireless NIC

You can also add wireless network capabilities using USB wireless network adapters, an example of which is shown in Figure 14.2. The USB NICs have the added benefit of being *placeable*—that is, you can move them around to catch the wireless signal as strongly as possible, akin to moving the "rabbit ears" on old pre-cable television sets.

Is the wireless network adapter in all your devices the only hardware you need to create a wireless network? Well, if your needs are simple—for example, if you're connecting a few laptops on a long train ride so you and your buddies can play a game together—then the answer is yes. If, however, you need to extend the capabilities of a wireless network—say, connecting a wireless network segment to a wired network—you need additional equipment. This typically means a wireless access point.

> It's the same concept, but 802.11 frames are not addressed and encapsulated the same way as 802.3 Ethernet frames.

A **wireless access point (WAP)** is a device designed to interconnect wireless network nodes with wired networks. A basic WAP operates like a hub and works at OSI Layer 1. Many WAP manufacturers combine multiple devices into one box, however, to create a WAP with a built-in switch and/or router, all rolled into one and working at several OSI layers. The eero device shown in Figure 14.3 is an example of this type of combo device.

> Many manufacturers drop the word "wireless" from wireless access points and simply call them *access points*. Furthermore, many sources abbreviate both forms, so you'll see the former written as *WAP* and the latter as *AP*. The CompTIA Network+ exam acronym list includes both terms.

Cross Check

Using Routers

You've seen wired routers before, and wireless routers function similarly, so cross-check your memory. Think way back to Chapter 1 and see if you can answer these questions. What can a router do for your network? Can you use a router to connect to the Internet? At what layer of the OSI seven-layer model do routers function? How do routers handle addressing?

Software

Every wireless network adapter needs two pieces of software to function with an operating system: a device driver to talk to the wireless NIC and a configuration utility. Installing drivers for wireless networking devices is usually automatic these days, but you should always consult your vendor's instructions before popping that card into a slot.

You also need a utility for configuring how the wireless hardware connects to other wireless devices. Every operating system has built-in wireless clients for configuring these settings. Figure 14.4 shows the Windows 10 Wi-Fi configuration page in the Settings app. Using this utility, you can determine important things like the **link state** (whether your wireless device is connected) and the **signal strength** (a measurement of how well your wireless device is connecting to other devices). You can also configure items such as your wireless networking *mode*, security encryption, power-saving options, and so on. I'll cover each of these topics in detail later in this chapter.

• **Figure 14.3** An eero device that acts as wireless access point, switch, and router

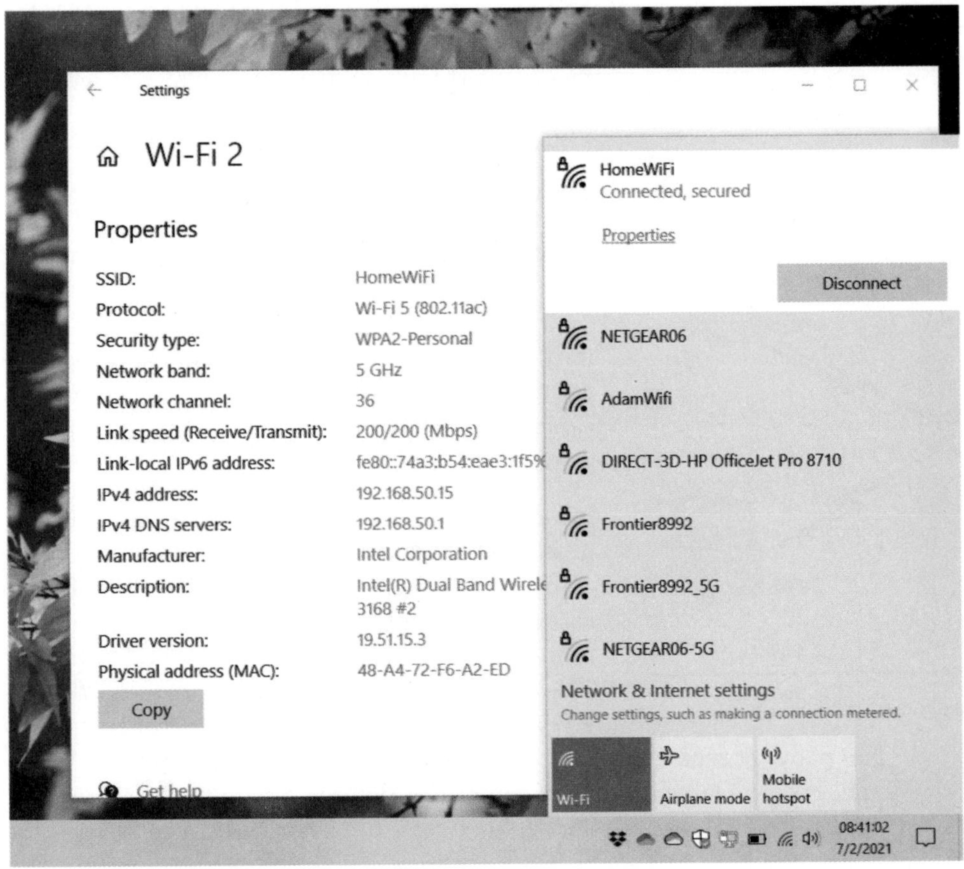

• **Figure 14.4** Wireless client configuration utility

You typically configure WAPs through browser-based setup utilities. The section "Implementing Wi-Fi" covers this process a bit later in this chapter. For now, let's look at the different modes that wireless networks use.

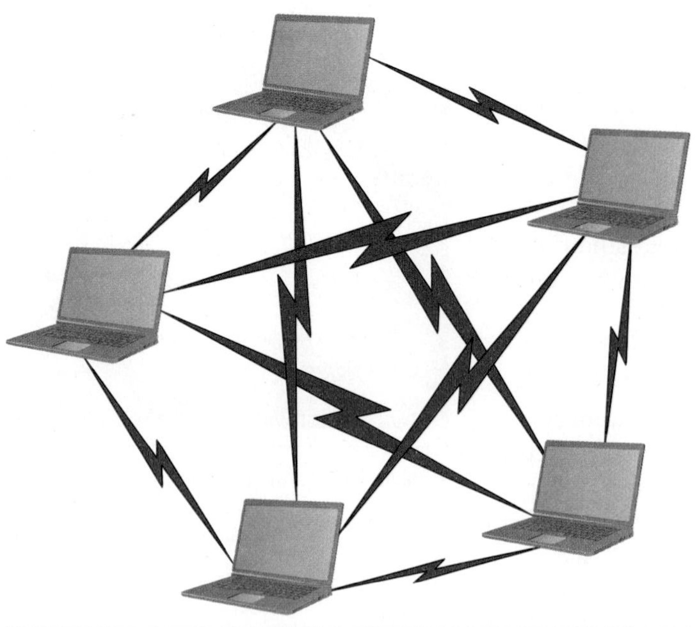

• **Figure 14.5** Wireless ad hoc mode network

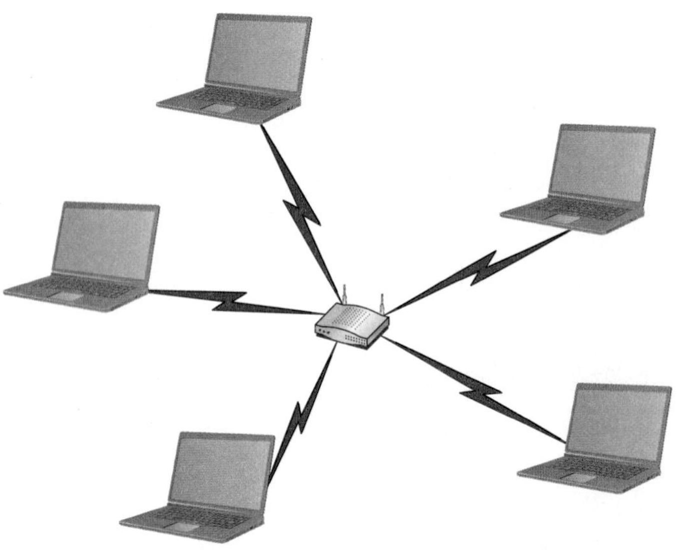

• **Figure 14.6** Wireless infrastructure mode network

Wireless Network Modes

802.11 networks operate in one of two modes. In the uncommon *ad hoc* mode, two or more devices communicate directly without any other intermediary hardware. The much more common *infrastructure* mode uses a WAP that, in essence, acts as a hub for all wireless clients. A WAP also bridges wireless network segments to wired network segments.

Ad Hoc Mode **Ad hoc mode** is sometimes called **peer-to-peer mode**, with each wireless node in direct contact with each other node in a decentralized free-for-all, as shown in Figure 14.5. Ad hoc mode does not use a WAP and instead uses a *mesh* topology, as discussed in Chapter 2.

Two or more wireless nodes communicating in ad hoc mode form an **independent basic service set (IBSS)**. This is a basic unit of organization in wireless networks. If you think of an IBSS as a wireless workgroup, you won't be far off the mark.

Ad hoc mode networks work well for small groups of computers (fewer than a dozen or so) that need to transfer files or share printers. Ad hoc networks are also good for temporary networks, such as study groups or business meetings.

Hardly anyone uses ad hoc networks for day-to-day work, however, simply because you can't use an ad hoc network to connect to other networks (unless one of the machines is running Internet Connection Sharing [ICS] or some equivalent).

Infrastructure Mode Wireless networks running in **infrastructure mode** use one or more WAPs to connect the wireless network nodes centrally, as shown in Figure 14.6. This configuration is similar to the physical *star* topology of a wired network. This creates a **wireless local area network (WLAN)**. You also use infrastructure mode to connect wireless network segments to wired segments. If you plan to set up a wireless network for a large number of computing devices, or you need to have centralized control over the wireless network, use infrastructure mode.

Cross Check

Topologies

The physical topology of a network represents the connectivity between nodes. This seems as good a time as any to cross-check your knowledge of topologies, so recall Chapter 2 and answer these questions. What are the four standard topologies? What are the hybrid topologies? If you connect a wireless network in infrastructure mode to a wired Ethernet network, what topology would that combined network have?

A single WAP servicing a given area is called a **basic service set (BSS)**. This service area can be extended by adding more access points. This is called, appropriately, an **extended service set (ESS)**.

Wireless networks running in infrastructure mode require a little more planning—such as where you place the WAPs to provide adequate coverage—than ad hoc mode networks, and they provide a stable environment for permanent wireless network installations. Infrastructure mode is better suited to business networks or networks that need to share dedicated resources such as Internet connections and centralized databases. (See "Implementing Wi-Fi" later in this chapter.)

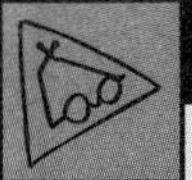

Tech Tip

EBSS vs. ESS

Many techs have dropped the word "basic" from the extended basic service set, the early name for an infrastructure-mode wireless network with more than one WAP. Accordingly, you'll see the initials for the extended basic service set as ESS. Using either EBSS or ESS is correct.

Range

Wireless networking range is hard to define. You'll see most descriptions listed with qualifiers such as "*around* 150 feet" and "*about* 300 feet." Wireless range is greatly affected by environmental factors. Interference from other wireless devices and solid objects affects range.

The maximum ranges listed in the sections that follow are those presented by wireless manufacturers as the *theoretical* maximum ranges. In the real world, you'll achieve these ranges only under the most ideal circumstances. Cutting the manufacturer's listed range in half is often a better estimate of the true effective range.

BSSID, SSID, and ESSID

Wireless devices connected together into a network, whether ad hoc or infrastructure, require some way to identify that network. Frames bound for computers within the network need to go where they're supposed to go, even when you have overlapping Wi-Fi networks. The jargon gets a little crazy here, especially because marketing has come into the mix. Stay with me.

The **basic service set identifier (BSSID)** defines the most basic infrastructure mode network—a BSS of one WAP and one or more wireless clients. With such a simple network, the Wi-Fi folks didn't see any reason to create some new numbering or naming scheme, so they made the BSSID the same as the MAC address for the WAP. Simple! Ah, but what do you do about ad hoc networks that don't have a WAP? The nodes that connect in an IBSS randomly generate a 48-bit string of numbers that looks and functions just like a MAC address, and that BSSID goes in every frame.

You could, if required, discover the MAC address for the WAP in a BSS and manually type that into the network name field when setting up a wireless computer. But that causes two problems. First, people don't want to remember strings of 48 binary digits, even if translated out as six hexadecimal octets, like A9–45–F2–3E–CA–12. People want names. Second, how do you connect two or more computers together into an IBSS when the BSSID has to be randomly generated?

The Wi-Fi folks created another level of naming called a **service set identifier (SSID)**, a standard name applied to the BSS or IBSS to help the connection happen. The SSID—sometimes called a **network name**—is up to a 32-bit identification string that's inserted into the header of each frame processed by a WAP. Every Wi-Fi device must share the same SSID to communicate in a single network. By default, a WAP advertises its existence by sending out a continuous **SSID broadcast**. It's the SSID broadcast that lets you see the wireless networks that are available on your wireless devices.

To really see the power of 802.11 in action, let's take it one step further into a Wi-Fi network that has multiple WAPs: an ESS. How do you determine the network name at this level? You use the SSID, but you apply it to the ESS as an **extended service set identifier (ESSID)**. In an ESS, every WAP connects to a central switch or switches to become part of a single broadcast domain.

With multiple WAPs in an ESS, clients connect to whichever WAP has the strongest signal. As clients move through the space covered by the broadcast area, they change WAP connections seamlessly, a process called **roaming**.

Most Wi-Fi manufacturers just use the term *SSID*, by the way, and not *ESSID*. When you configure a wireless device to connect to an ESS, you're technically using the ESSID rather than just the SSID, but the manufacturer often tries to make it simple for you by using only the letters *SSID*.

Transmission Frequency

One of the biggest issues with wireless communication is the potential for interference from other wireless devices. To solve this, different wireless devices must operate in specific transmission frequencies. Knowing these wireless frequency ranges will assist you in troubleshooting interference issues from other devices operating in the same wireless band. The original 802.11 standards use either 2.4-GHz or 5.0-GHz radio frequencies.

Transmission Methods

The original IEEE 802.11 wireless Ethernet standard defined methods by which devices may communicate using *spread-spectrum* radio waves. Spread-spectrum transmits data in small, discrete chunks over the different frequencies available within a certain frequency range.

The 802.11 standard defines three different spread-spectrum transmission methods: **direct-sequence spread-spectrum (DSSS)**, **frequency-hopping spread-spectrum (FHSS)**, and **orthogonal frequency-division multiplexing (OFDM)**. DSSS sends data out on different frequencies at the same time, whereas FHSS sends data on one frequency at a time, constantly shifting (or *hopping*) frequencies. DSSS uses considerably more bandwidth than FHSS—around 22 MHz as opposed to 1 MHz. DSSS is capable of greater data throughput, but it's also more prone to interference than FHSS. OFDM is the latest of these three methods, better at dealing with interference, and is used on all but the earliest 802.11 networks.

Channels

Every Wi-Fi network communicates on a **channel**, a portion of the available spectrum. For the 2.4-GHz band, the 802.11 standard defines 14 channels of 20-MHz each (that's the *channel bandwidth*), but different countries limit exactly which channels may be used. In the United States, for example, a WAP using the 2.4-GHz band may only use channels 1 through 11. These channels have some overlap, so two nearby WAPs should not use close channels like 6 and 7. Many WAPs use channels 1, 6, or 11 because they don't overlap. You can fine-tune a network by changing the channels on

WAPs to avoid overlap with other nearby WAPs. This capability is especially important in environments with many wireless networks sharing the same physical space. See the section "Configuring a Consumer Access Point" later in this chapter for more details on channel utilization.

The 5.0-GHz and 6.0-GHz bands offer many more channels than the 2.4-GHz band. In general there are around 40 different channels in the spectrums, and different countries have wildly different rules for which channels may or may not be used. The versions of 802.11 that use the 5.0- and 6.0-GHz bands use automatic channel switching, so from a setup standpoint we don't worry about channels when we talk about 5.0-GHz and 6.0-GHz 802.11 standards.

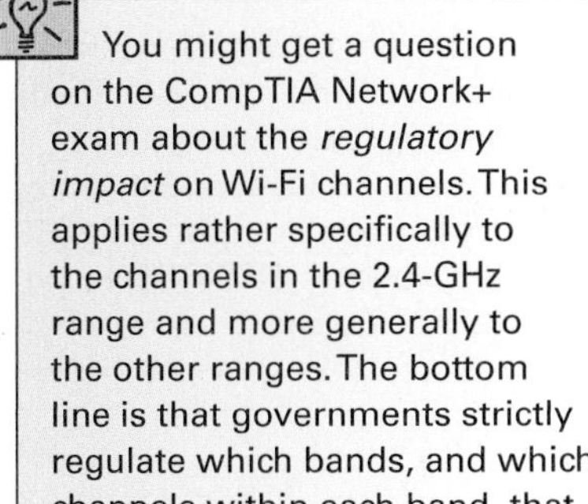

You might get a question on the CompTIA Network+ exam about the *regulatory impact* on Wi-Fi channels. This applies rather specifically to the channels in the 2.4-GHz range and more generally to the other ranges. The bottom line is that governments strictly regulate which bands, and which channels within each band, that Wi-Fi systems can use.

CSMA/CA

Because only a single device can use any network at a time in a physical bus topology, network nodes must have a way to access the network media without stepping on each other's frames. Wired Ethernet networks used *carrier-sense multiple access with collision detection (CSMA/CD)*, as you'll recall from Chapter 3, but Wi-Fi networks use **carrier-sense multiple access with collision avoidance (CSMA/CA)**. Let's compare both methods.

Wired Ethernet networks used CSMA/CD. Wi-Fi networks use CSMA/CA.

How do multiple devices share network media, such as a cable? Sharing is fairly simple: Each device listens in on the network media by measuring the level of voltage currently on the wire. If the level is below the threshold, the device knows that it's clear to send data. If the voltage level rises above a preset threshold, the device knows that the line is busy and it must wait before sending data. Typically, the waiting period is the length of the current frame plus a short, predefined silence period called an **interframe gap (IFG)**. So far, so good—but what happens when two devices both detect that the wire is free and try to send data simultaneously? As you probably guessed, frames transmitted on the network from two different devices at the same time will corrupt each other's signals. This is called a *collision*. Collisions are a fact of networking life. So how do network nodes deal with collisions? They both react to collisions after they happen, and take steps to avoid collisions in the first place.

Modern wired networks use switches running in full-duplex mode, so they don't have to worry about collisions. You'll recall that from back in Chapter 4. CSMA/CD is disabled with full-duplex mode. Wireless networks don't have this luxury.

With CSMA/CD, each sending node detects the collision and responds by generating a random timeout period for itself, during which it doesn't try to send any more data on the network—this is called a *backoff*. Once the backoff period expires (remember that I'm talking about only milliseconds here), the node goes through the whole process again. This approach may not be very elegant, but it gets the job done.

CSMA/CD won't work for wireless networking because wireless devices simply can't detect collisions, for two reasons. First, radio is a half-duplex transmission method. Wireless devices cannot listen and send at the same time. Second, wireless node A wanting to communicate with wireless node B can't hear the third, hidden node (Wi-Fi C) that's also trying to communicate with B. A collision might occur in that circumstance.

Wireless networks need another way to deal with potential collisions. The CSMA/CA access method, as the name implies, proactively takes steps

Current CSMA/CA devices use the Distributed Coordination Function (DCF) method for collision avoidance. Optionally, they can use Request to Send/Clear to Send (RTS/CTS) to avoid collisions.

As you read about the many speeds listed for 802.11, you need to appreciate that wireless networking has a tremendous amount of overhead and latency. WAPs send out almost continuous streams of packets that do nothing more than advertise their existence or maintain connections. Wireless devices may sometimes stall due to processing or timeouts.

The end result is that only a percentage of the total throughput speed is achieved in real data bits getting to the applications that need them. The *actual* number of useful bits per second is called the *goodput* of the wireless network.

Despite the *a* designation for this extension to the 802.11 standard, 802.11a was available on the market *after* 802.11b.

to avoid collisions, as does CSMA/CD. The difference comes in the collision avoidance.

The 802.11 standard defines two methods for collision avoidance: **Distributed Coordination Function (DCF)** and **Point Coordination Function (PCF)**. Currently, only DCF is implemented. DCF specifies rules for sending data onto the network media. For instance, if a wireless network node detects that the network is busy, DCF defines a backoff period on top of the normal IFG wait period before a node can try to access the network again. DCF also requires that receiving nodes send an acknowledgment (ACK) for every frame that they process. The ACK also includes a value that tells other wireless nodes to wait a certain duration before trying to access the network media. This period is calculated to be the time that the data frame takes to reach its destination based on the frame's length and data rate. If the sending node doesn't receive an ACK, it retransmits the same data frame until it gets a confirmation that the packet reached its destination.

The 802.11-1997 standard was the very oldest wireless standard (see Table 14.1). Over time, more detailed additions to 802.11 came along that improved speeds and took advantage of other frequency bands.

Table 14.1 802.11 Summary

Standard	Frequency	Spectrum	Speed	Range	Compatibility
802.11-1997	2.4 GHz	DSSS	2 Mbps	~300′	802.11

802.11b

The first widely adopted Wi-Fi standard—**802.11b**—supported data throughput of up to 11 Mbps and a range of up to 300 feet under ideal conditions. The main downside to using 802.11b was its frequency. The 2.4-GHz frequency is a crowded place, so you were more likely to run into interference from other wireless devices. Table 14.2 gives you the 802.11b summary.

Table 14.2 802.11b Summary

Standard	Frequency	Spectrum	Speed	Range	Backward Compatibility
802.11b	2.4 GHz	DSSS	11 Mbps	~300′	n/a

802.11a

The **802.11a** standard differed from the other 802.11-based standards in significant ways. Foremost was that it operated in a different frequency range, 5.0 GHz. The 5.0-GHz range is much less crowded than the 2.4-GHz range, reducing the chance of interference from devices such as telephones and microwave ovens. Too much signal interference can increase **latency**, making the network sluggish and slow to respond. Running in the 5.0-GHz range greatly reduces this problem.

The 802.11a standard also offered considerably greater throughput than 802.11b, with speeds up to 54 Mbps. Range, however, suffered somewhat and topped out at about 150 feet. Despite the superior speed of 802.11a, it never enjoyed the popularity of 802.11b.

Table 14.3 gives you the 802.11a summary.

Table 14.3	802.11a Summary				
Standard	Frequency	Spectrum	Speed	Range	Backward Compatibility
802.11a	5.0 GHz	OFDM	54 Mbps	~150′	n/a

802.11g

The **802.11g** standard offered data transfer speeds equivalent to 802.11a—up to 54 Mbps—and the wider 300-foot range of 802.11b. More importantly, 802.11g was backward compatible with 802.11b because they both used the 2.4-GHz band, so the same 802.11g WAP could service both 802.11b and 802.11g wireless nodes.

If an 802.11g network only had 802.11g devices connected, the network ran in *native mode*—at up to 54 Mbps—whereas when 802.11b devices connected, the network dropped down to *mixed mode*—all communication ran up to only 11 Mbps. Table 14.4 gives you the 802.11g summary.

Table 14.4	802.11g Summary				
Standard	Frequency	Spectrum	Speed	Range	Backward Compatibility
802.11g	2.4 GHz	OFDM	54 Mbps	~300′	802.11b

Later 802.11g manufacturers incorporated **channel bonding** into their devices, enabling the devices to use two channels for transmission. Channel bonding is not part of the 802.11g standard, but rather proprietary technology pushed by various companies to increase the throughput of their wireless networks. Both the NIC and WAP, therefore, had to be from the same company for channel bonding to work.

With the announcement of 802.11ax in 2018, the Wi-Fi Alliance added a fun marketing term, Wi-Fi 6, and then *retroactively* named earlier standards Wi-Fi 4 (as noted here) and Wi-Fi 5 (which you'll read about next). You might see either the standard names (802.11n, etc.) or the Wi-Fi Alliance names (Wi-Fi 4, and so on) on the CompTIA Network+ exam.

802.11n

The **802.11n** standard brought several improvements to Wi-Fi networking, including faster speeds and new antenna technology implementations. The Wi-Fi Alliance backnamed 802.11n as **Wi-Fi 4**.

The 802.11n specification requires all but handheld devices to use multiple antennas to implement a feature called **multiple input/multiple output (MIMO)**, which enables the devices to make multiple simultaneous connections called streams. With up to four antennas, 802.11n devices can achieve excellent speeds. They also implement channel bonding, combining two 20-MHz channels into a single 40-MHz channel to increase throughput even more. (The official standard supports throughput of up to 600 Mbps, although practical implementation drops that down substantially.)

Many 802.11n WAPs employ **transmit beamforming**, a multiple-antenna technology that helps get rid of **dead spots**—places where the radio signal just does not penetrate at all—or at least make them not so bad. The antennas adjust the signal once the WAP discovers a client to optimize the radio signal.

Like 802.11g, 802.11n WAPs can support earlier, slower 802.11b/g devices. The problem with supporting these older types of 802.11 is that 802.11n WAPs need to encapsulate 802.11n frames into 802.11b or 802.11g frames. This adds some overhead to the process. Adding any 802.11b devices to the network causes some slowdown overall, primarily because the faster devices have to wait for the slower devices to communicate.

To handle these issues, 802.11 WAPs transmit in three different modes: legacy, mixed, and greenfield. These modes are also sometimes known as connection types.

> You'll rarely see 802.11n used today for networking among computers, except in old installations. 802.11n is very much alive and well for peripherals such as wireless printers and in IoT devices.

Legacy mode means the 802.11n WAP sends out separate packets just for legacy devices. This is a terrible way to utilize 802.11n, but was added as a stopgap measure if the other modes didn't work. In **mixed mode**, also often called *high-throughput* or **802.11a-ht/802.11g-ht**, the WAP sends special packets that support the older standards yet also improve the speed of those standards via 802.11n's wider bandwidth. **Greenfield mode** is exclusively for 802.11n-only wireless networks. The WAP processes only 802.11n frames. Dropping support for older devices gives greenfield mode the best goodput but removes backward compatibility.

Table 14.5 summarizes 802.11n.

Table 14.5 802.11n Summary

Standard	Frequency	Spectrum	Speed	Range	Backward Compatibility
802.11n	2.4 GHz[1]	DSSS	100+ Mbps	~300′	802.11b/g/[2]

[1] Dual-band 802.11n devices could function simultaneously at both 2.4- and 5.0-GHz bands.
[2] Many dual-band 802.11n WAPs supported 802.11a devices as well as 802.11b/g/n devices. This was not part of the standard, but something manufacturers implemented.

802.11ac

802.11ac is a natural expansion of the 802.11n standard, incorporating even more streams, 80-MHz and 160-MHz channels, and higher speed. To avoid device density issues in the 2.4-GHz band, 802.11ac only uses the 5.0-GHz band. (See "What Wireless Is Already There?" later in this chapter for more on device density and how to deal with it.) The Wi-Fi Alliance backnamed 802.11ac as **Wi-Fi 5**. Table 14.6 summarizes 802.11ac.

Table 14.6 802.11ac Summary

Standard	Frequency	Spectrum	Speed	Range	Backward Compatibility
802.11ac	5.0 GHz	OFDM (QAM)	Up to 1 Gbps	~300′	802.11a

> For a transmitting method, the 802.11n and 802.11ac devices use a version of OFDM called *quadruple-amplitude modulated (QAM)*.

Current versions of 802.11ac include a version of MIMO called **multiuser MIMO (MU-MIMO)**. MU-MIMO gives a WAP the capability to transmit to multiple users simultaneously.

802.11ax

In 2021, IEEE released the **802.11ax** standard that brings improvements in high-density areas, like stadiums and conference halls. Marketed as **Wi-Fi 6** (operating at the 2.4-GHz and 5-GHz bands) and **Wi-Fi 6E** (operating at the 6.0-GHz band), 802.11ax implements orthogonal frequency-division multiple access (OFDMA) to increase overall network throughput by as much as 400 percent and decrease latency by 75 percent compared to 802.11ac. Table 14.7 summarizes 802.11ax.

Table 14.7 802.11ax Summary

Standard	Frequency	Spectrum	Speed	Range	Backward Compatibility
802.11ax	2.4 GHz, 5.0 GHz, 6.0 GHz	OFDMA (1024-QAM)	Up to 10 Gbps	~300′	802.11a, 802.11b, 802.11g, 802.11n, 802.11ac

The range of 802.11ax hits similar distances to previous Wi-Fi standards of ~300 feet because of limitations on power by the Federal Communications Commission (FCC) in the United States. That doesn't tell the whole story. Improvements in the standard mean the *throughput* at that range is vastly superior to its predecessors.

WPS

By around 2006, 802.11 was everywhere and it was starting to get popular for non-PC devices such as printers, scanners, and speakers. The challenge with these devices was that they lacked any kind of interface to make it easy to configure the wireless settings.

To make configuration easier, the wireless industry created a special standard called **Wi-Fi Protected Setup (WPS)**. WPS works in two modes: push button method or PIN method. (There were other modes, but they never were popular.) With the push button method, you press a button on one device (all WPS-compatible devices have a physical or virtual push button) and then press the WPS button on the other device. That's it. The two devices automatically configure themselves on an encrypted connection.

The PIN method was for connecting a PC to a WPS device (usually a WAP). You press the button on the WAP, locate the SSID on your device, and then enter an eight-digit PIN as the WPA personal shared key (more on WPA shortly). All WPS WAPs have the PIN printed on the device.

WPS is very easy to use but is susceptible to different forms of *WPS attacks*. By design, the WPS PIN numbers are short. WPS attacks, therefore, concentrate on hacking the PIN. By hacking the PIN, a bad actor can easily take control of the WAP, giving him or her access to the entire infrastructure.

Wi-Fi Security

One of the biggest problems with wireless networking devices is that right out of the box they provide *no* security. Vendors go out of their way to make setting up their devices easy, so usually the only thing that you have to do to join a wireless network is turn on your wireless devices and let them find each other. Setting up an *open* Wi-Fi network is relatively simple. Once you decide to add security, on the other hand, you need to decide how you plan to share access with others.

We need to use a number of techniques to make a wireless network secure, to *harden* it from malicious things and people. Wireless security is network hardening. (For details about network hardening techniques that apply to all kinds of networks, see Chapter 19.)

> All the methods used in wireless network security—authentication, encryption, MAC filtering—can be considered network hardening techniques.

You also need to consider that your network's data frames float through the air on radio waves instead of zipping safely along wrapped up inside network cabling. What's to stop an unscrupulous network tech with the right equipment from grabbing those frames out of the air and reading that data?

Wi-Fi has gone through numerous security techniques and authentication and encryption protocols and implementations since the original 802.11 rollout. This section starts with a brief review of encryption, then examines the ever-evolving security protocols, finishing with a discussion on a few other more or less effective security measures.

Data Encryption

Encrypting data packets enables wireless network security. **Encryption** electronically scrambles data packets and locks them with an encryption key before transmitting them onto the wireless network. The receiving network device must possess the decryption key to unscramble the packet and process the data. Thus, a hacker who grabs any data frames out of the air can't read those frames unless the hacker has the decryption key. Enabling wireless encryption through WPA2 or WPA3 (see below) provides a good level of security to data packets in transit.

WEP

The granddaddy of wireless security, **Wired Equivalent Privacy (WEP)**, uses a 64- or 128-bit encryption algorithm to scramble data frames. WEP sounded great on paper, but in practice it proved to be a horrible failure. Even with the strongest encryption enabled, WEP isn't a particularly robust security solution. In fact, WEP can be cracked in under a minute with just a regular laptop and open source software. The bottom line with WEP? Don't ever use it today.

WPA

Needless to say, the Wi-Fi developers scrambled to find a fix for the flaws in WEP. A full replacement called *802.11i* (discussed in the upcoming "WPA2" section) was designed to address the problems with WEP and to provide proper authentication. But the standard took a while to complete, so the wireless industry implemented an intermediate fix. They invented a sales term called **Wi-Fi Protected Access (WPA)** that adopted some features of the still-in-the-future 802.11i standard, fixing some of the weaknesses of WEP. WPA supports authentication using EAP. Let's take a look.

EAP One of the great challenges to authentication is getting the two ends of the authentication process to handle the many different types of authentication options. Even though *Point-to-Point Protocol (PPP)* for a time pretty much owned the username/password authentication business, proprietary forms of authentication using smart cards/tokens, certificates, and so on, began to show up on the market, threatening to drop practical authentication into a huge mess of competing standards.

Extensible Authentication Protocol (EAP) was developed to create a single standard to allow two devices to authenticate. Despite the name, EAP is not a protocol in the classic sense, but rather it is a PPP wrapper that EAP-compliant applications can use to accept one of many types of authentication. Although EAP is a general-purpose authentication wrapper, its only substantial use is in wireless networks. EAP comes in various types, but currently only seven types are in common use:

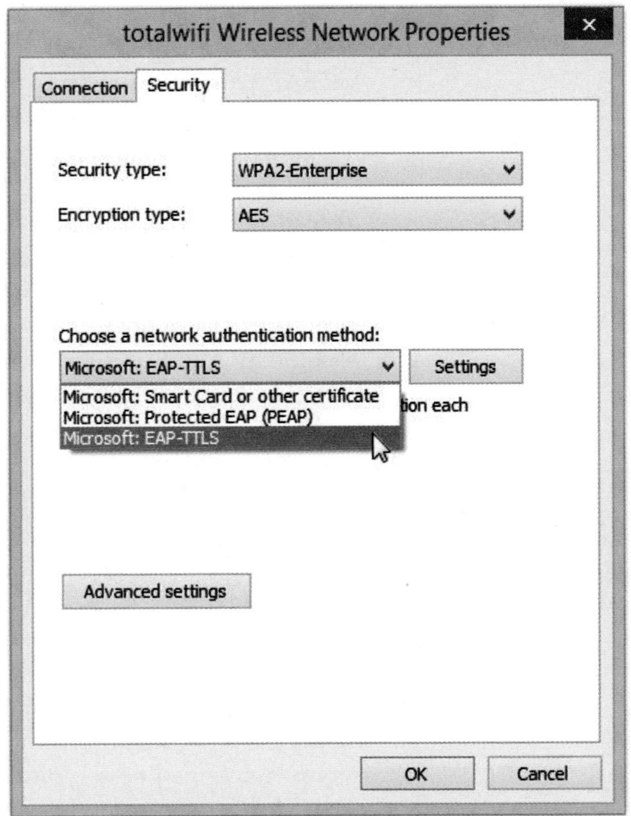

• **Figure 14.7** Setting EAP authentication scheme

- **EAP-PSK** Easily the most popular form of authentication used in wireless networks today, EAP-PSK (Pre-shared key) is nothing more than a shared secret code that's stored on both the wireless access point and the wireless client, encrypted using the powerful AES encryption, covered in Chapter 10. (See the *Encryption type* field in Figure 14.7.) Note that CompTIA loses the hyphen, so *preshared key*.
- **EAP-TLS** EAP with Transport Layer Security (TLS) defines the use of a RADIUS server as well as mutual authentication, requiring certificates on both the server and every client. On the client side, a smart card may be used in lieu of a certificate. EAP-TLS is very robust, but the client-side certificate requirement is an administrative challenge. Even though it's a challenge, the most secure wireless networks all use EAP-TLS. EAP-TLS is only used on wireless networks, but TLS is used heavily on secure Web sites.
- **EAP-TTLS** EAP-TTLS (Tunneled TLS) is similar to EAP-TLS but can use a single server-side certificate. EAP-TTLS is very common for more secure wireless networks.
- **EAP-MS-CHAPv2** More commonly known as Protected EAP (PEAP), EAP-MS-CHAPv2 uses a password function based on MS-CHAPv2 with the addition of an encrypted TLS tunnel similar to EAP-TLS. This is the most common implementation of EAP.
- **EAP-MD5** This is a very simple version of EAP that uses only MD5 hashes for transfer of authentication credentials. EAP-MD5 is weak and the least used of all the versions of EAP described.
- **LEAP** Lightweight EAP (LEAP) is a proprietary EAP authentication used almost exclusively by Cisco wireless products. LEAP is an interesting combination of MS-CHAP authentication between a wireless client and a RADIUS server.
- **EAP-FAST** *EAP Flexible Authentication via Secure Tunneling* is Cisco's replacement for LEAP. All current operating systems support EAP-FAST (assuming the right software is installed).

802.1X EAP was a huge success and almost overnight gave those who needed point-to-point authentication a one-stop-shop methodology to do so. EAP was so successful that there was a cry to develop an EAP solution for Ethernet networks. This solution is called 802.1X. Whereas traditional EAP is nothing more than an authentication method wrapped in PPP, 802.1X gets rid of the PPP (Ethernet is not a point-to-point protocol!) and instead puts the EAP information inside an Ethernet frame.

802.1X is a port-based authentication network access control mechanism for networks. In other words, it's a complete authentication standard designed to force devices to go through a full AAA process to get anywhere past the interface on a gateway system. Before 802.1X, a system on a wired network could always access another system's port. Granted, an attacker wouldn't be able to do much until he gave a username/password or certificate, but he could still send packets to any computer on the network. This wasn't good because it enabled attackers to get to the systems to try to do evil things. 802.1X prevented them from even getting in the door until they were authenticated and authorized.

> 802.1X is presented here in a wireless context, but note that the control mechanism is used in wired networks as well.

WPA-Enterprise uses 802.1X to provide a very robust authentication system using a RADIUS server and EAP. Let's look at the components and the process.

A **RADIUS server** either stores usernames and passwords or, more commonly today, consults Active Directory for authentication. A RADIUS server functions like a typical server, but the remote aspect of it requires you to learn new jargon.

> RADIUS stands for *Remote Authentication Dial-In User Service*. Say that five times.

Here's how it works. The client wireless computer, called a **supplicant**, contacts the WAP, called a **Network Access Server (NAS)**, and requests permission to access the network. The NAS collects the supplicant's username and password and then contacts the RADIUS server to see if the supplicant appears in the RADIUS server's security database. If the supplicant appears and the username and password are correct, the RADIUS server sends a packet back to the supplicant, through the WAP, with an Access-Accept code and an Authenticator section that proves the packet actually came from the RADIUS server. Then the remote user gets access to the network resources. That's some serious security! See Figure 14.8.

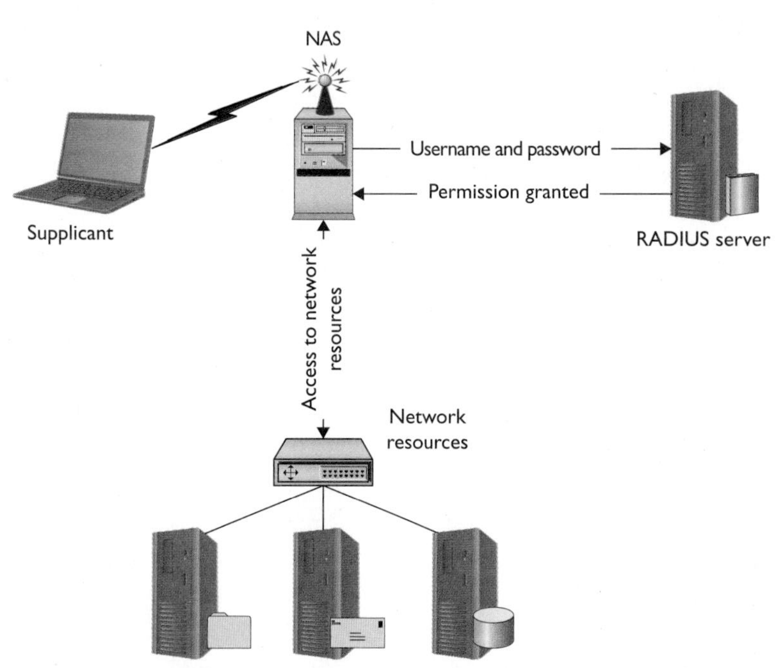

• **Figure 14.8** Authenticating using RADIUS

But here's where it gets tricky. What are the points of potential security failure here? All over the place, right? The connection between each of these devices must be secure; several protocols make certain of that security. PPP, for example, provides a secure connection between the supplicant and the NAS. IPsec often provides the security between the NAS and the RADIUS server. We then need some form of authentication standard that encrypts all this authentication process, and that's EAP. See Figure 14.9.

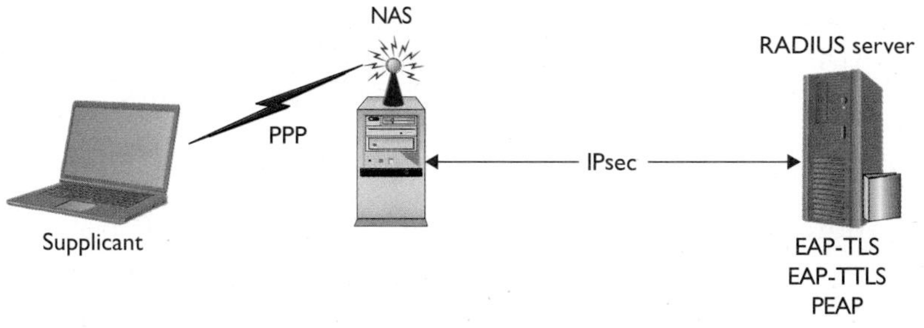

• **Figure 14.9** Authentication using RADIUS with protocols in place

TKIP WPA offers security enhancements such as dynamic encryption key generation (keys are issued on a per-user and per-session basis) and an encryption key integrity-checking feature.

WPA works by using an extra layer of security, called the **Temporal Key Integrity Protocol (TKIP)**, around the WEP encryption scheme. It's not, therefore, a complete replacement protocol for WEP and still uses RC4 for cipher initialization—hence the name **TKIP-RC4**. TKIP added a 128-bit encryption key that seemed unbreakable when first introduced. Within four years of introduction, however, researchers showed methods by which hackers could waltz through WPA security almost as quickly as through WEP security. Even with the enhancements offered by EAP, 802.1X, and TKIP, another solution had to be found.

WPA2

CCMP stands for *Counter Mode Cipher Block Chaining Message Authentication Code Protocol*. Whew! That's why we commonly just use the initials, CCMP. As you know from Chapter 10, AES stands for *Advanced Encryption Standard.*

zPA2 implemented the full IEEE **802.11i** standard to add much-needed security features. I already discussed the 802.1X authentication measure using EAP to provide secure access to Wi-Fi networks. 802.11i also replaced TKIP-RC4 with the much more robust **CCMP-AES**, a 128-bit block cipher that's much tougher to crack.

Implementing the full 802.11i standard took time because most of the installed Wi-Fi hardware couldn't be updated to handle AES encryption. WPA held the title of "most secure wireless option" for a number of years.

Eventually, enough devices were made that could support AES that the full 802.11i standard was implemented under the sales term **Wi-Fi Protected Access 2 (WPA2)**. A "WPA2-compliant device" is really just a marketing term for a device that fully supports the 802.11i standard. WPA2 is not hack-proof, but it definitely offers a much tougher encryption standard that stops the casual hacker cold.

The most common way to set up WPA2 encryption is to use a simple version called *WPA2 Pre-shared key (PSK)*, or **WPA2-Personal**. Basically, with the PSK version, you create a secret key that must be added to any device that is going to be on that SSID. There is no authentication with WPA2-PSK.

WPA2 attacks can happen, especially with wireless networks using WPA2-Personal passphrases. The attacks take place by using sophisticated methods that make assumptions about the passphrase, and the fact that certain passphrases are used quite often. The most important thing to do to prevent these attacks from succeeding is to use long passphrases (16 or more characters), thus making the network hard to crack. Otherwise, you need authentication. If you want authentication you move into what most wireless folks will call an enterprise setup. For example, when you use a RADIUS server for authentication with WPA2 to create an amazingly secure wireless network, it gets a fancy name: **WPA2-Enterprise**.

You might be asked a question that explores the two encryption options for WPA2-Personal, AES or TKIP. WPA2-Enterprise also has the same two options. Definitely use AES. TKIP is deprecated and you shouldn't ever use it today.

WPA3

WPA3 addresses weakness in WPA2's direct use of the Wi-Fi password to encrypt network traffic. WPA3 uses Simultaneous Authentication of Equals (SAE), a key exchange based on Diffie-Hellman that generates unique encryption keys between each client and WAP. This makes it difficult for an attacker to break the encryption key and capture Wi-Fi traffic right out of the air. The Wi-Fi Alliance announced and started certifying devices that use WPA3, the replacement for WPA2, in 2018, although industry adoption has been slow.

WPA3 does *not* appear in the CompTIA Network+ N10-008 exam objectives at the time of writing.

Additional Security Measures

Wireless networks have tried other techniques to secure networks beyond protocols for authentication and encryption. All seem plausibly effective in principle, but in practice, some fail and some help. Let's look at disabling SSID broadcast, MAC address filtering, isolation of networks, and geofencing.

Disabling SSID Broadcast An early "security" technique suggested was to disable the SSID broadcast. The theory was that only people who knew the SSID could connect, thus excluding the bad guys. This *security through obscurity* concept fails miserably at providing any security at all. Any wireless sniffing device will almost immediately discover "hidden" SSIDs. In practice, disabling SSID broadcast makes it harder for legitimate users to access a wireless network. It provides zero security.

WAPs use an access control list (ACL) to enable or deny specific MAC addresses. Note that a WAP's ACL has *nothing* to do with ACL in NTFS; it's just the same term used for two different things.

MAC Filtering Most WAPs support **MAC filtering**, a method that enables you to limit access to your network based on the physical addresses of wireless NICs. MAC address filtering creates a type of "accepted users" list—an *access control list (ACL)*—to restrict access to your wireless network. This is a common mitigation technique for undesired access to a network. A table stored in the WAP lists the MAC addresses that are permitted to participate in the wireless network, called a *whitelist*. Any network frames that don't contain the MAC address of a node listed in the table are rejected.

Many WAPs also enable you to deny specific MAC addresses from logging onto the network, creating a *blacklist*. This works great in close quarters, such as apartments or office buildings, where your wireless network signal goes beyond your perimeter. You can check the WAP and see the MAC addresses of every node that connects to your network. Check that list against the list of your computers, and you can readily spot any unwanted interloper. Putting an offending MAC address in the "deny" column effectively blocks that system from piggybacking onto your wireless connection.

MAC filtering with a whitelist means you allow only specific computers to join the network. When you deny specific computers, you create a blacklist. Whitelisting and blacklisting are labor-intensive processes, with whitelisting requiring far more work.

Although address filtering works, both whitelisting and blacklisting require way too much work for a network administrator and thus offer little practical security. Plus, a hacker can very easily *spoof* a MAC address—make the NIC report a legitimate address rather than its own—and access the network. Worse, a hacker doesn't have to connect to your network to grab your network traffic out of thin air! Avoid MAC address filtering as it offers no real security.

Isolation You can set up *wireless client isolation* or *guest network isolation* on better wireless access points to protect the rest of your network. Both features work similarly, blocking access to other wireless clients and the wired network, while allowing Internet access. In a typical Wi-Fi setup, every wireless client is part of the same WLAN and can communicate with each other. Isolation blocks this feature, making it ideal for the public portion of a wireless network. Figure 14.10 shows an access point configured for a guest network.

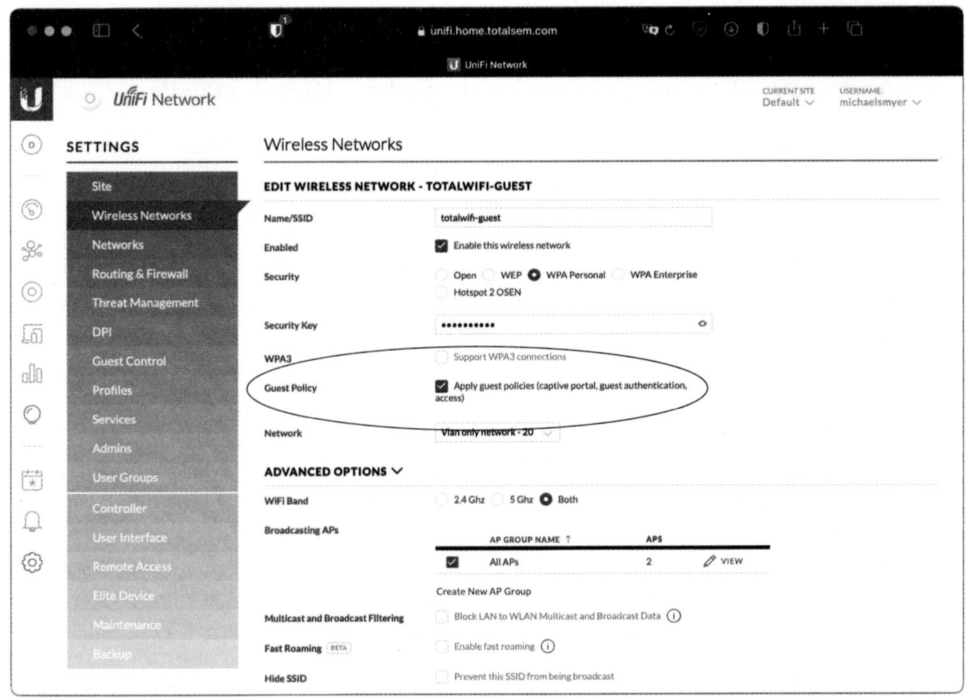

• **Figure 14.10** Guest network setting

Geofencing **Geofencing** uses various wireless methods—Wi-Fi, Bluetooth, cellular networks, Global Positioning System (GPS)—to create a perimeter or boundary around a specific physical area. Geofencing can be used to trigger alerts in a number of ways. A person with an unauthorized smartphone stepping inside the boundary, for example, can cause a flag to go up. Likewise, a person with a smartphone specifically tied to a system walking outside the boundary can stop the phone's access to the system.

The proliferation of mobile devices like smartphones, all connected to multiple wireless signals, makes geofencing a moving target as far as implementation. Internet-connected devices like smart lights at home can automatically turn on or turn off depending on the location of the smartphone user, for example. (You'll see a lot more about the Internet of Things in Chapter 17.)

Managing the wireless signal of a Wi-Fi network so that it doesn't go anywhere outside your network space is an important aspect of wireless security. Part of signal management requires proper antenna placement and adjustment of the power level of the signal. See "Placing the Access Points/Antennas" and "Signal/Power Levels" later in this chapter for the details.

Enterprise Wireless

A simple BSSID or ESSID is incredibly easy to set up. You can take a few cheap WAPs from your local electronics store, connect them to a switch, use a Web interface to configure each WAP, and start connecting clients.

Inexpensive SOHO WAPs and wireless routers have been around so long—almost as long as 802.11 itself—that for many of us this is what we think a "wireless network" means.

But as wireless networks become more important, complex, and busy, the cheap SOHO boxes just aren't going to work anymore. When you want dependable, robust, secure, administrable wireless networks, you need enterprise-class wireless equipment. In general, an enterprise wireless device differs from a SOHO device in five areas: robust device construction, centralized management, VLAN pooling, Power over Ethernet, and bringing personal wireless devices into the enterprise environment.

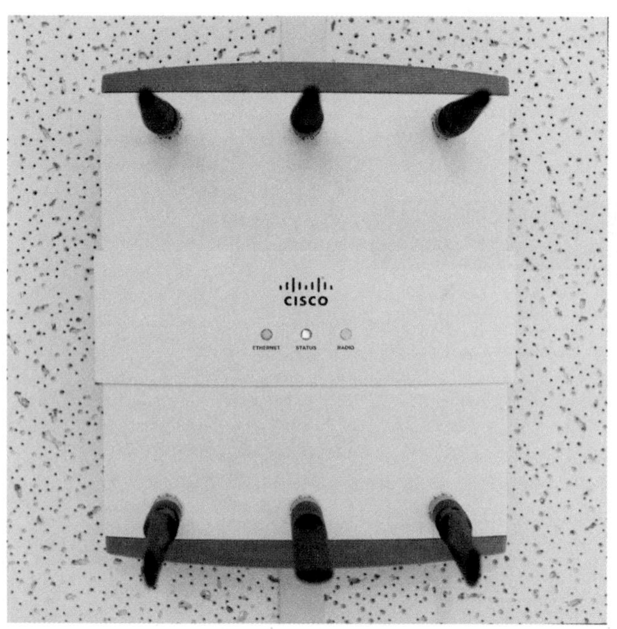

• **Figure 14.11** Enterprise WAP

Robust Device Construction

If you compare a typical SOHO WAP to an enterprise WAP, you'll notice immediately that the enterprise WAP is made of better materials (often metal instead of plastic). Enterprise WAPs for the most part will also be more configurable. Most enterprise WAPs enable you to swap out antennas and radios, so you can keep WAPs while upgrading them to the latest technologies. Figure 14.11 shows an enterprise WAP.

Enterprise Wireless Administration

An enterprise wireless infrastructure is almost certainly going to consist of a large number of WAPs. It's impossible to administer a large number of WAPs when you have to access each WAP individually. Imagine something as simple as changing the password on a WPA2-encrypted ESSID on a wireless network with 50+ WAPs (Figure 14.12). The job would take forever!

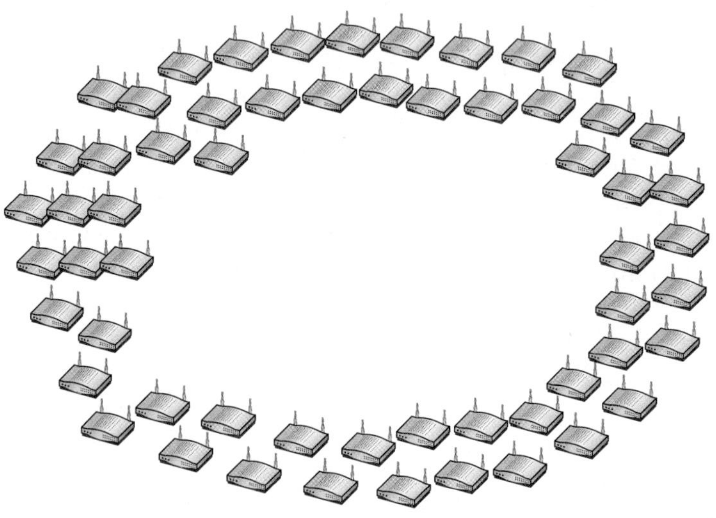

• **Figure 14.12** Configuring WAPs

The wireless industry long ago appreciated the complexity of enterprise-level wireless networks and created tools to make administration easier. The important point to any wireless network is that all of the WAPs, at least on a single SSID, connect to a single switch or group of switches. What if we offload the job of configuration to a switch that's designed to handle a number of WAPs simultaneously? We call these switches **wireless LAN controllers** (Figure 14.13).

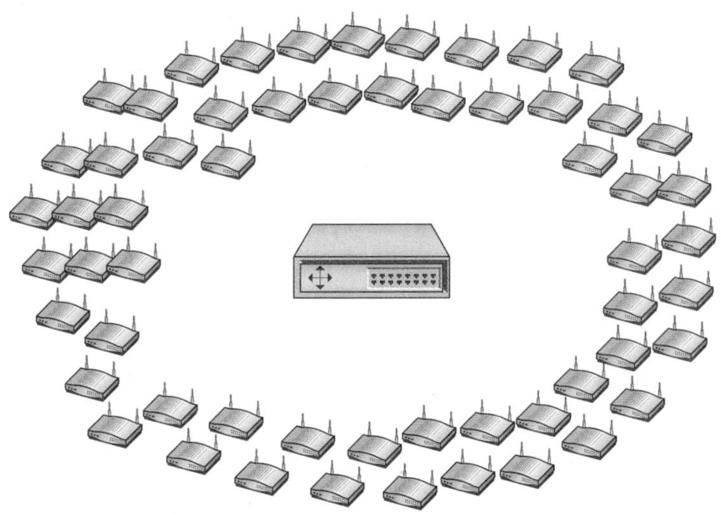

• **Figure 14.13** Wireless LAN controller

Wireless LAN controllers have a number of other names, such as wireless switch, wireless LAN switch, and so forth.

Any WAP that you can access directly and configure singularly via its own interface is called a **thick client**. A WAP that can only be configured by a wireless controller is called a **thin client**. For years, these centralized configuration methods were proprietary for each wireless manufacturer, making for little or no cross-brand interoperability. This incompatibility in thin and thick clients was a common wireless issue back in the day. Today, most manufacturers use the **Lightweight Access Point Protocol (LWAPP)** to ensure interoperability. Given LWAPP's broad acceptance, most WAPs will accept commands from any wireless controller.

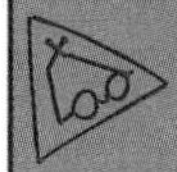

Tech Tip

Cloud-based AP Controls

Although it's not covered in the CompTIA Network+ N10-008 objectives, you should know that a lot of companies have adopted cloud-based AP control options. Companies big and small offer cloud AP solutions to organizations. Cisco's Meraki solution, for example, features Cisco APs provisioned and managed through the Meraki dashboard, a Web-based multi-site management tool.

The advantages of cloud-based wireless management mirror advantages in other aspects of networking, such as removing the need for dedicated hardware, applications, and technicians. You'll read a lot more about cloud solutions in all aspects of networking in Chapter 15.

VLAN Pooling

One of the big challenges to larger enterprise networks is the large number of clients that might be on a single SSID at any given moment. As the number of devices grows, you get a huge amount of broadcasts on the network. The traditional method to reduce this is to divide the WLAN into multiple broadcast domains and use routers to interconnect the domains. In many cases, though, the needs of the wireless network require a single domain; instead we create a pool of VLANs for a single SSID and randomly assign wireless clients to one of the VLANs. This is called **VLAN pooling**.

Power over Ethernet

Wireless access points need electrical power, but they're invariably placed in strange locations (like ceilings or high up on walls) where providing electrical power is not convenient. No worries! Many WAPs support one of the **Power over Ethernet (PoE)** standards that enables them to receive their power from the same Ethernet cables that transfer their data. The switch that connects the WAPs must support PoE, but as long as both the WAP and the switches to which they connect support PoE, you don't have to do anything other than just plug in Ethernet cables. PoE works automatically. As you might imagine, it costs extra to get WAPs and switches that support PoE, but the convenience of PoE for wireless networks makes it a popular option.

Look for a *cable connectivity* troubleshooting scenario that involves PoE or PoE+ on the CompTIA Network+ exam. Any break in the cable or problem with the PoE switch will cause the connected WAP to fail. No electricity means the lights go out, right? A failure of a wireless network that relies on PoE/PoE+ might not have anything to do with wireless components.

The original PoE standard—*802.3af*—came out in 2003 with great response from the industry. PoE switches support a maximum of 15.4 watts of DC power per port. In 2009, 802.3af was revised to output as much as 25.5 watts per port. This PoE amendment to 802.3 is called *802.3at*, PoE plus, or PoE+. In 2018, the IEEE released upgraded PoE again with the *802.3bt* standard. Switches that support PoE++ (or 4PPoE) can provide one of two power upgrades, with Type 3 supplying up to 51 watts per port and Type 4 supplying up to 71.3 watts per port.

Implementing Wi-Fi

Installing and configuring a Wi-Fi network requires a number of discrete steps. You should start with a site survey to determine any obstacles (existing wireless, interference, and so on) you need to overcome and to determine the best location for your access points. You'll need to install one or more access points, and then configure both the access point(s) and wireless clients. Finally, you should put the network to the test, verifying that it works as you intended.

Performing a Site Survey

As mentioned, the first step of installing a wireless network is the site survey. A **site survey** will reveal any obstacles to creating the wireless network and will help determine the best possible location for your access points. The main components for creating a site survey are a floor plan of the area you wish to provide with wireless and a site survey tool such as NETSCOUT's AirMagnet Survey Pro (Figure 14.14). **Wireless survey tools** help you discover any other wireless networks in the area and will integrate a drawing of your floor plan with interference sources clearly marked. This enables you to get the right kind of hardware you need and makes it possible to get the proper network coverage.

Check out the excellent Chapter 14 Show! Sim about third-party wireless utilities at http://totalsem.com/008. It's a cool sim about non-Microsoft implementations.

What Wireless Is Already There?

Discovering any wireless network signals other than your own in your space enables you to set both the SSID and channel to avoid networks that overlap. One part of any good site survey is a wireless analyzer. A **wireless analyzer** or **Wi-Fi analyzer** is any device that looks for and documents all existing wireless networks in the area. Wireless analyzers are handy tools that are useful for diagnosing wireless network issues and conducting site surveys. You can get dedicated, hand-held wireless analyzer tools or you can run site survey software on a laptop or mobile wireless device. Wireless survey tools like AirMagnet Survey Pro always include an analyzer as well. Figure 14.15 shows a screenshot of Acrylic Wi-Fi, a free and popular wireless analyzer.

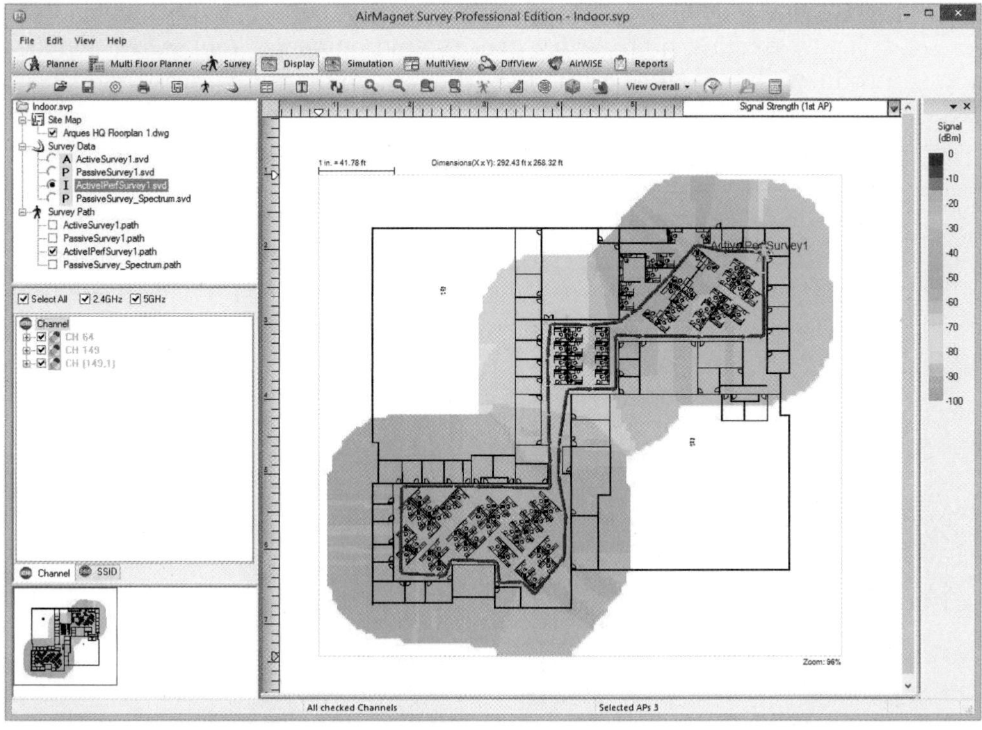

• **Figure 14.14** AirMagnet Survey Pro

Wireless networks send out radio signals on the 2.4-, 5.0-, or 6.0-GHz spectrum using one of a number of discrete channels. In early wireless networks, a big part of the setup was to determine the channels used nearby in order to avoid them. In modern wireless networks, we rarely adjust channels manually anymore. Instead we rely on powerful algorithms built into WAPs to locate the least congested channels automatically. The bigger

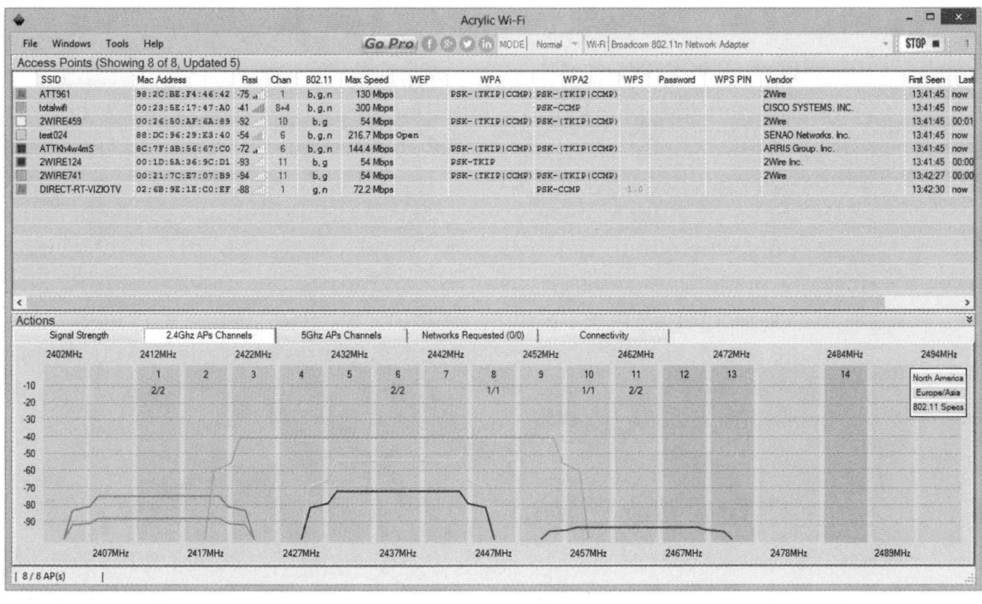

• **Figure 14.15** Acrylic Wi-Fi

challenge today is the preexistence of many Wi-Fi networks with lots of clients, creating high device density environments. You need a wireless solution that handles many users running on the few wireless frequencies available.

There are plenty of tools like AirMagnet Survey Pro to support a wireless survey. All good survey utilities share some common ways to report their findings. One of the most powerful reports that they generate is called a heat map. A *heat map* is nothing more than a graphical representation of the RF sources on your site, using different colors to represent the intensity of the signal. Figure 14.16 shows a sample heat map.

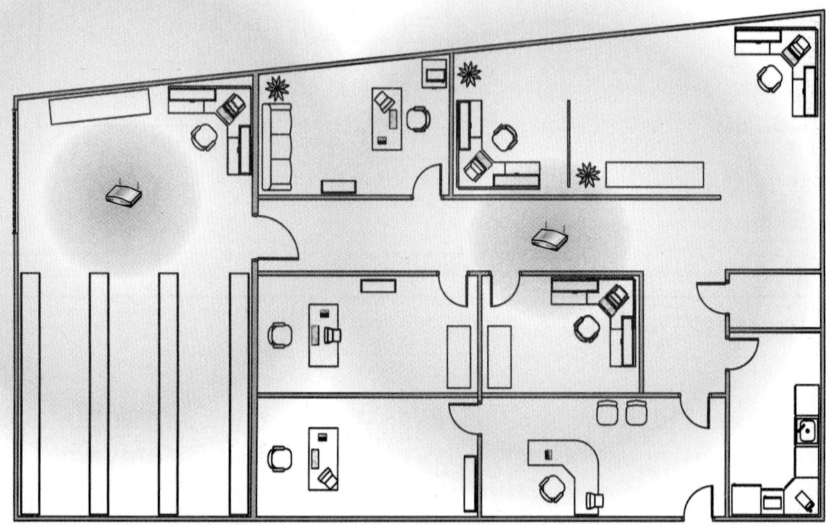

• **Figure 14.16** Site survey with heat map

Interference Sources

It might seem like overkill in a small network, but any network beyond a simple one should have a sketched-out site survey with any potential interference sources clearly marked (Figure 14.17). Refrigerators, reinforced walls, metal plumbing, microwave ovens—all of these can create horrible dead spots where your network radio wave can't easily penetrate. With a difficult or high-interference area, you might need to move up to 802.11ac or 802.11ax equipment with three or four antennas just to get the kind of coverage you want. Or you might need to plan a multiple WAP network to wipe out the dead zones. A proper site survey gives you the first tool for implementing a network that works.

Installing the Client

Because every Wi-Fi network needs clients (otherwise, what's the point?), you need to install Wi-Fi client hardware and software. Pretty much every

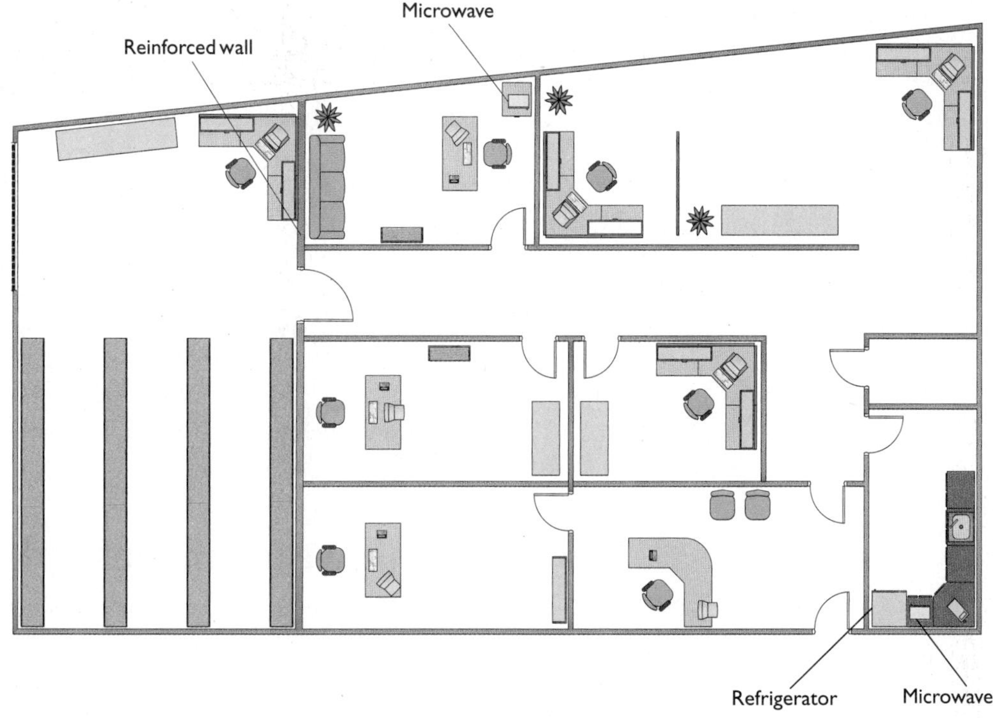

• **Figure 14.17** Site survey with interference sources noted

type of mobile device (smartphones, laptops, tablets, and so forth) comes with a built-in client, usually part of the operating system.

Desktop systems are a different story. Most desktops don't have built-in wireless, so you'll need to install a wireless NIC. You have a choice between installing a PCIe card or a USB device. With a PCIe NIC, power down the PC, disconnect from the AC source, and open the case. Following good CompTIA A+ technician procedures, locate a free slot on the motherboard, remove the slot cover, remove the NIC from its antistatic bag, install the NIC, and affix the retaining screw. See Figure 14.18. Often you'll need to attach the antenna. Button everything up, plug it in, and start the computer. If prompted, put in the disc that came from the manufacturer and install drivers and any other software necessary.

• **Figure 14.18** Wi-Fi NIC installed

With a USB NIC, you should install the drivers and software before you connect the NIC to the computer. This is standard operating procedure for any USB device, as you most likely recall from your CompTIA A+ certification training (or from personal experience).

> You might note the rather antique quality of the screenshot in Figure 14-19. That's because modern operating systems only grudgingly support ad hoc networks and only via complicated command-line command strings. Except for on the CompTIA Network+ exam, ad hoc mode is dead.

Setting Up an Ad Hoc Network

Although ad hoc networks are rare and not easily supported by modern operating systems, they are on the CompTIA Network+ exam. Plus, you

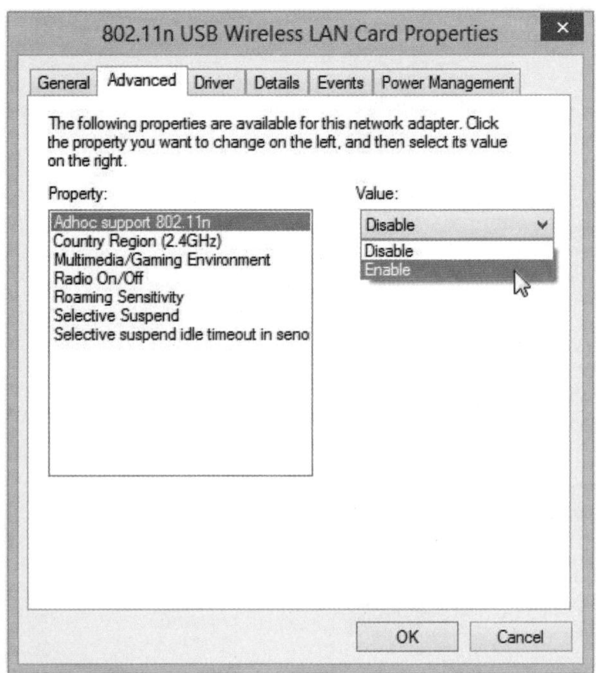

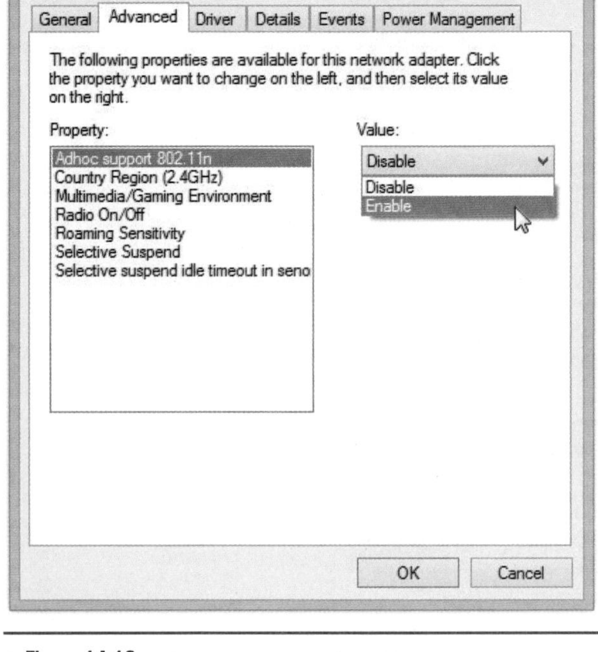

• **Figure 14.19** Enabling support for ad hoc networks on a wireless NIC

might end up dealing with some legacy gear and need to set one up in the real world, so let's look at the process.

Configuring NICs for ad hoc mode networking requires you to address four things: SSID, IP addresses, channel, and sharing. (Plus, of course, you have to set the NICs to function in ad hoc mode!) Each wireless node must be configured to use the same network name (SSID). Of course, no two nodes can use the same IP address, although this is unlikely because all operating systems use zeroconf (introduced in Chapter 6). If everything worked correctly, you will have a TCP/IP connection between the machines with no WAP. Figure 14.19 shows enabling support for ad hoc networks on a wireless NIC.

Setting Up an Infrastructure Network

Site survey in hand and Wi-Fi technology selected, you're ready to set up a wireless network in infrastructure mode. You need to determine the optimal location for your WAP, configure the WAP, and then configure any clients to access that WAP. Seems pretty straightforward, but the devil, they say, is in the details.

Placing the Access Points/Antennas

All wireless access points have antennas that radiate the 802.11 signal to the clients, so the optimal location for a WAP depends on the area you want to cover and whether you care if the signal bleeds out beyond the borders. You also need to use antennas that provide enough signal and push that signal in the proper direction and alignment. There are some interesting options here and you should know them both for modern networking and for the CompTIA Network+ exam.

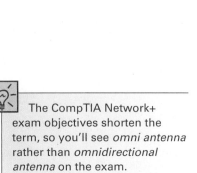

The CompTIA Network+ exam objectives shorten the term, so you'll see *omni antenna* rather than *omnidirectional antenna* on the exam.

Antenna placement on the WAPs is also very important. WAP antennas come in many shapes and sizes. In the early days it was common to see WAPs with two antennas. Some WAPs have only one antenna and some (802.11n, 802.11ac, and 802.11ax) have more than two (Figure 14.20). Even a WAP that doesn't seem to have antennas is simply hiding them inside the chassis.

• **Figure 14.20** An ASUS AX6000 WiFi 6 Gaming Router with four external antennas

There are three basic types of antennas common in 802.11 networks: omnidirectional, unidirectional, and patch. Each offers different solutions for coverage of specific wireless network setups. Plus, the signals emanating from the antennas have a feature called polarization that needs to be considered.

Omnidirectional In general, an **omnidirectional antenna** radiates signal outward from the WAP in all directions. For a typical network, you want blanket coverage and would place a WAP with an omnidirectional antenna in the center of the area (Figure 14.21). This has the advantage of ease of use—anything within the signal radius can potentially access the network. The standard straight-wire antennas that provide the most omnidirectional function are called **dipole antennas**.

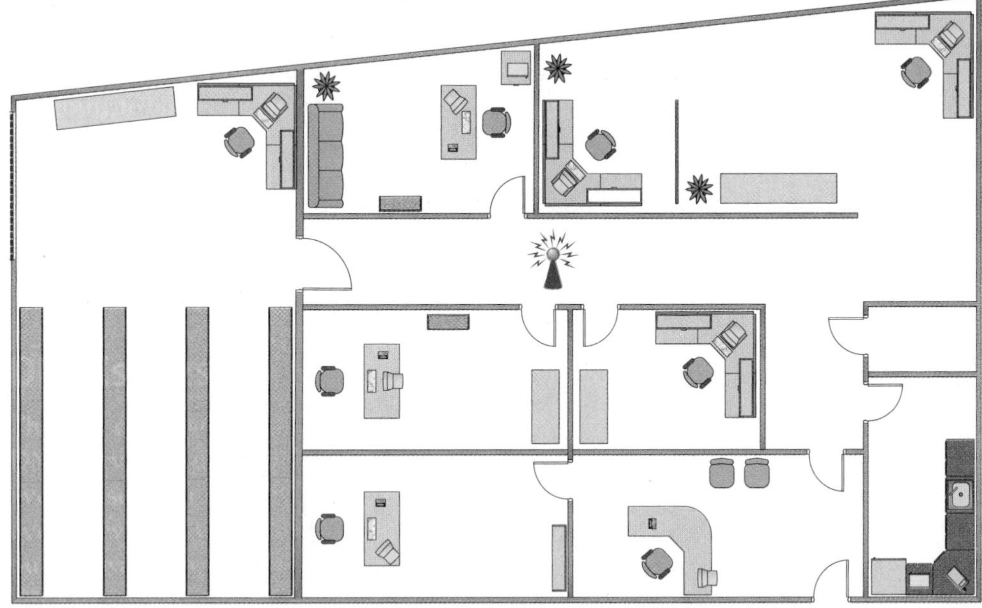

• **Figure 14.21** Office layout with WAP in the center

The famous little black antennas seen on older WAPs are all dipoles. A dipole antenna has two radiating elements that point in opposite directions. But if you look at a WAP antenna, it looks like it only points in one direction (Figure 14.22). If you open up one of these antennas, however, you'll see that it has two opposing radiating elements (Figure 14.23).

• **Figure 14.22** Typical WAP dipole antenna—where are the two elements?

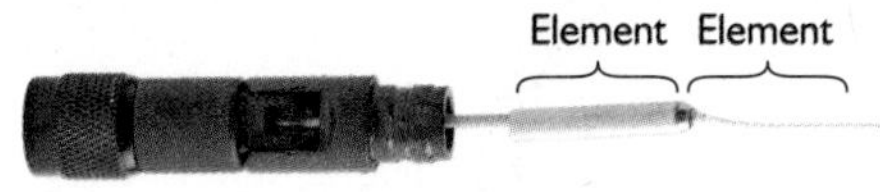

• **Figure 14.23** Same antenna from Figure 14.22 opened, showing the two elements

A dipole antenna doesn't radiate in a perfect ball. It actually is more of a doughnut shape, as shown in Figure 14.24. Note that this shape is great for outdoors or a single floor, but it doesn't send much signal above or below the WAP.

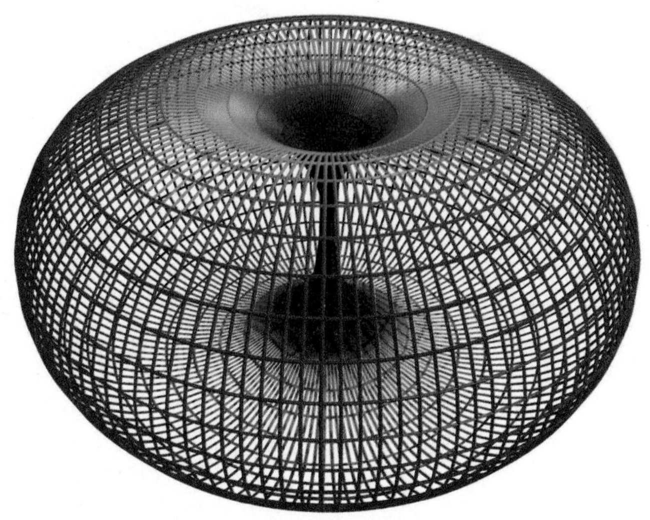

• **Figure 14.24** Dipole radiation pattern

The omnidirectional and centered approach does not work for every network, for three reasons. First, if the signal exceeds the size of the network space, that signal bleeds out. The signal can bleed out a lot in some cases, particularly if your specific space doesn't allow you to put the WAP in the center, but rather off-center. This presents a security risk as well, because someone outside your network space could lurk, pick up the signal, and do unpleasant things to your network. Second, if your network space exceeds the signal of your WAP, you'll need to get some sort of signal booster. Third, any obstacles will produce glaring dead spots in network coverage. Too many dead spots make a less-than-ideal solution. To address these issues, you might need to turn to other solutions.

An antenna strengthens and focuses the RF output from a WAP. The ratio of increase—what's called **gain**—is measured in decibels (dB). The gain from a typical WAP is 2 dB, enough to cover a reasonable area, but not a very large room. Increasing the signal requires a bigger device antenna. Some WAPs, especially outdoor models, have removable antennas. To increase the signal range for a single WAP using omnidirectional antennas, simply replace the factory-installed antennas with higher-gain models.

• **Figure 14.25** Yagi antenna

Unidirectional When you don't necessarily want to broadcast to the world, you can use one or more *directional antennas* to create a nicely focused network. A **unidirectional antenna**, as the name implies, focuses a radio wave into a beam of sorts. Unidirectional antennas come in a variety of flavors, such as parabolic, dish, and Yagi, to name a just a few. A *parabolic antenna* looks like a satellite dish. A *Yagi antenna* (named for one of its Japanese inventors) is often called a *beam antenna* and can enable a focused radio wave to travel a long way, even miles (Figure 14.25). If you need to connect in a narrow beam (down a hallway or from one faraway point to another), unidirectional antennas are the way to go.

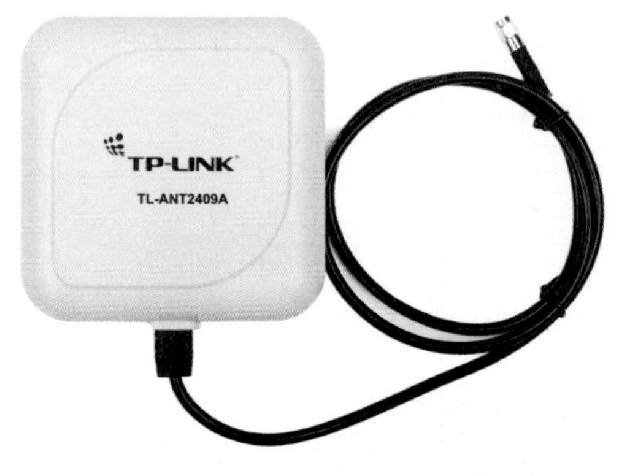

• **Figure 14.26** Patch antenna

Patch Antennas **Patch antennas** are flat, plate-shaped antennas that generate a half-sphere beam. Patch antennas are always placed on walls. The half-sphere is perfect for indoor offices where you want to fill the room with a strong signal but not broadcast to the room behind the patch (Figure 14.26).

Polarization and Antenna Alignment All radio signals have a property called **polarization**, which describes the orientation of the radio waves. The polarization of a Wi-Fi signal depends on the antenna, though linear polarization (meaning the waves all oscillate in the same direction) is the most common. In addition, these polarized antennas and emitted signals can be oriented in several ways, such as vertically, horizontally, and slanted (like a 45-degree angle).

When you adjust a Wi-Fi antenna or rotate the device it is attached to in physical space, you effectively change the angle (orientation) of its signal. When the receiving antenna aligns with the polarization of the transmitter, this creates the strongest signal. The greater the misalignment between receiver and transmitter, the weaker the signal. Misaligned polarization can lower a network's effective range and throughput. Let's look at a scenario with Ellen the network tech to show the impact of misalignment more clearly.

Ellen wants to connect two buildings in her organization via Wi-Fi. With both antennas aligned vertically, the connection will be strong and solid. If she sets one antenna to vertical and the other to horizontal, on the other hand, a 90-degree difference, the signal strength would drop by 18 decibels.

Every 3 dB equates to a doubling (or halving) of power, so –18 dB represents a 98.4 percent loss in power.

The math isn't important for the CompTIA Network+ exam, but the outcome is. In a worst-case cross-polarization scenario like Ellen's network, the connection would be 1/64 the comparable signal strength when compared with the same configuration using *common* (aligned) polarization. Ouch!

Know the concept of polarization and cross-polarization versus common polarization when setting up WAP antennas. When setting up a typical home or SOHO Wi-Fi network, don't worry about it at all.

Optimal Antenna Placement Optimal antenna placement varies according to the space to fill and security concerns. You can use the site survey and the same wireless analyzer tools to find dead spots, odd corners, and so on. Use the right kind of antenna on each WAP to fill in the space.

Configuring a Consumer Access Point

Consumer wireless access points often have a browser-based setup utility combined with routing and switching features. Typically, you open a Web browser on one of your network client workstations and enter the access point's IP address, such as 192.168.1.1, to bring up the configuration page. You need to supply an administrative password, included with your access point's documentation, to log in (Figure 14.27).

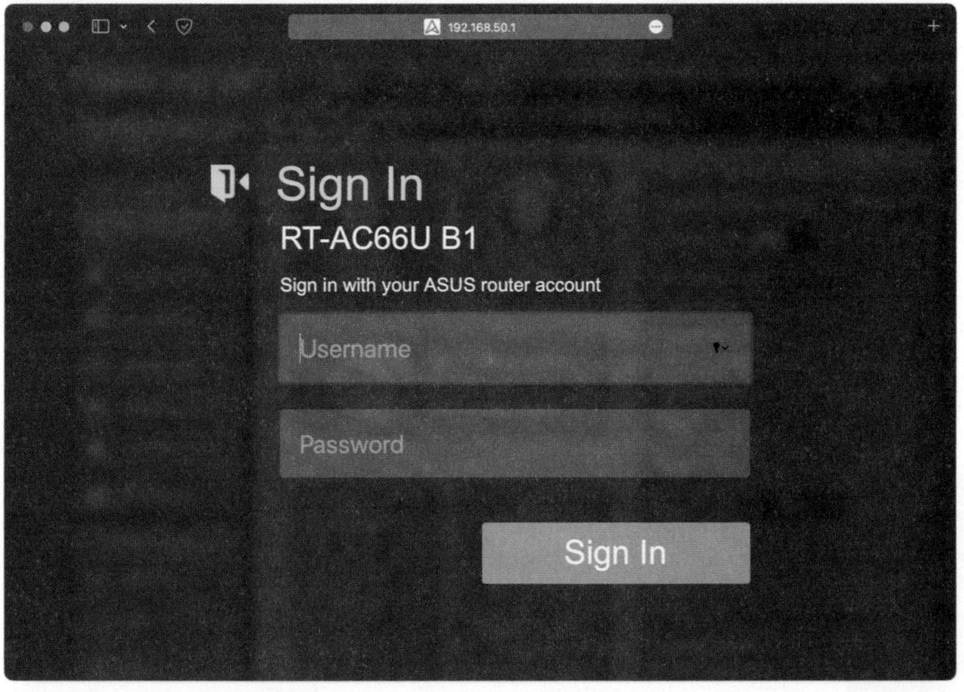

• **Figure 14.27** Security login for ASUS WAP

Once you've logged in, you'll see configuration screens for changing your basic setup, access point password, security, and so on. Different access points offer different configuration options. Figure 14.28 shows the home screen (Network Map in the menu) for an ASUS WAP/router.

Configuring the SSID and Beacon The SSID option is usually located somewhere obvious on the configuration utility. On the ASUS model shown in Figure 14.28, this option is right on the home screen. Configure your SSID to something unique.

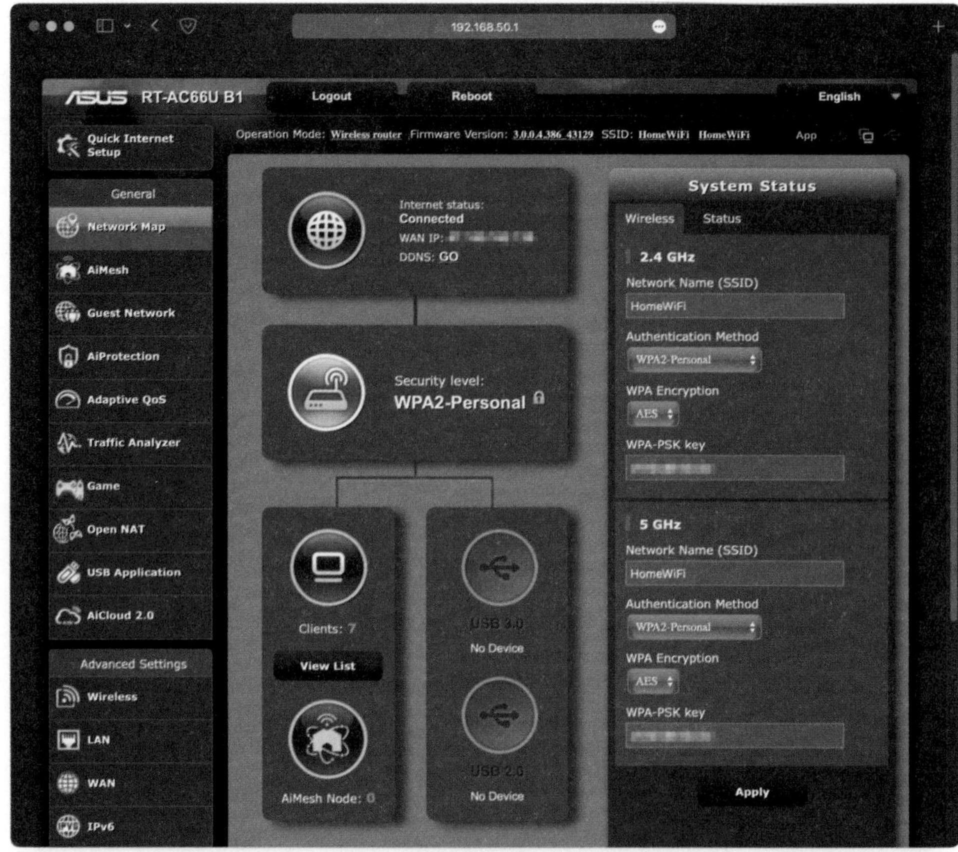

• **Figure 14.28** ASUS WAP home screen

The primary way we locate wireless networks is by using our clients to scan for SSIDs. All wireless networks have a function to turn off the SSID broadcast. You can choose not to broadcast the SSID, but this only stops casual users—sophisticated wireless intruders have tools to detect networks that do not broadcast their SSIDs. Turning off SSID broadcast forces users to configure the connection to a particular SSID manually.

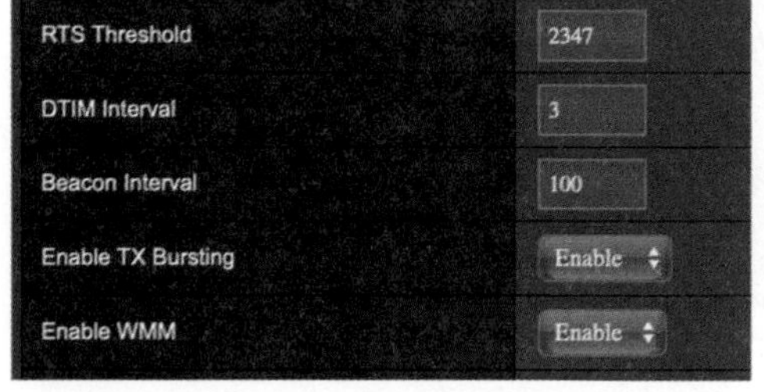

• **Figure 14.29** Setting for the beacon interval

Aside from the SSID, broadcast traffic includes the *beacon*, essentially a timing frame sent from the WAP at regular intervals. The beacon frame enables Wi-Fi networks to function, so this is fairly important. Beacon traffic also makes up a major percentage of network traffic because most WAPs have beacons set to go off every 100 ms! You can adjust the rate of the beacon traffic down and improve your network traffic speeds, but you lower the speed at which devices can negotiate to get on the network, among other things. Figure 14.29 shows the Beacon Interval setting on an ASUS WAP.

Configuring MAC Address Filtering You can use MAC address filtering to build a list of wireless network clients that are permitted or denied access to your wireless network based on their unique MAC addresses. Figure 14.30 shows the MAC address filtering configuration screen on the ASUS WAP. Simply enter the MAC address of a wireless client that you want to allow or deny access to your wireless network. (In Figure 14.30, I'm not using MAC filtering for security, but to make sure my Apple TV only uses the 5.0-GHz band.)

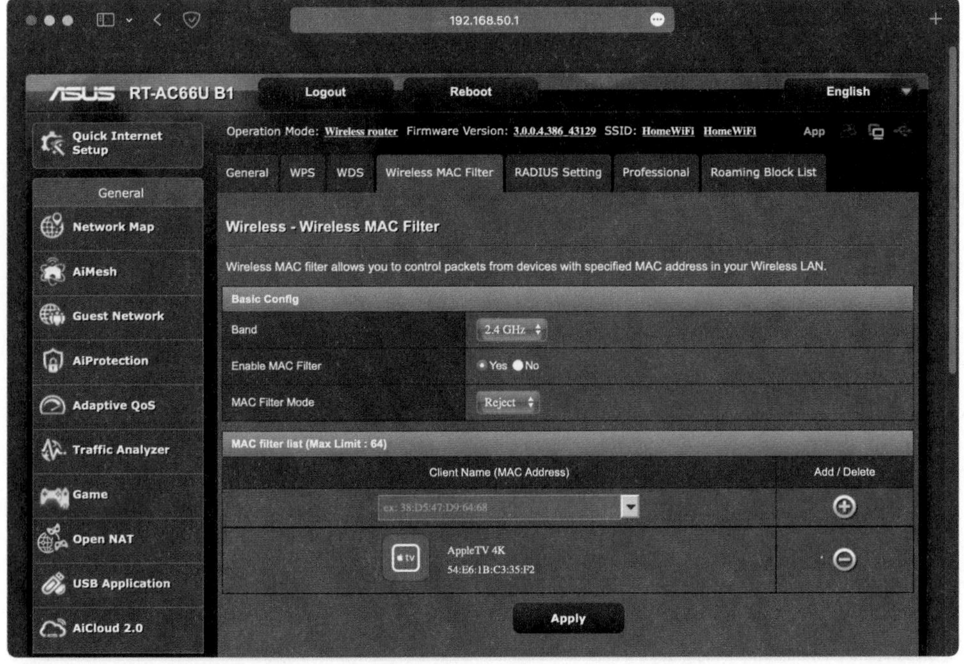

• **Figure 14.30** MAC address filtering configuration screen for an ASUS WAP

Configuring Encryption Enabling encryption ensures that data frames are secured against unauthorized access. To set up basic encryption, select an authentication method at the WAP and create a strong password—a *pre-shared key (PSK)*. Then configure all connected wireless clients on the network with the same key. Figure 14.31 shows the WPA2-Personal authentication and the pre-shared key settings screen for an ASUS WAP.

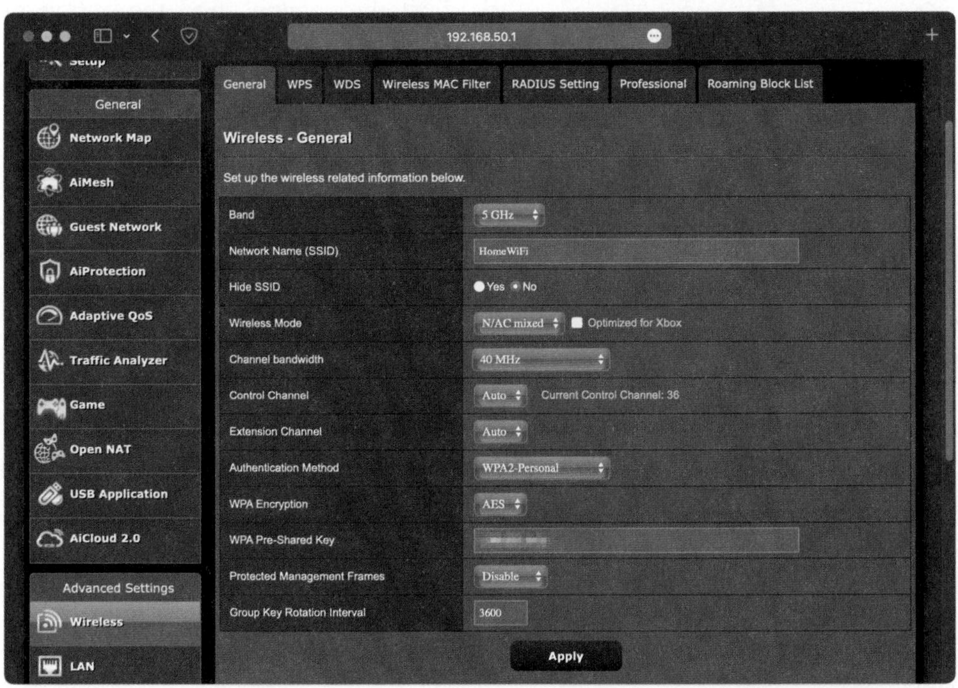

• **Figure 14.31** Security settings screen on an ASUS WAP

Most WAPs also support WPA2-Enterprise, allowing authentication using a RADIUS server (Figure 14.32). Always use the strongest encryption you can and choose a strong password if using WPA2-Personal.

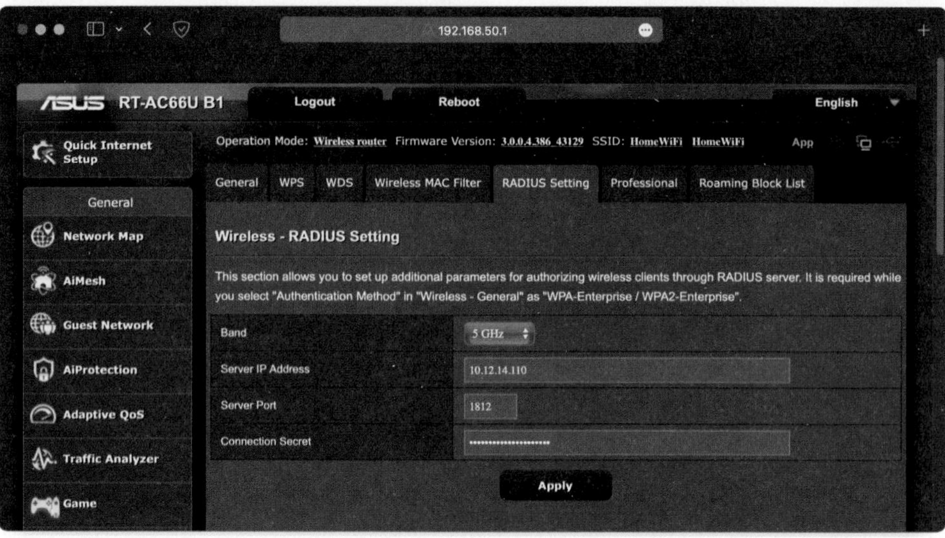

• **Figure 14.32** RADIUS settings

Configuring Channel and Frequency With most home networks, you can simply let the WAP automatically select the channel for each band, but in an environment with overlapping Wi-Fi signals, you'll want to manually set the channel for each band. Using a wireless analyzer, view the current channel utilization and then change your channel to something that doesn't conflict. To adjust the channel, find the option in the WAP configuration screens and simply change it. Figure 14.33 shows the 5.0-GHz channel menu in an ASUS WAP.

With dual-band WAPs, you can configure the SSID and security separately for 2.4 GHz or 5.0 GHz. This is useful if you want to force older 2.4-GHz devices onto their own SSID with a unique PSK. If you're not using one band, you can disable the radio. Figure 14.34 shows disabling the 2.4-GHz radio on an ASUS WAP.

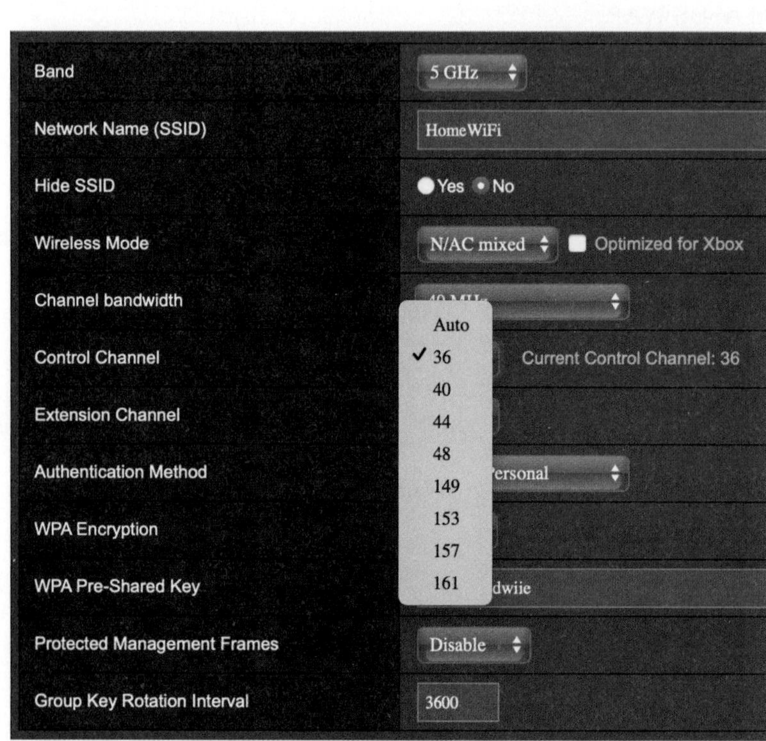

• **Figure 14.33** Changing the channel for the 5.0-GHz band

Configuring the Client

Infrastructure mode networks require that the same SSID be configured on all clients and access points. Normally, the client picks up a broadcast SSID and all you need to do is type in the PSK. With non-broadcasting networks, on the other hand, you need to type in a valid SSID as well as the PSK (Figure 14.35).

Wireless - Professional

Wireless Professional Setting allows you to set up additional parameters for wireless. But default values are recommended.

Band	2.4 GHz
Enable Radio	Yes No
Set AP Isolated	Yes No
Roaming assistant	Disable

• **Figure 14.34** Disabling the 2.4-GHz radio

Once you successfully connect a device to a wireless network, the client will store the settings for that wireless network in a profile. From now on, whenever the client sees a particular SSID, the device will automatically try to connect to that SSID using the encryption and key stored in the profile. Of course, if the wireless network changes in any way—for example, if the encryption password is changed—the device won't be able to access the network unless you delete the profile and reacquire the wireless network.

Extending the Network

Creating a basic service set network with a single WAP and multiple clients works in a relatively small area, but you can extend a Wi-Fi network in a few ways if you have difficult spaces—with lots of obstructions, for example—or a need to communicate beyond the ~300-foot range of the typical wireless network. Most commonly, you'd add one or more WAPs to create an extended service set. You can also install a wireless bridge to connect two or more wired networks.

Many companies make *wireless range extenders*, devices that pick up your Wi-Fi signal and rebroadcast it. Some look like a WAP; other models plug directly into an electrical outlet. Current wireless range extenders require very little setup and can extend your network between floors and into dead spots.

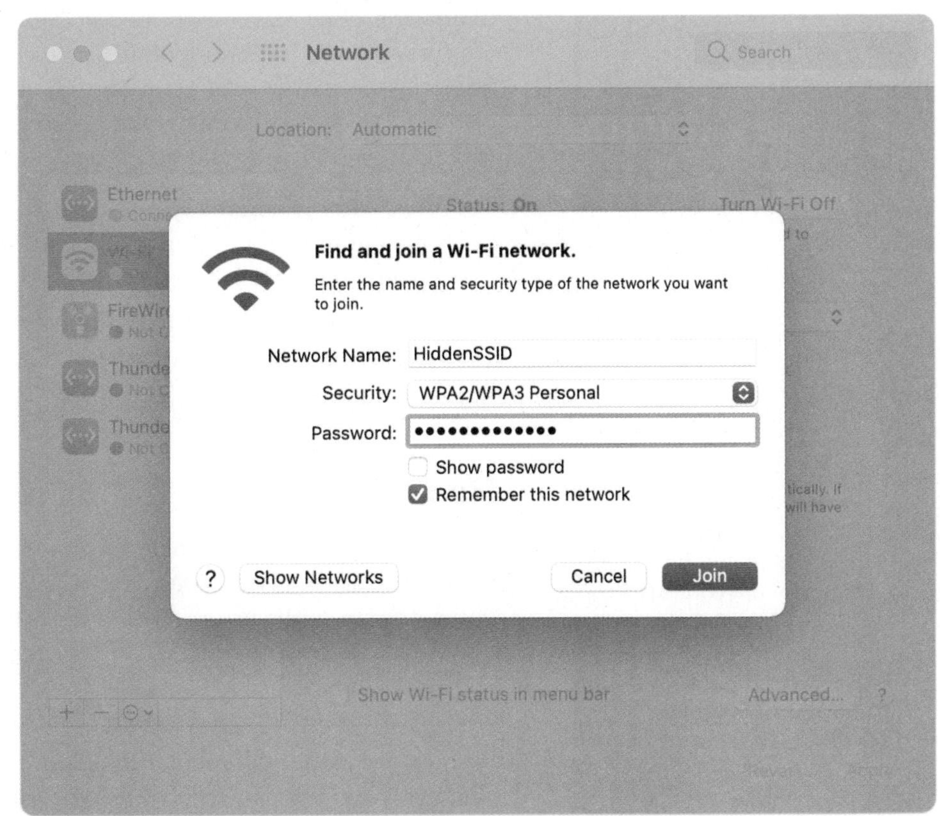

• **Figure 14.35** Typing in an SSID manually

Several Wi-Fi equipment manufacturers produce *mesh* networking gear in the consumer space to enable users to set up a multi-WAP network with ease. A typical mesh network product comes with three WAPs and a smartphone app. Creating a relatively secure network means opening the app, connecting to the first WAP, and then plugging in and connecting subsequent WAPs in the set. To add more coverage, just buy more mesh WAPs and apply the same process.

All mesh networks come preconfigured with security, such as WPA2. The lack of rigorous, manual control over security settings, on the other hand, makes mesh networks okay for the home but not suitable for a work environment. You won't find this sort of consumer gear on the CompTIA Network+ exam.

Adding a WAP

To add an additional WAP to a Wi-Fi network, you'll need to run a cable from a switch on the network to where you want to install it. Configuration is pretty straightforward. Both WAPs require the same ESSID, and if the WAPs are near each other, use separate channels.

Wireless Bridges

Dedicated **wireless bridges** connect two wired networks together or join wireless and wired networks together in the same way that wired switches do.

Wireless bridges come in two different flavors: point-to-point and point-to-multipoint. Point-to-point bridges can only communicate with a single other bridge and are used to connect two wired network segments. Point-to-multipoint bridges can talk to more than one other bridge at a time and can connect multiple network segments.

Verifying the Installation

Once you've completed the initial installation of a Wi-Fi network, test it. Move some traffic from one computer to another using the wireless connection. Never leave a job site without verifying the installation.

Troubleshooting Wi-Fi

Wireless networks are pretty magical when they work right, but the nature of no wires often makes them vexing things to troubleshoot when they don't.

As with any troubleshooting scenario, the first step in troubleshooting a wireless network is to break down tasks into logical steps. First, figure out the scope of the wireless networking problem. I like to break wireless problems into three symptom types:

- You can't get on the wireless network. Your client (or clients) may or may not think it's connected, but you can't access shared resources (Web pages, remote folders, and so on).
- Your wireless connections are way too slow. Your clients are accessing shared resources.
- Your wireless connection is doing weird things.

No Connection

Wi-Fi networks want to connect. You rarely if ever get an error on a device that says, "You may not speak to WAP55 that is supporting SSID X." Instead, you get more subtle errors such as repeated prompts for passwords, Automatic Private IP Addressing (APIPA)/zeroconf addresses, and such.

Be prepared for scenario questions that quiz you about the limits of the wireless standards. This includes throughput speeds (11-, 54-, 100+-Mbps), frequencies, distances, and channel usage. See the discussions earlier in the chapter for the limitations of each standard.

Channel Problems

If you're working with one of the older 802.11 versions using the 2.4-GHz channel, you may have problems with channels. One issue is **channel overlap**, where 2.4-GHz channels overlap with their nearest channel neighbors, causing interference. For example, channel 3 overlaps with channels 1, 2, 4, and 5. Some folks make the mistake of configuring an SSID and setting each WAP only one channel apart. This leads to connection problems, so always try to stick to using channels 1, 6, and 11 only.

You can use wireless scanning tools to check for *wireless channel utilization*. These are software tools that give you metrics and reports about nearby devices and which one is connected to which WAP. These tools enable you to discover overworked WAPs, saturated areas, and so on, so that you can deploy WAPs to optimize your network.

Security Type Mismatch

A *security type mismatch* defines one of two things: either you've connected manually to a wireless network and have set up the incorrect encryption type—an *encryption protocol mismatch*—or you've automatically accessed a particular SSID and entered the *incorrect passphrase*. Entering the wrong encryption type is rare, only happening when you set up a wireless connection manually. However, entering the wrong passphrase is the classic no-errors-but-won't-work issue. In older operating systems, you often would only get one chance to enter a key, and if you failed, your only clue was that your client got an APIPA/zeroconf address. More modern operating systems say something clearer, such as a message like *wrong passphrase*. Pretty much every wireless NIC is set to DHCP, and if you don't have the right password your client won't get past the WAP to talk to anything on the network, including the DHCP server.

- Symptoms: Not on network, continual prompting for password, APIPA/zeroconf address
- Solution: Enter the correct password

Signal/Power Levels

802.11 is a low-power radio and has a limited range. If the WAP doesn't have enough power, you'll have signal attenuation and your device won't be able to access the wireless network. (CompTIA blandly calls this *insufficient wireless coverage*.) All of the 802.11 standards have *distance limitations*; exceeding those limitations will reduce performance. Certainly a quick answer is to move closer to the WAP, but there are a number of issues that cause *power levels* to drop too low to connect beyond the obvious "you're too far away" from the WAP.

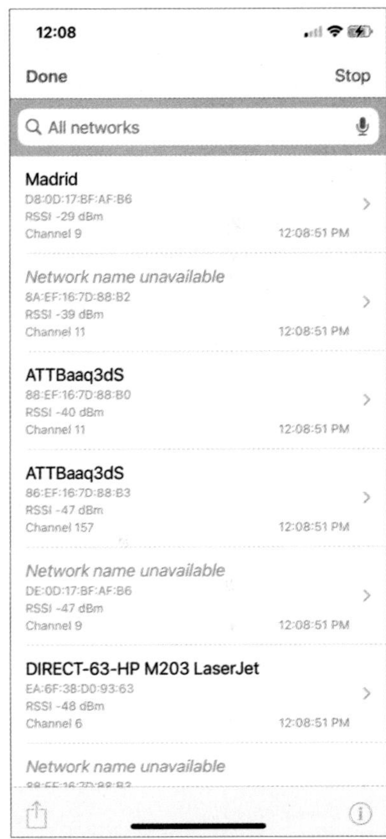

Figure 14.36 AirPort Utility showing RSSI strengths measured in decibel-milliwatts (dBm)

Manufacturers use scales called **received signal strength indication (RSSI)** to show the signal between a WAP and a receiver. Every manufacturer uses different RSSI numbers, but they usually show as "how many bars" you have. Running the Wi-Fi Scan feature of the AirPort Utility in my iPhone, for example, shows my WLAN RSSI as –29 dBm, whereas my neighbor's WLAN shows as –40 dBm (Figure 14.36). (We live close together in my neighborhood.) The closer to 0 dBm, the better the signal. The little symbol for Wi-Fi strength shows full strength to my WLAN.

If your WAP lacks enough signal power, you have a few choices: get closer to the WAP, avoid physical issues, turn up the power, use a better antenna, or upgrade to a newer 802.11 version (like 802.11ac) with features that enable the WAP to use the power it has more efficiently. I'm going to skip moving closer to the WAP as that's a bit obvious, but let's cover the other four.

Interference can also cause signal loss, but I choose to treat this as a separate issue later in this section. For now, we are talking about simple signal loss due to insufficient power.

A physical issue is what it sounds like: something physical in the way keeps the signal from reaching its destination. When installing a network, you must watch out for concrete walls, metal (especially metal studs), and the use of special RF-blocking window film. The solution is more careful

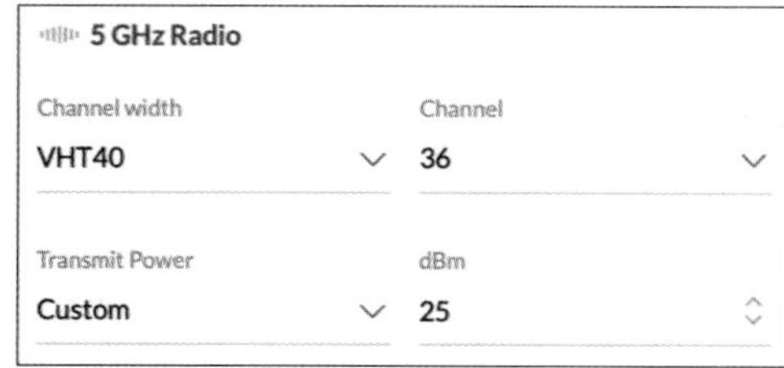

• **Figure 14.37** Transmit power configuration for an Ubiquiti WAP

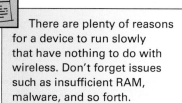

planning of WAP placement and realizing that even in the best-planned environment it is not at all uncommon to move WAPs based on the need to clear dead spots. We'll cover more about physical issues later in this chapter.

Some wireless devices make it easy to increase the power (Figure 14.37). It's tempting to think *cranking it up to 11* (a reference to *This Is Spinal Tap*) will fix all your Wi-Fi problems, but the unfortunate reality is more complex. If you have one WAP and live in the country, go ahead and crank the transmit power as high as it will legally go. But in a crowded urban environment, this can make Wi-Fi worse. Nearby WAPs will see your stronger signal and turn their own power up to compensate.

It's like being in a crowded restaurant. If everyone is talking at a moderate to low volume, everyone can converse without problems. But if one table starts to get boisterous, the table next to them has to get louder to be heard over the din. This cascades until everyone in the restaurant is practically shouting just so someone a few feet away can hear them.

The *effective radiated power (ERP)* is the signal strength coming out of an antenna. With a non-directional antenna, the signal in any direction will be the same. Use the *effective isotropic radiated power (EIRP)* to measure the relative signal strength coming out of a directional antenna, comparing the "strong" end signal with an omnidirectional antenna.

Too many 802.11 installations ignore the antennas, dropping in WAPs using their default antennas. In most cases the omnidirectional antennas that come with WAPs are very good—which is why they are so often the default antennas—but in many cases they are simply the incorrect antenna type and need to be replaced. If you're losing signal, don't forget to consider if the antenna is wrong for the wireless setup. Watch for scenarios on the CompTIA Network+ exam where replacing an omnidirectional antenna with one or more unidirectional antennas makes an easy fix. Also, look for incorrect antenna placement, where moving a few inches away from an obstacle can make big changes in performance.

The last power/signal issue is the fact that the MIMO features in 802.11n, 802.11ac, and 802.11ax are absolutely amazing in their ability to overcome dead spots and similar issues that on earlier versions of 802.11 can only be fixed with aggressive tweaking of WAP locations and antenna types. While MIMO and MU-MIMO aren't only to increase signal distance, it's almost certain you'll see a scenario where simply updating WAPs to 802.11ac or 802.11ax will automatically fix otherwise tricky problems.

Slow Connection

Slow wireless connections are far more difficult to troubleshoot than no connection at all. Unlike a disconnection, where you have obvious and clear clues, a slowdown is just…slow. In these situations you are clearly connected to an SSID, you have a good IP address, and the client itself runs well; but data transfer is slow: Web pages load slowly, applications time out, and you sense a general, hard-to-measure, irritating slowness.

In general, you can trace the cause of this slowness to one of several issues: you have too many devices overworking your WAPs; there are physical problems with signals going between your WAP and your clients; or there is too much RFI on the network. Let's look at these three issues.

There are plenty of reasons for a device to run slowly that have nothing to do with wireless. Don't forget issues such as insufficient RAM, malware, and so forth.

Overworked WAPs

An individual WAP has a very specific amount of bandwidth that depends on the version of 802.11 and the way it is configured. Once you hit the maximum bandwidth, you're going to have network slowdowns as the overworked WAP tries to handle all of the incoming wireless connections.

We overwork WAPs in many different ways, but one of the most common is by attaching too many devices to a single SSID over time, what's called *device saturation*. This creates *overcapacity* issues, such as slow speeds and inability to connect to the network. Avoid device saturation by adding more capacity. Careful placement of extra WAPs in high-demand areas is a huge step in the right direction. Usually the best, but most expensive, method is to upgrade your hardware: leaping from the 802.11n to the 802.11ac standard alone makes a massive difference in eliminating device saturation.

Jitter is the loss of packets due to an overworked WAP. Jitter shows up as choppy conversations over a video call, strange jumps in the middle of an online game—pretty much anything that feels like the network has missed some data. *Latency* is when data stops moving for a moment due to a WAP being unable to do the work. This manifests as a Word document that stops loading, for example, or an online file that stops downloading.

> Expect a scenario question on specific statistics or sensors to use to ensure wireless network availability on the CompTIA Network+ exam. Some of the performance metrics—specifically *network metrics*—you'll need to look for are bandwidth, latency, and jitter.

Speaking of 802.11ac, the biggest single issue causing device saturation is the imbalance of many devices using the 2.4-GHz band versus few devices using the 5.0-GHz band. In almost every midsized or larger wireless network, the 2.4-GHz band is filled to capacity, even with careful use of multiple channels. We call this **bandwidth saturation** and it's a huge issue with 802.11 networks. There is no answer other than to move to the 5.0-GHz band using primarily 802.11ac or 802.11ax.

Physical Issues

Any physical item placed on or near the straight-line path between a WAP and a wireless client can cause problems with a wireless signal. The problem depends on what is in the way and how it affects the radio signals as they encounter the physical item. Let's take a moment to discuss physical issues.

Absorption Nonmetallic building materials such as brick, sheetrock, and wood absorb radio signals, greatly reducing or in some cases eliminating a Wi-Fi signal completely. This phenomenon is called **absorption**.

Reflection Metallic materials like pipes, radiators, metal doors, and windows frames will reflect (or bounce) radio waves, sending them in unsuspected directions and keeping them from getting to their target device. This phenomenon is called **reflection** or **bounce**.

Refraction Glass is notorious for bending radio waves as the waves pass through them. What may look like a straight line between a WAP and client suddenly may run into problems if a glass door is placed between them. This phenomenon is called **refraction**.

> The CompTIA Network+ exam objectives differentiate between the attenuation described here—*RF attenuation*—and the signal loss caused by inadequate cable connecting an antenna to a WAP. The latter is referred to as *antenna cable attenuation/signal loss* and the fix is pretty straightforward. Use a better cable.

The result of all these physical problems is **attenuation**, the progressive loss of radio signal strength as the radio wave passes through different mediums (even things like air and rain reduce signal strength).

Be careful here! Different materials may cause more than one of these effects. A concrete wall may both absorb and reflect radio, whereas a metal framed door with glass inserts may both reflect and refract a radio wave.

Dealing with Physical Issues

Physical effects prevent clear, strong radio signals from reaching their target devices. These attenuation effects are different in every case and therefore tricky to predict during a site survey, requiring serious troubleshooting after the installation of a wireless network. A solid concrete wall is easy to predict as a problem (and a workaround created with specific WAP placement, for example). A room full of thick-walled, metal-framed room dividers might not be as easy to identify during a survey and won't come to light as a physical problem until the users start complaining about slow connections.

When a tech suspects a physical problem, the first step is another site survey. Find physical barriers that prevent hosts at specific locations that need good access. Often a quick look-around is all that's needed to identify and move a physical barrier or to move or add WAPs or antennas as needed. Secondly, the tech can install WAPs with multiple antennas, creating *multipath*.

Captive Portal

Many public facilities (such as airports) employ a **captive portal** to control access to their public Wi-Fi networks *and* control the amount of bandwidth each user can use. An attempt to connect to the network opens a Web browser that insists you follow the terms of service (*acceptable use policy*) and that sort of thing. Depending on how the organization sets it up, that captive portal can result in a seemingly slow connection. Higher security standards in your Web browser can also block this content and thus your access to the network.

Interference

Radio frequency interference (RFI) is an equally big problem when it comes to wireless network slowdowns. The 802.11 standard is pretty impressive in its ability to deal with noisy RF environments, but there's a point where any environment gets too noisy for 802.11. Interference comes from a number of sources, but basically we can break them down into two categories: RFI from non-Wi-Fi sources and RFI from Wi-Fi networks.

Non-Wi-Fi sources of RFI include CFL and LED lighting, low-power RF protocols like Bluetooth/Zigbee/Z-Wave, cordless phones, and microwaves. In general these devices can work nicely with 802.11 networks, but too many devices, especially devices too close to 802.11 equipment, can cause problems. The only way to eliminate this type of interference is to shut down or move the devices.

When it comes to 802.11-based interference, we are looking mainly at other WAPs generating signals that interfere with ours. The most common problem is that the limited number of channels means it's easy to have two WAPs on the same channel physically near each other. The extreme limitation of three nonoverlapping channels in 2.4 GHz is one reason why it's common to abandon the band in modern network designs.

To identify and measure interference, scan for RF sources using some form of RF scanner. A **spectrum analyzer**, for example, such as those used in wired and wireless networks, can measure electrical signals for frequency, power, harmonics, distortion, and more. We measure RFI with the

signal-to-noise ratio (SNR), essentially comparing the signal strength and the overall interference in the space. Figure 14.38 shows the popular AirMagnet WiFi Analyzer PRO reporting SNR. Use a channel that's not overwhelmed.

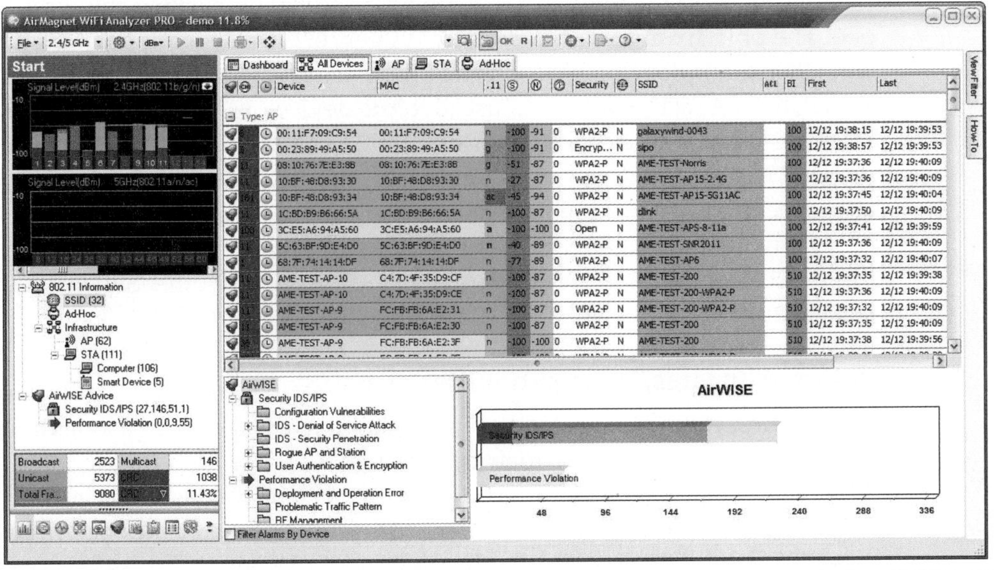

• **Figure 14.38** SNR on AirMagnet

Weird Connection

There are a number of situations where devices are connected to a wireless network and run at a good speed, but something is wrong—in some cases, dangerously wrong from a security perspective. Let's look at a few of these situations.

Open Networks

Open (nonencrypted) 802.11 networks are the bane of users and administrators. The two biggest challenges are how to avoid unintentionally logging into an open network with an SSID identical to one you have in another location, and how to provide security in an open network environment.

It's very common for your wireless device to access open networks with WAPs that use manufacturer default SSID names such as Linksys or D-Link. The danger with these is that bad guys know that most wireless devices, once they have created a profile to connect to one of these default open SSIDs, will then automatically connect to them again should they ever see one—and bad guys love to use this as a tool to attack these devices.

The second issue with any open wireless is that all of the data is transferred in the clear. It's easy for bad guys to listen in on your transmissions. The only way to avoid this is either to use a VPN or to use a Web browser add-on, like HTTPS Everywhere, that tries to connect you via HTTPS to every Web page.

The eavesdropping issue has declined in recent years because modern browsers default to HTTPS unless you specify HTTP in the URL. You have to *work* to connect to a nonsecure Web site these days, in other words.

Wrong SSID

It's easy to access the wrong SSID. Some 802.11 clients are notorious for moving their list of discovered SSIDs in such a way that you think you are clicking one SSID when you are actually accidentally clicking the wrong one. The only fix to this is to practice diligence when logging onto a new SSID. For example, who hasn't seen SSIDs such as the infamous "attwifi"? This SSID is AT&T's attempt to use all of its devices as hotspots. Sadly, it's a simple process to create an evil twin SSID (described in the upcoming section "Rogue Access Point") to mimic the attwifi SSID and get otherwise unsuspecting people to log into it.

Manually entering an SSID can obviously result in a typo. Luckily, in these cases your typo won't accidentally land you onto another SSID. You'll just get an error.

Untested Updates/Incompatibilities

802.11 is an ever-evolving standard, and manufacturers learned a long time ago to work hard to ensure their devices could evolve with the standard. This means that anyone supporting any 802.11 network is going to find themselves continually updating client firmware/software and WAP firmware. These updates are almost always good, but you need to stay aware of problems.

First, always research and test any update, especially firmware updates, which aren't too easy to reverse. Untested updates that go into your production network can potentially wreak havoc. If at all possible, run updates on a test network first.

Incompatibilities are related to untested updates in that they tend to appear at the same time an update appears. Make sure you are extremely clear on backward compatibility of different 802.11 versions. Also be aware that even in the same type of network there might be incompatibilities. A few years ago I bought what I thought was a dual-band (2.4- and 5.0-GHz) 802.11n WAP. I invested serious money in upgrading my 802.11n NICs in a few clients to accept dual band. Sadly, it wasn't until I was installing the new WAP that I read in the instructions that the WAP only supported one of the two bands at a time, and was totally incompatible with my new, expensive wireless NICs. Ouch! Too bad I didn't test the WAP before I tried to run it in my production environment.

Rogue Access Point

A **rogue access point (rogue AP)** is simply an unauthorized access point. Rogue access points have tortured every wireless network since the day Linksys came out with the first cheap wireless router back in the early 2000s. Most rogue APs aren't evil: just a user wanting to connect to the network who installs a WAP in a handy location into the wired network. Evil rogue APs are far more nefarious, acting as a backdoor to a network or a man-in-the-middle attack, grabbing usernames and passwords, among other items.

The most infamous form of rogue AP is called an evil twin. An **evil twin** is a rogue AP that intentionally mimics an existing SSID in order to get people to connect to it instead of the proper WAP. Evil twins work best in unsecured networks such as those you see in airports and hotels.

Client Disassociation Issues

Association describes the connection between an AP and a wireless client, a part of the typical 802.11 process. A couple of issues can cause association problems that result in very slow connection times or forced disassociation, meaning a client abruptly loses the Wi-Fi connection.

A few years ago, a popular Wi-Fi manufacturer upgraded AP firmware, which worked great for most users. Some users, however, immediately started complaining that the association process—that previously happened in a couple of seconds—took minutes and often failed altogether. Another firmware upgrade fixed the issue, but didn't quite fix the disgruntled users!

More common, especially in public Wi-Fi settings, is a *deauth attack* (deauth = deauthentication) designed to force a device off a legitimate AP and have the device join the attacker's AP. The attacker can then try to capture usernames and passwords. Chapter 19 goes into more detail on this and other attacks.

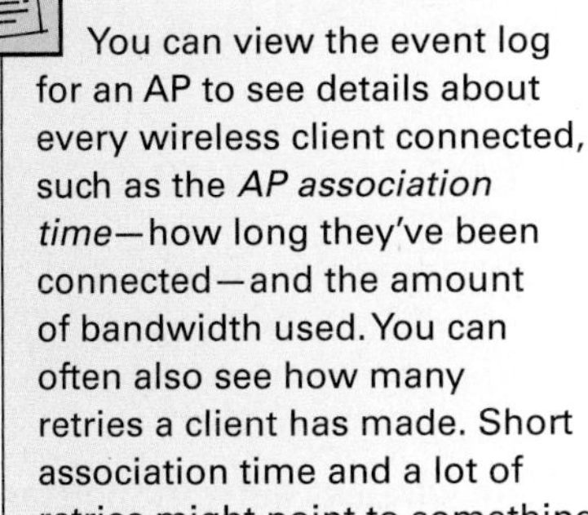

You can view the event log for an AP to see details about every wireless client connected, such as the *AP association time*—how long they've been connected—and the amount of bandwidth used. You can often also see how many retries a client has made. Short association time and a lot of retries might point to something negative happening.

Chapter 14 Review

■ Chapter Summary

After reading this chapter and completing the exercises, you should understand the following about wireless networking.

Explain wireless networking standards

- Wireless networks operate much like their wired counterparts, but they eliminate network cabling by using radio waves as a network medium.
- The wireless networking standard is IEEE 802.11, also known as Wi-Fi. 802.11 includes extensions to the standard such as 802.11a, 802.11b, 802.11g, 802.11n, 802.11ac, and 802.11ax.
- Modern versions of Windows, macOS, and Linux have wireless NIC configuration software built in. Third-party software might have more advanced features for more complex networks.
- A wireless network can operate in one of two modes: ad hoc or infrastructure.
- Ad hoc mode, also known as peer-to-peer mode, creates an independent basic service set (IBSS).
- Infrastructure mode is much more commonly used than ad hoc mode and allows wireless networks to connect to wired networks. A single wireless access point connecting computers in infrastructure mode is called a basic service set (BSS). If multiple WAPs are used, an extended basic service set (EBSS) is created, although most techs simply refer to it as an extended service set (ESS).
- Wireless networking ranges are also affected by environmental factors, interference from other wireless devices, and solid objects.
- The basic service set identifier (BSSID) identifies a single wireless network that acts as a broadcast domain.
- The service set identifier (SSID) configuration parameter enables you to set a basic level of access security. Properly configured SSIDs, or network names, exclude any wireless network device that does not share the same SSID.
- A Wi-Fi network with multiple WAPs applies the SSID to the ESS, creating an extended service set identifier (ESSID).
- The original 802.11 standards used the 2.4-GHz frequency band, whereas later standards use either 2.4-GHz, 5.0-GHz, or 6.0-GHz frequency bands. These frequencies enable the wireless networks to operate with less chance of interference from other wireless devices that are not part of the network.
- Spread-spectrum radio waves distribute data in small chunks over different frequencies to reduce interference from other wireless devices that are not part of the network. 802.11 networks use different forms of spread spectrum.
- Wi-Fi channels use a portion of the available frequency spectrum to tune out potential interference further. At 2.4 MHz, most WAPs use channels 1, 6, or 11. The 5.0-GHz and 6.0-GHz WAPs have a wider variety of channels, so overlap isn't a problem.
- Wi-Fi networks use carrier-sense multiple access with collision avoidance (CSMA/CA) to send frames. CSMA/CA is both proactive and reactive in that it attempts to avoid collisions before they happen rather than simply detecting them when they occur, and it retransmits frames that weren't acknowledged.
- Currently, only the Distributed Coordination Function (DCF) method of CSMA/CA is implemented. DCF uses IFS wait periods, backoff periods, and acknowledgments (ACK) to detect and avoid collisions and resend frames that collided with other frames.
- Wireless networking speeds range from 2 Mbps to a theoretical limit of 10 Gbps for 802.11ax. The speed is affected by the distance between wireless nodes, interference from other wireless devices such as wireless phones or baby monitors, and solid objects such as metal plumbing or air conditioning units.
- The 802.11b standard supported data throughput up to 11 Mbps over 300 feet on the 2.4-GHz frequency band.
- The 802.11a standard, which was released after 802.11b, supported data throughput up to 54 Mbps over 150 feet on the 5.0-GHz frequency band.
- The 802.11g standard supported data throughput up to 54 Mbps over 300 feet on the 2.4-GHz frequency band. 802.11g was also backward-compatible with 802.11b.
- The 802.11n standard supported data throughput up to 600 Mbps, theoretically, over 300 feet on the 2.4- or 5.0-GHz frequency band. 802.11n required MIMO

and transmit beamforming to achieve its greater data throughput. It was also backward-compatible with 802.11b, 802.11a, and 802.11g.

- 802.11n WAPs could transmit in three different modes: legacy, mixed, and greenfield. Legacy mode supported earlier standards; mixed mode enabled some earlier devices to work better than expected; and greenfield mode meant everything ran at the higher speed.
- The 802.11ac standard supports data throughput up to 1 Gbps over 300 feet on the 5.0-GHz frequency.
- The 802.1ax standard supports data throughput up to 10 Gbps over 300 feet on the 2.4-, 5.0-, or 6.0-GHz frequency.
- Wireless networks may be secured with MAC filtering, although this method can be easily hacked by spoofing.
- A RADIUS server stores usernames and passwords, enabling you to set a user's rights once in the network. A supplicant contacts a Network Access Server, which, in turn, contacts the RADIUS server.
- Data should be encrypted when being transferred across a wireless network. WEP offers no protection because it is easily hacked. WPA is better because it uses TKIP-RC4. WPA2, which uses CCMP-AES, is stronger than WPA. WPA3 uses Simultaneous Authentication of Equals along with strong encryption to make attacking the signal exceedingly difficult.
- Enterprise wireless networking equipment offers robust construction, durability, and centralized management. The latter can be specialized controller machines or through remote management software. Current enterprise networks can also rely on cloud-based AP controls.
- Better WAPs and switches can use Power over Ethernet (PoE) to provide electrical power to the WAP via the Ethernet cable that connects it with the switch. Both the WAP and the switch must have this capability built in for it to work.

Describe the process for implementing Wi-Fi networks

- The first step in creating a wireless network is to create a site survey, which identifies other wireless networks or objects that may cause interference and helps you to determine the best location for your WAPs.
- Wireless networking hardware must be installed in all the clients. Most laptops have wireless NICs built in, but a USB NIC can be used as an alternative. Desktop computers may use a PCIe card. Any computer with a USB port can use a USB wireless NIC.
- Configuring a NIC for ad hoc networking requires the SSID, IP address, channel, and sharing to be configured.
- Configuring a NIC for infrastructure networking requires planning the optimal placement of the WAP and its antennas. A replacement antenna can strengthen the wireless signal and extend the range. The WAP also needs to be configured with the proper settings for the SSID, security, and encryption options.
- A wireless network's range can be extended by adding multiple WAPs. The additional WAPs typically connect to each other via a hard cable.
- A wireless bridge connects two wired networks together.
- A point-to-point bridge can only communicate with a single other bridge, whereas a point-to-multipoint bridge can communicate with more than one other bridge at the same time.

Describe troubleshooting techniques for wireless networks

- Troubleshooting Wi-Fi networks falls into three categories: you can't get on the network, the connection is slow, and the wireless connection is weird.
- Channel overlap and frequency mismatch can cause network problems. The problem could also be a security-type mismatch or simply a wrong passphrase.
- WAPs have a distance limitation that can be overcome in several ways. Many WAPs can increase their power. If your WAP does not do so natively, you might still be able to succeed with a third-party tool. You can change out the antennas or reposition antennas for optimal performance.
- A slow wireless connection might be caused by overworked WAPs or interference from other sources. Solutions include adding more capacity with more WAPs and removing sources of interference. You can run a Wi-Fi analyzer to find such sources.
- Weird connections compromise security. Open networks, wrong SSIDs, and untested updates can create risk in Wi-Fi. Rogue access points can be used to grab usernames and passwords. Deauth attacks can result in clients getting kicked off a legitimate connection and joining a rogue AP, opening the potential for identity theft.

Key Terms

802.1X *(394)*
802.11 *(381)*
802.11a *(388)*
802.11a-ht *(390)*
802.11ac *(390)*
802.11ax *(390)*
802.11b *(388)*
802.11g *(389)*
802.11g-ht *(390)*
802.11i *(395)*
802.11n *(389)*
absorption *(415)*
ad hoc mode *(384)*
attenuation *(415)*
bandwidth saturation *(415)*
basic service set (BSS) *(385)*
basic service set identifier (BSSID) *(385)*
bounce *(415)*
captive portal *(416)*
carrier-sense multiple access with collision avoidance (CSMA/CA) *(387)*
CCMP-AES *(395)*
channel *(386)*
channel bonding *(389)*
channel overlap *(412)*
dead spot *(389)*
dipole antenna *(404)*
direct-sequence spread-spectrum (DSSS) *(386)*
Distributed Coordination Function (DCF) *(388)*
encryption *(392)*
evil twin *(418)*
extended service set (ESS) *(385)*
extended service set identifier (ESSID) *(386)*
Extensible Authentication Protocol (EAP) *(392)*
frequency-hopping spread-spectrum (FHSS) *(386)*
gain *(406)*
geofencing *(397)*
greenfield mode *(390)*
independent basic service set (IBSS) *(384)*
infrastructure mode *(384)*
interframe gap (IFG) *(387)*
jitter *(415)*
latency *(388)*
legacy mode *(390)*
Lightweight Access Point Protocol (LWAPP) *(399)*
link state *(383)*
MAC filtering *(396)*
mixed mode *(390)*
multiple input/multiple output (MIMO) *(389)*
multiuser MIMO (MU-MIMO) *(390)*
Network Access Server (NAS) *(394)*
network name *(385)*
omnidirectional antenna *(404)*
orthogonal frequency-division multiplexing (OFDM) *(386)*
patch antenna *(406)*
peer-to-peer mode *(384)*
Point Coordination Function (PCF) *(388)*
polarization *(406)*
Power over Ethernet (PoE) *(399)*
radio frequency interference (RFI) *(416)*
RADIUS server *(394)*
received signal strength indication (RSSI) *(413)*
reflection *(415)*
refraction *(415)*
roaming *(386)*
rogue access point (rogue AP) *(418)*
service set identifier (SSID) *(385)*
signal-to-noise ratio (SNR) *(417)*
signal strength *(383)*
site survey *(400)*
spectrum analyzer *(416)*
SSID broadcast *(386)*
supplicant *(394)*
Temporal Key Integrity Protocol (TKIP) *(395)*
thick client *(399)*
thin client *(399)*
TKIP-RC4 *(395)*
transmit beamforming *(389)*
unidirectional antenna *(406)*
VLAN pooling *(399)*
Wi-Fi *(381)*
Wi-Fi 4 *(389)*
Wi-Fi 5 *(390)*
Wi-Fi 6 *(390)*
Wi-Fi 6E *(390)*
Wi-Fi analyzer *(400)*
Wi-Fi Protected Access (WPA) *(392)*

Wi-Fi Protected Access 2 (WPA2) *(395)*
Wi-Fi Protected Setup (WPS) *(391)*
Wired Equivalent Privacy (WEP) *(392)*
wireless access point (WAP) *(382)*
wireless analyzer *(400)*
wireless bridge *(412)*
wireless LAN controller *(399)*
wireless local area network (WLAN) *(384)*
wireless network *(381)*
wireless survey tool *(400)*
WPA-Enterprise *(394)*
WPA2-Enterprise *(396)*
WPA2-Personal *(395)*

Key Term Quiz

Use the Key Terms list to complete the sentences that follow. Not all the terms will be used.

1. When a network uses the 802.11 standard, it is said to be a(n) ______________.
2. Matilda decides to upgrade her office's Wi-Fi 4 network to Wi-Fi 5, also known as ______________.
3. Serena needs to set up a wireless network that starts from the side wall of her office and focuses the signal only into the office, not to the business that shares the wall. She should install a WAP with a(n) ______________ to focus the wireless signal.
4. Of the three different spread-spectrum transmission methods, ______________ sends data out on different frequencies at the same time and, therefore, uses considerably more bandwidth.
5. Marketed as ______________, this standard operates in the 6.0-GHz band.
6. ______________ allowed devices on 802.11n networks to make multiple simultaneous connections, allowing for a theoretical throughput of 600 Mbps.
7. 802.11 implements ______________, which proactively avoids network packet collisions rather than simply detecting them when they occur.
8. Connecting two Wi-Fi computers through a WAP uses ______________, whereas connecting the two wirelessly together directly uses ______________.
9. A(n) ______________ is a rogue AP that intentionally mimics an existing SSID in order to get people to connect to it instead of the proper WAP.
10. When you want to extend a wireless network, simply add another ______________.

Multiple-Choice Quiz

1. With what technology can you avoid finding an AC outlet for a WAP?
   A. AES
   B. PoE
   C. Powered Wi-Fi
   D. TKIP
2. Sarah wants to connect a Wi-Fi client to an 802.11ax AP. What frequencies could she use? (Select the best answer.)
   A. 2.4-GHz band
   B. 5.0-GHz band
   C. 2.4- or 5-GHz band
   D. 2.4-, 5.0-, or 6.0-GHz band
3. Which of the following statements about SSIDs are true? (Select three.)
   A. All wireless networks use them.
   B. Only one wireless device uses them.
   C. They should be unique to your wireless LAN.
   D. They are broadcast, by default, by most wireless network devices.

4. What is the best way to connect multiple wireless segments together?
   - **A.** Use an 802.11g network adapter.
   - **B.** Use an 802.11i network adapter.
   - **C.** Use a point-to-multipoint wireless bridge.
   - **D.** Use a point-to-point wireless bridge.
5. Which of the following terms describes the loss of packets due to an overworked WAP?
   - **A.** Attenuation
   - **B.** Jitter
   - **C.** Reflection
   - **D.** Refraction
6. What process secures a wireless network by protecting data packets being transmitted?
   - **A.** Data packeting
   - **B.** Pulse encoding
   - **C.** Data encryption
   - **D.** MAC broadcasting
7. When setting up WPA2-PSK on his wireless network, Edsel has the option to choose TKIP or AES. Which should he implement?
   - **A.** Only AES
   - **B.** Only TKIP
   - **C.** Both AES and TKIP
   - **D.** Neither. He should implement RADIUS.
8. What is the progressive loss of radio signal passing through different media called?
   - **A.** Attenuation
   - **B.** EAP
   - **C.** RFI
   - **D.** SNR
9. Which of the following is the wireless network encryption method that offers the best security?
   - **A.** MAC filtering
   - **B.** WEP
   - **C.** WPA
   - **D.** WPA2
10. Which of the following is known as a basic service set in infrastructure mode?
   - **A.** A WAP
   - **B.** A WPA
   - **C.** A RADIUS server
   - **D.** A TKIP
11. Archer sets up a wireless network between two buildings. Both 802.11ax networks seem smoking fast within their buildings, but the connection between the buildings is dramatically slower. What could most likely be the problem?
   - **A.** Incorrect SSID
   - **B.** Incorrect antenna polarization
   - **C.** Insufficient PoE+
   - **D.** Invalid captive portals
12. What innovation enabled 802.11n networks to minimize dead spots?
   - **A.** Channel bonding
   - **B.** FIFO
   - **C.** MIMO
   - **D.** Transit beamforming
13. What's the optimal range for an 802.11ac connection?
   - **A.** 50 feet
   - **B.** 150 feet
   - **C.** 300 feet
   - **D.** 600 feet
14. To achieve maximum Wi-Fi coverage in a room, where should you place the WAP?
   - **A.** Place the WAP on the north side of the room.
   - **B.** Place the WAP in the center of the room.
   - **C.** Place the WAP near a convenient electrical outlet.
   - **D.** It doesn't matter where you place the WAP.
15. Dave has set up a Wi-Fi network for his café that works well for most patrons but works poorly on the patio. What's the least expensive option for making Wi-Fi work for the patio customers?
   - **A.** Add a wireless range extender close to the patio.
   - **B.** Exchange his 802.11n WAP for an 802.11ax WAP.
   - **C.** Reverse the polarity on the WAP's antennas.
   - **D.** Run another network drop to the patio and add a second WAP.

Essay Quiz

1. You are enrolled in a writing class at the local community college. This week's assignment is to write on a technical subject. Write a short paragraph about each of the wireless standards that can reach theoretical speeds of 100+ Mbps.
2. Prepare a short memo to your instructor (or friend) that outlines the basic differences between the WEP, WPA, WPA2, and WPA3 encryption methods. Use any standard memo format you are familiar with. Include a company or school logo on the top of the page to make the memo appear as if it were printed on company stationery (or "letterhead").
3. Write a few paragraphs describing the pros and cons of both wired and wireless networks. Specifically, compare 1000BASE-T to the 802.11ac standard. (Review Chapter 4 for more details on 1000BASE-T.) Then conclude with a statement of your own personal preference.

Lab Projects

• Lab Project 14.1

You just received a nice tax return and want to expand your home network. Your current wired home network setup consists of one macOS desktop with a Gigabit Ethernet connection to cable Internet (at 100 Mbps download). The portable devices in your house (phones, laptops, etc.) should connect via Wi-Fi. Because you're spending your own money buying equipment, you seek a solution that will satisfy your needs for a long time.

You want to buy your new equipment locally, so you can set it up right away. Use the Internet to explore local stores' prices and equipment. Also check out reviews of the items you are interested in obtaining. After you have done sufficient research, prepare an itemized price list with your choices arranged like the following table:

Item	Store/Model	Price	Quantity	Total
Wireless NICs, PCIe				
Wireless NICs				
Wireless access point				
Other				
Totals				

• Lab Project 14.2

You have been tasked with expanding your company's wireless network. Your IT manager asked you to create a presentation that explains wireless routers and their functions. She specifically said to focus on the 802.11ac and 802.11ax wireless network standards. Create a brief, yet informative, PowerPoint presentation that includes comparisons of these two technologies. You may include images of actual wireless bridges from vendor Web sites as needed, being sure to cite your sources. Include any up-to-date prices from your research as well.

Virtualization and Cloud Computing

"Above the cloud with its shadow is the star with its light. Above all things reverence thyself."

—Pythagoras

In this chapter, you will learn how to

- **Describe virtualization and cloud computing concepts**
- **Explain virtual networking concepts**
- **Explain how network virtualization and cloud computing work in modern networks**

Let's pretend you have an incredible idea for a new company. Oh my gosh, it's such a good idea! We can make millions! Let's do it! So, let's set up that Web site! Here we go . . . .

Hang on there, bucko! Not that long ago you had to go through a fairly onerous process of buying a beefy system, getting a static IP address from an ISP, installing and configuring the OS, installing and configuring the Web server software, and registering the Web site's domain. Then, of course, you had to build the Web site. You didn't have any other choices.

Building a Web site these days is easy if you don't need a lot of control. You pick a point-and-click service like Squarespace that'll register a domain for you; then pick a template, fill in some information about your company, even add a store to sell things! You can build a robust, functioning Web site without thinking about servers, operating systems, or IP addresses.

If your company is building the next killer app, as another example, you'll need more control than that! But you don't have to go hardware shopping, kill your back racking servers, and operate all that gear. You pick an online cloud provider like Amazon Web Services, Microsoft Azure, or Google Cloud and quickly set up a server that lives in someone else's rack.

How did we get from a place requiring so much manual effort to being able to set up Web sites and app servers by clicking a few buttons? Well, this is a combination of the two technologies you'll discover in this chapter: virtualization and the cloud. As you will soon see, virtualization and the cloud aren't at all the same thing, but they sure play well together!

Be warned: These examples of super-easy Web sites and app hosting explore only one aspect of the power of virtualization and the cloud. There's so much more, but hopefully this is enough to pique your interest to delve into this chapter with gusto!

This chapter begins with virtualization and cloud computing concepts to create a framework for discussion. The second section dives into how virtualization shapes many aspects of modern networking. The chapter finishes with practical applications of network virtualization and cloud computing. Let's get started.

Test Specific

Virtualization and Cloud Computing Concepts

Virtualization and cloud computing bring a host of jargon and specific concepts into play. Techs need to understand the basic concepts underlying the technologies to know how best to deploy them in current networking scenarios. This section looks first at virtualization and then cloud computing. The section finishes with a flourish, with a dive into infrastructure as code.

Virtualization

Virtualization usually refers to running software on a computer to create a **virtual machine (VM)**, an environment that imitates a physical machine. You can install and run an operating system in this environment as if it were its own physical computer. In a networking sense, a single physical machine could house multiple virtual machines, each running a different networking task, such as DHCP, DNS, firewall, VPN, and so on.

From the first day some nerdy type decided to take a PC and turn it into a server, there's been a big problem, *hardware underutilization*. **Hardware underutilization** means that a server (or a desktop PC, for that matter) isn't being used anywhere near its capability. Consider as an example a file server in an office LAN or a Web server sharing a single Web site. Each case shares the same issue: not enough users accessing the server (Figure 15.1).

• **Figure 15.1** Underutilization

No matter what a server is serving, traditionally we have a substantial amount of hardware underutilization. Sure, we've all experienced trying do something on the Internet and receiving a "Server busy" message or some error like that—*overutilization*—but in the vast majority of cases, underutilization is the problem.

For the record, virtual machines have been around for a long time, appearing on IBM mainframes back in the 1970s. It wasn't until 1998 when a company called VMware introduced ESX, its first hypervisor built to run on PCs. Other companies now compete with VMware for a piece of the VM market, but VMware is currently the leader in PC virtualization software.

So how do we fix hardware underutilization? Well, we need the servers to do more with the hardware they have. Luckily for us, PC processors, using roughly the same set of functions that enables your CPU to multitask many applications at once, can instead multitask a bunch of virtual machines. Virtualization enables one machine—called the **host**—to run multiple operating systems simultaneously. This is called hardware virtualization.

A virtual machine is a special program, running in protected space (just like programs run in protected space), that enables all the features of the server (RAM, CPU, drive space, peripherals) to run as though they are each separate computers (ergo, virtual machines). See Figure 15.2. The program used to create, run, and maintain the VMs is called a **hypervisor**.

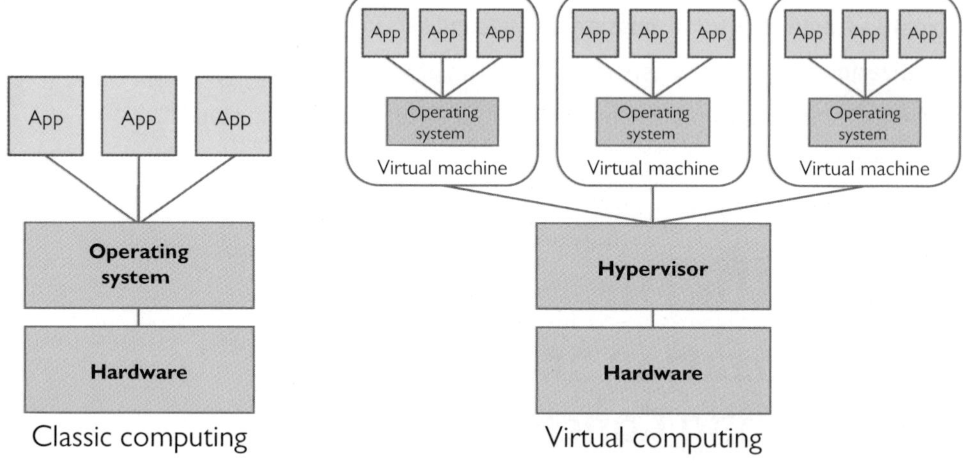

• **Figure 15.2** Classic computing versus computing with virtualization

You can install and run an operating system in this **guest** virtual environment as if it were its own physical computer. The VM is stored as a set of files that the hypervisor can load and save with changes. Figure 15.3 shows a macOS 11 host system using a program called Oracle VM VirtualBox to run an Ubuntu Linux guest.

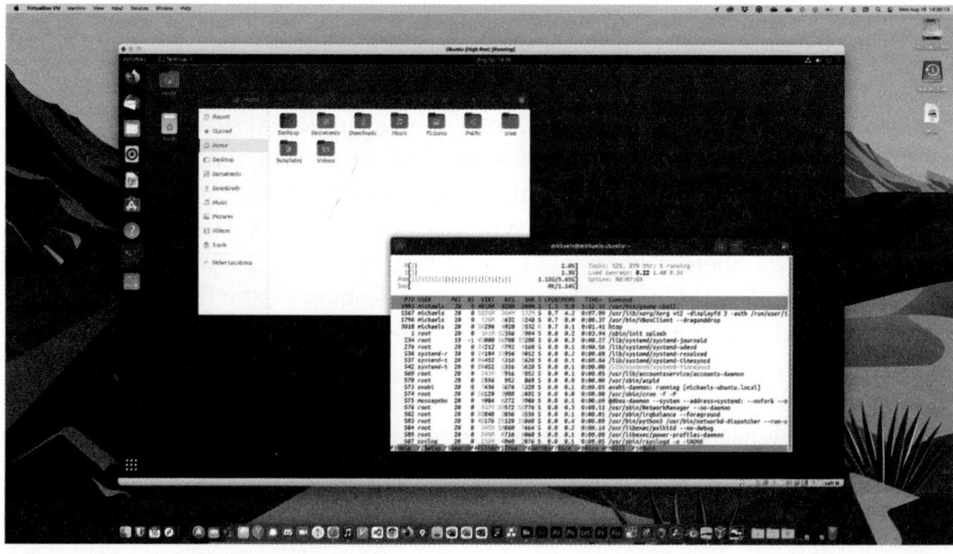

• **Figure 15.3** VirtualBox running Linux

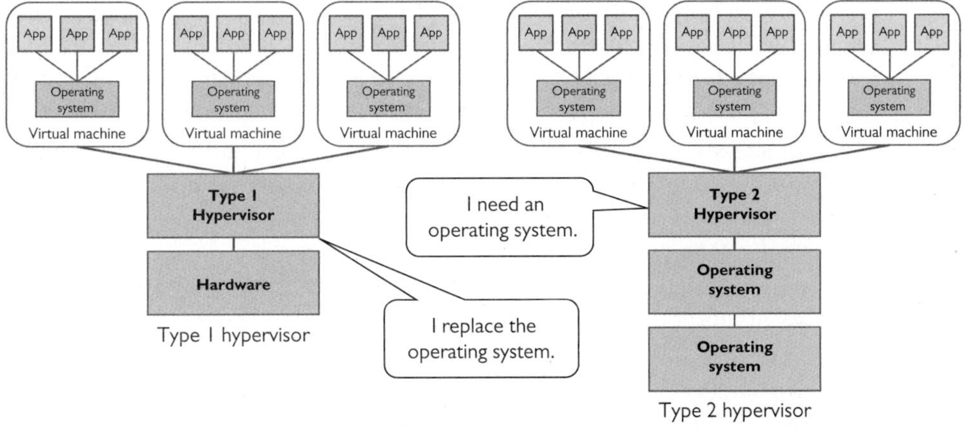

• **Figure 15.4** Hypervisor types

There are two types of hypervisors (Figure 15.4). A **Type 1 hypervisor** is installed on the system in lieu of an operating system. A **Type 2 hypervisor** is installed on top of the operating system. VMware sells both Type 1 and Type 2 hypervisors. Oracle's VM VirtualBox comes only as a Type 2 hypervisor.

Type 1 hypervisors are the most common for hard-working VMs. Type 2 hypervisors are popular for learning about virtualization and don't require a dedicated system.

Virtualization is an incredibly powerful tool that's taken over the Internet. Nearly every Web site is installed in a virtual machine running on a server. The chances of you ever hitting a Web site that uses classical Web hosting are almost nil. Long live virtualization!

This section explores three primary aspects of virtualization to provide a framework for understanding: abstraction, flexibility, and scaling.

Abstraction

Modern networks separate form from function on many levels, actions that are defined by the jargon word *abstraction*. It's a loaded term that has meanings in both English and networking, so let's break it down with some examples, then provide a working definition.

To **abstract** means to remove or separate. In networking terms, it means to take one aspect of a device or process and separate it from that device or process. You've seen this in hardware virtualization already in this chapter, with an operating system separated from hardware, being placed in a virtual machine. This is abstraction at work. The OS is abstracted (removed a step) from the bare metal, the computing hardware.

This same concept applies to more than VMs; it applies to how networks work in general. The whole idea of networking is to get data from one computer to another, right? Ethernet provides one form of connectivity. But the data coming from the sender originates much higher up the OSI protocol stack, eventually getting packaged into an IP packet. IP doesn't know Ethernet. IP is one step removed from the Ethernet frame that gets put on the wire.

Here's the key: applications can work with the Internet Protocol as a stand-alone *thing*, regardless of whether the network uses Ethernet or some other physical protocol to get data from source to destination.

The Internet Protocol is an abstraction that spares most applications from needing to know or care how their messages get from one place to another—and Ethernet is *also* an abstraction that spares IP from needing to know how to send those messages out on the wire. *Abstraction*—and particularly the process of abstracting something complicated into layers that let us focus on a few issues at a time—plays an important role in how network people manage complexity.

Abstraction is therefore both a concept and a noun, defining the process of separating functions into discrete units; those discrete units are *abstractions*.

Virtualization describes a specific kind of abstraction: a pattern that involves creating a *virtual* (software) version of something. Once upon a time, we created virtual (sometimes called *logical*) versions of real, physical things. But virtualization proved to be such a fruitful idea that we've kept right on virtualizing things that are already virtual. To keep your bearings, remember that most kinds of virtualization replace an existing component with a layer of software that is roughly indistinguishable to any programs, devices, or users that interact with it.

I hope a few examples drive these points home:

- Virtual memory replaces direct access to physical RAM with a layer of software that enables the OS to move a running program's memory to the swap file and back dynamically without the program's awareness.
- Hardware virtualization replaces all the physical devices an OS needs with software versions that the hypervisor controls. The hypervisor can use this control to redistribute the host's hardware resources among running VMs on-the-fly.
- One form of storage virtualization replaces a system's hard drive with a software block-storage device that can send reads and writes to other places, such as to a file or to a storage server accessible over the network.
- Network virtualization, the star of this particular show, creates software versions of networking functions—such as DNS, firewalls, and intrusion detection systems—that used to require dedicated network hardware boxes. The network operating system interacts with network functions just as it always did. Those functions—now software—in turn work with a hypervisor that interfaces with real hardware. Figure 15.5 shows this relationship shift.
- Taken to one extreme, you can use virtualization to create a fully functional network. A hypervisor can use a virtual network, in the form of a virtual switch, to enable multiple VMs it hosts to communicate without the frames ever leaving the host machine.

Tech Tip

Containerization

With containerization, *an operating system creates a self-contained environment for an application. This environment includes all the software the application needs to run as if it were the only application running on a clean operating system. Containerization isn't listed in the CompTIA Network+ objectives, but you'll see it in the real world. Containerization is a bit like hardware virtualization but essentially virtualizes the OS instead of the whole computer.*

Containers use fewer resources than VMs, but they're stuck with the same OS as their host and are less isolated from each other. The presence of terms like Docker, Kubernetes, k8s, k3s, LXC, and OCI indicates a technology uses containers; terms like cloud-native and microservices are also closely associated with containerization.

Flexibility

Replacing hardware components with software generally adds flexibility in how you use that virtual hardware. (You do get a performance decrease due to the added layer of software.) Most commonly, you'll see added flexibility in input and output devices, location of devices, and dividing or combining resources.

Reroute an Input or Output When you create a new virtual machine from scratch, you'll need to install an OS in it. Easy, right? On boring old physical

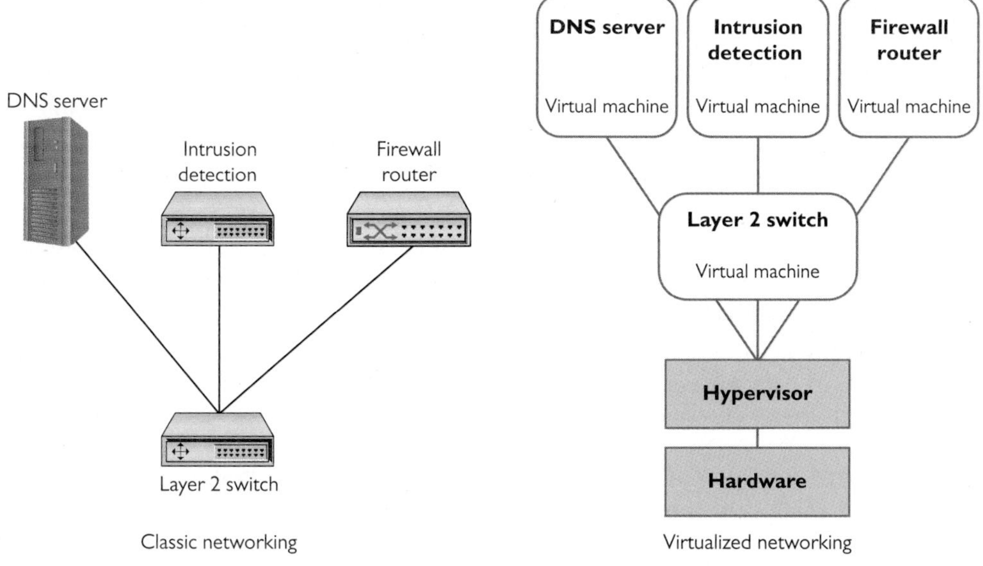

• **Figure 15.5** Classic versus virtualized networking

computers, you stick the installation media in a physical USB slot or optical drive. A VM has no such physical ports or drives. It has virtual equivalents that you can route input to from either the host's physical slot/drive or from a disk image file saved on the host. Figure 15.6 shows VirtualBox installation selecting an ISO image to install Windows 11.

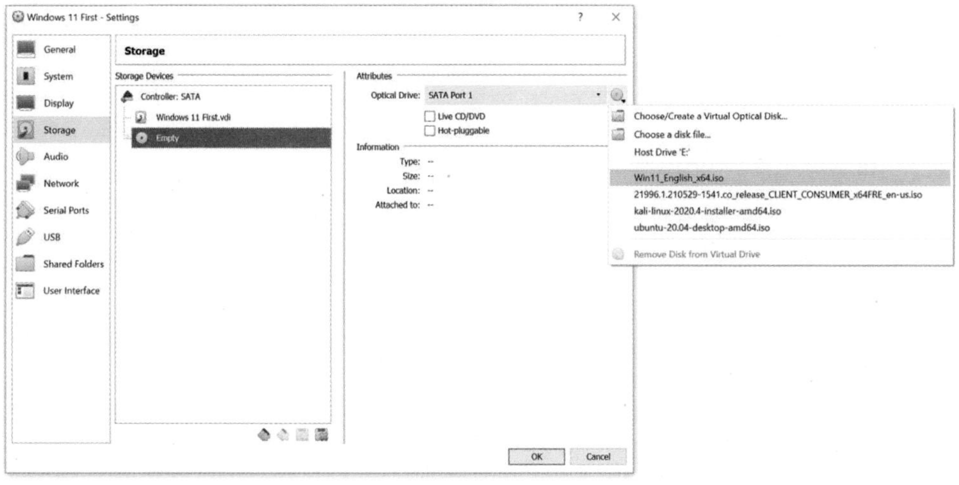

• **Figure 15.6** Selecting an ISO image for OS installation into a VM

Outputs can also get in on the game. If an application has no option for exporting a PDF but does have a print option, a virtual printer can save the output as a PDF without wasting ink or paper. A virtual printer can also capture a document you print while you're out and about and use the Internet to print out a hard copy back at your home or office.

Relocate Components Virtualization makes it possible to move systems and their parts around in all kinds of creative ways. With a classic server, you have a dedicated hardware box for the server hardware and operating system. That box contains the mass storage needed for the OS, applications, and data. What do you do if the server gets swamped with requests and needs more powerful hardware? In this scenario, you'd build another stand-alone server, install the OS and applications in the dedicated mass storage, and then migrate the data. That's a time-consuming process.

But virtual machines dramatically simplify the upgrade process. The VM is just a file. If it needs a faster processor or more RAM, just move the file to an upgraded machine running a compatible hypervisor.

Virtualization can also separate components that normally appear together. You can, for example, collect the hard drives that would normally live in each server case and relocate them to a small number of powerful centralized storage servers. This leads to the next point.

Divide and Combine Resources Virtualization enables you to pool resources and reallocate them as needed. Virtualizing a component such as RAM, a CPU, or a hard drive makes it possible to divide that resource up and give each VM its own fraction. It also means the inverse. A virtualized hard drive backed by multiple physical drives, for example, can function as a single drive larger than anything you could buy off the shelf.

Scaling

The benefits of aggressive virtualization become readily apparent at scale. Virtualizing servers and network hardware in a SOHO environment adds extra complexity without any obvious gains. Scale up to data center size, on the other hand, and virtualization provides tangible benefits.

If you're running a data center that hosts 100,000 physical servers, every server will have more-or-less fixed needs like rack space, power, network interface cards (NICs), cables, fans, and more—regardless of whether the server has a single CPU core and 256 MB of RAM or 32 cores and 64 GB of RAM. Powerful physical servers can host many VMs of different sizes (dozens if they are all small), making it possible to host 100,000 equivalent VMs using a fraction of these per-physical-machine resources. And this is just a start. A data center operator can analyze resource use and move VMs around to balance hardware use around the clock more efficiently or to power down idle systems. Even tiny tweaks can save millions of dollars a year at data center scale.

Just because new ideas often meet large-scale needs doesn't mean they aren't useful for the rest of us! Some ideas filter directly down into smaller networks, while others form the backbone of cloud computing services (which make extensive use of data centers) that customers can use. Let's look at cloud computing and the role virtualization plays in it.

Cloud Computing

Cloud computing moves the specialized machines used in classic and virtualized networking "out there somewhere," using the Internet to connect an organization to other organizations to manage aspects of the network. Some people like to point out that the cloud is just someone else's computer, and they're at least half right. But it's also been possible to rent someone else's computer from a traditional hosting service for decades, and the cloud is a bit more than a new name for this old idea. Cloud computing also doesn't necessarily mean *someone else's* computer—some organizations build their own cloud just for internal use. The cloud is more like a cafeteria of computing and networking resources—an *à la carte* data center enhanced by layers of powerful services and software.

The absolutely massive catalog of services available from large cloud service providers can seem like a hodge-podge of unrelated products sometimes. The early cloud ecosystem existed almost exclusively to supply building blocks for these Web applications. Economies of scale have enabled cloud service providers to create new ways to use, and sell, their computing resources to scratch all kinds of IT itches for their customers.

The Service-Layer Cake

Service is the key to understanding the cloud. At the hardware level, we'd have trouble telling the difference between the cloud and the servers and networks that comprise the Internet as a whole. We use the servers and networks of the cloud through layers of software that add great value to the underlying hardware by making it simple to perform complex tasks or manage powerful hardware.

End users mostly interact with the service-layer cake's sweet software icing—Web applications like Dropbox, Gmail, and Netflix. The rest of the cake, however, is thick with cool services that programmers, techs, and admins can use to build and support their applications and networks.

It's common to categorize cloud services into one of three *service models* that broadly describe the type of service provided to whoever pays the bill. I'll relate each of these service models to popular providers, but you should know that service models aren't a perfect way to characterize cloud service providers (because most of them offer many services that fit into different categories in the model). Service models are, however, a good shorthand to differentiate between services that meet the same general need in very different ways. Let's slice the cake open to take a closer look at these three service models (Figure 15.7), starting from the bottom.

• **Figure 15.7** A tasty three-layer cake

Infrastructure as a Service Large-scale global **infrastructure as a service (IaaS)** providers like Amazon Web Services (AWS) enable you to set up and tear down *infrastructure*—building blocks—on demand. Generally, IaaS providers just charge for what you use. For example, you can launch a few virtual servers (Figure 15.8) to host an internal application like a support ticket database, create a private network for communication between the servers, and support VPN connections from a few branch offices to the user-facing application server. Or you can relocate a file server that has run

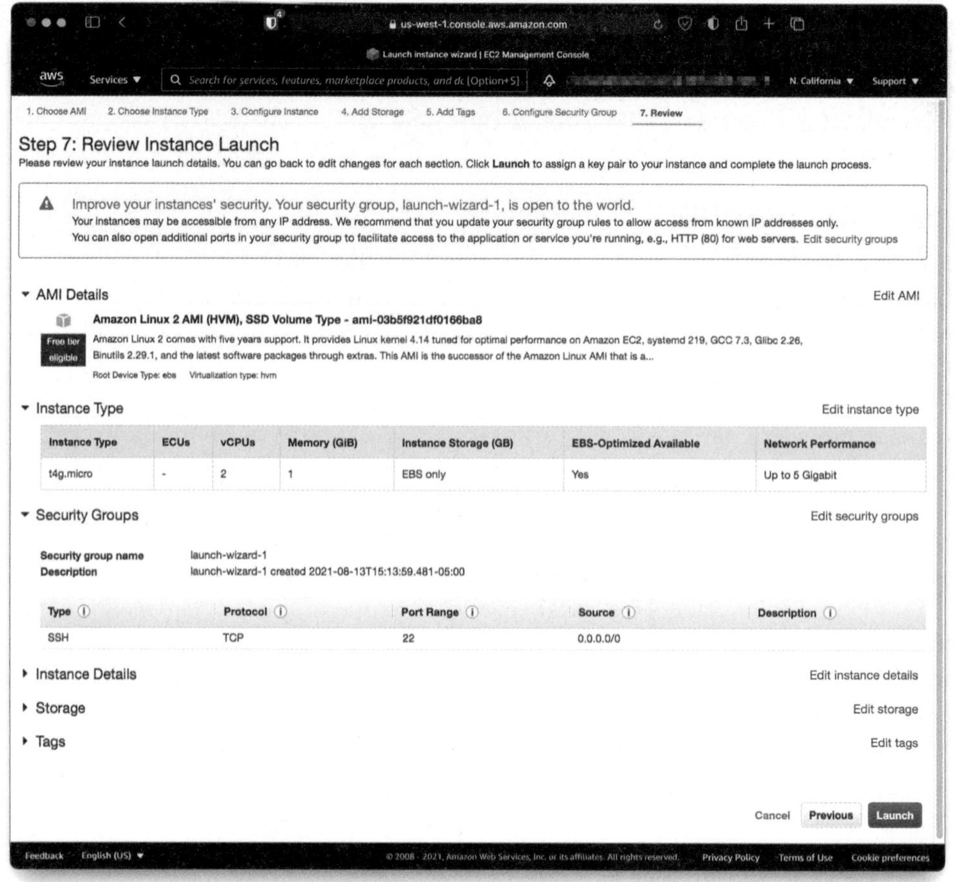

• **Figure 15.8** Creating an instance on AWS EC2

out of drive bays to have effectively unlimited data storage (Figure 15.9) billed by how much you store, how long you store it, and how often it gets transferred or downloaded.

The beauty of IaaS is that you no longer need to purchase and administer expensive, heavy hardware. You pay to use the provider's powerful infrastructure as a service while you need it and stop paying when you release the resources. IaaS doesn't spare you from needing to know what you're doing, though! You'll still have to understand your organization's needs, what components can meet them, and how to configure or integrate them to meet the goal. But it's a tasty layer!

Platform as a Service A **platform as a service (PaaS)** provider gives you some form of infrastructure, which could be provided by an IaaS, but on top of that infrastructure the PaaS provider builds a *platform*: a complete deployment and management system to handle every aspect of meeting some goal. For most PaaS providers in this middle cake layer, the customer's goal is running a Web application.

There are other kinds of PaaS, though, and the concept of a platform provides a good way to communicate whether the box a provider is selling contains Lego bricks or Ikea furniture parts (metaphorically speaking). In other words, a PaaS targeting Web apps will bundle different features than one targeting smartphone apps. The important point of PaaS is that

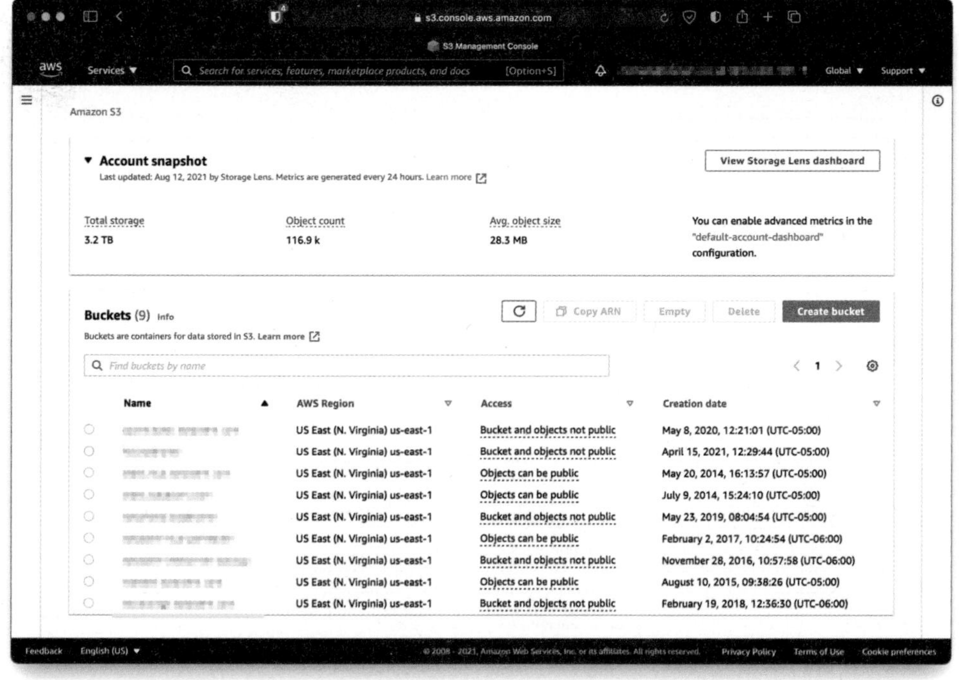

• **Figure 15.9** Amazon S3

the infrastructure underneath a PaaS is largely invisible to the customer. The customer cannot control it directly and doesn't need to think about its complexity.

Heroku, an early PaaS provider, creates a simple interface on top of the IaaS offerings of AWS, further reducing the complexity of developing and scaling Web applications. Heroku's management console (Figure 15.10) makes it easy to increase or decrease the capacity of an application with a single slider and set up add-ons that add a database, monitor your logs, track performance, and more. It could take days for a tech or developer unfamiliar with each software service to install, configure, and integrate a set of these services with a running application; PaaS providers help cut this down to minutes or hours.

Software as a Service **Software as a service (SaaS)** sits at the top layer of the cake, replacing applications once distributed and licensed via physical media (such as CD-ROMs in retail boxes) with subscriptions to equivalent applications from online servers. In the purest form, the application runs on the server; users don't install it—they just access it with a client (often a Web browser).

The popularity of the subscription model has also led developers of more traditional desktop software to muddy the water. Long the flagship of the retail brick-and-mortar Microsoft product line, the Office suite (Word, PowerPoint, Excel, etc.) migrated to a subscription-based Microsoft 365 service in 2011 (then called Office 365). In the old days, if you wanted to add Word to your new laptop, you'd buy a copy and install it (maybe even from a disc). These days, you pay Microsoft every month or year, log in to your Microsoft account, and either download Word to your laptop or just use Word Online. Only the latter is SaaS in the pure sense.

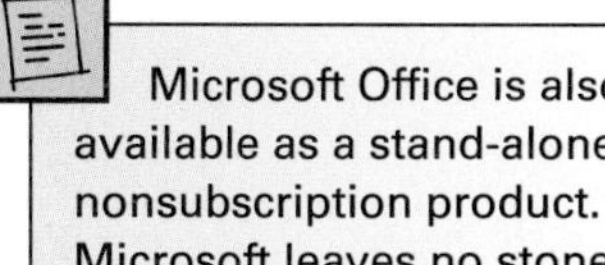

Microsoft Office is also available as a stand-alone, nonsubscription product. Microsoft leaves no stone unturned!

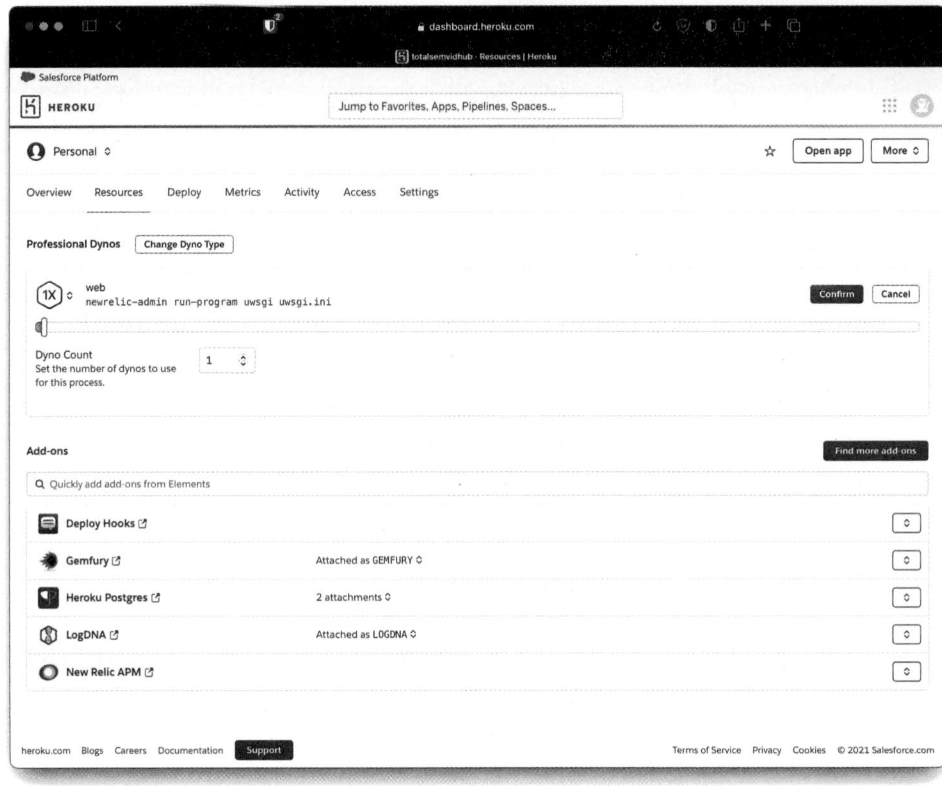

• **Figure 15.10** Heroku's management console

Cloud Deployment Models

Organizations have differing needs and capabilities, of course, so there's no one-size-fits-all cloud *deployment model* that works for everyone. When it comes to cloud computing, organizations have to balance cost, control, customization, and privacy. Some organizations also have needs that no existing cloud provider can meet. Each organization makes its own decisions about these trade-offs, but the result is usually a cloud deployment that can be categorized in one of four ways:

- Most folks usually just interact with a **public cloud**, a term used to describe software, platforms, and infrastructure that the general public sign up to use. When we talk about *the* cloud, this is what we mean.
- If a business wants some of the flexibility of the cloud, needs complete ownership of its data, and can afford both, it can build an internal cloud the business actually owns—a **private cloud**.
- A **community cloud** is more like a private cloud paid for and used by more than one organization with similar goals or needs (such as medical providers who all need to comply with the same patient privacy laws).
- A **hybrid cloud** deployment describes some combination of public, private, and community cloud resources. This can, for example, mean not having to maintain a private cloud powerful enough to meet peak demand—an application can grow into a public cloud instead of grind to a halt, a technique called *cloud bursting*.

Virtualization's Role in Cloud Computing

Virtualization profoundly impacts cloud computing. We've already seen a big financial reason for this—it helps the many massive data centers that comprise the cloud scale up efficiently. But virtualization's role is more foundational than dollar signs.

IaaS providers let their customers "create" as many servers as they need on demand, "destroy" those same servers as soon as they are done, and only bill them for the time and resources they used. The reason this arrangement works is because the providers can set up everything the customer selects in real time—and then release the resources for another customer just as quickly.

Human techs would have trouble reconfiguring networks and systems with the speed and confidence it takes to make this work for one customer, let alone keep it humming along smoothly for hundreds of thousands or even millions of them. The software-based flexibility of these virtualized components enables a cloud provider to integrate all of them with its own management systems, which orchestrate a dizzying swarm of automated tasks into the globe-spanning machines we call *a cloud*.

Infrastructure as Code

Organizations that develop networked applications and services have developed a philosophy over the years to address problems with scaling. **Infrastructure as code (IaC)**, in a nutshell, abstracts the infrastructure of an application or service into a set of configuration files or scripts. That's a mouthful! Let's break this process down into three parts so we can unpack yet another important concept. First, we'll look at the hurdles faced by the organizations. Second, we'll explore automation options. We'll finish with a concept called *orchestration* that helps organizations apply software-driven flexibility to problems.

Scaling Problems

As networked applications and services grow and mature, the organizations that develop them run into their own kinds of scaling problems. A few examples illustrate these problems.

- They have so many programmers that the programmers end up constantly stepping on each other's toes by making incompatible changes.
- Their applications grow so complex that no one person knows how to set up the components needed to test them.
- Their databases grow too big to fit on the beefiest servers money can buy.

The teams that build these applications initially had to blaze their own trails through this particular wilderness, but the approaches that have worked for them are filtering out to the rest of the industry in the form of tools, paid services, and efforts to spread the word about best practices.

Automation

When an application managed by a small number of people runs on a single server, manually configuring and tweaking that server can be convenient. But if that same application scales up to the point where several teams work on it and it runs on many servers spread around the world, the same convenience becomes a liability.

Over time, all-too-human mistakes and miscommunication tend to snowball until software that works fine on one server is a source of hard-to-troubleshoot bugs on another. The broad solution to this problem is to replace tasks people do manually with **automation**—using code to set up (*provision*) and maintain systems (installing software updates, for example) in a consistent manner, with no mistyped commands.

Multistep tasks that you have to perform frequently are a good place to start, but it can be even more important to automate infrequent tasks that you tend to forget the steps to complete. A little automation is better than nothing, but that's where IaC comes into play. By defining an application's or service's infrastructure (the servers and network components) in configuration files or scripts, organizations that apply IaC can more easily create identical copies of the needed infrastructure.

While this automation helps scale up the application to run on more servers, some of the big benefits of the IaC philosophy turn out to be just as important for small apps and teams:

- The ability to create identical copies of the necessary infrastructure makes it easy for people working on the application to create a *development environment* or *test environment*—separate temporary copies of the infrastructure used to develop new features and test out updates.
- You can save the code/scripts for creating and configuring the infrastructure in a source/version control system alongside the rest of the application's code, making it easier to ensure the infrastructure and application are compatible.
- You can also carefully review changes before rolling them out, helping catch configuration mistakes before they are applied to real, working systems.

Orchestration

Orchestration combines automated processes into bigger, multifaceted processes called *pipelines* or *workflows*. Orchestration streamlines development, testing, deploying, or maintaining, depending on the specific workflow.

Some of the best-run applications use a specific kind of orchestration called *continuous integration/continuous deployment (CI/CD)*. When developers check in changes to the application's code, they trigger an automatic multistep pipeline that can build the application, set up a temporary copy of the infrastructure the app needs, and run a bunch of automated checks to ensure it works. If these fail, the developers have to go back to square one. But if the new code passes the checks, the pipeline starts the process of deploying the new version.

Deploying can be as simple as just uploading the new code to each server, but these pipelines tend to incorporate lessons learned the hard way from botched deployments that knocked the service offline or deleted important data. The result can be a methodical sequence that eases into updates by backing up data, spinning up new copies of the infrastructure running the latest code, rotating them into use, and monitoring for signs deployment should stop and roll back the update. In either case, this pipeline orchestrates tasks across multiple systems and services to meet the high-level goal of rolling out application updates in a safe, consistent manner.

Another common kind of orchestration focuses on keeping a running service or application healthy. This usually involves monitoring a service and its components to identify any trouble—maybe a host froze, crashed, or is just responding slowly. When the monitoring system fires off a warning, it can trigger a pipeline that starts up a replacement host and swaps it into service as soon as it is ready.

Since organizations that depend on containerization can have hundreds or thousands of running containers to manage at any time, they often use *container orchestration* tools (such as Kubernetes) to automate most aspects of configuring, deploying, monitoring, and adapting the cluster as conditions change. Container orchestration is closely related to the IaC-style orchestration described here, but its scope is narrower.

Virtual Networking

Classic networking follows the same paradigm as classic computing. A dedicated computing device with a dedicated operating system performs each network function. Switches do switching; routers do routing. Even multilayer devices such as SOHO routers that perform switching, routing, and wireless networking are simply complex machines run by a dedicated operating system.

Virtualization is transforming networking, so that *software* performs the classic network functions. You saw an early version of this transformation with switches and virtual local area network (VLAN) capability back in Chapter 11. VLAN-capable switches use a software layer to create and modify VLANs.

This section explores sophisticated virtualization in networking, starting with virtual networking within VM hosts and then virtualization in switching and routing. We'll break out of the VM host and finish with *network function virtualization*. It'll take some backstory to clarify the last term, so let's get to it.

Virtual Networking Inside the VM Host

A hulking server hosting a few dozen VMs can have the same kind of complex networking requirements you'd have on a physical network that hosts a few dozen important servers. Some of the VMs may need to share a private network to collaborate; some may need to serve requests from the open Internet; others may need to be isolated from the network. And the server needs to rapidly reconfigure the network as VMs come and go.

Virtual networking inside the host is one way to meet these needs. Hypervisors tend to come with their own basic networking capabilities such as built-in switching. If you have networking needs that the built-in features don't cover, you can run other network functions as VMs (on the same hypervisor as any VMs they support, when you can).

Virtual Switches Here's the scenario. You have three virtual machines and you need these VMs to have access to the Internet. Therefore, you need to give them all legitimate IP addresses. The oldest and simplest way is to *bridge the NIC*. Each bridge is a software connection that passes traffic from

There is no difference between a virtual NIC and a physical NIC, once properly configured. Virtual NICs have MAC addresses just like a physical NIC. You set up everything about a vNIC—IP address, subnet mask, and so on—exactly as you do with a physical NIC.

the real NIC to a virtual one (Figure 15.11). This bridge works at Layer 2 of the OSI model, so each **virtual network interface card (vNIC)** gets a legitimate, unique MAC address.

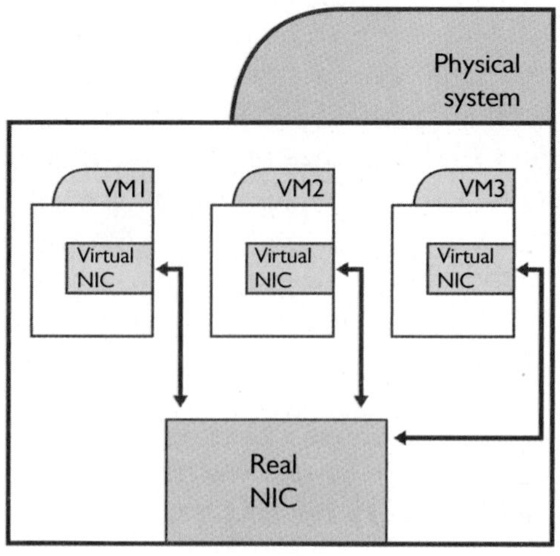

• **Figure 15.11** Bridged NICs

The technology at work here is the **virtual switch** (or **vSwitch**): software that does the same Layer 2 switching a hardware switch does, including features like VLANs (Figure 15.12). The big difference is what it means to "plug" into the virtual switch. When the NICs are bridged, the VMs and the host's NIC are all connected to the virtual switch. In this mode, think of the physical NIC as the uplink port on a hardware switch. This makes virtual switches a very powerful component for networking your VMs—but just like physical networks, we need more than just Layer 2 switching. That's where virtual routers and firewalls come in.

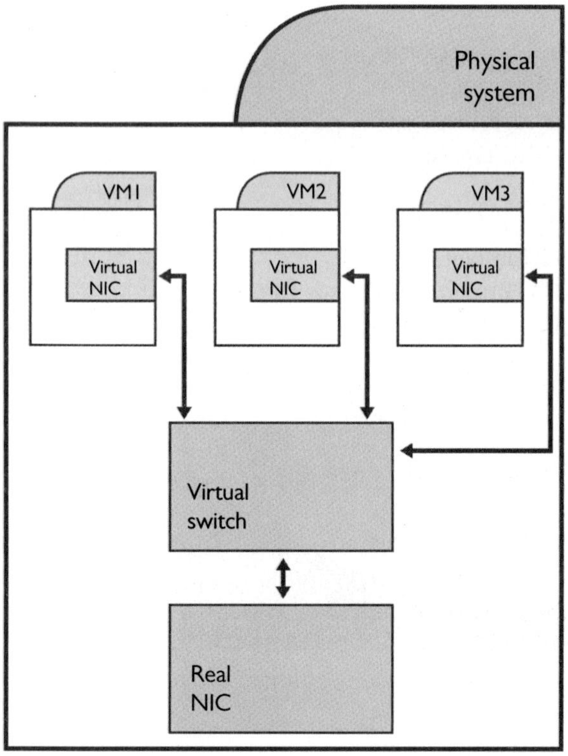

• **Figure 15.12** Virtual switch

Distributed Switches Just because a switch is virtual doesn't magically prevent it from needing the same management given to a real switch. Virtual switches normally use a Web interface for configuration, just like a regular switch. Yet virtual networks grow quite quickly, even more quickly than a physical network (no waiting for a new physical switch to arrive from the store; just spin up another virtual one!). With growth comes complexity, requiring careful configuration for every new virtual switch added to existing virtual switches in a large, complex single virtual network.

The centralized installation, configuration, and handling of every switch in a network is known as *distributed switching*. Every hypervisor has some form of central configuration of critical issues for switches, such as VLAN assignment and trunking.

Cross Check

Switches

You read about switches in Chapter 1, Chapter 3, and Chapter 11. Check your memory now. At what OSI layer do switches work? Why is that a trick question? How do you manage a switch?

Virtual Routers and Firewalls Similar to how virtual machines enable us to easily reallocate computing resources when demand changes, **virtual routers** let us dynamically reconfigure networks. This lets the network keep up when VMs are moved from host to host to meet demand or improve resource use. The virtual routers are just VMs like any other; we can allocate more resources to them as traffic grows, instead of having to buy bigger, better physical routers. When it comes to firewalls, the same rules apply: **virtual firewalls** can protect servers where inserting a physical one would be hard, costly, or impossible.

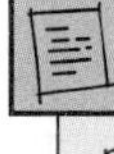

If you're interested in reading more about virtual routers and firewalls, a couple of interesting product lines to look at are Vyatta vRouter and Cisco Cloud Services Routers.

Breaking Out of the VM Host

An important concept to understand about virtual networking is that there's no rule that says it must stay inside the hypervisor. In one sense, the public cloud *really is* just someone else's computer. The same virtual network functions you can run as a VM in the cloud can also run as VMs on servers in your own network (or even inside your router, if it includes a hypervisor).

For instance, my network's VPN concentrator is a virtual machine running on my Dell R340 server (Figure 15.13). When a client connects to the VPN, their traffic is directed to a physical port on my router that is directly connected to one of the server's NICs. My hypervisor bridges this NIC to the VPN concentrator VM, enabling this "virtual" concentrator to handle real traffic between my physical network and remote clients.

If everyone who uses the VPN happened to only need access to servers hosted in the cloud, I could just as easily have set up a VPN concentrator as a VM running on AWS or Microsoft Azure. To integrate those cloud servers with my local network, I'd just set up a persistent tunnel from the office router to the concentrator.

Network Function Virtualization

In the early 2010s, several big telecommunications companies got together to figure out how their corner of the industry could take advantage of the practices cloud operators were using to manage their networks—such as IaC-style automation and orchestration. They hammered out a specification for a new network architecture called **network function virtualization (NFV)** that sweeps together these trends and applies them to network management.

NFV is a network architecture (a collection of patterns that generally—not specifically—describe how to design a network that achieves a specific set of goals), not an actual feature that you can implement. The first (and biggest) piece of an NFV architecture is the **network function virtualization infrastructure (NFVI)**: the hardware (*x*86-64 servers, storage arrays, and switches) and software (like hypervisors and controllers) that form the foundation of a virtual network.

Hardware switches are still a part of any "virtual" network; don't let that confuse you. Just because you can replace some hardware boxes with VMs, that doesn't mean you can eliminate all networking hardware! You still need a way to move network traffic between servers and up to the Internet.

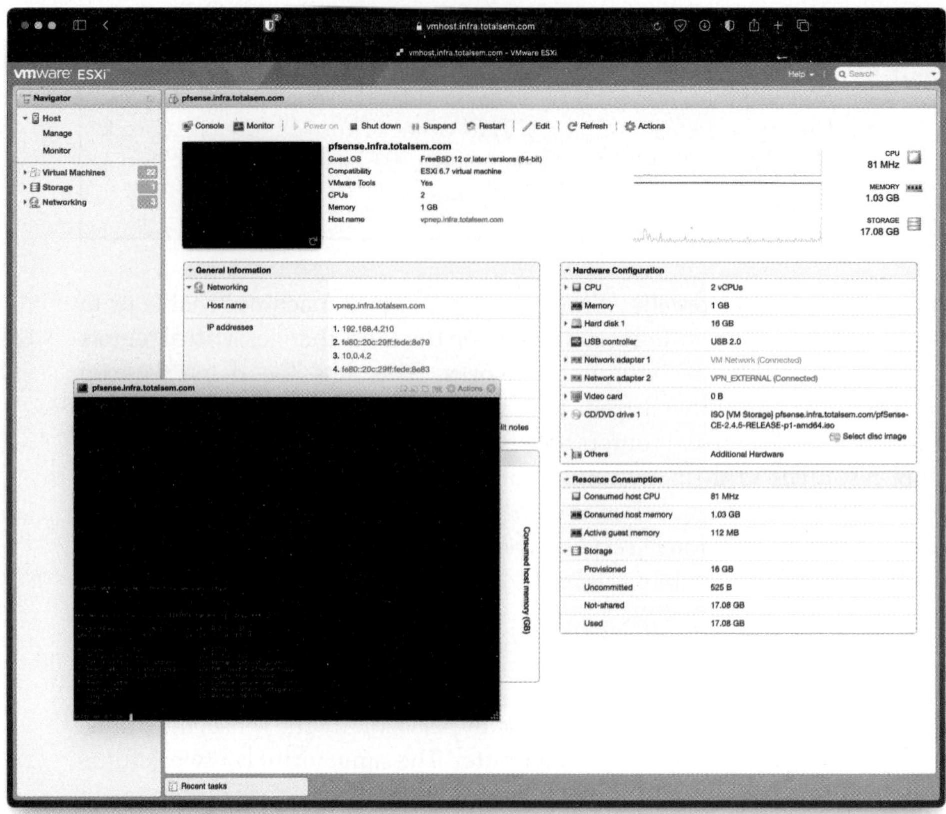

• **Figure 15.13** pfSense virtual machine acting as a VPN concentrator

The NVFI is where network functions (firewalls, load balancers, routers, and so on) run that are appropriately called **virtualized network functions (VNFs)**. At first glance, you might think that VNF is just a fancy term for a virtual machine like my VPN concentrator. That's almost right, but a VNF can be composed of one *or more* interconnected VMs (or containers)—called **VNF components (VNFCs)**—that collectively work as a VNF such as a VPN concentrator or firewall.

Big ISPs embrace virtual components and functions for a couple of reasons. For one, they give the ISP a way to consolidate the strange, proprietary, and often incompatible boxes (from many different vendors, for many different technologies) in their network into a small number of standard servers that are compatible with everything else in a normal data center. Second, since these functions are no longer limited to the original box, the ISP can adjust how much RAM or how many processors they can use in real time based on what their users are doing—or shift traffic around misbehaving components.

By saying the "ISP" adjusts the resources, though, it isn't usually a person sitting there clicking a mouse or flipping a switch. Real-time tweaks to networks like this—at this scale—are managed by fancy automation and orchestration tools. In NFV, this responsibility falls to the NFV orchestrator—a software conductor that does the work of creating, configuring, scaling, pausing, shutting down, and deleting the VNFs that run on the NFVI.

Just as the cool ideas developed for managing large data centers and cloud networks have trickled down into tools and practices used all around the industry, expect NFV (or at least parts of it) to turn up in smaller networks and projects as the concept continues to mature.

Network Function Virtualization versus Software-Defined Networking

> Some sources use the term *layer*, some use *plane*, and others mix them. I've also mixed them to make sure you're comfortable seeing both.

Virtual networking can already be a little hard to picture, especially something as loaded with jargon as NFV, so I want to take a moment to explain how network function virtualization—which uses software versions of network functions—is different from a similar sounding term: software-defined networking.

Traditionally, hardware routers and switches were designed with two closely integrated parts: a *control plane* that decides how to move traffic, and a *data plane* that executes those decisions. The control plane on a router is what you log into to configure the router and is what runs the software that actually speaks routing protocols like OSPF and BGP (discussed in Chapter 7) and builds the routing table that it gives to the data plane. The router's data plane (also known as the *forwarding plane*) reads incoming packets and uses the routing table to send them to their destination.

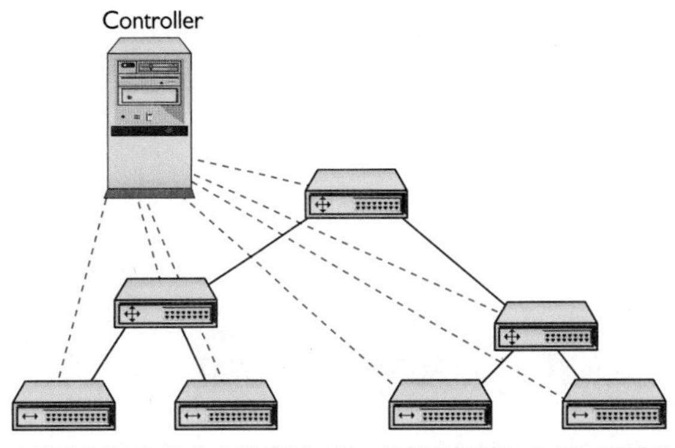

• **Figure 15.14** A controller controls traffic to all the routers and switches.

Software-defined networking (SDN) cuts the control layer of individual devices out of the picture and lets an all-knowing program (running on a server, probably in the cloud) called a *network controller* dictate how both physical and virtual network components move traffic through the network (Figure 15.14). SDN requires components (think routers, switches, firewalls) with a data layer (also called the *infrastructure layer*) designed to take instructions from the network controller instead of their own control plane.

While it's important enough that SDN allows for a master controller (such as the one shown in Figure 15.15—though large networks may also distribute the controller's workload over multiple servers), the revolutionary idea behind SDN is that the network controller is *programmable*. Programmers can write code (or use software designed by others) that controls how the entire network behaves.

To manage the complexity that comes with separating the infrastructure and control planes, SDN introduces a few new *planes* for us to keep straight. The most important are the *management plane* and the *application plane*.

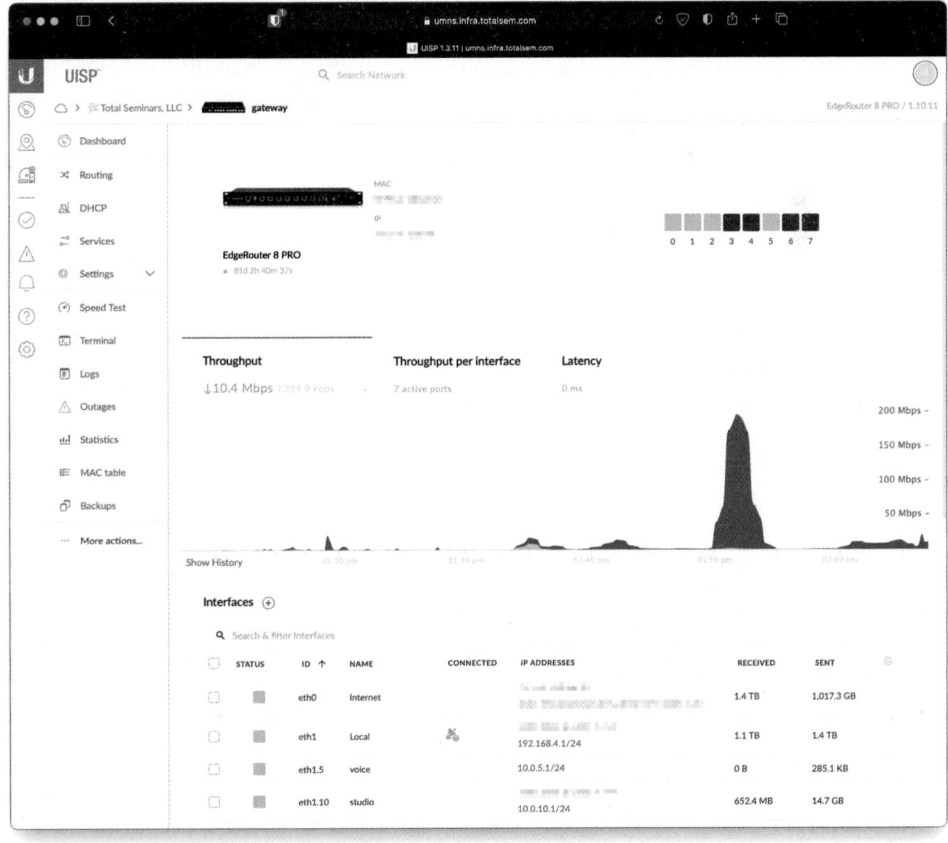

• **Figure 15.15** Management interface for UISP network controller from Ubiquiti

The CompTIA Network+ N10-008 objectives list four terms under software-defined networking—*application layer, control layer, infrastructure layer*, and *management plane*. This section uses "plane" more frequently than "layer," but that's what's referred to here. Note which terms you'll see on the exam.

The management (or administration) layer is responsible for setting up network devices to get their marching orders from the right controller. The application layer, which sits on top of this entire framework, is where the network-behavior-controlling software runs. Applications that run here often do jobs like load balancing, optimizing the flow of traffic, monitoring, enforcing security policy, threat protection, and so on.

Even though the term isn't in the name, SDN is yet another example of virtualization. The control plane is virtualized to outsource its role to the network controller. In NFV, in contrast, the *entire* network function is virtualized. NFV and SDN are separate, complementary ways to manage networks with software. You can use the two approaches separately, but an NFV architecture usually also takes advantage of SDN.

Putting Network Virtualization and Cloud Computing to Work

One thing that can make it hard for students to really sink their teeth into the latest ideas in enterprise networking is that many of them don't have access to racks full of enterprise-grade equipment. If you have the opportunity to get some hands-on learning in an environment like that, take it!

Virtualization and cloud computing have both really changed the game when it comes to the kinds of stuff we can play around with all on our own with just a computer, an Internet connection, and a little time. Unless you happen to live in a data center, an account at an IaaS provider (such as AWS or Azure) can enable you to set up lab networks that wouldn't even fit in most apartments or houses.

This section uses Rocket.Chat, an open source communication platform, as a long-form example for how to use cloud services to install and run any app. Rocket.Chat is cool because it's approachable. The program enables chatting among members, like Discord or Slack.

We'll begin with a look at how to set up Rocket.Chat (a program you can host yourself) on a local machine. Next, I'll review a few practical things you should know about managing cloud resources, and then step through how to set up Rocket.Chat in the cloud. Finally, I'll review two more things you should know about how to put virtualization and cloud services to work in your networks: virtual desktops for end users, and interconnecting cloud resources with your LAN.

Tech Tip

Cloud Accounts and Practice

Don't rule out playing around with cloud resources just because you don't have any money to spare. Many cloud platforms have free service tiers (at least for some basic services) or offer free credits when you create a new account. You may also be able to get free credits through any class, school, club/boot-camp/training, professional organization, or employer you're associated with. It doesn't hurt to ask.

A word of caution, though: only set up a cloud account if you understand the risks and are prepared to manage them. Once you connect a cloud account to a credit or debit card, spinning up a high-end resource and forgetting to shut it down can be a costly mistake. Make sure you understand how much anything you set up costs. Make sure you tear it down as soon as you're done. Make sure your account has a strong password. Make sure you close the account when you're done learning. Don't let someone break in and rack up a bank-account-draining bill at your expense.

Setting Up Rocket.Chat in a Local Hypervisor

Since Rocket.Chat is for communicating, the group of people you'd like to have access may affect where and how you decide to host it. If you're hosting it just for use inside a small office, you might want to host the whole app on a single in-house server. You'll need a more complex setup if you're hoping to serve a million of your closest friends, but for now, we'll keep it simple and use the excellent cross-platform hypervisor Oracle VM VirtualBox.

I'm going to use a pair of IaC tools for VirtualBox setup, but here's a quick summary of how you'd do it the most manual way just in case you don't remember it from CompTIA A+. First, download an ISO image for the OS installer of your choice. Click New to create a VM and follow the wizard to complete the following (Figure 15.16): name the VM, select an operating system, choose how much RAM to set aside for the VM, create a virtual hard drive for it, and (after clicking Create) select an installer image. Once this gets going, you can walk through a normal OS install inside the VM window and manually configure the OS or install software as needed.

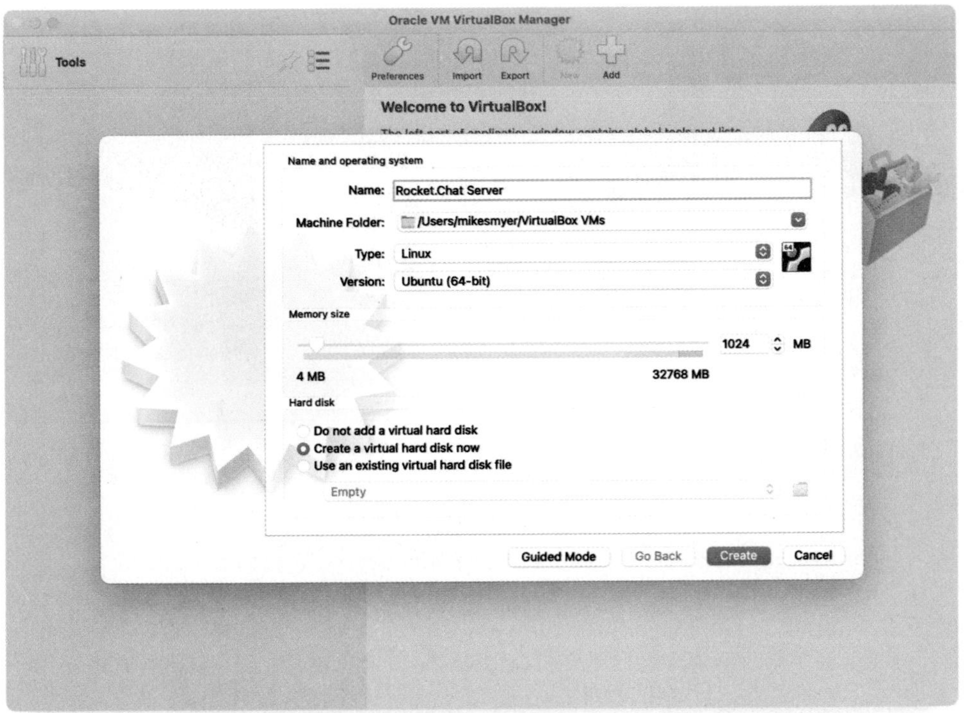

• **Figure 15.16** VirtualBox creating a new virtual machine

There's also a less-tedious (but still manual) way to set up a VM. Since VMs are just files on the host system, you can export a VM that already has an OS installed (and may be configured or include specific software) and then reuse it as a starting point on other systems. IaC tools and IaaS providers build on this basic idea—we don't install an OS from scratch every time we create a new VM!

The people working on Rocket.Chat are well aware of the bold new IaC world, so their installation instructions include how to use multiple automation tools, including the one used here. Vagrant, one of many open source IaC tools made by the great folks at HashiCorp, can create VMs in a few different hypervisors based on code that specifies things like what OS they should run, what system resources to allocate, how to network them, and any additional steps required to *provision* the VM with the needed configuration and software.

Unfortunately, Rocket.Chat's Vagrant instructions didn't work as of this writing. This won't be a surprise if you've done this kind of automation

Because IaC is more of a philosophy, "IaC tools" aren't all competing options that do the same well-defined thing a bit differently. There's a whole ecosystem of often-overlapping tools (plus some that aren't specific to IaC but still play an important role). An organization that embraces the philosophy will usually combine multiple tools to meet its goals.

already! There is a very real current that anyone who wants to take advantage of IaC has to swim against: automation is fragile and usually breaks or misbehaves when it runs into something unanticipated.

To get around this, I ended up combining Vagrant with Ansible—an IaC tool more focused on provisioning each VM based on what role the VM should have. Like most IaC tools, you use Vagrant and Ansible from the command line. I didn't take advantage of Ansible's full power for this example, but role-based provisioning enables you to set up one VM as a database server and another as a Web server, for example. To keep it simple, I just built a single VM that runs both the Web and database servers (see Figure 15.17).

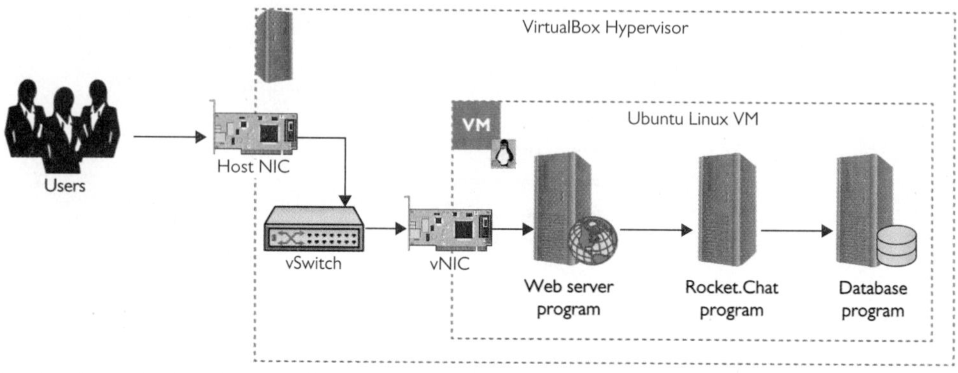

• **Figure 15.17** Diagram of my Rocket.Chat server VM

Ansible is one of the provisioners that Vagrant understands how to control, so all I had to do to set up this server was run `vagrant up` in the bottom terminal panel. Figure 15.18 shows the results of running that command. The top-left panel in my editor references a set of Ansible rules for setting up Rocket.Chat. The top-right panel is my Vagrantfile, which

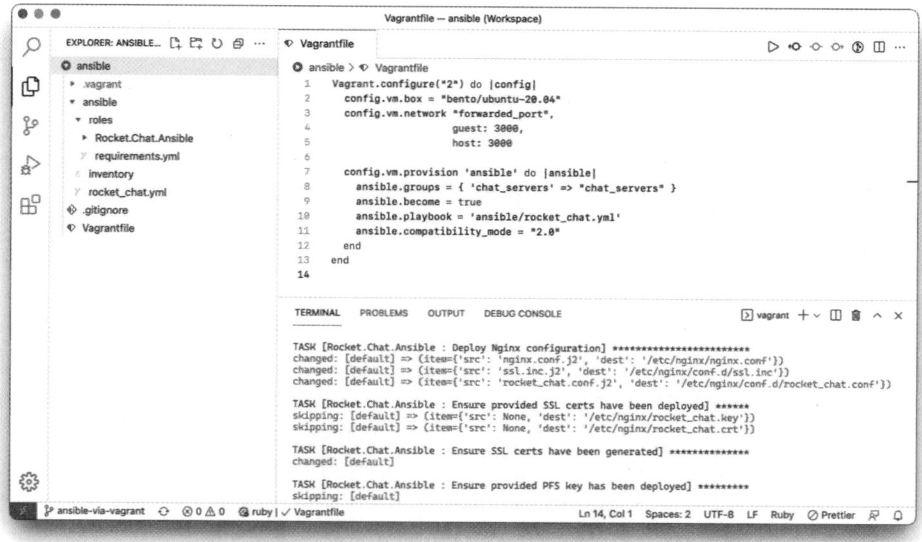

• **Figure 15.18** Creating a Rocket.Chat VM on a system with Vagrant and Ansible

describes the VM and tells Vagrant how to provision it with my Ansible rules. After this command finishes, I have a complete Rocket.Chat server running on my local computer; you can even see that I'm connecting to it from localhost in Figure 15.19.

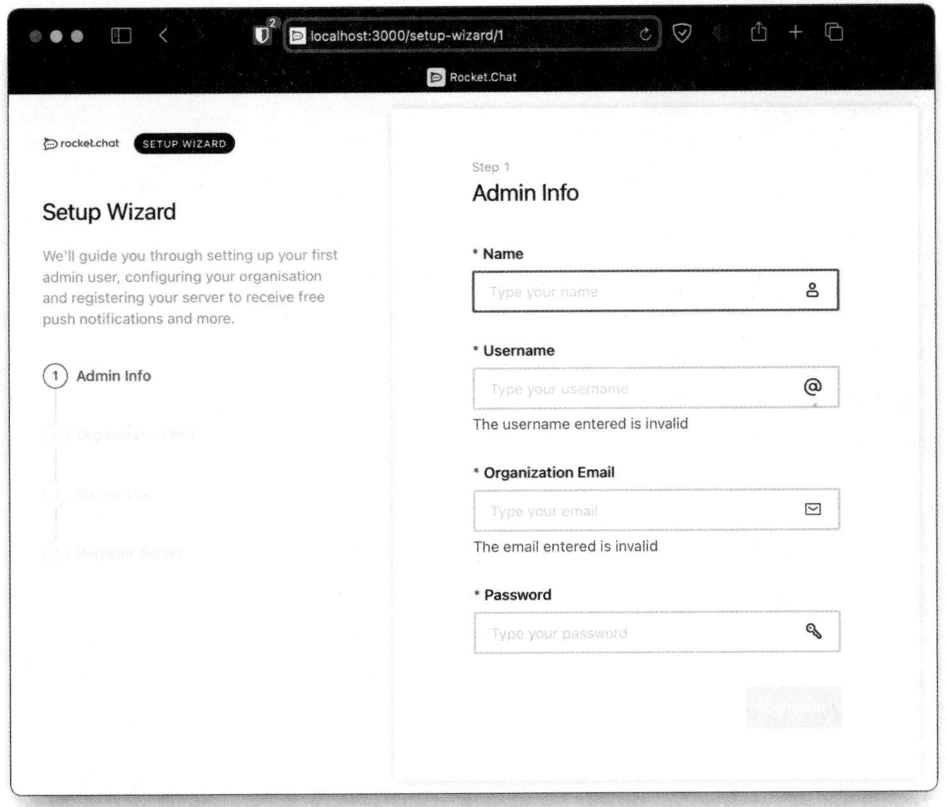

• **Figure 15.19** Setting up a brand-new Rocket.Chat server (running from localhost)

What makes this process so powerful is that I didn't have to log into the VM and install any software manually—everything was done completely automatically. Everything is controlled by the Vagrant and Ansible code, so anytime I need to spin up a Rocket.Chat server on a computer, I can run this little bit of code and, in a few minutes, start chatting (see Figure 15.20).

This section uses an open source programming-oriented text editor from Microsoft called Visual Studio Code (often abbreviated VS Code). One cool feature of VS Code is a built-in terminal for quick access to the command line.

Managing Cloud Resources

In a moment we'll look at how to move the Rocket.Chat install up into the cloud, but first I want to circle back to a few things I left out when I introduced cloud computing. I told you all about what cloud computing is, but we didn't really get into the nuts-and-bolts stuff you need to know about how cloud resources work. Specifically, I want to outline a few practical things you should know about scaling and security in the cloud.

Scaling

One of the cool things that virtualization enables people to do (especially in the cloud) is to take the same virtual machine and run it with more or less of its host machine's resources, or even move it to a more powerful machine.

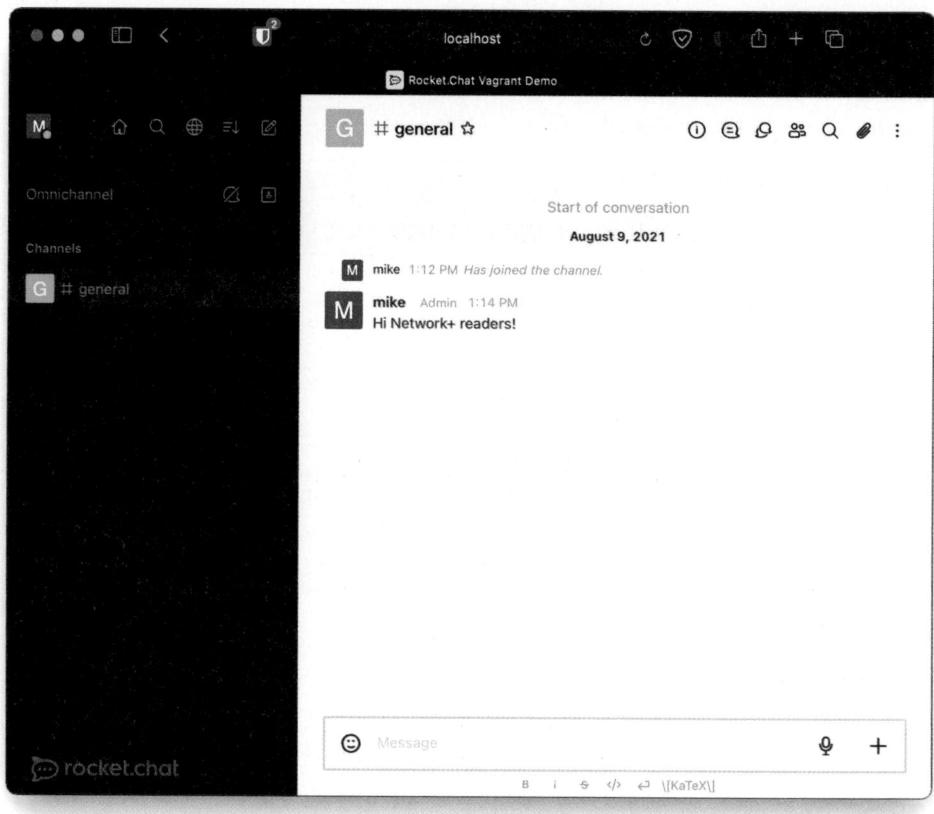

• **Figure 15.20** Chatting in Rocket.Chat

This **scalability** enables you to scale "up" an application or service without needing to run it on more than one server.

Virtualization also supports another way to scale an application "out" by starting up new instances in separate VMs. This benefit is called **elasticity**, because cloud providers (especially PaaS providers) make it simple to increase the number of running instances as demand grows and reduce the number of instances as demand shrinks. Don't think that elasticity is less important just because "scale" isn't in the name. If an application or service supports scaling out, this is a hugely popular way to scale.

If you're wondering why you need two ways to scale or what the difference is, the explanation is rather complicated, because it depends on the application or service. Some apps need tons of RAM, and others just a little. Some make efficient use of multiple CPUs, and others don't. Some are easy to run on multiple servers at once, and others need to be extensively modified.

Security Implications

Like almost all of networking, cloud computing has a long list of security implications. This section explores five areas of importance to cloud computing: account security, privacy, multitenancy, intrusion, and logging. Chapter 19 takes a deeper look at security issues.

Account Security When you (or your organization) sign up with a cloud provider, you get at least one extremely powerful account—like root on steroids—that someone could use to steal your organization's data, delete all of its infrastructure, or rack up a huge bill mining cryptocurrency. Just like with any other system, the *principle of least privilege* applies.

Cloud providers have authorization systems that enable you to set up separate credentials with explicit, limited permissions for the humans, servers, apps, tools, and services that need to manage your cloud account's resources. Setting up separate credentials for every distinct use case makes it easier to keep track of the purpose of each, restrict the permissions to limit the damage a compromised credential could do, and revoke a credential if it gets compromised, without disrupting other uses.

Cloud providers generally have one or more ways to log, monitor, and fire alerts based on account activity and changes to resources.

Privacy The cloud provider (or someone working for it) may have access to your data. These providers have some rules and practices in place to limit the likelihood that someone on their end goes browsing through your data, but those assurances may not be enough if your organization has sensitive data. In this case, your organization might choose to use the cloud provider but encrypt all the data it stores there, or use a private cloud model (entirely, or just for the sensitive resources).

Multitenancy **Multitenancy** is the ability to support multiple customers on the same infrastructure at the same time—and it's both a blessing and a curse. The blessing, and one of the great benefits of cloud computing, is that if you need a teeny-tiny server that does almost no work, you can pay for a likewise teeny-tiny fraction of the resources of a huge server for a few pennies a day. The curse, though, is that you have neighbors, and you don't get much say in who they are.

Your server may run really well on a quiet system with polite neighbors, or struggle for CPU time on a system where every neighbor keeps demanding more server resources. And then there's the question of *malicious* neighbors (or perhaps just nice neighbors who have been hacked). Hypervisors do a good job of isolating one VM from another, but this isn't perfect (and containers are less isolated).

There is a steady stream of new exploits that could enable a bad neighbor to snoop on your app or service. This isn't a big deal if you're just hosting some cat videos, but it can be a huge problem if you work with tightly regulated data such as patient medical records. In the latter case, the regulations may require you to pay a little more for *dedicated* instances (potentially using more secure facilities, networks, or hardware) that spare you from sharing the same infrastructure with other tenants.

Intrusion Just like an internal network, outright intrusion is a risk in the cloud. Even if everyone in your organization is trained about how to keep the LAN secure, integrating cloud resources with your LAN creates new risks. This is especially true if your organization focuses on securing the network perimeter and defaults to trusting every device inside the network.

Imagine a scenario, for example, where your organization maintains an always-on connection to enable servers or users to access cloud resources. Someone who compromises the least secure device on either end may be able to use it as a jumping-off point to attack devices on the other end.

Logging All kinds of devices and servers produce many logs. These logs can be great when you're debugging or looking into a security incident, but they may also contain sensitive information. Your organization may,

Once again, it's perfectly possible to do this work manually. You can use a browser to log in to an IaaS provider such as AWS or Azure and step through the forms for setting up VMs and networking them one by one. Then, you can log in to each VM and manually install the software it needs.

for example, need to set up policies and invest some effort to make sure the logs you need are collected from the devices and services that produce them and retained without violating customer privacy.

Setting Up Rocket.Chat on IaaS

With that cloud primer out of the way, I think we're ready to launch Rocket .Chat into the cloud using IaaS provided by AWS. This time I'll automate the process with Terraform, another command-line IaC tool developed by the fine folks at HashiCorp. Terraform, like Vagrant, will be able to use Ansible to provision the servers.

Terraform works on a code specification that describes your infrastructure at a high level—it can manage resources across multiple providers (and even include your private cloud or local devices). A single Terraform command can set up, update, or tear down complex, globe-spanning, multicloud infrastructure. I may be making this all sound simple and easy, but it's not a shortcut. A lot of hard work and thought goes into building up these specs!

Over a couple afternoons, I hammered out a Terraform spec that I could use to take my LAN Rocket.Chat server and break it up into separate components that will make it easier to grow the service. Some of these components run on their own virtual machines in AWS, and in other cases I made use of AWS services designed to meet specific needs such as DNS and load balancing. I simplified it a bit for clarity, but the service map in Figure 15.21 should give you an idea of the infrastructure.

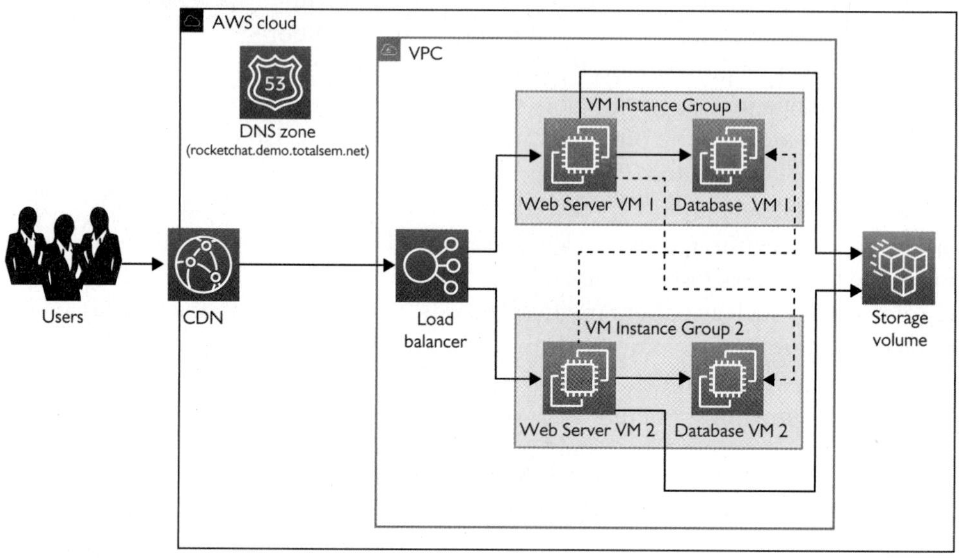

• **Figure 15.21** Service map for my Rocket.Chat infrastructure on AWS

When I run `terraform apply`, Terraform processes my specification to decide what resources it needs to create, shows me what it'll do, and confirms I want it to get to work. As it works, it stores information about the resources it has created. I can go grab a coffee or stare thoughtfully at the trees while Terraform gets everything ready for the big dance. When I come back, it's all already running (and pennies are flowing from my bank to Amazon's). I can open my browser and load the setup page just like I did locally (see Figure 15.22).

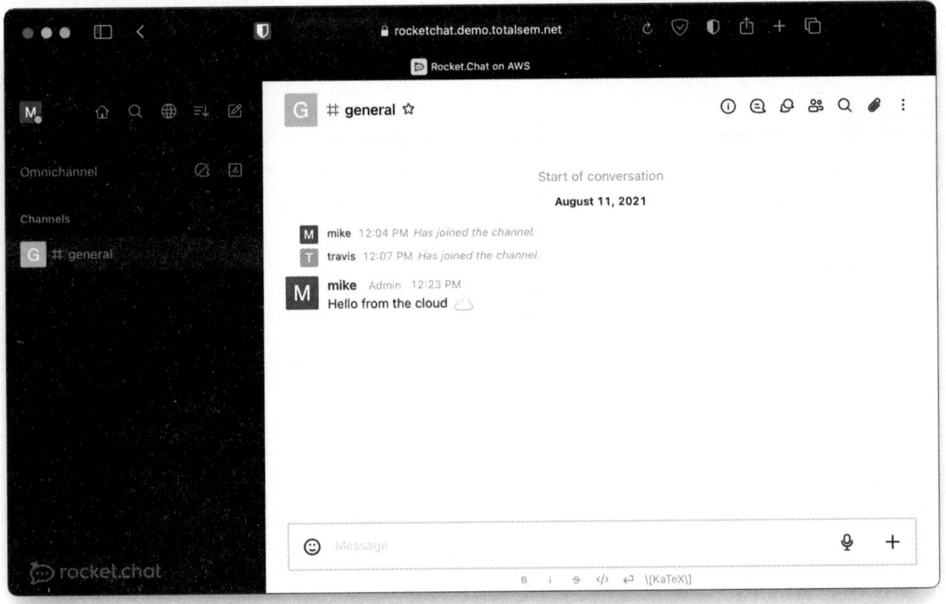

• **Figure 15.22** Rocket.Chat running on AWS

When I come back and change the code specification later, I can just run `terraform plan` to get Terraform to show me a change plan I can use to ensure my change does what I expect. Figure 15.23 shows part of Terraform's plan after I reduced the number of instances it was set to deploy from two to one, and Figure 15.24 shows an updated service map. When I don't need the chat server any more (as soon as I finish this demo and post a few memes), I can run `terraform destroy` to free up these resources for other AWS users (and save my money).

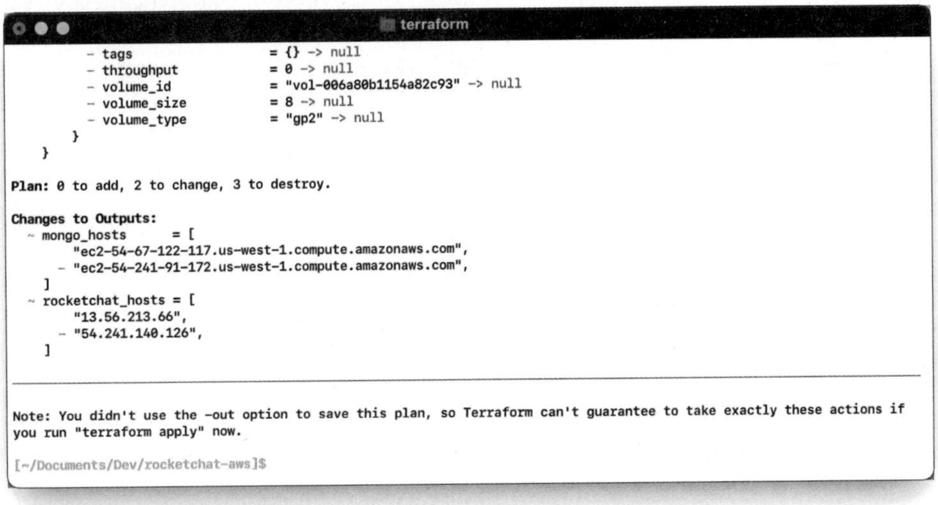

```
terraform
          - tags                    = {} -> null
          - throughput              = 0 -> null
          - volume_id               = "vol-006a80b1154a82c93" -> null
          - volume_size             = 8 -> null
          - volume_type             = "gp2" -> null
        }
    }

Plan: 0 to add, 2 to change, 3 to destroy.

Changes to Outputs:
  ~ mongo_hosts      = [
        "ec2-54-67-122-117.us-west-1.compute.amazonaws.com",
      - "ec2-54-241-91-172.us-west-1.compute.amazonaws.com",
    ]
  ~ rocketchat_hosts = [
        "13.56.213.66",
      - "54.241.140.126",
    ]

Note: You didn't use the -out option to save this plan, so Terraform can't guarantee to take exactly these actions if
you run "terraform apply" now.
[~/Documents/Dev/rocketchat-aws]$
```

• **Figure 15.23** Terraform's plan to delete the database and chat servers that comprise an instance

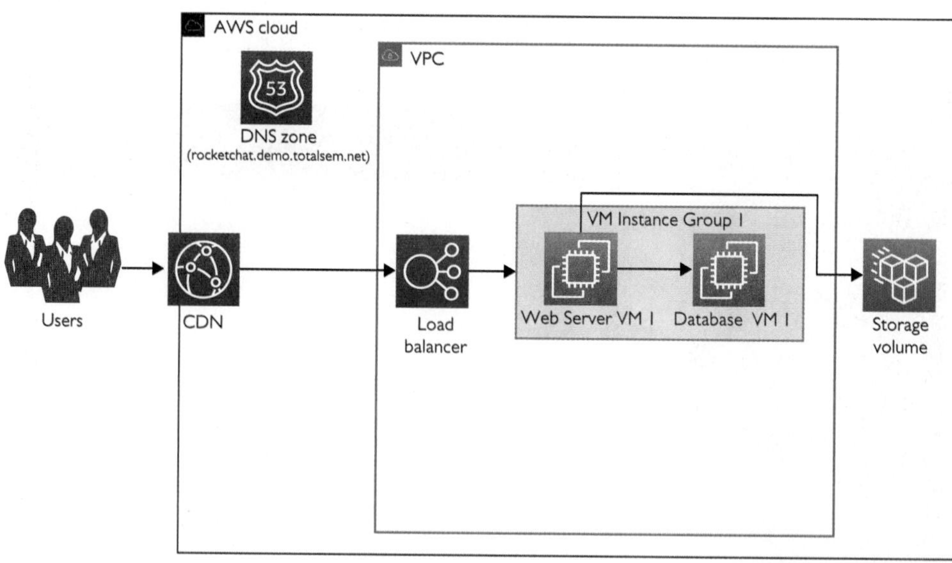

• **Figure 15.24** New service map after Terraform changes

Desktop as a Service

I've talked a lot about how cool it is to use virtualization and cloud networking for managing servers and the applications that run on them, but they aren't the only way to benefit from the *everything-as-a-service* trend that virtualization and cloud computing started. **Desktop as a service (DaaS)** enables you to move user workstations into the cloud and manage them as flexibly as other cloud infrastructure.

Oddly, the CompTIA Network+ N10-008 objectives list DaaS as a cloud service model right alongside IaaS, PaaS, and SaaS. DaaS isn't really a service model—it's just a kind of service. You can find different virtual desktop services that give you building blocks like IaaS does, a full platform like PaaS does, or a completely managed service like you'd expect from SaaS. DaaS is probably the wrong answer to any questions about service models—but be sure to read questions and answers that refer to DaaS carefully.

DaaS isn't really a new idea—it's just the latest form of a kind of virtualization we've been doing for a while now. Desktop virtualization replaces direct access to a system's local desktop environment with a client that can access an OS running in a VM. You could technically run that VM on the same device, but benefits like flexible management come from centralizing the desktop VMs on a smaller number of servers—a pattern called **virtual desktop infrastructure (VDI)**. This server/client VDI pattern is roughly what cloud providers bundle up and sell as DaaS.

Even though you can accomplish the same goals with in-house VDI, cloud services have some distinct benefits. For example, DaaS makes it possible to onboard new employees even when there's no space on the internal servers. The ability to host virtual desktops closer to users all around the world, even when you don't have an office nearby, can also help them have a smooth experience because of the reduction in lag. Some services also have distinct options or features—Windows 7 on Azure Virtual Desktop, for example, comes with free security updates from Microsoft until early 2023 for users that need to support legacy apps a little longer.

Figure 15.25 shows a virtual desktop running in the DaaS for AWS: Amazon WorkSpaces. If you want to support these workspaces for your users, they'll need a way to log in. AWS and other providers typically have some kind of directory service you can use to manually set up accounts—and that's what I used to configure the account for this desktop, as shown in Figure 15.26. If you have many users, you'll likely end up leaning on your existing directory service (such as Active Directory), which may be running in the cloud or hosted on your LAN.

A **virtual desktop** is a VM running a desktop OS used as a replacement for a desktop environment on a physical workstation.

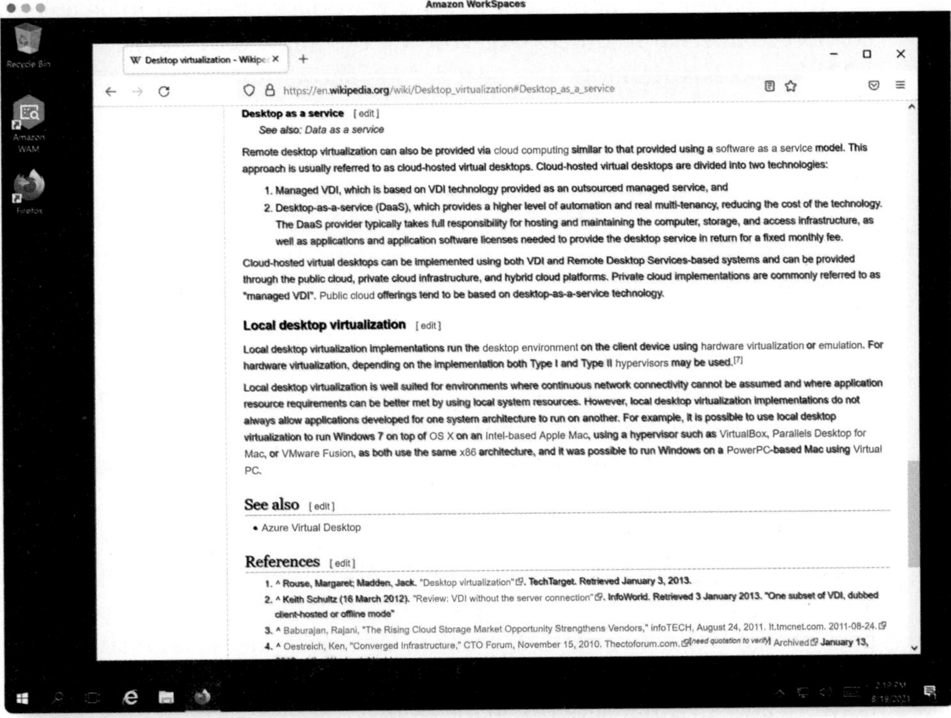

• **Figure 15.25** Amazon WorkSpaces virtual desktop

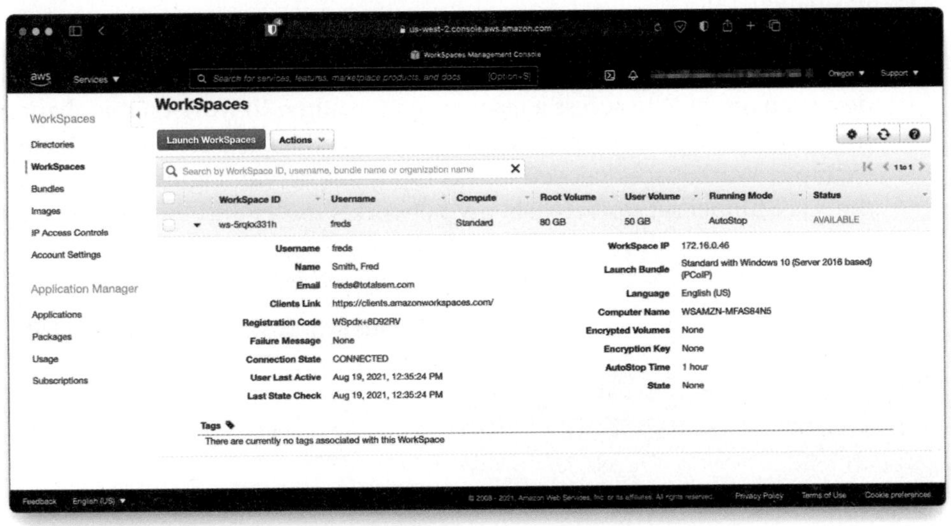

• **Figure 15.26** WorkSpaces configuration in Management Console

WorkSpaces is a building-blocks-style DaaS, so I also need to set up one or more virtual networks for my virtual desktops. This is enough for very simple needs, though you may also need to allow to pass through your firewall whatever protocols your client uses. There isn't a hard-and-fast rule here—Azure uses Microsoft's own proprietary Remote Desktop Protocol (RDP), while AWS uses a different proprietary protocol named PC-over-IP (PCoIP).

You'll have a bit more work to do if your desktops need to be able to connect to internal resources—or you want to allow only devices on your LAN to access a desktop. The next section shows how I can interconnect this virtual network with my LAN to meet needs like these.

Interconnecting Local and Cloud Resources

Unless your organization manages to chug along just fine without any cloud resources—or only needs to use resources that can be publicly accessible—it'll probably have to support interconnecting resources running locally with those running in the cloud. This chapter mentioned that the security implications of an always-on connection are problematic. Let's look also at two *connectivity options* that the exam objectives focus on: a virtual private network (VPN) and a private-direct connection to the cloud provider.

Virtual Private Network

The most convenient way to connect a network to the public cloud is through a VPN. As discussed back in Chapter 13, a VPN creates an encrypted tunnel between two networks over another, less-secure network. A **site-to-site VPN** can establish a permanent tunnel (often using IPsec) between a local network and a virtual network in the cloud.

VPN tunnels are relativity simple to set up because they use off-the-shelf technology like IPsec. This makes them easy to integrate with existing site-to-site WAN infrastructure or even an SD-WAN service (like you saw in Chapter 13).

There are many reasons you might want or need to interconnect these networks. The reasons all basically boil down to making it easier for a device on one side to access a resource on the other. To work on this chapter from the Amazon WorkSpace I showed you in the DaaS section earlier, for example, WorkSpaces needed access to my file server. Figure 15.27 shows the VPN tunnel set up between my network's router and the AWS Virtual

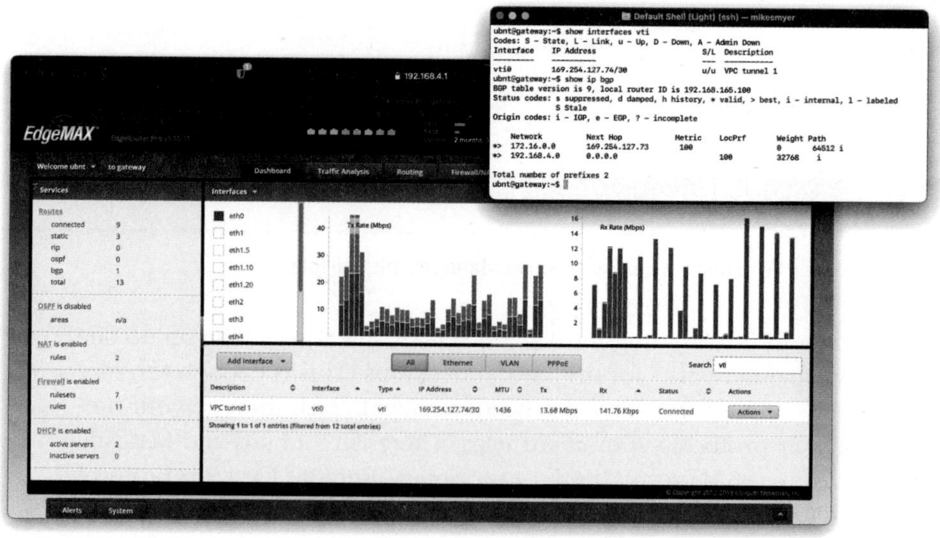

• **Figure 15.27** VPN activity on my network's router and its BGP routing table

Private Cloud network to which my virtual desktop is attached. Once I have the tunnel set up and the routes propagate, I can copy down my working files as shown in Figure 15.28.

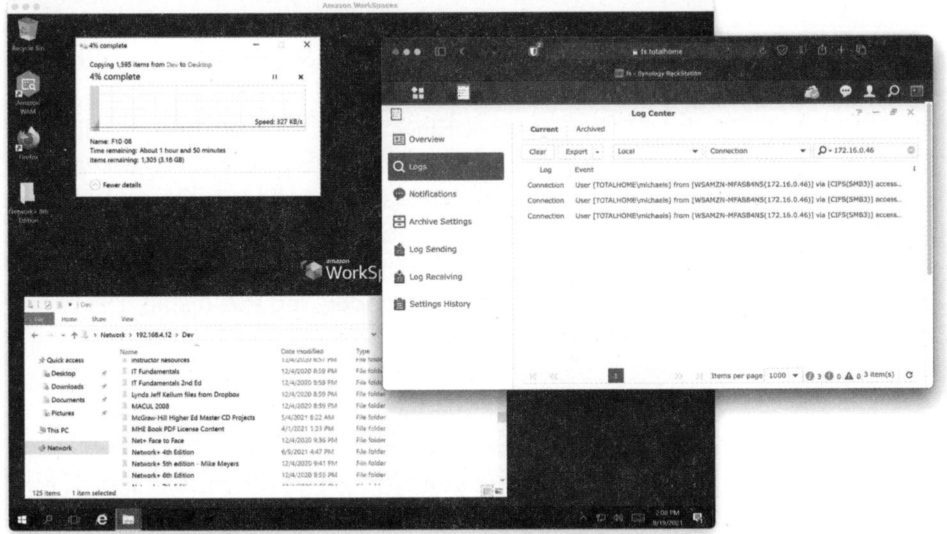

• **Figure 15.28** Transferring files from my on-premises file server to my virtual desktop

Private Direct Connection

VPNs are easy to set up, but big-time organizations often need big-time pipes. Providers such as AWS and Azure offer **private direct connections**—private direct links between your network and the cloud provider's—to meet this need. These connections take one of two forms: a physical port on the cloud provider's switch, which enables you to run fiber between your equipment and the cloud provider's, or a leased line that you contract through a third party. The main thing to keep in mind is that the traffic for a private direct connection never goes over the public Internet. It's a private line between your data center and your cloud provider.

You might see a question on the CompTIA Network+ exam that calls on you to identify a *private-direct connection to cloud provider.* That's a specific high-end (and expensive) data connection, as discussed here.

Chapter 15 Review

Chapter Summary

After reading this chapter and completing the exercises, you should understand the following about virtualization and cloud computing.

Describe virtualization and cloud computing concepts

- Abstracting something complicated into layers helps us manage complexity by focusing on a few issues at a time. For example, Internet Protocol and Ethernet deal with part of the problem of how to get messages from one place to another.
- Virtualization is an abstraction pattern that involves creating a software version that is more or less indistinguishable to anyone or anything that needs to interact with it.
- Replacing components with software often means making them more flexible, enabling you to reroute inputs or outputs to new locations, relocate components, and divide or combine resources in new ways.
- A big driver of virtualization's popularity is how this flexibility supports large-scale operations such as data centers. Being able to consolidate and pool resources enables them to save on redundant components and take advantage of economies of scale.
- Cloud computing provides services that combine *à la carte* computing and networking resources with layers of value-adding software that simplify performing complex tasks and managing powerful hardware.
- Cloud services are commonly categorized into one of three service models: infrastructure as a service (IaaS), platform as a service (PaaS), and software as a service (SaaS).
- You can create building blocks like virtual servers on demand with IaaS providers, pay only for what you use, and avoid having to purchase and administer expensive, heavy hardware.
- PaaS providers combine the infrastructure needed to run a modern Web application with simple administrative controls. PaaS trades some of the flexibility of IaaS in order to drastically cut the time and knowledge needed to build and run a Web application.
- True SaaS roughly replaces applications once distributed and licensed via physical media with access (sometimes a subscription) to equivalent applications running on a centralized server, which users access with a client such as a Web browser. In a less true form, some traditional desktop applications have also moved to a SaaS-like subscription model. You still install the software locally, but you pay a monthly or yearly subscription to continue using it.
- Four cloud deployment models describe who a cloud provides services to: public cloud, private cloud, community cloud, and hybrid cloud. The public cloud includes software, platforms, and infrastructure that the general public can sign up to use. A private cloud is internal to an organization. Organizations with shared goals or needs may create a shared community cloud. A hybrid cloud deployment describes combining resources from the other three models.
- The software-based flexibility of virtualized components makes it easier to automate provisioning and maintenance tasks.
- The infrastructure as code (IaC) philosophy aims to define needed infrastructure in configuration files and use automation to create or duplicate the infrastructure from the definition.
- Orchestration, which embodies the IaC philosophy, is a higher level of automation that composes automated tasks into longer sequences that better meet the needs of an organization or its employees—such as monitoring the health of a service and automatically replacing components that freeze or crash.

Explain virtual networking concepts

- Network virtualization covers a few different patterns, but they all involve software versions of network functions (such as switches, routers, and firewalls) that were traditionally hardware network appliances.
- A single VM host can contain multiple fully virtual networks with virtual NICs for each VM and virtual switches to interconnect them as needed.

- A virtual network function (such as a VPN concentrator) can run in a VM on the same hypervisor as the hosts it serves, on another nearby server, on your router (if it includes a hypervisor), or even in the cloud.
- Network function virtualization (NFV) is a network architecture that applies IaC-style automation and orchestration to network management.
- NFV has a foundation of hardware (such as generic servers and switches) and software (like hypervisors and controllers) called network function virtualization infrastructure (NFVI). NFV runs virtualized network functions (VNFs) such as firewalls, load balancers, and routers on the NFVI.
- NFV enables an organization such as a big ISP to consolidate all kinds of hard-to-manage proprietary boxes down into VMs running on a smaller number of generic servers and then use orchestration to manage software and configuration updates and reallocate resources in response to real-time traffic.
- Traditional network devices have a closely integrated control plane that decides how to move traffic, and a data plane that executes these decisions. Software-defined networking (SDN) outsources the control plane's work to a centralized network controller.
- An SDN controller is programmable—it runs software applications that do jobs like load balancing, optimizing traffic flow, threat protection, and more.
- SDN and NFV sound similar, but they are separate, complementary ways to manage networks with software. SDN virtualizes the control plane to outsource its work, while NFV virtualizes the entire network function. You can use them separately, though NFV often takes advantage of SDN.

Explain how network virtualization and cloud computing work in modern networks

- Virtualization and cloud computing both provide a great opportunity to play with networking setups and scenarios you wouldn't have access to in the real world.
- You can often host an internal app for a small office on a single in-house computer, such as a server running Oracle VirtualBox. Manually create a VM, install an OS, then install and configure the desired software.
- Since VMs are just files on the host system, you can export a VM you've configured and reuse it as a starting point on other systems. You don't have to install an OS from scratch every time you create a VM!
- IaC tools can use a code definition that you write to create, network, and provision one or more VMs with the needed configuration and software. But be aware that automation is fragile and may break or misbehave if it runs into something unanticipated.
- IaC automation tools (such as Vagrant and Ansible) can be used to install and run a server (such as a Rocket.Chat server) on a hypervisor (such as VirtualBox) with a single CLI command. Vagrant focuses on creating and managing VMs on a local hypervisor, and provisioning them with other tools. Ansible focuses on provisioning servers based on what role they'll perform.
- A big advantage of deploying an application or service to the cloud is how easy it is to adjust the resources it has available and the capacity it can serve. Scalability gives us a way to scale "up" an application by adjusting the amount of resources like CPU and RAM available to each VM. Elasticity enables us to quickly scale "out" by running more (or fewer) instances of the application.
- Signing up with a cloud provider generally creates an extremely powerful account—often attached to a credit card or bank account—that, if compromised, can be used to rack up big bills, steal data, or destroy your organization's infrastructure in a hurry. Set up separate credentials for each use case and follow the principle of least privilege!
- While cloud providers usually have policies to limit the risk of unauthorized access, they and their employees technically have the opportunity to access your data. Organizations with sensitive data may need to encrypt their own data, or use a private cloud model to ensure privacy.
- Cloud providers generally take advantage of multitenancy—the ability to support multiple customers on the same infrastructure. Unless you set up dedicated instances, your cloud VMs might share hardware with neighbors who are malicious, hacked, or simply overusing shared resources.
- Carefully consider the security implications before you interconnect your LAN and cloud networks—the interconnection can create opportunities for an

intruder to enter your network through the most-vulnerable device on either side and jump to the other.

- It can be important to collect logs from separate systems and services running in your cloud in order to debug them or recognize an intrusion—but those same logs may also contain sensitive information. Your organization may need to go to some lengths to collect the right logs and retain them without violating customer privacy.
- Terraform, like Vagrant, can use Ansible to provision VMs. Terraform focuses on setting up and managing resources across different cloud providers and local hypervisors.
- You can move user workstations to the cloud with a Desktop as a Service (DaaS) provider. These providers are mostly just bundling up an older desktop-virtualization pattern called virtual desktop infrastructure (VDI), but different services may have unique options.
- You'll still need some sort of authorization system for DaaS desktops, whether you use the cloud provider's lightweight directory service or integrate with an existing Active Directory server.
- The simple way to interconnect cloud and local resources is to establish a permanent site-to-site VPN tunnel. Organizations who need more bandwidth can take advantage of a private direct connection.

Key Terms

abstract *(429)*
abstraction *(430)*
automation *(438)*
cloud computing *432)*
community cloud *(436)*
desktop as a service (DaaS) *(452)*
elasticity *(448)*
guest *(428)*
hardware underutilization *(427)*
host *(428)*
hybrid cloud *(436)*
hypervisor *(428)*
infrastructure as a service (IaaS) *(433)*
infrastructure as code (IaC) *(437)*
multitenancy *(449)*
network function virtualization (NFV) *(441)*
network function virtualization infrastructure (NFVI) *(441)*
orchestration *(438)*
platform as a service (PaaS) *(434)*
private cloud *(436)*
private direct connection *(455)*
public cloud *(436)*
scalability *(448)*
site-to-site VPN *(454)*
software as a service (SaaS) *(435)*
software-defined networking (SDN) *(443)*
Type 1 hypervisor *(429)*
Type 2 hypervisor *(429)*
virtual desktop *(452)*
virtual desktop infrastructure (VDI) *(452)*
virtual firewall *(441)*
virtual machine (VM) *(427)*
virtual network interface card (vNIC) *(440)*
virtual router *(441)*
virtual switch (vSwitch) *(440)*
virtualization *(427)*
virtualized network function (VNF) *(442)*
VNF component (VNFC) *(442)*

Key Term Quiz

Use the Key Terms list to complete the sentences that follow. Not all the terms will be used.

1. A(n) ______________ is a complete environment for a guest operating system to function as though that operating system were installed on dedicated hardware.
2. Using code to perform a task consistently is an example of ______________.
3. John's hypervisor enables all five of the virtual machines on his system to communicate with each other through the ______________ without going outside the host system.

4. A(n) ______________ provider hosts virtual user workstations in the cloud.

5. ______________ describes supporting multiple customers on the same infrastructure at the same time.

6. With ______________, an application's servers and network components are defined in configuration files or scripts.

7. ______________ is a network architecture that leverages IaC concepts.

8. ______________ composes automated tasks into longer sequences.

9. In ______________, a controller is responsible for deciding how traffic will move through the network.

10. The easiest way to interconnect your LAN with cloud resources is a(n) ______________.

Multiple-Choice Quiz

1. Which of the following is a closely integrated plane (or layer) that is moved to its own server by SDN?
   - **A.** Application
   - **B.** Control
   - **C.** Infrastructure
   - **D.** Management

2. Which of the following describes the ability to adjust the capacity of a service or application by increasing or decreasing the number of running instances?
   - **A.** Cloud bursting
   - **B.** Elasticity
   - **C.** Flexibility
   - **D.** Orchestration

3. When a virtual machine is not running, how is it stored?
   - **A.** Firmware
   - **B.** RAM drive
   - **C.** Optical disc
   - **D.** Files

4. Which of the following do hypervisors tend to have built in?
   - **A.** NFVI
   - **B.** Virtual private network
   - **C.** Virtual RAM
   - **D.** vSwitch

5. Which of the following might require an organization to scale an application "up" instead of "out"?
   - **A.** The application is not designed to work in a hybrid cloud deployment.
   - **B.** The application is designed to use as much RAM as you configure it to use.
   - **C.** The application is not designed to run on multiple instances simultaneously.
   - **D.** The application is designed to run on a PaaS provider.

6. Which of these is *not* an example of NFVI?
   - **A.** Container
   - **B.** CPU
   - **C.** Hypervisor
   - **D.** Switch

7. Of the following programs used in this chapter, which is not an IaC tool?
   - **A.** Ansible
   - **B.** Terraform
   - **C.** Vagrant
   - **D.** VirtualBox

8. Tom has a great idea for a new photo-sharing service for real pictures of Bigfoot, but he doesn't own any servers. Where can he quickly create a new server to build his dream?
   - **A.** Public cloud
   - **B.** Private cloud
   - **C.** Community cloud
   - **D.** Hybrid cloud

9. Ford logs into his Microsoft account and continues work on his Great American Novel with the Web version of Microsoft Word. What is this type of service called?
   A. Software as a service
   B. Infrastructure as a service
   C. Platform as a service
   D. Desktop as a service
10. After the unforeseen failure of his Bigfoot-picture-sharing service, bgFootr—which got hacked when he failed to stay on top of his security updates—Tom has a great new idea for a new service to report UFO sightings. What service could he use to host this app without having to play system administrator?
   A. Software as a service
   B. Infrastructure as a service
   C. Platform as a service
   D. Desktop as a service
11. BigCorp is a successful Bigfoot-tracking company with an internal service to manage all of its automated Bigfoot surveillance stations. A Bigfoot migration has caused a massive increase in the amount of audio and video sent back from BigCorp's stations. In order to add short-term capacity, BigCorp can create new servers in the public cloud. What cloud computing model does this describe?
   A. Public cloud
   B. Private cloud
   C. Community cloud
   D. Hybrid cloud
12. Which of these virtualized network components is most likely to run in its own VM?
   A. Virtual LAN
   B. Virtual NIC
   C. Virtual router
   D. Virtual switch
13. A network of hospitals wants to create a centralized records service but has to observe serious governmental regulations on patient privacy. Which two of the following would best meet the network's needs?
   A. Public cloud
   B. Private cloud
   C. Community cloud
   D. Hybrid cloud
14. Each vNIC gets a Layer 2 ______________.
   A. pooled virtual IP address
   B. pooled virtual MAC address
   C. unique IP address
   D. unique MAC address
15. Which of the following is not a potential advantage of virtual machines over physical machines?
   A. Maximize application performance
   B. Allocate resources more efficiently
   C. Consolidate multiple physical machines
   D. Scale application capacity more easily

Essay Quiz

1. A company has three discrete physical servers: a file server running Linux, an e-mail server running the latest version of Windows Server, and a DNS and DHCP server running an earlier version of Windows Server. Make a case for either keeping the separate hardware, virtualizing these servers and consolidating them on a single in-house host, or virtualizing these servers and moving them to the cloud (and against the other two options).
2. Write a short essay comparing Infrastructure as a Service with Platform as a Service.

Lab Projects

• Lab Project 15.1

Unless you happen to have it already, download and install Oracle VirtualBox from www.virtualbox.org/wiki/Downloads and download an Ubuntu ISO installer image from https://ubuntu.com/download. I recommend using the desktop version if this is your first rodeo—but don't let that stop you from downloading the server version if you're feeling adventurous. Once you've got both of these, open VirtualBox and create some virtual machines using the Ubuntu installer.

With multiple VMs running simultaneous, attempt to ping from one VM to the other. You can even try and see if file sharing will work. Now that you know you can communicate between VMs, try and communicate with the larger LAN. Can you ping other hosts on the physical LAN? Can you ping hosts on the Internet? Play around and see what works and what doesn't. Can you figure out why?

• Lab Project 15.2

Now that you're comfortable with building VMs manually in VirtualBox, build an open source routing lab using VirtualBox, Vagrant, and Ubuntu. Start by installing a copy of Vagrant (www.vagrantup.com) and then download my Vagrantfile from the "Lab 15.2 files" entry in the Book Resources tab of your online content (see Appendix C for instructions), and move it to a new directory named **lab15-2**.

Next, open a command prompt and `cd` to lab15-2. Once lab15-2 is your working directory, type `vagrant up` and press ENTER. This will start the process of downloading and configuring three Linux VMs and two virtual networks in VirtualBox. One VM is a router and the other two are clients. The provisioning process will take a bit (especially the first time you run it).

Once provisioning is complete, create an SSH connection to the first client by running `vagrant ssh client1`. From here, try pinging client2 by running `ping -c 4 192.168.20.100`. You should now see four successful pings in your command prompt. To close the SSH session, run the `exit` command. To shut down the VMs, run the `vagrant halt` command after you've exited the VMs terminal. To remove the VMs, run `vagrant destroy`.

Now that you've successfully pinged between two VMs through a router. Open the Vagrantfile in a text editor such as Notepad or VS Code and look at the source code. It may seem intimidating at first, but see if you can figure out what it's doing. Can you change the IP addresses of the systems? Can you add a client? Play around and see what you can build!

chapter 16

Data Centers

"Big data is at the foundation of all of the megatrends that are happening today, from social to mobile to the cloud to gaming."

—Chris Lynch

In this chapter, you will learn how to

- **Describe classic data center architecture and design**
- **Describe modern data center architecture and design**
- **Explain high availability concepts and procedures**
- **Explain best practices for documentation in the data center**

Ah, the data center—those mythical buildings that store all the data that powers our Internet sojourns. Virtually every public server—from Web, game, and e-mail servers, to DNS and certificate servers—sits in a data center, ready to respond to requests from client systems (Figure 16.1).

Test Specific

In a nutshell, a **data center** is a networked group of servers in a dedicated space—a building or part of a building—that provides data storage, Web hosting, application hosting, cloud services, and more for remote client organizations.

• **Figure 16.1** We live in data centers!

A data center is so much more than just a big building full of servers. A data center requires all the networking hardware to secure and effectively connect the many servers to the Internet. The data center also provides the environmental controls and physical security to protect the servers and ensure uptime. Finally, the data center contains tools necessary to protect the data center from catastrophes such as fire and natural disasters (Figure 16.2).

You'll see data centers referred to as a single word, *datacenters*, in the CompTIA Network+ N10-008 objectives, and as two words—*data center* or *data centre*—throughout the industry. There is no standard, so when doing research, search on all the terms.

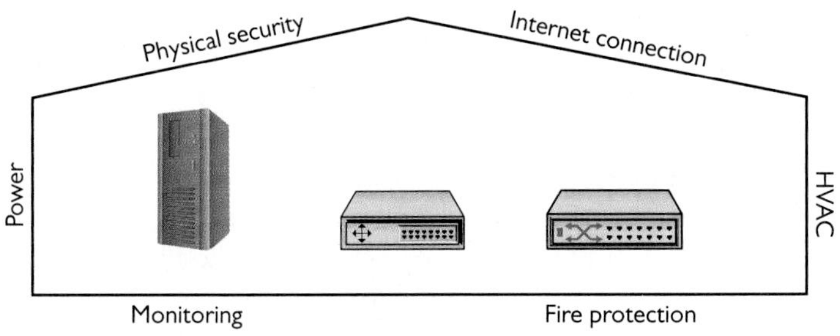

• **Figure 16.2** Data centers support the servers.

This chapter introduces you to what it takes to build and maintain a modern data center. We'll begin by observing classic data center architecture and design, exploring terms such as *tiers* and *traffic flows*. Next, you'll see how virtualization and other technologies have changed important aspects of the data center with *software-defined networking*. Third is an interesting tour of *high availability*—making sure the resources offered by the data center's servers are available when clients request them. The chapter closes by covering infrastructure support and documentation.

Classic Data Center Architecture and Design

Data centers, as a location to connect, protect, and support servers, isn't a new concept. Arguably, the earliest generations of mainframe-based data centers date back to the late 1960s, but for purposes of this discussion, it makes sense to start with data centers populated with Internet-connected, PC-based servers from the 1990s. In smaller organizations, the data center typically is co-located at the same facility as the users it supports. In larger enterprises with multiple locations (aka branch offices), the data center is a separate, dedicated building, connected to the enterprise's locations using dedicated connections. These external connections in the early years had names like T1/E1, OCx, ATM, and frame relay. Today these connections are usually Ethernet, MPLS, or SD-WAN (Figure 16.3).

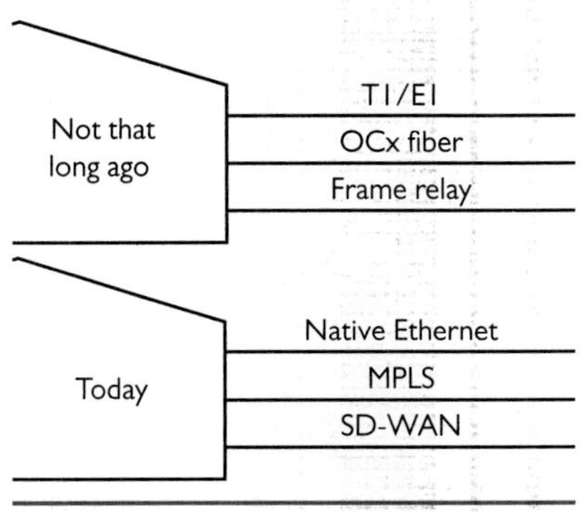

• **Figure 16.3** Data center connection technologies

All these external connections are useless unless all the servers in the data centers have the internal connections necessary to get to those external connections. In other words, the data center needs a well-planned and proven architecture to ensure a reliable and efficient flow of data from the servers out to the clients.

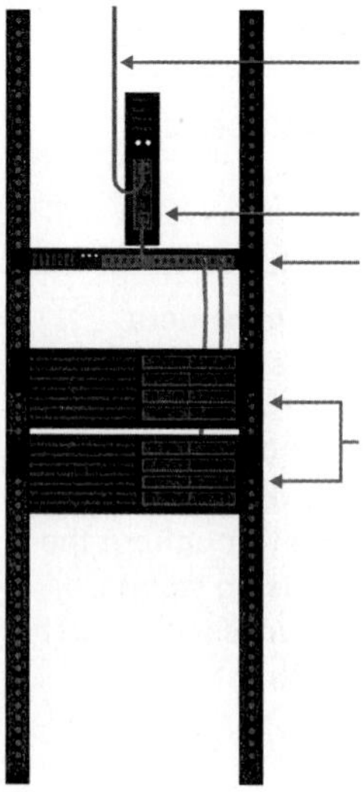

• **Figure 16.4** Simple data center

> **Cross Check**
>
> **WAN Connections**
>
> You read about WAN connections back in Chapter 13, so cross check your knowledge now. What are the advantages of MPLS over previous technologies? Would you replace MPLS with SD-WAN, or vice versa? Why? Finally what is metro Ethernet and what advantages or disadvantages does it have over competing technologies?

Tiers

In a simple world where a data center consists of a couple of servers, there isn't much in the way of architecture. You have servers, a switch, a router, and an ISP connection that might look something like Figure 16.4.

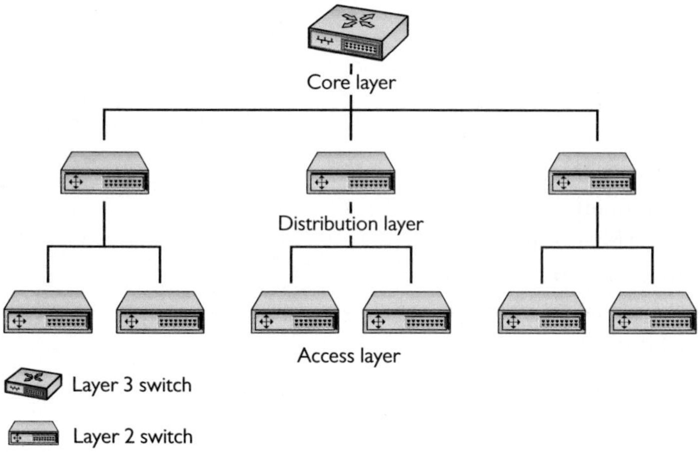

As the number of servers in your data center begins to grow, you need to have a structured approach to organizing your servers, switches, and routers, as well as many support systems (air conditioning systems and power especially). After decades of different architectures, the architecture most commonly adopted by traditional data centers is Cisco's **three-tiered architecture**. A three-tiered architecture consists of three layers: access layer, distribution layer, and core layer (Figure 16.5).

• **Figure 16.5** Three-tiered architecture

Access/Edge

The **access layer**—also referred to as the *edge layer*—acts as the primary connection between the data center connectivity and the users (keep in mind that "users" in the data centers are servers). The access layer is the cables and the access switches closest to the systems. A common implementation of access switches is **top-of-rack switching**, in which every equipment rack has one Layer 2 switch (or two for redundancy) sitting at the top of the rack, connecting to all the systems on the rack (Figure 16.6). Top-of-rack switches are *co-resident* in the rack with servers, as compared to switches that reside in a separate rack.

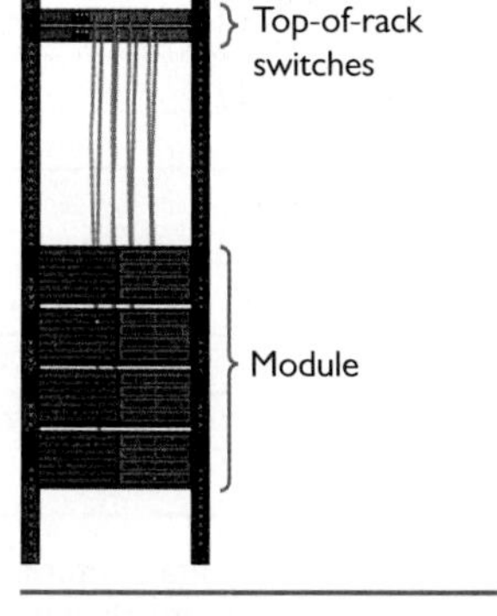

• **Figure 16.6** Typical rack with switch

Top-of-rack switches—*dedicated switches*—help keep cable runs short and well organized. Top-of-rack switching does not require that the switches be physically at the top of the rack (although they usually are). Each group of computers connected to the same access switch is known as a **module**.

Distribution/Aggregation Layer

Data centers have tens, hundreds, or in some cases thousands of racks in a single facility. With top-of-rack switches on all the racks, you need to provide a method to interconnect and distribute data to all the systems, acting as the connection between the access layer and the core layer. The **distribution layer**—also referred to as the *aggregation layer*—provides that connectivity. Distribution switches are usually multilayer and conduct forwarding from Layer 2 on the access side to Layer 3 for the core side. Cisco best practices recommend always having two distribution switches for each access switch. The two switches provide redundancy in case of the failure of the distribution switch or the cables that connect the distribution and access switches. Every group of modules that share the same connection to their distribution switches is known as a **pod** (Figure 16.7).

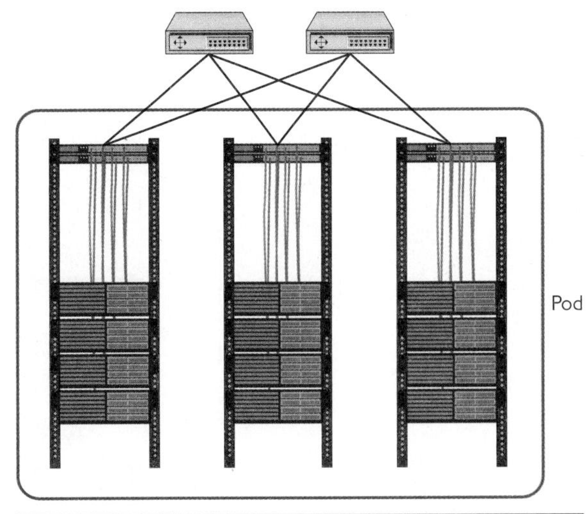

• **Figure 16.7** Distribution layer

Core

The **core layer** ties together all the switches at the distribution layer and acts as the point of connection to the external connections, including the Internet. All systems at this level run exclusively at OSI Layer 3 (Network layer). The interconnections here are the highest speed and the highest bandwidth and are therefore defined as the *backbone*. Just as with distribution, Cisco best practices recommend always having two core switches accessible to each access switch. Again, the redundancy here is warranted because of the criticality of the core switches.

Traffic Flows

All the switches, cables, and routers that populate your typical data center have a single job: to move a lot of data. To help those who design data centers, the industry has established common terms to define the movement of the data into/out of and around the data center. These are called *traffic flows*.

North-South

North-south traffic describes data moving into and out of the data center. While there is some variance in terms, the industry defines north-south traffic as any data leaving and entering the data center. Breaking down this term even more, *northbound traffic* leaves the data center and *southbound traffic* enters the data center.

> Network devices involved in north-south traffic include edge routers, edge firewalls, and load balancers.

East-West

East-west traffic is defined as any traffic that moves between systems within the data center. Unlike north-south traffic, there is no separate east traffic or

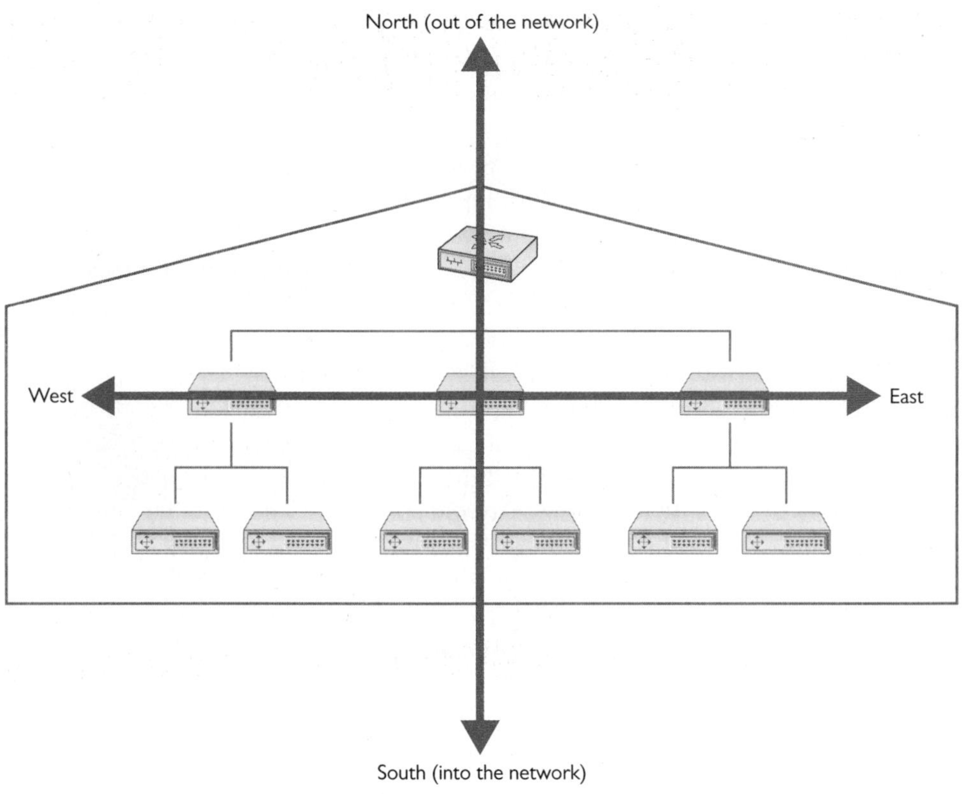

• **Figure 16.8** Traffic flows

> Network devices involved in east-west traffic include internal routers, internal firewalls, and switches.

west traffic. It's all just east-west. Examples of east-west traffic are backup traffic, intrusion detection system (IDS) alerts, and logs. Figure 16.8 shows traffic flows.

Data Storage

All that data moving north, south, east, and west sometimes needs to rest someplace, and that's where data storage comes into play. For the most part, all data storage in a classic data center focuses on the mass storage devices that store the terabytes or petabytes of ones and zeroes that make up the data. *Mass storage devices* in a traditional data center include *hard drives* and *tape backups*. Tape backups are rare (or completely gone), making hard drives and solid-state drives (SSDs) the main technologies used to store data in data centers.

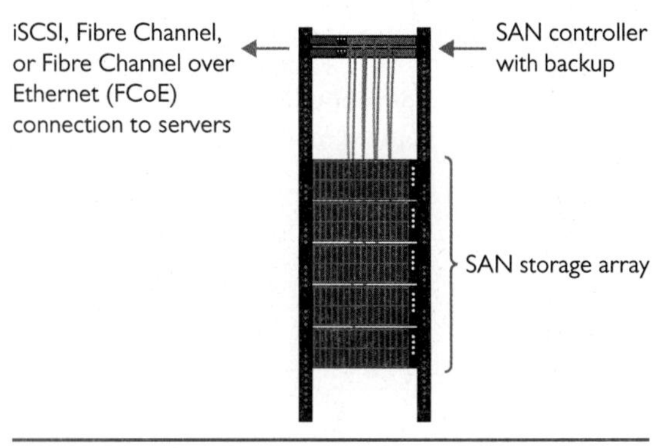

• **Figure 16.9** SAN in action

So, where are all these mass storage devices located in the data center, and what are their jobs? To be sure, every system is going to have a boot drive, in most cases a single M.2 drive mounted to the motherboard, but that drive does no more than boot the operating system. For the actual data storage, most traditional data centers use a **storage area network (SAN)**, a network that connects individual systems to a centralized bank of mass storage (Figure 16.9). But don't think of a SAN as simply a networked hard drive! You might remember from CompTIA A+ that hard drive storage is broken up into tiny sectors, also known as *blocks*. You might also remember that to access the hard drive, you have to plug it into an interface like SATA, which your operating system uses to read and write to blocks on the disk. A SAN is a *pool of mass storage devices*, presented over a network as any number of logical disks. The interface it presents to a client computer pretends to be a hard disk and enables the client's operating system to read and write blocks over a network.

Think of a drive accessed through the SAN as a **virtual disk**. Much as the hypervisor convinces the operating system it runs on its own hardware, the SAN convinces the OS it is interacting with a physical hard drive. Just like with a traditional hard disk, we have to format a virtual disk before we can use it. But unlike a traditional hard disk, the virtual disk the SAN presents could be mapped to a number of physical drives in various physical locations or even to other forms of storage.

One of the benefits of using a SAN is that, by just reading and writing at the block level, it avoids the performance costs of implementing its own file system. The SAN leaves it up to the client computers to implement their own file systems—these clients often use specialized shared file system software designed for high volume, performance, reliability, and the ability to support multiple clients using one drive.

When it comes to the infrastructure to support a SAN, there are currently two main choices:

- **Fibre Channel (FC)** is, for the most part, its own ecosystem designed for high-performance storage. It has its own cables, protocols, and switches, all increasing the costs associated with its use. While more recent developments like *Fibre Channel over Ethernet (FCoE)* make Fibre Channel a little more flexible within a local wired network, long-distance FC is still clumsy without expensive cabling and hardware.
- **Internet Small Computer System Interface (iSCSI)** is built on top of TCP/IP, enabling devices that use the SCSI protocol to communicate across existing networks using cheap, readily available hardware. Because the existing networks and their hardware weren't built as a disk interface, performance can suffer. Part of this performance cost is time spent processing frame headers. We can ease some of the cost of moving large amounts of data around the network at standard frame size by using **jumbo frames**. Jumbo frames are usually 9000 bytes long—though technically anything over 1500 qualifies—and they reduce the total number of frames moving through the network.

Moving a server's data storage physically apart from the server adds some risk. If the SAN fails, the server won't function. To address this risk, most SAN solutions provide more than one connection or path between the server and the SAN, what's called **multipathing**. If either connection fails, the other connection continues to keep the server connected to the SAN. A SAN is developed with high availability in mind, so it often includes features such as redundant controllers and power supplies, plus shared memory. All this is in addition to multipathing. (See "High Availability in the Data Center" later in the chapter for more details.)

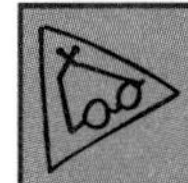

Tech Tip

SAN vs. NAS

A lot of newer techs or techs-in-training confuse the terms SAN and NAS. Both are mass storage technologies and use the same three letters, so it's understandable. But let's clear up the difference right now.

SANs are high-end data storage structures that create usable and configurable storage blocks for virtual drives, virtual desktops, and more. You're reading about them in this chapter.

Network attached storage (NAS) refers to a generally much smaller dedicated network appliance with two, four, six, or eight hard disk drives configured into some sort of array. A NAS attaches to a network switch (usually) via Ethernet and appears as available storage on the network. A NAS is used for local backups, media serving on the LAN, and other personal duties.

The physical connections between the systems and the SAN are usually fiber optics.

Where Is the Classic Data Center?

So, where does the data center physically exist? That answer varies based on where and how an organization stands in terms of growth. A tiny company might leave all of its data sitting on a single computer in the founder's garage. As a company grows and its data requirements grow, it faces choices. Does it build an **on-premises data center**, a dedicated data center at the company's site?

For many organizations, the next step is to build a rack in an empty room and load it with a few servers and mass storage devices, in essence, building a mini data center. That is perfectly fine for small organizations, but as data and server needs progress even further, a true data center is required. It's time to take the servers and move them into a proper, secure, reliable, classic data center.

But where to place this beast? On-premises data centers are wildly expensive in terms of both the building and the associated maintenance and upkeep. Back in the day, there really weren't any other viable choices. Over time, however, clever entrepreneurs (or folks who had already built data centers and had extra capacity) began to offer public, third-party data centers where anyone could place their own servers, a process known as **co-location**.

Expect a question on the CompTIA Network+ exam that compares branch office versus on-premises data center versus colocation (with no hyphen). That would be remote connections to a data center versus an on-site data center versus a data center hosted by a third party.

There's one more step in the growth of an organization that will affect the data center: multiple locations. As an organization grows into multiple locations, there's usually a central location (often corporate headquarters) that contains an organization's single data center. This data center serves outlying offices, called **branch offices**. The branch offices themselves store very little data.

The Modern Data Center

The first few decades of traditional data centers were populated with dedicated, monolithic hardware. Servers served one Web site or one function such as DNS. Routers and switches were dedicated boxes that performed only a single job, routing or switching. Monolithic devices worked well back in the day, but the introduction of virtualization and software-defined networking changed the data center dramatically, creating the *modern data center*.

Virtualization

Virtualization redefined the architecture of the data center. Where once physical servers ran single copies of Web servers and other individual applications, physical servers today are nothing more than hypervisors, running 2, 3, perhaps even 20 virtual servers each. There might be a few non-virtual (*bare-metal*) systems, but these apply almost always to very special situations such as SAN controllers. If you have a server in a data center today, it most likely is virtualized.

Software-Defined Networking

Virtualization doesn't stop with servers. Interconnections that once used dedicated switches have moved to software-defined networking (SDN) devices (that you read about in Chapter 15), making far more flexible and powerful data center architectures. There are still physical switches out in the data center; it's just that they've been relegated to act as only the *underlayment*, the path for mainly virtualized VLAN trunks to move far more complex architectures.

Spine and Leaf

Virtualization and SDN freed the data center from the three-tiered model. In particular, virtualization removes the need for the distribution/aggregation layer. With a **spine-and-leaf architecture**, every spine switch connects to every leaf switch in a two-tiered mesh network (Figure 16.10). The mesh network removes the need for dedicated connections between the spine *backbone* switches, because traffic moves seamlessly from spine to leaf to spine, regardless of how many spine or leaf switches are on the network.

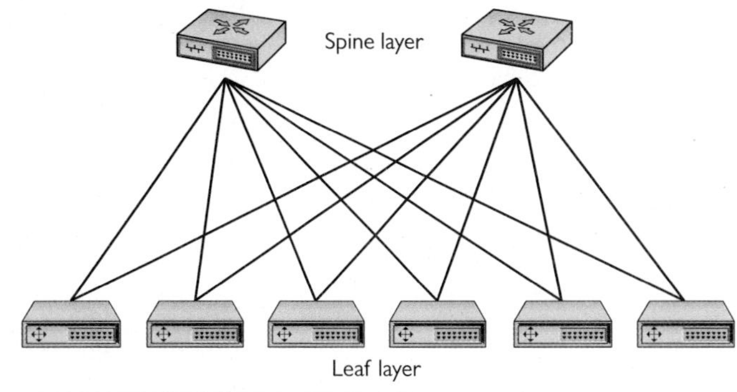

• **Figure 16.10** Spine-and-leaf architecture

Spine-and-leaf architecture has some real benefits compared to three-tiered architecture. First, spine-and-leaf architecture reduces the number of necessary devices. Every step from the spine to leaf is a single hop, which reduces latency and creates completely predictable connections. Also, there's no longer a concern for loops, making Spanning Tree Protocol (STP) unneeded. Virtual servers today rely heavily on data from other servers in the same data center, adding far more east-west traffic than is easily handled by three-tiered architecture. Spine-and-leaf architecture handles east-west traffic with ease. Spine-and-leaf architecture uses protocols such as *Equal-Cost Multipath (ECPM)* to provide load balancing across the paths so that no single connection gets overwhelmed.

Finally, spine-and-leaf architecture makes adding capacity simpler than in a three-tiered architecture. You can add another spine switch and connect it to every leaf switch through the mesh network; new leaf switches that are added simply slot in to reduce the load on all the other leaf switches.

> Spine-and-leaf configurations have multiple, interconnected top-of-rack structures.

> The CompTIA Network+ objectives refer to a spine-and-leaf architecture network as a software-defined network. This is odd terminology. Data centers certainly use SDN, but that includes both three-tier and spine-and-leaf-type data centers. Don't miss it if you see this on the exam.

High Availability in the Data Center

If there's one thing that a data center must do well, it is to provide the right data to the right host at the right time, without ever dropping or failing. Unfortunately, things fail in life: CPUs melt, rodents chew cables, and power supplies die. Therefore, it's important to ensure systems keep working without interruption or downtime; in other words, to make sure critical systems have **high availability (HA)**. Some of the concepts of HA have been covered previously in the book and even in this chapter, such as *multipathing* within a SAN; as the concepts come into play here, I'll point to where you read about them previously. HA in this section explores load balancing, redundancy, and facilities and infrastructure support.

Load Balancing

As a concept, **load balancing** means to share among two or more systems the effort to enable some process to work. You saw this concept way back in Chapter 11 in the context of using multiple servers as a server cluster that manifests as a single entity. Special-purpose load balancers help apportion the work among the various servers. You've seen the concept used in spine-and-leaf data centers earlier that rely on protocols like ECPM to balance the work among the various switches so that no single connection gets swamped. Load balancing in its many forms is one pillar of high availability.

Clustering solutions are commonly *active-active* examples of high availability in that all members of the cluster are active at the same time.

Clustering, in the traditional sense, means to have multiple pieces of equipment, such as servers, connected in a manner that appears to the user and the network as one logical device, providing data and services to the organization. Clusters usually share high-speed networking connections as well as data stores and applications and are configured to provide redundancy if a single member of the cluster fails.

Redundancy

Redundancy ensures high availability on many levels through the use of additional equipment and connection options. If one device or connection goes down, another takes its place.

With *redundant hardware/clusters*, you put into place primary switches, routers, firewalls, and other network gear, then have at the ready backup machines to step up in case the primary machine fails. Core to building high availability into a network is *failover*, the ability for backup systems to detect when a master has failed and then to take over.

If you're going to use multiple devices to do one job, there must be a way to make multiple devices look like a single device to the rest of the devices. This is commonly done by having multiple devices share a single external MAC address or IP address while using their own internal MACs or IPs to communicate with each other. You'll see this concept over and over again.

Building with high availability in mind extends to more than just servers; a default gateway, for example, is a critical node that can be protected by adding redundant backups. Protocols that support HA and redundancy are referred to as *first hop redundancy protocols (FHRPs)* and include the open standard **Virtual Router Redundancy Protocol (VRRP)** and the Cisco-proprietary **Hot Standby Router Protocol (HSRP)** and **Gateway Load Balancing Protocol (GLBP)**. The nice thing about VRRP, HSRP, and GLBP is that, conceptually, they perform the same function. They take multiple routers and gang them together into a single virtual router with a single *virtual IP (VIP)* address that clients use as a default gateway. This includes making redundant firewalls on the redundant routers! GLBP takes things a step further, providing full load balancing as well.

VRRP and HSRP are examples of *active-passive* high availability in that only one router is active at a time. All other routers are passive until the active router fails.

Redundancy applies to connections as well as systems. What's an absolutely critical connection point for a data center? *Connection to the Internet* should never be a single point of failure for a data center (or for any organization, for that matter). It's common for a data center to use *multiple Internet service providers (ISPs)* so that if one service goes down, the other ISP provides continued Internet connectivity. Sometimes the other ISP is a hot standby, so the Internet connection switches, a failover. Other setups have the secondary ISP actively engaged and available for excess traffic, and is in place to be the sole service if necessary. Employing multiple ISPs is a measure of fault tolerance.

It's very common for ISPs to share common lines and such, especially when they are servicing the same physical location. It's therefore critically important to ensure **path diversity**, where the lines out of your ISP follow *diverse paths* to other routers. A common method for path diversity in smaller centers, for example, uses a fiber connection for the primary path and a very fast cellular connection as a failover. Use of both a fiber ISP and a different cable ISP can also lead to path diversity.

Facilities and Infrastructure Support

Data centers require proper support for facilities and infrastructure, which means ensuring proper power, clean cool air for components, and emergency procedures are in place. All of these add to high availability and, in the case of the last item, disaster recovery.

Different rack manufacturers have specific rules and standards for rack electrical grounding. Refer to the specific manufacturer's installation instructions and consider hiring professional installers when placing your racks.

Power

Rack-mounted equipment has a number of special power needs. At an absolute minimum, start with a proper power source. A single small rack can get away with a properly grounded, 20-amp dedicated circuit. Larger installations can require larger, dedicated power transformers supplied by the local power grid.

When you get down to individual racks, it's always a good idea to provide each rack with its own rack-mounted **uninterruptible power supply (UPS)**—a battery backup and power conditioner. You then connect a **power distribution unit (PDU)**—a rack-mounted set of outlets for devices—to that UPS. If you're using *power converters* for devices that require DC rather than AC, always use a single power converter per rack.

The more demanding equipment room also demands more robust power and *battery backup*. A single, decent UPS might adequately handle brief power fluctuations for a single rack, for example, but won't be able to deal with a serious power outage. For that kind of *power redundancy*—keeping the lights on and the servers rolling—you'd need to connect **power generators** to the equipment room, devices that burn some petroleum product to produce electricity when the main grid goes dark.

Environment

Racks with servers, switches, routers, and such, go into closets or server rooms and they dump heat. The environment within this space must be monitored and controlled for both temperature and humidity. Network components work better when cool rather than hot.

The placement of a rack should *optimize the airflow* in a server area. All racks should be placed so that components draw air in from a shared cool row and then exhaust the hot air into a hot row.

The **heating, ventilation, and air conditioning (HVAC)** system should be optimized to recirculate and purify the hot air into cool air in a continuous flow. What's the proper temperature and humidity level? The ideal for the room, regardless of size, is an average temperature of 68 degrees Fahrenheit and ~50 percent humidity. A proper **fire suppression system**—one that can do things like detect fire, cut power to protect sensitive equipment, displace oxygen with fire-suppressing gasses, alert relevant staff, and activate sprinklers in a pinch—is an absolute must for any server closet or room. You need to extinguish any electrical spark quickly to minimize server or data loss.

Emergency Procedures

A data center must have proper **emergency procedures** in place before the emergencies happen. This is essential risk management. Here are five essential aspects that should be covered:

- Building layout
- Fire escape plan
- Safety/emergency exits
- Fail open/fail close
- Emergency alert system

Exit plans need to cover *building layout*, *fire escape plans*, and the locations of *emergency exits*. Exit signs should be posted strategically so people can quickly exit in a real emergency.

Secured spaces, such as server rooms, need some kind of default safety mechanism in case of an emergency. Emergency exits like stairways also require safety mechanisms like fail safe locks. Locked doors need to *fail open* (doors default to open in case of emergency) or *fail closed* (doors lock in case of emergency). *Fail safe locks*, such as maglocks, require power to stay locked. When the power goes out, they automatically open. The contrasting locks are called *fail secure*. They're locked by default and require power to open. If they power goes out, they stay locked.

Finally, nothing beats a properly loud **emergency alert system** blaring away to get people moving quickly. Don't forget to have annual fire drills and emergency alert mixers to make certain all employees know what they need to know.

Documenting the Data Center

A properly organized data center requires extensive documentation that describes every aspect of the organization, from physical layout to electrical structure, from networking standards and installations to climate control systems. This documentation includes the people necessary to maintain, repair, and replace every piece of equipment. Every applicable government standard needs to be included in the proper place in the documentation. And at least annually, the data center (and its documentation) should be reviewed and audited for efficiency and compliance. As you might imagine at this point, properly documenting a data center is a major *continuous* undertaking and not a task that should be shirked at all.

Here's the scenario. The Wapi Lava Corporation (WLC), based in Pocatello, Idaho, has a midsize data center (nicknamed "Hot Flo") in the basement of a downtown building. The city of Pocatello was chosen because of the availability of inexpensive electricity, good connectivity with the West Coast and solid links to the Midwest, and very low probability of natural disasters. This section explores the data center documentation in three categories:

- Network diagrams
- Baseline configurations
- Assessments

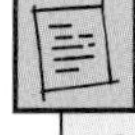

The fictitious Wapi Lava Corporation is named after the Wapi Lava Field, a very inactive volcanic site around 30 miles outside the city of Pocatello. It hasn't erupted in more than 2000 years. (It's pronounced *WAH-pie*.)

Network Diagrams

Good data center documentation contains all sorts of diagrams, mapping out physical and logical systems. These documents include dimensions, standards followed, locations, connectivity, technology manufacturers and model numbers, licensing, essential personnel, and more.

Physical Network Diagrams

Physical network diagrams map out physical aspects of the data center, including floor plans, rack diagrams, and documents describing the physical components and connectivity in the centralized wiring rooms on each floor.

Physical network diagrams rely on a few standard tools for layout, such as Microsoft Visio, Wondershare Edraw, or my current favorite, diagrams.net. Figure 16.11 shows some of the icons available in diagrams.net.

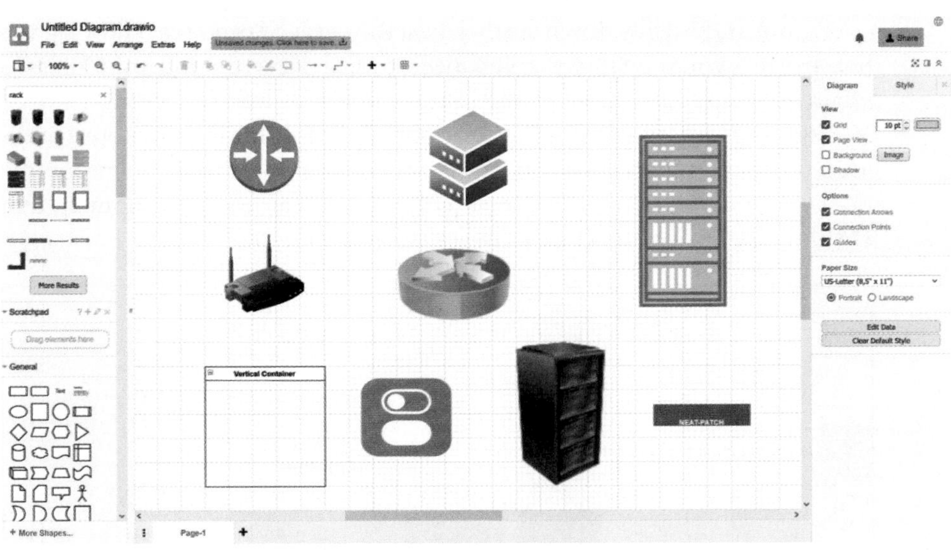

• **Figure 16.11** Icon options in the diagrams.net app

Floor Plans

A data center *floor plan* includes the dimensions and locations of rooms, like the simple floor plans you read about way back in Chapter 5, but expand dramatically to include details. Floor plans include locations of—and detailed information about—racks, hot and cold aisles, raised floors, ceiling heights, air conditioning units, ductwork, and so on. Floor plan documentation can take many pages, illustrations, and discussion.

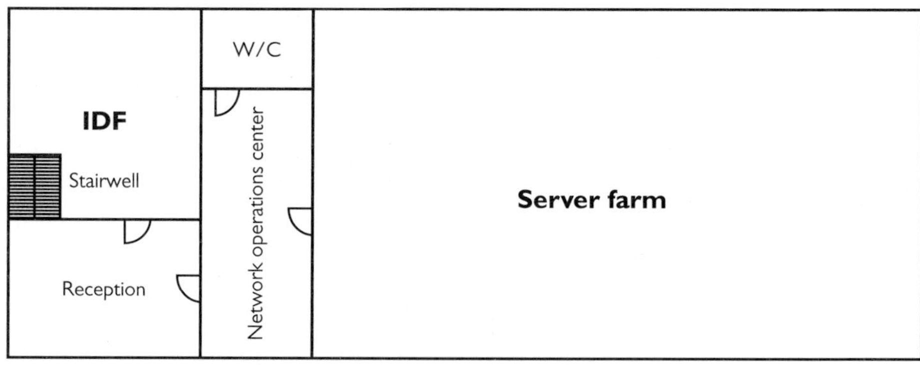

• **Figure 16.12** Basic layout of WLC's data center lower floor

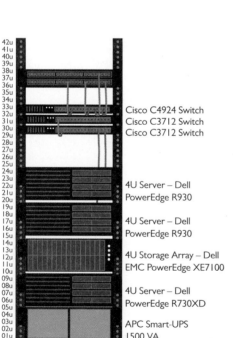

Figure 16.12 shows the basic layout of the lower level of Hot Flo. Note the three major sections. There is a wiring room in the west (left), a network operations center in the center, and the server farm in the east (right).

The wiring room is the **intermediate distribution frame (IDF)** that serves as the wiring focal point for all the devices on that floor. This is also called a *telecommunications* room, like you read about in Chapter 5. The **network operations center (NOC)** houses network engineers and technicians who maintain the applications housed in the data center, such as databases, Web servers, and so forth. The vast majority of the lower level is the **server farm**, with row upon row of racks holding stacks of servers. Each rack is topped with two switches.

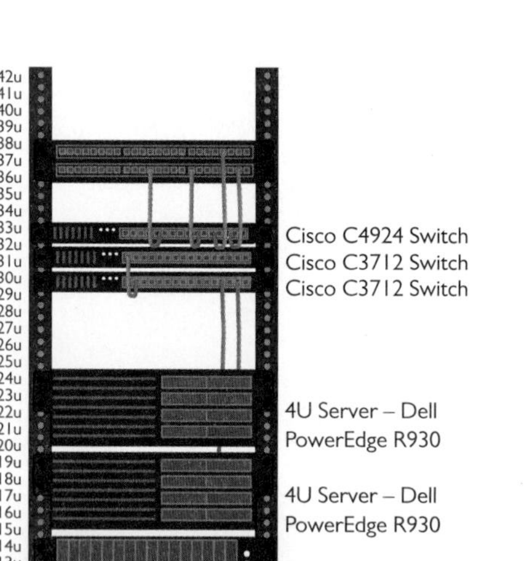

• **Figure 16.13** Floor plan details of server farm

Figure 16.13 drills down further into the server farm area, showing the hot aisles—where heat can go away from the servers—and cold aisles—where the air conditioning vents pump cold air for thirsty servers.

Figure 16.14 shows the upper-floor layout—although without individual offices mapped—with both a telecommunications room for the floor and a **main distribution frame (MDF)** that holds all the equipment that enables Hot Flo's connection to the outside world.

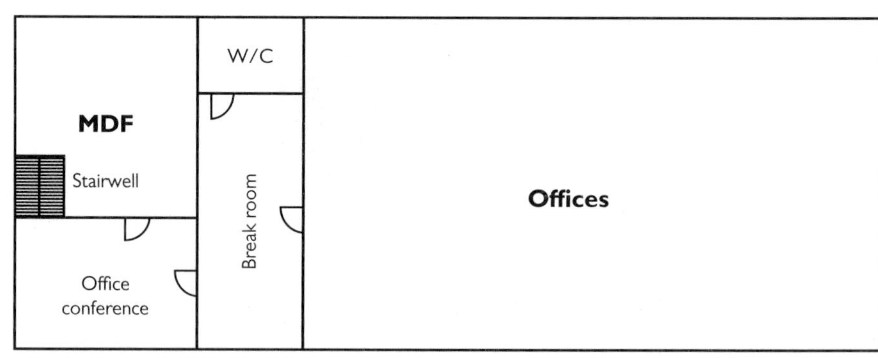

• **Figure 16.14** Upper-level floor plan of WLC's data center

Cisco C4924 Switch
Cisco C3712 Switch
Cisco C3712 Switch
4U Server – Dell PowerEdge R930
4U Server – Dell PowerEdge R930
4U Storage Array – Dell EMC PowerEdge XE7100
4U Server – Dell PowerEdge R730XD
APC Smart-UPS 1500 VA

• **Figure 16.15** Rack diagram

Rack Diagrams

Drilling down for more details, each rack (in the server farm and the IDFs and MDF) has a detailed **rack diagram** with a ton of details. Figure 16.15 shows one such rack. Note that the location and make and model of each component on the rack is labeled. Appended to this illustration is further documentation that has the current firmware version, date of purchase, upgrade history, service history, technician in charge of servicing, vendor contact, licensing information, and more.

MDF/IDF Documentation

The main distribution frame and intermediate distribution frames provide connectivity to the outside world (MDF) and network connectivity within each floor (IDF). They require unique and detailed documentation of the overall layout and connections, plus specific rack diagrams for their various components. Figure 16.16 shows the MDF documentation. The figure provides details about the demarc connection and the rack holding the patch panels and switches that provide further connectivity within the data center, and the uninterruptible power supply providing clean power to the rack components. The make and model of each component are clearly labeled.

Just as with the server farm rack described earlier, further documentation accompanies the MDF racks that detail firmware versions, service and upgrade records, assigned technicians, vendor contacts, and so on.

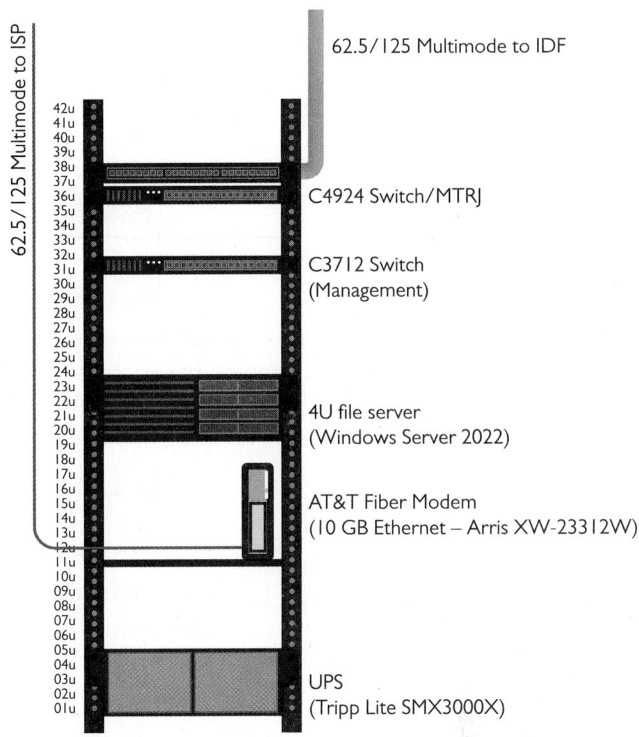

• **Figure 16.16** Basic MDF layout

Logical Network Diagrams

Essential network documentation includes **logical network diagrams**, line drawings that show the connectivity among the many devices in the network. Figure 16.17 shows the server farm portion of the WLC data center. Accompanying the logical drawing would be pages of additional documentation, including specific wiring standards used, vendor information, and so on.

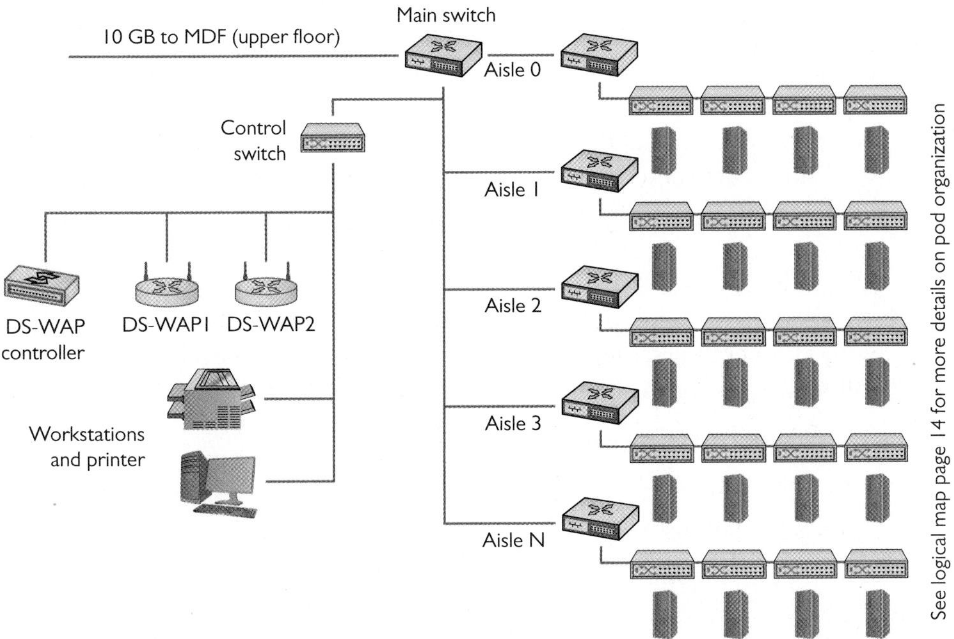

• **Figure 16.17** Logical network diagram showing the WLC data center server farm

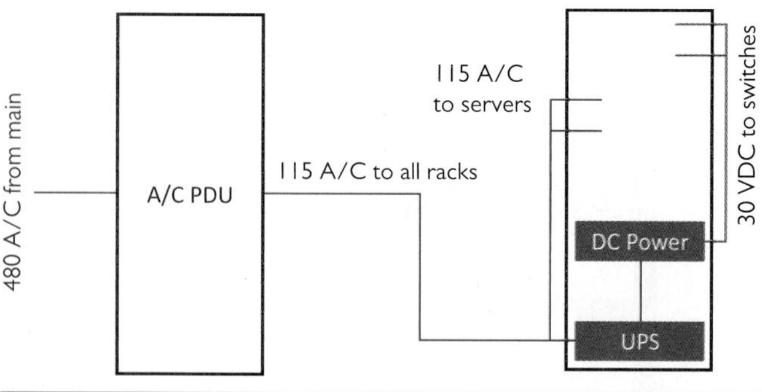

• **Figure 16.18** Wiring diagram showing the electrical components and connections in the server farm of the WLC data center

This definition of baseline configuration reflects the best practices outlined in NIST Special Publication 800-128, *Guide for Security-Focused Configuration Management of Information Systems.*

Wiring Diagrams

Wiring diagrams can show any number of types of wiring, from the full electrical map in Figure 16.18 to a detailed layout of the physical space with drops to each workstation and full cable runs. Wiring diagrams and the detailed additional documents provide absolutely essential network documentation for the data center.

Baseline Configurations

Once the data center is up and running and efficiently humming along, the **baseline configuration** documents all the components of the data center. Note that this is a *network baseline* rather than a *performance baseline*—the latter examines throughput, bandwidth, and the like. A *baseline configuration* describes all the pieces, including portable computers, servers, switches, routers, and so on, plus all the software packages installed on everything. The baseline configuration also includes network topology and placement of devices in the organization.

The baseline configuration provides the foundation for future upgrades. When any upgrades happen, the organization should update the baseline configuration documentation to the new baseline.

Assessments

Periodically, every data center should be assessed for overall efficiency and effectiveness. Is every component performing up to expectations? Does the current performance meet the goals of the organization? Is everything in the network in compliance with current national or international laws and regulations?

The assessments can be conducted by an external party or an internal division. The benefit of the former is that an external party has no preconceptions or bias toward any specific system or individuals (in theory). The benefit of the latter is that an internal division has much more familiarity with how data center operations are supposed to work to accomplish the organization's goals.

Site Surveys

A periodic **site survey** queries everything about the data center. This starts with an overall assessment and then drills down into each category. The following categories should be included in the **site survey report**:

- Layout and space utilization
- Infrastructure installed
- Expectations for the organization
- Future requirements
- Concerns about current performance

Drilling down, inspections should cover exhaustive details. For layout and space utilization, for example, examiners should inspect, and create detailed reports that include, at least the following:

- General layout
- Space utilization
- Thermal management
- Electrical distribution
- Cabling types and paths
- Racks, cabinets, server locations
- Labeling compliance with ANSI/TIA 606-C

Every category examined by the site survey team would get equally granular into aspects pertaining to that category.

The site survey final documentation—the **site survey report**—provides not only a picture of the current state of the data center, but also recommendations for improvements in any number of areas. The site survey is an essential piece of data center maintenance and development.

Audit and Assessment Reports

Annually at least, a data center should have a thorough **audit** that assesses compliance with every applicable law and regulation for the industry. This audit should be conducted by an outside organization that specializes in auditing, to avoid any potential conflict of interest or bias. The laws and regulations that almost certainly apply include the following:

- **ISO 27001** Standard that helps organizations manage and secure assets by making and implementing an information security management system (ISMS). An ISMS enables organizations to categorize and organize their many security controls—measures put in place to lock down the many systems employed.
- **ISO 27002** Standard that helps organizations manage security policies on every level.
- **Health Insurance Portability and Accountability Act (HIPAA)** U.S. federal law that regulates how organizations manage health information data to protect the privacy of individuals and other entities.
- **Payment Card Industry Data Security Standard (PCI DSS)** Standard for protecting credit card and other financial information exchanged between the organization and outside entities. The data center absolutely needs to be PCI DSS compliant.

The standards mentioned here are the tip of the iceberg when it comes to the laws and regulations governing organizations such as data centers. The highly detailed and technical nature of each of these laws and regulations makes yet another compelling case for using an outside firm to do the audit. At the end of an audit, the auditing firm produces an **assessment report** that details all findings and recommendations for upgrades, fixes for compliance, and so on.

Chapter 16 Review

Chapter Summary

After reading this chapter and completing the exercises, you should understand the following about data centers.

Describe classic data center architecture and design

- A data center is a networked group of servers in a dedicated space that provides data storage, Web hosting, application hosting, cloud services, and more, to remote client organizations. A data center can be co-located at the same facility as the users it supports, which is common in smaller organizations, or it can be a separate, dedicated building, which is common in larger, geographically dispersed organizations. Clients connect through Ethernet, MPLS, or SD-WAN technologies.
- Traditional data centers use a three-tiered architecture. The *access layer* provides connectivity between the data center and users. The *distribution layer* interconnects racks of servers and other rack-mounted gear through top-of-rack switching. The *core layer* ties together all the switches at the distribution layer and acts as the point of connection to the external connections, including the Internet.
- Traffic flows in the data center run north-south, describing data moving into and out of the data center, or they run east-west, describing data moving between systems in the data center.
- Data center data storage relies on storage area networks (SANs), pools of mass storage devices that present as any number of logical disks or virtual disks. SANs typically rely on Fibre Channel or iSCSI technology for interconnectivity. SANs use multipathing, redundant controllers and power supplies, and shared memory to provide high availability.

Describe modern data center architecture and design

- Modern data center design leverages advances in virtualization and software-defined networking (SDN) to replace the distribution layer common in the three-tiered network design with a virtualized mesh network. This produces a two-tiered spine-and-leaf model that reduces both the number of machines and the complexity of connectivity. Spine-and-leaf architecture handles east-west traffic with ease.
- Spine-and-leaf architecture uses protocols such as Equal-Cost Multipath (ECPM) to provide load balancing across the paths. Additionally, adding capacity is a matter of adding and connecting spine or leaf switches.

Explain high availability concepts and procedures

- Data centers are designed to withstand problems through various redundant and backup systems for all critical functions. High availability (HA) implementations ensure reliable uptime.
- Load balancing uses multiple systems to share the work to ensure high availability of a specific resource. Server clusters with load balancers that appear as a single unit are one example. Spine-and-leaf use of protocols like Equal-Cost Multipath (ECPM) for balancing the load among the spine and leaf connections is another example.
- Redundancy ensures HA through additional equipment and connection options. Routers using failover protocols, such as the router grouping protocols VRRP and HSRP, are a great example. Use of multiple Internet service providers, especially with path diversity, likewise provides redundancy and high availability.

- Data centers ensure HA and disaster recovery through proper support for facilities and infrastructure, which means ensuring proper power, clean cool air for components, and emergency procedures are in place.
- Power for rack-mounted gear is supplied by sufficient juice from the local power grid or backup generators. Racks uses power distribution units (PDUs) connected to uninterruptible power supplies (UPSs) for powering specific gear.
- Properly set up and maintained heating, ventilation, and air conditioning (HVAC) systems keep systems and components cool and dry. Fire suppression systems keep them from cooking.
- Emergency procedures keep people safe; everything else is replaceable, after all. Having exit plans in place and emergency alert systems mitigate loss in a disaster event.

Explain best practices for documentation in the data center

- Data center documentation covers every aspect of the data center operations, including layout, hardware, electrical, HVAC systems, internal and external personnel, and more. Physical and logical network diagrams map out hardware and connectivity among the various components of the data center. These include floor plans, rack diagrams, IDF/MDF layouts, and wiring diagrams.
- A baseline configuration describes all the hardware and software currently in use in the data center. Changes over time should be reflected in updated baseline configurations, because the configuration has new components.
- Annual assessments, generally performed by external specialist companies, help ensure the organization's compliance with all laws and regulations pertinent to that organization's operation. Audits produce assessment reports that can in turn be used as roadmaps to upgrades, fixes, and so on.

Key Terms

access layer *(464)*
assessment report *(477)*
audit *(477)*
baseline configuration *(476)*
branch office *(468)*
clustering *(470)*
co-location *(468)*
core layer *(465)*
data center *(463)*
distribution layer *(465)*
east-west traffic *(465)*
emergency alert system *(472)*
emergency procedures *(472)*
exit plan *(472)*
Fibre Channel (FC) *(467)*
fire suppression system *(472)*
Gateway Load Balancing Protocol (GLBP) *(470)*
heating, ventilation, and air conditioning (HVAC) *(471)*
high availability (HA) *(469)*
Hot Standby Router Protocol (HSRP) *(470)*
intermediate distribution frame (IDF) *(474)*
Internet Small Computer System Interface (iSCSI) *(467)*
jumbo frame *(467)*
load balancing *(470)*
logical network diagram *(475)*
main distribution frame (MDF) *(474)*

module *(465)*
multipathing *(467)*
network operations center (NOC) *(474)*
north-south traffic *(465)*
on-premises data center *(468)*
path diversity *(471)*
pod *(465)*
power distribution unit (PDU) *(471)*
power generator *(471)*
rack diagram *(474)*
redundancy *(470)*
server farm *(474)*
site survey *(476)*
site survey report *(476)*
spine-and-leaf architecture *(469)*
storage area network (SAN) *(466)*
three-tiered architecture *(464)*
top-of-rack switching *(464)*
uninterruptible power supply (UPS) *(471)*
virtual disk *(467)*
Virtual Router Redundancy Protocol (VRRP) *(470)*
Wiring diagrams *(476)*

Key Term Quiz

Use the Key Terms list to complete the sentences that follow. Not all the terms will be used.

1. The ________________ acts as the primary connection between the data center connectivity and the users.
2. Each group of computers connected to the same access switch is known as a(n) ___________.
3. In a three-tiered architecture, the _____________ is the connection between the access layer and the core layer.
4. ________________ flow describes data going into and out of the data center.
5. A(n) _______________ is a network that connects individual systems to a centralized bank of mass storage.
6. In a(n) __________________ data center, a virtualized mesh network interconnects the switches.
7. _______________ is the concept designed to ensure systems keep working without interruption or downtime.
8. The open standard ____________________ enables multiple routers to appear with a single virtual IP address as a default gateway.
9. A(n) ______________________ is a line drawing showing connectivity among the many devices in the network.
10. An auditing firm produces a(n) ____________________ that details all finding about an organization's compliance with laws, rules, and regulations.

Multiple-Choice Quiz

1. Which of the following data center implementations connects the access and core layers through the distribution layer?
   A. North-south traffic flow
   B. Spine-and-leaf architecture
   C. Three-tiered architecture
   D. Top-of-rack switching

2. Which SAN feature provides high availability through more than one connection between the server and the SAN?
   A. Fibre Channel
   B. iSCSI
   C. Multipathing
   D. Multiplaning

3. Blackwell Held, LLC, leases space in the Wapi Lava Corporation's data center. Which term describes this type of scenario?
   A. Branch office
   B. Co-location
   C. Leased-line
   D. On-premises

4. Which of the following protocols provides load balancing in a spine-and-leaf data center?
   A. ECPM
   B. HSRP
   C. STP
   D. VRRP

5. Joan's data center has two ISPs, one fiber and one cable. What aspect of security does this represent?
   A. Active-active
   B. Clustering
   C. Multipathing
   D. Redundancy

6. Which open standard protocol enables redundant routers to appear as a single router for high availability?
   A. HSRP
   B. RRPX
   C. VRRP
   D. XRRP

7. Brenda wants to add a second ISP to her small data center for high availability. What should she consider?
   A. Fiber
   B. Multipath
   C. Multitenancy
   D. Path diversity

8. Which device provides multiple electrical outlets conveniently located on a rack?
   A. Power generator
   B. PDF
   C. PDU
   D. Surge suppressor

9. Which of the following provides the most power redundancy?
   A. Power generator
   B. PDF
   C. PDU
   D. UPS
10. Brad and Stacy are arguing over the HVAC settings in the server farm. Brad says the temperature should stay at 68 degrees Fahrenheit. Stacy claims the humidity has to stay around 50 percent. Who's right?
   A. Only Brad is correct.
   B. Only Stacy is correct.
   C. Both Brad and Stacy are correct.
   D. Neither Brad nor Stacy is correct.
11. Stacy has the door installed for the server room to open in case of emergency. What is this feature?
   A. Emergency alert system
   B. Exit plan
   C. Fail closed
   D. Fail open
12. Which of the following documentation includes dimensions and locations of rooms plus the physical objects—racks, raised floors, AC units, and so on—in the space?
   A. Floor plan
   B. Logical network diagram
   C. Rack diagram
   D. System diagram
13. Which document contains details about all the hardware and software installed in a data center and provides the foundation for future upgrades?
   A. Baseline configuration
   B. Logical network diagram
   C. Performance baseline
   D. System diagram
14. Which documentation would contain information about the demarc?
   A. Baseline configuration
   B. IDF documentation
   C. MDF documentation
   D. Rack diagram
15. Which of the following is a review of an organization's compliance with applicable laws, rules, and regulations?
   A. Audit
   B. Baseline configuration
   C. Performance baseline
   D. Site survey

Essay Quiz

1. Your boss has decided that the company needs a small data center. Write a short essay describing three to five essential aspects of the new data center and back up your arguments with some examples or details.

Lab Project

• Lab Project 16.1

Get access (with permission!) to any kind of rack-mounted gear and analyze (but don't touch) the components. What kind of servers are there? What about switches? Are the latter at the top of the rack? Does the rack connect with other racks? Does the rack have a dedicated UPS? What about a PDU?

Integrating Network Devices

"The currency of real networking is not greed but generosity."

—Keith Ferrazzi

In this chapter, you will learn how to

- Explain the Internet of Things
- Describe unified communication features and functions
- Describe the function and major components of an ICS/SCADA network

Thus far, the book has discussed classic networks small and big, with clients connected via wires or wireless to switches, LANs, servers, routers, and WANs. This chapter explores all the other networked devices and systems you'll find in modern homes and businesses. CompTIA Network+ exam objective 2.1 lumps together devices as varied as networked printers and industrial control systems, so here's a (somewhat realistic) scenario to make discussing them all together here.

The Bayland Widgets Corporation (BWC) makes widgets at its campus of three buildings, networked together to form a **campus area network (CAN)**, shown in Figure 17.1. One building is the commercial office, where the sales and managerial staffs operate. The second is a factory space for building the new widget. The final building is the warehouse and shipping facility.

Cross Check

MAN

We talked about another network type way back in Chapter 13, so check your knowledge here. What is a MAN? How does it differ from the CAN described here?

The commercial space houses the primary servers, but a fiber-based network connects all three buildings, all of which have communications equipment installed. Plus, the factory and warehouse have robots and other mechanical systems that need computer-based controls.

As a kind of mass experiment, management decided at the beginning of the year that all employees should work from home for a year and a half, with intermittent solo office visits. This has created a challenge for the typical employee, but not as much for the techs who run the factory.

Emily, a top BWC performer, has adjusted well to working from home. She upgraded her home to include many network- and Internet-based features, including home automation devices, a faster Internet connection, and various mobile devices such as a smartwatch and upgraded smartphone.

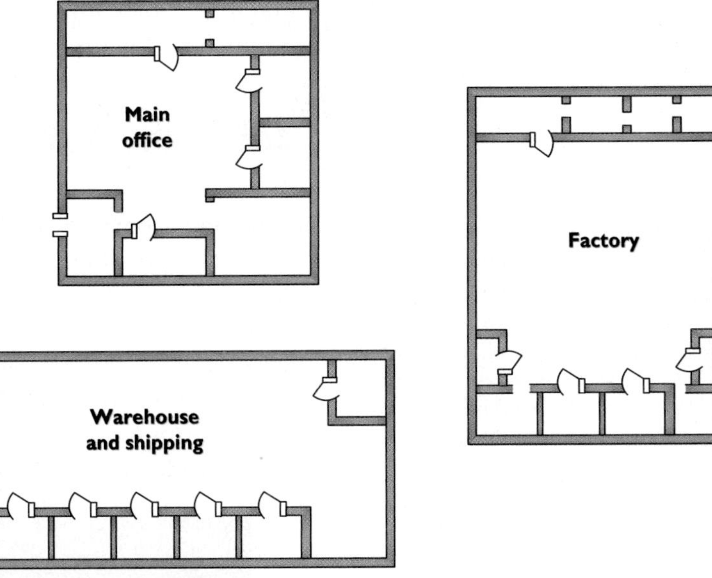

• **Figure 17.1** The BWC campus

Emily is working at the office a couple of days a week, but all that integration with her home devices doesn't stop at her office door. Her smart doorbell and wireless cameras let her know when packages arrive from Amazon or FedEx. She can interact with the delivery people remotely. She can monitor and control the temperature in her house with her smartphone from anywhere.

The other half of the scenario explores the steps BWC has taken to improve and maintain the production facilities on its campus. Because of the robust automation and remote management tools already in place before the work-from-home mandate came through, the techs simply shifted to home systems and connected to the office via virtual private networking (VPN).

This chapter explores the current scene at the BWC campus, including how Emily and her coworkers interact with personal Internet-connected devices at the office. The campus design includes unified communications features and functions. The chapter finishes by exploring the functions and major components of BWC's ICS/SCADA network.

Parts of this chapter cover topics that relate to exam-specific content but go outside the current scope of the Network+ N10-008 exam objectives. The pandemic that struck the world in 2020 fundamentally altered many of the ways in which people do business, bringing things like unified communication and video teleconferencing out of the shadows and into everybody's home office space. As a network tech, you need to know these topics to support modern networking needs.

Test Specific

Internet of Things

Marketing geniuses came up with the term **Internet of Things (IoT)** to describe the huge variety of devices you can access and control via the Internet (discounting personal computers, routers, and servers) and devices that connect directly to Internet resources. The term applies to lights you can turn on or off by using an app on your smartphone, air conditioning systems that you can monitor and control from a PC, and devices that can query the Internet for information. This section looks at *personal IoT* devices, like Emily has at her home.

IoT Home Automation

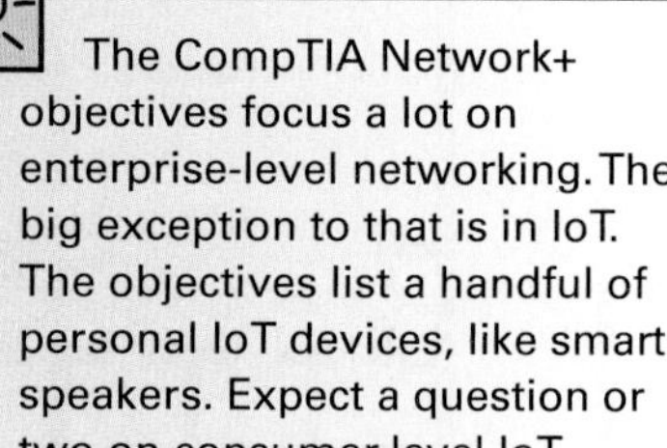

The CompTIA Network+ objectives focus a lot on enterprise-level networking. The big exception to that is in IoT. The objectives list a handful of personal IoT devices, like smart speakers. Expect a question or two on consumer-level IoT.

IoT technologies enable you to integrate a surprising variety of devices into a home automation system that you can control. (And they're all called "smart" to distinguish them from their "dumb" unconnectable siblings.) You can control smart bulbs to change the lighting in your house. You can access smart refrigerators on your drive home from the office to check levels of milk or bread. Smart thermostats enable you to vary the temperature in your home (Figure 17.2). If Emily is working on the premises of BWC and a sudden cold snap comes in, with a quick app access, she can flip the heater on in her house so that it's nice and cozy when she gets home.

• **Figure 17.2** Smart thermostat

• **Figure 17.3** Smart speaker

Many smart systems, like the Amazon Echo products, can connect to the music library of your choice, and you can sprinkle smart speakers throughout your home to give you a seamless soundtrack for your life (Figure 17.3). Integrated home audio systems used to require extensive wiring and power considerations for speakers, plus a central control area. Smart speakers handle voice commands and interconnect wirelessly.

Many IoT devices can connect directly to Internet resources to answer questions. The Amazon Echo Show pictured in Figure 17.4, for example, will answer the burning questions of the day, such as "Alexa, when was Miley Cyrus born?" and general important information, such as "Alexa, show me a recipe for chocolate chip cookies." (By default, Amazon devices respond to the name "Alexa," similarly to how Google devices respond to "OK Google" and Apple devices to "Hey, Siri!") Figure 17.4 shows a response to the second command.

Smart printers or *multifunction devices (MFDs)* connect directly to the Internet, not so much to control efficient communication but to enable it.

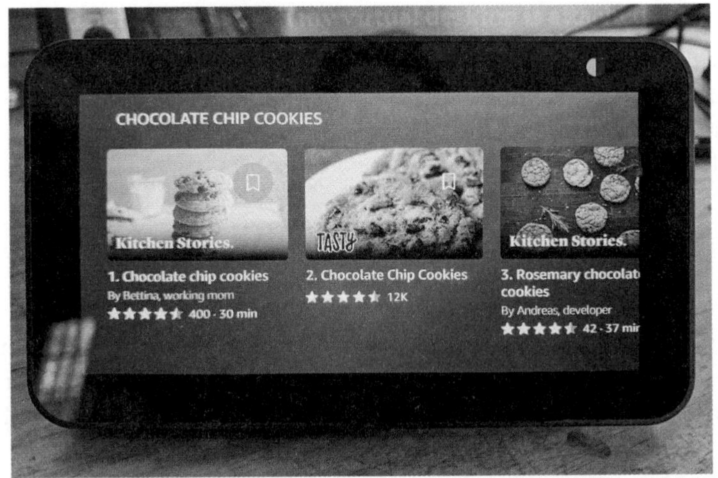

• **Figure 17.4** Amazon Echo Show responding to a command

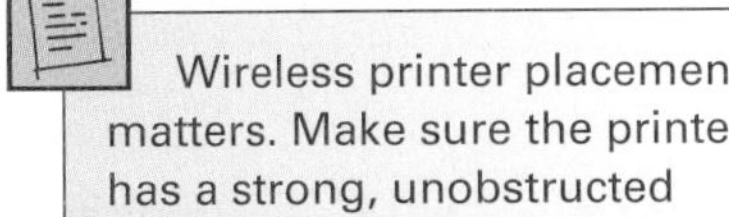

Wireless printer placement matters. Make sure the printer has a strong, unobstructed connection to the nearest WAP.

You can print from a smartphone directly, for example, via AirPrint (on Apple iOS devices, like iPhones and iPads). You can scan a document, save it as an Adobe Postscript file (PDF), and immediately upload it to an Internet location, from the print device.

Smart garage door openers enable you to open or close the garage door from an app. Normally you'd use the app in a local setting, like in the old dark days. But in a pinch, you can monitor, open, and close the door for a delivery that you wouldn't want left on the front porch, for example. A smart garage door opener is an example of a *physical access control device* installed at a house.

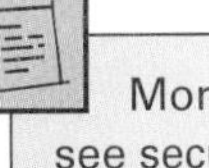

More commonly you'll see security gates, door locks, turnstiles, and such described as examples of physical access control devices.

IoT Home Security

IoT makes setting up and monitoring a robust home security system very simple. The Ring system from Amazon, for example, can be configured with any number of wireless cameras with motion sensors to automatically record movement—and can tell the difference between a squirrel and a person! You can add the Ring smart doorbell, which comes with a bell button, naturally, and a camera, microphone, and speaker (Figure 17.5). This enables you to "answer the door" and interact with visitors without being there in person. Many companies make IoT security systems.

• **Figure 17.5** Ring smart doorbell

IoT Communications Technologies

Using wireless technology for personal IoT such as home automation has many challenges. First is the huge number of IoT devices that a modern home might potentially use, from thermostats to washing machines to power outlets and light bulbs. Second, homes, unlike offices, are filled with small rooms, narrow staircases, and other obstacles that make regular radio-based wireless difficult.

Zigbee and Z-Wave

IoT developers have come up with many protocols to create a mesh network of many low-powered devices. The open source **Zigbee** protocol, for example, supports over 64,000 devices at either the 2.4-GHz or 915-MHz band. The proprietary **Z-Wave** protocol supports a mere 232 devices, but operates at the 908- and 916-MHz band.

Wi-Fi

802.11 Wi-Fi certainly plays a role in IoT communications. The base station of an IoT system often connects to a Wi-Fi network to get on the Internet. Amazon Echo devices, for example, can connect to Wi-Fi (or Ethernet) to access the Amazon servers for information, streaming, and so on. But the devices communicate among themselves via a Zigbee mesh.

Wi-Fi also comes into play with enterprise IoT, where manufacturers are happy not to worry about power consumption when the trade-off is much higher speed. Also, Wi-Fi 6 was developed with IoT in mind, so it will undoubtedly make inroads into the IoT space.

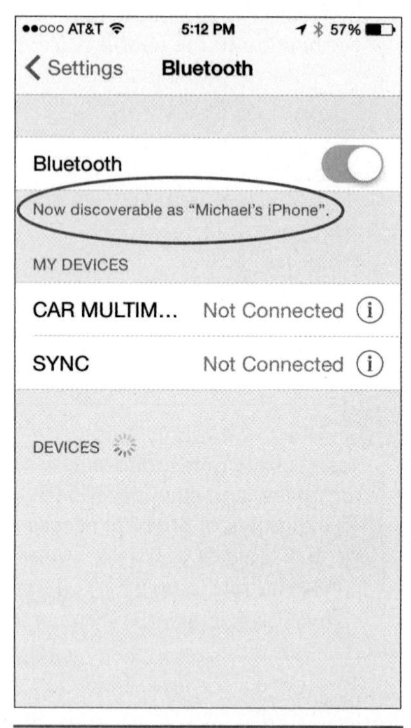

• **Figure 17.6** Setting up discoverable mode

Bluetooth

Bluetooth, that wonderful technology that connects headsets to smartphones and connects keyboards to laptops, is a wireless networking protocol developed to simplify connections between devices. You bring two Bluetooth-aware devices into close proximity, perform a quick pairing between the two, and they connect and work. Connected Bluetooth devices create a **personal area network (PAN)**, and security concerns apply to all the devices and communication within that PAN.

Bluetooth has two important tools to make using it more secure. First, all of today's Bluetooth devices are not visible unless they are manually set to *discovery* or *discoverable mode*. If you have a Bluetooth headset and you want to pair it to your smartphone, there is some place on the phone where you turn on this mode, as shown in Figure 17.6.

The beauty of discoverable mode is that you have a limited amount of time to make the connection, usually two minutes, before the device automatically turns it off and once again the device is no longer visible. Granted, there is radio communication between the two paired devices that can be accessed by powerful, sophisticated Bluetooth sniffers, but these sniffers are expensive and difficult to purchase, and are only of interest to law enforcement and very nerdy people.

> Some devices that use Bluetooth don't require a PIN. Bluetooth speakers, for example, offer no security risk so they automatically pair.

The second tool is the requirement of using a personal identification number (PIN) during the pairing process. When one device initiates a discoverable Bluetooth device, the other device sees the request and generates a PIN (of four, six, or eight numbers, depending on the device). The first device must then enter that code and the pairing takes place.

Bluetooth in IoT—including in every automobile infotainment system these days, it seems—offers two very different protocols for connectivity. The older, standard Bluetooth offers great range and speeds but uses a lot (relatively) of power to run. Newer IoT devices tap into **Bluetooth Low Energy (BLE)** networking technology introduced with Bluetooth 4.0 and carried over into current Bluetooth 5 devices. BLE, as the name implies, uses a lot less electricity than its predecessor. BLE runs at the same 2.4-GHz radio frequency as Bluetooth classic, but uses different modulation (so devices designed for one standard cannot work with the other standard).

Hardening IoT Devices

Hardening IoT devices decreases the danger of loss or downtime on the devices and increases the protection of personal information and company data. Generally, hardening means to keep the devices current (software and firmware), use physical security precautions, and apply internal security options.

Consider a scenario in which an organization uses many 802.11 PTZ (pan/tilt/zoom) cameras to monitor secure areas throughout three locations. These cameras are on the one and only SSID in each location. Each SSID uses WPA2 PSK encryption. Due to location, these cameras must use 802.11 for communication. All cameras must be accessible not only in each location but also in headquarters. Your job as a consultant is to provide a list of actions the organization should take to harden these cameras. Here's a list of actions you should consider:

- Limit physical access to the cameras.
- Place all cameras in their own SSID.
- Put all the camera feeds on their own VLAN.
- Use a very long pre-shared key (PSK).
- Set up routine queries for camera firmware updates from the manufacturer.
- Use username ACLs to determine who may access the cameras.

Expect a question on the CompTIA Network+ exam that explores *IoT access considerations*. Such considerations should be limiting physical access and restricting network access.

The CompTIA Network+ objectives spell out VoIP phone, so *Voice over Internet Protocol (VoIP) phone*. Expect a question or two on VoIP technologies.

Unified Communication

Some years ago, TCP/IP-based communications began to replace the traditional PBX-style phone systems in most organizations. This switch enabled companies to minimize wire installation and enabled developers to get more creative with the gear. Technologies such as **Voice over IP (VoIP)** made it possible to communicate by voice right over an IP network, even one as big as the Internet. Today, TCP/IP communications encompass a range of technologies, including voice, video, and messaging. On the cutting edge (led by Cisco) is the field of **unified communication (UC)**. Bayland Widgets implements UC throughout its CAN.

It Started with VoIP

Early VoIP systems usually required multiple cables running to each drop to accommodate the various services offered. Figure 17.7 shows a typical workstation drop for a **VoIP phone** that connects via two RJ-45 connections, one for data and the other exclusively for VoIP.

• **Figure 17.7** Workstation drop

Many VoIP systems, such as Skype, are complete Internet services that rely on nothing more than software installed on computers and the computers' microphone/speakers. All of the interconnections to the PSTN are handled in the cloud. While very popular for individuals, these systems, called **unified voice services**, were often considered unacceptable in office environments where people wanted a more classic "phone experience."

The CompTIA Network+ objectives list SIP ports 5060 and 5061 without mentioning TCP, UDP, or TLS. RTP is not mentioned in the objectives at all.

These drops would often even go to their own separate switches, and from there into separate **VoIP gateways** or **voice gateways** that would interface with old-school PBX systems or directly into the telephone network if the latter used **VoIP PBX**. These are the typical purposes and use case scenarios for *computer telephony integration (CTI)*.

Virtually all VoIP systems use the **Real-time Transport Protocol (RTP)**, as well as the **Session Initiation Protocol (SIP)**. Because CompTIA typically throws in questions about port numbers, here's the scoop on both. RTP uses UDP, but doesn't have a hard-and-fast port. Many applications use the Internet Engineering Task Force (IETF) recommendations of ports 6970 to 6999. SIP uses TCP or UDP ports 5060 and 5061, with the latter for encrypted traffic over Transport Layer Security (TLS).

This first-generation VoIP setup that required a separate wired network gave people pause. There really wasn't a critical need for physical separation of the data and the VoIP network, nor did these early VoIP systems handle video conferencing and text messaging. This prompted Cisco to develop and market its Unified Communications family of products.

Unified Communication Features

Of course, VoIP isn't the only communications game in town. As organizations were implementing VoIP, they realized a number of additional communications tasks would benefit from centralized management. Enter unified communication, which adds various additional services to the now-classic VoIP. These services include

- Presence information
- Video conferencing/real-time video
- Fax
- Messaging
- Collaboration tools/workflow

Along with some other real-time communication-oriented tools, these are categorized as *real-time services (RTS)*.

• **Figure 17.8** Presence at work

Most of these services should be fairly self-explanatory, but I'd like to elaborate on two of them. *Presence information services* simply refers to technologies that enable users to show they are present for some form of communication. Think of presence as a type of flag that tells others that you are present and capable of accepting other forms of communication (such as a video conference). See Figure 17.8.

Video teleconferencing (VTC) enables people to communicate via voice and video simultaneously over an IP network. Done with high-quality gear and a high-speed network, VTC simulates face-to-face meetings. **Real-time video** technologies attempt to make delays in reception imperceptible. Networks across the globe have embraced VTC and real-time video through platforms such as Zoom and GoToMeeting to make meetings possible and avoid direct physical interaction.

UC Network Components

A classic UC network consists of three core components: UC devices, UC servers, and UC gateways. Let's take a quick peek at each of these.

A **UC device** is what we used to call the VoIP telephone. In a well-developed UC environment, the UC device handles voice, video, and more (Figure 17.9).

A **UC server** is typically a dedicated box that supports any UC-provided service. In small organizations this might be a single box, but in larger organizations there will be many UC servers. UC servers connect directly to every UC device on the LAN. It's not uncommon to see all the UC servers (as well as the rest of the UC devices) on a separate VLAN.

A **UC gateway** is an edge device, sometimes dedicated but often nothing more than a few extra services added to an existing edge router. That router interfaces with remote UC gateways as well as with PSTN systems and services.

• **Figure 17.9** Cisco Unified IP Phone

UC Protocols

Unified communication leans heavily on SIP and RTP protocols but can also use H.323 or MGCP. **H.323** is the most commonly used video presentation protocol (or *codec*), and it runs on TCP port 1720. **Media Gateway Control Protocol (MGCP)** is designed from the ground up to be a complete VoIP or video presentation connection and session controller; in essence, it takes over all the work from VoIP the SIP protocol used to do and all the work from video presentation done by H.323. MGCP uses TCP ports 2427 and 2727.

The CompTIA Network+ exam might ask about VoIP endpoints. These are defined as the client and server machines and can be software or hardware.

Several companies offer cloud-based IC management solutions that use SIP to provide services. Called *SIP trunking*, the service can connect PBX systems from multiple locations seamlessly over the Internet via virtual connections called *SIP trunks*.

VTC and Medianets

All forms of communication over IP networks have some degree of sensitivity to disruption and slowdowns, but video teleconferencing is particularly susceptible. No one wants to sit in on a video conference that continually stops and jitters due to a poor or slow Internet connection. Medianets help to eliminate or reduce this problem. A **medianet** is a network of (typically) far-flung routers and servers that provide—via *quality of service (QoS)* and other tools—sufficient bandwidth for VTC. Plus, medianets work with UC servers (or sometimes by themselves) to distribute video conferences.

Medianets can be wildly complex or very simple. A medianet could be two gateway routers with enough QoS smarts to open bandwidth for active VTCs as soon as they are detected. A medianet could be a huge multinational company with its own group of high-powered edge routers, spanning the globe with an MPLS-based VLAN, working with UC servers to support tens of thousands of voice and video conversations going on continually throughout its organization.

Medianets are all about the quality of service. But this isn't the simple QoS that you learned about back in Chapter 11. VTC is the ultimate real-time application and it needs a level of QoS for performance that very few other applications need.

Be sure to remember all your TCP port numbers for the different VoIP/UC protocols!

- RTP uses UDP, often the IETF-recommended ports 6970 to 6999.
- SIP uses TCP or UDP ports 5060 and 5061.
- H.323 uses TCP port 1720.
- MGCP uses ports 2427 and 2727.

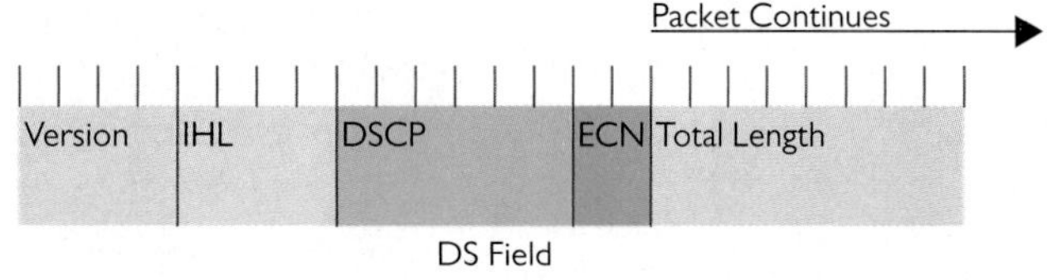

• **Figure 17.10** DS field

When we talk about QoS for medianets, we need to develop the concept of **differentiated services (DiffServ)**. DiffServ is the underlying architecture that makes all the QoS stuff work. The cornerstone of DiffServ is two pieces of data that go into every IP header on every piece of data: DSCP and ECN. DSCP stands for *differentiated services code point* and ECN stands for *explicit congestion notification*. These two comprise the differentiated services (DS) field (Figure 17.10).

The first six bits are DSCP, making a total of eight classes of service. A **class of service (CoS)** is just a value you may use (think of it like a group) to apply to services, ports, or whatever your QoS device might use. Figure 17.11 shows a sample from my home router. My router has four QoS priority queues and I can assign a CoS to every port.

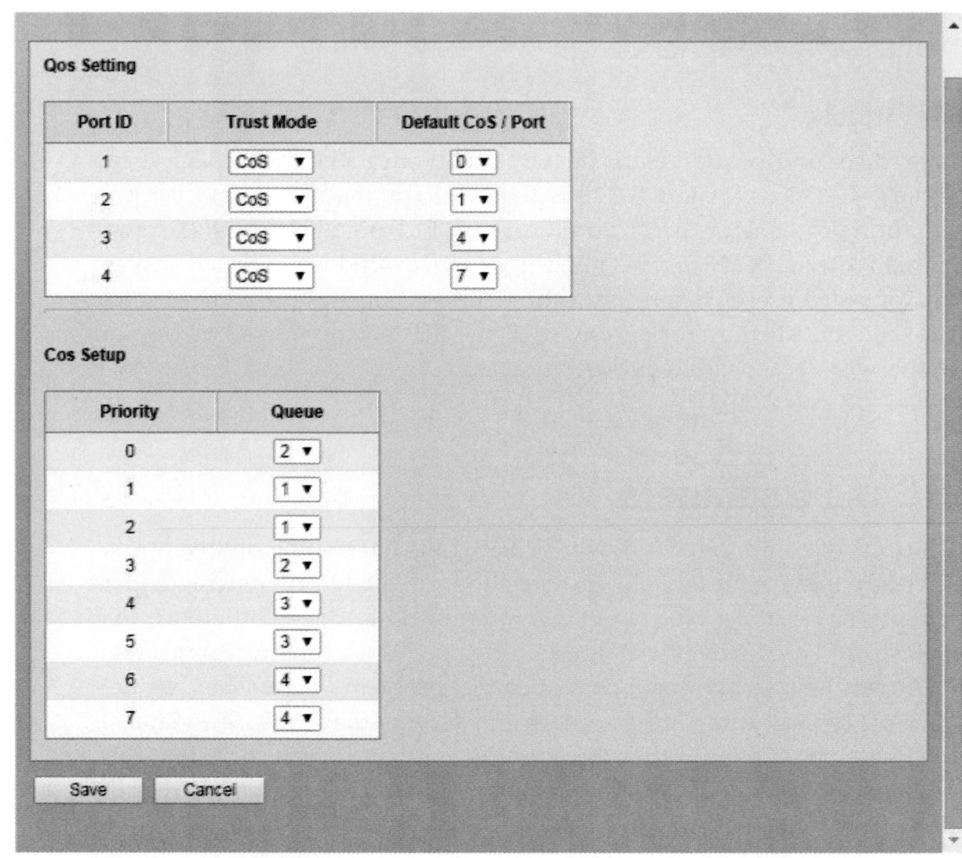

• **Figure 17.11** CoS settings on router

ECN is a 2-bit field where QoS-aware devices can place a "congestion encountered" signal to other QoS-aware devices. The following four values may show in that field:

- **00** Not QoS aware (default)
- **01** QoS aware, no congestion
- **10** QoS aware, no congestion (same as 01)
- **11** QoS aware, congestion encountered

UCaaS

Unified communication as a service (UCaaS) bundles up most (if not all) of an organization's communication needs—things like calls, meetings, messaging, and more—in a single service. For the most part, users communicate through an app they install on their computer or smartphone (though the service can reach beyond this—it might forward calls to regular phone lines, provide VoIP service, or send faxes). The heavy lifting happens on remote servers in the cloud, and UCaaS providers enable companies to subscribe to their services.

Zoom, WebEx by Cisco, and Microsoft Teams are all examples of UCaaS that integrate multiple kinds of real-time communication. These services typically integrate with whatever collaboration and productivity suite your company uses. Some of the big draws for organizations are predictable per-user licensing costs and getting rid of in-house communication servers. Figure 17.12 shows the Teams management interface where you can manage users and app integrations, view usage statistics, and more.

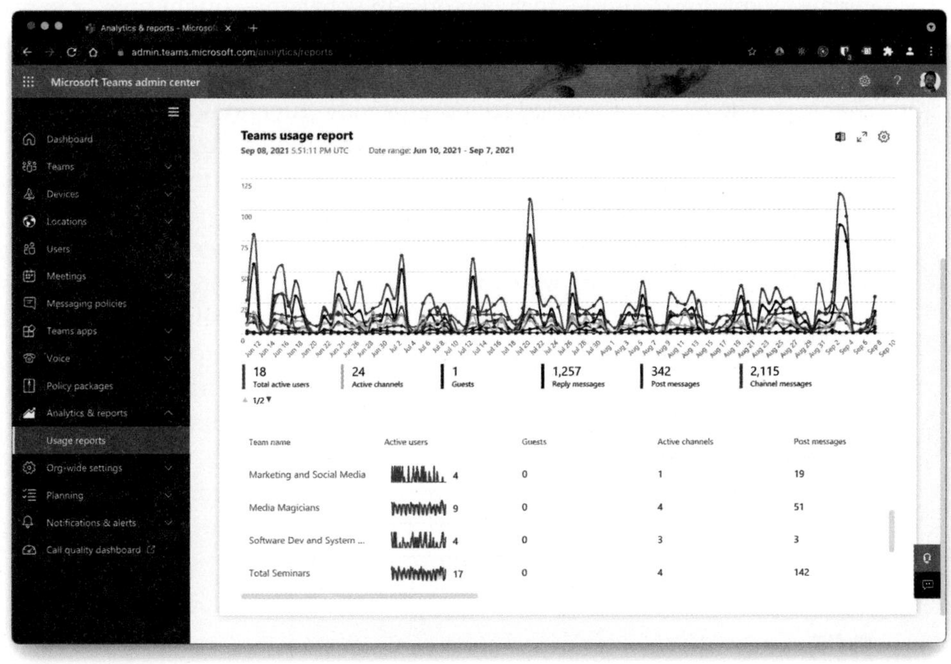

• **Figure 17.12** Microsoft Teams management interface showing usage statistics

ICS

Pretty much any industry that makes things, changes things, or moves things is filled with equipment to do the jobs that have to be done. From making mousetraps to ice cream, any given industrial plant, power grid, or pipeline is filled with stuff that needs to be monitored and stuff that needs to be controlled.

Here are some examples of things to monitor:

- Temperature
- Power levels

- Fill quantity
- Illumination
- Mass

And these are some examples of the things to control:

- Heaters
- Voltage
- Pumps
- Retractable roofs
- Valves

For Bayland Widgets, it's all about the robots that control the factory, the machines that help automate packing and shipping, and the air-conditioning controls for both buildings.

In the early days of automation, you might have a single person monitoring a machine that produced something. When the temperature hit a certain point, for example, that person—the **operator**—might open a valve or turn a knob to make changes and keep the machine functioning properly. As machines became more complex, the role of the operator likewise changed. The operator needed to monitor more functions and, sometimes, more machines. Eventually, computers were brought in to help manage the machines. The overall system that monitors and controls machines today is called an **industrial control system (ICS)**.

The ICS isn't a new concept. It's been around for over 100 years using technology such as telescopes and horns to monitor and using mechanisms and pneumatics to control from a distance. But ICSs really started to take off when computers were combined with digital monitors and controls. Over the last few years many ICSs have taken on more and more personal-computer aspects such as Windows- or Linux-based operating systems, Intel-style processors, and specialized PCs. Today, ICS is moving from stand-alone networks to interconnect with the Internet, bringing up serious issues for security. Competent network techs know the basic ICS variations and the components that make up those systems.

DCS

An ICS has three basic components: input/output (I/O) functions on the machine, a controller, and the interface for the operator. Input and output work through sensors and actuators. *Sensors* monitor things like temperature, for example, and the *actuator* makes changes that modify that temperature. The *controller*, some sort of computer, knows enough to manage the process, such as "keep the temperature between 50 and 55 degrees Fahrenheit." The operator watches some kind of monitor—the *interface*—and intervenes if necessary (Figure 17.13). Let's scale this up to a factory and add a little more complexity.

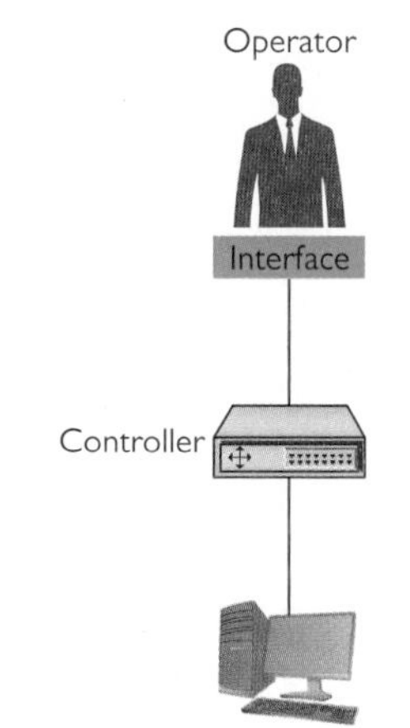

• Figure 17.13 A simple ICS

What if you have multiple machines that accomplish a big task, like in a factory that produces some finished product? The widgets at Bayland Widgets, for example, are produced in stages, with the machine at each stage needing monitoring and control. In the early days of computers, when computers were really expensive, the controller was a single computer.

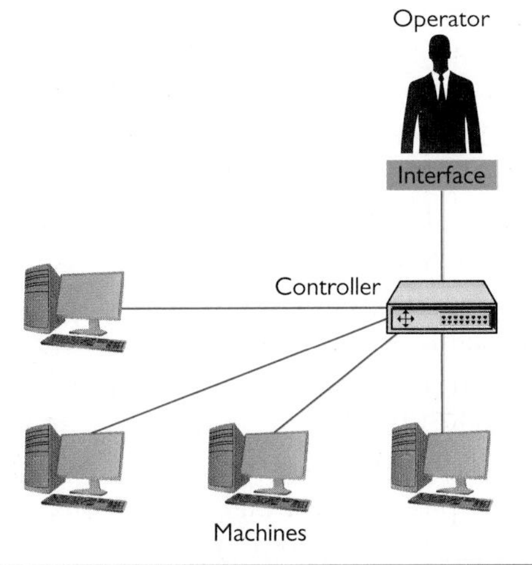

• **Figure 17.14** An early computer-assisted ICS

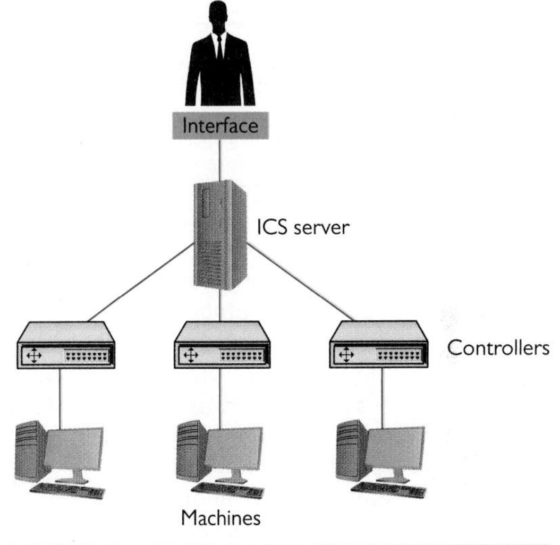

• **Figure 17.15** A simple DCS

All the sensors from each of the machines had to provide feedback to that single controller. The controller would compute and then send signals to the various actuators to change things, managing the process. See Figure 17.14.

As computing power increased and costs decreased, it made much more sense to put smaller controllers directly on each machine, to distribute the computing load. This is a **distributed control system (DCS)**.

In a modern DCS, each of the local controllers connects (eventually) to a centralized controller—called the **ICS server**—where global changes can be managed (Figure 17.15). Operators at the ICS server for Bayland Widgets, for example, could direct the controllers managing the robots to change production from green widgets to blue widgets.

Operators interact with controllers through a control or computer called a **human–machine interface (HMI)**. Early HMIs were usually custom-made boxes with gauges and switches. Today, an HMI is most likely a PC running a custom, touch-screen interface (Figure 17.16). It's important to appreciate that HMIs are not general purpose. You wouldn't run Microsoft Office on an HMI, even if the PC on which it is built is capable of such things. It's very common for an HMI to show a single interface that never changes.

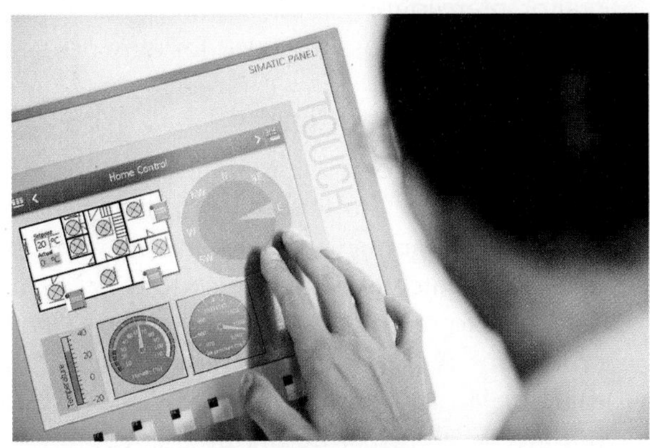

• **Figure 17.16** SIMATIC HMI Basic Panel with a touch screen (© Siemens AG 2014, All rights reserved)

• **Figure 17.17** Siemens SIMATIC S7-1500 PLC (© Siemens AG 2014, All rights reserved)

PLC

A DCS makes sense for a process that requires a continuous flow. The sensors provide real-time feedback to the controllers; the controllers are sophisticated enough to keep the machines functioning properly, making changes via the actuators. In a process that follows specific, ordered steps, in contrast, a different kind of system would make more sense.

A classic **programmable logic controller (PLC)** is a computer that controls a machine according to a set of ordered steps (Figure 17.17). Take for example a machine that produces cakes. Each step in the process of producing a cake follows a certain pattern (add ingredients, mix, bake, etc.) that has to go in order and in the proper timing. The PLC monitors sensors (like timers and oven temperatures) and tells the machine when to do the next step in the process.

ICS predates Ethernet and the TCP/IP protocols, but the predominance of Ethernet and TCP/IP has created a number of ICS solutions that use Ethernet and TCP/IP instead of proprietary cabling systems and communication protocols. If you were going to build an ICS from scratch today, odds are good that you would use Ethernet as your interconnection of choice.

SCADA

A **supervisory control and data acquisition (SCADA)** system is a subset of ICS. Generally, a SCADA system has the same basic components as a DCS, but differs in two very important ways. First, a SCADA system is designed for large-scale, distributed processes such as power grids, pipelines, and railroads. Second, due to the distance involved, a SCADA system must function with the idea that remote devices may or may not have ongoing communication with the central control.

Remote Terminal Unit

In general, a SCADA system is going to be a DCS using servers, HMIs, sensors, and actuators. The big difference is the replacement of controllers with devices called **remote terminal units (RTUs)**. RTUs provide the same function as a controller but have two major differences. First, an RTU is designed to have some amount of autonomy in case it loses connection with the central control. Second, an RTU is designed to take advantage of some form of long-distance communication such as telephony, fiber optic, or cellular WANs (Figure 17.18). As you might imagine, the fear of interception is a big deal with SCADA systems these days, so let's discuss the need for network segmentation.

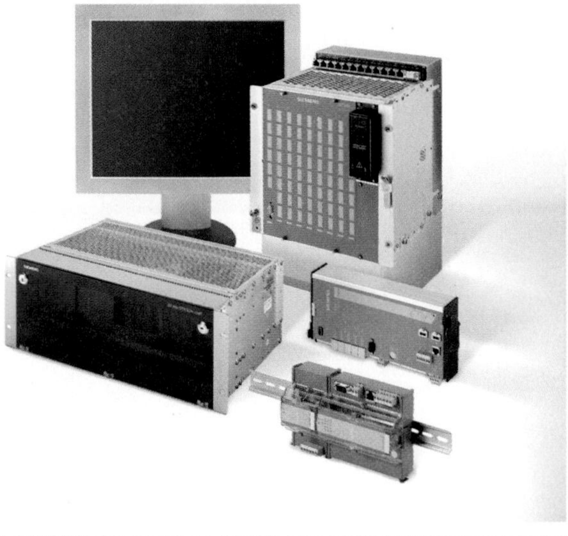

• **Figure 17.18** Substation Automation and RTUs (© Siemens AG 2014, All rights reserved)

Network Segmentation

It's pretty easy to say that a network failure isn't a happy occurrence. On the lowest end, losing your network in your home is going to make someone very unhappy when they can't watch the latest episode of *Bridgerton* on Netflix. Taking it to the other extreme, many ICSs are incredibly crucial for the needs of everyday living. From the DCSs that run an oil refinery to the SCADA systems keeping our electrical infrastructure up and running, the potential downside of a catastrophic failure is far worse than that of missing a show!

Security isn't the only reason we segment networks. We also reduce network congestion and limit network problems through segmentation. We segment to optimize performance. We segment to be in compliance with standards, laws, or best practices. We also segment for easier troubleshooting.

Network segmentation is done for security, performance optimization, load balancing, and compliance.

One of the best tools to help us understand network segmentation is the OSI seven-layer model, in particular the first three layers:

- **Layer 1 (Physical)** Physically separating your network from every other network
- **Layer 2 (Data Link)** Separating a physically connected network into separate broadcast domains (think VLANs here)
- **Layer 3 (Network)** Separating broadcast domains by using different subnets or blocking IP routes
- **Above Layer 3** VPNs, separate SSIDs, separate Windows domains, virtualization

The CompTIA Network+ exam covers a number of situations where network segmentation is important.

Segmentation and Industrial Control Systems

All forms of ICS are by definition closed networks. A *closed network* is any network that strictly controls who and what may connect to it. However, there are two places where we begin to see connectivity. In many SCADA systems, it is very convenient to use public wireless networks to connect RTUs, and, in some cases, we connect SCADA servers to the Internet to provide intranet access. The biggest single line of defense for these two scenarios are virtual private network (VPN) connections. It's impossible to find any form of SCADA/ICS that doesn't use a VPN in the cases where it must be open to the public Internet.

Chapter 17 Review

Chapter Summary

After reading this chapter and completing the exercises, you should understand the following about building a real-world network.

Explain the Internet of Things

- Internet of Things (IoT) describes all the other devices connected to and controllable via the Internet, meaning not the servers, routers, and PCs. Other IoT devices can access Internet resources directly to answer questions and provide information. Home automation IoT devices take many forms, from smart light bulbs to smart thermostats and smart speakers.
- IoT permeates home security, from smart cameras to smart doorbells that enable you to interact remotely with visitors using two-way communications, including video.
- Quite a few protocols enable IoT manufacturers to create mesh networks that interconnect many devices seamlessly. Two popular protocols are Zigbee and Z-Wave.
- Other IoT devices rely on 802.11 Wi-Fi for Internet connectivity and Bluetooth or Bluetooth Low Energy protocols to connect devices.
- Hardening IoT devices decreases the danger of loss or downtime on the devices and increases the protection of personal information and company data.

Describe unified communication features and functions

- Unified communication (UC) is the support of voice, video, and texting over IP networks. Unified communication is a natural evolution of VoIP technologies.
- VoIP uses the Real-time Transport Protocol (RTP) on UDP ports (unspecified, but many companies use the IETF recommendations of ports 6970 to 6999) and uses the Session Initiation Protocol (SIP) on TCP or UDP ports 5060 and 5061.
- UC improves over traditional VoIP by providing presence information, video conferencing/real-time video, fax, messaging, and collaborative tools/workflow.
- A UC network has UC devices, UC servers, and UC gateways.
- The most common UC protocols beyond RTP and SIP are H.323, which uses TCP port 1720, and MGCP, which uses ports 2427 and 2727.
- Video teleconferencing (VTC) is especially sensitive to network slowdowns. Medianets handle this problem using quality of service (QoS).
- Differentiated services (DiffServ) are the underlying IP-level functions that make QoS work. There are two fields in every QoS-aware IP field: ECN (explicit congestion notification) and DSCP (differentiated services code point). ECN is used to communicate congestion on sessions. DSCP is used to define a class of service (CoS) for the IP packet.
- Unified Communication as a Service (UCaaS) solutions, like Microsoft Teams, provide subscription-based real-time communication that relies on servers in the cloud and secure high-speed Internet.

Describe the function and major components of an ICS/SCADA network

- ICS stands for industrial control system. An ICS consolidates the monitoring and control of a process into one or more control areas.
- An ICS has three basic components: input/output (I/O) functions on the machine, a controller, and the interface for the operator.
- A distributed control system (DCS) has controllers distributed among the various machines to handle the I/O. The DCS controllers connect to the ICS server for managing global changes.
- The human–machine interface (HMI) is how the ICS manifests itself to the operator(s) of the system.
- A programmable logic controller (PLC) has a parallel function to the controllers in a DCS but works in a different way. A PLC controls a machine according to a set of ordered steps.
- A supervisory control and data acquisition (SCADA) system is designed for large-scale, distributed processes such as power grids.

- SCADA systems use remote terminal units (RTUs). An RTU uses some form of remote communication technology and is designed to have some amount of autonomy in case it loses connection with the central control.
- ICS/DCS/SCADA and other networks are traditionally good candidates for network segmentation.

Key Terms

Bluetooth *(488)*
Bluetooth Low Energy (BLE) *(488)*
campus area network (CAN) *(484)*
class of service (CoS) *(492)*
differentiated services (DiffServ) *(492)*
distributed control system (DCS) *(495)*
H.323 *(491)*
human–machine interface (HMI) *(495)*
ICS server *(495)*
industrial control system (ICS) *(494)*
Internet of Things (IoT) *(485)*
Media Gateway Control Protocol (MGCP) *(491)*
medianet *(491)*
operator *(494)*
personal area network (PAN) *(488)*
programmable logic controller (PLC) *(496)*
Real-time Transport Protocol (RTP) *(490)*
real-time video *(490)*
remote terminal unit (RTU) *(496)*
Session Initiation Protocol (SIP) *(490)*
supervisory control and data acquisition (SCADA) *(496)*
UC device *(491)*
UC gateway *(491)*
UC server *(491)*
unified communication (UC) *(489)*
Unified Communication as a Service (UCaaS) *(493)*
unified voice services *(490)*
video teleconferencing (VTC) *(490)*
voice gateway *(490)*
Voice over IP (VoIP) *(489)*
VoIP gateway *(490)*
VoIP PBX *(490)*
VoIP phone *(489)*
Zigbee *(488)*
Z-Wave *(488)*

Key Term Quiz

Use the Key Terms list to complete the sentences that follow. Not all the terms will be used.

1. ______________ describes devices that are accessible and controllable over the Internet.
2. ______________ made it possible to communicate by voice over an IP network.
3. The term ______________ refers to technologies that include voice, video, and messaging.
4. Connected Bluetooth devices create a(n) ______________.
5. IoT systems using the ______________ protocol run at either the 2.4-GHz or 915-MHz band and support over 64,000 devices.
6. The ______________ protocol supports video presentations and uses TCP port 1720.
7. A(n) ______________ is a network of (typically) far-flung routers that provides sufficient bandwidth for VTC.
8. ______________ is the underlying architecture for QoS in medianets.
9. A(n) ______________ uses an HMI to manipulate DCS controllers.
10. ______________ enables people to communicate simultaneously via voice and video over an IP network.

Multiple-Choice Quiz

1. What is a network composed of a number of geographically close buildings called?
   A. CAN
   B. LAN
   C. MAN
   D. PAN
2. Devices using which of the following protocols form a mesh network using the 908- and 916-MHz bands?
   A. 802.11 Wi-Fi
   B. Bluetooth
   C. Zigbee
   D. Z-Wave
3. The central component of any ICS is what?
   A. Sensors
   B. PLCs
   C. ICS server
   D. HMI
4. Which of the following differentiates a PLC from a DCS controller?
   A. Sequential control
   B. Sensors
   C. Operator
   D. Actuator
5. RTP runs on which ports?
   A. ICMP ports 5004, 5005
   B. UDP ports 5004, 5005
   C. TCP ports 5004, 5005
   D. RTP uses undefined UDP ports.
6. SIP uses which ports? (Select two.)
   A. 4005
   B. 5060
   C. 4050
   D. 5061
7. Unified communication expands on which classic technology?
   A. VTC
   B. VoIP
   C. VPN
   D. VLAN
8. In a well-developed UC environment, what are the individual phones called?
   A. UC devices
   B. UC servers
   C. UC gateways
   D. UC nodes
9. MGCP replaces which of the following protocols? (Select two.)
   A. TCP
   B. SIP
   C. H.320
   D. H.323
10. In a medianet, what does DSCP define?
    A. Network congestion
    B. Differentiated services
    C. Explicit congestion notification
    D. Classes of service
11. Of the following, which would most likely have an industrial control system implementation?
    A. An apartment complex
    B. A coffee shop
    C. A city park
    D. A bottling company
12. Which of the following would most clearly differentiate a DCS from a SCADA system?
    A. Multiple control rooms
    B. Distances greater than 10 km
    C. Unified control room
    D. More than ten devices to be controlled
13. An ICS will commonly interface to the human operator via which service?
    A. RTU
    B. HMI
    C. Relay
    D. Control unit

14. Which of the following devices is unique to a SCADA system?
    A. RTU
    B. HMI
    C. Relay
    D. Control unit

15. Which of the following is a motivation for network segmentation? (Select two.)
    A. Load balancing
    B. Redundancy
    C. Ease of use
    D. Security

Essay Quiz

1. Using the examples of a milk-bottling factory and a nuclear power plant, write a short essay describing the differences between a DCS and a PLC.

Lab Project

• Lab Project 17.1

Select a home (yours, a family member's, classmate's, etc.) and map out what improvements could be made with IoT devices. Think in terms of energy efficiency, ease of access to streaming entertainment content and information, and communication. You'll need to do some research! Write down a path to upgrading, including devices and functions and cost.

Network Operations

"There is no such thing as perfect security, only varying levels of insecurity."

—Salman Rushdie

In this chapter, you will learn how to

- **Describe the industry standards for risk management**
- **Discuss contingency planning**

Companies need to manage risk, to minimize the dangers posed by internal and external threats. The chapter tackles risk management first. Companies also need policies for expected dangers and procedures for things that will happen eventually. This is contingency planning. Let's get started.

Test Specific

Risk Management

IT **risk management** is the process of how organizations deal with the bad things (let's call them attacks) that take place on their networks. The entire field of IT security is based on the premise that somewhere, at some time, something will attack some part of your network. The attack may take as many forms as your paranoia allows: intentional, unintentional, earthquake, accident, war, meteor impact...whatever.

What do we do about all these attacks? You can't afford to build up a defense for every possible attack—nor should you need to, for a number of reasons. First, different attacks have different probabilities of taking place. The probability of a meteor taking out your server room is very low. There is, however, a pretty good chance that some clueless user will eventually load malware on their company-issued laptop. Second, different attacks/ potential problems have different impacts. If a meteor hits your server room, you're going to have a big, expensive problem. If a user forgets his password, it's not a big deal and is easily dealt with.

The CompTIA Network+ certification covers a number of issues that roughly fit under the idea of risk management. Let's run through each of these individually.

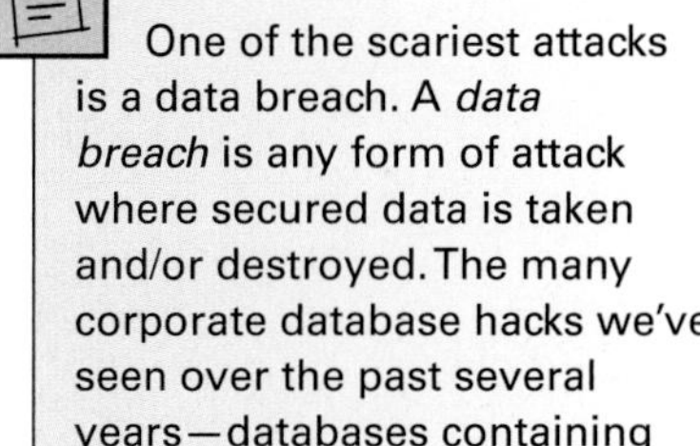

One of the scariest attacks is a data breach. A *data breach* is any form of attack where secured data is taken and/or destroyed. The many corporate database hacks we've seen over the past several years—databases containing information about user passwords, credit card info, and other personal identification—are infamous examples of data breaches.

Hardening and Security Policies

A **security policy** is a written document that defines how an organization will protect its IT infrastructure. There are hundreds of different security policies, but for the scope of the CompTIA Network+ certification exam we need to identify only a few of the most common policies. These policies include internal and external ones that affect just about every organization. This section covers the following policies:

- Acceptable use policies
- Network access policies
- Mobile deployment models
- Onboarding and offboarding policies
- Externally imposed policies

Acceptable Use Policies

An **acceptable use policy (AUP)** defines what is and what is not acceptable to do on an organization's computing devices. It's arguably the most famous type of security policy because it is the one document that pretty much everyone who works for any organization is required to read and, in many cases, sign before they can start work. The following are some provisions contained in a typical acceptable use policy:

- **Ownership** Equipment and any proprietary information stored on the organization's computers are the property of the organization.
- **Network access** Users will access only information they are authorized to access.

Many organizations require employees to sign an acceptable use policy, especially if it includes a consent to monitoring clause.

- **Privacy/consent to monitoring** Anything users do on the organization's computers is not private. The organization will monitor what is being done on computers at any time.
- **Illegal use** No one may use an organization's computers for anything that breaks a law. (This is usually broken down into many subheadings, such as introducing malware, hacking, scanning, spamming, and so forth.)

Network Access Policies

Companies need a policy that defines who can do what on the company's network. The **network access policy** defines who may access the network, how they may access the network, and what they can access. Network access policies may be embedded into policies such as VPN policy, password policy, encryption policy, and many others, but they need to be in place.

A common security concept that informs or guides many network access policies is the **principle of least privilege**, the idea that users should only have access to network resources required to do their job and nothing more. Managing permissions for every user individually is an endless chore, especially in large organizations, so it's better to do it by role.

Look for a scenario question on network hardening techniques that involve specific access to resources. Implementing role-based access is considered a best practice for hardening networks.

Sales representatives need access to the customer database to do their jobs, but they definitely do not need access to the accounting database. Instead of adding access to the customer database for every sales representative's account, a **role-based access** approach would establish a sales-representative role, associate each representative's account with the role, and assign all of the necessary privileges to the role.

Let's now look at a few network access policies specifically or indirectly covered on the CompTIA Network+ exam objectives.

- **Password policy** Password policies revolve around strength of password and rotation frequency (how often users have to change their passwords, password reuse, and so on.) See "Training" later in this chapter for more information on best practices, but keep in mind that some organizations will go far beyond those recommendations.
- **Data loss prevention policy** Data loss prevention (DLP) can mean a lot of things, from redundant hardware and backups, to access levels to data. A DLP policy takes into consideration many of these factors and helps minimize the risk of loss or theft of essential company data.
- **Remote access policy** A remote access policy (such as a VPN policy) enforces rules on how, when, and from what devices users can access company resources from remote locations. A typical restriction might be to not allow access from an open wireless portal, for example.

Policies reinforce an organization's IT security. Policies help define what equipment is used, how data is organized, and what actions people take to ensure the security of an organization. Policies tell an organization how to handle almost any situation that might arise (such as disaster recovery, covered later in this chapter).

Mobile Deployment Models

A long, long time ago, organizations had near total control over the devices on their networks by default. The hardware was huge, heavy, stationary, and often all had to come from a single vendor for compatibility—if your job required one, you used whatever the company bought. Organizations like having all of that control, but it doesn't come easy in a world where mobile and portable devices far outnumber stationary computers.

Organizations want to keep their networks and data secure, but it isn't as easy as purchasing the same device for everyone anymore. Users have strong opinions about their devices. Some will *want* to keep their work and personal use on separate devices, and others will refuse to carry two devices everywhere they go. Some will use any device they're given, and others will be frustrated if they have to learn to use Linux or macOS when they prefer Windows—or an Android device when they'd prefer an iPhone.

Each organization has to find its own way to balance what it wants with what its staff wants—but deployment models give us a shorthand for describing the main ways organizations approach the problem. This section explores four models: BYOD, COBO, COPE, and CYOD.

BYOD A **bring your own device (BYOD)** deployment lets employees use their existing portable devices at work. Employees get devices they prefer, which can increase employee happiness and productivity. The organization saves money on hardware, but the extra device variety comes with its own challenges. Many *BYOD challenges* revolve around security, support, and privacy.

Users might unwittingly bring in devices that are already compromised, putting the security of other devices—not to mention the organization's data—at risk. Someone could steal important company information if the user takes their device to a shady repair shop. A user might ask the support staff for help accessing a critical application from a brand new device that runs an unfamiliar OS, frustrating everyone involved. Finally, users expect more privacy on their own devices: monitoring software that is acceptable on a device the company owns may violate user privacy if installed on their personal phone.

How does the organization navigate these challenges? Generally, it'll compile a *BYOD policy*—a document each user who wants to bring their own device must agree to—that spells out details such as:

- Which devices are eligible. These may be general types of device, a more specific list of required features, or a very specific list of allowed models.
- What steps must be taken to prepare and secure a device before it can join the network. For example, it may need to be registered, pass a scan for malware or otherwise banned applications, and have monitoring or security software installed.
- To what extent the organization will provide technical or financial support for the device or associated data service.
- Notifying the user of any ongoing obligations they have, such as notifying the organization if the device is lost, stolen, or shows signs of malware.
- Notifying the user of any legal risks they are accepting or rights they are giving up. For example, that their device may be confiscated as evidence in the event of a lawsuit, or that the organization may wipe the device (including user data) if the device is believed lost or the user leaves the organization.

The CompTIA Network+ objectives don't mention deployment models, but they do want you to know about *bring your own device (BYOD) policy.* I think BYOD is easier to keep straight when you know the alternatives, but only BYOD itself should show up on the exam. The rest are also common in the real world—many organizations will even mix approaches.

COBO In a **corporate-owned, business only (COBO)** deployment model, the corporation owns all the mobile devices and issues them to employees. The corporation is solely responsible for the maintenance of the devices, the applications, and the data.

COBO is very rigid—nothing but company-approved software is used on the issued mobile devices. This is often a challenge as it requires employees to carry both the corporate device and their own device.

COPE **Corporate-owned, personally enabled (COPE)** is almost identical to COBO in that the organization issues mobile devices. With COPE, however, employees are presented with a whitelist of preapproved applications that they may install.

CYOD An organization offering **choose your own device (CYOD)** options provides employees free choice within a catalog of mobile devices. The organization retains complete control and ownership over the mobile devices, although the employees can install their own apps on the mobile devices.

Onboarding and Offboarding Policies

Every time someone joins or leaves an organization, there is a lot of important work to do. When they join, they'll need some combination of a workspace, keys, badges, hardware, accounts, and training. If they're an employee, they'll also need a process in place to make sure they get paid!

It doesn't always happen this way, but it's best for everyone involved if there's a smooth **onboarding** procedure to ensure new members get everything they need to settle in efficiently—and a careful **offboarding** procedure to reverse these when they leave the organization. The first step to ensuring it works like this is a good *onboarding and offboarding policy* that lays out what should happen, when it should happen, and who is responsible for doing it.

This process may involve multiple departments, and the people doing the work can differ depending on the size and structure of the organization. If the processes are all manual, a Network+ tech might be closely involved in multiple steps; if it's highly automated, an administrator may push a button and let the computers do the rest. Let's take a look at one role that may involve you: enrolling devices with your organization's *mobile device management (MDM)* system during onboarding, and removing them during offboarding.

Enrollment practices are also all over the map. The user might visit a URL to enroll their own device (especially in BYOD deployments), or an IT administrator might have to physically connect to a device to enroll it. The method tends to depend on both the device OS and the organization's MDM—but the result is pretty much the same.

An enrolled device is registered with the MDM (which can configure devices, deploy applications, and enforce security policies) and associated with its user. Unenrolling a device entails scrubbing the organization's data (and potentially software) from the device and either deactivating it within the MDM to await a new user or removing it from the MDM entirely.

Externally Imposed Policies

Government laws and regulations impose policies on organizations. International export controls, for example, restrict the export of some kinds of hardware and software—along with more obvious things like weapons—to specific countries. Laws such as the Health Insurance Portability and

Accountability Act of 1996 (HIPAA) regulate how an organization should store and secure specific types of data, who is allowed to access the data, whether employees can travel to other countries with devices containing the data, and more.

Most organizations devote resources to ensure they are in *compliance* with externally imposed policies. Just about every research university in the United States, for example, has export control officers who review all actions that risk violating federal laws and regulations. It's a really huge subject that the CompTIA Network+ only lightly touches.

Adherence to Policies

Given the importance of policies, it's also imperative for an organization to adhere to its policies strictly. This can often be a challenge. As technologies change, organizations must review and update policies to reflect those changes.

> **Try This!**
>
> **Checking Out Real-World Security Policies**
>
> Security policies can be interesting, so try this! Go to the SANS Institute Web site and check out all the free, cool, sample security policies:
>
> https://www.sans.org/security-resources/policies

Change Management

An IT infrastructure is an ever-changing thing. Applications are updated, operating systems change, server configurations adjust; change is a tricky part of managing an infrastructure. Change needs to happen, but not at the cost of losing security. The process of creating change in your infrastructure in an organized, controlled, safe way is called **change management**.

Change management usually begins with a **change management team**. This team, consisting of people from departments across your organization, is tasked with the job of investigating, testing, and authorizing all but the simplest changes to your network.

Changes tend to be initiated at two levels: strategic-level changes, typically initiated by management and major in scope (for example, we're going to switch all the servers from Windows to Linux), and infrastructure-level changes, typically initiated by a department by making a request to the change management team. The CompTIA Security+ exam explores change management in more detail, so for now I'll focus on the latter type of change, where *you* are the person who needs to understand enough about the process to propose a change to the change management team. Let's go over what to expect when dealing with change management.

Initiating the Change

The first part of many change processes is a request from a part of the organization. Let's say you're in charge of IT network support for a massive art department. There are over 150 graphic artists, each manning a powerful macOS workstation. The artists have discovered a new graphics program that they claim will dramatically improve their ability to do what they do.

After a quick read of the program's features on its Web site, you're also convinced that this a good idea. It's now your job to make this happen.

To begin, create a **change request**. Depending on the organization, this can be a highly official document or, for a smaller organization, nothing more than a detailed e-mail message. Whatever the case, you need to document the reason for this change. A good change request will include the following:

- **Type of change** Software and hardware changes are obviously part of this category, but this could also encompass issues like backup methods, work hours, network access, workflow changes, and so forth.
- **Configuration procedures** What is it going to take to make this change happen? Who will help? How long will it take?
- **Rollback process** If this change in some way makes such a negative impact that going back to how things were before the change is needed, what will it take to roll back to the previous configuration?
- **Potential impact** How will this change impact the organization? Will it save time? Save money? Increase efficiency? Will it affect the perception of the organization?
- **Notification** What steps will be taken to notify the organization about this change?

Dealing with the Change Management Team

With your change request in hand, it's time to get the change approved. In most organizations, change management teams meet at fixed intervals, so there's usually a deadline for you to be ready at a certain time. From here, most organizations rely heavily on a well-written change request form to get the details. The **approval process** usually consists of considering the issues listed in the change request, but also management approval and funding.

Making the Change Happen

Once your change is approved, the real work starts. Equipment, software, tools, and so forth, must be purchased. Configuration teams need to be trained. The change committee must provide an adequate **maintenance window**: the time it will take to implement and thoroughly test the coming changes. As part of that process, the committee must authorize downtime for systems, departments, and so on. Your job is to notify people who will be affected by the change and provide alternative workplaces or equipment if possible.

Documenting the Change

The ongoing and last step of the change is **change management documentation**. All changes must be clearly documented, including but not limited to the following:

- Network configurations, such as server settings, router configurations, and so on
- Additions to the network, such as additional servers, switches, and so on
- Physical location changes, such as moved workstations, relocated switches, and so on

Updating SOP

Organizations have *standard operating procedures (SOP)* that detail how to do most tasks within the organization. Any changes to procedures made during the change management process should be reflected in an updated SOP.

Patching and Updates

Best practices with *patch and firmware management* require both aggressive updates when manufacturers release patches and research to know when patches might cause problems. Patching and updating software and firmware is of critical importance in hardening networks. Bad actors know about system flaws and will attack the network through those unpatched gaps. (You'll see a lot more about attacking systems in Chapter 19.)

When we talk about patching and updates, we aren't just talking about the handy tools provided to us by Microsoft Windows or Ubuntu Linux. Almost every piece of software and firmware on almost every type of equipment you own is subject to patching and updating: printers, routers, wireless access points, desktops, programmable logic controllers (PLCs)... everything needs a patch or update now and then.

Cross Check

PLC

You'll remember PLCs from Chapter 17, so cross-check your memory now. What do these devices do for a modern network? How do they differ from a typical PC?

What Do We Update?

In general, specific types of updates routinely take place. Let's cover each of these individually, starting with the easiest and most famous: operating system (OS) updates.

OS updates are easily the most common type of update. Individuals install automatic updates on their OSs with impunity, but when you're updating a large number of systems, especially critical nodes like servers, it's never a good idea to apply all OS updates without a little bit of due diligence beforehand. Most operating systems provide some method of network server–based patching, giving administrators the opportunity to test first and then distribute patches when they desire.

All systems use device drivers, and they are another part of the system we often need to patch. In general, we apply driver updates to fix an incompatibility, incorporate new features, or repair a bug. Since device drivers are only present in systems with full-blown operating systems, all OS-updating tools include device drivers in their updates. Many patches will include feature changes and updates, as well as security vulnerability patches.

All software of any complexity has flaws. New hardware can expose flaws in the software it interacts with; newer applications create unexpected interactions; security standards change over time. All of these factors mean that responsible companies patch their products after they release them. When a major vulnerability is discovered, vendors tend to respond quickly by creating a fix and distributing an update or patch. Updating devices to protect them against vulnerabilities is a best practice for hardening networks.

Lesser vulnerabilities get patched as part of a regular patch cycle. You may have noticed that on the second Tuesday or Wednesday of each month, Microsoft-based computers reboot. Since October of 2003, Microsoft has sent out patches that have been in development and are ready for deployment on the second Tuesday of the month. This has become known as *Patch Tuesday*. These patches are released for a wide variety of Microsoft products, including operating systems, productivity applications, utilities, and more.

Firmware updates enable programming upgrades that make network devices more efficient, more secure, and more robust. Manufacturers release patches to firmware that unlock new features and fix or refine current features. Updating firmware regularly is part of network hardening best practices. The process for firmware upgrades varies among the many devices, but often it's a routine initiated via the browser-based interface or through a central management system.

How to Patch

In a network environment, patching is a routine but critical process. Here are a few important steps that take place in almost every scenario of a network patch environment:

- **Research** As a critical patch is announced, it's important to do some research to verify that the patch is going to do what you need it to do and that people who have already installed the patch aren't having problems.
- **Test** It's always a good idea to test a patch on a test system when possible.
- **Configuration backups** Backing up configurations is critical, especially when backing up firmware. The process of backing up a configuration varies from platform to platform, but almost all PCs can back up their system setups, and switches and routers have well-known "backup-config" style commands.

Upgrading vs. Downgrading

Patches, whether major or minor, require thorough testing before techs or administrators apply them to clients throughout the network. Sometimes, though, a hotfix might slip through to patch a security hole that then breaks other things inadvertently. In those cases, by following good **patch management** *procedures, you can roll back—the Windows terminology—or downgrade by removing the patch. You can then push an upgrade when a better patch is available.*

A single system may have many patches over time. When necessary, you might find yourself having to roll back the update, returning to an earlier version. This is usually pretty easy on PCs because OSs track each update. With firmware, the best way to handle this is to track each upgrade and keep a separate copy of each version to make it easy to revert to a safe version (some devices may do this automatically).

Training

End users are probably the primary source of security problems for any organization. We must provide *employee training* so they know what to look for and how to act to avoid or reduce attacks. Training users is a critical piece of managing risk. While a formal course is preferred, it's up to the IT department to do what it can to make sure users have an understanding of the following:

- **Security policies** Users need to read, understand, and, when necessary, sign all pertinent security policies.
- **Passwords** Make sure users understand best practices, especially when it comes to *password complexity/length*. Best practices according to the U.S. National Institute of Standards (NIST) include a minimum of eight characters for human-generated passwords. New passwords should be rejected if they appear in a database of previously breached passwords. Recent standards also reverse course on a lot of requirements people used to think were a good idea. For example, NIST now discourages expiring passwords and complexity requirements. A lot of online services require regular password changes and a certain password complexity, such as a combination of upper- and lowercase letters, numbers, and nonalphanumeric symbols; complexity can make passwords stronger, but NIST says the *requirements* only lead to formulaic passwords that are easier to crack.
- **Physical workplace and system security** Make sure users understand how to keep their workstations secure through screen locking and not storing written passwords in plain sight. Some organizations require their users to power down systems and clear documents off their desks at the end of the day. It's also important to report suspicious behavior or missing keys and equipment, shred paper documents as soon as possible, verify the identity of visitors, and avoid leaving data storage devices sitting around. Users shouldn't enable unauthorized access to secure areas by letting someone follow them in, leaving doors propped open, or leaving locks unlocked.
- **Social engineering** Users need to recognize typical social-engineering tactics and know how to counter them.
- **Malware** Teach users to recognize malware attacks and train them to deal with them.

Common Agreements

Dealing with third-party vendors is an ongoing part of any organization. When you are dealing with third parties, you must have some form of agreement that defines the relationship between you and the third party. This section explores five *common agreements*: a service-level agreement, a memorandum of understanding, a multi-source agreement, a statement of work, and a nondisclosure agreement.

Service-Level Agreement

A **service-level agreement (SLA)** is a document between a customer and a service provider that defines the scope, quality, and terms of the service to be provided. In CompTIA terminology, SLA requirements are a common part of business continuity and disaster recovery (both covered a little later in this chapter).

SLAs are common in IT, given the large number of services provided. Some of the more common SLAs in IT are provided by ISPs to customers. A typical SLA from an ISP defines the following:

- **Service provided** The minimum and/or maximum bandwidth and describes any recompense for degraded services or downtime.
- **Equipment** What equipment, if any, the ISP provides. It also specifies the type of connections to be provided.
- **Technical support** The level of technical support that will be given, such as phone support, Web support, and in-person support. This also defines costs for that support.

Memorandum of Understanding

A **memorandum of understanding (MOU)** is a document that defines an agreement between two parties in situations where a legal contract wouldn't be appropriate. An MOU defines the duties the parties commit to perform for each other and a time frame for the MOU. An MOU is common between companies that have only occasional business relations with each other. For example, all of the hospitals in a city might generate an MOU to accept each other's patients in case of a disaster such as a fire or tornado. This MOU would define costs, contacts, logistics, and so forth.

Multi-source Agreement

Manufacturers of various network hardware agree to a **multi-source agreement (MSA)**, a document that details the interoperability of their components. For example, two companies might agree that their gigabit interface converters (GBICs) will work in Cisco and Juniper switches.

Statement of Work

A **statement of work (SOW)** is in essence a legal contract between a vendor and a customer. An SOW defines the services and products the vendor agrees to supply and the time frames in which to supply them. A typical SOW might be between an IT security company and a customer. An SOW tends to be a detailed document, clearly explaining what the vendor needs to do. Time frames must also be very detailed, with milestones through the completion of the work.

Nondisclosure Agreement

Any company with substantial intellectual property will require new employees—and occasionally even potential candidates—to sign a **nondisclosure agreement (NDA)**. An NDA is a legal document that prohibits the signer from disclosing any company secrets learned as part of his or her job.

Security Preparedness

Managing risk effectively requires determined preparedness for incidents. If you decide to pursue the next logical CompTIA certification, CompTIA Security+, you'll find an incredibly detailed discussion of how the IT security industry spends inordinate amounts of time and energy creating a secure IT environment. CompTIA Network+ requires you to understand security risk assessments and business risk assessments.

Security Risk Assessments

CompTIA uses the term *security risk assessments* to categorize some fundamental aspects of risk assessment, notably threat assessment, vulnerability assessment, penetration testing, and posture assessment. Each of these subcategories pokes around at potentially bad things that can happen to an organization's *assets*. Anything of value to an organization is an **asset**. Organizations analyze potentially bad things to protect against them and to mitigate if or when bad things happen.

Threat Assessment *Threat* describes the potential or capability of an event or bad actor to cause damage to company assets. A *threat assessment*, therefore, is the organization analyzing what's out there.

Bayland Widgets Corporation (BWC), for example, has a factory for making widgets. The factory and all of its control systems are extremely important assets. The proprietary *widgetXplus* technology that makes BWC's widgets the best in the world is also a key corporate asset. What are the threats?

A **threat actor**—a person, organization, or even a nation state that has both the capability and intent to harm, steal, copy, or otherwise diminish an asset—could infiltrate the BWC network and steal the widgetXplus technology details. That's a threat. A disgruntled employee could change key programming details in the factory system right before quitting just to derail the production line. That's a threat too. Security-conscious organizations assess threats and rate them according to both the likelihood they might happen and the amount of pain they would cause if they do. Which leads us to the next section.

Vulnerability Assessment Every asset has some weakness that makes it potentially susceptible to a threat—a **vulnerability**. The BWC factory technicians control a lot of the systems remotely, for example, across the Internet. That Internet connection presents a potential weak spot in keeping out threat actors. If security controls aren't sufficient to stop the latest attack, then that connection is a clear vulnerability. The CompTIA Network+ exam objectives don't follow up with the next step, but you should know that assigning a monetary or intrinsic value to an asset helps the organization prioritize its security. (You'll get all this in gory detail in CompTIA Security+.)

Given the huge number of potential vulnerabilities out there, it's impossible for even the most highly skilled technician to find them by manually inspecting an organization's infrastructure. The best way to know the infrastructure's vulnerabilities is to run some form of program—a **vulnerability scanner**—that will inspect a huge number of potential vulnerabilities and create a report—a *vulnerability assessment*—for the organization to then act upon.

There is no single vulnerability scanner that works for every aspect of an organization's infrastructure. Instead, good network techs have a number of utilities that work for their type of network infrastructure. Here are a few of the more popular vulnerability scanners and where they are used.

Network security folks rely on a command-line tool named **Nmap** (*Network Mapper*) for network scanning, discovery, and auditing. Nmap can do a ton of things. First, **Nmap** is a **port scanner**, a software tool for testing a network for vulnerabilities. **Port scanning** queries individual nodes, looking for open or vulnerable ports and creating a report. Nmap can enable managing upgrades, monitoring hosts, monitoring uptime, network inventory, and more. Written by Gordon Lyon, Nmap is very popular, free, and well maintained. Figure 18.1 shows sample output from Zenmap, a GUI front-end to the `nmap` command.

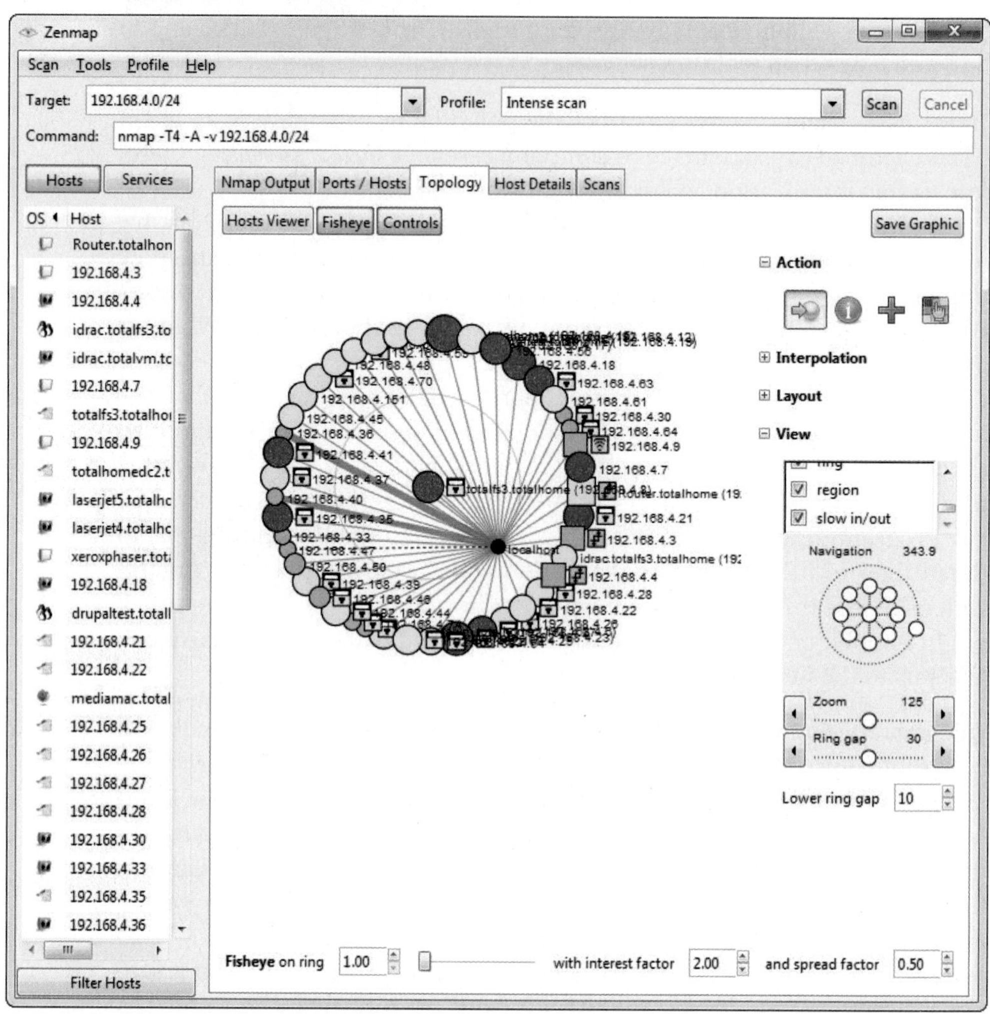

• **Figure 18.1** Nmap output

When you need to perform more serious vulnerability testing, it's common to turn to more aggressive and powerful comprehensive testers. There are plenty out there, but two dominate the field: Nessus and OpenVAS. **Nessus** (Figure 18.2), from Tenable Network Security, is arguably the first truly comprehensive vulnerability testing tool and has been around for almost two decades. Nessus is an excellent, well-known tool. Once free to everyone, Nessus is still free for home users, but commercial users must purchase a subscription.

OpenVAS is an open source fork of Nessus that is also extremely popular and, in the opinion of many security types, superior to Nessus.

You need to be careful not to use the term **vulnerability scanning** to mean "just running some program to find weaknesses." Vulnerability scanning is a part of a more strategic program called **vulnerability management**, an ongoing process of identifying vulnerabilities and dealing with them. The tools used for vulnerability scanning are an important part of the overall process of vulnerability management.

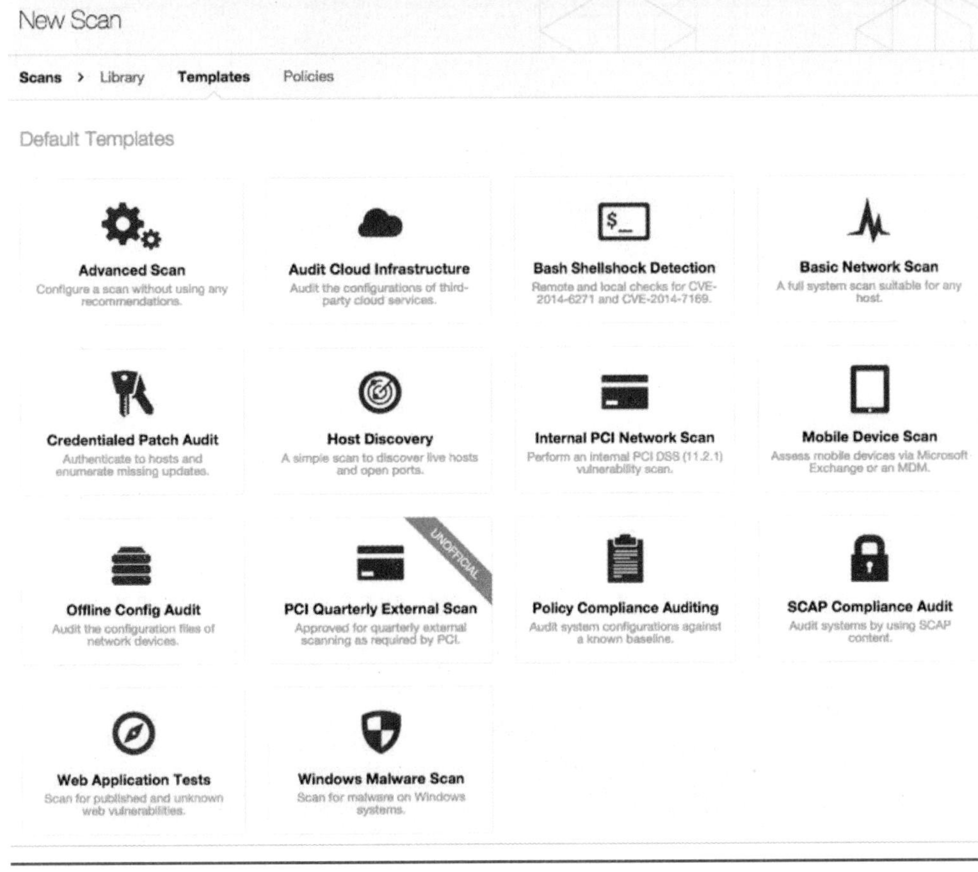

Figure 18.2 Nessus output

Penetration Testing

Once you've run your vulnerability tools and hardened your infrastructure, it's time to see if your network can stand up to an actual attack. The problem with this is that you don't want *real* threat actors making these attacks. You want to be attacked by an authorized hacker (also known as a "white hat" hacker), who will find the existing vulnerabilities and exploit them to get access. Instead of hurting your infrastructure or stealing your secrets, this hacker reports findings so that you can further harden your network. This is called **penetration testing (pentesting)**.

A legal pentest requires lots of careful documentation that defines what the pentester is to test, the level of testing, time frames, and documentation.

Unlike vulnerability testing, a good pentest requires a skilled operator who understands the target and knows potential vulnerabilities. To that end, there are a number of tools that make this job easier. Two examples are Aircrack-ng and Metasploit.

Aircrack-ng is an open source tool for pentesting pretty much every aspect of wireless networks. It's powerful, relatively easy to use (assuming you understand 802.11 wireless networks in great detail), and completely free.

Metasploit is a unique, open source tool that enables the pentester to use a massive library of attacks as well as tweak those attacks for unique penetrations. Metasploit is the go-to tool for pentesting. You simply won't find a professional in the pentesting arena who does not use Metasploit. Metasploit isn't pretty (Figure 18.3), but it gets the job done.

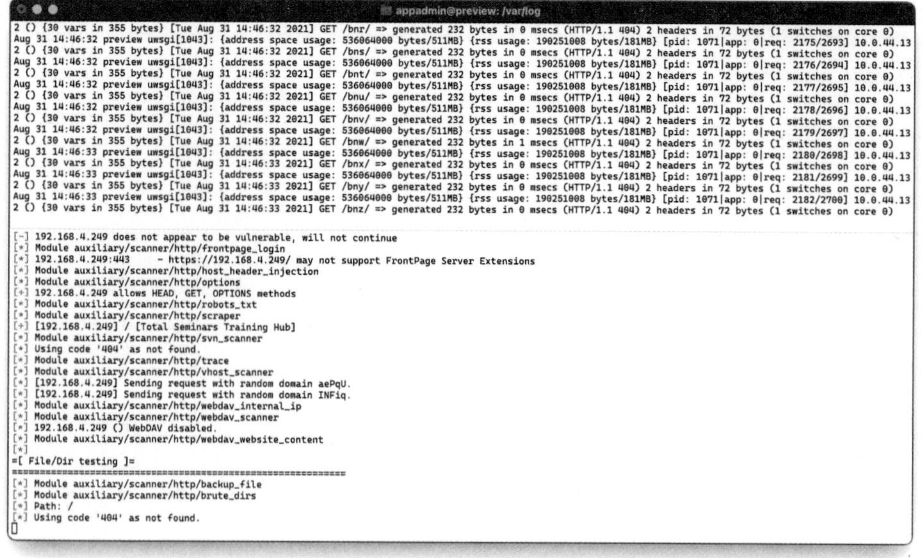

appadmin@preview: /var/log
2 () {30 vars in 355 bytes} [Tue Aug 31 14:46:32 2021] GET /bnr/ => generated 232 bytes in 0 msecs (HTTP/1.1 404) 2 headers in 72 bytes (1 switches on core 0)
Aug 31 14:46:32 preview uwsgi[1043]: {address space usage: 536064000 bytes/511MB} {rss usage: 190251008 bytes/181MB} [pid: 1071|app: 0|req: 2175/2693] 10.0.44.13
2 () {30 vars in 355 bytes} [Tue Aug 31 14:46:32 2021] GET /bns/ => generated 232 bytes in 0 msecs (HTTP/1.1 404) 2 headers in 72 bytes (1 switches on core 0)
Aug 31 14:46:32 preview uwsgi[1043]: {address space usage: 536064000 bytes/511MB} {rss usage: 190251008 bytes/181MB} [pid: 1071|app: 0|req: 2176/2694] 10.0.44.13
2 () {30 vars in 355 bytes} [Tue Aug 31 14:46:32 2021] GET /bnt/ => generated 232 bytes in 0 msecs (HTTP/1.1 404) 2 headers in 72 bytes (1 switches on core 0)
Aug 31 14:46:32 preview uwsgi[1043]: {address space usage: 536064000 bytes/511MB} {rss usage: 190251008 bytes/181MB} [pid: 1071|app: 0|req: 2177/2695] 10.0.44.13
2 () {30 vars in 355 bytes} [Tue Aug 31 14:46:32 2021] GET /bnu/ => generated 232 bytes in 0 msecs (HTTP/1.1 404) 2 headers in 72 bytes (1 switches on core 0)
Aug 31 14:46:32 preview uwsgi[1043]: {address space usage: 536064000 bytes/511MB} {rss usage: 190251008 bytes/181MB} [pid: 1071|app: 0|req: 2178/2696] 10.0.44.13
2 () {30 vars in 355 bytes} [Tue Aug 31 14:46:32 2021] GET /bnv/ => generated 232 bytes in 0 msecs (HTTP/1.1 404) 2 headers in 72 bytes (1 switches on core 0)
Aug 31 14:46:32 preview uwsgi[1043]: {address space usage: 536064000 bytes/511MB} {rss usage: 190251008 bytes/181MB} [pid: 1071|app: 0|req: 2179/2697] 10.0.44.13
2 () {30 vars in 355 bytes} [Tue Aug 31 14:46:32 2021] GET /bnw/ => generated 232 bytes in 1 msecs (HTTP/1.1 404) 2 headers in 72 bytes (1 switches on core 0)
Aug 31 14:46:33 preview uwsgi[1043]: {address space usage: 536064000 bytes/511MB} {rss usage: 190251008 bytes/181MB} [pid: 1071|app: 0|req: 2180/2698] 10.0.44.13
2 () {30 vars in 355 bytes} [Tue Aug 31 14:46:33 2021] GET /bnx/ => generated 232 bytes in 0 msecs (HTTP/1.1 404) 2 headers in 72 bytes (1 switches on core 0)
Aug 31 14:46:33 preview uwsgi[1043]: {address space usage: 536064000 bytes/511MB} {rss usage: 190251008 bytes/181MB} [pid: 1071|app: 0|req: 2181/2699] 10.0.44.13
2 () {30 vars in 355 bytes} [Tue Aug 31 14:46:33 2021] GET /bny/ => generated 232 bytes in 0 msecs (HTTP/1.1 404) 2 headers in 72 bytes (1 switches on core 0)
Aug 31 14:46:33 preview uwsgi[1043]: {address space usage: 536064000 bytes/511MB} {rss usage: 190251008 bytes/181MB} [pid: 1071|app: 0|req: 2182/2700] 10.0.44.13
2 () {30 vars in 355 bytes} [Tue Aug 31 14:46:33 2021] GET /bnz/ => generated 232 bytes in 0 msecs (HTTP/1.1 404) 2 headers in 72 bytes (1 switches on core 0)
[-] 192.168.4.249 does not appear to be vulnerable, will not continue
[*] Module auxiliary/scanner/http/frontpage_login
[*] 192.168.4.249:443 - https://192.168.4.249/ may not support FrontPage Server Extensions
[*] Module auxiliary/scanner/http/host_header_injection
[*] Module auxiliary/scanner/http/options
[+] 192.168.4.249 allows HEAD, GET, OPTIONS methods
[*] Module auxiliary/scanner/http/robots_txt
[*] Module auxiliary/scanner/http/scraper
[+] [192.168.4.249] / [Total Seminars Training Hub]
[*] Module auxiliary/scanner/http/svn_scanner
[*] Using code '404' as not found.
[*] Module auxiliary/scanner/http/trace
[*] Module auxiliary/scanner/http/vhost_scanner
[*] [192.168.4.249] Sending request with random domain aePqU.
[*] [192.168.4.249] Sending request with random domain INFiq.
[*] Module auxiliary/scanner/http/webdav_internal_ip
[*] Module auxiliary/scanner/http/webdav_scanner
[*] 192.168.4.249 () WebDAV disabled.
[*] Module auxiliary/scanner/http/webdav_website_content
[*]
=[File/Dir testing]=
==
[*] Module auxiliary/scanner/http/backup_file
[*] Module auxiliary/scanner/http/brute_dirs
[*] Path: /
[*] Using code '404' as not found.

• **Figure 18.3** Metasploit output

Linux distros come with many network diagnostic and pentesting tools available. Just about every security tech has a **Kali Linux** bootable USB drive, for example, a distro customized for pentesting.

> Seriously, get a copy of Kali Linux. It's an awesome distro. Just be careful to use your own lab for practicing pentesting (because of those pesky laws and stuff that you don't want to break). Get Kali here: https://www.kali.org/get-kali/

Posture Assessment Cybersecurity professionals use the term **risk posture** to describe the overall risk for an organization. BWC's risk posture, for example, includes threats from threat actors to vulnerable assets, like the factory systems and intellectual property used to make BWC products. Other risk factors need to be included as well, such as the potential for changes in laws or regulations that could negatively affect the company, natural disasters that could take out physical plants, and personal disasters such as the death or disablement of key corporate personnel. That took a morbid turn, but to make a point.

A *posture assessment*, to use CompTIA's term, covers it all—all the various threats and risks to which the company is exposed. And such an assessment includes the cost of negative events in both money and time. A proper risk assessment details how the company is vulnerable and can protect against potential negative events.

Business Risk Assessments

CompTIA uses the term *business risk assessments* to include a subset of risk assessment focused on operations in the organization, such as process assessment and vendor assessment. A business risk assessment looks at other aspects of overall risks facing an organization.

Process Assessment A **process assessment** examines various actions performed by an organization to produce desired results. For BWC, for example, one essential process is producing its patented widgets so that the corporation can grow and provide livelihoods for its employees. Another essential process is the research and development into making new and improved products in the future. A third essential process is the procurement of the materials used to create the final product. Another process is the sales force that interacts with other companies to sell widgets.

Within each of these broad-stroke processes are many subprocesses. An essential subprocess in sales, for example, is recruiting the best salespeople BWC can find. A corollary to that is the subprocess of all the support people and equipment that go into making a sales force effective.

In a risk management scenario, a process assessment codifies and ranks essential processes, then examines the likelihood of weakness in the process. A sales force in BWC's home state of Texas, for example, would have a much lower likelihood of weakness than a brand new team that just started in the first branch office in Mexico. The same kind of assessment would apply all across the board to all essential processes.

Vendor Assessment Many organizations rely on *third parties* to provide important pieces that make up their final product. BWC doesn't own a titanium factory to create the raw material used in its best widgets. BWC buys the titanium from a *vendor*. BWC also sources some of the servo motors used in its widgets from a vendor that specializes in servo motors.

Proper risk assessment—or in this case, business risk assessment—takes into consideration any potential problems outside of the control of the organization. A **vendor risk assessment** examines all aspects of a third party's security controls, processes, procurement, labor policies, and more to see what risks that vendor poses to the organization.

Contingency Planning

Despite the best efforts of competent techs, bad things happen. Anything that negatively affects an organization, that hurts or compromises its people, systems, or ability to function as an entity, is an **incident**. Incidents can and will vary in size and scope, from something as simple as an attack that was caught and stopped to something serious such as a data breach that affects confidentiality of customer records or a hurricane that wipes out a data center that seriously adversely affects availability. Whatever the case, organizations should develop a set of **contingency plans**—documents about how to limit damage and recover quickly—to respond to these incidents.

The CompTIA Network+ exam covers several aspects of contingency planning that we can divide into three groups based on the severity and location of the incident: incident response, disaster recovery, and business continuity. Incidents that take place within the organization that can be stopped, contained, and remediated without outside resources are handled by **incident response** planning. If an incident can no longer be contained, causing significant damage or danger to the immediate infrastructure, it is covered under *disaster recovery*. Last, if the disaster requires actions offsite from the primary infrastructure, it is under the jurisdiction of *business continuity*.

While related but not directly connected to contingency planning, we also need to take a look at forensics. Let's hit all these, but keep in mind that this is only the lightest touch on these very complex aspects of contingency planning. The goal of the CompTIA Network+ certification is only to introduce you to these concepts so that you progress to the next level (hopefully, CompTIA Security+).

Incident Response

The cornerstone of incident response is the incident response team—usually one or more trained, preassigned **first responders** with policies in place for what to do. Depending on the type of event, the team may be responsible for things like: deciding whether it qualifies as an incident the team should address, ignore, or escalate; evaluating the scope and cause of the issue; preventing further disruption; resolving the cause; restoring order to affected systems; and identifying ways to prevent a recurrence. Most incidents are handled at this level. Organizations should have detailed *incident response policies* and a detailed **incident response plan** that will guide the actions of the team in various incident scenarios. However, if an incident is so vast that the incident response team cannot stop, contain, or remediate it, disaster recovery comes into play.

Disaster Recovery

Disaster recovery is a critical part of contingency planning that deals directly with recovering your primary infrastructure from a disaster. A *disaster* is an event such as a hurricane or flood that disables or destroys substantial amounts of infrastructure.

Disaster recovery starts before a disaster occurs, with an organization developing a **disaster recovery plan**. An organization considers likely disasters and creates plans for how to deal with them. The actual plans vary by the type of disaster. In many cases an organization has a *disaster recovery team*, whose goal is to get the IT infrastructure up and running at the primary business location(s). One of the big jobs here is figuring out what kind of system and data **backups**—copies of essential information that can be restored—your organization will need to get up and running, how often backups should be made, and making sure those backups are available quickly in the face of any negative event.

Network Device Backup/Restore

Network devices can have both configuration data and state data that should be backed up in case of a catastrophe. *Configuration data* includes all the customized settings for a router, switch, load balancer, intrusion detection/prevention system (IDS/IPS), firewall, or other network device. Having a solid backup of what is essentially a text file enables network professionals to replace and restore settings to a failed device quickly. *State data* is a different animal. Replacing a router and updating its configuration to match its predecessor is great, but the router still needs to interact with other routers to get into convergence—its state. Another form of "state" involves things like Active Directory. Replacing an AD server and giving it the same configuration as the previous system won't do much good without restoring the actual Active Directory database that holds user accounts and critical policy data. Adding the latter can restore the AD server's state.

Backup Plan Assessments

A proper assessment of a backup plan records how much data might be lost and how long it would take to restore. A **recovery point objective (RPO)** sets an upper limit to how much lost data the organization can tolerate if it must restore from a backup, effectively dictating how frequently backups must be taken. Most restored systems have some amount of lost data based on when the last backup took place. Real-time backups, which are really just redundant servers, are the exception. Likewise, the **recovery time objective (RTO)** sets an upper limit to how long the organization can tolerate an outage before full functionality must be restored.

The CompTIA Network+ objectives directly refer to two hardware-specific disaster recovery items, MTBF and MTTR. I'll throw MTTF into the middle just for fun. Here's the scoop on these *redundancy and high availability concepts*.

The **mean time between failures (MTBF)** factor, which typically applies to hardware components, represents the manufacturer's best guess (based on historical data) regarding how much time will pass between major failures of that component. This assumes that more than one failure will occur, which means that the component will be repaired rather than replaced. Organizations take this risk factor into account because it may affect likelihood and impact of the risks associated with critical systems.

The **mean time to failure (MTTF)** factor indicates the length of time a device is expected to last in operation. In MTTF, only a single, definitive failure will occur and will require that the device be replaced rather than repaired.

Finally, the **mean time to repair (MTTR)** is the amount of time it takes to fix a system after it fails. That includes time to replace components, repair parts, and restore the system to its fully functional state.

Disaster recovery handles everything from restoring hardware to backups, but only at the primary business location. Anything that requires moving part of the organization's business offsite until recovery is complete is a part of business continuity.

Business Continuity

When a disaster disables, wipes out, floods, or in some other way prevents the primary infrastructure from operating, the organization should have a plan of action to keep the business going at remote sites. The planning and processes necessary to make this happen are known as *business continuity (BC)*. Organizations plan for BC with **business continuity planning (BCP)**. As you might expect, the goal of the team doing BCP is to produce a worthwhile **business continuity plan** that details risks to critical systems, cost to replace or repair such systems, and how to make those replacements or repairs happen in a timely fashion. Good BCP will deal with many issues, but one of the more important ones—and one that must be planned well in advance of a major disaster—is the concept of backup sites.

Every business continuity plan includes setting up some form of secondary location that enables an organization to continue to operate should its primary site no longer function. CompTIA identifies four types of secondary site: cold, warm, hot, and cloud.

- A **cold site** is a location that consists of a building, facilities, desks, toilets, parking—everything that a business needs…except computers. A cold site generally takes more than a few days to bring online.
- A **warm site** starts with the same components as a cold site, but adds computers loaded with software and functioning servers—a complete hardware infrastructure. A warm site lacks current data and may not have functioning Internet/network links. Bringing this site up to speed may start with activating your network links, and it most certainly requires loading data from recent backups. A warm site should only take a day or two to bring online.

- A **hot site** has everything a warm site does, but also includes very recent backups. It might need just a little data restored from a backup to be current, but in many cases a hot site is a complete duplicate of the primary site. A proper hot site should only take a few hours to bring online.
- As organizations increasingly migrate servers and services to the cloud, a cloud-site backup becomes a viable alternative to any of the traditional options. With a **cloud site**, everything of note is stored in the cloud, including servers, client machine images, applications, and data. If some disaster hits, an organization can quickly move to a new location unaffected by the disaster and access its resources as soon as it has Internet connectivity. In the increasingly decentralized workplace today, having a cloud-based system makes disaster "recovery" almost a moot point.

Business continuity isn't just about backup sites, but this aspect is what the CompTIA Network+ exam focuses on. Another term related to continuity planning is **succession planning**: identifying people who can take over certain positions (usually on a temporary basis) in case the people holding those critical positions are incapacitated or lost in an incident or disaster.

Forensics

Computer forensics is the science of gathering, examining, analyzing, preserving, and presenting evidence stored on a computer or any form of digital media that is presentable in a court of law. Computer forensics is a highly specialized science, filled with a number of highly specialized skills and certifications. Three of the top computer forensic certifications are the Certified Forensic Computer Examiner (CFCE), offered by the International Association of Computer Investigative Specialists (IACIS); the Certified Computer Examiner (CCE), from the International Society of Forensic Computer Examiners (ISFCE); and the GIAC Certified Forensic Analyst (GCFA), offered by the Global Information Assurance Certification (GIAC) organization. Achieving one of these challenging certifications gets you well on your way to a great career in forensics.

The CompTIA Network+ exam doesn't expect you to know computer forensics—that's a topic for the Security+ Exam—but it's still a good idea for you, as the typical technician, to understand enough of forensics that you know what to do in the rare situation where you find yourself as the first line of defense.

In general, CompTIA sees you as either the first responder or the technician responsible for supporting the first responder. The first responder in a forensic situation is the person or robot whose job is to react to the notification of a computer crime by determining the severity of the situation, collecting information, documenting findings and actions, and providing the information to the proper authorities. In a perfect world, a first responder has a toolbox of utilities that enables him or her to capture the state of the system without disturbing it. At the very least the first responder needs to secure the state of the media (mainly hard drives) as well as any volatile memory (RAM) in a way that removes all doubt of tampering either intentionally or unintentionally.

One of the first mistakes any first responder can make is to turn off or reboot a computer. There's a very hot debate in the forensics community about what to do when you seize devices. Most experts say to pull the plug, because a normal shutdown routine destroys or contaminates potential evidence. Temp files, log files, hard drive data, virtual memory...all these could be wiped. Just pull the plug.

Like so many aspects of computer security, there isn't a single school of thought on how exactly you should do computer forensics. There are, however, a number of basic attitudes and practices shared by every school of thought, especially at the very basic level covered by the CompTIA Network+ exam.

In general, when you are in a situation where you are the first responder, you need to

- Secure the area
- Document the scene
- Collect evidence

Secure the Area

The first step for a first responder is to secure the area. In most cases someone in authority has determined the person or persons who are allegedly responsible and calls you in to react to the incident. As a first responder, your job is to secure the systems involved as well as secure the immediate work areas.

The main way you secure the area is by your presence at the scene. If possible, you should block the scene from prying eyes or potential disturbance. If it's an office, lock the door, define the area of the scene, and mark it off in some way if possible.

Keep in mind that an incident is rarely anything as exciting (or scary) as catching a user committing a felony! In most cases an incident involves something as simple as trying to determine if a user introduced malware into a system or if a user was playing *World of Warcraft* during work hours. In these cases it's often easy to do your job. Simply observe the system and, if you identify an issue, provide that information in-house. The rules for forensics still apply. If, however, you're responding to one of the scarier scenarios, it's important for you as a first responder to understand when you need to *escalate* an issue. Given that *you* were called in to react to a particular incident, most escalation situations involve you discovering something more serious than you expected.

It's always a good idea to use a camera to document the state of the incident scene, including taking pictures of the operating state of computers and switches and the location of media and other devices.

Document the Scene

Once you have secured the area, it's time to *document the scene*. You need to preserve the state of the equipment and look for anything that you might need to inspect forensically.

While it's obvious you'll want to locate computers, switches, WAPs, and routers, be sure to take copious notes, paying particular attention to electronic media. Here are a few items you will want to document:

- Smartphones
- Optical media
- External hard drives
- USB drives
- Cameras
- VoIP phones

Collect Evidence

With the scene secured and documented, it's time to start the *evidence/data collection*. The moment you take something away from an incident scene or start to handle or use any devices within the incident scene, there is a chance that your actions could corrupt the evidence you are collecting. You must handle and document all evidence in a very specific manner. **Chain of custody**, as the name implies, is the paper trail of who has accessed or controlled a given piece of evidence from the time it is initially brought into custody until the incident is resolved. From the standpoint of a first responder, the most important item to keep in mind about chain of custody is that you need to document what you took under control, when you did it, what you did to it, and when you passed it to the next person in line.

From a strict legal standpoint, the actual process of how you obtain evidence and collect data is a complex business usually left to certified forensic examiners. In general it boils down to using specialized utilities and tools, many of which are unique for the type of data you are retrieving. The tools used also differ depending on different OSs, platforms, and the personal tastes of the examiners. Every forensic examiner has a number of these tools in his or her unique forensic toolkit.

If you need to transport any form of evidence, make sure to document for chain of custody as well as inventory. In other words, make a list of who has what equipment/evidence at any one time. Pack everything carefully. You don't want a dropped case to destroy data! If you are transporting evidence, don't leave the evidence at any time. Delay your lunch break until after you hand the evidence over to the next person! Follow the proper procedures for *data transport* to avoid any problems with the evidence.

The end result of your forensics work is a **forensics report**. In general, this is where you report your findings. A good forensics report includes the following:

- Examiner's name and title
- Examiner's qualifications
- Objective for the forensics
- Any case or incident numbers
- Tools used
- Where the examination took place
- Files found
- Log file output
- Screenshots

Forensics reports and evidence will be used in many circumstances. A forensics expert will present the report and evidence to the hiring entity. A company might review the report and discover potential criminal activity therein, and place a legal hold on the document and evidence. A **legal hold** is the process of an organization preserving and organizing data in anticipation of or in reaction to a pending legal issue. The data and the reports must be preserved in such a way that, should a legal authority want access to that data, they can reasonably access it. A forensic examiner will likely be called to court as an expert witness or for testimony.

Chapter 18 Review

Chapter Summary

After reading this chapter and completing the exercises, you should understand the following about network operations.

Describe the industry standards for risk management

- The field of IT security is based on the premise that there is a looming attack on some part of a network. Security attacks take many forms, including intentional, unintentional, accidental, natural disasters, acts of war, and others.
- A security policy is a document that defines how an organization will protect its IT infrastructure.
- An acceptable use policy specifies what is and is not permitted to be done on an organization's computers. Acceptable use policies cover topics including ownership of equipment and information, authorized access, privacy and monitoring consent, and illegal use.
- Network access policies define who can access the network, how it can be accessed, and what resources of the network can be accessed.
- The principle of least privilege means to give users only the access levels they need to perform their jobs.
- BYOD deployment uses employees' existing mobile devices for use by the corporation, and a BYOD policy lays out the related requirements and procedures.
- In a COBO deployment model, the corporation owns all the devices.
- With COPE, the organization issues a mobile device, but employees are presented with a whitelist of preapproved applications that they may install.
- CYOD provides employees free choice within a catalog of mobile devices.
- Onboarding is the process of bringing new users into the organization, and offboarding is the process of removing them. Onboarding and offboarding policy addresses the steps in this process, when they should happen, and who should take them.
- Change management teams investigate, test, and authorize most IT changes. IT changes come from two major sources: major strategic-level changes, and areas of infrastructure that need localized changes that are dealt with by the change management team.
- Change requests can be made with a formal document or via a less formal communication such as an e-mail message.
- Change requests should specify the type of change, the configuration procedures, a rollback process, the potential impact, and a notification process.
- Most hardware and software require occasional patches. Patches are issued for operating systems, device drivers, computers, and firmware. Before applying patches, research and test them. Keep configuration backups so equipment can be quickly reconfigured after a patch is applied.
- Effective risk management requires that users receive training in risk mitigation. Users should understand and follow security policies, use good password practices, maintain system and workplace security, recognize social-engineering tactics, and recognize malware.
- Common agreements define relationships between an organization and its third-party vendors. Examples include a service-level agreement, a memorandum of understanding, a multi-source agreement, a statement of work, and a nondisclosure agreement.
- Preparation for incidents is a multifaceted process with the goal of analyzing IT vulnerabilities to prevent a security breach. Among other issues, security preparedness calls for threat assessment, vulnerability assessment, penetration testing, and posture assessment. Popular vulnerability scanners include Nmap, Nessus, and OpenVAS.
- Once vulnerabilities have been identified and secured, penetration testing, also called pentesting, should be performed to exploit security holes. A pentester reports his or her findings, which can be used to further harden a network. Kali Linux is a popular distro used by security professionals to perform penetration analysis.

- Business risk assessments focus on the processes and systems. Process assessment examines the various processes that enable organizations to produce, ranking them in order of importance. Vendor assessment analyzes any risks in third-party supply chains.

Discuss contingency planning

- An incident is an event in which the security of an IT infrastructure is compromised.
- Organizations must have contingency plans to respond to an incident in such a way that the organization can continue to function. Incidents that take place within the organization that can be stopped, contained, and remediated without outside resources are handled by incident response planning. Disaster recovery deals with providing methods of recovering your primary infrastructure from a disaster.
- Disaster recovery starts with a plan and includes system and data backups.
- Business continuity planning prepares for a disaster that requires the business to continue functioning at remote sites. The types of remote site are cold, warm, hot, and cloud.
- Computer forensics is the science of gathering, examining, analyzing, preserving, and presenting computerized data. Technicians are often first responders or supporters of first responders to a security incident and should follow good forensic practices.
- In the event of an incident, secure the area, document the scene, and collect evidence.

Key Terms

acceptable use policy (AUP) *(503)*
Aircrack-ng *(515)*
approval process *(508)*
asset *(513)*
backup *(518)*
bring your own device (BYOD) *(505)*
business continuity plan *(519)*
business continuity planning (BCP) *(519)*
chain of custody *(522)*
change management *(507)*
change management documentation *(508)*
change management team *(507)*
change request *(508)*
choose your own device (CYOD) *(506)*
cloud site *(520)*
cold site *(519)*
corporate-issued, personally enabled (COPE) *(506)*
computer forensics *(520)*
contingency plan *(517)*
corporate-owned, business only (COBO) *(506)*
disaster recovery *(518)*
disaster recovery plan *(518)*
first responder *(517)*
forensics report *(522)*
hot site *(520)*
incident *(517)*
incident response *(517)*
incident response plan *(518)*
Kali Linux *(516)*
legal hold *(522)*
maintenance window *(508)*
mean time between failures (MTBF) *(519)*
mean time to failure (MTTF) *(519)*
mean time to repair (MTTR) *(519)*
memorandum of understanding (MOU) *(512)*
Metasploit *(515)*
multi-source agreement (MSA) *(512)*
Nessus *(514)*
network access policy *(504)*
Nmap *(514)*
nondisclosure agreement (NDA) *(512)*
offboarding *(506)*
onboarding *(506)*
patch management *(510)*
penetration testing (pentesting) *(515)*
port scanner *(514)*
port scanning *(514)*
principle of least privilege *(504)*
process assessment (516)
recovery point objective (RPO) *(518)*
recovery time objective (RTO) *(518)*
risk management *(503)*

risk posture *(516)*
role-based access *(504)*
security policy *(503)*
service-level agreement (SLA) *(511)*
statement of work (SOW) *(512)*
succession planning *(520)*
threat actor *(513)*
vendor risk assessment *(517)*
vulnerability *(513)*
vulnerability management *(515)*
vulnerability scanner *(513)*
vulnerability scanning *(515)*
warm site *(519)*

Key Term Quiz

Use the Key Terms list to complete the sentences that follow. Not all terms will be used.

1. A(n) _______________ is a written statement that defines how an organization will protect its IT infrastructure.
2. A document submitted to the change management team to ask for a modification to the infrastructure is a(n) _______________.
3. A(n) _______________ is a document that defines the scope, quality, and terms of services to be provided by a service provider.
4. An event in which the security of an infrastructure is compromised is called a(n) _______________.
5. The umbrella term that defines how an organization will continue to operate after a disaster is _______________.
6. A person whose job it is to react to the notification of a computer crime is called a(n) _______________.
7. _______________ is a critical part of contingency planning that deals with the aftermath of an event that destroys substantial amounts of infrastructure.
8. Should a primary facility fail, a(n) _______________ provides all of the resources and computers, but not proper data, to bring an organization back to functionality.
9. _______________ is the science of gathering, examining, analyzing, preserving, and presenting evidence stored on a computer that is acceptable in a court of law.
10. Among other things, _______________ is a free utility that's primarily used as a port scanner.

Multiple-Choice Quiz

1. Risk management is a concept that would most likely address which of the following situations?
   - **A.** A user needs to change a password.
   - **B.** A power surge has damaged a switch.
   - **C.** A file server is having more RAM installed.
   - **D.** A user needs the access code to connect to the company wireless network.
2. What issues should be addressed in an acceptable use policy?
   - **A.** ESD handling procedures
   - **B.** Procedures to be followed if malware is detected
   - **C.** How to operate the fire suppression system
   - **D.** Ownership of data on company computers
3. As technologies change, what should organizations do?
   - **A.** Encourage users to bring in new devices for immediate addition to the infrastructure.
   - **B.** Reject new technologies generally in favor of the tried and true.
   - **C.** Ask users to test new technologies in their areas and report their results to IT managers.
   - **D.** Update policies to reflect changes in technologies.

4. Which of the following is true about change management?
   - **A.** Change happens naturally over time as technologies improve.
   - **B.** Once IT infrastructure is established and working, there is seldom need for change.
   - **C.** Change needs to happen, but not at the cost of security.
   - **D.** Change management should be handled by individual department heads for their own area of the network.
5. Before applying a major patch to production equipment, what should be done?
   - **A.** The patch should be tested.
   - **B.** The patch should be checked for malware.
   - **C.** The patch should be applied to equipment in the least-important department and then, if no ill effects are encountered, deployed to the rest of the organization.
   - **D.** Drivers should be updated on all of equipment to be patched.
6. A popular network hardware company is looking to validate the security of a test network built with devices the company is developing in secret. Which of these documents are they most likely to use to compel an outside pentesting team to help them keep this secret?
   - **A.** An offboarding policy
   - **B.** A nondisclosure agreement (NDA)
   - **C.** A service-level agreement (SLA)
   - **D.** An acceptable use policy (AUP)
7. Which document defines the service provided, equipment provided, and level of technical support?
   - **A.** Service-level agreement (SLA)
   - **B.** Memorandum of understanding (MOU)
   - **C.** Statement of work (SOW)
   - **D.** Privacy/consent to monitoring section of the security policy manual
8. As part of security preparedness planning, which two tasks should be performed?
   - **A.** Configuration backup and patch testing
   - **B.** Prepare SOW documentation and enforce external policies
   - **C.** Vulnerability scanning and penetration testing
   - **D.** Review the network access policy and update role-based access controls
9. What is the next step after completing vulnerability scanning and hardening the infrastructure?
   - **A.** Perform a posture assessment.
   - **B.** Run Nessus.
   - **C.** Perform penetration testing.
   - **D.** Run OpenVAS.
10. In terms of risk management, the compromising of an IT infrastructure's security is known as what?
    - **A.** An accident
    - **B.** An incident
    - **C.** Malware
    - **D.** An exploit
11. A cold backup site has which one of the following resources?
    - **A.** Desks
    - **B.** Computers
    - **C.** Archived data
    - **D.** Current data
12. Which of these describes a recovery point objective? (Select the *best* answer.)
    - **A.** A system for rewarding teams who quickly restore failed systems
    - **B.** How long it will take to restore the latest backup
    - **C.** The maximum number of hours between backups
    - **D.** How long it will take to reach an off-site backup point and return
13. Which of the following tasks should be performed by first responders? (Select two.)
    - **A.** Power down the computer and remove the RAM.
    - **B.** Power down the computer and remove the mass storage drives.
    - **C.** Secure the area.
    - **D.** Document the scene.
    - **E.** Prepare a forensics report.

14. What is a paper trail of who has accessed or controlled a piece of evidence called?
   A. Legal hold
   B. Handoff trail
   C. Handling trail
   D. Chain of custody

15. Which deployment model uses employee-owned mobile devices for corporate use?
   A. BYOD
   B. COBO
   C. COPE
   D. CYOD

Essay Quiz

1. From this list of forensic certifications, select two: CFCE, CCE, GCFA. Research the requirements of each and write an essay documenting the differences in requirements and benefits of achieving these two certifications.

2. Write a short essay comparing patch management with change management.

Lab Project

• Lab Project 18.1

Search some of the major security policy organizations—such as NIST and SANS—for "security policies" and document five different types of security policies.

chapter 19

Protecting Your Network

"The superior man, when resting in safety, does not forget that danger may come."

—Confucius

In this chapter, you will learn how to

- **Explain concepts of network security**
- **Discuss common security threats in network computing**
- **Discuss common vulnerabilities inherent in networking**
- **Describe methods for hardening a network against attacks**
- **Explain how firewalls protect a network from threats**

The very nature of networking makes networks vulnerable. A network must allow multiple users to access serving systems. At the same time, the network must be protected from harm. Doing so is a big business and part of the whole risk management issue touched on in Chapter 18. This chapter concentrates on threats, vulnerabilities, network hardening, and firewalls.

Test Specific

Security Concepts

IT security is a huge topic and the Network+ exam objectives go into a fair amount of detail on IT security concepts and practices. Before we get into the nitty-gritty, let's break down a few critical concepts that will help us in this chapter.

CIA

There are three goals that are widely considered the foundations of the IT security trade: **confidentiality, integrity, and availability (CIA)**. Security professionals work to achieve these goals in every security program and technology. These three goals inform all the data and the systems that process it. The three goals of security are called the **CIA triad**. Figure 19.1 illustrates the three goals of confidentiality, integrity, and availability.

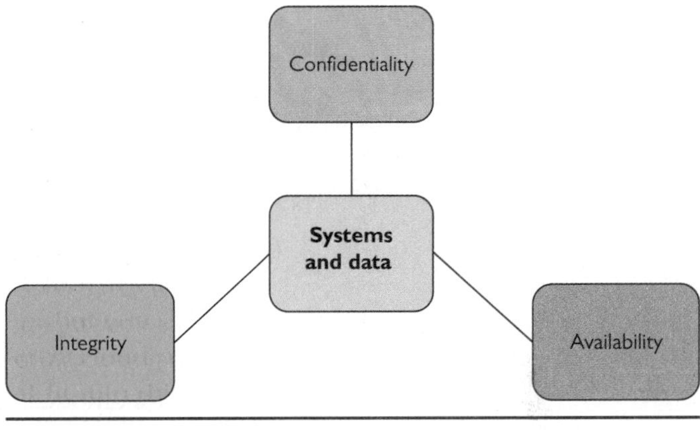

• **Figure 19.1** The CIA triad

> The CIA triad is put into practice through various security mechanisms and controls. Every security technique, practice, and mechanism that is implemented to protect systems and data ensures at least one goal of the CIA triad.

Confidentiality

Confidentiality is the goal of keeping unauthorized people from accessing, seeing, reading, or interacting with systems and data. Confidentiality is a characteristic met by keeping data secret from people who aren't allowed to have it or interact with it in any way, while making sure that only those people who do have the right to access it can do so. Systems achieve confidentiality through various means, including the use of permissions to data, encryption, and so on.

Integrity

Meeting the goal of *integrity* requires maintaining data and systems in a pristine, unaltered state when they are stored, transmitted, processed, and received, unless the alteration is intended due to normal processing. In other words, there should be no unauthorized modification, alteration, creation, or deletion of data. Any changes to data must be done only as part of authorized transformations in normal use and processing. Integrity can be maintained by the use of a variety of checks and other mechanisms, including hashing, data checksums, comparison with known or computed data values, and cryptographic means.

Availability

Maintaining *availability* means ensuring that systems and data are available for authorized users to perform authorized tasks, whenever they need them. Availability is, to some degree, a trade-off between security and ease of use. An extremely secure system that's not functional is not available in practice. Availability is ensured in various ways, including system redundancy, data backups, business continuity, and other means—but it also means not letting security goals render the system useless to the humans who need to use it.

During the course of your study, keep in mind the overall goals in IT security. First, balance three critical elements: functionality, security, and the resources available to ensure both. Second, focus on the goals of the CIA triad—confidentiality, integrity, and availability—when implementing, reviewing, managing, or troubleshooting network and system security. The book returns to these themes many times, tying new pieces of knowledge to this framework.

Zero Trust

Trust is a big deal when it comes to IT security. Who do you trust? How do you establish trust relationships between systems, organizations, and people? This is a massive conversation. In the traditional network security model, we trusted everyone who was already connected to the network, and focused our energy on protecting our sites and networks from everyone and everything outside it.

A better model for today's world starts with no automatic trust at all, a concept called **zero trust**. Quoting NIST Special Publication (SP) 800-207, *Zero Trust Architecture*: "Zero trust is a cybersecurity paradigm focused on resource protection and the premise that trust is never granted implicitly but must be continually evaluated."

In this model, there is no "trusted" network where you assume everyone connected is supposed to be connected, every device is malware free, and every resource is accessible. With a zero-trust architecture, you treat all traffic a device encounters as if it's hostile—like there's no difference between your office LAN and public Wi-Fi at the airport. In practice, this means that any user, device, or application that accesses a resource on your network should be explicitly authenticated and authorized to do so.

This is a major shift in thinking about how to design networks, but it has advantages. In particular, it reduces the risk that attackers can use one compromised device to attack other systems on the network. This doesn't mean you can completely prevent lateral movement, but hosts in a proper zero-trust environment will always have their guard up.

Defense in Depth

The CompTIA Network+ exam objectives expect you to understand multiple topics covered in this chapter as they relate to a defense-in-depth philosophy. I recommend thinking about how *everything* here relates to defense in depth—but pay extra attention to the discussions on network segmentation enforcement, screened subnets, separation of duties, network access control, and honeypots.

Zero trust is one instance of a whole philosophy of security-centric thinking that replaces a more traditional focus on building networks with a crunchy perimeter and an easy-to-abuse interior with a focus on security at every node and layer. As a philosophy, **defense in depth** acknowledges that you can't build a completely secure perimeter—so you should design your security posture with the assumption that every single defense can be beaten.

Because defense in depth is a philosophy and not a package deal you can buy from Microsoft, understanding what counts toward supporting that philosophy can be a little tricky. The fact of the matter is that almost everything counts. That said, when you see specific things all working together in a single organization—things like strong physical security, network segmentation, separation of duties, strong passwords, great password hygiene, and rigorous patch management—you can be pretty sure somebody in charge understands the value of defense in depth.

Separation of Duties

Much as a defense-in-depth approach acknowledges that all defenses can be beaten, it's also important to acknowledge that people are flawed—there's a very real risk employees will make a mistake or be tempted to abuse their power. **Separation of duties** is all about trying to manage this risk by identifying how people could abuse or misuse a system, determining what access they'd need to do so, and then splitting up that access so that no individual has the ability to do it alone.

If you've ever seen a scene in a movie where access to a secure area or weapon requires two keys or access cards, you've seen a simple kind of separation of duties. In the real world, separation of duties is usually nowhere near this exciting. For example, the person responsible for designing or implementing your organization's IT security shouldn't also be responsible for performing a security audit on it.

Network Threats

A network **threat** is any form of *potential* attack against your network. Don't think only about Internet attacks here. Sure, hacker-style threats are real, but there are so many others. A threat can be a person sneaking into your offices and stealing passwords, or an ignorant employee deleting files they should not have access to in the first place. Traditionally, most of the threats we focus on are *external threats* posed by people and systems outside of our organizations—but a strong security posture also means being prepared for *internal threats* posed by members of your organization.

Just by reading the word "potential" you should know that this list could go on for pages. This section includes a list of common network threats. CompTIA does not include all of these in the Network+ exam objectives (because they're covered in CompTIA A+ or Security+), but I've included them here to give a real-world sense of scope:

- Spoofing
- Packet/protocol abuse
- Zero-day attacks
- Rogue devices
- ARP cache poisoning
- Denial of service (with a lot of variations on a theme)
- On-path attack/man-in-the-middle
- Session hijacking
- Password attacks (brute force and dictionary)
- Compromised system
- Insider threat/malicious employee
- VLAN hopping
- Administrative access control
- Malware

- Social engineering
- And more!

It's quite a list, but before we dive in, I want to nail down some general terms that come up a lot when we discuss threats.

Threat Terminology

The **Common Vulnerabilities and Exposures (CVE)** database hosted by MITRE Corporation at https://cve.mitre.org/ compiles a huge list of known vulnerabilities with publicly released software. Many vulnerability scanners use this database to find software that needs to be updated or replaced.

In a very general sense, every threat pairs up with one or more **vulnerabilities**—weaknesses that the threat takes advantage of to work. That said, most of the time a vulnerability refers to an IT-specific weakness, like a problem with hardware, software, or configuration.

We can fix some vulnerabilities by just correcting our configuration or updating software as soon as a patch is available. But sometimes the best we can do is *mitigate* a vulnerability by taking other steps to minimize the risk—this is especially common when the vulnerability is really a design problem with the hardware or protocols we're using.

An **exploit** is an actual procedure for taking advantage of a vulnerability. When a vulnerability is widespread, well known, and easy to take advantage of, working exploits often turn up in hacking and penetration-testing tools that make it easy for people who can't even spell exploit to abuse one. Other vulnerabilities require the stars to align for anyone to exploit them, and might even lurk undiscovered for decades.

Finally, let's circle back to talk about a term that has been flying under the radar. A simple definition of an **attack** is when someone tries to compromise your organization or its systems (especially their confidentiality, integrity, or availability). But the word *attack* also gets thrown around a lot to categorize different tactics, threats, and exploits. I'll use it both ways in this chapter, but don't let it mislead you—unless your organization is neglecting security, most serious efforts to compromise it will string together multiple tactics and exploits that target more than one vulnerability.

Spoofing

Spoofing is the process of pretending to be someone or something you are not by placing false information into your packets. Any data sent on a network can be spoofed. Here are a few quick examples of commonly spoofed data:

- Source MAC address (*MAC spoofing*) or IP address (*IP spoofing*), to make you think a packet came from somewhere else.
- Address Resolution Protocol (ARP) message (*ARP spoofing*) that links the attacker's MAC address to a legitimate network computer, client, or server; to make you think that the message is from a trusted source. (See "ARP Cache Poisoning" later in the chapter for the gory details.)
- E-mail address, to make you think an e-mail came from somewhere else.
- Web address, to make you think you are on a Web page you are not on.
- Username, to make you think a certain user is contacting you when in reality it's someone completely different.

Generally, spoofing isn't so much a threat as it is a tool to make threats. If you spoof my e-mail address, for example, that by itself isn't a threat. If you use my e-mail address to pretend to be me, however, and to ask my employees to send to you their usernames and passwords for network login? That's clearly a threat. (And also a waste of time; my employees would *never* trust me with their usernames and passwords.)

One of the nastier spoofing attacks targets DNS servers, the backbone of naming on all networks today. In **DNS cache poisoning**, an attacker poisons a DNS server's cache to point clients to an evil Web server instead of the correct one.

The CompTIA Network+ exam objectives refer to DNS cache poisoning as simply *DNS poisoning*. Expect to see the shortened term on the exam.

To prevent DNS cache poisoning, the typical use case scenario is to add *Domain Name System Security Extensions (DNSSEC)* for domain name resolution. All the DNS root and top-level domains (plus hundreds of thousands of other DNS servers) use DNSSEC.

Packet/Protocol Abuse

No matter how hard the Internet's designers try, it seems there is always a way to take advantage of a protocol by using it in ways it was never meant to be used. Anytime you do things with a protocol that it wasn't meant to do and that abuse ends up creating a threat, this is *protocol abuse*. A classic example involves the Network Time Protocol (NTP).

The Internet keeps time by using NTP servers. Without NTP providing accurate time for everything that happens on the Internet, anything that's time sensitive would be in big trouble.

No computer's clock is perfect, so NTP is designed for each NTP server to have a number of peers. *Peers* are other NTP servers that one NTP server can compare its own time against to make sure its clock is accurate. Occasionally a person running an NTP server might want to query the server to determine what peers it uses. The command used on just about every NTP server to submit queries is called **ntpdc**. The `ntpdc` command puts the NTP server into interactive mode so that you can then make queries to the NTP server. One of these queries is called **monlist**. The `monlist` query asks the NTP server about the traffic going on between itself and peers. If you query a public NTP server with `monlist`, it generates a lot of output:

```
$ ntpdc -c monlist fake.timeserver5.org
remote address          port local address      count m ver rstr avgint  lstint
===============================================================================
time.apple.com           123 192.168.4.78          13 4  4   1d0    319     399
ntp.notreal.com          123 46.3.129.78         1324 4  4     1      0       0
123.212.32.44            123 32.42.77.82            0 0  0     0      0       0

<a few hundred more lines here>

ntpdc>
```

A bad guy can hit multiple NTP servers with the same little command—with a spoofed source IP address—and generate a ton of responses from the NTP server to that source IP address. Enough of these requests will bring the spoofed source computer—now called the target or victim—to its knees. We call this a denial of service attack (covered a bit later), and it's a form of protocol abuse.

If that's not sinister enough, hackers can also use evil programs that inject unwanted information into packets in an attempt to break another system. We call these *malformed packets*. Programs such as Scapy let you generate malformed packets and send them to anyone. You can use this to exploit a vulnerable server. What will happen if you broadcast a DHCP request with corrupt or incorrect data in the Options field? Well, if your DHCP server happens to have an unpatched vulnerability and reads the malformed request, it will break in some way: crashing the server, corrupting data, or giving an attacker remote access! This is an exploit created by packet abuse.

Zero-Day Attacks

As I mentioned earlier, some vulnerabilities are known and others lurk undiscovered. If that sounds a little sinister, the reality is actually a lot worse. There are plenty of unreported, unfixed vulnerabilities that *someone* knows about—and there's a whole black-market trade where nefarious characters sell and buy them for their own purposes.

When we're lucky, new vulnerabilities come to light due to the tireless efforts of security researchers who discover these problems and try to report them in a responsible way that gives the developer time to come up with a patch or workaround. If we're a little less lucky, the developer dawdles, prompting the researcher to publicly disclose the vulnerability so that users, at least, can start taking the problem seriously.

What about when we aren't so lucky? Someone launches a **zero-day attack**—an attack that leverages a previously unknown vulnerability that we've had zero days to fix or mitigate.

Rogue Devices

Some network devices—especially routers, switches, access points, firewalls, and DHCP servers—have a lot of power and require trust. Attackers love to usurp this trust and power by tricking your clients into believing rogue devices under the attackers' control are legitimate.

You'll recall *rogue DHCP servers* from way back in Chapter 6. Those cause problems when someone plugs a DHCP server into the LAN and it starts doing its job, doling out IP information...that has nothing to do with the accurate local information. And then people can't get to resources and help desk gets swamped with calls... and it's just a bad day.

DHCP Snooping

In order to defang rogue DHCP servers, **DHCP snooping** creates a database (called the DHCP snooping binding database) of MAC addresses for all of a network's known DHCP servers (connected to trusted ports) and clients (connected to untrusted ports). If a system connected to an untrusted port starts sending DHCP server messages, the DHCP snoop–capable switch will block that system, stopping all unauthorized DHCP traffic and sending some form of alarm to the appropriate person.

RA-Guard

DHCP snooping does a great job of protecting IPv4 networks, but DHCP is much less important in IPv6 networks. How do we protect against rogue router advertisements on our IPv6 networks? That's where **Router Advertisement Guard (RA-Guard)** comes in. Similar to DHCP snooping, RA-Guard enables the switch to block router advertisements and router redirect messages that are not sent from trusted ports or don't match a policy. The ability to define a policy for valid RA messages enables administrators to validate that a router advertisement contains what it should—such as only using prefixes from a set list.

ARP Cache Poisoning

ARP cache poisoning attacks target ARP caches on hosts and MAC address tables on switches. As we saw back in Chapter 6, the process and protocol used in resolving an IP address to an Ethernet MAC address is called Address Resolution Protocol (ARP).

Every node on a TCP/IP network has an *ARP cache* that stores a list of known IP addresses and their associated MAC addresses. On a Windows system you can see the ARP cache using the `arp -a` command. Here's part of the result of typing `arp -a` on my system:

```
C:\Users\Mike>arp -a
Interface: 202.13.212.205 --- 0xc
  Internet Address      Physical Address      Type
  202.13.212.1          d0-d0-fd-39-f5-5e     dynamic
  202.13.212.100        30-05-5c-0d-ed-c5     dynamic
  202.13.212.101        00-02-d1-08-df-8d     dynamic
  202.13.212.208        00-22-6b-a0-a2-9b     dynamic
```

If a device wants to send an IP packet to another device, it must encapsulate the IP packet in an Ethernet frame on wired LANs. If the sending device doesn't know the destination device's MAC address, it sends a special broadcast called an *ARP request*. In turn, the device with that IP address responds with a unicast packet to the requesting device. Figure 19.2 shows a Wireshark capture of an ARP request and response.

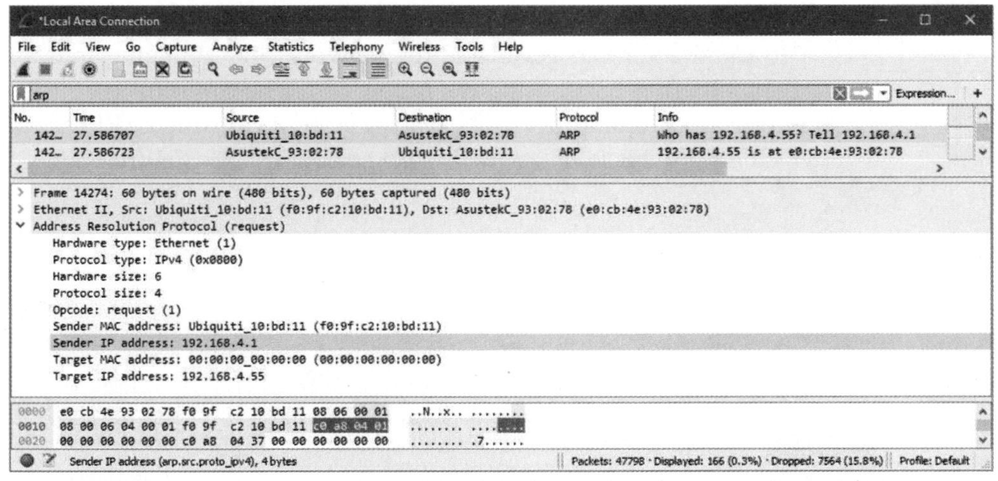

• **Figure 19.2** ARP request and response

The problem with ARP is that it has no security. Any device that can get on a LAN can wreak havoc with ARP requests and responses. For example, ARP enables any device at any time to announce its MAC address without first getting a request. Additionally, ARP has a number of very detailed but relatively unused specifications. A device can just declare itself to be a "router." How that information is used is up to the writer of the software used by the device that hears this announcement. More than a decade ago, ARP poisoning caused a tremendous amount of trouble.

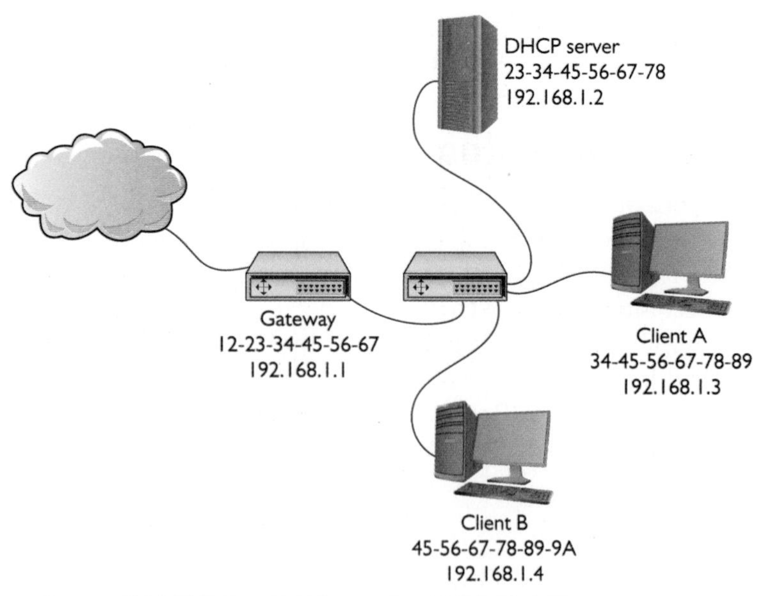

• **Figure 19.3** Our happy network

ARP Cache

Name	MAC	IP
Gateway	12-23-34-45-56-67	192.168.1.1
DHCP	23-34-45-56-67-78	192.168.1.2
Client A	34-45-56-67-78-89	192.168.1.3
Client B	45-56-67-78-89-9A	192.168.1.4

• **Figure 19.4** Each computer's ARP cache should look about the same.

Poisoning in Action

Here's how an ARP cache poisoning attack works. Figure 19.3 shows a typical tiny network with a gateway, a switch, a DHCP server, and two clients. Assuming nothing has recently changed with the computers' IP addresses, each system's ARP cache should look something like Figure 19.4. (ARP caches don't store computer names, but I've added them for clarity.)

If a bad actor can get inside the network (like plugging into an unused Ethernet port), using the proper tools, he can send false ARP frames that each computer reads, placing evil data into their ARP caches (which is why this is called ARP cache poisoning). See Figure 19.5.

Name	MAC	IP
Gateway	~~12-23-34-45-56-67~~ FE-ED-DC-CB-BA-A9	192.168.1.1
DHCP	23-34-45-56-67-78	192.168.1.2
Client A	34-45-56-67-78-89	192.168.1.3
Client B	45-56-67-78-89-9A	192.168.1.4

• **Figure 19.5** Every system's ARP cache is now poisoned.

Once the poisoning starts, the evil computer can perform an on-path attack (aka man-in-the-middle attack), reading every packet going through it, as shown in Figure 19.6.

Before cache poisoning

Gateway

Client A

Gateway

Client A

After cache poisoning

Evil computer

• **Figure 19.6** ARP cache poisoning enables an on-path attack.

Dynamic ARP Inspection

Clearly, we'd like to avoid ARP cache poisoning attacks. Fortunately, help is available. **Dynamic ARP Inspection (DAI)** technology in switches relies on ARP information that DHCP snooping collects in the DHCP snooping binding database—it's essentially a list of known-good IP and MAC addresses (Figure 19.7).

Known Good Systems

Name	MAC	IP
Gateway	12-23-34-45-56-67	192.168.1.1
DHCP	23-34-45-56-67-78	192.168.1.2
Client A	34-45-56-67-78-89	192.168.1.3
Client B	45-56-67-78-89-9A	192.168.1.4

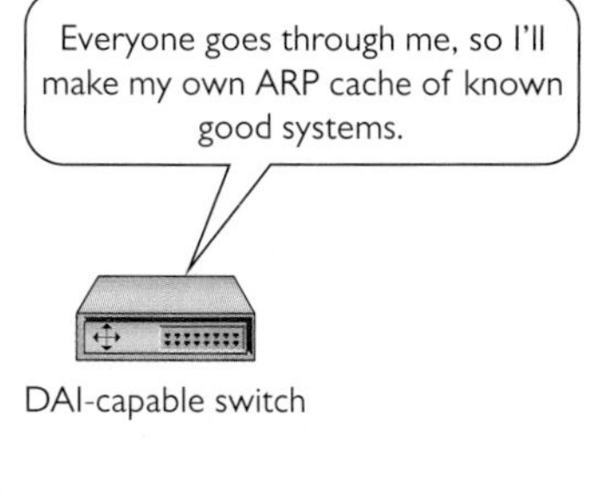
Everyone goes through me, so I'll make my own ARP cache of known good systems.
DAI-capable switch

• **Figure 19.7** DAI consulting the DHCP snooping binding database

I'm the gateway! Here are my MAC and IP addresses!
Evil computer
FE-ED-DC-CB-BA-A9

Uh, no. I don't know your MAC... BLOCKED!!!
DAI-capable switch

• **Figure 19.8** DAI in action

Now if an ARP poisoner suddenly decides to attack this network, the DAI-capable switch notices the unknown MAC address and blocks it (Figure 19.8).

Denial of Service

Hundreds of millions of servers on the Internet provide a multitude of different services. Given the amount of security now built in at so many different levels, it's more difficult than ever for a bad guy to cripple any one particular service by exploiting a weakness in the servers themselves. So what's a bad guy (or gal, group, or government) to do to shut down a service he doesn't like, even if he is unaware of any exploits on the target servers? Why, denial of service, of course!

The CompTIA Network+ objectives for network hardening say best practices are to implement Dynamic ARP Inspection (DAI) and enable DHCP snooping.

A **denial of service (DoS)** attack is a targeted attack on a server (or servers) that provides some form of service on the Internet (such as a Web site) with the goal of making that service unable to process any incoming requests. DoS attacks come in many different forms. The simplest example is a *physical attack,* where a person physically attacks the servers by going to where the servers are located and shutting them down or disconnecting their Internet connections, in some cases permanently. Physical DoS attacks are good to know for the exam, but they aren't very common unless the service is very small and served in only a single location.

The most common form of DoS is when a bad guy uses his computer to flood a targeted server with so many requests that the service is overwhelmed and ceases functioning. These attacks are most commonly performed on Web and e-mail servers, but any Internet service's servers can be attacked via some DoS method.

The secret to a successful DoS attack is to use up so much of a victim's resources that they can't serve legitimate requests. The important thing to understand about DoS attacks is that there are a million and one ways to waste resources—and they can be combined in some really creative ways—so it may help to distinguish between tactics that focus on wasting resources with an overwhelming volume of requests and tactics that waste resources in much more targeted ways.

Internet-service servers are robust devices, designed to handle a massive number of requests per second. These robust servers make it tricky for a single bad guy at a single computer to send enough requests to slow them down. The main way to send enough traffic to swamp a server is to get help. In theory this might mean a bad guy and a million of his friends all sign up to spray their target with packets—a **distributed denial of service (DDoS)** attack. In reality, DDoS operators usually don't own these computers, but instead use malware (discussed later) to take control of computers. A single computer under the control of an operator is called a **zombie** or **bot**. A group of computers under the control of one operator is called a **botnet**. Various *command and control (C2)* protocols are used to automate server controls over botnets, thus limiting the need for people once the initial zombification happens.

Zombified computers aren't always immediately obvious. DDoS operators often wait weeks or months after a computer's been infected to take control of it. Anti-malware software, training, and procedures can help keep your devices from becoming someone else's digital weapon.

A botnet isn't the only way for an attacker to get help, though. Another tactic is to send requests that spoof the target server's IP address as the source IP address to otherwise normally operating servers, such as DNS or NTP servers, using **reflection** to aim their resources at your target. Reflection is often combined with **amplification**—a tactic that focuses on sending small requests that trigger large responses reflected at your target—because it helps the attacker use their own limited resources efficiently to deliver a much larger volume to the target.

Sometimes it's best to work smart instead of hard—and that's the bread and butter of low-and-slow DoS tactics. With a low-and-slow attack, the bad guys send a small number of cleverly crafted packets to the victim that keep the target busy for as long as possible. These come in all kinds of shapes and sizes because they generally take advantage of some characteristic of the service they attack.

For example, Web servers can be vulnerable to a R.U.D.Y. (R U Dead Yet) attack where the attacker fills out a Web form with a ton of content and opens a connection to submit it. Instead of being polite, the attacker takes their sweet time trickling a few bytes at a time to the server, tying up a connection it needs to serve legitimate traffic. If the attacker opens enough of these requests, they can deny access to the service to everyone else.

Deauthentication Attack

A **deauthentication (deauth) attack**—a form of DoS attack—targets 802.11 Wi-Fi networks specifically by sending out a frame that kicks a wireless client off its current WAP connection. A rogue WAP nearby presents a great and often automatic alternative option for connection. The rogue WAP connects the client to the Internet and then proceeds to collect data from that client.

The deauth attack targets a specific Wi-Fi frame called a deauthentication frame, normally used by a WAP to kick an unauthorized WAP off its network. The attacker flips this narrative on its head, using the good disconnect frame for evil purposes. (And here you thought only wired networks got all the love from DoS attacks.) Refer to Chapter 14 to refresh your memory on Wi-Fi security.

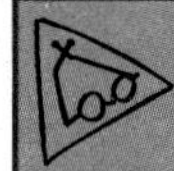

Tech Tip

Unintentional DoS Attack

A friendly or unintentional DoS attack is just as it's named: a system is brought down unintentionally. The most common form of friendly DoS occurs on a super-busy server: an organization's infrastructure isn't strong enough to keep up with legitimate demand. This is very common on the Web when a popular site makes a reference to a small site or someone mentions the small site on a radio or TV program, resulting in a massive increase in traffic to the small site. This unintentional DoS attack goes by many names, such as **slashdotting** *or the Reddit hug of death.*

DHCP Starvation Attack

Deauth attacks aren't the only way attackers can use DoS to shift legitimate clients over to rogue devices. DHCP is vulnerable to something very similar, even though it looks a little different in practice. Because DHCP servers hand out IP address leases for a set amount of time, and have a limited number of leases to give out, they're vulnerable to **DHCP scope exhaustion**: they just plain run out of open addresses.

An attacker can use this limitation to their advantage by spoofing packets to the DHCP server, tricking it into giving away all of its leases—a **DHCP starvation attack**. Much like a deauth attack, DHCP starvation is usually not the end objective, but just a technique used to encourage clients to switch to a rogue DHCP server that the attacker controls.

On-Path Attack

In an **on-path attack**—traditionally called a **man-in-the-middle** attack—an attacker taps into communications between two systems, covertly intercepting traffic thought to be only between those systems, reading or in some cases even changing the data and then sending the data on. Man-in-the-middle attacks are commonly perpetrated using ARP poisoning. But a classic man-in-the-middle attack would be to spoof the SSID and let people connect to the rogue WAP controlled by the attacker. The attacker could then listen in on that wireless network, gathering up all the conversations and gaining access to passwords, shared keys, or other sensitive information. Though heavily mitigated today by TLS and certificate pinning, attacks like this show why many organizations are moving to a zero-trust model of network security.

Session Hijacking

Somewhat similarly to man-in-the-middle attacks, **session hijacking** tries to intercept a valid computer session to get authentication information. Unlike man-in-the-middle attacks, session hijacking only tries to grab authentication information, not necessarily listen in for additional information.

Password Attacks

In a **password attack**, a bad actor uses various methods to discover a password, often comparing various potential passwords against known hashes of passwords. The methods vary from the simplest brute-force approach to more sophisticated approaches like dictionary attacks.

Brute Force

Brute force is an attack where a threat agent guesses every permutation of some part of data. Most of the time the term "brute force" refers to an attempt to crack a password, but the term applies to other attacks. You can brute force a search for open ports, network IDs, usernames, and so on. Pretty much any attempt to guess the contents of some kind of data field that isn't obvious (or is hidden) is considered a brute-force attack.

Dictionary

A **dictionary attack** uses a list of known words and partial words as the starting point for cracking passwords. People tend to create passwords they can remember. Eduardo's password is 3L!t3juaN, which looks pretty good at first blush. But a typical dictionary attack can be set up to do all kinds of substitution checks automatically, such as the number 3 for the letter e, for example, or ! for the letter i. Running a scan that does all the permutations for "elite one" would crack Eduardo's password pretty quickly with the power of modern computers.

Physical/Local Access

Not all threats to your network originate from faraway bad guys. There are many threats that lurk right in your LAN. This is a particularly dangerous place as these threats don't need to worry about getting past your network edge defenses such as firewalls or WAPs. You need to watch out for problems with hardware, software, and, worst of all, the people who are on your LAN.

Insider Threats

The greatest hackers in the world will all agree that being inside an organization, either physically or by access permissions, makes evildoing much easier. Malicious employees are a huge threat because of their ability to directly destroy data, inject malware, and initiate attacks. These are collectively called **insider threats**.

Trusted and Untrusted Users A worst-case scenario from the perspective of security is *unsecured access to private resources*. A couple of terms come into play here. There are trusted users and untrusted users. A **trusted user** is an account that has been granted specific authority to perform certain or all administrative tasks. An **untrusted user** is just the opposite, an account that has been granted no administrative powers.

Trusted users with poor password protection or other security leakages can be compromised. Untrusted users can be upgraded "temporarily" to accomplish a particular task and then forgotten. Consider this situation: A user accidentally copied a bunch of files to several shared network repositories. The administrator does not have time to search for and delete all of the files. The user is granted deletion capability and told to remove the unneeded files. Do you feel a disaster coming? The newly created trusted user could easily remove the wrong files. Careful management of trusted users is the simple solution to these types of threats.

Every configurable device, like a managed switch, has a default password and default settings, all of which can create an inadvertent insider threat if not addressed. People sometimes can't help but be curious. A user might note the IP address of a switch on his network, for example, and try to connect with Secure Shell (SSH) "just to see." Because it's so easy to get the default passwords/settings for devices with a simple Google search, that information is available to the user. One change on that switch might mean a whole lot of pain for the network tech or administrator who has to fix things.

Dealing with such authentication issues is straightforward. Before bringing any system online, change any default accounts and passwords. This is particularly true for administrative accounts. Also, disable or delete any "guest" accounts (make sure you have another account created first!). Finally, apply the *principle of least privilege*—always assign the most-limited privileges that will be sufficient.

Malicious Users Much more worrisome than accidental accesses to unauthorized resources are **malicious users** who consciously attempt to access, steal, or damage resources. Malicious users or *actors* may represent an external or internal threat.

What does a malicious user want to do? If they are intent on stealing data or gaining further access, they may try *packet sniffing*. This is difficult to detect, but as you know from previous chapters, encryption is a strong defense against sniffing.

One of the first techniques that malicious users try is to probe hosts to identify any open ports. There are many tools available to poll all stations on a network for their up/down status and for a list of any open ports (and, by inference, all closed ports too). Nmap is the de facto tool for troubleshooting hosts, but can be used for malevolent activities.

Having found an open port, another way for a malicious user to gain information and additional access is to probe a host's open ports to learn details about running services. This is known as **banner grabbing**. For instance, a host may have an exposed SSH server running. Using a utility like Nmap or Netcat, a malicious user can send an request to port 22. The server may respond with a message indicating the type and version of SSH server software that is running; for example:

```
$ nc -v ci.home.totalsem.com 22
Connection to ci.home.totalsem.com port 22 [tcp/ssh] succeeded!
SSH-2.0-OpenSSH_7.6p1 Ubuntu-4ubuntu0.5
```

With that information, the malicious actor can then learn about vulnerabilities of that product and continue their pursuit. The obvious solution to port scanning and banner grabbing is to not run unnecessary services (resulting in an open port) on a host and to make sure that running processes have current security patches installed.

In the same vein, a malicious user may attempt to exploit known vulnerabilities of certain devices attached to the network. MAC addresses of Ethernet NICs have their first 24 bits assigned by the IEEE. This is a unique number assigned to a specific manufacturer and is known as the **organizationally unique identifier (OUI)**, sometimes called the vendor ID. By issuing certain messages such as broadcasted ARP requests, a malicious user can collect all of the OUI numbers of the wired and wireless nodes attached to a network or subnetwork. Using common lookup tools, the malicious user can identify devices by OUI numbers assigned to particular manufacturers. The past few years have seen numerous DDoS attacks using zombified Internet of Things (IoT) devices, such as security cameras.

VLAN Hopping

An older form of attack that still comes up from time to time, called VLAN hopping, enables an attacker to access a VLAN they'd otherwise have no access to. The mechanism behind **VLAN hopping** is to take a system that's connected to one VLAN and, by abusing VLAN commands to the switch, convince the switch to change your switch port connection to a trunk link.

Administrative Access Control

All operating systems and many switches and routers come with some form of **access control list (ACL)** that defines what users can do with a device's shared resources. An access control might be a file server giving a user read-only privileges to a particular folder, or a firewall only allowing certain internal IP addresses to access the Internet. ACLs are everywhere in a network. In fact, you'll see more of them from the standpoint of a firewall later in this chapter.

> The CompTIA Network+ exam does not test you on the details of file system access controls. In other words, don't bother memorizing details like NTFS permissions, but do appreciate that you have fine-grained controls available.

Every operating system—and many Internet applications—are packed with administrative tools and functionality. You need these tools to get all kinds of work done, but by the same token, you need to work hard to keep these capabilities out of the reach of those who don't need them.

Make sure you know the **administrative accounts** native to Windows (administrator), Linux (root), and macOS (root). You must carefully control these accounts. Clearly, giving regular users administrator/root access is a bad idea, but far more subtle problems can arise. I once gave a user the Manage Documents permission for a busy laser printer in a Windows network. She quickly realized she could pause other users' print jobs and send her print jobs to the beginning of the print queue—nice for her but not so nice for her coworkers. Protecting administrative programs and functions from access and abuse by users is a real challenge and one that requires an extensive knowledge of the operating system and of users' motivations.

> Administering your super accounts is only part of what's called *user account control*. See "Controlling User Accounts" later in this chapter for more details.

Unused Components and Devices

In many organizations, unused components and devices can be an easily overlooked risk. Your old laptops, desktops, hard drives, printers, and network hardware can easily have sensitive data sitting there for the taking—or they could be just the thing an attacker needs to access your network without arousing suspicion. Every computing device and IT system has a **system life cycle**, from shiny and new, to patched and secure, to "you're still using that old junk?", to safely decommissioned.

Organizations that are serious about archiving or destroying sensitive data as needed typically have *system life cycle policies* that cover everything from how to plan and provision new IT systems to **asset disposal**.

These policies might cover where and how to archive important data before decommissioning components, how to ensure no one else can recover sensitive data from your old devices, and whether you should donate old devices to a worthy nonprofit organization or send them through a shredder.

The big thing to keep in mind here is that there are all kinds of devices and systems out in the world, and they have all kinds of different components and wiping procedures. You don't necessarily *have* to send your devices through a shredder, but a lot of people default to physical destruction as a surefire way to *sanitize devices for disposal* instead of effectively leaving all of your HR department's files out by the curb for anyone who's curious. In many cases, performing a *factory reset/wipe configuration* is sufficient—especially when it comes to networking gear and devices that use full-disk encryption. In every case, you should follow your organization's policy!

Malware

The term **malware** describes any program or code (macro, script, and so on) that's designed to do something on a system or network that you don't want to have happen. Malware comes in many forms, such as viruses, worms, macros, Trojan horses, rootkits, adware, and spyware. We'll examine all these malware flavors in this section. Stopping malware, by far the number one security problem for just about everyone, is so important that we'll address that topic in its own section later in this chapter, "Anti-Malware Programs."

Crypto-malware/Ransomware

Crypto-malware uses some form of encryption to lock a user out of a system. Once the crypto-malware encrypts the computer, usually encrypting the boot drive, in most cases the malware then forces the user to pay money to get the system decrypted. When any form of malware makes you pay to get the malware to go away, we call that malware **ransomware**. If a crypto-malware uses a ransom, we commonly call it *crypto-ransomware*.

Crypto-ransomware is one of the most troublesome malwares today, first appearing around 2012 and still going strong. Zero-day variations of crypto-malware, with names such as CryptoWall or WannaCry, are often impossible to clean.

Virus

A **virus** is a program that has two jobs: to replicate and to activate. *Replication* means it makes copies of itself, often as code stored in boot sectors or as extra code added to the end of executable programs. A virus is not a stand-alone program, but rather something attached to a host file, kind of like a human virus. *Activation* is when a virus does something like erase the boot sector of a drive. A virus only replicates to other applications on a drive or to other drives, such as flash drives or optical media. It does not replicate across networks. Plus, a virus needs human action to spread.

Worm

A **worm** functions similarly to a virus, though it replicates exclusively through networks. A worm, unlike a virus, doesn't have to wait for someone to use a removable drive to replicate. If the infected computer is on a network, a worm immediately starts sending copies of itself to any other computers it can locate on the network. Worms can exploit inherent vulnerabilities in program code, attacking programs, operating systems, protocols, and more. Worms, unlike viruses, do not need host files to infect.

Macro

A **macro** is any type of virus that exploits application macros to replicate and activate. A *macro* is also programming within an application that enables you to control aspects of the application. Macros exist in any application that has a built-in macro language, such as Microsoft Excel, that users can program to handle repetitive tasks (among other things).

Logic Bomb

A **logic bomb** is code written to execute when certain conditions are met, usually with malicious intent. A logic bomb could be added to a company database, for example, to start deleting files if the database author loses her job. Or, the programming could be added to another program, such as a Trojan horse.

Trojan Horse

A **Trojan horse** is a piece of malware that looks or pretends to do one thing while, at the same time, doing something evil. A Trojan horse may be a game, like poker, or a free screensaver. The sky is the limit. The more "popular" Trojan horses turn an infected computer into a server and then open TCP or UDP ports so a remote user can control the infected computer. They can be used to capture keystrokes, passwords, files, credit card information, and more. Trojan horses do not replicate.

Rootkit

It's easier for malware to succeed if it has a good way to hide itself. As awareness of malware has grown, anti-malware programs make it harder to find new hiding spots. A **rootkit** takes advantage of very low-level system functions to both gain privileged access and hide from all but the most aggressive of anti-malware tools. Rootkits make their happy little homes deep in operating systems, hypervisors, and even firmware. At this level, they can evade or even actively undermine malware scanners that need to execute on the infected system.

Adware/Spyware

There are two types of programs that are similar to malware in that they try to hide themselves to an extent. **Adware** is a program that monitors the types of Web sites you frequent and uses that information to generate targeted advertisements, usually pop-up windows. Adware isn't, by definition, evil, but many adware makers use sneaky methods to get you to use adware, such as using deceptive-looking Web pages ("Your computer is infected with a virus—click here to scan NOW!"). As a result, adware is often considered malware. Some of the computer-infected ads actually install a virus when you click them, so avoid these things like the plague.

Spyware is a function of any program that sends information about your system or your actions over the Internet. The type of information sent depends on the program. A spyware program will include your browsing history.

A more aggressive form of spyware may send keystrokes or all of the contacts in your e-mail. Some spyware makers bundle their product with ads to make them look innocuous. Adware, therefore, can contain spyware.

The CompTIA Network+ exam objectives categorize common types of attacks as *technology-based* and *human and environmental*. It's doubtful you'll get a question based on category, but note that most of the attacks discussed so far in the chapter fall into the first category. The social engineering and related attacks (discussed next) are in the latter category.

Social Engineering

A considerable percentage of attacks against your network fall under the heading of **social engineering**—the process of using or manipulating people inside the networking environment to gain access to that network from the outside. The term "social engineering" covers the many ways humans can use other humans to gain unauthorized information. This unauthorized information may be a network login, a credit card number, company customer data—almost anything you might imagine that one person or organization may not want a person outside of that organization to access.

Social engineering attacks aren't considered hacking—at least in the classic sense of the word—although the goals are the same. Social engineering is where people attack an organization through the people in the organization or physically access the organization to get the information they need.

The most classic form of social engineering is the telephone scam in which someone calls a person and tries to get him or her to reveal his or her username/password combination. In the same vein, someone may physically enter your building under the guise of having a legitimate reason for being there, such as a cleaning person, repair technician, or messenger. The attacker then snoops around desks, looking for whatever he or she has come to find (one of many good reasons not to put passwords on your desk or monitor). The attacker might talk with people inside the organization, gathering names, office numbers, or department names—little things in and of themselves, but powerful tools when combined later with other social engineering attacks.

Social engineering attacks are commonly used together, so if you discover one of them being used against your organization, it's a good idea to look for others.

These old-school social engineering tactics are taking a backseat to a far more nefarious form of social engineering: phishing.

Phishing

In a **phishing** attack, the attacker poses as some sort of trusted site, like an online version of your bank or credit card company, and solicits you to update your financial information, such as a credit card number. You might get an e-mail message, for example, that purports to be from PayPal telling you that your account needs to be updated and provides a link that looks like it goes to https://www.paypal.com. Upon clicking the link, however, you end up at a site that claims to list a legitimate phone number for PayPal support, but is actually https://paypal-customer-service.example.com, a phishing site. Or the e-mail might have fabricated documents attached—like a speeding ticket or an invoice—designed to spur you into taking action.

Shoulder Surfing

Shoulder surfing is the process of surreptitiously monitoring people when they are accessing any kind of system, trying to ascertain password, PIN codes, or personal information. The term shoulder surfing comes from the classic "looking over someone's shoulder" as the bad guy tries to get your password or PIN by watching which keys you press. Shoulder surfing is an old but still very common method of social engineering.

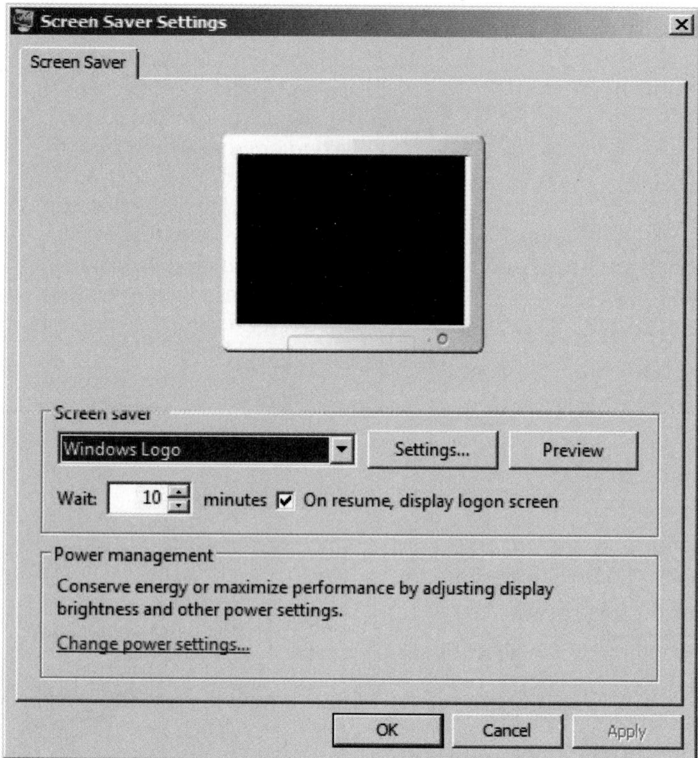

• **Figure 19.9** Applying a password-protected screensaver to a server

Physical Intrusion

You can't consider a network secure unless you provide some physical protection to your network. I separate physical protection into two different areas: protection of servers and protection of clients.

Server protection is easy. Lock up your servers to prevent physical access by any unauthorized person. Large organizations have special server rooms, complete with card-key locks and tracking of anyone who enters or exits. Smaller organizations should at least have a locked closet. While you're locking up your servers, don't forget about any network switches! Hackers can access networks by plugging into a switch, so don't leave any switches available to them.

Physical server protection doesn't stop with a locked door. One of the most common mistakes made by techs is to walk away from a server while still logged in. Always log off from your server when you're not actively managing the server. As a backup, add a password-protected screensaver (Figure 19.9).

Locking up all of your client systems is difficult, but your users should be required to perform some physical security. First, all users should lock their computers when they step away from their desks. Instruct them to press the WINDOWS KEY-L combination to perform the lock. Hackers take advantage of unattended systems to get access to networks.

Second, make users aware of the potential for dumpster diving and make paper shredders available. Last, tell users to mind their work areas. It's amazing how many users leave passwords readily available. I can go into any office, open a few desk drawers, and invariably find little yellow sticky notes with usernames and passwords. If users must write down passwords, tell them to put them in locked drawers!

Tech Tip

Lock Them Down

A Windows PC should be locked down when it's not actively being used. The simplest thing to teach your users to do is to press the WINDOWS KEY-L *combination when they get up from their desks. The effects from the key combination vary according to both the version of Windows and whether a system is a member of a workgroup or domain, but all will require the user to log in to access his or her account (assuming the account is password protected in the first place, of course!).*

Cross Check

Wireless Threats

You've just read about some threats common to all networks, but back in Chapter 14 you learned about some threats specific to wireless networks, so cross-check this out. Do you remember what a rogue access point (AP) does? What about an evil twin? Are these common wireless threats today?

Common Vulnerabilities

If a threat is an action that threat agents do to try to compromise our networks, then a vulnerability is a potential weakness in our infrastructure that a threat might exploit. Note that I didn't say that a threat will take advantage of the vulnerability, only that the vulnerability is a weak place that needs to be addressed.

Some vulnerabilities are obvious, such as connecting to the Internet without an edge firewall or not using any form of account control for user files. Other vulnerabilities are unknown or missed, and that makes the study of vulnerabilities very important for a network tech. This section explores a few common vulnerabilities.

Using a firewall or ACL to block/filter ports can lead to a common network service issue, that of *blocked services, ports, or addresses*. A typical scenario you might need to troubleshoot at a client level is a newly installed Internet-aware application (like a game) that can't access the Internet. Aggressively filtering ports—by an overly zealous tech or user—can block legitimate network access.

A similar scenario on the server side can occur when one tech blocks ports and doesn't properly document his or her actions. Another tech wouldn't necessarily know the ports are blocked in the firewall and could look to other issues when confronted with an application that can't access the network.

Unnecessary Running Services

A typical system running any OS is going to have a large number of important programs running in the background, called **services**. Services do the behind-the-scenes grunt work that users don't need to see, such as wireless network clients and DHCP clients. There are client services and server services.

As a Windows user, I've gotten used to seeing zillions of services running on my system, and in most cases I can recognize only about 50 percent of them—and I'm good at this! In a typical system, not all these services are necessary, so you should *disable unneeded network services*.

From a security standpoint, there are two reasons it's important not to run any unnecessary services. First, most OSs use services to listen on open TCP or UDP ports, potentially leaving systems open to attack. Second, bad guys often use services as a tool for the use and propagation of malware.

The problem with trying not to run unnecessary services is the fact that there are just so many of them. It's up to you to research services running on a particular machine to determine if they're needed or not. It's a rite of passage for any tech to review the services running on a system, going through them one at a time. Over time you will become familiar with many of the built-in services and get an eye for spotting the ones that just don't look right. There are tools available to do the job for you, but this is one place where you need skill and practice.

Closing unnecessary services closes TCP/UDP ports. Every operating system has some tool for you to see exactly what ports are open. Figure 19.10 shows an example of the `netstat` command in macOS.

```
michaels@mediamac-2: ~ — ~ — zsh — 90×41

michaels@mediamac-2 ~                                                          [9:45:48]
> $ netstat -n
Active Internet connections
Proto Recv-Q Send-Q  Local Address          Foreign Address        (state)
tcp4       0   1238  192.168.4.78.17500     192.168.4.53.9941      ESTABLISHED
tcp4     262      0  192.168.4.78.17500     192.168.4.27.59229     ESTABLISHED
tcp4       0      0  192.168.4.78.62253     192.168.4.36.17500     ESTABLISHED
tcp4       0      0  192.168.4.78.62252     192.168.4.42.17500     ESTABLISHED
tcp4       0      0  192.168.4.78.62251     192.168.4.53.17500     ESTABLISHED
tcp4       0      0  192.168.4.78.62250     192.168.4.35.17500     ESTABLISHED
tcp4       0      0  192.168.4.78.62249     192.168.4.57.17500     ESTABLISHED
tcp4       0      0  192.168.4.78.62248     23.23.249.59.443       ESTABLISHED
tcp4       0      0  192.168.4.78.62245     108.160.165.138.443    ESTABLISHED
tcp4       0      0  192.168.4.78.62211     72.246.57.9.80         ESTABLISHED
tcp4       0      0  192.168.4.78.62210     23.205.120.9.80        ESTABLISHED
tcp4       0      0  192.168.4.78.62201     23.205.120.32.80       ESTABLISHED
tcp4       0      0  192.168.4.78.62200     23.205.120.32.80       ESTABLISHED
tcp4       0      0  192.168.4.78.62199     216.38.160.128.80      ESTABLISHED
tcp4       0      0  192.168.4.78.62197     173.194.115.45.80      ESTABLISHED
tcp4       0      0  192.168.4.78.62194     216.38.160.130.80      ESTABLISHED
tcp4       0      0  192.168.4.78.62191     173.194.115.45.80      ESTABLISHED
tcp4       0      0  192.168.4.78.62183     173.194.115.96.443     ESTABLISHED
tcp4       0      0  192.168.4.78.62170     74.125.227.188.80      ESTABLISHED
tcp4       0      0  192.168.4.78.62169     173.194.115.97.443     ESTABLISHED
tcp4       0      0  192.168.4.78.62161     173.194.115.57.443     ESTABLISHED
tcp4       0      0  192.168.4.78.62160     173.194.115.98.443     ESTABLISHED
tcp4       0      0  192.168.4.78.62150     173.194.115.96.80      ESTABLISHED
tcp4       0      0  192.168.4.78.62145     193.182.8.59.4070      ESTABLISHED
tcp4       0      0  127.0.0.1.62107        127.0.0.1.62109        ESTABLISHED
tcp4       0      0  127.0.0.1.62109        127.0.0.1.62107        ESTABLISHED
tcp4       0      0  127.0.0.1.62105        127.0.0.1.62106        ESTABLISHED
tcp4       0      0  127.0.0.1.62106        127.0.0.1.62105        ESTABLISHED
tcp4      85      0  192.168.4.78.62102     50.57.203.128.443      CLOSE_WAIT
tcp4       0      0  192.168.4.78.62048     54.243.247.94.443      ESTABLISHED
tcp4       0      0  127.0.0.1.3705         127.0.0.1.60713        ESTABLISHED
tcp4       0      0  127.0.0.1.60713        127.0.0.1.3705         ESTABLISHED
tcp4       0      0  127.0.0.1.3705         127.0.0.1.60712        ESTABLISHED
tcp4       0      0  127.0.0.1.60712        127.0.0.1.3705         ESTABLISHED
tcp4       0      0  192.168.4.78.60542     108.160.167.175.80     ESTABLISHED
tcp4       0      0  192.168.4.78.60529     192.168.4.19.445       ESTABLISHED
```

• **Figure 19.10** The `netstat` command in action

Unpatched/Legacy Systems

Unpatched systems—including operating systems and firmware—and legacy systems present a glaring security threat. You need to deal with such problems on live systems on your network. When it comes to unpatched OSs, well, patch or isolate them! There's a number of areas in the book that touch on proper patching, especially Chapter 18, so we won't go into more detail here.

Look for questions on hardening network systems that discuss disabling unnecessary systems, patching and upgrades for software, and upgrading firmware. This is *patch and firmware management*.

Firmware updates enable programming upgrades that make network devices more efficient, more secure, and more robust, as you read in Chapter 18. Follow the procedures listed there to update firmware when necessary.

Legacy systems are a different issue altogether. *Legacy* means systems that are no longer supported by the OS maker and are no longer patched. In that case you need to consider the function of the system and either update if possible or, if not possible, isolate the legacy system on a locked-down network segment with robust firewall rules that give the system the support it needs (and protect the rest of the network if the system does get compromised). Equally, you need to be extremely careful about adding any software or hardware to a legacy system, as doing so might create even more vulnerabilities.

Unencrypted Channels

The open nature of the Internet has made it fairly common for us to *use secure protocols* or channels such as VPNs, SSL/TLS, and SSH. It never ceases to amaze me, however, how often people use **unencrypted channels**—especially in the most unlikely places. It was only a few years ago I stumbled upon a tech using Telnet to do remote logins into a very critical router for an ISP.

In general, look for the following insecure protocols and unencrypted channels:

- Using Telnet instead of SSH for remote terminal connections.
- Using HTTP instead of HTTPS on Web sites.
- Using insecure remote desktops like VNC.
- Using any insecure protocol in the clear. Run them through a VPN!

Cleartext Credentials

Older protocols offer a modicum of security—you often need a valid username and password, for example, when connecting to a File Transfer Protocol (FTP) server. The problem with such protocols (FTP, Telnet, POP3) is that they aren't encrypted, and clients send **cleartext credentials** (usernames and passwords) to the server.

Let's get one thing straight. If anyone's listening, they'll know your username and password. Unless you absolutely cannot avoid it, you shouldn't be *depending* on the security of any application or protocol that stores or sends credentials in the clear. If you ignore this advice and the bad guys intercept your credentials, expect to get mocked on Twitter and Reddit.

Another place where cleartext credentials can pop up is poor configuration of applications that would otherwise be well protected. Almost any remote control program has some "no security" setting. This might be as obvious as a "turn off security" option or it could be a setting such as Password Authentication Protocol (PAP) (which, if you recall, means cleartext passwords). The answer here is understanding your applications and knowing ahead of time how to configure them to ensure good encryption of credentials.

RF Emanation

Radio waves can penetrate walls, to a certain extent, and accidental spill, called **RF emanation**, can lead to a security vulnerability. Avoid this by placing some form of filtering between your systems and the place where the bad guys are going to be using their super high-tech *Bourne Identity* spy tools to pick up on the emanations.

To combat these emanations, the U.S. National Security Agency (NSA) developed a series of standards called **TEMPEST**. TEMPEST defines how to shield systems and manifests in a number of different products, such as coverings for individual systems, wall coverings, and special window coatings. Unless you work for a U.S. government agency, the chance of you seeing TEMPEST technologies is pretty small.

Hardening Your Network

Once you've recognized threats and vulnerabilities, it's time to start applying security hardware, software, and processes to your network to prevent bad things from happening. This is called **hardening** your network. Let's look at three aspects of network hardening: physical security, network security, and host security.

Physical Security

There's an old saying: "The finest swordsman in all of France has nothing to fear from the second finest swordsman in all of France." It means that they do the same things and know the same techniques. The only difference between the two is that one is a little better than the other. There's a more modern extension of the old saying that says: "On the other hand, the finest swordsman in all of France can be defeated by a kid with a rocket launcher!" Which is to say that the inexperienced, when properly equipped, can and will often do something totally unexpected.

Proper security must address threats from the second finest swordsman as well as the kid. We can leave no stone unturned when it comes to hardening the network, and this begins with physical security. Physical threats manifest themselves in many forms, including property theft, data loss due to natural damage such as fire or natural disaster, data loss due to physical access, and property destruction resulting from accident or sabotage.

Let's look at physical security as a two-step process of prevention methods and detection methods. First, prevent and control access to IT resources to appropriate personnel. Second, track the actions of those authorized (and sometimes unauthorized) personnel.

Prevention and Control

The first thing we have to do when it comes to protecting the network is to make the network resources accessible only to personnel who have a legitimate need to fiddle with them. You need to use *access control hardware*. Start with the simplest approach: a **lock**. Locking the door to the network closet or equipment room that holds servers, switches, routers, and other network gear goes a long way in protecting the network. Key control is critical here and includes assigning keys to appropriate staff, tracking key assignments, and collecting the keys when they are no longer needed by individuals who move on. This type of access must be guarded against circumvention by ensuring policies are followed regarding who may have or use the keys. The administrator who assigns keys should never give one to an unauthorized person without completing the appropriate procedures and paperwork.

Locking down servers within the server room with unique keys adds another layer of physical security to essential devices. Additionally, all modern server chassis come with **tamper detection** features that will log in the motherboard's nonvolatile RAM (NVRAM) if the chassis has been opened. The log will show chassis intrusion with a date and time. And it's not just the server room (and resources with it) that we need to lock up. How about the front door? There are a zillion stories of thieves and saboteurs coming in through the front (or sometimes back) door and making their way straight to the corporate treasure chest. A locked front door can be opened by an authorized person, and an unauthorized person can attempt to enter through that already opened door, what's called **tailgating**. While it is possible to prevent tailgating with policies, it is only human nature to "hold the door" for that person coming in behind you. Tailgating is especially easy to do when dealing with large organizations in which people don't know everyone else. If the tailgater dresses like everyone else and maybe has a badge that looks right, he or she probably won't be challenged. Add an armload of gear, and who could blame you for helping that person by holding the door?

> **Piggybacking** is very similar to tailgating. The only difference is that while tailgating is done without the authorized person's consent or even realization, piggybacking means the authorized person is aware of the unauthorized person's attempt.

There are a couple of techniques available to foil a tailgater. The first is a **security guard**. Guards are great. They get to know everyone's faces. They are there to protect assets and can lend a helping hand to the overloaded, but authorized, person who needs in. They are multipurpose in that they can secure building access, secure individual room and office access, and perform facility patrols. The guard station can serve as central control of security systems such as video surveillance and key control. Like all humans, security guards are subject to attacks such as social engineering, but for flexibility, common sense, and a way to take the edge off of high security, you can't beat a professional security guard or two.

For areas where an entry guard is not practical, there is another way to prevent tailgating. An **access control vestibule**—traditionally called a **mantrap**—is an entryway with two successive locked doors and a small space between them providing one-way entry or exit. After entering the first door, the second door cannot be unlocked until the first door is closed and secured. Access to the second door may be a simple key or may require approval by someone else who watches the trap space on video. Unauthorized persons remain trapped until they are approved for entry, let out the first door, or held for the appropriate authorities.

Brass keys aren't the only way to unlock a door. This is the 21st century, after all. Twenty-five years ago, I worked in a campus facility with a lot of interconnected buildings. Initial access to buildings was through a security guard and then we traveled between the buildings with connecting tunnels. Each end of the tunnels had a set of sliding glass doors that kind of worked like the doors on the starship *Enterprise*. We were assigned **badges** with built-in radio frequency ID (RFID) chips. As we neared a door, the RFID chip was queried by circuitry in the door frame called a **proximity reader**, checked against a database for authorization, and then the door slid open electromechanically.

The CompTIA Network+ objectives refer to proximity readers as *badge readers*.

Smart cards today use microprocessor circuitry to enable authentication, among other things. They can certainly be used to gain access, but also to make transactions and more.

It was so cool and so fast that people would jog the hallways during lunch hours and not even slow down for any of the doors. A quarter century later, the technology has only gotten better. The badges in the old days were a little larger than a credit card and about three times as thick. Today, the RFID chip can be implanted in a small, unobtrusive **key fob**, like the kind you use to unlock your car.

If there is a single drawback to all of the physical **door access controls** mentioned so far, it is that access is generally governed by something that is in the possession of someone who has authorization to enter a locked place. That something may be a key, a badge, a key fob with a chip, or some other physical token. The problem here, of course, is that these items can be given or taken away. If not reported in a timely fashion, a huge security gap exists.

To move from the physical possession problem of entry access, physical security can be governed by something that is known only to authorized persons. A code or password that is assigned to a specific individual for a particular asset can be entered on an alphanumeric **keypad** that controls an electric or electromechanical door lock. There is a similar door lock mechanism called a cipher lock. A **cipher lock** is a door unlocking system that uses a door handle, a latch, and a sequence of mechanical push buttons. When the buttons are pressed in the correct order, the door unlocks and the door handle works. Turning the handle opens the latch or, if you pressed the wrong order of buttons, clears the unlocking mechanism so you can try again. Care must be taken by staff who are assigned a code to protect that code.

This knowledge-based approach to access control may be a little better than a possession-based system because information is more difficult to steal than a physical token. However, poor management of information can leave an asset vulnerable. Poor management includes writing codes down and leaving the notes easily accessible. Good password/code control means memorizing information where possible or securing written notes about codes and passwords.

All this talk about intangible asset control, like passwords, doesn't mean you should ignore tangible asset control. Many companies employ RFID and other electronic devices as *asset tags* for inventory control purposes. Plus they'll use low-tech physical security tools like special stickers or zip ties for *tamper detection* in its most basic use of the term.

Well-controlled information is difficult to steal, but it's not perfect because sharing information is so easy. Someone can loan out his or her password to a seemingly trustworthy friend or coworker. While most times this is probably not a real security risk, there is always a chance that there could be disastrous results. Social engineering or over-trusting can cause someone to share a private code or password. Systems should be established to reassign codes and passwords regularly to deal with the natural leakage that can occur with this type of security.

The best way to prevent loss of access control is to build physical security around a key that cannot be shared or lost. **Biometric** access calls for using a unique physical characteristic of a person to permit access to a controlled IT resource. Doorways can be triggered to unlock using fingerprint readers, facial recognition cameras, voice analyzers, retinal blood vessel scanners, or other, more exotic characteristics. While not perfect, biometrics represent a giant leap in secure access. For even more effective access control, *multifactor authentication* can be used, where access is granted based on more than one access technique. For instance, in order to gain access to a secure server room, a user might have to pass a fingerprint scan (inherence factor) and have an approved security fob (possession factor).

Smart Lockers

A **smart locker** is a locker that an organization can control via wireless or wired networking to allow temporary access to a locker so users can access items (Figure 19.11). First popularized by Amazon as a delivery tool, smart lockers are common anywhere an organization needs to give users access to…whatever they can fit into a locker!

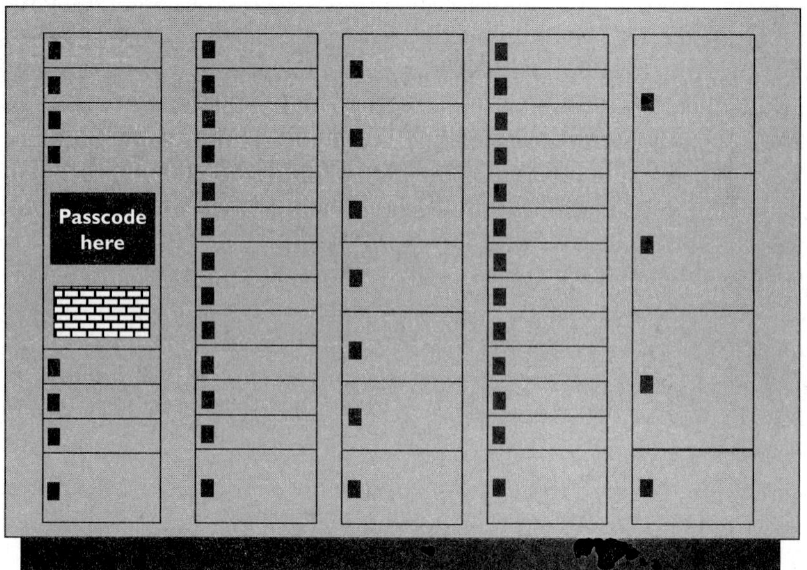

• **Figure 19.11** Typical smart locker

Cross Check

Multifactor Authentication

You encountered multifactor authentication way back in Chapter 10, so cross-check your knowledge and see if you can answer these questions. Clearly a key fob is *something you have*, a physical object. What are the other common authentication factors? What's an example of knowledge-based authentication? What's temporal authentication and can it apply to networks?

Let me point out something related to all of this door locking and unlocking technology. Physical asset security is important, but generally not as important as the safety of people. Designers of these door-locking systems must take into account safety features such as what happens to the state of a lock in an emergency like a power failure or fire. Doors with electromechanical locking controls can respond to an emergency condition and lock or unlock automatically, respectively called **fail secure** or **fail safe**. Users and occupants of facilities should be informed about what to expect in these types of events.

Monitoring

Okay, the physical assets of the network have been secured. It took guards, locks, passwords, eyeballs, and a pile of technology. Now, the only people who have access to IT resources are those who have been carefully selected, screened, trained, and authorized. The network is safe, right? Maybe not. You see, here comes the old problem again: people are human. Humans make mistakes, humans can become disgruntled, and humans can be tempted. The only real solution is heavily armored robots with artificial intelligence and bad attitudes. But until that becomes practical, maybe what we need to do next is to ensure that those authorized people can be held accountable for what they do with the physical resources of the network.

Enter video surveillance. With **video surveillance** of facilities and assets, authorized staff can be monitored for mistakes or something more nefarious. Better still, our kid with a rocket launcher (remember him?) can be tracked and caught after he sneaks into the building.

Many small office/home office (SOHO) video surveillance systems rely on **motion detection systems** that start and stop recordings based on actions caught by the camera(s). This has the advantage of saving a lot of storage space, hopefully only catching the bad guys on film when they're breaking into your house or stealing your lawn gnomes.

Let's look at two video surveillance concepts. *Video monitoring* entails using remotely monitored visual systems. **IP cameras** and **closed-circuit televisions (CCTVs)** are specific implementations of video monitoring. CCTV is a self-contained, closed system in which video cameras feed their signal to specific, dedicated monitors and storage devices. CCTV cameras can be monitored in real time by security staff, but the monitoring location is limited to wherever the video monitors are placed. If real-time monitoring is not required or viewing is delayed, stored video can be reviewed later as needed.

IP cameras have the benefit of being a more open system than CCTV. IP video streams can be monitored by anyone who is authorized to do so and can access the network on which the cameras are installed. The stream can be saved to a hard drive or network storage device. Multiple workstations can simultaneously monitor video streams and multiple cameras with ease.

Network Security

Protecting network assets is more than a physical exercise. Physically speaking, we can harden a network by preventing and controlling access to tangible network resources through things like locking doors and video monitoring. Next we will want to protect our network from malicious, suspicious, or potential threats that might connect to or access the network. This is called **access control** and it encompasses both physical security and network security. In this section we look at some technologies and techniques to implement network access control, including user account control, edge devices, posture assessment, persistent and non-persistent agents, guest networks, and quarantine networks.

Controlling User Accounts

A user account is just information: nothing more than a combination of a username and password. Like any important information, it's critical to control who has a user account and to track what these accounts can do. Access to user accounts should be restricted to the assigned individuals (no sharing, no stealing), and permissions for those accounts should follow the *principle of least privilege*—access to only the resources those individuals need, no more.

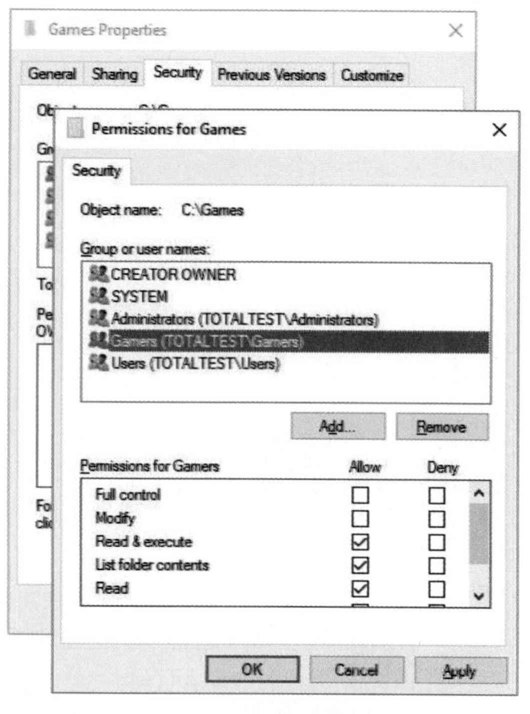

• **Figure 19.12** Giving a group permissions for a folder in Windows

Tight control of user accounts helps prevent unauthorized access or improper access. *Unauthorized access* means a person does something beyond his or her authority to do. *Improper access* occurs when a user who shouldn't have access gains access through some means. Often the improper access happens when a network tech or administrator makes a mistake.

Disabling unused accounts is an important first step in addressing these problems, but good user account control goes far deeper than that. One of your best tools for user account control is to implement groups. Instead of giving permissions to individual user accounts, give them to groups; this makes keeping track of the permissions assigned to individual user accounts much easier.

Figure 19.12 shows an example of giving permissions to a group for a folder in Windows Server. Once a group is created and its permissions are set, you can then add user accounts to that group as needed. Any user account that becomes a member of a group automatically gets the permissions assigned to that group.

Figure 19.13 shows an example of adding a user to a newly created group in the same Windows Server system.

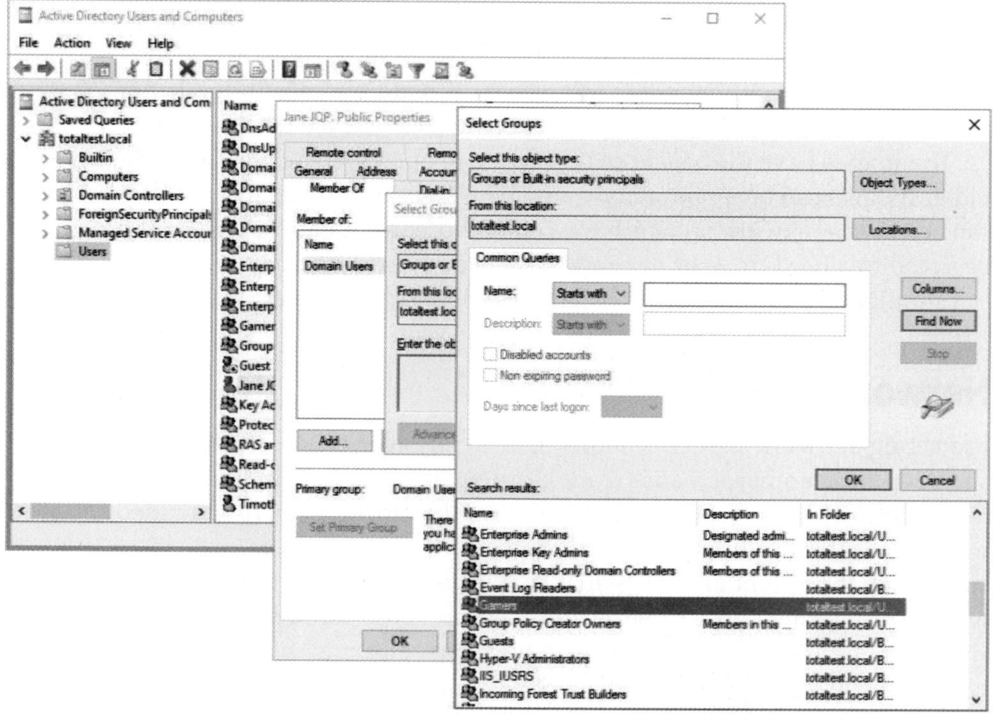

• **Figure 19.13** Adding a user to a newly created group

You should always put user accounts into groups to enhance network security. This applies to simple networks, which get local groups, and to domain-based networks, which get domain groups. Do not underestimate the importance of properly configuring both local groups and domain groups.

Groups are a great way to get increased complexity without increasing the administrative burden on network administrators because all network operating systems combine permissions. When a user is a member of more than one group, which permissions does he or she have with respect to any particular resource?

In all network operating systems, the permissions of the groups are *combined*, and the result is what is called the **effective permissions** the user has to access a given resource. Let's use an example from Windows Server. If Timmy is a member of the Sales group, which has List Folder Contents permission to a folder, and he is also a member of the Managers group, which has Read and Execute permissions to the same folder, Timmy will have List Folder Contents *and* Read and Execute permissions to that folder.

Combined permissions can also lead to *conflicting permissions*, where a user does not get access to a needed resource because one of his groups has a Deny permission for that resource while another allows it. At the group level, Deny always trumps any other permission (but a user permission will override this).

Watch out for *default* user accounts and groups—they can grant *improper access* or secret *backdoor access* to your network! All network operating systems have a default Everyone group, and it can easily be used to sneak into shared resources. This Everyone group, as its name implies, literally includes anyone who connects to that resource. Some versions of Windows give full control to the Everyone group by default. All of the default groups—Everyone, Guest, Users—define broad groups of users. Never use them unless you intend to permit all those folks to access a resource. If you use one of the default groups, remember to configure it with the proper permissions to prevent users from doing things you don't want them to do with a shared resource!

All of these groups only do one thing for you: they enable you to keep track of your user accounts. That way you know resources are only available for users who need those resources, and users only access the resources you want them to use.

Before I move on, let me add one more tool to your kit: diligence. Managing user accounts is a thankless and difficult task, but one that you must stay on top of if you want to keep your network secure. Most organizations integrate the creating, disabling/enabling, and deleting of user accounts with the work of their human resources folks. Whenever a person joins, quits, or moves, the network admin is always one of the first to know!

The administration of permissions can become incredibly complex—even with judicious use of groups. You now know what happens when a user account has multiple sets of permissions to the same resource, but what happens if the user has one set of permissions to a folder and a different set of permissions to one of its subfolders? This brings up a phenomenon called **inheritance**. I won't get into the many ways different network operating systems handle inherited permissions. Luckily for you, the CompTIA Network+ exam doesn't test you on all the nuances of combined or inherited permissions—just be aware they exist. Those who go on to get more advanced certifications, on the other hand, must become extremely familiar with the many complex permutations of permissions.

Edge

Access control can be broadly defined as exactly what it sounds like: one or more methods to govern or limit entry to a particular environment. Historically, this was accomplished and enforced with simply communicated rules and policies and human oversight. As systems grew in size and sophistication, it became possible to enforce the governing rules using automated technology, relieving managers to focus on other tasks. These control technologies began their developmental life as a central control system with peripheral actuators.

Let me show you what I mean. Take the example of the *Star Trek*–like security door system I talked about in the "Physical Security" section a little while ago. That system worked by having a computer with a database of doors, staff, and a decision matrix. Because it controlled many doors, it was centrally located and had wires running to and from it to every controlled door on the campus. Each door had two peripherals installed: a proximity reader with a status indicator, and a door open/close actuator. The proximity reader would read the data from the RFID chip carried by someone and send the data over a sometimes very long data cable to the control computer.

The computer would take the data and the door identifier and check to see if the data was valid, current, and authorized to pass through the door. If it did not meet authorization criteria, a data signal was sent back down the data line to cause a red LED to blink on the proximity reader. Of course, the door would not open. If all of the criteria were met for authorization, a good signal was sent down the data line to make a green LED glow, and power was sent down the line to operate the door actuator.

We've talked about the benefits of this system, so let's look at a few drawbacks. First, the system was proprietary. As systems like these were introduced, competition stymied any effort to create industry standards. Central control meant that large, powerful boxes had to be developed as central controllers. Expandability became an issue as controllers maxed out the number of security doors they could support. Finally, the biggest problem was the large amount of cabling needed to support large numbers of doors and potentially great distances from the central controller. The problem was made worse when facilities had to retrofit nonsecure doors for secure ones.

A lot of time and technology has passed since those days. Today's automated secure entry systems take advantage of newer technologies by leveraging existing network wiring. By using IP traffic and Power over Ethernet (PoE), the entire system can usually run over the existing wiring. Applications and protocols have been standardized so they can run on existing server hardware.

Also contributing to the simplification and standardization of these security systems are edge devices. An **edge** device is a piece of hardware that has been optimized to perform a task. Edge devices work in coordination with other edge devices and controllers.

The primary defining characteristic of an edge device is that it is installed closer to a client device, such as a workstation or a security door, than to the core or backbone of a network. In this instance, a control program that tracks entries, distributes and synchronizes copies of databases, and tracks door status can be run on a central server. In turn, it communicates with edge devices. The edge devices keep a local copy of the database and make their own decisions about whether or not a door should be opened.

Posture Assessment

Network access control (NAC) is a standardized approach to verify that a node meets certain criteria before it is allowed to connect to a network. Many product vendors implement NAC in different ways. Network Admission Control (also known as NAC) is Cisco's version of network access control.

Cisco's NAC can dictate that specific criteria must be met before allowing a node to connect to a secure network. Devices that do not meet the required criteria can be shunted with no connection or made to connect to another network. The types of criteria that can be checked are broad ranging and can be tested for in a number of ways. For the purposes of this text, we are mostly concerned about verifying that a device attempting to connect is not a threat to network security.

Cisco uses **posture assessment** as one of the tools to implement NAC. Posture assessment, as you'll recall from Chapter 18, is a way to expose or catalog all the threats and risks facing an organization. In the Cisco implementation, a switch or router that has posture assessment enabled and configured will query network devices to confirm that they meet minimum security standards before being permitted to connect to the production network.

Posture assessment includes checking things like type and version of anti-malware, level of QoS, and type/version of operating system. Posture assessment can perform different checks at succeeding stages of connection. Certain tests can be applied at the initial physical connection. After that, more checks can be conducted prior to logging in. Prelogin assessment may look at the type and version of operating system, detect whether keystroke loggers are present, and check whether the station is real or a virtual machine. The host may be queried for digital certificates, anti-malware version and currency, whether the machine is real or virtual, and a large list of other checks.

If everything checks out, the host will be granted a connection to the production network. If posture assessment finds a deficiency or potential threat, the host can be denied a connection or connected to a non-production network until it has been sufficiently upgraded.

Persistent and Non-persistent Agents

How does a host respond to a posture assessment query? Like a lot of things, the answer depends on the environment. Let's focus on a workstation to answer this question. A workstation requires something called an *agent* to answer a posture assessment query. An **agent** is a process or program running within the computer that scans the computer to create an inventory of configuration information, resources, and assets. When the workstation attempts to connect to the network through a posture assessment–enabled device, it is the agent that answers the security query.

Agents come in two flavors. The first is a small scanning program that, once installed on the computer, stays installed and runs every time the computer boots up. These agents are composed of modules that perform a thorough inventory of each security-oriented element in the computer. This type of agent is known as a **persistent agent**. If there is no agent to respond to a posture assessment query, the node is not permitted to connect to the production network.

Sometimes a computer needs to connect to a secure network via a Web site portal. Some portals provide VPN access to a corporate network, while others provide a less robust connection. In either case, it is important that these kinds of stations meet the appropriate security standards before they are granted access to the network, just as a dedicated, onsite machine must. To that end, a posture assessment is installed at the endpoint. The endpoint in this instance is the device that actually creates a secure attachment to the production network. At the workstation, a small agent that scans only for the queried conditions is downloaded and run. If the query is satisfied that the station needing access is acceptable, connection is granted and the node can access the production network. When the node disconnects from the network and leaves the portal site, the agent is released from memory. This type of agent is known as a **non-persistent agent**.

Cisco is not the only player in town and using an agent is not the only way to check a node for security compliance. To paraphrase Shakespeare: "There are more things in heaven and earth, Horatio…and they aren't all workstations." There are tablets, smartphones, other bring-your-own devices (BYOD), switches, printers, and plenty of other things that can connect to a network. For this reason, there needs to be a flexible, cross-platform method of checking for node security before granting access to a secure network. For these platforms, an 802.1X supplicant, in the form of either an agent or a client, can be installed in the device. You'll remember 802.1X from Chapter 14.

Further, a number of vendors support **agentless** posture assessments. Using a variety of techniques, hosts can be checked for things like a device fingerprint (set of characteristics that uniquely identifies a particular device), a CVE ID, or other agent-less responses. These techniques are easily implemented on a large variety of platforms and they work in a wide array of network environments.

Whether a station responds to a posture assessment query with or without an agent, the result is still one of three options: clearance into the network, connection denied, or redirect to a non-production network.

Network Segmentation

When it comes to securing your networks, one of the best tools in your toolkit is network segmentation: using hardware, VLANs, ACLs, firewalls, and anything else at your disposal to break your network up into logical segments that collect all of the clients or servers that need the same policy or security controls. Segmentation means that you can put all of the risky clients together, away from everyone else. It also means you can collect your critical servers—away from everyone else!

When you break a network up into logical segments like this, the responsibility of **network segmentation enforcement**—actually blocking or allowing traffic to enforce your segmentation policy—typically falls to network devices (such as firewalls and switches) at the boundary between segments. A more recent approach, *microsegmentation*, adds flexibility by doing segmentation enforcement at every network node (either at the switch connected to the host or in the host itself). Let's look at some simple examples of segmentation.

Because microsegmentation supports segmentation enforcement at each node, it plays an important role in zero-trust networking.

Envision that you are a customer at a coffee shop that welcomes its patrons to check e-mail on their portable devices while enjoying an iced latte. As you turn on your laptop to scan for Wi-Fi networks, two SSIDs appear. One SSID is named CoffeeGuest and the other is called CoffeePrivate. Some might try to hack into CoffeePrivate, but clearly the intent is for consumers to attach to CoffeeGuest and gain access to the Internet through that connection. The CoffeeGuest network is an example of a **guest network**.

A guest network can contain or allow access to any resource that management deems acceptable to be used by nonsecure hosts that attach to the guest network. Those resources might include an Internet connection, a local Web server with a company directory or catalog, and similar assets that are nonessential to the function of the organization.

In the preceding example, access to the guest network results from a user selecting the correct SSID. More in line with the goals of this book would be a scenario where a station attempts to connect to a network but is refused access because it does not conform to an acceptable level of security. In this case, the station might be assigned an IP address that only enables it to connect to the guest network. If the station needs access to the production network, the station could be updated to meet the appropriate security requirements. If it only requires the resources afforded by the guest network, then it's good to go.

Whenever a node is *denied* a connection to the production network, it is considered to be quarantined. It is common practice for suspicious nodes or nodes with active threats detected to be denied a connection or sent to a **quarantine network**.

So let's put it all together. An organization may have a multitude of production networks, a guest network, and a quarantine network. Who gets to go where? Stations that pass a profile query performed by an edge device with posture assessment features can connect to a production network. From there, access to the various networks and resources is determined by privileges granted to the login credentials.

If a station does not pass the posture query but does not appear to pose a threat, it will likely be connected to the guest network. Stations with active malware or that display a configuration that is conducive to hacking will be quarantined with no connection or connected to a quarantine network.

Device Hardening

Proper network hardening requires implementing device hardening. Many of the hardening techniques and best practices discussed for network access and server security apply to switches, routers, and network appliances. Let's look at five topics.

Network devices come with default credentials, the username and password combo that enables you to log into the device for configuration. *Changing default credentials* should be the first step in hardening a new device. As with any other system, *avoiding common passwords* adds security. *Change default passwords* every time.

Keep network devices up to date. That means upgrading firmware, patching and updating as necessary to close any security gaps exposed over time. Proper patch and firmware management is essential for network hardening.

Network devices such as routers include common services like Telnet and HTTP access, as well as services you don't normally see, like TCP and UDP small services, debugging and testing tools that primarily use ports 20 and lower. If enabled, these services can be used to launch DoS and other attacks. All modern devices have these disabled; hardening rules that apply to devices from every manufacturer insist on *disabling unnecessary services.*

> Attackers can use *traffic floods*—excessive or malformed packets—to conduct DoS attacks on networks and hosts, targeting vulnerable switches through their switch ports. Better switches today employ **flood guards** to detect and block excessive traffic. This enhances *switch port protection.*

Using secure protocols hardens network devices. Don't use Telnet to access a managed switch or router, for example, but use SSH so that the communication is encrypted.

Disabling unused ports on network devices *enhances port security* for access control. This includes standard IP ports and device ports, both physical and virtual for the latter. CompTIA notes this also as *disable unneeded switchports.*

Use targeted QoS filters for specific traffic. *Control Plane Policing,* for example, protects routers and switches from attacks that target the control plane of the devices. Enabling *Control Plane Policing* on Cisco devices, for example, helps manage the flow of control plane packets so the router or switch does not become overwhelmed in the face of a DoS attack.

Host Security

The first and last bastion of defense for an entire infrastructure's security is at the individual hosts. It's the first bastion for preventing dangerous things that users do from propagating to the rest of the network. It's the last bastion in that anything evil coming from the outside world must be stopped here.

We've talked about local security issues several times in this book and even in this chapter. User accounts and strong passwords that follow the password complexity/length principles laid out by the NIST, for example, obviously provide a first line of defense at the host level. So let's look at another aspect of host security: malware prevention and recovery.

Malware Prevention and Recovery

The only way to protect your PC permanently from getting malware is to disconnect it from the Internet and never permit any potentially infected software to touch your precious computer. Because neither scenario is likely these days, you need to use specialized anti-malware programs to help stave off the inevitable assaults. Even with the best anti-malware tools, there are times when malware still manages to strike your computer. When you discover infected systems, you need to know how to stop the spread of the malware to other computers, how to fix infected computers, and how to remediate (restore) the system as close to its original state as possible.

Malware Prevention If your PC has been infected by malware, you'll bump into some strange things before you can even run an anti-malware scan. Like a medical condition, malware causes unusual symptoms that should stand out from your everyday computer use. You need to become a PC physician and understand what each of these symptoms means.

Malware's biggest strength is its flexibility: it can look like anything. In fact, a lot of malware attacks can feel like normal PC "wonkiness"—

momentary slowdowns, random one-time crashes, and so on. Knowing when a weird application crash is actually a malware attack is half the battle.

A slow PC can mean you're running too many applications at once or you've been hit with malware. How do you tell the difference? In this case, it's the frequency. If it's happening a lot, even when all of your applications are closed, you've got a problem. This goes for frequent lockups, too. If Windows starts misbehaving (more than usual), run your anti-malware application right away.

Malware, however, doesn't always jump out at you with big system crashes. Some malware tries to rename system files, change file permissions, or hide files completely. Most of these issues are easily caught by a regular anti-malware scan, so as long as you remain vigilant, you'll be okay.

Some malware even fights back, defending itself from your many attempts to remove it. If your Windows Update feature stops working, preventing you from patching your PC, you've most likely got malware. If other tools and utilities throw up an "Access Denied" roadblock, you've got malware. If you lose all Internet connectivity, either the malware is stopping you or removing the malware broke your connection. In this case, you might need to reconfigure your Internet connection: reinstall your NIC and its drivers, reboot your router, and so on.

Even your browser and anti-malware applications can turn against you. If you type in one Web address and end up at a different site than you anticipated, a malware infection might have overwritten your hosts file and thus automatically changed the DNS resolver cache. Most browser redirections point you to phishing scams or Web sites full of free downloads (that are, of course, covered in malware). In fact, some free anti-malware applications are actually malware—what techs call a *rogue anti-malware* program. You can avoid these rogue applications by sticking to the recommended lists of anti-malware software found online.

Watch for security alerts in Windows, either from Windows' built-in security tools or from your third-party anti-malware program. Windows 10 includes a tool called Security and Maintenance (see Figure 19.14). You don't

> **Tech Tip**
>
> **Hijacked E-mail Accounts**
>
> *While it's not necessarily a malware attack, watch out for hijacked e-mail accounts, too, belonging either to you or to someone you know. Hackers can hit both e-mail clients and Webmail users. If you start receiving some fishy (or phishy) e-mail messages, change your Web-based e-mail password or scan your PC for malware.*

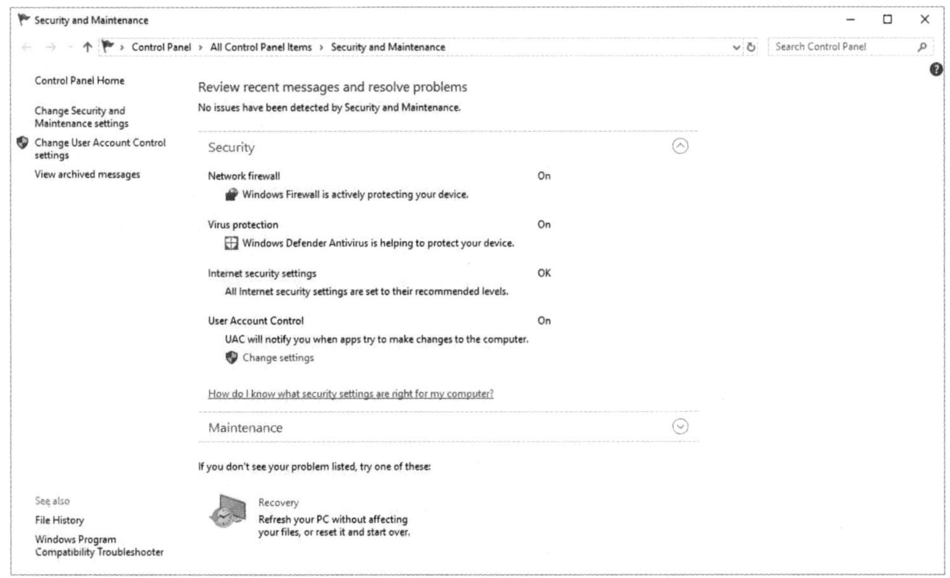

• **Figure 19.14** Windows 10 Security and Maintenance

actually configure much using these applets; they just tell you whether or not you are protected. These tools place an icon and pop up a notification in the notification area whenever Windows detects a problem.

Symptoms of a Compromised System A system hit by malware will eventually show the effects, although in any number of ways. The most common symptoms of malware on a *compromised system* are general sluggishness and random crashes. In some cases, Web browsers might default to unpleasant or unwanted Web sites. Frequently, compromised systems increase network outflow a lot, a spike in traffic that network monitoring software should flag automatically.

If you get enough compromised systems in your network, especially if those systems form part of a botnet or DDoS attack force, your network will suffer. The amount of traffic specifically doing the bidding of the malware on the systems can hog network bandwidth, making the network sluggish.

Watch for *top talkers*—systems with very high network output—and a network that doesn't seem nearly as fast as the specs say it should be. Monitor employee complaints about sluggish machines or poor network performance carefully and act as soon as you think you might have infected systems. You need to deal with malware—hopefully catching it before it strikes, but dealing with it swiftly when it does. Let's go there next.

> One of the most important malware mitigation procedures is to keep systems under your control patched and up to date through proper patch management—which includes testing patches before you deploy them to every device in your organization. Microsoft does a very good job of putting out bug fixes and patches as soon as problems occur. Microsoft isn't perfect, and sometimes patches introduce their own problems. Still, at the end of the day, a patched system will likely be more secure than an unpatched one.

Dealing with Malware You can deal with malware in several ways: anti-malware programs, employee training and awareness, patch management, and remediation.

At the very least, every computer should run an anti-malware program. If possible, add an appliance that runs anti-malware programs against incoming data from your network. Also remember that an anti-malware program is only as good as its updates—keep everyone's definition file (explained a bit later) up to date with, literally, nightly updates! Users must be trained to look for suspicious ads, programs, and pop-ups, and understand that they must not click these things. The more you teach users about malware, the more aware they'll be of potential threats. Your organization should have policies and procedures in place so everyone knows what to do if they encounter malware. Finally, a good tech maintains proper incident response records to see if any pattern to attacks emerges. He or she can then adjust policies and procedures to mitigate these attacks.

> The term *antivirus* is becoming obsolete (as are *anti-spyware* and similar terms). Viruses are only a small component of the many types of malware. Many people continue to use the term as a synonym for anti-malware.

Anti-Malware Programs An **anti-malware program** such as a classic **antivirus** program protects your PC in two ways. It can be both sword and shield, working in an active seek-and-destroy mode and in a passive sentry mode. When ordered to seek and destroy, the program scans the computer's boot sector and files for viruses and, if it finds any, presents you with the available options for removing or disabling them. Anti-malware programs can also operate as **virus shields** that passively monitor a computer's activity, checking for viruses only when certain events occur, such as a program executing or a file being downloaded.

Anti-malware programs use different techniques to combat different types of malware. They detect boot sector viruses simply by comparing the drive's boot sector to a standard boot sector. This works because most boot sectors are basically the same. Some anti-malware programs make a backup copy of the boot sector. If they detect a virus, the programs use that backup copy to replace the infected boot sector. Executable viruses are a little more difficult to find because they can be on any file in the drive. To detect executable viruses, the anti-malware program uses a library of signatures. A **signature** is the code pattern of a known virus. The anti-malware program compares an executable file to its library of signatures. There have been instances where a perfectly clean program coincidentally held a virus signature. Usually the anti-malware program's creator provides a patch to prevent further alarms.

Anti-malware software comes in multiple forms today. First is the classic **host-based anti-malware** that is installed on individual systems. Host-based anti-malware works beautifully, but is hard to administer when you have a number of systems. An alternative used in larger networks is **network-based anti-malware**. In this case a single anti-malware server runs on a number of systems (in some cases each host has a small client). These network-based programs are much easier to update and administer.

Last is **cloud/server-based anti-malware**. These servers store the software on a remote location (in the cloud or on a local server), but it's up to each host to access the software and run it. This has the advantage of storing nothing on the host system and making updating easier, but suffers from lack of administration as it's still up to the user on each host to run the anti-malware program.

Expect a question on the CompTIA Network+ exam that addresses the *security implications* of malware and cloud resources. Who is responsible for security, the provider or the customer? Framed this way, a typical correct answer puts cloud resource security on the provider, not the customer. The customer is responsible for host security.

Firewalls

Firewalls are devices or software that protect an internal network from unauthorized access by acting as a filter. That's right; all a firewall does is filter traffic that flows through its ports. Firewalls are essential tools in the fight against malicious programs on the Internet.

The most basic job of the firewall is to look at each packet and decide based on a set of *firewall rules* whether to **block** or **allow** the traffic. This traffic can be either **inbound traffic**, packets coming from outside the network, or **outbound traffic**, packets leaving the network.

Types of Firewalls

Firewalls come in many different forms. The types covered in this section are the common ones CompTIA wants you to be familiar with.

Software vs. Hardware Firewalls

The **network-based firewall** is often implemented in some sort of **hardware appliance** or is built into the router that is installed between the LAN and the wilds of the Internet. Most network techs' first encounter with a network-based firewall is the **SOHO firewall** built into most consumer-grade routers. These firewalls form the first line of defense, providing protection for the whole network. While they do a great job of protecting whole networks, they can't provide any help if the malicious traffic is originating from inside the network itself. That is why we have host-based firewalls.

A **host-based firewall** is a software firewall installed on a "host" that provides firewall services for just that machine. A great example of this type of

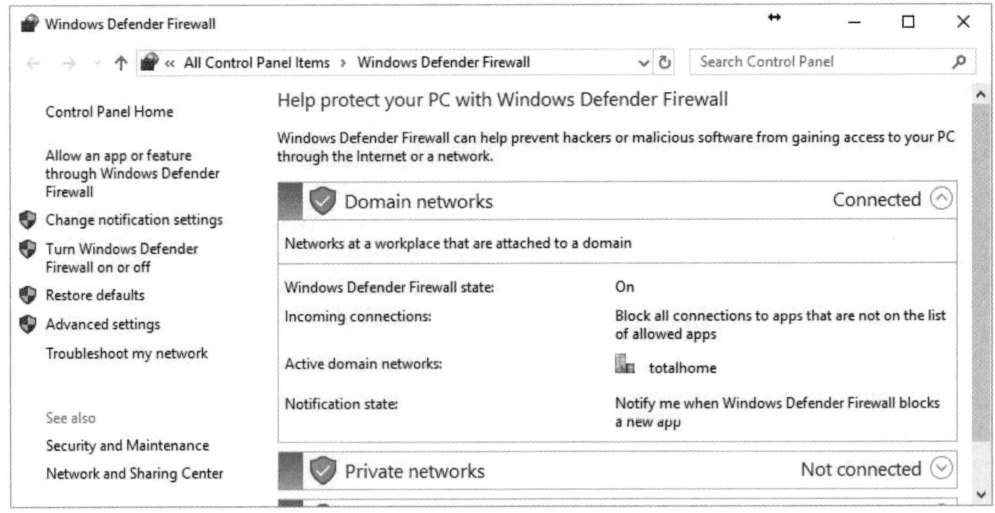

• **Figure 19.15** Windows Defender Firewall in Windows 10

firewall is Windows Defender Firewall, shown in Figure 19.15, which has shipped with every version of Windows since XP (though it was known as Windows Firewall before the Fall 2017 update to Windows 10). This makes the host-based firewall probably one of the most common types of firewalls you will encounter in your career as a network tech.

Advanced Firewall Techniques and Features

Knowing that a firewall can live in the network or on a host is all well and good, but firewalls are very sophisticated these days and you should be familiar with the features that separate a modern firewall from a simple *packet filter*. One of the first modern techniques added to firewalls is **stateful inspection**, or the capability to tell if a packet is part of an existing connection. In other words, the firewall is aware of the packet's state, as it relates to other packets. This is an upgrade to the older **stateless inspection** model where the firewall looked at each packet fresh, with no regard to the state of the packet's relation to any other packet.

Building on the stateful firewall, firewalls that are **application/context aware** operate at Layer 7 of the OSI model and filter based on the application or service that originated the traffic. This makes context-aware firewalls invaluable in stopping port-hopping applications such as BitTorrent from overloading your network.

Next-Generation Firewalls A **next-generation firewall (NGFW)** functions at multiple layers of the OSI model to tackle traffic no traditional firewall can filter alone. A Layer 3 firewall can filter packets based on IP addresses, for example. A Layer 5 firewall can filter based on port numbers. Layer 7 firewalls understand different application protocols and can filter on the contents of the application data. An NGFW handles all of this and more.

Implementing and Configuring Firewalls

Now that you have a solid understanding of what a firewall is and how it works, let's delve into the details of installing and configuring a hardware firewall on a network. We'll start with the now familiar Bayland Widgets network and their gateway (Figure 19.16).

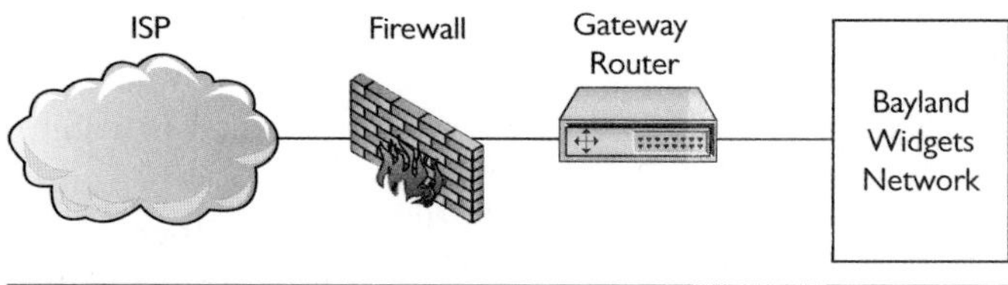

• **Figure 19.16** Bayland Widgets network gateway

The location of the firewall in the Bayland Widgets network is one of the most common locations for a firewall. By placing the firewall between the trusted internal network and the Internet, it can see all the traffic flowing between the two networks. This also means that the firewall's performance is critical for Bayland Widgets' connection speed. If the firewall becomes overloaded, it can easily bring a 1-Gbps Internet connection down to 100 Mbps or slower speeds—yikes! In this case, Bayland Widgets has chosen a powerful Cisco Adaptive Security Appliance (ASA) to provide the firewall.

Physically installing a firewall is just like installing other networking equipment such as routers and switches. The entry-level or SOHO models usually have a fixed number of ports, often with a fixed-purpose function (like dedicated ports for WAN traffic). Enterprise-grade hardware (typically supporting 200+ users) often is built around the idea of a flexible function that supports having cards added for different interface types and that can be reconfigured as the network changes. Once the hardware is plugged in, it's time to start configuring your firewall's settings.

Restricting Access via ACLs

Modern firewalls come with a massive number of features, and configuring them can be a daunting task for any network tech. But at its core, configuring a firewall is about defining which traffic can flow and which traffic shall not pass. These rules often take the form of an *access control list (ACL)*, a set of rules applied to an interface that allows or *denies* traffic based on things like source or destination IP addresses. ACLs can restrict access to network resources.

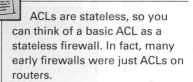

> ACLs are stateless, so you can think of a basic ACL as a stateless firewall. In fact, many early firewalls were just ACLs on routers.

Let's take a look at an ACL that you might find on a Cisco router or firewall:

```
access-list 10 deny 10.11.12.0 0.0.0.255
access-list 10 permit any
```

That looks rather cryptic at first glance, but what it's doing is very simple. The beginning of the first line, `access-list 10`, tells Cisco IOS that we want to create an ACL and its number is 10.

The end of the first line, `deny 10.11.12.0 0.0.0.255`, is the actual rule—an **explicit deny**—we want the firewall to apply. In this case, it means deny all traffic from the 10.11.12.0/24 subnet.

That's all well and good; any traffic coming from the 10.11.12.0/24 subnet will be dropped like a bad habit. But what's up with that second line, `access-list 10 permit any`? Well, that's there because of a very important detail about ACLs: they have an **implicit deny any**, or *automatically deny any packets that don't match a rule.* So in this case, if we stopped after the first line, *all* traffic—even the good stuff—would get blocked without a rule that explicitly permits it! So to make our ACL be a firewall instead of a brick wall, the last rule in this ACL permits through any traffic that wasn't dropped by the first rule.

Check out the excellent Chapter 19 "Implicit Deny" Show! over at https://totalsem.com/008. It's a good tool for reviewing filtering techniques.

Firewalls and other advanced networking devices offer all sorts of filtering. *Web filtering*, for example, enables networks to block specific Web site access. In contrast, *content filtering* enables administrators to filter traffic based on specific signatures or keywords (such as profane language). *IP filtering* blocks specific IP address traffic; *port filtering* blocks traffic on specific ports. All of these filtering options are fairly standard network hardening techniques.

Tech Tip

Bastion Hosts

A bastion host is designed to be fully exposed to and withstand attacks from the open Internet. A bastion host is exposed because it provides some service to clients external to the network.

Once the ACL has been created, it must be assigned to an interface to be of any use. One interesting feature of ACLs is that they don't just get plugged in to an interface. You must specify the rules that apply to each *direction* the traffic flows. Traffic flowing through an interface can be thought of as either *inbound*, traffic entering from the network, or *outbound*, traffic flowing from the firewall out to the network. This is an important detail because you can and often want to have different rules for traffic entering and leaving through an interface.

We've only looked at very simple ACLs here, but they are still very important in modern network security, providing the critical filtering to keep traffic flowing where it should and, maybe more importantly, from flowing where it shouldn't.

DMZ and Firewall Placement

The use of a single firewall between the network and the ISP in the example shown in Figure 19.16 is just one approach to firewall placement. That configuration works well in simple networks or when you want strong isolation between all clients on the inside of the firewall. But what happens when we have servers, like a Web server, that need less restricted access to the Internet? That's where the concepts of the DMZ and internal/external firewalls come in.

A **screened subnet**, also known as a **demilitarized zone (DMZ)**, is a network segment carved out by firewalls to provide a special place (a zone) on the network for any servers that need to be publicly accessible from the Internet. By definition, a DMZ uses **network segmentation** as a mitigation technique against attacks on the network.

The most common DMZ design is to create a DMZ by using two routers with firewalls to create a perimeter network. With a perimeter network (Figure 19.17), the two firewalls carve out areas with different levels of trust. The firewall that sits between the perimeter network and the Internet is known as an **external firewall**. It protects the public servers from known Internet attacks, but still allows plenty of traffic through to the public-facing servers.

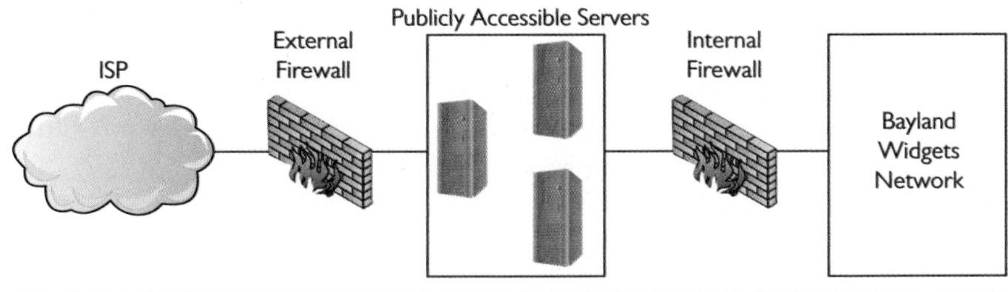

• **Figure 19.17** Tasty firewall sandwich

These servers are still publicly accessible, though, and are still more vulnerable to attack and takeover. That's acceptable for the public-facing servers, but the light protection afforded by the external firewall is unacceptable for internal systems. That's where the **internal firewall** comes in; it sits between the perimeter network and the trusted network that houses all the organization's private servers and workstations. The internal firewall provides extremely strong ACLs to protect internal servers and workstations.

Honeypots and Honeynets

As described, firewalls are bidirectional "filter" systems that can prevent access into a network or stop traffic flow out of a network. These systems work well, but nothing is foolproof. Any high-value network resource provides sufficient motivation for a nefarious actor to jump through the hoops to get at your goodies. Remember that malicious hackers have three primary weapons to gain access to computer assets: expertise, time, and money (to pay others with more expertise and to buy time).

To protect our network from expert hackers with too much time on their hands, we layer roadblocks to exhaust their time. We upgrade those roadblocks, and add more where practical, to defeat a hacker's expertise. We can also use something from our own arsenal that works in conjunction with our roadblocks: a detour.

Have you ever seen one of those sports-type movies where a ragtag team of misfits is playing a pro team? In the beginning of the game the pros are beating the brains out of the misfits. Then, when the misfits have had enough of a drubbing, the captain calls a play to "Let them through." The bad guy comes through and gets a pasting or two of his own. The network security equivalents to "Let them through" are honeypots and honeynets.

Now, "letting them through" is about choices. A network administrator may elect to make access to honeypots and honeynets an easy thing. Or, the network administrator may lay them out as a reward to a hacker after breaking through the normal protection barriers. This is a choice that depends on a lot of variables. In either case, a **honeypot** is a computer that presents itself as a sweet, tempting target to a hacker but, in reality, is a decoy. Honeypots can be as simple as a "real" network machine with decoy files in it. A text file called PASSWORDS.TXT with fake contents makes for an enticing objective.

Of course, there are much more sophisticated products that can run on a computer as a program or within a virtual machine. These products can mimic all of the features of a real computer asset, including firewalls and other roadblocks to keep a hacker occupied and wasting time on a resource that will yield no value in the end.

Scale up a honeypot to present a complete network as a decoy and you have a **honeynet**. A honeynet, like a honeypot, could be built by constructing an actual network, but that wouldn't be very cost effective. Honeynets can run on a single computer or within a virtual machine and can look like a simple network or a vast installation.

Honeypots and honeynets are useful tools not just in their diversionary value, but in that they can also monitor and report the characteristics of attacks that target them. First-hand knowledge of new attacks can be a great way to level up your defenses!

When deploying honeypots and honeynets, it is critical that they be segmented from any live or production networks. Pure isolation is the ideal goal. Network segmentation can be achieved by creating a disconnected network or assigning them to an isolated VLAN.

Troubleshooting Firewalls

The firewalls used in modern networks are essential and flexible tools that are critical for securing our networks. Yet, this flexibility means a *misconfigured firewall* becomes more likely, and with it the threat of a security breach. You should be familiar with a couple of issues that can crop up, *incorrect ACL settings* and *misconfigured applications*.

When troubleshooting firewalls, a common place for misconfigurations to pop up is in the ACLs. Because of implicit deny, all nonmatching traffic is blocked by default. So if a newly installed firewall refuses to pass any traffic, check to see if it's missing the *permit any* ACL rule.

The other source of firewall misconfigurations you should know about concerns applications. With firewalls, "application" means two different things depending on whether you are configuring a network-based firewall or a host-based firewall.

With a network-based firewall, "application," in most situations, can be read as "protocol." Because ACLs on modern firewalls can use protocols as well as addresses and ports, a careless entry blocking an application/protocol can drop access to an entire class of applications on the network.

With a host-based firewall, "application" has its traditional meaning. A host-based firewall is aware of the actual applications running on the machine it's protecting, not just the traffic's protocol. With this knowledge, the firewall can be configured to grant or deny traffic to individual applications, not just protocols, ports, or addresses. When dealing with *incorrect host-based firewall settings* here, symptoms are most likely to pop up when an application has been accidentally added to the deny list. When this happens, the application will no longer be able to communicate with the network. Fortunately, on a single system the fix is easy: open the firewall settings, look for the application's name or executable, and change the deny to allow.

> Expect a question on troubleshooting general networking issues such as *blocked services, ports, or addresses.* Think about the purpose of firewalls and know that misconfiguration can certainly cause these problems.

Chapter 19 Review

■ Chapter Summary

After reading this chapter and completing the exercises, you should understand the following about network protection.

Explain concepts of network security

- The CIA triad represents the three goals of IT security: confidentiality, integrity, and availability. These translate to keeping unauthorized people from an organization's resources, making sure nothing unauthorized changes those resources, and maintaining resources properly and managing change in an orderly, organized fashion.
- In a zero-trust model, nothing gets a free pass; rather, everything is assumed hostile unless explicitly authenticated and authorized. The zero-trust model seeks to minimize lateral (internal) attacks.
- In defense in depth, network administers assume breaches could happen to one system, such as perimeter security, and design the next system in line to handle the attack differently. Layers include strong physical security, separation of duties, strong passwords, patch management, and so on.

Discuss common security threats in network computing

- A network *threat* is any form of *potential* attack against a network. Threats try to take advantage of *vulnerabilities*, potential weak spots in a network's defense. An *exploit* is an actual procedure for taking advantage of a vulnerability. An *attack* occurs when a threat agent attempts to exploit a vulnerability.
- Spoofing is the process of pretending to be someone or something you are not by placing false information into your packets. An attacker spoofs by replacing the attacker's MAC address, IP address, username, e-mail address, and so forth with some other values.
- Abusing protocols is a common form of threat. A protocol is abused by forming communication in a way the protocol is not supposed to be used.
- A zero-day attack exploits a previously undiscovered vulnerability in a system.
- ARP cache poisoning attacks target the ARP caches on hosts and MAC address tables on switches by sending false ARP frames.
- ARP cache poisoning is a common method for on-path attacks. Technologies such as Dynamic ARP Inspection and DHCP snooping can help negate ARP cache poisoning.
- A denial of service (DoS) attack is a targeted attack by one or more systems against a server (or servers) that provides some form of service on the Internet. A distributed denial of service (DDoS) attack uses a vast number of zombified systems (called a botnet) to attack a more robust target.
- In an on-path attack (aka man-in-the-middle attack), an attacker taps into communications between two systems, covertly intercepting traffic thought to be only between those systems, reading or in some cases even changing the data and then sending it on.
- In a password attack, a bad actor uses various methods to discover a password, often comparing various potential passwords against known hashes of passwords. The methods vary from the simplest brute-force approach to more sophisticated approaches like dictionary attacks.
- Physical/local access threats are particularly dangerous as they take place inside your network. These threats include insider threats, VLAN hopping, administrative access controls, and unused or ready-to-retire devices.
- The term *malware* defines any program or code (macro, script, and so on) that's designed to do something on a system or network that you don't want to have happen. Malware comes in a number of different forms such as ransomware, viruses, worms, macros, logic bombs, Trojan horses, rootkits, and adware/spyware.
- Social engineering is the process of using or manipulating people inside the networking environment to gain access to that network from the outside. Phishing—using false e-mails and Web sites to collect usernames and passwords—is a particularly notorious form of social engineering. Techniques like tailgating can be used to gain physical entry into a secure location.

Discuss common vulnerabilities inherent in networking

- Unneeded running services give attackers opportunities to attack by exploiting open ports and propagating malware. Shut them down.
- Any open ports on a system give attackers a potential attack vector. Close the ports by shutting down the associated service.
- Unpatched systems should be patched. Firmware should be updated when necessary. Legacy systems should be updated if possible, and isolated if not.
- Be careful about using any protocols over unencrypted channels and use VPN or SSH tunnels whenever possible.
- Don't use protocols or applications with cleartext credentials.
- RF emanation from systems can potentially be exploited by sophisticated detectors to read information from a distance. The NSA defines a series of standards called TEMPEST to block RF emanation.

Describe methods for hardening a network against attacks

- Infrastructures must be physically secured. This includes the following measures: security guards, door locks with good access controls (key pads, badges, smart cards, biometrics, RFID readers), and access control vestibules (mantraps).
- Video surveillance of facilities and assets monitors authorized staff and unauthorized "guests" for mistakes or something more nefarious. Typically, this uses IP cameras and CCTVs. Motion detection systems trigger recording when an action is detected, thus saving storage space.
- Hardening a network requires securing both the edges of the network and the internal network.
- Network access control (NAC) is a standardized approach to verify that a node meets certain criteria before it is allowed to connect to the network.
- A safe network includes both persistent and non-persistent agents.
- A guest network can contain or allow access to any resource that management deems acceptable to be used by nonsecure hosts that attach to the guest network.
- It is common practice for suspicious nodes or nodes with active threats detected to be denied a connection—quarantined—or sent to a *quarantine network*.
- Device hardening has many aspects, from changing default credentials and avoiding common passwords, to keeping firmware upgraded, patched, and updated. Disabling unnecessary services, using secure protocols, and disabling unused ports also harden devices.
- A compromised system will exhibit traffic spikes and system slowdowns.
- Prevent malware by using anti-malware software.

Explain how firewalls protect a network from threats

- All firewalls can be placed into one of two categories: network-based (usually hardware) and host-based (usually software).
- Firewalls may inspect packets in two ways: stateful and stateless. Stateful inspection is aware of the connection the packets are using. Stateless inspection means to inspect a packet alone without any other reference.
- A stateless firewall applies its access control list (ACL) to determine which packets will or will not be filtered. Almost any aspect of a packet can be part of an ACL.
- ACLs consider traffic as either inbound or outbound to the router. A screened subnet (traditionally called a demilitarized zone, or DMZ) normally consists of two firewalls, one external and one internal.
- A honeypot or honeynet presents attackers with a false target on which to waste their time and resources.

Key Terms

access control *(553)*
access control list (ACL) *(542)*
access control vestibule *(550)*
administrative account *(542)*
adware *(544)*
agent *(557)*
agentless *(558)*
allow *(563)*
amplification *(538)*
anti-malware program *(562)*
antivirus *(562)*
application/context aware *(564)*
ARP cache poisoning *(535)*
asset disposal *(542)*
attack *(532)*
badge *(551)*
banner grabbing *(541)*
biometric *(552)*
block *(563)*
bot *(538)*
botnet *(538)*
brute force *(540)*
CIA triad *(529)*
cipher lock *(551)*
cleartext credential *(548)*
closed-circuit television (CCTV) *(553)*
cloud/server-based anti-malware *(563)*
Common Vulnerabilities and Exposures (CVE) *(532)*
confidentiality, integrity, and availability (CIA) *(529)*
crypto-malware *(543)*
deauthentication (deauth) attack *(539)*
defense in depth *(530)*
demilitarized zone (DMZ) *(566)*
denial of service (DoS) *(538)*
DHCP scope exhaustion *(539)*
DHCP snooping *(534)*
DHCP starvation attack *(539)*
dictionary attack *(540)*
distributed denial of service (DDoS) *(538)*
DNS cache poisoning *(533)*
door access control *(551)*
Dynamic ARP Inspection (DAI) *(537)*
edge *(556)*
effective permissions *(555)*
explicit deny *(565)*
exploit *(532)*
external firewall *(566)*
fail safe *(553)*
fail secure *(553)*
firewall *(563)*
flood guard *(560)*
guest network *(559)*
hardening *(549)*
hardware appliance *(563)*
honeynet *(567)*
honeypot *(567)*
host-based anti-malware *(563)*
host-based firewall *(563)*
implicit deny any *(565)*
inbound traffic *(563)*
inheritance *(555)*
insider threat *(540)*
internal firewall *(566)*
IP camera *(553)*
key fob *(551)*
keypad *(551)*
lock *(550)*
logic bomb *(544)*
macro *(544)*
malicious user *(541)*
malware *(543)*
man-in-the-middle *(539)*
mantrap *(550)*
monlist *(533)*
motion detection system *(553)*
network access control (NAC) *(557)*
network-based anti-malware *(563)*
network-based firewall *(563)*
network segmentation *(566)*
network segmentation enforcement *(558)*
next-generation firewall (NGFW) *(564)*
non-persistent agent *(558)*
ntpdc *(533)*
on-path attack *(539)*
organizationally unique identifier (OUI) *(542)*
outbound traffic *(563)*
password attack *(540)*
persistent agent *(558)*

phishing *(545)*
piggybacking *(550)*
posture assessment *(557)*
proximity reader *(551)*
quarantine network *(559)*
ransomware *(543)*
reflection *(538)*
RF emanation *(549)*
rootkit *(544)*
router advertisement (RA) guard *(534)*
screened subnet *(566)*
security guard *(550)*
separation of duties *(531)*
service *(547)*
session hijacking *(539)*
shoulder surfing *(545)*
signature *(563)*
slashdotting *(539)*
smart card *(551)*
smart locker *(552)*
social engineering *(545)*
SOHO firewall *(563)*
spoofing *(532)*
spyware *(544)*
stateful inspection *(564)*
stateless inspection *(564)*
system life cycle *(542)*
tailgating *(550)*
tamper detection *(550)*
TEMPEST *(549)*
threat *(531)*
Trojan horse *(544)*
trusted user *(540)*
unencrypted channel *(548)*
untrusted user *(540)*
video surveillance *(553)*
virus *(543)*
virus shield *(562)*
VLAN hopping *(542)*
vulnerability *(532)*
worm *(543)*
zero-day attack *(534)*
zero trust *(530)*
zombie *(538)*

Key Term Quiz

Use the Key Terms list to complete the sentences that follow. Not all terms will be used.

1. Various different camera technologies are used for physical security. CCTV is an older technology, whereas a(n) _______________ is much more modern.
2. _______________ is a standardized approach to verify that a node meets certain criteria before it is allowed to connect to the network.
3. An edge firewall usually manifests as a(n) _______________.
4. _______________ is the process of pretending to be someone or something you are not by placing false information into your packets.
5. A(n) _______________ is a potential attack on your network. A(n) _______________ is a weakness of your network that might enable the attack.
6. A(n) _______________ can take advantage of low-level functions to hide deep in an OS, hypervisor, or firmware.
7. Phishing is a form of _______________.
8. The process of applying security hardware, software, and processes to a network in defense of attacks is called _______________.
9. A(n) _______________ and a(n) _______________ both help prevent tailgating.
10. In a network access control (NAC) environment, a(n) _______________ is continually running on a client.

Multiple-Choice Quiz

1. Which term most closely describes collecting all of the network clients or servers that need the same security policies?
   - A. Hardening
   - B. Segmentation
   - C. Spoofing
   - D. Posturing
2. Which of the following prevents ARP cache poisoning?
   - A. DHCP
   - B. DAI
   - C. Edge firewall
   - D. DNS snooping
3. A computer compromised with malware to support a botnet is called a ______________.
   - A. Zombie
   - B. Reflection
   - C. DDoS
   - D. Locked node
4. A DoS attacker using ______________ would focus on sending the smallest amount of traffic possible.
   - A. Reflection
   - B. Inflection
   - C. Emanation
   - D. Amplification
5. A user's machine is locked to a screen telling her she must call a number to unlock her system. What kind of attack is this?
   - A. DDoS
   - B. Logic bomb
   - C. Ransomware
   - D. Session hijacking
6. An attack where someone tries to hack a password using every possible password permutation is called what?
   - A. Man-in-the-middle
   - B. Spoofing
   - C. Rainbow table
   - D. Brute force
7. Which Windows utility would show you open ports on a host?
   - A. `netstat`
   - B. `ping`
   - C. `ipconfig`
   - D. `nbtstat`
8. Which of the following protocols are notorious for cleartext passwords? (Select two.)
   - A. SSH
   - B. Telnet
   - C. HTTPS
   - D. POP3
9. The NSA's TEMPEST security standards are used to combat which risk?
   - A. RF emanation
   - B. Spoofing
   - C. DDoS
   - D. Malware
10. Bob is told by his administrator to update his anti-malware program before he runs it. What kind of anti-malware is he most-likely using?
    - A. Host-based
    - B. Network-based
    - C. Cloud-based
    - D. FTP-based
11. Randi inspects her router configuration and notices that Telnet is active, although she always uses SSH. By disabling Telnet, she has performed which of the following hardening actions?
    - A. Keeping system up to date
    - B. Blocking unused ports
    - C. Using secure protocols
    - D. Disabling unnecessary services
12. Janet, the new company intern, accidentally discovers that with a press of a button she can delete the entire company personnel database. Joy! What access-control concept has been violated? (Select the best answer.)
    - A. Improper access
    - B. Principle of least privilege

C. Unauthorized access

D. Unnecessary access

13. Everyone at Bayland Widgets Corp. is required to enter a secure door using their smart card. Bobby enters the secure door using his smart card. Betty Sue enters the same door before it closes for Bobby. What has she done?

   A. Drafting

   B. Drifting

   C. Miling

   D. Tailgating

14. Which of these enables a host to respond to a posture-assessment query?

   A. Administrative access

   B. An agent

   C. Multifactor authentication

   D. A proximity reader

15. Which type of firewall functions at multiple OSI layers?

   A. Packet filtering

   B. Content filtering

   C. APM

   D. NGFW

Essay Quiz

1. Research three major computer hacking events that have occurred over the past year or two. Identify the type of attack, the impact to each company, its employees, and its customers, and any other significant effects.
2. There are a lot of anti-malware packages available. Research the benefits and features that a small (< 15 computers) organization might need. Select a package that best suits the organization you have in mind and write up a proposal to convince your boss why the organization should use this product.
3. The IT department has discovered that many employees are responding to phishing attack e-mails. These responses expose company information and employee personnel to ne'er-do-wells. Create a training document to teach staff how to identify phishing attacks and how to respond to them.

Lab Projects

• Lab Project 19.1

You are the boss and head nerd for a small office and you control the edge firewall. Your network ID for the entire network is 192.168.4/24. Your computer's IP address is 192.168.4.23. You want to prevent users from accessing a public *Minecraft* server and playing during company time (9 to 5, Monday through Friday). However, you don't want to prevent them from playing outside of company time. You, however, like to play *Minecraft* all day long. You are going to write in plain English some ACLs.

1. Research the port that *Minecraft* servers use.
2. Your routers are all set to UTC/GMT time. What is 9–5 in UTC/GMT in your time zone?
3. Write in plain English an ACL rule that blocks the *Minecraft* port from all computers on 192.168.4.0/24 from 9 to 5 UTC/GMT.
4. Write in plain English an ACL rule that will give your computer access at all times.

• Lab Project 19.2

You have a user who uses Valve's Steam to play his games. Research all the ports needed by a Steam client, and then use Windows Firewall to block all of them. If you do not have a Windows system, then just write all of the ports on a piece of paper.

• Lab Project 19.3

The CompTIA Network+ objectives give the concept of hardening your network only the lightest of touches. Do some research and list at least five aspects of network hardening that aren't listed in the CompTIA Network+ objectives.

Network Monitoring

"I'm still passionately interested in what my fellow humans are up to. For me, a day spent monitoring the passing parade is a day well-spent."

—Garry Trudeau

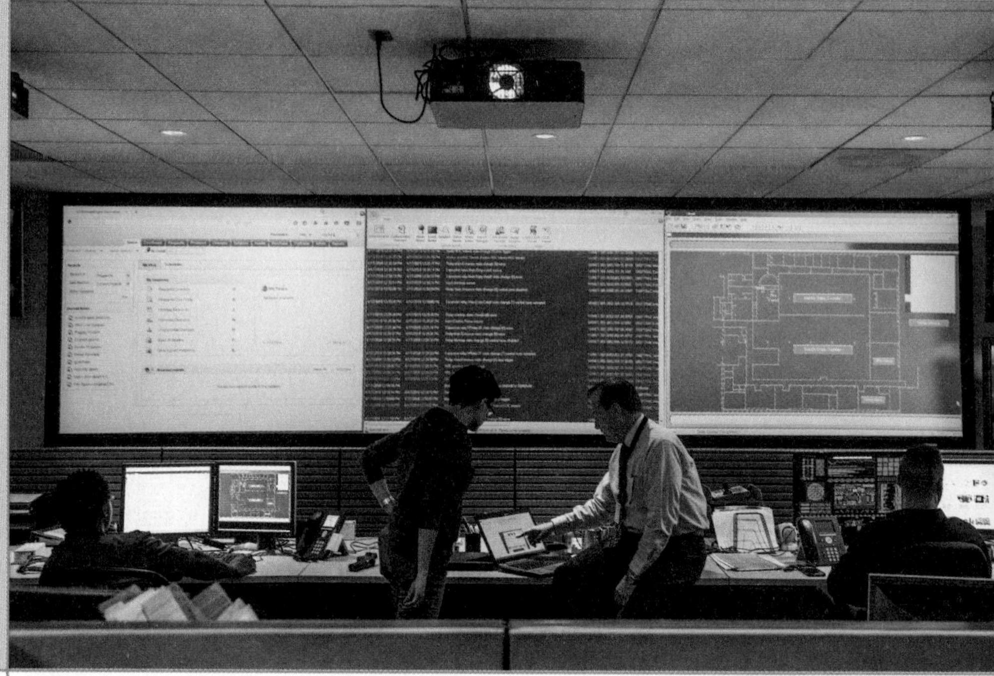

In this chapter, you will learn how to

- **Explain how SNMP works**
- **Describe network monitoring tools**
- **Discuss a scenario that uses management and monitoring tools**

A modern network doesn't behave properly without regular or irregular intervention from network technicians. Techs need to install network management tools and then deploy other tools to monitor, troubleshoot, and optimize networks over time. Because IP networks dominate today, we have a standard set of free tools to accomplish these goals.

This chapter looks first at network management tools, then examines the monitoring tools available and in common use. The chapter finishes with scenarios that call for deploying specific tools, analyzing their output, and fixing problems. For that final section, we'll revisit the Bayland Widgets Corporation and their campus area network (CAN) first discussed back in Chapter 13.

Cross Check

CAN, MAN, LAN, WAN, WLAN

You encountered the acronym soup of networking terms back in Chapters 4, 13, 14, 17…so cross-check your memory now. What do these terms mean? How do they differ? How do these networks communicate?

Test Specific

SNMP

A quick Google search for *network monitoring tools* finds literally hundreds of products out there, ranging from complex and expensive to simple and free (Figure 20.1). One thing most of them have in common is the underlying protocol that enables them to work. The **Simple Network Management Protocol (SNMP)** is the de facto network management protocol for TCP/IP networks (and it includes a truckload full of jargon terms to describe the various components).

An SNMP system—which creates a **managed network**—consists of at least three components:

- Managed devices
- SNMP manager
- SNMP agent

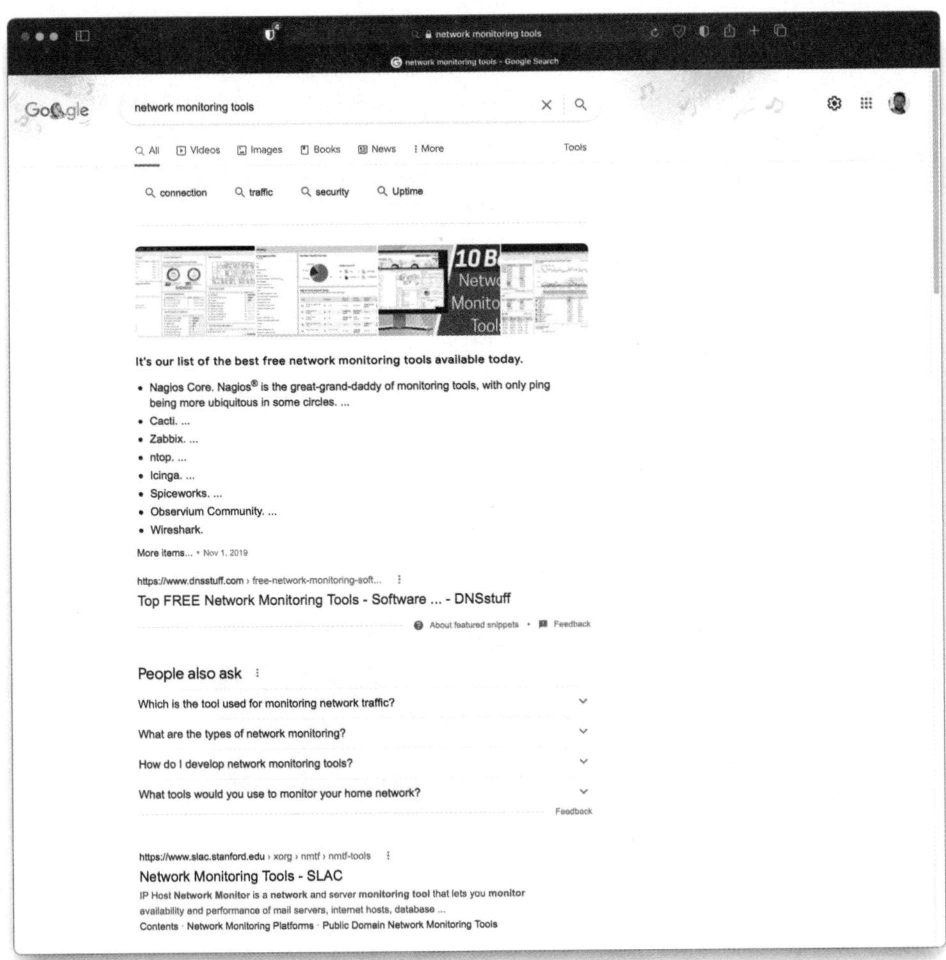

• **Figure 20.1** Google results for network monitoring tools

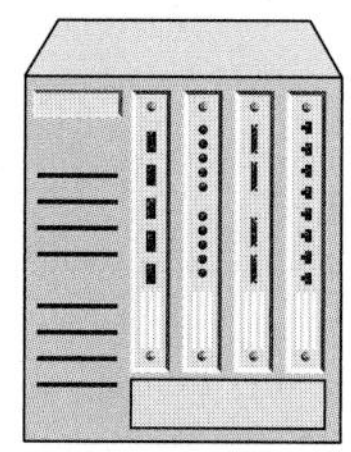

"I'm running an NMS to manage all these devices."

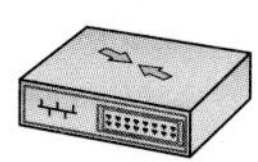

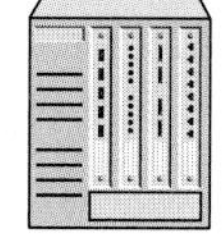

"We run agent software to respond to the NMS."

• **Figure 20.2** SNMP components

> There is some disagreement in the tech community about the exact definitions of network management system and SNMP managers. Some sources state they are the same thing, others state that the manager runs as part of the NMS, and yet others say the NMS runs as part of the SNMP manager. As most definitions equate the two terms, I have done the same.

> An SNMP PDU is not related to the PDU discussed earlier with OSI. It's the typical tech sector practice of repurposing an excellent term.

The **SNMP manager**, also known as the **network management system (NMS)**, requests and processes information from **agent** software that runs on **managed devices**. Managed device types include workstations, printers, video cameras, routers, switches, and more. Figure 20.2 illustrates the basic SNMP hardware.

The kind of information the SNMP manager can monitor from managed devices varies a lot, primarily because SNMP is an *extensible protocol*, meaning it can be adapted to accommodate different needs. Developers can create software that queries pretty much any aspect of a managed device, from current CPU load on a workstation to how much paper is left in a printer. SNMP uses **management information bases (MIBs)** to categorize the data that can be queried (and subsequently analyzed). *Object identifiers (OIDs)* uniquely number individual data pieces within a MIB.

Once set up properly, an SNMP-managed network runs regular queries to managed devices and then gathers that information in a format usable by SNMP operators. We need to add a little more jargon to go through the steps of the process.

An SNMP system has up to eight core functions (depending on the version of SNMP), of which four merit discussion here: Get, Response, Set, and Trap. The common term for each of these functions is **protocol data unit (PDU)**.

When an SNMP manager wants to query an agent, it sends a **Get** request, such as *GetRequest* or *GetNextRequest*. An agent then sends a **Response** with the requested information. Figure 20.3 illustrates the typical SNMP process.

An NMS can tell an agent to make changes to the information it queries and sends, called **variables**, through a **Set** PDU, specifically *SetRequest*.

An agent can solicit information from an NMS with the **Trap** PDU. An agent can send a *Trap* with or without prior action from the SNMP manager, at least from SNMPv2 to the current SNMPv3.

I've just dropped a lot of jargon on you, so here's a scenario that will make the process and terms a little more understandable. The Bayland Widgets art department has a color laser printer for producing brochures (Figure 20.4). Their CompTIA Network+ certified technicians maintain that laser printer, meaning they replace toner cartridges, change paper, and install the printer maintenance kits. (They're also CompTIA A+ certified, naturally!)

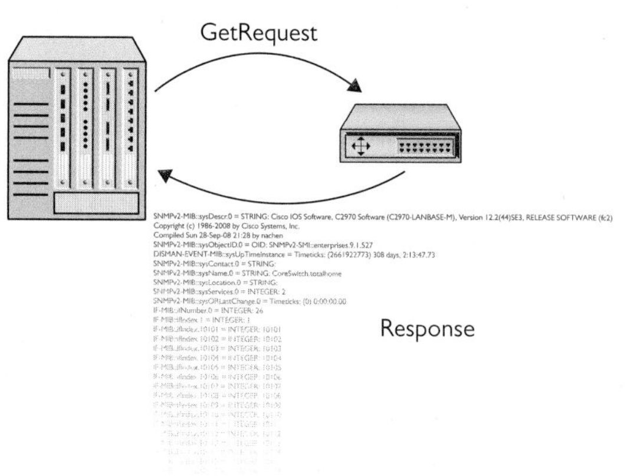

• **Figure 20.3** Simple SNMP process

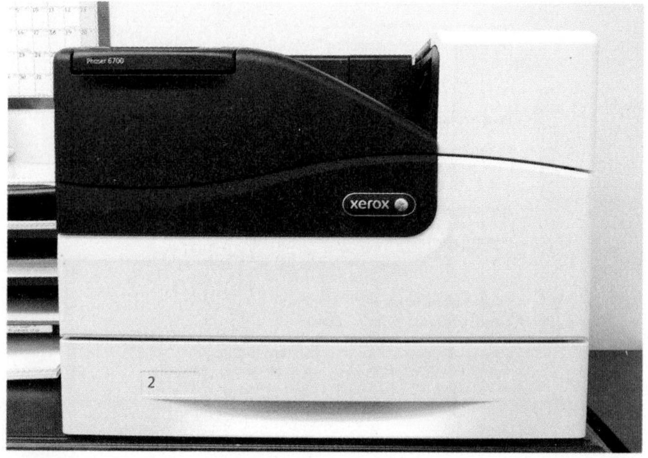

• **Figure 20.4** The Bayland Widgets art department printer

To manage this printer, nicknamed "Kitty," the techs use an SNMP network management system. At regular intervals, the NMS sends a *GetRequest* to the printer agent about the number of pages printed. According to the *Response* sent from the printer agent to the NMS, the techs can determine if the printer needs maintenance (that is, if it's at the point in its usage cycle where the printer maintenance kit parts need to be replaced).

At irregular intervals, the printer agent has to tell the techs that the printer is out of toner or out of paper. Although this information could come from the Get/Response interaction, it makes more sense that it come from the printer agent without a query. Kitty needs to yell "Help!" when she's out of toner. Otherwise the techs have to deal with irate artists, and that's just never going to be pretty. Kitty yells for help by sending a *Trap* to the NMS. Figure 20.5 illustrates the interaction.

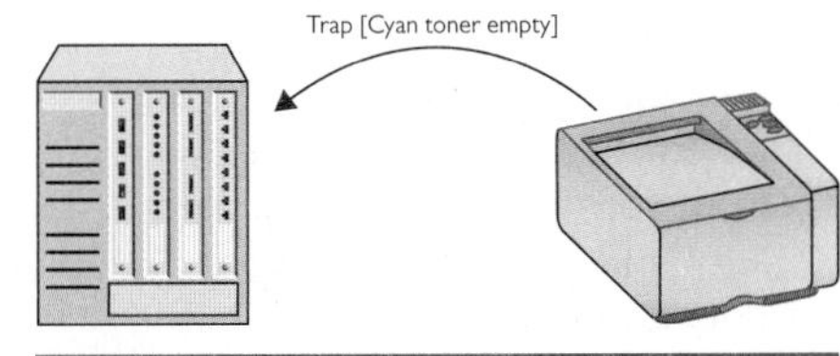

• **Figure 20.5** Trap in action

The BWC network techs don't sit at the SNMP manager, waiting for Kitty the printer to send messages about toner or ink. Instead, the manager software has the *event management* capability to send **alerts**: *notifications* directly to the techs when their intervention is required. These notifications can have a variety of forms. When the SNMP system was initially rolled out, one snarky manager suggested using text messages via **Short Message Service (SMS) alerts** that would cause techs' smartphones to meow upon receipt. That idea was nixed pretty early in favor of **e-mail alerts** (without any lolcat pictures attached).

SNMP has (as of this writing) three major versions. SNMP version 1 (SNMPv1) appeared in three requests for proposals (RFPs) all the way back in 1988. SNMPv2c was a relatively minor tweak to version 1. SNMPv3 added additional security with support for encryption and robust authentication, plus it provided features to make administering a large number of devices easier.

SNMP uses User Datagram Protocol (UDP) ports 161 and 162 for nonsecure communication. The NMS receives/listens on port 162. The agent receives/listens on port 161. When security is added via Transport Layer Security (TLS), the standard ports used are 10162 and 10161, respectively.

If you find yourself troubleshooting SNMP issues, the Net-SNMP package contains a number of utilities for working with the protocol on macOS/Linux. With `snmpwalk`, for example, you can quickly query any SNMP device directly from a computer's terminal.

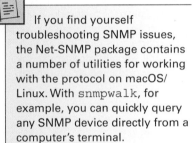

SNMP managers use UDP ports 162 or 10162 (with TLS). Agents use ports 161 or 10161 (with TLS).

The CompTIA Network+ objectives use the term *Secure SNMP* to refer to the addition of TLS and the different ports. RFC 6353, "Transport Layer Security (TLS) Transport Model for the Simple Network Management Protocol (SNMP)," provides guidelines for implementing TLS and DTLS (Datagram TLS). If you see "Secure SNMP" on an exam question, know that it simply refers to using SNMP over a tunnel secured with TLS or DTLS.

Monitoring Tools

The biggest trick to monitoring a network is to start by appreciating that even the smallest network has a dizzying amount of traffic moving though it every second. Even more, this traffic is moving through all kinds of different aspects of the network, from individual interfaces coming from a single NIC in a system to everything moving through a massive router on the edge of your infrastructure.

To be able to do the monitoring, the troubleshooting, and the optimizing necessary to keep our networks in top shape, we need the right monitoring tools at the right places looking for the right things. There are hundreds of different monitoring tools available, but for the scope of the CompTIA Network+ exam, we can break them down into four major types: packet sniffers, protocol analyzers, interface monitors, and performance monitors.

Check out the Chapter 20 "SNMP Monitoring" Show! and Click! sims at https://totalsem.com/008. The pair offer a great, practical introduction to SNMP tools.

Various names are used to describe utilities that analyze packets: *packet sniffer*, *packet analyzer*, *protocol analyzer*, and *network analyzer*. There's so much overlap here! That can be attributed to the fact that so many protocol analyzers come with sniffers as well. Bottom line, don't rely on the name of the monitoring tool to determine all it can do. Read the tech specs.

Look for specific terms on the CompTIA Network+ exam, such as *protocol analyzer*, *packet capture*, and *NetFlow analyzers*. You'll see a lot of terms in the real world used as synonyms.

Packet Sniffers

A **packet sniffer** (or just *sniffer*) is a program—a software tool—that queries a network interface and collects (captures) packets in a file called (surprisingly) a **capture file**. These programs might sit on a single computer, or perhaps on a router or a dedicated piece of hardware. The typical scenario for their use is one where network access/probing by a bad actor is suspected.

Packet sniffers need to capture all the packets they can, so it's typical for them to connect to an interface in *promiscuous mode* or, in the case of a switch, a *mirrored port*. This ensures they get as much data as possible. They run silently and transparently in the background.

Packet sniffers are essential information-gathering tools, but we also need a tool to enable analysis of the captured packets. For this reason, you don't really see packet sniffers as a stand-alone product. Instead, they are usually packaged with a protocol analyzer (see next section).

Protocol Analyzers

A **protocol analyzer** is a program that processes capture files from packet sniffers and analyzes them based on our monitoring needs. (You'll also hear the tool referred to as *packet analyzer*, though the exam uses the former term.) A good protocol analyzer can filter and sort a capture file based on almost anything and create an output to help us do monitoring properly. In other words, a protocol analyzer performs *packet/traffic analysis*. A typical question a protocol analyzer might answer is "What is the IP and MAC address of the device sending out DHCP Offer messages and when is it doing this?"

Protocol Analyzing with Wireshark

There are other protocol analyzers available out there, but you'd be hard-pressed to find a network administrator/technician/whatever who isn't familiar with the powerful and open source **Wireshark**. It was originally written by Gerald Combs, who still maintains the program with the help of hundreds of contributors. This probably won't be a surprise if you've noticed all of the Wireshark screenshots in earlier chapters, but I *love* Wireshark—it's my go-to protocol analyzer.

Try This!

Play Along with Wireshark

It's never too late to learn how to use protocol analyzers, so try this! Open your copy of Wireshark—you've already downloaded Wireshark (www.wireshark.org), right?—and just play. There's no danger to doing so, and it's actually a lot of fun!

The default Wireshark screen has become the standard most other protocol analyzers are based on. You select an interface to begin the capture and let the capture begin (Figure 20.6).

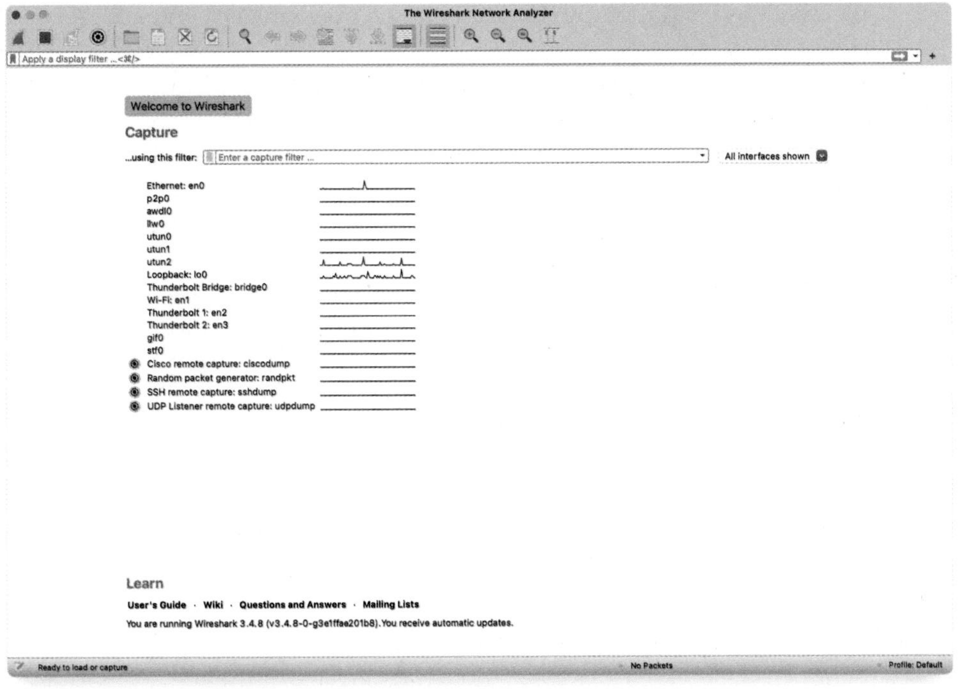

• **Figure 20.6** Wireshark default window

When you stop the capture, you'll see something like Figure 20.7. Wireshark's screen breaks into three parts. The top part is a numbered list of all the packets in the capture file, showing some of the most important information. The second part is a very detailed breakdown of the packet that is currently highlighted in the top pane. The bottom pane is the hex

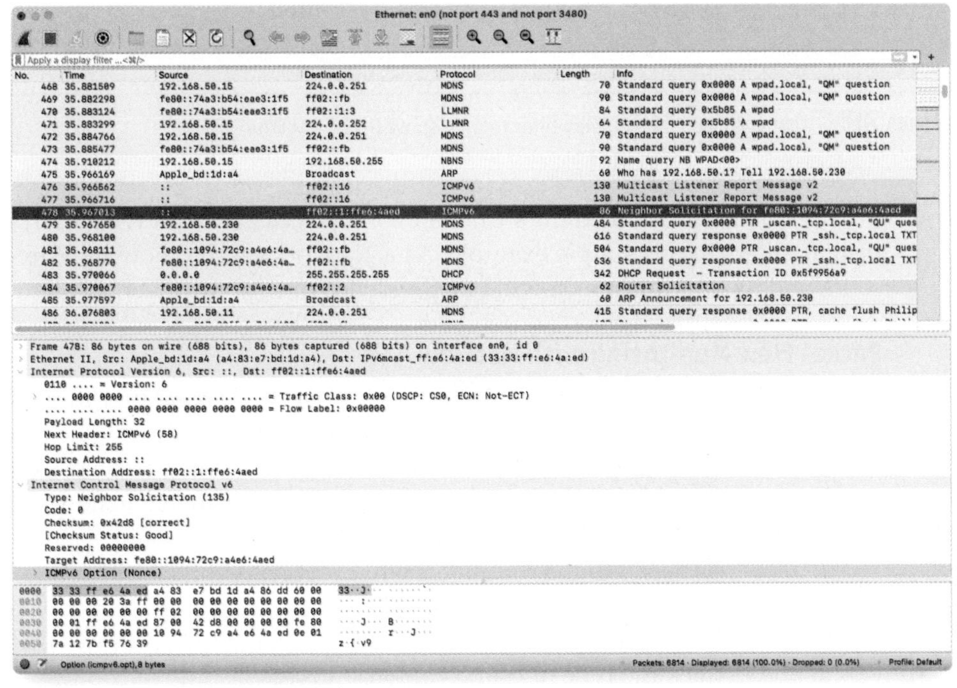

• **Figure 20.7** Wireshark capturing packets

representation and the ASCII representation of whatever part of the second pane is detailed.

The downside to a capture is that Wireshark is going to grab everything coming into the NIC unless you filter the firehose of traffic. To that end, Wireshark offers two types of filtering: simplified *capture filters* that let you exclude packets from ever getting captured, and sophisticated *display filters* that let you filter the already captured packets. Unfortunately, these two filter types have similar but incompatible syntax. Figure 20.8 shows both types of filters in action, a capture filter to exclude port 443 and 3480 traffic (you can see this in the title of the window) and a display filter to only show DHCP packets.

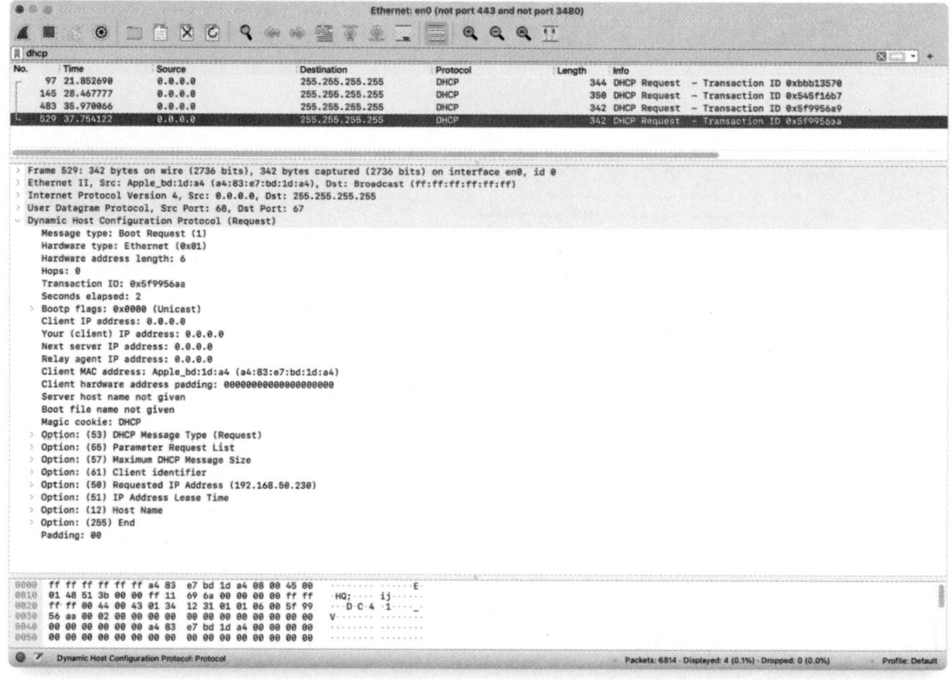

• **Figure 20.8** Using Wireshark's display filter to only show DHCP packets

I've not even scratched the surface of what you can do with Wireshark's display filters in this simple example. As a Network+ tech, knowing Wireshark and its filtering syntax will pay dividends over your career!

Packet Flow Monitoring with NetFlow

Packet flow monitoring, accomplished with a set of tools related to general packet sniffers and analyzers, tracks traffic flowing between specific source and destination devices. Cisco developed the concept of packet flow monitoring and subsequently included it in routers and switches. The primary tool is called **NetFlow**.

NetFlow has been around for quite a while and has evolved into a powerful tool that just about every owner of Cisco equipment uses. NetFlow is similar to SNMP, but different. NetFlow is based on the idea of flows that you define to track the type of traffic you wish to see.

A single **flow** is a sequence of packets from one specific place to another. Each of these flows is then cached in a **flow cache**. A single entry in a flow cache normally contains information such as destination and source addresses, destination and source ports, the source on the device running that flow, and total number of bytes of that flow.

Analyzing the flow data—CompTIA calls it *NetFlow data*—enables administrators to build a clear picture of the volume and flow of traffic on the network. This in turn enables them to optimize the network (by adding capacity where needed or other options).

Most of the heavy lifting of NetFlow is handled by the **NetFlow collectors**. NetFlow collectors store information from one or more devices' NetFlow caches, placing it into a table that can then be analyzed by **NetFlow analyzers**.

There are many different companies selling different NetFlow analyzers, and which tool you should choose is often a matter of features and cost. Figure 20.9 shows a screenshot of a popular tool called LiveAction.

> To use NetFlow you must enable NetFlow on that device. If the device doesn't support NetFlow, you can use standalone probes that can monitor maintenance ports on the unsupported device and send the information to the NetFlow collector.

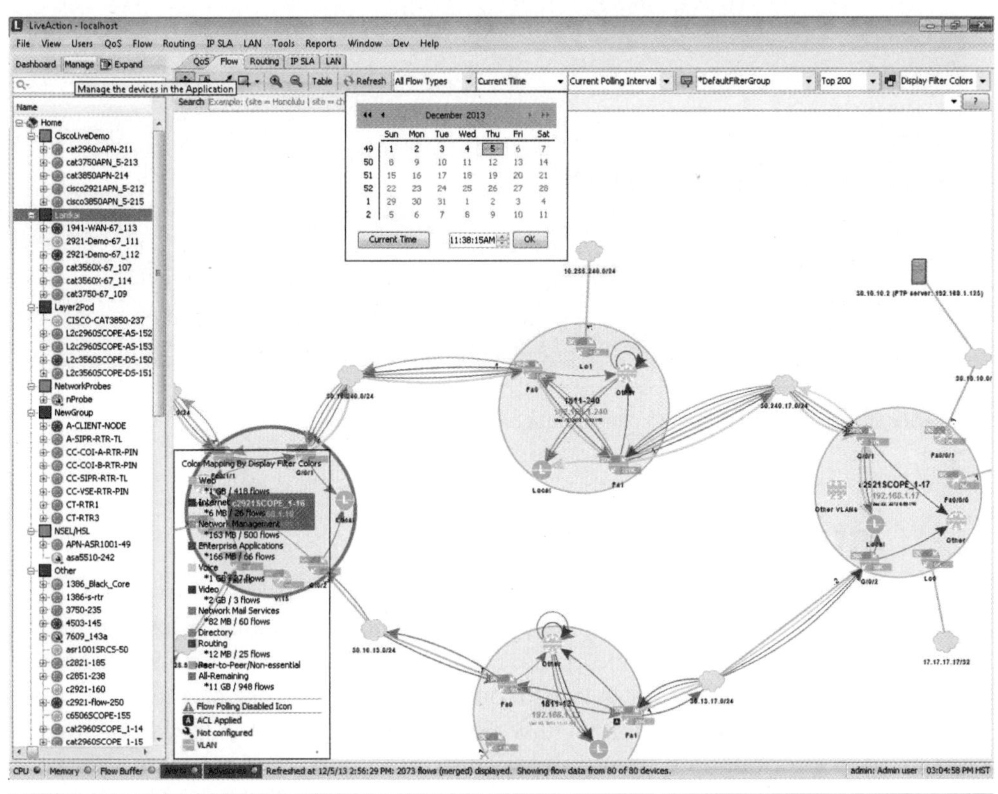

• **Figure 20.9** LiveAction in action!

Cisco's NetFlow started the idea of traffic flows that can then be collected and analyzed. Just about every other form of competing flow-monitoring concept (names like sFlow, NetStream, and IPFIX) builds on the idea of the flow.

Sensors

Various hardware and software sensors can monitor performance and environmental factors. *Performance metrics/sensors* such as *device/chassis sensors,*

You saw network metrics measuring latency and jitter back in Chapter 14 in the context of wireless networking.

for example, can show *temperature*, *central processing unit (CPU)* and *memory* usage, and more. *Network metrics* can show *bandwidth* use, such as *latency* and *jitter*, among other things. See "Putting It All Together" later in this chapter for a discussion of specific tools.

Environmental sensors can monitor environmental factors, such as external *temperatures*, *humidity* levels in the server room, issues with *electrical load*, and more. (You'll see this interaction as *environmental factors and sensors* in the objectives.) Many of the available tools for monitoring sensor data are graphical. The well-loved Zabbix Dashboard, for example, will show all sorts of data about a switch or rack (Figure 20.10).

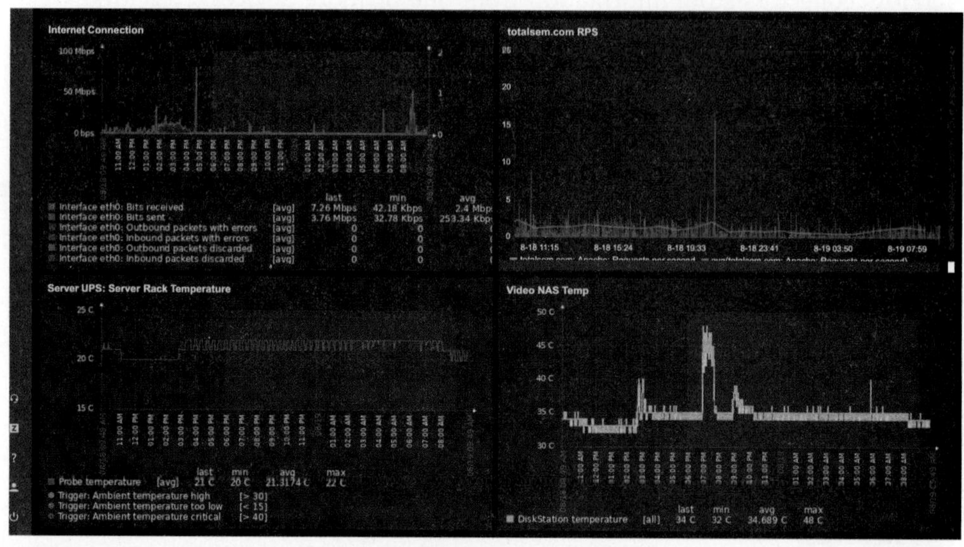

• **Figure 20.10** Zabbix reporting sensor data and other information

The CompTIA Network+ objectives mention sensors for physical flooding, which you'd find in very specific industries and deal with liquid levels and such. That's not sensor data typical in a data center.

Interface Monitors

If you want to know how hard your network is working, turn to an interface monitor. **Interface monitors** track the bandwidth and utilization of one or more interfaces on one or more devices. Think of them as the traffic monitors for your network. A typical question you might ask an interface monitor is "How hard is the Gigabit Ethernet port 17 on the backbone switch working right now, in megabits per second?"

Interface monitors track the quantity and utilization of traffic through a physical port or ports on a single device. At a high level, you generally do interface monitoring through a graphical tool, such as Zabbix, that aggregates all kinds of information, including information about the interfaces, and enables you to set up alerts and visualize what's going on. When you're troubleshooting, though, it's often helpful to access the same information for the interfaces on a specific device. Figure 20.11 shows a small section of a Junos OS—Juniper device operating system—`show interfaces` command. It goes on for another 100+ lines, providing a ton of detail.

Cisco devices also have a `show interfaces` command in IOS that provides similar levels of detail. Some of the highlights or **metrics** (performance

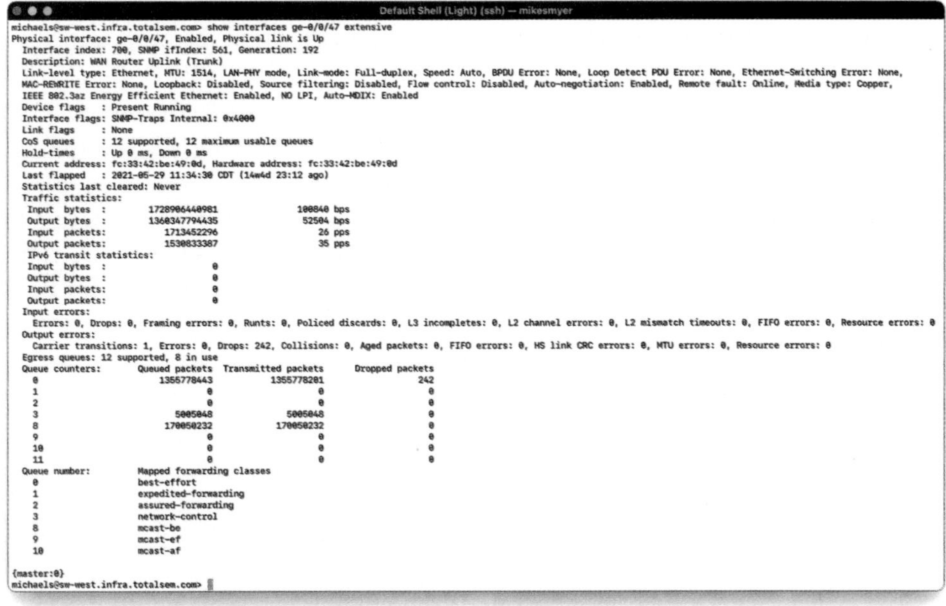
Default Shell (Light) (ssh) — mikesmyer
michaels@sw-west.infra.totalsem.com> show interfaces ge-0/0/47 extensive
Physical interface: ge-0/0/47, Enabled, Physical link is Up
Interface index: 700, SNMP ifIndex: 561, Generation: 192
Description: WAN Router Uplink (Trunk)
Link-level type: Ethernet, MTU: 1514, LAN-PHY mode, Link-mode: Full-duplex, Speed: Auto, BPDU Error: None, Loop Detect PDU Error: None, Ethernet-Switching Error: None,
MAC-REWRITE Error: None, Loopback: Disabled, Source filtering: Disabled, Flow control: Disabled, Auto-negotiation: Enabled, Remote fault: Online, Media type: Copper,
IEEE 802.3az Energy Efficient Ethernet: Enabled, NO LPI, Auto-MDIX: Enabled
Device flags : Present Running
Interface flags: SNMP-Traps Internal: 0x4000
Link flags : None
CoS queues : 12 supported, 12 maximum usable queues
Hold-times : Up 0 ms, Down 0 ms
Current address: fc:33:42:be:49:0d, Hardware address: fc:33:42:be:49:0d
Last flapped : 2021-05-29 11:34:30 CDT (14w4d 23:12 ago)
Statistics last cleared: Never
Traffic statistics:
Input bytes : 1728906440981 100840 bps
Output bytes : 1360347794435 52504 bps
Input packets: 1713452296 26 pps
Output packets: 1530833387 35 pps
IPv6 transit statistics:
Input bytes : 0
Output bytes : 0
Input packets: 0
Output packets: 0
Input errors:
Errors: 0, Drops: 0, Framing errors: 0, Runts: 0, Policed discards: 0, L3 incompletes: 0, L2 channel errors: 0, L2 mismatch timeouts: 0, FIFO errors: 0, Resource errors: 0
Output errors:
Carrier transitions: 1, Errors: 0, Drops: 242, Collisions: 0, Aged packets: 0, FIFO errors: 0, HS link CRC errors: 0, MTU errors: 0, Resource errors: 0
Egress queues: 12 supported, 8 in use
Queue counters: Queued packets Transmitted packets Dropped packets
0 1355778443 1355778201 242
1 0 0 0
2 0 0 0
3 5005048 5005048 0
8 170050232 170050232 0
9 0 0 0
10 0 0 0
11 0 0 0
Queue number: Mapped forwarding classes
0 best-effort
1 expedited-forwarding
2 assured-forwarding
3 network-control
8 mcast-be
9 mcast-ef
10 mcast-af
{master:0}
michaels@sw-west.infra.totalsem.com>

• **Figure 20.11** Junos OS `show interfaces` result sample

and use option numbers) include the following *interface statistics/status* and *interface errors or alerts*:

- **Link state (up/down)** A specific port status.
- **Speed/duplex** The speed and duplex status of a port; Figure 20.11 shows full-duplex and Gigabit Ethernet, for example.
- **Send/receive traffic** What's happening on the network; Figure 20.11 shows traffic statistics.
- **Cyclic redundancy checks (CRCs) and CRC errors** Information about packets received that had reported errors.
- **Protocol packet and byte counts** Network packet types and quantity that have recently passed through the network device.
- **Giants** Packets received that exceeded the maximum size; that's the Ethernet MTU: 1514 in Figure 20.11.
- **Runts** Packets received that are shorter than Ethernet's minimum size of 64 bytes; runts were at zero in Figure 20.11.
- **Encapsulation errors** Some Layer 3 packets missing essential Layer 2 information.
- **Uptime/downtime** Overall time that a switch or device has been up and functional or down and dysfunctional (and needing therapy?).

The list presented here only scratches the surface of the quantity and specific details of network device information you can glean from interface monitors such as the `show interfaces` command in Junos OS and IOS. But these are the likely things you will see on the CompTIA Network+ 008 exam.

Performance Monitors

A **performance monitor** tracks the performance of some aspect of a system over time and lets you know when things aren't normal. Performance monitors are usually tied to a particular operating system or application, as the performance monitoring requires very detailed understanding of the low-level aspects of the system. A typical question you might ask a performance monitor is "How many requests per second occurred on my Web server over the last hour?"

The two most common performance monitoring tools are Windows' **Performance Monitor** (perfmon.exe) and **syslog** (found in macOS and Linux). Although they perform the same job, I want to introduce both tools to you because they do that job very differently…and use very different terms to describe the same things. As we next look at certain aspects that are common to any good performance monitor, I'll use the terminology for both tools.

This section explores the processes and expected outputs for log reviewing and reviewing baselines. We'll start with definitions of logs and then move into the active processes of reviewing.

Logs

Performance monitors use system log files to track performance over time. **Logs** store information about the performance of some particular aspect of a system. Different programs refer to the monitored aspect with different terms. Performance Monitor calls them *counters*; syslog calls them *facilities*. A log file might record the percentage of utilization over time of a specific Ethernet port, for example, or the average throughput of a network connection.

Network device logs can provide a lot of information useful in troubleshooting. Devices can log traffic, SSH connections, and more, assuming they're set up to do so. Part of device configuration is to set up the device logging—local logging—to capture the data you'll need. The worst time to discover that logging wasn't set up properly is when devices go down and you're troubleshooting.

Baselines

The only way to know when a problem is brewing on your network is to know how things perform when all's well with the network. Part of any proper performance monitor is the facility to create a **baseline**: a log of performance indicators such as CPU usage, network utilization, and other values to give you a picture of your network and servers when they are working correctly. A major change in these values can point to problems on a server or the network as a whole.

A typical scenario for baselines is for techs and administrators to create and use appropriate documentation and diagrams for how the network optimally performs. They use this information to manage the network over time. The CompTIA Network+ exam objectives use the phrase *network performance baselines* to describe the documentation and diagrams needed in this process.

All operating systems come with some form of baseline tools. Performance Monitor is the common tool used to create a baseline on Windows systems.

Log Management

Any system that generates electronic log files has two issues. The first is security. Log files are important for the information they provide. The second is maintenance. Log files are going to continue to grow until they fill the mass storage they are stored on. The job of providing proper security and maintenance for log files is called **log management**.

Logs often contain private or sensitive data and thus must be protected. Access to active logs must be carefully controlled. It's very common to give read access rights only to specific users, to make sure only the correct users have access to the log files. In many cases the logging application has only write access to the files—it's not a good idea to give root access to critical log files.

Generally, log files by default simply grow until they fill the space they are stored on. To prevent this, it's common to make log files *cyclical*—when a file grows to a certain size, it begins to cycle. *Cycling* just means that as a new record appears in the file, the oldest record in the file is deleted. It's also common for log files to be re-created on a time basis. Depending on the utility, you can set a new log file to be created daily, weekly, hourly—whatever is most convenient for the administrators. These files can then be backed up.

There are many laws today that require retention of log files for a certain period of time. It's important to check with your legal department to see if any files need to be kept longer than your standard backup time frames.

Putting It All Together

Up to this point in the chapter, we've looked at management and monitoring tools as distinct things, easy to label and easy to differentiate. And in a small office/home office network, that kind of simplicity makes sense. If you have a Windows-based network with a single server running Windows Server, then of course you'd use Performance Monitor to baseline and monitor your network over time. The CompTIA Network+ competencies lead to this modular thinking as well. Once you scale up past the one-server network, though, things get a lot more...*chaotic* isn't quite the right word... *nuanced* is better. Let's take a look.

Scenario: Monitoring and Managing

This scenario revisits the Bayland Widgets CAN and applies the network managing and monitoring tools to see how their techs would use these tools to manage, monitor, maintain, and troubleshoot their network.

Figure 20.12 shows the BWC campus layout with its three main buildings. The main office has servers and various individual offices. The factory houses the robots and control systems that produce the company's widgets. The warehouse and shipping building does exactly as it's named.

Internally, each building is wired with Gigabit Ethernet. In addition, the buildings interconnect with 10-Gigabit fiber into access switches. Add onto that a campus-wide Wi-Fi network (802.11ac) and, not pictured, the router that gives them access to the Internet.

Since we're talking about managing and monitoring the whole network here, let's list all the types of networked devices:

- Routers (wired and wireless)
- Switches

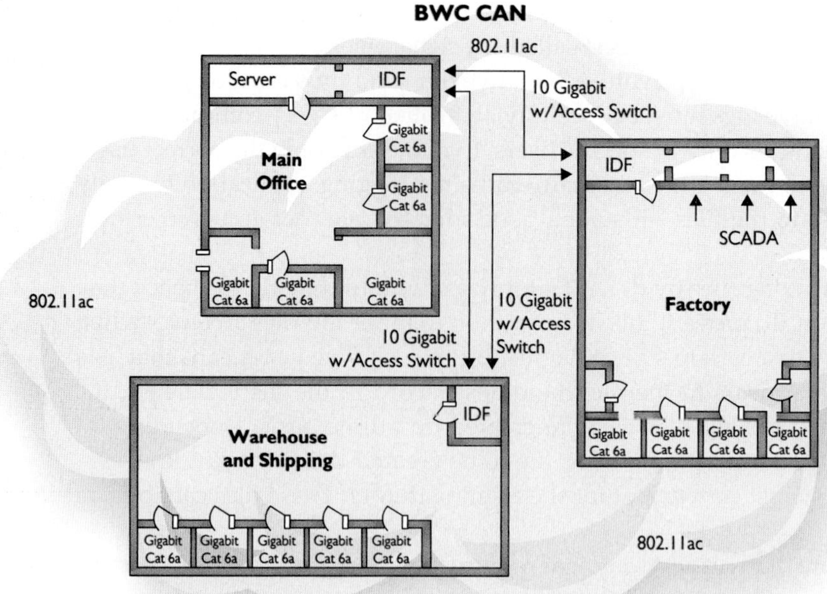

• **Figure 20.12** Diagram of Bayland Widgets' campus area network

- Wireless access points
- Servers
- Workstations
- Printers
- Phones

Note that I've left out the industrial control systems that run the factory and shipping automation. Plus, I've left out the security systems and other essential components of a functional CAN. This list focuses on the core networking devices that a CompTIA Network+ tech would encounter.

Modern networking tools enable skilled network administrators to manage networks as complex at Bayland Widgets' network fairly easily, after those tools have been set up properly. The tools used must be customized for the network. Plus, the various tools aren't really interchangeable. Just like you wouldn't use a hammer when you need to turn a screw, you wouldn't use a protocol analyzer when you want to check toner levels in a laser printer.

Bayland Widgets could dedicate an area in the main office as a **network operations center (NOC)**, a centralized location for techs and administrators to manage all aspects of the network. From that NOC, they could use various programs on the SNMP-managed network to query devices. A **graphing** program could create graphs and diagrams that display any set of the data received.

Graphing applications like **Cacti** and Grafana would show everything about a specific switch, for example, to determine utilization of that switch in many aspects—that is, how well it handles its current workload. Figure 20.13 shows Cacti with four graphs depicting network device CPU utilization, memory usage, traffic (bandwidth usage) on the WAN interface, and traffic to the file server.

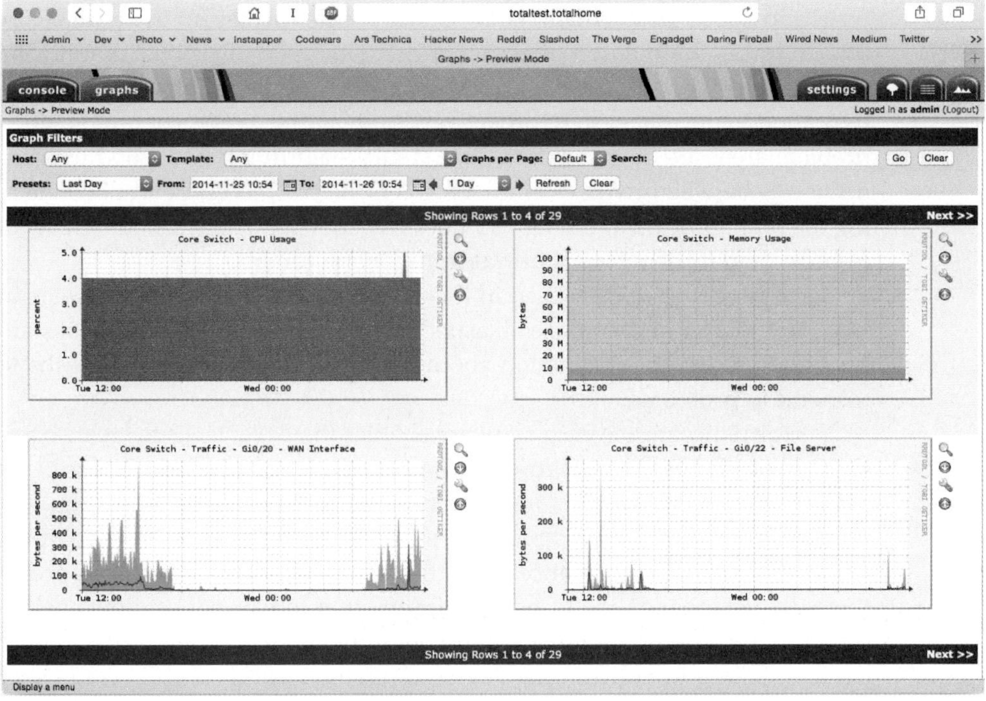

• **Figure 20.13** Cacti showing switch utilization graphs

With a different query, Cacti can graph available storage on a file server (Figure 20.14), or wireless channel utilization.

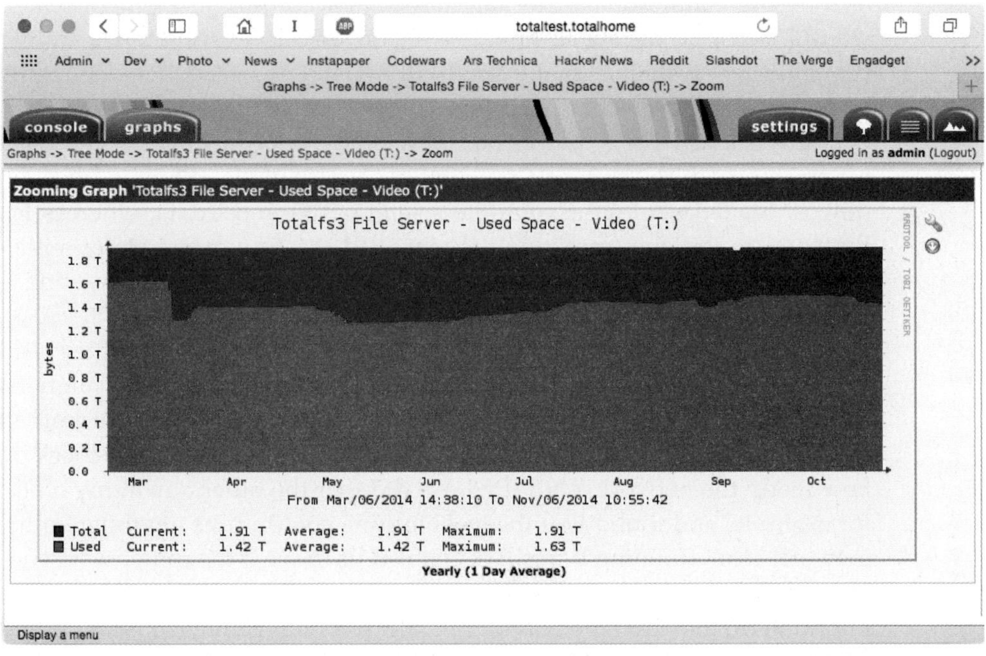

• **Figure 20.14** Cacti showing file server storage utilization graph

Applications like Cacti enable you to see very quickly essential facts about your network hardware. You can see available storage, network device CPU usage, network device memory usage, and more. This level of monitoring is especially critical for wireless, where you can quickly spot problems like high channel utilization and frequent retries. These tools are a tech's friend!

A tool like *iPerf/iPerf3* can actively measure the available and maximum bandwidth on a network. The iPerf utility works with TCP, UDP, and SCTP; it functions in IPv4 and IPv6 networks. Check out https://iperf.fr for more details.

The default destination port for syslog is UDP port 514. That's what you'll see on the CompTIA Network+ exam. Telcos use TCP port 601 these days for syslog. Tuck the latter fact in your back pocket; you won't see it on the exam.

Cycling through the various network monitoring tools enables network administrators to see very quickly if a specific server or other device has problems. They could analyze the campus Wi-Fi network with a Wi-Fi analyzer and spot a problematic WAP. Going a little further up the food chain, BWC admins could add to their network toolboxes more robust monitoring and alerting with a tool like Zabbix or SolarWinds and, after proper configuration, have that system proactively send alerts via SMS or e-mail when problem areas are detected. If the **link status**—signifying how good the connection is between two systems—between the two access servers connecting the main office and the factory goes red, that's a whole different level of priority than if Kitty the art printer runs low on toner.

Each type of tool discussed in this chapter enables the network team at BWC to monitor and analyze all aspects of the network. The SNMP system offers very specific information about managed devices, enabling techs to respond to problems.

Performance monitoring software enables the BWC techs to create baselines when the network is functioning correctly. In a scenario where complaints about network performance come in from one portion of the network (Accounting, for example), that same software can be used to compare current network performance with the historical, normal performance. If there's a discrepancy, the techs can turn to other tools—packet flow analyzers and interface monitors—to figure out if the issue is excess traffic, failing devices, failing interfaces on a device, or an overworked **bottleneck** (a spot where traffic slows precipitously). The appropriate tools can troubleshoot cable connectivity issues such as specification discrepancies and limitations in throughput, speed, and distance.

A syslog server enables the collection of messages from many devices on the network. Syslog listens on UDP port 514, logging messages coming from clients. Syslog enables *log reviews*, including *traffic logs* and *audit logs*. Syslog can automatically tag messages according to *logging levels* or *severity levels*, according to how it's set up. Severity levels range from 0 (Emergency—system is totally down) to 7 (Debug—used when debugging a program) and everything in between.

Network analyzers and packet flow analyzers can discover the busiest machines on the network, potentially sources of overall network slowdowns. **Top talkers** are the computers sending the most data, whereas **top listeners** are the ones receiving the most. If BWC is worried about a malware problem, finding that the computer assigned to Joe in Accounting is the top talker might track down that spam infestation.

The network techs turn to a packet sniffer/analyzer tool when they need to go deep into the traffic. Here's an example of when Wireshark might be the tool to start. BWC wants to move the network to IPv6 and turn off all IPv4 traffic. Turning off IPv4 on a test machine would be a good check on how ready the network is for IPv6. We did that the other day in my office, for example, and found that the test machine couldn't see anything on the network at all. Running Wireshark enabled us to see if the router was sending out IPv6 router advertisements with DNS. When we confirmed that information, the next step was more old-fashioned. Had we misconfigured the test workstation's IPv6 settings?

Accomplished techs use a variety of managing and monitoring tools to maintain a healthy network. Use each type of tool when that tool is appropriate. Often, you'll need to use multiple tools during a longer troubleshooting scenario.

SIEM

The Bayland Widgets people could use an approach called **security information and event management (SIEM)** to monitor and manage their network. SIEM is an industry-standard term, but there are many products of various types that are marketed as SIEM solutions. SIEM is a mashup of two processes: security event management (SEM) and security information management (SIM).

As the name implies, SIEM is a two-part process that begins with the security event monitoring component. SEM is based on real-time monitoring of security events. The SEM framework calls for monitoring the entire enterprise, often through edge devices at monitor points, then saving the logged events to a location that supports single viewpoint review and analysis of the events. In addition to active event monitoring, another task of SEM is to collect and centralize otherwise disparately located security and event logs.

Once logs are created and saved, the second part of SIEM, security information management, kicks in: here, the log files are reviewed and analyzed by automated and human interpreters.

One place SIEM comes into play is with *file integrity monitoring (FIM)*, checking for changes in all sorts of aspects of files. These include

- Attributes and file size
- Configuration values
- Content
- Credentials
- Hash values
- Privileges and security settings

Any changes discovered could indicate that an attack has occurred or is happening right now. The verification process compares a baseline or known good copy of the file with the current file, checking for differences.

SIEM systems are complex solution suites that are found in large, enterprise environments. Depending on the organization, they may be self-implemented and managed or may be administered under contract by a vendor in the form of a managed security service provider (MSSP).

Chapter 20 Review

Chapter Summary

After reading this chapter and completing the exercises, you should understand the following about network monitoring.

Explain how SNMP works

- An SNMP-managed network consists of three core components: SNMP agents, SNMP managers, and managed devices. SNMP agent software running on managed devices organizes information in management information bases (MIBs). The SNMP manager, also known as the NMS, queries the agent for this information and processes it.
- An SNMP system has up to eight core functions, or PDUs. The Get, Response, Set, and Trap PDUs are used for queries to agents, responses from agents, setting of parameters, and actions from agents.
- An SNMP system can have all sorts of features. It can be set up to send SMS or e-mail alerts, for example, so techs will know when some part of the system needs maintenance.
- SNMP uses UDP ports 161 and 162 for unsecured communication. The NMS receives on port 162. The agent receives on port 161. When security is added via TLS, the standard ports used are 10162 and 10161, respectively.

Describe network monitoring tools

- Monitoring tools enable network techs and admins to gather information about all kinds of aspects of the network. This in turn enables them to manage, troubleshoot, and optimize network traffic.
- Packet sniffers, protocol analyzers, and packet flow analyzers capture files and produce information on IP addresses, types of data flowing between connections, and much more. Tools in this category are Wireshark and NetFlow.
- Interface monitors track the bandwidth and utilization of one or more interfaces on one or more devices. They reveal information such as percentage of utilization, packet drops, errors, and more.
- Performance monitors track the performance of some aspect of a system over time and let you know when things aren't normal. They enable you to create baselines so you know how a system should run, then keep logs for analysis so that you can track down problem areas. Typical performance monitoring tools are Performance Monitor in Windows and syslog in macOS and Linux.

Discuss a scenario that uses management and monitoring tools

- SNMP tools enable network pros to manage just about any aspect of a network. Graphing programs like Cacti and Grafana can display information as diverse as traffic on an individual switch port, to device CPU usage, to available file storage on a server. More powerful tools like Zabbix can be customized to send alerts when monitored systems need help.
- The SIEM approach to monitoring and managing networks offers a range of tools for accomplishing its tasks. SIEM actively monitors at the enterprise level and makes log files available for analysis by automated and human interpreters.

Key Terms

agent *(578)*
alert *(579)*
baseline *(586)*
bottleneck *(590)*
Cacti *(588)*
capture file *(580)*
e-mail alert *(579)*
flow *(583)*
flow cache *(583)*
Get *(578)*
graphing *(588)*
interface monitor *(584)*
link status *(590)*
log *(586)*
log management *(587)*
managed device *(578)*
managed network *(577)*
management information base (MIB) *(578)*
metrics *(584)*
NetFlow *(582)*
NetFlow analyzer *(583)*
NetFlow collector *(583)*
network management system (NMS) *(578)*
network operations center (NOC) *(588)*
packet sniffer *(580)*
performance monitor *(586)*
Performance Monitor (Windows) *(585)*
protocol analyzer *(580)*
protocol data unit (PDU) *(578)*
Response *(578)*
security information and event management (SIEM) *(591)*
Set *(578)*
Short Message Service (SMS) alert *(579)*
Simple Network Management Protocol (SNMP) *(577)*
SNMP manager *(578)*
syslog *(586)*
top listener *(590)*
top talker *(590)*
Trap *(578)*
variable *(578)*
Wireshark *(580)*

Key Term Quiz

Use the Key Terms list to complete the sentences that follow. Not all the terms will be used.

1. A(n) _______________ requests and processes information from managed devices.
2. An SNMP system uses _______________ PDUs for querying agents.
3. An agent uses _______________ PDUs to solicit information from an NMS.
4. The _______________ is a physical place where techs and administrators can manage all aspects of a network.
5. Runts and giants are examples of _______________.
6. A primary tool for capturing and analyzing the flow of packets from one device to another is called _______________.
7. Use a(n) _______________ program to track the quantity and utilization of traffic through a physical port or ports on a single device.
8. Raphael can compare the results of a current Performance Monitor output with the _______________ to see if the network is performing correctly.
9. Performance monitors use a(n) _______________ to store some form of performance information about a system.
10. Graphing programs like _______________ can show everything about specific switches, such as bandwidth usage.

Multiple-Choice Quiz

1. In an SNMP-managed network, which software does an SNMP manager run?
   A. Agent
   B. NMS
   C. SNMP manager
   D. MIB
2. In an SNMP-managed network, which software does a managed device run?
   A. Agent
   B. NMS
   C. SNMP manager
   D. MIB
3. Which PDU enables a tech to change the variables queried of a managed device?
   A. Get
   B. Response
   C. Set
   D. Trap
4. How does an SNMP-managed system categorize data that can be queried?
   A. MIBs
   B. PDUs
   C. UDP
   D. QoS
5. An analysis of a network shows a lot of traffic on one machine on port 162. What kind of machine is it?
   A. Managed device
   B. SNMP manager
   C. PDU
   D. MIB
6. A newly hired networking consultant announces at the Monday staff meeting, "Now you techs can't hide from your duties. All problems with managed devices will be reported to your cell phones." What did the consultant add to the network management system?
   A. PDU alerts
   B. Agent responses
   C. SMS alerts
   D. Trap alerts
7. The boss at a small business has learned that the existing management system for this network is using unsecured SNMP traffic. Due to the sensitive nature of SNMP traffic, that data needs to be secured. What's the minimum SNMP version required on all the business's network devices?
   A. SNMPv2
   B. SNMPv2c
   C. SNMPv3
   D. SNMPv4
8. An SNMP agent uses which port with TLS?
   A. 161
   B. 162
   C. 10161
   D. 10162
9. Jason is concerned about the communication between two workstations and wants to capture and analyze that traffic to see if anything illicit is going on. Which tool would best serve his needs?
   A. Interface monitor
   B. Packet flow monitor
   C. Packet sniffer
   D. Performance monitor
10. Jill suspects a switch on Level 12 has a bottlenecked port, with too much traffic. Which tool would enable her to check that port specifically?
    A. Interface monitor
    B. Packet sniffer
    C. Protocol analyzer
    D. Packet flow monitor
11. Bart has a choice of tools to view his managed network, but he primarily wants to see graphs of various types of data, such as the overall traffic and the current capacities of the file servers. Which tool offers him the best option?
    A. Cacti
    B. `snmpwalk`
    C. NetFlow
    D. Wireshark

12. Cindy's newly installed Windows network runs great! She needs to create a baseline now for later analysis. Which tool should she use?
    - A. Cacti
    - B. Performance Monitor
    - C. Syslog
    - D. Wireshark
13. What component in NetFlow stores information from NetFlow caches?
    - A. Flow cache
    - B. LiveAction
    - C. NetFlow collectors
    - D. NetFlow PDUs
14. Where does a packet sniffer put information it collects?
    - A. Trap
    - B. Capture file
    - C. Management information base
    - D. Flow cache
15. John is conversing with another tech who consistently uses the term "network analyzer" when discussing network monitoring tools. What sort of tool is he using?
    - A. Interface monitor
    - B. Protocol analyzer
    - C. Performance analyzer
    - D. Performance monitor

Essay Quiz

1. Write a short essay comparing a protocol analyzer, like Wireshark, to an SNMP manager like Zabbix. Do they complement each other or overlap when you're trying to understand things such as overall network traffic? What about when assessing the performance of a specific network device, such as a managed switch?
2. Similarly to question 1, compare Wireshark with NetFlow and address the same questions. Do they complement or overlap?

Lab Projects

• Lab Project 20.1

If you haven't already, download a copy of Wireshark and run it. Capture packets for a few minutes, adding traffic by surfing various Web sites. Once you have a nice set of information, stop the capture and analyze the packets. How does the DHCP or ARP traffic manifest? Are there any errors?

• Lab Project 20.2

If you have access to a managed switch, open a terminal and log into its command-line interface. Poke around and explore the status of various interfaces with `show interfaces` or the equivalent command for your switch (you may need to ask your instructor or consult the documentation). What information does your switch expose about its interfaces? Can you modify the command to reveal more metrics?

Network Troubleshooting

"This is the end / Beautiful friend / This is the end."

—Jim Morrison

In this chapter, you will learn how to

- **Describe appropriate troubleshooting tools and their functions**
- **Analyze and discuss the troubleshooting process**
- **Resolve common network issues**

Have you ever seen a tech walk up to a network and seem to know all the answers, effortlessly typing in a few commands and magically making the system or network work? I've always been intrigued by how they do this. Observing such techs over the years, I've noticed that they tend to follow the same steps for similar problems—looking in the same places, typing the same commands, and so on.

When someone performs a task the same way every time, I figure they're probably following a plan. They understand what tools they have to work with, and they know where to start and what to do second and third and fourth until they find the problem.

This chapter's lofty goal is to consolidate my observations on how these "übertechs" fix networks. I'll show you the primary troubleshooting tools and help you formulate a troubleshooting process and learn where to look for different sorts of problems. Then you'll apply this knowledge to resolve common network issues.

Troubleshooting Tools

While working through the process of finding a problem's cause, you sometimes need tools. These tools are the software and hardware tools that provide information about your network and enact repairs. I covered a number of tools already: hardware tools like cable testers and crimpers and software utilities like ping and tracert. The trick is knowing when and how to use these tools to solve your network problems.

Almost every new networking person I teach will, at some point, ask me: "What tools do I need to buy?" My answer shocks them: "None. Don't buy a thing." It's not so much that you don't need tools, but rather that different networking jobs require wildly different tools. Plenty of network techs never crimp a cable. An equal number never open a system. Some techs do nothing all day but pull cable. The tools you need are defined by your job.

No matter what the problem, always consider the safety of your data first. Ask yourself this question before performing any troubleshooting action: "Can what I'm about to do potentially damage my data?"

This answer is especially true with software tools. Almost all the network problems I encounter in established networks don't require me to use any tools other than the classic ones provided by the operating system. I've fixed more network problems with ping, for example, than with any other single tool. As you gain skill in this area, you'll find yourself hounded by vendors trying to sell you the latest and greatest networking diagnostic tools. You may like these tools. All I can say is that I've never needed a software diagnostics tool that I had to purchase.

Hardware Tools

In multiple chapters in this book, you've read about tools used to configure a network. These **hardware tools** include cable testers, TDRs, OTDRs, certifiers, voltage event recorders, protocol analyzers, cable strippers, multimeters, tone probes/generators, and punchdown tools. Some of these tools can also be used in troubleshooting scenarios to help you eliminate or narrow down the possible causes of certain problems. Let's review the tools as listed in the CompTIA Network+ exam objectives (plus a couple I think you should know).

Read this section! The CompTIA Network+ exam is filled with repair scenarios, and you must know what every tool does and when to use it.

Cable Testers, TDRs, and OTDRs

The vast majority of cabling problems occur when the network is first installed or when a change is made. Once a cable has been made, installed, and tested, the chances of it failing are pretty small compared to all of the other network problems that might take place. If you're having trouble connecting to a resource or experiencing performance problems after making a connection, a bad cable likely isn't the culprit. Broken cables don't make intermittent problems, and they don't slow down data. They make permanent disconnects.

Network techs define a "broken" cable in numerous ways. First, a broken cable might have an *open circuit*, where one or more of the wires in a cable simply don't connect from one end of the cable to the other. The signal lacks *continuity*. Second, a cable might have a *short*, where one or more of the wires in a cable connect to another wire in the cable. (Within a normal cable, no wires connect to other wires.)

The CompTIA Network+ exam objectives use the terms *open/short*. More commonly, techs would refer to these issues as *open circuits* and *short circuits*.

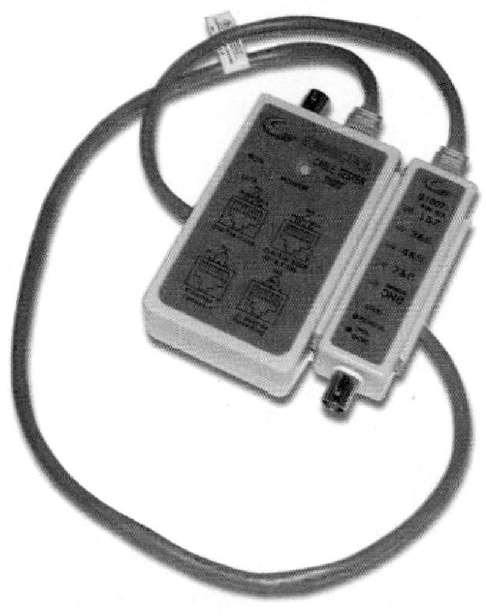

• **Figure 21.1** Classic cable tester

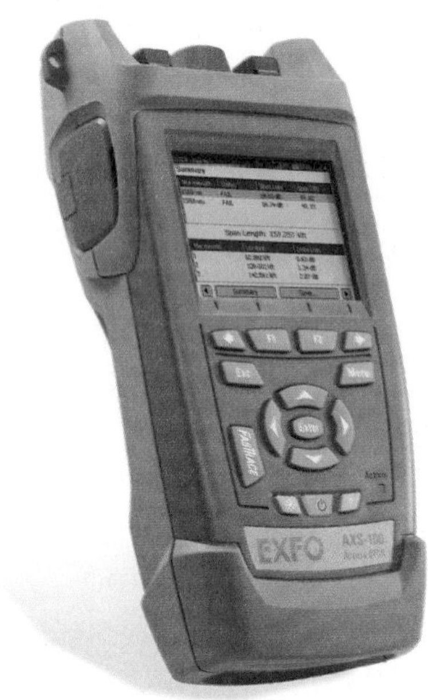

• **Figure 21.2** An EXFO AXS-100 OTDR (photo courtesy of EXFO)

> The CompTIA Network+ exam objectives use the term *fiber light meter*. The more accurate term in this context is either *power meter* or *optical power meter*. You may see any of these terms on the exam.

Third, a cable might have a *wire map problem*, where one or more of the wires in a cable don't connect to the proper location on the jack or plug. This can be caused by improperly crimping a cable, for example. Fourth, the cable might experience *crosstalk*, where the electrical signal bleeds from one wire pair to another, creating interference.

Fifth, a broken cable might pick up *noise*, spurious signals usually caused by faulty hardware or poorly crimped jacks. Finally, a broken cable might have *impedance mismatch*. Impedance is the natural electrical resistance of a cable. When cables of different types—think thickness, composition of the metal, and so on—connect and the flow of electrons is not uniform, it can cause a unique type of electrical noise, called an *echo*.

Network technicians use three different devices to deal with broken cables. **Cable testers** can tell you if you have a continuity problem or if a wire map isn't correct (Figure 21.1). **Time domain reflectometers (TDRs)** and **optical time domain reflectometers (OTDRs)** can tell you where the break is on the cable (Figure 21.2). A TDR works with copper cables and an OTDR works with fiber optics, but otherwise they share the same function. If a problem shows itself as a disconnect and you've first checked easier issues that would manifest as disconnects, such as loss of permissions, an unplugged cable, or a server shut off, then think about using these tools.

Certifiers

Certifiers test a cable to ensure that it can handle its rated amount of capacity. When a cable is not broken but it's not moving data the way it should, turn to a certifier. Look for problems that cause a cable to underperform. A bad installation might increase crosstalk, attenuation, or interference. A certifier can pick up an impedance mismatch as well. Most of these problems show up at installation, but running a certifier to eliminate cabling as a problem is never a bad idea. Don't use a certifier for disconnects, only slowdowns. All certifiers need some kind of **loopback adapter** on the other end of the cable run to provide termination and return of a signal. A loopback adapter is a small device with a single port.

Fiber Light Meter

The extremely transparent fiber-optic cables allow light to shine but have some inherent impurities in the glass that can reduce light transmission. Dust, poor connections, and light leakage can also degrade the strength of light pulses as they travel through a fiber-optic run. To measure the amount of light loss, technicians use an **optical power meter**, also referred to as a **fiber light meter** (see Figure 21.3).

• **Figure 21.3** FiberLink® 6650 Optical Power Meter (photo courtesy of Communications Specialties, Inc.)

The fiber light meter system uses a high-powered source of light at one end of a run and a calibrated detector at the other end. This measures the amount of light that reaches the detector.

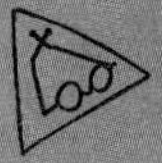

Tech Tip

Never Buy Cheap Tools

There's an old adage used by carpenters and other craftspeople that goes, "Never buy cheap tools." Cheap tools save you money at the beginning, but they often break more readily than higher-quality tools and, more importantly, make it harder to get the job done. This adage definitely applies to multimeters! You might be tempted to go for the $10 model that looks pretty much like the $25 model, but chances are the leads will break or the readings will lie on the cheaper model. Buy a decent tool, and you'll never have to worry about it.

Voltage Quality Recorder/Temperature Monitor

Networks need the proper temperature and adequate power, but most network techs tend to view these issues as outside of the normal places to look for problems. That's too bad, because both heat and power problems invariably manifest themselves as intermittent problems. Look for problems that might point to heat or power issues: server rooms that get too hot at certain times of the day, switches that fail whenever an air conditioning system kicks on, and so on. You can use a **voltage quality recorder** and a **temperature monitor** to monitor server rooms over time to detect and record issues with electricity or heat, respectively. They're great for those "something happened last night" types of issues.

Cable Strippers and Snips

A **cable stripper** (Figure 21.4) helps you to make UTP cables. You'll need a crimping tool (a **cable crimper**) as well. Cable strippers include a tool for cutting wires. You can also cut wires with a **snip**, a tool designed to cut through metal like wires. You don't need these tools to punch down 66- or 110-blocks. You would use a punchdown tool for that (as described in a bit).

• **Figure 21.4** A cable stripping and crimping tool

Multimeters

Multimeters test voltage (both AC and DC), resistance, and continuity. They are the unsung heroes of cabling infrastructures because no other tool can tell you how much voltage is on a line. They are also a great fallback for continuity testing when you don't have a cable tester handy.

Tone Probes and Tone Generators

Tone probes and their partners, **tone generators**, have only one job: to help you locate a particular cable. You'll never use a tone probe without a tone generator. You'll recall these from way back in Chapter 5, when we explored the classic Fox and Hound toner set from Triplett Corporation. The tone generator connects to a cable. The tone probe scans the wires and ports on the far end to see which connects.

Punchdown Tools

Punchdown tools (Figure 21.5) put UTP wires into 66- and 110-blocks. The only time you would use a punchdown tool in a diagnostic environment is a quick repunch of a connection to make sure all the contacts are properly set.

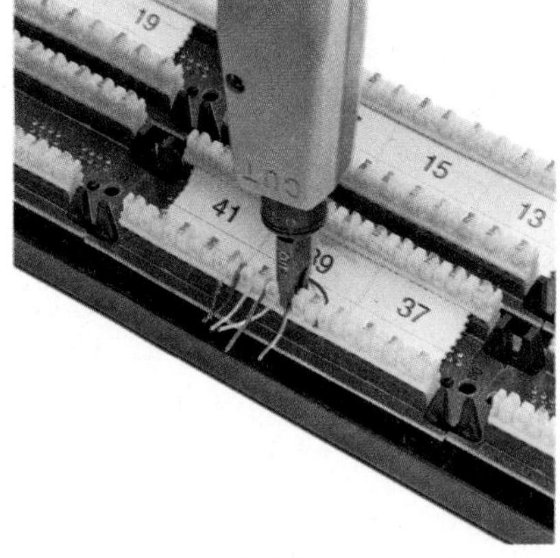

• **Figure 21.5** A punchdown tool in action

Try This!

Shopping Spree

As more and more people have networks installed in their homes, the big-box hardware stores stock an increasing number of network-specific tools. Everybody loves shopping, right? So try this! Go to your local hardware store—big box, like Home Depot or Lowes, if there's one near you—and check out their tools. What do they offer? Write down prices and features and compare with what your classmates found.

Software Tools

Make the CompTIA Network+ exam (and real life) easier by separating your software tools into two groups: those that come built into every operating system and those that are third-party tools. Typical built-in tools are hostname, tracert/traceroute, ipconfig/ifconfig/ip, arp, ping, arping, pathping, nslookup/dig, mtr, route, and netstat/ss. Third-party tools fall into the categories of packet sniffers, port scanners, throughput testers, and looking glass sites. And because nothing is quite as simple as built-in vs. third-party, we have to add terminal emulators, which are both. We'll start with terminal emulators.

Try This!

Playing Along in Windows

This section contains many command-line tools that you've seen earlier in the book in various places. Now is a great time to refresh your memory about how each one works, so after I review each command, run it yourself. Then type `help` followed by the command to see the available switches for that command. Run the command with some of the switches to see what they do. Running the command is more fun than just reading about it; plus, you'll solidify the knowledge that you need to master.

The CompTIA Network+ exam tests your ability to recognize the output from all of the built-in tools (except arping, mtr, and ss). Take some time to memorize example outputs from all of these tools.

Terminal Emulator

Network techs rely on a *command-line interface (CLI)* for troubleshooting and configuring at all levels, from simple commands to complex scripts. A CLI is a *shell*, a way to interact with an operating system, just as a graphical user interface (GUI) is a *shell*. A **terminal emulator** program enables access to various CLI shells.

Every modern operating system offers one or more terminal emulators. macOS has Terminal.app, for example. The terminal emulator enables you to modify how the CLI text renders. This manifests as different colors and fonts on the screen, in the simplest sense, to compatibility modes for working with legacy systems.

hostname

The **hostname** utility does exactly what it says on the label—it prints out the hostname of the current system. There are other places to check the hostname (especially in the GUI), but being able to check the hostname from the shell may save your skin if you're troubleshooting over SSH. The command is also useful if you have to run a script on many systems that needs access to each system's hostname (for example, to gather information about how many systems are configured and save the details in a file named for each host).

The utility isn't terribly interesting on its own, but here's sample `hostname` output from a Windows system:

```
C:\>hostname
mikes-desktop
```

tracert/traceroute

The **traceroute** utility (the command in Windows is **tracert**) is used to trace all of the routers between two points. Use traceroute to diagnose where the problem lies when you have problems reaching a remote system. If a traceroute stops at a certain router, you know the problem is either the next router or the connections between them.

When sending a traceroute, it's important to keep a significant difference between Windows and UNIX/Linux systems in mind. Windows tracert sends only ICMP packets, while UNIX/Linux traceroute sends UDP datagrams by default, but can also send TCP segments.

Because many routers block ICMP packets, if traceroute fails from a Windows system, running it on a Linux or UNIX system may return more complete results. The reverse is true as well. Routers could be blocking UDP (many in fact do block UDP-based traceroutes), and then the ICMP version becomes the more informative one.

Here's sample `traceroute` output:

```
traceroute to fs.totalhome (192.168.4.12), 64 hops max, 52 byte packets
 1  10.0.44.129 (10.0.44.129)  24.540 ms  29.325 ms  25.628 ms
 2  fs.totalhome (192.168.4.12)  25.859 ms  26.075 ms  24.943 ms
```

The `traceroute` command defaults to either IPv4 or IPv6 depending on the OS installed and the network connection installed. In either case, you can force traceroute to use IPv6 with the `-6` flag. In addition, on macOS/Linux, you can use the IPv6-specific `traceroute6` command.

ipconfig/ifconfig/ip

The **ipconfig** (Windows), **ifconfig** (macOS and UNIX), and **ip** (Linux) utilities tell you almost anything you want to know about a computer's IP settings. Make sure you know that typing `ipconfig` alone only gives basic information. Typing `ipconfig /all` gives detailed information (like DNS servers and MAC address).

Here's sample `ipconfig` output:

```
Ethernet adapter Main:

   Connection-specific DNS Suffix  . :
   IPv6 Address. . . . . . . . . . . : 2001:470:bf88:1:fc2d:aeb2:99d2:e2b4
   Temporary IPv6 Address. . . . . . : 2001:470:bf88:1:5e4:c1ef:7b30:ddd6
   Link-local IPv6 Address . . . . . : fe80::fc2d:aeb2:99d2:e2b4%8
   IPv4 Address. . . . . . . . . . . : 192.168.4.27
   Subnet Mask . . . . . . . . . . . : 255.255.255.0
   Default Gateway . . . . . . . . . : fe80::223:4ff:fe8c:b720%8
                                       192.168.4.1

Tunnel adapter Local Area Connection* 6:

Media State . . . . . . . . . . . : Media disconnected
Connection-specific DNS Suffix  . :
```

And here's sample `ifconfig` output:

```
lo0: flags=8049<UP,LOOPBACK,RUNNING,MULTICAST> mtu 16384
        options=3<RXCSUM,TXCSUM>
        inet6 ::1 prefixlen 128
        inet 127.0.0.1 netmask 0xff000000
        inet6 fe80::1%lo0 prefixlen 64 scopeid 0x1
        nd6 options=1<PERFORMNUD>
gif0: flags=8010<POINTOPOINT,MULTICAST> mtu 1280
stf0: flags=0<> mtu 1280
en0: flags=8863<UP,BROADCAST,SMART,RUNNING,SIMPLEX,MULTICAST> mtu 1500
        options=10b<RXCSUM,TXCSUM,VLAN_HWTAGGING,AV>
        ether 3c:07:54:7a:d4:d8
        inet6 fe80::3e07:54ff:fe7a:d4d8%en0 prefixlen 64 scopeid 0x4
        inet 192.168.4.78 netmask 0xffffff00 broadcast 192.168.4.255
        inet6 2601:e::abcd:3e07:54ff:fe7a:d4d8 prefixlen 64 autoconf
        inet6 2601:e::abcd:b84e:9fad:3add:c73b prefixlen 64 autoconf temporary
        nd6 options=1<PERFORMNUD>
        media: autoselect (1000baseT <full-duplex,flow-control>)
        status: active
```

And finally, here's Linux's `ip address` output:

```
1: lo: <LOOPBACK,UP,LOWER_UP> mtu 65536 qdisc noqueue state UNKNOWN group default
    link/loopback 00:00:00:00:00:00 brd 00:00:00:00:00:00
    inet 127.0.0.1/8 scope host lo
       valid_lft forever preferred_lft forever
    inet6 ::1/128 scope host
       valid_lft forever preferred_lft forever
2: eth0: <BROADCAST,MULTICAST,UP,LOWER_UP> mtu 1500 qdisc pfifo_fast state UNKNOWN group
default qlen 1000
    link/ether 00:0c:29:e0:b2:85 brd ff:ff:ff:ff:ff:ff
    inet 192.168.4.19/24 brd 192.168.4.255 scope global eth0
       valid_lft forever preferred_lft forever
    inet6 2601:e:0:abcd:8cfb:6220:ec23:80a/64 scope global temporary dynamic
       valid_lft 86221sec preferred_lft 14221sec
    inet6 2601:e:0:abcd:20c:29ff:fee0:b285/64 scope global dynamic
       valid_lft 86221sec preferred_lft 14221sec
    inet6 fe80::20c:29ff:fee0:b285/64 scope link
       valid_lft forever preferred_lft forever
```

arp

You get three for the price of one with sims in this chapter! Check out the Chapter 21, "Who Made That NIC," sims at https://totalsem.com/008. You'll find a Show!, a Click!, and a Challenge! on the subject that will help you solidify the usefulness of the tools for your technician's toolbox.

Computers use Address Resolution Protocol (ARP) to resolve IP addresses to MAC addresses. As the computer learns various MAC addresses on its LAN, it jots them down in the ARP table. When Computer A wants to send a message to Computer B, it determines B's IP address and then checks the ARP table for a corresponding MAC address.

The **arp** utility enables you to view and change the ARP table on a computer. Here's sample output from `arp -a`:

```
Interface: 192.168.4.57 --- 0xc
  Internet Address      Physical Address      Type
  192.168.4.1           b8-9b-c9-7d-e7-76     dynamic
  192.168.4.2           00-87-b6-7e-ae-23     dynamic
  192.168.4.8           67-ab-cc-aa-fe-ed     dynamic
  192.168.4.12          23-b5-94-17-d7-33     dynamic
  192.168.4.13          4b-4b-4c-4d-4e-46     dynamic
  192.168.4.14          55-55-55-55-55-55     dynamic
```

ping, pathping, and arping

The **ping** utility uses Internet Message Control Protocol (ICMP) packets to query by IP address or by name. It works across routers, so it's generally the first tool used to check if a system is reachable. Unfortunately, many devices block ICMP packets, so a failed ping doesn't always point to an offline system.

The `ping` utility defaults to either IPv4 or IPv6 depending on the OS installed and the network connection installed. In either case, you can force ping to use IPv6 with the `-6` flag. In addition, on macOS/Linux, you can use the IPv6-specific `ping6` command.

Here's sample `ping` output:

```
Pinging 192.168.4.19 with 32 bytes of data:
Reply from 192.168.4.19: bytes=32 time<1ms TTL=64
Reply from 192.168.4.19: bytes=32 time<1ms TTL=64
Reply from 192.168.4.19: bytes=32 time<1ms TTL=64
Reply from 192.168.4.19: bytes=32 time<1ms TTL=64

Ping statistics for 192.168.4.19:
     Packets: Sent = 4, Received = 4, Lost = 0 (0% loss),
Approximate round trip times in milli-seconds:
     Minimum = 0ms, Maximum = 0ms, Average = 0ms
```

If `ping` doesn't work, you can try **arping**, which uses ARP frames instead of ICMP packets. The only downside to arping is that ARP frames do not cross routers because they only consist of frames, and never IP packets, so you can only use arping within a broadcast domain. Windows does not have arping. UNIX and UNIX-like systems, on the other hand, support the arping utility.

Next is sample `arping` output:

```
ARPING 192.168.4.27 from 192.168.4.19 eth0
Unicast reply from 192.168.4.27 [00:1D:60:DD:92:C6]   0.875ms
Unicast reply from 192.168.4.27 [00:1D:60:DD:92:C6]   0.897ms
Unicast reply from 192.168.4.27 [00:1D:60:DD:92:C6]   0.924ms
Unicast reply from 192.168.4.27 [00:1D:60:DD:92:C6]   0.977ms
```

The `ping` command has the word *Pinging* in the output. The `arping` command has the word *ARPING*. You'll see ping on the CompTIA Network+ exam; you won't see arping.

The ping and traceroute utilities are excellent examples of *connectivity software*, applications that enable you to determine if a connection can be made between two computers.

Microsoft has a utility called **pathping** that combines the functions of ping and traceroute and adds some additional functions.

Here is sample `pathping` output:

```
Tracing route to xeroxpaser.totalhome [182.168.4.17]
Over a maximum 30 hops:
  0  local-PC.totalhome [192.168.4.53]
  1  xrxphsr.totalhome [192.168.4.17]
Computing statistics for 25 seconds...
            Source to Here    This Node/Link
Hop  RTT    Lost/Sent - Pct   Lost/Sent - Pct Address
  0                                           local-PC.totalhome
[192.168.4.53]
                              0/ 100 - 0%    :
  1    0ms     0/ 100 - 0%    0/ 100 - 0%   xrxphsr.totalhome
[192.168.4.17] Trace complete
```

nslookup/dig

The **nslookup** (all operating systems) and **dig** (macOS/UNIX/Linux) utilities help diagnose DNS problems. These tools are very powerful, but the CompTIA Network+ exam won't ask you more than basic questions, such as how to use them to see if a DNS server is working. When working on Windows systems, the nslookup utility is your only choice by default. On macOS/UNIX/Linux systems, you should prefer the dig utility. Both utilities will help in troubleshooting your DNS issues, but dig provides more verbose output by default. You need to be comfortable working with both utilities when troubleshooting networks.

Running the networking commands several times will help you memorize the functions of the commands as well as the syntax. The CompTIA Network+ exam is also big on the switches available for various commands, such as `ipconfig /all`.

Following is an example of the `dig` command:

```
dig mx totalsem.com
```

This command says, "Show me all the MX records for the totalsem.com domain."

Here's the output for that `dig` command:

```
; <<>> DiG 9.10.6 <<>> mx totalsem.com
;; global options: +cmd
;; Got answer:
;; ->>HEADER<<- opcode: QUERY, status: NOERROR, id: 25734
;; flags: qr rd ra; QUERY: 1, ANSWER: 1, AUTHORITY: 0,
ADDITIONAL: 3

;; OPT PSEUDOSECTION:
; EDNS: version: 0, flags:; udp: 4000
;; QUESTION SECTION:
;totalsem.com.                IN    MX

;; ANSWER SECTION:
totalsem.com.          1798   IN    MX     0 totalsem.com.mail.
protection.outlook.com.

;; ADDITIONAL SECTION:
totalsem-com.mail.protection.outlook.com. 9 IN A
104.47.55.110
totalsem-com.mail.protection.outlook.com. 9 IN A
104.47.70.110

;; Query time: 422 msec
;; SERVER: 192.168.4.11#53(192.168.4.11)
;; WHEN: Wed Aug 25 09:56:50 CDT 2021
;; MSG SIZE  rcvd: 126
```

mtr

My Traceroute (mtr) is a dynamic (keeps running) equivalent to traceroute; like pathping it combines traceroute and ping. mtr is a UNIX/Linux tool; you can find a Windows version called WinMTR, but you should run the native mtr instead through the Windows Subsystem for Linux (WSL) in Windows 10/11. Both pathping and mtr run a traceroute all along a path, but pathping stops when it hits a site that doesn't respond, whereas mtr keeps going to the end if it can. Both tools help pinpoint problems, but mtr is more robust and precise.

Here's a sample of `mtr` output:

```
                                  My traceroute  [v0.86]
linux-workstation (::)                                               Wed Aug 25 10:02:59 2021
Keys:  Help   Display mode   Restart statistics   Order of fields   quit
                                                         Packets               Pings
 Host                                                  Loss%   Snt   Last   Avg  Best  Wrst StDev
 1. 2603:300c:d:cd01::1                                 0.0%    66    0.3   0.2   0.2   0.3   0.0
 2. 2001:558:4081:8d::1                                 0.0%    65    9.3  11.6   8.6  17.7   1.9
 3. ae-251-1204-rur02.airport.tx.houston.comcast.net    0.0%    65   16.7  13.4   9.2  29.6   4.3
 4. 2001:558:2c0:242d::1                                0.0%    65   12.9  15.8  10.1  34.8   5.0
 5. ae-68-ar01.bearcreek.tx.houston.comcast.net        40.0%    65   12.4  14.2  11.6  23.5   2.6
 6. ae-3-sur01.wallisville.tx.houston.comcast.net       0.0%    65   19.4  16.9  10.9  30.8   4.5
 7. be-33662-cr02.dallas.tx.ibone.comcast.net          46.2%    65   18.5  20.5  16.3  28.1   2.7
 8. be-3312-pe12.1950stemmons.tx.ibone.comcast.net     62.5%    65   25.2  20.4  17.7  25.2   1.9
 9. 2001:559::a06                                       0.0%    65   20.8  20.1  16.6  26.4   1.9
10. 2607:f8b0:8327::1                                   0.0%    65   18.6  19.0  16.0  28.6   2.6
11. 2001:4860:0:1::5694                                 3.1%    65   16.1  19.6  16.1  26.4   2.5
    2001:4860:0:1::5696
12. 2001:4860:0:1::5693                                 0.0%    65   19.4  19.4  16.7  25.2   2.1
    2001:4860:0:1::5691
13. dfw28s29-in-x0e.1e100.net                           0.0%    65   18.4  19.9  17.1  27.8   2.1
```

route

The **route** utility enables you to display and edit the local system's routing table. To show the routing table, just type `route print` or `netstat -r`.

Here's a sample of `route print` output:

```
===========================================================================

Interface List
8 ...00 1d 60 dd 92 c6 ...... Marvell 88E8056 PCI-E Ethernet Controller
1 ........................... Software Loopback Interface 1
===========================================================================
IPv4 Route Table
===========================================================================
Active Routes:
Network Destination        Netmask          Gateway       Interface  Metric
0.0.0.0                    0.0.0.0      192.168.4.1    192.168.4.27      10
127.0.0.0                255.0.0.0         On-link        127.0.0.1     306
127.0.0.1          255.255.255.255         On-link        127.0.0.1     306
127.255.255.255    255.255.255.255         On-link        127.0.0.1     306
169.254.0.0            255.255.0.0         On-link     192.168.4.27     286
169.254.214.185    255.255.255.255         On-link  169.254.214.185     276
169.254.255.255    255.255.255.255         On-link     192.168.4.27     266
192.168.4.0        255.255.255.0           On-link     192.168.4.27     266
192.168.4.27       255.255.255.255         On-link     192.168.4.27     266
192.168.4.255      255.255.255.255         On-link     192.168.4.27     266
224.0.0.0          240.0.0.0               On-link        127.0.0.1     306
224.0.0.0          240.0.0.0             On-link  169.254.214.185       276
224.0.0.0          240.0.0.0             On-link  192.168.4.27          266
255.255.255.255    255.255.255.255       On-link  127.0.0.1             306
255.255.255.255    255.255.255.255       On-link  169.254.214.185       276
255.255.255.255    255.255.255.255       On-link  192.168.4.27          266
===========================================================================
```

```
Persistent Routes:

None

IPv6 Route Table
===========================================================================
Active Routes:
 If Metric Network Destination      Gateway
  9    281 ::/0                     fe80::f29f:c2ff:fe10:bd11
  1    331 ::1/128                  On-link
  9    281 2603:300c:d:cd01::/64    On-link
  9    281 2603:300c:d:cd01:1121:e26a:b122:a58e/128
                                    On-link
  9    281 2603:300c:d:cd01:7c79:438f:ff47:35a1/128
                                    On-link
  9    281 2603:300c:d:cd01:956a:3afa:5f62:225d/128
                                    On-link
  9    281 2603:300c:d:cd01:ac86:4d41:dc52:7aad/128
                                    On-link
 26    281 fe80::/64                On-link
  9    281 fe80::/64                On-link
 40   5256 fe80::/64                On-link
 49   5256 fe80::/64                On-link
 56   5256 fe80::/64                On-link
 64   5256 fe80::/64                On-link
  9    281 fe80::1121:e26a:b122:a58e/128
                                    On-link
 40   5256 fe80::2cfa:5ffd:42ea:6fb5/128
                                    On-link
 56   5256 fe80::4c4b:6106:d29e:8b5/128
                                    On-link
 26    281 fe80::4ce7:a9fe:8406:11aa/128
                                    On-link
 49   5256 fe80::ac1e:33c2:7eba:f1d0/128
                                    On-link
 64   5256 fe80::e87a:7895:960:1da8/128
                                    On-link
  1    331 ff00::/8                 On-link
 26    281 ff00::/8                 On-link
  9    281 ff00::/8                 On-link
 40   5256 ff00::/8                 On-link
 49   5256 ff00::/8                 On-link
 56   5256 ff00::/8                 On-link
 64   5256 ff00::/8                 On-link
===========================================================================
Persistent Routes:
  None
```

netstat and ss

The **netstat** utility displays information on the current state of all the running IP processes on a system. It shows what sessions are active and can also provide statistics based on ports or protocols (TCP, UDP, and so on). Typing `netstat` by itself only shows current sessions. Typing `netstat -r` shows the routing table (identical to Windows' `route print`). If you want to know about your current sessions, netstat is the tool to use.

Here's sample `netstat` output:

```
Active Connections

Proto     Local Address           Foreign Address        State
TCP       127.0.0.1:27015         MikesPC:51090          ESTABLISHED
TCP       127.0.0.1:51090         MikesPC:27015          ESTABLISHED
TCP       127.0.0.1:52500         MikesPC:52501          ESTABLISHED
TCP       192.168.4.27:54731      72-165-61-141:27039    CLOSE_WAIT
TCP       192.168.4.27:55080      63-246-140-18:http     CLOSE_WAIT
TCP       192.168.4.27:56126      acd4129913:https       ESTABLISHED
TCP       192.168.4.27:62727      TOTALTEST:ssh          ESTABLISHED
TCP       192.168.4.27:63325      65.54.165.136:https    TIME_WAIT
TCP       192.168.4.27:63968      209.8.115.129:http     ESTABLISHED
```

Windows still comes with netstat, but the *ss* utility—part of the *iproute2* utility suite, along with ip and all its switches—has completely eclipsed it on the Linux side. The ss utility is faster and more powerful than netstat. Unlike netstat, however, you won't find ss on the CompTIA Network+ exam. Here's sample output from **ss**, filtered to show only TCP connections:

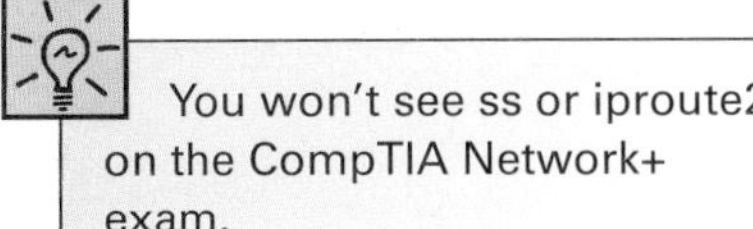

You won't see ss or iproute2 on the CompTIA Network+ exam.

```
State       Recv-Q Send-Q      Local Address:Port          Peer Address:Port
CLOSE-WAIT  28     0           10.0.2.15:52161             91.189.92.24:https
CLOSE-WAIT  28     0           10.0.2.15:46117             91.189.92.11:https
ESTAB       0      0           10.0.2.15:55542             74.125.239.40:http
```

Packet Sniffer/Protocol Analyzer

A **packet sniffer**, as you'll recall from Chapter 20, intercepts and logs network packets, a process called *packet capture*. You have many choices when it comes to packet sniffers. Some sniffers come as programs you run on a computer, while others manifest as dedicated hardware devices. Most packet sniffers come bundled with a **protocol analyzer**, the tool that takes the sniffed information and figures out what's happening on the network. Arguably, the most popular GUI packet sniffer and protocol analyzer is **Wireshark** (Figure 21.6).

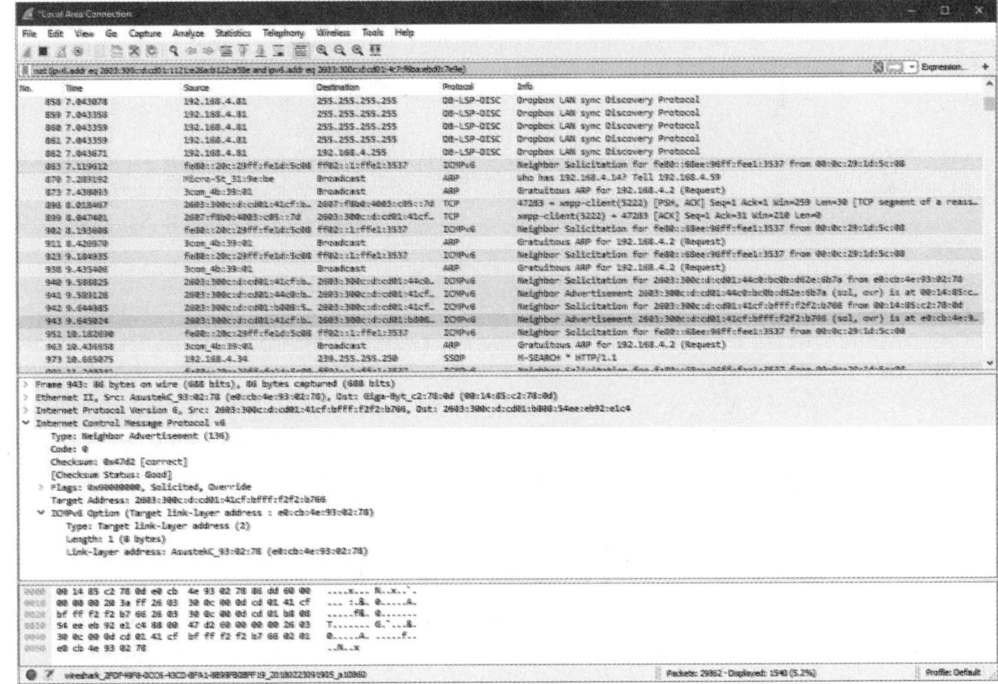

• **Figure 21.6** Wireshark in action

> Sometimes a GUI tool like Wireshark won't work because a server has no GUI installed. In situations like this, **tcpdump** is the go-to choice. This great command-line tool not only enables you to monitor and filter packets in the terminal, but can also create files you can open in Wireshark for later analysis. Even better, it's installed by default on most UNIX/Linux systems.

Port Scanners

As you'll recall from back in Chapter 18, a **port scanner** is a program that probes ports on another system, logging the state of the scanned ports. These tools are used to look for unintentionally opened ports that might make a system vulnerable to attack. As you might imagine, they also are used by hackers to break into systems.

Most network techs rely on **Nmap** as their port scanning tool of choice, as you'll recall. Nmap was originally designed to work on UNIX systems, so Windows folks used alternatives like **Angry IP Scanner** by Anton Keks (Figure 21.7). Nmap has been ported to just about every operating system these days, however, so you can find it for Windows.

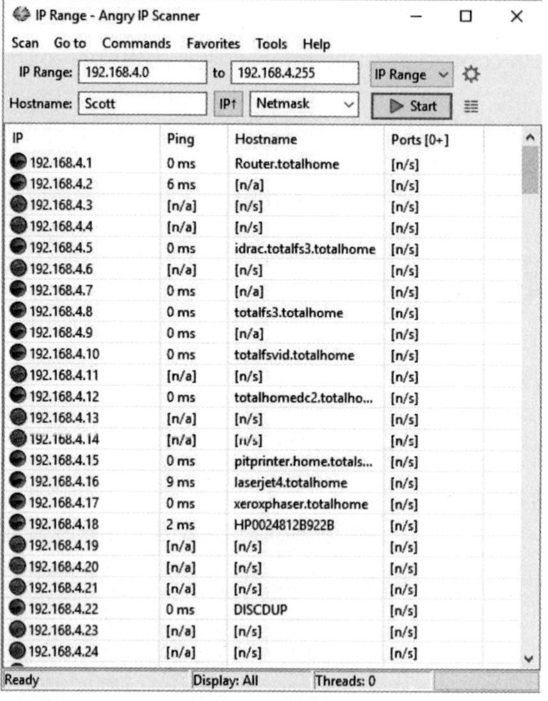

• **Figure 21.7** Angry IP Scanner

Throughput Testers

Throughput testers enable you to measure the data flow in a network. Which tool is appropriate depends on the type of network throughput you want to test. Most techs use one of several **speed-test sites** for checking an Internet connection's throughput, such as MegaPath's Speakeasy Speed Test (Figure 21.8): www.speakeasy.net/speedtest. The CompTIA Network+ exam objectives refer to throughput testers as **bandwidth speed testers**.

Looking Glass Sites

Sometimes you need to perform a ping or traceroute from a location outside of the local environment. **Looking glass sites** are remote servers accessible with a browser that contain common collections of diagnostic tools such as ping and traceroute, plus some Border Gateway Protocol (BGP) query tools.

Most looking glass sites allow you to select where the diagnostic process will originate from a list of locations, as well as the target destination,

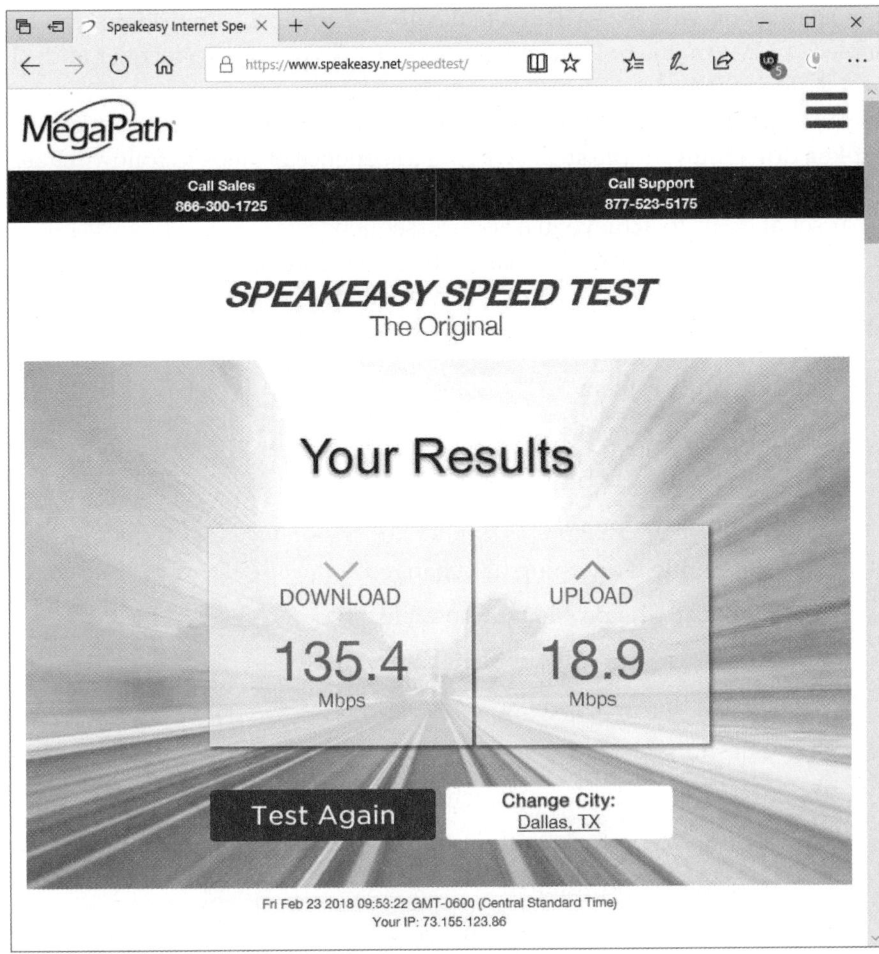

• **Figure 21.8** Speed Test results from Speakeasy

which diagnostic, and sometimes the version of IP to test. A Google search for "looking glass sites" or "looking glass servers" will provide a large selection from which to choose.

The Troubleshooting Process

Troubleshooting is a dynamic, fluid process that requires you to make snap judgments and act on them to try and make the network go. Any attempt to cover every possible scenario here would be futile at best, and probably also not in your best interest. If an exhaustive listing of all network problems is impossible, then how do you decide what to do and in what order?

Before you touch a single console or cable, you should remember two basic rules. For starters, to paraphrase the Hippocratic Oath, "First, do no harm." If at all possible, don't make a network problem bigger than it was originally. This is a rule I've broken thousands of times, and you will too.

But if I change the good doctor's phrase a bit, it's possible to formulate a rule you can actually live with: "First, do not trash the data!" My gosh, if I had a dollar for every megabyte of irreplaceable data I've destroyed, I'd be rich! I've learned my lesson, and you should learn from my mistakes.

The second rule is: "Always make good backups!" Computers can be replaced; data that is not backed up is, at best, expensive to recover and, at worst, gone forever.

No matter how complex and fancy, any troubleshooting process can be broken down into simple steps. Having a sequence of steps to follow makes the entire troubleshooting process simpler and easier, because you have a clear set of goals to achieve in a specific sequence.

The CompTIA Network+ exam objectives contain a detailed troubleshooting methodology that provides a good starting point for our discussion. Here are the basic steps in the troubleshooting process:

1. Identify the problem.
    a. Gather information.
    b. Question users.
    c. Identify symptoms.
    d. Determine if anything has changed.
    e. Duplicate the problem, if possible.
    f. Approach multiple problems individually.
2. Establish a theory of probable cause.
    a. Question the obvious.
    b. Consider multiple approaches:
        i. Top-to-bottom/bottom-to-top OSI model.
        ii. Divide and conquer.
3. Test the theory to determine the cause.
    a. If the theory is confirmed, determine the next steps to resolve the problem.
    b. If the theory is not confirmed, reestablish a new theory or escalate.
4. Establish a plan of action to resolve the problem and identify potential effects.
5. Implement the solution or escalate as necessary.
6. Verify full system functionality and, if applicable, implement preventive measures.
7. Document findings, actions, outcomes, and lessons learned.

Identify the Problem

First, *identify the problem*. That means grasping the true problem, rather than what someone tells you. A user might call in and complain that he can't access the Internet from his workstation, for example, which could be the only problem. But the problem could also be that the entire wing of the office just went down and you've got a much bigger problem on your hands. You need to gather information, question users, identify symptoms, determine if anything has changed on the network, duplicate the problem (if possible), and approach multiple problems individually. Following these steps will help you get to the root of the problem.

Gather Information, Question Users, and Identify Symptoms

Gather information about the situation. If you are working directly on the affected system and not relying on somebody on the other end of a telephone to guide you, you will *identify symptoms* through your observation of what is (or isn't) happening.

If you're troubleshooting over the telephone (always a *joy*, in my experience), you will need to *question users*. These questions can be *close-ended*, which is to say there can only be a yes-or-no-type answer, such as "Can you see a light on the front of the monitor?" You can also ask *open-ended* questions, such as "What have you already tried in attempting to fix the problem?"

The type of question you ask at any given moment depends on what information you need and on the user's knowledge level. If, for example, the user seems to be technically oriented, you will probably be able to ask more close-ended questions because they will know what you are talking about. If, on the other hand, the user seems to be confused about what's happening, open-ended questions will allow him or her to explain in his or her own words what is going on.

Determine If Anything Has Changed

Determine if anything has changed on the network recently that might have caused the problem. You may not have to ask many questions before the person using the problem system can tell you what has changed, but, in some cases, establishing if anything has changed can take quite a bit of time and involve further work behind the scenes. Here are some examples of questions to ask:

- "What exactly was happening when the problem occurred?"
- "Has anything been changed on the system recently?"
- "Has the system been moved recently?"

Notice the way I've tactfully avoided the word *you*, as in "Have *you* changed anything on the system recently?" This is a deliberate tactic to avoid any implied blame on the part of the user. Being nice never hurts, and it makes the whole troubleshooting process more friendly.

You should also *internally* ask yourself some isolating questions, such as "Was that machine involved in the software push last night?" or "Didn't a tech visit that machine this morning?" Note you will only be able to answer these questions if *your* documentation is up to date. Sometimes, isolating a problem may require you to check system and hardware logs (such as those stored by some routers and other network devices), so make sure you know how to do this.

Avoid aggressive or accusatory questions when trying to get information from a user.

Duplicate the Problem

One of the first steps in trying to determine the cause of a problem is to understand the extent of the problem. Is the problem specific to one user or is it network-wide? Sometimes this entails trying the task yourself, both from the user's machine and from your own or another machine.

For example, if a user is experiencing problems logging into the network, you might need to go to that user's machine and try to use his or her username to log in. In other words, try to *duplicate the problem*. Doing this tells you whether the problem is a user error of some kind, as well as enables you to see the symptoms of the problem yourself. Next, you probably want to try logging in with your own username from that machine, or have the user try to log in from another machine.

In some cases, you can ask other users in the area if they are experiencing the same problem to see if the issue is affecting more than one user. Depending on the size of your network, you should find out whether the problem is occurring in only one part of your company or across the entire network.

What does all of this tell you? Essentially, it tells you how big the problem is. If nobody in an entire remote office can log in, you may be able to assume that the problem is the network link or router connecting that office to the server. If nobody in any office can log in, you may be able to assume the server is down or not accepting logins. If only that one user in that one location can't log in, the problem may be with that user, that machine, or that user's account.

Eliminating variables is one of the first tools in your arsenal of diagnostic techniques.

Approach Multiple Problems Individually

If you encounter a complicated scenario, with various machines off the network and potential server room or wiring problems, break it down. *Approach multiple problems individually* to sort out root causes. Methodically tackle them and you'll eventually have a list of one or more problems identified. Then you can move on to the next step.

Establish a Theory of Probable Cause

Once you've identified one or more problems, try to figure out what could have happened. In other words, *establish a theory of probable cause*. Just keep in mind that a *theory is not a fact*. You might need to chuck the theory out the window later in the process and establish a revised theory.

This step comes down to experience—or good use of the support tools at your disposal, such as your knowledge base. You need to select the most *probable* cause from all the *possible* causes, so the solution you choose fixes the problem the first time. This may not always happen, but whenever possible, you want to avoid spending a whole day stabbing in the dark while the problem snores softly to itself in some cozy, neglected corner of your network.

Don't forget to *question the obvious*. If Bob can't print to the networked printer, for example, check to see that the printer is plugged in and turned on.

Consider multiple approaches when tackling problems. This will keep you from locking your imagination into a single train of thought. You can use the OSI seven-layer model as a troubleshooting tool in several ways to help with this process. Here's a scenario to work through.

Martha can't access the database server to start her workday. The problem manifests this way: She opens the database client on her computer, then clicks on recent documents, one of which is the current project that management has assigned to her team. Nothing happens. Normally, the database client connects to the database that resides on the server on the other side of the network.

Try a *top-to-bottom* or *bottom-to-top OSI model* approach to the problem. Sometimes it pays to try both. Here are some ideas on how this might help.

7	Application	Could there be a problem with the API that enables the database application to connect to the database server? Sure.
6	Presentation	Could there be a problem with encryption between the application and the database server? Maybe, but Martha would probably see an error message rather than nothing.
5	Session	Could a database authentication failure be preventing access? Again, this could be the problem, but Martha would probably see an error message here as well.
4	Transport	Perhaps extreme traffic on the network could block an acknowledgment segment? This seems a bit of a reach, but worth considering.
3	Network	Someone might have changed the IP address of the database server.
2	Data Link	The MAC address of the database server or Martha's machine might be blacklisted.
1	Physical	A disconnected cable or dead NIC can make for a bad day.

You might imagine the reverse model in some situations. If the network was newly installed, for example, running through some of the basic connectivity at Layers 1 and 2 might be a good first approach.

Another option for tackling multiple options is to use the *divide and conquer* approach.

On its face, divide and conquer appears to be a compromise between top-to-bottom OSI troubleshooting and bottom-to-top OSI troubleshooting. But it's better than a compromise. If we arbitrarily always perform top-to-bottom troubleshooting, we'll waste a lot of time at Layers 7 through 3 to troubleshoot Data Link layer and Physical layer issues.

Divide and conquer is a time saver that comes into play as part of developing a theory of probable cause. As you gather information for troubleshooting, a general sense of where the problem lies should manifest. Place this likely cause at the appropriate layer of the OSI model and begin to test the theory and related theories at that layer. If the theory bears out, follow the appropriate troubleshooting steps. If the theory is wrong, move up or down the OSI model with new theories of probable causes.

Test the Theory to Determine the Cause

With the third step, you need to *test the theory to determine the cause*, but do so without changing anything or risking any repercussions. If you have determined that the probable cause for Bob not being able to print is that the printer is turned off, go look. If that's the case, then you should plan out your next step to resolve the problem. Do not act yet! That comes next.

If the theory is not confirmed, you need to *reestablish a new theory or escalate the problem.* Go back to step two and determine a new probable cause. Once you have another idea, test it.

The reason you should hesitate to act at this third step is that you might not have permission to make the fix or the fix might cause repercussions you don't fully understand yet. For example, if you walk over to the print server room to see if the printer is powered up and online and find the door padlocked, that's a whole different level of problem. Sure, the printer is turned off, but management has done it for a reason. In this sort of situation, you need to escalate the problem.

To *escalate* has two meanings: either to inform other parties about a problem for guidance or to pass the job off to another authority who has control over the device/issue that's most probably causing the problem. Let's say you have a server with a bad NIC. This server is used heavily by the accounting department, and taking it down may cause problems you don't even know about. You need to inform the accounting manager to consult about what to do next. Alternatively, you'll come across problems over which you have no control or authority. A badly acting server across the country is the responsibility of another person (hopefully) to whom you need to hand over the job.

Regardless of how many times you need to go through this process, you'll eventually reach a theory that seems right. *If the theory is confirmed, determine the next steps you need to take to resolve the problem.*

Establish a Plan of Action and Identify Potential Effects

By this point, you should have some ideas as to what the problem might be. It's time to "look before you leap" and *establish a plan of action to resolve the problem.* An action plan defines how you are going to fix this problem. Most problems are simple, but if the problem is complex, you need to write down the steps. As you do this, think about what else might happen as you go about the repair. *Identify the potential effects* of the actions you're about to take, especially the unintended ones. If you take out a switch without a replacement switch at hand, the users might experience excessive downtime while you hunt for a new switch and move them over. If you replace a router, can you restore all the old router's settings to the new one or will you have to rebuild from scratch?

Implement the Solution or Escalate as Necessary

Once you think you have isolated the cause of the problem, you should decide what you think is the best way to fix it and then *implement the solution*, whether that's giving advice over the phone to a user, installing a replacement part, or adding a software patch. Or, if the solution you propose requires either more skill than you possess at the moment or falls into someone else's purview, *escalate as necessary* to get the fix implemented.

If you're the implementer, follow these guidelines. All the way through implementation, try only one likely solution at a time. There's no point in installing several patches at once, because then you can't tell which one fixed the problem. Similarly, there's no point in replacing several items of hardware (such as a hard disk and its controller cable) at the same time, because then you can't tell which part (or parts) was faulty.

As you try each possibility, always *document* what you do and what results you get. This isn't just for a future problem either—during a lengthy troubleshooting process, it's easy to forget exactly what you tried two hours before or which thing you tried produced a particular result. Although being methodical may take longer, it will save time the next time—and it may enable you to pinpoint what needs to be done to stop the problem from recurring at all, thereby reducing future call volume to your support team—and as any support person will tell you, that's definitely worth the effort!

Then you need to test the solution. This is the part everybody hates. Once you think you've fixed a problem, you should try to make it happen again. If you can't, great! But sometimes you will be able to re-create the problem, and then you know you haven't finished the job at hand. Many techs want to slide away quietly as soon as everything seems to be fine, but trust me on this, it won't impress your customer when her problem flares up again 30 seconds after you've left the building—not to mention that you get the joy of another two-hour car trip the next day to fix the same problem, for an even more unhappy client!

In the scenario where you are providing support to someone else rather than working directly on the problem, you should have *her* try to re-create the problem. This tells you whether she understands what you have been telling her and educates her at the same time, lessening the chance that she'll call you back later and ask, "Can we just go through that one more time?"

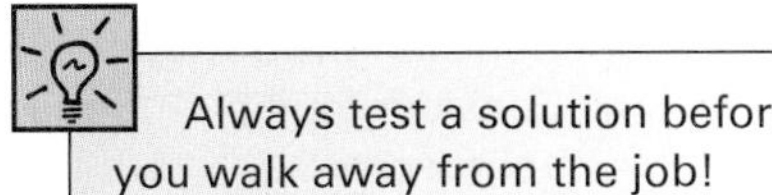
Always test a solution before you walk away from the job!

Verify Full System Functionality and Implement Preventive Measures

Okay, now that you have changed something on the system in the process of solving one problem, you must think about the wider repercussions of what you have done. If you've replaced a faulty NIC in a server, for instance, will the fact that the MAC address has changed (remember, it's built into the NIC) affect anything else, such as the logon security controls or your network management and inventory software? If you've installed a patch on a client PC, will this change the default protocol or any other default settings that may affect other functionality? If you've changed a user's security settings, will this affect his or her ability to access other network resources? This is part of testing your solution to make sure it works properly, but it also makes you think about the impact of your work on the system as a whole.

Make sure you *verify full system functionality*. If you think you've fixed the problem between Martha's workstation and the database server, have her open the database while you're still there. That way you don't have to make a second tech call to resolve an outstanding issue. This saves time and money and helps your customer do his or her job better. Everybody wins.

Also at this time, if applicable, *implement preventive measures* to avoid a repeat of the problem. If that means you need to educate the user to do or not do something, teach him or her tactfully. If you need to install software or patch a system, do it now.

Document Findings, Actions, Outcomes, and Lessons Learned

It is *vital* that you *document findings, actions, outcomes, and lessons learned* of all support calls, for two reasons: First, you're creating a support database to serve as a knowledge base for future reference, enabling everyone on the support team to identify new problems as they arise and know how to deal with them quickly, without having to duplicate someone else's research efforts.

Memorize these problem analysis steps:

1. Identify the problem.
   a. Gather information.
   b. Question users.
   c. Identify symptoms.
   d. Determine if anything has changed.
   e. Duplicate the problem, if possible.
   f. Approach multiple problems individually.
2. Establish a theory of probable cause.
   a. Question the obvious.
   b. Consider multiple approaches:
      i. Top-to-bottom/bottom-to-top OSI model.
      ii. Divide and conquer.
3. Test the theory to determine the cause.
   a. If the theory is confirmed, determine the next steps to resolve the problem.
   b. If the theory is not confirmed, reestablish a new theory or escalate.
4. Establish a plan of action to resolve the problem and identify potential effects.
5. Implement the solution or escalate as necessary.
6. Verify full system functionality and, if applicable, implement preventive measures.
7. Document findings, actions, outcomes, and lessons learned.

Second, documentation enables you to track problem trends and anticipate future workloads, or even to identify a particular brand or model of an item, such as a printer or a NIC, that seems to be less reliable or that creates more work for you than others. Don't skip this step—it *really* is essential!

Resolving Common Network Service Issues

Network problems fall into several basic categories, and most of these problems you or a network tech in the proper place can fix. Fixing problems at the workstation, work area, or server is a network tech's bread and butter. The same is true of other *nearby* problems such as connecting to local resources. Problems connecting to *far-flung* resources can also often be resolved at the local level, but sometimes you'll need to escalate them. Finally, network performance issues can require patient detective work to locate the trouble. The knowledge from the previous chapters combined with the tools and methods you've learned in this chapter should enable you to fix just about any network!

There are a couple of stumbling blocks when it comes to resolving network issues. First, at almost any level of problem, the result—as far as the end user is concerned—is the same. He or she can't access resources beyond the local machine. Whether a user tries to access the local file server or do a Google search, if the attempt fails, "the network is down!" You need to fall back on the most important question a tech can ask: What can cause this problem? Then methodically work through the troubleshooting steps and tools to narrow possibilities. Let's look at a scenario to illustrate the narrowing process.

"We Can't Access Our Web Server in Istanbul!"

Everyone in the local office appears to have full access to local and Internet Web sites. No one, however, can reach a company-operated server at a particular remote site in Istanbul. There has been a recent change to the firewall configuration, so it is up to a technician, Terry, to determine if the firewall change is the culprit or if the problem lies elsewhere.

Terry has come up with three possible theories: the remote server is down, the remote site is inaccessible, or the local firewall is preventing communication with the server. He elects to test his theories with the "quickest to test" approach. His first test is to confirm that all of the local office workstations cannot reach the remote server. Using different hosts, he uses the ping and ping6 utilities. First, he pings localhost to confirm the workstation has a working IP stack, then he attempts to ping the remote server and gets no response. Next, he tries the tracert and traceroute utilities on the different hosts. Traceroute shows a functional path to the router that connects the remote office to the Internet but does not get a response from the server.

So far, everything seems to confirm that the local office cannot get to the remote server. Just to be able to say he tried everything, Terry runs the mtr utility from a Linux box and lets it run for an extended time. At the same time, he runs the pathping utility from a Windows computer. Neither utility can contact the server. He tries all of these utilities on some other company resources and Internet sites and has no problems connecting.

Confident that the reported symptom is confirmed, Terry puts in a call to the remote site to ask about the status. The virtual PBX sends Terry to voicemail for every extension that he calls. This could point to a network disconnection at the site or to everyone being out of the office there. Since it is 3:00 a.m. at the remote site, Terry does not have a clear answer.

The next quick test to perform is to see if the site is reachable from outside of the local office. This will confirm or eliminate his theory of a local *incorrect host-based firewall settings* issue.

Terry sits down at a computer and searches on Google for a looking glass site. He selects one from the results list and browses to the site. Once in the site, he selects the location of a source router to perform a diagnostic test, and then he selects the type of test to run; in this case, he chooses a ping test. He enters the target server address of the company's remote server and submits the test parameters. After a moment, the looking glass server sends a set of pings, none of which receives a response. He tries the test from a few other source router locations and gets the same results.

To complete his tests, Terry uses the looking glass site to ping some additional hosts at the remote site and is pleased to discover that they are all reachable. Now Terry knows that the site is accessible, so it must be that the server is down. When the office opens, he will contact the technician there and offer whatever help and information that he can. In the meantime, he informs the rest of the organization of the server's status.

Narrowing the problem to a single source—an apparently down server—doesn't get all the way to the bottom of the problem (although it certainly helps!). What could cause an unresponsive server?

- Local power outage, like a blown circuit breaker
- Failed NIC on the server
- Network cable disconnected
- Improper network configuration on the server
- A changed patch cable location in the rack
- Failed component in the server
- Server shutdown
- A whole lot of other possibilities

Let's look at some network troubleshooting considerations to keep in mind, and then review a number of specific problems from a hands-on view, then expand our view to nearby problems, expand it further to consider far-flung issues, and finish with performance issues that could crop up anywhere.

Network Troubleshooting Considerations

Any time trouble pops up with our networks, it can be easy to get pulled right into the details of the first user report, pick a thread, start pulling on it, and see where it takes you. Sometimes this is exactly what you'll have to do to track down the source of a problem—but occasionally you can end up having trouble seeing the forest for the trees. The CompTIA Network+

objectives specifically call out a small number of *considerations* to keep in mind as you troubleshoot so that you'll notice cases where they might help you narrow down possibilities or find the problem faster.

Device Configuration Review

Whenever you run into network trouble, it's a good idea to consider the possibility that someone (or maybe even just an update) has changed a *device configuration* recently. This might've been a documented change, or maybe someone else was trying to troubleshoot a different problem and forgot to revert or document the change. If a user had sufficient permissions on the system, they may have fiddled with settings themselves to try and get things working again.

There's a risk here that someone trying to fix a problem has changed the settings to something that won't work no matter what you do. Especially with user devices, make sure they are configured correctly before you start looking at the network itself.

Most managed network devices, such as a switch or a router, enable you to get to a terminal—such as through SSH—and type commands to show the current configuration of the device. The information would include the users and hostname, configured protocols such as Spanning Tree Protocol or BGP, and configuration of individual interfaces (such as trunking, VLAN assignment, and more).

The specific commands for *show config*—the overall category of commands—differ among the many operating systems used on these devices. A tech might ask, "Did you run a show config on that router?" and the specific command would vary from device to device.

Interface Status

While it seems simple enough, checking the *interface status* of the systems involved can help resolve many networking issues quickly. So instead of looking first for a more complex cause to your problem, don't forget to consider the interface status of the devices you're troubleshooting.

The shorthand command to display the current interface status from a terminal is *show interface*. IOS and Junos OS lengthen the precise command to `show interfaces`, which you saw back in Chapter 11. On physical devices, the command would show the status of a specific port, such as type of hardware, MAC address, description, media type, number of packets, and more.

> The CompTIA Network+ objectives place *show interface*, *show config*, and *show route* under the subobjective "Basic network platform commands." That would make the casual reader think these were specific commands. Although some operating systems might use the specific language, all of them vary to some degree. It's best to think about the three terms as shorthand or categories of commands.

Routing Tables

If you are troubleshooting a Layer 3 problem, consider the *routing tables* of the various routers, firewalls, and other devices that the packets are moving through. Checking the routing tables directly enables you to see how the packets will be forwarded through the network. This can help point to a direct problem with the routes themselves or indicate that the packets are taking a path through the network you didn't know about.

The shorthand command to display routing table information at a terminal is *show route*, though the specific commands vary by OS. Junos OS uses `show route`. A common version of IOS uses `show ip route`. Regardless, the information displayed is the same, the routing tables for that device. The command shows where the router thinks a packet should go.

VLAN Assignment

Like the other considerations just described, doing a quick review of the *VLAN assignments* is good practice when troubleshooting. You could be dealing with a simple incorrect port assignment, or more complex problems. While this will be most important when troubleshooting Layer 2 issues, VLAN assignment also plays a role in problems further up the OSI stack.

Network Performance Baselines

One of the best things you can do to keep a network in good shape is to invest time now to set up performance monitoring via a network monitoring system (NMS) or take periodic benchmarks and learn what kind of performance and access patterns are normal when all is well. When your future self is unsettled by a few vague complaints about speed or reliability, having access to historical **network performance baselines** can be the difference between knowing where to look and having to let the problem fester until you have enough user reports to connect the dots. The baselines may even help you proactively spot failing or misconfigured devices, catch compromised hosts up to no good, or plan for extra capacity before performance falls off a cliff.

Hands-On Problems

Hands-on problems refer to things that you can fix at the workstation, work area, or server. These include physical problems and configuration problems.

A *power failure* or *power anomalies*, such as dips and surges, can make a network device unreachable. We've addressed the fixes for such issues a couple of times already in this book: manage the power to the network device in question and install an uninterruptible power supply (UPS).

A *hardware failure* can certainly make a network device unreachable. Fall back on your CompTIA A+ training for troubleshooting. Check the link lights on the NIC. Try another NIC if the machine seems functional in every other aspect. Ping the localhost.

Pay attention to link lights when you have a "hardware failure." The *network connection light-emitting diode (LED) status indicators*—link lights—can quickly point to a connectivity issue. Try known-good cables/NICs if you run into this issue.

Hot-swappable *transceivers* (which you read about way back in Chapter 4) can go bad. The key when working with small form-factor pluggable (SFP) or the much older gigabit interface converter (GBIC) transceivers is that you need to check both the media and the module. In other words, a seemingly *bad SFP/GBIC* could be *the cable connected to it or the transceiver.* As with other hardware issues, try known-good components to troubleshoot.

Outside invisible forces can cause problems with copper cabling. You've read about electromagnetic interference (EMI) and radio frequency interference (RFI) previously in the book. *EMI and RFI can disrupt signaling on a copper cable,* especially with the very low voltages used today on those cables. These are crazy things to troubleshoot.

An interference problem might manifest in a scenario like this one. John can use e-mail on his laptop successfully over the company's wireless network. When he plugs in at his desk in his cubicle, however, e-mail messages just don't get through.

Cross Check

Interference at the Demarc

You read about interference causing problems at the demarc in an office building back in Chapter 13, so cross-check your knowledge now. What kind of interference could cause problems? How would you avoid the problems?

Typically, you'd test everything before suspecting EMI or RFI causing this problem. Test the NIC on the laptop by plugging into a known-good port. You'd use a cable tester on the cable. You'd check for continuity between the port in John's office to the switch. You'd glance at the cabling certification documents to see that, yes, the cable worked when installed.

Only then might a creative tech at her wit's end notice the recently installed, high-powered WAP on the wall outside Tom's office across from John's cubicle. RFI strikes!

If the installation is new and unproven, a perfectly fine network device might be unreachable because of *interface errors*, meaning that the installer didn't install the wall jack correctly. The resulting *incorrect termination* might be a mismatched standard (568A rather than 568B, for example). The cable from the wall to the workstation might be bad or might be a *crossover* cable rather than *straight-through* cable. That's an *incorrect cable type*, according to the CompTIA Network+ objectives. Try another cable.

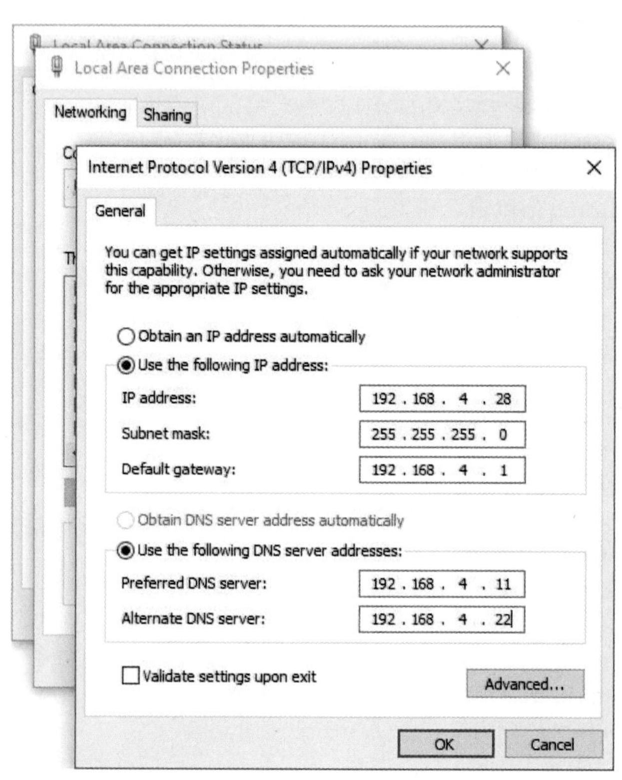

• **Figure 21.9** TCP/IP settings in Windows Server

Aside from obvious physical problems, other hands-on problems you can fix manifest as some sort of misconfiguration. *IP setting issues*, such as setting a PC to an *incorrect IP address* that's not on the same network ID as other resources, would result in a "dead-to-me" network. A similar fate would result from inputting *incorrect gateway* IP address information. The same is true with an *incorrect subnet mask* setting—that is, the subnet mask isn't accurate. If it has an *incorrect DNS* server address, the system might have trouble resolving all DNS names. (This may be more subtle, such as only internal DNS names failing, if the address is a valid DNS server—just not the right one.) The system will go nowhere, fast.

The fix for these sorts of problems should be pretty obvious to you at this point. Go into the network configuration for the device and put in correct numbers. Figure 21.9 shows TCP/IP settings for a Windows Server machine.

Some problems that you can fix at the local machine don't point to messed-up hardware or invalid settings, but reflect the current mix of wired and wireless networks in the same place. Here's a scenario that applies to Windows versions *before* Windows 10. Tina has a wireless network connection to the Internet. She gets a shiny new printer with an Ethernet port, but with no Wi-Fi capability. She wants to print from both her PC and her laptop, so she creates a small LAN: a couple of Ethernet cables and a switch. She plugs everything in, installs drivers, and all is well. She can print from both machines. Unfortunately, as soon as she prints, her Internet connection goes down.

The funny part is that the Internet connection didn't go anywhere, but her *simultaneous wired/wireless connections* created a network failure. The wired and wireless NICs can't actually operate simultaneously and, by default, the wired connection takes priority in the order in which devices are accessed by network services.

To fix this problem, open **Network Connections** in the Control Panel. Press the ALT key to activate the menu bar, then select **Advanced | Advanced Settings** (Figure 21.10). Change the connection priority in the Advanced Settings options by selecting the one Tina wants to take priority and clicking the up arrow to move it up the list.

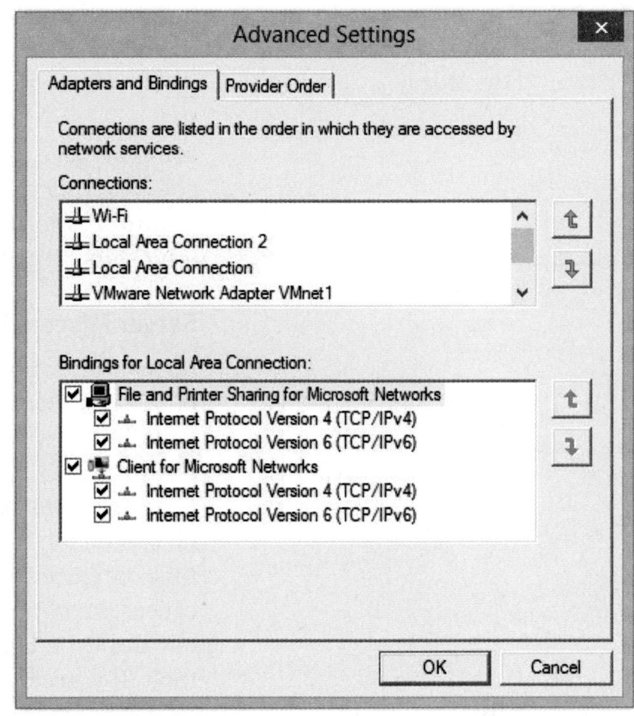

• **Figure 21.10** Network Connections Advanced Settings

Nearby Problems

Incorrect configuration of any number of options in devices can stop a device from accessing nearby resources. These problems can be simple to fix, although tracking down the culprit can take time and patience.

One of the most obvious errors occurs when you're duplicating machines and using static IP addresses. As soon as you plug in the duplicated machine with its *duplicate IP address*, the network will howl. No two computers can have the same IP address on a broadcast domain. The fix for the problem is to change the IP address on the new machine either to an unused static IP address or to DHCP.

A related issue comes from *duplicate MAC addresses*, something that can happen when working with virtual machines or, rarely, as a result of a manufacturing error. The effect is the same as duplicate IP addresses. Either put the devices on different VLANs or swap out NICs to avoid duplication.

An expired IP address can cause a system not to connect. Release/renew to obtain a proper IP address from the DHCP server. If the DHCP server's scope of IP addresses has been claimed, that release/renew won't work. You'll get an error that points to *DHCP scope exhaustion*. The only fix for this is to make changes at the DHCP server.

> Windows 10 does not have this simultaneous wired/wireless connection issue at all, so the problem is irrelevant as long as your clients have updated computers. You might see this issue in an exam question, though hopefully CompTIA has let it go.

Client Misconfigurations

Most clients use DHCP for IP address, subnet mask, and default gateway settings. With manual configuration, on the other hand, errors can creep in and cause a device to fail to connect to network resources. A typical scenario is with a bring your own device (BYOD) environment, where an employee brings in a manually configured laptop—forgetting that it's tuned to his

> A *DHCP starvation attack*, like you read about in Chapter 19, causes *DHCP scope exhaustion*.

home network—and complains about not being able to access the LAN or the Internet.

Anything that doesn't match the LAN settings will cause a client to fail to connect. An IP address that doesn't match the subnet, for example, will bring no love. An error in the subnet mask settings will stop client access cold. A DNS server setting that's not accurate can cause name resolution failure. If the default gateway address is incorrect—an *incorrect gateway* issue—then there's no Internet for the client.

Server Misconfigurations

Misconfigurations of server settings can block all or some access to resources on a LAN. *Misconfigured DHCP* settings on a host above can cause problems, but they will be limited to the host. If these settings are misconfigured on the DHCP server, however, many more machines and people can be affected. A *misconfigured DNS* server might direct hosts to incorrect sites or no sites at all. It might appear as an *unresponsive service* and just do nothing. Misconfigured DNS settings on a client results in *names not resolving* and causes the network to appear to be down for the user.

You'll be clued into such misconfiguration by using ping and other tools. If you can ping a file server by IP address but not by name, this points to *DNS issues*. Similarly, if a computer fails in *discovering neighboring devices/nodes*, like connecting to a networked printer, DHCP or DNS misconfiguration can be the culprit. To fix the issue, go into the network configuration for the client or the server and find the misconfigured settings.

Cross Check

DNS Settings

You learned about DNS in detail in Chapter 9, so dust off those memories and see if you can answer these questions: What might cause a DNS server to go down? What's a DNS root server? What are the authoritative top-level domain servers? Does DNS use a flat name space or a hierarchical name space? What's the difference?

Adding VLANs

When you add VLANs into the network mix, all sorts of fun network issues can crop up. As an example, suppose Bill has a 24-port managed switch segmented into four VLANs, one for each group in the office: Management, Sales, Marketing, and Development (Figure 21.11).

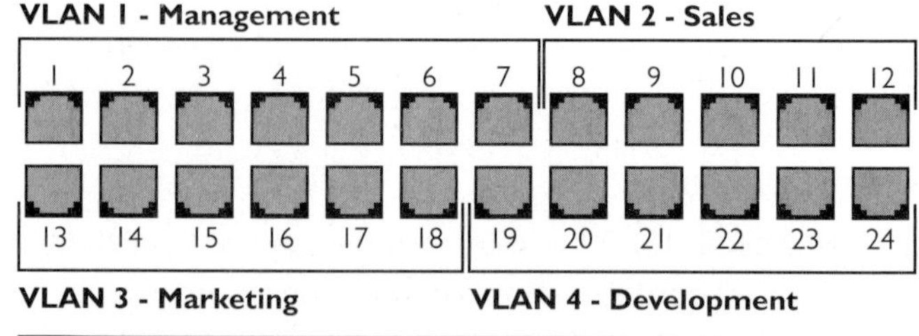

• **Figure 21.11** Bill's VLAN assignments

Bill thought he'd assigned six ports to each VLAN when he set up the switch, but by mistake he assigned seven ports to VLAN 1 and only five ports to VLAN 2. Merrily plugging in the patch cables for each group of users, Bill gets called up by his boss asking why Cindy over in sales suddenly can see resources reserved for management. This obviously points to an *interface misconfiguration* that resulted in a *VLAN mismatch*, a lovely phrase meaning Bill put somebody into the *incorrect VLAN*.

Similarly, after fixing his initial mistake and getting the VLANs set up properly, Bill needs to plug the right patch cables into the right ports. If he messes up and plugs the patch cable for Cindy's computer into a VLAN 1 port, the intrepid salesperson would again have access to the Management resources. Such *cable placement errors* show up pretty quickly and are readily fixed. Keep proper records of patch cable assignments and plug the cables into the proper ports.

Link Aggregation Problems

Ethernet networks (traditionally) don't scale easily. If you have a Gigabit Ethernet connection between the main switch and a very busy file server, that connection by definition can handle up to 1-Gbps bandwidth. If that connection becomes saturated, the only way to bump up the bandwidth cap on that single connection would be to upgrade both the switch and the server NIC to the next higher Ethernet standard, 10-Gigabit Ethernet. That's a big jump and an expensive one, plus it's an upgrade of 1000 percent! What if you needed to bump up bandwidth by only 20 percent?

The scaling issue became obvious early on, so manufacturers came up with ways to use multiple NICs in tandem to increase bandwidth in smaller increments, what's called **link aggregation** or **NIC teaming**, which you'll recall from way back in Chapter 11. Numerous protocols enable two or more connections to work together simultaneously, such as the vendor-neutral IEEE 802.1AX-2020 specification *Link Aggregation Control Protocol (LACP)* and the Cisco-proprietary *Port Aggregation Protocol (PAgP)*. Let's focus on the former for a common network issue scenario.

To enable LACP between two devices, such as the switch and file server just noted, each device needs two or more interconnected network interfaces configured for LACP. When the two devices interact, they will make sure they can communicate over multiple physical ports at the same speeds and form a single logical port that takes advantage of the full combined bandwidth (Figure 21.12).

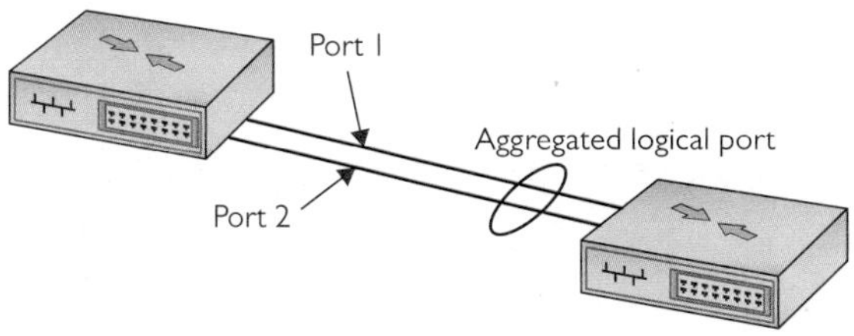

• **Figure 21.12** LACP

Those ports can be in one of two modes: active or passive. *Active* ports want to use LACP and send special frames out trying to initiate creating an aggregated logical port. *Passive* ports wait for active ports to initiate the conversation before they will respond.

So here's the common network error with LACP setups. An aggregated connection set to active on both ends (*active-active*) automatically talks, negotiates, and works. A connection set to active on one end and passive on the other (*active-passive*) talks, negotiates, and works. But if you set both ends to passive (passive-passive), neither will initiate the conversation and LACP will not engage. Setting both ends to passive when you want to use LACP is an example of *NIC teaming misconfiguration*.

NIC teaming provides many more benefits than just increasing bandwidth, such as redundancy. You can team two NICs in a logical unit but set them up with one NIC as the primary—*live*—and the second as the hot spare—*standby*. If the first NIC goes down, the traffic will automatically flow through the second NIC. In a simple network set up for redundancy, you'd make one connection live and the other as standby on each device. Switch A has a live and a standby, Switch B has a live and a standby, and so on.

The key here is that multicast traffic to the various devices needs to be enabled on every device through which that traffic might pass. If Switch C doesn't play nice with multicast and it's connected to Switch B, this can cause multicast traffic to stop. One "fix" for this in a Cisco network is to turn off a feature called IGMP snooping, which is enabled by default on Cisco switches. IGMP snooping is normally a good thing, because it helps the switches keep track of devices that use multicast and filter traffic away from devices that don't.

The problem with turning off IGMP snooping is that the switches won't map and filter multicast traffic. Instead of only sending to the devices that are set up to receive multicast, the switches will treat multicast messages as broadcast messages and send them to everybody. This is a NIC teaming misconfiguration that can seriously degrade network performance.

A better fix would be to send a couple of network techs to change settings on Switch C and make it send multicast packets properly.

Broadcast Storms

A **broadcast storm** is the result of one or more devices sending a nonstop flurry of broadcast frames on the network. The first sign of a broadcast storm is when every computer on the broadcast domain suddenly can't connect to the rest of the network. There are usually no clues other than network applications freezing or presenting "can't connect to…" types of error messages. Every activity light on every node is solidly on. Computers on other broadcast domains work perfectly well.

The trick is to isolate; that's where escalation comes in. You need to break down the network quickly by unplugging devices until you can find the one causing trouble. Getting a packet analyzer to work can be difficult, but you should at least try. If you can scoop up one packet, you'll know what node is causing the trouble. The second the bad node is disconnected, the network returns to normal. But if you have a lot of machines to deal with and a bunch of users who can't get on the network yelling at you, you'll need help. Call a supervisor to get support to solve the crisis as quickly as possible.

Switching Loops

Also known as a *bridging loop*, a **switching loop** is when you connect and configure multiple switches together in such a way that causes a circular path to appear. Switching loops are rare because switches use the Spanning Tree Protocol (STP), but they do happen. The symptoms are identical to a broadcast storm: every computer on the broadcast domain can no longer access the network.

The good part about switching loops is that they rarely take place on a well-running network. Someone had to break something, and that means someone, somewhere is messing with the switch configuration. Escalate the problem, and get the team to help you find the person making changes to the switches.

Multicast Flooding

Related to broadcast storms, though not as destructive, is *multicast flooding*. Multicast is a Layer 3 technology and, therefore, switches see multicast traffic as broadcasts that they dutifully forward to every port in the broadcast domain. Multicast flooding is not much of an issue when you're dealing with something like phone intercoms, but it becomes much more of a problem if you are using multicast for things like high-bandwidth video. In that case, you can easily send hundreds of megabits of traffic to every host on the LAN.

To mitigate problems with multicast flooding, you can move all the systems that need to participate in the multicast group to their own VLAN or physically separate network. This will minimize the flooding to hosts on that broadcast domain. But do note that this still can saturate any any trunk lines carrying that VLAN's traffic.

Another approach to mitigating multicast issues is to enable *IGMP snooping* on your switches. This will let your switches forward multicast traffic only to ports with hosts that are members of a multicast group. IGMP snooping works by letting the switch "listen" for when the host joins a multicast group, and only then will the switch forward frames from that multicast to that host.

Time Issues

Most devices these days rely on the NIST time servers on the Internet to regulate time. Every once in a while (like on the CompTIA Network+ exam), you'll see a scenario where machines, isolated from the Internet (and thus removed from a time server and the ubiquitous *Network Time Protocol*, or *NTP*), will get out of sync. This can result in *incorrect time* issues that stop services from working properly. Did I mention that this is rare? The CompTIA Network+ objectives call this *NTP issues*.

Collisions

While **collisions**—two devices trying to speak on the same wire at the same time—once plagued wired networks, this problem is *almost* entirely behind us on modern networks. There is still at least one kind of misconfiguration—in theory and on a CompTIA exam in your near future—that can cause collisions.

If the port on one end of a connection is explicitly set to use a specific bandwidth and duplex setting, it will no longer auto-negotiate settings with its partner port at the other end. While newer high-speed Ethernet standards only support or default to full-duplex connections, older/slower standards default to half-duplex connections. When one side is set to use something like 10BASE-T at full duplex, its partner will fall back to 10BASE-T at half duplex—and collisions can result because of this *duplexing issue*.

Because collisions have become so rare, we don't have as many tools to diagnose them when they do crop up. But, if you do have a port that has fallen back to half-duplex mode, creating the potential for collisions, you can configure your network monitoring software to notify you. Once you know where the problem device is, you can then use the troubleshooting steps to try and determine why it is no longer auto-negotiating.

Low Optical Link Budget

For those coming from UTP cable land, installing and troubleshooting fiber adds a few wrinkles that we don't have to worry about with copper. One of those wrinkles is your *optical link budget*, which is the difference between the maximum power a transceiver can transmit and the minimum power it needs to receive a signal. This budget, basically, is how much the signal can attenuate before you run into trouble.

Attenuation is affected by factors such as the number and type of connectors, cable length and quality, and how many times the cable is spliced or patched. Assuming your network was properly designed and installed, you should not run into optical link budget issues. Otherwise, these issues might accumulate until eventually the light is too dim for the receiver on the other end to cleanly detect the signal, at which point it may start having frame errors or completely lose connectivity.

If you suspect a problem, a good place to start is with the diagnostics built into more advanced switches. These diagnostics will tell you about the module's minimum, maximum, and current transmit/receive power. If you have a network monitoring system set up, it should trigger an alarm if any of these thresholds are exceeded. Here is the diagnostics output from my Juniper switch:

```
Virtual chassis port: vcp-255/2/3
    Laser bias current                     :  6.204 mA
    Laser output power                     :  0.3300 mW / -4.81 dBm
    Module temperature                     :  30 degrees C / 86 degrees F
    Module voltage                         :  3.3460 V
    Receiver signal average optical power  :  0.3190 mW / -4.96 dBm
    . . .
    Laser output power high alarm threshold   :  1.9950 mW / 3.00 dBm
    Laser output power low alarm threshold    :  0.1170 mW / -9.32 dBm
    Laser output power high warning threshold :  1.5840 mW / 2.00 dBm
    Laser output power low warning threshold  :  0.1860 mW / -7.30 dBm
    Laser rx power high alarm threshold       :  1.9953 mW / 3.00 dBm
    Laser rx power low alarm threshold        :  0.0490 mW / -13.10 dBm
    Laser rx power high warning threshold     :  1.5849 mW / 2.00 dBm
    Laser rx power low warning threshold      :  0.0776 mW / -11.10 dBm
```

Beyond what is built into the switch, you'll want to turn to dedicated hardware diagnostic devices such as optical power meters and fiber inspectors. These tools can be used by technicians to help hunt down the source of any attenuation issues in the fiber run.

Licensed Feature Issues

I want to let you in on a little industry secret: once you move beyond SOHO gear, many of the features on network devices require specific licenses. For example, my office's Juniper switches require a separate license to use Open Shortest Path First (OSPF) routing.

Licensing is important to keep in mind when you are purchasing new equipment or want to start using additional features your exiting gear supports. There is no technical fix for *licensed feature issues*—you just need to make sure you have bought (or have an active subscription for) the correct license to enable the features you need and have registered those licenses on the devices.

Far-flung Problems

Problems that stop users from accessing resources over longer distances such as across a WAN like the Internet—or even a large LAN—can originate at the local machine, the remote machine, and in switches and routers along the way. As you might infer from the opening scenario, some of these common network problems you can fix, and some you cannot. We discussed many remote connectivity problems and solutions way back in Chapter 13, so I won't rehash them here.

This section starts with router configuration issues, problems with misconfigured multilayer network appliances, issues with certificates, and company security policies. The following section goes into bigger problems that require escalation.

Router Problems

Routers enable networks to connect to other networks, which you know well by now. Problems with routers simply make those connections not work. (Recall that physical problems with routers or router interface modules were covered in Chapter 7 and Chapter 13.) Loss of power or a bad module can certainly wreck a tech's day, but the fixes are pretty simple: provide power or replace the module.

Router configuration issues can be a bit trickier. The ways to mess up a router are many. You can specify the wrong routing protocol, for example, or misconfigure the right routing protocol.

An access control list (ACL) might include addresses to block that shouldn't be blocked or allow access to network resources for nodes that shouldn't have it. *Incorrect ACL settings* can lead to *blocked TCP/UDP ports* that shouldn't be blocked. A misconfiguration can lead to a *missing route* that makes some destinations unreachable for users.

As you'll recall from Chapter 16, if you want to prevent downtime due to a failure on your default gateway, you should consider implementing *Virtual Router Redundancy Protocol (VRRP)* or, if you are a Cisco shop, *Gateway Load Balancing Protocol (GLBP)*.

Improperly configured routers aren't going to send packets to the proper destination. The symptoms are clear: every system that uses the misconfigured router as a default gateway is either not able to get packets out or not able to get packets in, or sometimes both. Web pages don't come up, FTP servers suddenly disappear, and e-mail clients can't access their servers. In these cases, you need to verify first that everything in your area of responsibility works. If that is true, then escalate the problem and find the person responsible for the router.

One excellent tool for determining a router problem beyond your LAN is tracert/traceroute. Run `traceroute` to your default gateway. (You can also use ping to check connectivity.) If that fails, you know you have a local issue and can potentially do something about it. If the traceroute comes back positive, run it to a site on the Internet. A solid connection should return something like the output shown in Figure 21.13. A failed route will return a failed response.

```
Default Shell (Light) (-zsh) — mikesmyer
┌─[mikesmyer in ~][12:00:05] took 1m31s
└─>$ traceroute explainshell.com
traceroute to explainshell.com (174.138.81.104), 64 hops max, 52 byte packets
 1  192.168.50.1 (192.168.50.1)  0.560 ms  0.296 ms  0.307 ms
 2  * * *
 3  te0-5-0-12---0.lcr01.hfmn.tx.frontiernet.net (172.102.49.246)  7.030 ms  7.567 ms
    te0-5-0-12---0.lcr01.nsby.tx.frontiernet.net (172.102.49.182)  7.118 ms
 4  ae8---0.scr01.dlls.tx.frontiernet.net (74.40.3.21)  11.946 ms
    ae9---0.scr02.dlls.tx.frontiernet.net (74.40.3.29)  11.092 ms
    ae8---0.scr01.dlls.tx.frontiernet.net (74.40.3.21)  13.648 ms
 5  ae1---0.cbr05.dlls.tx.frontiernet.net (45.52.201.123)  11.482 ms  11.254 ms  11.857 ms
 6  * * *
 7  * * *
 8  * * *
 9  * * *
10  * * *
11  * * *
12  * * *
13  174.138.81.104 (174.138.81.104)  51.726 ms  52.026 ms  51.203 ms

┌─[mikesmyer in ~][12:03:25] took 2m
└─>$
```

• **Figure 21.13** Good connection

Some extra problems show up when you zoom out and look at entire chains or webs of routers. At this scale, individual routers—and how they interact with others—shape the health of the network. At any given hop, unexpected behavior could create hard-to-troubleshoot problems. Let's take a look at two specific cases of unexpected inter-router communication: asymmetric routing and routing loops.

Asymmetric Routing *Asymmetric routing*—when packets take one path to their destination but the response takes a different path back—isn't necessarily a problem for everyone all the time, but it could still give you a headache. Some networks intentionally use asymmetric routes for performance reasons, but the different routes may confuse security and NAT devices that assume they'll see both halves of a symmetric conversation—or mislead you about the nature of a connectivity problem that is only impacting packets sent in one direction.

Diagnosing a problem asymmetric route often involves using packet captures and traceroute to determine how the packets are actually flowing through the network. Some advanced networking devices will also detect asymmetric routes automatically and give you a heads-up about potential issues.

Routing Loops Since individual routers don't really see the forest for the trees, they'll happily forward a packet down a path that they *think* is correct but actually leads it back around to a router it has already passed through, causing a *routing loop*. Once this happens, the packets are doomed either to time out or to get dropped after the packet takes as many hops as its time to live (TTL) metric allows.

Routing loops are generally a misconfiguration problem between routers, and different routing protocols have different features that attempt to keep these loops from developing in the first place.

Appliance Problems

Many of the boxes that people refer to as "routers" contain many features, such as routing, Network Address Translation (NAT), switching, an intrusion detection system (IDS), a firewall, and more. These complex boxes, such as the *Cisco Adaptive Security Appliance (ASA)*, are called *network appliances*.

One common issue with network appliances is technician error. By default, for example, NAT rules take precedence over an appliance's routing table entries. If the tech fails to set the NAT rule order correctly, traffic that should be routed to go out one interface (like to the DMZ network) can go out an *incorrect interface* (like to the inside network).

Users on the outside would expect a response from something but instead get nothing, all because of a NAT *interface misconfiguration*.

The fix for such problems is to set up your network appliance correctly. Know the capabilities of the network appliance and the relationships among its services. Examine rules and settings carefully.

Look for a question on the CompTIA Network+ exam that explores incorrect network-based firewall settings creating general networking issues. Trace the steps and who performed them to find the problem.

Certificate Issues

TLS/SSL certificates have expiration dates and companies need to maintain them properly. If you get complaints from clients that the company Web site is giving their browsers *untrusted TLS/SSL certificate* errors, chances are that the certificate has expired. The fix for that is pretty simple—update the certificate.

Company Security Policy

Implemented company security policies can make routine WAN connectivity actions completely fail. Here's a scenario.

Mike is the head of his company's IT department and he has a big problem: the amount of traffic running between the two company locations is on a dedicated connection and is blowing his bandwidth out of the water! It's so bad that data moving between the two offices often drops to a crawl four to five times per day. Why are people using so much bandwidth?

As he inspects the problem, Mike realizes that the sales department is the culprit. Most of the data is composed of massive video files the sales department uses in their advertising campaign. He needs to make some security policy decisions. First, he needs to set up a throttling policy that defines in terms of megabits per second the maximum amount of bandwidth any single department can use per day. Second, he needs to add a *blocking policy*. If anyone goes over this limit, the company will block all traffic of that type for a certain amount of time (one hour). Third, he needs to update his company's *fair access policy* or *utilization limits* security policies to reflect these new limits. This lets employees, especially those pesky sales folks, know what the new rules are.

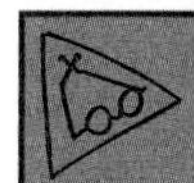

Tech Tip

Escalating

No single person is truly in control of an entire Internet-connected network. Large organizations split network support duties into very skill-specific areas: routers, cable infrastructure, user administration, and so on. Even in a tiny network with a single network support person, problems will arise that go beyond the tech's skill level or that involve equipment the organization doesn't own (usually it's their ISP's gear). In these situations, the tech needs to identify the problem and, instead of trying to fix it on his or her own, escalate the issue.

In network troubleshooting, problem escalation should occur when you face a problem that falls outside the scope of your skills and you need help. In large organizations, escalation problems have very clear procedures, such as who to call and what to document. In small organizations, escalation often is nothing more than a technician realizing that he or she needs help.

Network Performance Issues

Connectivity problems are great! I mean, they're bad for users, and bad for productivity—but most of them have a clear resolution. Once someone tracks down the problem and implements a solution, we can close the ticket and move on. In contrast, *network performance issues* can be a bit more like stepping on abandoned chewing gum on a hot summer day.

A performance problem could just as easily be caused by a pipe that's just too small, a router that's running too hot, new sources of interference, ailing network devices, too many coworkers watching Netflix or Twitch while they work, poor QoS policies, backups running during your daytime peak instead of at night, an office that's simply outgrowing its infrastructure, or a compromised host exfiltrating petabytes of your organization's most precious data.

Network performance baselines are great to have for many kinds of troubleshooting—but they're *really* great when it comes to spotting performance issues before people are cranky enough to start complaining. In all of these cases, monitoring is your friend. Monitor everything you can!

Monitor your devices and network, obviously—but don't be shy about throwing in anything you have instruments and storage space to track. Things like temperature, humidity, the weather, indoor and outdoor air quality, the quality of electricity from your power company, the number of active Wi-Fi clients, the amount of ambient noise, and the number of active DHCP leases. Once you have all this data feeding into your NMS, make sure to set up thresholds so that you are notified when critical systems are running outside of their optimal performance range.

You won't need most of this data most of the time. But it's the kind of thing that can help you work your way back from complaints on Monday afternoons about Wi-Fi in the break room to the WAP on the ceiling going on the fritz when your water delivery service props the door open for 10 minutes on a muggy, sweltering Friday afternoon.

Troubleshooting Is Fun!

The art of network troubleshooting can be a fun, frolicsome, and frequently frustrating feature of your network career. By applying a good troubleshooting methodology and constantly increasing your knowledge of networks, you too can develop into a great troubleshooting artist. Developing your artistry takes time, naturally, but stick with it. Begin the training. Use the Force. Learn new stuff, document problems and fixes, and talk to other network techs about similar problems. Every bit of knowledge and experience you gain will make things that much easier for you when crunch time comes and a network disaster occurs—and as any experienced network tech can tell you, it will occur, even on the most robust network.

Chapter 21 Review

Chapter Summary

After reading this chapter and completing the exercises, you should understand the following about network troubleshooting.

Describe appropriate troubleshooting tools and their functions

- Before starting work on any problem, always ask yourself if what you are about to do can potentially harm your data.
- The vast majority of cabling problems take place when the network is first installed or when changes, if any, take place. Cables rarely go bad after they have been made, installed, and tested.
- Broken cables don't create intermittent problems—they make permanent disconnects. A TDR can tell you where a break is on a cable.
- Certifiers test a cable to ensure that it can handle its rated amount of capacity. If a cable isn't broken, yet isn't moving data the way it should, test it with a certifier. Use a certifier for slowdowns, not disconnects. With optical fiber, use an optical power meter (a fiber light meter) to measure the amount of light loss.
- Heat and power problems manifest as intermittent network problems. Use a voltage quality recorder to measure power and use a temperature monitor to ensure proper temperature.
- A multimeter tests voltage and can tell you how much voltage is on a line.
- A tone generator and a tone probe work as a pair to help you locate a particular cable.
- A punchdown tool places UTP wires into 66-blocks and 110-blocks. In a diagnostic environment, you'll find it useful to repunch a connection to make sure all the contacts are properly set.
- Software tools can be organized in two categories: those that come built into your operating system and those that are provided by a third party.
- Terminal emulators enable techs to access command line interface shells, such as Terminal.app in macOS. Network techs use the CLI for troubleshooting, diagnostics, configuration, and more.
- The hostname utility prints the hostname of the current system. It can be especially helpful if you're using a script to automatically gather information about many systems, for example.
- The traceroute utility (called tracert in Windows) is used to trace all the routers between two points. Use it to diagnose problems reaching a remote system.
- The ipconfig (Windows), ifconfig (macOS/UNIX), and ip (Linux) utilities give you information about a computer's IP settings. Using `ipconfig` with the `/all` switch gives additional detailed information, including DNS server addresses and MAC addresses.
- The ping utility uses ICMP packets to show if you can reach a computer on the LAN or a remote computer.
- Because some devices block the ICMP packets, arping can be used instead of ping. However, arping is available only on UNIX/Linux systems—and it can't cross routers, so it can't be used where ICMP is blocked to test *remote* connectivity.
- The nslookup utility is used to diagnose DNS problems and is the only DNS utility on Windows by default.
- The dig tool is the preferred utility on UNIX/Linux systems, but Microsoft does not provide dig with Windows.
- The mtr utility, which is not available on Windows, is similar to traceroute except that it keeps running until shut down. It's comparable to pathping, but pathping stops when it doesn't receive a response, whereas mtr continues, if possible, to the end of the route.

- The route utility enables you to display and edit the local system's routing table.
- Running `netstat` or `ss` (UNIX/Linux) displays information on the current state of all the running IP processes on your computer. Use netstat or ss when you want to know about your current sessions.
- A packet sniffer intercepts and logs network packets. Wireshark and tcpdump are popular packet sniffers.
- A port scanner probes ports on another system, logging the state of scanned ports. It can be used to find an unintentionally open port so you can secure it. Hackers like to use port scanners to look for openings into machines. Once they have found these openings, they can attempt to exploit any vulnerabilities they have found.
- Throughput testers and speed-test sites enable you to gauge the overall upload and download speeds of a connection.
- Looking glass sites enable you to run various diagnostic tools from outside your network.

Analyze and discuss the troubleshooting process

- There is no reference guide to troubleshooting every possible network problem, because such a guide would be obsolete the moment it was created.
- A basic troubleshooting model may include the following steps:
  1. Identify the problem.
  2. Establish a theory of probable cause.
  3. Test the theory to determine the cause.
  4. Establish a plan of action to resolve the problem and identify potential effects.
  5. Implement the solution or escalate as necessary.
  6. Verify full system functionality and, if applicable, implement preventive measures.
  7. Document findings, actions, outcomes, and lessons learned.
- First, identify the problem. You need to gather information, question users, identify symptoms, determine if anything has changed on the network, duplicate the problem (if possible), and approach multiple problems individually. Following these steps will help you get to the root of the problem.
- When establishing the symptoms, you may need to ask the user reporting the trouble both closed- and open-ended questions.
- Isolating the cause of the problem includes identifying the scope of the problem, such as determining if it affects a single system or the entire network.
- When trying to determine what recent changes may have caused the problem, it is important to recognize things that are not causes. Re-creating the problem yourself removes user error as a possible cause, and experiencing the problem on another computer removes the possibility of changed settings on the first computer as the cause.
- Once you have determined possible causes, you should establish a theory of probable cause. The ability to identify the most probable cause improves with experience. Consider multiple approaches when tackling problems. Try a top-to-bottom or bottom-to-top OSI model approach.
- With the third step, you need to test the theory to determine the cause, but do so without changing anything or risking any repercussions.
- Next, establish a plan of action and identify potential effects. With complex problems, write down the steps you need to take. Review before implementing.
- When implementing a solution, be sure to try only one thing at a time. If you perform multiple activities or make multiple changes, you won't know which action actually solved the problem—and you won't know which action made things worse.
- Once a solution has been implemented, test it by trying to re-create the problem. If you can re-create the error, you haven't fixed the problem.
- If you have fixed a problem, you need to recognize what potential problems you may have caused. For example, replacing a NIC in a server may get the server back online, but the new NIC has a different MAC address, which may introduce a whole new set of problems.

- Problems, symptoms, and solutions should be documented so the solutions can be used later in a knowledge base. Additionally, the documentation will help you track problem trends.
- Verify end-to-end connectivity on a local network. Users need connections to appropriate resources. Ports need to be open. ACLs need to be set up properly.

Resolve common network issues

- Network problems fall into several basic categories, and most of these problems you or a network tech in the proper place can fix. You should know how to fix problems at the workstation, work area, and server. The same is true of connecting to nearby resources. Problems connecting to remote resources can often be resolved at the local level, but sometimes they need to get escalated.
- Consider several additional aspects of networking that can have an impact on troubleshooting. Review device configuration settings for errors, for example. Review the interface status by running some type of *show interface* command. Examine routing tables for incorrect entries. Problems with accessing another system can come from errors in VLAN assignment. Compare the current problematic networking system against a recent network performance baseline to help point to problem areas.
- Hands-on problems refer to things that you can fix at the workstation, work area, or server. These include physical problems, such as power and hardware failures, and configuration problems, such as improper IP addressing or default gateway information, mixing wired and wireless networks, and more.
- Incorrect configuration of any number of options in devices can stop a device from accessing nearby resources over a LAN. These run the gamut from server misconfigurations—DHCP or DNS settings—to VLAN assignment errors.
- On fancier networks, incorrectly setting up network devices to use link aggregation can cause that aggregation to fail. NIC teaming can cause all sorts of problems if combined with other misconfigurations, such as turning off IGMP snooping on Cisco switches.
- Look for spikes in traffic on the network that slow or stop communication. The can be the result of broadcast storms, switching loops, or multicast flooding.
- Use dedicated hardware diagnostic tools such as optical power meters to sleuth out problems on fiber optic networks, such as insufficient power transmitting a signal over a specific segment. Such could cause attenuation and frame errors.
- Pay attention to any additional licensing fees required for desired features on better network devices. Factor those into the operating budget.
- Far-flung issues include router configuration errors and errors in complex network appliance settings causing traffic to flow in unintended ways. Company security policies can readily derail or stop common networking activity.
- Network performance issues are all over the map. The best thing you can do is set up extensive monitoring and alerting to catch issues early.

Key Terms

Angry IP Scanner *(608)*
arp *(602)*
arping *(603)*
bandwidth speed tester *(608)*
broadcast storm *(624)*
cable crimper *(599)*
cable stripper *(599)*
cable tester *(598)*
certifier *(598)*
collision *(625)*
dig *(604)*
fiber light meter *(598)*

hardware tool *(597)*
hostname *(600)*
ifconfig *(601)*
ip *(601)*
ipconfig *(601)*
link aggregation *(623)*
looking glass site *(608)*
loopback adapter *(598)*
multimeter *(599)*
My Traceroute (mtr) *(604)*
netstat *(606)*
network performance baseline *(619)*
NIC teaming *(623)*
Nmap *(608)*
nslookup *(604)*
optical power meter *(598)*
optical time domain reflectometer (OTDR) *(598)*
packet sniffer *(607)*
pathping *(603)*
ping *(603)*
port scanner *(608)*
protocol analyzer *(607)*
punchdown tool *(599)*
route *(605)*
snip *(599)*
speed-test site *(608)*
switching loop *(624)*
tcpdump *(608)*
temperature monitor *(599)*
time domain reflectometer (TDR) *(598)*
tone generator *(599)*
tone probe *(599)*
traceroute *(601)*
tracert *(601)*
voltage quality recorder *(599)*
Wireshark *(607)*

Key Term Quiz

Use the Key Terms list to complete the sentences that follow. Not all the terms will be used.

1. Use ______________ to locate a problem between two routers.
2. Use a(n) ______________ to put wires into 66- and 110-blocks.
3. A(n) ______________ tests cables to ensure they can handle their rated capacity.
4. If ICMP packets are being blocked, you can use ______________ to test connectivity to another system.
5. ______________ is a popular packet sniffer/protocol analyzer/packet analyzer.
6. To view IP settings on a Linux computer, use the ______________ command.
7. Use a(n) ______________ to test AC/DC voltage, resistance, and continuity.
8. Numerous protocols enable two or more connections to work together simultaneously, a process called NIC teaming or ______________.
9. ______________ uses ICMP packets to test connectivity between two systems.
10. The ______________ command, like `dig`, is used to diagnose DNS problems.

Multiple-Choice Quiz

1. Jordan says she can't access files on the server anymore. No other user has reported this problem, and she can ping the server from another computer successfully. Typing `ping 127.0.0.1` from Jordan's computer is also successful. Using ping to try to reach the server or any other computer from Jordan's computer fails. A check of IP settings on Jordan's computer shows that her static IP address and other information is good. What is the most likely cause of the problem?
   - **A.** The router that Jordan's computer connects to is down.
   - **B.** Jordan's network card is bad.
   - **C.** The DHCP server is down.
   - **D.** Jordan's Ethernet cable has become unplugged from her computer.
2. You are trying to locate which patch cable in the main switch traces back to a particular computer. Which tool should you use?
   - **A.** Tone probe
   - **B.** Cable tester
   - **C.** Punchdown tool
   - **D.** Butt set
3. The Windows tracert tool fails sometimes because many routers block _______________ packets.
   - **A.** ping
   - **B.** TCP
   - **C.** UDP
   - **D.** ICMP
4. What is the first step in the troubleshooting model?
   - **A.** Implementing the solution
   - **B.** Testing the solution
   - **C.** Identifying the problem
   - **D.** Establishing the symptoms
5. Kay's computer has lost all network access. Which tool should you use to test for a break on the cable?
   - **A.** Certifier
   - **B.** TDR
   - **C.** Voltage event recorder
   - **D.** Crimper
6. Which command shows you detailed IP information, including DNS server addresses and MAC addresses?
   - **A.** `ipconfig`
   - **B.** `ipconfig -a`
   - **C.** `ipconfig /all`
   - **D.** `ipconfig /dns`
7. Which tool uses ICMP packets to test connectivity between two systems?
   - **A.** arp
   - **B.** arping
   - **C.** netstat
   - **D.** ping
8. Which tools can you (and hackers) use to discover vulnerabilities on your network? (Select three.)
   - **A.** Port scanner
   - **B.** Nmap
   - **C.** IP Scanner
   - **D.** arp
9. Asking a user "Can you start your e-mail program?" is what type of question?
   - **A.** Closed-ended
   - **B.** Open-ended
   - **C.** Leading
   - **D.** Unprofessional

10. If you want to see which other computers on your network are currently connected to yours, what command should you use?
    A. `ping`
    B. `ws`
    C. `netstat`
    D. `tracert`
11. One of your users calls you with a complaint that she can't reach the site www.twitter.com. You try and access the site and discover you can't connect either, but you can ping the site with its IP address. What is the most probable culprit?
    A. The workgroup switch is down.
    B. Twitter is down.
    C. The gateway is down.
    D. The DNS server is down.
12. A brand-new employee is complaining on his second day of work that he can't log into his computer. What is the most probable cause?
    A. The server is down.
    B. His network card is bad.
    C. He forgot or is mistyping his password.
    D. A port on the switch is bad.
13. When should you use a cable tester to troubleshoot a network cable?
    A. When you have a host experiencing a very slow connection
    B. When you have an intermittent connection problem
    C. When you have a dead connection and you suspect a broken cable
    D. Never
14. Which tools should you use to diagnose problems with DNS?
    A. Nmap or Wireshark
    B. nslookup or dig
    C. ping or pathping
    D. tracert or pathping
15. Which Windows command displays the local system's routing table?
    A. `route print`
    B. `print route`
    C. `tracert /print`
    D. `tracert /p`

Essay Quiz

1. You and a coworker are working late trying to fix a problem on the server. Your coworker suggests applying three hot fixes and swapping out the network card for another. He wants to do all these things at the same time, however, to finish the job quicker. Explain to him why that's not a good idea.
2. Because of your outstanding troubleshooting skills, you have been selected by your supervisor to train a new intern. Explain to her the steps of a basic troubleshooting model.
3. You've read in this chapter: "First, do no harm." Explain in your own words what this phrase means to you. Then, think of a situation in which you were either the technician or the "victim" in a troubleshooting case where harm was done. What happened?

Lab Projects

• Lab Project 21.1

You've learned about many free software tools in this chapter—some available only for Windows, some only for macOS/UNIX/Linux, and some available for all. Make a chart with five columns and label them as follows: Tool Name, Description, Useful Switches/Options, Supported Operating System(s), and Built-In or Third Party. Fill in the chart with the tools from this chapter and use it as a study guide.

• Lab Project 21.2

Using the chart you created in the previous lab activity, run each of the tools to gain some familiarity with the interface, switches, and output. Do you use any of the tools listed in your chart on a regular (or semi-regular) basis? Which tools are the easiest for you to understand? Which tools do you not completely understand? If any tools are still unclear to you, ask your instructor or search the Internet for clarification on the tool's usage. Once you've run each of the tools, compare your findings with classmates or verify with your instructor to make sure your research resulted in correct information!

Exam Objective Map

Exam N10-008

Exam N10-008 Objectives	Chapter(s)	Page(s)
1.0 Networking Fundamentals		
1.1 Compare and contrast the Open Systems Interconnection (OSI) model layers and encapsulation concepts.		
OSI model		
Layer 1 – Physical	1	5
Layer 2 – Data Link	1	13
Layer 3 – Network	1	15
Layer 4 – Transport	1	17
Layer 5 – Session	1	21
Layer 6 – Presentation	1	22
Layer 7 – Application	1	23
Data encapsulation and decapsulation within the OSI model context	1	23
Ethernet header	1, 6	9, 134
Internet Protocol (IP) header	1, 6	9, 130
Transmission Control Protocol (TCP)/User Datagram Protocol (UDP) headers	6	131, 132
TCP flags	6	132
Payload	1, 6	9, 130
Maximum transmission unit (MTU)	7	204
1.2 Explain the characteristics of network topologies and network types.		
Mesh	2	33
Star/hub-and-spoke	2	32
Bus	2	31
Ring	2	31
Hybrid	2	33
Network types and characteristics		
Peer-to-peer	1	25
Client-server	1	25
Local area network (LAN)	4, 6, 13	72, 133, 352
Metropolitan area network (MAN)	13	357
Wide area network (WAN)	6, 13	133, 352
Wireless local area network (WLAN)	14	384
Personal area network (PAN)	17	488
Campus area network (CAN)	13, 17	352, 484
Storage area network (SAN)	16	466

Exam N10-008 Objectives	Chapter(s)	Page(s)
Software-defined wide area network (SDWAN)	13	357
Multiprotocol label switching (MPLS)	13	355
Multipoint generic routing encapsulation (mGRE)	13	371
Service-related entry point	5	98
Demarcation point	5	97
Smartjack	5	98
Virtual network concepts		
vSwitch	15	440
Virtual network interface card (vNIC)	15	440
Network function virtualization (NFV)	15	441
Hypervisor	15	428
Provider links		
Satellite	13	361
Digital subscriber line (DSL)	13	358
Cable	13	360
Leased line	13	354
Metro-optical	13	357
1.3 Summarize the types of cables and connectors and explain which is the appropriate type for a solution.		
Copper	2, 3	35, 55
Twisted pair	2	37
Cat 5	2	38
Cat 5e	2	38
Cat 6	2	38
Cat 6a	2	38
Cat 7	2	38
Cat 8	2	38
Coaxial/RG-6	2	35
Twinaxial	2	36
Termination standards	3	54
TIA/EIA-568A	3	54
TIA/EIA-568B	3	54
Fiber	2	39
Single-mode	2	40
Multimode	2	40
Connector types	2, 4	41, 74
Local connector (LC), straight tip (ST), subscriber connector (SC), mechanical transfer (MT), registered jack (RJ)	2, 4	41, 73
Angled physical contact (APC)	4	74
Ultra-physical contact (UPC)	4	74
RJ11	2	39
RJ45	2	39
F-type connector	2	35
Transceivers/media converters	4	75
Transceiver type	4	78

Exam N10-008 Objectives	Chapter(s)	Page(s)
Small form-factor pluggable (SFP)	4	78
Enhanced form-factor pluggable (SFP+)	4	78
Quad small form-factor pluggable (QSFP)	4	80
Enhanced quad small form-factor pluggable (QSFP+)	4	80
Cable management	5	102
Patch panel/patch bay	5	93, 96
Fiber distribution panel	5	99
Punchdown block	5	93
66	5	94
110	5	93
Krone	5	95
Bix	5	95
Ethernet standards	3, 4	52, 69
Copper	3, 4	55, 77
10BASE-T	3	52
100BASE-TX	4	69
1000BASE-T	4	72
10GBASE-T	4	77
40GBASE-T	4	80
Fiber	4, 13	70, 354
100BASE-FX	4	70
100BASE-SX	4	71
1000BASE-SX	4	73
1000BASE-LX	4	73
10GBASE-SR	4	76
10GBASE-LR	4	76
Coarse wavelength division multiplexing (CWDM)	13	354
Dense wavelength division multiplexing (DWDM)	13	354
Bidirectional wavelength division multiplexing (WDM)	13	354
1.4 Given a scenario, configure a subnet and use appropriate IP addressing schemes.		
Public vs. private	6, 7	166, 185
RFC1918	6	166
Network address translation (NAT)	7	181
Port address translation (PAT)	7	182
IPv4 vs. IPv6	6, 12	130, 336
Automatic Private IP Addressing (APIPA)	6	163
Extended unique identifier (EUI-64)	12	336
Multicast	6	146
Unicast	6	146
Anycast	6, 12	146, 338
Broadcast	6	146
Link local	12	336
Loopback	6	166
Default gateway	6	141

Exam N10-008 Objectives		Chapter(s)	Page(s)
IPv4 subnetting		6	147
Classless (variable-length subnet mask)		6	151
Classful		6	146
A		6	146
B		6	146
C		6	146
D		6	146
E		6	146
Classless Inter-Domain Routing (CIDR) notation		6	145
IPv6 concepts		12	333
Tunneling		12	346
Dual stack		12	345
Shorthand notation		12	334
Router advertisement		12	339
Stateless address autoconfiguration (SLAAC)		12	340
Virtual IP (VIP)		16	470
Subinterfaces		11	314
1.5 Explain common ports and protocols, their application, and encrypted alternatives.			
Protocols	**Ports**		
File Transfer Protocol (FTP)	20/21	8	230
Secure Shell (SSH)	22	8, 10	225, 291
Secure File Transfer Protocol (SFTP)	22	10	297
Telnet	23	8	224
Simple Mail Transfer Protocol (SMTP)	25	8	225
Domain Name System (DNS)	53	8, 9	214, 243
Dynamic Host Configuration Protocol (DHCP)	67/68	8	215
Trivial File Transfer Protocol (TFTP)	69	8	215
Hypertext Transfer Protocol (HTTP)	80	8	232
Post Office Protocol v3 (POP3)	110	8	225
Network Time Protocol (NTP)	123	8	215
Internet Message Access Protocol (IMAP)	143	8	225
Simple Network Management Protocol (SNMP)	161/162	10, 20	298, 577
Lightweight Directory Access Protocol (LDAP)	389	10	299
Hypertext Transfer Protocol Secure (HTTPS) [Secure Sockets Layer (SSL)]	443	8	233
HTTPS [Transport Layer Security (TLS)]	443	8	233
Server Message Block (SMB)	445	9	244
Syslog	514	20	586
SMTP TLS	587	10	297
Lightweight Directory Access Protocol (over SSL) (LDAPS)	636	10	299
IMAP over SSL	993	10	297
POP3 over SSL	995	10	297
Structured Query Language (SQL) Server	1433	8	229
SQLnet	1521	8	230

Exam N10-008 Objectives		Chapter(s)	Page(s)
MySQL	3306	8	230
Remote Desktop Protocol (RDP)	3389	13	365
Session Initiation Protocol (SIP)	5060/5061	17	490
IP protocol types		8, 10, 13	214, 299, 371
Internet Control Message Protocol (ICMP)		8	216
TCP		8	214
UDP		8	214
Generic Routing Encapsulation (GRE)		13	371
Internet Protocol Security (IPSec)		10	295
Authentication Header (AH)/Encapsulating Security Payload (ESP)		10	295
Connectionless vs. connection-oriented		6, 8	131, 215
1.6 Explain the use and purpose of network services.			
DHCP		6, 11	156, 315
Scope		6	159
Exclusion ranges		6	161
Reservation		6	160
Dynamic assignment		6	154
Static assignment		6	154
Lease time		6	158
Scope options		6	159
Available leases		6	158
DHCP relay		6, 11	160, 315
IP helper/UDP forwarding		6, 11	160, 315
DNS		9	243
Record types		9	256
Address (A)		9	257
Canonical name (CNAME)		9	258
Mail exchange (MX)		9	258
Authentication, authorization, accounting, auditing (AAAA)		9	257
Start of authority (SOA)		9	256
Pointer (PTR)		9	258
Text (TXT)		9	259
Service (SRV)		9	259
Name server (NS)		9	256
Global hierarchy		9	246
Root DNS servers		9	246
Internal vs. external		9	253
Zone transfers		9	249
Authoritative name servers		9	249
Time to live (TTL)		9	255
DNS caching		9	255
Reverse DNS/reverse lookup/forward lookup		9	250
Recursive lookup/iterative lookup		9	253

Exam N10-008 Objectives	Chapter(s)	Page(s)
NTP	8	215
Stratum	8	215
Clients	8	215
Servers	8	215
1.7 Explain basic corporate and datacenter network architecture.		
Three-tiered	16	464
Core	16	465
Distribution/aggregation layer	16	465
Access/edge	16	464
Software-defined networking	15	443
Application layer	15	444
Control layer	15	444
Infrastructure layer	15	444
Management plane	15	444
Spine and leaf	16	469
Software-defined network	16	469
Top-of-rack switching	16	464
Backbone	16	469
Traffic flows	16	465
North-South	16	465
East-West	16	465
Branch office vs. on-premises datacenter vs. colocation	16	468
Storage area networks	16	466
Connection types	16	467
Fibre Channel over Ethernet (FCoE)	16	467
Fibre Channel	16	467
Internet Small Computer Systems Interface (iSCSI)	16	467
1.8 Summarize cloud concepts and connectivity options.		
Deployment models	15	436
Public	15	436
Private	15	436
Hybrid	15	436
Community	15	436
Service models	15	433
Software as a service (SaaS)	15	435
Infrastructure as a service (IaaS)	15	433
Platform as a service (PaaS)	15	434
Desktop as a service (DaaS)	15	452
Infrastructure as code	15	437
Automation/orchestration	15	438
Connectivity options	15	454
Virtual private network (VPN)	15	454
Private-direct connection to cloud provider	15	455
Multitenancy	15	449

Exam N10-008 Objectives	Chapter(s)	Page(s)
Elasticity	15	448
Scalability	15	448
Security implications	15, 19	448, 563
2.0 Network Implementations		
2.1 Compare and contrast various devices, their features, and their appropriate placement on the network.		
Networking devices		
Layer 2 switch	11	316
Layer 3 capable switch	7, 11	174, 316
Router	1, 7, 11	15, 173, 316
Hub	1, 3	9, 52
Access point	14	382
Bridge	3, 14	58, 412
Wireless LAN controller	14	399
Load balancer	11	317
Proxy server	11	323
Cable modem	13	360
DSL modem	13	359
Repeater	3	52
Voice gateway	17	490
Media converter	3	56
Intrusion prevention system (IPS)/intrusion detection system (IDS) device	11	321
Firewall	11, 19	321, 563
VPN headend	13	370
Networked devices		
Voice over Internet Protocol (VoIP) phone	17	489
Printer	17	484
Physical access control devices	17	487
Cameras	17	487
Heating, ventilation, and air conditioning (HVAC) sensors	16	471
Internet of Things (IoT)	17	485
Refrigerator	17	486
Smart speakers	17	486
Smart thermostats	17	486
Smart doorbells	17	487
Industrial control systems/supervisory control and data acquisition (SCADA)	17	496
2.2 Compare and contrast routing technologies and bandwidth management concepts.		
Routing	7	172
Dynamic routing	7	186
Protocols [Routing Internet Protocol (RIP), Open Shortest Path First (OSPF), Enhanced Interior Gateway Routing Protocol (EIGRP), Border Gateway Protocol (BGP)]	7	190–195
Link state vs. distance vector vs. hybrid	7	195
Static routing	7	186
Default route	7	177
Administrative distance	7	195

Exam N10-008 Objectives	Chapter(s)	Page(s)
Exterior vs. interior	7	172
Time to live	7	205
Bandwidth management		
Traffic shaping	11	320
Quality of service (QoS)	11, 17	319, 491
2.3 Given a scenario, configure and deploy common Ethernet switching features.		
Data virtual local area network (VLAN)	11	310
Voice VLAN	11	315
Port configurations		
Port tagging/802.1Q	11	312
Port aggregation	11	320
Link Aggregation Control Protocol (LACP)	11	320
Duplex	11	308
Speed	11	308
Flow control	11	309
Port mirroring	11	323
Port security	11	309
Jumbo frames	11, 16	309, 467
Auto-medium-dependent interface crossover (MDI-X)	3	61
Media access control (MAC) address tables	3	59
Power over Ethernet (PoE)/Power over Ethernet plus (PoE+)	14	399
Spanning Tree Protocol	3, 21	61, 624
Carrier-sense multiple access with collision detection (CSMA/CD)	3	56
Address Resolution Protocol (ARP)	6, 19	134, 535
Neighbor Discovery Protocol	12	338
2.4 Given a scenario, install and configure the appropriate wireless standards and technologies.		
802.11 standards	14	381
a	14	388
b	14	388
g	14	389
n (WiFi 4)	14	389
ac (WiFi 5)	14	390
ax (WiFi 6)	14	390
Frequencies and range		
2.4GHz	14	386
5GHz	14	387
Channels		
Regulatory impacts	14	387
Channel bonding	14	389
Service set identifier (SSID)	14	385
Basic service set	14	385
Extended service set	14	385
Independent basic service set (Ad-hoc)	14	384
Roaming	14	386

Exam N10-008 Objectives	Chapter(s)	Page(s)
Antenna types		
Omni	14	404
Directional	14	406
Encryption standards		
WiFi Protected Access (WPA)/WPA2 Personal [Advanced Encryption Standard (AES)/ Temporal Key Integrity Protocol (TKIP)]	14	392
WPA/WPA2 Enterprise (AES/TKIP)	14	394
Cellular technologies		
Code-division multiple access (CDMA)	13	363
Global System for Mobile Communications (GSM)	13	362
Long-Term Evolution (LTE)	13	363
3G, 4G, 5G	13	363, 364
Multiple input, multiple output (MIMO) and multi-user MIMO (MU-MIMO)	14	389, 390
3.0 Network Operations		
3.1 Given a scenario, use the appropriate statistics and sensors to ensure network availability.		
Performance metrics/sensors	20	583
Device/chassis	20	583
Temperature	20	584
Central processing (CPU) usage	20	584
Memory	20	584
Network metrics	14, 20	415, 584
Bandwidth	14, 20	415, 584
Latency	14	415
Jitter	14	415
SNMP	20	577
Traps	20	578
Object identifiers (OIDs)	20	578
Management information bases (MIBs)	20	578
Network device logs	20	586
Log reviews	20	590
Traffic logs	20	590
Audit logs	20	590
Syslog	20	586
Logging levels/severity levels	20	590
Interface statistics/status	20	585
Link state (up/down)	20	585
Speed/duplex	20	585
Send/receive traffic	20	585
Cyclic redundancy checks (CRCs)	20	585
Protocol packet and byte counts	20	585
Interface errors or alerts	20	585
CRC errors	20	585
Giants	20	585

Exam N10-008 Objectives	Chapter(s)	Page(s)
Runts	20	585
Encapsulation errors	20	585
Environmental factors and sensors	20	583
Temperature	20	584
Humidity	20	584
Electrical	20	584
Flooding	20	584
Baselines	20	586
NetFlow data	20	582
Uptime/downtime	20	585
3.2 Explain the purpose of organizational documents and policies.		
Plans and procedures		
Change management	18	507
Incident response plan	18	507
Disaster recovery plan	18	518
Business continuity plan	18	519
System life cycle	19	542
Standard operating procedures	18	509
Hardening and security policies	18	503
Password policy	18	504
Acceptable use policy	18	503
Bring your own device (BYOD) policy	18	505
Remote access policy	18	504
Onboarding and offboarding policy	18	506
Security policy	18	503
Data loss prevention	18	504
Common documentation		
Physical network diagram	16	473
Floor plan	5, 16	100, 473
Rack diagram	16	474
Intermediate distribution frame (IDF)/main distribution frame (MDF) documentation	16	474
Logical network diagram	16	475
Wiring diagram	16	476
Site survey report	16	476
Audit and assessment report	16	477
Baseline configurations	16	476
Common agreements		
Non-disclosure agreement (NDA)	18	512
Service-level agreement (SLA)	18	511
Memorandum of understanding (MOU)	18	512
3.3 Explain high availability and disaster recovery concepts and summarize which is the best solution.		
Load balancing	16	470
Multipathing	16	467
Network interface card (NIC) teaming	11	320

Exam N10-008 Objectives	Chapter(s)	Page(s)
Redundant hardware/clusters	16	470
Switches	16	470
Routers	16	470
Firewalls	16	470
Facilities and infrastructure support	5, 16	119, 471
Uninterruptible power supply (UPS)	5, 16	119, 471
Power distribution units (PDUs)	5, 16	92, 471
Generator	5, 16	120, 471
HVAC	16	471
Fire suppression	16	472
Redundancy and high availability (HA) concepts	16, 18	469, 519
Cold site	18	519
Warm site	18	519
Hot site	18	520
Cloud site	18	520
Active-active vs. active-passive	16	470
Multiple Internet service providers (ISPs)/diverse paths	16	470
Virtual Router Redundancy Protocol (VRRP)/First Hop Redundancy Protocol (FHRP)	16	470
Mean time to repair (MTTR)	18	519
Mean time between failure (MTBF)	18	519
Recovery time objective (RTO)	18	518
Recovery point objective (RPO)	18	518
Network device backup/restore	18	518
State	18	518
Configuration	18	518
4.0 Network Security		
4.1 Explain common security concepts.		
Confidentiality, integrity, availability (CIA)	19	529
Threats	19	531
Internal	19	541
External	19	541
Vulnerabilities	19	532
Common vulnerabilities and exposures (CVE)	19	532
Zero-day	19	534
Exploits	19	532
Least privilege	18	504
Role-based access	18	504
Zero Trust	19	530
Defense in depth	19	530
Network segmentation enforcement	19	558
Screened subnet [previously known as demilitarized zone (DMZ)]	19	566
Separation of duties	19	531

Exam N10-008 Objectives	Chapter(s)	Page(s)
Network access control	10, 19	284, 557
Honeypot	19	567
Authentication methods	10	284
Multifactor	10	284
Terminal Access Controller Access-Control System Plus (TACACS+)	10	290
Single sign-on (SSO)	10	291
Remote Authentication Dial-in User Service (RADIUS)	10	289
LDAP	10	299
Kerberos	10	290
Local authentication	10	284
802.1X	14	394
Extensible Authentication Protocol (EAP)	14	392
Risk Management		
Security risk assessments	18	513
Threat assessment	18	513
Vulnerability assessment	18	513
Penetration testing	18	515
Posture assessment	18	516
Business risk assessments	18	516
Process assessment	18	516
Vendor assessment	18	517
Security information and event management (SIEM)	20	591
4.2 Compare and contrast common types of attacks.		
Technology-based		
Denial-of-service (DoS)/distributed denial-of-service (DDoS)	19	538
Botnet/command and control	19	538
On-path attack (previously known as man-in-the-middle attack)	19	539
DNS poisoning	19	533
VLAN hopping	19	542
ARP spoofing	19	532
Rogue DHCP	6, 19	165, 534
Rogue access point (AP)	14	418
Evil twin	14	418
Ransomware	19	543
Password attacks	19	540
Brute-force	19	540
Dictionary	19	540
MAC spoofing	19	532
IP spoofing	19	532
Deauthentication	19	539
Malware	19	543
Human and environmental		
Social engineering	19	545

Exam N10-008 Objectives	Chapter(s)	Page(s)
Phishing	19	545
Tailgating	19	550
Piggybacking	19	550
Shoulder surfing	19	545
4.3 Given a scenario, apply network hardening techniques.		
Best practices		
Secure SNMP	20	579
Router Advertisement (RA) Guard	19	534
Port security	19	560
Dynamic ARP inspection	19	537
Control plane policing	19	560
Private VLANs	11	316
Disable unneeded switchports	19	560
Disable unneeded network services	19	547
Change default passwords	19	559
Password complexity/length	18	511
Enable DHCP snooping	19	537
Change default VLAN	11	310
Patch and firmware management	18, 19	509, 548
Access control list	10, 14, 19	284, 396, 542
Role-based access	10, 18	285, 504
Firewall rules	19	563
Explicit deny	19	565
Implicit deny	19	565
Wireless security	14	391
MAC filtering	14	396
Antenna placement	14	405
Power levels	14	397
Wireless client isolation	14	397
Guest network isolation	14	397
Preshared keys (PSKs)	14	409
EAP	14	392
Geofencing	14	397
Captive portal	14	416
IoT access considerations	17	489
4.4 Compare and contrast remote access methods and security implications.		
Site-to-site VPN	13	370
Client-to-site VPN	13	370
Clientless VPN	13	370
Split tunnel vs. full tunnel	13	370
Remote desktop connection	13	365
Remote desktop gateway	13	365
SSH	8, 10, 13	225, 291, 367

Exam N10-008 Objectives	Chapter(s)	Page(s)
Virtual network computing (VNC)	13	366
Virtual desktop	15	452
Authentication and authorization considerations	13	365
In-band vs. out-of-band management	11	308
4.5 Explain the importance of physical security.		
Detection methods	19	549
Camera	19	553
Motion detection	19	553
Asset tags	19	551
Tamper detection	19	550
Prevention methods	19	549
Employee training	18	511
Access control hardware	19	550
Badge readers	19	551
Biometrics	19	552
Locking racks	5	93
Locking cabinets	5	93
Access control vestibule (previously known as a mantrap)	19	550
Smart lockers	19	552
Asset disposal	19	542
Factory reset/wipe configuration	19	543
Sanitize devices for disposal	19	543
5.0 Network Troubleshooting		
5.1 Explain the network troubleshooting methodology.		
Identify the problem	21	610
Gather information	21	611
Question users	21	611
Identify symptoms	21	611
Determine if anything has changed	21	611
Duplicate the problem, if possible	21	611
Approach multiple problems individually	21	612
Establish a theory of probable cause	21	612
Question the obvious	21	612
Consider multiple approaches	21	612
Top-to-bottom/bottom-to-top OSI model	21	613
Divide and conquer	21	613
Test the theory to determine the cause	21	613
If the theory is confirmed, determine the next steps to resolve the problem	21	614
If the theory is not confirmed, reestablish a new theory or escalate	21	613
Establish a plan of action to resolve the problem and identify potential effects	21	614
Implement the solution or escalate as necessary	21	614
Verify full system functionality and, if applicable, implement preventive measures	21	615
Document findings, actions, outcomes, and lessons learned	21	615

Exam N10-008 Objectives	Chapter(s)	Page(s)
5.2 Given a scenario, troubleshoot common cable connectivity issues and select the appropriate tools.		
Specifications and limitations	20	590
Throughput	20	590
Speed	20	590
Distance	20	590
Cable considerations		
Shielded and unshielded	2	37
Plenum and riser-rated	2	41
Cable application		
Rollover cable/console cable	7	196
Crossover cable	3	61
Power over Ethernet	14	399
Common issues		
Attenuation	5	111
Interference	5	108
Decibel (dB) loss	5	111
Incorrect pinout	5	108
Bad ports	5	118
Open/short	5	108
Light-emitting diode (LED) status indicators	21	619
Incorrect transceivers	5	112
Duplexing issues	21	625
Transmit and receive (TX/RX) reversed	5	93
Dirty optical cables	5	112
Common tools		
Cable crimper	21	599
Punchdown tool	21	599
Tone generator	21	599
Loopback adapter	21	598
Optical time-domain reflectometer (OTDR)	21	598
Multimeter	21	599
Cable tester	21	598
Wire map	5	109
Tap	11	323
Fusion splicers	5	113
Spectrum analyzers	14	416
Snips/cutters	5, 21	104, 599
Cable stripper	5, 21	104, 599
Fiber light meter	21	598
5.3 Given a scenario, use the appropriate network software tools and commands.		
Software tools		
WiFi analyzer	14	400
Protocol analyzer/packet capture	20, 21	580, 607

Exam N10-008 Objectives	Chapter(s)	Page(s)
Bandwidth speed tester	21	608
Port scanner	21	608
iperf	20	590
NetFlow analyzers	20	583
Trivial File Transfer Protocol (TFTP) server	8	215
Terminal emulator	21	600
IP scanner	21	608
Command line tool		
ping	21	603
ipconfig/ifconfig/ip	21	601
nslookup/dig	21	604
traceroute/tracert	21	601
arp	21	602
netstat	21	606
hostname	21	600
route	21	605
telnet	8	224
tcpdump	21	608
nmap	21	608
Basic network platform commands	21	618
show interface	11, 21	308, 618
show config	21	618
show route	21	618
5.4 Given a scenario, troubleshoot common wireless connectivity issues.		
Specifications and limitations		
Throughput	14	388
Speed	14	388
Distance	14	388
Received signal strength indication (RSSI) signal strength	14	413
Effective isotropic radiated power (EIRP)/power settings	14	414
Considerations		
Antennas	14	404
Placement	14	404
Type	14	404–406
Polarization	14	406
Channel utilization	14	413
AP association time	14	419
Site survey	14	400
Common issues		
Interference	14	416
Channel overlap	14	412
Antenna cable attenuation/signal loss	14	415
RF attenuation/signal loss	14	415

Exam N10-008 Objectives	Chapter(s)	Page(s)
Wrong SSID	14	418
Incorrect passphrase	14	413
Encryption protocol mismatch	14	413
Insufficient wireless coverage	14	413
Captive portal issues	14	416
Client disassociation issues	14	419
5.5 Given a scenario, troubleshoot general networking issues.		
Considerations		
Device configuration review	21	618
Routing tables	21	618
Interface status	21	618
VLAN assignment	21	618
Network performance baselines	21	618
Common issues		
Collisions	21	625
Broadcast storm	21	624
Duplicate MAC address	21	621
Duplicate IP address	21	621
Multicast flooding	21	625
Asymmetrical routing	21	628
Switching loops	21	624
Routing loops	21	628
Rogue DHCP server	6	165
DHCP scope exhaustion	21	621
IP setting issues	21	620
Incorrect gateway	21	620
Incorrect subnet mask	21	620
Incorrect IP address	21	620
Incorrect DNS	21	620
Missing route	21	627
Low optical link budget	21	626
Certificate issues	21	629
Hardware failure	21	619
Host-based/network-based firewall settings	19, 21	568, 617, 629
Blocked services, ports, or addresses	19	547
Incorrect VLAN	21	623
DNS issues	21	604
NTP issues	21	625
BYOD challenges	18	505
Licensed feature issues	21	626
Network performance issues	21	629

Create Your Study Plan

Congratulations on completing the Network+ Pre-Assessment test on the Total Seminars Training Hub! You should now take the time to analyze your results with these two objectives in mind:

- Identifying the resources you should use to prepare for the CompTIA Network+ exam
- Identifying the specific topics you should focus on in your preparation

Review Your Overall Score

Use the following table to help you gauge your overall readiness for the CompTIA Network+ exam based on the number of questions you answered correctly on the Network+ Pre-Assessment test.

Number of Answers Correct	Recommended Course of Study
0–26	Spend a significant amount of time reviewing the corresponding chapters from this book to make sure you understand the topics completely.
27–39	Review your scores in the specific exam domains shown in the next table to identify the particular areas that require your focused attention, and then use this book to review that material.
40–50	Use this book to refresh your knowledge and prepare yourself mentally for the actual exam.

Review Your Score by CompTIA Network+ Exam Domain

Domain	Weight	Number of Questions in Pre-Assessment Test	Priority for Additional Study		
			High	Medium	Low
1.0 Networking Fundamentals	24%	12	0–6 correct	7–9 correct	10–12 correct
2.0 Network Implementations	19%	9	0–5 correct	6–7 correct	8–9 correct
3.0 Network Operations	16%	8	0–4 correct	5–6 correct	7–8 correct
4.0 Network Security	19%	10	0–5 correct	6–8 correct	9–10 correct
5.0 Network Troubleshooting	22%	11	0–6 correct	7–9 correct	10–11 correct

Appendix C: About the Online Content

This book comes complete with

- TotalTester Online customizable practice exam software with more than 100 practice exam questions and a pre-assessment test
- The Appendix B "Create Your Study Plan" in PDF format for online reference after taking the pre-assessment
- A video introduction to the N10-008 CompTIA Network+ certification
- More than an hour of sample video training episodes from Mike Meyers' CompTIA Network+ Certification video series
- More than 20 sample simulations from Total Seminars' TotalSims for Network+
- Links to a collection of Mike Meyers' favorite tools and utilities for network troubleshooting
- Link to files for Chapter 15 labs
- The Glossary in PDF format for online reference

System Requirements

The current and previous major versions of the following desktop browsers are recommended and supported: Chrome, Microsoft Edge, Firefox, and Safari. These browsers update frequently, and sometimes an update may cause compatibility issues with the TotalTester Online or other content hosted on the Training Hub. If you run into a problem using one of these browsers, please try using another until the problem is resolved.

Your Total Seminars Training Hub Account

To get access to the online content you will need to create an account on the Total Seminars Training Hub. Registration is free, and you will be able to track all your online content using your account. You may also opt in if you wish to receive marketing information from McGraw Hill or Total Seminars, but this is not required for you to gain access to the online content.

Privacy Notice

McGraw Hill values your privacy. Please be sure to read the Privacy Notice available during registration to see how the information you have provided will be used. You may view our Corporate Customer Privacy Policy by visiting the McGraw Hill Privacy Center. Visit the **mheducation.com** site and click **Privacy** at the bottom of the page.

Single User License Terms and Conditions

Online access to the digital content included with this book is governed by the McGraw Hill License Agreement outlined next. By using this digital content you agree to the terms of that license.

Access To register and activate your Total Seminars Training Hub account, simply follow these easy steps.

1. Go to this URL: **hub.totalsem.com/mheclaim**
2. To register and create a new Training Hub account, enter your e-mail address, name, and password on the **Register** tab. No further personal information (such as credit card number) is required to create an account.

   If you already have a Total Seminars Training Hub account, enter your e-mail address and password on the **Log in** tab.
3. Enter your Product Key: `3sng-jnxw-sbjc`
4. Click to accept the user license terms.
5. For new users, click the **Register and Claim** button to create your account. For existing users, click the **Log in and Claim** button.

   You will be taken to the Training Hub and have access to the content for this book.

Duration of License Access to your online content through the Total Seminars Training Hub will expire one year from the date the publisher declares the book out of print.

Your purchase of this McGraw Hill product, including its access code, through a retail store is subject to the refund policy of that store.

The Content is a copyrighted work of McGraw Hill, and McGraw Hill reserves all rights in and to the Content. The Work is © 2022 by McGraw Hill.

Restrictions on Transfer The user is receiving only a limited right to use the Content for the user's own internal and personal use, dependent on purchase and continued ownership of this book. The user may not reproduce, forward, modify, create derivative works based upon, transmit, distribute, disseminate, sell, publish, or sublicense the Content or in any way commingle the Content with other third-party content without McGraw Hill's consent.

Limited Warranty The McGraw Hill Content is provided on an "as is" basis. Neither McGraw Hill nor its licensors make any guarantees or warranties of any kind, either express or implied, including, but not limited to, implied warranties of merchantability or fitness for a particular purpose or use as to any McGraw Hill Content or the information therein or any warranties as to the accuracy, completeness, correctness, or results to be obtained from, accessing or using the McGraw Hill Content, or any material referenced in such Content or any information entered into licensee's product by users or other persons and/or any material available on or that can be accessed through the licensee's product (including via any hyperlink or otherwise) or as to non-infringement of third-party rights. Any warranties of any kind, whether express or implied, are disclaimed. Any material or data obtained through use of the McGraw Hill Content is at your own discretion and risk and user understands that it will be solely responsible for any resulting damage to its computer system or loss of data.

Neither McGraw Hill nor its licensors shall be liable to any subscriber or to any user or anyone else for any inaccuracy, delay, interruption in service, error or omission, regardless of cause, or for any damage resulting therefrom.

In no event will McGraw Hill or its licensors be liable for any indirect, special or consequential damages, including but not limited to, lost time, lost money, lost profits or good will, whether in contract, tort, strict liability or otherwise, and whether or not such damages are foreseen or unforeseen with respect to any use of the McGraw Hill Content.

TotalTester Online

TotalTester Online provides you with a simulation of the CompTIA Network+ exam. Exams can be taken in Practice Mode or Exam Mode. Practice Mode provides an assistance window with hints, references to the book, explanations of the correct and incorrect answers, and the option to check your answer as you take the test. Exam Mode provides a simulation of the actual exam. The number of questions, the types of questions, and the time allowed are intended to be an accurate representation of the exam environment. The option to customize your quiz allows you to create custom exams from selected domains or chapters, and you can further customize the number of questions and time allowed.

To take a test, follow the instructions provided in the previous section to register and activate your Total Seminars Training Hub account. When you register, you will be taken to the Total Seminars Training Hub. From the Training Hub Home page, select your certification from the Study drop-down menu at the top of the page to drill down to the TotalTester for your book. You can also scroll to it from the list of Your Topics on the Home page, and then click the TotalTester link to launch the TotalTester. Once you've launched your TotalTester, you can select the option to customize your quiz and begin testing yourself in Practice Mode or Exam Mode. All exams provide an overall grade and a grade broken down by domain.

Pre-Assessment

In addition to the sample exam questions, the TotalTester also includes the CompTIA Network+ Pre-Assessment test to help you assess your understanding of the topics before reading the book. To launch the pre-assessment test, click **Network+ Pre-Assessment**. The Network+ Pre-Assessment test is 50 questions and runs in Exam Mode. When you complete the test, you can review the questions with answers and detailed explanation by clicking **See Detailed Results**.

Create Your Study Plan

Once you've completed the pre-assessment test, you can refer to Appendix B, "Create Your Study Plan," to get a recommended study plan based on your results. The appendix can be found at the back of the book or you can access it online under **Meyers' Network+ Guide to M&T Networks 6e (N10-008) Resources**.

Playing the CompTIA Network+ Introduction Video

You can watch the video introduction to the CompTIA Network+ exam online. Select **Meyers' Network+ Guide to M&T Networks 6e (N10-008) Resources** from the list of "Your Topics" on the Home page. Click the Resources tab, and then select the **Network+ Intro** button.

Mike's CompTIA Network+ Video Training Sample

Over an hour of training videos, starring Mike Meyers, are available for free. Select **Meyers' Network+ Guide to M&T Networks 6e (N10-008) Resources** from the list of "Your Topics" on the Home page. Click the TotalVideos tab. Along with access to the videos, you'll find an option to purchase Mike's complete video training series.

TotalSims Sample for CompTIA Network+

From your Total Seminars Training Hub account, select **Meyers' Network+ Guide to M&T Networks 6e (N10-008) Resources** from the list of "Your Topics" on the Home page. Click the TotalSims tab. The simulations are organized by chapter, and there are over 20 free simulations available for reviewing topics referenced in the book, with an option to purchase access to the full TotalSims for Network+ (N10-008) with over 120 simulations.

Mike's Cool Tools

Mike loves freeware/open source networking tools! Access the utilities mentioned in the text by selecting **Meyers' Network+ Guide to M&T Networks 6e (N10-008) Resources** from the list of "Your Topics" on the Home page. Click the Resources tab, and then select **Mike's Cool Tools**.

Technical Support

For questions regarding the TotalTester or operation of the Training Hub, visit **www.totalsem.com** or e-mail **support@totalsem.com**.

For questions regarding book content, visit **www.mheducation.com/customerservice**.

3G Third-generation wireless data technologies for cell phones and other mobile devices. 3G matured over time until Evolved High-Speed Packet Access (HSPA+) became the final wireless 3G data standard. It transferred at theoretical maximum speeds up to 168 megabits per second (Mbps), although real-world implementations rarely passed 10 Mbps.

4G Fourth-generation wireless data technologies for cell phones and other mobile devices. Most popularly implemented as Long Term Evolution (LTE), a wireless data standard with theoretical download speeds of 300 Mbps and upload speeds of 75 Mbps.

4to6 Internet connectivity technology that encapsulates IPv4 traffic into an IPv6 tunnel to get to an IPv6-capable router.

5G Fifth-generation wireless data technologies for cell phones and other mobile devices. Cellular carriers started rolling out 5G in 2019. Depending on the frequency bands used and the 5G modems in the devices, the speed ranges from 30 Mbps to well over 1 Gbps.

6in4 An IPv6 tunneling standard that can go through IPv4 network address translation (NAT).

6to4 An IPv6 tunneling protocol that doesn't require a tunnel broker. It is generally used to directly connect two routers because it normally requires a public IPv4 address.

8 position 8 contact (8P8C) Four-pair connector used on the end of network cable. Often erroneously referred to as an RJ-45 connector.

10 Gigabit Ethernet (10 GbE) A very fast Ethernet designation that runs at 10 Gbps, with a number of fiber-optic and copper standards.

10BASE-FL Fiber-optic implementation of Ethernet that runs at 10 Mbps using baseband signaling. Maximum segment length is 2 km.

10BASE-T An Ethernet LAN designed to run on UTP cabling. Runs at 10 Mbps and uses baseband signaling. Maximum length for the cabling between the NIC and the hub (or the switch, the repeater, and so forth) is 100 m.

10GBASE-ER/10GBASE-EW A 10 GbE standard using 1550-nm single-mode fiber. Maximum cable length up to 40 km.

10GBASE-LR/10GBASE-LW A 10 GbE standard using 1310-nm single-mode fiber. Maximum cable length up to 10 km.

10GBASE-SR/10GBASE-SW A 10 GbE standard using 850-nm multimode fiber. Maximum cable length up to 300 m.

10GBASE-T A 10 GbE standard designed to run on Cat 6a UTP cabling. Maximum cable length of 100 m.

40GBASE-T A 40 GbE standard designed to run on Cat 8 UTP cabling. Maximum cable length of 30 m.

40 Gigabit Ethernet (40 GbE) Ethernet designation that runs at 40 Gbps, primarily used in switch-to-switch trunks and data center servers. 40 GbE can use either single-mode fiber or OM3 (or greater) multimode fiber. Transceivers use the *quad small form-factor pluggable plus (QSFP+)* port.

66 block Patch panel used in telephone networks; displaced by 110 blocks in networking.

100BASE-FX An Ethernet LAN designed to run on fiber-optic cabling. Runs at 100 Mbps and uses baseband signaling. Maximum cable length is 400 m for half-duplex and 2 km for full-duplex.

100BASE-T An Ethernet LAN designed to run on UTP cabling. Runs at 100 Mbps, uses baseband signaling, and uses two pairs of wires on Cat 5 or better cabling.

100BASE-TX The technically accurate but little-used name for 100BASE-T.

100 Gigabit Ethernet (100 GbE) Ethernet designation that runs at 100 Gbps, primarily implemented in backbones and machine-to-machine connections. Employs both MMF and SMF with various connectors. A typical connector, the QSFP28, has four 25 Gb channels.

110 block A connection gridwork used to link UTP and STP cables behind an RJ-45 jack or patch panel. Also known as a *110-punchdown block*.

110-punchdown block *See* 110 block.

110-punchdown tool *See* punchdown tool.

802 committee The IEEE committee responsible for all Ethernet standards.

802.1Q IEEE trunk standard that enables switches from different manufacturers to transfer VLAN traffic to each other.

802.1X A port-authentication network access control mechanism for networks.

802.3 (Ethernet) *See* Ethernet.

802.3ab The IEEE standard for 1000BASE-T.

802.3z The umbrella IEEE standard for all versions of Gigabit Ethernet other than 1000BASE-T.

802.11 *See* IEEE 802.11.

802.11a A wireless standard that operates in the frequency range of 5 GHz and offers throughput of up to 54 Mbps.

802.11ac A wireless standard that operates in the frequency range of 5 GHz and offers throughput of up to 1 Gbps. 802.11ac is marketed as *Wi-Fi 5*.

802.11a-ht Along with the corresponding 802.11g-ht standard, technical terms for mixed mode 802.11a/802.11g operation. In mixed mode, both technologies are simultaneously supported.

802.11ax Wireless standard that brings improvements in high-density areas such as stadiums and conferences in comparison to previous standards. Marketed as both *Wi-Fi 6* and *Wi-Fi 6E*. Wi-Fi 6 operates at the 2.4-GHz and 5-GHz bands, while Wi-Fi 6E operates at the 6-GHz band. 802.11ax offers a maximum throughput of up to 10 Gbps.

802.11b The first popular wireless standard, operates in the frequency range of 2.4 GHz and offers throughput of up to 11 Mbps.

802.11g Older wireless standard that operates on the 2.4-GHz band with a maximum throughput of 54 Mbps. Superseded by 802.11n.

802.11g-ht Along with the corresponding 802.11a-ht standard, technical terms for mixed mode 802.11a/802.11g operation. In mixed mode, both technologies are simultaneously supported.

802.11i A wireless security standard branded as WPA2. *See* Wi-Fi Protected Access 2 (WPA2).

802.11n An 802.11 standard (marketed as *Wi-Fi 4*) that increases transfer speeds and adds support for multiple input/multiple output (MIMO) by using multiple antennas. 802.11n can operate on either the 2.4- or 5-GHz frequency band and has a maximum throughput of 400 Mbps. Superseded by 802.11ac, but used with many IoT devices.

1000BASE-LX A Gigabit Ethernet standard using single-mode fiber cabling, with a 5-km maximum cable distance.

1000BASE-SX A Gigabit Ethernet standard using multimode fiber cabling, with a 220- to 500-m maximum cable distance.

1000BASE-T A Gigabit Ethernet standard using Cat 5e/6 UTP cabling, with a 100-m maximum cable distance.

1000BASE-X An umbrella Gigabit Ethernet standard. Also known as *802.3z*. Comprises all Gigabit standards with the exception of 1000BASE-T, which is under the 802.3ab standard.

A record DNS record that maps hostnames to their IPv4 addresses.

AAA (Authentication, Authorization, and Accounting) *See* Authentication, Authorization, and Accounting (AAA).

AAAA record DNS record that maps hostnames to their IPv6 addresses.

absorption Quality of some building materials (such as brick, sheetrock, and wood) to reduce or eliminate a Wi-Fi signal.

abstraction To remove an aspect of a device or process to treat it as a separate unit. Also, the removed aspect of a device or process.

acceptable use policy (AUP) A document that defines what a person may and may not do on an organization's computers and networks.

access control All-encompassing term that defines the degree of permission granted to use a particular resource. That resource may be anything from a switch port to a particular file to a physical door within a building.

access control list (ACL) A clearly defined list of permissions that specifies what actions an authenticated user may perform on a shared resource.

Access Control Server (ACS) Cisco program/process/server that makes the decision to admit or deny a node based on posture assessment. From there, the ACS directs the edge access device to allow a connection or to implement a denial or redirect.

access control vestibule An entryway with two successive locked doors and a small space between them providing one-way entry or exit. This is a security measure taken to prevent unauthorized entry. Traditionally called a *mantrap*.

access layer One tier of a three-tiered architecture commonly used in data centers. The access layer acts as the primary connection between the data center's connectivity and the servers.

access port Regular port in a switch that has been configured as part of a VLAN. Access ports are ports that hosts connect to. They are the opposite of a trunk port, which is only connected to a trunk port on another switch.

Active Directory A form of directory service used in networks with Windows servers. Creates an organization of related computers that share one or more Windows domains.

activity light An LED on a NIC, hub, or switch that blinks rapidly to show data transfers over the network.

ad hoc mode A wireless networking mode where each node is in direct contact with every other node in a decentralized free-for-all. Ad hoc mode is similar to the mesh topology.

Address Resolution Protocol (ARP) A protocol in the TCP/IP suite used with the command-line utility of the same name to determine the MAC address that corresponds to a particular IP address.

administrative account Specialized user account that has been granted sufficient access rights and authority to manage specified administrative tasks. Some administrative accounts exist as a default of the system and have all authority throughout the system. Others must be explicitly assigned the necessary powers to administer given resources.

administrative distance Feature of multi-protocol routers that enables the router to determine the most reliable route—among its protocols—to the same destination.

ADSL (asymmetric digital subscriber line) *See* asymmetric digital subscriber line (ADSL).

Advanced Encryption Standard (AES) A block cipher created in the late 1990s that uses a 128-bit block size and a 128-, 192-, or 256-bit key size. AES has never been cracked.

adware A program that monitors the types of Web sites you frequent and uses that information to generate targeted advertisements, usually pop-up windows.

agent In terms of posture assessment, refers to software that runs within a client and reports the client's security characteristics to an access control server to be approved or denied entry to a system.

agentless In terms of posture assessment, refers to a client that has its posture checked and presented by non-permanent software, such as a Web app program, that executes as part of the connection process. Agentless software does not run directly within the client but is run on behalf of the client.

aggregation A technique used in IPv4 and IPv6 address space planning to combine subnets, thus reducing the number of entries in routing tables and using IP address space more efficiently.

air gap The act of physically separating a network from every other network.

Aircrack-ng An open source tool for penetration testing many aspects of wireless networks.

alert (SNMP) Proactive message sent from an SNMP manager as a result of a trap issued by an agent. Alerts may be sent as e-mail, SMS message, voicemail, or via other avenues.

algorithm A set of rules for solving a problem in a given number of steps.

allow Permission for data or communication to pass through or to access a resource. Specific allowances through a firewall are called *exceptions*.

American Registry for Internet Numbers (ARIN) A Regional Internet Registry (RIR) that parcels out IP addresses to large ISPs and major corporations in North America.

amplification *See* amplified DoS attack.

amplified DoS attack The type of DoS attack that sends a small amount of traffic to a server, which produces a much larger response from the server that is sent to a spoofed IP address, overwhelming a victim machine.

angled physical contact (APC) Fiber-optic connector that makes physical contact between two fiber-optic cables. It specifies an 8-degree angle to the curved end, lowering signal loss. APC connectors have less connection degradation from multiple insertions compared to other connectors.

Angry IP Scanner Open-source cross-platform GUI port scanner. Can be used as an alternative to Nmap for less demanding scanning tasks.

ANSI/TIA-568 Technical standards published by the Telecommunications Industry Association (TIA) and accredited by the American National Standards Institute (ANSI) for cabling in commercial buildings. Replaced the TIA/EIA-568 standards. Part of the standards include pin and pair assignments in twisted pair networking cable, such as that used in Ethernet networks. *See also* T568A and T568B.

ANSI/TIA-606 Labeling standard/guidelines published by the Telecommunications Industry Association (TIA) and accredited by the American National Standards Institute (ANSI) for cabling in commercial buildings. Replaced the TIA/EIA-606 standard/guidelines.

anti-malware program Software that attempts to block several types of threats to a client, including viruses, Trojan horses, worms, and other unapproved software installation and execution.

antivirus Software that attempts to prevent viruses from installing or executing on a client. Some antivirus software may also attempt to remove the virus or eradicate the effects of a virus after an infection.

anycast A method of addressing groups of computers as though they were a single computer. Anycasting starts by giving a number of computers (or clusters of computers) the same IP address. Advanced routers then send incoming packets to the closest of the computers.

Application layer *See* Open Systems Interconnection (OSI) seven-layer model.

application log Tracks application events, such as when an application opens or closes. Different types of application logs record different events.

Application Programming Interface (API) Shared functions, subroutines, and libraries that allow programs on a machine to communicate with the OS and other programs.

application/context aware Advanced feature of some stateful firewalls where the content of the data is inspected to ensure it comes from, or is destined for, an appropriate application. Context-aware firewalls look both deeply and more broadly to ensure that the data content and other aspects of the packet are appropriate to the data transfer being conducted. Packets that fall outside these awareness criteria are denied by the firewall.

approval process One or more decision makers consider a proposed change and the impact of the change, including funding. If the change, the impact, and the funding are acceptable, the change is permitted.

archive The creation and storage of retrievable copies of electronic data for legal and functional purposes.

archive bit An attribute of a file that shows whether the file has been backed up since the last change. Each time a file is opened, changed, or saved, the archive bit is turned on. Some types of backups turn off the archive bit to indicate that a good backup of the file exists on tape.

Area ID (OSPF) 32-bit numeric identifier assigned to OSPF areas. Can manifest as an integer between 0 and 4,294,967,295, or in a form similar to an IPv4 address (for example, "0.0.0.0"). The Area ID will be 0 in networks with a single area. *See also* areas (OSPF) *and* Open Shortest Path First (OSPF).

areas (OSPF) Within the OSPF routing protocol, areas are administrative groupings of interconnected routers used to control how routers reroute traffic if a link drops. *See also* Area ID (OSPF) *and* Open Shortest Path First (OSPF).

ARP *See* Address Resolution Protocol (ARP).

ARP cache poisoning A man-in-the-middle attack (on-path attack) where the attacker associates his MAC address with someone else's IP address (almost always the router), so all traffic will be sent to him first.

The attacker sends out unsolicited ARPs, which can be either requests or replies.

arping A command used to discover hosts on a network, similar to ping, but that relies on ARP rather than ICMP. The arping command won't cross any routers, so it only works within a broadcast domain. *See also* Address Resolution Protocol (ARP) *and* ping.

assessment report After a data center audit, the auditing company produces this report to detail all findings, upgrade recommendations, and compliance fixes.

asset disposal Reusing, repurposing, or recycling computing devices that follows system life cycle policies in many organizations.

asset management Managing each aspect of a network, from documentation to performance to hardware.

asymmetric digital subscriber line (ADSL) A fully digital, dedicated connection to the telephone system that provides download speeds of up to 9 Mbps and upload speeds of up to 1 Mbps.

asymmetric-key algorithm An encryption method in which the key used to encrypt a message and the key used to decrypt it are different, or asymmetrical.

attenuation The degradation of signal over distance for a networking cable.

audit (data center) An assessment of a data center's compliance with laws, regulations, and standards for information security, such as HIPAA or PCI DSS. An audit should be made by an outside organization that specializes in auditing to avoid any potential conflict of interest or bias.

authentication The process of verifying the credentials of a user attempting to access a system. The most common set of credentials is a username and password.

Authentication, Authorization, and Accounting (AAA) A security philosophy wherein a user trying to connect to a network must first present some form of credential in order to be authenticated and then must have limitable permissions within the network. The authenticating server should also record session information about the client.

Authentication Server In Kerberos, the system that authenticates (but does not authorize) the client. After verifying the submitted credentials, the server gives the client a Ticket-Granting Ticket. *See also* Ticket-Granting Ticket (TGT).

authoritative DNS server DNS server that holds the primary zone file for a particular domain or domains.

authoritative name servers Another name for authoritative DNS servers. *See* authoritative DNS server.

authorization A step in the AAA philosophy during which a client's permissions are decided upon. *See also* Authentication, Authorization, and Accounting (AAA).

Automatic Private IP Addressing (APIPA) A networking feature in operating systems that enables clients to self-configure an IP address and subnet mask automatically when a DHCP server isn't available.

Autonomous System (AS) An organizational concept within the Border Gateway protocol (BGP) that defines one or more networks that share a unified "policy" regarding how they exchange traffic with other Autonomous Systems.

back up To save important data in a secondary location as a safety precaution against the loss of the primary data.

backup Archive of important data that the disaster recovery team can retrieve in case of some disaster.

backup designated router (BDR) In OSPF networks, a second router set to take over if the designated router fails. *See also* designated router (DR).

backup generator An onsite generator that provides electricity if the power utility fails.

badge A card-shaped device used for authentication; something you have, a possession factor.

bandwidth (computing) The amount of digital data that can be transferred over a medium in a fixed amount of time. For networks, most often expressed in bits per second.

bandwidth saturation When the frequency of a band is filled to capacity due to a large number of devices using the same bandwidth.

bandwidth speed tester Web site for measuring an Internet connection throughput, both download and upload speeds.

banner grabbing When a malicious user gains access to an open port and uses it to probe a host to gain information and access, as well as learn details about running services.

baseband Digital signaling that has only one signal (a single signal) on the cable at a time. The signal must be in one of three states: one, zero, or idle.

baseline Static image of a system's (or network's) performance when all elements are known to be working properly.

baseline configuration Reference record of all the hardware (including portable computers, servers, switches, routers, etc.) and software currently in use in a data center. The baseline configuration also includes network topology and placement of devices in the organization.

basic NAT A simple form of NAT that translates a computer's private or internal IP address to a global IP address on a one-to-one basis.

Basic Service Set (BSS) In wireless networking, a single access point servicing a given area.

Basic Service Set Identifier (BSSID) The MAC address of a wireless access point (WAP).

baud One analog cycle on a telephone line.

baud rate The number of bauds per second. In the early days of telephone data transmission, the baud rate was often analogous to bits per second. Due to advanced modulation of baud cycles as well as data compression, this is no longer true.

bidirectional (BiDi) transceiver Full-duplex fiber-optic connector that relies on wave division multiplexing (WDM) to differentiate wave signals on a single fiber, creating single strand fiber transmission.

bidirectional wavelength division multiplexing (BWDM) An older, less popular version of WDM, mostly replaced by *dense wavelength division multiplexing (DWDM)*.

biometric Human physical characteristic that can be measured and saved to be compared as authentication in granting the user access to a network or resource. Common biometrics include fingerprints, facial scans, retinal scans, voice pattern recognition, and others.

biometric device Device that scans fingerprints, retinas, or even the sound of the user's voice to provide a foolproof replacement for both passwords and smart devices.

block Access that is denied to or from a resource. A block may be implemented in a firewall, access control server, or other secure gateway. *See also* allow.

block cipher An encryption algorithm that encrypts data in "chunks" of a certain length at a time.

blocks Contiguous ranges of IP addresses that are assigned to organizations and end users by IANA. Also called *network blocks*.

BNC connector A connector used for 10BASE-2 coaxial cable. All BNC connectors have to be locked into place by turning the locking ring 90 degrees.

BNC coupler Passive connector used to join two segments of coaxial cables that are terminated with BNC connectors.

bonding Two or more NICs in a system working together to act as a single NIC to increase performance.

Bootstrap Protocol (BOOTP) Early protocol that provided dynamic IP addressing (this job has generally been replaced by DHCP) and diskless booting.

Border Gateway Protocol (BGP) An exterior gateway routing protocol that enables groups of routers to share routing information so that efficient, loop-free routes can be established. BGP connects Autonomous Systems on the Internet. The current version is BGP-4.

botnet A group of computers under the control of one operator, used for malicious purposes. *See also* zombie.

bottleneck A spot on a network where traffic slows precipitously.

bounce A signal sent by one device taking many different paths to get to the receiving systems.

bps (bits per second) A measurement of how fast data is moved across a transmission medium. A Gigabit Ethernet connection moves 1,000,000,000 bps.

branch office (data center) A multilocation organization's remote office served by centralized data centers. Branch offices themselves store very little data onsite.

bridge A device that connects two networks and passes traffic between them based only on the node address, so that traffic between nodes on one network does not appear on the other network. For example, an Ethernet bridge only looks at the MAC address. Bridges filter and forward frames based on MAC addresses and operate at Layer 2 (Data Link layer) of the OSI seven-layer model. While wired bridges were made obsolete by switches, wireless bridges are still in use today. *See also* wireless bridge.

bridge loop *See* switching loop.

bridged connection An early type of DSL connection that made the DSL line function the same as if you snapped an Ethernet cable into your NIC.

bring your own device (BYOD) Mobile deployment model wherein users bring their own network-enabled devices to the work environment. These cell phones, tablets, notebooks, and other mobile devices must be easily and securely integrated and released from corporate network environments using onboarding and offboarding technologies.

broadband Analog signaling that sends multiple signals over the cable at the same time. The best example of broadband signaling is cable television. The zero, one, and idle states exist on multiple channels on the same cable. *See also* baseband.

broadcast A frame or packet addressed to all machines; always limited to a broadcast domain.

broadcast address The address a NIC attaches to a frame when it wants every other NIC on the network to read it. In TCP/IP, the general broadcast address is 255.255.255.255. In Ethernet, the broadcast MAC address is FF-FF-FF-FF-FF-FF.

broadcast domain A network of computers that hear each other's broadcasts.

broadcast storm The result of one or more devices sending a nonstop flurry of broadcast frames on the network.

brute force A type of attack wherein every permutation of some form of data is tried in an attempt to discover protected information. Commonly used to crack short passwords.

buffer (fiber-optic cable) A component of a fiber-optic cable that adds strength to the cable.

bus topology A network topology that uses a single bus cable that connects all of the computers in a line. Bus topology networks must be terminated to prevent signal reflection. True bus topologies are no longer used.

business continuity planning (BCP) The process of defining the steps to be taken in the event of a physical corporate crisis to continue operations at another location. Includes the creation of documents to specify facilities, equipment, resources, personnel, and their roles.

byte Eight contiguous bits; a fundamental data unit in contemporary computing. Bytes are counted in powers of two and each byte represents a decimal value between 0 and 255.

cable certifier A very powerful cable testing device used by professional installers to test the electrical characteristics of a cable and then generate a certification report, proving that cable runs pass ANSI/TIA standards.

cable drop Location where the cable comes out of the wall at the workstation location.

cable modem A bridge device that interconnects a cable company's DOCSIS service to a user's Ethernet network. In most locations, the cable modem is the demarc.

cable stripper Device that enables the creation of UTP cables.

cable tester A generic name for a device that tests the functionality of cables. Some common tests are for continuity, electrical shorts, crossed wires, or other electrical characteristics.

cable tray A device for organizing cable runs in a drop ceiling.

cached lookup (DNS) A DNS response served from a cache of previous responses. *See* DNS caching.

cache-only DNS server (caching-only DNS server) DNS server that does not have any forward lookup zones. Resolves names of systems on the Internet for the network, but is not responsible for telling other DNS servers the names of any clients.

caching engine A server dedicated to storing cache information on a network. These servers can reduce overall network traffic dramatically.

Cacti Network graphing program.

campus area network (CAN) A network installed in a medium-sized space spanning multiple buildings.

canonical name (CNAME) record A DNS record that stores a fully qualified domain name. A common use is to provide an alias for another hostname.

captive portal A Wi-Fi network implementation used in some public facilities that directs attempts to connect to the network to an internal Web page for that facility; generally used to force terms of service on users.

capture file A file in which the collected packets from a packet sniffer program are stored.

card Generic term for devices designed to snap into an expansion slot.

carrier-sense multiple access with collision avoidance (CSMA/CA) Access method used only on wireless networks. Before hosts transmit, they first listen for traffic. If the transmitting host does not hear any traffic, it will transmit its frame. It will then listen for an acknowledgment frame from the receiving host. If the transmitting host does not hear the acknowledgment, it will wait for a randomly determined period of time and try again.

carrier-sense multiple access with collision detection (CSMA/CD) Obsolete access method that Ethernet systems used in wired LAN technologies, enabling frames of data to flow through the network and ultimately reach address locations. Hosts on CSMA/CD networks first listened to hear if there was any data on the wire. If there was none, the hosts sent out data. If a collision occurred, then both hosts waited for a randomly determined time period before retransmitting the data. Full-duplex Ethernet made CSMA/CD obsolete.

Cat 3 Category 3 wire, a standard for UTP wiring that can operate at up to 16 Mbps.

Cat 5 Category 5 wire, a standard for UTP wiring that can operate at up to 100 Mbps.

Cat 5e Category 5e wire, a standard for UTP wiring with improved support for 100 Mbps using two pairs and support for 1000 Mbps using four pairs.

Cat 6 Category 6 wire, a standard for UTP wiring with improved support for 1000 Mbps; supports 10 Gbps up to 55 meters.

Cat 6a Category 6a wire, a standard for UTP wiring with support for 10 Gbps up to 100 meters.

Cat 7 Category 7 wire, a standard (unrecognized by ANSI/TIA) for UTP wiring with support for 10+ Gbps at 600 MHz maximum frequency.

category (Cat) rating A grade assigned to twisted pair cable to help network installers get the right cable for the right network technology. Cat ratings are officially rated in megahertz (MHz), indicating the highest-frequency bandwidth the cable can handle.

CCMP-AES A 128-bit block cipher used in the IEEE 802.11i (WPA2) standard. *See* Advanced Encryption Standard (AES).

central office Building that houses local exchanges and a location where individual voice circuits come together.

certificate A digitally signed electronic document issued by a trusted third party—a *certificate authority (CA)*—attesting to the identity of the holder of a specific cryptographic public key. *See* digital signature *and* public-key infrastructure (PKI).

certifier A device that tests a cable to ensure that it can handle its rated amount of capacity.

chain of custody A document used to track the collection, handling, and transfer of evidence.

Challenge Handshake Authentication Protocol (CHAP) A remote access authentication protocol. It has the serving system challenge the remote client, which must provide an encrypted password.

change management The process of initiating, approving, funding, implementing, and documenting significant changes to the network.

change management documentation A set of documents that defines procedures for changes to the network.

change management team Personnel who collect change requests, evaluate the change, work with decision makers for approval, plan and implement approved changes, and document the changes.

change request A formal or informal document suggesting a modification to some aspect of the network or computing environment.

channel A portion of the wireless spectrum on which a particular wireless network operates. Setting wireless networks to different channels enables separation of the networks.

channel bonding Wireless technology that enables wireless access points (WAPs) to use two channels for transmission.

channel overlap Drawback of 2.4-GHz wireless networks where channels shared some bandwidth with other channels. This is why only three 2.4-GHz channels can be used in the United States (1, 6, and 11).

Channel Service Unit/Data Service Unit (CSU/DSU) A piece of equipment that connects a T-carrier leased line from the telephone company to a customer's equipment (such as a router). It performs line encoding and conditioning functions, and it often has a loopback function for testing.

checksum A simple error-detection method that adds a numerical value to the end of each packet, enabling the receiver to detect corruption that can occur as a packet moves through the network. *See also* hash.

choose your own device (CYOD) Mobile deployment model where corporate employees select among a catalog of approved mobile devices. The organization retains complete control and ownership over the mobile devices, although employees can install their own apps.

CIA triad Widely considered to be the foundation of IT security; stands for confidentiality, integrity, and availability. It is put into practice through various security methods and controls. Every security technique, practice, and mechanism put into place to protect systems and data relates in some fashion to ensuring confidentiality, integrity, and availability

cipher A series of complex and hard-to-reverse mathematics run on a string of ones and zeroes to make a new set of seemingly meaningless ones and zeroes.

cipher lock A door unlocking system that uses a door handle, a latch, and a sequence of mechanical push buttons.

ciphertext The output when plaintext is run through a cipher algorithm using a key.

circuit switching The process for connecting two phones together on one circuit.

Cisco IOS Cisco's proprietary operating system for routers and switches. Originally stood for Internetworking Operating System.

cladding The part of a fiber-optic cable that makes the light reflect down the fiber.

class of service (CoS) A prioritization value used to apply to services, ports, or whatever a quality of service (QoS) device might use.

class license Contiguous chunk of IP addresses passed out by the Internet Assigned Numbers Authority (IANA). Classful addressing was phased out after the introduction of Classless Inter-Domain Routing and is no longer used.

classful Obsolete IPv4 addressing scheme that relied on the original class blocks, such as Class A, Class B, and Class C.

classless IPv4 addressing scheme that does not rely on the original class blocks, such as Class A, Class B, and Class C.

Classless Inter-Domain Routing (CIDR) The basis of allocating and routing classless addresses, not restricting subnet masks to /8, /16, or /24, which classful addressing did. Based on *variable-length subnet masking (VLSM)*, where subnets can be allocated according to the needs of an organization, such as /26 for a network with 254 or fewer node, or /30 for a network with only two nodes. *See also* subnetting.

classless subnet A subnet that does not fall into the common categories such as Class A, Class B, and Class C.

cleartext Readable data transmitted or stored in unencrypted form.

cleartext credentials Any login process conducted over a network where account names, passwords, or other authentication elements are sent from the client or server in an unencrypted fashion.

client A computer program that uses the services of another computer program; software that extracts information from a server. A Netflix or Hulu application running on a Smart TV is a client for the provider's streaming services. Also, a machine that accesses shared resources on a server.

client/server A relationship in which a client obtains services from a server on behalf of a user. In classic terms, a network architecture (topology) where one computer shares resources (the server) and other computers on the network access those resources (clients).

client/server application An application located on a client that makes use of services provided by a server. This server can be external or located on the client system.

client/server network A network that has dedicated server machines and client machines.

client-to-site VPN A type of VPN connection where a single computer logs into a remote network and becomes, for all intents and purposes, a member of that network.

clock strata Tiers of NTP time sources layered according to relative accuracy. A number indicates the accuracy of each tier (called a stratum), counting up from the most-accurate Stratum 0.

closed-circuit television (CCTV) A self-contained, closed system in which video cameras feed their signal to specific, dedicated monitors and storage devices.

cloud computing The cloud is like a cafeteria of computing and networking resources that are managed by someone else and enhanced by layers of powerful services and software. Cloud computing is the act of using these resources and services.

cloud/server-based anti-malware Anti-malware software that offloads a significant amount of processing from individual hosts to local or cloud-based servers.

clustering Multiple pieces of interconnected equipment, such as servers, that appear to the network as a single (logical) device. Clustering provides redundancy and fault tolerance.

coarse wavelength division multiplexing (CWDM) An optical multiplexing technology in which a few signals of different optical wavelength could be combined to travel a fairly short distance.

coaxial cable A type of cable that contains a central conductor wire surrounded by an insulating material, which in turn is surrounded by a braided metal shield. It is called coaxial because the center wire and the braided metal shield share a common axis or centerline.

code-division multiple access (CDMA) Early cellular telephone technology that used spread-spectrum transmission. Obsolete.

cold site A location that consists of a building, facilities, desks, and everything that a business needs except computers.

collision The result of two nodes transmitting at the same time on a multiple access network such as a wireless network. Both frames may be lost or partial frames may result.

collision domain A set of connected hosts that all share one medium to transmit and receive. The shared medium can result in a collision if two hosts transmit at the same time. Characteristic of early, half-duplex, non-switched Ethernet.

co-location A process in which an organization places its own server hardware in a public, third-party data center. Also written without the hyphen as *colocation*.

command A request, typed from a terminal or embedded in a file, to perform an operation or to execute a particular program.

community cloud A private cloud paid for and used by more than one organization with similar goals or needs (such as medical providers who all need to comply with the same patient privacy laws).

compatibility issue When different pieces of hardware or software don't work together correctly.

compatibility requirements With respect to network installations and upgrades, requirements that deal with how well the new technology integrates with older or existing technologies.

computer forensics The science of gathering, preserving, examining, and presenting evidence stored on a computer or any form of digital media that is presentable in a court of law.

concentrator A device that brings together at a common center connections to a particular kind of network (such as Ethernet) and implements that network internally.

configuration management A set of documents, policies, and procedures designed to help an organization maintain and update its network in a logical, orderly fashion.

configuration management documentation Documents that define the configuration of a network. These would include wiring diagrams, network diagrams, baselines, and policy/procedure/configuration documentation.

configurations The settings stored in devices that define how they are to operate.

connection Generically, a link that enables two computers to communicate.

connectionless A type of communication characterized by sending packets that are not acknowledged by the destination host. Connectionless protocols are generally faster than connection-oriented protocols. UDP is the quintessential connectionless protocol in the TCP/IP suite.

connection-oriented Network communication between two hosts that includes negotiation between the hosts to establish a communication session. Data segments are then transferred between hosts, with each segment being acknowledged before a subsequent segment can be sent. Orderly closure of the communication is conducted at the end of the data transfer or in the event of a communication failure. TCP is the only connection-oriented protocol in the TCP/IP suite.

console port Connection jack in a switch or router used exclusively to connect a computer that will manage the device.

content filter An advanced networking device that implements content filtering, enabling administrators to filter traffic based on specific signatures or keywords (such as profane language).

content switch Advanced networking device that works at least at Layer 7 (Application layer) and hides servers behind a single IP address.

contingency planning The process of creating documents—a contingency plan—that set out how to limit damage and recover quickly from an incident.

continuity The physical connection of wires in a network.

continuity tester Inexpensive network tester that can only test for continuity on a line.

convergence Point at which the routing tables for all routers in a network are updated.

core (fiber-optics) The central glass of the fiber-optic cable that carries the light signal.

core layer One tier of a three-tiered architecture commonly used in data centers. The core layer ties together all the switches at the distribution layer and interconnects with external networks such as the Internet.

corporate-owned business only (COBO) Deployment model where the corporation owns all the mobile devices issued to employees. Employees have a whitelist of preapproved applications they can install.

corporate-owned personally enabled (COPE) Deployment model that is very similar to COBO, in that the organization issues mobile devices. With COPE, however, employees are presented with a whitelist of preapproved applications that they may install.

cost (routing metric) A metric for the desirability of a particular route. Can incorporate factors that affect performance such as bandwidth.

counter A predefined event that is monitored and recorded to a log file. Logs store information about the performance of some particular aspect of a system. Different programs refer to the monitored aspect with different terms. Performance Monitor calls them counters; syslog calls them *facilities*. *See* syslog.

CRC (cyclic redundancy check) *See* cyclic redundancy check (CRC).

crimper Also called a *crimping tool*, the tool used to secure a crimp (or an RJ-45 connector) onto the end of a cable.

crossover cable A specially terminated UTP cable used to interconnect routers or switches, or to connect network cards without a switch. Crossover cables reverse the sending and receiving wire pairs from one end to the other.

crosstalk Electrical signal interference between two cables that are in close proximity to each other.

crypto-malware Malicious software that uses some form of encryption to lock a user out of a system. *See also* ransomware.

CSMA/CA (carrier-sense multiple access with collision avoidance) *See* carrier-sense multiple access with collision avoidance (CSMA/CA).

CSMA/CD (carrier-sense multiple access with collision detection) *See* carrier-sense multiple access with collision detection (CSMA/CD).

CSU/DSU (Channel Service Unit/Data Service Unit) *See* Channel Service Unit/Data Service Unit (CSU/DSU).

customer-premises equipment (CPE) The primary distribution box and customer-owned/managed equipment that exists on the customer side of the demarc.

cyclic redundancy check (CRC) A mathematical method used to check for errors in long streams of transmitted data with high accuracy. The CRC is found in the Frame Check Sequence (FCS).

data backup The process of creating extra copies of data to be used in case the primary data source fails.

data center A dedicated space—a building or part of a building—housing a networked group of servers that provides data storage, Web hosting, application hosting, cloud services, and more.

Data Link layer *See* Open Systems Interconnection (OSI) seven-layer model.

Data Over Cable Service Interface Specification (DOCSIS) The standard protocol used by cable modem networks to facilitate data transfer.

datagram A connectionless transfer unit created with User Datagram Protocol designed for quick transfers over a packet-switched network.

datagram TLS (DTLS) VPN A virtual private network solution that optimizes connections for delay-sensitive applications, such as voice and video. A DTLS VPN uses TLS to provide encryption for enhanced security.

dead spot A place that should be covered by the network signal but where devices get no signal.

deauthentication (deauth) attack A form of DoS attack that targets 802.11 Wi-Fi networks specifically by sending out a frame that kicks a wireless client off its current WAP connection. A rogue WAP nearby presents a stronger signal, which the client will prefer. The rogue WAP connects the client to the Internet and then proceeds to intercept communications to and from that client.

decapsulation The process of stripping all the extra header information from a packet as the data moves up a protocol stack.

decibel (dB) A measurement of the quality of a signal.

dedicated circuit A circuit that runs from a breaker box to specific outlets.

dedicated line A telephone line that is an always open, or connected, circuit. Dedicated telephone lines usually do not have telephone numbers.

dedicated server A machine that does not use any client functions, only server functions.

default A software function or operation that occurs automatically unless the user specifies something else.

default gateway In a TCP/IP network, a router that accepts traffic for all routes unknown to a client or another router. In SOHO networks, this is usually the only router in the network and provides the interface to the ISP's network.

defense in depth Using multiple layers of security to protect against threats to the network.

demarc A device that marks the dividing line of responsibility for the functioning of a network between internal users and upstream service providers. Also, *demarcation point*.

demarc extension Any cabling that runs from the network interface to whatever box is used by the customer as a demarc.

demilitarized zone (DMZ) *See* screened subnet.

demultiplexer Device that can extract and distribute individual streams of data that have been combined to travel along a single shared network cable.

denial of service (DoS) An attack that floods a networked resource with so many requests that it becomes overwhelmed and ceases functioning. DoS prevents users from gaining normal use of a resource.

dense wavelength division multiplexing (DWDM) An optical multiplexing technology in which a large number of optical signals of different optical wavelength could be combined to travel over relatively long fiber cables.

designated router (DR) The main router in an OSPF network that relays information to all other routers in the area.

desktop as a service (DaaS) A cloud computing service that enables a user or organization to virtualize user workstations and manage them as flexibly as other cloud resources.

destination (header field) A field common to many packet-switched network protocols. Contains the address of the intended recipient (in the address format—such as a MAC or IP address—appropriate for the protocol).

destination port A fixed, predetermined number that identifies which process the data in a TCP segment or UDP datagram is intended for. The destination port number is contained in the destination field of segments and datagrams.

device driver A subprogram to control communications between the computer and some peripheral hardware.

device ID The last six digits of a MAC address, identifying the manufacturer's unique serial number for that NIC.

DHCP four-way handshake (DORA) DHCP process in which a client gets a lease for an IPv4 address—Discover, Offer, Request, and Acknowledgment.

DHCP lease Created by the DHCP server to allow a system requesting DHCP IP information to use that information for a certain amount of time.

DHCP relay A router feature that, when enabled, accepts DHCP broadcasts from clients and then sends them via unicast addresses directly to the DHCP server. In common terms, DHCP communications can cross from one network to another through a router that has DHCP relay configured. Also known as a DHCP relay agent.

DHCP scope The pool of IP addresses that a DHCP server may allocate to clients requesting IP addresses or other IP information like DNS server addresses.

DHCP snooping Switch process that monitors DHCP traffic, filtering out DHCP messages from untrusted sources. Typically used to block attacks that use a rogue DHCP server.

DHCPv6 IPv6 version of DHCP. A *stateful* DHCPv6 server works similarly to an IPv4 DHCP server, while a *stateless* DHCPv6 server provides configuration information and lets the host pick its own address via *stateless address autoconfiguration (SLAAC). See* Dynamic Host Configuration Protocol (DHCP).

differential backup Similar to an incremental backup in that it backs up the files that have been changed since the last backup. This type of backup does not change the state of the archive bit.

differentiated services (DiffServ) The underlying architecture that makes quality of service (QoS) work.

dig (domain information groper) See domain information groper (dig).

digital signature A hash of a message which has been encrypted and attached to the message. The hash is encrypted with the signer's private key. The recipient can decrypt the hash with the signer's public key and use the hash to confirm the message was not altered. This both verifies a sender's identity and the integrity of the message. *See also* certificate *and* hash.

digital subscriber line (DSL) A high-speed Internet connection technology that uses a regular telephone line for connectivity. DSL comes in several varieties, including asymmetric (ADSL) and symmetric (SDSL), and many speeds. Typical home-user DSL connections are ADSL with a download speed of up to 9 Mbps and an upload speed of up to 1 Kbps.

dipole antenna The standard straight-wire antenna that provides most omnidirectional function.

direct current (DC) A type of electric circuit where the flow of electrons is in a complete circle.

directional antenna An antenna that focuses its signal more toward a specific direction; as compared to an omnidirectional antenna that radiates its signal in all directions equally.

direct-sequence spread-spectrum (DSSS) A spread-spectrum broadcasting method defined in the 802.11 standard that sends data out on different frequencies at the same time.

disaster recovery The means and methods to recover primary infrastructure from a disaster. Disaster recovery starts with a plan and includes data backups.

discretionary access control (DAC) Authorization method based on the idea that there is an owner of a resource who may at his or her discretion assign access to that resource. DAC is considered much more flexible than mandatory access control (MAC).

disk mirroring Process by which data is written simultaneously to two or more disk drives. Read and write speed is decreased but redundancy, in case of catastrophe, is increased. Also known as *RAID level 1*.

disk striping Process by which data is spread among multiple (at least two) drives. It increases speed for both reads and writes of data, but provides no fault tolerance. Also known as *RAID level 0*.

disk striping with parity Process by which data is spread among multiple (at least three) drives, with parity information as well to provide fault tolerance. The most commonly implemented type is RAID 5, where the data and parity information is spread across three or more drives.

dispersion Diffusion over distance of light propagating down fiber cable.

distance vector Set of routing protocols that calculates the total cost to get to a particular network ID and compares that cost to the total cost of all the other routes to get to that same network ID.

distributed control system (DCS) A small controller added directly to a machine used to distribute the computing load.

Distributed Coordination Function (DCF) One of two methods of collision avoidance defined by the 802.11 standard and the only one currently implemented. DCF specifies strict rules for sending data onto the network media. *See also* Point Coordination Function (PCF).

distributed denial of service (DDoS) Multicomputer assault on a network resource that attempts, with sheer overwhelming quantity of requests, to prevent regular users from receiving services from the resource. Can also be used to crash systems. DDoS attacks are usually executed using botnets consisting of compromised systems referred to as zombies.

distributed switching The centralized installation, configuration, and handling of every switch in a virtualized network.

distribution layer One tier of a three-tiered architecture commonly used in data centers. The distribution layer interconnects racks of servers and other rack-mounted gear through top-of-rack switching. Modern data center design leverages advances in virtualization and software-defined networking (SDN) to replace the distribution layer common in the three-tiered network design with a virtualized mesh network.

DNS cache poisoning Also known as *DNS poisoning*, an attack that adds or changes information in a DNS server's cache to point hostnames to incorrect IP addresses, under the attacker's control. When a client requests an IP address from this DNS server for a Web site, the poisoned server hands out an IP address of an attacker machine, not the legitimate site. When the client subsequently visits the attacker site, they become vulnerable to a number of threats including malware.

DNS caching A feature of DNS servers that temporarily stores information about previous DNS lookups to speed up future requests.

DNS domain A specific branch of the DNS name space. Top-level DNS domains include .com, .gov, and .edu.

DNS forwarding DNS server configuration that sends (forwards) DNS requests to another DNS server.

DNS record A piece of data, such as an IP address, attached to a name in the DNS tree. Each record type helps different aspects of DNS do their job. For example: A records store the IP address of a domain, NS records store the name server for a given DNS entry, and MX records direct e-mail to specific e-mail servers.

DNS resolver cache *See* resolver cache.

DNS root servers Servers at the top of the hierarchy of DNS servers running the Internet. There are only 13 root servers.

DNS server Software that responds to DNS queries, often running on a system dedicated to this purpose.

DNS tree A hierarchy of DNS domains and individual computer names organized into a tree-like structure, the top of which is the root.

document A medium and the data recorded on it for human use; for example, a report sheet or book. By extension, any record that has permanence and that can be read by a human or a machine.

documentation A collection of organized documents or the information recorded in documents. Also, instructional material specifying the inputs, operations, and outputs of a computer program or system.

domain A term used to describe a grouping of users, computers, and/or networks. In Microsoft networking, a domain is a group of computers and users that shares a common account database and a common security policy. For the Internet, a domain is a group of computers that shares a common element in their DNS hierarchical name.

domain controller A Microsoft Windows Server system specifically configured to store user and server account information for its domain. Often abbreviated as "DC." Windows domain controllers store all account and security information in the *Active Directory* domain service.

domain information groper (dig) Command-line tool in non-Windows systems used to diagnose DNS problems.

Domain Name System (DNS) A TCP/IP name resolution system that resolves hostnames to IP addresses, IP addresses to hostnames, and other bindings, like DNS servers and mail servers for a domain.

domain users and groups Users and groups that are defined across an entire network domain.

door access controls Methodology to grant permission or to deny passage through a doorway, whether computer-controlled, human-controlled, token-oriented, or by other means.

dotted decimal notation Shorthand method for discussing and configuring binary IP addresses using a base 10 numbering system.

drive mirroring The process of writing identical data to two hard drives on the same controller at the same time to provide data redundancy.

DSL Access Multiplexer (DSLAM) A device located in a telephone company's central office that connects multiple customers to the Internet.

DSL modem A device that enables customers to connect to the Internet using a DSL connection. A DSL modem isn't really a modem—it's more like an ISDN terminal adapter—but the term stuck, and even the manufacturers of the devices now call them DSL modems.

dual stack Networking device, such as a router or PC, that runs both IPv4 and IPv6.

dynamic addressing A way for a computer to receive IP information automatically from a server program. *See also* Dynamic Host Configuration Protocol (DHCP).

Dynamic ARP Inspection (DAI) Uses information collected by DHCP snooping to spot and ignore suspicious ARPs to prevent ARP cache poisoning and other malevolent efforts.

Dynamic DNS (DDNS) A protocol that enables DNS servers to get automatic updates of IP addresses of computers in their forward lookup zones, mainly by talking to the local DHCP server.

Dynamic Host Configuration Protocol (DHCP) A protocol that enables a DHCP server to set TCP/IP settings automatically for a DHCP client.

dynamic multipoint VPN (DMVPN) A virtual private network solution optimized for connections between multiple locations directly.

dynamic NAT (DNAT) Type of network address translation (NAT) in which many computers can share a pool of routable IP addresses that number fewer than the computers.

dynamic port numbers Port numbers 49152–65535, recommended by IANA to be used as ephemeral port numbers.

dynamic routing Process by which routers in an internetwork automatically exchange information with other routers. Requires a dynamic routing protocol, such as OSPF or EIGRP.

EAP-TLS (Extensible Authentication Protocol with Transport Layer Security) A protocol that defines the use of a RADIUS server as well as mutual authentication, requiring certificates on both the server and every client.

EAP-TTLS (Extensible Authentication Protocol with Tunneled Transport Layer Security) A protocol similar to *EAP-TLS* but only uses a single server-side certificate.

east-west traffic Any network activity that moves between systems within the data center. Network devices seen in east-west traffic include internal routers, internal firewalls, and switches.

edge device A hardware device that has been optimized to perform a task in coordination with other edge devices and controllers.

edge router Router that connects one Autonomous System (AS) to another.

effective permissions The permissions of all groups combined in any network operating system.

elasticity A popular way to scale an application by starting up new instances. Cloud providers make it simple to increase the number of instances as demand grows and reduce the number of instances as demand shrinks.

electromagnetic interference (EMI) Interference from one device to another, resulting in poor performance in the device's capabilities. This is similar to having static on your TV while running a hair dryer, or placing two monitors too close together and getting a "shaky" screen.

e-mail Messages, usually text, sent from one person to another via computer. E-mail can also be sent automatically to a large number of addresses, known as a *mailing list*.

e-mail alert (SNMP) Notification sent by e-mail as a result of an event. A typical use is a notification sent from an SNMP manager as a result of an out-of-tolerance condition in an SNMP managed device.

e-mail client Program that runs on a computer and enables a user to send, receive, and organize e-mail.

e-mail server Also known as a *mail server*, a server that accepts incoming e-mail, sorts the e-mail for recipients into mailboxes, and sends e-mail to other servers using SMTP.

emergency alert system An essential component of a data center's emergency procedures. The emergency alert system informs employees that there is an emergency, enabling them to respond or evacuate.

emergency procedures The policies and procedures a data center implements to enable effective and safe responses to a wide variety of potential emergencies.

emulator Software or hardware that converts the commands to and from the host machine to an entirely different platform; for example, a program that enables you to run Nintendo games on your PC.

encapsulation The process of putting the packets from one protocol inside the packets of another protocol. An example of this is IP encapsulation in Ethernet, which places IP packets inside Ethernet frames.

encryption A process that attempts to make some data unreadable to anyone but the owner or intended recipient. Generally, the data is scrambled and unscrambled with cryptographic keys. Encryption plays a critical role in securing traffic sent across open networks such as the Internet.

endpoint (TCP/IP) *See* socket.

endpoints (TCP/IP) *See* socket pairs.

Enhanced Data rates for GSM Evolution (EDGE) Early cellular telephone technology that used a SIM card; obsolete.

Enhanced Interior Gateway Routing Protocol (EIGRP) Cisco's proprietary hybrid protocol that has elements of both distance vector and link state routing.

enhanced quad small form-factor pluggable (QSFP+) Interface and module specification for hot-pluggable network transceivers up to 40 Gbps. *See also* transceiver.

enhanced small form-factor pluggable (SFP+) Interface and module specification for hot-pluggable network transceivers up to 10 Gbps. *See also* transceiver.

environmental monitor Device used in telecommunications rooms that keeps track of humidity, temperature, and more.

ephemeral port In TCP/IP communication, an arbitrary port number chosen by a sending computer for the receiving computer to use as the destination port when it responds. IANA suggests operating systems use 49152-65535 as ephemeral ports, but the actual range varies from OS to OS—anything greater than 1024 may be ephemeral on some platforms.

ephemeral port number *See* ephemeral port.

equipment rack A metal structure used in equipment rooms to secure network hardware devices and patch panels. Most racks are 19" wide. Devices designed to fit in such a rack use a height measurement called *units*, or *simply U*.

Ethernet Open and vendor-neutral Layer 2 network protocol standardized under the IEEE 802.3 umbrella, enabling any company to make interoperable Ethernet equipment. Originally created in the 1970s by Xerox and transferred to the IEEE.

evil twin An attack that lures people into connecting to a rogue access point by broadcasting the same SSID as the target network's access points.

Evolved High-Speed Packet Access (HSPA+) The final wireless 3G data standard, transferring theoretical maximum speeds up to 168 Mbps, although real-world implementations rarely passed 10 Mbps.

executable viruses Viruses that are literally extensions of executables and that are unable to exist by themselves. Once an infected executable file is run, the virus loads into memory, adding copies of itself to other EXEs that are subsequently run.

Exim E-mail server for every major platform; fast and efficient.

exit plan Documents and diagrams that identify the best way out of a building in the event of an emergency. It may also define other procedures to follow.

Extended Service Set (ESS) A single wireless access point servicing a given area that has been extended by adding more access points.

Extended Service Set Identifier (ESSID) An SSID applied to an Extended Service Set as a network naming convention.

Extended Unique Identifier, 48-bit (EUI-48) The IEEE term for the 48-bit MAC address assigned to a network interface. The first 24 bits of the EUI-48 are assigned by the IEEE as the organizationally unique identifier (OUI).

Extended Unique Identifier, 64-bit (EUI-64) A process that generates the last 64 bits of the IPv6 address using a calculation based on a device's 48-bit MAC address.

Extensible Authentication Protocol (EAP) Authentication wrapper that EAP-compliant applications can use to accept one of many types of authentication. While EAP is a general-purpose authentication wrapper, its only substantial use is in wireless networks.

external connections A network's connections to the wider Internet. Also a major concern when setting up a SOHO network.

external firewall The firewall that sits between the perimeter network and the Internet and is responsible for bearing the brunt of the attacks from the Internet. *See also* firewall.

external threats Any theoretical source of harm to an organization or its IT operations from outside of the organization itself. External threats such as hackers and malware take advantage of vulnerabilities that exist in the network.

fail close Defines the condition of doors and locks in the event of an emergency, indicating that the doors should close and lock.

fail open Defines the condition of doors and locks in the event of an emergency, indicating that the doors should be open and unlocked.

far-end crosstalk (FEXT) Crosstalk on the opposite end of a cable from the signal's source.

Fast Ethernet Nickname for the 100-Mbps Ethernet standards. Originally applied to 100BASE-TX.

fault tolerance The capability of any system to continue functioning after some part of the system has failed. RAID is an example of a hardware device that provides fault tolerance for hard drives.

F-connector A screw-on connector used to terminate small-diameter coaxial cable such as RG-6 and RG-59 cables.

Federal Communications Commission (FCC) In the United States, regulates public airwaves and rates PCs and other equipment according to the amount of radiation emitted.

fiber light meter Device that measures the intensity of light pulses within or at the terminal ends of fiber-optic cables.

fiber-optic cable A high-speed physical medium for transmitting data that uses light rather than electricity to transmit data and is made of high-purity glass fibers sealed within a flexible opaque tube. Much faster than conventional copper wire.

Fibre Channel (FC) A self-contained, high-speed storage environment with its own storage arrays, cables, protocols, cables, and switches. Fibre Channel is a critical part of storage area networks (SANs).

file hashing When the download provider hashes the contents of a file and publishes the resulting message digest.

file server A computer designated to store software, courseware, administrative tools, and other data on a local area network (LAN) or wide area network (WAN). It "serves" this information to other computers via the network when users enter their personal access codes.

File Transfer Protocol (FTP) Classic protocol for file transfer over TCP/IP networks using ports 20 and 21. Has been mostly displaced by protocols such as HTTP(S) and SSH File Transfer Protocol.

fire ratings Ratings developed by Underwriters Laboratories (UL) and the National Electrical Code (NEC) to define the risk of network cables burning and creating noxious fumes and smoke.

fire suppression system System designed to detect and respond quickly to the presence of fire in a server closet or data center. A good fire suppression system should be able to detect fire, cut power to protect sensitive equipment, displace oxygen with fire-suppressing gases, alert relevant staff, and activate sprinklers (potentially—sprinklers will harm equipment).

firewall A network security device or software that restricts incoming and outgoing network traffic based on pre-defined rules. Individual systems can have their own host-based firewalls, while the broader network can be protected by firewalls running on standalone devices or inside other network devices.

First Hop Redundancy Protocol (FHRP) A method of ensuring high data availability by taking multiple routers and grouping them into a virtual router with a single virtual IP address that clients use as a default gateway. Common FHRP protocols are the open standard *Virtual Router Redundancy Protocol (VRRP)* and Cisco's proprietary *Hot Standby Router Protocol (HSRP)* and *Gateway Load Balancing Protocol (GLBP)*.

first responder The person or robot whose job is to react to the notification of a possible computer crime by determining the severity of the situation, collecting information, documenting findings and actions, and providing the information to the proper authorities.

flat name space A naming convention that gives each device only one name that must be unique. NetBIOS used a flat name space. TCP/IP's DNS uses a hierarchical name space.

flat-surface connector Early fiber-optic connector that resulted in a small gap between fiber-optic junctions due to the flat grind faces of the fibers. It was replaced by angled physical contact (APC) connectors.

flood guard Technology in modern switches that can detect and block excessive traffic.

flow A stream of packets from one specific place to another.

flow cache Stores sets of flows for interpretation and analysis. *See also* flow.

forensics report A document that describes the details of gathering, securing, analyzing, transporting, and investigating evidence.

forward lookup zone In Windows Server DNS, the database that stores the DNS records (A, AAAA, CNAME, etc.) for a particular domain. Generically referred to as the *zone file* outside of Windows Server DNS.

forward proxy server Server that acts as middleman between clients and servers, making requests to network servers on behalf of clients. Results are sent to the proxy server, which then passes them to the original client. The network servers are isolated from the clients by the forward proxy server.

FQDN (fully qualified domain name) *See* fully qualified domain name (FQDN).

frame A defined series of binary data that is the basic container for a discrete amount of data moving across a network. Generally, the components of a frame can be broken down into the *header* (MAC addresses and type), the *payload* (the actual data being transmitted), and the *trailer* (the frame check sequence [FCS]). Frames are created at Layer 2 of the OSI model.

frame check sequence (FCS) A sequence of bits placed at the very end (trailer) of a frame that is used to check the primary data for errors by implementing a cyclic redundancy check (CRC).

FreeRADIUS Open source RADIUS server software for UNIX/Linux systems.

freeware Software that is distributed for free with no license fee.

frequency mismatch Problem in older wireless networks with manual settings where the WAP transmitted on one channel and a wireless client was set to access on a different channel.

frequency-hopping spread-spectrum (FHSS) A spread-spectrum broadcasting method defined in the 802.11 standard that sends data on one frequency at a time, constantly shifting (or *hopping*) frequencies.

FUBAR Fouled up beyond all recognition.

full backup Archive created where every file selected is backed up, and the archive bit is turned off for every file backed up.

full-duplex Any communication system that enables a device to send and receive data simultaneously.

fully meshed topology A mesh network where every node is directly connected to every other node.

fully qualified domain name (FQDN) The complete DNS name of a system, from its hostname to the top-level domain name. Textual nomenclature to a domain-organized resource. It is written left to right, with the hostname on the left, followed by any hierarchical subdomains within the top-level domain on the right.

Each level is separated from any preceding or following layer by a dot (.).

gain The strengthening and focusing of radio frequency output from a wireless access point (WAP).

Gateway Load Balancing Protocol (GLBP) A Cisco-proprietary version of an FHRP that provides increased data availability through redundancy and load balancing. *See* First Hop Redundancy Protocol (FHRP).

gateway router A router that acts as both a small network's default gateway and its interface to the ISP's network. Most common in a SOHO context, though the term is falling out of use.

general logs Logs that record updates to applications.

geofencing The process of using a mobile device's built-in GPS capabilities and mobile networking capabilities to set geographical constraints on where the mobile device can be used.

Get (SNMP) A query from an SNMP manager sent to the agent of a managed device for the status of a management information base (MIB) object.

giga The prefix that generally refers to the quantity 1,073,741,824. One gigabyte is 1,073,741,824 bytes. With frequencies, in contrast, giga- often refers to one billion. One gigahertz is 1,000,000,000 hertz.

Gigabit Ethernet *See* 1000BASE-T.

gigabit interface converter (GBIC) Modular port that supports a standardized, wide variety of gigabit interface modules.

gigabyte 1024 megabytes.

global hierarchy (DNS) Tiered arrangement of DNS name servers that distribute the work of storing and translating domain names to IP addresses.

global routing prefix The first 48 bits of an IPv6 unicast address, used to get a packet to its destination. *See also* network ID.

Global System for Mobile (GSM) Early cellular telephone networking standard; obsolete.

global unicast address A public IPv6 address that every system needs in order to get on the Internet.

graphing Type of software that creates visual representations and graphs of data collected by SNMP managers.

greenfield mode One of three modes used with 802.11n wireless networks wherein everything is running at higher speed.

Group Policy A feature of Windows Active Directory that enables an administrator to apply policy settings to network users *en masse*.

groups Collections of network users who share similar tasks and need similar permissions; defined to make administration tasks easier.

guest (virtualization) In terms of virtualization, an operating system running as a virtual machine inside a hypervisor.

guest network A network that can contain or allow access to any resource that management deems acceptable to be used by insecure hosts that attach to the guest network.

H.323 A VoIP standard that handles the initiation, setup, and delivery of VoIP sessions.

hackers In general use, people who break into computer systems. Those with malicious intent are sometimes considered *black hat* hackers and those who do so with a positive intent and permission from their target (such as vulnerability testing) are regularly referred to as *authorized*, *white hat*, or *ethical* hackers. Of course, there are middle-ground hackers who do so without permission but also without malicious intent: *gray hats*.

half-duplex A form of communication where a device can either send or receive data at any given moment rather than do both simultaneously.

hardening Applying security hardware, software, and processes to your network to prevent bad things from happening.

hardware appliance Physical network device, typically a "box" that implements and runs software or firmware to perform one or a multitude of tasks. Could be a firewall, a switch, a router, a print server, or one of many other devices.

hardware tools Tools such as cable testers, time-domain reflectometers (TDRs), optical TDRs (OTDRs), certifiers, voltage event recorders, protocol analyzers, cable strippers, multimeters, tone probes/generators, butt sets, and punchdown tools used to configure and troubleshoot a network.

hash The fixed-length value that a hash function computes from its input. Hashes have many important jobs in computing, but in networking they are primarily used for authentication and ensuring data integrity.

hash function A mathematical algorithm that converts a sequence of binary digits of any length into a fixed-length value. Any given input always results in the same output.

header First section of a frame, packet, segment, or datagram; contains key information about the data being transmitted such as destination and source addresses.

heating, ventilation, and air conditioning (HVAC) All of the equipment involved in heating and cooling the environments within a facility. These items include boilers, furnaces, air conditioners and ducts, plenums, and air passages.

hex (hexadecimal) A base 16 numbering system (i.e., one with 16 symbols). It uses 10 digits (0 through 9) and 6 letters (A through F) to represent the 0s and 1s of binary numbers in a more human-friendly format. Hexadecimal 9 is equal to decimal 9, and hexadecimal A is equal to decimal 10.

hierarchical name space A naming scheme where the full name of each object includes its position within the hierarchy. An example of a hierarchical name is www.totalseminars.com, which includes not only the hostname but also the domain name. DNS uses a hierarchical name space scheme for fully qualified domain names (FQDNs).

high availability (HA) A collection of technologies and procedures that work together to keep an application available at all times.

history logs Logs that track the history of how a user or users access network resources, or how network resources are accessed throughout the network.

home automation The process of remotely controlling household devices, such as lights, thermostats, cameras, and washer and dryer.

honeynet A network containing one or more honeypots created to in order to lure in hackers.

honeypot A resource that an administrator sets up for the express purpose of attracting a computer hacker, often using fake data and deliberate vulnerabilities as bait. If a hacker takes the bait, the network's important resources are unharmed and network personnel can analyze the attack to predict and protect against future attacks, making the network more secure.

hop The passage of a packet through a router.

hop count An older metric used by routers that use RIP. The number of routers that a packet must cross to get from a router to a given network. Hop counts were tracked and entered into the routing table within a router so the router could decide which interface was the best one to forward a packet.

horizontal cabling Cabling that connects the equipment room to the work areas.

host A single device (usually a computer) on a TCP/IP network that has an IP address; any device that can be the source or destination of a data packet. Also, a computer running multiple virtualized operating systems.

host ID The portion of an IP address that defines a specific machine in a subnet.

host-based anti-malware Anti-malware software that is installed on individual systems, as opposed to the network at large.

host-based firewall A software firewall installed on a "host" that provides firewall services for just that machine, such as Windows Firewall.

hostname (command) Command-line tool that returns the hostname of the computer it is run on.

hostname (DNS) An individual computer name in the DNS naming convention.

hosts file The predecessor to DNS, a static text file that resides on a computer and is used to resolve DNS hostnames to IP addresses. Automatically mapped to a host's DNS resolver cache in modern systems. The hosts file has no extension.

host-to-host Type of VPN connection in which a single host establishes a link with a remote, single host.

host-to-site Type of VPN connection where a host logs into a remote network as if it were any other local resource of that network.

hot site A complete backup facility to continue business operations. It is considered "hot" because it has all resources in place, including computers, network infrastructure, and current backups, so that operations can commence within hours after occupation.

hotspot A wireless access point that is connected to a cellular data network, typically 4G. The device can route Wi-Fi to and from the Internet. Hotspots can be permanent installations or portable. Many cellular telephones have the capability to become a hotspot.

Hot Standby Router Protocol (HSRP) A Cisco-proprietary version of an FHRP that provides increased data availability through redundancy. *See* First Hop Redundancy Protocol (FHRP).

HTML (HyperText Markup Language) *See* HyperText Markup Language (HTML).

hub An electronic device that sits at the center of a star topology network, providing a common point for the connection of network devices. In a 10BASE-T Ethernet network, the hub contained the electronic equivalent of a properly terminated bus cable. Hubs have been replaced by switches.

human-machine interface (HMI) In a distributed control system (DCS), a computer or set of controls that exists between a controller and a human operator. The human operates the HMI, which in turn interacts with the controller.

hybrid cloud A conglomeration of public and private cloud resources, connected to achieve some target result. There is no clear line that defines how much of a hybrid cloud infrastructure is private and how much is public.

hybrid topology A mix or blend of two different topologies. A star-bus topology, for example, is a hybrid of the star and bus topologies.

hypertext A document that has been marked up to enable a user to select words or pictures within the document, click them, and connect to further information. The basis of the World Wide Web.

HyperText Markup Language (HTML) An ASCII-based script-like language for creating hypertext documents like those on the World Wide Web.

Hypertext Transfer Protocol (HTTP) Extremely fast protocol used for network file transfers on the World Wide Web.

Hypertext Transfer Protocol over TLS (HTTPS) A secure form of HTTP in which hypertext is encrypted by Transport Layer Security (TLS) before being sent onto the network. It is commonly used for Internet business transactions or any time a secure connection is required. Also referred to as HTTP over SSL, reflecting the precursor technology to TLS called Secure Sockets Layer (SSL). *See also* Hypertext Transfer Protocol (HTTP) *and* Secure Sockets Layer (SSL).

hypervisor In virtualization, a layer of programming that creates, supports, and manages a virtual machine. Also known as a *virtual machine monitor (VMM)*.

ICS (industrial control system) *See* industrial control system (ICS).

ICS (Internet Connection Sharing) *See* Internet Connection Sharing (ICS).

ICS server Unit in a distributed control system (DCS) that can be used to manage global changes to the controllers.

IEEE (Institute of Electrical and Electronics Engineers) *See* Institute of Electrical and Electronics Engineers (IEEE).

IEEE 802.3 IEEE working group that defines the standards for wired Ethernet networks.

IEEE 802.11 A family of standards for wireless local area networks marketed as Wi-Fi.

IEEE 1284 The IEEE standard for a now-obsolete parallel communication technology.

IETF (Internet Engineering Task Force) *See* Internet Engineering Task Force (IETF).

ifconfig A command-line utility for Linux servers and workstations that displays the current TCP/IP configuration of the machine, similar to ipconfig for Windows systems. The newer command-line utility, ip, has replaced ifconfig on most Linux systems, but it is still the default for MacOS.

IMAP (Internet Message Access Protocol) *See* Internet Message Access Protocol Version 4 (IMAP4).

impedance The amount of resistance to an electrical signal on a wire. It is used as a relative measure of the amount of data a cable can handle.

implicit deny any A rule for access control lists that blocks all access by default (implicitly), unless the access is specifically permitted based on details like IP addresses, e-mail addresses, or type of application. The list of permitted entries is often referred to as a whitelist.

in-band management Technology that enables managed devices such as a switch or router to be managed by any authorized host that is connected to that network.

inbound traffic Describes the direction of a flow of packets relative to some point of reference. Relative to the entire network, packets coming in from outside the network.

incident Any negative situation that takes place within an organization.

incident response Reaction to any negative situations that take place within an organization that can be stopped, contained, and remediated without outside resources.

incremental backup Backs up all files that have their archive bits turned on, meaning they have been changed since the last backup. This type of backup turns the archive bits off after the files have been backed up.

Independent Basic Service Set (IBSS) A basic unit of organization in wireless networks formed by two or more wireless nodes communicating in ad hoc mode.

Independent Computing Architecture (ICA) Remote access protocol developed by Citrix. Once formed the basis of Windows Terminal Services, though Microsoft now uses its own Remote Desktop Protocol (RDP) for the same purpose.

industrial control system (ICS) System that monitors and controls machines such as those in a factory or chemical plant—or even just a large HVAC system in an office building.

infrastructure as a service (IaaS) Cloud service model that provides on-demand access to infrastructure such as servers, switches, and routers at rates based on resource use. Large-scale, global IaaS providers use virtualization to minimize idle hardware, protect against data loss and downtime, and respond to spikes in demand. *See also* cloud computing.

infrastructure as code (IaC) An automation philosophy that defines the infrastructure (servers and network components) an application or service requires in configuration files or scripts well enough that it is easy to create identical copies of the needed infrastructure.

infrastructure mode Mode in which wireless networks use one or more wireless access points to connect the wireless network nodes centrally. This configuration is similar to the *star topology* of a wired network.

inheritance A method of assigning user permissions, in which folder permissions flow downward into subfolders.

insider threats Potential for attacks on a system by people who work in the organization.

Institute of Electrical and Electronics Engineers (IEEE) A worldwide professional association for electrical and electronics engineering and related disciplines. Regularly develops networking standards such as the IEEE 802 family of LAN standards.

insulating jacket The external plastic covering of a fiber-optic cable.

integrity Protecting data from being changed or deleted without authorization. In networks, integrity is mainly verified with checks that ensure data sent to a recipient is unchanged when it is received at the destination host.

interface identifier (interface ID) The second half (64 bits) of an IPv6 address.

interface monitor A program that tracks the bandwidth and utilization of one or more interfaces on one or more devices in order to monitor traffic on a network.

interframe gap (IFG) A short, predefined silence originally defined for CSMA/CD; also used in CSMA/CA.

intermediate distribution frame (IDF) The room where all the horizontal runs from all the work areas on a given floor in a building come together.

Intermediate System to Intermediate System (IS-IS) A link-state dynamic routing protocol similar to, but not as popular as, OSPF. IS-IS has had support for IPv6 since its inception and is the *de facto* standard for Internet service providers (ISPs).

internal connections The connections between computers in a network.

internal firewall The firewall that sits between the perimeter network and the trusted network that houses all the organization's private servers and workstations. The internal firewall provides strong access control lists to protect internal servers and workstations. *See also* firewall.

internal network A network under the control of an organization.

internal threats All the things that a network's own users do to create problems on the network. Examples include accidental deletion of files, accidental damage to hardware devices or cabling, malicious users, and abuse of rights and permissions.

Internet Assigned Numbers Authority (IANA) The organization originally responsible for assigning public IP addresses. IANA no longer directly assigns IP addresses, though it does still oversee Autonomous System Number (ASN) assignment. IANA assigns blocks of IP addresses to the five Regional Internet Registries (RIRs) and delegates the work of assigning individual addresses to the RIRs. *See also* Autonomous System (AS) *and* Regional Internet Registries (RIRs).

Internet Authentication Service (IAS) Popular RADIUS server for Microsoft environments.

Internet Connection Sharing (ICS) Technique enabling more than one computer to access the Internet simultaneously using a single Internet connection. When you use Internet connection sharing, you connect an entire LAN to the Internet using a single public IP address. Also known simply as Internet sharing,

Internet Control Message Protocol (ICMP) A TCP/IP protocol used to handle many low-level functions such as error or informational reporting. ICMP messages are usually request and response pairs such as echo requests and responses or router solicitations and responses. There are also unsolicited "responses" (advertisements) that consist of single packets. ICMP messages are connectionless.

Internet Corporation for Assigned Names and Numbers (ICANN) Standards organization that sits at the very top of the Internet hierarchy, with the authority to create new top-level domains (TLDs) for use on the Internet.

Internet Engineering Task Force (IETF) A standards organization that develops Internet standards, including those for TCP/IP.

Internet Group Management Protocol (IGMP) Protocol that routers use to communicate with hosts to determine a "group" membership in order to determine which computers want to receive a multicast. Once a multicast has started, IGMP is responsible for maintaining the multicast as well as terminating at completion.

Internet Information Services (IIS) A Web server developed by Microsoft.

Internet Message Access Protocol Version 4 (IMAP4) Protocol for retrieving e-mail from an SMTP server. An alternative to POP3. Currently in its fourth revision, IMAP4 retrieves e-mail from an e-mail server like POP3, but has several features that make it a superior e-mail tool. IMAP4 enables users to create folders on the e-mail server and multiple clients to access a single mailbox. IMAP uses TCP port 143.

Internet of Things (IoT) The billions of everyday objects that can communicate with each other, specifically over the Internet. These include smart home appliances, automobiles, video surveillance systems, and more.

Internet Protocol (IP) Layer 3 protocol responsible for logical addressing and routing packets across networks, including the Internet. It does not guarantee reliable delivery of packets across the network, leaving that task to higher level protocols. IP has two versions, *IPv4*, and *IPv6*.

Internet Protocol Security (IPsec) Network layer encryption protocol.

Internet Protocol version 4 (IPv4) First version of the Internet Protocol introduced in 1980. IPv4 consists of a protocol, header, and address specification. Its 32-bit addresses are written as four sets of numbers between 0 and 255 separated by a period (often called *dotted decimal* format). No IPv4 address may be all 0s or all 255s. Examples of IPv4 addresses include 192.168.0.1 and 64.176.19.164.

Internet Protocol version 6 (IPv6) Second version of the Internet Protocol developed as the address-space limitations of IPv4 became clear. While standardization started in the 1990s, the transition from IPv4 to IPv6 is still ongoing. Its 128-bit addresses consist of eight sets of four hexadecimal numbers, each number being a value between 0000 and ffff, using a colon to separate the numbers. No IP address may be all 0s or all ffffs. An example is: fe80:ba98:7654:3210:0800:200c:00cf:1234.

Internet Small Computer System Interface (iSCSI) A protocol that enables the SCSI command set to be transported over a TCP/IP network from a client to an iSCSI-based storage system. iSCSI is popular with storage area network (SAN) systems.

interVLAN routing A feature on managed switches to provide routing between VLANs.

intranet A private TCP/IP network inside a company or organization.

intrusion detection system (IDS)/intrusion prevention system (IPS) An application (often running on a dedicated IDS box) that inspects incoming packets, looking for active intrusions. The difference between an IDS and an IPS is that an IPS can react to an attack by blocking traffic, while an IDS can only notify a person or device of the attack.

ip Linux terminal command that displays the current TCP/IP configuration of the machine; similar to Windows' ipconfig and macOS's ifconfig.

IP *See* Internet Protocol (IP).

IP address The numeric address of a computer connected to a TCP/IP network, such as the Internet. IPv4 addresses are 32 bits long, written as four octets of 8-bit binary. IPv6 addresses are 128 bits long, written as eight sets of four hexadecimal characters. IP addresses must be matched with a valid subnet mask, which identifies the part of the IP address that is the network ID and the part that is the host ID.

IP addressing The processes of assigning IP addresses to networks and hosts.

IP camera Still-frame or video camera with a network interface and TCP/IP transport protocols to send output to a network resource or destination.

IP exclusion range Range of IP addresses deliberately excluded from the pool of addresses a DHCP server may issue to clients.

IP filtering A method of blocking packets based on IP addresses.

IP helper Refers variously to an IP helper address (also known as the UDP helper address) or a command for configuring IP helper addresses. An IP helper address specifies an IP address on another subnet to which a router will forward all UDP broadcasts. Most often used to enable one DHCP server to serve many subnets, but also makes it possible to pass along broadcasts for protocols such as TFTP, Time Service, TACACS, DNS, NetBIOS, and others. *See also* DHCP relay.

ipconfig A command-line utility for Windows that displays the current TCP/IP configuration of the machine; similar to macOS's ifconfig and UNIX/Linux's ip.

IPsec VPN A virtual private networking technology that uses IPsec tunneling for security.

ISP (Internet service provider) An organization that provides access to the Internet in some form, usually for a fee.

IT (information technology) The business of computers, electronic communications, and electronic commerce. IT uses computers to create, exchange, and process various types of data.

Java A network-oriented programming language invented by Sun Microsystems (acquired by Oracle) and commonly used for writing programs that can be downloaded to your computer through the Internet and immediately run. Using small Java programs (called *applets*), Web pages can include functions such as animations, calculators, and other fancy tricks.

jitter A delay in completing a transmission of all the frames in a message; caused by excessive machines on a network.

jumbo frames Frames (usually 9000 bytes long—though technically anything over 1500 bytes qualifies) that make large data transfer easier and more efficient than using the standard frame size.

K- Most commonly used as the suffix for the binary quantity 1024. For instance, 640K means 640 × 1024 or 655,360. Just to add some extra confusion to the IT industry, K is often misspoken as "kilo," the metric value for 1000. For example, 10 KB, spoken as "10 kilobytes," means 10,240 bytes rather than 10,000 bytes. Finally, when discussing frequencies, K means 1000. So, 1 KHz = 1000 kilohertz.

kbps (kilobits per second) Data transfer rate. 1 kilobit per second is equal to 1000 bits or 125 bytes per second.

Kerberos An open authentication standard best known for serving as the authentication protocol in Windows Domains.

Key Distribution Center (KDC) System for granting authentication in Kerberos. The KDC stores secret keys for users and services.

key fob Small device that can be easily carried in a pocket or purse or attached to a key ring. This device is used to identify the person possessing it for the purpose of granting or denying access to resources such as electronic doors.

key pair Name for the two keys—one public and one private—that are generated in asymmetric-key encryption systems.

keypad The device in which an alphanumeric code or password that is assigned to a specific individual for a particular asset can be entered.

kilohertz (KHz) A unit of measure that equals a frequency of 1000 cycles per second.

Krone LSA-PLUS (Krone) A proprietary connector developed in the 1970s by The Krone Group (a German telecommunications company) that is an alternative to the 110 punchdown block. Krone connectors enable networking as well as audio interconnections.

LAN (local area network) *See* local area network (LAN).

last mile The connection between a central office and individual users in a telephone system.

latency A measure of a signal's delay.

layer A grouping of related tasks involving the transfer of information. Also, a particular level of the OSI seven-layer model, for example, Physical layer, Data Link layer, and so forth.

Layer 2 switch Any device that filters and forwards frames based on the MAC addresses of the sending and receiving machines. What is normally called a "switch" is actually a "Layer 2 switch."

Layer 2 Tunneling Protocol (L2TP) A VPN protocol developed using Cisco's L2F and Microsoft's PPTP tunneling protocols that can be run on almost any connection imaginable. LT2P has no authentication or encryption but is often used with IPsec to provide security.

Layer 3 switch A switch that can also route packets (it filters and forwards data packets based on the IP addresses of the sending and receiving machines). *See also* multilayer switch.

LC connector A duplex type of small form factor (SFF) fiber connector, designed to accept two fiber cables. Also known as *local connector* or *Lucent connector*.

LED (light emitting diode) Solid-state device that emits photons at luminous frequencies when current is applied.

legacy mode One of three modes used with 802.11n wireless networks where the wireless access point (WAP) sends out separate packets just for legacy devices.

legal hold The process of an organization preserving and organizing data in anticipation of or in reaction to a pending legal issue.

light leakage The type of interference caused by bending a piece of fiber-optic cable past its maximum bend radius. Light bleeds through the cladding, causing signal distortion and loss.

light meter An optical power meter used by technicians to measure the amount of light lost through light leakage in a fiber cable.

lights-out management (LOM) Special "computer within a computer" features built into better servers, designed to give you access to a server even when the server itself is shut off.

Lightweight Access Point Protocol (LWAPP) Protocol used in wireless networks that enables interoperability between thin and thick clients and WAPs.

Lightweight Directory Access Protocol (LDAP) A protocol used to query and change a database used by the network. LDAP uses TCP port 389 by default.

Lightweight Extensible Authentication Protocol (LEAP) A proprietary EAP authentication used almost exclusively by Cisco wireless products. LEAP is an interesting combination of MS-CHAP authentication between a wireless client and a RADIUS server.

link aggregation Connecting multiple NICs in tandem to increase bandwidth in smaller increments. *See also* NIC teaming.

Link Aggregation Control Protocol (LACP) IEEE specification of certain features and options to automate the negotiation, management, load balancing, and failure modes of aggregated ports.

link light An LED on NICs, routers, and switches that lights up to show good connection between the devices. Link lights are called *light-emitting diode (LED) status indicators* on the CompTIA Network+ exam.

link state Type of dynamic routing protocol that announces only changes to routing tables, as opposed to entire routing tables. Compare to distance vector routing protocols. Examples of link-state routing protocols include OSPF and IS-IS. *See also* distance vector.

link status A network analyzer report on how good the connection is between two systems.

link-local address The address that a computer running IPv6 gives itself after first booting. The first 64 bits of a link-local address are always fe80::/64. Link-local addresses are used for communicating on a local network.

Linux Family of open source operating systems inspired by UNIX. Very popular for cloud infrastructure, embedded systems, enterprise servers, and mobile devices.

listening port A port that is currently accepting incoming IP packets and passing them to the application that opened the port.

load balancing The process of taking several servers and making them look like a single server, spreading processing and supporting bandwidth needs.

local Refers to the computer(s), server(s), and/or LAN that a user is physically using or that is in the same room, building, or subnet which can span multiple buildings.

local area network (LAN) Network that generally (but not always) belongs to one household or organization and covers a limited place (anything from two devices in an apartment up to thousands of devices on a multibuilding school or business campus).

local authentication Authenticating a user account against a password database stored on the system itself (as opposed to on a remote authentication server).

local connector (LC) *See* LC (connector).

local user accounts The accounts unique to a single Windows system. Stored in the local system's registry.

localhost The hosts file alias for the loopback address of 127.0.0.1, referring to the current machine.

lock A physical device that prevents access to essential assets of an organization, such as servers, without a key.

log Stores information about the performance of some particular aspect of a system. Different programs refer to the monitored aspect with different terms. Performance Monitor calls them *counters*; syslog calls them *facilities*.

log management The process of providing proper security and maintenance for log files to ensure the files are organized and safe.

logic bomb Code written with malicious intent designed to execute when certain conditions are met.

logical address A programmable network address (an IP address, for example), unlike a physical address that is burned into ROM.

logical addressing As opposed to physical addressing, the process of assigning organized blocks of logically associated network addresses to create smaller manageable networks called subnets. IP addresses are one example of logical addressing.

Logical Link Control (LLC) The aspect of the NIC that talks to the operating system, places outbound data coming "down" from the upper layers of software into frames, and creates the FCS on each frame. The LLC also deals with incoming frames by processing those addressed to the NIC and erasing ones addressed to other machines on the network.

logical network diagram A document that shows the broadcast domains and individual IP addresses for all devices on the network. Only critical switches and routers are shown.

logical topology A network topology defined by signal paths as opposed to the physical layout of the cables. *See also* physical topology.

Long Term Evolution (LTE) A wireless data standard with theoretical download speeds of 300 Mbps and upload speeds of 75 Mbps. LTE is marketed as a 4G (fourth generation) wireless technology.

looking glass site A server or Web site that enables technicians outside of a network to inspect information on or run diagnostic tools within that network. A technician might use their ISP's looking glass to troubleshoot a routing issue.

loopback adapter *See* loopback plug.

loopback address Sometimes called the localhost, a reserved IP address used for internal testing: 127.0.0.1.

loopback plug Network connector that connects back into itself for physical loopback testing.

loopback test A test that sends data out of a NIC and checks to see if it comes back. Software versions that don't test the actual port are commonly included in the device's own diagnostics. Hardware or physical loopback tests that include the port require a loopback plug.

MAC (media access control) address Unique 48-bit address assigned to each network card. IEEE assigns blocks of possible addresses to various NIC manufacturers to help ensure that each address is unique. The Data Link layer of the OSI seven-layer model uses MAC addresses to locate machines.

MAC address filtering A method of limiting access to a wireless network based on the physical addresses of wireless NICs.

MAC filtering *See* MAC address filtering.

MAC reservation IP address assigned to a specific MAC address in a DHCP server.

MAC-48 The unique 48-bit address assigned to a network interface card. This is also known as the *MAC address* or the *EUI-48*.

macro Programming within an application that enables users to control aspects of it (generally to handle repetitive tasks). Also, any type of malware that exploits application macros to replicate and activate.

mailbox Special holding area on an e-mail server that separates out e-mail for each user.

main distribution frame (MDF) The room in a building that stores the demarc, telephone cross-connects, and LAN cross-connects.

maintenance window The time it takes to implement and thoroughly test a network change.

malicious user A user who consciously attempts to access, steal, or damage resources.

malware Any program or code (macro, script, and so on) that's designed to do something on a system or network that you don't want to have happen. Some examples of malware include spyware, rootkits, worms, and ransomware.

man-in-the-middle attack *See* on-path attack.

managed devices Networking devices, such as routers and advanced switches, that are extensively configurable.

managed device (SNMP) A component of a *managed network*. Managed devices send information to an *SNMP manager* to be processed.

managed network Network that is monitored by the SNMP protocol consisting of SNMP managed devices, management information base (MIB) items, and SNMP manager(s).

managed switch *See* managed devices.

management information base (MIB) SNMP's management database. *See* Simple Network Management Protocol (SNMP).

mandatory access control (MAC) A security model in which every resource is assigned a label that defines its security level. If the user lacks that security level, they do not get access.

mantrap *See* access control vestibule.

manual tunnel A simple point-to-point connection between two IPv6 networks.

maximum transmission unit (MTU) Specifies the largest size of a data unit in a communications protocol, such as Ethernet.

MB (megabyte) 1,048,576 bytes.

MD5 (Message-Digest Algorithm Version 5) An older hashing function that has been cracked and *should* have been replaced by now—especially in any security context.

mean time between failures (MTBF) A factor typically applied to a hardware component that represents the manufacturer's best guess (based on historical data) regarding how much time will pass between major failures of that component.

mean time to failure (MTTF) Indicates the length of time a device is expected to last in operation. In MTTF, only a single, definitive failure will occur and will require that the device be replaced rather than repaired.

mean time to repair (MTTR) The estimated amount of time it takes to replace or fix a failed system.

Mechanical Transfer Registered Jack (MT-RJ) A type of small form factor (SFF) fiber connector.

Media Access Control (MAC) The part of a NIC that prepares outgoing frames, processes incoming frames, and controls the physical layer interface. The MAC is responsible for tasks such as addressing outgoing frames and validating the length and FCS of incoming frames.

Media Access Control (MAC) address table A database every switch maintains, listing the MAC address and port of each connected device.

media converter A device that lets you interconnect different types of Ethernet cable.

Media Gateway Control Protocol (MGCP) A protocol that is designed to be a complete VoIP or video presentation connection and session controller. MGCP uses TCP ports 2427 and 2727.

medianet A network of far-flung routers and servers that provides sufficient bandwidth for video teleconferencing (VTC) via quality of service (QoS) and other tools.

mega- A prefix that usually stands for the binary quantity 1,048,576. One megabyte is 1,048,576 bytes. One megahertz, however, is 1,000,000 hertz.

memorandum of understanding (MOU) A document that defines an agreement between two parties in situations where a legal contract is not appropriate.

mesh topology Topology in which each computer has a direct or indirect connection to every other computer in a network. Any node on the network can forward traffic to other nodes. Popular in cellular and many wireless networks.

Metasploit A tool that enables a penetration tester to use a massive library of exploits and payloads as well as tweak them for specific penetrations.

Metaverse Iteration of the Internet that relies on virtual reality (VR) environments to create a 3-D experience for user interaction. Early attempts at creating this space include Second Life (video game) and many science fiction stories, such as *Neuromancer*, *The Matrix*, and *Snow Crash*. Facebook uses the term *Metaverse*. NVIDIA refers to the space as the *Omniverse*.

metric Relative value that defines the "cost" of using a particular route (to determine the best one).

metro Ethernet A metropolitan area network (MAN) based on the Ethernet standard.

metropolitan area network (MAN) Multiple computers connected via cabling, radio, leased phone lines, or infrared that are within the same city. A perfect example of a MAN is the Tennessee city Chattanooga's gigabit network available to all citizens, the Chattanooga Gig.

MHz (megahertz) A unit of measure that equals a frequency of 1 million cycles per second.

mirroring Also called *drive mirroring*, reading and writing data at the same time to two drives for fault-tolerance purposes. Considered *RAID level 1*.

mixed mode Also called *high-throughput*, or *802.11a-ht/802.11g-ht*, one of three modes used with 802.11n wireless networks wherein the wireless access point (WAP) sends special packets that support older standards yet can also improve the speed of those standards via 802.

modal distortion A light distortion problem unique to multimode fiber-optic cable.

model A simplified representation of a real object or process. In the case of networking, models represent logical tasks and subtasks that are required to perform network communication.

modem (modulator-demodulator) A device that converts both digital bit streams into analog signals (modulation) and incoming analog signals back into digital signals (demodulation). Most commonly used to interconnect telephone lines and computers.

modulation techniques The various multiplexing and demultiplexing technologies and protocols, both analog and digital.

modulator-demodulator (modem) *See* modem (modulator-demodulator).

module (data center) A group of computers connected to the same access switch.

monlist A query that asks an NTP server about the traffic between itself and peers.

motion detection system A feature of some video surveillance systems that starts and stops recordings based on actions caught by the camera(s).

mounting bracket Bracket that acts as a holder for a faceplate in cable installations.

MS-CHAP Microsoft's dominant variation of the CHAP protocol, uses a slightly more advanced encryption protocol.

MTU (maximum transmission unit) *See* maximum transmission unit (MTU).

multicast Method of sending a packet in which the sending computer sends it to a group of interested computers.

multicast addresses A set of IP addresses reserved for one-to-many communication, such as in streaming video conferencing.

multifactor authentication (MFA) A form of authentication where a user must use two or more factors to prove his or her identity. Methods of multifactor authentication involve knowledge factors (like passwords or pin numbers), possession factors (like a badge or smart card), and inherence factors (like fingerprints or voice).

multilayer switch A switch that has functions that operate at multiple layers of the OSI seven-layer model.

multimeter A tool for testing voltage (AC and DC), resistance, and continuity.

multimode Type of fiber-optic cable with a large-diameter core that supports multiple modes of propagation. The large diameter simplifies connections, but has drawbacks related to distance.

multimode fiber (MMF) Type of fiber-optic cable that uses LEDs.

multipathing An availability solution in which more than one connection or path between a server and SAN is maintained in order to ensure continued availability in the event that one connection goes down.

multiple input/multiple output (MIMO) Feature in 802.11n and later WAPs that enables them to make multiple simultaneous connections. *See also* multiuser MIMO (MU-MIMO).

multiplexer Device that merges information from multiple input channels to a single output channel.

Multiprotocol Label Switching (MPLS) Router feature that labels certain data to use a desired connection. It works with any type of packet switching (even Ethernet) to force certain types of data to use a certain path.

multisource agreement (MSA) A document that details the interoperability of network hardware from a variety of manufacturers.

multitenancy The ability to support multiple customers on the same infrastructure at the same time. Enables customers with small computing needs to only pay for what they actually need in exchange for sharing the same infrastructure with other customers. Comes with the risk those customers will hog shared resources or compromise the infrastructure (by accident or on purpose).

multiuser MIMO (MU-MIMO) Feature of 802.11ac and later networking that enables a WAP to broadcast to multiple users simultaneously. *See also* multiple input/multiple output (MIMO).

MX record DNS record that SMTP servers use to determine where to send mail for a given domain.

My Traceroute (mtr) Terminal command in Linux that dynamically displays the route a packet is taking. Similar to traceroute.

name resolution A method that enables one computer on the network to locate another to establish a session. All network protocols perform name resolution by providing some form of *name server*.

name server DNS servers that hold the actual name and IP DNS records in a kind of database called a zone.

NAT (network address translation) *See* network address translation (NAT).

NAT translation table Special database in a NAT router that stores destination IP addresses and ephemeral source ports from outgoing packets and compares them against returning packets. A NAT translation table also maps internal sockets to their external counterparts.

NAT64 A transition mechanism that attaches the bytes of an IPv4 address onto the end of an IPv6 address for network traversal.

native VLAN The VLAN designation assigned to all frames without 802.1Q tags entering a trunk port on a switch. In addition, any frames that are part of the native VLAN will not receive an 802.1Q tag when they leave the trunk port.

near-end crosstalk (NEXT) Crosstalk at the same end of a cable from which the signal is being generated.

neighbor advertisement IPv6 packet sent in response to a multicast neighbor solicitation packet, telling the requesting system the MAC address of the system it solicited.

neighbor discovery *See* Neighbor Discovery Protocol (NDP).

Neighbor Discovery Protocol (NDP) IPv6 protocol that performs the same functions as ARP in IPv4 and plays a role in features such as SLAAC. It consists of five ICMP control message types: neighbor solicitation, neighbor advertisement, router solicitation, router advertisement, and redirect.

neighbor solicitation IPv6 process of finding a MAC address of a local host, given its IPv6 address.

Nessus Popular and extremely comprehensive vulnerability testing tool.

NetBEUI (NetBIOS Extended User Interface) Microsoft's first networking protocol, designed to work with NetBIOS. NetBEUI is long obsolesced by TCP/IP. NetBEUI did not support routing.

NetBIOS (Network Basic Input/Output System) A protocol that operates at the Session layer of the OSI seven-layer model. This protocol creates and manages connections based on the names of the computers involved.

NetBIOS over TCP/IP (NetBT) A Microsoft-created protocol that enables NetBIOS naming information to be transported over TCP/IP networks. The result is that Microsoft naming services can operate on a TCP/IP network without the need for DNS services.

NetBIOS/NetBEUI *See* NetBEUI; *see also* NetBIOS.

NetFlow The primary tool used to monitor packet flow on a network.

NetFlow collector Component process of NetFlow that captures and saves data from a NetFlow-enabled device's cache for future NetFlow analysis.

netstat A command-line utility used to examine the TCP/IP connections open on a given host. Once universal, though it is being replaced by ss in Linux.

network A collection of two or more devices interconnected by telephone lines, coaxial cables, satellite links, radio, and/or some other communication technique. A computer *network* is a group of computers that are connected together and communicate with one another for a common purpose. Computer networks support "people and organization" networks, users who also share a common purpose for communicating.

network access control (NAC) Control over information, people, access, machines, and everything in between.

network access policy Rules that define who can access the network, how it can be accessed, and what resources of the network can be used.

network access server (NAS) System that controls the modems in a RADIUS network.

network address translation (NAT) A means of translating a system's IP address into another IP address before sending it out to a larger network. NAT manifests itself by a NAT program that runs on a system or a router. A network using NAT provides the systems on the network with private IP addresses. The system running the NAT software has two interfaces: one connected to the network and the other connected to the larger network.

The NAT program takes packets from the client systems bound for the larger network and translates their internal private IP addresses to its own public IP address, enabling many systems to share a single IP address.

network appliance Feature-packed network box that incorporates numerous processes such as routing, network address translation (NAT), switching, intrusion detection and prevention systems, firewall, and more.

network attached storage (NAS) A dedicated file server that has its own file system and typically uses hardware and software designed for serving and storing files.

network blocks Also called *blocks*, contiguous ranges of IP addresses that are assigned to organizations and end users by IANA.

network closet An equipment room that holds servers, switches, routers, and other network gear.

network design The process of gathering together and planning the layout for the equipment needed to create a network.

network diagram An illustration that shows devices on a network and how they connect.

network function virtualization (NFV) A network architecture that applies infrastructure-as-code (IaC)-style automation and orchestration to network management.

network function virtualization infrastructure (NFVI) The foundation of hardware (such as generic servers and switches) and software (like hypervisors and controllers) that power network function virtualization (NFV).

network ID A number used in IP networks to identify the network on which a device or machine exists.

network interface A device by which a system accesses a network. In most cases, this is a NIC or a modem.

network interface card (NIC) Traditionally, an expansion card that enables a PC to link physically to a network. Modern computers now use built-in NICs, no longer requiring physical cards, but the term "NIC" is still very common.

network interface unit (NIU) Another name for a demarc. *See* demarc.

Network layer Layer 3 of the OSI seven-layer model. *See also* Open Systems Interconnection (OSI) seven-layer model.

Network Management Software (NMS) Tools that enable you to describe, visualize, and configure an entire network.

network management system (NMS) *See* SNMP manager.

network map A highly detailed illustration of a network, down to the individual computers. A network map shows IP addresses, ports, protocols, and more.

network name Another name for the *Service Set Identifier (SSID).*

network operations center (NOC) A centralized location for techs and administrators to manage all aspects of a network.

network performance baseline Network performance and access patterns under normal conditions. A network performance baseline can be acquired through continuous performance monitoring or periodic benchmarks and is used to aid in network troubleshooting.

network prefix The first 64 bits of an IPv6 address that identifies the network.

network protocol Special software that exists in every network-capable operating system that acts to create unique identifiers for each system. It also creates a set of communication rules for issues like how to handle data chopped up into multiple packets and how to deal with routers. TCP/IP is the dominant network protocol suite today.

network segmentation Separating network assets through various means, such as with VLANs or with a DMZ, to protect against access by malicious actors.

network share A shared resource on a network.

network technology The techniques, components, and practices involved in creating and operating computer-to-computer links.

network threat Any number of things that share one essential feature: the potential to damage network data, machines, or users.

Network Time Protocol (NTP) Protocol that gives the current time.

network topology Refers to the way that cables and other pieces of hardware connect to one another.

network-based anti-malware A single source server that holds current anti-malware software. Multiple systems can access and run the software from that server. The single site makes the software easier to update and administer than anti-malware installed on individual systems.

network-based firewall Firewall, perhaps implemented in a gateway router or as a proxy server, through which all network traffic must pass inspection to be allowed or blocked.

next hop The next router a packet should go to at any given point.

next-generation firewall (NGFW) Network protection device that functions at multiple layers of the OSI model to tackle traffic no traditional firewall can filter alone.

NIC teaming Connecting multiple NICs in tandem to increase bandwidth in smaller increments. *See also* link aggregation.

Nmap A popular open-source network scanner designed to scan a network and create a map of hosts and services by sending out packets and examining the responses. Frequently used as a vulnerability scanner.

node A member of a network or a point where one or more functional units interconnect transmission lines.

noise Undesirable signals bearing no desired information and frequently capable of introducing errors into the communication process.

non-persistent agent Software used in posture assessment that does not stay resident in client station memory. It is executed prior to login and may stay resident during the login session but is removed from client RAM when the login or session is complete. The agent presents the security characteristics to the access control server, which then decides to allow, deny, or redirect the connection.

nonrepudiation Not being able to deny having sent a message.

normal backup A full backup of every selected file on a system. This type of backup turns off the archive bit after the backup.

north-south traffic Data traffic entering and leaving a data center. Network devices seen in north-south traffic include edge routers, edge firewalls, and load balancers.

ns (nanosecond) A billionth of a second. Light travels a little over 11 inches in 1 ns.

NS records Records that list the authoritative DNS servers for a domain.

nslookup A command-line tool used to query DNS servers manually for specific records. Used when a tech needs to see if a DNS record exists and confirm its value.

NTFS (NT File System) A file system for hard drives that enables object-level security, long filename support, compression, and encryption. NTFS 4.0 debuted with Windows NT 4.0. Later Windows versions continue to update NTFS.

NTFS permissions Groupings of what Microsoft calls special permissions that have names like Execute, Read, and Write, and that allow or disallow users certain access to files.

ntpdc Command that puts the NTP server into interactive mode in order to submit queries.

OEM (Original Equipment Manufacturer) Contrary to the name, does not create original hardware, but rather purchases components from manufacturers and puts them together in systems under its own brand name. Dell, Inc. and Gateway, Inc., for example, are for the most part OEMs. Apple, Inc., which manufactures most of the components for its own Mac-branded machines, is not an OEM. Also known as *value-added resellers (VARs)*.

offboarding The process of confirming that mobile devices leaving the control of the organization do not store any proprietary applications or data.

offsite A term used to describe resources that are stored and maintained at a location other than the primary office or facility. Examples of resources that can be offsite include servers and data backups.

Ohm rating Electronic measurement of a cable's or an electronic component's impedance.

omnidirectional antenna Technology used in most WAPs that send wireless signals in all directions equally.

onboarding The process of verifying that new mobile devices appearing in the organization's infrastructure are secure and safe to use within the organization.

on-path attack Traditionally known as a *man-in-the-middle attack*. An attacker taps into communications between two systems, covertly intercepting traffic thought to be only between those systems, reading or in some cases even changing the data and then sending the data on.

on-site A term used to describe resources that are stored and maintained at the primary office or facility rather than an external location.

open port *See* listening port.

Open Shortest Path First (OSPF) An interior gateway routing protocol developed for IP networks based on the shortest path first or *link state algorithm*.

open source Applications and operating systems that offer access to their source code; this enables developers to modify applications and operating systems easily to meet their specific needs.

Open Systems Interconnection (OSI) An international standard suite of protocols defined by the International Organization for Standardization (ISO) that implements the OSI seven-layer model for network communications between computers.

Open Systems Interconnection (OSI) seven-layer model An architecture model based on the OSI protocol suite, which defines and standardizes the flow of data between computers. The following lists the seven layers:

- **Layer 1** The *Physical layer* defines hardware connections and turns binary into physical pulses (electrical or light). Cables operate at the Physical layer.
- **Layer 2** The *Data Link layer* identifies devices on the Physical layer. MAC addresses are part of the Data Link layer. Switches operate at the Data Link layer.
- **Layer 3** The *Network layer* moves packets between computers on different networks. Routers operate at the Network layer. IP operates at the Network layer.

- **Layer 4** The *Transport layer* breaks data down into manageable chunks with TCP. UDP also operates at the Transport layer.
- **Layer 5** The *Session layer* manages connections between machines. Sockets operate at the Session layer.
- **Layer 6** The *Presentation layer*, which can also manage data encryption, hides the differences among various types of computer systems.
- **Layer 7** The *Application layer* provides tools for programs to use to access the network (and the lower layers). HTTP, SSL/TLS, FTP, SMTP, DNS, DHCP, and IMAP are all examples of protocols that operate at the Application layer.

OpenSSH A series of secure programs developed by the OpenBSD organization to fix the limitation of Secure Shell (SSH) of only being able to handle one session per tunnel.

operating system (OS) The set of system software that manages a computer's hardware and software resources and provides an interface between the PC and the user. Examples are Microsoft Windows, Apple macOS, and Manjaro Linux.

operator In a distributed control system, a human who runs the computer-controlled resources through a human–machine interface. *See also* human–machine interface (HMI).

optic A removable module that enables connectivity between a device and a cable.

Optical Carrier (OC) Specification used to denote the optical data carrying capacity (in Mbps) of fiber-optic cables in networks conforming to the SONET standard. The OC standard is an escalating series of speeds, designed to meet the needs of medium-to-large corporations. SONET establishes OCs from 51.8 Mbps (OC-1) to 39.8 Gbps (OC-768).

optical power meter *See* fiber light meter.

optical time-domain reflectometer (OTDR) Tester for fiber-optic cable that determines continuity and reports the location of cable breaks.

orchestration A higher level of automation in which smaller automated tasks are composed into longer sequences. These sequences (sometimes called pipelines, processes, or workflows) better represent whatever the organization or its employees are trying to accomplish. Also, arrangement of music for multiple instruments.

organizationally unique identifier (OUI) The first 24 bits of a MAC address, assigned to the NIC manufacturer by the IEEE.

orthogonal frequency-division multiplexing (OFDM) A spread-spectrum broadcasting method that combines the multiple frequencies of DSSS with FHSS's hopping capability.

OS (operating system) *See* operating system (OS).

oscilloscope A device that gives a graphical/visual representation of signal levels over a period of time.

OSPF (Open Shortest Path First) *See* Open Shortest Path First (OSPF).

outbound traffic Describes the direction of a flow of packets relative to some point of reference. Relative to the entire network, packets leaving the network from within it.

out-of-band management Method to connect to and administer a managed device such as a switch or router that does not use a standard network-connected host as the administrative console. A computer connected to the console port of a switch is an example of out-of-band management.

overlay tunnel Enables two IPv6 networks to connect over an IPv4 network by encapsulating the IPv6 packets within IPv4 headers, transporting them across the IPv4 network, then decapsulating the IPv6 data.

packet Basic component of communication over a network. A group of bits of fixed maximum size and well-defined format that is switched and transmitted as a complete whole through a network. It contains source and destination address, data, and control information. *See also* frame.

packet analyzer A program that reads the capture files from packet sniffers and analyzes them based on monitoring needs.

packet filtering A mechanism that blocks any incoming or outgoing packet from a particular IP address or range of IP addresses. Also known as *IP filtering*.

packet sniffer A tool that intercepts and logs network packets.

pad Extra data added to an Ethernet frame to bring the data up to the minimum required size of 64 bytes.

partially meshed topology A mesh topology in which not all of the nodes are directly connected.

passive optical network (PON) A fiber architecture that uses a single fiber to the neighborhood switch and then individual fiber runs to each final destination.

Password Authentication Protocol (PAP) The oldest and most basic form of authentication and also the least safe because it sends all passwords in cleartext.

patch antenna Flat, plate-shaped antenna that generates a half-sphere beam; used for broadcasting to a select area.

patch bay A dedicated block with A/V connections (instead of twisted pair and fiber network connections).

patch cables Short (2 to 5 foot) UTP cables that connect patch panels to switches.

patch management The process of regularly updating operating systems and applications to avoid security threats.

patch panel A panel containing a row of female connectors (ports) that terminate the horizontal cabling in the equipment room. Patch panels facilitate cabling organization and provide protection to horizontal cabling. *See also* vertical cross connect.

path diversity Increases availability by ensuring lines out of your network follow *diverse paths* to other networks. A common method for path diversity in smaller centers, for example, uses a fiber connection for the primary and a very fast cellular connection as a failover. Use of both a fiber ISP and a different cable ISP can also lead to path diversity.

Path MTU Discovery A method for determining the highest MTU that can pass through all hops in a route without fragmentation.

path vector Routing protocol in which routers maintain path information. This information gets updated dynamically. *See* Border Gateway Protocol (BGP).

pathping Command-line tool that combines the features of the ping command and the tracert/traceroute commands.

payload The primary data that is encapsulated in a *frame* or other *protocol data unit (PDU)* and sent from a source network device to a destination network device.

PBX (private branch exchange) A private phone system used within an organization.

peer-to-peer (P2P) A network in which each machine can act as either a client or a server.

peer-to-peer mode *See* ad hoc mode.

penetration testing (pentesting) An authorized, network hacking process that identifies and exploits real-world weaknesses in network security and documents the findings.

Performance Monitor (perfmon.exe) The Windows logging utility.

permissions Sets of attributes that network administrators assign to users and groups that define what they can do to resources.

persistent agent In network access control systems, a small scanning program that, once installed on the computer, stays installed and runs every time the computer boots up. Composed of modules that perform a thorough inventory of each security-oriented element in the computer.

persistent connection A connection to a shared folder or drive that the computer immediately reconnects to at logon.

personal area network (PAN) The network created among Bluetooth devices such as smartphones, tablets, printers, keyboards, mice, and so on.

phishing A social engineering technique where the attacker poses as a trusted source and tries to inspire the victim to act based on a false premise (usually communicated via e-mail, phone, or SMS). A successful attack typically obtains confidential information or introduces malware into the network.

physical address An address burned into a ROM chip on a NIC. A MAC address is an example of a physical address.

physical contact (PC) connector Family of fiber-optic connectors that enforces direct physical contact between two optical fibers being connected.

Physical layer *See* Open Systems Interconnection (OSI) seven-layer model.

physical network diagram A document that shows all of the physical connections on a network. Cabling type, protocol, and speed are also listed for each connection.

physical topology The manner in which the physical components of a network are arranged.

piggybacking An authorized person helping an unauthorized person follow them into a secure area.

ping A small ICMP message sent to check for the presence and response of another system. Also, a command-line utility that uses these messages to check the "up/down" status of an IP addressed host. *See also* Internet Control Message Protocol (ICMP).

ping -6 A command-line utility to check the "up/down" status of an IP addressed host. The –6 switch included on the command line, using the Windows version of ping, specifies that the host under test has an IPv6 address.

ping6 Linux command-line utility specifically designed to ping hosts with an IPv6 address.

plain old telephone service (POTS) *See* public switched telephone network (PSTN).

plaintext Describes the data passed through a cipher (even if it is already encrypted). Running plaintext through a cipher algorithm using a key generates the encrypted ciphertext.

platform Hardware environment that supports the running of a computer system.

platform as a service (PaaS) Cloud service model that provides a complete deployment and management system with all the tools needed to administer and maintain a Web application. *See also* cloud computing.

plenum Usually a space between a building's false ceiling and the floor above it. Most of the wiring for networks is located in this space. Plenum is also a fire rating for network cabling.

plenum-rated cable Network cable type that resists burning and does not give off excessive smoke or noxious fumes when burned.

pod (data center) A group of modules that share the same connection to their distribution switches in a data center.

Point Coordination Function (PCF) A method of collision avoidance defined by the 802.11 standard but has yet to be implemented. *See also* Distributed Coordination Function (DCF).

point-to-multipoint topology Topology in which one device communicates with more than one other device on a network.

Point-to-Point Protocol (PPP) A protocol that enables two devices to connect, authenticate with a username and password, and negotiate the network protocol the two devices will use.

Point-to-Point Protocol over Ethernet (PPPoE) A protocol that was originally designed to encapsulate PPP frames into Ethernet frames. Used by DSL providers to force customers to log into their DSL connections instead of simply connecting automatically.

point-to-point topology Network topology in which two computers are directly connected to each other without any other intervening connection components such as hubs or switches.

Point-to-Point Tunneling Protocol (PPTP) A legacy protocol intended to provide a secure data link between computers (a VPN). It has long been included in Windows but has fallen out of favor because it has multiple security vulnerabilities.

pointer record (PTR) A type of DNS record that points IP addresses to hostnames. *See also* reverse lookup zone.

polyvinyl chloride (PVC) A material used for the outside insulation and jacketing of most cables. Also a fire rating for a type of cable that has no significant fire protection.

port (logical connection) In TCP/IP, 16-bit numbers between 0 and 65535 assigned to a particular TCP/IP process or application. For example, Web servers use port 443 (HTTPS) to transfer Web pages to clients. The first 1024 ports are called *well-known ports*. They have been preassigned and generally refer to TCP/IP processes and applications that have been around for a long time.

port (physical connector) In general, the portion of a computer through which a peripheral device may communicate, such as video, USB, serial, and network ports. In the context of networking, the jacks found in computers, switches, routers, and network-enabled peripherals into which network cables are plugged.

port address translation (PAT) The most commonly used form of network address translation, where the NAT uses the outgoing IP addresses and port numbers (collectively known as a socket) to map traffic from specific machines in the network. *See also* network address translation (NAT).

port aggregation A method for joining two or more switch ports logically to increase bandwidth.

port authentication Function of many advanced networking devices that authenticates a connecting device at the point of connection.

port blocking Preventing the passage of any TCP segments or UDP datagrams through any ports other than the ones prescribed by the system administrator.

port bonding The logical joining of multiple redundant ports and links between two network devices such as a switch and storage array.

port filtering *See* port blocking.

port forwarding Preventing the passage of any IP packets through any ports other than the ones prescribed by the system administrator.

port mirroring The capability of many advanced switches to mirror data from any or all physical ports on a switch to a single physical port. Useful for any type of situation where an administrator needs to inspect packets coming to or from certain computers.

port number Number used to identify the requested service (such as SMTP or FTP) when connecting to a TCP/IP host. Some example server port numbers include 80 (HTTP), 21 (FTP), 25 (SMTP), 53 (DNS), and 67 (DHCP).

port scanner A program that probes ports on another system, logging the state of the scanned ports.

port scanning The process of querying individual nodes, looking for open or vulnerable ports and creating a report.

Post Office Protocol Version 3 (POP3) One of the two protocols that receive e-mail from SMTP servers. POP3 uses TCP port 110.

Post Office Protocol Version 3 over SSL (POP3S) Secure version of the POP3 protocol. Uses TLS on port 995.

PostScript A language defined by Adobe Systems, Inc., for describing how to create an image on a page. The description is independent of the resolution of the device that will create the image. It includes a technology for defining the shape of a font and creating a raster image at many different resolutions and sizes.

posture assessment Process by which a client presents its security characteristics via an agent or agent-less interface to an access control server. The server checks the characteristics and decides whether to grant a connection, deny a connection, or redirect the connection depending on the security compliance invoked.

power converter Device that changes AC power to DC power.

power distribution unit (PDU) A rack-mounted set of outlets for devices installed in the rack. Connected to the rack's uninterruptible power supply (UPS).

power generator Backup generator that provides power redundancy by burning petroleum fuel to provide electricity if the main power goes out in a data center or equipment room.

Power over Ethernet (PoE) A standard that enables wireless access points (WAPs) to receive their power from the same Ethernet cables that transfer their data.

power redundancy Secondary source of power in the event that primary power fails. The most common redundant power source is an uninterruptible power supply (UPS).

PPP (Point-to-Point Protocol) *See* Point-to-Point Protocol (PPP).

PPPoE (PPP over Ethernet) *See* Point-to-Point Protocol over Ethernet (PPPoE).

preamble A 7-byte series of alternating ones and zeroes, followed by a 1-byte *start frame delimiter*, always precedes a frame. The preamble gives a receiving NIC time to realize a frame is coming and to know exactly where the frame starts.

prefix delegation An IPv6 router configuration that enables it to request an IPv6 address block from an upstream source, then to disseminate it to local clients.

prefix length The IPv6 term for subnet mask. In all cases, the prefix length is /64.

Presentation layer *See* Open Systems Interconnection (OSI) seven-layer model.

primary name server The name server where records are added, deleted, and modified. The primary name server sends copies of this zone file to secondary name servers in a process known as a zone transfer.

private cloud Software, platforms, and infrastructure that an organization owns and operates for internal use.

private direct connections Links between an organization's network and the cloud provider. The traffic for a private direct connection never goes over the public Internet, but rather over a private line between an organization's data center and a cloud provider.

private IP addresses Groups of IP addresses set aside for internal networks; Internet routers block these addresses, such as 10.*x.x.x* /8, 172.(16–31).*x.x* /16, and 192.168.(0–255).*x* /24.

private port numbers *See* dynamic port numbers.

program A set of actions or instructions that a machine is capable of interpreting and executing. Used as a verb, it means to design, write, and test such instructions.

programmable logic controller (PLC) A computer that controls a machine according to a set of ordered steps.

promiscuous mode A mode of operation for a NIC in which the NIC processes all frames that it sees on the cable regardless of the frame's destination address.

prompt A character or message provided by an operating system or program to indicate that it is ready to accept input.

proprietary Term used to describe technology that is unique to, and owned by, a particular vendor.

Protected Extensible Authentication Protocol (PEAP) An authentication protocol that uses a password function based on MS-CHAPv2 with the addition of an encrypted TLS tunnel similar to *EAP-TLS*.

protocol An agreement that governs the procedures used to exchange information between cooperating entities; usually includes how much information is to be sent, how often it is sent, how to recover from transmission errors, and who is to receive the information.

protocol analyzer A tool that monitors the different protocols running at different layers on the network and that can give Application, Session, Network, and Data Link layer information on every frame going through a network.

protocol data unit (PDU) A single unit of information consisting of protocol control information and some form of data. Different layers of the OSI model use different PDUs. For example, a layer 2 PDU would be called a frame, while a layer 3 PDU is known as a packet.

protocol stack The actual software that implements the protocol suite on a particular operating system.

protocol suite A set of protocols that are commonly used together and operate at different levels of the OSI seven-layer model.

proximity reader Sensor that detects and reads a token that comes within range. The polled information is used to determine the access level of the person carrying the token.

proxy ARP The process of making remotely connected computers act as though they are on the same LAN as local computers.

proxy server A device that fetches Internet resources for a client without exposing that client directly to the Internet. Most proxy servers accept requests for HTTP, FTP, IMAP, and SMTP resources. The proxy server often caches, or stores, a copy of the requested resource for later use.

PSTN (public switched telephone network) *See* public switched telephone network (PSTN).

public cloud Software, platforms, and infrastructure delivered through networks that the general public can use.

public switched telephone network (PSTN) Also known as *plain old telephone service (POTS)*, the most common type of phone connection, which takes your sounds, translated into an analog waveform by the microphone, and transmits them to another phone.

public-key cryptography A method of encryption and decryption that uses two different keys: a public key for encryption and a private key for decryption.

public-key infrastructure (PKI) The system for creating and distributing digital certificates issued by trusted third parties such as DigiCert, GoDaddy, or Sectigo.

punchdown tool A specialized tool for connecting UTP wires to a 110-block. Also called a *110-punchdown tool*.

PVC-rated cable Type of network cable that offers no special fire protection; burning produces excessive smoke and noxious fumes.

quad small form-factor pluggable (QSFP) Bidirectional (BiDi) fiber-optic connector used in 40GbE networks.

quality of service (QoS) Policies that control how much bandwidth a protocol, PC, user, VLAN, or IP address may use.

quarantine network Safe network to which are directed stations that either do not require or should not have access to protected resources.

raceway Cable organizing device that adheres to walls, making for a much simpler, though less neat, installation than running cables in the walls.

rack diagram A diagram with information about the make and model of every component on a rack including details such as firmware versions, date of purchase, upgrade history, and service history.

rack monitoring system Set of sensors in an equipment closet or rack-mounted gear that can monitor and alert when an out-of-tolerance condition occurs in power, temperature, and/or other environmental aspects.

radio frequency interference (RFI) The phenomenon where a Wi-Fi signal is disrupted by a radio signal from another device.

Radio Guide (RG) rating Ratings developed by the U.S. military to provide a quick reference for the different types of coaxial cables.

RADIUS server A system that enables remote users to connect to a network service.

ransomware Crypto-malware that uses some form of encryption to lock a user out of a system. Once the crypto-malware encrypts the computer, usually encrypting the boot drive, it informs the user that they must pay to get the system decrypted. Whether or not the data is actually decrypted upon payment depends primarily on the motive of the threat actor.

real-time processing The processing of transactions as they occur, rather than batching them. Pertaining to an application, processing in which response to input is fast enough to affect subsequent inputs and guide the process, and in which records are updated immediately. The time lag from input to output must be sufficiently brief for acceptable timeliness. Timeliness is a function of the total system: missile guidance requires output within a few milliseconds of input, whereas scheduling of steamships requires a response time in days. Real-time systems are those with a response time of milliseconds; interactive systems respond in seconds; and batch systems may respond in hours or days.

Real-time Transport Protocol (RTP) Protocol that defines the type of packets used on the Internet to move voice or data from a server to clients. The vast majority of VoIP solutions available today use RTP.

real-time video Communication that offers both audio and video via unicast messages.

reassembly The process where a receiving system verifies and puts together packets into coherent data.

recovery point objective (RPO) An upper limit to how much lost data an organization can tolerate if it must restore from a backup. Effectively dictates how frequently backups must be taken.

recovery time objective (RTO) The amount of time needed to restore full functionality from when the organization ceases to function.

recursive lookup (DNS) When a client requests a type of record belonging to an FQDN, and its DNS server does any legwork needed in order to return the record. This is in contrast to an *iterative lookup*, where the client itself asks each server down the DNS hierarchy (starting at the root) until it locates the authoritative DNS server that returns the record.

Reddit hug of death The massive influx of traffic on a small or lesser-known Web site when it is suddenly made popular by a reference from the media. *See also* slashdotting.

redundant array of independent [or inexpensive] disks [or devices] (RAID) A way to create a fault-tolerant storage system. RAID has six levels. Level 0 uses byte-level striping and provides no fault tolerance. Level 1 uses mirroring or duplexing. Level 2 uses bit-level striping. Level 3 stores error-correcting information (such as parity) on a separate disk and data striping on the remaining drives. Level 4 is level 3 with block-level striping. Level 5 uses block-level and parity data striping.

reflection Used in DDoS attacks. The attacker sends requests to normal servers with the target's IP address spoofed as the source. The normal servers respond to the spoofed IP address (the target system), overwhelming it with *reflected* traffic without identifying the true initiator.

reflective DDoS *See* reflection.

refraction Bending of radio waves when transmitted through glass.

Regional Internet Registries (RIRs) Entities under the oversight of the Internet Assigned Numbers Authority (IANA). RIRs parcel out IP addresses from blocks delegated to them by IANA.

registered jack (RJ) Type of connector used on the end of telephone and networking cables. *See* RJ-11 *and* RJ-45, *respectively*.

registered ports Port numbers from 1024 to 49151. IANA assigns these ports for anyone to use for their applications.

regulations Rules of law or policy that govern behavior in the workplace, such as what to do when a particular event occurs.

remote Refers to computers, servers, and/or networks that are located in some other physical location.

remote access The capability to access a computer from outside a building in which it is housed. Remote access requires communications hardware, software, and actual physical links.

remote access server (RAS) Refers to both the hardware component (servers built to handle the unique stresses of a large number of clients calling in) and the software component (programs that work with the operating system to allow remote access to the network) of a remote access solution.

Remote Authentication Dial-In User Service (RADIUS) An AAA standard created to support ISPs with hundreds if not thousands of modems in hundreds of computers to connect to a single central database. RADIUS consists of three devices: the RADIUS server that has access to a database of user names and passwords, a number of network access servers (NASs) that control the modems, and a group of systems that dial into the network.

Remote Desktop Protocol (RDP) A Microsoft-created remote access protocol.

Remote Installation Services (RIS) A tool introduced with Windows 2000 that can be used to initiate either a scripted installation or an installation of an image of an operating system onto a PC.

remote terminal A connection on a faraway computer that enables you to control that computer as if you were sitting in front of it and logged in. Remote terminal programs all require a server and a client. The server is the computer to be controlled. The client is the computer from which you do the controlling.

remote terminal unit (RTU) In a SCADA environment, has the same functions as a controller plus additional autonomy to deal with connection loss. It is also designed to take advantage of some form of long-distance communication.

repeater A device that takes all of the frames it receives on one Ethernet segment and re-creates them on another Ethernet segment. Repeaters operate at Layer 1 (Physical) of the OSI seven-layer model. They do not check the integrity of the Layer 2 (Data Link) frame so they may repeat incorrectly formed frames. They were replaced in the early 1980s by bridges that perform frame integrity checking before repeating a frame.

resistance The tendency for a physical medium to impede electron flow. It is classically measured in a unit called *ohms*. *See also* impedance.

resolver A DNS component that queries name servers and translates DNS names to IP addresses.

resolver cache A cache used by Windows DNS clients to keep track of DNS information.

resource (networking) Some device, software, or data accessible via a network connection. Examples include files on a fileserver, a shared printer directly connected to another workstation, an inventory tracking application hosted on local servers, and a remotely hosted e-mail server.

Response (SNMP) Answer from an agent upon receiving a Get protocol data unit (PDU) from an SNMP manager.

reverse lookup zone A DNS setting that resolves IP addresses to FQDNs. In other words, it does exactly the reverse of what DNS normally accomplishes using forward lookup zones.

reverse proxy server A connectivity solution that gathers information from its associated servers and shares that information to clients. The clients don't know about the servers behind the scenes. The reverse proxy server is the only machine with which they interact.

RF emanation The transmission, intended or unintended, of radio frequencies. These transmissions may come from components that are intended to transmit RF, such as a Wi-Fi network card, or something less expected, such as a motherboard or keyboard. These emanations may be detected and intercepted, posing a potential threat to security.

RG-6 A grade of coaxial cable used for cable television and modern cable modem Internet connections. RG-6 has a characteristic impedance of 75 ohms.

RG-59 A grade of coaxial cable used for cable television and early cable modem Internet connections. RG-59 has a characteristic impedance of 75 ohms.

ring topology A network topology in which all the computers on the network attach to a central ring of cable.

RIP (Routing Information Protocol) A routing protocol with several shortcomings, such as a maximum hop count of 15 and a routing table update interval of 30 seconds (causing every router on a network to send out its table at once). Also known as RIPv1.

RIPv2 Second version of RIP. Adds support for CIDR and fixes some problems in RIPv1, but the maximum hop count of 15 still applies.

riser Fire rating that designates the proper cabling to use for vertical runs between floors of a building.

risk management The process of how organizations evaluate, protect, and recover from threats and attacks that take place on their networks.

Rivest Cipher 4 (RC4) A streaming symmetric-key algorithm. No longer secure due to the many vulnerabilities that have been discovered since its initial implementation.

Rivest, Shamir, Adleman (RSA) *See* RSA (Rivest, Shamir, Adleman).

RJ (registered jack) Connectors used for UTP cable on both telephone and network connections.

RJ-11 Type of connector with four-wire UTP connections; usually found in telephone connections.

RJ-45 Type of connector with eight-wire UTP connections; usually found in network connections and used for 10/100/1000BASE-T networking.

roaming A process where clients seamlessly change wireless access point (WAP) connections, depending on whichever WAP has the strongest signal covered by the broadcast area.

rogue access point (rogue AP) An unauthorized wireless access point (WAP) installed in a computer network. A rogue access point may be part of an attack, or the result of a well-meaning user bringing in hardware from home. *See also* evil twin.

rogue DHCP server An unauthorized DHCP server installed in a computer network. The rogue DHCP server might be in an unauthorized device installed by a well-meaning user, or it could be malicious as in an *on-path attack*.

role-based access control (RBAC) The most popular authentication model used in file sharing, defines a user's access to a resource based on the roles the user plays in the network environment. This leads to the idea of creation of groups. A group in most networks is nothing more than a name that has clearly defined accesses to different resources. User accounts are placed into various groups.

rollback The process of downgrading—undoing—a recently applied patch or updated.

ROM (read-only memory) The generic term for nonvolatile memory that can be read from but not written to. This means that code and data stored in ROM cannot be corrupted by accidental erasure. Additionally, ROM retains its data when power is removed, which makes it the perfect medium for storing BIOS data or information such as scientific constants.

root directory The directory that contains all other directories.

rootkit A type of malware that takes advantage of very low-level operating system functions to hide itself from all but the most aggressive of anti-malware tools.

route (command) A command to display and edit the local system's routing table.

route redistribution Occurs in a multiprotocol router, which learns route information using one routing protocol and disseminates that information using another routing protocol.

router A device that connects separate networks and forwards packets from one network to another based only on the network address for the protocol being used. For example, an IP router looks only at the IP network ID. Routers operate at Layer 3 (Network) of the OSI seven-layer model.

router advertisement (IPv6) Router's response to a client's router solicitation, also sent at regular intervals, that gives the client information to configure itself (prefix, prefix length, and more).

router solicitation (IPv6) Query from a host to find routers and get information to configure itself.

Routing and Remote Access Service (RRAS) Windows' remote access server that provides VPN and dial-up services. Supports the PPTP, L2TP, or L2TP/IPsec protocols.

Routing Information Protocol (RIP) *See* RIP (Routing Information Protocol).

routing loop A situation where one or more routes through interconnected routers create a closed loop, causing the routers to respond slowly and the packets to go undelivered.

routing table A list of various networks and the next hop to reach them. Routers direct traffic for each network to the next hop. This table can be built either manually or automatically.

RSA (Rivest, Shamir, Adleman) An asymmetric cryptography algorithm used to encrypt/decrypt messages and generate digital signatures.

run A single piece of installed horizontal cabling.

SC connector Fiber-optic connector used to terminate single-mode and multimode fiber. It is characterized by its push-pull, snap mechanical coupling, known as "stick and click." Commonly referred to as *subscriber connector*, *standard connector*, and sometimes, *Siemon connector*.

scalability The capability to support network growth.

scanner A device that senses alterations of light and dark. It enables the user to import photographs, other physical images, and text into the computer in digital form.

screened subnet A lightly protected or unprotected subnet positioned between an outer firewall and an organization's highly protected internal network. Screened subnets are used mainly to host public servers (such as Web servers). Traditionally known as a *demilitarized zone (DMZ)*.

SDSL (symmetric digital subscriber line) *See* symmetric digital subscriber line (SDSL).

secondary name server Authoritative DNS server for a domain. Unlike a primary name server, no additions, deletions, or modifications can be made to the zones on a secondary name server, which always gets all information from the primary name server in a process known as a zone transfer.

Secure Copy Protocol (SCP) One of the first SSH-enabled programs to appear after the introduction of SSH. SCP was one of the first protocols used to transfer data securely between two hosts and thus might have replaced FTP. SCP works well but lacks features such as a directory listing.

Secure Hash Algorithm (SHA) A popular family of cryptographic hashing algorithms including SHA-1, SHA-2, SHA-3. SHA-1 is no longer secure and should be replaced—especially in any security context.

Secure Shell (SSH) A terminal emulation program that looks exactly like Telnet but encrypts the data. SSH has replaced Telnet on the Internet.

Secure Sockets Layer (SSL) A protocol developed by Netscape for securing Web sites. Final version was 3.0 before the name was changed to TLS in 1999. *See also* Transport Layer Security (TLS).

security The practice of enhancing a network's resilience against unwanted access or attack.

security considerations In network design and construction, planning how to keep data protected from unapproved access. Security of physical computers and network resources is also considered.

security guard Person responsible for controlling access to physical resources such as buildings, secure rooms, and other physical assets.

security information and event management (SIEM) A two-part process consisting of security event management (SEM), which performs real-time monitoring of security events, and security information management (SIM), where the monitoring log files are reviewed and analyzed by automated and human interpreters.

security log A log that tracks anything that affects security, such as successful and failed logons and logoffs.

security policy A set of procedures defining actions employees should perform to protect the network's security.

segment (network) In early Ethernet, the bus cable to which the computers on an Ethernet network connect. In modern networks, a generic way of referring to any subset of a network—including a subnet or VLAN. Not to be confused with a *TCP segment*.

segmentation In a TCP/IP network, the process of chopping requested data into chunks that will fit into a packet (and eventually into the NIC's frame), organizing the packets for the benefit of the receiving system, and handing them to the NIC for sending.

separation of duties A method of defense in depth in which a single user can't perform a particular task without direct involvement or observation by another party. One example is a server room that requires at least two employees to be badged in at any given time.

server Software that serves requests from client programs—and, by proxy, the hardware devices that host this software.

server farm Section of a data center dedicated to storing and operating racks of servers and equipment.

Server Message Block (SMB) *See* SMB (Server Message Block).

server-based network A network in which one or more systems function as dedicated file, print, or application servers, but do not function as clients.

service level agreement (SLA) A document between a customer and a service provider that defines the scope, quality, and terms of the service to be provided.

Service Set Identifier (SSID) A 32-bit identification string, sometimes called a *network name*, that's inserted into the header of each data packet processed by a wireless access point.

services Background programs in an operating system that do the behind-the-scenes grunt work that users don't need to interact with on a regular basis.

session A networking term used to refer to the logical stream of data flowing between two programs and being communicated over a network. Many different sessions may be emanating from any one node on a network.

session hijacking The interception of a valid computer session to get authentication information.

Session Initiation Protocol (SIP) A signaling protocol for controlling voice and video calls over IP. SIP competes with H.323 for VoIP dominance.

Session layer *See* Open Systems Interconnection (OSI) seven-layer model.

session software Handles the process of differentiating among various types of connections on a PC.

Set (SNMP) The PDU with which a network management station commands an agent to make a change to a management information base (MIB) object.

shell Generally refers to the user interface of an operating system. A shell is the command processor that is the actual interface between the kernel and the user.

shielded twisted pair (STP) A cabling for networks composed of pairs of wires twisted around each other at specific intervals. The twists serve to reduce interference (also called *crosstalk*). The more twists, the less interference. The cable has metallic shielding to protect the wires from external interference. *See also* unshielded twisted pair (UTP) for the more commonly used cable type in modern networks.

short circuit Allows electricity to pass between two conductive elements that weren't designed to interact together. Also called a *short*.

Short Message Service (SMS) alert A proactive message regarding an out-of-tolerance condition of an SNMP managed device sent as an SMS text.

shoulder surfing The process of surreptitiously monitoring people when they are accessing any kind of system in order to pilfer passwords, PIN codes, or sensitive information. A tried-and-true method of social engineering.

signal strength A measurement of how well your wireless device is connecting to other devices.

signal-to-noise ratio (SNR) A measurement that expresses how much of a received transmission is discernable signal and how much is noise. Helps understand the amount of interference (such as RFI) when designing and troubleshooting Wi-Fi networks.

signaling topology Another name for logical topology. *See* logical topology.

signature (malware) Specific pattern of bits or bytes that is unique to a particular virus. Virus scanning software maintains a library of signatures and compares the contents of scanned files against this library to detect infected files.

Simple Mail Transfer Protocol (SMTP) The main protocol used to send electronic mail on the Internet. SMTP uses TCP port 25.

Simple Mail Transfer Protocol Secure (SMTPS) Uses TCP port 587 to secure SMTP communication with TLS. SMTPS is not an extension of SMTP or a propriety protocol.

Simple Network Management Protocol (SNMP) A set of standards for communication with network devices (switches, routers, WAPs) connected to a TCP/IP network. Used for network management.

single point of failure One component or system that, if it fails, will bring down an entire process, workflow, or organization.

single sign-on (SSO) A process whereby a client performs a one-time login to a gateway system. That system, in turn, takes care of the client's authentication to any other connected systems for which the client is authorized to access.

single-mode fiber (SMF) Fiber-optic cables that use lasers.

site survey A process that informs wireless network design by mapping out the physical space to identify requirements, obstacles, and sources of interference.

site-to-site VPN A type of VPN connection using two VPN concentrators to connect two separate LANs permanently.

slashdotting The massive influx of traffic on a small or lesser-known Web site when it is suddenly made popular by a reference from the media. *See also* Reddit hug of death.

small form factor (SFF) A description of later-generation, fiber-optic connectors designed to be much smaller than the first iterations of connectors. *See also* LC connector *and* Mechanical Transfer Registered Jack (MT-RJ).

small form-factor pluggable (SFP) A Cisco module that enables you to add additional features to its routers.

small office/home office (SOHO) *See* SOHO (small office/home office).

smart card Device (such as a credit card) that you insert into your PC or use on a door pad for authentication.

smart device Device (such as a credit card, USB key, etc.) that you insert into your PC in lieu of entering a password.

smart jack Type of network interface unit (NIU) that enables ISPs or telephone companies to test for faults in a network, such as disconnections and loopbacks.

smart locker A locker that an organization can control wirelessly to grant specific users temporary access. The lockers provide a secure way to deliver equipment to a specific user, keep items safe while users are away, or drop off items for someone else to retrieve later.

SMB (Server Message Block) Protocol used by Microsoft clients and servers to share file and print resources.

SMTP (Simple Mail Transfer Protocol) *See* Simple Mail Transfer Protocol (SMTP).

sneakernet Saving a file on a portable medium and walking it over to another computer.

sniffer Diagnostic program that can order a NIC to run in promiscuous mode. *See also* promiscuous mode.

snip *See* cable stripper.

SNMP (Simple Network Management Protocol) *See* Simple Network Management Protocol (SNMP).

SNMP manager Software and station that communicates with SNMP agents to monitor and manage management information base (MIB) objects.

snmpwalk SNMP manager PDU that collects management information base (MIB) information in a tree-oriented hierarchy of a MIB object and any of its subordinate objects. The snmpwalk command queries the object and then automatically queries all the objects that are subordinated to the root object being queried.

social engineering The process of using or manipulating people inside an organization to gain unauthorized access. Common social-engineering techniques include phishing and impersonation.

socket A combination of a port number, Layer 4 protocol, and an IP address that uniquely identifies a connection.

socket pairs Each pair consists of two linked sockets, one at each end of a TCP/IP session between two hosts.

software Programming instructions or data stored on some type of binary storage device.

software as a service (SaaS) Cloud service model that provides centralized applications accessed over a network. *See also* cloud computing.

software-defined networking (SDN) Programming that allows a master controller to determine how network components will move traffic through the network. Used in virtualization.

SOHO (small office/home office) A classification of networking equipment, usually marketed to consumers or small businesses, which focuses on low price and ease of configuration. SOHO networks differ from enterprise networks, which focus on flexibility and maximum performance.

SOHO firewall Firewall, typically simple, that is built into the firmware of a SOHO router.

solid core A cable that uses a single solid wire to transmit signals.

SONET (Synchronous Optical Network) An American fiber carrier standard for connecting fiber-optic transmission systems. SONET was proposed in the mid-1980s and is now an ANSI standard. SONET defines interface standards at the Physical layer of the OSI seven-layer model.

Spanning Tree Protocol (STP) A protocol that enables switches to detect and prevent switching loops automatically. *See also* switching loop.

spectrum analyzer A tool used to scan for radio frequency (RF) sources in order to identify interference.

speed-test site A Web site used to check an Internet connection's throughput, such as www.speakeasy.net/speedtest.

spine-and-leaf architecture Data center architecture in which every spine switch connects to every leaf switch in a two-tiered mesh network. The mesh network removes the need for dedicated connections between the spine backbone switches, because traffic moves seamlessly from spine to leaf to spine, regardless of how many spine or leaf switches are on the network.

split pair A condition that occurs when signals on a pair of wires within a UTP cable interfere with the signals on another wire pair within that same cable.

spoofing A security threat where an attacker makes some data seem as though it came from somewhere else, such as sending an e-mail with someone else's e-mail address in the sender field.

spyware Any program that sends information about your system or your actions over the Internet.

SQL (Structured Query Language) A language created by IBM that relies on simple English-like statements to perform database queries. SQL enables databases from different manufacturers to be queried using a standard syntax.

SRV record DNS record that associates servers for individual protocols with a domain. SRV records specify a host, port, protocol, and other details for a specific service. For example, VoIP clients can readily discover a domain's associated SIP server.

SSH File Transfer Protocol (SFTP) A replacement for FTP released after many of the inadequacies of Secure Copy Protocol (SCP)—such as the inability to see the files on the other computer—were discovered. Not to be confused with Simple File Transfer Protocol, FTP over SSH, or FTPS.

SSID broadcast A wireless access point feature that announces the WAP's SSID to make it easy for wireless clients to locate and connect to it. By default, most WAPs regularly announce their SSID.

SSL (Secure Sockets Layer) *See* Secure Sockets Layer (SSL).

SSL VPN A type of VPN that formerly used SSL encryption but now uses TLS. The two most common types of SSL VPNs are SSL portal VPNs and SSL tunnel VPNs. In portal VPNs, clients connect to the VPN server using a standard Web browser; in tunnel VPNs they use a dedicated VPN client. Despite the fact that SSL is no longer in use, the SSL VPN moniker stuck.

ST connector Fiber-optic connector used primarily with 2.5-mm, single-mode fiber. It uses a push-on, then twist-to-lock mechanical connection commonly called stick-and-twist although ST actually stands for *straight tip*.

star topology A network topology in which all computers in the network connect to a central wiring point.

star-bus topology A hybrid of the star and bus topologies that uses a physical star, where all nodes connect to a single wiring point (such as a hub) and a logical bus that maintains the Ethernet standards. One benefit of a star-bus topology is *fault tolerance*.

star-ring topology A hybrid topology which uses a physical star and logical ring. Star-ring ultimately lost market-share in favor of the more popular star-bus topology.

start frame delimiter (SFD) One-byte section of an Ethernet packet that follows the preamble and precedes the Ethernet frame.

start of authority (SOA) record DNS record that defines the primary name server in charge of a domain. Also includes parameters that control how secondary name servers check for updates to the zone file, such as the serial number which indicates whether the zone file has updates to fetch.

stateful (DHCP) Describes a DHCPv6 server that works very similarly to an IPv4 DHCP server, passing out IPv6 addresses, subnet masks, and default gateways as well as optional items like DNS server addresses.

stateful filtering/stateful inspection A method of filtering in which all packets are examined as a stream. Stateful devices can do more than allow or block; they can track when a stream is disrupted or packets get corrupted and act accordingly.

stateless (IPv6) Describes a DHCPv6 server that only passes out information like DNS servers' IP addresses, but doesn't give clients IPv6 addresses.

stateless address autoconfiguration (SLAAC) A process that enables network clients to determine their own IPv6 addresses without the need for DHCP.

stateless filtering/stateless inspection A method of filtering where the device that does the filtering looks at each IP packet individually, checking the packet for IP addresses and port numbers and blocking or allowing accordingly.

statement of work (SOW) A contract that defines the services, products, and time frames for the vendor to achieve.

static addressing The process of assigning IP addresses by manually typing them into client computers.

static NAT (SNAT) A type of network address translation (NAT) that maps a single routable IP address to a single machine, allowing you to access that machine from outside the network and *vice versa*.

static routes Entries in a router's routing table that are not updated by any routing protocols. Static routes must be added, deleted, or changed by a router administrator. Static routes are the opposite of dynamic routes.

static routing A process by which a router uses manually entered static routes to forward traffic to other networks.

storage A device or medium that can retain data for subsequent retrieval.

storage area network (SAN) A server that can take a pool of hard disks and present them over the network as any number of logical disks.

STP (Spanning Tree Protocol) *See* Spanning Tree Protocol (STP).

straight-through cable UTP or STP cable segment that has the wire and pin assignments at one end of the cable match the wire and same pin assignments at the other end. Straight-through cables are used to connect hosts to switches or to connect switches to routers and are the connective opposite of crossover cables.

straight tip connector *See* ST connector.

stranded core A cable that uses a bundle of tiny wire strands to transmit signals. Stranded core is not quite as good a conductor as solid core, but it will stand up to substantial handling without breaking.

stream cipher An encryption method that encrypts a single bit at a time. Popular when data comes in long streams (such as with older wireless networks or cell phones).

stripe set Two or more drives in a group that are used for a striped volume.

structured cabling Standards defined by the American National Standards Institute/Telecommunications Industry Association (ANSI/TIA) that define methods of organizing the cables in a network for ease of repair and replacement.

subnet Each independent network in a TCP/IP internetwork.

subnet ID Portion of an IP address that identifies bits shared by all hosts on that network.

subnet mask The value used in TCP/IP settings to divide the IP address of a host into its component parts: network ID and host ID.

subnetting Taking a block of IP addresses and chopping it into multiple smaller groups. *See also* Classless Inter-Domain Routing (CIDR).

subscriber connector (SC) *See* SC connector.

subscriber identity module (SIM) card Small storage device used in cellular phones to identify the phone, enable access to the cellular network, and store information such as contacts.

succession planning The process of identifying people who can take over certain positions (usually on a temporary basis) in case the people holding those critical positions are incapacitated or lost in an incident.

supervisory control and data acquisition (SCADA) A system that has the basic components of a distributed control system (DCS), yet is designed for large-scale, distributed processes and functions with the idea that remote devices may or may not have ongoing communication with the central control.

supplicant A client computer in a RADIUS network.

switch A Layer 2 (Data Link) multiport device that filters and forwards frames based on MAC addresses.

switch port protection Various methods to help modern switches deal with malicious software and other threats. Includes technologies such as flood guards.

switching loop A circular path caused by connecting multiple switches together in a circuit. Switches use Spanning Tree Protocol (STP) to detect loops and disable the associated port. Also known as a *bridge loop* or *bridging loop*.

symmetric DSL (SDSL) Type of DSL connection that provides equal upload and download speed and, in theory, provides speeds up to 15 Mbps, although the vast majority of ISPs provide packages ranging from 192 Kbps to 9 Mbps.

symmetric-key algorithm Any encryption method that uses the same key for both encryption and decryption.

Synchronous Digital Hierarchy (SDH) European fiber carrier standard equivalent to SONET.

Synchronous Optical Network (SONET) *See* SONET (Synchronous Optical Network).

syslog System log collector in macOS and Linux. Useful for auditing, performance monitoring, and troubleshooting.

system life cycle Description of typical beginning and end of computing components. Handling such devices at the end includes system life cycle policies and asset disposal.

system log A log file that records issues dealing with the overall system, such as system services, device drivers, or configuration changes.

T568A One of two four-pair UTP crimping standards for 10/100/1000BASE-T networks. *See also* ANSI/TIA-568.

T568B One of two four-pair UTP crimping standards for 10/100/1000BASE-T networks. *See also* ANSI/TIA-568.

tailgating An unauthorized person attempting to follow an authorized person into a secure area.

tamper detection A feature of modern server chassis that will log in the motherboard's nonvolatile RAM (NVRAM) if the chassis has been opened. The log will show chassis intrusion with a date and time. Alternatively, the special stickers or zip ties that break when a device has been opened.

TCP segment The connection-oriented payload of an IP packet. A TCP segment works at the Transport layer.

TCP three-way handshake A three-packet conversation between TCP hosts to establish and start a data transfer session. The conversation begins with a SYN request by the initiator. The target responds with a SYN response and an ACK to the SYN request. The initiator confirms receipt of the SYN-ACK with an ACK. Once this handshake is complete, data transfer can begin.

tcpdump A command-line packet sniffing tool.

TCP/IP suite The collection of all the protocols and processes that make TCP over IP communication over a network possible.

telecommunications room A central location for computer or telephone equipment and, most importantly, centralized cabling. All cables usually run to the telecommunications room from the rest of the installation.

Telecommunications Industry Association (TIA) The standards body that defines most of the standards for computer network cabling. Many of these standards are defined under the ANSI/TIA-568 standard. Since the Electronics Industry Association (EIA) was accredited by the American National Standards Institute (ANSI) to develop the standards, the name changed from TIA/EIA to ANSI/TIA after the EIA closed up shop in 2011.

telephony The science of converting sound into electrical signals, moving those signals from one location to another, and then converting those signals back into sounds. This includes modems, telephone lines, the telephone system, and any products used to create a remote access link between a remote access client and server.

Telnet A program that enables users on the Internet to log onto remote systems from their own host systems. Telnet is no longer used due to its lack of encryption.

temperature monitor Device for keeping a telecommunications room at an optimal temperature.

TEMPEST The NSA's security standard that is used to combat radio frequency (RF) emanation by using enclosures, shielding, and even paint.

Temporal Key Integrity Protocol (TKIP) *See* TKIP-RC4.

Terminal Access Controller Access Control System Plus (TACACS+) A proprietary protocol developed by Cisco to support Authorization, Authentication, and Accounting (AAA) in a network with many routers and switches. It is similar to RADIUS in function, but uses TCP port 49 by default and separates AAA into different parts.

terminal emulation Software that enables a PC to communicate with another computer or network as if it were a specific type of hardware terminal.

termination Endpoint in a network segment. *See* demarc.

TFTP (Trivial File Transfer Protocol) *See* Trivial File Transfer Protocol (TFTP).

threat Any form of potential attack against a network.

three-tiered architecture A traditional type of data center architecture consisting of the *access layer* that provides connectivity between the data center and users, the *distribution layer* that interconnects racks of servers, and the *core layer* that ties together all the switches at the distribution layer and acts as the point of connection to the external connections, including the Internet.

TIA/EIA (Telecommunications Industry Association/Electronics Industry Association) *See* Telecommunications Industry Association (TIA).

TIA/EIA 568A *See* T568A.

TIA/EIA 568B *See* T568B.

TIA/EIA 606 *See* ANSI/TIA-606.

Ticket-Granting Ticket (TGT) Sent by an Authentication Server in a Kerberos setup if the credentials sent by the client match those in its database. The client uses the TGT to request authorization for network resources from the Ticket-Granting Server.

time-domain reflectometer (TDR) Advanced cable tester that tests the length of cables and their continuity or discontinuity, and identifies the location of any discontinuity due to a bend, break, unwanted crimp, and so on.

time to live (TTL) A field in the IP header that indicates the number of hops a packet can make before it hits its demise and gets discarded by a router.

TKIP-RC4 The extra layer of security that Wi-Fi Protected Access (WPA) adds on top of Wired Equivalent Privacy (WEP); uses RC4 for cipher initialization. TKIP-RC4 has been replaced by CCMP-AES, which is much more difficult to crack.

TLS (Transport Layer Security) *See* Transport Layer Security (TLS).

tone generator *See* toner.

tone probe *See* toner.

toner Generic term for two devices used together—a tone generator and a tone locator (probe)—to trace cables by sending an electrical signal along a wire at a particular frequency. The tone locator then emits a sound when it distinguishes that frequency. Also referred to as *Fox and Hound*.

top listener Host that receives the most data on a network.

top talker Host that sends the most data on a network.

top-level domain (TLD) names Peak of the hierarchy for naming on the Internet; these include the .com, .org, .net, .edu, .gov, .mil, and .int names, as well as international country codes such as .us, .eu, etc.

top-level domain servers A set of DNS servers—just below the root servers—that handle the top-level domain names, such as .com, .org, .net, and so on.

top-of-rack switching An implementation of access switches in which every equipment rack uses one (or two for redundancy) Layer 2 switches sitting at the top of the rack, connecting to all the systems on the rack. Top-of-rack switches are *co-resident* in the rack with servers, as compared to switches that reside in a separate rack.

topology The pattern of interconnections in a communications system among devices, nodes, and associated input and output stations. Also describes how computers connect to each other without regard to how they actually communicate.

tracert (also traceroute) A command-line utility used to follow the path a packet takes between two hosts.

tracert –6 (also traceroute6) A command-line utility that checks a path from the station running the command to a destination host. Adding the –6 switch to the command line specifies that the target host uses an IPv6 address. `traceroute6` is a Linux command that performs a traceroute to an IPv6 addressed host.

traffic analysis The process of extracting knowledge from traffic flows on a network. *See also* protocol analyzer.

traffic shaping Controlling the flow of packets into or out of the network according to the type of packet or other rules.

traffic spike Unusual and usually dramatic increase in the amount of network traffic. Traffic spikes may be the result of normal operations within the organization or may be an indication of something more sinister.

trailer The portion of an Ethernet frame that is the frame check sequence (FCS).

transceiver Interchangeable network modules that make it easy to change the media (and associated Ethernet standards) a network device uses. Most often used to provide fiber-optic interfaces for switches, routers, and NICs.

Transmission Control Protocol (TCP) A Layer 4 connection-oriented protocol within the TCP/IP suite. TCP provides a reliable communications channel over an unreliable network by ensuring all packets are accounted for and retransmitted if any are lost.

Transmission Control Protocol/Internet Protocol (TCP/IP) A set of communication protocols developed by the U.S. Department of Defense that enables dissimilar computers to share information over a network. IP provides an address scheme and delivers packets between hosts, while TCP ensures the data is transferred reliably and accurately.

transmit beamforming A multiple-antenna technology in 802.11n WAPs that helps get rid of dead spots.

Transport layer *See* Open Systems Interconnection (OSI) seven-layer model.

Transport Layer Security (TLS) In TLS, hosts use public-key cryptography to securely negotiate a cipher and symmetric key over an unsecured network, and the symmetric key to encrypt the rest of the session. Current name for the historical SSL protocol.

trap (SNMP) Out-of-tolerance condition in an SNMP managed device.

Trivial File Transfer Protocol (TFTP) A protocol that transfers files between servers and clients. Unlike FTP, TFTP requires no user login. Devices that need an operating system, but have no local hard disk (for example, diskless workstations and routers), often use TFTP to download their operating systems.

Trojan horse A virus that masquerades as a file with a legitimate purpose, so that a user will run it intentionally. A common example would be a fake antivirus program that introduces some kind of malicious program under the guise of protecting the computer.

trunk port A port on a switch configured to carry all data, regardless of VLAN number, between all switches in a LAN.

trunking The process of transferring VLAN data between two or more switches.

trusted user An account that has been granted specific authority to perform certain or all administrative tasks.

tunnel An encrypted link between two programs on two separate computers.

tunnel broker In IPv6, a service that creates the actual tunnel and (usually) offers a custom-made endpoint client for you to use, although more advanced users can often make a manual connection.

Tunnel Information and Control (TIC) protocol One of the protocols that sets up IPv6 tunnels and handles configuration as well as login.

Tunnel Setup Protocol (TSP) One of the protocols that sets up IPv6 tunnels and handles configuration as well as login.

twisted pair Twisted pairs of cables, the most overwhelmingly common type of cabling used in networks. The two types of twisted pair cabling are UTP (unshielded twisted pair) and STP (shielded twisted pair).

The twists serve to reduce interference, called *crosstalk*; the more twists, the less crosstalk.

two-factor authentication A method of security authentication that requires two separate means of authentication; for example, some sort of physical token that, when inserted, prompts for a password. Also called *multifactor authentication (MFA)*.

TXT record Freeform type of DNS record that holds a text value. Most commonly used for SPF, DKIM, and DMARC.

type (Ethernet field) Part of an Ethernet frame that describes/labels the frame contents.

U (unit) *See* unit (U).

UC device One of three components of a unified communication (UC) network, it is used to handle voice, video, and more.

UC gateway One of three components of a unified communication (UC) network, it is an edge device used to add extra services to an edge router.

UC server One of three components of a unified communication (UC) network, it is typically a dedicated box that supports any UC-provided service.

UDP (User Datagram Protocol) *See* User Datagram Protocol (UDP).

UDP datagram A connectionless networking container used in UDP communication.

ultra-physical contact (UPC) connector Fiber-optic connector that makes physical contact between two fiber-optic cables. The fibers within a UPC are polished extensively for a superior finish and better junction integrity.

unencrypted channel Unsecure communication between two hosts that pass data using cleartext. A Telnet connection is a common unencrypted channel.

unicast A message sent from one computer to one other computer.

unicast address A unique IP address that identifies a specific host on a network.

unidirectional antenna An antenna that focuses all of its transmission energy in a single, relatively narrow direction. Similarly, its design limits its ability to receive signals that are not aligned with the focused direction.

unified communication (UC) A system that rolls many different network services into one. Instant messaging (IM), telephone service, and video conferencing are a few examples.

unified threat management (UTM) A firewall that is also packaged with a collection of other processes and utilities to detect and prevent a wide variety of threats. These protections include intrusion detection systems, intrusion prevention systems, VPN portals, load balancers, and other threat mitigation apparatus.

unified voice services Complete self-contained Internet services that rely on nothing more than software installed on computers and the computers' microphone/speakers to provide voice telecommunication over the Internet. All of the interconnections to the public switched telephone network (PSTN) are handled in the cloud.

uniform resource locator (URL) An address that defines the type and the location of a resource on the Internet. URLs are used in almost every TCP/IP application. An example of HTTPS URL is https://www.totalsem.com.

uninterruptible power supply (UPS) A device that supplies continuous clean power to a computer system the whole time the computer is on. Protects against power outages and sags. The term *UPS* is often used mistakenly when people mean standby power supply or system (SPS).

unit (U) The unique height measurement used with equipment racks; 1 U equals 1.75 inches.

UNIX A family of computer software operating systems (including macOS and Linux) descended from or heavily influenced by AT&T's UNIX.

unsecure protocol Also known as an *insecure protocol*, transfers data between hosts in an unencrypted (cleartext) format. If these packets are intercepted between the communicating hosts, their data is completely exposed and readable.

unshielded twisted pair (UTP) A popular cabling for telephone and networks composed of pairs of wires twisted around each other at specific intervals. The twists serve to reduce interference (also called *crosstalk*). The more twists, the less interference. The cable has no metallic shielding to protect the wires from external interference, unlike its cousin, STP. Gigabit Ethernet (1000BASE-T) uses UTP, as an example.

UTP is available in a variety of grades, called categories, as defined in the following:

- **Category 1 UTP** Regular analog phone lines, not used for data communications
- **Category 2 UTP** Supports speeds up to 4 Mbps
- **Category 3 UTP** Supports speeds up to 16 Mbps
- **Category 4 UTP** Supports speeds up to 20 Mbps
- **Category 5 UTP** Supports speeds up to 100 Mbps
- **Category 5e UTP** Supports speeds up to 100 Mbps with two pairs and up to 1000 Mbps with four pairs
- **Category 6 UTP** Improved support for speeds up to 10 Gbps
- **Category 6a UTP** Extends the length of 10-Gbps communication to the full 100 meters commonly associated with UTP cabling
- **Category 7 UTP** A standard (unrecognized by TIA) for UTP wiring with support for 10+ Gbps.

untrusted user An account that has been granted no administrative powers.

uplink port Port on a switch that enables you to connect two switches together using a straight-through cable.

upload The transfer of information from a user's system to a remote computer system. Opposite of *download*.

UPS *See* uninterruptible power supply (UPS).

URL *See* uniform resource locator (URL).

user Anyone who uses a computer. You.

user account A record on a network server used to save information that identifies a user to the application, operating system, or network, including name, password, username, groups to which the user belongs, and other information based on the user and the OS or NOS being used. Usually defines the rights and roles a user has on a system.

User Datagram Protocol (UDP) Connectionless protocol in the TCP/IP suite. Has less overhead and better performance than TCP, but also a higher risk of errors. Fire-and-forget UDP datagrams do a lot of important behind-the-scenes work in a TCP/IP network.

user profile A collection of settings that corresponds to a specific user account and may follow the user, regardless of the computer at which he or she logs on. These settings enable the user to have customized environment and security settings.

user-level security A security system in which each user has an account, and access to resources is based on user identity.

UTP coupler A simple, passive, double-ended connector with female connectors on both ends. UTP couplers are used to connect two UTP cable segments together to achieve longer length when it is deemed unnecessary or inappropriate to use a single, long cable.

variable (SNMP) Value of an SNMP management information base (MIB) object. That value can be read with a Get PDU or changed with a Set PDU.

variable-length subnet masking (VLSM) *See* Classless Inter-Domain Routing (CIDR).

vertical cross-connect Main patch panel in a telecommunications room. *See also* patch panel.

very-high-bit-rate DSL (VDSL) The latest form of DSL with download and upload speeds of up to 100 Mbps. VDSL was designed to run on copper phone lines, but many VDSL suppliers use fiber-optic cabling to increase effective distances.

video surveillance Security measures that use remotely monitored visual systems that include IP cameras and closed-circuit televisions (CCTVs).

video teleconferencing (VTC) The classic, multicast-based presentation where one presenter pushes out a stream of video to any number of properly configured and properly authorized multicast clients.

virtual desktop infrastructure (VDI) Technologies that use virtual machines to provide and manage virtual desktops. VDI can provide benefits like flexible management when the desktop VMs are centralized on a smaller number of servers.

virtual disk Block-level storage provided via a storage area network (SAN) that functions for the client computer as a physical, directly attached hard drive.

virtual firewall A firewall that is implemented in software within a virtual machine in cases where it would be difficult, costly, or impossible to install a traditional physical firewall.

virtual IP (VIP) address A single IP address shared by multiple systems. This is commonly the single IP address assigned to a home or organization that uses NAT to have multiple IP stations on the private side of the NAT router. Virtual IP addresses are also used by *First Hop Redundancy Protocol (FHRP)*.

virtual local area network (VLAN) A common feature among managed switches that enables a single switch to support multiple Layer 2 broadcast domains and provide isolation between hosts on different VLANs. Critical for modern network performance and security.

virtual machine (VM) A virtual computer accessed through a class of programs called a hypervisor or virtual machine monitor. A virtual machine runs *inside* your actual operating system, essentially enabling you to run two or more operating systems at once.

virtual machine monitor (VMM) *See* hypervisor.

Virtual Network Computing (VNC) A remote access program and protocol.

virtual network interface card (vNIC) Software-based NIC that functions identically to a physical NIC and uses a software connection to pass traffic from the real NIC to the virtual one.

virtual PBX Software that functionally replaces a physical PBX telephone system.

virtual private network (VPN) A network configuration that enables a remote user to access a private network via the Internet. VPNs employ an encryption methodology called *tunneling*, which protects the data from interception.

virtual router A router that is implemented in software within a virtual machine. The scalability of a virtual machine makes it easy to add capacity to the router when it is needed. Virtual routers are easily managed and are highly scalable without requiring the purchase of additional network hardware.

Virtual Router Redundancy Protocol (VRRP) Open standard FHRP that provides high availability by taking multiple routers and grouping them together into a single virtual router with a single virtual IP address that clients use as a default gateway. *See* First Hop Redundancy Protocol (FHRP).

virtual switch Software that performs Layer 2 switching within a hypervisor and enables virtual machines (VMs) to communicate with each other without going outside of the host system.

virtualization Generally, the process of running software (called a hypervisor) on a *host* computer to create a virtual machine (VM) that models (virtualizes) the hardware you'd find on a physical computer. Also, a pattern that involves replacing existing components with software (virtual) versions that are roughly indistinguishable to any programs, devices, or users that interact with them.

virtualized network functions (VNFs) Network functions such as firewalls, load balancers, and routers that are run using network function virtualization infrastructure (NFVI).

virtualized network function components (VNFCs) Virtual machines (or containers) that can be interconnected to work collectively as a VNF, such as a VPN concentrator or firewall.

virus A program that can make a copy of itself on a system without the user being aware of it. All viruses carry some payload that may or may not do something malicious. Computer viruses generally require a host file or program to run.

virus definition or data files Enables the virus protection software to recognize the viruses on your system and clean them. These files should be updated often. Also called *signature files*, depending on the virus protection software in use.

virus shield Anti-malware program that passively monitors a computer's activity, checking for viruses only when certain events occur, such as a program executing or a file being downloaded.

VLAN hopping A Layer 2 attack that enables an attacker to access hosts on a VLAN the attacker is not a part of. Traditionally this attack used switch spoofing or double tagging.

VLAN pooling A method to load-balance wireless network clients associated with a single SSID. Distributes clients across many VLANs to avoid excessive levels of broadcast traffic.

VLAN Trunking Protocol (VTP) Cisco proprietary protocol to automate the process of syncing VLANs across switches.

Voice over IP (VoIP) Using an IP network to conduct voice calls.

VoIP gateway Interface between a traditional switched telephone network and a VoIP service provider.

VoIP PBX A private branch exchange that uses VoIP instead of the traditional switched telephone circuits.

volt (V) Unit of measurement for voltage.

voltage The pressure of the electrons passing through a wire.

voltage event recorder Tracks voltage over time by plugging into a power outlet. Also known as a *voltage quality recorder*.

VPN concentrator A server program that supports many VPN connections (L2TP, SSL VPN, etc.). Typically part of a VPN-capable router.

VPN tunnel A connection over the Internet between a client and a server; the VPN tunnel enables the client to access remote resources as if they were local, securely.

vulnerability A potential weakness in an infrastructure that a threat actor might exploit.

vulnerability management The ongoing process of identifying vulnerabilities and dealing with them.

vulnerability scanner A tool that scans a network for potential attack vectors.

WAN (wide area network) A geographically dispersed network created by linking various computers and LANs over long distances, generally using leased phone lines. There is no firm dividing line between a WAN and a LAN.

warm site Facility with all of the physical resources, computers, and network infrastructure to recover from a primary site disaster. A warm site does not have current backup data and it may take a day or more to recover and install backups before business operations can recommence.

wattage (watts or W) The amount of amps and volts needed by a particular device to function.

wavelength In the context of laser pulses, the distance the signal has to travel before it completes its cyclical oscillation and starts to repeat. Measured in nanometers, wavelength can be loosely associated with colors.

Web server A server that speaks the HTTP protocol, often secured with TLS. Historically used to deliver only HTML Web sites, has since became the backbone for almost all network-based apps.

Web services Applications and processes that can be accessed over a network, rather than being accessed locally on the client machine. Web services include things such as Web-based e-mail, network-shareable documents, spreadsheets and databases, and many other types of cloud-based applications.

well-known port numbers Port numbers from 0 to 1023 that are used primarily by client applications to talk to server applications in TCP/IP networks.

wide area network (WAN) *See* WAN (wide area network).

Wi-Fi 4 *See* 802.11n.

Wi-Fi 5 *See* 802.11ac.

Wi-Fi 6 *See* 802.11ax.

Wi-Fi The most widely adopted wireless networking type in use today. Technically, only wireless devices that conform to the extended versions of the 802.11 standard—802.11a, b, g, n, ac, and ax—are Wi-Fi certified.

Wi-Fi analyzer *See* wireless analyzer.

Wi-Fi Protected Access (WPA) A wireless security protocol that addresses weaknesses and acts as an upgrade to WEP. WPA offers security enhancements such as dynamic encryption key generation (keys are issued on a per-user and per-session basis), an encryption key integrity-checking feature, user authentication through the industry-standard Extensible Authentication Protocol (EAP), and other advanced features that WEP lacks. WPA has been replaced by the more secure WPA2.

Wi-Fi Protected Access 2 (WPA2) Consumer name for the IEEE 802.11i standard and the replacement for the WPA protocol. It uses the Advanced Encryption Standard algorithm, making it much harder to crack than its predecessor.

Wi-Fi Protected Access 3 (WPA3) Wireless encryption standard that is replacing WPA2. Uses Simultaneous Authentication of Equals (SAE), a key exchange based on Diffie-Hellman that generates unique encryption keys between each client and WAP.

Wi-Fi Protected Setup (WPS) Automated and semi-automated process to connect a wireless device to a

WAP. The process can be as simple as pressing a button on the device or pressing the button and then entering a PIN code. WPS is particularly vulnerable to brute force attacks.

Windows Defender Firewall The firewall that has been included in Windows operating systems since Windows XP SP2; originally named Internet Connection Firewall (ICF) but renamed in subsequent versions of Windows.

Windows domain A group of computers controlled by a computer running a Windows Server operating system with the Active Directory Domain Controller role installed.

wire map A test for copper cables that checks not only for continuity but also that all the wires on both ends of the cable connect to the right spot. A wire map will also pick up shorts and crossed wires.

wire scheme *See* wiring diagram.

Wired Equivalent Privacy (WEP) An early wireless security protocol for Wi-Fi that uses the RC4 encryption algorithm. No longer used due to major security vulnerabilities.

wired/wireless considerations The planning of structured cabling, determining any wireless requirements, and planning access to the Internet when building or upgrading networks.

wireless access point (WAP) Connects wireless network nodes to wireless or wired networks. Many WAPs are combination devices that act as high-speed hubs, switches, bridges, and routers, all rolled into one.

wireless analyzer Any device that finds and documents all wireless networks in the area. Also known as a *Wi-Fi analyzer*.

wireless bridge Device used to connect two wireless network segments together, or to join wireless and wired networks together in the same way that wired bridge devices do.

wireless controller Central controlling device for thin client WAPs.

wireless LAN (WLAN) A complete wireless network infrastructure serving a single physical locale under a single administration.

wireless network *See* Wi-Fi.

wireless survey tool A tool used to discover wireless networks in an area; it also notes signal interferences.

Wireshark A popular packet sniffer.

wiring diagram A document, also known as a *wiring schematic*, that usually consists of multiple pages and that shows the following: how the wires in a network connect to switches and other nodes, what types of cables are used, and how patch panels are configured. It usually includes details about each cable run.

wiring schematic *See* wiring diagram.

work area In a basic structured cabling network, often simply an office or cubicle that potentially contains a PC attached to the network.

Workgroup A convenient method of organizing computers under Network/My Network Places in Windows operating systems.

workstation Computer that a person physically uses to accomplish their work. Often a general computer, but workstations for some occupations need specialized hardware. Traditionally, workstations were stationary computers that were small and cheap enough for it to be practical to set one up at an employee's physical workstation (in contrast to shared mini/mainframe computers that took up one or more server racks).

worm A form of malware. Unlike a classic virus, a worm does not infect other files on the computer. Instead, it autonomously replicates by infecting systems over a network by taking advantage of security weaknesses in networking protocols.

WPA *See* Wi-Fi Protected Access (WPA).

WPA2 *See* Wi-Fi Protected Access 2 (WPA2).

WPA2-Enterprise A version of WPA2 that uses a RADIUS server for authentication.

WPA3 *See* Wi-Fi Protected Access 3 (WPA3).

WPS *See* Wi-Fi Protected Setup (WPS).

WWW (World Wide Web) A vast network of servers and clients communicating through the Hypertext Transfer Protocol (HTTP). Commonly accessed using graphical Web-browsing software such as Mozilla Firefox and Google Chrome.

XOR (eXclusive OR) An operation commonly used in cryptography. XOR takes two input bits and outputs one bit. If the input bits are the same, the output is 0, while if they are different, the output is 1.

Yost cable Cable used to interface with a Cisco device.

zero-configuration networking (zeroconf) Automatically generated IP addresses in the 168.254.0.0/16 subnet when a DHCP server is unreachable.

zero-day attack New attack that exploits a vulnerability that has yet to be identified.

zero trust A cybersecurity paradigm focused on resource protection and the premise that trust is never granted implicitly but must be continually evaluated.

Zigbee Wireless home automation control standard.

zombie A single computer under the control of an operator that is used in a botnet attack. *See also* botnet.

Z-Wave Wireless home automation control standard.

INDEX

A

B

C

E

F

G

H

I

J

K

L

M

N

O

P

Q

R

S

T

U

V

W

X

Y

Z

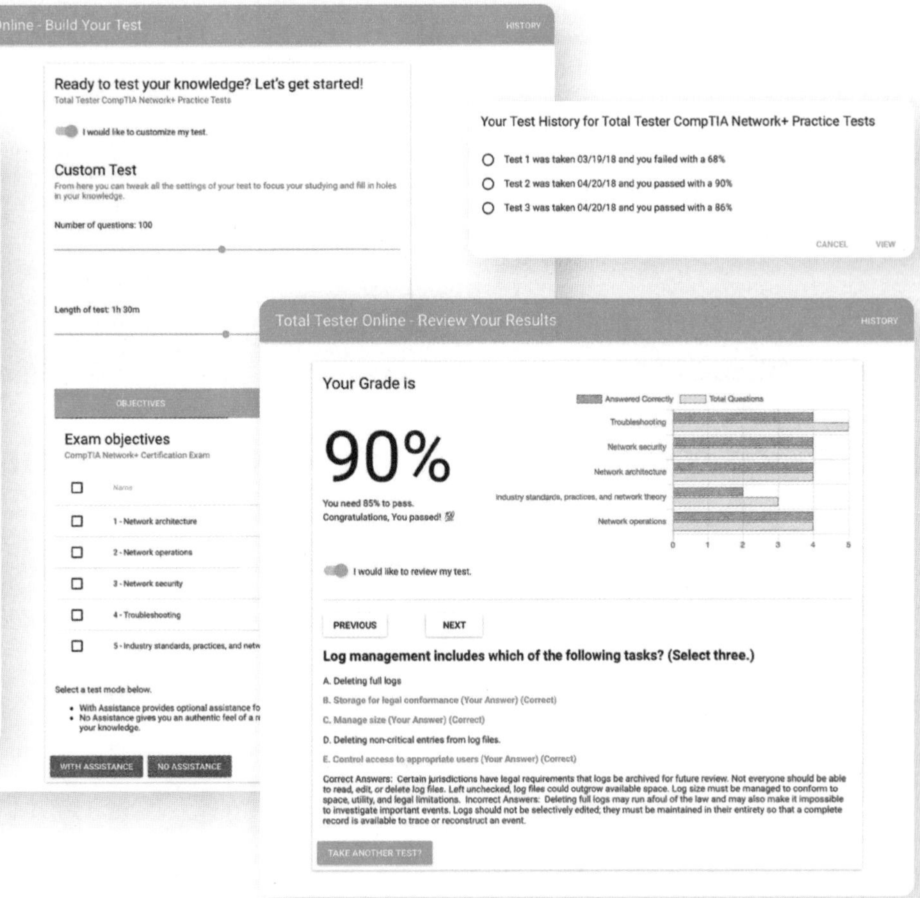

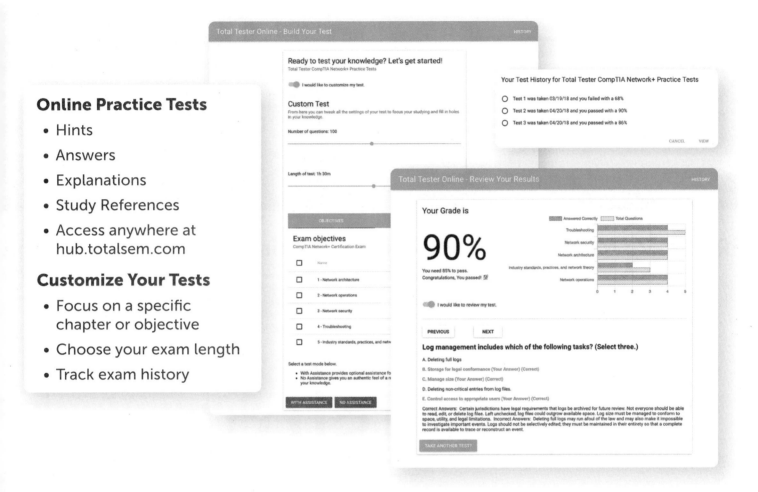

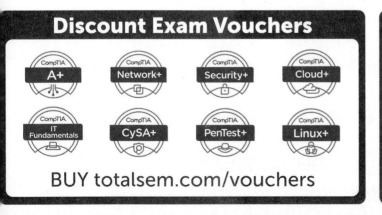